CHILD AND FAMILY LAW

CHILD AND FAMILY LAW

Elaine E. Sutherland
LLB, LLM
Senior Lecturer, School of Law, University of Glasgow

T&T CLARK
EDINBURGH
1999

T&T CLARK LTD
59 GEORGE STREET
EDINBURGH EH2 2LQ
SCOTLAND

First published 1999

ISBN 0 567 00537 2

British Library Cataloguing-in-Publication Data
A catalogue record for this book is available from the British Library

Typeset by Fakenham Photosetting Limited, Fakenham, Norfolk
Printed and bound in Great Britain by MPG Books, Bodmin

To the members of my family

CONTENTS

PREFACE

This book is intended for everyone with an interest in child and family law. It explores and analyses the current legal position in Scotland, considering how we arrived there and where we might go in the future. Where appropriate, reference is made to approaches and solutions found in other jurisdictions. The intention is that it will be of assistance to practising lawyers and members of related professions and that students of law and other disciplines will find it helpful.

The approach I have taken is to begin by looking at some of the fundamental issues in child and family law, preparing the ground, if you like, for further discussion later in the book. The next step is to consider legal personality as a means of identifying the building blocks of families, the people involved. Child law is then examined, before moving on to adult relationships and concluding with some of the special issues relating to older family members. To some extent, this order corresponds with individual experience. To state the obvious, we are all children before we are adults and we are all young before we are old. However, there was a more subtle motive for the order selected. Traditional family law had a tendency to treat children as an afterthought, to be dealt with after a lengthy examination of marriage and divorce. Such an approach is neither realistic nor philosophically sound.

Children are now recognised as people with rights of their own, rights that are independent of the adults around them. How those rights can be implemented continues to present challenges and precisely how the Children (Scotland) Act 1995 will operate has not yet been fully explored. All of this provides great scope for the academic and the practitioner alike.

Although many of the issues surrounding adult relationships have been explored in depth over the years, it should not be thought that this area of law is a dead letter. The present solutions are not wholly satisfactory and we must remain open to new ways of approaching old problems. Perhaps the greatest challenges relate to the recognition which ought to attach to non-marital relationships in general and same-sex relationships in particular.

In the face of an increasingly ageing population, society has tended either to ignore any suggestion that special consideration ought to be given to older members of the community or to regard the demographic changes simply as a problem. To see a whole section of the community in such a negative light both insults the individuals involved and takes us no closer to accommodating any special needs they may have. For this reason, the book concludes with a short chapter intended to stimulate discussion of some of the issues which may be relevant to older members of the family.

The debt I owe to many authors cannot be underestimated and particular thanks go to Dr Eric M. Clive for *The Law of Husband and Wife in Scotland*, now in its fourth edition, and Sheriff A. B. Wilkinson and Professor Kenneth McK. Norrie for *The Law of Parent and Child in Scotland*, the second edition of which is currently in preparation. Recognition must also go to the many students I have taught over the years. Their enthusiasm has been encouraging and their searching questions have provided endless stimulation. Thanks go to the School of Law, University of Glasgow, for granting me study leave and to Lewis and Clark Law School, Portland, Oregon, for providing me with the facilities and environment in which to work on the book. To borrow an expression from the youth of America, the library and research facilities at Lewis and Clark are 'to die for'.

The fact that thanks are due to so many people is a tribute, not only to the wealth of talent we have in this field in Scotland today, but also to the generous way in which those people share their expertise. Many thanks go to Professor Robert Black, Alison Cleland, Dr Graeme Laurie, Dr Eric M. Clive, Tom Guthrie, Sheriff Graham Johnston, Brian Lister, Professor Emeritus J. K. Mason, Dr David Nichols, Professor Robert Rennie, Joan Rose, and the staff at various government agencies and non-departmental public bodies, including the General Register Office for Scotland, the Scottish Children's Reporter Administration, the Scottish Courts Administration, and the Scottish Office.

Tributes are due to Rob Dunbar for contributing paragraphs 14.128 to 14.154, dealing with the tax consequences of marital breakdown, and to Professor Norrie for allowing me to use his excellent flow chart illustrating the procedural steps to be followed in respect of a child protection order. Patricia McKeating's technical assistance with the various flow charts and diagrams proved indispensable. Lesley-Anne Barnes, Kirsty Hood and Emily Wiewiorka have earned eternal gratitude for their contributions as research assistants at various stages.

Thanks go to all at T & T Clark who helped me in the course of publication. A special word of gratitude is extended to Dorothy Amos who was my editor and whose diligence, professionalism and support were exemplary. I would also like to thank my colleague, Dr Jane Mair, who prepared the index.

Mention must also be made of Nermal who, in the course of the book's progress, developed into a fully-fledged research cat. Ensuring that I did not sleep past 5 a.m. and keeping me company during the long hours at the word processor, he demonstrated a level of maturity and loyalty that many might not expect from one of his much-maligned species.

The final, and very special, word of thanks goes to John P. Grant whose support and encouragement, often in the face of my rather obsessive attachment to the project, was unflagging. His legal analysis, constructive criticism, incisive observations and imaginative suggestions were of enormous help and his inimitable sense of humour was indispensable. How anyone can write a book without that level of support is beyond me.

Responsibility for the final work, and the many opinions expressed, is my own. I have attempted to state the law as at 1st November 1998 and, occasionally, it has been possible to incorporate more recent developments.

Elaine E. Sutherland
Glasgow
February 1999

TABLE OF CASES

LEGISLATION

Statutes

References to paragraph numbers include references to footnotes belonging to those paragraphs.
Footnote numbers in headings are taken as being related to the paragraph that follows.

Statutory Instruments

1997

Rules of Court

International Instruments

CHAPTER 1

THE FUNCTIONS OF CHILD AND FAMILY LAW
AND THE ROLE OF THE STATE

1.1 More than any other part of the legal system, child and family law could tell a visitor from Mars how our society is organised. In its ideal form, child and family law is the expression of our most profound beliefs about how we live our lives. It embodies our history, our culture, our philosophy and our politics. It is a reflection of our past, a statement of our present and an expression of our hopes for the future. The place of different family members, both children and adults, within the group, and how we accommodate any special needs they may have, whether resulting from age, disability or other cause, all say something about us as individuals and as a society. What kinds of relationship are considered important and for what purposes tell us more. How we deal with problems and disputes may be the real test both of the preferred models and our entire social structure. At the outset, any discussion of this area of law asks more questions than it answers, but it is in the course of asking the questions that we can begin to work towards a greater understanding of child and family law.

1.2 Is child and family law singular or plural? At one time, traditional books on family law discussed children almost as an afterthought, as an adjunct to adult relationships. Recognition of the importance of the rights and needs of children has meant that they have rightly moved to a more central position in legal thinking. With this has come an holistic approach to the needs of children and young people and an appreciation that any discussion of the relevant law is incomplete if it fails to take account of such matters as the role of the state in setting parameters for child rearing and the child in conflict with the law. Thus, it can be argued, child law has become a discipline in its own right, distinct from family law. None the less, most children live within the family structure and the relationship between children and the adults with whom they live can, quite legitimately, be viewed as family law. Of course, what is family law is not always easy to define. Some matters, like which personal relationships are recognised by the legal system and which are ignored, are usually 'family law' issues.[1] But a great many other areas of the law, like social security, taxation and succession, impact upon family life and no consideration of how a modern family functions would be complete without at least noting them. The best answer to the question 'Is child and family law singular or plural?' is that it

---

1 Equally, recognition or non-recognition of particular relationships may be a civil liberties issue.

is both. More important for our present purpose, perhaps, is that it does not matter. In this book, the approach taken is that narrow compartmentalisation of areas of law should be avoided. If something is relevant to the topic in hand, it should be discussed.

1.3 Of course, not every issue which is relevant to family life will be discussed at length here. This work concentrates on children and families, and many areas of law merit an in-depth analysis and books in their own right.[2] Many specialised books exist and reference will be made to them at the relevant times. In addition, it should be remembered that this is a book about law. While the impact of other disciplines, like philosophy, economics, psychology and medicine, are all relevant to how children and families function, they are largely beyond the scope of this book. In the name of being interdisciplinary, one too often finds lawyers playing at being psychologists or economists when their training does not equip them for that role.[3]

1.4 Child and family law is dynamic. It has a past, a present and a future, and an understanding of all of those dimensions is essential to any coherent appreciation of the subject. Where we have come from helps us to understand where we are and, in some respects, how far we have progressed. Of course, change is not always progress. It is all the more important, then, that we should understand how family law operated in the past. For this reason, reference will frequently be made to how the law has dealt with particular issues in the past. The law as it is now will be the focus of this book, always bearing in mind that the law is not static. The common law may have reached a particular conclusion at a given time, but it is normally capable of responding to changing circumstances.[4] Simply because a statute has been interpreted in a particular way, on one occasion, does not mean that it cannot be interpreted differently in a subsequent case.[5] No-one would argue that all of our present child and family law is ideal. Thus, it is necessary to consider how

2 Some works do attempt to cover the whole of Scots law or, at least, the whole of Scots private law and have done so very well. See for example, T. B. Smith, *A Short Commentary on the Law of Scotland* (W. Green & Son,1962), D. M. Walker, *Principles of Scottish Private Law* (4th edn, Oxford University Press, 1988), and the late W. A. Wilson, A. D. M. Forte, The Lord Rodger of Earlsferry, A. Paton, L. Dunlop, P. Hood and A. R. W. Young, *Gloag and Henderson: The Law of Scotland* (10th edn, W. Green, 1995). In a world where the sheer volume of law seems ever-increasing, it might be questioned that such all-encompassing works will continue to be written. *The Laws of Scotland: Stair Memorial Encyclopaedia*, first published in 25 volumes in the 1980s and 1990s, is one way to accommodate the problem.

3 Some lawyers are also self-taught or otherwise trained in other disciplines and, where that is the case, they can make enormous contributions in each. In addition, much can be gained from lawyers and others working together in interdisciplinary groups where knowledge, expertise and experience are shared. While learning about other disciplines can only enrich, it is the pretence of expertise and proficiency that is dangerous.

4 For example, for a long time the common law did not accept that a husband could be charged with raping his wife. By 1989, however, it was accepted that marriage did not imply a blanket consent to sexual intercourse and, thus, that such a charge was competent – *S v HM Advocate* 1989 SLT 469, discussed in chapter 11, para 15.

5 For example, the Damages (Scotland) Act 1976 allows a person to recover damages where a relative has died 'in consequence of personal injuries sustained by him'. Initially, there were conflicting decisions on whether the phrase could apply where the deceased had been injured while in the womb – see *Hamilton v Fife Health Board* 1992 SLT 1026 and *McWilliams v Lord Advocate* 1992 SLT 1045. The issue was resolved by the Inner House in *Hamilton v Fife Health Board* 1993 SLT 624, discussed in chapter 2, para 6.

it could be improved and proposals for reform of the law will be considered. In the context of law reform, no single body has made a greater contribution than the Scottish Law Commission and frequent reference will be made to its work.[6] Many of its recommendations have already been implemented and a number of others await legislative action. In addition, it is important to bear in mind that, while some ideas for reform may come from within Scotland, others come from elsewhere. How similar issues are addressed in other jurisdictions can provide invaluable guidance, not only in suggesting alternative solutions, but also in helping us to avoid some of the pitfalls that can accompany these solutions.[7]

1.5 In one sense, child and family law impacts upon all of our lives all the time. When the lay person thinks of law, he or she will often think of such matters as divorce, adoption or disputes between parents over their child.[8] From time to time, specific provisions require an individual to comply with some part of child and family law. Thus, for example, a parent may be required to register the birth of a child or an individual may be required to give notice to the district registrar that he or she intends to get married. On other occasions, simply knowing what the law provides may be important in helping people to plan their lives. Knowing whether the parents' marital status affects the decisions they may make about their child's future, or what effect marriage has on property, might help individuals to decide whether or not to get married. For the organised person, knowing about the law of intestate succession may help him or her to decide whether or not to make a will. However, these situations aside, it may be that the law is of little practical importance to individuals when all is going well in their lives.

6 Usually, the Commission examines a particular area of law, using its own highly-qualified staff and produces a Discussion Paper (formerly known as a Consultative Memorandum), setting out the history of the present law, the problems with it, comparative solutions found elsewhere, and its own provisional proposals for reform. Quite apart from the law reform proposals contained therein, the Discussion Papers provide valuable discussion of the existing law. The Commission then allows interested individuals and bodies time to consider its work and invites responses. Sometimes, the Commission consults more widely with members of the public through opinion polls or public meetings. As a result of responses it receives, the Commission then formulates its own firm recommendations and usually provides draft legislation embodying its proposals. The provision of draft legislation should ensure that not only the government of the day has ready-made material to present to Parliament, but also that private members can use the Commission's proposals.

7 The International Society of Family Law, founded in 1973, has contributed much in this context in bringing together some 500 members from 49 countries. In addition, it publishes The International Survey of Family Law each year and organises regular local, and triennial international, conferences on particular topics. A selection of the papers delivered at the triennial conferences are published in individual volumes. See for example, J. Eekelaar and T. Nhlapo (eds), *The Changing Family: Family Forms and Family Law* (Hart Publishing, 1998), which contains some of the papers from the 1996 conference in Durban, South Africa. A wealth of useful information on the comparative position can be gleaned from the many books and journals. More recently, a number of Internet bulletin boards on child and family law have come into existence, facilitating international exchange of information and discussion.

8 Perhaps only criminal law ranks more immediately in the public perception of 'law', as reflected both in media reporting and in popular culture, as expressed in novels, plays and movies. The common ground may be that child, family and criminal law are the areas most likely to touch people's own lives in an immediate and significant way.

People often live their lives concerned about how they will pay the bills, whether their jobs are secure, what their children are doing and where they will go on holiday. The law only becomes relevant when some problem or dispute emerges. It may be only then that they realise what the law provides and how it can, or cannot, help them. This dual nature of child and family law, important to people and yet not immediately so, becomes relevant when we consider the functions of family law and the role of the state.

1.6 Not only do lay people often think of child and family law issues when they think of law, most people have strong views on many of these issues. Bring up the subject of abortion, assisted reproduction, children's rights, single parents, divorce or voluntary euthanasia, with any group of people and opinions will fly. Religion, cultural background, political preferences and personal morality all contribute to individual beliefs about how we should live. Not only do individual views differ, but compromise between the conflicting opinions may not always be possible. This has a host of consequences for the legal system. If law is the expression of the democratic will of the people, how are these diverse views to be accommodated? If the law cannot meet the needs of the whole, or at least a substantial part, of the community, what is its value? Are there certain minimum standards that can be imposed legitimately, irrespective of there being significant opposition to them? Should different systems be provided for different groups of people? Again, these issues will be addressed when we consider the functions of family law and the role of the state. What constitutes a family, who are family members and what are the functions and goals of family law are all questions which are capable of a variety of answers. Indeed, the questions themselves are interrelated, since defining a family in a particular way may require that family law should fulfil a particular function. Conversely, determining that family law ought to have a particular goal may have implications for how we define a family. One thing is clear. If the 'right answer' is something that is accepted universally, then there are very few, if any, right answers. There is simply a whole range of options, and it is for a given society to express its own preferences and to ensure that they find expression in that society's legal system.

1.7 A common refrain from politicians, religious leaders and the media is that, 'things are getting worse'. When applied to family law, this theme finds expression in lamenting the decline of the family and 'family values', although the latter term is rarely defined. It is claimed that more children are born to unmarried women than ever before; more children are growing up with one parent in a different household; an increasing number of children are involved in criminal activity; marriage is on the decline; and the divorce rate is increasing. The first question to ask is whether these claims are true. The most striking feature of the living arrangements of adults in Scotland is variety. In 1997, 31% of households were one-person households.[9] About 17% of adults were cohabiting outside marriage.[10] The

---

9 Office for National Statistics, Regional Trends 33 (The Stationery Office, 1998), hereinafter, 'Regional Trends 33', Table 3.19. This was the highest percentage for the UK outside London.
10 Regional Trends 33, Table 3.17.

number of marriages solemnised that year was at its lowest since 1917[11] and the number of divorces, while down from the previous year, was still broadly in line with the figures for the last 15 years at 12,220.[12] While no official statistics are available, a recent National Opinion Poll survey found that, in 17% of heterosexual couples, the male partner was the homemaker while the female partner was the breadwinner.[13] 1997 saw births increase slightly on the figure for 1996, when the birth rate was at its lowest since civil registration began in 1855. Of the 59,440 children born in 1997, 38% were to unmarried parents.[14] 6,558 children under the age of 16 were affected by divorce in 1996, children being present in 34% of divorces.[15] Thus, the statistical evidence points to diversity in family structures and impermanence in some. In these respects, developments in Scotland are part of a world trend, at least in post-industrial countries.[16]

1.8 However, caution should be exercised when statistics are cited in support of particular conclusions. Bare statistics often fail to tell the whole story. Many children born to unmarried parents live with both parents, while some children born within marriage do not. A whole host of children live with a parent and the parent's new partner, whether heterosexual or homosexual, and others live within an extended family group. The fact that there are more cases of child abuse and neglect reported now than in the past does not necessarily mean that more abuse and neglect is actually happening. Refinements in our perceptions and definitions of the problem, combined with improved procedures for identifying and reporting it, may well explain at least some of the increase. Any correlation between children living with one parent rather than two and an increased likelihood of the child becoming involved with criminality or drugs cannot be explained by the parent's living arrangements alone. Poverty is more likely to accompany a one-adult household than one where two adults are present. Thus, the real correlation may be between poverty and crime or drugs.

1.9 Nor are all the trends discouraging. The fact that many people cohabit as an alternative or prelude to marriage is sometimes presented as some kind of moral decline. Why? Giving people choice about the nature of their relationship is arguably promoting freedom. Allowing couples the opportunity to assess their compatibility before they embark on marriage can be seen as promoting responsibility. The fact that a significant number of couples divorce is, of course, sad, insofar as it reflects people who have ceased to be happy together. But the fact that they are able to leave the

11 There were 29,611 marriages: Registrar General for Scotland, Annual Report 1997 (General Register Office for Scotland, 1998), hereinafter 'Annual Report 1997', Table 7.1.
12 Annual Report 1997, Table 8.1.
13 'Homing in on the house husbands', *The Herald*, Wednesday, 2 April, 1997, p 15, col 8.
14 Annual Report 1997, Table 3.1.
15 Registrar General for Scotland, Annual Report 1996 (General Register Office for Scotland, 1997), Table 8.8. The comparative figures are not provided in the Annual Report 1997.
16 See, M. A. Glendon, *The Transformation of Family Law: State, Law and the Family in the United States and Western Europe* (University of Chicago Press, 1989).

unhappy relationship is hardly cause for unqualified gloom. There are no accurate statistics recording the number of unhappy couples who stayed together in the past because of social or economic pressure or the general unavailability of divorce. If the present law makes divorce easier to obtain, it makes it easier for people to get out of a situation in which they are unhappy and go on to rebuild their lives.

1.10 When we hear that 'things are getting worse' perhaps what we should remember, above all, is that such a refrain is nothing new.[17] The tendency to look to the past and see halcyon days when everything was better is clearly a trait of long standing, but it is misplaced. The rosy view of the past is frequently inaccurate[18] and, in any event, we are not living in the past. We are living in the present and whatever system of child and family law we develop must cope with the challenges and problems of the present.

1.11 What has caused the changes in family structures cannot be separated from general economic, social and political changes.[19] Everything from the agricultural and industrial revolutions to the development of technology has had an impact on how we live, both individually and in family groups. Industrialisation heralded migration to cities and the move away from the extended family towards smaller family groups. The changing position of women in society, resulting from female suffrage and, later, the feminist movement, has had a tremendous impact.[20] Children are now recognised as the holders of rights and are no longer simply recipients of protection. Recognition of cultural diversity and the need to eliminate discrimination has played its part. Medical developments have contributed to changing family patterns and reassessment of family relationships. The increased availability and efficiency of birth control and abortion have made it possible for women to control their fertility in terms of limiting family size, while the development of reproductive technology has made it possible for people to have children when, in the past, they could not have done so. Improved diagnostic and other medical provision has meant that people live longer and this, combined with the lower birth rate, has resulted in an increased number of older people in society. The welfare state, in its various forms, has had an impact on the family, as have private pension schemes and private medical provision. Many of these changes have improved our quality of life and increased freedom of choice for many. Of course, not all change is necessarily for the better. Nor is every improvement an unqualified blessing. Again, however, we must recognise that

---

17 Many of the older texts on child and family law reveal that writers throughout history appear to have felt similarly despondent about the apparent decline in society. For example, writing in 1832, Alison regretted the 'vast increase in juvenile delinquency' – A. J. Alison, *Principles and Practice of the Criminal Law of Scotland* (1832–33), at p 663.

18 For a 'warts and all' account of life in Scotland in the recent past, see, T. C. Smout, *A Century of the Scottish People 1830–1950* (Fontana Press, 1969).

19 The connection is not unique to Scotland. See, J. Eekelaar and T. Nhlapo (eds), *The Changing Family: Family Forms and Family Law* (Hart Publishing, 1998).

20 In *The End of Order* (The Social Market Foundation, 1997), F. Fukuyama attributes the decline of the nuclear family and the undermining of marriage to the increase in female control of fertility and women's economic independence.

there will often be no going back and it is for today's children and the family, as it is constituted at present, that the legal system must cater.

What is a family?

1.12 In one of the most quoted definitions in legal history, Lord Atkin gave a succinct and useful answer to the question 'Who is my neighbour?'.[21] Would that someone had asked him to define the family. The term is capable of definition at various different levels and it is a great deal easier to reject suggested definitions than to accept any one as universally satisfactory. Consider which of the following, if any, you regard as a family, why, and who the family members are.

Anne and Ahmed, a married couple, and their two children who live together;

Barbara and Brian, both in their 70s, who married last year and have no intention of having children;

Diane and David, an unmarried couple, who live together with their two children;

Fatima and Fred, a married couple who live together with Fatima's son, Fergus, Fred's daughter, Fiona, and Flora, an elderly family friend who helps to look after the children but is not related to any of them;

George, and his three-year-old daughter, Gillian, who live with George's mother, Gertrude, and her cohabitant, Gerald;

Sarah and Stephanie, two lesbians who live together with Sarah's ten-year-old son, Sam, by a previous relationship (Sam also spends substantial periods of time with his father and his father's wife and children);

Vera and Vernon, a brother and sister who are adults and live together;

Wendy, Wesley and William, three unrelated friends who share a flat, eat meals and socialise together, rely on each other for emotional support, help each other out financially, but have no romantic or sexual involvement with each other.

1.13 A traditional answer might be that a family is a group of people related to each other through blood or marriage. That certainly conveys notions of kinship but it may, at the same time, both include too broad a group of individuals and exclude others inappropriately. Thus, in the examples above, Anne, Ahmed and their children would qualify, as would any blood relative of either of the adults, however distant and uninvolved in their lives. Similarly, Barbara and Brian would be regarded as a family. Vera and Vernon, being siblings, would also qualify on the basis of their blood relationship. On the other hand, Diane and David would not be members of a family in respect of each other, since they are not related to

---

21 *Donoghue* v *Stevenson* 1932 SC (HL) 31, at p 44.

each other by either blood or marriage, although each of them would be members of the same family as their children. To deny a family relationship between Diane and David seems absurd, given the similarity of their relationship to that of Anne and Ahmed. What, then, of Sarah and Stephanie? Applying the traditional definition, they would not qualify, yet how they live their lives may not be that different from the previous two couples.

1.14   Perhaps it would help if we were to consider what functions families serve and then assess which of the above examples serve some or all of them. One function of the family, both in traditional and contemporary society, is often stated to be procreation and the nurturing of children. That certainly allows us to include some of the examples above in a way that is consistent with common sense. Thus, Diane and David would be recognised as a family as, perhaps, would Fatima and the individuals mentioned along with her, and George and the others in his group. Similarly, Sarah and Stephanie would gain recognition. However, is Flora really a member of Fatima's family? Certainly, she participates in the child-rearing function but so too would a nanny or a day-care provider. Does Gerald's membership of George's family depend on whether he helps to take care of Gillian? In addition, Barbara and Brian would be excluded from being a family, since they have made clear they will neither procreate nor raise children. Similarly, Vera and Vernon would be excluded. However, neither society nor the legal system would deny that there is a relationship between Brian and Barbara or Vera and Vernon. Clearly, procreation and child rearing cannot be the sole test of family.

1.15   There is no reason why a family should have only one function, and another, very valid function, might be mutual support and comfort. This would bring Barbara and Brian and Vera and Vernon back into the picture, but it would also add Wendy and her flatmates as a family group, something most people might find stretching the notion of family too far. Emotional ties are often seen as part of any definition of the family although, of course, liking each other has never been a prerequisite for belonging to a family group. Economic support may be a more reliable indicator and, indeed, the legal system does view the family as an economic unit for some purposes. What both emotional and economic support suggest is the notion of family as a mutually-supportive, co-operative effort. In some cases, that will make some families difficult to distinguish from very close friendships.

1.16   Perhaps another way to approach the question of defining a family is to consider what people usually believe it to be. One popular image of the family is that of the nuclear family. This is the happy family from the cornflakes advertisement, consisting of a married couple with their smiling daughter and son, a cat, a dog and sometimes a sweet little granny thrown in. It may be the advertising executive's dream, but it is hardly reality for many people living in Scotland today. Far less is it the reality when the legal system is most often called upon to play an active role in family life. Again, it begs the question whether children are essential to any definition of family. Nor does it encompass the reality that some people belong to more than one family. In the example of Sarah and Stephanie, Sam may be seen as a member of their family group, but he is also a member of his father's family. On the other hand, Sam's father would almost certainly not regard himself as a member of the same family as Sarah and Stephanie.

1.17 It is hardly surprising that Scots law has no single definition of a 'family'. Instead, it goes no further than defining specific individual relationships like 'relative', 'couple' or 'child'. Different pieces of legislation recognise individual relationships for particular purposes. On occasions, a very broad definition of relative is provided. For example, for the purpose of claiming damages for death, a 'relative' includes: a spouse or former spouse; a cohabitant; a parent or child (including a person 'accepted' as a child of the family); ascendants and descendants; siblings; and aunts and uncles.[22] However, it is more usual to define adult relationships in terms of marriage or, at least heterosexual, marriage-like, models. Thus, for example, occupancy rights in the family home are extended to couples who are living together as if they were man and wife.[23] As far as children are concerned, only those of the adults in the relationship, or those 'accepted' or 'treated' as if they were,[24] are usually included and often only marriage-like relationships are accepted as the foundation of the family.[25] In its proposals for a Child and Family Code,[26] the Scottish Law Commission offers no definition of the family. Again, it defines specific terms like 'parent', 'child' and 'cohabitant'.

1.18 What the above discussion indicates is that there is almost certainly no satisfactory single definition of a family. Two approaches to defining the

22 Damages (Scotland) Act, 1976, s 10(1) and Sched. 1.
23 Matrimonial Homes (Family Protection) (Scotland) Act 1981, s 18.
24 The Family Law (Scotland) Act 1985, s 1(1)(d) places an obligation to aliment a child on any person who has 'accepted' the child as a member of his or her family. More often the link arises where an adult has 'treated' a child as a family member. So, for example, in divorce proceedings, the court must consider whether it should make one of a variety of orders in respect of a child of the parties or a child who has been treated by both of them as a child of the family – Children (Scotland) Act 1995, s 12. For a discussion of the difference between acceptance and treatment, see chapter 6, para 64.
25 See, *X, Y and Z* v *United Kingdom*, 75/1995/581/667, judgment delivered on 22 April 1997. There, X, a female to male transsexual and Y, who had a child by donor insemination, argued that their rights under arts 8 and 14 of the European Convention had been breached by English law's refusal to recognise X as the child's father. The European Court found that 'family life' was not confined to notions of families based on marriage. However, it found that the state's interest in maintaining coherence in family law and in prioritising the interests of children justified caution in changing the law. Given that X could act as a social parent and gain legal recognition through a residence order, it found no violation of art 8 and found no need to examine the issues in respect of art 14.
26 Report on Family Law (Scot Law Com No 135, 1992), para 19.4. The Report will be referred to frequently throughout this book, simply as the 'Report on Family Law'. Many of the recommendations contained in it on matters of child law have already been implemented in the Children (Scotland) Act 1995. Others await implementation. Recognising that Parliamentary time often determines how and when law reform proceeds, the Commission envisaged that specific aspects of its proposals might be implemented at different times. The whole might then be brought together in a Child and Family Code, using the expedited procedure available for a consolidating statute.

family are often juxtaposed. The first embraces a clearly-defined notion of the family and recognises only that as having consequences in family law. This formal notion of the family brings with it the benefits of certainty, but at a cost. The price is a failure to recognise legitimate voluntary relationships and to offer the members of some groups the same rights as the members of other, substantially similar, groups. The second way to approach defining a family looks more to the function being fulfilled by the relationships and to recognise those which serve some family-like function. The benefits of the functionalist approach lie in its flexibility and adaptability. It can respond more readily to changing social and economic conditions. In reality, people live in lots of different types of groups. Those people may benefit from recognition of their relationships for a whole range of purposes, both while the relationship is functioning well and when problems occur. It then falls to the legal system, through child and family law and otherwise, to cope with the specific issues presented by the diverse range of groupings which present themselves in practice. In terms of 'coping', what, then, are the legitimate functions of child and family law? By asking that question, we are, of course, adopting a functionalist approach to the matter of definition.

What are the functions of child and family law?

1.19 Child and family law could promote a particular moral or religious view of personal relationships at the expense of all others. Historically, that was very much the approach of Scots law.[27] Thus, marriage was the only acceptable form of adult union and only children born to married parents were given full recognition. Children born outside marriage were barely recognised as being related to their parents at all and suffered other, more general, legal disabilities. Clearly, we have moved on from that absolutist position. A wider range of adult relationships is now recognised and the link between children, their parents and other adults is open to more flexible interpretation. Scotland is increasingly a multi-cultural society, inhabited by individuals who embrace different moral positions and who subscribe to a variety of religions or none at all. Ideally, the legal system should serve all of these people and, if it is to do so, this suggests a flexible approach to the whole notion of the family. Of course, a fundamental problem arises when the beliefs of one group conflict with those of another.

1.20 Does the idea of law, as the expression of the democratic will of the people, help us here? Provided that what we mean by democracy is the expression of the will of the majority, coupled with maximum tolerance for minority views, it can produce a system of child and family law which meets

---

27 For example, in his *Institutions of the Law of Scotland* (1693), Viscount Stair discusses law and Christian teachings as if they were one and the same, with occasional disparaging references to non-Christians. Discussing the parental obligation to provide financial support for children he quotes from I Tim 5:8 and goes on to make the following observation, 'If he provide not for his own family, he is worse than an infidel'. Prior to the Reformation, family law matters were determined under the canon law of the Roman Catholic church and, after the Reformation, by the Commissary Court. However, the Reformation did nothing to reduce the influence of Christianity on the law. For example, the prohibited degrees of marriage were based on Leviticus, chapter 18.

the needs of all. However, it is a constant danger in any democratic system that only the voice of the majority will prevail, at the expense of minority interests. This probably explains, for example, the continued failure by the legal system to recognise lesbian and homosexual relationships. In addition, it may be that there is no compromise to be reached between the adherents of particular views as witnessed, for example, by the abortion debate.[28] What then, can child and family law seek to do?

1.21 Delivering the annual James Wood Lecture in 1989,[29] Dr Eric M. Clive analysed family law reform in Scotland from the perspectives of liberty, equality and protection. While these are laudable goals, he noted that they cannot always be reconciled fully in the instant case. None the less, the progress of Scots law has been more in the direction of promoting these ends than otherwise. So, for example, it can be argued that individual liberty is provided for in allowing heterosexual adults a choice of the kind of relationship they enter and in providing that cohabitation and marriage have different consequences. Children now have a right to have their views taken into account when major decisions are being taken which affect them. Equality for men and women has been achieved, at least on a theoretical level. Thus, young men and women now achieve increased legal capacity at the same age and married women now own and control property like all other sane, competent adults. A coherent system exists to protect children from exploitation and abuse and to protect adults from domestic violence. Of course, in all of these cases, other factors detract from full realisation of the goals of liberty, equality and protection.[30]

1.22 Liberty, in the sense of choice of personal relationships, is not extended to lesbian and homosexual couples. While children's rights are increasingly recognised, the extent to which children themselves are aware of their rights is open to question.[31] In addition, meaningful access to the legal system is beyond the reach of many children and much more needs to be done in terms of creating a child-friendly legal system. One need only look at the comparative earnings of men and women,[32] the kind of

---

28 In reality, the issue of abortion has long since ceased to be the subject of debate, in the sense of meaningful discussion. Indeed, it is impossible to see how the views of the pro-choice and anti-abortion lobbies can be reconciled.

29 'Family Law Reform in Scotland: Past, Present and Future' 1989 JR 133.

30 Many of the themes mentioned here are explored more fully in the chapters which follow.

31 The Scottish Child Law Centre has done much to improve the quality and availability of information for children in this respect through its telephone advice line, publications and conferences and a number of other organisations seek to inform children, parents and the public about children's rights. The Scottish Office publication, You Matter, attempts to convey relevant information in a child-friendly way. It is encouraging to see the various agencies working with each other and with government agencies. See for example, Your Children Matter, commissioned by the Scottish Office and written by Maureen Lynch of Family Mediation Scotland.

32 Regional Trends 33, n 9 above, Table 8.6 shows average male and female incomes in graph form. While it is clear that women in Scotland and the rest of the UK earn significantly less than men, this method of presenting the information makes precise figures difficult to ascertain. In 1995–96, the average female income was just over £10,000, while the average male income was just over £17,000.

employment most frequently associated with one sex or the other and which sex dominates senior legal positions,[33] to be aware that equality between the sexes has not been achieved. Despite recent legislation, real equality for people with disabilities continues to be a goal rather than reality. Other groups, like older people, receive even less protection from discrimination, although experience and affluence may help at least some older people to lobby for change and combat ageism. The protection from violence offered to children and adults is imperfect, as is witnessed by the fact that it continues. Despite all of this, it does appear that child and family law has gone some way towards promoting liberty, equality and protection and this suggests that it is capable of continuing to do so in the future.

1.23 Each of these terms has a certain fluidity about it and further clarification of what might be encompassed within each is worth exploring. Liberty, including, as it does, notions of tolerance, flexibility and diversity can be one of the most valuable ways to ensure that child and family law meets the needs of as wide a range of individuals in society as possible. It cannot, of course, be absolute. Absolute liberty for one individual may result in harm to others or to particular groups. Nor does liberty require the law to become value-free.[34] Thus, for example, it is sometimes permissible to restrict the freedom of one individual to enter the family home in order to protect other family members from domestic violence. Similarly, equality is a desirable and laudable goal, but substantive justice requires that it should not be assumed where it does not exist. Thus, for example, we cannot assume that every individual is equally able to protect his or her own rights and interests. Again, the protection of others may require that all people are not treated equally. Protection, the third of the desirable goals, must again be monitored to ensure that it does not become a form of oppression. As we shall see, children are often denied access to particular activities or products in the name of protecting the child or others. Thus, the opportunity to apply for a driving licence is deferred until a person reaches the age of 17. This goes some way towards protecting both society and the individual, but it also places a restriction on the co-ordinated, responsible 15-year-old who could drive a car as safely as many adults. When we turn to consider child abuse, we shall see that, where abuse is suspected, the only way to explore the suspicion may be through examination of the child's family circumstances and physical examination of the child. It may also involve the temporary removal of the child from the home. If the suspicion turns out to be wrong, the child and the family have been put through a great deal in the name of protection.

---

33 According to information published in the 1998 Scottish Law Directory, there are just over 500 female partners in Scottish law firms; ten female QCs; one female Senator of the College of Justice; no female Sheriffs Principal and only six female sheriffs.

34 It is sometimes argued that law has become the means by which we avoid moral discourse – C. E. Schneider, 'Moral Discourse and the Transformation of American Family Law' 83 Mich L Rev 1803 (1985); A. Freeman and E. Mensch, 'The Politics of Virtue: Animals, Theology and Abortion' 25 Ga. L. Rev. 923 (1991). For a rebuttal of these views from a feminist perspective, see L. J. Lacey, 'Mimicking the Words, But Missing the Message: The Misuse of Cultural Feminist Themes in Religion and Family Law Jurisprudence' 35 BC L Rev 1 (1993).

1.24 Perhaps the key to making the goals of liberty, equality and protection work is to ensure that they operate as a balance against each other to produce a coherent whole. This notion of balancing is, again, nothing new to child and family law. Another fundamental debate in the field involves the rights of the individual and the rights of the group. Is it the purpose of the law here to structure child and family law such that it promotes the welfare of the individual over the group or the group over the individual? This brings us back to the modern refrain that 'things are getting worse', this time in its incarnation that attributes the decline of the family to the pursuit of individualism. Adults usually form relationships in the belief that they will bring happiness. When they do not, an individual may leave the relationship, despite the fact that this has an impact on the former partner and the children who have been born by the time of the separation. For some critics, this epitomises the pursuit of self at the expense of the family unit, an offence which is aggravated if the absconding individual has the temerity to go on to form a new relationship and to have more children. For child and family law, the picture is not so simple. There are the interests of lots of individuals and at least two groups to be considered in this scenario. The trick for the legal system is balancing those interests. Is that, then, the fundamental function of child and family law?

The role of the state

1.25 It is fairly uncontentious that the state does and should fulfil a whole range of functions in respect of children and the family. These include: record keeping; the regulation of services like day care and residential care for children and adults; and the machinery for the resolution of disputes. The extent to which the state should provide financial and other support to families causes slightly more debate. These various functions will be discussed presently. The very fact that whole tomes are devoted to child and family law illustrates the fact that the state regulates a great deal of family life. It is in this arena that we encounter one of the most stimulating debates of contemporary jurisprudence.

The public/private divide

1.26 What has come to be known as the 'public/private divide' has generated a vast literature of its own[35] and discussion of it contains a number of interrelated strands but, essentially, what it comes down to is this. Whereas the state feels free to regulate the 'public' sphere of government and the workplace,[36] it has often been less willing to intervene in the 'private' arena of the family and family relations. One manifestation of this is that, while labour practices and labour relations, including wages, are governed by

---

35 The following are a broad sample of publications in the context of child and family law: F. Olsen, 'The Myth of State Intervention in the Family' 18 U Mich. J L R 835 (1985); K. O'Donovan, *Sexual Divisions in Law* (Weidenfeld and Nicolson, 1985); R. Gavison, 'Feminism and the Public/Private Distinction' 45 Stan L Rev 1 (1992); S. E. Boyd (ed), *Challenging the Public/Private Divide: Feminism, Law and Public Policy* (University of Toronto Press, 1997).
36 In its most extreme form, the public/private divide distinguishes between government workplaces and private industry, regarding state regulation of the latter as less legitimate.

legislation, work done in the home, like childcare and care of older family members, is unpaid, unregulated and, largely, unrecognised. The fact that most of the latter services are provided by women results in such women being disadvantaged, both economically and in terms of influencing decision-making. If a person's major contribution to society takes place in this 'private' sphere, that person is disempowered and undervalued.

1.27 A second strand of separating the public and private spheres is tied to the idealised notion of the family as a nurturing, supportive environment.[37] According to this view, family members will take care of each other and the state has no business interfering. Thus, individuals should be free to make private arrangements regarding such matters as property, without state oversight. According to this thinking, such notions as equality of bargaining power, which might be appropriate in the 'public' sphere, are unnecessary in the 'private', loving, sphere of the family. Taken to its most extreme, this argument would lead to the absurd conclusion that the state has less legitimate interest in intervening in domestic violence than in violence between strangers. Not only does the public/private divide limit the state's power to intervene, it absolves the state of responsibility. It may be the state's responsibility to ensure that roads are safe and that building regulations set standards for construction, but it need not concern itself with ensuring that there are enough places in day care to accommodate all the children who need them because such matters will be provided for by the family. Similarly, the family can be relied upon to provide for any special needs that individual family members may have as a result of disability, infirmity or old age.

1.28 It is hardly surprising that 'considerable feminist energy has been directed to the deconstruction of ... the state/family aspects of the public/private divide'.[38] In Scotland, this has met with some success. No-one would contend seriously that violence between family members is a private matter which should be unregulated. Thus, not only may the criminal law become relevant when violence occurs within the family, but a person can be ejected from his or her own home if the safety of another family members justifies such action. Where there is concern about a child's welfare, there is a whole range of mechanisms for state intervention. In cases of dispute over other aspects of a child's upbringing, any person with an interest, including the child, may take the matter to a court for adjudication. A variety of presumptions govern the ownership of property in the home, at least where married couples are concerned. On divorce, the courts have extensive powers to reallocate the parties' property. All of these issues are discussed later in this book but, for our present purpose, what is important is that, in many respects, the family is anything but a private sphere.

1.29 However, vestiges of the idea of privacy linger on, sometimes overtly, sometimes more subtly. Where heterosexuals cohabit, rather than

37 This idealised notion of the family involves seeing the, usually female, provider of free services as a saintly mother-figure, something which is presumably intended to compensate for the fact that the position is unpaid.
38 Boyd, above, at p 10.

marry, there is only very limited regulation of the relationship and protection of the partners. This is sometimes defended as leaving people freedom of choice between cohabitation and marriage. In addition, it is argued, cohabitants can always make their own, individually-negotiated contracts, governing their relationships. Where the partners involved are lesbians or homosexuals, the legal system ignores the relationship almost entirely. The law may have given children the right to participate when important decisions are being taken about their lives, but it does little to help them use the legal system, should they want to turn that right to practical effect.[39] The legal system refuses to outlaw so-called 'reasonable chastisement' of children by their parents, thus condoning conduct that would constitute assault in any other setting. The parental right to choose which state school a child should attend is enshrined in statute, but the statute does little to ensure that the child participates in the decision. Perhaps it is in the context of children that the notion of privacy holds its most pervasive sway. There is a belief that parents should be able to raise 'their' children in accordance with their own beliefs, free from state interference except where clear abuse or neglect is present. The rights of adults may still be inhibited by the public/private divide; the rights of children are in danger of being crushed by it.

1.30 Perhaps the greatest challenge to liberal thinking and the public/private divide comes when cultural and religious diversity are added to the debate. We live in a multi-cultural society where a variety of religions are adhered to and atheism is accepted. Religious freedom is rightly viewed as a fundamental liberty. Certain practices are deemed unacceptable and prohibited or regulated by the legal system. What happens when the two are on a collision course? What happens when a particular religious practice offends against some other norm? Which prevails? It is worth exploring a few examples here. The idea that children should obey their parents or that wives should obey their husbands has a substantial religious history. The former still features in our legal system through the concept of a child being beyond parental control,[40] while the latter has long since been abandoned. Female genital mutilation, also known as female circumcision,[41] is a practice having cultural and, arguably, religious roots. It has

---

39 This issue is discussed fully in chapter 3, along with the restrictions placed on children, in the name of child protection, and the extent to which some of these measures are intended as guidance on child rearing, for the benefit of parents.
40 The issue of a child being beyond parental control (or 'beyond the control of any relevant person', as the statute puts it) is not simply a matter of children obeying parents. As currently understood, it relates to child protection and the child's safety. See chapter 9, para 26.
41 The term 'female circumcision' developed because one form of female genital mutilation (FGM), the clitoridectomy (removal of the prepuce, the protective foreskin of the clitoris) resembles male circumcision. However, two other forms of FGM, excision (removal of the prepuce, the clitoris and the labia minora) and infibulation (removal of the prepuce, the labia minora and the labia majora and stitching together of most of the vulva), cannot be likened to procedures carried out on males. This is a good example of how chosen terminology can often indicate an individual's views on a particular issue. Contrast also 'affirmative action' and 'positive discrimination'.

been subject to international condemnation[42] and was prohibited in the UK in 1985.[43] On the other hand, circumcision of male babies[44] remains perfectly legal. Facial scarring of children, as part of a cultural rite of passage, will generally be regarded as child abuse.[45] Where a particular form of dress is required of children or adults, as part of religious or cultural norms, the courts have shown themselves capable of respecting religious and cultural diversity at the same time as balancing this consideration with other factors, like safety.[46] It seems clear that, while the legal system can accommodate some religious or cultural diversity, reliance on religious or cultural freedom does not provide carte blanche for freedom of action. Again, the private sphere is being eroded but, frequently, only very reluctantly.

1.31 It becomes clear that the state's role in respect of the family, like child and family law itself, involves balancing competing interests and principles. Clearly, the state has some role in the family beyond the most simple one of record keeping. How much further it should go in defining, assisting, supporting and directing children and families, is a matter for ongoing debate. That the state has a significant role in respect of children and families has one major consequence. The traditional distinction between private law and public law loses much of its meaning. Private law, or the law which governs relationships between individuals, and public law, or the law which regulates government and its interaction with individuals, co-exist and overlap when issues concerning children and families arise. Some aspects of the state's role are explored below and, as we shall see, while it is convenient to distinguish the different roles, again, they overlap.

Record keeping

1.32 Perhaps the least contentious of all state functions in the context of children and families is record keeping. Since the introduction of a national system for the registration of births, deaths and marriages in 1854,[47] central

---

42 The United Nations Convention on the Elimination of All Forms of Discrimination Against Women, 18 December 1979, 19 I L M 33, requires states to eliminate discrimination against women, including abolishing discriminatory laws, customs or practices. The Declaration on the Elimination of Violence Against Women (UN Doc A/48/629), passed by the General Assembly in December 1993 (GA Res 48/104), includes FGM as one of the examples of violence against women. The United Nations Fourth Conference on Women, held in Beijing in September 1995, discussed the issue.

43 Prohibition of Female Circumcision Act 1985.

44 For different views on the practice, see P. Leach, *Children First* (Michael Joseph, 1990) at p 204 and M. Freeman, 'The Convention: An English Perspective' in M. Freeman (ed), *Children's Rights: A Comparative Perspective* (Dartmouth, 1996) at p 107.

45 *R v Adesanya*, *The Times*, 16 July 1974.

46 For example, in *Mandla v Dowell Lee* [1983] 2 AC 548, the headmaster of a private school who refused to admit a Sikh boy unless he removed his turban and cut his hair was found to have discriminated unlawfully in terms of the Race Relations Act 1976. On the other hand, in *Singh v British Rail Engineering Ltd* [1986] ICR 22, where the appellant was unable to comply with his employer's requirement that he should wear protective headgear, because he felt unable to remove his turban, it was held that the employer was justified, none the less, in imposing the requirement.

47 Registration of Births, Deaths and Marriages (Scotland) Act 1854. That Act was amended and the results have now been consolidated in the Registration of Births, Deaths and Marriages (Scotland) Act 1965.

registers of births, deaths and marriages have been kept by the Registrar General in Edinburgh. Individuals can obtain access to these registers and may purchase copies of certificates of birth, death or marriage. From an individual point of view, such records are valuable as a source of verification and evidence of identity and family history. In addition, they enable social planning by organisations and state and other agencies. For academics the records and other publications derived from them[48] are an invaluable source of data giving information about our past as well as the present and projections for the future. Other collected statistics, including those on civil and criminal court business,[49] social work statistics[50] and a whole range of social trends,[51] are similarly fascinating, and reference will be made to them throughout this book.

Supporting children and families

1.33 That the state accepts a role in supporting children and their families is evidenced by the fact that a whole chapter of the Children (Scotland) Act 1995 is devoted to the duties of the local authority in this respect.[52] Thus, the local authority is obliged to produce service plans and publish information about the services it provides for children. It has a host of responsibilities: to provide day care for pre-school children; to look after children who are not being taken care of otherwise; to provide for children with special needs and disabilities, and to provide after-care for children it has looked after. It is worth noting that the assistance to be rendered here is to children and their families. What of people who do not have children? We shall see in the chapters that follow that the state, often through the local authority, is charged with other responsibilities to individuals and particularly towards individuals who demonstrate some special need, whether that need is caused by infirmity, disability or old age. Arguably, the law in many of these instances deals with individual needs, but its impact on

---

48 The Registrar General for Scotland produces Annual Reports, giving the statistics for a particular year and analysing them in the light of the statistics for previous years. The most recent is the Annual Report 1997 (General Register Office for Scotland, 1998).

49 Civil Judicial Statistics and Criminal Proceedings in the Scottish Courts are published annually by Scottish Courts Administration and the Scottish Office respectively and are available from the Stationery Office. For summaries and other interesting information, see the Scottish Office website on <www.scotland.gov.uk>.

50 A host of annual publications analyse statistics relating to the courts, tribunals and social work provision. Some are produced by Social Work Services Group. See for example, its Statistical Bulletins. Sometimes the job of reporting and analysing particular statistics is transferred from one agency to another. For example, the statistics on children's hearings were dealt with by Social Work Services Group until 1997 (see, Statistical Bulletin, Referrals of Children to Reporters and Children's Hearings 1995 (No SWK/CH/1997/20, May 1997, Scottish Office)). They are now handled by the Scottish Children's Reporters Administration (see, Statistical Bulletin, Disposal Statistics 1996/97: Referrals of Children to Reporters and Children's Hearings: April 1, 1996 to March 31, 1997 (No SCRA/IM/1998/21, September 1998, SCRA)).

51 See for example, Regional Trends, produced by the Office for National Statistics, Regional Trends 33 (1998, The Stationery Office), which draws together statistics from a number of sources and presents them for UK-wide comparison. A General Household Survey will be undertaken in 1999 and will produce useful statistics on a wide range of child and family law issues.

52 Chapter 1 of Part II, comprising ss 16–38.

families and supporting families is obvious. In addition, the local authority is charged with providing housing, again, an issue of central concern in families remaining together. The advent of community care and the idea that individuals should be given assistance to remain at home rather than living in an institution has much to commend it in terms of autonomy and privacy. However, for it to work properly, sufficient resources must be allocated to providing the necessary support. The danger is that either inadequate support will be given or that the responsibility for support will be placed on family members who are in no position to offer it or who can only do so at enormous personal and financial cost.

1.34 Of course, a crucial question in all of this is who pays for the services. It is one thing to find state provision of services, it is quite another to find that a charge is made for them and that they are thus put beyond the reach of individuals who need them. Certainly, not all services are provided free of charge. Where a charge is made, this will often be means-tested, the intention being that those who can afford to will pay for or contribute towards the cost of the service, while those who have fewer resources will not. It is often suggested that means-testing discourages some people from taking advantage of services to which they are entitled and, in any event, any test must be carefully formulated and applied. However, in terms of payment for services, this tells us two things. First, the state generally accepts some responsibility for providing services to children and family members. Second, it will sometimes pay for these services.

1.35 As far as more general financial support for individuals and families is concerned, state benefits are available through both contributory and non-contributory schemes. As a general rule, non-contributory benefits place greater emphasis on the family unit[53] than do contributory benefits. The trend in recent years has been to emphasise the importance of family members bearing the responsibility to support each other, with the state having the 'role of last resort'. Thus, for example, the Child Support Act 1991 ('the 1991 Act') introduced a scheme for the assessment and collection of sums of money from parents for the support of their children. That parents should support their children is not a new concept, but before the 1991 Act the system was administered largely through the courts. When the new system was introduced, it was amid great political rhetoric about parents taking responsibility for their children, but there is considerable doubt that it has improved the lot of children, their families or, indeed, that there has been any saving to the public purse.[54]

---

53 For this purpose, the family is usually defined in terms of the nuclear family or family members who live together and heterosexual cohabitants are treated in the same way as married couples.

54 One of the goals of the 1991 Act was to reduce the amount of legal aid devoted to pursuing aliment through the courts and to reduce the amount of state benefits paid to a parent who was caring for the child by ensuring that the other parent paid his or her share. Undoubtedly, legal aid for actions of aliment has been reduced. However, in order to implement the new system, the Child Support Agency, with a substantial staff, was created and appeals from the decisions of this body go to the Child Support Appeal Tribunal and, thereafter, to the Child Support Commissioners and, occasionally, the courts. While legal aid is not available to provide an individual with legal representation at the Tribunal or

Child protection

1.36 Undoubtedly the state plays a major role in protecting children and, indeed, the UK, being a party to various international instruments which require the state to fulfil this responsibility, has accepted the obligation to do so.[55] Few, if any, would doubt that this is a legitimate function of government, but precisely what the state should involve itself in is sometimes a matter of contention. As we shall see in chapters 3 and 7, there are a host of ways in which the state attempts to protect children. In the international arena, it helps to formulate standards and subscribes to agreements. In the domestic setting, it: provides services for children and their families; legislates on matters affecting children; provides the machinery to monitor and ensure compliance with standards set, for services for children; establishes the machinery for investigation of alleged child abuse and neglect and, where necessary, for the removal of children from their homes, either temporarily or permanently; and, ultimately, looks after children where there is no other person capable of, or suited to, doing so. The very vast array of legislation aimed at child protection comprises a substantial portion of this book. At this stage, suffice it to say that it seeks to protect children: by denying them access to various commodities or activities deemed inappropriate for or dangerous to children; by requiring children to participate in, for example, education; by defining certain conduct by children or, more particularly, by adults, as unacceptable and, as such, grounds for intervention through the civil or the criminal law, or both; and by setting minimum standards of care which are deemed acceptable. What becomes apparent is that much of this cannot be value-free. What is 'acceptable' in terms of standards of care and what is good for children as opposed to harmful are not matters of universally-accepted truth. As we shall see, this poses one of the most challenging problems for the state in balancing the protection of children against respect for their freedom and rights and the rights of their families.

Protecting adults

1.37 We have touched upon the fact that the state provides assistance to and services for adults and particularly for adults who have special needs. That this is a legitimate state function cannot be doubted if one accepts that it is a function of any society to protect its weakest members. That the individual's protection should be provided for in a manner consistent with full regard for the liberty and rights of the recipient is axiomatic. Of course, how this is accommodated in practice can be more problematic. But what of the adult individual who is healthy and competent? Does the state have

---

before the Commissioners, preliminary advice can be sought under the legal advice and assistance scheme and, in any event, these bodies cost money to run. The whole system for child support is about to be overhauled. On child support, see chapter 6, paras 37–59.

55 For example, by signing and ratifying the UN Convention on the Rights of the Child, the UK agreed to be bound by its provisions insofar as ratification was not subject to reservations. Similarly, the European Convention on Human Rights requires the state to protect certain rights in respect of adults and children. For an example of the UK's failure to live up to its obligations, see the discussion of 'reasonable chastisement', in chapter 6, para 19.

any obligation or, indeed, any right, to protect him or her either from his or her own actions or from the actions of others? A libertarian would probably answer with a resounding negative. That is not the approach taken by the state in Scotland today. Sometimes, the state is satisfied by giving public warnings about particular dangers and, in addition, it may try to make something less attractive by taxing it heavily. Cigarettes are an obvious example here, where the state finds itself in the convenient position of being able to claim a clear conscience on the basis that it warns of the dangers and discourages consumption by substantial taxes, at the same time as collecting these very taxes and using them to balance the budget. In addition, adults are denied access to all sorts of substances and activities deemed harmful to the individual. Not only is it illegal to possess marijuana, but, at the time of writing, selling beef on the bone attracts the full force of criminal sanctions.[56] It matters not that you are informed fully about the risks of consuming a particular commodity; the state will take it upon itself, on occasions, to decide that you should not be permitted to run that risk.

1.38 One justification for intervention in the lives of adults is that none of us lives in isolation and our conduct has repercussions for the rest of society. Thus, where we choose to harm our health, we become a burden to the health service, at a cost to the public purse. Even if our conduct does not create a direct cost, state intervention can sometimes be justified on the basis of the general moral climate and standards of behaviour. In the context of the family, state intervention takes the form of determining which adult individuals should be permitted to form relationships and what conduct is deemed unacceptable within relationships. Thus, for example, the law on incest and the prohibited degrees for marriage determine that certain relationships are unacceptable. Other conduct may result in divorce or exclusion from the family home. In addition, the law acknowledges that personal relationships may provide scope for the rules to apply differently. Thus, while spouses are free to contract with each other, the law is more prepared to accept that undue influence may have been brought to bear on one of the parties by the other. Again, these matters are explored at length in later chapters.

Regulation, licensing and scrutiny of services

1.39 As we have seen, the state, often through the medium of the local authority, provides a host of services for children and families. In addition, services are provided by other agencies, commercial organisations and private companies and sometimes the local authority sub-contracts for the provision of services. Where it provides the service itself, the local authority or other state organ can monitor the quality of service and the suitability and qualifications of staff. Of course, no such system is fail-safe.[57] None the less,

---

56 In *MacNeill (PF for Selkirk)* v *Sutherland* 1998 SCCR 474, the respondent, a hotelier, was charged with contravention of the Beef Bones Regulations 1997, made under the Food Safety Act 1990, after a much-publicised dinner at his hotel where beef on the bone was served. Initially, the sheriff dismissed the complaint but the High Court allowed the appeal by the Crown.

57 See for example, the instances and allegations of children and older people being abused by staff in institutions, discussed in chapters 7 and 15, paras 29 and 29–34, respectively.

at least where the state is running the facility, it has some control over how it operates. Concern that services provided outside the state system might be inadequate, whether for financial, organisational, or other reasons, has led to widespread regulation of such services. The state, again often through the local authority, sets standards, approves, registers and monitors a variety of such services including child-minding, day care for children, adult day centres and adult residential facilities. In addition, legislation provides for special vetting of individuals who will be in charge of children.

Providing for the resolution and adjudication of disputes

1.40 A fundamental function of the state in any orderly society is ensuring that disputes are resolved and that a system for fair and impartial adjudication is available to all. In Scotland, a sophisticated system of tribunals and courts exist for that purpose and they are often called upon to resolve issues of child and family law. Whether they are freely open to all is subject to question, since they are certainly not open free to all. Of course, any adult can represent himself or herself in court but, to make full use of the legal system, the individual must have both knowledge of the law and proficiency in its use. Many individuals cannot get access to legal advice because they cannot afford to pay for it themselves and they are not eligible for legal aid. Thus, the value of the courts and, to a lesser extent, tribunals, is diminished for them. In the context of child and family law particularly, it is worth remembering that courts and tribunals are not the only way in which disputes can be resolved. Increasingly, the cost, delay and acrimony associated with litigation is causing individuals and the state to look at other approaches and alternative dispute resolution, or ADR, as it is known, employs a number of techniques. ADR is being used increasingly in the resolution of family disputes and this chapter concludes with an examination of the various techniques and services that are available.

Negotiating, concluding and observing international obligations

1.41 Since the state, rather than the individual, is the major player in the international arena, it is not surprising that a legitimate role for the state is the fulfilment of our international obligations, not only abroad but also at home. A host of international agreements deal with child and family law issues and they will be referred to throughout the following chapters. Perhaps one of the best known is the United Nations Convention on the Rights of the Child, not least because of the speed with which it was ratified by an unprecedented number of countries. The European Convention on Human Rights and Fundamental Freedoms,[58] adopted in the aftermath of

58 Despite its title, the European Convention is an international instrument and not the product of European Law. Cases arising under the Convention are heard by a specially constituted court, the European Court of Human Rights, which sits in Strasbourg. European Law is the product of the European Community/Union and cases arising under it are heard either in domestic courts or in the European Court of Justice, which sits in Luxemburg. The issue is further complicated by the fact that some provisions of the European Convention on Human Rights have been adopted into European Law, a complication which will shortly become moot.

the Second World War and now enacted into domestic legislation,[59] has had a very considerable impact on child and family law in the UK already, an impact which can only increase in the future. The work of the Council of Europe and the European Union generally has also contributed to both the debates on and the substance of child and family law in Scotland. Another major contribution to domestic child and family law has come from the Hague Conference on Private International Law, a standing body which recognises the increased international mobility of individuals and seeks to produce international instruments which address conflict of law issues and to facilitate recognition of rights held in one country in the courts of others.[60] That child and family law receives so much attention in the international arena is hardly surprising. Personal relationships and the problems we encounter are fairly universal human experiences. We can learn from the way these issues are addressed in other jurisdictions and sharing our solutions with the world may save much re-invention of wheels. The contribution to domestic law of discussions on the Internet, the many international conferences on child and family law and, in particular, the work of the International Society of Family Law, is thus of considerable, if less quantifiable, importance.

Alternative Dispute Resolution

1.42 Litigation is one method of resolving disputes and, in the public perception, it is often viewed as the main or, sometimes, the only, way lawyers and the legal system can be of service. Any such perception is – and always was – inaccurate. Lawyers have a long history of negotiating settlements on behalf of clients and of using arbitration as alternatives to the court process. However, there is no doubt that, since the 1970s, increasing attention has been devoted to finding ways to resolve disputes other than through litigation, and alternative dispute resolution (ADR) has become an area of study in its own right.[61] There are a number of reasons for this shift of emphasis and, clearly, cost has been a factor. Concern over the increasing cost of litigation, both to individual litigants and to the public purse, has led to attempts to find a less expensive method of dispute resolution. Increasing pressure on court time, and the resulting delay, has fuelled the search. However, the interest in ADR should not be seen as solely a reaction to other problems. The idea of individuals taking charge

59 Human Rights Act 1998. The fact that the UK has ratified an international instrument does not mean that individuals can found upon its terms in a domestic court if they are inconsistent with a clear provision of domestic law. If domestic law is ambiguous on the issue, it is generally presumed that it is in line with our international obligations – *Kaur* v *Lord Advocate* 1980 SC 319; *Salomon* v *Commissioners of Customs and Excise* [1967] 2 QB 116; *IRC* v *Collco Dealings Ltd* [1962] AC 1. The value of enacting international obligations in domestic legislation is that it enables UK nationals to use the provisions directly in domestic courts. See K. Campbell, 'Human Rights Brought Home' 1998 SLT (News) 269.

60 For a discussion of the development of the Hague Conference, see, A. Dyer, 'The Internationalization of Family Law' 30 UC Davis L Rev 625 (1997).

61 On ADR generally, see E. Brunet and C. B. Craver, *Alternative Dispute Resolution: The Advocate's Perspective* (Michie, 1997); E. W. Trachete-Huber and S. K. Huber, *Mediation and Negotiation: Reaching Agreement in Law and Business* (Anderson Publishing Co, 1998).

of the resolution of their own disputes has the attraction of empowering those individuals at a time when their lives often appear chaotic. It reinforces personal responsibility. 'Bargaining in the shadow of the law',[62] a phrase associated with the birth of the ADR movement, sums up what is going on very well. The legal system does not bow out of disputes. Substantive law remains in place to regulate rights and responsibilities and it is in the context of knowing what the law provides for that the dispute is resolved. What ADR provides is a different mechanism, or route, to the resolution of disputes. It is worth noting, however, that, once the parties have reached a resolution of the dispute through ADR, they may be precluded from using the more traditional legal method of litigation as freely as they might have done before.[63] For this reason, various methods of ADR are sometimes described as 'private ordering'.[64]

1.43 There are a variety of methods of ADR and, while some have overlapping characteristics, it would be a mistake to see ADR as a monolithic entity.[65] In arbitration, a neutral third party decides the matters in dispute and it is similar to litigation insofar as a third party imposes a solution on the disputants. It is distinct from litigation in being private, rather than public, and may have cost and time advantages. In negotiation, the parties or, more often, their solicitors, arrive at an agreed solution by the process of bargaining. Like arbitration, there is the advantage of privacy and there may be savings in terms of time and cost. However, what distinguishes negotiation from litigation and arbitration is the fact that the parties retain control over the outcome. It is this feature which negotiation shares with mediation and the hope is that where the parties retain autonomy, they will be more committed to making the agreed solution work. ADR is not confined to the resolution of family disputes. Nor are all the methods of ADR used in such disputes. Arbitration, for example, appears not to have been adopted.

1.44 Early in the life of distinctly-identified ADR, it became apparent that it has particular application in the context of disputes involving the personal relationships of family members.[66] It was appreciated that strict

---

62 The phrase is taken from the title of what has come to be regarded as one of the seminal articles on ADR, at least in the context of family disputes – R. H. Mnookin and L. Kornhauser, 'Bargaining in the Shadow of the Law' 88 Yale LJ 950 (1979).

63 This theme is explored later, in the context of particular kinds of agreements. However, it is worth noting that where a married couple concluded an ante-nuptial marriage agreement, the court's power to reopen the agreement is limited. On the other hand, regardless of what parents agree in respect of future arrangement for their children, the court always has the power to look at the case afresh.

64 Mnookin and Kornhauser, above at p 950, attribute to Professor L. Fuller the definition of 'private ordering' as '"law" that the parties bring into existence by agreement'. See L. L. Fuller, 'Mediation: Its Forms and Functions' 44 S Cal L Rev 305 (1970).

65 J. H. Folberg, 'Divorce Mediation – A Workable Alternative' in H. A. Davidson and L. E. Ray (eds), *Alternative Means of Family Dispute Resolution* (American Bar Association, 1982).

66 H. A. Davidson and L. E. Ray (eds), *Alternative Means of Family Dispute Resolution* (American Bar Association, 1982). In 1982, the International Society on Family Law devoted its triennial conference to the issue of family dispute resolution. For a selection of the papers presented there, see J. M. Eekelaar and S. N. Katz, *The Resolution of Family Conflict* (Butterworths, 1984). For a more recent update, see 'Roundtable: Opportunities for and Limitations of Private Ordering in Family Law' 73 Ind L J 535 (1998), which

adherence to an adversarial system may not be the best way to resolve matters, particularly if the parties are to be expected to co-operate in the future over such issues as arrangements for the children. In the emotionally-charged atmosphere of personal relationships, it may be that the adversarial system exacerbates conflict. In addition, a formal and public setting may not be the preferred arena for many of the parties involved. If a way could be found to resolve family disputes by building in an element of voluntarism, it was believed that the parties might be more committed to making the arrangement work because it was of their own making. It was in this context that mediation emerged as a favoured model of ADR in child and family disputes.[67]

Mediation

1.45 In the field of family law, mediation began to have a significant impact in Scotland in the 1980s and the Scottish Family Conciliation Service was established in 1987. Now renamed Family Mediation Scotland,[68] it is the umbrella organisation for the 12 mediation groups operating around the country. The service offered is aimed primarily at helping couples and families[69] to find a solution over the future arrangements for children which is acceptable to everyone involved, including the children. This service is free of charge although, given the constant financial pressure under which the local organisations operate, donations are welcome. Some local mediation services also offer 'all issues' mediation, dealing with property and other disputed matters, but only in cases where there are children. There is a charge for this service and mediators offering it receive additional training. Referrals to the organisation's services exceeded 5,000 in the year 1997–98 and, while about a third of the cases were self-referrals, other agencies, solicitors and the courts all refer significant numbers of cases to the various local Family Mediation groups.[70]

1.46 In addition, and for a long time, many solicitors had been committed to trying to resolve matrimonial disputes in as non-adversarial a way as possible. Indeed, the line between negotiation between two solicitors on behalf of their clients and those same solicitors acting as quasi-mediators

records a roundtable discussion between a number of leading academics in the field. That volume contains other relevant articles which were presented at the Symposium.

67 H. J. Folberg and A. Taylor, *Mediation: A Comprehensive Guide to Resolving Disputes without Litigation* (Jossey-Bass, 1984); H. H. Irving and M. Benjamin, *Family Mediation: Contemporary Issues* (Sage Publications, 1995); L. Parkinson, *Conciliation in Separation and Divorce* (1986); E. W. Trachete-Huber and S. K. Huber, n 61 above, chapter 8.

68 There was a fear that the use of the word 'conciliation' led to confusion with the concept of 'reconciliation'. 'Mediation' was thought to convey more clearly that the goal was to help the parties to resolve outstanding disputes over arrangements for the future rather than to attempt reconciliation.

69 Mediation services do not confine themselves to disputes between the parents of a child and will assist in cases involving other individuals: for example, disputes between parents and grandparents over contact.

70 Of the 5,328 referrals in 1997–98, some 34% were self-referrals, with 3% coming from other agencies, 7% from solicitors and 2.5% from the courts – Family Mediation Scotland: Eleventh Annual Report 1997–98 (Family Mediation Scotland, 1998). The relatively low referral rate from solicitors may be explained by their use of solicitors affiliated to CALM as well as the services of Family Mediation.

has always been blurred. It was not surprising when, in 1994, Comprehensive Accredited Lawyer Mediators (CALM) was launched to bring together solicitors who were accredited by the Law Society of Scotland as family mediators.[71] Members of CALM are happy to take referrals from other solicitors or the parties themselves, and deal with the whole range of matters which can arise in matrimonial breakdown. Parties are encouraged to have their own solicitors and the mediators charge for the service although, since 1995, legal aid has been available to meet the cost if the parties are eligible for it.

1.47 In the early days of mediation it is probably fair to say that there was a degree of wariness or even suspicion, particularly from some solicitors. Cynics suggested that solicitors simply feared the loss of lucrative business, but that would be to misrepresent the genuine and deep-seated concerns surrounding the whole process of mediation. At a general level, concern was directed at such matters as: the training of mediators; the force or, more particularly, the lack of force attached to their codes of practice; a perception that non-lawyers might have problems with the concept of confidentiality; the possibility that the mediator might have his or her own agenda and would not, therefore, be truly neutral; and the fact that, by offering an alternative, mediation detracts from the need to reform the existing court structure as it applies generally.[72] As far as professional competence is concerned, it should be noted that Family Mediation Scotland is committed to rigorous training of its mediators and sets great store by compliance with its Code of Practice. Similarly, the Law Society of Scotland will only accredit lawyer-mediators who have been trained for the job. The issue of confidentiality and mediation was examined by the Scottish Law Commission[73] and has resulted in the Civil Evidence (Family Mediation) (Scotland) Act 1995.[74] Similar efforts have been made in other jurisdictions to ensure appropriate professional standards are in place for mediators.[75] Two further matters require special mention.

1.48 First is the concern over the issue of power imbalance in the mediation process. Where the parties start from a position of inequality, is it the mediator's role to attempt to redress the balance and, if so, can a mediator ever be fully effective in achieving an equitable balance? The

71 A. H. Dick and M. Jeffrey, 'Lawyer Mediator: Interface or Interloper' 1995 SLT (News) 305.
72 See F. E. Raitt, 'Mediation as a Form of Alternative Dispute Resolution' (1995) 40 JLSS 182 and A. Oswald, 'Mediation in Family Disputes' (1996) 41 JLSS 115. For a US perspective, see C. A. McEwan, N. H. Rogers and R. J. Maiman, 'Bringing in the Lawyers: Challenging the Dominant Approaches to Ensuring Fairness in Divorce Mediation' 79 Minn L Rev 1317 (1995).
73 The Commission's Discussion Paper No 92 on Confidentiality in Family Mediation, published in 1991, was followed by the Report on Evidence: Protection of Family Mediation (Scot Law Com No 136, 1992).
74 The Act makes evidence of what happened during mediation inadmissible in certain civil proceedings.
75 See for example: *Divorce and Family Mediation: Standard of Practice* (American Bar Association, 1986) (excerpt in Brunet and Craver, n 61 above, at pp 273–276); T. Fisher, 'Training for Family Mediators' [1995] Fam Law 570.

debate here has, perhaps inevitably, been viewed from a feminist perspective. Initially, mediation found favour with some feminist commentators as an alternative to what was seen as an essentially patriarchal court system which rendered women powerless. Indeed, one commentator argued that mediation expressed her perception of the feminist approach to problem-solving in stressing co-operation, negotiation and participation.[76] Fairly quickly, however, the feminist tide turned against mediation[77] and, on balance, feminists have remained suspicious of, if not hostile to, it.[78] Particular concern centres on any use of mediation in cases where there has been a history of domestic violence where mediation can be yet another tool in the aggressor's harassment of the victim.[79] Certainly, in Scotland, it is acknowledged that there are cases where mediation is wholly inappropriate and the early screening process operated by Family Mediation should protect individuals from exposure to risk. There are signs in more recent literature that attempts are being made to address the concerns of the feminist critics.[80]

1.49 The second point deserving of special mention is the position of children in the mediation process. As we shall see, when an important decision is being taken about a child, the decision-maker is required to take account of any views the child concerned wishes to express.[81] Concern has been expressed in other jurisdictions that, where the child's future is resolved in mediation, he or she will not have been given adequate opportunity to have an input into the arrangements agreed.[82] As far as Scotland is concerned, the responsibility to take the child's views into

---

76 J. Rifkin, 'Mediation from a feminist perspective: Promise and problems' 2 Law and Inequality 21 (1984).

77 A. Bottomley, 'What is happening to Family Law? A Feminist Critique of Conciliation' in J. Brophy and C. Smart, *Women-in-law: Explorations in law, family and sexuality* (Routledge, 1985); M. L. Leitch, 'The Politics of Compromise: A Feminist Perspective on Mediation' 14 Mediation Quarterly 163 (1986); L. Woods, 'Mediation: A Backlash to Women's Progress on Family Law Issues' 19 Clearinghouse Review 431 (1985).

78 T. Grillo, 'The Mediation Alternative: Process Dangers for Women' 100 Yale LJ 1545 (1991); D. Majury, 'Unconscionability in an Equality Context' (1991) 7 Fam L Q 123.

79 R. Busch and N. Robertson, 'Innovative Approaches to Child Custody and Domestic Violence in New Zealand: the Effects of Law Reform on the Discourses of Battering' in P. Jaffe (ed), *Children Exposed to Domestic Violence* (Sage, 1998); B. J. Hart, 'Gentle Jeopardy: The Further Endangerment of Battered Women and Children in Custody Mediation' 7 Mediation Quarterly 317 (1990); M. Hester and L. Radford, *Domestic violence in child contact arrangements in England and Denmark* (The Policy Press, 1996); L. Lehrman, 'Mediation of Wife Abuse Cases: the Adverse Impact of Informal Dispute Resolution on Women' 7 Harvard Women's Law Journal 57.

80 'Towards a Feminist-Informed Model of Therapeutic Family Mediation' in Irving and Benjamin, n 67 above.

81 Section 6 of the Children (Scotland) Act 1995 places the obligation on a person exercising parental responsibilities or rights and s 11(7) places a similar obligation on the court. The right of the child to have his or her views taken into account is discussed fully in chapter 3.

82 J. Fortin, *Children's Rights and the Developing Law* (Butterworths, 1998) at pp 162–167. It should be noted that the Children Act 1989, governing the position in England and Wales has no equivalent of s 6 of the 1995 Act. See also, C. Bruch, 'And how are the children? The effects of ideology and mediation on child custody and children's well-being in the United States' (1995) Int J L and Fam 106.

account lies first with the parents and the fact that they are using mediation in no way diminishes that responsibility. However, given the general concern over parental compliance with the obligation, it may be that mediators should take a more active role in ensuring that the child has been given the opportunity to express his or her views.[83] Indeed, the whole issue of children and their part in the decision-making process about future arrangements for them is part of a much larger debate. Essentially, this centres on giving children a voice at the same time as ensuring that they are not burdened with inappropriate responsibility and guilt.

1.50 Despite these concerns, mediation has much to offer in appropriate cases and, indeed, that may be the point. It is the finding of the appropriate forum for a particular dispute that remains important. It is clear that mediation, in general, is gaining acceptance in Scotland, with family mediation being the most prevalent.[84] Members of the legal profession appear to have overcome initial reservations and are now more willing to embrace mediation either in making referrals or as providers.[85] Clear support for mediation has been signalled from the bench.[86] As we shall see, where parental responsibilities and rights are in dispute in a divorce action, the court may refer the dispute on that point to a mediator accredited to a specified family mediation organisation at any stage.[87] Thus, it appears, mediation now forms an integral part of the dispute resolution landscape in Scotland in certain kinds of child and family law matters. How much further we wish to go with mediation remains to be seen. Other jurisdictions have certainly given mediation a more central place in the divorce process.[88] Some have even made it mandatory for divorcing couples to attend at least a few sessions.[89] Whether mediation is appropriate in child protection cases[90] raises further questions. What is clear is that, whatever we do, it must be as a result of considered reflection and a clear appreciation of what will work in Scotland.

---

83 *Giving Children a Voice in Family Mediation* (National Family Mediation and the Gulbenkian Foundation, 1994).

84 *Alternative Dispute Resolution in Scotland* (CRU, 1996).

85 B. Clark and R. Mays, 'The Legal Profession and ADR' 1996 JR 389.

86 See for example, *Harris* v *Martin* (IH) 1995 SCLR (Notes) 580, at p 584, where Lord President Hope made the following observation in a dispute between unmarried parents over access, as it then was – 'There may well be a role for an experienced mediator to play in reassuring the defender and helping her to address the practical arrangements which hitherto she has refused to face up to.'

87 Rules of the Court of Session 1994 (RSC), r 49.23; Ordinary Cause Rules 1993 (OCR), r 33.22. See *Harris* v *Martin*, above; *Harvey* v *Duff* 1995 GWD 5–229; *Patterson* v *Patterson* (Sh Ct) 1994 SCLR (Notes) 166.

88 It is anticipated that the Family Law Act 1996 will have this effect in England and Wales. See, Looking to the Future: Mediation and the Grounds for Divorce – the Government's Proposals, Cm 2799 (1995). For a discussion of some of the concerns surrounding the way this has been done and the dangers of inadequate funding, see S. M. Cretney, 'Family Law – A Bit of a Racket?' (The Joseph Jackson Memorial Lecture) (1996) NLJ 91.

89 For example, in California, mediation is mandatory in disputes over child custody and visitation cases – Cal Civ Code, s 4607. It might be argued, however, that 'mandatory mediation' is an oxymoron.

90 A. E. Barsky, 'Mediation in Child Protection Cases' in Irving and Benjamin, n 61 above.

CHAPTER 2

NATURAL LEGAL PERSONALITY

2.1 The Scottish legal system recognises two kinds of legal personality, natural personality and juristic personality.[1] Natural personality is that which attaches to individual human beings[2] and this chapter will examine when natural legal personality begins and ends and some of the significant attributes of natural legal persons. Juristic personality is that which attaches to those entities which owe their existence to the legal system and obvious examples are charities, trades unions and limited companies. The law governing these juristic legal persons is dealt with extensively elsewhere and will not be covered here.

2.2 It is stating the obvious to note that people are the building blocks of families, but that fact means that it is essential to be aware of the attributes of an individual to which the legal system attaches importance and for what purposes. The point at which the law recognises legal personality as beginning and ending can matter for decisions others may make (eg the withdrawal of medical treatment). A person's age may be of no importance in some contexts (eg a child's legal rights in succession), but central to others (eg the child's right to consent to or veto his or her own adoption). A person's gender may be wholly irrelevant for some purposes (eg the right to vote), but crucial for others (eg who may marry whom).

WHEN DOES LEGAL PERSONALITY BEGIN?

2.3 When life begins, is a matter which has long exercised philosophers,

---

1 T. B. Smith, *A Short Commentary on the Law of Scotland* (W. Green, 1962) at p 245.
2 Scots law has long recognised legal personality as attaching to all human beings and, as early as 1778, explicitly rejected slavery and the attendant notion of one person being the property of another person – *Knight* v *Wedderburn* (1778) Mor 14545. Lest we be tempted to become too complacent about our civilised past, it is worth remembering the conditions of servitude imposed on colliers and salters, and through the process of 'arling', on their children, in the 17th and early 18th centuries – see T. C. Smout, *A History of the Scottish People 1560–1830* (Fontana Press, 1969), pp 168–170. While legislation seeks to protect animals and provision can be made for them through trusts and wills, they are regarded by the legal system as property and do not have legal personality. Thus, for example, they cannot own property. None the less, 'animal rights' is a popular topic. See for example, G. L. Francione, *Animals, Property and the Law* (Temple U Press, 1995); G. L. Francione, *Rain Without Thunder: The Ideology of the Animal Rights Movement* (Temple U Press, 1996; R. Gardner (ed), *Animal Rights: The Changing Debate* (New York U Press, 1996); P. Singer, *Animal Liberation* (2nd edn, Avon Books, 1990); P. Singer and T. Regan (eds), *Animal Rights and Human Obligations* (Prentice Hall, 1989); A. Watson, 'Rights of Slaves and Other Owned-Animals' 3 Animal Law 1 (1997).

theologians and the medical profession, and is not one which lawyers can determine any more definitively than anyone else. Instead, the legal system defines when it will accept legal personality as beginning. The general rule is very simple: legal personality begins when a person is born alive.[3] Once a person has been born alive, he or she has legal personality until death, however short the interval between birth and death is. Delivery of a stillborn foetus is not a live birth and the foetus never acquires legal personality.[4]

2.4 As with most, apparently straightforward, legal principles, this proved too simplistic an approach to accommodate various practical problems which emerged, and it requires some qualification. Thus, under the *nasciturus* principle,[5] where a child is born alive, legal personality can be backdated to a time prior to the child's birth, if this will benefit the child. In addition, other aspects of the law, discussed below, have a bearing on any coherent notion of when legal personality begins.

The *nasciturus* principle

2.5 The *nasciturus* principle has its origins in Roman law[6] and has long been accepted in Scotland. As often happens, the principle has developed over time and should not be restricted to its original, narrow ambit.[7] It allows a child who is born alive to acquire rights arising out of events which occurred prior to the child's birth. Essentially, it allows a backdating of legal personality where this will be of benefit to the child. A prerequisite for the principle to apply is that the child should live, albeit the duration of that life is short. Initially, it was thought that the backdating covered only the time between conception and birth, but there is no reason why the period prior to conception should be excluded. Thus, a child might be able to recover damages for injuries which resulted from negligent pre-conception screening of a parent or for injuries suffered due to a parent's exposure to hazardous chemicals. However, it should be noted that cases in respect of pre-conception harm will have a much-reduced prospect of success if they come within the ambit of wrongful life actions.[8] Since the principle is premised on the idea of achieving justice for the child, it was thought to be well established that it would only apply where its application would benefit the child, rather than some other person.[9]

---

3 Smith, n 1 above.
4 A 'stillborn child' is defined as one which has never breathed or shown signs of life after being expelled from its mother and a separate register is kept of such births – Registration of Births, Deaths and Marriages (Scotland) Act 1965, ss 21 and 56(1). The terminology used here is unfortunate since the use of the word 'child' denotes a living person, that is, the very being which does not result from a stillbirth.
5 The Latin maxim encapsulating this principle is *nasciturus pro iam habetur quotiens de eius commoda agitur.*
6 *Digest,* I, v, 7 and 26.
7 Cf A. Rodger, 'Report of the Scottish Law Commission on Antenatal Injury' 1974 JR 83.
8 See paras 2.36–2.38, below.
9 *Elliot* v *Joicey* 1935 SC (HL) 57, per Lord Macmillan, at p 71. It is interesting to note that it was not until this case reached the House of Lords that it was realised that Scots, rather than English, law was the proper law to apply.

2.6 However, in *Hamilton* v *Fife Health Board*,[10] the parents of a child who died at three days old as a result of negligent delivery procedures, were successful in recovering damages under the Damages (Scotland) Act 1976 ('the 1976 Act'), which allows relatives of a person who dies as a result of his or her injuries the right to recover from the person responsible for the injuries. The hospital board argued that the injury was sustained prior to birth and was, therefore, not an injury to a 'person' resulting in death, for which relatives could recover. At first instance,[11] this argument was accepted and the court further took the view that, since there was no possible benefit to the deceased child, the *nasciturus* principle could not apply. On appeal, while the decision was reversed by the Inner House, the court proceeded on the basis that the child's right to raise an action had accrued when the child was born alive and that the parents had a right to recover under the 1976 Act as relatives of such a person.[12] In taking the view that it was not necessary to apply the *nasciturus* principle in order to achieve this result, the court was following an earlier Outer House[13] decision where recovery was allowed in similar circumstances without resort to the *nasciturus* principle.

2.7 The *nasciturus* principle has been applied to allow a posthumous child to succeed to the father's estate.[14] While there is no reported case on the point, it could apply equally to the child's right to succeed to the mother's estate where, for example, she had died prior to the child's birth and her body had been maintained on a 'life support' machine. Statute provides expressly that a child, born as a result of either the implantation of a stored embryo or the use of stored sperm after the genetic father's death, has no succession rights in the father's estate.[15] No similar provision is required in respect of genetic mothers, since the woman who carries the child (and no other woman) is always treated in law as the child's mother.[16] It has long been accepted that posthumous children can recover damages under the *nasciturus* principle for the death of a parent.[17]

The child and ante-natal injury

2.8 The Scottish Law Commission was sufficiently confident that Scots law would allow the child to recover in delict from a third party in respect of his or her own ante-natal injury, that it concluded legislation was

10 1993 SLT 624.
11 1992 SLT 1026.
12 Section 1(1).
13 *McWilliams* v *Lord Advocate* 1992 SLT 1045.
14 *Jervey* v *Watt* (1762) Mor 8170 (posthumous child entitled to *legitim*); *Hardman* v *Guthrie* (1826) 6 S 920 (posthumous child could benefit from a legacy in favour of 'children'); *Findlay's Trustees* v *Findlay* (1886) 14 R 167 (posthumous child can benefit from the *condictio si testator sine liberis decesserit*).
15 Human Fertilisation and Embryology Act 1990, s 28(6)(b).
16 Human Fertilisation and Embryology Act 1990, s 27(1).
17 See, for example, *Leadbetter* v *National Coal Board* 1952 SLT 179.

unnecessary.[18] Various theories can be advanced in support of recovery, including, application of the *nasciturus* principle; viewing of the injury as crystallising (taking effect) at the moment of birth;[19] and simple public policy. Despite some early resistance,[20] many other jurisdictions have long permitted recovery for ante-natal injury.[21]

2.9 Of course, a pregnant woman is in a unique position in relation to the foetus she is carrying. The question of whether a mother would be liable in delict to the child for injury caused by her deliberate or negligent conduct during pregnancy has never been litigated in Scotland.[22] The Scottish Law Commission was in no doubt that such recovery was competent[23] and, in the light of the law of delict[24] and subsequent recognition of the ante-natal environment in other contexts,[25] it is difficult to reach any other conclusion. If a third party owes a duty of care to the foetus, that duty crystallising into a right of action when a child is born alive, there is no reason in law why the pregnant woman, who is in the closest proximity to the foetus, should not owe the same duty of care and bear the same attendant liability for breach of that duty. The fiction that the pregnant woman and the foetus are one loses all credibility once third party liability is accepted.

2.10 The only real case against maternal liability for ante-natal injury lies in public policy. It has been variously argued that to accept such liability would create friction between the child and the mother, who might well be caring for the (sometimes disabled) child; that no real benefit would accrue to the child, since any damages would come from the family coffers; that liability would place unreasonable restrictions on the freedom of action of pregnant women; and that it gives foetal rights priority over the rights of women. It has been suggested that some women might seek abortions in order to avoid liability, although there is no evidence to support such a notion. Furthermore, there is the difficulty of defining exactly what kind of conduct by the pregnant woman would attract liability. Not only would it have to be shown that there was a causal link between the pregnant woman's action and the injury, it would have to be established that she

18 Report on Liability for Antenatal Injury (Scot Law Com No 30, 1973), Cmnd 5371, paras. 8–13. This contrasts with the position in England and Wales, where the Law Commission concluded that the common law was sufficiently uncertain to warrant legislation – Report on Injuries to Unborn Children (Law Com No 60, 1974), paras 3 and 8. The Congenital Disabilities (Civil Liability) Act 1976 now governs the situation there.
19 *Watson* v *Fram Reinforced Concrete Co (Scotland) Ltd and Winget Ltd* 1960 SC (HL) 92.
20 *Walker* v *Great Northern Railway Company of Ireland* (1891) 28 IrLR 69; *Deitrich* v *Inhabitants of Northampton* 138 Mass 14 (1884).
21 *Montreal Tramways* v *Leveille* (1933) 4 DLR 337; *Duval* v *Seguin* (1972) 26 DLR 3d 418; *Watt* v *Rama* 1972 VR 353; *Bonbrest* v *Kotz* 65 Fed Supp 138 (1946); *Smith* v *Brennan* 157 A 2d 497 (NJ, 1960).
22 J. K. Mason, *Medico-Legal Aspects of Reproduction and Parenthood* (2nd edn, Dartmouth, 1998) (hereinafter 'Mason'), at pp 172–178.
23 Report on Liability for Antenatal Injury, above, para 25. While the Commission felt that recovery was competent on general delictual principles, it reserved its position on the desirability of such actions.
24 A child can sue a parent in delict – see for example, *Young* v *Rankin* 1934 SC 499.
25 See paras 2.12–2.17, below.

knew or ought to have known the likely consequences of her action. It seems likely that the consumption of controlled substances or excessive quantities of alcohol would attract liability, but other possibilities include smoking cigarettes, taking prescribed medication, engaging in dangerous sports and, possibly, eating a non-nutritious diet while pregnant. As every new research study on foetal health emerges, the list will grow longer. Of course, it is only worth raising an action against a defender who has the resources to meet any award of damages, either directly or by virtue of being covered by insurance and, thus, many mothers will not qualify as worthwhile defenders. While maternal liability for ante-natal injury has been accepted in other jurisdictions,[26] acceptance is far from universal.[27]

2.11 It is sometimes suggested that maternal liability for ante-natal injury is inconsistent with permitting a woman to terminate a pregnancy. However, liability only becomes an issue if the woman decides to proceed with the pregnancy and subsequently gives birth to a child. Prior to that time, and within the constraints of the conditions under which terminations may be performed lawfully, there is nothing to prevent her from seeking an abortion. To put it another way, her duty of care only arises when she decides to proceed with the pregnancy. Thus, acceptance of maternal liability for ante-natal injury need place no additional restriction on the woman's right to make the choice between continuing the pregnancy or termination.

Regulating the ante-natal environment

2.12 Liability for ante-natal injury raises the related issue of regulating the ante-natal environment.[28] It is stating the obvious, perhaps, to note that there is a societal interest in attempting to provide the optimum environment for the birth of healthy children. While it had to steer the difficult course between protecting the lives and health of children and accommodating the possibility of abortion,[29] the United Nations Convention on

---

26 *Grodin* v *Grodin* 301 NW 869 (1981), where the child successfully sued his mother in respect of damage to his teeth caused by his mother taking tetracyclene while pregnant, the woman having failed to tell her doctor that she might be pregnant when he prescribed the drug; *Lynch* v *Lynch* [1992] 3 Med LR 62 (NSW, Australia), where a child succeeded in her claim against her mother in respect of cerebral palsy contracted *in utero* due to the woman's negligent driving while participating in a cattle muster.

27 Initially, the Law Commission for England and Wales favoured recovery – Injuries to Unborn Children, (Working Paper No 47, 1973), para 27. However, after consultation, it rejected maternal liability, except where the woman was driving a motor vehicle and was, thus, covered by insurance – Report on Injuries to Unborn Children, above, para 63. The Commission's proposals were accepted in the subsequent legislation – Congenital Disabilities (Civil Liability) Act 1976, ss 1(1) and 2. See also, *Stallman* v *Youngquist* 531 NE 2d 355 (Ill, 1985), where the court refused to allow recovery on the basis that to do so would restrict the freedom of pregnant women unduly.

28 E. E. Sutherland, 'Regulating pregnancy: should we and can we?', in E. E. Sutherland and R. A. McCall Smith, *Family Rights: Family Law and Medical Advance* (EUP, 1990).

29 See chapter 3, para 13, below, for a discussion of how the conflict over the issue of abortion was resolved during the negotiation of the Convention.

the Rights of the Child[30] acknowledges this. Of course, yet again, the real challenge lies in achieving an acceptable balance between taking steps to protect the foetus and acknowledging the rights of pregnant women.

2.13 To the extent that potential civil liability may make some pregnant women behave in particular ways, ante-natal conduct is regulated already. In addition, free health education and ante-natal care contribute, in a relatively non-invasive manner, to improving ante-natal care for both the foetus and the pregnant woman. Furthermore, the woman faces the very real prospect that evidence of her conduct (particularly drug abuse) during pregnancy, might result in the removal of her child from her care.[31] Regulation of the ante-natal environment has reached its most extreme position in the USA, where the possibility of 'protective incarceration' of pregnant drug-abusing women,[32] and the threat of criminal liability attaching to the pregnant woman's ante-natal conduct,[33] have become reality.[34]

---

30 Article 24, which addresses child health, acknowledges the importance of the ante-natal environment in making specific mention of taking steps to diminish infant mortality, and providing pre-natal care and preventative health care.

31 *McGregor v L* 1981 SLT 194. A child was removed on a similar basis in England – *Re D (A minor)* v *Berkshire County Council* [1987] 1 All ER 20.

32 In *United States* v *Vaughn* (DC Super Ct Aug 23, 1988, cited by Roberts, below), a woman convicted of forging cheques was sentenced to imprisonment for the duration of her pregnancy. There, the judge expressed the view that he was determined 'to keep her locked up until the baby is born' in order to prevent her having access to drugs. However, in *Cox v Court* 537 NE 2d 721 (Ohio, 1988), the court reversed a juvenile court order placing a pregnant woman in a secure drug facility in order to protect the foetus from the woman's drug abuse and in *TH* v *Department of Health and Rehabilitation Services* 661 So 2d 403 (Fla, 1995), the court concluded that it lacked the authority to order the mother of a cocaine-dependent child to undergo bi-monthly drug-testing. See C. L. Glaze, 'Combatting Prenatal Substance Abuse: The State's Current Approach and the Novel Approach of Court-Ordered Protective Custody of the Fetus' 80 Marq L Rev 793 (1997). For a discussion of a similar case in Manitoba involving the detention and treatment of a pregnant woman who was addicted to glue-sniffing, see R. D. Bell, 'Prenatal Substance Abuse and Judicial Intervention in Pregnancy: Winnipeg Child and Family Services *v* G (DF)' 55 U Toronto Fac L Rev 321 (1997).

33 In *State* v *Johnson* 1991 Fla App LEXIS 3583, a woman addicted to crack cocaine was convicted of two counts of delivering a controlled substance to a minor after two of her children tested positive for cocaine at birth. A number of other prosecutions have proceeded on the basis of criminal statutes aimed at countering child endangerment and have been unsuccessful. See, *Reyes* v *Superior Court of San Bernadino County* 75 Cal App 3d 214 (1977), where the court refused to accept that the word 'child' in the statute included the foetus in the prosecution of a woman who had used heroin during pregnancy and *State* v *Gray* 584 NE 2d 710 (1992), where there was another unsuccessful attempt at prosecution in similar circumstances. However, in *Whitner* v *State* 492 SE 2d 777 (SC, 1997) prosecution for child endangerment was held competent where it was alleged that the mother had ingested cocaine during the last trimester of her pregnancy.

34 For a very full discussion of these developments, see S. L. Best, 'Fetal Equality?: The Equality State's Response to the Challenge of Protecting Unborn Children' 32 Land and Water L Rev 193 (1997); C. Hunt, 'Criminalizing Prenatal Substance Abuse: A Preventive Means of Ensuring the Birth of a Drug-Free Child' 33 Idaho L Rev 451 (1997); A. M. Leonard, 'Fetal Personhood, Legal Substance Abuse and Maternal Prosecutions: Child Protection or "Gestational Gestapo"?' 32 New Eng L Rev 615 (1998); M. D. Mills, 'Fetal Abuse Prosecutions: The Triumph of Reaction over Reason' 1998 DePaul L Rev 989 (1998); D. Roberts, 'Punishing Drug Addicts Who Have Babies: Women of Color, Equality and the Right of Privacy' 104 Harv L Rev 1419 (1991);

Of course, incarcerating pregnant women in the attempt to prevent them having access to drugs presumes that such drugs will not be available in the prison, a proposition which is, at best, questionable. Criminal liability relies on the deterrent effect of the threat of prosecution, as a means of controlling the behaviour of pregnant women. When one considers that the women who have been prosecuted were already breaking the law by taking the drugs in the first place, such a deterrent effect must be questioned.

2.14 A recent decision of the Inner House, where a husband sought to prevent his wife having a termination, not only denies that the foetus is capable of holding rights during the time in the womb and, thus, interdict is not available to protect any 'rights', but also indicates an aversion to control of the ante-natal environment.[35] While the latter comments are *obiter*, they give some indication of current judicial attitudes in Scotland on control of the ante-natal environment and suggest that protective incarceration would be unlikely here. However, we will see that third parties have been prosecuted successfully for conduct during the ante-natal period which resulted in a child's death.[36] A possible extension of this idea to the prosecution of women for their own ante-natal conduct may be only a matter of time.

2.15 A further aspect of regulating the ante-natal environment arises in respect of court-ordered caesarian delivery. As yet, the courts in Scotland have not had the opportunity to consider the matter, but it has arisen in other jurisdictions. In England[37] and in some states in the USA,[38] courts have ordered caesarian deliveries to be carried out in the face of opposition from the pregnant woman. The earlier English cases often involved speedy court decisions[39] although, as Mason has pointed out, haste is sometimes an 'inevitable concomitant' of the medical condition presenting at the time.[40] In any event, the Court of Appeal came to the conclusion eventually that 'while pregnancy increased the personal responsibilities of a woman it did not diminish her entitlement to decide whether or not to undergo medical treatment',[41] always assuming that she was mentally competent.

2.16 Scots law recognises that the consent of a competent and conscious

D. Roberts, *Killing the Black Body: Race, Reproduction and the Meaning of Liberty* (Pantheon, 1997), chapter 4; D. Roberts, *Women, Pregnancy and Substance Abuse* (Center Women's Policy, 1991).

35 *Kelly* v *Kelly* 1997 SLT 896, at p 901I. The case is discussed fully at para 2.25, below.
36 See para 2.21, below.
37 *Re S (Adult: Refusal of Treatment)* [1992] 4 All ER 671; *Norfolk and Norwich Healthcare (NHS) Trust* v *W* [1996] 2 FLR 613; *In re MB (Caesarian Section)* [1997] 2 FCR 541.
38 *Jefferson Griffin Spalding County Hospital Authority* 274 SE 2d 457(Ga, 1981), where ironically, the woman was delivered of a healthy baby by vaginal delivery, the order having been obtained against the pregnant woman's wishes and in the light of medical evidence that there was a 99% chance that the baby would not survive such a delivery. Not all courts are prepared to take this interventionist approach – *Baby Boy Doe* v *Mother Doe* 632 NE 2d 326 (Ill, 1994).
39 The decision in *Re S*, above, was taken in the course of an 18–minute hearing.
40 Mason, n 22 above, at p 155. See, pp 153–157 for a full discussion of the English cases prior to *St George's Healthcare NHS Trust* v *S*, below.
41 *St George's Healthcare NHS Trust* v *S, R* v *Collins and Others, ex parte S* [1998] TLR 299.

adult is a prerequisite to treating that person and that courts will not order a person to undergo a medical procedure if he or she does not wish to do so, regardless of the motive for refusal.[42] For a court to order a woman to undergo a caesarian delivery in the face of her opposition would be a clear example of placing foetal rights above those of the woman and, it is submitted that present indications are that the Scottish courts would not favour such an approach. Would it make any difference if the court was faced with a young, as opposed to an adult, pregnant woman? A young woman below the age of 16 years can consent to such surgery, provided that the attending physician is of the opinion that she understands the nature and possible consequences of the treatment.[43] It is generally accepted in Scotland that this right to consent carries with it the right to refuse and this view is reinforced by the fact that the Children (Scotland) Act 1995 preserves the position of a competent young person's consent as a prerequisite to treatment, even in the face of a court order or the decision of a children's hearing.[44] This being the case, it seems unlikely that the court would compel a competent woman below the age of 16 to undergo a procedure which an adult woman would be entitled to refuse.

2.17 The liability of the father for ante-natal injury is, again, unlitigated. His special relationship with the foetus after conception arises from nothing other than the fact that he may be in proximity to the pregnant woman more often than anyone else. Arguably, his liability is the same as that attaching to any third party. Thus, were it to be established, for example, that secondary smoke was harmful to the foetus, resident potential fathers might be wise to regulate their conduct accordingly. The liability of parents in respect of pre-conception conditions is discussed presently.

Other recognition of the ante-natal period

2.18 As we saw earlier, in *Hamilton*,[45] the courts have concluded that parents can recover damages in respect of ante-natal injury where the child subsequently dies, regardless of the fact that the child lived for only a very short time.[46] Since the successful claim proceeded under the Damages (Scotland) Act 1976, similar claims would be open to other relatives.[47] However, where a stillbirth results from ante-natal injury, since there has never been a living child, no claim under the statute is competent.[48] It is

---

42 *Whitehall v Whitehall* 1958 SC 252.
43 Age of Legal Capacity (Scotland) Act 1991, s 2(4).
44 Section 90. The Scottish legislation is in different terms to that operating in England and Wales and may avoid the position reached there by somewhat convoluted legal reasoning. For a more full discussion, see chapter 3, para 70.
45 *Hamilton v Fife Health Board* 1993 SLT 624, discussed at para 2.6, above.
46 *McWilliams v Lord Advocate* 1992 SLT 1045; *Hamilton v Fife Health Board* 1993 SLT 624.
47 Section 10(2) and Sched 1, para 1, which define 'relative' for the purpose of the Act, and includes: ascendants and descendants, nieces and nephews, and cousins. While it would be competent for a grandparent to raise an action for damages, such claims seem unlikely.
48 The 'parents' would have a claim, at common law, for their own suffering.

entirely understandable that the bereaved relatives in such cases find it difficult to comprehend this fine legal distinction since their sense of loss is no less than that of parents whose child dies after a few hours. The law here is ripe for consideration by the Scottish Law Commission.

2.19 Child protection legislation recognises the ante-natal situation in looking at prior parental conduct when considering whether a child born today may be at risk. Any prior behaviour may be relevant, including the mother's conduct while she was pregnant. It is competent for the local authority to seek a child protection order in respect of a child where the child has never lived with the parents, but where their past conduct suggests that the child is likely to suffer significant harm and that the order is necessary to protect the child.[49] The case will then be referred to the children's reporter who will arrange a children's hearing.[50] Where parents have failed to protect a child from abuse in the past, any subsequent child they have may be referred to the children's reporter who will consider whether it is necessary to convene a children's hearing to explore the need to place the child under compulsory measures of supervision.[51]

The ante-natal period and the criminal law

2.20 Scots criminal law has long recognised the foetus as warranting special protection. The offence of concealment of pregnancy dates from a statute of 1690[52] and originally raised a presumption of murder, where a woman concealed her pregnancy throughout the whole gestation period, failed to seek assistance at the time of delivery, and the child was dead or missing.[53] The current statute has reduced the presumption to one of culpable homicide.[54]

2.21 The general principle is that murder and culpable homicide can only be committed in respect of a living person. A charge of murder is competent where the child is still partially inside the mother's body.[55] Destruction of a non-viable foetus in the womb will normally amount to abortion and, unless performed within the permitted parameters, will constitute an offence.[56] It has been suggested that destruction of a viable foetus is criminal.[57] Where injury is inflicted on the foetus or pregnant woman and the child, subsequently born alive, dies as a result of these

---

49 Children (Scotland) Act 1995, s 57(1). On child protection orders, see chapter 7, paras 77–88.
50 1995 Act, s 65(2).
51 Children (Scotland) Act 1995, s 52(2). See, *McGregor* v *H* 1983 SLT 626, where an older child had been removed from the parents' care; *A* v *Kennedy* 1993 SLT 1188, where another child had died eight and a half years earlier as a result of being wilfully assaulted and mistreated at the parents' home.
52 Child Murder Act 1690 (c 50) APS ix, 195.
53 G. H. Gordon, *The Criminal Law of Scotland* (2nd edn, W. Green, 1978), para 27–01.
54 Concealment of Birth (Scotland) Act 1809 (c 14).
55 *HM Advocate* v *Scott* (1892) 19 R (J) 63.
56 See para 2.23 below.
57 *HM Advocate* v *McAllum* (1858) 3 Irv 187, per Lord Justice-Clerk Inglis, at p 200. In England and Wales statute provides for the specific offence of killing a foetus capable of being born alive – Infant Life (Preservation) Act 1929.

injuries, criminal responsibility will attach. Thus, the driver of a car which collided with another vehicle in which a pregnant woman was the passenger was convicted of causing death by reckless driving, when the baby died the following day as a result of injuries sustained in the collision.[58]

Abortion

2.22   At common law, the procuring of an abortion was always a criminal offence, subject to the defence that the abortion was necessary to save the pregnant woman's life or to protect her physical or mental health.[59] Since the passing of the Abortion Act 1967 ('the 1967 Act'), it is no longer an offence to procure or participate in an abortion in certain circumstances. The 1967 Act has been amended fairly extensively by the Human Fertilisation and Embryology Act 1990.[60]

2.23   No offence is committed where the abortion is performed by a registered medical practitioner[61] and in a National Health Service hospital or place approved by the Secretary of State,[62] provided that at least one of the conditions set out in the 1967 Act is satisfied. The various conditions are as follows

(i) Two registered medical practitioners must have formed the opinion in good faith that continuation of the pregnancy would involve greater risk to the physical or mental health of the woman or any existing children in her family than would a termination.[63] Such a termination is only permitted up to the 24th week of pregnancy and this is the only condition where a time-limit applies.[64] This condition is very broad indeed and it should be noted that the comparison is between *the risk* to the woman or her existing children of termination and the birth itself. There is no requirement of *grave* risk, as is the case in respect of the second condition, discussed below, nor *serious* risk. Mason argues that this condition might be used to justify the termination of a pregnancy where the woman was sufficiently distressed by the sex of the healthy foetus she was carrying. As he rightly points out, '[a]bortion on the ground of sex may well be unethical, and ecologically unsound, but it is certainly not illegal'.[65]

---

58 *McCluskey* v *HM Advocate* 1989 SLT 175. A similar conclusion was reached in England in *Attorney General's Reference (No. 3 of 1994)* [1997] 3 All ER 936. See also, *Kwok Chak Ming* (1963) Hong Kong LR 349 and *Commonwealth v Cass* 467 NE 2d 1324 (Mass, 1984).

59 G. H. Gordon, n 53 above, at paras 28–01–28–04.

60 On abortion generally, see I. Kennedy and A. Grubb, *Medical Law* (2nd ed, Butterworths, 1994), chapter 12; Mason, n 22 above, chapter 5; J. K. Mason and R. A. McCall Smith, *Law and Medical Ethics* (4th edn, Butterworths, 1996), chapter 5.

61 See, *Royal College of Nursing* v *DHSS* [1981] AC 800, where it was clarified that this requirement is satisfied where the overall procedure is the responsibility of a registered medical practitioner, albeit the component parts may be carried out by nursing staff.

62 1967 Act, s 1.

63 1967 Act, s 1(1)(a).

64 The time-limit was introduced by the Human Fertilisation and Embryology Act 1990. Formerly, no time-limit applied in Scotland.

65 Mason, n 22 above, at p 117.

(ii) The termination is necessary to prevent 'grave permanent injury to physical or mental health of pregnant woman'.[66] Terminations under this condition may be authorised by a single practitioner and are not subject to any time-limit. Again, this condition could be applied to terminating a pregnancy because the foetus was not of the preferred sex and would only be satisfied where the woman's feelings on the matter were sufficiently strong as to affect her mental health.[67]

(iii) Continuation of pregnancy would involve risk to the life of pregnant woman greater than termination.[68] Again, terminations under this condition may be authorised by a single practitioner and are not subject to any time-limit.

(iv) Two registered medical practitioners form the view that there is substantial risk that if the child was born alive it would suffer from such physical or mental abnormalities as to be seriously handicapped.[69] This condition is not subject to any time-limit but requires authorisation by two qualified medical practitioners.

2.24 Some health care professionals have a conscientious objection to abortion and the 1967 Act excuses them from participating in an abortion unless the treatment is directed at saving the life or health of the pregnant woman.[70]

2.25 The decision to seek a termination lies, at first instance, with the pregnant woman, who must fulfil the conditions outlined above. That the potential father has no standing to prevent the abortion from taking place is well established in England.[71] In 1997, the Scottish courts had the opportunity to consider the matter for the first time. In *Kelly* v *Kelly*,[72] the husband of a pregnant woman sought interdict to prevent his wife having a termination. Given the clear indication from England that a husband has

---

66 1967 Act, s 1(1)(b).
67 The European Convention on Human Rights and Biomedicine, art 14, prohibits the use of techniques aimed at medically assisted procreation from being used to choose a future child's sex except where the aim is to avoid serious hereditary sex-related disease. The Convention was opened for signature on 4 April 1997.
68 1967 Act, s 1(1)(c).
69 1967 Act, s 1(1)(d).
70 Section 4. The exemption applies only to participating in the treatment and does not extend to a medical secretary who was dismissed following her refusal to type a letter referring a patient for an abortion – *Janaway* v *Salford Area Health Authority* [1989] AC 537.
71 *Paton* v *British Pregnancy Advisory Service Trustees* [1979] QB 276, where a husband was unsuccessful in seeking an injunction to prevent his wife from having an abortion. Mr Paton continued to pursue the matter, at least in principle, claiming that his rights under art 8 (respect for family life) of the European Convention on Human Rights and Fundamental Freedoms had been violated. That claim was rejected by the Commission – *Paton* v *United Kingdom* (1980) 3 EHRR 408. See also, *C* v *S* [1987] 1 All ER 1230 and *Tremblay* v *Daigle* (1989) 62 DLR (4th) 634, where non-marital partners in England and Canada, respectively, had a similar lack of success in preventing abortions.
72 1997 SLT 896. It should be noted that this case dealt solely with interim interdict since the husband, having lost at that stage, decided not to pursue the case. Thus, the court never had the opportunity to consider full interdict. It is understood that Ms Kelly had a termination.

no standing to prevent an abortion proceeding, the case was argued on a different basis. For Mr Kelly it was argued that a child can claim damages for ante-natal injury on the basis of the *nasciturus* principle, that such claims could be made by the child's guardian, that the interdict was competent to prevent a wrong occurring, and that he was therefore entitled to seek interdict in the present circumstances (as the potential child's guardian). The Second Division rejected his claim on the basis that, while a living child had a right of action in respect of injuries sustained in the womb, the foetus has no legal persona and, thus, can have no rights which are capable of being protected by interdict. In particular, the court took the view that Scots law confers no right on the foetus to a continued existence in the womb, since such a right would conflict with the woman's right to seek a termination under the 1967 Act. The position of at least one Scottish court in the 'foetal rights v women's rights' debate seems clear and refreshingly insightful. While, very sensibly, no attempt was made in *Kelly* to found on any right the husband might have *qua* husband, it is unlikely that such an argument would have succeeded. An aggrieved husband in such a situation would almost certainly have an action for divorce on the basis that his wife's behaviour, in having a termination against his wishes, made it unreasonable to expect him to continue to live with her.[73]

2.26 It is generally acknowledged that, provided the medical practitioner is selected with reasonable care, it is relatively easy to obtain an abortion, although there are regional variations within Scotland. Since the passing of the 1967 Act there has been an unrelenting campaign by anti-abortion groups either to restrict the conditions in which abortion is legal or to outlaw it altogether. It should be noted that any attempt to prevent legal abortions from being carried out by, for example, blocking the entrance to a particular clinic or hospital, is an offence.[74] In addition, interdict would often be available to prevent groups or individuals interfering with free access to hospitals or clinics.[75] Abortion, unlike most other health matters,[76] will not be devolved to the Scottish Parliament and the reason given in the White

---

73 Divorce (Scotland) Act 1976, s 1(2)(b).

74 At the very least, such conduct would be a breach of the peace. Depending upon the circumstances, other attempts to interfere with individuals' free movement might constitute assault. The Scottish courts would take the same view as those in the USA, where it has been held to be no defence to a charge of murder that the victim had been performing abortions.

75 Given the ferocity with which some anti-abortion campaigners in the USA seek to prevent women from gaining access to abortion clinics, it is not surprising that there has been considerable litigation there. See for example, *National Organisation for Women (NOW) v Scheidler* 114 S Ct 798, rehearing denied 114 S Ct 1340 (1994), where NOW was successful in bringing an action against a coalition of anti-abortion groups whom, it claimed, were members of a nationwide conspiracy to close abortion clinics through a pattern of racketeering activity in violation of the Racketeer Influenced and Corrupt Organisations Act. See also, *Schenck v Pro-Choice Network of Western New York* 117 S Ct 1169 (1997), where the Supreme Court upheld a federal court injunction against anti-abortion protesters demonstrating outside family planning clinics.

76 Other health issues reserved to the UK Parliament, for the same reason, are human fertilisation and embryology, genetics, xenotransplantation and vivisection; Scotland's Parliament, Cm 3658, 1997, paras 2.4 and 3.3 and Scotland Act 1998, Sched 5.

Paper was the 'need for a common approach'[77] throughout the UK. It is curious indeed that abortion should receive this special treatment when other matters, such as transport, the police and the environment do not. Perhaps the real reason for the UK Parliament retaining control of abortion lies in the strength of the anti-abortion lobby in parts of Scotland and a desire to avoid the unseemly future prospect of a trail of pregnant women heading over the border to England in pursuit of terminations.

Wrongful birth or conception

2.27 For many people who decide that they do not want to have any more children or, indeed, that they do not want to have children at all, having a sterilisation operation (female) or a vasectomy (male) seems a more certain option than simply relying on contraception. Like all medical procedures, there are risks involved and, from the point of view of controlling reproduction, the most significant risk is the possibility that the operation will be unsuccessful. Where this happens, the couple involved is likely to consider an action in delict against the surgeon and the hospital involved. Two distinct causes of action may arise. First, there is the possibility that the operation itself was performed negligently. Second, while the operation may have been performed with reasonable care, the health care professionals involved may have been negligent in failing to warn the couple of the possibility that the operation would not be a success and the advisability of using contraception until the success or otherwise of the operation could be established.

2.28 Initially, the courts in England accepted that in either of the above situations, the parents of the unplanned child had the right to recover damages in respect of the mother's pain and suffering but not for the costs associated with raising the child.[78] The refusal to award damages under the latter head was based on what has come to be known as the 'joys and blessings' view of the birth of a child; essentially, that the joy associated with the birth of a child (or, at least, a healthy child) outweighs the economic costs involved. In later cases the naivety of this view was accepted and recovery for the costs of raising the child was allowed.[79] In one case, this included the cost of providing private education.[80] Of course, the result was that hospitals became a great deal more careful in warning patients of the risk that the operation would not be successful.[81]

2.29 For some time, the comparative dearth of cases in Scotland suggested that either health care professionals were a lot more careful here, both in carrying out operations and in issuing warnings, or that when they

77 Above, para 3.3.
78 *Udale* v *Bloomsbury Area Health Authority* [1983] 2 All ER 522, where damages were awarded for the woman's pain and suffering and loss of earnings, but the claim for the cost of raising the child was firmly rejected.
79 *Thake* v *Maurice* [1986] QB 644; *Emeh* v *Kensington and Chelsea and Westminster Area Health Authority* [1985] QB 1012.
80 *Benarr* v *Kettering Area Health Authority* (1988) 138 New LJ.
81 *Gold* v *Haringey Health Authority* [1987] 2 All ER 888.

got it wrong the case was settled without the need for litigation.[82] For a time, it was thought that the position in Scotland was the same as that arrived at in England and for much the same reasons.[83] In 1997, the whole question returned to centre-stage with two conflicting Outer House decisions, before the Inner House was able to clarify matters the following year. The result is that Scots law does, indeed, permit recovery in respect of the birth of a healthy baby, where the requisite negligence precedes the birth. How we arrived back at the position many believed we occupied, prior to 1997, warrants brief examination of the cases.

2.30 The journey began with Lord Gill's decision, in the Outer House, in *McFarlane* v *Tayside Health Board*.[84] There, the pursuers decided that their family of four children was large enough and the husband underwent a vasectomy. Aware of the risk of post-operative spontaneous recanalisation of the divided vas, they continued to practice contraception until they were informed by the hospital that the husband's sperm count was negative and that they could dispense with such precautions. Thereafter, the wife became pregnant and subsequently gave birth to a healthy baby girl. The McFarlanes raised an action against the health board claiming damages for the wife's pain, suffering and distress, her loss of earnings, the cost of moving to a larger house and the cost of raising the child. The court was presented with a wealth of authority from England and the USA as well as the limited Scottish case-law. It is worth noting that the defenders expressly renounced any argument that the pursuers could have mitigated their loss by means of abortion or adoption.[85]

2.31 Taking a course which has been rejected elsewhere and at home, the Lord Ordinary dismissed the action on a number of grounds. First, while he acknowledged that pregnancy 'causes discomfort, pain and sickness', he felt that these 'are natural processes resulting in a happy outcome' and, consequently, pregnancy could not be regarded as a form of personal injury. Even if it were a form of personal injury, he did not feel that the court should 'dissociate pregnancy and labour from their outcome'.[86] Thus, Ms McFarlane's claim under that head fell. Secondly, he turned to the costs associated with the child and, applying the general principles of delict,

---

82 Two cases, *Pollock* v *Lanarkshire Health Board* (1987) and *Lindsay* v *Greater Glasgow Health Board* (1990), both based on the lack of warning of failure, were settled out of court. They are discussed briefly in Mason and McCall Smith, *Law and Medical Ethics* (4th edn, Butterworths, 1994), at pp 82–83, where it is suggested that the settlement reached in *Lindsay* was £50,000.

83 In *Allan* v *Greater Glasgow Health Board* 1998 SLT 580, the case failed on its merits but the Lord Ordinary expressed the view, albeit *obiter*, that, as a matter of principle, and taking account of both the law of delict and public policy considerations, recovery under all heads of damage was competent. It should be noted that the case was decided on 23 November 1993 and the delay in it finding its way into the mainstream Scottish law reports was probably due to an oversight that was noticed when the issue again became the subject of litigation. See also, *Cameron* v *Greater Glasgow Health Board* 1993 GWD 6–433.

84 1997 SLT 211.

85 1997 SLT 211, at p 212E. That argument was made and rejected in England in *Emeh* v *Kensington and Chelsea and Westminster Area Health Authority* [1985] 1 QB 1012.

86 1997 SLT 211, at p 214H–J.

pointed out that, where there had been negligence and loss, that loss must be offset against any benefits derived. Rejecting the idea that there might be partial recovery for the economic consequences of the birth, since this would require placing a value on the life of a child, he concluded that 'the value of a child should be held to outweigh all'[87] of the costs associated with her and, accordingly that the action failed. Anticipating the possibility of an appeal, the Lord Ordinary went on to express the view that, even if he was wrong in holding the claim for the costs of raising the child to be irrelevant, it still fell on the issue of causation. He made the following, somewhat puzzling, statement

> 'On the assumption that there had been negligence but for which the child would not have been conceived, that negligence would not be the proximate and effective cause of the financial losses. It was simply a *causa sine qua non*. The *causa causans* was the parents' natural love and affection for the child'.[88]

This suggests that parents have a discretion about such matters as housing, feeding, clothing and educating their children. They do not. A whole host of statutes, most notably the Children (Scotland) Act 1995, place parents under an obligation to fulfil these responsibilities and failure to do so attracts both civil and criminal penalties. As we shall see presently, Lord Gill was correct to anticipate an appeal.

2.32 Prior to the appeal in *McFarlane* being heard by the Inner House, another case, presenting rather different circumstances, was heard in the Outer House. In *Anderson* v *Forth Valley Health Board*,[89] the pursuers, a married couple, had two sons. When the elder boy was about four years old, it was discovered that he suffered from a form of Duchenne muscular dystrophy, a genetically-transmitted condition which affects only males, but can be passed on through the female line. Further tests revealed that the younger boy also suffered from the condition. The parents raised an action against the health board alleging that, on the basis of information about her family history disclosed by the wife, they ought to have been referred for genetic counselling. Had this been done, they alleged that they would have opted to have only female children and, thus, have avoided giving birth to two children suffering from Duchenne muscular dystrophy. They sought damages for anxiety, upset and distress, caused by the birth of their two children, and for the patrimonial loss caused by the wife having to give up work to look after the children and the husband being unable to work overtime as a result of the additional child-care responsibilities involved in looking after the boys. Allowing a proof before answer, Lord Nimmo Smith, rejected the 'joys and blessings' argument in the following terms.

> 'The birth and upbringing of a child no doubt bring both advantages and

---

87 Ibid, at p 215G–H. At p 216A, the Lord Ordinary makes a curious reference to 'the contingent benefit of financial support in later life' which a child brings to parents. The Family Law (Scotland) Act 1985 abolished the obligation on children to aliment their parents. Thus, any support parents can hope for in later life from their children relies on the, wholly discretionary, generosity of the children.
88 Ibid, at p 217D–E.
89 1998 SLT 588.

disadvantages, both happiness and distress; and most people most of the time would regard the former as outweighing the latter. But it seems to me to be a question of fact and degree in the circumstances of any particular case where the balance rests. It may be regarded as being within the range of reasonable responses to the birth of a child that in one case his parents may accept it as an unmixed blessing ... while in another it is seen as nothing less than an unmitigated disaster'.[90]

2.33 It was in the context of these widely-divergent views from the lower courts that the Inner House heard the appeal in *McFarlane* and was able to reach unanimity in overturning the Lord Ordinary's decision.[91] Turning first to Ms McFarlane's claim in respect of the pregnancy, the court took the view that, it was unnecessary to categorise it as personal injury, since it constituted 'manifestations of damnum to an interest'.[92] On the issue of the cost of raising the child, the court noted the parental obligation to do so. Finally, on the issue of children as an unmitigated blessing, the court gave what can be regarded for the time being, at least, as the definitive view, in the following words

> 'The proposition that the blessing of a child is an overriding benefit is one-sided. It ignores the fact that couples such as the pursuers can and do seek sterilisation and rely on its effectiveness precisely in order to avoid the additional expenditure which the birth of another child will entail'.[93]

2.34 Thus, the position in Scotland at present would appear to be that, while children may be a blessing, that blessing is not necessarily unmitigated. Consequently, where the parents have sought to avoid the child's conception and there has been negligence on the part of health care professionals resulting in the birth of a child, the health board responsible for the professionals will be liable. This is so regardless of the fact that the resulting child is healthy. In addition, it should be noted that the health board may be liable in a second situation.

2.35 Where a child is born with disabilities that could have been foreseen in the circumstances, and the parents were not warned, it is at least arguable that they would have an action in delict against whoever failed to inform them of the risk, their measure of damages being the additional cost of raising the child.[94] Cases here include both pre-conception harm, for example, negligent screening of the parents who then pass a genetic condition on to the child[95] and negligence that occurs post- conception, for example, a failure to diagnose the pregnant woman as having been infected with rubella (german measles). Essentially, by not being informed of the likely dangers, the pregnant woman (and to some extent her partner) has

90 Ibid, at p 605D–E.
91 1998 SC 389.
92 Above, at p 394D.
93 Above, at pp 395I–396A *per* Lord Justice-Clerk Cullen.
94 For the position in the USA, see *Jorgensen* v *Meade-Johnson Laboratories* 483 F 2d 237 (1973); *Renslow* v *Mennonite Hospital* 367 NE 2d 1250 (Ill, 1977); *Yeager* v *Bloomington Obstetrics and Gynaecology Inc* 585 NE 2d 696 (Ind, 1992).
95 See *Anderson* v *Forth Valley Health Board*, n 89 above.

been deprived of the opportunity to seek a termination.[96] This claim by the child's parents should be distinguished from the child's claim for 'wrongful life'.

Wrongful life

2.36 Attempts by the child to recover damages in respect of his or her disabilities have proved almost universally unsuccessful, where the child attempts to argue that, had the likelihood of his or her condition been known, he or she would either not have been conceived or would have been aborted while a foetus. Essentially, the child is really arguing that, had all the relevant facts been known, he or she would not have been born at all. With few exceptions,[97] the courts in the USA have rejected such actions on the basis that they are unwilling to take the view that no life at all would be preferable to life with disabilities, that the measure of damages is impossible to assess, and judicial antipathy towards what might be perceived as promoting abortion.[98] The only English case on the point rejected the child's claim on the same grounds[99] and such actions may now be precluded by statute[100] there.

2.37 How the Scottish courts would approach a case of this kind is unknown and, indeed, the Scottish Law Commission was unwilling to commit itself on the matter.[101] Undoubtedly, making judgments based on some lesser quality of life attributable to disabilities, and quantifying that loss, is a sensitive issue, but it is one which the courts grapple with all the time in personal injury cases. The fear that to allow such claims would promote abortion is probably exaggerated and, in any event, the possibility is present already in the widespread provision of ante-natal screening. Perhaps most important of all is the fact that hospitals (and others, like diagnostic laboratories) are in a better position to provide for the additional costs associated with life with disabilities, than are individual

---

96 *Gregory* v *Pembrokeshire Health Authority* [1989] 1 Med LR 81. See also, *McLelland* v *Greater Glasgow Health Board* 1998 SCLR 1081, where, in addition to a substantial award being made for the cost of the child's upbringing, each of the parents was awarded damages in respect of their shock and distress on discovering that their son suffered from Down's syndrome. Despite the woman having alerted health care professionals to the fact that there was a history of the condition in her family, full tests were not carried out during her pregnancy.

97 *Curlender* v *Bio-Science Laboratories* 165 Cal Rptr 477 (1980), where the pre-conception tests carried out on the parents to reveal their status as carriers of Tay-Sachs disease were performed negligently and the child was born with the condition. See also *Turpin* v *Sortini* 182 Cal Rptr 377 (1982), where the claim was restricted to special damages; *Harbeson* v *Parke-Davis* 659 P 2d 483 (Wash, 1983); and *Gallacher* v *Duke University* 638 F Supp 979 (NC, 1988).

98 *Gleitman* v *Cosgrove* 296 NYS 2d 687 (1967); *Ellis* v *Sherman* 515 A 2d 1327 (Pa, 1986); *Crowe* v *Forum Group Inc* 575 NE 2d 630 (Ind, 1991).

99 *McKay* v *Essex Area Health Authority* [1982] 2 All ER 771, where the child's mother had been infected with rubella but, it was alleged, the tests she underwent to establish this had been negligently performed or negligently interpreted. The child was born severely disabled, but her action was unsuccessful.

100 Congenital Disabilities (Civil Liability) Act 1976, s 1(2)(b). Cf J. E. S. Fortin, 'Is the "Wrongful Life" Action Really Dead?' [1987] JSWL 306.

101 Report on Liability for Antenatal Injury, above, para 22.

families. If the professionals are negligent, they should bear such costs and have every opportunity to insure against liability. In the end of the day, the practical difference between an action by the parents and an action by the child may not be all that significant in terms of making additional funding available.

2.38 Were wrongful life actions to be allowed in Scotland, would the child have any action against his or her parents? Again, cases could arise from both pre-conception and post-conception circumstances. Should potential parents who have family histories of particular conditions face liability if they do not undergo pre-conception screening?[102] Where a man knows that he is HIV positive and, none the less, proceeds to father a child, should the child who is born infected have any claim against him? Where a pregnant woman is informed that the foetus she is carrying has been infected with rubella, but decides to proceed with the pregnancy, should the child have a right of action against the mother? To allow such claims would effectively deny some people the opportunity to have children and is setting the rights of the child well above those of adults. In addition, it might well fall foul of the European Convention on Human Rights and Fundamental Freedoms.[103]

THE END OF LEGAL PERSONALITY

2.39 Essentially, legal personality ends at death.[104] However, this state-ment is sometimes qualified by acknowledging the post-mortem effects of a person's action. Thus, a will made or a trust deed executed while a person was alive will have effect after the person has died. An executor has the right to deal with the deceased's property, to continue litigation begun by the deceased, and to raise an action for damages in respect of solatium for injuries suffered by the deceased.[105] In all of these cases, what continues is inexorably linked to something that happened while the person was alive. Thus, the qualification does not alter the basic proposition.

What do we mean by death?

2.40 At one time, establishing death was a simple process and could be defined in terms of the heart stopping or breathing ceasing. However, neither of these events need be permanent in every case and stimulation of the heart, cardiac massage and artificial ventilation can reverse apparent

---

102 The issue of genetic screening and counselling brings with it a whole range of complex issues for family members and the professionals involved. For excellent discussions of the issues, see G. T. Laurie, 'The Most Personal Information of All: An Appraisal of Genetic Privacy in the Shadow of the Human Genome Project' 10 Int J Law, Policy and the Family 74 (1996) and I. Pullen, 'Patients, families and genetic information' in E. E. Sutherland and R. A. McCall Smith (eds), *Family Rights: Family Law and Medical Advance* (EUP, 1990) at p 42.
103 Article 12 acknowledges the right to marry and found a family.
104 Stair, *Institutions*, IV, 45, 17. All deaths must be registered – Registration of Births, Deaths and Marriages (Scotland) Act 1965, s 23.
105 Damages (Scotland) Act 1976, s 2, as substituted by the Damages (Scotland) Act 1993, s 3.

death. In addition, bio-scientific developments[106] and the advent of such concepts as brain death[107] have made any definition of death considerably more complicated.[108] This raises a host of interesting dilemmas, most notably surrounding the treatment of and, more significantly, withdrawal of treatment from, patients. In order to keep the issue in perspective, perhaps the words of Mason and McCall Smith should be borne in mind: 'In practice, it is astonishing how often the moment of death is perfectly clear. One can tell immediately when a loved one or carefully observed patient "dies"'.[109]

2.41 The dilemmas surrounding the end of a person's life[110] and, particularly, any medical involvement in that process, attract sincere, strongly-held opinions, which are as polarised as those surrounding the abortion debate. This is less than encouraging for legislators, since it suggests that any hope of reaching consensus on how the law ought to approach the matter is a forlorn one. At the outset, it may be helpful (at least to some) to draw a distinction between withdrawal of medical treatment from a patient (ie doing little or nothing) and assisting suicide (ie doing something to promote a person's death).

Withdrawal of medical treatment

2.42 Where a competent, adult patient requests the withdrawal of medical treatment, or requests that treatment should be confined to a specific limited type (eg relief of pain), there is no legal problem. Treatment of an adult against his or her wishes normally constitutes an assault and, once the patient's views are known, they must be respected. Arguably, the position is no different where a child or young person expresses clear views, provided that the patient understands the options available and the consequences of his or her decision. Where the patient is no longer competent, the decision on treatment must be made by someone else.

2.43 While the courts have shown themselves willing to consider evidence of 'what the patient would have wanted', at present, there is nothing an individual can do in advance, to determine what will happen. The Scottish Law Commission considered empowering people to make arrangements for the future through the mechanism of 'advance statements' (perhaps

---

106 Given the degree of uncertainty surrounding whether it is effective, cryogenic preservation with the intention of later resuscitation will not be discussed here.

107 For a discussion of the concept of brain death and problems associated with its application, see A. Halevy and B. Brody, ' Brain Death: Reconciling Definitions, Criteria and Tests', *Annals of Internal Medicine* 119 (1993) 519; R. D. Truog, 'Is It Time To Abandon Brain Death?' Hastings Centre Report 27, no 1 (1997) 29.

108 For an excellent discussion, see J. K. Mason and R. A. McCall Smith, n 60 above, pp 281–290.

109 Ibid, at p 281. See also, *Re A* [1992] 3 Med LR 303, where the court accepted that 'death' meant brain stem death.

110 For a fascinating discussion of the legal issues surrounding death in England and Wales, see 'Dispatchings' in B. Hale (The Hon Mrs Justice, formerly Professor Brenda Hoggett), *From the Test Tube to the Coffin: Choice and Regulation in Private Life*, The Hamlyn Lectures, Forty-Seventh Series (Sweet and Maxwell, 1996).

better known as 'living wills'). It recommended that such statements should be valid, subject to exceptions and the possibility of revocation.[111]

2.44 However, where the patient is in a permanent vegetative state (PVS), a recent decision of the Inner House and subsequent action by the Lord Advocate have helped the families and doctors of such patients. In *Law Hospital NHS Trust* v *Lord Advocate*,[112] the patient had been in PVS for over four years. There was medical evidence that she was wholly unconscious, unaware of her surroundings, dependent on artificial feeding and, perhaps most significantly, that there was no prospect of her condition improving. The pursuers sought declarator that it would not be unlawful for them to discontinue all life-sustaining and medical treatments and to provide only such treatments as would allow her to die peacefully. Given the uncertain state of the law, what the hospital trust was seeking was the court's protection from both civil and criminal liability. Since all of Mrs J's relatives were in agreement with the hospital trust that cessation of treatment was desirable, the question of civil liability was not a live issue in this case.[113] However, the possibility of criminal liability posed greater problems, since decisions on prosecution lie with the Lord Advocate.

2.45 How, then, did the Inner House resolve the civil issue raised by the case? It concluded that it had jurisdiction to hear applications for the discontinuation of treatment where a patient was in PVS and that, in future, cases of this kind should be brought by way of petition rather than declarator. The court indicated that the test to be applied was that the 'best interests' of the patient must be served and that the 'best interests' test should be 'viewed negatively, namely, that it is not in the best interests of the patient to be kept alive by artificial means, where the court is satisfied that the diagnosis is so clear and the prognosis so futile that the [patient] has no interest in being kept alive'.[114] The case was remitted back to the Lord Ordinary, who pronounced declarator and the patient subsequently died.

2.46 In order to avoid continuing uncertainty with regard to criminal liability, the Lord Advocate issued a policy statement[115] indicating that he would not authorise prosecution of a medical practitioner (or any person acting on the instructions of such a practitioner) who withdrew treatment from a patient in PVS provided that the action was taken in good faith and with the authority of the court. Thus, any fear of prosecution would

---

111 Report on Incapable Adults (Scot Law Com No 151, 1995), paras 5.41–5.59 and recs 68–74. See also, Consultation Paper, Managing the Finances and Welfare of Incapable Adults (Scottish Office, 1997).

112 (IH) 1996 SCLR 491. There had already been considerable debate in Scotland, following the earlier English decision in *Airedale NHS Trust* v *Bland* [1993] AC 789. For an excellent discussion of these cases and others, see, J. K. Mason and G. T. Laurie, 'The Management of the Persistent Vegetative State in the British Isles' 1996 JR 263.

113 None the less, who could consent on behalf of another, in order to protect clinicians, was an issue requiring resolution.

114 (IH) 1996 SCLR 491, per Lord Milligan at p 517F–G.

115 1996 SLT 869.

seem to have been removed in such cases. A postscript seems worth exploring, if only to dismiss it. Since private prosecution remains competent, a medical practitioner might, in theory, face prosecution by either a relative of the patient or one of the various groups who pursue their own perception of morality through all available channels. However, for a private prosecution to be brought there must either be the concurrence of the Lord Advocate (who would presumably refuse) or the permission of the High Court. Since the matter has been explored and decided as a matter of public policy, it seems inconceivable that the High Court would grant permission.

2.47 Thus it seems that the first step has been taken in addressing the issues surrounding PVS and serious or terminal illness. How far the principles set out in *Law Hospital NHS Trust* v *Lord Advocate* will be extended remains to be seen. One possible area of extension would seem to be the treatment of seriously handicapped neonates[116] and young children, an area of the law described by Mason as 'an example of the cyclical nature of medical jurisprudence'.[117]

Assisted suicide and euthanasia

2.48 There have been a number of attempts to legalise physician-assisted suicide in other jurisdictions but, to date, most have had no long-term success.[118] The common belief that euthanasia is 'legal' in the Netherlands is inaccurate. However, where a physician causes a patient's death at the latter's request or assists the patient to commit suicide, where the patient 'is "suffering unbearably" and "with no prospect of improvement", and subject to a number of procedural safeguards ... Dutch case law and prosecutorial policy recognises a defence of necessity'.[119] The legislation of

---

116 A neonate is defined as a child within the first month of life – J. K. Mason and R. A. McCall Smith, *Butterworths Medico- Legal Encyclopaedia* (Butterworths, 1987) at p 371. In England and Wales, a separate certificate of death with the somewhat unwieldy title 'Medical certificate of Cause of Death of a Live-Born Child Dying within the first twenty-eight days of life', must be completed where such a child dies, reflecting this definition of a neonate. No equivalent dedicated certificate exists in Scotland.

117 Mason, n 22 above, at p 281 and, more generally, chapter 11. See also, *Withholding or Withdrawing Life Saving Treatment in Children: A Framework for Practice* (Royal College of Paediatrics and Child Health, 1997); J. Wise, 'When life saving treatment should be withdrawn in children' (1997) 315 Brit Med J 834; and *Re C (Medical Treatment)* [1998] 1FLR 384, where the High Court authorised a hospital to discontinue ventilation of a 16-month-old child in the face of parental opposition. The child was suffering from spinal muscular atrophy and was conscious, but had no hope of recovery and was facing the likelihood of increased suffering.

118 The Rights of the Terminally Ill Act 1996 (NT), which permitted physician-assisted suicide in the Northern Territory, Australia, operated for only nine months and was brought to an end when the Senate passed the Euthanasia Law Act on 25 March 1997.

119 J. Griffiths, 'Recent Developments In The Netherlands Concerning Euthanasia And Other Medical Behaviour That Shortens Life' (1994) 1 Medical Law International 137, at p 138. The author examines the legal position in the Netherlands and the unique data available there, and argues that other related methods of shortening life deserve more attention in the light of the practical issues surrounding effective control of decision-making.

1993, far from authorising euthanasia, simply prescribes the form of reporting deaths in such circumstances.

2.49 After a somewhat troubled history, the Death with Dignity Act[120] has now started operating in Oregon, USA, and a number of individuals have used its provisions to enable them to end their own lives. The Act requires the physician and the patient to comply with a number of, fairly rigorous, conditions before the physician can prescribe a lethal prescription of drugs for the patient to take. Only patients over the age of 18 may benefit from the Act's provisions and a physician must certify that the patient has less than six months to live. Once the patient requests a lethal prescription, the physician, if willing to participate in the process and satisfied that the patient qualifies, must refer the patient to a second doctor for confirmation that the patient has less than six months to live and is mentally competent. If there is doubt about mental competence, the patient must also be referred to a psychiatrist. The patient must then make a written request for lethal medication and the patient's signature must be witnessed by two witnesses. The patient's doctor cannot act as a witness and one of the witnesses must be a non-relative, who is neither an heir of the patient nor an employee of the health care facility where the patient is being treated. At least 48 hours must elapse from the time of the written request, and 15 days from the first oral request, before the patient can make a further oral request. The physician must then offer the patient the opportunity to change his or her mind and, assuming the patient does not wish to do so, the physician can write the prescription. Some doctors have conscientious objections to participating in assisted suicide while others are afraid of the personal consequences of doing so. In the light of attacks on doctors who perform abortions in the USA, these fears may be well-founded. None the less, the Act provides an example how the legal system can empower a patient to end his or her own life and build in safeguards designed to minimise the possibility of abuse. A number of other jurisdictions in the USA are considering similar legislation.

2.50 In Scotland, assisted suicide, regardless of whether the assistance is given by a doctor or someone else, is illegal. Depending on the circumstances, the accused may be charged with murder or culpable homicide and it may be some reflection of the attitude of prosecutors that, even where the original charge is murder, the accused's guilty plea to the lesser charge is often accepted.[121] In addition, there are cases which illustrate leniency in sentencing where it is accepted that the accused acted out of concern for

---

120 The Death With Dignity Act was first approved by a ballot of the electorate by 51% to 49% in 1994. The legislation was blocked thereafter by challenges in the courts, but, in 1997, an attempt to have the Act repealed was defeated, this time by 60% to 40%, again by a ballot of the electorate. The injunction was then lifted and the Act began operating early in 1998. For a discussion of the Act and the challenges it presents to the professionals involved, see J. Woolfrey, 'What Happens Now? Oregon and Physician-Assisted Suicide' 28 Hastings Center Report 9 (1998).

121 See for example, *HM Advocate* v *Brady* 1997 GWD 1–18 where a man was convicted of culpable homicide for killing his brother who had been suffering from Huntington's disease. He killed his brother after the brother had made many requests to him and other relatives to be assisted in dying and the court accepted that he was motivated by nothing

the deceased in killing him or her. However, such decisions are no guarantee that a particular prosecutor or court would take an equally compassionate and lenient attitude in the future. Clearly, the time has come to address this controversial area of the law.

Presumption of Death

2.51 It is sometimes the case that, while no body can be produced, all the circumstances point to the fact that a person has died. Thus, where a person has boarded an aeroplane which crashes into the ocean with no survivors, it is reasonable to presume that the person has died. However, as we will see, the law now accepts less dramatic circumstances as indicating death, as for example, where a person has been missing for a long period of time and no one comes forward to indicate that the person is alive. There may be sound reason why the fact of the person's death should be established. A spouse may want to deal with the missing person's property or to claim on insurance policies. Business partners may want to take certain steps that would require the missing person's consent, were he or she alive.

2.52 The common law embraced a very strong presumption of life and a person was presumed to live to a very advanced age. Stair[122] set life expectancy as high as 100 years, which seems rather over-optimistic in the light of prevailing conditions at the time. However, even under the common law, there was provision allowing for the presumption of life to be rebutted by proof that the person had died.[123] The matter has long been regulated by statute.[124] The current statute, the Presumption of Death (Scotland) Act 1977 ('the 1977 Act'), does not preclude actions under the common law. However, since the common law requires proof beyond reasonable doubt, while the 1977 Act permits proof on the balance of probabilities, common law actions are now unknown.

2.53 An action to have a person declared dead may be brought in either the sheriff court or the Court of Session by any person having an interest.[125] A declarator is competent in two situations.[126] The first arises where there is a clear indication that a person died at a particular time, as in the case of the passenger on the crashed aeroplane, and the action can be raised immediately after the crash. The second situation arises where the person 'has not been known to be alive for a period of at least seven years' and, obviously, such actions must only be raised after that period of time has

other than love for his brother. It is perhaps a reflection of changing attitudes that, while he had been charged originally with murder which carries a mandatory life sentence, the prosecution accepted his plea of guilty to the lesser charge of culpable homicide. In the event, Mr Brady was admonished, a sentence which does not involve any imprisonment at all. For the position in England, see *Re B* [1981] 1 WLR 1421; *R v Cox*, 19 September 1992, 12 BMLR 38.

122 Stair, *Institutions*, IV, 45, 17.
123 *Fife* v *Fife* (1855) 17 D 951; *Fairholme* v *Fairholme's Trustees* (1858) 20 D 813.
124 The, now repealed, Presumption of Life Limitation (Scotland) Acts 1881 and 1891, took a more euphemistic and delicate approach to the issue.
125 Section 1(1). The sheriff may remit the case to the Court of Session and must remit the case if so directed by the court.
126 Above.

elapsed. Where it is established that either of the two conditions is satisfied, the court must grant the declarator providing that the person died, in the first case, at a specific date or, in the second case, at the date seven years after the person was last known to be alive.

2.54 Once a person has been declared dead, the decree is conclusive on all matters and effective against any person for all purposes including any rights in property.[127] Such a decree terminates the missing person's marriage for all time and the limited provisions allowing for variation or recall of the decree do not revive the marriage.[128] Only criminal liability is unaffected by a declarator of death. In the unlikely event that the person declared dead reappears, he or she remains liable under the criminal law and, conversely, may be the victim of a crime.

2.55 In order to accommodate the possibility that the person declared dead might reappear, the 1977 Act contains provision for variation or recall of the decree.[129] Where the missing person reappears within five years, the court can make such order as is 'fair and reasonable in all the circumstances of the case' regulating property rights, but such orders do not affect any rights acquired by a third party in good faith and for value.[130] Because of the possibility of a subsequent variation or recall affecting property rights, trustees are required to arrange insurance to cover the possibility before they make payments as a result of a declarator of death. Similarly, before insurers pay any capital sum arising from the death, they may require the payee to insure against subsequent variation or recall.

Presumption of survivorship

2.56 Where two people die in a common calamity, it may be impossible to ascertain which of them survived the other and the common law created no presumptions to govern the situation.[131] The Succession (Scotland) Act 1964 ('the 1964 Act') introduced a general presumption that the younger person survives the elder.[132] However, there are two exceptions to this rule. First, where the two persons were husband and wife, neither is presumed to survive the other.[133] This prevents the estates of both of them being inherited by the survivors of only one. The second exception applies where the elder person has left property to the younger, whom failing to a third party. Where the younger person has died intestate, the elder person is presumed to have survived the younger (for the purpose of that particular legacy only) and the property passes to the third party.[134] It should be noted

---

127 Section 3.
128 Section 4(5).
129 Section 4.
130 Section 5.
131 *Drummond's JF* v *HM Advocate* 1944 SC 298; *Ross's JF* v *Martin* 1955 SC (HL) 56.
132 Section 31(1)(b).
133 Section 31(1)(a).
134 Section 31(2).

that the whole scheme introduced by the 1964 Act applies only in cases of doubt and if it can be established, on the balance of probabilities, that one person did in fact survive the other, the usual rules of succession apply.[135] For this reason, it is quite common in wills for the testator to provide that a particular beneficiary will only inherit if he or she survives the testator by, for example, thirty days. This ensures that either the beneficiary will enjoy the property or that it will pass to other people chosen by the testator.

WHAT IS IT ABOUT PEOPLE THAT MATTERS?

Name

2.57   The general principle in Scotland is that a person may use any name he or she likes,[136] although to use a particular name for a fraudulent purpose will attract criminal penalties.[137] Certain conventions surround the use of names, but it should be stressed that these are no more than conventions and have no legal standing.

Children's names

2.58   Deciding on a child's forenames is a feature of parental rights. Thus, where a child is born to parents who are married at the time of the birth, the parents have equal rights to select the child's forenames. Such a child will usually take the father's last name as a matter of convention. Where parents make a particularly eccentric choice of forenames as, for example, choosing all the names of the members of their favourite football team, the registrar has no power to refuse to register the child as having these names. Arguably, to burden a child with such a long name is not in the child's best interests and the parents' choice could be challenged in court.[138] However, where both parents agree on the (albeit eccentric) choice of name, it may be that no other individual is sufficiently concerned to raise the action on the child's behalf.

2.59   Disagreement between parents on the choice of name is far from unknown and, ultimately, if they cannot resolve their dispute, either of them could apply to the court for a determination.[139] The court would then have to take a decision based on what would serve the child's interests, although how it is to make a choice between 'Fiona' or 'Jane', for example, is difficult to fathom and it is thought that the courts would be anxious to encourage parents to reach a compromise. Where the mother has not been

---

135   *Lamb* v *HM Advocate* 1976 SC 110.
136   *Johnston, Petitioner* (1899) 2 F 75, at p 76, 'Any person in Scotland may, without the authority of the court, call himself what he pleases.'
137   *Clark* v *Chalmers* 1961 JC 60.
138   Under s 11 of the Children (Scotland) Act 1995, the court can make an order on the way in which parental rights are exercised and the action can be brought by a wide variety of individuals. For a discussion of parental responsibilities and rights, see chapters 5 and 6.
139   1995 Act, s 11.

married to the child's father, she faces no such need to compromise, since unless she has executed a parental rights agreement with him, he will have no parental rights.[140] She may choose the child's forenames and the child will usually use her last name, again, as a matter of convention.

2.60 Another area which sometimes gives rise to disagreement, although rarely to litigation,[141] is the question of changing a child's name at a later stage.[142] This occurs most often when the parents divorce and the mother, with whom the child is living, remarries. She may wish to change the child's last name to that of her new partner and the child's father may object. Again, the court must apply the welfare principle but, here, it has something more to work on than simple preference. On the one hand, it may be in the child's interest in avoiding embarrassment to be known by the same name as the adults (and possibly half-siblings) with whom he or she is living. In addition, the change can be argued to facilitate the child's integration into that family. On the other hand, it may be argued to be in the child's interest to keep his or her identity in respect of both parents.[143] In addition to applying the welfare principle, the court would have to take account of any view the child wishes to express, in the light of the child's age and understanding.[144] A child who wishes to change his or her name may raise an action to do so independently of the parents once the child is old enough to understand what is involved in instructing a solicitor and there is a presumption that a child of 12 years or older has sufficient understanding.[145]

2.61 In the absence of disagreement requiring resolution by a court, the Registrar General will accept a change to a child's name, known as a 'substitution', provided that the child is known by the new name prior to his or her first birthday and that the change is registered before the child is two years old.[146] Thereafter, one change of forename and one change of last name may be recorded in respect of a child until he or she reaches the

---

140 1995 Act, s 3(1). Where the father has obtained parental rights, whether by court order or with the mother's consent, the court retains its power to grant or refuse a specific issue order in respect of the child's name. See *Dawson v Wearmouth* [1998] 1 All ER 271 for differing judicial attitudes to the question in England.

141 For a rare example, see *GSF v GAF* 1995 SCLR 189. It should be noted that the case was decided under the law as it was prior to the Children (Scotland) Act 1995. For a discussion of the history of last names and tests the courts have applied or might apply in the USA, see L. Kelly, 'Divining the Deep and Inscrutable: Towards a Gender-Neutral, Child-Centred Approach to Child Name Change Proceedings' 99 W Va L Rev 1 (1996).

142 In 1997, 109 changes of name were recorded in respect of children under two years old and 473 were recorded in respect of children aged between two and 16 years old – Annual Report 1997, p 139.

143 The United Nations Convention on the Rights of the Child, art 8(1), recognises the child's right to preserve his or her identity and specifically mentions the child's name and family relations as part of that identity. See *Dawson v Wearmouth*, n 140 above.

144 1995 Act, s 11(7)(b).

145 Age of Legal Capacity (Scotland) Act 1991, s 2(4A), see chapter 3, para 63, below.

146 Registration of Births, Deaths and Marriages Act 1965, s 43(3). Only one such change is permitted. See, *Stair Memorial Encyclopaedia*, vol 19, para 1425.

age of 16, provided that the new name has been used by the child for not less than two years.[147]

Adult's names

2.62 Many women adopt their husband's last name on marriage. This convention is of relatively recent adoption in Scotland and is thought to be one which was imported from England in the 19th century.[148] However, many married women do not change their names on marriage. Since there is no requirement that they should do so, there is no need to justify their decision, but common reasons include the woman's desire to retain her identity or to continue the benefits of an established professional reputation and, sometimes, an affinity with the traditions of Scots law. Nor is there anything to prevent a husband replacing his own last name with that of his wife or for the couple to use a combination of both names. The only difficulty with combined last names appears to be a practical one, if it were to continue for several generations. A person who is cohabiting outside marriage may use his or her partner's last name and, again, the couple may use a combination of both names.

2.63 An adult may wish to change his or her name for a whole variety of reasons.[149] Examples include simply not liking a forename, wishing to revert to a former last name on divorce or the, increasingly likely, wish to select one of several last names by which he or she has been known throughout childhood. A person can do this, in a practical sense, by simply using the chosen names. However, sometimes a person might wish more formal recognition of the change of name.[150] The Registrar General will record a change of first or last name or both upon a person demonstrating that he or she has used the new name for the previous two years.[151] Any extract or abbreviated certificate issued thereafter shows the original name along with the new name.

Age

Calculation of age

2.64 At common law, age was calculated *de momento in momentum*, that is from the exact time of birth.[152] The potential for problems with this

---

147 1965 Act, s 43(4).
148 For a fascinating discussion of this development and the older Scottish approach, see E. M. Clive, *The Law of Husband and Wife in Scotland* (4th edn, 1997) at paras 11.019–11.021.
149 In 1997, 565 changes of name were recorded in respect of individuals aged 16 or over – Annual Report 1997, p 139.
150 The procedure for changing one's name by deed poll found in England and Wales does not apply in Scotland.
151 The following are accepted as proof of use of a particular name: original letters, bank statements, club membership cards, medical records and benefit books. If none of these is available, sworn statements from two unrelated householders are accepted.
152 Stair, *Institutions*, I, vi, 33.

approach were highlighted by the Scottish Law Commission[153] and, as a result of its recommendations[154] the Age of Legal Capacity (Scotland) Act 1991 now provides that a person attains a particular age at the beginning of the relevant anniversary of his or her birth.[155] Where a person is born on 29 February in a leap year, the relevant anniversary is 1 March in any year other than a leap year.[156] Thus, a person who was born at 22.30 hours on 29 February 1996 will attain the age of 16 years at 00.01 hours on 29 February 2012, and the age of 18 years at 00.01 hours on 1 March 2014.

Young people and the significance of age

2.65 A person's age is significant for a whole variety of legal purposes. The period of time during which distinctions are drawn most frequently lies between birth and adulthood. Adulthood is attained when a person reaches the age of majority at 18.[157] Prior to this time a variety of different ages are important for different purposes and sometimes the child's actual level of maturity, as opposed to chronological age, will be relevant. Thus, for example, when a child will be held responsible for his or her own actions in the context of the criminal law is determined largely by reference to the child's age,[158] whereas, in the context of delictual liability, the determining factor is the child's maturity and understanding.[159] In addition, the legal system recognises that, due to their vulnerability or inexperience, children may require special treatment through protective legislation and that legislation is usually couched in terms of the child's age.[160] A child or young person's general capacity to participate in the legal system is determined, in some cases, by reference to the child's chronological age and in others by reference to his or her capacity to understand.[161] Clearly, in the latter case, this will be linked to the individual child's level of maturity. These matters are considered in detail in later chapters and, as we shall see, when the law uses actual age as the determinant in respect of protection from different dangers, a host of inconsistencies are apparent. As a general rule, the age of 16 is emerging as being one of increasing significance in terms of the

---

153 Legal Capacity of Minors and Pupils (Scot Law Com Consultative Memorandum No 65, 1985) para 5.138. One example given by the Commission is of a person marrying on his or her 16th birthday at a time of day prior to that of his or her birth. The marriage would be void since the person would not have attained the age of 16 by the common law method of calculation. For an example of the difficulty created by the common law, see *Drummond* v *Cunningham-Head* (1624) Mor 3465, where a person who signed a bond of caution within a matter of hours of attaining majority was able to reduce it.

154 Report on the Legal Capacity of Minors and Pupils (Scot Law Com No 110, 1987), rec 19(a).

155 Section 6(1).

156 Section 6(2).

157 Age of Majority (Scotland) Act 1969, s 1(1).

158 The age of criminal responsibility is currently eight years old – Criminal Procedure (Scotland) Act 1995, s 41. It is worth noting that, where the child is below the age of 16, the case will almost always be dealt with by a children's hearing rather than a criminal court. For a detailed discussion of the children's hearings system, see chapter 9.

159 See chapter 3, paras 81–82.

160 See chapter 3, paras 91–100.

161 Age of Legal Capacity (Scotland) Act 1991. The Act is discussed at length in chapter 3 at paras 60–78.

autonomy and responsibility of young people. A person may marry, leave school and home, engage in full-time employment and transact as an adult from that age.[162] However, children in Scotland acquire considerable capacity from the age of 12. Thus, for example, a person may make a will,[163] and consent to or veto his or her own adoption from that age.[164] In addition, there is a presumption that a person aged 12 or over has sufficient understanding to express views on such matters as the future arrangements for his or her own care[165] and to instruct a solicitor.[166] Of course, this does not preclude a younger child from demonstrating sufficient understanding and children as young as 8 years old have instructed solicitors.

Adulthood and age

2.66 Once a person becomes an adult, the individual's chronological age is of little legal significance. Broadly, there are two exceptions to this general principle. First, specific legislation may provide for an age limit as a qualification for a particular purpose. Thus, for example, a person cannot stand for election to the Westminster[167] or Scottish[168] Parliaments until he or she is 21 years old.

2.67 The second area where age acquires significance relates to older members of the community. Unlike young people, older people are not subject to any blanket scheme relating to their capacity and simply being over a particular age has no significance in terms of capacity. However, it is increasingly recognised that, as the law stands at present, ageing brings with it certain restrictions and entitlement to benefits. Thus, there is a fixed age at which most people must retire[169] and various ages at which individuals become entitled to receive a pension from the state. The fact that such landmarks exist and apply to the population as a whole suggests that this group merits special attention. The position of older members of the family is discussed in chapter 15.

Gender

Determining gender

2.68 A person's gender is determined at birth, using chromosomal,

---

162 While a person between the ages of 16 and 18 has virtually the same capacity as an adult, he or she gains the benefit of additional protection through the possibility of setting transactions aside – 1991 Act, ss 1(1)(b) and 3(1), discussed in chapter 3 at paras 75–78. This may mean that adults will be less willing to transact with such young people.
163 1991 Act, s 2(2).
164 1991 Act, s 2(3).
165 Children (Scotland) Act 1995, ss 6 and 11(7)(b) and (10).
166 1991 Act, s 2(4A), added by the Children (Scotland) Act 1995, Sched 4, para 53(3).
167 Union With Scotland Act 1706. That Act uses the term 'twenty-one years' and was unaffected by the Age of Majority (Scotland) Act 1969 which lowered the age of majority to 18.
168 Scotland Act 1998, s 5.
169 The idea of a mandatory retirement age, particularly when coupled with entitlement to benefits, can be seen as protective of, and beneficial to, older people. However, increasing numbers of older people would prefer not to be compelled to retire at a particular age

gonadal and genital factors,[170] and is registered accordingly.[171] At this stage it is not possible to consider such factors as social role acceptance or psychological gender. Roman law regarded the hermaphrodite as belonging to the gender he or she more closely resembled and, in cases of doubt, to be male.[172] Since then, such have been the advances in chromosomal testing that it is now possible to reveal a more complex picture of what can be seen as 'categories' of gender. None the less, Scots law currently permits of only two categories – male and female.

2.69 Where an error has occurred in the original determination of gender, any person with an interest may apply to the Registrar General to have the error corrected. Appeal from refusal to do so lies to the sheriff, whose decision is final. In either case, any correction will be recorded in the Register of Corrected Entries. However, such changes apply only to the correction of errors and there is no provision for recording a change of gender, even where that change has occurred naturally.[173] It has been argued that a petition to the *nobile officium* would be competent to acknowledge that a change in gender had occurred.[174]

Change of gender

2.70 Many other jurisdictions acknowledge that sex-realignment treatment, including surgery, can bring about a change of gender,[175] either for specific purposes or more generally. In England, in the now infamous, case of *Corbett* v *Corbett*,[176] the court rejected the idea that such surgery could render a (former) male into a female. Since marriage could only be contracted between a male and a female, it thus concluded that the transsexual's purported marriage to a man was invalid. Challenge to this notion of fixed gender, particularly in the context of family relationships, then moved to the European arena.[177]

2.71 In *Rees* v *United Kingdom*,[178] while the European Commission on Human Rights took the unanimous view that the failure by the UK to

and the whole system can be seen as a form of age-based discrimination. In the USA, for example, there is no mandatory retirement age and an employer cannot terminate an employee's contract solely on the ground of age.

170 Mason, n 22 above, at pp 5–7 and J. K. Mason, *Forensic Medicine for Lawyers* (3rd edn, 1995), at pp 227–228.

171 Registration of Births, Deaths and Marriages (Scotland) Act 1965, s 13(1).

172 *Digest*, I, v, 9. The only Scottish authority to consider the question followed this view – see Forbes, *The Institutes of the Law of Scotland*, I, 1, 1, 18.

173 *X, Petitioner* 1957 SLT (Sh Ct) 61.

174 T. B. Smith, n 1 above, at p 250.

175 For example, Germany and the Netherlands have specific legislation regulating change of gender and its recognition for most purposes. In the USA, state law is somewhat inconsistent – see *MT* v *JT* 355 A 2d 204 (NJ 1976) (marriage allowed); *B* v *B* 355 NYS 2d 712 (1974) (marriage not recognised); *Re Ladrach* 513 NE 2d 828 (Ohio, 1987) (marriage license refused). See Mason, above, pp 8–14.

176 [1971] P 83. For the application of the same approach in the context of criminal law, see *R* v *Tan* [1983] 2 All ER 12.

177 For an excellent discussion of both the medical and legal aspects of the issue, see J. K. Mason, 'United Kingdom *v* Europe: Current Attitudes to Transsexualism' (1998) 2 *Edinburgh Law Review* 107.

178 (1986) 9 EHRR 56.

recognise change of gender constituted a breach of art 8 of the European Convention on Human Rights,[179] guaranteeing the right to respect for privacy in family life, the European Court of Human Rights rejected the claim by twelve votes to three. Neither the Commission nor the court found there to be any breach of art 12, guaranteeing the right to marry and found a family. In *Cossey* v *United Kingdom*[180] a similar decision was reached, but by a narrower majority. The court continued to move in the direction of recognition of transsexualism in *B* v *France*,[181] although it should be noted that the decision there turned, at least to some extent, on the peculiar publicity that the French administrative system gives to an individual's gender through his or her social security number.[182] B, who began life as a male but had undergone sex-realignment surgery, appealed against the refusal of the Cour de Cassation to declare her to be female and to order the appropriate change to her documentation. B's appeal was upheld by a majority of fifteen to six on the basis that art 8 had been violated. So much for the trend towards recognition of transsexualism insofar as it can benefit the adult as an individual and, one suspects, might, be developed to benefit the adult as a partner in marriage.

2.72 What of the position of the transsexual as a parent? This issue came before the European Court in *X, Y and Z* v *United Kingdom*.[183] There, X, a female-to-male transsexual, and Y had lived in a stable relationship for 15 years. Y had given birth to three children as a result of donor insemination. Along with Z, one of the children, they argued that their rights under arts 8 and 14[184] of the European Convention had been breached by English law's refusal to register X as the children's father.[185] While the Commission expressed the view that there had been a violation of art 8, the court disagreed by a majority of fourteen to six. The court's view was prompted, at least in part, by the fact that the law on transsexualism was in a state of transition. However, the fact that X could take a number of practical steps, including making a will and applying for joint residence, to put himself in the position of a parent, led the court to conclude that the disadvantages of the present situation were not all that great. It was also persuaded by the fact that any change in the law, treating X as the child's father, would have the effect of inconsistency, since he would still be regarded as female for

---

179 ETS No 5 (1950).

180 (1991) 13 EHRR 622.

181 (1993) 16 EHRR 1.

182 In France, an individual's *carte d'identite* is used for a host of purposes all the time and, thus, where it reveals a gender inconsistent with the individual's appearance and social persona, the infringement of privacy is arguably greater than would be the case in respect of a birth certificate, which is rarely produced in public, in the UK.

183 Application No. 75/1995/581/667 (1997).

184 Article 14 provides that the rights under the Convention shall be afforded without discrimination on the basis of a whole host of grounds, including sex. It will be remembered that art 8 provides for the right to respect for privacy in family life.

185 Where a woman has a child by donor insemination in the course of treatment services provided for her and a man together by a licensed person and the man is not the donor, he is treated in law as the child's father – Human Fertilisation and Embryology Act 1990, s 28(3). See chapter 4, para 44 for a full discussion of this provision.

other legal purposes.[186] Curiously, both the Commission and the court agreed that a decision on art 8 rendered redundant any decision on art 14, guaranteeing the benefits of the Convention without discrimination on a number of grounds including a person's sex. In the past, the fact that one of the applicants in a case was a child has sometimes helped to secure rights for adults,[187] but here the court was again swayed by the lack of consensus amongst member states.

2.73 It is worth noting that the issue of transsexualism has not been the subject of litigation in Scotland since 1957[188] and, in that case, no sex-realignment surgery was involved. Any logically consistent approach to transsexualism requires that it should be recognised for all purposes or for none at all. It is to be hoped that the courts take on board both the enormous scientific developments which have taken place, the trend towards recognition as illustrated by the European Court's decisions and English case-law in the context of employment,[189] and the needs of individual litigants, in adopting an open and permissive approach to an issue in which there is little legitimate public interest. In the context of adult relationships, it is difficult to see any public interest in denying individuals the gender with which they identify and which, often, they have gone to considerable lengths to achieve. In the context of parenthood, the opportunity to recognise an individual's role in a child's life, through clothing that person with parental responsibilities and rights provides a partial practical solution, but it does not create a child-parent relationship.[190]

Significance of gender: civil law

2.74 The development of Scots private law reflects a gradual removal of almost all of the consequences attaching to gender and we have now reached the point where gender is largely insignificant for civil law purposes.[191] People of the same gender may not contract a marriage and, so, to the limited extent that marriage itself attracts any significant

---

186 Van Bueren points out the 'unsatisfactory as well as circular' nature of this argument, since it is the case-law from the European Court which sanctions such an anomaly – G. Van Bueren, 'Annual Review of International Family Law' in A. Bainham (ed), *The International Survey of Family Law 1996* (Martinus Nijhoff, 1998) at p 6.

187 See G. Van Bueren, 'Annual Review of International Family Law' in A. Bainham (ed), *The International Survey of Family Law 1995* (Martinus Nijhoff, 1997) at p 13.

188 *X, Petitioner*, n 173 above. *The Scotsman*, 1 September 1998, p 7 reported the case of Alexandra MacRae, a male to female transsexual, whom the Scottish Prison Service has permitted to serve her sentence in the female unit of a prison. According to the report, this is the first time that a transsexual had been accommodated in this way and it may signal a welcome openness on the part of the authorities.

189 *M v Chief Constable of the West Midlands Police* (1996) IT case 08964/96. See also the decision of the European Court of Justice in *P v S* [1996] 2 CMLR 247 and *P v S and another* [1996] ICR 795.

190 See *X, Y and Z v United Kingdom*, n 183 above. For a discussion of parental responsibilities and rights, see chapters 5 and 6.

191 Of course, this is not to suggest that gender is insignificant. For a fascinating discussion of gender and why women do not achieve parity with men in the private practice of law in Canada, see J. Hagen and F. Kay, *Gender in Practice: A Study of Lawyers' Lives* (OUP, 1995). For a discussion of the position in the USA, see C. F. Epstein, R. Saute, B.

consequences, gender has a lingering importance. The issue of same-sex relationships will be considered later in the context of adult relationships.[192]

2.75 Not only does gender have only limited consequences for civil law purposes, but discrimination on the basis of gender has long been regulated by legislation. The Equal Pay Act 1970 and the Sex Discrimination Acts 1975 and 1986 contain extensive prohibitions on both direct and indirect discrimination on the grounds of sex in the contexts of employment, housing, education and the provision of services.

Significance of gender: criminal law

2.76 So far as the common law is concerned, the gender of an alleged offender is significant for criminal law purposes only insofar as the individual's gender is an essential element of the crime itself. Thus, only a man can commit rape, although a woman can be art and part to the commission of rape.[193] Specific legislation aimed at the protection of girls and young women provides for sexual offences where the crime can only be committed in respect of female victims.[194]

2.77 Until 1980, consensual sexual acts between homosexuals constituted criminal offences. It was perhaps a reflection of changing social attitudes that prosecutions of consenting adults was unknown latterly. In 1980,[195] statute intervened to provide that consensual sexual acts in private between two men over the age of 21 would no longer constitute an offence and, in 1995,[196] the age of consent for homosexuals was reduced to 18, while the age of consent to heterosexual acts remained at 16. To date, attempts to remove this example of discriminatory treatment under the criminal law have been unsuccessful.[197]

Sexual preference

2.78 An individual's sexual preference has no general impact on his or her civil capacity, save for the obvious exception of marriage. Scots law simply does not countenance same-sex marriage[198] and thus, such couples cannot gain the automatic consequences of marriage.[199] In addition, it is significant that, within the UK, there is no equivalent of either sex

Oglensky and M. Gever, 'Glass Ceilings and Open Doors: Women's Advancement in the Legal Profession' 64 Fordham L Rev 291 (1995) and Note, 'Why Law Firms Cannot Afford to Maintain the Mommy Track' 109 Harv L Rev 1375 (1996).

192 See chapter 10, paras 19–21, below.
193 G. H. Gordon, n 53 above, paras 33-01–33-04.
194 These offences are discussed in chapter 3, paras 96–97.
195 Criminal Justice (Scotland) Act 1980, s 80.
196 Criminal Law (Consolidation) (Scotland) Act 1995, s 13.
197 On June 22, 1998, the House of Commons voted by 336 votes to 129 to reduce the age of consent for homosexuals to sixteen, but the amendment to the Crime and Disorder Bill was defeated in the House of Lords.
198 Marriage (Scotland) Act 1977, s 5(4)(e), discussed in chapter 10, para 2 below.
199 Same-sex marriage and registered partnerships, along with other ways in which lesbian and gay couples can gain recognition of their relationships and some of the benefits available to heterosexual couples, are discussed in chapter 10, para 3, below.

discrimination or race relations legislation in respect of lesbians or homosexuals and, thus, such protection from discrimination as is afforded by that legislation is not available to this particular group. In a number of countries, including Germany and South Africa, discrimination on the basis of sexual orientation is prohibited in the constitution while in others, including some Canadian provinces, Denmark, France, Israel, the Netherlands and Sweden have specific anti-discrimination provisions in legislation. Developments in the USA in this respect have been interesting. As recently as 1986, the Supreme Court upheld a Georgia statute which criminalises private, consensual sexual activity between homosexuals.[200] None the less, a number of states prohibit discrimination on the basis of sexual preference, either generally or in respect of employment and the supply of specific services, like housing. However, such is the strength of feeling on the issue, that the picture is changing constantly.[201] That some inroads have been made in the UK in the fight against homophobia is evidenced by the decriminalisation of homosexuality and the recent decision permitting a homosexual to adopt a child.[202] However, the disappointing decision of the European Court of Justice in *Grant* v *South-West Trains*[203] suggests that debate on this issue will continue. None the less, a comprehensive review of the law in this area is long overdue.

Birth status

2.79   At one time whether a child was legitimate, illegitimate, legitimated

---

200 *Bowers* v *Hardwick* 478 US 186, rehearing denied 478 US 1039 (1986).
201 For example, in Maine, one of the first states to apply anti-discrimination laws to sexual preference, the legislation was repealed by popular ballot in February 1998. On the other hand, in the same month in Oregon, where there is no such state anti-discrimination law, the city of Portland passed an ordinance, banning companies that do not have a formal sexual preference anti-discrimination policy from contracting with the city. In *Romer* v *Evans* 116 S Ct 1620 (1996), the Supreme Court held that Colorado's repeal of its anti-discrimination law was unconstitutional. In *Curran* v *Mount Diablo Council of the Boy Scouts of America* 72 Cal Rptr 2d 410 (1998), the Supreme Court of California held that the Boy Scouts' refusal to admit Mr Curran as an assistant scout leader because he was homosexual did not violate the state's constitution. However, the decision was based on the very narrow ground that the Boy Scouts were a private organisation and not a business. The same court issued a similar decision on the same day, upholding the Boy Scouts' refusal to admit atheists who declined to repeat a promise which included the word 'God' – *Randall* v *Orange County Council, Boy Scouts of America* 72 Cal Rptr 2d 453 (1998) (rehearing denied 13 May 1998). In this constantly-changing area of the law it is difficult to keep up-to-date, but the current position in Europe is discussed in the ILGA *Euroletter* – <http://fglb.qrd.org:8080/fqrd/assocs/ilga/euroletter>. The situation in the USA is discussed in the following recent articles; L. Kramer, 'Same-Sex Marriage, Conflict of Laws, and the Unconstitutional Public Policy Exemption' 106 Yale L J 1965 (1997); M. A. Provost, 'Disregarding the Constitution in the Name of defending Marriage: The Unconstitutionality of the Defense of Marriage Act' 8 Seton Hall Const L J 157 (1997); and B. A. Robb, 'The Constitutionality of the Defense of Marriage Act in the Wake of Romer v Evans' 32 New Eng L Rev 263 (1997).
202 *T, Petitioner* 1997 SLT 724, discussed in chapter 8, paras 16–17 below.
203 [1988] IRLR 207, discussed in chapter 10, para 2. For a discussion of the earlier stages of this case and developments in Europe, see P. L. Spackman, 'Grant *v* South-West Trains: Equality for Same-Sex Partners in the European Community' 12 Am U J Int'l L & Pol'y 1063 (1997).

or, latterly, adopted was of very considerable significance in determining the child's relationship with his or her parents, the consequences in respect of other family members and, indeed, in respect of an individual's capacity in society generally. Many of these distinctions have been eroded or eliminated over the centuries by a process of piecemeal legislation. None the less, significant differences remain, most notably between children, depending on whether their parents have ever been married. This issue will be discussed at length in chapters 4, 5 and 6. For the present, it is worth bearing in mind that the United Nations Convention on the Rights of the Child prohibits *'discrimination of any kind, irrespective of the child's or his or her parent's* or legal guardian's race, colour, *sex*, language, religion, political or other opinion, national, ethnic or social origin, property, disability, *birth* or *other status'*.[204]

Marital status

2.80 While marital status has no general impact on an individual's capacity in terms of the civil law, nor on his or her responsibility in criminal law, marriage itself still attracts a number of important consequences. These are discussed in chapter 11.

Mental and physical incapacity

2.81 At the outset, it is important to note the breadth of conditions and disabilities encompassed within the term 'incapacity', and the impact of these conditions and disabilities on an individual's ability to make decisions and to be self-sufficient varies enormously. The special facilities that are required by a person who wears a hearing aid and, thereby, suffers little hearing loss, are quite different to the facilities required to enable a person confined to a wheelchair to use public transport to the full. What is required to provide adequate protection for an individual suffering from dementia might result in unnecessary and unreasonable restrictions being placed on a young adult with fairly minor mental incapacity, if the same régime were to be applied. It follows that the need for the law to make special provision and, perhaps more significantly, the legitimacy for it doing so, requires that there should be a degree of flexibility consistent with recognising the variety of situations which present themselves.

2.82 Concern that the needs of all persons suffering from incapacity should be met has received increasing world attention in the latter half of the 20th century.[205] In 1971, the United Nations adopted the Declaration on the Rights of Mentally Retarded Persons.[206] While the terminology of the Declaration itself is somewhat dated, it none the less recognised the need to enable individuals to realise their full potential at the same time as providing the necessary protection and guidance. Many countries[207] have enacted legislation giving effect to the principles set out in the Declaration.

204 Article 2, italics added.
205 T. Degener, *Human Rights and Disabled Persons* (Martinus Nijhoff, 1994).
206 UN General Assembly 26th Session, resolution 2856.
207 For example, Alberta, Canada; New Zealand; USA.

In 1982, the General Assembly of the United Nations adopted the World Programme of Action Concerning Disabled Persons[208] and this was developed further in the World Conference on Human Rights (June 1993) Vienna Declaration[209] and through the Standard Rules on the Equalisation of Opportunities for Persons with Disabilities. The needs of children with disabilities are expressly recognised in the United Nations Convention on the Rights of the Child.[210] The Council of Europe has produced recommendations aimed at ensuring that procedures are put in place to ensure that speedy emergency protection is available for children, and vulnerable adults.[211]

2.83 Within Scotland,[212] a number of developments have been aimed at improving the position of individuals with disabilities. The, somewhat discredited, policy of 'care in the community', as set out in the White Paper, Caring for People: Community Care in the Next Decade and Beyond,[213] recognised the need to accommodate diversity. It emphasised the need where possible to provide

> 'the services and support which people who are affected by problems of ageing, mental illness, mental handicap or physical or sensory disability need to be able to live as independently as possible in their own homes, or in 'homely' settings in the community'.[214]

The policy itself found much support from individuals with incapacities, the professions and the community as a whole. What has created disquiet is the failure to provide the necessary resources to carry it out. The Disability Discrimination Act 1995 marked another step forward in meeting the needs of people with disabilities in the provision of employment, education, and access to goods and services.[215] The Children (Scotland) Act 1995 makes special provision for children affected by disability and places the local authority under special duties towards them.[216] Other legislation governs assessing the needs of individuals who appear to be in need of

---

208 UN General Assembly, resolution 37/52, 3 December 1982.
209 32 ILM 1661 (1993).
210 Article 23 provides that 'a mentally or physically disabled child should enjoy a full and decent life, in conditions which ensure dignity, promote self-reliance and facilitate the child's active participation in the community' and recognises the disabled child's right to special care including provision for 'education, training, health care services, rehabilitation services, preparation for employment and recreation opportunities in a manner conducive to the child's achieving the fullest possible social integration and individual development, including his or her cultural and spiritual development'.
211 Emergency Measures in Family Matters, Recommendation No R(91)9, 9 September 1991. The Council of Europe is continuing its work in this area, with a view to the preparation of an international convention. In addition, the Hague Conference on International Law is preparing a Convention on Incapable Adults.
212 For a more full account of the background to proposals for reform of Scots law, see Scottish Law Commission, Report on Incapable Adults (Scot Law Com No 151, 1995), Cm 2962, paras 1.1–1.6. See also, Consultation Paper Managing the Finances and Welfare of Incapable Adults (Scottish Office, 1997).
213 Cm 849 (1989).
214 Ibid, para 1.1.
215 See para 2.86.
216 See para 2.84.

'community care services'.[217] None the less, it is acknowledged that aspects of the law, not least in respect of guardianship and the protection of individuals with disabilities, are far from satisfactory and proposals for reform of the law in these respects are discussed presently.[218]

Physical incapacity

2.84 Physical incapacity has no effect on an individual's legal capacity. However, there are circumstances where a particular disability will give an individual additional rights or require that some special procedure should be followed. For example, the parents of a child with 'pronounced, specific or special needs' can require the local authority to assess and meet these needs.[219] Thus, a child with speech difficulties[220] or dyslexia[221] may be entitled to additional educational provision aimed at the particular problem. Other individuals may have disabilities which entitle them, or the person caring for them, to additional state benefits.

2.85 Perhaps the best example of a special procedure being provided for a person suffering from physical incapacity is that of notarial execution of deeds. Notarial execution is now governed by the Requirements of Writing (Scotland) Act 1995, which altered the previous law in a number of important respects, and the procedure outlined here applies to deeds executed on or after 1 August 1995.[222] Where an individual is temporarily or permanently blind or unable to write, a formal legal document may be executed on his or her behalf by a 'relevant person': that is, a solicitor, an advocate, a justice of the peace or a sheriff clerk.[223] Briefly, notarial execution works as follows. The granter, the relevant person and the

---

217 Social Work (Scotland) Act 1968, s 12A. See, for example, the Carers (Recognition and Services) Act 1995 and the Disabled Persons (Services, Consultation and Representation) Act 1986.
218 See paras 2.92 and 2.93.
219 Education (Scotland) Act 1980, s 1(5)(c) and (d) as amended by the Education (Scotland) Act 1981, s 3. The local authority cannot take its own resource limitations into account in assessing and meeting the educational needs of children – *R v East Sussex County Council, ex parte Tandy* [1998] 2 All ER 769.
220 *R v Lancashire County Council, ex parte C M (A Minor)* 1989 Fam Law 395.
221 *R v Hampshire Education Authority, ex parte J* (1985) 84 LGR 547.
222 1995 Act, s 9 and Sched 3. Prior to that date, notarial execution was governed by the Conveyancing (Scotland) Act 1924, s 18(1) and Sched 1. The validity of deeds executed under the older procedure may be relevant for many years to come. For a full discussion of the position under the 1924 Act and the 1995 Act, see I. J. S. Talman (ed), *Halliday's Conveyancing Law and Practice in Scotland* (2nd edn, W. Green, 1996), at paras 3-37–3-41 and paras 3-151–3.158, respectively.
223 1995 Act, s 9(6). Care should be taken to ensure that the relevant person does not have a disqualifying interest. Where the document confers a benefit (in money or money's worth and whether directly or indirectly) on the relevant person or his or her spouse or child, the document will be invalid to the extent of the benefit. On the rigour with which this rule was applied in the past, see *Crawford's Trustees* v *Glasgow Royal Infirmary* 1955 SC 367. Where the deed is executed abroad, notarial execution may be effected by a person authorised to do so in the foreign jurisdiction. Scottish notaries who are not also solicitors may no longer effect notarial execution in Scotland. Prior to the 1995 Act, a Church of Scotland minister acting in his or her own parish could execute testamentary writings *only*, notarially – Church of Scotland (Property and Endowments) Amendment Act 1933, s 13. This is no longer possible.

witness meet together. The granter declares that he or she is blind or unable to write and the relevant person reads the document to him or her, unless the granter expressly dispenses with such a reading. The granter then authorises the relevant person to subscribe the document, subscription takes place in the sight of the witness, and the witness then signs the document as well.[224] While a blind person can sign a document himself or herself, notarial execution is thought to be preferable since it reduces the possibility of fraud.

2.86 In the past, the widespread failure to give recognition to physical incapacity was, in itself, a form of discrimination. If an individual faces restrictions or limitations because of his or her disability, and steps are not taken to accommodate that individual's needs, he or she may be disadvantaged. The Disability Discrimination Act 1995 ('the 1995 Act') seeks to tackle this problem. It defines 'disability' as 'a physical or mental impairment which has a substantial and long-term adverse effect [on a person's] ability to carry out normal day-to-day activities'.[225] It is unlawful for an employer with 20 or more staff to discriminate against a disabled person because of a reason relating to his or her disability,[226] unless the employer can show that the discrimination is justified.[227] Less favourable treatment is justified only if it is both material to the circumstances of the particular case and substantial.[228] However, the employer is obliged to make reasonable adjustments to accommodate the disabled person.[229] Trade organisations are under similar obligations.[230] The providers of goods, services and facilities to the public are not permitted to discriminate against disabled persons and, again, the onus falls on the provider to justify any discrimination.[231] In the context of higher education, institutions are required to take account of the needs of disabled people and to publish statements about their facilities in this respect. Exactly how the 1995 Act will operate is untested as yet. However, taking the example of a university, it appears that the institution will have to do a great deal more to accommodate people with disabilities *qua* employer and provider of services such as museums and art galleries, than it will *qua* provider of education.

---

224 In the case of a testamentary writing, the relevant person should sign the document on every page –1995 Act, s 3(2).
225 Section 1(1). The Secretary of State has exercised the power, conferred by s 3 of the Act to issue guidelines on a host of matters, including interpretation of the definition of disability. Copies of the guidelines which, while disclaiming authoritative status will undoubtedly be used in interpreting the Act (see, s 3(3)), are available from HMSO. The Supreme Court of the USA has recently decided, by a narrow majority, that a person fell within the ambit of 'disability' for the purpose of the Americans With Disabilities Act where she was HIV positive but showed no symptoms of illness – *Bragdon* v *Abbott* 118 S Ct 2196 (1998). It should be noted that the decision turned on the relatively narrow facts of that particular case and, arguably, the case does not offer protection to all persons who are HIV positive. See also the very strong dissenting opinion in the case.
226 Section 4.
227 Section 5(1)(b).
228 Section 5(3).
229 Section 6.
230 Sections 13–15.
231 Sections 19–21.

Mental incapacity

2.87 Adults with full legal capacity are entitled to take decisions for themselves, and Scots law starts from the presumption that an individual has full legal capacity until the contrary is established.[232] Where a person is mentally incapacitated, there are a number of mechanisms providing for the guardianship of adults.[233] Some of these, most notably the appointment of a tutor-at-law,[234] can provide for a guardian who deals with both the welfare of the incapacitated person and the management of his or her property, while others, like the tutor-dative, who had this joint role in the past, have recently been appointed with personal welfare powers only.[235] Others, like mental health guardians,[236] are simply restricted personal guardians with no control over the incapacitated person's property. Yet others, like the curator bonis, are restricted to managing property. Still others, like Department of Social Security appointees[237] and hospital managers,[238] are confined to the management of specific property. While a person has capacity, he or she can appoint another person, known as an attorney, to manage his or her financial affairs. In all of this, there is virtually no role for relatives of the incapacitated person unless they hold a specific appointment.[239] That this fragmentation of the guardian's role is less than ideal was highlighted by the Scottish Law Commission when it pointed out that 'most adults' welfare and finances are inextricably

232 *Lindsay* v *Watson* (1843) 5 D 1194.
233 For an excellent discussion of the mechanisms, their development and their short-comings, see Scottish Law Commission, Mentally Disabled Adults: Legal Arrangements for Managing their Welfare and Finances (Discussion Paper No. 94, 1991) at paras 2.3–2.26 and 4.2–4.26, (summarised in Report on Incapable Adults (Scot Law Com No 151, 1995), Cm 2962, at paras 1.7–1.26) and David Nichols, 'Legal Arrangements for Managing the Finances of Mentally Disabled Adults in Scotland', 1992 (3) J Soc Wel & Fam L 193.
234 Tutors-at-law were thought to be obsolete until relatively recently, when a father was appointed tutor-at-law to his adult daughter *Britton* v *Britton's Curator Bonis* (OH) 1992 SCLR 947. She had sustained brain injury when she was knocked down as a two year-old and, while she already had a curator bonis managing her financial affairs (the assets being derived from compensation for the accident), the court accepted that it would be helpful to developing her own capacity if her affairs were managed by someone involved in her day-to-day life.
235 Like the tutor-at-law the office of tutor-dative is of considerable antiquity, but, unlike the tutor-at-law appointment was never limited to the nearest male agnate. The office of tutors-dative was thought to be obsolete until a number of recent cases demonstrated how it might usefully assist in the care of incapable persons and the appropriate modern procedure has been clarified to some extent. With the exception of *Chapman, Petitioner* 1993 SLT 955, the cases are unreported. However they are discussed in – A. D. Ward, 'Revival of Tutors-Dative' 1987 SLT (News) 69 and A. D. Ward, 'Tutors to Adults: Developments' 1992 SLT (News) 325; Adrian D. Ward, *The power to act: the development of Scots law for mentally handicapped people* (Scottish Society for the Mentally Handicapped, 1990).
236 Appointment is under the Mental Health (Scotland) Act 1984, s 36.
237 Social Security (Claims and Payments) Regulations 1987, r 33, SI 1987 No 1968.
238 Mental Health (Scotland) Act 1984, s 94.
239 Specific provision permits certain payments to be made to the individual looking after the mentally incapable person and this will often be a relative. See Mental Health Act 1983, s 142 (payments from government departments) and Industrial and Provident Societies Act 1965, s 22 (payments from such societies).

connected and decisions in one area may well have repercussions in the other'.[240]

2.88 Quite apart from this, rather confusing, array of possible appointments, the present law is defective in a number of other respects. Only the nearest male agnate of a mentally incapacitated person is entitled to be appointed as tutor-at-law.[241] With the offices of tutor-at-law and tutor-dative, being only recently revived, it is necessary to search fairly ancient case-law in order to establish their exact powers and responsibilities. Appointment in both cases requires application to the Court of Session, a somewhat expensive process. In terms of property, the appointment of a curator is something of an 'all or nothing' affair, with the curator taking over the management of all of a person's property until the appointment is recalled. In addition to its lack of flexibility, curatory is expensive. Other mechanisms, like the attorney and the hospital manager, may be criticised as being, respectively, unsupervised or too informal. It is hardly surprising that the Scottish Law Commission described the present law as 'fragmented [and] archaic'[242] and concluded that it 'fails to provide an adequate remedy in many common situations'.[243]

2.89 So far, we have considered the private arrangements which can be made for the guardianship of a mentally incapacitated person. Separate from, but to some extent linked to this, is consideration of what, if any, public powers exist to protect vulnerable adults. The Mental Health (Scotland) Act 1984 permits a doctor to authorise the detention in hospital of an individual where the doctor believes that, due to the person's mental disorder, there is urgent necessity in order to protect the disordered person or for the protection of the public.[244] In addition, there is provision for the following

a person authorised by the local authority or the Mental Welfare Commission may demand admission to premises where the mentally disordered person is;[245]

a mental health officer or medical commissioner may obtain a warrant from a sheriff or a justice of the peace to effect forcible entry to premises and to remove a disordered person to a place of safety;[246]

a police officer may take a mentally disordered person to a place of safety if the person is in need of care or control and is found in a public place;[247]

---

240 Report on Incapable Adults, n 233 above, at para 1.23.
241 Curators Act 1585. In addition, he must be at least 25 years old and fit to act. If the nearest male agnate is unwilling to act or incapable of so doing, no other person can be appointed tutor-at-law.
242 Report on Incapable Adults, above, at para 1.15.
243 Ibid.
244 Section 24. Detention can be for up to 72 hours. In addition, a nurse may authorise detention in hospital for up to two hours so that the patient may be examined in order to establish whether an emergency application is necessary, s 25.
245 Section 117(1).
246 Section 117(2).
247 Section 118.

the local authority has a duty to protect the property of a mentally disordered person where the person has been admitted to hospital, is subject to guardianship or has been removed from the home, if no one else is doing this.[248]

In addition, the local authority can apply to the sheriff for authorisation to remove from the home a person suffering from a chronic disease who lacks proper care and attention and take him or her to a hospital.[249]

2.90 Again, the Scottish Law Commission examined this area of the law and found it to be inadequate in a number of respects.[250] Most of the powers concentrate on mentally disordered people and do not provide protection to other vulnerable groups of adults. The powers tend to go for the 'all or nothing' response of removal and, as such, both lack the flexibility necessary to accommodate all the circumstances which may present themselves and are out of step with the modern approach of regarding removal to an institution as the last resort. The individual powers highlighted above were also criticised in a number of specific respects.[251]

Reform of the law

2.91 As a result of its consideration of the law governing both the guardianship of incapable adults and the protection of vulnerable adults, and after extensive consultation, the Commission produced two, free-standing reports containing extensive recommendations for reform. As is the Commission's usual practice, each Report makes life easy for the legislature by providing a draft Bill. The draft Bills await legislative action.[252]

2.92 In the 'Report on Incapable Adults', the Commission recommends a comprehensive scheme governing the personal welfare and property of incapable adults and designed to cover both short-term and long-term needs with the maximum of flexibility. Consistent with respect for individual autonomy, the proposals provide for a competent adult to make arrangements, by means of a power of attorney, for personal welfare and property matters to be taken care of in the event of his or her incapacity. There are various schemes to enable those looking after incapable adults to deal with personal welfare and property issues without the need to report to the courts as well as other measures which would require legal proceedings. In addition to the court's powers to appoint guardians, provision is recommended for inexpensive administration of small estates by a Public Guardian.[253]

248 National Assistance Act 1948, s 48, as amended by the 1984 Act, s 92(2).
249 1948 Act, s 47.
250 Scottish Law Commission, Mentally Disordered and Vulnerable Adults: Public Authority Powers (Discussion Paper No 96, 1993).
251 For a summary of these, see Report on Vulnerable Adults (Scot Law Com No 158, 1997), paras 2.4–2.7.
252 See also, Consultation Paper, Managing the Finances and Welfare of Incapable Adults (Scottish Office, 1997).
253 In England and Wales, the Lord Chancellor's Department has been considering this area of the law; see the Consultation Paper, Who Decides? Making decisions on behalf of

2.93 In the 'Report on Vulnerable Adults', the Commission recommends legislation which would cover not only the mentally disordered but other potentially vulnerable groups. A vulnerable person is defined as one who is unable to safeguard his or her own welfare, property or financial affairs and is in need of care and attention due to age or infirmity, or suffering from illness or mental disorder or substantially handicapped by any disability. Given that existing child protection legislation tends to cease when the young person reaches 16,[254] the Commission's recommendation would pick up at that stage. Broadly, the scheme proposed by the Commission provides for a duty to investigate cases where a vulnerable adult or a person suspected of being vulnerable seems to be ill-treated, inadequately cared for or financially exploited. This would include a power to inspect premises where the person is living, to examine documents relating to his or her financial affairs, and to carry out an examination or assessment of the person. Ultimately, there would be the power to remove the risk of abuse from the vulnerable person or, as a last resort, to remove the person to a place of safety.

Links with a place

2.94 Having a link with a particular place can be of significance for a host of civil legal purposes, including an individual's nationality, domicile and habitual residence. In addition, such links, combined with such other matters as parentage and registration, are significant for immigration purposes. So far as the criminal law is concerned, an individual's links with a particular place are largely irrelevant, save for the fact that most countries will not permit the extradition of their own nationals to stand trial in other countries. The Race Relations Act 1976 prohibits discrimination against a person on the basis of race, colour, nationality, or ethnic or national origins and makes it an offence to incite racial hatred. Fascinating though they are, these matters are largely outwith the scope of this book.

Insolvency

2.95 A person whose estate has been sequestrated suffers certain restrictions on his or her freedom to borrow money or to participate in various business activities.[255] Thus, it is an offence for such a person to obtain credit of £250.00 or more without disclosing his or her status to the creditor.[256] Similarly, it is an offence for such a person to act as director or liquidator of a company or to take part in the promotion, formation or management of a company.[257] In addition, while he or she remains undischarged, such a

mentally incapable adults (December 1997, Lord Chancellor's Department) paras 1.10–1.13, where the question is asked whether the same system should apply throughout the UK.
254 This is not always the case. The jurisdiction of the children's hearings system can extend beyond 16 and the local authority owes certain duties to persons over that age.
255 On insolvency, see W. W. McBride, *Bankruptcy* (2nd edn, W. Green, 1995); W. A. Wilson, *The Scottish Law of Debt* (2nd edn, W. Green, 1991).
256 Bankruptcy (Scotland) Act 1985, s 67.
257 Company Directors Disqualification Act 1986, s 11.

person is disqualified from being elected to Parliament or, if already elected, from sitting or voting therein.[258] From the point of view of the family, perhaps the most important aspect of insolvency legislation is the restriction placed on a trustee in bankruptcy who seeks to sell the debtor's home where it is occupied by the family.[259]

Imprisonment

2.96 Apart from the obvious deprivation of liberty and the restrictions attendant thereto, imprisonment itself does not affect an individual's capacity to participate in the legal process. Thus a prisoner retains the capacity to enter contracts and to marry. Indeed, the European Court of Human Rights has found it to be a breach of the Convention to restrict a prisoner's freedom to marry.[260] The main restriction on a prisoner's capacity to be a player in the legal process is the denial of the right to vote.[261]

2.97 Considerable attention began to focus on women in prison in Scotland due largely to a sharp rise in the incidence of suicide and self-harm in recent years. Between 1995 and 1997 seven women hanged themselves in Cornton Vale prison.[262] This represented a dramatic departure from the usual Scottish experience. In 1997, the Prison and Social Work Inspectorate reviewed the use of custody for women offenders and considered alternative community disposals. Such was the urgency with which the matter was rightly regarded that it reported within four months, making a number of recommendations.[263] Many of its recommendations, including the setting up of a steering group in Glasgow to direct an inter-agency project examining issues arising from female offending and the disposal of offenders, were implemented swiftly.

2.98 Clearly family life will often be affected by the enforced absence of one of the family members and, while imprisonment does not amount to 'wilful desertion'[264] for the purpose of divorce, engaging in criminal conduct in the knowledge that imprisonment might result could justify a sufficiently distressed spouse in seeking a divorce on the ground of the offender's behaviour.[265] In addition, any period of imprisonment could count towards the two- or five-year periods of non-cohabitation.[266] The

---

258 Insolvency Act 1986, s 427.
259 Bankruptcy (Scotland) Act 1985, s 40.
260 *Hamer* v *United Kingdom* [1982] 4 EHRR 139.
261 Representation of the People Act 1983, s 3.
262 Of the seven women who died, five were on remand and three of them were under 21 years old. The incidence of self-harm had also been rising and at least four incidents could have been fatal but for the swift intervention of the staff. See Women Offenders – A Safer Way, below, at p 1.
263 Social Work Services and Prisons Inspectorate for Scotland, Women Offenders – A Safer Way: A Review of Community Disposals and the Use of Custody for Women Offenders in Scotland (The Scottish Office, 1998).
264 E. M Clive, *The Law of Husband and Wife in Scotland* (4th edn, W. Green, 1997), at para 21.040.
265 Divorce (Scotland) Act 1976, s 1(2)(b).
266 Divorce (Scotland) Act 1976, s 1(2)(d) and (e).

separation of parent and child occasioned by the parent's imprisonment results in the parent being unavailable to fulfil parental responsibilities or to exercise parental rights fully and, while contact can be maintained by letter, telephone and prison visits, the facilities available in most of Scotland's prisons do nothing to enhance the quality of visits.[267]

267 More Than A Box Of Toys (Save the Children Scotland 1997), points out that, while 1,600 children make prison visits every week, most prisons make inadequate arrangements for parents and children to have time together outside the formal visiting room; have no play supervisor to keep the children amused while the parents talk; and one in five does not even have a box of toys. The position is not universally bleak, with Greenock offering a specially designed visits centre and a similar facility is planned for Barlinnie in 1998.

CHAPTER 3

CHILDREN: RIGHTS AND POWERS, RESPONSIBILITIES AND RESTRICTIONS

3.1 It is often said that the idea of children, as people with rights, as opposed to their being the objects of protection, is a relatively new phenomenon. In one sense this is true. Like most other developed legal systems, Scots law has long sought to protect children from the dangers inherent in, or posed by, the adult world, but many rights have only found expression in recent legislation. Thus, while there is nothing new in an official body being responsible for taking care of children where no other person is doing so,[1] widespread recognition of the child's right to be consulted in the decision-making process only found statutory expression in the Children (Scotland) Act 1995.[2] None the less, this popular belief proves to be too simplistic, both in an historical context, and in respect of the contemporary position, when we analyse what we mean by the concepts of 'children's rights' and 'child protection'.[3]

3.2 A good example of the recognition of children having rights, and one

---

1 See G. Nicholls, *A History of the Scotch Poor Law* (1856); G. A. Mackay, *Practice of the Scottish Poor Law* (1907). For an excellent discussion of general developments here, see K. Marshall, 'The History and Philosophy of Children's Rights in Scotland' in Cleland and Sutherland (eds), *Children's Rights in Scotland: Scots Law Analysed in the Light of the UN Convention on the Rights of the Child* (W. Green, 1996).

2 As we shall see, it had become a matter of good practice to consider the child's views in many contexts before the passing of the 1995 Act. So, for example, where the parents were in dispute over future child-care arrangements, most courts took the child's views into account. However, benefitting from a discretionary practice is not the same thing as having a right. Historically, children have always had significant rights in respect of adoption.

3 An extensive body of literature exists on the subject of children's rights, the needs of children to be protected, and the interaction of children's rights with the rights of others. The following are a sample of those the present author regards as amongst the best: P. Alston, S. Parker and J. Seymour (eds), *Children, Rights and the Law* (Clarendon Press, 1992); D. M. Dickens, 'The Modern Function and Limits of Parental Rights' (1981) 97 LQR 462; J. Eekelaar, 'The Emergence of Children's Rights' (1986) 6 Oxford L Stud 161; M. Freeman, *The Rights and Wrongs of Children* (Frances Pinter, 1983); B. Hafen, 'Children's Liberation and the New Egalitarianism: Some reservations about Abandoning Youth their Rights' B Y U L Rev 605 (1976); N. MacCormick, 'Children's Rights: A Test Case' in *Legal Right and Social Democracy: Essays in Legal and Political Philosophy* (Clarendon Press, 1982); M. Minow, 'Rights for the Next Generation: A Feminist Approach to Children's Rights' 9 Harv W L J 1 (1986); M. Wald, 'Children's Rights: A Framework for Analysis' 12 UC Davis L Rev 225 (1979).

of ancient standing,[4] is the way in which minor children[5] could participate in the legal system, either with the agreement of their curators (guardians), or independently. Thus, a minor with a curator could contract, in some circumstances, and could make a will.[6] These examples of children's ability to be effective participants are sometimes described as 'powers' rather than 'rights', but, that distinction is not wholly satisfactory. The power to participate in the legal system can equally be seen as reflecting respect for the child's evolving capacity and recognising the child's right to participate in decision-making.

3.3 What were conceived of, originally, as measures aimed at protecting children may be seen as restricting the child's freedom of action when examined in a modern context. Early legislation controlling the use of child labour was undoubtedly aimed at protecting children from the excesses of the industrial revolution.[7] However, to restrict unduly the right of older children to engage in safe employment for short periods of time may be to deny them the fulfilment and limited independence of earning a small income. To deny a driving licence to anyone below the age of 17 may protect children from harming themselves and others, but it may restrict the freedom of young people and particularly those living in rural areas.[8] In each case, it might be argued that the child's evolving capacity is not being recognised. What these examples of 'protective measures' or 'restrictions' illustrate is the tension that exists between protecting a child's welfare at the same time as recognising his or her rights. We will return to discuss this tension presently.

3.4 What, then, of children's responsibilities? As we shall see, children have the capacity to enter into various kinds of transactions and, where the

---

4 See Wilkinson and Norrie, *Parent and Child* (W. Green, 1993), pp 37–51 and the *Stair Memorial Encyclopaedia*, vol 10, paras 1049–1114.
5 Minors were young people below the age of majority but, in the case of females, over the age of 12, and in the case of males, over the age of 14, years. If the minor had a curator, the curator's consent was normally required for the minor's legal transactions to be valid. However, where the minor was living an independent life, he or she could transact as an adult. Such independent minors were described as being 'forisfamiliated'. For a discussion of forisfamiliation, see Wilkinson and Norrie, above, pp 44–45, and *Stair Memorial Encyclopaedia*, vol 10, paras 1098–1104.
6 See para 3.65, below and the references therein.
7 In many parts of the world, it remains the case that children are employed in a wholly unacceptable manner and exploited mercilessly. It is estimated that some 120 million children between the ages of five and 14 currently work full-time, with a further 130 million working part-time – ILO, Combatting the Most Intolerable Forms of Child Labour: A Global Challenge (ILO, 1997). See also, Final Report of the [Oslo] International Conference on Child Labour (ILO, 1997); A. Giampetro-Meyer, T. Brown and N. Kubasek, 'The Exploitation of Child Labor: An Intractable Legal Problem?' 16 Loy L A Int'l & Comp L J 657 (1994); and M. Moran, 'Ending Exploitative Child Labor Practices' 5 Pace Int'l Rev 287 (1993).
8 In many states in the USA, a young person can apply for a 'hardship licence' on the basis that, due to the circumstances of the particular case, he or she would be restricted unreasonably by not being allowed to drive. In Texas, for example, such applications are open to a person aged 14 or older. Of course, the young person then has to pass a driving test before being permitted to drive.

transaction is valid, the child is responsible for it.[9] In addition, the law has long regarded some children as being responsible for their actions in the context of both delict and criminal law. Once it has been established that a child has committed an offence, most children will be dealt with in the children's hearings system which has treatment, rather than a punishment, as its underlying philosophy.[10] This seeks to assess what the individual child's problems are and to help him or her to overcome them and, as such, is rightly viewed by many as enlightened and humane. However, since each child's circumstances, rather than the offence, determine what will happen, there is no opportunity for the child to experience the predictability of the kind of tariff adult offenders face. Thus, it is quite possible that two children who commit an offence together will be subject to very different disposals. It has been argued that such an approach does not accord with notions of justice.[11]

3.5 What the above is intended to illustrate is that notions of children's rights, powers, responsibilities and restrictions are part of a complex, interlocking structure. None the less, in examining the various aspects of the structure, it is often helpful to use these very terms. Nor should the complexity be seen as an obstacle; it is simply the challenge which makes this area of study so fascinating. In this chapter, we will look first at international activity and then examine specific examples of how children's rights, powers, responsibilities and restrictions operate.

CHILDREN'S RIGHTS

The World Scene[12]

3.6 The acceptance that children have rights – and real attempts to define the content of these rights – is a process which in a world context can best be described as somewhat uneven and haphazard.[13] Since the beginning of this century, various groups[14] and organisations formulated statements of

---

9 See para 3.62, below.

10 The children's hearing system is discussed in detail in chapter 9.

11 In the USA, *In re Gault* 387 U S 1 (1967) is often cited as signalling the Supreme Court's rejection of different treatment of young people within the criminal justice system. In fact, what that case attacked was a specific example of a juvenile being denied basic due process protection, albeit the opportunity was taken to question some of the fundamental assumptions of the system operating at the time. As the court made clear in *McKiever* v *Pennsylvania* 404 U S 528 (1971) at p 533, *Gault* did not 'spell the doom of the juvenile justice system or ... deprive it of its "informality, flexibility or speed"'.

12 Much of the discussion contained in this section and that dealing with the drafting of the United Nations Convention on the Rights of the Child substantially reproduces what was said by the present author in, 'The Convention Comes To Scotland' in Cleland and Sutherland, n 1 above. However, the whole area of children's rights is so dynamic that much has been added. In addition, other international developments are discussed.

13 For a thorough analysis of the various attempts, see P. Veerman, *The Rights of the Child and the Changing Image of Childhood* (Martinus Nijhoff, 1992).

14 See for example, The Declaration of the Rights of the Child, proposed to the 'Prolet Cult', Moscow, 1918, discussed in Veerman, above, at pp 281–285.

the rights of children[15] and young people.[16] While some of these concentrated on particular areas of concern, for example, employment, others were more general in nature.

3.7 However, the first step in establishing a truly international document resulted from the work and determination of Eglantyne Jebb,[17] the founder of Save the Children International Union and the British Save the Children Fund. She sought the creation of a Code for Children which should

> 'not be a piece of legislation but rather a document defining the duties of adults towards children, which each country would recognise either by means of State intervention or by private action'.[18]

Her efforts resulted in the Declaration of Geneva. The document had already been signed by an impressive number of heads of state and governments in individual ceremonies around the world prior to the historic ceremony in the Geneva Museum of Art and History in 1924, but it gained further recognition when it was endorsed by the League of Nations later that year. The League urged member states to be guided by it and Guiseppe Motta, the chairman of the League's Assembly, called it the 'Children's Charter of the League of Nations'.

3.8 As early as 1946, the International Union for Child Welfare began lobbying the Economic and Social Council of the United Nations to adopt the Declaration of Geneva and there followed a period of deliberation when various amendments to the Declaration were discussed.[19] In 1959, the United Nations adopted the Declaration of the Rights of the Child.[20] Being a resolution of the General Assembly, the Declaration is not a legally-binding instrument, although, from its terms, it was clearly intended to have normative effect.

3.9 During the 1970s the 'children's rights movement' began to gather force to the extent that, by 1983, Freeman was prompted to observe that, '"Children's rights" has become something of a "hurrah" idea'.[21] 'Hurrah' idea or not, the essential problems with recognition of these rights remained the content of the rights themselves and the mechanisms that could be employed effectively in order to ensure that these rights were enforceable. In addressing the content of children's rights, Farson saw the child's right to self-determination as the cental issue and viewed notions of protecting the child's welfare as a restriction on this.[22] His vision of children's rights included not only the more traditional rights of education and justice, but the more controversial rights to sexual freedom and choice

---

15 See for example, The Children's Charter, President Hoover, 1930; The Children's Charter, International Council of Women, 1922, discussed in Veerman, above.
16 See for example, The Declaration of the Rights of Adolescents, Youth Workers International and the International Union of Socialist Youth Organisations, Salzburg, 1922, discussed in Veerman, above.
17 Her work is discussed in Veerman above, pp 88–91 and 155–156.
18 Quoted in Veerman above, at p 155.
19 See Veerman above, at pp 159–168.
20 UN Doc A/4054 (1959) (hereinafter, the 'Declaration').
21 M. D. A. Freeman, *The Rights and Wrongs of Children* (Frances Pinter, 1983), at p 6.
22 R. Farson, *Birthrights* (Penguin, 1978).

of living arrangements. Holt[23] took a similar approach and included the right to use drugs in his list.[24]

3.10 Unsurprisingly enough, the 'liberation school' met with much criticism, not least for its failure to recognise the need to protect children.[25] It would be all too easy from the perspective of the 1990s, confronted, as we are, by the problems of drug-dependency and HIV, to dismiss the liberation school as a collection of cranks. None the less, the writings of the time focused attention on the need to address the crucial issues of the content of children's rights and, in particular, the extent to which freedom and equality with adults could be accommodated. The 1980s saw greater emphasis being placed on children's rights in the context of the responsibilities placed on parents and others, the concept of welfare, and attempts to reconcile apparent conflict through the notion of the evolving capacity of children.[26]

3.11 Twenty years after the adoption of the Declaration, as part of the celebrations for the International Year of the Child, the Polish government proposed the drafting of a Convention to elevate the principles embodied in the Declaration to the status of enforceable rights.[27] It submitted two draft models to the Commission on Human Rights, the United Nations body which drafts such instruments. The first model, which substantially repeated the Declaration and added an enforcement mechanism, was much criticised as being too imprecise. The second, much more detailed, model formed the basis of deliberations for the drafting of what was to become the Convention.

The United Nations Convention on the Rights of the Child

Drafting the Convention[28]

3.12 It might be thought that the drafting of the Convention did not get off to a good start. As Van Bueren points out, the majority of member states had opposed the call for a binding treaty on the rights of the child in 1959 and, while their opposition was withdrawn in 1979, 'a withdrawal of opposition ... is not the same as enthusiastic support'.[29] She continues, however, with the encouraging observation that 'delegates began to realise

---

23 J. Holt, *Escape from Childhood* (Penguin, 1975).
24 Above at p 201.
25 Freeman above, pp 22–24; Hafen, n 3 above.
26 Alston, n 3 above, Eekelaar, n 3 above, and Freeman, above. See also, Scottish Law Commission, Legal Capacity with Responsibilities of Minors and Pupils (Scot Law Com Consultative Memorandum No 65, 1985); Report on Responsibilities and Rights of Minors and Pupil (Scot Law Com No 110, 1987).
27 For a discussion of the different enforcement mechanisms employed in international conventions, see J. P. Grant, 'A Paper Tiger?: Monitoring and Enforcing the Convention' in Cleland and Sutherland, n 1 above, p 241.
28 See C. P. Cohen and H. A. Davidson (eds), *Children's Rights in America: UN Convention on the Rights of the Child compared with United States Law* (American Bar Association, 1990); G. Van Bueren, *The International Law on the Rights of the Child* (Martinus Nijhoff, 1995); Veerman, n 13 above.
29 Van Bueren above, at p 13.

the importance of their work'. While much of the Convention has its origins in the second Polish draft presented to the Commission on Human Rights in 1979, some articles were the result of drafts tabled by government delegations or sponsored by non-governmental organisations.[30] During the first reading deliberative process, most articles were amended to some extent, while amendment during the second reading stage appears to have varied from intense to haphazard.[31] Drafting of the Convention proceeded on the basis of consensus, consensus being described by Cohen as 'a process which does not so much denote support, as it does a lack of objection'.[32]

3.13 A good illustration of what the drafting process involved can be found in relation to art 1. Since all lawyers know that the very definition of terms used is an essential prerequisite for discussing substantive issues, it is hardly surprising that finding an acceptable definition of 'the child' provoked much debate throughout the drafting process,[33] and indeed continues to reflect division of opinion amongst states which have signed or ratified the Convention.[34] Debate focused on three issues: the beginning of childhood; the end of childhood; and the age of majority, although it was the first of these which proved to be the most controversial. The second Polish model referred to a child as 'every human being from the moment of his[35] birth to the age of 18 years'.[36] This prompted a sharp division during the deliberations of the working group between states who wanted to protect the child from the moment of conception and those whose domestic law permitted abortion. Agreement was reached by the adoption of the proposal by the Moroccan government to delete the words 'from the moment of birth'. During the second reading, Malta and Senegal, supported by the observer from the Holy See, proposed the insertion of the words 'moment of conception', but the proposal was dropped in the face of strong opposition. To some extent, the willingness of Malta and Senegal to concede the matter resulted from the agreement to include in the preamble to the Convention mention of the child's need for 'appropriate legal protection before as well as after birth'. While the preamble must be read in the light of the substantive articles in the Convention, this mention of the

30 For a discussion of the activities of non-governmental organisations, see C. P. Cohen, 'The Role of Non-Governmental Organisations in the Drafting of the Convention on the Rights of the Child', 12 *Human Rights Quarterly* 137 (1990). Indeed, Van Bueren suggests that the initial reluctance of some governments to accord high priority to the drafting of the Convention had the beneficial result that the working group was able to adopt its own methods of working including close co-operation with non-governmental organisations – above, at p 13, n 97.
31 Cohen, 'A Guide to Linguistic Interpretation of the UN Convention on the Rights of the Child' in Cohen and Davidson above, 33 at p 40.
32 Above, at p 42.
33 Above, at pp 41–43. See also, Van Bueren above, at pp 32–38.
34 Ratification document of the Holy See and The UK Reservation and Declarations (CRC/C/2/Rev 4, p 32) which provides 'The United Kingdom interprets the Convention as applicable only following a live birth'.
35 Gender neutrality found its way into the Convention in the course of the drafting process.
36 UN Doc E/CN 4/1 1542 (1980), paras 30–31.

pre-birth period injected a point of principle enabling consensus. In effect, each state is left to decide the matter for itself.

3.14 From the point of view of Scots law, it is significant that the UK delegation to the negotiations included no Scots lawyer. This explains why the difficulties which arose later in respect of art 37(d), which requires that every child deprived of his or her liberty should have prompt access to legal and other appropriate assistance, were not noticed at an earlier stage. The way in which the children's hearings system operated at the time raised real problems over compliance with that provision and the UK was forced to enter a reservation in respect of the system. Had there been a Scots lawyer present, the difficulty would have been noticed and attempts would have been made to avoid the ensuing embarrassment. Subsequent changes to the hearings system, introduced by the Children (Scotland) Act 1995 and the rules made thereunder, enabled the UK to withdraw its reservation in respect of the children's hearings system.[37]

3.15 The Convention was adopted unanimously by the General Assembly of the United Nations on 20 November 1989. Having received ratification by more than the required twenty states, it came into force on 2 September 1990.

Structure of the Convention

3.16 The Convention is unique in a number of respects. Not only does it deal with an unprecedented range of rights, it also applies both during peace and in time of war. It came into force more quickly than any other UN human rights convention. Various attempts have been made to categorise the many different rights embodied in the Convention and one of the clearest is provided by Muntarbhorn[38] who classified the rights as follows

'1 *General rights* (the right to life, prohibition against torture, freedom of expression, thought and religion, the right to information and to privacy).

2. *Rights requiring protective measures* (including measures to protect children from economic and sexual exploitation, to prevent drug abuse, and other forms of abuse and neglect).

3 *Rights concerning the civil status of children* (including the right to acquire nationality, the right to preserve one's identity, the right to remain with parents, unless the best interests of the child dictate otherwise, and the right to be reunited with the family).

4 *Rights concerning government and welfare* (including the child's right

---

37 Reservation F was withdrawn on 18 April 1997.
38 V. Muntarbhorn, 'The Convention on the Rights of the Child: reaching the unreached?' (1992) 91 Bulletin of Human Rights 66, quoted in M. D. A. Freeman, 'Laws, Conventions and Rights', (1993) 7 Children and Society 37, at pp 43–44. See also, L. J. LeBlanc, *The Convention on the Rights of the Child: United Nations Lawmaking on Human Rights* (University of Nebraska Press, 1995), where the author discusses the Convention in terms of survival rights, membership rights, protection rights and empowerment rights.

to a reasonable standard of living, the right to health and basic services, the right to social security, the right to education and the right to leisure).

5 *Rights concerning children in special circumstances* or in "especially difficult circumstances". These extend to such children as handicapped children, refugee children and orphaned children. Included are special regulations on adoption, the cultural concerns of minority and indigenous children, and rehabilitative care for children suffering from deprivation, as well as a prohibition on the recruitment of soldiers under 15 years of age.

6 *Procedural considerations*, particularly the establishment of an international committee of ten experts to monitor implementation of the Convention.'

3.17 In all of this, the importance of a particular provision will depend on the circumstances confronting the individual child. The right to have one's views taken into account may be of little significance to a child whose immediate concern is the elimination of the suffering he or she is experiencing due to malnutrition or disease. The rights of a child during armed conflict may be of little immediate concern to the Scottish child who wants to participate in the decision about where he or she goes to school. None the less, it is the fact that the Convention provides for the rights of all children around the world in the diverse circumstances in which they find themselves that makes it so special. The precise impact of the rights conferred by the Convention and their impact on Scots law will be discussed in the following chapters. However, it is worth taking a little time to examine three principles, fundamental to the Convention – the rights to freedom from discrimination, to protection and to participation.

Fundamental Principles

3.18 Central to the Convention is the principle that the child is entitled to be protected from all forms of discrimination. While art 2(1) confines its prohibition on discrimination to that in respect of the rights set out in the Convention, art 2(2) is broader in scope and requires states to 'take all appropriate measures to ensure that the child is protected against all forms of discrimination or punishment on the basis of the status, activities, expressed opinions, or beliefs of the child's parents, legal guardians, or family members'. Thus, the ambit of art 2(2) goes beyond the specific rights covered by the Convention and includes any other matters.

3.19 It is when one considers the remaining two fundamental principles of the Convention, the right to protection and the right to participation, that what is sometimes seen as the internal conflict in the Convention becomes apparent. Article 3 provides as follows

'1 In all actions concerning children, whether undertaken by public or private social welfare institutions, courts of law, administrative authorities or legislative bodies, the best interests of the child shall be a primary consideration.

2 States Parties undertake to ensure the child such protection and care as is necessary for his or her well-being, taking into account the rights and duties of his or her parents, legal guardians, or other individuals legally responsible for him or her, and, to this end, shall take all appropriate legislative and administrative measures.

3 States Parties shall ensure that the institutions, services and facilities responsible for the care or protection of children shall conform with the standards established by competent authorities, particularly in the areas of safety, health, in the number and suitability of their staff, as well as competent supervision.'

3.20 It is worth noting that the Convention, unlike the Declaration and Scots law, requires that the child's welfare should be 'a primary' rather than 'the primary' or 'the paramount' consideration. How the position of the child's best interests came to be watered down in this way has never been satisfactorily explained and there is the danger that it would permit a state to find another primary consideration, such as economic interests, which takes precedence. However, Van Bueren[39] has suggested that, since art 3 embodies a broad principle of interpretation, there may be occasions (such as the granting to parents of a decree of divorce) when the child's interests are only one of a number of legitimate concerns. Furthermore, at various points throughout the Convention, the principle of 'the best interests of the child' is restated in other ways. In art 18, which recognises the parental responsibility for the upbringing and development of the child, it is noted that '[t]he best interests of the child will be their basic concern'. Interestingly, when the matter of adoption is being addressed in art 21, the best interests of the child is stated to be 'the paramount consideration'. A very real concern about the concept of the 'best interests of the child' is that there is so little consensus about what this involves when applied in particular cases and that it can become nothing more than a shorthand phrase for the views of a particular dominant group of adults.

3.21 Having attempted to guarantee protection for the child, art 12 of the Convention turns to the right of participation. It provides

'1 States Parties shall assure to the child who is capable of forming his or her own views the right to express those views freely in all matters affecting the child, the views of the child being given due weight in accordance with the age and maturity of the child.

2 For this purpose, the child shall in particular be provided the opportunity to be heard in any judicial and administrative proceedings affecting the child, either directly, or through a representative or an appropriate body, in a manner consistent with the procedural rules of national law.'

This principle reflects acceptance of the fact that the holding of rights can become something of an empty concept in the absence of the opportunity

39 Above, at p 46.

to participate in the exercise of these rights.[40] However, it should be noted that the child is given nothing more than the right to have his or her voice heard and any views expressed taken into account. Article 12 does not give the child autonomy. To leave unfettered decision-making power with children would fly in the face of the responsibility of the adult members of any community, not only to protect children from other adults, but to protect them from their own inexperience.

3.22 While participation is a child's right, protection and, to some extent, decision-making are adult responsibilities. This right to participation becomes all the more meaningful when the nature of a child's evolving capacity is emphasised, as it is in both art 12 and art 5. Recognising the role of family members in providing direction and guidance to the child, Article 5 again notes the evolving nature of the child's capacity. Indeed, it can be argued that it is through enabling a child to exercise this evolving capacity that he or she will become fully able to participate in the community as an adult.

Ratification and Reservations

3.23 The UK signed the Convention on 19 April 1990 and ratified it on 16 November 1991. Ratification was subject to a number of Reservations and Declarations.[41] The reservations relate to the following matters: confining the Convention's application to the period after the child's birth; restrictions on the meaning of the word 'parent'; citizenship and the right of entry into the UK; employment legislation; the mixing of adult and young offenders; and the children's hearings system.

3.24 While the ratification of the Convention does not make its provisions directly applicable in Scotland or, indeed, any other part of the UK, it is accepted that every attempt will be made to honour our international obligations. Where, for example, a statute is ambiguous, it will be interpreted in a way that will lead to compliance with rather than the flouting of such obligations.[42] However, where Scots law on a particular point is clear, the fact that it is in breach of the Convention will not diminish the validity of Scots law within Scotland.[43]

3.25 While it represents a landmark in the development of children's rights, the Convention should not be seen as an end point, but rather as the foundations for future developments. In one sense, the Convention has this built into its own provisions, since States Parties are required to report

---

40 See M. G. Flekkoy and N. H. Kaufman, *Rights and Responsibilities in Family and Society* (Jessica Kingsley, 1987), which examines the child's right to self-expression and the development of the decision-making function, and K. Marshall, *Children's Rights in the Balance* (The Stationery Office, 1997) which looks at children's rights and focuses on participation in the decision-making process.

41 CRC/C/2/Rev 4, p 32. The full text of the UK Reservations and Declarations in reproduced in Cleland and Sutherland n 1 above, at Appendix 2.

42 See for example, *Mortensen v Peters* (1906) 8 F (J) 93; *Waddington v Miah* [1974] 1 WLR 683; *R v Secretary of State for the Home Department ex parte Brind* [1991] 2 WLR 588.

43 See for example, *Kaur v Lord Advocate* 1980 SC 319; *Salomon v Commissioners of Customs and Excise* [1967] 2 QB 116; *IRC v Collco Dealings Ltd* [1962] AC 1.

their progress to the UN Committee on the Child at regular intervals.[44] In addition, the United Nations continues its work on children's rights. There are proposals to add to the substantive provisions of the Convention through two optional protocols, one on the sale of children, child prostitution and child pornography,[45] and the other on children in armed conflict.[46]

Report of the UN Committee on the Rights of the Child

3.26 The Convention requires[47] each State Party to submit its first report to the Committee on the Rights of the Child within two years of the Convention entering into force in that state. While the United Kingdom's First Report[48] was two months late and had some lamentable shortcomings, which will be discussed presently, it is worth noting that many other states were either late in reporting or have completely failed to do so. Given that future reports are required 'thereafter every five years', one might speculate on when the second report from these countries will be due. Is it five years from when they should have submitted the first report or five years from when they actually do so (assuming that they do so eventually)? The following table gives some idea of the extent to which States Parties have complied with the obligation to report[49]:

Total number of reports due	176
Those submitted on time	2
Reports submitted less than one year late	54
Reports submitted more than one year late	53
No report yet submitted	67

3.27 States are required to report on 'the measures they have adopted which give effect to the rights [in the Convention] ... and on the progress made on the enjoyment of those rights'.[50] This system of self-reporting is not without its dangers. As Grant[51] has pointed out, '[i]t is not surprising

---

44 See para 3.26, below.
45 Report of the Special Rapporteur [Mrs. Ofelia Calcetas-Santos] on the Sale of Children, Child Prostitution and Child Pornography, January 1996 (UN Doc E/CN 4/1996/100). This optional protocol is already in draft form – see E/CN 4/1998/103 (March 1998).
46 Impact of Armed Conflict on Children, Report of the Expert of the Secretary-General, Ms Graca Machel, August 1996 (UN Doc A/51/306); followed by Children in Armed Conflict, Interim Report by the Special Rapporteur of the Secretary-General, Mr Olara A. Otunna, March 1998 (UN Doc E/CN 4/1998/119).
47 Article 44(1)(a).
48 The UK's First Report to the UN Committee on the Rights of the Child (February 1994, HMSO). The Report was due on 14 January and the Committee records it as having been received on 15 March, CRC/C/44.
49 The figures are taken from CRC/C/67, 1 July 1997 and, of course, the position will change from day to day.
50 Article 44(1).
51 'Could do better: The Report on the UK's Compliance with the Convention on the Rights of the Child', 1995 JR 533 at p 538.

that states assess themselves favourably, emphasising the positive and down-playing (or ignoring completely) the negative'. The Committee on the Rights of the Child appeared to be seeking a more inquisitorial role when, at its first session, it adopted reporting guidelines[52] and provisional rules of procedure.[53] Amongst other things, the rules gave the Committee the powers to indicate the form and content of reports[54] and to request reports from specialised agencies and other UN organs.[55] Despite this, the UK submitted a report which makes little reference to Scotland and, when it does, takes the approach of 'tagging it on' to a discussion of the position in England and Wales. The Committee's Concluding Observations,[56] adopted in February 1995, make no specific reference to Scotland, despite the fact that the Committee had before it the findings of the Children's Rights Development Unit (CRDU). The CRDU was set up as an independent charity to monitor the implementation of the Convention throughout the UK. The Unit's Scottish section produced the 'Scottish Agenda for Children',[57] which addressed a number of areas of the law in Scotland from the perspective of compliance with the Convention. The 'Scottish Agenda for Children' informed the 'UK Agenda for Children' which was presented to the Committee. The Committee encouraged input from non-governmental organisations and met with representatives of the CRDU and the Scottish Child Law Centre on 17 October 1994 in Geneva.

3.28 The Committee's Concluding Observations were divided into three categories: 'positive aspects'; 'principal subjects of concern'; and 'suggestions and recommendations'. As far as Scotland is concerned, the positive aspects include: initiatives taken to combat bullying in schools; attempts to address the issue of child sexual abuse; the government's commitment to legislation on adoption; and the commitment to extending pre-school education. The first, and most general, of the principal subjects of concern raised by the Committee was the very broad ambit of the UK's reservations to the Convention and their compatibility with its object and purpose. It will be remembered that one of these reservations related to the children's hearings system (and has now been withdrawn), although there is no specific mention of the system itself. This is particularly interesting since the Committee goes on to express concern about the low age of criminal responsibility in the UK. One wonders whether, had the Committee understood the non-punitive philosophy underlying the hearings system, it might have been prompted to make a positive comment. Other areas of concern included: expenditure in the social sector; insufficient attention being given to the child's right under art 12 to express his or her opinion;

---

52 CRC/C/L2.
53 CRC/C/4.
54 Rule 66(3).
55 Rule 70.
56 CRC/C/15/Add34.
57 1994. Copies can be obtained from the Scottish Child Law Centre (see Appendix for the address).

the rising number of children living in poverty; and the imprecise nature of 'reasonable chastisement'.

3.29 Under the heading of 'suggestions and recommendations' the Committee urged the UK to review its reservations and to establish a permanent national organisation to implement the Convention. It urged 'regular and closer co-operation between the Government and ... those non-governmental organisations closely involved in monitoring ... respect for the rights of the child'. It recommended the adoption of measures to ensure that the administration of juvenile justice was more 'child-oriented'. Again, one wonders what it might have said if it had known something of the children's hearings system. Urgent consideration of measures to deal with the impact of sexual exploitation and drug abuse on children is called for, as are measures to counteract poverty, homelessness and socio-economic and ethnic factors affecting health. On a more specific level, education on the responsibilities towards children, campaigns to lower the incidence of teenage pregnancy, and measures to prohibit the physical punishment of children, are all recommended.

Other International Instruments

3.30 Quite apart from the UN Convention, which is capable of global application, there are various regional instruments which recognise children's rights.[58] These include the American Declaration on the Rights and Duties of Man[59] and the American Convention on Human Rights,[60] adopted by the Organisation of American States, and the African Charter on Human and People's Rights[61] and the African Charter on the Rights and Welfare of the Child,[62] adopted by the Organisation of African Unity. In addition, children's rights are recognised, directly[63] or indirectly,[64] in a

---

58 See G. Van Bueren, *The International Law on the Rights of the Child* (Kluwer Academic Publishers, 1995), particularly at pp 22–25; P. Veerman, *The Rights of the Child and the Changing Image of Childhood* (Martinus Nijhoff, 1992).

59 OAS (1948). This is in similar, although not identical terms, to the Universal Declaration of Human Rights adopted by the United Nations a few months later.

60 OASTS No 36 (1969). This is similar in ambit to the European Convention on Human Rights but is more child-centred For example, art 19 recognises the special position of children.

61 OAU Doc CAB/LEG/67/3 rev 5 (1981), also known as the Banjul Charter. The emphasis here is on the family, reflecting as it does, African customary law. However, art 18, having required the elimination of discrimination against women, goes on to require states to protect the rights of women and children as stipulated in international declarations and conventions.

62 OAU Doc CAB/LEG/24 9/49 (1990), which not only seeks to reflect African culture, but raises standards in some respects.

63 For example, the Constitution of the Republic of South Africa 1996 (which replaced the interim Constitution of 1993) contains both provisions which affect the rights of children as people and specific rights which apply only to children. See J. D. van der Vyver, 'Constitutional Protection of children and young persons' in J. A. Robinson (ed), *The Law of Children and Young Persons in South Africa* (Butterworths, 1997).

64 While the USA has not ratified the UN Convention on the Rights of the Child, a matter which has caused considerable consternation amongst children's rights activists there, the Constitution of the United States of America contains many provisions which are significant for the rights of children. See C. P. Cohen and H. A. Davidson (eds),

variety of foreign domestic constitutions. While none of these instruments applies in Scotland, they merit attention when considering children's rights in a world context and, since they sometimes contain provisions which differ from those applying here, demonstrate social, cultural, religious and political considerations which have an impact elsewhere.

3.31 From a domestic point of view, we shall see that the European Convention on Human Rights has had an impact on children's rights, albeit often somewhat indirectly, through recognition of the rights of parents and other family members. With the passing of the Human Rights Act 1998[65] the direct impact of the European Convention can be expected to increase. Instead of having to go through the time-consuming process of taking a case to the European Court,[66] it will be possible to use the provisions of the Convention in the Scottish courts. A whole *corpus* of law, interpreting the Convention, has grown up over the years and a thorough understanding of it will be essential to the Scots practitioner in the future. The European Convention deals primarily with civil and political rights and the European Social Charter of 1961 embodies the corresponding economic and social rights. The Social Charter underwent a process of revision in the early 1990s and the revised version was adopted by the Committee of Ministers in 1996.[67] While the revised Charter has a variety of provisions impacting upon children's rights, arts 7 and 11 are of particular importance. They contain extensive provisions governing child protection, both within the family and more generally, criminal responsibility and juvenile justice, education and training, and employment.[68]

3.32 Following the adoption of the UN Convention on the Rights of the Child, the Council of Europe sought to support it. This was done, in part, by simply urging member states to ratify the Convention, if they had not already done so, and by developing a European strategy for children.[69] The UN Convention inspired the Council to set up the Childhood Policies

---

Children's Rights in America: UN Convention on the Rights of the Child compared with United States Law (American Bar Association, 1990). Ratification remains a contentious issue in the USA, in part, for constitutional reasons, see: A. D. Rentelin, 'Who's Afraid of the CRC: Objections to the Convention on the Rights of the Child' 3 ILSA J Int'l & Comp L 629 (1997).

65 Essentially, the Act embodies the European Convention, subject to some amendments. A number of Protocols to the Convention are not included in the Act, but the UK was not a party to them in any event.

66 A number of Scottish litigants did take this course and their success had far-reaching implications for domestic law. See for example, *Campbell and Cosans* v *United Kingdom* (1982) 4 EHRR 293 (corporal punishment in schools) and *McMichael* v *United Kingdom* [1995] 20 EHRR 205 (child protection procedures).

67 ETS No. 163. The revised European Social Charter was opened for signature on 3 May 1996 and will come into force after it has been ratified by three states.

68 See Directorate of Human Rights, *Children and Adolescents: protection within the European Social Charter*, Human rights, Social Charter monographs, No 3 (Council of Europe Publishing, 1996).

69 See for example, recommendation 1286 (1996) of the Parliamentary Assembly of the Council of Europe on a European strategy for children.

Project, a four-year programme (1992–95), to reflect the policy implications of the Convention at a European level.[70] A significant result of this activity was the adoption of the European Convention on the Exercise of Children's Rights.[71] Given the experience with the UN Convention, it is interesting to note that this Convention does not permit reservations to be made.[72] The Convention is far more limited in its scope than many other instruments on children's rights and deals exclusively with promoting the right of children to participate in judicial proceedings dealing with family matters. It recognises the right to be fully informed about what is happening as an inherent part of participation, as well as the child's right to be assisted in expressing his or her own views and to be represented.

Recognition in Scots law

3.33 In the wake of the UN Convention, one way to analyse a particular legal system's approach to children's rights is to compare that approach with the Convention itself and, indeed, that is precisely what the UN Committee on the Child does in its reports on individual countries. Another international standard against which we might measure children's rights is the European Convention on Human Rights, albeit that Convention is not concerned primarily with the rights of children. Of course, the passage of the Human Rights Act will afford domestic courts ample opportunity, in the future, to consider whether Scots law meets the standards of the European Convention, not as an international instrument but as a part of domestic law. In addition, the recognition of children's rights in any one jurisdiction might be measured against that accorded in other jurisdictions or we might assess our own legal system in the light of an abstract standard. A number of such studies exist.[73] For the present, we will take a brief look at Scots law in the light of the UN Convention's core provisions, before examining how children fare within the legal system in Scotland.

Non discrimination

3.34 Throughout the UK, legislation prohibits discrimination on the grounds of race, colour, nationality, ethnic or national origins, sex, marital

---

70 In order to illustrate the 'extraordinary richness' of the instruments of the Council of Europe concerning children, the project recommended that these should be published in a single volume and *The Rights of the Child: a European perspective* (Council of Europe Publishing, 1996) resulted.

71 The Convention was opened for signature on 25 January 1996 and will come into force three months after it has been ratified by three member states, at least two of which must be members of the Council of Europe – Article 21.

72 Article 24.

73 This has been done in a variety of jurisdictions. See for example, Cleland and Sutherland, *Children's Rights in Scotland* (W. Green, 1996); C. P. Cohen and H. A. Davidson, *Children's Rights in America* (ABA, 1990); J. Fortin, *Children's Rights and the Developing Law* (Butterworths, 1998) (England and Wales); S. J. Fox, 'Beyond the American Legal System for the Protection of Children's Rights' 31 Fam L Q 237 (1997); M. Freeman (ed), *Children's Rights: A Comparative Perspective* (Dartmouth, 1996) (individual chapters devoted to a variety of jurisdictions).

status or disability, albeit the ambit of the protection is sometimes incomplete.[74] Thus, as a general rule, Scots law is broadly in line with the spirit of the Convention when it comes to discrimination. However, one aspect of the law, as it affects children, stands in stark contrast to this, generally sound, position. Scots law continues to level discriminatory treatment against children born outside marriage.[75] Article 19(1) requires that both parents should have common responsibilities for the upbringing and development of the child. As we shall see, the Children (Scotland) Act 1995 ('the 1995 Act') denies automatic parental responsibilities to non-marital fathers.[76] As a result, many children have one, rather than two adults with responsibilities towards them. As we have seen, art 2 takes two distinct approaches to discrimination. First, it prohibits discrimination in respect of the rights specified in the Convention. Second, it tackles the general problem by requiring the States Parties to 'take all appropriate measures to ensure the child is protected against discrimination'. The effect is that Scots law is in breach of art 2(1) in denying the rights under art 19(1) to one group of children, those born outside marriage, by discriminating on the basis of 'the child or his or her parent's ... birth or other status'. In denying such a child the right to equal succession to a title or honour,[77] a right quite understandably not specifically covered by the Convention, Scots law is in breach of art 2(2).

Welfare as the primary consideration

3.35 As we have seen, it can be argued that Scots law goes further than the Convention by treating the child's welfare as the 'paramount', rather than simply 'a primary' consideration in most circumstances.[78] Norrie has described the whole debate on this issue as a 'rather sterile argument'[79] and, it must be admitted, he has a point. None the less, it should be noted that Scots law permits of deviation from the paramountcy of welfare principle on occasions. For example, the paramountcy of welfare principle can be displaced 'for the purpose of protecting members of the public from serious harm'.[80] Similarly, in considering whether to detain a child in secure accommodation, one of the criteria is the likelihood of the child injuring 'himself [or herself] or some other person'.[81] In any event, it can be concluded that, at the very least, Scots law meets the standard set by the UN Convention in recognising the child's welfare. As we shall see in the following chapters, what actually does serve a child's welfare can often be a contentious issue. There are many competing views on what is 'good' for children and what will have an adverse effect on their well-being and development. Frequently, these views are based on nothing more than

---

74 See chapter 2, paras 79 and 94, above.
75 The present discrimination, its historical roots, and why it matters, is discussed in detail in chapter 5, paras 42–52.
76 Children (Scotland) Act 1995, s 3(1)(b).
77 Law Reform (Parent and Child) (Scotland) Act 1986, s 9(1)(c).
78 See para 3.20, above.
79 K. McK. Norrie, *Children (Scotland) Act 1995* (W. Green, 1995), at p 35.
80 Children (Scotland) Act 1995, s 16(5).
81 Children (Scotland) Act 1995, s 70(10)(b).

conventional wisdom and it is encouraging that empirical research is being conducted in this area[82] and that, on occasions, courts pay attention to it.[83]

The right to participate in the decision-making process

3.36 What of the remaining key provision of the Convention, the child's right to express his or her views freely and to have them taken into account in the decision-making process? It was art 12 of the Convention which led to specific provision being made in the 1995 Act for taking account of children's views in certain circumstances. Essentially, there are two strands to recognition of the child's views, First, is the general provision set out in s 6 of the 1995 Act, which provides as follows

'(1) A person shall, in reaching any major decision which involves –
(a) his [or her] fulfilling a parental responsibility or the responsibility [the responsibilities of a person with care or control of a child]; or
(b) his [or her] exercising a parental right or giving consent by virtue of [being a person with care or control of a child],
have regard so far as is practicable to the views (if he [or she] wishes to express them) of the child concerned, taking account of the child's age and maturity, and of those of any other person who has parental responsibilities or parental rights in relation to the child (and wishes to express those views); and without prejudice to the generality of this subsection a child of twelve years of age or more shall be presumed to be of sufficient age and maturity to form a view'.[84]

3.37 The 1995 Act does not define 'major decision' and there has been much discussion of what kinds of parental decisions would fall within the ambit of s 6. Opponents of children's rights sometimes use this section to raise the spectre of interference in private family life through children challenging parental requests that they should help with the washing up or tidy their rooms. Ultimately, it will be for the courts to decide, but it is probably safe to assume that those sorts of minor day-to-day decisions would not be regarded as 'major'. On the other hand, deciding where the family will live or which school the child will attend, may well be major decisions. The significant point to note here is that s 6 does not give

82　See for example, H. Sweeting and P. West, Young People and Their Families: Analyses of Data from the Twenty-07 Study Youth Cohort, Working Paper No 49 (Medical Research Council, 1995), which examined a 15-year-old cohort in the West of Scotland, first surveyed in 1987 and interviewed again in 1993 and 1997. The data produced has been used to examine associations between aspects of family life, lifestyle indicators and future life chances. See: H. Sweeting and P. West, 'Family Life and Health in Adolescence: A Role for Culture in the Health Inequalities Debate' (1995) 40 Soc Sci Med 163 and H. Sweeting, P. West and A. Richards, 'Teenage Family Life, Lifestyles and Life Chances: Association with Family Structure, Conflict with Parents and Joint Family Activity' 12 Int'l J Law, Policy and the Family 15 (1998). A host of other studies conducted elsewhere in the world have examined similar issues and a number of them are discussed in the second of the articles cited. See also, K. Kiernan, 'Lone Motherhood, Employment and Outcomes for Children' (1996) Int'l J Law and the Family 231. Until 1987 the International Journal of Law and the Family was the International Journal of Law, Policy and the Family.

83　See for example, Lord President Hope's willingness, in *T, Petitioner* (IH) 1996 SCLR 897, to consider the evidence on whether the fact that a parent was living in a homosexual relationship would have any impact on a child who lived in the household.

84　The terms in square brackets indicate additions or paraphrasing.

children autonomy. It simply requires that their views must be taken into account in the decision-making process. This leads some authors to conclude that the 1995 Act is 'not concerned with children's rights'.[85] That is to misunderstand the dynamics of the UN Convention and the attempts of the 1995 Act to comply with it. The Convention seeks respect for a variety of rights. As we have seen, some of these rights, like the primacy of welfare and the right to be heard, are themselves capable of creating a certain tension. It is only through working to make these very rights operate together that we can hope to reach the level of sophistication needed to achieve a system which is effective for children. Section 6 provides a good example of how this can be done. The child's right to participate is recognised, while the final decision lies with the relevant adults who are obliged to take the decision, taking account of the paramountcy of the child's welfare. To put it another way – and this is a theme which will be repeated throughout this book – participation is a child's right, decision-making is an adult responsibility. In addition, the child's evolving capacity is recognised in the requirement to take account of the child's age and maturity, when considering the child's views. Marrying together the various strands in the Convention is not a simple matter and s 6 does an admirable job. All that now remains is for these subtleties to be worked though into judicial decisions.

3.38 It is often said that rights are of no value unless they can be enforced. It is in the nature of family relationships that resort to law is often and, certainly, should be, a last resort. Of course, high-handed parents who did not listen to their children before the 1995 Act was passed may well continue in their old ways. Many parents and children will not know of s 6 and some adults who are aware of it will ignore it. Very young children will be able to do little about enforcing their rights. However, as we shall see, children have standing to raise an action seeking, amongst other things, to have the court regulate the exercise of parental rights or responsibilities.[86] Where they have sufficient understanding, they can instruct solicitors to act for them.[87] Thus, it would be quite possible for a child to force his or her views into the decision-making process in the face of parental intransigence. Of course, children's rights operate in a world where other people have rights and the rights of those other people require recognition. As a result, s 6 goes on to provide that, where a third party deals in good faith with a child's representative, the transaction cannot be challenged on the ground that the appropriate views were not sought.[88]

3.39 The second way in which the 1995 Act recognises the child's right to participate in the decision-making process is by requiring courts and other agencies to take account of any views the child wishes to express when these bodies are taking a decision about the child. When it is considering

85 L. Edwards and A. Griffiths, *Family Law* (W. Green, 1997) at paras 4.21–4.23, where the cases cited predate the 1995 Act.
86 1995 Act, s 11. The child's right to raise an action and the role of the court are discussed in chapter 5.
87 Age of Legal Capacity (Scotland) Act 1991, s 2(4A), discussed at para 3.63, below.
88 Section 6(2).

whether to make any order in relation to parental responsibilities or rights, a court must have regard to any views the child wishes to express.[89] When a court or a children's hearing is exercising any of its functions under Part II of the 1995 Act, there is, again, a requirement to have regard to any views the child wishes to express.[90] A local authority is required to take a similar approach in respect of a child it is looking after.[91]

Other Convention provisions

3.40 In addition to the core provisions, the Convention is concerned with a wide range of rights and how well Scots law accommodates many of them is discussed in texts devoted to the subject. However, since children live in a world governed by adults, the way in which children's rights operate must be understood in the context of adult participation. The Convention embodies this understanding, first, by emphasising the role of the family in the lives of children and, second, in placing obligations on States Parties to ensure that children's rights are observed. In the chapters which follow, frequent reference will be made to the Convention and how it applies to particular issues.

Children and the legal system

3.41 Children become involved in the legal system in a variety of ways. They may be pursuers or defenders in civil actions. Occasionally, they are defenders in criminal proceedings. In either civil or criminal proceedings, they may be called as witnesses. In addition, the court may be required to obtain their consent[92] or to give them an opportunity to express their views, particularly in family matters. How child-friendly is the legal system? It should be remembered that courts are intimidating places for most lay adults. If we were to make no special arrangements for children who become involved in the legal system, their ability to participate effectively would be greatly diminished. For these reasons, additional adults often become involved in court and other proceedings where children are involved. However, the extent to which they provide support for the child depends on the particular function being carried out. We will consider the role of these additional adults and the mechanisms for eliciting children's views before we examine the special position of child witnesses in court proceedings and the protection from publicity afforded to children in the legal process.

Is there support for children in the legal system?

3.42 A host of different individuals may enter the picture when a child becomes involved in court proceedings, depending upon the nature of the proceedings and the child's place in them. As we shall see, a child may

89 Section 11(7)(b). This provision is discussed in chapter 5, paras 130–134.
90 Section 16(2). This provision is discussed in chapter 7, para 64 and chapter 9, para 83.
91 Section 17(3) and (4). This provision is discussed in chapter 7, para 56.
92 For example, a child of 12 years old or over must consent before he or she can be adopted unless the child is incapable of giving consent – Adoption (Scotland) Act 1978, s 12(8) and s 18(8). See chapter 8, paras 12–13.

instruct a solicitor in civil proceedings, where he or she has the capacity to understand what it means to do so, and a child aged 12 or older is presumed to have this capacity.[93] This innovation of the 1995 Act undoubtedly strengthens the position of children as active participants in the legal process. However, it is subject to a variety of constraints. Before this power will be of real assistance to a child with a legal problem, he or she must be aware: that the problem is one where legal advice may be beneficial (ie the child must identify the problem as *legal* in nature); that he or she may have rights at all; that he or she can consult a solicitor; and of how to go about contacting a solicitor, and the right kind of solicitor, at that. It is doubtful that many children have this, rather sophisticated, understanding of the system. Clearly, greater education of children about their rights is needed if they are to make full use of the provision. To the extent that a solicitor provides support to any client, that support is there for the child where he or she actually has a solicitor of his or her own. It is fair to say that solicitors who specialise in this kind of work are acutely aware that a young client will usually require reassurance and support.

3.43 The idea of a solicitor instructed by the child to act as the child's representative is fairly new. Of greater antiquity is the curator *ad litem*, appointed by a court to act on the child's behalf.[94] However, it is important to distinguish the curator's role from that of a legal representative.[95] The curator is an officer of the court and is bound to protect the child's interests. He or she is not there to take instructions from the child. Yet another player may enter the legal process when a child is referred to a children's hearing – the safeguarder. Dating, in theory, from the Children Act 1975[96] and, in practice, from 1984,[97] safeguarders are appointed by a children's hearing or a sheriff 'to safeguard the interests of the child' in proceedings relating to the hearing.[98] While some safeguarders believe that

93 Age of Legal Capacity (Scotland) Act 1991, s 2(4A) See para 3.63, below, for a full discussion of the child's capacity in this respect. In other jurisdictions with a longer history of providing representation for children, there has been greater opportunity to consider some of the problems involved. See: M. Guggenheim, 'Reconsidering the Need for Counsel for Children in Custody, Visitation and Child Protection Proceedings' 29 Loy U Chi L J 299 (1998); P. Margulies, 'The Lawyer as Caregiver: Child Client's Competence in Context' 64 Fordham L Rev 1473 (1996); L. E. Shear, 'Children's Lawyers in California Family Law Courts' 34 Fam and Conciliation Courts Review 256 (1996).
94 See Stair, *Institutions*, I, v, 12 and I, v, 31 and Fraser, *A Treatise on the Law of Scotland Relating to Parent and Child*, p 213.
95 For a discussion of this distinction, see C. Kelly, 'The Role of the Curator *Ad Litem* contrasted with the Role of the Solicitor' in *Listening to the Voice of the Child* (Scottish Child Law Centre, 1995). Other chapters in that volume explore other aspects of children being given the opportunity to express themselves within the legal system.
96 Section 66 of the 1975 Act added s 34A to the Social Work (Scotland) Act 1968.
97 The relevant provision was not brought into force until 1984 – Social Work (Panels of Persons to Safeguard the Interests of Children) (Scotland) Regulations 1984, SI 1984 No 1442. The Children Act 1975 provides one of the worst examples of a statute being brought into force in bits and pieces or, in respect of some sections, not at all. It is a great relief that the 1995 Act did not suffer the same fate and has been implemented in a well-organised manner.
98 1995 Act, s 41(1). The 1995 Act continues the tradition, established in the earlier legislation, whereby the word 'safeguarder' does not appear at all. The word does appear, however, in the Children's Hearings Rules.

they are duty-bound to give full expression to the child's views, or to assist the child in doing so, the safeguarder's obligation to protect the child's interests is undisputed.[99]The fundamental point to appreciate here, in respect of both curators and safeguarders, is that representing a person's interests, even if one does air that person's views, is not the same thing as representing a client on the basis of the client's instructions. Again, curators and safeguarders can provide the child with additional support, where they attend the proceedings. For completeness, it should be noted that, in adoption proceedings, two other adult roles emerge, with the same person often playing both parts. A curator *ad litem* is appointed by the court to report on the circumstances of the child and the prospective adopters, while the reporting officer is concerned primarily with ensuring that the relevant consents have been given and understood.[100] Giving support to the child is not a feature of either role.

3.44 If this array of possible participants is bewildering to adults, what must it be like for a child, confronted with one of these individuals? What are the child's expectations of what the adult will be able to do for him or her?[101] The truth is often that children will not understand what the adult is there to do and, in any event, the provision of support to children is not central to many of the functions. The position does not get any better when we turn to consider the opportunities for a child to express his or her views when a court is taking a decision about that child's future.

Giving children the opportunity to express their views

3.45 As we shall see, when a court is making a decision on parental responsibilities or rights, it is bound to take account of any views the child wishes to express, in the light of the child's age and maturity.[102] Cases of this kind are most often heard in the sheriff court and some sheriffs have always been happy to see the child, either alone or accompanied by a neutral person, in chambers.[103] Depending upon the sheriff's skills and the individual child's personality, this can result in open communication of the child's views and their incorporation into the final decision. However, not all sheriffs are comfortable with this arrangement and not all children express themselves well in such a setting. The requirement to take account of the child's views in decisions on parental responsibilities and rights was an innovation of the Children (Scotland) Act 1995 and heralded a welcome recognition of the need to consult children in the decision-making process.

---

99 E. E. Sutherland, 'The Role of the Safeguarder' in *Listening to the Voice of the Child*, n 95 above.
100 Wilkinson and Norrie, *Parent and Child*, pp 564–566. Adoption is discussed fully in chapter 8.
101 A. Cleland, 'The Child's Right to be Heard and Represented in Legal Proceedings' in Cleland and Sutherland, at p 60, cites an example of the kind of disappointment and confusion experienced by many children. One young woman had expressed the desire to return home but the curator did not believe this was in her best interests and, accordingly, could not recommend such a course of action. The child responded, '[b]ut I thought you were my lawyer and my Dad says your lawyer does what you tell him to'.
102 1995 Act, s 11(7)(b).
103 See B. Kearney, 'Private Interviewing of Children by Judges – The Presence of the Child in Court' in *Listening to the Voice of the Child*, n 95 above.

However, if it is to have any substance, we must find a way to make the rule work in practice. In the attempt to do just that, the procedure to be followed in such actions was amended and a new means of eliciting the views of children was introduced.

3.46 In every application which includes an order in relation to parental responsibilities or rights, whether it is by the pursuer in the initial writ, by the defender in the defences, or by a minuter in the process, there must be a crave to intimate the proceedings on the child affected.[104] The sheriff then decides whether to make an order for intimation on the child, taking account of such matters as the age of the child and the nature of the order sought. Even if the sheriff dispenses with intimation to the child, at the initial stage, he or she may order intimation to the child at any time.[105] While practice varies from court to court and, indeed, from sheriff to sheriff, intimation is not usually ordered on a child who is likely to be too young to understand the proceedings. In addition, intimation may be dispensed with subject to the *proviso* that, if circumstances change, the sheriff retains the residual power to order intimation. Essentially, the procedure involves written intimation to the child of the action and of his or her right to express a view if he or she wishes to do so, along with a reply form and information on how the child can go about seeking advice. The onus then falls on the child who wishes to exercise this right to respond to the sheriff clerk. Where a child returns the form which he or she has received as part of the intimation, or where the child indicates in some other way (eg by telephone) that he or she wishes to express a view about the proceedings, the sheriff may not grant any order without giving the child an opportunity to put his or her point of view. The sheriff must take such steps as are necessary to ascertain the child's views. That may be by the child completing and returning the form sent along with the intimation. However, instead, the child may: instruct a solicitor to represent him or her in court; ask a third party, like a schoolteacher or a friend, to write to the court on his or her behalf; or request a private interview with the sheriff.[106] If the child expresses his or her views in writing, the document can be placed in a sealed envelope and kept within the court process, to be accessed only by the sheriff. Similarly, where the child expresses views orally, they can be recorded and retained in this way.

3.47 While there is no doubt that this new procedure was an attempt to facilitate children having an opportunity to express their views, it is open to a number of criticisms. It is quite possible that the letter intimating the action to the child may be intercepted by a, sometimes well-intentioned, adult, often the parent with whom the child is living. There is considerable doubt over whether a child will necessarily read the letter or, if he or she does, whether its contents and their importance will be understood. If a child does read and understand the document, how sure can we be that the response is not the product of subtle or explicit pressure from an influential

104 OCR 33.7(1)(h).
105 OCR 33.15.
106 OCR 33.19.

adult? In addition, communication of important personal information in this way is highly insensitive and wholly inappropriate to children. It fails to see them as individuals and to distinguish between different age groups and the evolving nature of understanding and resilience that is inherent in growing up. Perhaps the central point to be made here is that the onus of using the legal system should not be put on children. Rather the legal system should go to the child, offering support and assistance in a child-friendly way, appropriate to the age and maturity of each child.

3.48 In addition to intimation to the child, a special step in the procedure, the child welfare hearing, was created in the attempt to resolve disputes over the future arrangements for children at as early a stage as possible. Where an order for parental responsibilities or rights is at issue, the court must arrange a child welfare hearing. The child may receive intimation of the child welfare hearing in order that he or she can have a voice in the proceedings. Broadly, a child welfare hearing involves bringing all the parties together in the court to discuss any issues that might be resolved at an early stage. The child will be included in the discussion where he or she has already received intimation of the action or where the sheriff believes that the child's presence is desirable. Thereafter, the sheriff has a very flexible role in the proceedings and may seek to facilitate a thorough discussion or take some other course of action. For example, he or she may: appoint a curator for the child; order a report from a suitable person on the child's background, with a request that the reporter make recommendations on the matters in dispute; or fix a preliminary hearing or proof in relation to the issues affecting the child. Such a hands-on approach has not been easy to accommodate within the traditional adversarial system where, historically, judicial involvement is normally limited to hearing the evidence and submissions and making a decision.

3.49 It is encouraging to find new procedures being devised in the attempt to enable children to participate in decision-making and to expedite cases in which they are involved. However, if children are to be given a full opportunity to participate in the legal system, either as initiators of actions or by having their views taken into account fully, we must look for other ways to facilitate that participation more effectively.[107] Children must be offered both professional and personal support when they are participating in what is, after all, a very adult forum. Attempts to provide children with this level of support have been made in other jurisdictions.[108] The time has come, in Scotland, for a thorough re-examination of the roles of the various

---

107 For one possible approach, see E. E. Sutherland, 'A Voice for the Child and the Children (Scotland) Act 1995, Part I' (1996) 41 JLSS 391. A three-year study into young people's access to legal services was conducted by the Scottish Child Law Centre between 1995 and 1998 and the findings make fascinating reading – R. Gallacher, Children and Young People's Voices on The Law, Legal Services, & Systems in Scotland (Scottish Child Law Centre, 1998).
108 See A. Cleland, 'Representing Children – A Global View' (1994) 39 JLSS 366. In the USA, many states have a system of Court-Appointed Special Advocates (CASAs), lay persons and lawyers who are given training to enable them to accompany and assist children throughout the court process – see, H. A. Davidson, 'The Child's Right to be Heard and Represented in Judicial Proceedings' 18 Pepp L Rev 255 (1991).

individuals currently used in proceedings involving children, with particular emphasis being placed on how we might provide better support for children. That is the challenge presented by the UN Convention and the 1995 Act.

Child witnesses

3.50 The first matter to be considered when a child is called as a witness is the child's competency to give evidence at all. Essentially, this requires establishing that the child is of sufficient maturity to appreciate the difference between truth and falsehood and to give an accurate account of the events to which he or she will speak. It is a matter for the judge to assess and usually involves him or her in talking to the child about what it means to tell the truth. If the judge is satisfied that the child has sufficient understanding, he or she must decide whether it is necessary to administer the oath. It is quite competent for the oath to be replaced by an admonition to the child to tell the truth, and it then falls to the judge or the jury, as the case may be, to decide what weight to attach to the child's evidence. While the Scottish Law Commission explored the possibility of a statutory formulation of the common law rules on competency, it concluded that the matter had been stated sufficiently clearly in *Rees* v *Lowe*[109] and, thus, that no statutory provision was necessary. However, concern remains that a child's evidence may be devalued, at least in the eyes of jurors, by the fact that competency is tested at all. In addition, the competency test itself may place stress on child witnesses and the abolition of the competency test is being considered.[110]

3.51 A further complication in respect of 'something a child has said' arises in the context of hearsay evidence. Since 1988,[111] hearsay evidence has been admissible in civil cases in Scotland. However, it is well established[112] that, where, as in the case of a very young child, the competency of the witness has not been tested in accordance with the ordinary rules in such cases, hearsay evidence is not admissible.[113] This led to some debate over statements made by a child to a third party and whether any account could be taken of them, where the child's competency had not been tested.[114] Suppose, for example, a child comes home from visiting the non-resident parent and makes allegations that the non-resident parent hit him. If such a statement cannot be treated as evidence, can any account be taken of it or must the court simply pretend that no such statement was made?

---

109 1990 SLT 507.
110 Consultation Paper on Further Measures to Support Child Witnesses in Civil and Criminal Proceedings (Scottish Courts Administration, 1997).
111 Civil Evidence (Scotland) Act 1988, s 2.
112 *F* v *Kennedy (No 1)* 1993 SLT 1277.
113 *Rees* v *Lowe*, n 109 above. It has been suggested that the child must be examined in court to establish competency before any evidence from the child can be led, see *L* v *L* 1996 SLT 767. That this is the effect of the legislation has, it is submitted rightly, been doubted – D. H. Sheldon, 'Children's Evidence, Competency and the New Hearsay Provisions' 1997 SLT (News) 1.
114 This was one of the many issues explored in *Sanderson* v *McManus* 1997 SC (HL) 55. The case is discussed in chapter 5, para 101.

The question was resolved by the House of Lords where Lord Hope gave the following guidance

> 'It would be artificial to leave out of account what the child said, so long as the evidence was that these statements were spontaneous. What the child said was simply another aspect of the child's behaviour which the court was entitled to take into account when having regard to his welfare'.[115]

3.52 There has long been concern that giving evidence in court in both civil and criminal proceedings causes children particular stress and anxiety.[116] The problem arises in a variety of situations, from the child who has witnessed some event in which he or she had no direct interest, to the child who has been the victim of an offence. The stress itself may come from nothing more than the fact that courts are formal, sombre places, unfamiliar to children, or it may be caused by the child anticipating facing the adult who has harmed him or her. Legislative innovation in respect of child witnesses has been greatest in the context of criminal proceedings, perhaps because they provide the greatest potential for the child to feel intimidated, but also because securing fairness to the accused may make members of the judiciary less likely to act on their own initiative. The Scottish Law Commission examined the problems and made proposals for reform in 1990.[117] As a result of its proposals, the then Lord Justice-General issued a 'Memorandum on Child Witnesses',[118] offering guidance to judges on how to minimise the anxiety and distress caused to children giving evidence. It suggests that judges should consider such matters as: the removal of wigs and gowns by the judge, counsel, and solicitors; positioning the child at a table along with the judge and lawyers, rather than placing the child in the witness box; permitting a relative or other supporting person to sit alongside the child while he or she is giving evidence; and clearing the court of all persons who do not have a direct interest in the case.

3.53 The Commission's proposals were given further effect in 1990,[119] when provision was made for children giving evidence in criminal proceedings to do so by means of a live television link rather than being present in the courtroom itself. Permission for the child to give evidence in this way must be sought from the court 14 days before the trial begins. It is unfortunate that, to date, the appropriate equipment is only available in Edinburgh and Glasgow and the opportunity to give evidence by television link is consequently denied to many children in Scotland. In addition, there is no parallel provision for civil proceedings, which include child protection cases. Clearly, from a child's point of view, giving evidence of abuse or neglect in order to ensure that he or she is not returned to a particular

---

115 *Sanderson* v *McManus*, above, at p 61C. Lord Weir had made a similar point in the Inner House – see 1996 SLT 750 at p 766I.
116 J. Spencer and R. Flin, *The Evidence of Children: the Law and the Psychology* (2nd edn, Blackstone, 1993).
117 Report on the Evidence of Children and Other Potentially Vulnerable Witnesses (Scot Law Com No 125, 1990).
118 26 July 1990. Technically, the Memorandum applies only to criminal proceedings but, in practice, it is accepted as guidance in all courts.
119 Law Reform (Miscellaneous Provisions) (Scotland) Act 1990, ss 56–60. The procedure is now contained in the Criminal Procedure (Scotland) Act 1995, s 271.

household can be every bit as traumatic as giving the same evidence to secure the conviction of the abuser. The use of live television links has met with a generally favourable response in Australia,[120] England and Wales[121] and New Zealand.[122] The Scottish Office commissioned a study of the experience in Scotland and the detailed report which resulted, while favouring the availability of live television links, highlights some of the problems associated with it and makes recommendations on a variety of matters surrounding the evidence of children generally.[123]

3.54 In 1993,[124] two further techniques, designed to ease the burden on child witnesses were introduced. The first provides for the child giving evidence prior to the trial and for the video recording of that process. The second provides for courts giving permission for the erection of a screen in the court to conceal the accused from the sight of the child while the latter is giving evidence. While this statute applies only to criminal proceedings, video recorded statements have been admissible as evidence in civil proceedings since the removal of the hearsay rule.[125]

3.55 It is encouraging to note that efforts to alleviate the stress placed on child witnesses continues. The possible extension of live television links and the use of screens in civil cases is under consideration and the issue of testing the competency of child witnesses and how this can be done best is being discussed.[126] The challenge remains to find the appropriate balance between protecting and supporting child witnesses, on the one hand, and fairness to the other parties in the proceedings, on the other. In all of this, it must be remembered that, unless any special procedures adopted to accommodate child witnesses are perceived as being 'fair', the child's evidence itself may be taken less seriously and this, in turn, would disempower children in the legal process.

Protection from publicity

3.56 It is inherent in the nature of a democratic society that the way the legal system operates should be open to public scrutiny. For this reason, members of the public are normally free to sit in court and observe

---

120 J. Cashmore and N. De Haas, The Use of Closed-Circuit Television for Child Witnesses in the ACT (Report for the Australian Law Commission, 1992). For a summary of these findings, see J. Cashmore, 'The use of closed-circuit television in the ACT' in K. Murray and S. Asquith (eds), *Children's Evidence and Technology*, Centre Occasional Series No 1, Centre for the Study of the Child & Society, (University of Glasgow, 1992).

121 G. M. Davies and E. Noon, *An Evaluation of the Live Link for Child Witnesses* (Home Office, 1990); G. M. Davies and E. Noon, 'Video Links: The Impact on Child Witness Trials' in N. J. Clark and G. M. Stephenson (eds), *Children, Evidence and Procedure* (British Psychological Society, 1993).

122 L. Whitney and A. Cook, The Use of Closed-Circuit Television in New Zealand: The First Six Trials (New Zealand Department of Justice, 1990).

123 K. Murray, *Live Television Link: An Evaluation of its Use by Child Witnesses in Scottish Criminal Trials* (Scottish Office, 1995).

124 Prisoners and Criminal Proceedings (Scotland) Act 1993, ss 33–35. Again, the relevant provisions are now found in the Criminal Procedure (Scotland) Act 1995, s 271.

125 Civil Evidence (Scotland) Act 1988, ss 1 and 2.

126 Consultation Paper on Further Measures to Support Child Witnesses in Civil and Criminal Proceedings (Scottish Courts Administration, 1997).

proceedings and members of the press are free to report both civil and criminal cases. However, it is acknowledged that the right of the individual to protect his or her privacy may justify restricting publicity of the individual's identity in some cases. The protection here is not confined to children and, for example, restrictions may be placed on reporting aspects of matrimonial proceedings.[127] None the less, the legal system has long accepted that children merit special attention when it comes to the issue of privacy.[128]

3.57 In civil proceedings, the court has a wide-ranging power to prohibit reporting of the name, address, or school or of 'any particulars calculated to lead to the identification' of any child who is involved in the proceedings as a party, a witness or as a person in respect of whom the proceedings are taken.[129] In addition, the court may prohibit the publication of any photograph of the child. The fact that a direction may be made to protect the identity of a child 'in respect of whom the proceedings are taken' means that children who are the subject of a dispute over parental responsibilities or rights may benefit from the provision.[130] It should be noted that the prohibition on publicity in civil cases, unlike that afforded to children in criminal cases, requires action on the part of the court. While members of the press may be present at children's hearings, they are prohibited from identifying the child involved.[131]

3.58 In criminal proceedings, the prohibition on disclosing the identity of any child involved is automatic:[132] that is, it applies unless it is lifted by the court. The provision confines itself to children under the age of 16 and protects the identity of the child-accused, the child-victim and, subject to one exception, the child-witness. Where a child-witness is under the age of 16 and no one against whom the proceedings are being taken is below that age, the prohibition does not apply unless the court so directs.[133] The prohibition on reporting may be dispensed with, in whole or in part, by the court where it is satisfied that to do so 'is in the public interest'.[134] It was

127 Judicial Proceedings (Regulation of Reports) Act 1926.
128 B. McCain, A. J. Bonnington and G. A. Watt, *Scots Law for Journalists* (6th edn, W. Green, 1995), chapter 12.
129 The Children and Young Persons (Scotland) Act 1937, s 46, as amended by the Children and Young Persons Act 1963, s 57.
130 *C v S* 1989 SLT 168. Similar provisions exist in England and Wales in the Administration of Justice Act 1960, s 12. However, the need to protect the child from publicity will not necessarily prevail over all reporting of a particular case. See *In re G (Minors) (Celebrities: Publicity)* [1998] TLR 657 where the Court of Appeal reversed the decision of the Family Division, prohibiting publication of even a summary of the case, in a dispute between well-known parents over residence of children. Thorpe LJ observed that there was 'an inevitable tendency for the Family Division judge at first instance to give too much weight to welfare and too little weight to freedom of speech'. It may be no coincidence that sketchy details of the dispute between Paula Yates and Bob Geldof over the arrangements for their children were published in various newspapers the following day.
131 Children (Scotland) Act 1995, s 43(3)(b) and 44.
132 Criminal Procedure (Scotland) Act 1995, s 47(1).
133 Criminal Procedure (Scotland) Act 1995, s 47(3)(a).
134 Criminal Procedure (Scotland) Act 1995, s 47(3)(b).

particularly unfortunate that this was done in one case prior to the accused's appeal against conviction being heard, since her conviction was overturned on appeal.[135] Once the proceedings are completed (ie after any appeal has been heard) the Secretary of State may dispense with reporting restrictions, again, either in whole or in part, and if such dispensation is in the public interest.[136] A proposal was mooted to amend the legislation to remove the automatic reporting restrictions where an under-16-year-old was convicted of a serious offence.[137] It is to be hoped that nothing comes of this proposal. While there may be a legitimate public interest in knowing that young people sometimes commit serious offences, the legitimate public interest in knowing the identity of the particular young offender is questionable. Protecting the young offender from publicity acknowledges that these young people will often themselves be vulnerable, albeit their conduct may mean they elicit little public sympathy. It is suggested that publicity could only serve to add to the pressure on offenders (and their families) and inhibit their future development and rehabilitation. It is worth noting that the UN Convention requires that child-offenders should be 'treated in a manner consistent with the promotion of the child's sense of dignity and worth' and that account should be taken of their 'age and the desirability of promoting the child's reintegration and the child's assuming a constructive role in society'.[138] In addition, it must be remembered that, however heinous the offence, these offenders are still children whose welfare deserves consideration.

POWERS OF CHILDREN

3.59 While we have seen that a child acquires legal personality at birth[139] and, thus, becomes a player in terms of the legal system, there are obvious practical reasons why he or she cannot participate actively from that time. Thus, the law has always recognised that the child should have either no capacity, or limited capacity, to act independently until he or she reaches a particular age. The common law achieved this by developing a scheme derived from Roman law, which divided all children and young people into two categories, pupils and minors, with guardians, known as tutors or curators, respectively. Pupils were girls up to the age of 12 and boys up to the age of 14 years old, whereupon young people became minors. Capacity depended on whether the young person was a pupil or a minor and, once a minor, on the degree of independence they had in their lives.[140] When it examined the law in this area, the Scottish Law Commission concluded that a modern approach should satisfy three goals: protection of young people, fairness to third parties dealing with them and clarity in the provisions

---

135 *Codona v HM Advocate* 1996 SLT 1100.
136 Criminal Procedure (Scotland) Act 1995, s 47(3)(c).
137 Consultation Paper on Identification of Children: Proposals to Amend section 47 of the Criminal Procedure (Scotland) Act 1995 (Scottish Office, 1996).
138 Article 40.
139 T. B. Smith, *A Short Commentary on the Law of Scotland* (W. Green, 1962), at p 245.
140 For a discussion of the position at common law, see Wilkinson and Norrie, *Parent and Child*, pp 37–51 and the *Stair Memorial Encyclopaedia*, vol 10, paras 1049–1114.

themselves. It found the then-existing law to be wanting in all respects, that it was out of touch with modern social and economic reality, and that the sexist distinction in when a young person achieved minority was no longer acceptable.[141]

3.60 As a result of the Commission's recommendations, much of the common law was replaced by the Age of Legal Capacity (Scotland) Act 1991 ('the 1991 Act').[142] The distinction between pupils and minors has been swept away and the new scheme focuses on the age of 16, as being a more realistic landmark in the lives of young people today, combined with a notion of evolving capacity.[143] The general principle is that a person below the age of 16 years has no legal capacity to enter into any transaction and that a person over that age has full legal capacity.[144] The Commission recognised that, if that general principle was left in this stark form, the result would have been to ignore practical reality that young people under the age of 16 do enter into transactions all the time. Furthermore, various powers that young people had at common law would have been abolished and the protection afforded to young adults would have been removed. Thus, the 1991 Act goes on to provide a host of exceptions to the general principle of incapacity below the age of 16 and to provide special protection to persons who transact between the ages of 16 and 18.

Children and young persons under the age of sixteen

3.61 While the general rule is that a person below the age of 16 has no legal capacity to enter any legal transaction[145] and any purported attempt to do so is void,[146] there are a number of exceptions to the rule.

Common transactions

3.62 Children have the capacity to enter a transaction provided that two conditions are satisfied. First, the transaction itself must be of a kind commonly entered into by persons of the child's age and circumstances and, secondly, the terms of the transaction must not be unreasonable.[147] The aim here is to have a flexible provision, capable of meeting the diverse circumstances which might occur in terms of the range of children and young people it covers, their varying lifestyles and time itself. It is, perhaps, one of the best examples of statutory drafting showing itself to be capable of the kind of adaptability found in Scots common law. The reality is that children enter into transactions all the time, although what will be deemed to be a 'usual transaction' for a child of a particular age in given

---

141 Legal Capacity of Minors and Pupils (Scot Law Com Consultative Memorandum No 65, 1985), paras 2.12–2.19 and Report on the Legal Capacity and Responsibility of Minors and Pupils (Scot Law Com No 110, 1987).
142 Section 1(3) lists matters not affected by the Act and these include delictual and criminal responsibility.
143 It is interesting to note that the idea of evolving capacity is one which was echoed several years later in the UN Convention on the Rights of the Child.
144 Section 1(1).
145 Section 1(1)(a).
146 Section 2(5).
147 Section 2(1).

circumstances is, as yet, untested in the courts.[148] However, it seems reasonable that a ten-year-old might buy sweets, comics and small toys, while a 14-year-old might enter into transactions involving the expenditure of larger sums of money, buying such items as a CD or a pair of jeans. Whatever the nature of the transaction, its terms must not be unreasonable. Reasonableness is not defined in the 1991 Act, but would arguably apply to such factors as market conditions. Thus, while a pair of designer jeans might cost a great deal more than a pair bearing a generic label, the transaction itself would not be unreasonable if the young person buying designer jeans paid the usual price for such an item. This is the most sweeping and practically significant of the exceptions to the general rule.

Instructing a solicitor in connection with a civil matter

3.63 A person under the age of 16 has the capacity to instruct a solicitor in connection with a civil matter provided that the child or young person has a general understanding of what it means to do so and a child of 12 years or older is presumed to have sufficient understanding.[149] Of course, this does not preclude a younger child from demonstrating sufficient understanding and children as young as eight years old have instructed solicitors. The 1991 Act is silent on the question of who assesses the child for this purpose.[150] In practice, it is the solicitor receiving instructions who makes this assessment. At first glance, this seems curious, since the solicitor might be viewed as having some interest in gaining a client. However, the 1991 Act provides a parallel in allowing the treating physician to assess a child's understanding for the purpose of medical treatment.[151] In addition, and quite apart from relying on the proven ethics of the legal profession, one might question that any solicitor would benefit from being instructed by an incoherent client. In any event, the other party in any court proceedings could always challenge the child's competency to instruct. The child's capacity to instruct a solicitor includes the capacity to sue and defend in civil proceedings. None of this has any bearing on the child's capacity in relation to any criminal matter.[152]

3.64 This provision demonstrates a real commitment to recognising children as holders of rights and not simply objects of protection, since they can now take the initiative in pursuing their rights. Another attraction of the provision is that children will almost always be eligible for legal aid, whereas their parents may be unable or unwilling to finance their pursuit of their rights, particularly if the parents' rights are in conflict with the child's.

148 Some caution should be used in seeking too much guidance from the, often charming, cases found in the common law, since the provision there related to the purchase of 'necessaries', albeit that term was interpreted very flexibly.
149 Section 2(4A), added to the 1991 Act by the Children (Scotland) Act 1995, Sched 4, para 53(3).
150 In England and Wales, both the solicitor and the court must be satisfied that the child has sufficient understanding – Family Proceedings Rules 1991, r 9.2A(1)(b). It must be remembered, however, that there, children must obtain leave of the court to raise an action at all.
151 See paras 3.67–3.71, below.
152 Section 2(4)(c).

All of this assumes, of course, that children have both an appreciation of their rights and access to legal services: a somewhat optimistic assumption. As we have seen, the current state of Scots law is less than satisfactory in this respect.[153]

Making a will

3.65 A young person of 12 years old or over has the capacity to make a will.[154] At common law, a young person acquired this capacity in respect of moveable property on reaching minority and heritage was added later by statute.[155] Thus, the 1991 Act has made no practical difference so far as young women are concerned, but it has removed the sexism that was inherent in the concept of minority. In practice, very few young people make a will.

Consenting to adoption

3.66 A young person has the right to consent to or veto his or her own adoption from the age of 12 years old.[156] Again, this was something a minor child had the right to do at common law. The court has the power to authorise an adoption where the young person is incapable of giving consent.[157]

Consenting to surgical, dental or medical treatment

3.67 A person below the age of 16 has the capacity to consent to any surgical, medical or dental procedure or treatment where the qualified practitioner attending him or her is of the opinion that the young person understands the nature and possible consequences of the procedure or treatment.[158] There were two schools of thought on when a young person acquired the right to consent, at common law, to his or her own medical treatment. On one view, the power to consent on the young person's behalf was derived from guardianship and, thus, vested in the young person when he or she attained minority at 12 or 14.[159] The other view was that it derived from custody and, thus, vested in the guardian until the young person was 16.[160] It is submitted that the former view is preferable.

3.68 Whatever might have been the position before the 1991 Act, this provision attracted considerable public attention when the legislation was progressing through Parliament, not least because it came in the wake of the infamous *Gillick* case[161] in England. There, a mother sought an

---

153 See paras 3.42–3.44, above.
154 Section 2(2).
155 Succession (Scotland) Act 1964, s 28.
156 Section 2(3).
157 Adoption (Scotland) Act 1978, ss 12(8) and 18(8).
158 Section 2(4).
159 See for example, K. McK. Norrie, 'The *Gillick* Case and Parental Rights in Scots Law' 1985 SLT (News) 157.
160 See for example, J. M. Thomson, 'The *Gillick* Case and Parental Rights in Scots Law: Another View' 1985 SLT (News) 223.
161 *Gillick* v *West Norfolk and Wisbech Area Health Authority* [1985] 3 All ER 402. The case is discussed extensively in Mason and McCall Smith, *Law and Medical Ethics* (4th edn, Butterworths, 1996) at pp 94 and 179.

assurance from her local health board that none of her daughters under the age of 16 would be given advice or treatment on contraception or abortion without her prior consent. When the health board refused to give this assurance, she pursued a course of much-publicised litigation to have the courts uphold what she perceived to be her right as a parent to control this aspect of her daughters' lives. Ultimately, the House of Lords concluded that a young person below the age of 16 did have the capacity to consent to his or her own treatment where he or she was sufficiently mature to understand the nature of that treatment, although there was some doubt about whether the treatment also had to be in the young person's best interest. What the *Gillick* case and the debate surrounding this provision in the 1991 Act illustrate is the extent to which strong opinion on a single issue can influence, and sometimes skew, rational debate on matters of more general principle. Thus, concern over young women having access to advice on contraception dominated the debate on the more general issue of consent to medical treatment.

3.69 In any event, the 1991 Act makes it clear that a young person in Scotland does have the capacity to consent to his or her own treatment, subject to the test that he or she understands what is happening. That being the case, other individuals with parental responsibilities and rights in respect of the young person have no power to veto that consent. Thus, parents have no power to prevent their 15-year-old daughter from having an abortion provided that this is what she wants and that she understands what is involved. Arguably, the same principle holds true across the board. So, for example, where a young person wishes to donate an organ for transplantation into another person, provided that the young person understands all the short- and long-term problems and risks involved, he or she can consent to do so.[162]

3.70 Logic suggests that the power to consent carries with it the power to refuse and this is the position taken by most commentators discussing the 1991 Act.[163] According to that view, where a competent young person refuses treatment, no one else can nullify that refusal by consenting on his or her behalf. However, developments in England and Wales, albeit

162 The issue of organ donation by young people has barely been touched upon in the UK, but has been explored more extensively in the USA, often in the context of parents seeking the court's permission for the donation. See for example, *Hart v Brown* 289 A 2d 386 (Conn, 1972) (where the court gave permission for a kidney to be removed from a seven-year-old boy, for transplant in his twin); *Little v Little* 576 SW 2d 493 (Tex, 1979) (where the court authorised the removal of a kidney from a mentally incompetent 14-year-old girl, for transplant in her younger brother). However, in *Curran v Bosze* 566 NE 2d 1319 (Ill, 1990), the court refused to order three-year-old twins to undergo tests with a view to donating bone marrow to their half-brother. Since bone marrow donation is less intrusive than organ donation, this decision was somewhat surprising but was prompted, in part, by the opposition of the twin's mother whose support through the procedure was thought to be central to its impact on the children. See also, *In the Marriage of GWW and CWM* 21 Fam LR 612, where the Family Court of Australia authorised bone marrow harvesting from a nine-year-old boy for use in his aunt.
163 J. Blackie and H. Patrick, 'Medical Treatment' in Cleland and Sutherland, n 1 above; Mason and McCall Smith, n 161 above, p 229; Wilkinson and Norrie, n 4 above, pp 184–185.

applying different legislation, have muddied the waters on the issue of the minor's power to refuse medical treatment there[164] and it remains to be seen whether this muddying will be adopted by the Scottish courts. Certainly, a strong case can be made for rejecting the English approach in Scotland. Firstly, the clear words of the 1991 Act, in giving the child who understands what is happening the power to consent, can be argued to remove any power to consent that the parent may have had prior to the legislation. Admittedly, the 1991 Act does not actually say this. Secondly, it can be argued that the power to refuse is supported by the later amendment to the 1991 Act found in the Children (Scotland) Act 1995 which provides that, even in the face of a court order or the decision of a children's hearing, when authorising medical examination of the child, the consent of a competent young person is a prerequisite to such an examination.[165] If the young person has the power to refuse in these circumstances, consistency requires recognition of a more general power to refuse. Thirdly, there is the less convincing argument that the competent child's refusal can only be overridden where to do so would be in the child's best interests and to force a person to be treated against his or her wishes will rarely be in his or her interests. Undoubtedly, the Scottish courts will have the opportunity to consider this matter in due course. The paradigm case for the court will be in dealing with a life or death case. For example, where a sane, competent, 14-year-old anorexic young person is refusing life-saving treatment, should the court order the treatment to be carried out?[166] It remains to be seen whether the courts will be persuaded by the reasoning adopted south of the border or, indeed, will find some other way, perhaps founded on the notion of best interests or public policy, to override what would be an unpopular result in some quarters.

3.71 It is understandable that case-law around the world, and the media attention it attracts, surrounding young people and medical treatment focuses on the dramatic cases. In order to keep some sense of perspective, it is worth remembering that the issue of consent does not arise in the vast majority of cases when a young person is being treated. Thus, when the school nurse bathes a seven-year-old's grazed knee, or a dentist fits a retainer on the teeth of a ten-year-old, it may be that neither the children

164 The Court of Appeal went through a process of somewhat convoluted reasoning in addressing the issue of the young person's right to refuse medical treatment in *Re R (A Minor) (Wardship: Consent to Treatment)* [1991] 4 All ER 177 and *Re W (A Minor) (Medical Treatment)* [1992] 4 All ER 627. In *re R*, Lord Donaldson introduced the notion of 'key holders' all of whom could open the door to consent. Thus, while the young person herself held the key to consent to treatment, where she refused, that consent could be provided by another key holder, like a parent. In *re W*, he replaced the notion of key holders with that of 'flak-jackets' which could offer protection to the young person in the face of her refusal to accept life-saving treatment. The cases, and the issues involved, are discussed in A. Bainham, 'The Judge and the Competent Minor' (1992) 108 LQR 194 and Mason and McCall Smith, n 161 above, pp 322–323.
165 Section 90.
166 J. L. Rosato, 'The Ultimate Test of Autonomy: Should Minors have the Right to make Decisions regarding Life-Sustaining Treatment?' 49 Rutgers L Rev 1 (1996) and A. Elton, P. Honig, A. Bentovim and J. Simons, 'Withholding consent to life-saving treatment: three cases' (1995) 310 Brit Med J 373.

nor the adults involved give any thought to who has the power to consent to the procedure.

Transactions entered into before the commencement of the Act

3.72 Where the transaction was entered into before the 1991 Act came into force on 25 September 1991, the common law rules will apply.[167]

Parental responsibilities and rights

3.73 While parental responsibilities and rights are usually held in respect of a person under 16,[168] such young people may themselves be parents. Where this happens, the young parent may hold and exercise parental responsibilities and rights in respect of his or her own child[169] and may be appointed as guardian to the child.[170]

Other matters not affected

3.74 While the 1991 Act supersedes all prior legislation governing the capacity of pupils and minors,[171] it makes clear that its provisions do not affect certain other matters. Thus, legislation laying down an age limit expressed in years remains valid.[172] A number of age limits will be explored presently but, typically, they restrict the access young people have to particular commodities or activities and include such matters as the sale of cigarettes and alcohol and the obtaining of a driving licence. Delictual and criminal responsibility remain unaffected[173] by the 1991 Act and, while these matters are not 'transactions' at all, it was as well to put the matter beyond all possible doubt.

Sixteen- to eighteen-year-olds

3.75 Young people over the age of 16 have full legal capacity to enter into any transaction[174] and, at first sight, this may suggest that they are on the same footing as adults. However, the common law always recognised these 'beginners' in terms of exercising capacity as being entitled to some additional protection from their own inexperience and greater vulnerability to exploitation.[175] The 1991 Act continues to recognise this need to protect young people, by providing that a person under the age of 21 may apply to the court to have a transaction which he or she entered while between the ages of 16 and 18 set aside.[176] The purpose of allowing a person

---

167 Section 1(3)(a).
168 See chapter 5.
169 Section 1(3)(g).
170 Section 5(2).
171 Section 1(4).
172 Section 1(3)(d).
173 Section 1(3)(c).
174 Section 1(1)(b).
175 This is one explanation for the prohibition on sending circulars offering credit to a person under the age of 18 and on taking an article in pawn from such a person – Consumer Credit Act 1974, ss 50 and 114. Documents in connection with student loans are excluded from the prohibition on sending credit-related circulars to people under the age of 18 – Education (Student Loans) Act 1990, s 3.
176 Section 3(1).

under 21 to challenge the transaction is to allow time for the young person to reflect upon the transaction itself and, perhaps, to become aware of the right to challenge it. Where a person could have challenged a transaction, the application can be made instead by that person's executor, trustee in bankruptcy, trustee acting under a trust deed for creditors or curator bonis.[177]

3.76 In order to mount a successful challenge, the young person must demonstrate that the transaction was a 'prejudicial transaction' and, in order to do this, must satisfy two criteria. First, it must be shown that the transaction was not one which an adult, exercising reasonable prudence, would have entered into in the circumstances at the time the transaction was entered into.[178] Second, it must be shown that the transaction itself has caused or is likely to cause substantial prejudice to the young person.[179] To turn these criteria on their head, the first thing to establish is that the applicant for reduction has suffered, or is likely to suffer, loss. However, that alone will not be enough. In addition, it must be shown that a reasonable adult would not have done exactly the same in the circumstances. An example here might be buying shares in a particular company. If the young person has suffered loss when the price of the shares fell, his or her claim would still fail if all the indications at the time were enough to convince other prudent adult investors to buy them.

3.77 Regardless of their impact on the young person, certain transactions and other activities are explicitly exempted from applications for reduction under the 1991 Act. It should be remembered that this does not bar applications for reduction on the many other grounds available to anyone, irrespective of age, including misrepresentation, fraud, and coercion. A young person's exercise of testamentary capacity cannot be the subject of an application for reduction under the 1991 Act.[180] Since any person can change his or her testamentary writings throughout his or her lifetime, simply by executing a new will, reduction would seem to be unnecessary in such circumstances in any event. In other cases where reduction is not available using the 1991 Act, the young person will have been given a degree of protection anyway either by a court or by professional ethics. Thus, consent to adoption,[181] action taken in the course of civil proceedings[182] and consent to any surgical, medical or dental procedure[183] are exempted. Where the particular transaction was entered into by the young person in the course of a trade, occupation or profession, it cannot be reduced using the 1991 Act.[184] This exemption exemplifies the balance that the Commission sought to achieve between protecting young people and fairness to third parties dealing with them. Where a young person chooses

177 Section 3(4).
178 Section 3(2)(a).
179 Section 3(2)(b).
180 Section 3(3)(a) and (b).
181 Section 3(3)(c).
182 Section 3(3)(d).
183 Section 3(3)(e).
184 Section 3(3)(f).

to engage in commercial activity and to gain the benefits that may come with that, there is a degree of natural justice in expecting that young person to stand by his or her own transactions. In any event, if such transactions were reducible, third parties would be less willing to deal with young people, thus denying them the opportunity to participate fully in the business world. Some transactions and activities are exempted from reduction under the 1991 Act on an application of the general principle of personal bar. Where a young person has induced the other party to enter the transaction by fraudulent misrepresentation as to his or her age or any other material fact,[185] reduction is not available. Similarly, where the young person has ratified the transaction after reaching the age of 18, knowing that it could be set aside, reduction is barred.[186]

3.78 Furthermore, in the attempt to achieve a degree of certainty, the 1991 Act provides a mechanism whereby a transaction can be given prior approval by a court where it would otherwise be the kind of transaction which could be subject to reduction.[187] The application is made to the sheriff by all of the parties to it, including the young person. Provided that the court is satisfied that it is not a prejudicial transaction, it can ratify the transaction and, thereafter, no application to reduce it can be made under the 1991 Act.[188]

RESPONSIBILITIES OF CHILDREN

3.79 Not only do children have the capacity to become players in the legal system, in certain circumstances, they can also acquire responsibilities. Thus, for example, where a child has the capacity to contract, he or she acquires not only rights but responsibilities under the contract. Where a 16-year-old marries,[189] he or she takes on the responsibilities that attach to marriage, including the liability to aliment one's spouse.[190] Two particular areas of potential responsibility, delict and the criminal law, warrant special attention.

Delict

3.80 As we have seen, once a child is born, he or she will have a right of action in delict for any harm sustained as a result of a negligent act or omission which occurred while that child was a foetus.[191] It is not surprising, then, that a child will have a similar claim in respect of the delictual acts of others which occurred after the child's birth. The child's parents are not placed in any special position, in this respect, and a child can sue his or her parents in delict.[192]The fact that a pursuer in an action of delict is a child does become relevant, however, in the context of contributory negligence;

185 Section 3(3)(g).
186 Section 3(3)(h).
187 Section 4.
188 Section 3(3)(j).
189 A person acquires the capacity to marry at 16 – Marriage (Scotland) Act 1977, s 1.
190 Family Law (Scotland) Act 1985, s 1(1)(a) and (b).
191 See chapter 2, paras 8–11.
192 *Young* v *Rankin* 1934 SC 499.

that is, when the defender argues that the harm was caused, at least in part, by the child's own conduct. At one time it was thought that the standard of care to be expected of a child was the same as that expected of an adult.[193] It is now well established that the law will take the far more reasonable approach of assessing the child in the light of that child's age and experience.[194] Thus, a child of five, living in an urban environment, can be expected to have some appreciation of the dangers of traffic.[195]

3.81 There is no minimum age for delictual liability in Scotland and the older authorities suggest that a pupil child (girls below 12, and boys below 14, years old) could be liable.[196] The Age of Legal Capacity (Scotland) Act 1991 explicitly excludes the law of delict from its ambit[197] and, thus, the position remains that even a young child could be held responsible for his or her delictual acts. However, since there must be something negligent or deliberate about a person's act or omission before he or she can be liable in delict at all, a child's age will often be relevant in ascertaining whether a child had any appreciation of the likely consequences of a particular act. Thus, neither the baby who drops a rattle from a pram, causing a passer-by to trip and sustain injury, nor the toddler who pushes another child causing the latter to fall and sustain a fractured skull, is likely to be held liable for these acts. As far as older children are concerned, it should be remembered that it is only worth raising an action against a person with sufficient resources to pay any damages awarded. Since most children have no significant assets and are not covered by insurance, they do not make attractive defenders.

3.82 Where the parent instigates the child's delictual act or has been negligent in, for example, failing to supervise the child, liability may attach to the parent.[198] However, in the absence of fault (in the delictual sense) on the part of the parent, he or she has no automatic responsibility for the delicts of his or her children. The Scottish Law Commission took the opportunity to invite views on whether, in the absence of fault, parents should be so liable.[199] As a result of the responses it received, the Commission very wisely recommended no change to the law.[200]

Criminal law

3.83 Children receive such general protection as is afforded to everyone

---

193 *Grant* v *Caledonian Railway Co* (1870) 9 M 258, per Lord President Inglis at 270 and per Lord Ardmillan at p 264.
194 *Campbell* v *Ord & Maddison* (1873) 1 R 149; *Banner's Tutor* v *Kennedy's Trustees* 1978 SLT (Notes) 83.
195 *McKinnell* v *White* 1971 SLT (Notes) 61, per Lord Fraser at 62.
196 Craig, *Jus feudale*, 2, 12, 14; *Davie* v *Wilson* (1854) 16 D 956, per Lord Robertson at 960, where the action founded upon an allegedly deliberate act, sadly missing the opportunity to explore the pupil's liability for negligence.
197 Section 1(3)(c).
198 The parent's liability here would result from his or her own conduct.
199 Legal Capacity and Responsibility of Minors and Pupils (Scot Law Com Consultative Memorandum No 65, 1985), para 6.12.
200 Report on the Legal Capacity and Responsibility of Minors and Pupils (Scot Law Com No 110, 1987), para 13.

by the criminal law and thus, for example, taking a child's property may be theft; striking a child will often be an assault;[201] and killing a child will be culpable homicide or murder. In addition, the legal system regards certain behaviour as criminal simply because a child is involved. Thus, for example, anyone who neglects or ill-treats a child in his or her care commits an offence;[202] certain sexual offences can only be committed in respect of young people;[203] and selling certain commodities, like cigarettes, alcohol and firearms, is prohibited where the purchaser is below a particular age. As we shall see, these offences are usually aimed at protecting children, although some involve elements of protecting other members of the community or setting standards for what might be described as 'good parenting'. Here we are concerned with the child's responsibility for his or her own allegedly criminal acts.

3.84 An examination of the early approach of Scots law to juvenile justice reveals that, in common with most other jurisdictions, there was little recognition that children might require any special treatment. After some earlier doubt, Scots common law fixed on seven as the age of criminal responsibility.[204] While pupil children were generally thought to be exempt from capital punishment,[205] and the cases show numerous examples of 'leniency' in sentencing being shown on account of the minority of the offender,[206] it was not until 1908[207] that a clear distinction was drawn between juvenile and adult offenders.

3.85 In 1925, the first separate Scottish inquiry into the care and protection of children and the treatment of juvenile offenders was set up under the chairmanship of George Morton, KC,[208] and looking at the way the law treated 'children who are wronged' along with 'children who did wrong' was to become the pattern for approaching such issues in Scotland. The Morton Committee recommended that the age of criminal responsibility

---

201 An exception to the general protection from assault, afforded to children, is right of parents (and certain other persons) under what is described as 'reasonable chastisement'. This invidious concept is discussed in chapter 6, paras 18–19.

202 Children and Young Persons (Scotland) Act 1937, s 12. Again, this is subject to the concept of reasonable chastisement – 1937 Act, s 12(7).

203 See paras 3.96–3.100, below.

204 D. Hume, *Commentaries on the Law of Scotland Respecting Crimes* (1819, reprinted 1986, the Law Society of Scotland), I, 35; A. Alison, *Principles of the Criminal Law of Scotland* (1832, reprinted 1989, the Law Society of Scotland and Butterworths), p 666.

205 Hume was unwilling to elevate this idea to one of general principle irrespective of 'how deliberate soever the wickedness, or how incorrigible the obstinacy, or how cunning the malice of the offender' above, at p 34.

206 'Leniency' is used here in the context of the time as the following examples cited by Hume above, at pp 32–34 illustrate: *Duff and Millar*, March 1701 (two boys aged 14 and 12 convicted of housebreaking along with an adult were sentenced to be scourged at the gibbet while the adult was sentenced to death); *Alexander Livingston*, 1749 (a 12-year-old boy convicted of killing another boy by stabbing him was sentenced to transportation); and *Main and Atchieson* 25 March 1818 (two boys of 15 who were convicted of housebreaking and sentenced to death, had their sentences reduced to transportation).

207 Children Act 1908, which applied to Scotland, England and Wales.

208 Report of the Departmental Committee on Protection and Training (HMSO, 1928).

should be raised to eight.[209] Its second, more major, recommendation was that jurisdiction over all cases of children and juvenile offenders should be transferred to specially constituted Justice of the Peace juvenile courts where the cases would be heard by justices who were specially qualified by their knowledge and experience to hear such cases.[210] As far as modern juvenile justice is concerned, the turning point was the report of the Kilbrandon Committee in 1964.[211] The Committee's recommendations were implemented in the Social Work (Scotland) Act 1968 and the children's hearings system was established. The hearings system is now governed by the Children (Scotland) Act 1995 which introduced some changes to the original model.

3.86 The current age of criminal responsibility remains eight[212] and the fact that Scotland has one of the lowest ages for criminal responsibility in the world was not lost on the United Nations Committee on the Rights of the Child.[213] It listed this as one of its principal areas of concern when it reported on the UK's compliance with the Convention. As was suggested earlier, it may be that the Committee did not understand the full implications of the children's hearings system, since the UK's own report centred on the position in England and Wales, with the Scottish position being presented very much as an aside. Had the UN Committee appreciated the philosophy and practice of juvenile justice in Scotland it might have taken a different approach. None the less, since it remains possible for a child to be prosecuted in a criminal court, the fact that the age of criminal responsibility is so low is a valid concern.

3.87 Where a child is alleged to have committed an offence, he or she will almost always be dealt with in the children's hearings system. The hearings system is discussed fully in chapter 9, but it is worth giving a brief outline of its salient features, as they impact upon children who offend.[214] The system deals with both children who have offended and children who are in need of care and protection and, in both cases, the child is referred to the Principal Reporter. The Principal Reporter decides whether the child may be in need of compulsory measures of supervision and, if so, arranges a

209 Above, at p 48. The Report gives only a brief explanation for this very minor change and one is left with the impression that the Committee would have liked to raise the age further. It may have been that the Committee, like so many since, was conscious of what would be politically acceptable.
210 While this recommendation was also accepted, in principle, in the Children and Young Persons (Scotland) Act 1937, s 1, it required implementation by an order from the Secretary of State and only four such orders, covering a small part of Scotland, were ever made.
211 Report of the Committee on Children and Young Persons, Scotland, (Cmnd 2306 1964).
212 Research conducted in Scotland, in the late 1970s demonstrated that a number of children under the age of eight were engaging in activity which would have been criminal, had they been older. While some of the children or, at least, their families, were known to the social work department, a number were not. See, J. P. Grant and S. A. M. McLean, 'Police Contact with Children under Eight Years of Age' 1981 J Soc Welf L 140.
213 CRC/C/15/Add34.
214 The following paragraphs outline the hearings system in very broad terms and reference to the relevant statutory provisions has been omitted. Reference should be made to chapter 9.

hearing for the child. If the child denies the offence, or the parents do not accept that the child committed it, or the child appears not to understand what is being alleged, the case must be referred to a court if it is to proceed, where guilt or otherwise will be established according to the ordinary rules of evidence. If the child is found guilty, the case will be sent back to the hearing for disposal. If the child accepts that he or she committed the offence, the case can proceed before the hearing without going to a court at all.

3.88 A fundamental innovation of the hearings system is that, rather than what should happen to a child being decided by a court, the decision is taken by a children's hearing comprising three lay members of the community, after a round-table discussion with the child and the family of all the relevant circumstances and not simply the offence. In order to assist it, the hearing will have a variety of reports about the child's background from the local authority's social work department, the child's school and, in some cases, other relevant professionals. A further point to note is that the hearing takes its decision based on what will serve the child's best interests and, thus, is based on a non-punitive, treatment, model of juvenile justice. The hearing can: decide that no action is necessary; make a supervision requirement; or require that the child should comply with other conditions. An appeal may be taken to the sheriff against the decision of a hearing and further appeal on a point of law may be taken to the Sheriff Principal and the Court of Session. Where a supervision requirement is made, the decision of a hearing must be reviewed by a future hearing within a year and it is possible for the case to be reviewed at an earlier stage.

3.89 Despite the fact that the vast majority of children who offend are dealt with by the hearings system, prosecution of children in the criminal courts is provided for in a limited range of circumstances. Prosecution of a person under the age of 16 may only take place on the instructions of the Lord Advocate or at his or her instance.[215] Where convicted, the child can be sentenced by the court. However, provision is made for involving the children's hearing system in disposals. If the child is already on supervision, the High Court may, and the sheriff must, remit the case to the Principal Reporter for advice as to the treatment of the child.[216] If the child is not already on supervision, the court in question may remit the case to the Principal Reporter for disposal or for advice.[217] This course of action does not apply to cases where the penalty for the case is fixed by law[218] and, thus, a child convicted of murder will not benefit from the provision.[219]

3.90 In Scotland, the number of children committing very serious offences, and particularly those involving the death of another person, has been very small, but then, in world terms, Scotland is a very small country.

---

215 Criminal Procedure (Scotland) Act 1995, s 42. Special procedures govern the arrest and detention of children under the age of 16 – 1995 Act, ss 43–46.
216 1995 Act, s 49(3).
217 1995 Act, s 49(1).
218 1995 Act, s 49(5).
219 A. Normand, 'The Scottish System' in P. Cavadino, *Children Who Kill* (Waterside Press, 1996).

Media attention has highlighted a number of cases in other jurisdictions, over the last few years, where the crimes of individual young people have been such as to astound their own communities and attract worldwide attention. What has come to be known as the 'Bulger case' in England is one such example.[220] In the USA, concern has surrounded the highly-publicised cases of teenagers who have gained access to firearms and have gone on to kill, the victims usually being members of their own families or people they knew.[221] While the magnitude of destruction is often part of the reason for the reaction to these offences, the fact that the offenders are young is a central feature. It offends our image of childhood, as a time of innocence, to be confronted with young people committing such serious offences. As societies, we simply do not know how to deal with these young offenders and we must be careful not to grasp at simplistic solutions out of sheer desperation.[222] One such quick-fix response, summed up in the catchy slogan '[c]ommit an adult crime, do adult time', has proved popular with voters in some areas of the USA.[223] There are different mechanisms by which this can be achieved[224] but, essentially, it involves trying and sentencing the juvenile as an adult. The popular appeal of such a solution fails to take account of the defects inherent in it. By trying juveniles as adults, cases become bogged down in the adult criminal court system and greater delays result, thus losing the benefit of a swift response, regarded as essential in dealing with young offenders. Most significant, however, is that adult sentencing lacks the rehabilitative component of juvenile justice. The result is a higher rate of recidivism amongst juveniles processed through the adult system.[225] If ever there was a case of society shooting itself in the

---

220 In that case, two ten-year-old boys took a toddler, James Bulger, to a remote spot and killed him.

221 In 1998, Kip Kinkel allegedly killed his parents and spent the night at home with their bodies, before going to school and shooting a number of fellow pupils in Springfield, Oregon. In the few years prior to that case, similar incidents occurred in Pearl, Mississippi, West Paducah, Kentucky, and Jonesboro, Arkansas. In total, 15 people died and a further 44 were physically injured. These figures do not include witnesses to the incidents, who suffered psychological trauma, nor the accused themselves.

222 See P. Cavadino, *Children Who Kill*, above, which provides a worldwide review of children who kill and how different legal systems deal with them.

223 For a discussion of this trend, see E. K. Klein, 'Dennis the Menace or Billy the Kid: An Analysis of the Role of Transfer to Criminal Court in Juvenile Justice' 35 Am Crim L Rev 371 (1998).

224 Under the 'judicial waver' model, the prosecutor requests transfer of the case and the final decision lies with the judge. Under the 'statutory exclusion' model, the legislature removes certain offences from the jurisdiction of the juvenile courts, thus ensuring trial in criminal court. The 'prosecutorial discretion' model leaves it to the discretion of the prosecutor to file the case in a particular court.

225 D. Bishop and C. Frazier reviewed prosecutorial transfers in Florida from 1979 to 1987 – Juvenile Justice: Juveniles Processed in Criminal Court and Case Dispositions (US General Accounting Office, 1995). J. Fagan compared cases transferred in New York with cases relating to similar crimes that were dealt with in juvenile court – J. Fagan 'Separating the Men from the Boys: The Comparative Advantages of Juvenile Versus Criminal Court Sanctions on Recidivism Among Adolescent Offenders' in J. C. Howell (ed), *A Sourcebook: Serious, Violent, Chronic Juvenile Offenders* (Sage, 1995). Both studies found a higher rate of recidivism amongst transfer cases and that the young people re-offended within a shorter time of release. Transferred youths were more likely to commit serious offences when they re-offended.

foot, this is it. In the name of 'doing something about' a problem and, one suspects, satisfying the public desire for retribution, a system can emerge which is less effective in dealing with juvenile crime and results in more serious crime in the future.[226] One does not have to belong to the 'liberal' camp to appreciate why this is a bad idea.

RESTRICTIONS

3.91 Think back to your own childhood and one of the memories that will almost certainly surface is of being told that you would have to wait until you were older to be allowed to do a particular thing. When specific statutory age limits are examined, a host of inconsistencies appear and this is often because particular legislation was passed in response to a perceived problem at a given time. None the less, the overall result is a badly designed mosaic. In the paragraphs below, we will take a brief look at some of these age limits, how they apply and the rationale behind them.

3.92 In the attempt to protect children from the dangers posed by the adult world, the legal system seeks to deny children and young people access to a whole host of perceived dangers. Often, the mechanism employed is to make it an offence for an adult to sell a named commodity to a person below a particular age. Sometimes the young person will also commit an offence by seeking to buy the commodity. Thus, for example, it is an offence for any person to sell cigarettes to a person under the age of 16.[227] Alcohol is similarly treated with the age limit being 18 and, in this case, the seller, any person purchasing alcohol for the young person and the young person may be liable for contravention.[228] In addition, the presence of young people on licensed premises is regulated.[229] Running on through the generally accepted vices, we come to gambling. The general age limit here is 18,[230] with concessions being made to allow young people to

---

226 In addition, transfers fail to accommodate the case of very young offenders accused of serious crimes. In Chicago, in August 1998, two boys, aged seven and eight years old, were charged with the murder of an 11-year-old girl. The very thought of these children being tried in an adult court conjures up the worst Dickensian images.

227 Children and Young Persons (Scotland) Act 1937, s 18, as amended by the Protection of Children (Tobacco) Act 1986 and the Children and Young Persons (Protection from Tobacco) Act 1991. The prohibition covers the sale of cigarettes and any product containing tobacco and intended for oral or nasal use, thus, including chewing tobacco and a product known as Skol Bandits, which had a brief spell of popularity in the 1980s and lay behind the 1986 Act.

228 The offences here include selling or supplying alcohol to a person below the age of 18, the young person buying or attempting to buy it and the employment of young people on licensed premises – Licensing (Scotland) Act 1976, ss 68–73 as amended by the Law Reform (Miscellaneous Provisions) (Scotland) Act 1990.

229 The licensee is prohibited from allowing a person below the age of 14 to be on licensed premises unless he or she has been granted a children's certificate – Licensing (Scotland) Act 1976, ss 68–73 as amended by the Law Reform (Miscellaneous Provisions) (Scotland) Act 1990. This exception allows for so-called 'family rooms' in bars.

230 Betting Gaming and Lotteries Act 1963, ss 21 and 22, as amended by the Gaming Act 1968 and the National Lottery Etc. Act 1993. The offences include having 'any betting transaction' with a person below 18, knowingly allowing a person below 18 to take part in gambling on licensed premises, or employing such a person 'in the effecting of any betting transaction or in a licensed betting office'.

participate in state-sanctioned gambling from the age of 16.[231] Of course, such prohibitions assume that, by making particular conduct criminal, people will not engage in it; an assumption which is, at the very least, questionable. Not all regulation relates to activities which are regarded by some sections of the community as decadent. Thus, there is extensive regulation of the employment of children.[232] The legislation in this area began during the industrial revolution when many children were exploited mercilessly. While there is undoubtedly a need for regulation of the employment of young people,[233] the whole system is in need of thorough overhaul in order to achieve an appropriate balance between protecting young people and allowing them the freedom to develop and acquire responsibility.[234]

3.93 Other forms of regulation relate to the fact that children are likely to be present at a particular place. So, for example, where entertainment is being provided for children, the organiser is obliged to ensure adequate adult supervision.[235] Yet other age limits aim to protect the public as well as the child, and one has only to look at the fact that a person cannot obtain a licence to drive a car until he or she is 17 years old, to appreciate that the protection is aimed more broadly than at the child driver.[236] A similar explanation can be found for restrictions on holding a pilot's licence[237] and

231 The best-known form of gambling available to 16-year-olds is the National Lottery and here, the age limit was set by a regulation made under the relevant statute – National Lottery Etc. Act 1993, s 12 and SI 1994 No 189. However, this is not the first time that the age limit for gambling has been lowered, since premium bonds can also be sold to 16-year-olds; Premium Savings Bonds Regulations 1972, SI 1972 No 765. It must be conceded, however, that premium bonds are a more benign form of gambling, since they do not involve the loss of the original stake.

232 Regulation is spread across a number of statutes, including the following: Employment of Women, Young Persons and Children Act 1920; Children and Young Persons Act 1933; Children and Young Persons Act 1963; Children and Young Persons (Scotland) Act 1937; Employment Act 1989; and the Education Act 1996. The local authority has the power to regulate aspects of employment of young people within its area and local authorities across Scotland have amended their regulations to ensure compliance with the Protection of Young People At Work Directive, Directive No 94/33. Broadly, employment of a person below the age of 13 is prohibited and, thereafter, employment is heavily regulated in terms of hours, types of work and conditions.

233 See: M. Gillespie and P. Hunter, 'The School of Hard Knocks: Employment of Children' in Sutherland and Cleland; M. Lavalette, J. McKechnie, S. Hobbs and J. Murray, *The Forgotten Workforce: Scottish Children at Work* (Scottish Low Pay Unit, 1991); J. McKechnie, S. Lindsay and S. Hobbs, *Still Forgotten: Child Employment in Dumfries and Galloway* (Scottish Low Pay Unit, 1994).

234 A review of children and employment was announced by the government in December 1997 and it is expected to report shortly.

235 Children and Young Persons (Scotland) Act 1937, s 23. Entertainment provided at a private dwelling house is not covered by the legislation, but where, for example, a child attends a birthday party at another child's home and the former is injured as a result of inadequate supervision, the parent who hosted the party may be liable in delict.

236 The Road Traffic Act 1988, ss 101 and 108 regulate the holding of licences in respect of particular vehicles and these can be summarised as follows: invalid carriages and motor cycles (16); small passenger and goods vehicles and agricultural tractors (17); medium sized goods vehicles (18) and other motor vehicles (21).

237 It is an offence for a person under the age of 16 to pilot a glider and 17 is the minimum age at which a person may act as a member of the flight crew of an aeroplane, or apply for

purchasing or possessing firearms.[238] It is not clear whether it is the desire to protect animals or parents that lies behind the prohibition on selling a pet to a person who appears to be below the age of 12.[239]

3.94 Some legislation seems to be seeking to educate parents through setting standards for what might be described as 'good parenting' by, for example, making it an offence to give alcohol to a child below the age of five, except for medical purposes,[240] or to leave a child below the age of seven in a room with an unguarded fire.[241] There is extensive regulation of substitute care for children where this is provided by a foster carer,[242] a childminder or through day care.[243] A popular myth should be dispelled at this point. The law does not provide for any fixed age at which a young person may babysit for other children in the children's own home, nor does it set a clear limit on when an older child may look after a younger sibling. Were a parent to leave a child with a young carer who could not reasonably be expected to shoulder the responsibility, the parent's conduct might amount to neglect[244] and any child so left might be referred to a children's hearing.[245]

3.95 Sometimes age limits are imposed, not by the legal system, but by a particular trader. Often the trader is simply seeking to protect his or her own position and to avoid problems with irate parents. Thus, for example, there is no statutory age limit which applies to having one's ears (or other body parts) pierced.[246] However, most commercial enterprises appear to operate a policy of refusing to do this for anyone below the age of

---

a balloon or airship licence. In order to apply for a licence to fly a helicopter or to be a flight engineer, a person must be at least 21 years old. See Air Navigation Order 1995, SI 1995 No 1038.

238 The provisions here are somewhat complex and apply different age limits to different circumstances. It is an offence to *sell or let* a firearm or ammunition to a person below the age of 17 and for a young person to *purchase or hire* firearms or ammunition, while it is an offence for an unsupervised person under the age of 15 to have an assembled shotgun *in his or her possession* – Firearms Act 1968, ss 22(1) and (3) and 24(1). However, 14 is the age limit applied in respect of *giving or lending* a firearm, ammunition or an air rifle to a young person – 1968 Act, ss 24(2) and (3). Possession of an air rifle in a public place is an offence if the young person is under the age of 17 – 1968 Act, s 22(5). Of course, the potential for young people to injure themselves or others when they have access to firearms or air rifles is greatly increased. In addition, many cats, dogs and birds experience untold suffering as a result of the legal latitude in allowing young people access to weapons.

239 Pet Animals Act 1951, s 7. Certainly, the fact that a person below the age of 18 cannot hold a licence to keep a 'dangerous animal' contains elements of protection of children and protection of the community – Dangerous Wild Animals Act 1976, s 1.

240 Children and Young Persons (Scotland) Act 1937, s 16.

241 Children and Young Persons (Scotland) Act 1937, s 22.

242 Foster Children (Scotland) Act 1984, discussed in chapter 7, para 54.

243 Children Act 1989, ss 72–77, discussed in chapter 6, paras 23–24.

244 Children and Young Person (Scotland) Act 1937, s 12(1).

245 Children (Scotland) Act 1995, s 52(2)(c).

246 In contrast, it is an offence to tattoo a person who is below the age of 18 – Tattooing of Minors Act 1969, s 1.

(somewhere about) 16 years old, without parental consent.[247] In chapter 7 we will return to the role of the state in protecting children and promoting their welfare. When considering statutory age-related regulation, remember, reference should be made to the appropriate statutory provisions, including any statutory instruments, for details of the precise restriction or offence and whether it is adults or the child involved (or both) who commit any offences. Two areas of age-related regulation merit more detailed attention.

Sexual and related offences

3.96 The desire to protect young people, and particularly young women, from sexual exploitation has resulted in a number of offences being created. With the exception of the regulation of homosexual conduct, the child or young person commits no offence although sexual activity may result in the young person being referred to a children's hearing.[248] It is an offence for a man to have sexual intercourse with a young woman under the age of 13.[249] A similar offence applies where the young woman is over the age of 13 but under the age of 16,[250] but a special bar on prosecution and a number of defences apply in such cases. No prosecution can be commenced more than one year after the commission of the offence where the victim was between the ages of 13 and 16.[251] Where the young woman is in this age group, it is a defence for the accused to show that he had reasonable cause to believe she was his wife.[252] Where the accused is under the age of 24, it is a defence for him to show that he had reasonable cause

247 Applying the law to this example is not without its problems. Piercing does not come within the exception governing consent to medical treatment since, while it might be regarded as a 'surgical procedure', the 'treatment' is not being carried out by a 'qualified medical practitioner' – Age of Legal Capacity (Scotland) Act 1991, s 2(4). If contracting to have the piercing carried out is simply 'a transaction', it will only come within the 'common transactions' exemption for under 16-year-olds if it is the kind of transaction commonly entered into by a young person of that age and in these circumstances – 1991 Act, s 2(1)(a). Clearly, something can only become common for people of a particular age if it is available to them and applying the statutory provision here becomes rather circular. It is probably attributing too detailed an understanding of the legal provisions to them, but it would certainly explain why practitioners in this field are cautious about carrying out piercing on young people.
248 One of the grounds on which a child may be referred to a hearing is that he or she 'is falling into bad associations or is exposed to moral danger' – Children (Scotland) Act 1995, s 52(2)(b). In addition, a child may be referred to a hearing where he or she is a member of the same household as a child who has been the victim of sexual abuse or where he or she is a member of the same household as a sex offender.
249 Criminal Law (Consolidation) (Scotland) Act 1995, s 5(1). Section 5 includes 'attempts' as well as the successful commission of the offence.
250 Criminal Law (Consolidation) (Scotland) Act 1995, s 5(3).
251 Criminal Law (Consolidation) (Scotland) Act 1995, s 5(4). This may explain a case where the father pursued an action in respect of his parental rights where he was 34 and the child's mother was 15 years old when the child was born – McMillan v Brady, 1997 GWD 4–130.
252 Criminal Law (Consolidation) (Scotland) Act 1995, s 5(5)(a). In many parts of the world, marriage is permitted below the age of 16. If we take the example of a 20-year-old man and his 14-year-old wife, who were domiciled, and validly married, in such a country, no offence would be committed were they to engage in sexual intercourse in Scotland.

to believe the young woman was over the age of 16.[253] This defence is only available to an accused who has not been charged with a like offence before, presumably on the basis that, having been in trouble over this kind of behaviour before, a man can be expected to be more vigilant in the future.

3.97 It is an offence at common law to use lewd, indecent or libidinous practice or behaviour towards a girl below the age of 12 and statute governs the criminal nature of such conduct towards young women aged between 12 and 16.[254] A number of other offences relate to allowing a child to be in a brothel[255] and the procuring or encouragement of young women for the purpose of prostitution.[256]

3.98 Until 1980, a consensual sexual act between male homosexuals constituted a criminal offence. That year, statute intervened to provide that consensual acts in private between two men over the age of 21 would no longer be a criminal offence.[257] In 1995, the age of consent to such acts was reduced to 18.[258] Despite efforts to reduce the age of consent to 16,[259] in line with the age of consent for heterosexual activity, 18 remains the relevant age. It can be anticipated that the removal of this discriminatory treatment of young people on the basis of their sexual orientation will continue to be the subject of concern and attempts at law reform. For the present, it should be noted that the non-criminal nature of the conduct only applies where no more than two people take part in the activity and does not protect conduct in public toilets.[260] There are various offences relating to living on the earnings of a male prostitute, soliciting or importuning of male prostitution, and running a brothel, to which no age limit applies.[261]

3.99 It is an offence to take or to permit the taking of indecent photographs of a person below the age of 16 and the original statutory provision was amended to include 'pseudo-photographs' and such material as computer graphics are now included.[262] Clearly, this provision is aimed at combatting child pornography. Another cause for international, as well as domestic, concern – that of so-called 'sex tourism' – was tackled by the

---

253 Criminal Law (Consolidation) (Scotland) Act 1995, s 5(5)(b).
254 Criminal Law (Consolidation) (Scotland) Act 1995, s 6.
255 Criminal Law (Consolidation) (Scotland) Act 1995, s 12.
256 Criminal Law (Consolidation) (Scotland) Act 1995, ss 7, 10 and 11. In some cases, the offence aims to protect women up to the age of 21 and, in others, there is no age limit specified. Thus, for example, it is an offence to procure, or attempt to procure, any woman or girl to become a common prostitute in any part of the world – s 7(1)(b).
257 Criminal Justice (Scotland) Act 1980, s 80.
258 Criminal Law (Consolidation) (Scotland) Act 1995, s 13. It is a defence for an accused to show that: he is under 24 years old; had reasonable cause to believe that the other man was 18; and that he has not been charged with a similar offence before – s 13(8).
259 In 1998 an attempt was made to amend the Crime and Disorder Bill to reduce the age of homosexual consent to 16. It had initial success in the House of Commons but was defeated in the House of Lords.
260 Criminal Law (Consolidation) (Scotland) Act 1995, s 13(2).
261 Criminal Law (Consolidation) (Scotland) Act 1995, s 13(9) and (10).
262 Civic Government (Scotland) Act 1982, s 52, as amended by the Criminal Justice and Public Order Act 1994, s 84.

Sex Offenders Act 1997.[263] Where a person commits an act outside the UK that was an offence under the law of the country where the act was committed and would have constituted a listed sexual offence[264] if it had been done in Scotland, he or she may be tried in Scotland for the offence. Provision is made giving the courts in England, Wales and Northern Ireland similar jurisdiction.[265] Prosecution is only competent where the defender is a British citizen or is resident in the UK.

3.100 It is understandable that residents of a neighbourhood may feel some disquiet at the prospect of a sex offender moving into the district on being released from prison. For example, many women would feel unhappy at the prospect of a convicted rapist living next door. When the offender has been convicted of an offence against a child, the disquiet becomes magnified with parents, in particular, sometimes marshalling local concern in the attempt to force the offender to move away. No one would doubt that children must be protected from exposure to people who may harm them. However, some of the measures which have been proposed or adopted in Scotland and elsewhere in order to provide that protection are based on the presumption that sex offenders can never be 'cured' and, as such, can never be rehabilitated fully into society. Such a presumption is open to question and acceptance of it poses a serious breach of the civil liberties of such offenders. Achieving the appropriate balance between the protection of children, on one hand, and respecting the rights of an offender who has served his or her sentence, on the other, poses a difficult challenge to the legal system. At present, persons convicted of certain sex offences must notify the police of their names (including all names used) and their home addresses (and all changes of address).[266] The length of time for which a person must give such notification depends on the penalty to which the offender was sentenced. Where the sentence was to imprisonment for life or a term of 30 months or more, notification must be given indefinitely, while a person sentenced to imprisonment for six months or less need only make notification for five years following release.[267] Parallel provisions govern persons found not guilty by reason of insanity, those detained in a hospital rather than a prison and young offenders.[268] It is an offence for a person to fail to notify the police as required.[269] What the police do with this information is not specified. However, further legislation aimed at ensuring that persons convicted of sex offences against children do not have the opportunity to have unsupervised contact with children through, for example, employment or voluntary work has been

263 Section 8 of the 1997 Act adds a new 16B to the Criminal Law (Consolidation) (Scotland) Act 1995.
264 'Listed sexual offence' includes: intercourse with a girl below the age of 16; homosexual acts with a person below the age of 16; rape of a girl below the age of 16; lewd, indecent or libidinous behaviour or practices; and conspiracy or incitement to commit any such offences – 1995 Act, s 16B(7).
265 Sex Offenders Act 1997, s 7.
266 Sex Offenders Act 1997, s 2.
267 Sex Offenders Act 1997, s 1(4).
268 Sex Offenders Act 1997, s 5.
269 Sex Offenders Act 1997, s 3.

proposed.[270] As yet, we have not seen any official proposal to introduce a requirement, along the lines of the 'Megan's Laws'[271] in the USA, that sex offenders should make their status known in any community in which they go to live on release.

The experiment with curfews

3.101 Much media attention has been devoted to the recent experimental schemes in parts of Scotland dubbed 'curfews on children' by the press. Typically, a curfew provides that certain persons are not permitted to be on the streets at certain times. Usually, breaching a curfew will be an offence in itself. As such, curfews are a limitation on the individual's liberty to move around freely. It appears that what was introduced in various areas of Hamilton involved a concentration of police resources to inquire why any child under the age of 16 was out alone after 9 pm. The scheme was introduced, in part, in response to complaints from local adults about the behaviour of some young people and concern that their presence on the streets, particularly in the evenings and at night, was a real problem. It was always described as a pilot project and is the subject of independent evaluation.[272]

3.102 In the first six months of the scheme's operation, of the 229 children approached by police officers, 200 were returned to their parents, 25 were given advice on safety or found not to be in danger, and four were charged with offences.[273] Arguably, what is involved is not a curfew at all, since the vast majority of the children were not regarded as having committed any offence simply by being on the streets after 9 pm. In addition, the police have the power to arrest anyone suspected of having committed an offence. As far as children are concerned, the police play an integral part in the whole system aimed at child protection and it would not be unreasonable for them to approach a young child out alone to establish whether the child was at risk, abandoned or neglected. Thus, in approaching at least some of these children, the police officers involved were exercising the ordinary powers they have. What is extraordinary, of course, is that a strategy was employed, involving approaches to all persons under 16 out alone after 9 pm; and that advance notice was given of intention to do so. When resources are diverted to target a particular group for attention, then

270 In Sex Offenders: A Ban on Working With Children (Home Office and Scottish Office Consultation Paper, 1997), the creation of an offence along these lines was explored.
271 The history of these laws began, in 1996, with the rape and murder of seven-year-old Megan Kanka by a man who had a history of sex offences against children. In response to public concern that parents had not been warned of the offender's arrival in their neighbourhood, the first community registration and notification law was passed. Since then, similar legislation has been passed in many parts of the USA. For a lengthy discussion of the legal issues surrounding such laws, see 'Symposium: Critical Perspectives on Megan's Law: Protection vs Privacy' 13 N Y L. Sch J Hum Rts 1 (1997) which records the contributions of various distinguished speakers and the discussion which took place at the symposium.
272 Professor Powers of Stirling University has been funded by the Scottish Office to conduct a study of the project and his report is expected shortly.
273 *The Scotsman*, 17 April 1998, pp 1 and 2. Until Professor Power's report is published, information regarding the scheme must be gleaned from the press.

undoubtedly that group is faced with discriminatory treatment. The real question is whether such schemes achieve anything which would justify discrimination. Two obvious goals might be achieved. First, the protection of children themselves might be improved and, second, crime and disruptive behaviour by young people might be reduced. Whether achieving either or both of these goals would justify the measures taken in order to do so is a matter of judgment and one on which there will almost certainly not be unanimity. Yet again, we are confronted with the delicate balancing of children's rights, child protection and the rights of others. The verdict on the scheme will have to await evaluation. If it is adjudged to be a 'success',[274] it may be that the pilot project will be extended to other areas or, possibly, the whole country. The idea of subjecting children to a curfew has been tried in other jurisdictions,[275] with mixed reactions.[276]

THE REAL QUESTION

Does Scots law recognise and respect children's rights?

3.103 Perhaps the question we should be asking ourselves at this stage is, 'does Scots law recognise and respect children's rights?'. Before we can answer that question, we need to ask 'which rights?'. Thus far, we can see examples of real efforts by the legal system to recognise and accommodate particular rights. We have also seen examples of when the legal system fails to do so. In addition, we have seen that, because some of the rights themselves have to be balanced with each other, a certain tension is created. Ensuring that children are adequately protected and that their welfare is ensured, is not always easy to achieve in a manner consistent with respecting the child's evolving capacity and right to participate in the decision-making process. As we have seen, protecting children may involve placing restrictions on their freedom of action. Children's rights must also be put in the context of responsibilities and this chapter has highlighted some of the key fields where children can acquire responsibilities. As the UN Committee on the Child pointed out, when it reported in 1995, Scots law was failing to meet some of the obligations created by the Convention. Some of the Committee's concerns were addressed in the Children (Scotland) Act 1995 and the Committee will have another opportunity to comment on our progress in 1999. Given that there are a great many more areas of the law, as it affects children, to be explored, perhaps it is too early to reach any firm conclusion on the current state of Scots law.

---

274 Preliminary figures suggest that the second of the goals discussed above was achieved since, during the first six months of the scheme's operation, reported crimes allegedly committed by young people under 16 fell by 33% and complaints about disorderly behaviour by young people fell by 48%. The impact of the scheme on child protection will be more difficult to measure since it involves assessing how many children avoided harm by not being on the streets or by being returned home.

275 In the USA, it has been estimated that child curfews of some kind are operating in some 1,000 localities – R. E. Shepherd, Jr, 'Juvenile Justice' 12 Crim Just 43 at p 43 (1997).

276 G. Z. Chen, 'Youth Curfews and the Trilogy of Parent, Child and State Relations' 72 NYUL Rev 131 (1997); K. H. Federle, 'Children Curfews and the Constitution' 73 Wash ULQ 1315 (1995); S. A. Kizer, 'Juvenile Curfew Laws: Is There a Standard?' 45 Drake L Rev 749 (1997).

CHAPTER 4

CHILDREN, PARENTS AND OTHER FAMILY MEMBERS

4.1 As we saw in chapter 1, there is no single model of a family in Scotland today. Instead, there is a vast array of diverse family types. The result for children is that they may be living in a wide variety of family settings. While 38% of children born in 1997 were to unmarried parents,[1] 81% of the births were registered jointly by the child's parents, with 70% of these parents living at the same address.[2] This suggests that the traditional notion of unmarried parenthood meaning lone parenthood is far from accurate.[3] Of course the fact that a child is born to married parents is no guarantee that he or she will grow up living with both parents since many children experience parental divorce.[4] Given that about a quarter of divorcees remarry,[5] while others go on to cohabit with a new partner, it can be assumed that some of their children will find their way into either *de jure* or *de facto* step-families. This is borne out by the fact that about half of all adoptions are step-parent adoptions.[6] In addition, many children live in extended families or apart from family members.

4.2 Perhaps all that can be said is that children, like adults, live in a diverse range of settings. What distinguishes children, and particularly young children, from adults is that, while adults can choose whether or not to keep in touch with a former partner and his or her extended family, and can make their own decisions about how much contact they want to have

---

1 Registrar General for Scotland, Annual Report 1997 (General Register Office for Scotland, 1998), Tables 3.1.
2 Annual Report 1997, Table 3.2 and p 32.
3 While the trend towards children being born outside of marriage is clear and distinct, the phenomenon is not new in Scotland. In the years 1861–1865, the percentage of births outside marriage varied from 4.24% in Ross and Cromarty to 15.65% in rural Wigtownshire. In the period 1911–1915, Wigtownshire again led the field at 14.91%, with the lowest level (4.05%) being recorded in the urban centre of Renfrew. For a discussion of family patterns and, indeed, a thorough challenge to many unfounded assumptions, see, T. C. Smout, *A Century of the Scottish People 1830–1950,* pp 165–180.
4 6,658 children under 16 were affected by divorce in 1996 alone, with children being present in 34% of divorces – Registrar General for Scotland, Annual Report 1996, (General Register Office for Scotland, 1997) Figure 8.1. The equivalent figures are not given in the Annual Report 1997, but would be of the same order. As we shall see, cohabiting couples need do nothing formal to end their relationships, so there are no accurate figures for the number of children affected each year by the termination of such relationships.
5 Annual Report 1997, Table 7.4.
6 Annual Report 1997, Table 9.2.

with a new partner's family, children are far more dependent on the arrangements adults make. Albeit Scots law recognises the child's right to have his or her views taken into account when a major decision affecting him or her is being taken,[7] the reality is often that adults make the decisions. Whether the parent who no longer lives with the child actually keeps in touch or whether the parent with whom the child lives and the non-resident parent's family co-operate over the child maintaining family ties is, at least at first instance, very much up to the adults.

4.3 In assessing how well the law copes with the diverse family types in which children find themselves, it would be wonderful to take a truly child-centred approach: that is, one without reference to the nature of adult relationships. However, since the law itself often defines the child-adult relationship in terms of adult relationships, that is not possible. In addition, the simple fact that children live with adults means that adult relationships are often very relevant to the child's position. In this chapter, we will examine the legal provisions which define the child-parent link and how adequately the law accommodates reproductive technology. The various techniques will be explored along with the applicable law, before we move on to introduce some of the other people who may play a significant part in the life of a particular child.

PARENTAGE[8]

Maternity

4.4 That disputes over the maternity of a child were virtually unknown in Scots law is evidenced by the dearth of case-law on the matter. A striking exception can be found in *Douglas* v *Duke of Hamilton*,[9] which is worth reading, not least because the facts would not have been out of place in a novel by Sir Walter Scott. While the advent of surrogacy[10] has raised questions surrounding the true meaning of motherhood, the position remains that disputes over maternity are rare. Maternity may be important for immigration purposes and the advent of DNA profiling has been of assistance in resolving disputed cases in this context.[11]

4.5 Cases have arisen in other jurisdictions where it has been alleged that,

---

7 Children (Scotland) Act 1995, s 6. There is no machinery to monitor compliance with this provision and it might be questioned that many children or adults are aware of it. An aggrieved child who had not been consulted could take the matter to the court, but this raises all the questions and problems surrounding the ability of children to use the legal system – see chapter 3, paras 42–49.

8 For a wide-ranging discussion of parenthood, its regulations and its implications, around the world, see J. Eekelaar and P. Sarcevic (eds), *Parenthood in Modern Society: Legal and Social Issues for the Twenty-First Century* (Martinus Nijhoff, 1993).

9 (1769) 2 Pat 143.

10 Surrogacy is discussed at paras 4.53–4.62, below.

11 For a discussion of DNA profiling, see paras 4.18–4.19. In J. J. Rankin, 'DNA Fingerprinting' (1988) 33 JLSS 124, the author discusses the case of a Ghanaian boy who was refused readmission to the UK to rejoin his mother because immigration officials suspected that he was not the person he claimed to be. The results of DNA profiling were sufficient to convince the Home Office as to his identity and he was given the right of entry.

due to an error at the hospital, two women have gone home with each other's baby, the mistake being discovered at a later stage. Any dispute would, of course, be over both the maternity and the paternity of the children. In *Twigg* v *Mays*,[12] probably the most publicised case of this kind, a Florida court refused to grant parental rights to the biological parents of a child who had been the victim of just such an error. The facts of the case are probably deserving of the court's description of them as being 'exceptionally delicate and unique'.[13] Briefly, the very sad story is as follows. The Twiggs left hospital in December 1978 with a baby they believed to be their daughter and whom they called Arlena. Some ten years later, Arlena died during surgery to correct a congenital heart defect. During her final illness, Arlena had blood tests which revealed that the Twiggs could not be her biological parents. In the course of enquiries after Arlena's death, it became apparent that only one other white female had been born in the same hospital at the time of Arlena's birth and eventually the Twiggs located that child, then known as Kimberley Mays. Tests showed that there was a 95% chance that the Twiggs, rather than Richard Mays and his late wife, were Kimberley's biological parents. Prior to the blood tests being conducted on Kimberley, it had been agreed that the Twiggs would seek visitation (contact) rather than custody (residence).[14] Initially, they did have a number of meetings with Kimberley which appear to have gone well. However, co-operation between the families broke down fairly quickly amid accusations and counter-accusations and the dispute degenerated into a rather unpleasant battle.[15] Eventually, the Twiggs sought a declaration that they were Kimberley's biological parents, that they were her natural guardians and concluded for custody, with reasonable visitation being allowed to Richard Mays, the man whom Kimberley had believed, for almost all of her life, was her father. Kimberley counterclaimed seeking to terminate any rights which the Twiggs claimed or possessed. The Twiggs' action was dismissed without any finding as to parentage on the basis that it would be detrimental to Kimberley to declare them to be her parents or to require her to have any contact with them.[16] Thus, Robert Mays' status as the legal father remained unchanged. It is tempting to analyse this case as one of social parenthood prevailing over biological parenthood or, on one interpretation of the

12 The earlier stage of the case, *Mays* v *Twigg* 543 So 2d 241 (Fla, 1989) gives the fullest available account of the facts. The final stage of the case, *Twigg* v *Mays* (Fla Cir Ct 18 August 1993) appears only to be reported at 1993 WL 330624.
13 543 So 2d 241 (Fla, 1989) at p 242.
14 The Twiggs did reserve the right to seek custody of Kimberley if it was shown that Richard Mays was unfit to care for her or if there was a change of circumstances – 1993 WL 330624, at p 1.
15 Richard Mays stopped the visits, claiming that Kimberley's school work was suffering, while the Twiggs accused him of trying to prevent them from forming a relationship with her. In addition, the Twiggs accused Richard Mays, his late wife and her parents of swapping the babies deliberately. See 1993 WL 330624.
16 It appears that, after the case, Kimberley did, in fact, go to live with the Twiggs; E. P. Miller, Note, '*Deboer* v *Schmidt* and *Twigg* v *Mays*: Does the 'Best Interests of the Child' Standard Protect the Best Interests of Children?' 20 J Contemp L 497 (1994), at p 505, n 36.

concept, as a victory for children's rights. In reality, it may be no more than a particular interpretation of 'the best interests of the child' as applied in one jurisdiction.[17] The case caused widespread concern and academic discussion,[18] not least because it happened to coincide with other cases giving rise to debate about the nature of parenthood,[19] the rights of a child to initiate termination of parental rights,[20] and the interpretation of the child's 'best interests'.

4.6 Were such a case to arise in Scotland, the correct procedure would be to obtain a declarator of parentage on the basis of evidence which satisfied a court on the balance of probabilities.[21] As we shall see, there would be difficulties in a case of this kind over obtaining consent to the blood testing of the child in order to establish parentage, where the child was too young to give consent and the presumptive parents were unwilling to do so.[22] Of course, other evidence would be relevant. Were the facts similar to those in *Twigg* v *Mays*, evidence of the circumstances surrounding the birth of both children and the fact that the applicants were not the parents of the baby they had taken home from the hospital, could be led. Whether this would

17 The court in Florida took a course which would be incompetent in Scotland as a result of a previous decision of the Supreme Court in that state. In *Department of Health and Rehabilitative Service* v *Privette* 617 So 2d 305 (Fla. 1993), the court had ruled that, where a child is born legitimate, the child is entitled to maintain that status if it is in his or her best interests to do so. Applying that reasoning to the instant case, Mr Mays' status as Kimberley's father would not be disturbed unless it was in her best interests to do so.

18 A number of excellent articles discuss this case and compare it with others in the attempt to find a coherent analysis of how courts should approach issues of parentage, family, children's rights and best interests. The following are a selection of the many: C. G. Baunach, Note, 'The Role of Equitable Adoption in a Mistaken Baby Switch' 31 U Louisville J Fam L 501 (1992/93); S. Cannon, 'Finding Their Own "Place To Be": What Gregory Kingsley's and Kimberley Mays' "Divorces" from their Parents have done for Children's Rights' 39 Loy L Rev 837 (1994); J. Mcmillen, Note, 'Begging the Wisdom of Solomon: Hiding Behind the Issue of Standing in Custody Disputes to Treat Children as Chattel without Regard for their Best Interests' 39 St Louis U L J 699 (1995); E. P. Miller, above; J. L. Richards, 'Redefining Parenthood: Parental Rights versus the Rights of the Child' 40 Wayne L Rev 1227 (1994). On 5 August 1998, the *New York Times* reported the case of two little girls who left a Virginia hospital in 1995 with the wrong mothers, the error only coming to light when one of the children, Callie, had a DNA test in the course of an attempt to get child support from the man believed to be her father. In a further twist to the story, it appears that the other child, Rebecca, was 'orphaned' when the couple who believed they were her parents were killed in a car accident. She has been cared for since then by 'relatives'.

19 As a result of the decision in *Deboer* v *Schmidt (In re Clausen)* 501 NW 2d 193 (Mich, 1993), perhaps better known as the 'Baby Jessica' case, a little girl was forcibly removed from the care of the only 'parents' she had ever known to be returned to her biological parents. The television-viewing public was outraged as it witnessed the event. The case is discussed, in the context of adoption, in chapter 8, paras 8.84–8.85.

20 In *Kingsley* v *Kingsley* 623 So 2d 780 (Fla, 1993) a 12-year-old boy sought to have his mother's parental rights over him terminated in order that he could be adopted by his foster carers. The case is discussed, in the context of the child's standing to raise such actions, in chapter 5, para 5.84.

21 Law Reform (Parent and Child) (Scotland) Act 1986, s 7. Declarators of parentage are discussed at paras 4.14–4.27, below.

22 1986 Act, s 6. As we shall see, the court's power to consent to the taking of a sample of blood, bodily fluid or body tissue arises only where there is no person entitled to give consent, where it is not practicable to obtain that person's consent, or where the person

be sufficient to displace parentage, as registered, would depend on the facts of the individual case, but the Scottish courts could not refuse to determine parentage by applying a best interests test. However, the best interests test would become central when the court turned to consider the future arrangements for the child's care. As we shall see, the court has a very flexible power to entertain applications, made by a broad range of persons, for an order in relation to parental responsibilities and rights. It might be that, in the very unusual circumstances of this kind of case, it would regard persons claiming to be a child's biological parents as persons who claim 'an interest',[23] without their having established parentage where, for example, consent to the testing of the child was being withheld. Any decision on such matters as where the child lived and with whom the child had contact would be taken on the basis of the child's best interests in the light of the child's views on the matter and existing arrangements.[24]

Paternity

4.7 Unlike disputes over maternity, paternity disputes have always been far more common. Undoubtedly, the trail of litigation stretching back throughout our legal history was often prompted by single mothers seeking to get some financial support for the child from the putative father, and that continues to be the case today. However, sight should not be lost of the importance of establishing parentage as part of the child's well-recognised right to preserve his or her identity.[25] Simply knowing who one's parents are may be important to the individual child. The common law recognised the importance of establishing paternity and developed presumptions to assist in disputed cases.[26] Statute has replaced the common law but has continued aspects of the old presumptions.

Presumptions of paternity

4.8 The presumptions governing paternity are now contained in s 5 of the Law Reform (Parent and Child) (Scotland) Act 1986 ('the 1986 Act'). These presumptions merely provide a legal starting point and all of them are rebuttable; that is, they can be displaced by proof on a balance of

who could give consent 'is unwilling to accept the responsibility of giving or withholding consent' – s 6(3). The court has no power to override the refusal of such a person to give consent. In addition, where the child had the capacity to consent, but refused to do so, s 6(3) would be of no assistance.

23 Children (Scotland) Act 1995, s 11(1) and (3). Who qualify as such persons is discussed in chapter 5, para 79.

24 1995 Act, s 11(7). How courts determine issues of this kind is discussed in detail in chapter 5.

25 The United Nations Convention on the Rights of the Child, art 8, recognises this right. See, A. Bissett-Johnson 'Name, Nationality and Identity' in Cleland and Sutherland (eds), *Children's Rights in Scotland* (W. Green, 1996), and K. O'Donovan, 'Right to Know One's Parentage' 1988 Int'l J of Law and the Family 27. In 1996, the International Journal of Law and the Family became the International Journal of Law, Policy and the Family.

26 A. B. Wilkinson and K. McK. Norrie, *Parent and Child* at pp 126–127; *Stair Memorial Encyclopaedia*, vol 10, paras 1155–1156.

probabilities.[27] A man is presumed to be the father of a child in the following circumstances

If he was married to the child's mother at any time from the child's conception to his or her birth[28]

4.9 The common law presumed that a woman's husband was the father of her child, the presumption being encapsulated in the Latin maxim *pater est quem nuptiae demonstrant*. The 1986 Act essentially restates that, not unreasonable, assumption. It applies to all kinds of marriage and regular, irregular and voidable marriages are all sufficient to trigger its application.[29] Indeed, it might be said that the presumption applies to what might be described as a 'non-marriage', in the sense that a child born to parents whose marriage is subsequently declared void will also benefit from it.[30] Often the couple will have been married for some time before the child's birth and will remain so, albeit perhaps only temporarily, at the time of any dispute over paternity.[31] However, it does not matter that they married the day before the child was born;[32] the presumption applies. Nor does it matter if a couple who were married at the time of conception, or at a subsequent date, divorce prior to the birth.[33] Again, the presumption will apply. Where a man marries a woman who already has a child, there is no presumption that he is that child's father.[34] The presumption can be rebutted by proof on the balance of probabilities.[35]

4.10 This presumption is of particular importance, given the fact that only 'married fathers' have automatic parental responsibilities and rights. Thus, for example, where a married woman is living with another man and a dispute arises over the paternity of her child, her husband can probably consent to blood samples being taken from the baby, but her cohabitant cannot.[36] Where the mother is unwilling or unable to give consent,[37] this can lead to problems if the husband refuses.

---

27 Section 5(4).
28 Section 5(1)(a).
29 Section 5(2). For a discussion of what these terms mean see chapter 10, paras 16, 73 and 78–80.
30 Section 5(2).
31 Sometimes evidence adduced in the paternity dispute and any finding that the husband is not the child's father will be used to establish adultery in divorce proceedings.
32 At common law, there was a presumption that a man who married a woman knowing her to be pregnant was the father of the child – *Gardner* v *Gardner* (1877) 4 R (HL) 56; *Imre* v *Mitchell* 1958 SC 439.
33 Similarly, if the husband dies prior to the child's birth, he will still be presumed to be the father.
34 This was also the position at common law – *Smith* v *Dick* (1869) 8 M 31. In one case where a man was held to be the child's father in such circumstances, the fact that the child had long been reputed to be his son was central to the decision – *James* v *McLennan* 1971 SLT 162.
35 *Russell* v *Wood* 1987 SCLR 207.
36 See para 4.23, below.
37 A pre-1986 Act case arising out of facts along these lines is *Docherty* v *McGlynn* 1985 SLT 237, where the mother had died.

Where the above provision does not apply, if both he and the mother have acknowledged that he is the father and he has been registered as such[38]

4.11   At common law, where a couple agreed that a particular man was the child's father, there was nothing they could do to have this recognised in law short of obtaining a declarator. That was so even if the man was registered as the father.[39] The 1986 Act made the law much more user-friendly and now, provided that both parents agree that a particular man is the child's father and he is registered as such, he will be presumed to be the child's father. This provision is of particular importance to unmarried, cohabiting, couples.

4.12   Of course, as with the other presumptions, rebuttal, by proof on the balance of probabilities, is competent. Where a man has been registered as a child's father and later has doubts, he can raise an action for declarator of non-parentage and, if successful, an entry will be made in the Register of Corrected Entries, amending the original registration of birth.[40]

Where the court has declared him to be the father of a child[41]

4.13   As we will see, the court can grant declarator of parentage or non-parentage; that is, it can declare that a particular man is or is not a child's father. Where the court has done so, the declarator will be presumed to be accurate unless displaced by a later successful challenge.

Establishing parentage or non-parentage

Declarators

4.14   Disputes over a child's parentage will almost always be about paternity rather than maternity but the same procedure, through the mechanism of declarator, applies to resolving the dispute in either case. An action for declarator of parentage or non-parentage may be raised in either the Court of Session or the sheriff court.[42] The issue of parentage may also be determined incidentally to other proceedings.[43] Frequently, the action will be raised by the child's mother. However, an unmarried man may raise an action for declarator of parentage, to establish that he is a child's father, or a woman's husband may raise the action for declarator of non-parentage, to establish that he is not the father of her child (ie to displace the *pater est* presumption). While the action is usually raised fairly soon after a child is born, the issue may arise at a much later stage and, of course, such actions may be raised by the child or on the child's behalf. Other

---

38 Section 5(1)(b).
39 *MacKay* v *MacKay* 1946 SC 78.
40 It may be that, once a DNA test has demonstrated that the man is not the child's father, he will not have to go to the expense of obtaining a declarator, if the mother accepts that the registration ought to be corrected.
41 Section 5(3).
42 Section 7(1). For an action to be raised in Scotland at all or in a particular sheriffdom, there must be a real connection between the parties and the jurisdiction – s 7(2) and (3).
43 Section 7(5).

people may have an interest in a particular child's parentage and they too may raise the action. For example, the children of a person who has died may wish to establish that a putative sibling is not a child of the deceased and, thus, is not entitled to share in the succession to property.

Evidence

4.15 The court must be satisfied as to the sufficiency of evidence,[44] but corroborated evidence is no longer required.[45] In order to rebut any of the presumptions discussed above, the pursuer must prove his or her case on a balance of probabilities.[46] Where there is an equal chance that either of two men is the father of an unmarried woman's child, paternity cannot be established against either of them.[47] However, if either man has acknowledged paternity and been registered as the father, the presumption under s 5(1)(b) of the 1986 Act would apply, and the evidence that another man was equally likely to be the father would be insufficient to rebut it. The advent of DNA profiling makes such a situation unlikely today but, if there is any doubt, men should perhaps be wary of rushing to register their paternity.

4.16 The kind of evidence led in parentage cases has changed quite dramatically with the arrival of DNA profiling. This made it possible, for the first time, to establish that a person *is* the father of a child, and it will be discussed presently. Previously, the scientific evidence available through the older kind of blood test could only establish that a man was *not* the father of the child.[48] Thus, while such blood tests helped in establishing non-parentage, they were of limited value in establishing parentage.[49] For this reason, extensive use was made of other evidence to establish paternity. For example, evidence of an established relationship or, better still, cohabitation, between the child's mother and the alleged father helped to support a case for his paternity. Other circumstantial evidence of the behaviour of the couple[50] and the views of friends and relatives would also be relevant. Only in exceptional circumstances (and a long time ago) has

---

44 Civil Evidence (Scotland) Act 1988, s 8(1).
45 1988 Act, s 1(1). Corroboration by false denial, an archaic rule whereby if the defender was found to have lied on oath about a material fact, that lie was held to corroborate the allegation of paternity, has also been abolished – 1988 Act, s 1(2).
46 1986 Act, s 5(4).
47 *Robertson* v *Hutchison* 1935 SC 708.
48 *Imre* v *Mitchell*, 1958 SC 439.
49 Of course, if there were only two candidates and one was excluded, the inference was obvious – *Docherty* v *McGlynn* 1985 SLT 237. On blood tests, see B. E. Dodds, 'Parentage Testing' in J. K. Mason (ed), *Paediatric Forensic Medicine and Pathology* (Chapman & Hall, 1989).
50 See for example, *Antoniewicz* v *Barty (Wood's Executor)* 27 June 1991, unreported, but mentioned in Wilkinson and Norrie, n 26 above, at p 147. There, the alleged father had died four days before he was due to provide a sample for a DNA test. Evidence was led that, while the child's mother was pregnant, he placed his hand on her stomach and asked about 'his baby' and that he had settled an action for aliment shortly after the child's birth.

evidence of a physical resemblance between the child and the alleged father been admitted.[51]

4.17 Evidence of the gestation period (the time between conception and birth) was usually used to suggest that a particular man was not the father of the child and was often employed to rebut the *pater est* presumption. Essentially, the evidence here is one of both arithmetic and what the law liked to call 'opportunities of access'. Taking the date of the child's birth as a starting point, the likely date of conception is calculated. If the alleged father could not have had sexual intercourse with the mother around the date of conception, the inference is that he is not the child's father. While 280 days is now accepted as a normal gestation period, considerable variation can occur,[52] and other evidence, for example, the condition of the baby at birth, may be relevant.[53] None the less, where the gestation period would be either unreasonably short or unreasonably long for the defender to be the father, this evidence may support his denial.[54] While DNA profiling has now largely replaced the other forms of evidence used in paternity cases, the latter remains relevant and will continue to be used where the samples necessary for DNA profiling cannot be obtained.

DNA profiling

4.18 DNA profiling now provides a reasonably certain[55] way of establishing parentage. Its value is not confined to child and family law, and extensive use has been made of it in immigration and criminal cases. In the context of paternity, it has doubtless avoided injustices that must have occurred in the past, either because the evidence was insufficient to establish the father's paternity or because evidence that appeared sufficient resulted in a man who was not the child's father being declared as such. In addition, a great deal of stress has been avoided, and court time and (private or public) money saved, by reducing litigation surrounding paternity. Once a DNA test has established that a particular man is or is not the child's father, there is little point in litigating the matter.[56]

---

51 *Grant* v *Countess of Seafield* 1926 SC 274. Evidence of a different skin colour did not affect the decision more recently – *S* v *S* 1977 SLT (Notes) 65. Evidence of physical resemblance has been admitted in England – *C* v *C and C* [1972] 3 All ER 577.

52 J. K. Mason, *Forensic Medicine for Lawyers* (3rd edn, Butterworths, 1995) at pp 231–232. Stair was prepared to accept a maximum gestation period of 11 months while Erskine accepted a minimum of 6 months. For a discussion of the development of the thinking on gestation periods, see Wilkinson and Norrie n 26 above, at pp 129–130.

53 Where it is alleged that a baby was premature, birth weight and other indicators of physical development may be relevant – *Preston-Jones* v *Preston-Jones* [1951] AC 391.

54 In *Preston-Jones* v *Preston-Jones, supra,* a gestation period of either 186 or 360 days was held not to be unreasonable, while in *Currie* v *Currie* 1950 SC 10, 336 days, when taken with the other facts of the case, was indicative that the woman's husband was not her child's father.

55 There have been attempts to challenge the results of DNA profiling in criminal cases, where the standard of proof required is beyond reasonable doubt – see P. M. MacDonald, 'DNA Profiling – Less than the Whole Truth' 1990 SLT (News) 285.

56 Where the DNA test establishes paternity, the parents would be as well to acknowledge the fact and have the register of births corrected accordingly, since, if either of them continues to deny it, the other parent will almost certainly be able to obtain a declarator from the court which will have the same effect.

4.19 DNA (deoxyribonucleic acid) forms the chromosomes which carry an individual's genetic components and is found *inter alia* in blood and other body tissue, including hair follicles and nail clippings. With the exception of identical twins, each person has a unique DNA, hence its value as a means of identification and the popular, although somewhat inaccurate, expression 'DNA fingerprinting'. By taking samples of blood or tissue and subjecting the sample to radiation, a profile of the individual can be produced. Individual profiles can then be compared to establish any relationship between these individuals.[57] DNA profiling is now widely available. So much for the practicalities. What of the law? Essentially, the interesting legal issues surrounding DNA testing relate to consent to the necessary samples being taken at all and these issues apply to the older, and less satisfactory, type of blood tests as well.

Consent to testing

4.20 The first question concerns adults submitting to the tests. Fundamental to Scots law is the principle that a civil court[58] cannot compel a competent adult to submit to a blood test or, indeed, any other test involving bodily interference.[59] Nor, in the past, could the courts draw any inference from a person's refusal to submit to a test. Thus, an alleged unmarried father was well-advised to refuse to be tested, in the hope that the other evidence available would be insufficient to establish paternity. The Scottish Law Commission examined the matter[60] and, as a result of its recommendations,[61] the law has now been put on a more satisfactory footing. While it remains the case that the court cannot compel a person to submit to a test, it may now request a party to the proceedings[62] to do so and draw any contrary inference from refusal as it considers appropriate.[63] This does not mean that the pursuer will automatically succeed in establish-

---

57 For a more detailed explanation of genetics and genetic testing, see J. K. Mason, *Forensic Medicine for Lawyers*, (3rd edn, Butterworths, 1995) at pp 243–254.

58 The position in the context of criminal law is different and enables fingerprints and non-intimate samples to be taken without a person's consent – Criminal Procedure (Scotland) Act 1995, s 18.

59 *Whitehall* v *Whitehall* 1958 SC 252; *Torrie* v *Turner* 1990 SLT 718.

60 Evidence: Blood Group Tests, DNA Tests, and Related Matters (Scot Law Com Discussion Paper No 80, 1988).

61 Report on Evidence: Blood Group Tests, DNA Tests, and Related Matters (Scot Law Com No 120, 1989).

62 In a somewhat unusual case, Sheriff Principal Maguire found that it was competent for the court to request such a sample from the alleged grandmother of a child – *Mackay* v *Murphy* 1995 SLT (Sh Ct) 30. The alleged father of the child had died and the action was raised against his mother *in her capacity as her deceased son's executrix*. The alleged grandmother's solicitor argued that she was not a 'party to the proceedings' in her personal capacity any more than a bank or a solicitor would have been had either of them been the alleged father's executor and, thus, that it was incompetent to request a sample from her. While the sheriff accepted this argument, the Sheriff Principal rejected it with the passing observation that 'one should eventually be able to get blood from a solicitor'. There would be no point in requesting such a sample from the solicitor, since it would be of no assistance in establishing paternity unless, of course, the solicitor was related to the alleged father.

63 Law Reform (Miscellaneous Provisions) (Scotland) Act 1990, s 70.

ing paternity,[64] but it does reduce the incentive simply to keep one's head down.

4.21 The second issue arising from the testing of blood and other genetic material is who can consent to a sample being taken from the child. Where the child is of sufficient age and understanding to appreciate what is involved in the test and the likely consequences, he or she can consent.[65] While a court could draw a contrary inference from a child's refusal, it is submitted that it should not do so. The rationale underlying adult refusal and contrary inferences is that the adult is seeking to hide something and, often, to avoid the responsibilities that attach to parenthood. The child, on the other hand, has nothing to hide, since the contenders for paternity are already declared. The child does not face being burdened with responsibilities. Admittedly, one possible father may be more attractive than another, not only in personal terms, but also in terms of financial support and succession prospects. However, the child is unlikely to have the knowledge about the circumstances surrounding conception to be making a calculated choice to hide anything. In addition, the court is required to take decisions in the child's best interests.[66] While it may be in the child's interests to know the truth about his or her identity, it is doubtful that the truth will be served by applying a measure aimed at penalising non-co-operation.

4.22 Where a competent child refuses to submit to a test, can anyone else consent on the child's behalf? The Law Reform (Parent and Child) (Scotland) Act 1986, s 6(2), provides that 'any person having parental responsibilities' or 'having care and control' of the child can consent to the taking of a sample from a child below the age of 16.[67] However, it is submitted that this probably does not enable such a person to override a competent child's refusal to have a sample taken. The 1986 Act aimed to clarify the position on who could consent on behalf of young children and sought to avoid some uncertainty which had existed previously. It predated the Age of Legal Capacity (Scotland) Act 1991 which empowers the competent child in respect of consent to medical procedures.[68] If the right to consent carries with it the right to refuse and, as we have seen, a strong

---

64 For example, in *Smith* v *Greenhill* 1994 SLT (Sh Ct) 22, the pursuer claimed to be the father of a married woman's child. She had also had intercourse with her husband around the time of conception and the husband refused to submit to a blood test. Despite the opportunity to draw a contrary inference, the court did not feel that the husband's refusal was sufficient to rebut the *pater est* presumption.

65 Age of Legal Capacity (Scotland) Act 1991, s 2(4). See chapter 3, paras 67–71.

66 Children (Scotland) Act 1995, s 11(7)(a). While that provision relates to court orders in respect of parental responsibilities and rights, the duty to regard the child's welfare as the paramount consideration must apply by analogy since establishing parentage is one of the starting points for parental responsibilities and rights.

67 As amended by the Children (Scotland) Act 1995, Sched 4, para 38(3). A person can have such responsibilities automatically (the mother and the married father), as a result of a court order, and, in the case of an unmarried father, by virtue of a parental responsibilities and rights agreement with the mother.

68 1991 Act, s 2(4).

case can be made for such a proposition,[69] a person with parental responsibilities cannot consent if the competent child refuses.

4.23 In most cases of disputed parentage, the child will be too young to be in a position to consent to any tests and the necessary consent will have to come from elsewhere. Any person who has parental responsibilities in respect of the child under 16 or care and control of him or her may consent on the child's behalf.[70] All mothers have automatic parental responsibilities and rights from the moment of the child's birth[71] and, thus, the mother can consent. Only a father who was married to the mother at any time from the child's conception has these responsibilities and rights automatically[72] and, again, he can consent. Where the father was not married to the mother at the relevant time (or, indeed, at all), he will not normally have the power to consent unless he and the mother have executed a parental responsibilities and rights agreement.[73]

4.24 An interesting question arises when a married man claims not to be the father of his wife's child and she refuses to the child being tested. By virtue of the *pater est* presumption, the husband is presumed to be the child's father and has automatic parental responsibilities and rights. Thus, in terms of the 1986 Act, he can consent to a sample being taken from the child. However, the whole basis for his right to consent, his presumed paternity, is the very thing he is seeking to disprove. It can be argued that he is entitled to benefit from the presumption until that presumption is displaced. Support for this view is sometimes taken from *Docherty* v *McGlynn*,[74] where the mother had died, and both her husband and the man with whom she had been living claimed paternity of the child. However, there, the husband was seeking to uphold, rather than deny, the *pater est* presumption. None the less, *dicta* in *Docherty* support the husband's continued role in giving consent on the basis of the presumption[75] and cite, with approval, passages from *Imre* v *Mitchell*,[76] where a woman was seeking to establish that her husband was not the father of her child.

4.25 The court can consent to samples being taken from 'any person who is incapable of giving consent' in two situations.[77] It should be noted that this would not apply to enable the court to override the refusal of a competent child (or adult) to be tested, since the person refusing is not incapable of giving consent, he or she being merely unwilling to do so. The court is prohibited from consenting to the taking of a sample unless it is

---

69 See chapter 3, para 70.
70 1986 Act, s 6(2).
71 1995 Act, s 3(1)(a).
72 1995 Act, s 3(1)(b).
73 1995 Act, s 4.
74 1983 SLT 645.
75 At p 647 *per* Lord President Emslie, at p 650 *per* Lord Cameron and at p 651 *per* Lord Grieve.
76 1958 SC 439. There the woman sought to rely on her husband's consent to blood samples being taken from the child since, at the time, she could not consent. The point there was arguably one of the competency of evidence rather than consent; see Wilkinson and Norrie, n 26 above, at pp 155–156.
77 1986 Act, s 6(3).

satisfied that the taking of the sample 'would not be detrimental to the person's health'.[78]

4.26 The first situation where the court can consent is where there is no one entitled to give consent.[79] This would enable the court to authorise the testing of a child who had no capacity to consent, either because he or she was too young to understand what was happening, or because the child's mental disability precluded such comprehension, and there was no person with parental responsibilities. It would not entitle the court to authorise testing where a person with parental responsibilities refused to consent, again because there would be a person with capacity to consent in such circumstances. So, for example, where an unmarried man, who has acknowledged paternity and been registered as a child's father, has doubts and seeks a declarator of non-parentage, and the child's mother refuses to consent to a sample being taken from the child, the court cannot authorise the taking of a sample. The court might draw a contrary inference from the mother's refusal but it would not necessarily conclude that the presumption of paternity, triggered by acknowledgement and registration, had been displaced.

4.27 The second situation enables the court to consent to testing where there is a person with capacity to consent but, either, it is not reasonably practicable to obtain that person's consent, or that person is unwilling to accept the responsibility of giving or withholding consent.[80] Given modern methods of communication, it is difficult to imagine what would make obtaining consent all that difficult, even from someone in an inaccessible foreign spot. It is, however, more conceivable that a person with parental responsibilities might not want the responsibility for making the decision.

ASSISTED REPRODUCTION

4.28 Whatever difficulty parents in the past may have had in answering the question 'Where do babies come from?', at least the biological explanation was fairly straightforward. The advent of assisted reproduction has made the answer very much more complicated. Bio-science has advanced to the point where individuals and couples who are experiencing difficulty in having children can be helped through a range of treatment options.[81] The appropriate technique which may be effective in an individual case will depend on the nature of the problem and not all of the techniques are new.[82] However, since the techniques have a common goal,

---

78 1986 Act, s 6(4).
79 1986 Act, s 6(3)(a).
80 1986 Act, s 6(3)(b).
81 For a discussion of infertility in men and women and the corresponding treatment options, see J. K. Mason, *Medico-Legal Aspects of Reproduction and Parenthood* (Dartmouth, 1998) (hereinafter 'Mason'), chapters 8 and 9.
82 The earliest references to, albeit accidental, artificial insemination of a human female can be found in the Babylonian Talmud of the third century AD, where there is a discussion of a woman becoming pregnant as a result of bathing in water into which a man had ejaculated. For a discussion of this and other early examples of artificial insemination, see D. J. Cusine, *New Reproductive Techniques: A Legal Perspective* (Gower, 1988), at pp 11–14.

and aspects of the legislation govern a variety of them, it is convenient to consider them together. Broadly, they include: artificial insemination, donation of gametes (ova or sperm), *in vitro* (literally, 'in a glass') fertilisation and surrogacy. In addition, where a woman is experiencing difficulty in producing healthy ova, the problem can sometimes be resolved by hormone treatment. While this increases the likelihood of multiple births,[83] there are no legal issues involved beyond those associated with medical treatment generally, and, thus, such treatment does not warrant discussion here.

4.29 While the various bio-scientific advances have undoubtedly brought great benefits, not least in enabling many people to become parents who would not otherwise have had that opportunity, it was realised early on that the gains brought with them certain problems. The most important questions of all, of course, relate to the child who is born as a result of these techniques. Should he or she be informed of the circumstances of his or her conception? If so, to what other information should the child be entitled? What might be the impact of this knowledge? Who are the parents of a child born as a result of wholly or partially donated gametes? Should the donor have any responsibilities or rights? A host of other questions arise. Should some or all of the techniques be prohibited altogether? Should the state attempt to regulate the availability of some or all of them? Who should be eligible to benefit from these, sometimes expensive, procedures? To what extent should they be marketed for the commercial benefit of individuals or institutions?

4.30 Given that attitudes to assisted reproduction vary enormously, what are 'problems' depends, at least to some extent, on one's position on its availability at all. However, even for those most opposed to what they may see as interference with the natural order of things, the reality is that knowledge has advanced to the point where the techniques for assisting reproduction are available. Once we know how to do something, there is little point in the legal system simply rejecting an option that is attractive to a significant number of, often desperate, people. If the legal system will not regulate the use of these techniques, they will be carried out in an unregulated environment, arguably exposing the participants to the risk of greater exploitation than if a legal framework existed. The greater the opportunity for the particular technique to be carried out by the individuals themselves (artificial insemination, for example, requires no medical participation), the more likely it is that it will be done, regardless of what the legal system provides. Even where the involvement of physicians is required, simply outlawing something in the UK will not necessarily ensure that it does not happen[84] and, in any event, people may simply travel abroad in order to get a service they cannot get here. Sight must not be lost

---

83 For a discussion of the problems associated with multiple pregnancies and multiple births, see para 4.48, below.

84 Prior to the Abortion Act 1967, abortions were carried out throughout the country, sometimes with the involvement of doctors. Despite being prohibited by the Prohibition of Female Circumcision Act 1985, it is believed that female genital mutilation still takes place – see chapter 1, para 30 and chapter 6, para 13.

of the fact that the techniques provide the opportunity for many adults to fulfil what is for many a very strong human urge, the desire to procreate. It then remains for the legal system to create a framework for the use of the techniques, consistent with respecting the rights of everyone involved.[85]

4.31 Recent developments surrounding the cloning of Dolly, probably the best-known sheep in the world, at the Roslyn Institute near Edinburgh, have focused debate on the possibility of the cloning of humans. The prospect of being able to produce an exact genetic replica[86] of a human being is one which alarms, excites and generates academic[87] and political debate. Certainly, the bulk of political opinion appears to be opposed to the idea. It may be that the unique situation presented by cloning is such as to warrant its being treated differently to the existing forms of assisted reproduction. None the less, the arguments advanced in the preceding paragraph should, perhaps, be borne in mind before we embark on hasty legislation prompted by fears which are often more rooted in science fiction than in the reality of human behaviour and the choices people are likely to make. Human cloning is a matter for the future. Let us return to the, currently available, techniques and how they are regulated.

4.32 In 1982, a committee,[88] chaired by (now Dame) Mary Warnock, was set up

> 'To consider recent and potential developments in medicine and science related to human fertilisation and embryology; to consider what policies and safeguards should be applied, including consideration of the social, ethical and legal implications of these developments; and to make recommendations'.[89]

That the Committee had no easy task is evidenced by the three 'Expressions of Dissent' contained in the final report.[90] None the less, the Warnock Report and the recommendations contained therein form the basis of the

---

85 For a fascinating discussion of the legal issues surrounding reproduction in England and Wales, see, 'Hatchings' in B. Hale (The Hon Mrs Justice, formerly Professor Brenda Hoggett), *From the Test Tube to the Coffin: Choice and Regulation in Private Life*, The Hamlyn Lectures, Forty-Seventh Series (Sweet and Maxwell, 1996).

86 Of course, a clone cannot be a complete replica of a person in so far as the clone will not have had the personal, intellectual and sensory experiences of the original and, thus, cannot be seen as a duplicate in any real sense.

87 R. Chester, 'To Be, Be, Be ... Not Just To Be: The Legal and Social Implications of Cloning for Human Reproduction' 49 Fal L Rev 303 (1997); J. McLean, 'Human Cloning: A Dangerous Dilemma' (1998) 43 JLSS 24; S. A. Newman, 'Human Cloning and the Family: Reflections on Cloning Existing Children' 13 N Y L Sch J Hum Rts 523 (1997); J. A. Robertson, 'Liberty, Identity and Human Cloning' 76 Tex L Rev 1371 (1998). See also, in Europe, Group of Advisers on the Ethical Implications of Biotechnology to the European Commission, Ethical Aspects of Cloning Techniques (1997) and, in the USA, A Critique of Human Cloning: Report and Recommendations of the National Bioethics Advisory Commission (1997).

88 Given the Committee's title, The Committee of Inquiry into Human Fertilisation and Embryology, it is not surprising that it is known as the 'Warnock Committee'.

89 Report of the Committee of Inquiry into Human Fertilisation and Embryology, Cmnd 9314, 1984, para 1.2.

90 Above, pp 87–93.

bulk of the current legislation.[91] Such is the magnitude of the issues at stake and the speed with which biotechnology continues to advance, that it could not hope to answer all the questions that would arise, and the debate surrounding reproductive technology continues.[92]

Provision of infertility services

4.33 Not surprisingly, the Warnock Committee recommended that a statutory body should be set up to regulate the provision of fertility services and research in this area.[93] The Human Fertilisation and Embryology Authority (HFEA) was created by the Human Fertilisation and Embryology Act 1990 ('the 1990 Act')[94] to supervise and control treatment services governed by the Act.[95] The system of supervision and control relies heavily on the fact that treatment may only be provided by centres holding a licence from the HFEA and licences will only be granted to centres which comply with the HFEA's Code of Practice.

Parentage

4.34 Following the Warnock Committee's recommendations,[96] the 1990 Act established clear rules on the parentage of children born as a result of various kinds of reproductive technology.[97] It should be noted that these are fixed rules and, unlike the presumptions on paternity, cannot be rebutted. Frequently, the rules provide that a person will be treated in law as the child's parent when that is not the biological reality.[98] Where a person is to be treated as the mother or father of a child as a result of the 1990 Act, the effect is stated to apply 'for all purposes'.[99] However, the 1990 Act itself contains two qualifications on this, apparently absolute, effect. First, it does not apply to the transmission of any title, coat of arms,

91 In response to the Warnock Report, the Government issued a White Paper, Human Fertilisation and Embryology: A Framework for Legislation, Cm 259, 1987. The Surrogacy Arrangements Act 1985 was passed shortly after the Warnock Committee reported and without the Report having been considered in full. However, the Human Fertilisation and Embryology Act 1990 can more accurately be described as having its origins in the Report, although not all of the recommendations were implemented. The 1990 Act has been amended by subsequent legislation including, the Human Fertilisation and Embryology (Disclosure of Information) Act 1992 and the Children (Scotland) Act 1995.
92 See for example, The Review of the Guidance on the Research Use of Foetuses and Foetal Material (the Polkinghorne Report) Cmd 762, 1989.
93 Warnock Report, rec 1.
94 Section 5.
95 For a detailed discussion of the role of the HFEA and its regulations in respect of the various kinds of infertility treatment, see Mason, n 81 above, chapters 8 and 9.
96 Warnock Report, recs 50–55.
97 In the USA, these issues are dealt with on a state by state basis although the Uniform Parentage Act provides a model. See, A. E. King, 'Solomon Revisited: Assigning Parenthood in the Context of Collaborative Reproduction' 5 UCLA Women's L J 329 (1995); R. Rao, 'Reconceiving Privacy: Relationships and Reproductive Technology' 45 UCLA L Rev 1077 (1998).
98 The artificial creation of the child-parent relationship is not new and is found in adoption legislation. See chapter 8.
99 Section 29(1).

honour or dignity,[100] although property which devolves along with such aristocratic trappings can transmit to the child.[101] Second, while references in enactments, deeds and other instruments are to be construed as if a child-parent relationship existed,[102] it is open to any person executing a deed to provide that this is not to be the effect. The rules creating the child-parent relationship will be examined in the paragraphs that follow and, thereafter, the techniques will be explored and the rules on parentage will be applied to them.

4.35   Where a woman is carrying, or has carried, a child as a result of an embryo or sperm and eggs being placed in her, that woman and no other woman is to be treated as the mother of the child.[103] While this provision seeks to 'cover all bases', its exact wording is unfortunate, since it would be more correct to describe a woman as carrying a foetus, rather than a child. The provision applies whether the woman was in the UK or elsewhere when the embryo or gametes were placed in her.[104] There are two ways by which the carrying woman can be displaced as the child's mother. The first is where the child is adopted by the ordinary method of adoption,[105] whereby the adopters take over as the child's parents and the child's legal link with birth relatives is severed.[106] The second is through the special provision, created by the 1990 Act and confined to surrogacy, whereby the couple who commissioned a surrogate to carry a foetus, genetically linked to one or both of the couple, can apply for a special kind of parental order.[107] This parental order is, effectively, a form of accelerated, and less regulated, adoption.

4.36   The provision dealing with paternity is a little more complicated than that on maternity. It applies not only where a child is being or has been carried by a woman as a result of an embryo, or sperm and eggs being placed in her, but also where the woman has been inseminated artificially.[108] Again, it would be more correct to say that a foetus, rather than a child, has been carried by the woman. Where the woman was married at the time of the treatment but the embryo was created using sperm from someone other than her husband, her husband is treated as the child's father unless it can be shown that he did not agree to the treatment.[109] Thus, the onus is placed firmly on the husband to rebut consent.

4.37   Where no man would be treated as the child's father by the application of the provision dealing with husbands, discussed above, the 1990 Act goes on to deal with another possibility. Where a man and a

---

100 Section 29(5)(a).
101 Section 29(5)(b).
102 Section 29(3).
103 Section 27(1).
104 Section 27(3).
105 Section 27(2).
106 There are a number of qualifications which apply to this description of the effect of adoption and they are discussed fully in chapter 8.
107 Section 30. For a discussion of this provision, see paras 4.63–4.67, below.
108 Section 28(1).
109 Section 28(2).

woman are treated together, in the course of treatment services[110] provided by a person who is licensed to provide such services, the man concerned will be treated as the father of the child. All the conditions laid down in the subsection must be satisfied for the father-child relationship to be created. The relevant man must be involved in the woman's treatment;[111] unlike the husband, it is not enough that he is simply her partner. The provision applies only to heterosexual couples and a lesbian couple cannot benefit from it, regardless of the degree of involvement of the mother's partner. The provision does not apply to treatment provided by an unlicensed person, nor to a child born as a result of do-it-yourself donor insemination.[112]

4.38 An interesting question arises from the interaction of the two provisions on paternity. Where a married woman, who is living with a male partner other than her husband, conceives a child through donor insemination, the insemination having been carried out by a duly-licensed person and her cohabitant having been involved in the treatment, whom does the law regard as the child's father? Initially, her husband would be treated as such. If it could be demonstrated that he had not consented to the treatment, he would be displaced as the father and only then could the provision creating the father-child relationship between the cohabitant come into play. Of course, a woman in this situation might have some difficulty getting treatment at all were she to disclose all the facts to the provider.[113]

The techniques

Partner insemination

4.39 Artificial insemination is the process whereby semen obtained from a donor is injected into the woman's uterus. Where a married woman is inseminated artificially with her husband's semen, there is no conflict between the biological and legal paternity of the child and the method of effecting insemination does not matter. The husband is the father in both senses of the word. Where an unmarried woman is inseminated using her partner's semen, the artificial nature of the insemination is not the source of any problem. Since the couple are not married, the simplest way for the man to gain legal recognition as the child's father is for the couple to acknowl-

110 'Treatment services' are defined as 'medical, surgical or obstetric services provided to the public or a section of the public for the purpose of assisting women to carry children' – s 2(1). It is interesting that the 1990 Act departs from the usual legislative practice on definitions by providing a handy table (in s 47) indicating where particular definitions can be found.
111 See *Re Q (A Minor) (Parental Order)* [1996] 1 FLR 369, where the embryo carried by a surrogate was a product of the commissioning woman's egg and semen from an anonymous donor. The anonymous donor was not treated as the child's father and the surrogate was not married. None the less, the court was not prepared to conclude that the treatment had been provided to the surrogate and the commissioning woman's husband such as to enable him to be treated as the child's father under s 28(3).
112 For a discussion of donors involved in the do-it-yourself type of donation in the USA and their subsequent involvement with the resulting children, see para 4.46, below.
113 The availability of and access to treatment is left to the discretion of individual clinics.

edge his paternity and register the child accordingly.[114] However, as an unmarried father, he will gain no parental responsibilities or rights unless the couple execute a parental responsibilities and rights agreement.[115]

4.40 It is possible for a husband's semen to be collected, frozen and stored, under licence, with a view to its later use. This option is particularly attractive where the husband is scheduled to receive treatment, for example, radiography, which might render him sterile; the intention being that the semen can be used later to inseminate his wife. Where the whole process is successful and the husband is alive, there is no problem. However, concern surrounds the use of stored semen where the donating husband has died. Should the widow be able to use his semen in order to have their child after her husband's death?[116] This problem first came to world-wide attention when a widow in France sought to use her late husband's semen in this way. The court ultimately approved her choice, despite the opposition of some of the husband's relatives, although it added that any child born would have no succession rights in respect of the father's estate.[117] The 1990 Act envisages the storage of semen and ova and requires individuals to make their wishes on future use of stored gametes clear at the time of donation.[118] Furthermore, even where the necessary consent has been given, the 1990 Act provides that where a child's birth is occasioned by the use of stored semen after the donor's death, the child will not be treated as the donor's child.[119] Thus, the child will have no right to succeed to the deceased's estate nor will the child have any action in respect of the donor's wrongful death.

4.41 In the UK, use of stored semen requires the agreement of the HFEA and a recent English case highlighted the problems that can arise with the present legislation. In *R v Human Fertilisation and Embryology Authority, ex parte Blood*,[120] Ms Blood and her husband had decided to start a family. Before she conceived, her husband contracted meningitis and lapsed into a coma. At Ms Blood's request, semen was removed from him and stored. Mr Blood then died, without having the opportunity to record his wishes on the use of the semen. Ms Blood applied to the HFEA for permission to

---

114 Law Reform (Parent and Child) (Scotland) Act 1986, s 5(1)(b). See para 4.11, above.
115 Children (Scotland) Act 1995, ss 3(1)(b) and 4. See paras 5.53–5.66, below.
116 See, J. J. Berry, 'Life After Death: Preservation of the Immortal Seed' 72 Tul L Rev 231 (1997); L. C. Nolan, 'Posthumous Conception: A Private or Public Matter?' 11 B Y U. J Pub L 1 (1997); R. Rao, 'Reconceiving Privacy: Relationships and Reproductive Technology' 45 UCLA L Rev 1077 (1998); A. R. Schiff, 'Arising from the Dead: Challenges of Posthumous Procreation' 75 N C L Rev 901 (1997).
117 *Parpalaix* v *Cecos* Gaz Pal 1984 2e sem jur 560. In the event, the attempts at artificial insemination were unsuccessful. In *Hart* v *Shalala* (E D La 1994), discussed in Berry, above, the mother of a posthumous child, conceived using her late husband's sperm, sought declaratory relief from the state of Louisiana and the federal government to obtain death benefits for the child. She was successful before an administrative law judge but this decision was overturned by the Social Security Appeals Council. Before the case was heard in federal district court, the Commissioner of Social Security ordered the immediate payment of benefits.
118 Sched 3, para 2(2).
119 Section 28(6).
120 [1997] 2 All ER 687.

use her husband's stored semen to have their child or to be allowed to export it to be used in Belgium where the law does not contain the same restrictions as those contained in the 1990 Act.[121] The HFEA refused both applications. Refusal was prompted, in the first case, by the fact that semen had been stored in contravention of the 1990 Act and, in the second case, by the HFEA's belief that it could not exercise its discretion to allow export where the result would be to defeat the provisions of the 1990 Act. Ms Blood sought judicial review of the HFEA's decision. Ultimately, she was successful and her appeal was allowed but what is important is why. The Court of Appeal concluded that the HFEA was correct to refuse its consent to treatment in this country and to export on the basis that the 1990 Act had been breached. However, applying European law, it found that nationals of one member state have a directly enforceable right to receive medical treatment in another member state and that the refusal to allow export infringed that right. Thus, Ms Blood was entitled to take the semen to Belgium and to receive treatment there.[122] While this case undoubtedly demonstrates the value of having a good lawyer who is capable of lateral thinking, it leaves the law in the UK in a somewhat unsatisfactory state.

4.42 As a result of that case, Professor McLean was invited to review the law in this area. Her Report recommended that the law should continue to require explicit consent for the removal of gametes; that it should be permissible for gametes to be removed from an incompetent person where it is in that person's best interests to do so; that, pending the restoration of that person's competence, the HFEA should have the power to waive written consent to storage of the gametes; that the 1990 Act be amended to provide that the HFEA's discretion to permit export of gametes should not extend to authorising export where the gametes have been obtained unlawfully; and that consideration should be given to amending the 1990 Act to provide that the gametes donor should be regarded as the father of the posthumous child, albeit no succession rights should accrue to the child.[123]

4.43 A further, and highly controversial, use of artificial insemination relates to sex selection of children. While sex selection for purely social or preference reasons is generally, and justifiably, condemned, selection can be used to reduce the possibility of a parent passing on a particular

---

121 Sections 3, 4 and 12 and Sched 3 of the Act, read together, require that a person must give consent in writing to the storage of his or her gametes and must indicate, amongst other things, what is to happen to the gametes in the event of his or her death.

122 Ms Blood's treatment was successful and she gave birth to a boy in December 1998. *The Sunday Times*, 20 September 1998, p 25, reported the birth of a daughter to a 57-year-old Israeli woman, Simi Hermon, whose pregnancy had been brought about by the use of her deceased husband's sperm and an ovum purchased from an anonymous donor. Ms Hermon's case differs from that of Ms Blood in two respects. Ms Hermon's husband had donated sperm while they were attempting to have a child, although it is not clear from the report whether he had left documentary evidence of his intention. In addition, Ms Hermon was unable to produce ova of her own.

123 *Review of the Consent Provisions of the Human Fertilisation and Embryology Act 1990* (Department of Health, 1998) (McLean Report). The final report was preceded by a process of consultation; *Consent and the Law: Review of the current provisions of the Human Fertilisation and Embryology Act 1990* (Department of Health, 1997).

disease.[124] The available techniques are far from guaranteed and Mason and McCall Smith estimate a success rate of 70% at best.[125]

Donor insemination (DI)[126]

4.44　The technique for donor insemination is exactly the same as that for partner insemination, save only that the semen is donated by a third party and not the woman's partner.[127] For a married or cohabiting couple who are experiencing difficulty in having a child due to the male partner's infertility, donor insemination is a relatively simple[128] way for them to have a child who is biologically linked to the woman and, by dint of the provisions discussed above, is treated in law as the male partner's child. Such opposition as there is to donor insemination derives either from the view that we should not interfere with nature or that the creation of a child using donated sperm is some kind of interference in the marital (or quasi-marital) relationship. It is submitted that the latter issue is one properly left to the couple involved. In any event, the Scottish courts accepted long ago that donor insemination does not constitute adultery for the purpose of divorce.[129] Were a wife to seek or receive donor insemination without her husband's consent, her action would probably amount to 'unreasonable behaviour' enabling her distressed husband to obtain a divorce.[130]

124 Indeed, the European Convention on Human Rights and Biomedicine, art 14, prohibits the use of the techniques for sex selection other than in this specific situation.
125 J. K. Mason and R. A. McCall Smith, *Law and Medical Ethics* (4th edn, Butterworths, 1994) at p 53.
126 Donor insemination is also known as artificial insemination by donor (AID), but the new terminology is thought to be preferable in avoiding any possible confusion with AIDS (acquired immune deficiency syndrome). However, both terms are still widely used and Mason, for example, prefers to use AID since he considers any confusion to be 'improbable' – Mason, n 81 above, chapter 8, n 22.
127 Another option is available, whereby the partner's semen is mixed with that of the donor, leaving ambiguity about the biological paternity of the child. Essentially, this allows the couple to believe that the child might be the male partner's. One has to question whether couples who prefer this option are completely comfortable with what they are doing, a matter which might be significant to their attitude to the child in the future. Of course, the truth can be established by DNA profiling. See Mason, n 81 above, pp 222–223 where he discusses this form of insemination under the heading 'Evading the issue' and makes the valid point that one advantage may be that it 'salves the conscience of those couples who register the resultant child as their own'.
128 While the technique itself is relatively simple and, indeed, can be performed by the parties themselves, it is not unproblematic. There is some risk of disease, including HIV, being transmitted through semen – see C. L. R. Barratt and I. D. Cooke, 'Risks of Donor Insemination' (1989) 299 BMJ 1178.
129 *McLennan* v *McLennan* 1958 SC 105. There, the husband raised an action for divorce, founding on the birth of a child, who could not have been his child, as evidence of his wife's adultery. Her defence was that the child had been conceived through donor insemination. The court accepted that, if she established the alleged donor insemination, it would not amount to adultery. In the event, the wife did not produce the necessary evidence and the husband obtained a decree of divorce. Of course, DI is only non-adulterous where there is, in fact, no intercourse. Were intercourse to take place, the fact that the sole motive was DI would not negate the adulterous nature of the conduct – Divorce (Scotland) Act 1976, s 1(2)(a). For a discussion of adultery, see chapter 13, paras 23–34.
130 Divorce (Scotland) Act 1976, s 1(2)(b). See chapter 13, paras 35–46 for a discussion of this ground for divorce.

4.45 Whether donor insemination ought to be provided to unmarried couples, whether heterosexual or homosexual, and single women, is yet another contentious issue, but the Royal College of Obstetricians and Gynaecologists has issued guidelines to its members suggesting that donor insemination should only be made available to married women and with the written consent of their husbands.[131] This, somewhat extreme, position denies the diversity of relationships and lifestyles found in our society. While it can be argued that the paramountcy of the child's welfare mandates that the child's rights, rather than the adults' desire for parenthood or 'right' to procreate, should determine the matter, such a solution begs more questions than it answers. Whether a future with unmarried parents or a single parent is, in fact, deleterious to a child's welfare is open to question. As the many children who experienced parental divorce illustrate, marriage is not guaranteed to last and nor is apparently stable cohabitation. The 1990 Act certainly does not prohibit donor insemination being made available to single women. It simply requires that consideration should be given to the child's need for a father[132] in a provision described by Mason as 'so imprecise as to be either all-embracing or meaningless'.[133] The courts have indicated some movement towards accepting homosexual and lesbian parents. In any event, since artificial insemination is possible without the help of the medical profession, it is perhaps naive of the profession to wash its hands of the issue by opting for the simple solution. The 1990 Act does a little better, but it also limits those who will be treated as a child's parents on the basis of narrow, heterosexual, couple-based, parameters.

4.46 Mention has been made of do-it-yourself donor insemination and it should be remembered that, where this is the background to a child's conception, the rules in the 1990 Act governing the woman's husband or male partner being treated as the child's father do not apply.[134] Where a woman makes her own arrangements for donation, and it should be remembered that this can be done without sexual intercourse taking place, the donor will be treated by the legal system as the child's father. Were the woman to disclose the donor's identity, he could face the financial responsibilities of parenthood.[135] In addition, the donor could seek declarator of paternity.[136] Whether he would be successful in applying for parental responsibilities or rights would be determined in the light of the child's best interests, any views the child wished to express and the nature

---

131 See Mason and McCall Smith, n 125 above, at p 54, where the authors cite some of the literature on the subject and observe, quite rightly, that 'much of the literature in this area is partisan'.

132 Section 13(5).

133 At p 219, where the author admits to having changed his view on the provision of fertility services to single women. See also, H. H. Harlow, 'Paternalism Without Paternity: Discrimination Against Single Women Seeking Artificial Insemination by Donor' 6 S Cal L Rev & Women's Stud 173 (1996).

134 Section 28, discussed at paras 4.36–4.38.

135 For a discussion of the parental responsibility for aliment and child support, see chapter 6, paras 29–80.

136 Law Reform (Parent and Child) (Scotland) Act 1986, s 7.

of the existing arrangements for the child's care.[137] Examples can be found in the USA of sperm donors in this sort of situation being granted the equivalent of parental rights where the surrounding circumstances suggest that this was in the child's interests.[138]

In vitro *fertilisation (IVF)*

4.47 IVF is more technically demanding than artificial insemination and is not open to a do-it-yourself approach. Essentially, it involves the fertilisation of the ovum in laboratory conditions and the transfer of the resulting embryo into the uterus.[139] Where the ovum and sperm have come from determines biological parentage but, as we have seen, the 1990 Act provides rules for determining the child-parent relationship as far as the law is concerned. Despite the need to maintain openness of mind in terms of who ought to be able to benefit from the technique, it is simplest to illustrate the application of the rules on parentage by reference to a married couple receiving treatment through IVF. Where the couples' gametes are used to produce the embryo which is subsequently transferred to the wife, biological and legal parentage coincide. Where either the ovum or sperm has been donated by a third party, the rules set out in the 1990 Act apply to determine who will be treated in law as the child's parents. The paradigm here is where both the ovum and sperm are donated by third parties but the embryo is carried by the wife who subsequently gives birth. In such a case, she and her husband will be treated as the parents of a child to which they are not biologically related at all.

4.48 A particular problem associated with IVF can be described, broadly, as 'overproduction' and occurs in two separate contexts. First, the process requires that more embryos should be produced than will be implanted, since not all of the embryos will be useable. The status of superfluous embryos is, itself, a matter for concern and one which brings us right back to the question of defining life; the very issue which is at the heart of the abortion debate.[140] In addition, where the embryos are stored, the question of control of their future use may arise. We will return to this matter, and the relevant provisions of the 1990 Act, presently. The second difficulty which arises with IVF is that, in order to maximise the likelihood of a successful pregnancy, it is necessary to implant more than one embryo in the womb. This increases the prospect of a multiple pregnancy with all the

---

137 Children (Scotland) Act 1995, s 11(7).
138 See, for example, *Jhordan C* v *Mary K* 224 Cal Rptr 530 (Ct App, 1986), where the father provided the mother with sperm for self-insemination and they had an oral agreement that he surrendered all parental rights. Despite this, he had been allowed to form a relationship with the child by regular visits and the court refused to divest him of his parental rights. Similarly, in *Thomas S* v *Robin Y* 618 N Y S 2d 357 (App Div, 1994), a donor had agreed to relinquish parental rights but, none the less, established a relationship with the child. The court allowed him visitation rights.
139 Strictly speaking, IVF refers to the fertilisation process, while embryo transfer (ET) refers to the subsequent transfer. For a discussion of the actual techniques involved and the distinction which is sometimes drawn between a 'human embryo' and a 'pre-embryo', see Mason, n 81 above, at pp 229–230.
140 See Mason, n 81 above, at pp 107–111 and 234–235 where he addresses the issue of life in the contexts of abortion and superfluous embryos, respectively.

attendant risks to the pregnant woman, the foetuses and any resulting children. In addition, there are resource considerations, both surrounding the multiple birth itself, and in the longer term issue of care of and support for the children. As a practical matter this second difficulty can be overcome by what Mason refers to, perhaps a little euphemistically, as 'reduction of the pregnancy'. He goes on to clarify that this means 'the excess early foetuses are given toxic injections and die within the uterus' and to use the more graphic term 'selective foeticide'.[141] Where a woman is carrying more than one foetus, anything done with the intention of procuring a miscarriage of any foetus comes within the legal protection of the Abortion Act 1967, provided that the conditions laid down in that Act are satisfied.[142] Of course, while such a solution will be acceptable to many of the individuals involved, universal acceptance of the practice is unlikely.

4.49 To return to the question of storage and future use of embryos, it should be noted that the extensive legislative provision in the UK may have helped us to avoid some of the problems which have arisen in other jurisdictions. A brief examination of some of these cases highlights the nature of the problems associated with storage. In Australia, a couple, who had arranged for the creation of embryos using the wife's ova, died before the embryos could be implanted in her. After tremendous public concern had been expressed, the Parliament passed a statute to permit these embryos to be placed in volunteers.[143]

4.50 In *Davis* v *Davis*,[144] what might become a more common scenario was at the centre of the dispute.[145] There, the couple had donated gametes but had divorced before the embryos had been used. The former wife wanted to use some of the embryos in order to have a child, while the former husband wanted them destroyed. As the case proceeded through the various levels of the court system in Tennessee, different courts analysed the problem using, essentially, three different conceptual frameworks. The first, the 'right to life' approach, treated the embryos as human lives and determined the case as if it were a custody (residence) dispute. Perhaps inevitably, that court found that the best interests of the embryos would be served by an award of custody to the woman who wished them to be implanted. The appellate court rejected that approach and treated the dispute as one over marital property, awarding 'joint control' of the property to the former spouses. Of course, this approach did not get the court any further in deciding whether or not the embryos could be implanted. The Tennessee Supreme Court sought to steer a middle course

---

141 At p 233.
142 1990 Act, s 37(5).
143 Information about this case is difficult to find, but Mason and McCall Smith are of the view that implantation did not take place – see, Mason and McCall Smith, n 125 above, at p 65.
144 1989 Tenn App LEXIS 641 (Tenn Cir Ct, 21 September 1989); 1990 WL 130807 (Tenn App, 13 September 1990); 842 SW 2d 588 (Tenn Sup Ct, 1992).
145 A similar case appears to have arisen in Australia, see Mason and McCall Smith, n 125 above, at p 66.

between these approaches and avoided referring to the embryos as either 'lives' or 'property'. Instead, it viewed them as having a 'special significance' greater than inanimate objects but less than people. It devised a six-step test for determining what should happen to the embryos[146] and concluded that, in this case, the interests of the former husband in not procreating outweighed his former wife's interests in using the embryos. Ms Davis was unsuccessful in her attempt to take the case to the US Supreme Court[147] and, thus, the matter remains one which will be resolved on a state by state basis.

4.51 In *AZ* v *BZ*,[148] a court in Massachusetts was faced with much the same kind of dispute and considered many of the same issues. However, there were two significant differences in this case. First, the couple had already had twins as a result of IVF. Second, they had executed written agreements on seven different occasions providing that, in the event of separation or divorce, any remaining embryos would be available to the wife for implantation. Despite the agreements which, admittedly, were several years old and appear to have predated the marital decline, the court felt able to give greater weight to the views of the person who did not wish to procreate, thus avoiding burdening that person with unwanted responsibilities. In addition, it felt that the 'changed conditions' of the couple's relationship were relevant. The argument that a person should not be forced into paternity had been rejected earlier by a court in New York on the basis that participation in an *in vitro* programme indicated an intention to procreate.[149] However, the court in Massachusetts felt that the continued desire of both parents for parenthood was central to applying this consideration. Equally, it might have applied the same notion of 'changed conditions' as it had in respect of the contractual agreements. While, at the time of participating in the programme, a person may have wished parenthood to result, that person may have changed his or her mind in the context of marital breakdown or divorce.[150]

4.52 In the light of the legislation, it is unlikely that there would be the

---

146 842 SW 2d 588 (Tenn Sup Ct, 1992) at p 604. Briefly, the steps are as follows. (1) The court must consider the wishes of the interested parties including the gametes providers above any other authority like the health care organisation or clinic. (2) If the gametes providers cannot agree, the court should enforce any prior contractual agreement between them. (3) The court must balance the interests of the parties in use and non-use of the embryos. (4) The party who wished the embryos destroyed should prevail unless the other party had no other way of having a child. (5) The court should consider the argument of the party who wanted the embryo implanted either in herself or in a willing third party. (6) If the couple were in dispute over whether or not to donate the embryos to a third party, the party opposed to donation should prevail.

147 Cert denied 61 US, LW 3437.

148 Suffolk County Prob Ct, 25 March 1996.

149 *Kass* v *Kass* 1995 WL 110368 (NY, Nassau County Sup Ct, 19 January 1995). That decision was overturned by the Appellate Division of the Supreme Court of New York (663 NYS 2d 581 (1997)), a decision affirmed by the Court of Appeals (91 NY 2d 554 (1998)) on the basis that the parties' signed agreement donating the embryos to the IVF programme should determine the matter.

150 For an excellent discussion of these cases, see, D. I. Steinberg, 'Divergent Conceptions: Procreational Rights and Disputes over the Fate of Frozen Embryos' 75 BU Pub Int L J

same opportunity for this sort of dispute to come before the courts in the UK. The 1990 Act provides for the giving of necessary consent for the storage and use of embryos. Each person whose gametes have contributed to the embryo must give consent in writing to the future use of the embryo and the conditions under which it can be used and such consent can be withdrawn.[151] Thus, where a couple contribute to the creation of an embryo and they separate or divorce, either of them could veto subsequent use of it. In addition, each contributor must specify the maximum period of storage of the embryo, if this is less than the statutory maximum, and must indicate what is to happen to it in the event of his or her death or incapacity.[152]

Surrogacy

4.53 The first thorny issue to tackle here is exactly what we mean by surrogacy. At its simplest, what is known as 'full surrogacy' involves a woman ('the surrogate') agreeing to carry a foetus, produced from the gametes obtained from a couple ('the commissioning couple'), with the intention that the child will be handed over to the couple to be raised by them as their child. In such a case, the commissioning couple are the biological parents, and the woman who carries the foetus is, in strict biological terms, an unrelated host. The position in law will be examined presently. Frequently, surrogacy does not take this absolute form and, instead, the sperm is donated[153] by the husband of the commissioning couple and used to fertilise the surrogate's own ovum. This is known as 'partial surrogacy' and the husband and the surrogate are the biological parents of the child. Yet another option involves sperm donated by an anonymous third party being used to impregnate the surrogate and an agreement that she will hand the child over to the commissioning couple. In all, Cusine[154] identifies nineteen possible permutations in what might, or might not, be described as surrogacy arrangements.

315 (1997). See also L. Kuo, 'Lessons Learned from Great Britain's Human Fertilisation and Embryology Act: Should the United States Regulate the Fate of Unused Human Embryos?' 19 Loy L A. Int'l & Comp L J 1027 (1997); Rao, above, at pp 1082–1083.

151 1990 Act, Sched 3, paras 1, 2(1) and 6(3).
152 1990 Act, Sched 3, paras 2(2) and 8(2).
153 Two Bible stories recount examples of what might be described as surrogacy. In the first (Genesis 16: 1–16), Abraham's wife, Sarah, was unable to have children and, at her suggestion, Abraham had a child with her maid, Hagar. The story goes on to recount a degree of tension developing between the two women. In Genesis 21 we hear that Sarah gave birth to a son (Isaac) when she was 90 and Abraham was 100. In the second story (Genesis 30: 1–24), Jacob's first wife, Rachel, was unable to have children and encouraged him to have two sons with her maid. When Jacob's second wife, Leah, discovered that she could no longer have children she took a leaf out of Rachel's book and suggested he attempt to father children with her maid, Zilpah. Again, the process was successful. In what must give hope to many childless women, it appears that both Rachel and Leah went on to recover their fertility. Common to these stories is the fact that there was no artificial element to the insemination; the maids in question were inseminated by sexual intercourse. Such conduct constitutes adultery, although, where the wife participates in the arrangement, the defence of *lenocinium* would be open to the husband – see chapter 13.
154 D. J. Cusine, *New Reproductive Techniques: A Legal Perspective* (Gower, 1988) at p 109.

4.54 Surrogacy has attracted more controversy than other techniques used to assist in reproduction. This is, in part, because of the greater degree of active involvement of a third party. Undoubtedly, this increases the potential for problems and disputes. The matter of how much, if any, control the couple should have over the surrogate's lifestyle, aimed at ensuring optimum conditions for the birth of a healthy baby, raises fundamental questions of human liberty. The possibility of a relative acting as a surrogate has led to further debate. Where a woman is capable of producing healthy ova but is not able to carry a foetus to term, one solution might be for the ovum to be fertilised *in vitro*, using her husband's semen, and for the embryo to be implanted into and carried by her mother or sister. While such examples of family assistance may be viewed as loving and selfless acts and, indeed may create a special bond of affection between the 'grandmother' or 'aunt'[155] and the child, the confusion that it can impose on family relationships has caused some concern.

4.55 A whole range of issues arise in the context of surrogacy and parenthood. The first difficulty can occur when, having given birth, the surrogate refuses to hand the child over to the commissioning couple. Whether she is in fact the child's biological mother or not, she is treated in law as the child's mother by virtue of having carried the foetus[156] and, thus, starts off with full parental rights.[157] The fact that no other woman is to be treated in law as the child's mother[158] means that, even where the child has resulted from the use of an ovum taken from the commissioning woman, she has no automatic standing in respect of the child. How this provision will interact with the possibility of the commissioning woman seeking a declarator of parentage, based on DNA evidence, under s 7 of the Law Reform (Parent and Child) (Scotland) Act 1986, is untested as yet. It might be argued that, since the 1990 Act states quite unambiguously that, in such circumstances, 'no other woman is to be treated as the mother of the child', there is nothing that the biological mother can do. This argument seems particularly strong when one applies the general rule that a later statute overrules an earlier one. However, the 1990 Act made no attempt to amend the 1986 Act to rule out actions for declarator of parentage in such cases. Arguably, then, the later statute was not seeking to preclude the possibility of such actions. What the courts decide on this point may not be crucial to the child's future, since, as we shall see, actions in respect of parental responsibilities and rights can be raised by a variety of persons, including non-parents, however defined.[159] Any decision would be taken on the basis that the child's welfare is the paramount consideration. Since the child involved will be a baby, the opportunity to consider the child's views will not arise. However, given that the court is directed not to make any

---

155 Applying s 27 of the 1990 Act, the woman who carried the foetus will be treated in law as the child's mother. Thus, the surrogate in such cases is both the child's mother in legal terms and the child's grandmother (or aunt) in biological terms.
156 1990 Act, s 27(1).
157 Children (Scotland) Act 1995, s 3(1)(a).
158 1990 Act, s 27(1).
159 1995 Act, s 11. See chapter 5, paras 73–75.

order unless to do so would be better than not making the order, the deck would seem to be stacked in the surrogate's favour.

4.56 Where the surrogate is married, and some have been, the position of her husband is interesting.[160] In terms of the 1990 Act, he will be treated in law as the child's father, unless it can be shown that he did not consent to his wife's treatment.[161] This would make him a 'married father' with the attendant parental responsibilities and rights. Where the commissioning man is also the child's biological father, he will face the same statutory problems as confronted the commissioning woman and the court will arrive at a solution in the same way. Where the surrogate is not married, there would seem to be less likelihood of problems arising. Any partner of the surrogate would only be treated as the child's father if he had been treated along with her,[162] an unlikely possibility where a commissioning man donated semen for the impregnation. In the light of the decision in *Re Q (A Minor) (Parental Order)*,[163] it is questionable that the commissioning man would be regarded as being treated along with the surrogate.

4.57 The anguish caused by cases where the surrogate changed her mind about handing over the baby is well documented in other jurisdictions,[164] but it was not until *C v S*,[165] in 1996, that a Scottish court had the opportunity to consider the matter. There, a couple paid £8,000 to an unemployed woman who was living on benefits for 'loss of earnings and inconvenience' associated with her being inseminated with the husband's sperm and bearing the child who was to be handed over to them. The woman subsequently changed her mind about agreeing to adoption, thus making it impossible for the couple to use the expedited 'parental order' procedure.[166] The couple then applied to adopt the child in the ordinary way. The court dispensed with the woman's agreement to the adoption (something that could not have been done if the couple had been applying for a parental order) and granted the adoption order. It is interesting to note that, while the court concluded that the payment contravened the Human Fertilisation and Embryology Act 1990, and such a contravention might bar the adoption on public policy grounds, this did not create an absolute statutory bar to adoption. Perhaps most significant of all was the

---

160 A further complication with a married surrogate, who is having marital relations with her husband, would be real uncertainty about the child's biological paternity. Of course, this matter could be resolved using DNA profiling.

161 Section 28(2). This assumes, of course, that the surrogacy was achieved by way of 'treatment'. Where a 'do-it-yourself' approach was taken, a married surrogate's husband would be regarded as the child's father, at first instance, under the *pater est* presumption – Law Reform (Parent and Child) (Scotland) Act 1986, s 5(1)(a), discussed above at paras 4.36. The presumption is rebuttable.

162 Section 28(3).

163 [1996] 1 FLR 369, discussed at para 4.37, above.

164 *Re C (A Minor)* [1985] FLR 846; *Matter of Baby M* 537 A 2d 1227 (1988); *Johnson* v *Calvert* 851 P 2d 776 (1993).

165 1996 SLT 1387.

166 The procedure for parental orders is discussed at paras 4.63–4.67. However, at this stage it should be noted that parental orders are inapplicable where the surrogate does not consent. Unlike the procedure for adoption, there is no possibility of dispensing with her consent.

conclusion that the court's duty to safeguard and promote the child's welfare outweighed any public policy considerations relating to payment and, thus, should prevail in permitting the adoption to proceed.

4.58 A different, but none the less unfortunate, difficulty can arise with surrogacy arrangements. It may be that, after the birth, neither the commissioning couple nor the surrogate wants the child.[167] It is submitted that, in practice, the solution would be for the local authority to look after the child until suitable adopters can be found.[168] Given the dearth of babies available for adoption and the very great demand for them, making satisfactory adoption arrangements should present no problems.

Surrogacy and commercialism

4.59 Of greater offence to public sensibilities is the idea of commercial involvement in surrogacy arrangements. The opposition to commercial provision of assisted reproduction and profit for participants is founded on the idea that creating life is somehow too important or too special to be tainted by commerce. The possibility of a clinic setting itself up to broker surrogacy arrangements for profit is seen as, at the very least, distasteful, and at worst, an exploitation of poor and desperate women. The idea of a surrogate being paid a large sum of money to carry the foetus is sometimes viewed as tantamount to selling babies although, particularly where the surrogate is not biologically related to the child, there is a distinction. Our society seems to have no difficulty in accepting that many women sell their time and presence, often very cheaply, in the name of employment. One wonders why, then, there is such opposition to a woman making a free choice about earning money for herself and her family by another use of her time and assets.[169] The opposition seems particularly patronising when it comes from individuals who make a very good living from their own talents; talents developed and fostered by the wide-ranging opportunities they have often had. It is worth remembering that payment is sometimes made for the donation of semen and IVF is often offered in expensive private clinics. Where payment is part of the picture, it may mean that the affluent childless will find it easier to enlist the assistance of a surrogate than will the poor childless. That such a situation is unjust is undeniable, but it should not blind us to the bigger issues surrounding commercial

---

167 In one of the worst examples of this kind of breakdown of a surrogacy arrangement in the USA, the child concerned was disabled and the ensuing unseemly battle was played out on the Phil Donoghue television chat-show.

168 In any event, the local authority is obliged to look after any child who has been abandoned and may do so for any other child if it considers that to do so would safeguard or promote the child's welfare – Children (Scotland) Act 1995, s 25(1)(b) and (2).

169 Certain kinds of work appear to be more socially acceptable than others, with prostitution being regarded by some as at the 'least acceptable' end of the scale. A piece of conventional wisdom has developed which suggests that 'feminist writers' equate commercial surrogacy with prostitution, although it appears that the same few writers are cited over and over again in support of this proposition; A. Dworkin, *Right-Wing Women* (Perigree Books, 1983); G. Corea, *The Mother Machine: Reproductive Technologies from Artificial Insemination to Artificial Wombs* (Perennial Library, 1985). For a thought-provoking discussion of why the two should not be equated, see J. M. Sera, 'Surrogacy and Prostitution: A Comparative Analysis' 5 Am U J Gender & L 315 (1997).

surrogacy. It may be that the various arguments on the matter lie behind the legislation governing surrogacy and the fact that some commercial activity is criminal while other involvement is not.

4.60 In an attempt to pacify public concern, brought into focus by the birth of Baby Cotton[170] as a result of a commercial surrogacy arrangement, the Surrogacy Arrangements Act 1985 ('the 1985 Act') was pushed through Parliament before the recommendations of the Warnock Committee could be considered in depth.[171] The 1985 Act makes it an offence to negotiate a surrogacy arrangement on a commercial basis[172] or to be involved in advertising such arrangements.[173] However, and it is a big 'however', it is not illegal for the surrogate and the commissioning couple to enter into a surrogacy arrangement, nor is any payment made to or for the benefit of the surrogate regarded as a commercial payment. Later in 1985, a Private Members Bill was introduced in an attempt to criminalise all involvement in surrogacy arrangements.[174] The Bill was unsuccessful.

4.61 While neither the surrogate nor the commissioning couple commit any offence by making a surrogacy arrangement, any agreement made is unenforceable.[175] Thus, the surrogate cannot be compelled to hand the child over, nor can she enforce any agreement for the payment of money, regardless of what the parties have agreed. Of course, the court may grant parental responsibilities or rights to the commissioning couple or to one of them, despite opposition from the surrogate, but any such order will be made under the court's general jurisdiction to determine these matters in the light of the child's welfare, and not on the strength of any agreement.

4.62 As in so many other areas of the law, the real interest for lawyers is in trying to minimise the scope for problems and in dealing with disputes when they arise. However, sight should not be lost of the fact that many surrogacy arrangements are concluded to the satisfaction of the adults involved. This is perhaps evidenced best by the fact that the 1990 Act makes specific provision for the making of parental orders in favour of the commissioning couple with the agreement of the surrogate. Furthermore, as we saw, payment to a surrogate will not necessarily prevent the child

---

170 K. Cotton and D. Wynn, *Baby Cotton: for love and money* (Dorling Kindersley, 1985). In that English case, it was the local authority, rather than the surrogate, which opposed the biological father's involvement with the child. In the event, the High Court examined what would be in the child's best interests, granted care and control to the father and gave him permission to take the child out of the country – *Re C (A Minor)* [1985] FLR 846.

171 The Warnock Committee was, itself, divided on the issue of surrogacy. The majority favoured criminalising all surrogacy agencies, whether profit-making or not, and the minority preferring state-controlled provision. For a full discussion, see J. K. Norrie, 'Legal Regulation of Human Reproduction in Great Britain' in S. A. M. McLean (ed), *Law Reform and Human Reproduction* (Gower, 1992).

172 Sections 1(8) and 2(3).

173 Section 3. The offence can be committed by persons involved in running such agencies or by proprietors, editors and publishers who engage in advertising.

174 Surrogacy Arrangements (Amendment) Bill 1985 (Bill No 116).

175 In its original form, the 1985 Act was somewhat ambiguous on the enforceability of surrogacy agreements and the position was clarified by the 1990 Act, s 36, which amended it to provide, '[n]o surrogacy arrangement is enforceable by or against any of the persons making it' – 1985 Act, s 1A.

being adopted by the commissioning couple through the ordinary adoption process.[176] The continuing concern surrounding surrogacy is evidenced by the fact that the whole matter was considered again by a Committee of academics, chaired by Professor Brazier, which recommended that payment to surrogates should be restricted to expenses only, that all surrogacy agencies should be registered and governed by a Code of Practice, and that parental orders should be available only where the Code of Practice had been complied with.[177]

Parental orders and gametes donors

4.63 Mention has been made of the special provision for the making of a parental order[178] in favour of gametes donors, essentially an order which is similar to an adoption order but less regulated. It should be stressed at the outset that such an order is available only where a host of conditions are satisfied and is, in any event, at the discretion of the court.[179] Some of the conditions are self-explanatory, while others require further exploration. They are

The application must be made by a married couple[180]

4.64 Only a married couple can apply for this kind of order. It is not available to cohabiting couples, whether heterosexual or homosexual, nor to a married or single person alone. Accordingly, the applicants are referred to as the 'husband' and 'wife' in the section.

The child concerned must have been carried by a woman other than the wife as the result of the placing in her of an embryo or sperm and eggs or her artificial insemination[181]
Essentially, this condition restricts applications to cases where the child is a product of full or partial surrogacy.

The gametes of the husband or the wife, or both, were used to bring about the creation of the embryo[182]
At least one of the applicants must be the biological parent of the child.

The husband and wife must apply for the order within six months of the child's birth[183]

---

176 *C* v *S* 1996 SLT 1387.
177 Professors Brazier, Golombok and Campbell, issued a consultation document and questionnaire in October 1997 – Surrogacy: Review for the UK Health Ministers of current arrangements for payment and regulation. The team's Report was published a year later – Surrogacy Review for Health Ministers of Current Arrangements for Payments and Regulation (1998, Cm 4068).
178 Only three such orders were made in 1997; Annual Report 1997, p 139.
179 1990 Act, s 30(1) provides that the court 'may' make a parental order where the conditions are satisfied, which indicates that such an order could be refused. For example, the court might refuse an order where, despite the conditions being satisfied, it did not believe the order to be in the child's best interests.
180 Section 30(1).
181 Section 30(1)(a).
182 Section 30(1)(b).
183 Section 30(2). In order to cover children born before the Act came into force, this subsection provides that couples had six months from that date to apply for an order.

The child's home must be with the couple both at the time of the application and at the time of the order being made[184]

The husband or the wife, or both, must be domiciled in the UK or in the Channel Islands or the Isle of Man at the time of the application and at the time of the order being made[185]

Both the husband and the wife must have attained the age of eighteen by the time any order is made[186]

Both the woman who carried the child and the father of the child (including a man treated as such by virtue of s 28 of the Act) have freely, and with full understanding of what is involved, agreed unconditionally to the making of the order[187]

4.65 This condition is similar to that found in the context of adoption. Since the effect of the parental order is to displace the people who would have been treated as the child's parents but for the order, it is not surprising to find a parallel provision. A person's consent is not required if he or she cannot be found or is incapable of giving agreement, and the agreement of the woman who carried the child is ineffective if it is given less than six weeks after the child's birth.[188] However, unlike adoption legislation, there is no provision for dispensing with agreement on the ground that it is being withheld unreasonably.

The court must be satisfied that no money or other benefit (other than for expenses reasonably incurred) has been given or received by the husband or the wife for: the making of the order, any agreement required, the handing over of the child to them, or the making of any arrangements with a view to the making of the order[189]

4.66 Essentially this condition seeks to avoid commercial surrogacy. However, while a prohibited payment might prevent a parental order being granted, it seems that this may only slow down, but not bar, the child's eventual adoption through the ordinary adoption process. It will be recalled that in *C* v *S*,[190] while a parental order would not have been possible, in any event, due to the surrogate's lack of consent, the commissioning couple were permitted to adopt the child and the payment issue did not prevail over the court's duty to promote the child's welfare. What was not possible by parental order became permissible under the ordinary rules on adoption.

4.67 An application for a parental order may be made in the Court of

184 Section 30(3)(a).
185 Section 30(3)(b).
186 Section 30(4).
187 Section 30(5).
188 Section 30(6). Again, similar provisions are found in the Adoption (Scotland) Act 1978.
    See chapter 8.
189 Section 30(7).
190 1996 SLT 1387.

Session or the sheriff court.[191] If granted, its effect will be that the child will be 'treated in law' as the child of the applicants.[192] While, unlike the provisions in ss 27 and 28, there is no statement that they shall be so treated 'for all purposes', the inference is that they will be. What is less clear is whether the provision governing effects that are to be excluded in respect of those sections (relating to titles, honours and deeds) also apply here. Section 29 applies expressly to ss 27 and 28, but nothing is said about it applying to parental orders. Thus, it might be concluded that it does not apply and so, for example, a child who has been the subject of a parental order made in favour of members of the aristocracy could succeed to the title. However, s 30 itself provides for regulations to be made applying the 'enactments about adoption' to parental orders.[193] The clear implication is that a parental order is a form of adoption and thus, it could be argued, the ordinary rules on adoption, which prevent adopted children from succeeding to titles, apply to parental orders. Clearly, the best solution would be for regulations to be made clarifying the matter.

Freezing and storage of semen, ova and embryos

4.68   Given that assisted reproduction involves the harvesting and use of gametes, the Warnock Committee believed it was essential that provision should be made for these and associated matters[194] and the 1990 Act makes extensive provision in this respect. Before a person's gametes, or an embryo produced from such gametes, can be stored, the donor must consent.[195] Consent to the use of an embryo must specify whether the use is for the donor, the treatment of another person or for research.[196] A maximum period of storage must be stated if this is less than the statutory maximum and the consent must indicate what is to happen to the gametes or embryos in the event of the death or incapacity of the donor.[197] There is extensive regulation of the licensing of those who may store such matter, what they may and may not do with it, and the penalties for contravention.[198] The extensive and detailed regulation of reproductive technology and its commercial application in the UK can be contrasted with the, considerably less, regulation in the USA[199] although the matter varies from state to state.[200]

4.69   As with any human endeavour, errors can occur. The opportunities

---

191 Section 30(8)(b).
192 Section 30(1).
193 Section 30(9).
194 Warnock Report, paras 10.1–10.15.
195 1990 Act, Sched 3, paras 2 and 8.
196 Sched 3, paras 2 and 5.
197 Sched 3, paras 2 and 8.
198 See, in particular, 1990 Act, ss 3 and 4 and the HFEA, Code of Practice (2nd revision, 1995).
199 For a very full discussion of the need for greater regulation, see K. A. Byers, 'Infertility and *In Vitro* Fertilization: A Growing Need for Consumer-Oriented Regulation of the *In Vitro* Fertilization Industry' 18 J Legal Med 265 (1997).
200 Virginia, for example, has rather greater regulation than many other states – Byers, above, at pp 296–299.

for commercial exploitation make it all the more likely that some individuals will misuse the trust that has been placed in them for financial gain. Any breach of trust is upsetting to the victim. To find that one's solicitor or accountant has had his or her 'fingers in the till' may engender a sense of betrayal. When what has been taken and misused is something as personal as one's own reproductive material, the outrage and distress of the victims is magnified many times. The full details of a recent example of the kind of problem that can occur are still unfolding, but a general picture is emerging.[201] A number of women believed that their ova were being stored at the University of California at Irvine's Center for Reproductive Health, for the exclusive use of the individual woman who donated them. It appears that some of these ova were used to bring about pregnancies in women other than the donors. According to one report

> 'Over seventy women who received fertility treatment at [the clinic] were either inadvertent donors or recipients of stolen eggs or embryos. At least ten children are products of reproductive material allegedly stolen by doctors at the clinic. As a result, over eighty lawsuits and three custody suits have been filed against the university and the doctors'.[202]

It is also alleged that the (previously eminent and respectable) doctors at the clinic

> 'prescribed an unapproved fertility drug, concealed over $900,000 in revenue from the University of California, performed nonconsensual research on patients and stole embryos from younger patients to increase the likelihood of older and more problematic patients becoming pregnant [and that] the eggs of one woman allegedly ended up in a Wisconsin zoology laboratory'.[203]

Shortly before the allegations were published, the University closed the clinic. While, at the time, there was no criminal statute applicable to the theft of the ova or embryos,[204] federal charges relating to mail fraud were laid. Before the prosecutions could proceed, two of the accused doctors sold their homes and left the US. Thus, it is unlikely that the full facts of the case will ever be known, although the litigation underway may reveal more details.

4.70 The real value of the allegations, for our present purpose, is in alerting us to problems that could occur. It is tempting to suggest that, in the highly-regulated setting of the UK, such things could not happen, but it is always dangerous to take such a self-satisfied position. More significantly, were such events to unfold in Scotland, would the legal system be able to deal with them? It is submitted that, quite apart from offences under the

---

201 Not surprisingly, many of the reports are to be found in newspapers and magazines, with little appearing in the academic journals as yet. Citation here will be confined to the latter category although it should be appreciated that the academic articles often refer to the more popular sources of information.
202 R. S. Snyder, 'Reproductive Technology and Stolen Ova: Who Is The Mother?' 16 Law and Ineq 289 (1998) at p 290. See also, S. J. Paine, P. K. Moore and D. L. Hill, 'Ethical Dilemmas in Reproductive Medicine' 18 Whittier L Rev 51 (1996), which concludes with a series of questions and answers relating to the issues raised by the allegations.
203 Byers, above, at p 309.
204 Not surprisingly, the case has generated legislative activity in California and elsewhere.

1990 Act, the very flexibility of the criminal law would provide responses, assuming that the accused remained within the jurisdiction. Fraud and theft seem obvious avenues for prosecution, although, inevitably, theft charges would run into problems over whether the stolen matter was defined as property or not. More important, however, is how the system would deal with disputes over children produced from 'stolen embryos'. Again, the 1990 Act appears to provide a response. The woman who carried the foetus to term is regarded as the mother of the child for all legal purposes and the 1990 Act makes no exception for improperly obtained gametes.[205] Similarly, the provisions which result in that woman's husband or partner being treated as the child's father are couched in absolute terms.[206] Notional parentage, it seems, would not present a problem. It would, of course, remain open to the biological parents to claim to be persons having an interest for the purpose of applications in relation to parental responsibilities and rights.[207]

Unresolved problems

4.71 While the legal system has made strenuous efforts to provide a framework for the use of techniques to assist reproduction, problems remain. Those surrounding the use of stored gametes after the donor's death have been discussed above. As we saw, while the Surrogacy Arrangements Act 1985 sought to remove commercialism from surrogacy, it has not been completely effective. In addition, the sad truth is that people will often do more for money than they would have done for nothing and services will be provided for gain where there would otherwise have been no provision. As long as treatment for infertility remains available free, it may be that the time has come to accept that commercial provision is inevitable and to take the opportunity to regulate it in order to avoid, or, at least, minimise, the exploitation of those involved. The recommendations of the Brazier Committee can be expected to contribute to this debate. Many other issues remain unresolved, but two seem of particular importance.

4.72 The first concerns the child's right to information about the circumstances of his or her conception and, in the case of surrogacy, gestation. As we will see, it has long been accepted that secrecy should be avoided in the context of adoption[208] but there, at least, there is documentary evidence of the adoption having taken place. Where reproduction has been assisted using a technique other than surrogacy, there will be no such evidence readily available to the child. While many parents will tell the child the truth about his or her background, some undoubtedly will not. This denies the child fundamental information about his or her identity and, families being what they are, there is a real possibility of the 'skeleton coming out of the cupboard' in less than ideal circumstances. Even where the child is told

---

205 Section 27.
206 Section 28.
207 Children (Scotland) Act 1995, s 11.
208 J. Triseliotis, *In Search of Origins* (Routledge and Kegan Paul, 1973). See chapter 8, paras 20–21.

of the broad facts surrounding conception, the other information made available is very limited. While the Human Fertilisation and Embryology Authority is required to provide a person of 18 or over with information about the fact that he or she resulted from donated gametes or a donated embryo, other medical information, and the extent to which he or she might be related to an intended spouse, there is no provision for disclosure of the identity of the donor.[209] Thus, unlike adopted children, children produced by assisted reproduction do not have the opportunity to trace genetic parents and, thus, other relatives. Given that many sperm donors donated with the understanding that their identity would not be disclosed, any change in the law here would be a fairly radical intrusion on their liberty.[210] However, the child's fundamental right to knowledge about his or her identity[211] requires that this information ought to be available. Reconciling the rights of the parties involved is problematic, particularly if, as is suspected, any future legislation which provides donor children with the same rights to information as adopted children, results in fewer donors coming forward.

4.73 The second issue which is inadequately addressed in both policy and legislation is the availability of assisted reproduction to single women and same sex couples.[212] While single women and lesbian couples can make use of do-it-yourself artificial insemination, and a number have, other techniques are largely unavailable to them in the UK. The rules on parentage provided by the 1990 Act are premised on the notion of traditional marriage and make only minimal concession to unmarried heterosexual couples. Parental orders are available only to married (by definition heterosexual) couples. Imaginative use of the ordinary rules on adoption may enable one partner in a homosexual relationship to adopt a child who has resulted from a surrogacy arrangement but, as we shall see, the current law on adoption does not permit joint adoption by an unmarried couple. Arguments supporting the present legal régime rely largely on the notion that it is in the child's interests to be raised in a traditional family and that

209 1990 Act, s 31.
210 The 1990 Act, specifically prohibits the Authority giving information about the identity of the donor where it could not have been required to give this information at the time of donation – s 31(5). For the case against donor anonymity, see, K. D. Katz, 'Ghost Mothers: Human Egg Donation and the Legacy of the Past' 57 Alb L Rev 733 (1994), where the author makes her position very clear: 'If gametes donors are unwilling to have their sons and daughters meet them face to face one day, they should not participate in the creation of children by artificial insemination or egg donation' (at p 779). See also, Rao, above, and H. S. W. Swanson, 'Donor Anonymity in Artificial Insemination: Is It Still Necessary?' 27 Colum J L & Soc Probs 151 (1993).
211 The United Nations Convention on the Rights of the Child, art 8, talks of 'the child's right to preserve his or her identity, including nationality, name and family relations as recognised by law'. There may be a certain circularity in the definition. It should be remembered that, just as parental remarriage or cohabitation can bring with it a host of step-relatives, tracing biological parents can bring knowledge of a multitude of other blood relatives.
212 The Warnock Committee considered this issue and, while it did not believe hard and fast rules to be appropriate and, thus, made no recommendations, it favoured treatment being available to heterosexual couples, whether married or not – Warnock Report, paras 2.5–2.13.

the state should not set out to assist adults to have children in other settings. While the focus on what will serve the child is laudable, arguments of about what is better for children are often based on unfounded assumptions and generalisations. It may be that reform of the law and practice in respect of surrogacy requires rethinking the law on child-parent relationships in general. None the less, we have arrived at the point where many children already live in single-parent families or in families where the significant adults are in a same-sex relationship. Adoption in a homosexual setting has already been permitted.[213] The issue may often come down to one of how to use limited resources. However, to deny adults who do not fit into the traditional model of the family the opportunity of help to become parents, when science makes that help available to more conventional adults, is increasingly difficult to defend.

IMPLICATIONS OF PARENTHOOD

4.74 Thus far, this chapter has focused on the question of establishing parentage, either as a biological fact or as a legal fiction. As we have seen, the distinction between the two is of considerable significance in the context of the child's identity. When we examine the issue of adoption, we will see that the question of identity is, again, important.[214] However, the law must also concern itself with other matters. The practicalities of day-to-day life require the legal system to address such issues as where a child lives; with whom a child has contact; who bears financial responsibility for the child; and who makes decisions, particularly in respect of a young child whose youth may preclude or limit the child's own role in decision-making.[215] These issues are discussed in detail in the following chapters. The central point to note here is that, as far as the responsibilities and rights, in the broadest sense,[216] are concerned, parenthood is simply the starting point.

4.75 The Children (Scotland) Act 1995 provides that the fact of parenthood may or may not confer automatic parental responsibilities and rights, as defined by the Act.[217] However, a host of other people may apply to the

---

213 See *T, Petitioner* 1997 SLT 724, where a homosexual adopted a child, having made it clear that he would be raising the child along with his male partner. This case is discussed more fully in chapter 8.
214 See chapter 8, paras 20–21.
215 It should be remembered, of course, that before anyone takes a 'major decision' in the course of fulfilling his or her parental responsibilities or exercising his or her parental rights, he or she is obliged to have regard to any views the child wishes to express, taking account of the child's age and maturity – Children (Scotland) Act 1995, s 6. Children of 12 years old and above are presumed to be of sufficient age and maturity to form a view although younger children will often be capable of doing so. For a full discussion of the place of the child's views in the decision-making process, see chapter 3, paras 36–39.
216 As we shall see (chapter 5, paras 7–29 and 30–39), 'parental responsibilities' and 'parental rights' are subject to reasonably broad but, none the less, specific, definition in the Children (Scotland) Act 1995, ss 1(1) and 2(1).
217 Mothers and married fathers have automatic parental rights while unmarried fathers do not. They may acquire them by concluding a parental responsibilities and rights agreement with the child's mother – 1995 Act, ss 3(1) and 4. They can, of course, apply for them – 1995 Act, s 11. See chapter 5, paras 40–67.

court, not only to ask to be given some or all of the responsibilities or rights, but to request the court to regulate the way in which parents (or others) exercise them.[218] While parenthood alone will bring with it financial responsibility for the child, non-parents can acquire similar responsibilities.[219] When we turn to consider child protection, we will see that it is not only parental conduct that is regulated.[220] How a variety of family members and third parties behave towards children is subject to considerable legal provision. Nor is it simply parents who have standing to be involved when the removal of a child from home is being considered by a state agency.[221] In short, the wider practical questions surrounding involvement in a child's life are frequently complicated. It is no surprise, then, that the legal system should apply concepts which are broader than simple parenthood in addressing these matters. When we turn, in the following chapters, to consider how the law does this, a crucial question to bear in mind is whether the legal system embraces sufficient flexibility to accommodate the diversity of cases presenting themselves. First, however, we will take a brief look at other family members and the role the law may allow them in the child's life.

THE POSITION OF OTHER FAMILY MEMBERS

4.76 The importance of other family members in the lives of individual children will depend, at least to some extent, upon the practical arrangements of the particular family. In some cases, the extended family may be very significant indeed, particularly where several generations live in the same household or spend time together. In other cases, the effects of geographic mobility, busy lives and family feuds may mean that the children have little or nothing to do with the extended family. In addition, divorce, cohabitation and remarriage mean that many children acquire *de facto* or *de jure* step-parents, step-siblings and other step-relatives. At this stage, it is important to bear in mind that the term 'parental responsibilities and rights' might be said to be something of a misnomer. Not only can these responsibilities and rights be held by persons other than parents, persons with an interest can apply to the court to have their exercise regulated.[222] Thus, the term is simply a convenient shorthand way of referring to responsibilities and rights that may be held by parents, but may

---

218 1995 Act, s 11. See chapter 5, paras 72–97.
219 While child support is payable only by parents, parents and others and, in particular, a person who has 'accepted' a child into his or her family, may be responsible for alimenting a child. See chapter 6, paras 61–66.
220 As we saw in chapter 3 (paras 3.91–3.100), there are numerous legal provisions, aimed primarily at protecting children, which can have an impact on many members of the community. In addition, the definitions of child abuse and neglect (chapter 7, paras 5–13) indicate that it is the risk to the child that is important, rather than its source.
221 The concept of the 'relevant person' is widely used in this context and includes not only parents, but persons who have parental responsibilities or rights and any person who ordinarily has charge of, or control over, the child 1995 Act, s 93(2)(b)(iii). See chapter 7, para 32.
222 Children (Scotland) Act 1995, s 11.

also be held by other people.[223] In addition, the nature of a child's biological or social relationship with certain other people may be such as to place restrictions on the kind of relationship they may have. So, for example, marriage between certain related individuals is prohibited. The position of the most frequently encountered 'others' is highlighted below. All of the issues touched upon in the following paragraphs will be examined in greater detail in later chapters. However, for the present, it is important to have a broad, general, idea of the significance of these other people.

Grandparents

4.77 It comes as a surprise to many grandparents to discover that they have no automatic parental responsibilities or rights.[224] Usually, the reality of their legal position only becomes apparent to them when a dispute arises within the family. Let us take a fairly typical example of a four-year-old granddaughter whose parents divorce amid a degree of acrimony. The girl lives with her mother and has little contact with her father, and, thus, as a practical matter, the paternal grandparents have no real opportunity to see her while she is with their son. In the course of the divorce, they were rather explicit in their support of their son and, as a result, are not on friendly terms with their former daughter-in-law. She refuses to let them see their granddaughter, although they had a good relationship with the child in the past and are convinced that she would like to spend time with them. As things stand, they have no right whatsoever to see the little girl. Aside from negotiating a mutually acceptable solution, they will have to go to a court to seek contact.[225] Not enough emphasis can be placed on the need for individuals in this position to see litigation as a last resort, since it is likely to exacerbate, rather than alleviate, any existing hostility. A better course of action would be to discuss the matter and to seek assistance, through, for example, mediation, in order to resolve the dispute.

4.78 A grandparent has no standing to oppose the adoption of a grand-child unless he or she is also the child's guardian.[226] As a general rule, grandparents no longer have an obligation to support grandchildren. Like anyone else, they can acquire the obligation by accepting the child into their family or by being enriched as a result of succession to property which belonged to a person who did owe the child an obligation of aliment.[227] Any civil or criminal responsibility that grandparents have in terms of caring for

---

223 Lord Hope made a similar observation in respect of the term 'parental rights' as it was used in the Law Reform (Parent and Child) (Scotland) Act 1986 – *F* v *F* 1991 SLT 357 at p 361.
224 See, E. E. Sutherland, *Grandparents and the Law in Scotland* (Age Concern Scotland, 1993) (new edition in preparation) for a lay person's guide to the law here.
225 Children (Scotland) Act 1995, s 11.
226 For an example of the problems that can arise as a result, see *F* v *F* 1991 SLT 357, discussed in chapter 8, para 36.
227 Family Law (Scotland) Act 1985, s 1(1)(d) and (4). As part of its wider proposals for reform of the law on succession, the Scottish Law Commission has recommended the abolition of the continuing right to aliment from a person enriched by succession – Report on Succession (Scot Law Com No 124, 1990) paras 9.4–9.5, rec 55 and draft Bill, clause 27.

a child or, for example, ensuring that the child receives education, will arise from their position as carer and not as grandparent. The relationship between grandparents and a grandchild is relevant for the purpose of the law on succession and incest and for the prohibited degrees of relationship in the context of marriage.

Brothers and sisters

4.79 Siblings have no automatic parental responsibilities or rights in respect of each other but, as we shall see, may apply to the court for an order in respect of them.[228] Where the parents have died or are otherwise incapable of discharging their functions, an older sibling might apply for a residence order in respect of younger siblings and, while this is the stuff of movies, it is fairly uncommon in practice. The fact that a parent's parental rights may have been terminated will not prevent a sibling from applying for parental responsibilities or rights.[229]

4.80 In other respects, siblings are in much the same position as grandparents in: having no automatic standing when a brother or sister is being adopted; no independent responsibility for the care of siblings; and no general obligation to aliment a sibling. The relationship between siblings is relevant for the purpose of the law on succession and incest and for the prohibited degrees of relationship in the context of marriage. No special legal relationship is created between step-siblings.

Aunts, uncles and other relatives

4.81 Aunts, uncles and other relatives are in much the same position as grandparents and brothers and sisters.

Step-parents

4.82 The simple fact of becoming a step-parent brings with it no automatic parental responsibilities or rights although a step-parent could apply to the court as a person with an interest. Many step-parents play a significant role in the lives of step-children without ever having the matter regulated.[230] Others prefer a more formal role and approximately half of all adoptions are by step-parents. The prevalence of step-parent adoption was undoubtedly a factor in a special procedure being created for such adoptions.[231] While a step-parent has no liability to pay child support, where he or she accepts a step-child into the family, a duty to pay aliment may be created.[232]

---

228 Children (Scotland) Act 1995, s 11.
229 Under the Law Reform (Parent and Child) (Scotland) Act 1986, there was some doubt on this point initially – *AB* v *M and Central Regional Council* 1988 SLT 652 and *M* v *A, B and Lothian Regional Council* 1989 SLT 426. The position was clarified in *F* v *F*, above.
230 For a fascinating discussion of her research into the experiences of step-families in Australia, see G. Ochiltree, *Children in Stepfamilies* (Prentice Hall, 1990).
231 The Children (Scotland) Act 1995, s 97 amended the Adoption (Scotland) Act 1978 to create this special procedure which is discussed in chapter 8, paras 31–32.
232 Family Law (Scotland) Act 1985, s 1(1)(d).

4.83   Certain restrictions on marriage flow from being a step-parent.[233] A person cannot marry the son, daughter or grandchild of a former spouse, unless both intending spouses have attained the age of 21, and the younger party has not at any time before attaining the age of 18 lived in the same household as the other party and been treated by the other party as a child of the family.[234] It is an offence for a step-parent or former step-parent to have sexual intercourse with a step-child or former step-child, but only in certain circumstances.[235] The step-relationship is of no significance for succession purposes and a step-parent who wants a step-child to inherit property should make provision in a will to that effect.

Parents' cohabitants

4.84   Like a step-parent, a cohabitant acquires no parental responsibilities or rights simply by virtue of moving into the home where the child lives. The cohabitant can apply to the court for responsibilities and rights but the special provisions on adoption by a step-parent do not apply to cohabitants.[236] A cohabitant can acquire the obligation to aliment a child where he or she accepts the child into his or her family.[237]

4.85   Unlike a step-parent, a former cohabitant faces no restriction on marrying the child of a former partner. Nor is a former cohabitant prohibited from having sexual relations with a partner's child, provided that the 'child' is over the age of 16.[238] It should be noted, however, that it is a separate offence for a person over the age of 16 to have sexual intercourse with a child under the age of 16 where the parties are members of the same household and the older person is in a position of trust or authority in relation to the child.[239] Being the cohabitant of a child's parent has no consequence for succession purposes and, again, making provision in a will might be considered in appropriate circumstances.

Family friends

4.86   Obviously, these people are not 'family members' at all and, in the usual course of events, they have no special legal relationship with a child.[240] However, they merit mention in passing here because of an issue which

233   Marriage (Scotland) Act 1977, s 2(1A).
234   This provision is discussed in chapter 10, para 29.
235   Criminal Law (Consolidation) (Scotland) Act 1995, s 2. The relevant circumstances are, either, that the step-child is under the age of 21 or that, prior to the age of 18, the step-child has lived in the same household as the step-parent and been treated as a child of the step-parent's family. A number of defences apply to this offence. See chapter 11, para 79.
236   The procedure under the Adoption (Scotland) Act 1978, s 15(1) (as amended by the Children (Scotland) Act 1995, s 97) is open only to a person 'who is married to' the child's parent.
237   Family Law (Scotland) Act 1985, s 1(1)(d).
238   It is an offence for any man to have sexual intercourse with a girl under the age of 16 – Criminal Law (Consolidation) (Scotland) Act 1995, s 5.
239   Criminal Law (Consolidation) (Scotland) Act 1995, s 3(1). Again, certain defences apply. See chapter 11, para 80.
240   While becoming a god-parent to a child may have religious and social significance, it has no legal consequences.

comes up with reasonable frequency in practice. Some parents, and particularly lone parents, give thought to how their child will be cared for if they should die before the child reaches adulthood. In some cases, the parent may be anxious that the child should be looked after by a valued family friend rather than by relatives or the local authority and wants to know how he or she can ensure that this will happen. The short answer is that the parent cannot 'ensure' that any such arrangement will be complied with. However, the parent can take steps to appoint the family friend as the child's guardian and to confer parental responsibilities and rights on the friend. Provided that the parent was entitled to act as the child's legal representative at the time of the parent's death, a written appointment of a person as the child's guardian is valid if it is signed by the appointing parent.[241] Should the parent die, the guardian then takes on all parental responsibilities and rights.[242] If any other person has parental responsibilities or rights at the time of the parent's death, he or she retains them.[243] The reason that a parent cannot 'ensure' that such an arrangement is given effect to is twofold. First, the court retains the power to remove or restrict the exercise of parental responsibilities and rights and to confer them on some other person.[244] Thus, for example, a grandparent might challenge the appointment of a friend and request that he or she should be given parental responsibilities or rights instead. Second, the friend appointed as guardian must accept the appointment, either expressly or impliedly, by acting as such.[245] Of course, as a matter of practice, before a parent begins to make formal provision in this respect, it is essential that he or she has discussed the matter in depth with the family friend and secured the friend's agreement.

4.87 Assuming that the parent dies and the appointment is taken up by the family friend, he or she effectively steps into the parent's shoes and acquires all parental responsibilities and rights as defined under the 1995 Act. It should be noted, however, that the child-guardian relationship is not an exact replica of the child-parent relationship. Obviously this is so in the biological and social senses, but it is also the case in the legal sense. All that the guardian acquires are parental responsibilities *in terms of the 1995 Act*. Depending on the living arrangements of parties, the guardian may be deemed to have accepted the child into his or her family and, thus, have acquired the responsibility to aliment the child.[246] The appointment of a guardian has no effect for the purposes of the law on succession or incest or the prohibited degrees of relationship in the context of marriage.

---

241 Children (Scotland) Act 1995, s 7(1)(a). The appointment of guardians is discussed more fully in chapter 6, para 9.
242 1995 Act, s 7(5).
243 1995 Act, s 7(1)(b).
244 1995 Act, s 11.
245 1995 Act, s 7(3).
246 Family Law (Scotland) Act 1985, s 1(1)(d).

CHAPTER 5

PARENTAL RESPONSIBILITIES AND RIGHTS: DEFINITIONS AND ACQUISITION

5.1 Historically, parents had always been seen by Scots law as having certain rights over, and duties towards, their children.[1] Stair[2] refers to the parental right to expect obedience and aliment (financial support) from children and the obligation on parents to aliment children. The nature of these rights and obligations developed over time. So, for example, the parental right to obedience diminished and, arguably, has now disappeared[3] and the parental right to receive aliment was abolished by statute,[4] while other parental rights and obligations were added.[5] Mothers and fathers have long since been placed on an equal footing,[6] as far as children

---

1 At common law, fathers had a primary position in respect of children born in marriage, while mothers occupied a similar, but not identical position, in respect of children born outside marriage. For a thorough review of the common law and statutory provision, prior to the Children (Scotland) Act 1995, see A. B. Wilkinson and K. McK. Norrie, *Parent and Child* (Scottish Universities Law Institute Ltd, 1993) pp 1–5, 37–45, 163–164 and 380–381; *Stair Memorial Encyclopaedia*, vol 10, paras 147–148, 1174–1175, 1229–1239 and 1259–1264. See also, Lord Fraser, *Parent and Child* (3rd edn, 1906, J. Clark (ed)), the classic work of its time in the field.
2 *Institutions*, I, v, 7–8. Stair saw these obligations as deriving from the law of nature and enacted into the civil law and we get some idea of the importance he attached to the source and content of the obligations from the following passage: 'That there are natural obligations betwixt parents and children, not proceeding from the consent of either party, or from the constitution of any human law, but from the obedience man oweth to his Maker, who hath written this law in the hearts of parents and children, as to their interests and duties, with capital letters, is evident by the common consent of all the nations of the world, how barbarous soever', at I, v, 1.
3 Notions of filial obedience do not sit well with the child's rights to participate in decision-making and to freedom of expression – UN Convention, arts 12 and 13. It is interesting to note, however, that the first ground on which a child can be referred to a children's hearing is that the child is 'beyond the control' of a parent (or someone in a similar position) – Children (Scotland) Act 1995, s 52(1)(a). Since a parent can refer his or her own child to a hearing, there might be argued to be some vestige of obedience here. However, when one remembers that the grounds of referral are simply indicators that a child might need compulsory intervention in his or her life and that the hearings system, itself, is non-punitive, the true position becomes clear. For a discussion of the children's hearings system, see chapter 9.
4 Family Law (Scotland) Act 1985, s 1(1).
5 The introduction of compulsory education has created both an obligation on parents to ensure that their children are receiving education and the right to make certain choices about how that is achieved. See chapter 6, paras 14–17.
6 The father's primary position in respect of children born in marriage was watered down gradually by statute. The Conjugal Rights (Scotland) Amendment Act 1861, s 9, began the trend by providing that, in cases of divorce or separation, the court might determine

born in marriage are concerned, although the mother's primary position in respect of children born outside marriage remains.[7] By the time the Scottish Law Commission re-examined the whole area,[8] it was clear that the law was in need of major reform. The Commission's thoughts on the matter culminated in the 'Report on Family Law'[9] which forms the foundation of the present law.

5.2 The Commission identified a number of problems with the existing law. While some parental rights were quite clear, there was considerable ambiguity about the existence, content or scope of others.[10] While parental responsibilities were, again, sometimes obvious, others were not and there was no coherent statement of them.[11] The emphasis on parental rights rather than parental responsibilities was rather dated, particularly in the light of increased awareness, both nationally and internationally, of children's rights.[12] The duration of parental responsibilities and rights, and how they should apply in practice, was in need of clarification.

5.3 What the Commission recommended should replace the, somewhat flawed, law of the time is examined in detail below. However, a brief outline of its recommendations will serve to set the scene. Throughout its discussion, the Commission considered how the issues of responsibilities and rights were dealt with in other jurisdictions[13] and it was particularly conscious of the provisions of the United Nations Convention on the Rights of the Child. Indeed, many of its recommendations echo specific provisions of the Convention. The Commission recommended that there should be a statutory statement of parental responsibilities and parental rights and that it should be clear that parental rights exist in order to enable

issues of where the child lived and financial support on the basis of what was 'just and proper'. Later statutory intervention provided that the welfare principle, as well as the wishes of both parents, should be considered – Guardianship of Infants Act 1886, s 5. Full parental equality, in disputed cases, came with the Guardianship of Infants Act 1925, s 1 and more general parental equality was articulated in the Guardianship Act 1973, s 10.

7　At common law, the father had no right to apply to have a child live with him – *Corrie* v *Adair* (1860) 22 D 897; *Sutherland* v *Taylor* (1887) 15 R 224. He could answer a claim for aliment by offering to fulfil the obligation by having the child living in his home – *Grant* v *Yuill* (1872) 10 M 511. The mother's primary position was eroded first in 1891, when statute gave the father the right to apply to the court to have the child live with him – Custody of Children Act 1891. See also, Illegitimate Children (Scotland) Act 1930, s 2. Despite the fact that the Law Reform (Parent and Child) (Scotland) Act 1986 attempted to put children on substantially the same footing, irrespective of their parents' marital status, differences remain. These differences are discussed at length below.

8　The Commission's earlier work here can be found in Family Law: Illegitimacy (Scot Law Com Consultative Memorandum No 53, 1982), Report on Illegitimacy (Scot Law Com No 82, 1984), Parental Responsibilities and Rights, Guardianship and the Administration of Children's Property (Scot Law Com Discussion Paper No 88, 1990) and Report on the Legal Capacity and Responsibility of Minors and Pupils (Scot Law Com No 110, 1987).

9　Scot Law Com No 135, 1992.

10　Report on Family Law, paras 2.15–2.25.

11　Above, para 1.1.

12　Above, para 2.14.

13　The Commission made frequent reference to the Children Act 1989, operating in England and Wales and to the Report on Guardianship and Custody (Law Com No 172, 1988) on which that Act is based.

parents to fulfil their responsibilities. It recommended that these responsibilities and rights should attach to all parents, whether married or not.[14] In addition, it anticipated that other persons, like relatives or step-parents, might apply to be given certain parental responsibilities and rights or to have their exercise by the holders regulated. Provision was also made for yet others, like babysitters or day carers, who may become involved in a child's life, either temporarily or on a part-time basis. How parental responsibilities and rights were to be exercised was clarified in the Commission's proposals. For the first time, there was comprehensive recognition of the child's right to participate in decision-making. The role of the courts and the criteria they should apply were spelt out. Essentially, what it recommended was a system which would accommodate both the traditional model of family relationships and the diverse array of other relationships found in modern families. It was intended to provide the courts, which would continue to make decisions in disputed cases, with clear guidance, while retaining the flexibility to allow for tailor-made resolution of these disputes. Consistent with its usual approach, the Commission provided not only its thinking on these matters, but made firm recommendations for reform of the law and appended a draft Bill to its Report, expressing these recommendations in statutory language.

5.4 Under the then existing legislation, the Law Reform (Parent and Child) (Scotland) Act 1986 and, indeed, earlier statutes and the common law, the most commonly litigated parental rights were custody and access. Custody was normally the right of a parent (or other person) to have a child living with him or her and to exercise general control over the child's day-to-day life,[15] although there was sometimes the need to distinguish custody from care and control or guardianship.[16] Access was the right to have some contact with the child and spanned a wide range of involvement in the child's life.[17] In some cases, it amounted to no more than the right to spend every second Saturday afternoon with the child. In other cases, it might involve the child staying with a person for longer periods and going abroad on holiday with him or her.[18] There were a host of problems associated with these concepts and the way in which they operated, not

14 It should be noted that this was one of the Commission's recommendations which was not accepted by Parliament and, consequently, is not contained in the Children (Scotland) Act 1995.

15 For a full discussion of the concept of custody at common law and under subsequent statutes, see Wilkinson and Norrie, n 1 above, pp 68–81 and 197–225 and *Stair Memorial Encyclopaedia*, vol 10, paras 1274–1292.

16 A distinction was also drawn in some cases between custody, on the one hand, and care and control, on the other. In *Robertson* v *Robertson* 1981 SLT (Notes) 7, a rather unusual case, the court granted custody of an eight-year-old girl to her father, but provided that the girl was to live with her mother for most of the week. Effectively, the court split custody and care and control.

17 For a full discussion of access at common law and under subsequent statutes, see Wilkinson and Norrie, n 1 above, pp 226–235 and *Stair Memorial Encyclopaedia*, vol 10, paras 1293–1303.

18 In *Sinclair* v *Sinclair* 1987 GWD 16–587, another fairly unusual case, the court granted custody of a seven-year-old girl to her father and access for seven consecutive days every second week to her mother. Effectively, the child lived with each parent in alternate weeks.

least that lay persons who, it must be remembered, are most often the people who live with the results of legislation, frequently misunderstood what the terms actually meant.[19] It was common, even amongst lawyers, to talk of *awards* of custody or access or of a parent *winning* or *losing* one or other. The whole vocabulary came to be identified with conflict and confrontation and the tendency was to equate disputes over where a child should live with disputes over property. This kind of legal provision did an inadequate job of reflecting the continued involvement of both parents in the lives of their children even after parental separation or divorce.[20] Many organisations and individuals who responded to the Commission's Discussion Paper on 'Parental Responsibilities and Rights, Guardianship and the Administration of Children's Property',[21] felt that a change in the terminology was needed.[22] Accordingly, the Commission effectively abolished the terms *custody* and *access* and replaced them with *residence* and *contact*.[23] The Commission was not so naive as to think that this simple change in terminology would eradicate all the acrimony associated with the old custody battles.[24] However, it is to be hoped that the new formulation of the rights, the whole tenor of the 1995 Act and, particularly, its emphasis on responsibilities rather than rights, might help to change adult thinking over a period of time.

5.5 Most of the Commission's proposals were given effect in the Children (Scotland) Act 1995 ('the 1995 Act')[25] and form the basis of the present

19 In the Report on Family Law (at para 2.28), the Commission expressed concern that some parents who had custody seemed to think that meant they had all parental rights in respect of the child to the exclusion of the other parent. It quotes one solicitor who observed that, 'the parent who has custody tends to dictate matters to an extent far beyond that which one would necessarily think is reasonable'.

20 Above, paras 2.15–2.35.

21 No 88, 1990.

22 Included in the list were, the Family Charter Campaign, Family Conciliation Scotland (now Family Mediation Scotland), the Humanist Society of Scotland, the Law Society of Scotland, the Royal Scottish Society for the Prevention of Cruelty to Children, and the Scottish Child and Family Alliance; Report on Family Law above, paras 2.28 and 2.29.

23 Many of the cases referred to in this chapter were decided under the law prior to the Children (Scotland) Act 1995 and, accordingly, deal with the concepts of custody and access. Thus, these terms, along with residence and contact, will all be mentioned. It is important to remember, however, that it is the latter terms which are appropriate in Scotland today. When cases from other jurisdictions are being referred to, the language of that jurisdiction will be used. For example, in the USA, the terms custody and visitation are the concepts employed. Reference to cases from England and Wales are easier to accommodate, since residence and contact are now the appropriate terms there.

24 Report on Family Law, para 5.6.

25 Statutory references in the remainder of this chapter are to the 1995 Act unless otherwise stated. As often happens, the Act came into force in chunks: Children (Scotland) Act 1995 (Commencement No 1) Order 1995, SI 1995 No 2787; Children (Scotland) Act 1995 (Commencement No 2 and Transitional Provisions) Order 1996, SI 1996 No 2203; Children (Scotland) Act 1995 (Commencement No 2 and Transitional Provisions) (Amendment) Order 1996, SI 1996 No 2708; Children (Scotland) Act 1995 (Commencement No 2 and Transitional Provisions) (Amendment) Order 1997, SI 1997 No 137; Children (Scotland) Act 1995 (Commencement No 3) Order 1996, SI 1996 No 3201; Children (Scotland) Act 1995 (Commencement No 3) (Amendment and Transitional Provisions) Order 1997, SI 1997 No 744.

law. Where Parliament chose to ignore the Commission, the law is arguably the worse for it.[26] The starting point, and one which is consistent with the UN Convention on the Rights of the Child ('the UN Convention'),[27] is the premise that the family setting is generally the best place for the child, although the responsibilities and rights of the various individuals are subject to the paramountcy of the child's welfare.[28] It should be noted at the outset, that, while the 1995 Act talks of *parental* responsibilities and *parental* rights, these are simply convenient shorthand terms[29] and each may be owed or held by persons other than parents. A court will only intervene where such intervention would be better than not intervening and, again, the child's welfare is regarded as paramount.[30] Throughout, there is recognition that the child has a right to express his or her views, and to have them taken into account in the light of that child's age and maturity, when decisions are being taken.[31] These are known as the overarching principles[32] and, with some exceptions which will be explored at the relevant times,[33] run throughout the 1995 Act. Such is their importance – and, indeed, they can be regarded as something of a child lawyer's mantra – that they merit repeating. They are

The welfare of the child is the paramount consideration;

The child must be given the opportunity to express his or her views and account will be taken of these views in the light of the child's age and maturity;

The court will not make any order unless to do so will be better than making no order at all.

5.6 In chapter 4 we examined how parenthood is established and we noted that individuals other than parents can become involved in a child's life in a variety of ways. In this chapter, we will explore the nature and content of parental responsibilities and rights and how individuals acquire them. It must be stressed, once again, that, while the legislation talks in terms of parental responsibilities and rights and it is often convenient to discuss examples of it in operation by reference to a 'mother' and a 'father', these responsibilities and rights can apply to non-parents. Indeed, as we shall see,

---

26 There are two main areas where the Commission's proposals were not followed. The first concerns the position of the unmarried father – see para 5.44–5.67, below. The second concerned the so-called parental right to chastise (use physical violence towards) a child – see chapter 6, paras 18–19. In each case, Scots law is found wanting when measured against the UN Convention on the Rights of the Child.
27 Article 9.
28 Section 1(1) and 11(7)(a).
29 This point was made in respect of earlier legislation – F v F 1991 SLT 357, per Lord Hope, at p 361.
30 Section 11(7)(a).
31 Sections 6 and 11(7)(b).
32 That phrase was coined by Professor Norrie in his excellent annotations to the 1995 Act – K. McK. Norrie, *Children (Scotland) Act 1995* (W. Green, 1995) at p 6.
33 Briefly, deviation from these principles is sometimes permitted where public safety requires it and such deviations occur in the context of local authority powers, court decisions on removing a child from the home and, occasionally, in the context of children's hearings. These matters are discussed fully in chapters 7 and 9.

this is one of the strengths of the 1995 Act. How disputed cases are resolved will be considered. In chapter 6 specific examples of parental responsibilities and rights will be explored and the issue of child abduction and the particular problems of international child abduction will be addressed.

PARENTAL RESPONSIBILITIES

5.7 For the first time, the 1995 Act provides a clear statement of what responsibilities parents have towards their children. Parental responsibilities exist only so far as is practicable and in the interests of the child.[34] They are

To safeguard and promote the child's health, development and welfare[35]

5.8 This requires, not only that parents should protect the child's health, welfare and development, but the use of the word 'promote' conveys the idea that they should actively foster these interests.[36] Clearly, a parent is required to meet the child's basic physical needs for housing, food and clothing. The specific reference to the child's health, including, as it must, mental health, and development, draws attention to the child's need for what might be described as 'nurturing', and emphasises the duty on parents to provide children with attention, affection and a sense of self-worth. Developmental needs of children include physical, emotional and intellectual development, and ensuring that a child receives education is discussed as one of the specific parental responsibilities.[37] Providing for the child's welfare encompasses such matters as physical and psychological welfare and includes not only issues like safety, but also the provision of adequate medical care. This raises the thorny question of parents who reject a particular course of medical treatment for religious or other reasons. We are not talking here of parents who simply do not bother to seek medical attention for a sick child. On the contrary, the cases often reveal parents who have given very considerable thought and attention to their decision.[38] Indeed, the parents may be making a decision over a matter on which the medical profession is divided. So, for example, while immunisation against a variety of potentially life-threatening (or -impairing) illnesses is generally recommended by the medical profession, it is acknowledged that immunisation itself carries with it certain risks. None the less, where the parent's particular beliefs expose the child to having his or her health put at risk,

---

34 Section 1(1). For a discussion of these qualifications, see paras 5.26 and 5.27, below.

35 Section 1(1)(a).

36 When we come to consider the duties placed on a person who is looking after a child, but who does not have parental responsibilities or rights, we will see that they are obliged to 'do what is reasonable in all the circumstances to *safeguard* the child's health, development and welfare' – s 5(1) (emphasis added). Since such a person will normally be looking after the child temporarily, and in addition to the parent, it was not felt necessary that such a person be required to *promote* health, development and welfare. See para 6.24.

37 See para 6.14–6.17.

38 For example, in *Finlayson (Applicant)* 1989 SCLR 601, the parents' refusal to allow their haemophiliac son to be treated with donated plasma was prompted by their fear that he might contract HIV from it.

respect for parental autonomy cannot be allowed to override protection of the child's health, welfare and development.[39]

5.9   Obviously, the capacity of an individual parent to meet the various obligations will depend on the parent's personal and, to some extent, financial, resources. While the legal system does not demand 'perfect parenting', and the social work term 'good enough parent' is often used in assessing how adequately a parent is fulfilling his or her responsibilities, certain minimal standards are required. However, it is worth remembering that a parent's alleged failure to meet his or her responsibilities is usually raised in one of two distinct settings. The first is in the context of a dispute between family members, and often occurs in the course of the parents' divorce. In this setting, while fundamental issues of childcare and parenting may arise,[40] the real dispute may be over differences in opinion or lifestyles.[41] Here a court has to tread the delicate path of trying to avoid imposing particular and, often class-based, preferences and securing the best option for the child's future. The second context in which a parent's abilities may be questioned is when the local authority is considering whether a child is being exposed to harm or unacceptable risk of harm.[42] Since notions of child-rearing do not exist in a vacuum, neither the courts nor social workers can be entirely free from their own individual preferences but, again, it is the impact of the particular lifestyle on the child that matters.

To provide, in a manner appropriate to the stage of development of the child – (i) direction; (ii) guidance[43]

5.10   Central to this responsibility is the distinction between 'direction', suggesting, as it does, something in the nature of parental instruction, and 'guidance', which suggests a more advisory parental role. The distinction is inexorably linked to the notion of the child's evolving capacity, a constant theme in the UN Convention.[44] The line between direction and guidance will not always be clear-cut and there is a sense in which most parents will know what is appropriate when they are confronted with a given situation. However, as we have seen so often, the law is of little relevance to happy families that are functioning well. The real significance of this parental responsibility (and corresponding right) becomes apparent when disagreement emerges over a particular issue. The disagreement might be between

---

39 See *McKechnie* v *McKechnie* (Sh Ct) 1990 SCLR (Notes) 153, where a father was denied joint custody because of the court's fear that, as a Jehovah's Witness, he would refuse to consent to the child receiving a blood transfusion. The parental responsibility to provide medical treatment is discussed in chapter 6 at para 13, below, and the impact of parental religious preference in decisions on residence and contact is discussed at para 5.122, below.

40 See for example, *Early* v *Early* 1990 SLT 221, where the fact that the children's father had two convictions for child-neglect was raised.

41 See for example, *Clayton* v *Clayton* 1995 GWD 18-1000. The case is discussed at para 5.111.

42 See chapter 7, below.

43 Section 1(1)(b).

44 See in particular, art 5.

the child and the parent, the parents themselves, or may involve a third party. It should be remembered that the parental responsibility operates only where practicable and in the child's interests and alongside the child's rights to make decisions and the rights of third parties in certain contexts. How individual disputes will be resolved will depend on the particular issue, the nature of the dispute, the parties involved and, often, the age of the child. For example, a decision about which kindergarten a child attends is one where the parents may be seen as providing direction, and, indeed, it is more accurate to describe the parents as taking the decision. When the same child reaches the age of 14 and is selecting which subjects to study at school, the parental role will often have become more one of guidance than direction and will often include advice and assistance from others, like the specialist teachers at the child's school.

5.11 In formulating this parental responsibility, the Commission noted that the Convention provided for parental direction and guidance on the matter of the child's exercise of his or her rights. It took the view that the parental role ought to be broader and include direction and guidance on matters of the child's responsibilities and more general activities and decisions.[45] Accordingly, the responsibility provided for in the 1995 Act envisages parental involvement in the whole range of rights, powers, responsibilities and restrictions which may be relevant to the child.[46]

5.12 The duration of parental responsibilities will be discussed presently, but it should be noted, at this point, that the parental responsibility to provide direction lasts until the child is 16 years old whereas the responsibility to provide guidance continues until the child is 18.[47] This creates an apparent anomaly, because the corresponding parental *right* to provide guidance lasts only until the child is 16.[48] However, when one considers that guidance, by this time, will often amount to giving advice, it becomes clear that the anomaly is probably of little importance. Essentially what it comes down to is this: the parent is placed under an obligation to offer 'good advice', but the young person is free to behave like an adult in refusing to listen to it. As we shall see, the parental obligation to provide financial support for a child, through the mechanism of aliment, can last until the 'child' reaches the age of 25.[49] Once a child is over the age of 16, a parent can offer to discharge that obligation by maintaining the child in the parent's home.[50] Refusal of such an offer, where it would be reasonable to

---

45 Report on Family Law, para 2.4.
46 For a discussion of these terms, their interaction and examples of each of them, see chapter 3.
47 Section 1(2).
48 Section 2(7).
49 Family Law (Scotland) Act 1985, s 1(5)(b). Both aliment and child support, the other mechanism by which parents can be obliged to support their children, are discussed in chapter 6. For completeness at this stage, it is worth noting that any person who has accepted the child as a member of his or her family can also be obliged to aliment the child – 1985 Act, s 1(1)(d). In addition, any person enriched by succession to the property of a person who owed an obligation of aliment can be obliged to provide aliment up to the extent that he or she was enriched – 1985 Act, s 1(4).
50 1985 Act, s 2(8) and (9).

expect acceptance, provides the parent with a defence should the child raise an action for aliment. Where the parent of a young person between the ages of 16 and 18 and, indeed, beyond that age, is supporting the young person, the opportunity for the parent to offer guidance may be a little more realistic on the basis of the well-known aphorism 'he or she who pays the piper calls the tune'.[51]

If the child is not living with the parent, to maintain personal relations and direct contact with the child on a regular basis[52]

5.13 As we have seen, one of the Commission's main recommendations was that the concept of access should be replaced by that of contact, as a parental responsibility and a parental right. Some commentators suggested that it should be the child, rather than the parent, who had the right to contact and the Commission thought that, by making the maintenance of personal relations and direct contact a parental responsibility as well as a parental right, it achieved the same end.[53] Whether or not this is so, might take us deep into the realm of jurisprudential discourse on the nature of rights themselves.[54] For our present purpose, however, it is more useful to examine what might be encompassed within this particular parental responsibility. It should be noted that the 1995 Act refers to 'personal relations' as well as direct contact. This suggests communication on an emotional and psychological level, as well as simple presence. Essentially, a parent is required, at the very least, to keep in touch with a child, on a regular basis, where they are not living in the same household. In many cases, contact will involve a great deal more, including: seeing the child on a regular basis; spending quality time with the child; attending activities in which the child is involved, like soccer matches and concerts; being involved in discussions with the child and others, like the other parent and the child's school, about the child's present progress and plans for the future; and taking holidays with the child. Not every parent will do all of these things, but it is to be hoped that more will reach this level of involvement than will confine contact to telephone calls.

5.14 Of course, in some cases, the living arrangements of the family will be such that the child and the non-resident parent live far apart or in different countries. In such cases, and depending upon the financial resources available, face-to-face contact will be restricted, if not impossible. None the less, the progress of technology can offer much to assist in contact, particularly over long distance, through e-mail, Internet conferencing and, in the near future, telephones with visual as well as audio links.[55] Sadly, these forms of communication have resource implications,

---

51 Where the payment is made after a successful court action, it is sometimes the case that the young person is not seeing the parent at all.
52 Section 1(1)(c).
53 Report on Family Law, para 2.32.
54 See chapter 3, para 1, n 3 and authorities cited therein.
55 Each of these may be more or less appropriate, depending on the age of the child. For a young child, the benefit of seeing the person to whom he or she is talking may be important, whereas, for a teenager, e-mail brings the benefits of reasonably immediate communication in a medium with which young people are increasingly familiar.

but they will often provide avenues for communication at less than the cost of an airfare. It will be remembered that parental responsibilities apply only insofar as they are practicable and in the interests of the child and, so, a failure to maintain contact will not necessarily attract criticism of a parent, where he or she is precluded by circumstances from fulfilling his or her responsibility.[56]

5.15 It is worth remembering, at this point, that it is not only parents who can have parental responsibilities. As we shall see, any person claiming interest can make applications in relation to them and, thus, other family members can acquire the responsibility (and the right) to maintain personal relations and direct contact with a child. In addition, in certain circumstances, a person who has parental responsibilities can delegate that responsibility to another person.[57] As we shall see, this may have particular application where, for example, a parent's employment precludes meaningful, regular contact. The parent can arrange for other family members to effectively take over contact in his or her absence.

To act as the child's legal representative[58]

5.16 The responsibility (and right) of a parent to act as the child's legal representative dates from the common law and found expression through the ancient mechanisms of tutory, curatory and guardianship.[59] As the Commission pointed out

> 'it was odd to define the parent's role in terms of the guardian's role, given that parenthood was the primary relationship. Guardians are substitute parents, not the other way about'.[60]

Accordingly, it concluded that there should be a specific parental responsibility to act as the child's legal representative. What that involves is further defined and there are three strands to the responsibility, each of which warrants closer examination. Fundamental to understanding the parental obligation to act as legal representative is appreciating the child's independent capacity to act on his or her own behalf. The general rule is that children acquire capacity at the age of 16.[61] However, a child below that age may enter transactions of a kind commonly entered into by a person of that age and in those circumstances.[62] There are also a number of legal acts which a child below the age of 16 is entitled to perform for himself or herself, including making a will[63] and consenting to or vetoing his or her

---

56 See para 5.26, where this point is discussed more fully.
57 Section 3(5). The opportunity for delegation, but not abdication, of parental responsibility is discussed in chapter 6, para 7.
58 Section 1(1)(d).
59 For a full discussion of tutory and curatory at common law and under subsequent statutes, see Wilkinson and Norrie, n 1 above, pp 37–52 and *Stair Memorial Encyclopaedia*, vol 10, paras 1049–1120.
60 Report on Family Law, para 2.27.
61 Age of Legal Capacity (Scotland) Act 1991, s 1(1). The rules on capacity of children are discussed fully in chapter 3, paras 59–78.
62 1991 Act, s 2(1)(a). The statutory provision has been paraphrased to render it gender-neutral.
63 1991 Act, s 2(2).

own adoption.[64] In addition, a child can instruct a solicitor, where he or she has a general understanding of what it means to do so, and a child of 12 years old or older is presumed to have such understanding.[65]

5.17 What, then, is involved in the parental responsibility to act as the child's legal representative and how does this operate in conjunction with the child's independent capacity? First, the parental role involves administering any property belonging to the child.[66] Most children have little property and when we consider amounts of relatively small value, like pocket-money and modest birthday gifts, the child's independent capacity will often come into play. It will be remembered that, while the general rule is one of incapacity for children under the age of 16, the Age of Legal Capacity (Scotland) Act 1991 allows children under that age to enter transactions of a kind commonly entered into by a person of that age and in those circumstances. This is the 'common transactions' exception, and transactions are defined very widely, to include unilateral transactions.[67] So, for example, where an 11-year-old decides to alienate property by using her pocket-money to buy a birthday gift for a friend, that may well come within the child's own capacity. Were this altruistic child to be so moved by the plight of underprivileged children as to decide to give away all of his toys, the unusual nature of this activity might put it outwith the range of the child's capacity. In any event, this might be a case for the parental responsibility of direction or guidance to come into play. As we shall see, the Scottish Law Commission recommended a number of reforms to the law on the administration of a child's property. However, it was at pains to point out that nothing in its recommendations was 'intended to prevent children or young people under the age of 16 from handling pocket money or other small sums on their own behalf'.[68]

5.18 When the Commission examined the role of parents as administrators of their children's property, it believed it was unnecessary to invoke a complex legal machinery to cover parents administering relatively small sums of money. Accordingly, where the child's parents, as legal representatives, administered property on the child's behalf, the 1995 Act empowers them to do anything that the child could have done with that property, had the child been of full age and capacity.[69] Thus, they can invest money, buy and sell property, and give it away. However, their freedom of action is subject to two limitations. First, they must 'act as a reasonable and prudent person would act' on his or her own behalf.[70] Second, they are liable to account to the child for their intromissions with the property when they cease to be legal representatives,[71] usually when the child reaches 16

---

64 1991 Act, s 2(3).
65 1991 Act, s 2(4A).
66 Section 15(5)(a).
67 1991 Act, s 9.
68 Report on Family Law, para 4.2.
69 Section 10(1)(b). The court may limit a legal representative's freedom of action under a section 11 order.
70 Section 10(1)(a).
71 Section 10(1).

years of age. In accounting for their intromissions, legal representatives incur no liability in respect of funds they have used to safeguard and promote the child's health, development and welfare.[72] Thus, where a parent uses the child's funds for the child's private education, foreign travel or, riding lessons, such use would come within the ambit of this provision.

5.19 So much for the vast majority of children of modest means. Moving on up the scale, what of the more unusual cases of children who acquire substantial property? Frequently, where substantial property or sums of money are left or given to a child, the testator or donor will have set up a trust, with trustees to administer it. However, the Scottish Law Commission found that there were a number of circumstances in which a child could become entitled to a sizeable amount of property where no trust had been set up.[73] The most common of these are: where an award of damages is made to the child; where payment is to be made by the Criminal Injuries Compensation Board (CICB);[74] and on inheritance, in certain cases. The legal system had always sought to recognise the guardian's role as administrator of the child's property at the same time as protecting the property from abuse or mismanagement by a foolish, indigent or unscrupulous guardian.[75] When it examined the existing law, the Commission found the system to be unsatisfactory in a number of respects.[76] As we have seen it favoured a minimalist approach to regulation in respect of small sums of money. However, it concluded that some protection was warranted when larger sums were involved and its recommendations were implemented in the 1995 Act.

5.20 Where property, owned by or due to a child, is held by a person other than the child's parent or guardian and, but for s 9 of the 1995 Act, it would be payable to the child's parent[77] or guardian, the holder of the property may have to take special action, depending on the value of the property involved and the capacity in which the property is being held. If the holder is an executor or trustee and the property is worth more than £20,000, he or she *must* apply to the Accountant of Court for direction as to the administration of the property.[78] If the property is worth between £5,000 and £20,000, the executor or trustee *may* seek such direction.[79] Where the holder is not a trustee or executor, but the property is worth at least £5,000, he or she *may*, seek the guidance of the Accountant of Court.[80]

---

72 Section 10(2).
73 Report on Family Law, para 4.1.
74 Insofar as payments by the CICB were concerned, the Commission felt that the safeguards built into the scheme were adequate. It noted that the *ex gratia* nature of the payments allowed considerable scope for flexibility and that the question of obtaining a good discharge did not arise – Report on Family Law, para 4.9.
75 For a discussion of the law as it was before the 1995 Act, see Wilkinson and Norrie, n 1 above pp 362–367.
76 Report on Family Law, paras 4.1–4.23.
77 Section 9 covers only the possibility of payment to a parent with parental responsibilities – s 9(1)(c).
78 Section 9(2)(a).
79 Section 9(2)(b).
80 Section 9(3).

If the parent or guardian to whom the property would be transferred has been appointed a trustee under a trust deed, no application to the Accountant of Court is necessary, presumably on the basis that the trustor had sufficient faith in the parent or guardian.[81] On receipt of an application, the Accountant of Court may do one or more of the following: apply to the court for the appointment of a judicial factor; direct that all or part of the property be transferred to him or her; direct that some or all of the property be transferred to the parent or guardian.[82] Where a sum of money becomes payable to a child in any court proceedings, the court may make such order for the payment and management of the money as it thinks fit.[83] Without restricting the court's latitude, in this respect, the 1995 Act gives the example of the court appointing a judicial factor to manage the money or ordering the money to be paid directly to the child, to the child's parent or guardian, or to the sheriff clerk or the Accountant of Court.[84] A receipt from the person to whom the court orders payment is a good discharge of the obligation to make payment.[85]

5.21 The second strand to acting as the child's representative involves consenting to any transaction where the child is incapable of so acting on his or her own behalf.[86] Here, the 1995 Act draws attention to the interaction between the representative's capacity and the child's own capacity, quite expressly. Again, the 'usual transactions' exception provides illustrations of this interaction at work. So, for example, it would be quite usual for a ten year-old to control the spending of small sums of money on sweets, comics and the like, while an older child might purchase more expensive items like CDs and jeans. The point here is that the representative function only operates so long as the child needs a representative. When the child has the capacity to take charge of his or her own property, the representative is not required in respect of that property. Obviously, there are grey areas here and, indeed, the parental obligation to offer direction and guidance may come into play. Pointing out to a ten-year-old that, 'if you spend all your pocket-money on a new outfit for Barbie, you will have nothing left to buy sweets during the week', falls into that category and is consistent not only with offering guidance, but is part of promoting the child's development, another of the parental responsibilities.

5.22 There is also the parental role in litigation. Essentially, the duty of a legal representative is to sue and defend in civil proceedings[87] on behalf of

---

81 Section 9(4).
82 Section 9(5).
83 Section 13(1).
84 Section 13(2).
85 Section 13(3).
86 Section 15(5)(b).
87 Both the 1991 and 1995 Acts deal with civil proceedings. Criminal proceedings give rise to different considerations in terms of representation. Whether the child is entitled to representation will often depend on whether the criminal proceedings involve court proceedings. Where the child is alleged to have committed an offence and the proceedings which result are confined to a children's hearing (ie where the child and the parents accept the grounds for referral) representation of the child is unusual. Indeed, in these

a person who cannot do that for himself or herself. However, the 1995 Act anticipates that some children who are quite capable of instructing a solicitor themselves will prefer, none the less, to leave the matter to their parents. It provides that, where this is the case, they may consent to be represented in the proceedings by the person who would have had the responsibility to act as their legal representative, had they lacked the legal capacity to do so.[88] When such a child will elect to leave matters to a parent rather than take care of them personally will vary from case to case, but two situations may be contrasted. Take, on the one hand, the 14-year-old who is injured when she is knocked down by a negligent driver. Arguably she has the capacity to instruct a solicitor to raise the action for damages for her. However, she would rather concentrate on her convalescence and prefers that her parents take care of the action. On the other hand, the child may be considering litigation in which the parent has a direct interest, for example, where the child was injured in an accident where the parent was driving the car in a negligent manner. In such circumstances, it is submitted that, regardless of what the child wants, it would be inappropriate for the parent to act where there is a potential conflict of interest and the appointment of a curator *ad litem* will often be the solution here. Perhaps a more common example of the parent being an inappropriate representative is where the child is raising an action in respect of parental responsibilities and rights.[89]

Other parental responsibilities

5.23 When the Scottish Law Commission was consulting on its proposals for reform, it received expressions of concern over the possibility that parental financial obligations to children over the age of 16 might be brought to an end, were the Commission's proposals to be implemented.[90] It was never the Commission's intention to change the law on aliment but the fact that concern was expressed emphasises the need to stress that many other statutory parental obligations remained in place after the 1995 Act was passed. Other parental responsibilities which may have existed under the common law were, however, to be replaced. It should be remembered that one of the problems being addressed by the reforms was the very ambiguity surrounding the nature of parental responsibilities at common law. Accordingly, the 1995 Act provides as follows

'The parental responsibilities [listed above] supersede any analogous duties imposed on a parent at common law; but this section is without prejudice to any other duty so imposed [on a parent] under or by virtue of any other provision of this Act or of any other enactment'.[91]

circumstances, it is doubtful that the proceedings of the hearing are criminal proceedings at all – see chapter 9, para 37. Where the hearing leads to court proceedings (proof of the grounds for referral or appeal) or the child is prosecuted in the ordinary criminal court, the child is entitled to legal representation.

88 Section 15(6).
89 For a discussion of this possibility, see para 5.28, below.
90 Report on Family Law, para 2.8.
91 Section 1(4).

So, for example, the obligations in respect of aliment and child support are unaltered by the 1995 Act, as are obligations in respect of education.

5.24 It is interesting to note that the Law Commission for England and Wales rejected the idea of a statutory list of parental responsibilities as being 'superficially attractive' but a 'practical impossibility', due to their changing nature over time and the need to meet varying circumstances.[92] Arguably, that conclusion is erroneous. What the 1995 Act does is to clarify what was previously rather vague, at the same time as defining parental responsibilities in a sufficiently broad manner so as to ensure that they can be applied to the varying circumstances which present themselves at a given time and, indeed, over time. The criticism of listing parental responsibilities is all the more surprising when one observes that the Children Act 1989[93] contains a checklist of factors to which the court must have particular regard when reaching a decision on parental responsibilities and that this provision results from the recommendations of the Law Commission for England and Wales.[94] As we shall see, such a checklist was rejected by the Scottish Law Commission and the 1995 Act contains the overarching principles, but no list of factors which indicate how welfare will be served. Instead, the courts in Scotland must determine welfare, as they always have, on the facts and circumstances of each case.[95]

Duration of parental responsibilities

5.25 The responsibilities in respect of promoting health, development and welfare, providing direction, maintaining contact and legal representation all cease when the 'child' is 16.[96] The responsibility to provide guidance lasts a little longer, until the 'child' is 18.[97] The Scottish Law Commission grappled with the issue of age limits and, while it acknowledged that its proposal was 'less tidy' than simply having one age limit for all of the responsibilities, it concluded that the different nature of the responsibilities justified different ages.[98] The Commission's very full discussion of the issue rewards reading in the original and only a part of it will be repeated here.

---

92 Report on Guardianship and Custody (Law Com No 172, 1988) para 2.6. Its recommendation was accepted in the Children Act 1989, s 3(1).
93 Section 1(3) and (4).
94 Report on Guardianship and Custody (Law Com No 172, 1988) paras 3.17–3.21.
95 Of course, it might be suggested that, if the Scottish Law Commission favoured a list in the case of what parental responsibilities are, it would have been more consistent if it had recommended a list of relevant factors in the context of welfare. Why such a suggestion is simplistic becomes apparent when the Commission's reasons for rejecting such a list are understood – see para 5.106.
96 Section 1(2)(a). The lower age limit applying to most of the parental responsibilities is inconsistent with the UN Convention's definition of a 'child' as 'a human being below the age of 18 years' – art 1. It might be argued that the different age limits applied in respect of different parental responsibilities can, in itself, be seen as a recognition of the idea of a child's evolving capacity embodied in arts 5 and 12. The Commission was aware of the Convention's provisions and pointed out that art 41 provides that nothing in the Convention is to affect any provisions in a state's laws which are more conducive to the realisation of the rights of the child than the provisions of the Convention.
97 Section 1(2)(b).
98 Report on Family Law, paras 2.7–2.13.

On the one hand, it gave the example of a 17-year-old living away from home and engaged in full-time education and concluded that the responsibility to provide guidance should not necessarily end at 16, bearing in mind that the responsibility will exist only 'so far as practicable' and that the parental obligation of aliment would continue.[99] On the other hand, it felt that, by the age of 16, contact had become 'more of a question of a voluntary relationship between two adults'[100] and was so closely linked to the parental right to contact as to justify the lower age limit. This reasoning has attractions and demonstrates both internal consistency of thinking in the 1995 Act[101] and external consistency with other statutes.[102]

Qualifications on parental responsibilities

5.26 All of the parental responsibilities are subject to two conditions. They exist only so far as is practicable and in the interests of the child.[103] As we shall see, while a parent may begin parenthood having all the parental responsibilities and rights automatically, these may be removed or restricted by the court. Even where divorced or separated parents each retain all of the responsibilities and rights, if the child lives with one of them most of the time, the non-resident parent's opportunity to fulfil his or her responsibilities will be restricted, in practice. To put it another way, the fact that a parent has particular responsibilities, only so far as 'practicable', should ensure the injection of common sense into the interpretation of the 1995 Act. If a parent is exploring ancient ruins in the Amazonian jungle, that parent's opportunity to maintain regular contact with the child may be restricted and a failure to fulfil the responsibility might be excused on the basis that it is not practicable. Of course, going off on such an expedition without making appropriate alternative arrangements for the care of one's child is no excuse for a failure to fulfil parental responsibilities.

5.27 That parental responsibilities can be exercised only where such exercise would be consistent with the welfare of the child is yet another example of the centrality of the welfare principle in the care of children. While welfare is inherent in the court's decision-making process, the fact that specific mention has been made in s 1 of the 1995 Act simply reinforces the fact that welfare must be considered even in the absence of any court order. Whether or not the matter has been adjudicated by a court, parents must fulfil their responsibilities having regard to the welfare principle. Take, for example, separated parents who have not approached the court for regulation of their responsibilities and whose five-year-old son lives with his mother. The little boy has decided that he does not want to have anything to do with his father and throws screaming tantrums when his

---

99 In the Commission's draft Bill, the responsibilities to safeguard and promote health and to provide direction and guidance would have continued until the child was 18 – clause 1(2)(a).
100 Report on Family Law, para 2.11.
101 Parental rights cease when a child is 16, see below.
102 For example, the Age of Legal Capacity (Scotland) Act 1991 adopts both 16 and 18 as the age limits for particular purposes.
103 Section 1(1).

father telephones or visits. Try as she might, the mother cannot persuade the child to change his mind and the child has nightmares, stops eating, and shows other signs of distress, whenever contact is attempted. In that situation it may well not be in the child's interests for the father to attempt to maintain contact for the time being.[104]

Are parental responsibilities enforceable?

5.28 The 1995 Act provides that the child, or anyone acting on the child's behalf, will have title to sue or defend in proceedings in respect of parental responsibilities.[105] In its proposals, the Commission had not recommended that parental responsibilities should be enforceable in this way and its draft Bill was criticised on the grounds that responsibilities without sanctions to support them were somewhat meaningless. Valid as that criticism was, it is to be hoped that litigation on this point will be used sparingly. It would be perfectly reasonable for a court to take account of a parent's failure to discharge responsibilities when it was considering that parent's parental rights. So, for example, where a parent, who had shown no interest in the child for some time, sought to obtain a court order for contact, the court might well look at the failure to maintain contact in the past as one of the relevant factors in considering whether to grant the order. Of course, it should be remembered that the court's decision is predicated on the child's overall welfare, any views the child wishes to express and the nature of the existing arrangement. It would not proceed on the basis of punishing the parent for past neglect where future contact would be beneficial to the child.

5.29 However, any attempt to enforce parental responsibilities against an unwilling parent seems futile. It is difficult to imagine a case where, for example, contact, ordered by a court in the face of a parent's opposition, could be in the interests of a child. That the 1995 Act, at least on the face of it, countenances something which is tantamount to specific implement of a personal relationship (a remedy not normally competent) suggests that parental responsibilities and, by implication, children's rights, are to be held in very high order indeed. Cynics might argue, of course, that it is not children's rights but parental, rather than the state's, responsibilities which are being emphasised.

PARENTAL RIGHTS

5.30 Parental rights exist in order that parents can fulfil their parental responsibilities;[106] that is their *raison d'être*. This point is important for two reasons. First, since parental rights are tied to parental responsibilities in this way, they are subject to the same qualifications. They can only be

---

104 In the longer term, the child may change his mind and, failing that, other strategies, like attempting meetings at a grandparent's home could be tried and professional help could be sought in the attempt to overcome the child's aversion to contact. Of course, it may be that the child has some good reason for not wanting to have contact with his father.
105 Section 1(3).
106 Section 2(1).

exercised so far as is practicable and in the interests of the child. Second, by emphasising the subsidiary nature of parental rights, we might go some way towards ending the view of children as the property of their parents.[107] Indeed, it would probably have been more accurate to describe what are contained in s 2 of the 1995 Act as parental *powers* rather than parental *rights*, since they are not rights in the sense in which that term is usually understood.[108] The parental rights are

To have the child living with him or her or otherwise to regulate the child's residence[109]

5.31 This is the right of residence and it replaces the old notion of custody. It should be remembered that, as with other parental responsibilities and rights, while all is well in the family, residence is not an issue and the child simply lives with the parent or parents. Where this right becomes relevant between family members[110] is when a dispute arises, usually because the parents separate or have never lived together. Often one parent will seek an order for residence as a means of restricting the other parent's right to determine it. In addition, a third party, like a grandparent, may seek a residence order as a way of restricting the rights of the parents. Normally a person seeking a residence order will be intending that the child should live with him or her. However, it should be noted that the right includes regulating the child's residence in some other way. This might include a parent's decision to send a child to boarding school. Whether a court would grant such an order where the other parent was seeking to have the child live at home and attend school as a day pupil would, of course, be determined by the overarching principles. Indications are, however, that the boarding school would have to be offering something rather special that would serve the child's interests, before it would be preferred to life in the family setting.

To control, direct or guide, in a manner appropriate to the stage of development of the child, the child's upbringing[111]

5.32 This is the corollary of the parental responsibility to provide direction and guidance to a child. However, it should be noted that the word 'control' has been added and the addition warrants explanation, not least because of the chilling connotations of the term.[112] The Commission explained its choice of words in terms of the evolving nature of the parental

---

107 The attitude, 'he or she is my child, therefore, I have the right to ...', sometimes found amongst parents, and equating children with a car, has no place in modern child law.

108 The Commission itself pointed out that the word 'rights' was being used in a loose sense – Report on Family Law, para 2.15, n 4.

109 Section 2(1)(a).

110 The issue of where a child lives also arises in the context of protective removal of a child by the local authority (see chapter 7) and supervision requirements of a children's hearing (see chapter 9).

111 Section 2(1)(b).

112 Admittedly, the term is not always used negatively. Contrast the pejorative sense conveyed by the expression 'controlling person' with the more positive sentiment of 'she felt in control'.

role, already discussed above in respect of the parental responsibility. It said

> 'In the case of a very young child 'control' would be the appropriate concept. Later there might be a constantly changing mixture of control, direction and guidance. In the case of an older child it would generally be a case of guidance'.[113]

With respect, that does not explain the addition of the word control at all. It appears to add nothing to the concept of direction. If that is so, the addition is probably of no practical significance. A distinction can certainly be drawn between a parent saying to a 14-year-old 'you have school tomorrow, so I would advise against going to a party tonight', with the same parent saying, 'you have school tomorrow, so I forbid you to go to a party tonight'. The former is clearly guidance, but is the latter direction or control?

5.33   It should be noted that, whereas the parental *responsibility* in respect of direction ended when the child reached 16 and that in respect of guidance continued for a further two years, the parental *right* to control, direct and guide ends, uniformly, on the child's 16th birthday. The same observations as were made in relation to continuing parental influence, particularly where the parent is providing financial support, apply here.

If the child is not living with the parent, to maintain personal relations and direct contact with the child on a regular basis[114]

5.34   This parental right is the mirror-image of the parental responsibility to maintain personal relations and direct contact. Essentially, the parent is being given the right to do that which he or she is obliged to do. It should be remembered that the right is also subject to the qualification that it applies only insofar as it is practicable and, perhaps more significantly, where it is in the child's interests.

To act as the child's legal representative[115]

5.35   Again, the parental right simply reflects the parental responsibility to act as the child's legal representative and is subject to the same qualifications.

Other parental rights

5.36   As we saw in respect of parental responsibilities, the intention was to replace common law provisions but to save statutory responsibilities. Much the same thing has been done in respect of parental rights by the following provision.

> 'The parental rights [listed above] supersede any analogous rights enjoyed by a parent at common law; but this section is without prejudice to any other right so

---

113 Report on Family Law, para 2.30.
114 Section 2(1)(c).
115 Section 2(1)(d).

enjoyed [by a parent] under or by virtue of any other provision of this Act or of any other enactment'.[116]

So, for example, parental rights in respect of a child's education remain.

Duration of parental rights

5.37 All of the parental rights terminate when the child reaches the age of 16.[117] While 16 is not a universal cut-off point insofar as the child-parent relationship is concerned, there is much to be said for termination of parental rights at this stage. It is entirely consistent with many other legal provisions and the general social setting for many young people. Sixteen is a landmark in terms of a young person's contractual capacity and the capacity to marry and is the time when the young person may cease full-time education and seek full-time employment. We have noted the inconsistency with the UN Convention, which defines a child as being under the age of 18.[118] However, as we have seen, young people are not abandoned upon reaching 16. The parental responsibility to provide guidance continues until the young person is 18 and the obligation to aliment can last a great deal longer. The legal system is simply recognising the evolving nature of capacity, the varying maturity of young people and the differing nature of individual families. So, for example, one young person might strike out on her own, get a job, get married and take full charge of her life, all at the age of 16. It would be absurd to suggest her parents should have any right to determine her residence or control her actions although, of course, they may be offering advice on various decisions she makes. Another 16-year-old might continue to live with his parents while he attends university and is supported by them financially. As a practical matter, they may be on hand to offer advice more often but, again, it would be inappropriate that he should be subject to another person's right to make decisions for him. Both of these examples deal with young people whose lives appear, from the skeletal facts, to be going well. However, where a young person is experiencing problems through, for example, family dysfunction or his or her own problems with drugs, the answer does not lie in continuing parental rights beyond the age of 16. It lies in better support from other sources, like guidance counsellors, social workers and health care professionals and, as we shall see in chapter 7, some of this is provided.

Qualifications on parental rights

5.38 Since parental rights exist in order to enable a person to fulfil his or her parental responsibilities, the same qualifications apply to the former as apply to the latter. That means that parental rights may only be exercised where practicable and in the interests of the child. Take, for example, divorced parents where the children live with the mother and their father has regular and successful contact. The mother remarries and she and her

116 Section 2(5).
117 Section 2(7).
118 Article 1. See discussion in chapter 3, para 13.

new husband believe that there would be greater opportunities for themselves and the children in Australia. They decide to emigrate. This will have an enormous impact on the nature of any contact that the father can have with the children. Of course, he can write, telephone and the like, and he may even be able to afford occasional visits, but he will certainly not be able to see the children on the regular basis that has been possible to date. If he opposes the children's removal from Scotland, how will a court view his right to maintain personal relations and direct contact? The appropriate course of action would be for the court to look at the whole circumstances of the case as they impact upon the children's lives, consider any views the children wish to express, and assess the necessity for a court order to change the existing arrangements. It might be that, in a particular case, the court would agree with the mother and step-father, that the opportunities offered by emigration were sufficiently great that the children's best interests would be served by taking this course, albeit the father's contact would change.[119] Hard though such a decision is on the father in our case, it correctly recognises that parental rights apply only where they are in the child's interests and, when it comes to balancing benefits to the child, a particular parental right may have to take second place to those interests.

Are parental rights enforceable?

5.39 Practitioners may be surprised that this question is asked at all, since litigation on parental rights is so commonplace. For completeness, it should be noted that the 1995 Act provides that a parent, or anyone acting on his or her behalf, shall have title to sue or defend in proceedings in respect of parental rights.[120]

WHO HAS PARENTAL RESPONSIBILITIES AND RIGHTS AUTOMATICALLY?

5.40 Parental rights are held automatically by:

The child's mother[121]

5.41 All mothers acquire parental responsibilities and rights automatically from the moment of the child's birth. In the vast majority of cases, this is a perfectly reasonable approach. It is a fair assumption that most parents will act in their child's best interests and to endow every mother with the legal attributes of parenthood, from the moment of birth, simply acknowledges that. Of course, the law could require every parent to demonstrate 'fitness for parenthood' before clothing them with the trappings, but such an approach would be unduly cumbersome and, at least arguably, would breach both the European Convention on Human Rights[122] and the UN

---

119 See *Johnson* v *Francis* 1982 SLT 285 where this was the decision the court reached in such circumstances.
120 Section 2(4).
121 Section 3(1)(a).
122 For example, art 8, dealing with privacy and family life, and art 12, dealing with the right to found a family.

Convention on the Rights of the Child.[123] As we shall see presently, not all fathers benefit from being endowed with such automatic recognition, but that in no way diminishes the reasonableness of applying it in respect of mothers. It must be remembered that, where there is concern about the child's welfare, the mother's freedom to exercise her parental responsibilities and rights may be short-lived.[124] As we saw in chapter 4, the woman who gives birth to a child is treated in law as the child's mother and no other woman is so treated.[125] Thus, even where a surrogate gives birth to a child to whom she is not biologically related at all, she will acquire parental responsibilities from the moment of the child's birth.

The child's father, but only if he has been married to the mother at the time of the child's conception or subsequently[126]

5.42 All 'married fathers' are treated in the same way as are mothers, being endowed with automatic parental responsibilities and rights from the moment of the child's birth. In this context, 'marriage' includes one which is voidable and one which is void but which the parties believed in good faith to be valid at the time it was entered into.[127] 'Unmarried fathers' are treated differently. The term 'unmarried father' is used here to denote a man who is not married to the child's mother. Of course, he may be married to someone else. In any event, these unmarried fathers acquire no automatic parental responsibilities and rights. A small concession to their position as parents is made by allowing some unmarried fathers to acquire parental responsibilities and rights more easily than can third parties, provided that the child's mother agrees, but the fundamental position remains one of discriminatory treatment. The position of unmarried fathers is discussed presently. However, one point merits mention here. Where a woman has had a child as a result of a number of techniques available to assist reproduction, it may be the case that her husband or male partner is not biologically related to the child. As we saw in chapter 4, subject to certain conditions being satisfied, he will be treated as the child's father for all purposes and no other man will be so treated.[128] Whether that man acquires automatic parental responsibilities and rights depends not on any biological link between the child and him, but on whether he is married to the mother. If he and the mother are married, he acquires all parental responsibilities and rights automatically, despite his being unrelated to the

---

123 For example, art 18, requires states to recognise that parents have the primary responsibility for the upbringing of their child and to provide appropriate support, while art 9 requires that a child and the parents should not be separated except by competent authorities subject to judicial review.

124 See for example, *A v Kennedy* 1993 SLT 1188, where the first child had died, as a result of being wilfully assaulted and mistreated at his parents' home, eight and a half years before the second child was born. The Second Division upheld the reporter's right to refer the second child to a children's hearing. For a discussion of when one child can be referred to a hearing because of something that has happened to another child, see chapter 9, para 32.

125 Human Fertilisation and Embryology Act 1990, s 27, discussed in chapter 4, para 35.

126 Section 3(1)(b).

127 Section 3(2).

128 Human Fertilisation and Embryology Act 1990, s 28, discussed in chapter 4, para 36.

child. If he and the child's mother are not married, he is treated like any other unmarried father and acquires no automatic parental responsibilities and rights.

5.43 No other persons acquire parental responsibilities or rights automatically. However, it must be remembered, that this is no more than a starting point and the position may change subsequently. As we shall see, these parental responsibilities may be restricted or removed by a court.[129] A children's hearing may make a decision that has an enormous practical impact on the exercise of parental rights by, for example, requiring that the child should live somewhere other than with the parents.[130] Where the child is adopted subsequently, the original parental responsibilities and rights come to an end and the adopters acquire them afresh.[131] In addition, a host of persons may apply to the court for an order in relation to parental responsibilities and rights.[132] Indeed, where the mother will not co-operate with him, that may be the only avenue open to the unmarried father. Let us, consider the position of this pariah and why the legal system takes a discriminatory approach to him.

THE POSITION OF THE UNMARRIED FATHER

5.44 We have seen that the unmarried father is treated differently to mothers and married fathers. In order to understand how Scots law came to be in this shameful position, we must examine the concept of illegitimacy and its history and development, before exploring how we might have approached this issue and the small concession made to unmarried fathers in the 1995 Act.

The concept of 'illegitimacy'

5.45 Were it possible simply to ignore the parts of the legal system that are offensive, this section would not appear at all. Sadly, ignoring such areas will not make them go away and, indeed, vigilance over what is wrong is essential if reform is ever to come about. While the word 'illegitimate' has a particular meaning in a legal context, there is no escaping the notion it carries of something which is somehow unacceptable or illicit.[133] No child should ever be described in such terms. None the less, the distinction between legitimate and illegitimate children is one which is rooted in our legal history. The concept was known to Roman law and was embraced in both pre- and post-Reformation Scotland. The purpose was twofold. First,

---

129 Section 11.
130 Section 70. The children's hearings system is discussed fully in chapter 9.
131 Adoption (Scotland) Act 1978, s 39. Adoption is discussed fully in chapter 8.
132 Section 11.
133 As the Scottish Law Commission noted, '[I]t was offensive for the law to use terms which suggested that some people were legitimate or lawful, and some people illegitimate or unlawful' – Report on Family Law, para 17.3.

it helped to achieve a degree of certainty and stability in family structures and, for the small number of landed families, ensured the smooth transfer of property from one generation to the next.[134] Secondly, by making illegitimacy an unattractive status, the law reinforced accepted religious and moral beliefs. Insofar as the child was disadvantaged by the status,[135] the punishment was, of course, meted out to the one person who had no control over the circumstances of his or her birth. Illegitimacy is the status accorded to 'children not begotten of parents lawfully married'.[136] Thus, a child is illegitimate if he or she is born to an unmarried woman or to a married woman, where her husband is not the child's father. At common law, where a child was born illegitimate, he or she could be legitimated if the parents married subsequently and statute continued this rule.[137] The illegitimate child was often described as a *filius nullius* (no one's child),[138] but it would be a mistake to interpret this as meaning that there was no link between the child and his or her parents. A more accurate statement of the position was provided by Lord Jeffrey, in 1844, when he said that the child's father was 'liable in the burdens of paternity without any of the privileges'.[139] At common law, both parents were obliged to aliment the child,[140] this obligation transmitting to the deceased parent's estate.[141] The mother alone had the right to custody,[142] although the father could

---

134 Of course, the 'certainty' here is premised on the assumption that a married woman's child is, in fact, also her husband's child. The assumption is false in some cases, but it was not until the advent of DNA profiling that the magnitude of such erroneous assumptions could be established. Even today, most married couples do not undergo tests in order to establish the paternity of a child.

135 While most of the effects of illegitimacy resulted in some disadvantage to the child, this was not so universally. Thus, for example, the illegitimate child was not obliged to aliment his or her parents. Until the obligation placed on legitimate children to aliment their parents was abolished by the Family Law (Scotland) Act 1985, illegitimate children were, arguably, in a better position in this respect.

136 Stair, *Institutions*, III, 3, 44.

137 Initially, legitimation *per subsequens matrimonium* (by subsequent marriage) was only possible where the parents had been free to marry at the time of the child's conception, but this restriction was subsequently removed by statute – Legitimation (Scotland) Act 1968, s 1. Scots common law also adopted another form of legitimation from Roman law – letters of legitimation – granted here by the Crown. More restricted than its Roman original which appears to have endowed full legitimacy, letters of legitimation enabled the illegitimate person to make a will. This form of legitimation became obsolete when illegitimate persons acquired full capacity to test. For a discussion of the common law rules on legitimation and their statutory successor, see Wilkinson and Norrie, n 1 above, pp 18–28 and *Stair Memorial Encyclopaedia*, vol 10, paras 1171–1173.

138 *Corrie* v *Adair* (1860) 22 D 897, per Lord Justice-Clerk Inglis, at p 900.

139 *Weepers* v *Heritors and Kirk-Session of Kennoway* (1844) 6 D 1166, at p 1173.

140 Erskine, *Institute*, I, 6, 56; Bankton, *Institute*, I, 5, 64.

141 For a time, this had the (probably unintended) consequence that, where a parent died, an illegitimate child was placed in a more favourable position than was the legitimate child, since the latter's rights of succession were postponed until the former's right to aliment had been met – *Beaton* v *Beaton's Trustees* 1935 SC 187. It was not until 1968 that this anomaly was corrected by statute – Law Reform (Miscellaneous Provisions) (Scotland) Act 1968, s 4. Initially, the alimentary obligation was potentially lifelong. From 1930, the illegitimate child's claim to aliment ceased when the child reached 21 years old – Illegitimate Children (Scotland) Act 1930, s 1.

142 *Weepers* v *Heritors and Kirk-Session of Kennoway*, above.

meet a claim for aliment by offering to support the child in the father's home.[143] Initially, the illegitimate child was subject to a host of public disabilities and, for example, could not hold office in the pre-Reformation church,[144] could not hold judicial office[145] and could not make a will.[146]

5.46 Early law reform in this area was very much a piecemeal process, with individual statutes being directed at specific issues. In 1836, illegitimate persons were empowered to make a will determining the succession to their movable property[147] and, in 1926, a limited right of succession was created between the mother and the illegitimate child.[148] In 1940, illegitimate persons were accorded equal status with legitimate persons for the purpose of recovering damages and *solatium* for the death of a parent[149] and, in 1962, the child's parent acquired a similar right to damages in respect of the child's death.[150] In 1968, the law of succession was altered to create substantial equality regardless of the illegitimate link, at least within the child-parent relationship.[151] None the less, differences remained despite a growing movement favouring the abolition of illegitimacy as a status. By the 1970s, substantially more children were being born outside marriage and the social climate was changing. The following plea from a leading academic at the time, encapsulates the nature of the problem

'Imagine a city the size of Aberdeen, and you have some idea of the extent of the problem. If the citizens of Aberdeen were subjected to special discriminatory laws ... there would be an outcry and immediate reform'.[152]

5.47 By the early 1980s, the Scottish Law Commission had turned its attention to the issue. It produced a Consultative Memorandum in 1982[153] and, in the light of the responses it received, published its 'Report on Illegitimacy,'[154] containing detailed proposals for reform of the law and

143 The father's right here derives from the notion of his discharging the alimentary obligation in the least burdensome way – *Corrie* v *Adair*, n 138 above, per Lord Justice-Clerk Inglis, at p 900. The option was only open to the father once the child reached a particular age, which Lord Cowan believed to be seven years old, in the case of a boy, and ten, in the case of a girl – *Corrie* v *Adair*, above, at p 901. The age of seven was certainly consistent with the older distinction drawn between infancy (which lasted until the child reached seven) and pupillarity, the former being the time during which a widow could determine the residence of a legitimate child before the child's tutor acquired the right to make this decision – Craig, *Jus feudale*, 2, 20, 14.
144 Fraser, *Parent and Child*, (3rd edn) at p 51.
145 Hope, *Major Practicks*, IV, 8, 9 (Stair Society, 1937, vol 3, p 320).
146 Thus, unless the illegitimate person was survived by a spouse or children, property fell to the Crown as *ultimus haeres*. The Crown could waive its right by granting letters of legitimation. Statute first intervened in 1836 to allow an illegitimate person limited capacity to test – Bastards (Scotland) Act 1836.
147 Bastards (Scotland) Act 1836.
148 Legitimacy Act 1926, s 9.
149 Law Reform (Miscellaneous Provisions) (Scotland) Act 1940, s 2.
150 Law Reform (Damages and Solatium) (Scotland) Act 1962, s 2.
151 Law Reform (Miscellaneous Provisions) (Scotland) Act 1968, ss 1–6. That Act did not create complete equality and, for example, the illegitimate child was given no right of representation.
152 E. M. Clive, 'Legal Aspects of Illegitimacy in Scotland' 1979 SLT (News) 233, at p 233.
153 Family Law: Illegitimacy (Consultative Memorandum No 53, 1982).
154 Scot Law Com No 82, 1984.

draft legislation. It is a tribute to the coherence and good sense of its proposals that they prompted the Law Commission for England and Wales to reconsider its own proposals for law reform there.[155] Legislation followed in Scotland, setting the scene for substantial equality between children, irrespective of their parents' marital status.[156] However, the legislation did not create equality in terms of the position of parents, nor did it abolish the status of illegitimacy. Thus, vestiges of the distinction between legitimate and illegitimate children lingered on.

5.48 The Scottish Law Commission returned to the matter in its 'Report on Family Law'[157] in 1992. It believed that

> '[i]f the advantages of a codification of family law are to be fully realised, unnecessary and anachronistic concepts will have to be eliminated. Legitimacy, illegitimacy and legitimation now fall into this category. ... The separate status of illegitimacy is not only unnecessary but is also considered by many to be offensive. ... In the new Scottish family law children should just be children, and people should just be people, whether their parents were married to each other or not'.[158]

The Commission favoured the complete abolition of any distinction between children dependent upon their parents' marital status.[159] Sadly, Parliament did not.

5.49 In its initial form, the Children (Scotland) Bill would have amended the existing legal provision with the aim of 'completing the task' of abolishing the status of illegitimacy. When the Bill was progressing through Parliament, this proposed improvement was sabotaged, in part, by that ill-defined battle-cry 'family values' and, in part, by opponents raising the spectre of the child born as a result of incest or rape. We shall see presently why this latter concern should never have prevailed as it did. In any event, it is worth noting that the distinction between legitimate and illegitimate children remains important for the following purposes

the denial of automatic parental rights to certain unmarried fathers;[160]

the parent's right to appoint a guardian for the child in certain circumstances;[161]

---

155 Second Report on Illegitimacy (Law Com No 157, 1986).
156 The Law Reform (Parent and Child) (Scotland) Act 1986, s 1(1), provided, 'The fact that a person's parents are not or have not been married to one another shall be left out of account in establishing the legal relationship between the person and any other person; and accordingly any such relationship shall have effect as if the parents were or had been, married to one another'. The Act provided for exceptions to that general rule, see s 9.
157 Paras 17.1–17.15.
158 At para 17.4.
159 Report on Family Law, rec 88.
160 Section 3(1).
161 Only a person who is entitled to act as the child's legal representative can appoint a person to be the child's guardian in the event of the parent's death – s 7(1). Thus, until the unmarried father acquires the capacity to act as the child's legal representative, assuming he ever does, he cannot appoint a guardian to act in his stead.

the domicile of a child;[162]

the transmission of titles, coats of arms, honours or dignities;[163]

legitim or succession to the estate of person dying before commencement of the 1986 Act.[164]

Objections to the continued discrimination

5.50 Not only did the Scottish Law Commission recommend that the status of illegitimacy should be abolished, it addressed the role of parents and parental responsibilities and rights quite explicitly and concluded that unmarried fathers should be put in the same position as mothers and married fathers.[165] It considered that to deny parental responsibilities and rights to a father solely on the criterion of marital status was objectionable on a number of grounds. It failed to recognise the widespread existence of stable cohabitation; in emphasising the casual liaison, it placed undue importance on the circumstances of conception; and it denied the child the opportunity to have two automatic guardians. A point rarely made, but valid, none the less, is that being married to the child's mother is not a matter wholly within the control of the father. Unmarried fathers are often presented in the media as feckless creatures who are failing to face up to their responsibilities by 'doing the decent thing' – that is, marrying. Even assuming that the man does want to marry the woman in question, she may not want to marry him. In any event, the imminent arrival of a child is not, in itself, a good reason for marriage, nor does it guarantee any better future, overall, to the child or the parents. A recent worldwide survey[166] of the number of children born to young women between 15 and 19 years old found that 87% of children born to such women in the UK were born outside marriage. For each of these young women having a child outside marriage, there is an unmarried father. Aside from the 15-year-olds, who

---

162 Law Reform (Parent and Child) (Scotland) Act 1986, s 9(1)(a). A child born to married parents takes his or her domicile of origin from the father, whereas a child born to unmarried parents takes his or her domicile of origin from the mother. Increasingly, the concept of domicile is giving way to that of habitual residence. See for example, the Convention on Jurisdiction, Applicable Law, Recognition, Enforcement and Co-operation in respect of Parental Responsibility and Measures for Protection of Children, signed on 19 October 1996 at the Hague.

163 Law Reform (Parent and Child) (Scotland) Act 1986, s 9(1)(c). A similar provision applies in respect of children born as a result of assisted reproduction and is one of the few exceptions to such a child being treated as a person's child 'for all purposes' – Human Fertilisation and Embryology Act 1990, s 29.

164 Law Reform (Parent and Child) (Scotland) Act 1986, s 9(1)(d).

165 Report on Family Law, paras 2.36–2.50.

166 Into a New World: Young Women's Sexual and Reproductive Lives (International Planned Parenthood Federation, 1998). This compared with 62% in the USA and 10% in Japan. During the 1980s, in the USA, there was concern over the high proportion of young African-American women having children outside marriage. Between 1990 and 1996 the birthrate amongst African-American women aged between 15 and 17 fell by 20%. Why this has happened remains a matter for speculation, but it has been suggested that increased emphasis on educational opportunities and awareness of the dangers of HIV, rather than welfare changes, may provide the answer.

cannot marry in Scotland,[167] should the legal system really be attempting to drive them into marriage? As we shall see, youth at the time of marriage is one of the factors which increases the likelihood of divorce.[168] Even if the present discriminatory law were to have the effect of encouraging marriage – and it does not appear to do so – it would simply be storing up a different problem for the future.

5.51 Against this principle of giving automatic parental rights to unmarried fathers, it can be argued that it would leave many women open to harassment by the child's father, would offend many single mothers who are coping alone, and would create difficulties, particularly where the father reappeared having been out of touch for a period of time. None of these problems is unique to women who have never been married to their child's father. They are problems which are inherent in family dysfunction and it is the task of the legal system to deal with them. The spectre of the child resulting from rape or incest was also cited as a reason not to give the unmarried father the same status as other parents. Undoubtedly, such cases present special difficulties, but they account for a tiny proportion of children born to unmarried parents. It makes no sense to draft laws focused on the exceptional cases, while ignoring the more usual cases. A further point seems to have been missed in respect of children who result from an incestuous relationship. While in some cases, the way in which incest occurred amounted to abuse of the woman, this is not so universally. Some women are willing participants in incest and the legal system does not deny them automatic parental responsibilities and rights. Clearly, no rape victim should be put in the position of having to deal with the rapist through future contact. That is a separate issue to whether their child should have contact with the father.[169] It can be argued that contact with such a father would not be in the child's interests and, indeed, addressing the circumstances of his or her conception with the child poses special and very delicate problems. The fact that a man has been convicted of rape does not result in automatic termination of his parental responsibilities and rights in respect of his other children. It might be possible, in appropriate cases, to arrange for contact between the child and the father without involving the mother. For the present writer, this is one of those occasions where logic and intellectual coherence do not accord with instinct. None the less, the point remains that such exceptional cases are precisely that – exceptional. For the vast majority of other cases involving unmarried fathers, it must be remembered that such considerations do not apply. A more general point should be emphasised here. Since parental responsibilities are explicitly stated to apply only where they are in the interests of the child, and parental rights are subsidiary to responsibilities, cases of unworthy fathers (and unworthy mothers) could be accommodated.

5.52 Quite apart from what might be described as social arguments, the present legal provision in Scotland is in flagrant breach of our international

---

167 Marriage (Scotland) Act 1977, s 1.
168 See chapter 13, para 21.
169 The Commission's measured consideration of the matter rewards reading; Report on Family Law, para 2.47.

obligations. The United Nations Convention on the Rights of the Child is quite explicit in outlawing discrimination founded on *the child and the parent's sex, birth,* or *other status.*[170] The present position of Scots law manages discrimination on three levels. It denies the child born outside marriage two automatic legal guardians on the basis of the child's birth status, the parents' marital status and, in the latter case, only in respect of the father. Arguably, there is also a breach of art 18 which requires 'recognition of the principle that both parents have common responsibilities for the upbringing and development of the child'.

Parental Responsibilities and Rights Agreements

5.53 Despite the considered views of the Scottish Law Commission, unmarried fathers were not accorded equal responsibilities and rights by the 1995 Act. As a small concession to the many responsible men who find themselves in this position, a new procedure has been introduced by s 4 of the 1995 Act to enable an unmarried father to acquire parental responsibilities and rights. This provision recognises the special position of the child's father, since he is the only person with whom the mother can reach this kind of agreement. It is not available, for example, to other relatives or step-parents.[171] It should be noted, at the outset, that this provision was not part of the Scottish Law Commission's recommendations, since these recommendations would have rendered it unnecessary. As we shall see, there are various aspects of s 4 which are curious, if not inexplicable. With all due respect to the draftsperson, who had to produce a legislative provision while the Bill was going through Parliament, it may be that the section would have benefited from more considered reflection. The Scottish Office has produced a user-friendly booklet, detailing the nature of the agreements, how people go about making them, and a copy of the form to be completed.[172] What, then, are the detailed requirements of such agreements?

Both the mother and the father of the child must agree

5.54 Central to the unmarried father's acquisition of parental responsibilities and rights is the agreement of both parents. If the mother does not wish him to have these responsibilities and rights, that is an end of the matter in so far as an agreement is concerned. Under adoption legislation, there is provision for dispensing with the mother's agreement where, for example, it is being withheld unreasonably.[173] There is no parallel here, so the mother is free to agree or not as she chooses. It is interesting that the opportunity was not taken to provide, as, again, is provided in the adoption

---

170 Article 2.
171 As we shall see, it is possible for a person with parental responsibilities or rights to arrange for them to be carried out by another person, but this does not absolve the original holder if there is a failure to fulfil any responsibility – s 3(4)and (5), discussed in chapter 6, para 7.
172 Copies of the booklet can be obtained from Citizens Advice Bureaux, Registrars' Offices and the Scottish Office Home Department.
173 Adoption (Scotland) Act 1978, ss 16(2)(b) and 18(1)(b).

legislation, that the mother's agreement is ineffective if given less than six weeks after the birth of the child.[174] On the other hand, the mother cannot foist parental responsibilities and rights on an unwilling father, since he too must agree.[175] No other person can consent in the mother's stead and so, in the unusual case of a mother dying before an agreement can be registered, the unmarried father will not be able to use this special procedure.[176]

5.55 In many cases, the opportunity for parents to agree that both of them shall have parental responsibilities and rights will simply allow the law to reflect the practical reality of their lives, without the need to go to court. So, for example, where both parents are living together with the child, such agreements may be particularly appropriate. However, the provision applies equally to parents who are not or, indeed, never have, lived with each other. Despite the fact that much has been made here of the injustice inherent in the way the law treats unmarried fathers, it is the case that some mothers should be careful about agreeing to the child's father having parental responsibilities and rights. Where the mother has real concerns about how the father will behave in the future, it makes no sense for her to weaken her legal position and, thus, her ability to protect her child from whatever she may fear could happen. Since the form for recording the agreement comes in the package explaining what is involved, it is fairly simple for individuals to complete the whole process by themselves. The folder produced by the Scottish Office does explain that individuals should seek advice from a Citizens Advice Bureau, a law centre or a solicitor, but the ease with which the whole process could be completed leaves it open to exploitation. As with any agreement, it would be open to challenge on such grounds as duress or force and fear. As we shall see presently, revoking the agreement requires going to court and, given the novelty of the provision, how willing the courts will be to revoke these agreements is a matter for speculation.

5.56 Nothing is said in s 4 of the 1995 Act about the possibility of conditional arrangements. Can the mother make her agreement conditional on the father doing, or not doing, something? Two examples illustrate the point here. In terms of a positive condition, a mother might be prepared to agree to the father having parental responsibilities and rights as a way to secure his agreement to pay for private day care and, later, private education for the child in addition to his general child support and alimentary obligations. Particularly where the couple are not living together, the mother might want to provide that, while the father will

---

174 Adoption (Scotland) Act 1978, ss 16(4) and 18(4). The six weeks are intended to give the mother time to reflect upon her decision and to avoid her making such an important decision at a time when she might be particularly vulnerable.
175 Of course, the mother can seek to establish the father's paternity in court, regardless of his wishes – see chapter 4, para 14, above – and paternity alone will render him liable to contribute to the child's financial support – see chapter 6, paras 29–80, below.
176 See the facts of *Docherty* v *McGlynn* 1985 SLT 237, where a dispute about paternity arose between the widower and the former cohabitant of a woman who had died shortly after the birth of the child. Where the mother is incapable of giving consent due, for example, to mental illness, the father will again have to seek parental responsibilities and rights from the court.

receive the whole package of responsibilities and rights, he agrees that the child will live with the mother and residence will be a matter for her to determine. Can she impose a negative condition, that the father will not exercise his responsibility or right in respect of residence? The agreement must be in the prescribed form and that form makes no provision for conditions to be attached to consent. Thus, it appears that conditions cannot form part of the agreement that is registered. However, it would be possible to record any conditions in a separate agreement. What force would they have? It is submitted that their enforceability depends on the nature of the condition. If the condition relates to simple payment of money, it may enforceable.[177] If it relates to action (or non-action) in respect of the child, the court will be bound to look to the overarching principles in determining whether to enforce it. Of course, as a practical matter, it is always easier to enforce a condition if it can be complied with before the corresponding consent is given. In the unusual case of a woman seeking to secure her child's financial future she could always require the father, if he was sufficiently affluent, to make the financial arrangements, for example, through a trust, before she gives her consent to his acquisition of parental responsibilities and rights.

The mother, herself, must have full parental responsibilities and rights

5.57 The mother can only consent to the father's acquisition of parental responsibilities and rights if she herself has not been deprived of any of them. The court may make an order restricting or removing a person's parental responsibilities or rights.[178] Where this has been done in respect of the child's mother, she is no longer in a position to agree to the child's father acquiring any responsibilities or rights at all. It should be noted that her capacity to consent is only affected where she has been deprived of some or all of her responsibilities or rights. The fact that her opportunity to exercise them has been restricted by, for example, a supervision order from a children's hearing, does not so deprive her and so she can reach agreement with the child's father in such circumstances.[179] In one respect, this makes sense. Let us suppose that the mother's right to have the child living with her has been removed and she is limited to contact. It would be absurd if she could confer on the father something she does not have herself. On the other hand, the mother may have been deprived of some of her parental rights for reasons wholly unconnected with the father. None the less, he will have to go to court if he is to acquire responsibilities and rights in such circumstances. In addition, it might be asked why the mother cannot agree to the father acquiring whatever responsibilities she still has?

---

177 Of course, the court might refuse to enforce a separate agreement because it regarded it as unconscionable or contrary to public policy. Where, for example, the mother required the father to pay her £1 million, in return for her consent to agreeing to his having parental responsibilities and rights, such an argument might be made.

178 1995 Act, ss 11 and 86; Adoption (Scotland) Act 1978.

179 For a full discussion of the children's hearings system, see chapter 9. Where a child is subject to a supervision order, the father's opportunity to exercise his responsibilities and rights would, of course, be restricted by the order insofar as they were inconsistent with it.

The reason appears to lie in internal consistency within the provision. As we shall see presently, what the father can acquire by virtue of an agreement is very much 'all or nothing'.

5.58 One aspect of the provision is unclear. The 1995 Act gives the mother the opportunity to agree to the father's acquisition of parental responsibilities and rights where she 'has not been deprived' of any of her responsibilities or rights. If a mother has been deprived of a parental right at one time, but has regained it and now has what we might call 'the full set' of responsibilities and rights, is she then in a position to give valid consent? On a literal interpretation of the provision, it appears not. Despite her current standing, she has been deprived of a parental right at one time and so can never again consent. If this is, indeed, the correct interpretation, why Parliament should have wanted to take this extreme position is not clear. Would this incapacity apply if the removal of the parental right was only ever on an interim basis?

Which fathers can benefit?

5.59 Answering the question 'which fathers' can be a party to such an agreement, requires looking at two separate issues. The first relates to the meaning of the word 'father' in this context. Part I of the 1995 Act defines 'parent' as meaning genetic parent[180] and so, in most cases, agreement will be competent only with the child's biological father. However, that definition itself is subject to the provisions of the Adoption (Scotland) Act 1978 and the Human Fertilisation and Embryology Act 1990, dealing with who is treated as a parent. As we shall see,[181] the only couples who can adopt a child are married couples, so the issue of parental responsibilities and rights agreements does not arise for them, since, as the adopters, they each acquire the full range of responsibilities and rights on adoption. A single person can adopt, but a single woman cannot endow her partner with parental responsibilities and rights by an agreement, because her partner will not be the child's father.[182] Turning to assisted reproduction, the only case where a parental responsibilities and rights agreement would be relevant is where a single woman has given birth to the child and she has been treated along with her male partner in the course of treatment services being provided to her.[183] As we saw in chapter 4, her male partner will be treated as the child's father and thus, is eligible to participate in a parental responsibilities and rights agreement.[184] Where the woman's male partner has not been treated along with her or, indeed, where the woman's partner is female, parental responsibilities and rights agreements have no

180 Section 15(1).
181 Who may adopt a child is discussed in chapter 9, paras 26–34.
182 Of course, it is within the bounds of possibility that a woman might adopt a child where her partner was, in fact, the child's father. In such very unusual circumstances, the effect of the adoption order would be that the biological father was no longer regarded as a parent in legal terms and, thus, no agreement would be possible – 1978 Act, s 39(1)(c).
183 1990 Act, s 28(3).
184 See chapter 4, para 37 for a full discussion of this provision.

application and the partners, like the partners of single adopters would have to apply to the court for responsibilities and rights.

5.60 The second issue to consider in the context of 'which fathers' are eligible to conclude an agreement with the child's mother is the requirement, contained in s 4 itself, that he 'has no parental responsibilities or parental rights' already.[185] Again, this is a curious provision. Let us assume that the unmarried parents were not on good terms at the time of the child's birth. No agreement was possible because the mother would not agree and the father had no option but to seek contact by applying to the court. At a later stage, contact has been working well, the parents are getting on much better and are co-operating over matters concerning the child. Why Parliament thought they should not be able to conclude an agreement then is not at all clear. Let us take the scenario one step further. Suppose the parents resume their relationship and, ultimately, live together with the child. Since the father already has the limited parental responsibility and right of contact, the parents cannot reach agreement that he should have 'the full set'. Of course, any fresh application by him to the court for an order granting him the whole range of parental responsibilities and rights would presumably not be opposed by the child's mother, but quite why they should be put to the trouble and expense of the very kind of application which s 4 sought to avoid is something of a mystery.

Irrespective of the age of the parents

5.61 Section 4 provides that the parents may reach agreement 'whatever age they may be'. This is to ensure that, where either or both of them is under the age of 16, the courts do not have to adjudicate whether such an agreement falls within the 'usual transactions' exception to the general incapacity of persons under 16 provided for in the Age of Legal Capacity (Scotland) Act 1991.[186] Once a person under the age of 16 has parental responsibilities and rights, nothing in the 1991 Act prevents that person from fulfilling or exercising them.[187]

Agreement on partial responsibilities or rights not an option

5.62 A parental responsibilities and rights agreement is an 'all or nothing' proposition. The parents must agree to the father having all the responsibilities and rights. It is not possible for them to agree that the father should have some of the responsibilities and rights, even if a more limited agreement would reflect how the parents envisage the arrangement working in practice. Suppose, for example, that the parents anticipate that the father will have regular contact with the child, but that the mother will fulfil all other parental responsibilities. An agreement on contact might be enough to meet the circumstances of the case. Why should they have to agree to sharing 'the full set'? To some extent, this provision is consistent with seeing both parents as important in the child's life. Certainly, by giving

185 Section 4(1).
186 1991 Act, ss 1(1)(a) and 2(1), discussed in chapter 3, paras 61–62.
187 1991 Act, s 1(3)(g).

full responsibilities and rights to the father, he is put on an equal footing with other parents and, were the mother to die, the child would have a fully-empowered guardian in place. However, one wonders whether some mothers, who would have agreed to the father having limited parental responsibilities and rights, will not baulk at extending equal parental status to him. In such cases, either the parties can agree contact or the father can apply to the court.

The agreement must be in a form prescribed by the Secretary of State for Scotland

5.63 The Secretary of State has made regulations[188] prescribing the form of words to be used for such agreements and the Scottish Office package contains a copy of the very simple form and instructions to the parties on how to complete it.

The agreement must be registered in the Books of Council and Session while the mother still has the responsibilities and rights which she had at the time the agreement was made

5.64 The agreement must be registered in the Books of Council and Session[189] and the father acquires responsibilities and rights from the date of such registration.[190] It should be noted that the mother must still have full responsibilities and rights by this stage.[191] If any of them have been removed after the agreement was made but before registration, she cannot agree to the child's father acquiring any of them. Where a mother is aware of plans by, for example, the local authority, to apply to the court for removal of any of her parental rights, it appears that, provided she moves quickly enough and both makes and registers the agreement prior to such removal, she can endow the father with responsibilities and rights.

Irrevocability?

5.65 Such agreements, once made, are stated to be 'irrevocable' although, as is always the case with parental responsibilities and rights, the court retains its jurisdiction on the matter.[192] Thus, a father who has acquired parental responsibilities and rights by agreement with the mother can have those rights restricted or removed by the court just as this can happen to any other person who has parental responsibilities or rights. However, where the court makes an order in relation to parental responsibilities and rights, those which a father has by agreement are only removed or restricted to the extent necessary to comply with the court's order.[193] In addition, the court may revoke the parental responsibilities and rights

---

188 Parental Responsibilities and Parental Rights Agreement (Scotland) Regulations 1996, SI 1996 No 2549.
189 Section 4(2)(b).
190 Section 4(1) and (3).
191 Section 4(2)(b).
192 Section 4(4). In England see, for example, *Re P (terminating parental responsibility)* [1995] 1 FLR 1048.
193 Section 11(11).

agreement itself.[194] Thus, such an agreement is anything but irrevocable, albeit the parties to it cannot revoke it at will.

5.66 If the experience of a similar provision[195] in England and Wales is anything to go by, it is likely that comparatively little use will be made of this small concession to unmarried fathers.[196] In Scotland, in 1997, while 22,388 children were born to unmarried parents,[197] only 191 agreements were registered.[198] It should be remembered that, during the first years that such agreements are possible, a number of them will relate to older children whose parents are simply taking advantage of this new opportunity. Since it became possible to register agreements on 1 November 1996, there has been a steady increase in their use and it is anticipated that the number of agreements registered in 1998 will exceed that for 1997. None the less, when compared with the number of children born to unmarried parents, the number of agreements registered is very small indeed. Of course, many parents will have no idea that such agreements are possible, despite efforts made to publicise them. In addition, even where they are aware of the possibility, many people do not take steps to organise their respective responsibilities and rights in relation to children until disputes arise and that is precisely the stage at which the mother is least likely to agree to sharing responsibilities and rights. Simple inertia is likely to be the greatest obstacle to full use being made of such agreements, but maternal opposition will play its part. In the absence of agreement from the mother, it remains open to the unmarried father to apply to the court.[199]

Does it matter whether unmarried fathers have parental responsibilities or rights?

5.67 As is so often the case, in practice, it is of little importance whether an unmarried father has parental responsibilities or rights while relationships are going well. If he is living happily with the child and the child's mother, they probably function as any other happy family, blissfully unaware of the legal system and the way they are being treated by it. If the parents are not living together, they may well have worked out an amicable arrangement over their respective roles in the child's life. It is only when a dispute arises that the reality of the father's legal relationship with the child becomes apparent and significant. Where the father has no parental

---

194 Section 11(11).
195 Children Act 1989, s 4.
196 After initial enthusiasm in 1992 (4,422 agreements registered), 1993 (5,506) and 1994 (5,369), the number of agreements registered fell in 1995 (3,323) and 1996 (3,367), although agreements appear to have recovered popularity in 1997 (4,126). I am grateful to The Information, Management and Analysis Group, The Court Service, for providing this information.
197 Registrar General for Scotland, Annual Report 1997 (Registrar General for Scotland, 1998), Table 3.2. Some 81% of these births were registered by the parents jointly and, of the joint registrations, 70% of the parents registered themselves as living at the same address – Table 3.2 and p 32.
198 I am grateful to the staff at the Books of Council and Session, Registers of Scotland, for providing this information and for discussing the trend in the use of agreements.
199 Section 11.

responsibilities or rights, the mother can prevent him from having anything to do with the child. She can make arrangements for the child's care without consulting him.[200] If he takes the child away, he may be convicted of the ancient common law offence of plagium (child stealing).[201] Unless he has charge of the child, he is not a 'relevant person' for the various public law powers relating to child protection,[202] although he is accorded a measure of recognition within the children's hearings system if he is living with the child's mother.[203] If the child's mother dies, she may have appointed a guardian to take care of the child in her stead. That person then steps into her shoes and the father still has no special position.[204] If the mother has made no such arrangement, the father may find himself in dispute with other relatives over the child's future care.[205] In short, there are many reasons why a father who cannot reach agreement with the mother over parental responsibilities or rights will want to apply to the court.

THE ROLE OF THE COURT

5.68 As we have seen, a narrow range of people acquire parental responsibilities and parental rights automatically or by agreement. Family

200 In a case in 1997 which received only press coverage, a mother handed her child over to an unrelated couple in a private fostering arrangement, without informing the child's father. Provided the local authority had been notified and the couple had been approved, this was all quite legal.

201 See *Downie* v *HM Advocate* 1984 SCCR 365, a case prior to the 1995 Act, but relevant, none the less. There, an unmarried father who had no parental rights took his one-year-old daughter away from the child's mother in a public street. His claim that the charge of *plagium* (child stealing) was incompetent, because he was the child's father and had acted out of concern for her welfare, did nothing to prevent his conviction. This case is in stark contrast to the decision in the highly unusual case *Sherwin* v *Trumayne* 1992 GWD 29–1683. There, the father had abducted his young son despite the fact that the Irish court had awarded custody to the mother. Having cared for the child for over a year, he succeeded in obtaining custody in a Scottish court. Normally, the courts here will not consider the merits of a case of this kind where a competent foreign court has decided the matter. International child abduction is considered in chapter 6, paras 81–100.

202 Section 93(2)(b). For a full discussion of the term 'relevant person' see chapter 7, para 72.

203 This recognition is achieved through the Children's Hearings (Scotland) Rules 1996, SI 1996 No 3261, rather than the 1995 Act, which accord him the right to receive copies of all the same documents as a relevant person does and to attend the hearing – 1996 Rules, rr 5(3)(b) and 12(1). None the less, since he is not a relevant person, he has no right to accept or deny the grounds of referral, appeal against the hearing's decision, or call for a review. See chapter 9, para 20, for a more detailed discussion of this point.

204 Section 7(2), discussed in chapter 4, para 86.

205 See for example, *Breingan* v *Jamieson* 1993 SLT 186, where the father had lost custody (as it was then) some years earlier when he and his daughter's mother divorced. The child, who was seven when her mother died, was looked after by a maternal aunt and other relatives. In a dispute over her future custody, the father was unsuccessful in seeking to have her come to live with him and his new wife since she was happy and settled where she was. It is worth remembering the centrality of the child's welfare in such cases and sometimes the court will conclude that the father can serve this better than the other claimant. See *Kyle* v *Stewart* 1989 GWD 14–580, where the mother had given the child to her sister to care for shortly before taking a fatal overdose. In that case, the father did succeed in gaining custody. The aunt's youth and status, as a lone parent, were regarded as significant by the court. See also *Sherwin* v *Trumayne*, n 201 above.

relationships being what they are, disputes will sometimes arise between them over fulfilling their respective roles. In addition, a much broader group of people may be involved with a child and have an active interest in his or her life and well-being. Unmarried fathers who have not concluded parental responsibilities and rights agreements are one such group, but the range of 'others' is almost limitless. Relatives, including grandparents, aunts and uncles, and siblings, are fairly obvious candidates. Given the large number of children who encounter step-parents or quasi step-parents (a parent's cohabitant), they represent yet another category of significant persons in the lives of many children. Depending upon the individual's relationship with the child, he or she may wish to acquire some or all of the parental responsibilities or rights. In other cases, the interested person may simply be seeking to regulate how parental responsibilities or rights are exercised or fulfilled by another person. In order to accommodate the diverse range of relationships inherent in modern child and family law, these various 'others' are provided with an avenue for involvement in the child's life through the courts.

5.69 While the role of the courts should not be underestimated, it is essential at this point to remember that litigation should not normally be seen as the first step when concerns or disputes arise. Depending upon the nature of the particular problem, it may be wise to seek professional advice about what the law provides in the circumstances. However, the value of discussion, negotiation and, in appropriate cases, mediation, can be enormous. As we saw in chapter 1, alternative dispute resolution has gained increased recognition in recent years and the services available to family members and others, through the legal profession and other organisations, has expanded greatly.[206] Many families who may have thought that litigation was inevitable have discovered that their disputes could be resolved through mediation and at much less personal and financial cost. Once people find themselves in court, there is a sense in which the battle-lines are drawn and it is much more difficult to resolve disputes amicably. Having said that, the courts themselves have developed mechanisms, like options hearings, aimed at finding out if any apparently contentious issues can be resolved and retain the power to refer a case to mediation. While avoiding acrimonious litigation should always be the aim of the legal system, there is a pressing, pragmatic reason for such an approach in disputes involving children. Often the parties will continue to be involved in the child's life in the future and, if they are to have any hope of working together in the interests of the child's welfare, the less resentment stored up, the better.

5.70 In a significant number of cases, the court is either the appropriate or the inevitable forum for the resolution of issues surrounding parental responsibilities and rights. Who may apply to the court, for what and how, are matters that we shall explore in detail presently, along with the criteria

---

206 See chapter 1, paras 45–50 for a discussion of the development of mediation, in general, and the work of such organisations as CALM and Family Mediation Scotland, in particular.

for decision-making by the court. At the outset, it will be helpful to bear in mind that what is needed here is a sufficiently flexible and open system that anyone with a legitimate interest in a child's life is able to bring concerns before the court and a court endowed with powers that are adequate to meet every situation. That is a pretty tall order and requires not only adequate legislation, but an imaginative and flexible interpretation of it by the judiciary. Whether the provisions of the 1995 Act and the members of the judiciary, past and present, meet this exacting standard forms a part of the discussion below. In addition, it should be remembered that even where no application for an order in relation to parental responsibilities or rights has been sought, the court can make such order as it considers appropriate.[207]

Who can make applications in respect of parental responsibilities and rights?

5.71 The 1995 Act provides that the court may make an order *in relation to* parental responsibilities, parental rights, guardianship or the administration of a child's property.[208] The phrase 'in relation to' substantially repeats that found in earlier legislation and conveys two fundamental aspects of the provision and the court's role.[209] The first is that the court has very broad powers in granting any order it thinks fit in this very wide area.[210] The second point, and the one with which we are concerned primarily here, is that the orders the court can make need only be *dealing with* the various rights and responsibilities. It follows that, while the pursuer will often be applying to be given parental responsibilities or rights, he or she may be seeking to have another person's rights removed or regulated. This means, in turn, that there is scope for applications to be made by a wide range of persons. Who, then, may apply?

5.72 The following persons may make applications

Any person who does not have and never has had parental responsibilities or parental rights in relation to the child but claims an interest[211]

5.73 This is the most far-reaching, broad, category of potential applicants and covers anyone who has never had parental responsibilities or parental rights in relation to the child. Unmarried fathers who have not concluded an agreement with the child's mother, step-parents and relatives may all

---

207 Section 11(3)(b). Similarly, where the court refuses the order applied for, it may grant a different order where it considers such a course of action to be appropriate. In addition, the court may refer the child to the Principal Reporter. See para 5.87, for a discussion of what the court may do on its own initiative.

208 Section 11(1).

209 The Law Reform (Parent and Child) (Scotland) Act 1986, s 3(1) provided for applications for 'an order relating to' parental rights, parental responsibilities not being articulated expressly in that statute.

210 The 1995 Act, s 11(2) goes on to give examples of the kind of orders a court may make but these are stated expressly to be 'without prejudice to the generality' of the court's power overall.

211 Section 11(3)(i).

make applications under this provision. There are two qualifications. First, they must never have had parental responsibilities or rights. Where a person has had any such responsibility or right and has lost it, he or she may still be able to make an application to the court, depending on how the responsibility or right was lost, but not under this subsection. As we shall see, in some cases, like disputes between parents in the course of a divorce, the loss of responsibilities or rights does not prevent an individual from returning to the court at a future date to reopen the matter.[212] In other cases, like adoption, where the person's responsibilities and rights are extinguished by an adoption order, he or she cannot come back to the court to reopen the issue.[213]

5.74 The second qualification is that the applicant must 'claim an interest'. Again, this is similar to the phrase used in the previous legislation[214] and the courts had certain initial difficulty[215] with it, before the whole matter was resolved by the Inner House in *F* v *F*.[216] There, the paternal grandparents of two boys who had been freed for adoption and placed with prospective adopters applied for custody of them. The local authority challenged the competency of their application and the Inner House took the opportunity to clarify the position, finding the grandparents' application to be competent. Lord President Hope expressed the view that 'parental rights' was 'merely a convenient way of describing those rights [which were defined in the Act]' and went on to say, 'I do not think that it implies any limitation on those persons who may apply for them'.[217] His comments apply equally to parental responsibilities and parental rights, as defined by the 1995 Act, and are consistent with the whole thrust of the legislation. On any literal or, indeed, common-sense, approach, the phrase 'claims an interest' conveys the idea that anyone who can show some legitimate concern or connection with the child should be able to go to the court and ask to have the matter considered. This, after all, is only the first step. It merely allows a person to get a matter before the court. What happens thereafter will be determined according to the overarching principles. Usually, the applicant will be a member of the child's family, but there may be cases where a third party can satisfy the test. For example, a schoolteacher who became aware that parents planned to authorise the sterilisation of their learning-impaired daughter might raise an action in

---

212 Such a parent could apply under s 11(3)(a)(iii) which is discussed below.
213 See para 5.86, below, for a more detailed discussion of who is prevented from applying to the court.
214 The Law Reform (Parent and Child) (Scotland) Act 1986, s 3(1) provided for 'any person claiming interest' applying.
215 In *AB* v *M and Central Regional Council* 1988 SLT 652, Lord McCluskey refused to allow a 13-year-old girl to apply for access (as it was then) to her sisters who had recently been adopted on the basis that the provision was 'deliberately restricted to conferring a title on a person who can claim an interest as a parent to exercise the rights which any parent is entitled to claim'. A year later, in *M* v *Lothian Regional Council* 1989 SLT 426, Lord Cullen refused to follow this restrictive interpretation and took the view that there was no reason to confine applications to parents. The latter view was followed by the sheriff in a later case – *Whyte* v *Hardie* (Sh Ct) 1990 SCLR 23.
216 1991 SLT 357.
217 At p 361.

order that the court could decide whether such a course was, indeed, in the young woman's best interests.[218] A doctor, who did not feel that his young patient understood all of the consequences of abortion fully, might seek an order of the court authorising the termination where he or she believed that course of action was in the patient's best interests, despite parental opposition.

5.75 One of the great strengths of this provision is its flexibility. It allows for a range of people to be recognised as being relevant to a child's life without being tied to narrow stereotypical notions of the family. A number of other jurisdictions have passed statutes aimed at accommodating the child's relationship with particular people, sometimes because the precise wording of the pre-existing legislation in that jurisdiction produced unjust results by excluding individuals who had a significant connection with a child, like step-parents.[219] There is no need for this kind of piecemeal, specific-issue, approach in Scotland, because the 1995 Act is sufficiently all-encompassing. One area where this flexibility will be of particular use is that of homosexual and lesbian couples. As we have seen, while a lesbian may have a child as a result of assisted reproduction, her female partner will not be treated as a parent of the child, because the Human Fertilisation and Embryology Act 1990 accommodates only the male partner of the woman who bears the child.[220] While the courts have shown encouraging openness of mind in permitting a homosexual to adopt a child he planned to raise along with his male partner, the partner could not be accorded any legal status in the adoption, because only married couples can adopt together.[221] A homosexual or lesbian parent who has children resulting from a previous relationship may live with a same-sex partner subsequently and the partner may become a *de facto* step-parent to the children.[222] In all of these cases, the partner may apply to the court as a person claiming

218 In *Re D (A Minor) (Wardship: Sterilisation)* [1976] 1 All ER 326, an educational psychologist initiated proceedings to have D, a 12-year-old girl with a mental handicap, declared a ward of court in England (a procedure not found in Scots law) and asked the court to delay the sterilisation. In *Beagley v Beagley* 1984 SLT 202, a case which predates the 1986 Act, Lord Fraser of Tullybelton (at p 206) discussed the possibility of a schoolteacher or a close family friend having interest in respect of a child in certain circumstances. Caution should be exercised in relying on that case in other respects, since it predates the 1986 Act and is concerned primarily with issues that were somewhat debatable at the time and are now dealt with explicitly in the 1995 Act.
219 See for example, California's Step-Parent Visitation Statute, which started as Assembly Bill 2635 and became s 4351.5 of the California Family Code, which was passed in response to a number of cases where former step-parents were denied visitation rights. The background to this measure and its shortcomings are discussed in an excellent article, but one which suggests that journal editors might consider limiting the length of article titles – see D. L. Abraham, 'California's Stepparent Visitation Statute: For the Welfare of the Child, or a Court-Opened Door to Legally Interfere with Parental Autonomy: Where are the Constitutional Safeguards?' 7 S Cal Rev L & Women's Studies 125 (1997). See also, the Interstate Child Visitation Act 1995.
220 Section 28, discussed in chapter 4, paras 34–38.
221 *T, Petitioner* 1997 SLT 724. This case is discussed fully in chapter 8, para 17.
222 See for example, *Early v Early* 1989 SLT 114, where the issue of the mother's lesbianism and the fact that she was living with her new partner were central in her losing custody of her son.

interest in order to be given parental responsibilities and rights. Similarly, if the relationship breaks down, the former partner may apply in the same way as a former heterosexual partner.

Any person who has parental responsibilities or rights[223]

5.76 Where a person already has parental responsibilities and rights, he or she may, none the less, wish to apply to the court for regulation of them, or of someone else's parental responsibilities and rights. The most common scenario here is where married parents are separating or divorcing. Usually, by virtue of being married, they will begin any dispute with each of them having the full set of parental responsibilities and rights.[224] On separation, fresh arrangements will be made for the care of the children. It should be remembered that, at this point, there is normally no need for the parents to seek any change to their existing parental responsibilities and rights. If they can co-operate, each of them can continue with the same legal recognition of his or her status as a parent. In the past, seeking to regulate what was then custody and access was done almost as a matter of course in divorce. In making its recommendations the Scottish Law Commission was acutely aware of the need to recognise the continued involvement of both parents in the lives of their children, even after divorce;[225] something recognised as the child's right by the UN Convention on the Rights of the Child.[226] As we shall see, when the court is considering what, if any, order to make, one factor it must consider is whether making the order would be better than not making it.[227] Thus, the onus is on any applicant to show why the status quo should be changed.[228] With the passage of time, it is likely that such post-divorce regulation of the arrangements for children will become less common. None the less, there will always be cases where the parents cannot agree and one or other of them will go to the court to seek a change to the existing parental responsibilities and rights. Most often, the applicant will not be attempting to change the responsibilities and rights he or she has. The goal will be to remove or restrict his or her former partner's responsibilities and rights. Thus, for example, the mother with whom the children are living may seek to restrict her former husband's role in respect of residence and possibly guardianship. If successful, she will then be the sole person with responsibility for determining the children's residence and her former husband's role will effectively be restricted to contact. Where his responsibility to safeguard and promote the children's health, development and welfare,

---

223 Section 11(3)(a)(ii).
224 Section 3(1).
225 Report on Family Law para 5.16.
226 Article 18 talks of 'recognition of the principle that both parents have common responsibilities for the upbringing and development of the child'. While art 9 acknowledges that there are circumstances where a child will not be living with both parents, it emphasises the need for continued contact, unless contact would be contrary to the child's best interests.
227 Section 11(7)(a).
228 For a full discussion of the onus of proof, see para 5.101, below.

and to provide direction and guidance, fits into this picture, will be discussed presently.

5.77 It is not only the parents of a child who may have some of the parental responsibilities and rights and this provision allows any person who has any of them to apply to the court for the regulation of their own or another person's responsibilities and rights. Thus, for example, a grandparent who has a right of contact may wish to see the child more often, or on a different basis, to that provided for in the contact order. In such a case, he or she could apply under this provision. Similarly, a step-parent who had contact, but now believed it would be better for the child to live with him or her, might apply for a residence order. This reinforces the idea that the court's role in regulating parental responsibilities and rights is never at an end. It can continue throughout a young person's childhood. The fact that every child is developing and maturing, the very fluidity of personal relationships and the changing nature of individual circumstances, make it essential that the door should never be closed to looking afresh at the arrangements for the care of children. None the less, this can sometimes lead to parents continuing their battle with each other, through the medium of new applications to the court. While it may be true in opera that '[i]t isn't over until the fat lady sings', in disputes over the future arrangements for children, the point is that the fat lady never sings.

Any person who has had parental responsibilities or rights in relation to the child, but no longer has them and is not excluded by the Act[229]

5.78 At first sight, this appears to be a somewhat complex provision, but it becomes much clearer when the background to it is understood. It has its origins in the uncertainty and conflicting court decisions under the previous legislation. The story begins with *Beagley* v *Beagley* where, ultimately, the House of Lords[230] decided that a parent whose parental rights had been removed and vested in the local authority, by virtue of the child protection provisions in force at the time,[231] could not use an application for custody to attempt to recover those rights. Essentially, their Lordships were saying that a parent could not use a private law route to achieve what was barred by the public law route, once all the appeals under that public law route were exhausted. In *Borders Regional Council* v *M*,[232] the Inner House came to the same conclusion, where parental rights had been removed by the child being freed for adoption. On that occasion, the parent was not permitted to use the private law route of applying for parental rights in order to reverse the effects of a decision taken by the court in the context of adoption.

5.79 The position remained settled until the passage of the Law Reform (Parent and Child) (Scotland) Act 1986 which, it will be remembered, introduced the concept of any person claiming 'an interest' being able to

229 Section 11(3)(a)(iii).
230 1984 SC (HL) 69.
231 Social Work (Scotland) Act 1968, s 16.
232 1986 SC 63.

apply for parental rights. As we have seen, after some initial uncertainty in the lower courts, the Inner House established, in *F* v *F*,[233] that this very broad phrase was to mean precisely what it seemed to mean; that is, any person who could show a legitimate interest could apply. Indeed, Lord President Hope made it clear that, while adoption severed the legal relationship between the child and his or her birth family, nothing could alter biological reality and, thus, that birth relatives would retain interest to apply to the court in respect of parental rights even after an adoption petition had been granted.[234] Thus, the door was opened for parents who were unhappy about decisions removing their parental rights, either to vest them in the local authority or where the child had been adopted, to use the private law route of applying for parental rights to get themselves back into their child's life. This remained the position until the decision of the House of Lords in *D* v *Grampian Regional Council*, where a mother applied for custody of her two children, having been unsuccessful in opposing the local authority's application to have the children freed for adoption. By a majority, the Inner House[235] found her action to be competent, and the judgments reward careful reading for the sheer breadth of judicial reasoning employed. The House of Lords[236] overturned that decision and concluded that such applications by parents whose parental rights had been transferred to an adoption agency were not competent. By implication, once the adoption is completed, similar applications by birth parents would not be competent. Even the House of Lords was unwilling to close the door completely on a birth parent's future involvement with the child and Lord Jauncey envisaged that applications to the *nobile officium* of the Court of Session would remain open to them in extreme cases.[237] *D* v *Grampian Regional Council* was decided while the Bill that became the 1995 Act was progressing through Parliament and the Scottish Law Commission's original formulation, along the lines of the 1986 Act, was amended to give statutory effect to the decision of the House of Lords and put the matter beyond all doubt. The provision will make it almost impossible to argue that there is the necessary *lacuna* justifying the use of the *nobile officium* in even the most extreme case and, in that respect, the legislation goes a step further than Lord Jauncey, at least, envisaged.

5.80 Thus, it is now the case that an application for an order under s 11 of the 1995 Act may not be made by any person who had any parental responsibility or parental right but no longer has them because they have been:[238]

---

233 1991 SLT 357.
234 At p 361.
235 1994 SLT 1038.
236 1995 SLT 519.
237 At p 522H, he said, 'If there were to arise after the making of an adoption order exceptional circumstances affecting the welfare of the child which were unforeseen by Parliament and required intervention by the court it may be that an application by the divested parent to the *nobile officium* for an appropriate order would be entertained by the Court of Session'.
238 Section 11(3)(a)(iii) and (4).

extinguished by an adoption order,[239]

transferred to an adoption agency by an order freeing the child for adoption,

extinguished by an order under the Human Fertilisation and Embryology Act 1990, s 30(9);[240]

transferred to a local authority by a parental responsibilities order.[241]

5.81 The decision of the House of Lords in *D* v *Grampian Regional Council* and the terms of s 11(4) of the 1995 Act prevent people who were involved in a child's life at one time from raising issues of concern in the courts and, as such, are open to criticism. Remember, at this stage, we are only considering these people getting the case as far as a court. The final decision would be taken on the basis of the overarching principles. Had they still been permitted to apply to the court, it might have been only very rarely that, for example, parents, could reverse the effect of a parental responsibilities order. As we shall see presently, the 1995 Act denies local authorities the opportunity to apply for orders relating to parental responsibilities and rights and restricts them to the 'public law' procedures.[242] It might be argued that, as a corollary, parents should be similarly restricted. This argument has the attraction of a certain symmetry. It hints at 'fairness'. On the one hand is a local authority, staffed by professionals who are experienced in using procedures and the legal system. On the other hand, are the parents who are often the least competent individuals when it comes to such procedures. Even allowing for the parents getting legal advice, it is hardly a competition between equals. Given that it is the 'need to safeguard and promote the welfare of the child concerned throughout [the child's] life',[243] that is the paramount consideration, the relative position of the parents and the local authority may not be crucial. None the less, that those central to the life of the child should have the opportunity to address the court, as often as is necessary, seems desirable. In the context of adoption, there is the issue of not disrupting a child who is happy and settled in a new family and the broader question of 'open adoption' and these matters are discussed in chapter 8.

5.82 It should be remembered that this provision affects only persons who have had and have lost parental responsibilities or rights in respect of a child. Other relatives of that child are not affected by s 11(4) where they have never had parental responsibilities or rights. Their position remains that they may apply under s 11(3)(a)(i) and, in this respect, they receive the

---

239 Adoption is discussed in chapter 8.
240 It will be remembered that s 30 of the 1990 Act created a special kind of expedited adoption procedure for surrogacy cases – see chapter 4, paras 53–62.
241 Parental responsibilities orders, which are discussed in chapter 6, were created by the 1995 Act and replace the old procedure for assumption of parental rights discussed in the pre-1995 cases.
242 The parental responsibilities order available to the local authority, under Part II, Chapter 4, of the 1995 Act, replaces the old procedure for assumption of parental rights and is discussed in chapter 7, paras 89–93.
243 Section 95.

latitude afforded by the decision in *F* v *F*. Thus, for example, where a child has been adopted, it would remain competent for birth-siblings or birth-grandparents to apply for a contact order, so that they could visit the child and keep in touch. Of course, once the overarching principles are applied, other considerations might prevail, and it might be thought that contact would not be in the child's best interests. The point is, at least the other relatives will have had the opportunity to put their case.

The child[244]

5.83 In the past, there was some doubt about whether or not a child could competently apply to the court for an order regulating parental rights being exercised over him or her. While the Commission took the view that such an application was already competent, it thought the matter should be put beyond doubt.[245] Given that the Commission was acutely aware of the UN Convention on the Rights of the Child, which requires recognition of the child's evolving capacity[246] and the child's right to participate in the decision-making process,[247] the recommendation was unsurprising. Fortunately, on this occasion, Parliament accepted the wisdom of the Commission's position and the 1995 Act implements the recommendation. Thus, for example, where a child is unhappy about a decision that has been taken by a person exercising parental responsibilities or rights, the child can ask the court to resolve the matter. The prospect of children resorting to litigation in droves every time they are told they cannot do what they want is one which has been overplayed by the media and opponents of children's rights. It is always easy to produce silly and trivial examples of what 'might happen', and the prospect of children raising actions over being asked to help with the washing-up or tidy their rooms are the spectres often trotted out. In reality, it is unlikely that actions will be raised by children with any frequency. First, any person taking a major decision in the course of fulfilling parental responsibilities or exercising parental rights is obliged to take account of any views the child wishes to express.[248] Of course, that does not mean that parents are obliged to do what the child wants, but at least the discussion which one hopes will accompany the process of ascertaining the child's views should give the adult the opportunity to explain his or her preference. Second, as we have seen, children have limited access to legal services and only the most resourceful are ever likely to get as far as a solicitor. None the less, the opportunity for children to initiate proceedings in respect of parental responsibilities and rights will lead inevitably to the kind of cases that have arisen in other jurisdictions and which the media has sensationalised under the banner headlines 'Child Divorces Parents'.

244 Section 11(5).
245 Report on Family Law, para 5.11 and rec 31, draft Bill, clause 11(3).
246 Article 5.
247 Article 12.
248 Section 6, discussed in chapter 6, paras 3–6. While 'major decision' is not defined in the Act, asking a child to help with the washing-up or tidy his or her room is probably outwith the scope of the section. None the less, the climate created by highlighting the importance of children participating in the decision-making process, should have a knock-on effect to smaller decisions.

5.84 One such case, in the USA, was *Kingsley* v *Kingsley*,[249] where Gregory, a 12-year-old boy, sought to have his mother's parental rights over him terminated in order that he could be adopted by his foster carers. Sadly, Gregory's circumstances were far from unusual. His early years were spent to-ing and fro-ing between his estranged parents, an aunt and the care of the authorities in Missouri and Florida. Indeed, he had spent only seven months of the eight years immediately prior to the case with his mother. For the preceding three years, he had been living with foster carers, the Russes and, interestingly enough, Mr Russ was an attorney. Apparently, Gregory raised the issue of adoption and how this could be achieved with Mr Russ and, once he gained an understanding of the procedures involved, sought out an attorney to act for him in having his mother's parental rights terminated in order that his adoption by the Russes could go ahead. It was this initiative that singled the case out for media attention.[250] In the event, the County Court granted his application and approved his adoption. While that decision was reversed by the District Court of Appeal,[251] it did nothing to calm the fears of the media.

5.85 When can a similar case, with a child initiating the proceedings, be expected in Scotland? In England,[252] a 14-year-old young woman who had gone to live with her boyfriend and his parents, against the wishes of her parents, opposed her parents' application for a residence order, using a provision of the Children Act 1989[253] which is very similar to that found in the 1995 Act. Thus, the answer is that we may not have long to wait. It is a matter of concern that relations within the family have broken down to the extent that a young person feels the need to litigate in this way. However imperfect young people's awareness of their rights may be, and difficult as youth access to legal services is, it is encouraging that the opportunity exists for a sufficiently unhappy young person to take matters to a court for resolution.

249 623 So 2d 780 (Fla, 1993).
250 See S. A. Cannon, 'Finding Their Own 'Place To Be': What Gregory Kingsley's and Kimberley Mays' 'Divorces' from their Parents have done for Children's Rights' 39 Loy L Rev. 837 (1994), where the decision in Gregory's case is compared with that in *Twigg* v *Mays* (see chapter 4, para 5 for a discussion of that case and references to a sample of the extensive literature arising from the two cases). In the article, the author notes that Gregory was not the first child to institute proceedings to terminate parental rights. At note 46, he mentions the case of Walter Polovchak, a 12-year-old Ukranian boy, who made no allegations of abuse or neglect, but sued to terminate parental rights solely because he did not want to return to the Soviet Union with his parents. According to the author, the 'family values' lobbyists were conspicuously silent in denouncing this example of intrusion on parental authority.
251 Interestingly, while the District Court of Appeals concluded that Gregory had no standing to raise the action himself, it did not regard this point as crucial, since the procedural error was cured by the various petitions filed by other (adult) persons on his behalf. The central point of the appeal, and the one which resulted in the reversal of the adoption, was the fact that the trial court had approved the adoption before Gregory's mother's appeal against termination of her parental rights had been heard (623 So 2d 780 (Fla, 1993), at pp 783–790).
252 *Re CE (Section 37 Directions)* [1995] 1 FLR 26.
253 Under the legislation in England and Wales, the young person must obtain leave of the court to raise the action – 1989 Act, s 10(8). In Scotland, no such leave is required.

Who cannot make applications in respect of parental responsibilities and rights?

5.86   As we have seen, persons whose parental responsibilities and rights have been removed as a result of adoption proceedings or by the local authority obtaining a parental responsibilities order cannot use s 11 in order to have a 'second bite at the cherry'. What of the local authority? Should it be able to use a s 11 application as well as the very extensive powers conferred on it by Part II of the 1995 Act? Under the previous legislation a local authority succeeded in doing precisely that in *M* v *Dumfries and Galloway Regional Council*.[254] When it came to review the situation, the Scottish Law Commission recommended that a local authority should not be able to use the 'private law' route, rather than its extensive 'public law' powers, in this way.[255] Again, this recommendation was accepted and the 1995 Act provides that 'person' does 'not include a local authority'.[256] As we shall see in chapter 7, the local authority has separate and far-reaching powers to intervene in family life to provide for and protect children.

Action the court can take on its own initiative

5.87   Normally, the court will consider making an order because someone has made an application. However, the court can take the initiative by exercising one or both of two powers provided for under the 1995 Act. First, where no application has been made, or where the order sought by an applicant has been refused, the court can make a s 11 order, none the less.[257] The court must consider whether it is necessary to exercise this power in any action for divorce, judicial separation or declarator of nullity of marriage,[258] where there are children under the age of 16 involved.[259] In addition, it may also exercise it in other circumstances, like an action for declarator of parentage. Second, if it appears to the court that any of the

---

254 (Sh Ct) 1991 SCLR 481. In that case, the local authority successfully used the welfare principle in the 1986 Act to resist the parents' application for return of their daughter who was in the authority's care on a 'voluntary' basis under the Social Work (Scotland) Act 1968, s 15.

255 Report on Family Law, rec 28, draft Bill, clause 11(4).

256 Section 11(5).

257 Section 11(3)(b). In this respect, the 1995 Act expands the power, formerly held by the Court of Session, to make such orders in certain specified proceedings – Court of Session Act 1988, s 20 (repealed by the 1995 Act, Sched 5).

258 Section 12. Where the court considers it likely that it may have to make a s 11 order, but requires to give further consideration of the case, it may, in 'exceptional circumstances which make it desirable in the interests of that child that it should not grant decree', postpone its decision on the granting of the decree – s 12(2). This is a significant change to the previous legislation governing this situation. Under the Matrimonial Proceedings (Children) Act 1958, s 12, the court was bound to refuse the decree unless it was satisfied as to the arrangements made for the care and upbringing of the children.

259 Section 12 applies where there is a 'child of the family' and this term is defined as meaning a child of both parties to a marriage, or any other child who has been treated by both of them as a child of their family – s 12(4). Foster children are specifically excluded from the definition.

grounds for referring a child to a children's hearing[260] is satisfied in relation to a child, it may refer the matter to the Principal Reporter, who will consider whether it is necessary to refer the child to a hearing.[261] Again, the court must consider whether there is any need to exercise this power in the matrimonial proceedings listed above,[262] and may do so in a host of other actions.[263]

What can be applied for?

5.88 As the above discussion shows, almost anyone with a legitimate interest can apply to the court for an order in relation to parental responsibilities, parental rights, guardianship or the administration of a child's property. In addition, the court may make such an order, either at its own instance or in substitution of the order sought by an applicant. The next question to consider is what it is that these people may apply for or, to put it another way, what can the court order? The simple answer is that the court may make any order it thinks fit.[264] Thus, the court has enormous latitude in tailor-making orders to suit the needs of a particular case and no problem should arise which is beyond the power of the court to resolve. Of course, no court will make an order unless there is a reasonable prospect, in practice, that it can be complied with and this is where the difficulties may arise. It is the human resources available, in terms of such matters as a parent's personal skill, judgment and commitment, that determine whether he or she can fulfil his or her parental responsibilities fully and exercise his or her parental rights appropriately. Failing the parents, the availability of other persons both willing and able to take on this role, becomes central. The point to bear in mind is that, no amount of flexible legislation and judicial wisdom can make up for deficiencies in the people available to an individual child. All that the legal system can hope to do is to ensure that the court has the range of powers necessary to make the best use of the resources available and, where they are inadequate, ensure that the state, through one of its agencies, is there to step in. Arguably, the 1995 Act gives the court sufficient range. In addition to allowing the courts broad powers, the 1995 Act goes on to give examples of the kind of orders that are available,[265] while stressing that these examples are not intended to limit the court's general power. It is worth remembering that, when considering whether to make any order, the court is bound by the overarching principles. How it goes about applying them is considered presently. First, it should be noted that the examples of the order which might be considered, are

---

260 The provision applies to all of the grounds for referral except that relating to the child having committed an offence – s 54(1). The children's hearings system is discussed in detail in chapter 9.
261 Section 54.
262 Section 12(1). Again, it can delay its decision on the granting of the decree in exceptional circumstances.
263 Section 54(2).
264 Section 11(2).
265 Section 11(2).

*An order depriving a person of some or all of his or her parental
responsibilities or parental rights in relation to a child[266]*

5.89 The court is required by s 11(11) to be specific about precisely which
parental responsibilities or rights are being taken away from a person.
Under the previous law, the assumption was that where, for example,
custody was given to one parent, the other parent lost all rights in respect
of the child unless an award of access was made. The 1995 Act, which is
based on the premise that both parents should normally continue to be
involved in the child's life, changes all of that. The rule to apply now is that,
where a person has any responsibilities or rights in respect of a child, he or
she keeps them until they are removed expressly. This change is of
particular importance to practitioners who must take care to ask the court
for an order in precisely the terms they are seeking. It should be noted that
the court order relates to a particular child. It is not possible to achieve a
blanket removal of parental responsibilities and rights from a person in
respect of any children they may have.[267]

*An order imposing parental responsibilities and giving parental rights to a
person in respect of a child[268]*

5.90 Again, the order must be specific in terms of the responsibilities and
rights involved and in identifying the child concerned. Where the court
intends to confer all the responsibilities and rights on a person, it would be
more appropriate to appoint the person as the child's guardian under s
11(2)(h), below. It should be noted that conferring responsibilities and
rights on a non-parent does not put that person in the same position as the
parent for the purpose of such other matters as the law of succession.

5.91 Parental responsibilities and rights may only be conferred on a
person over the age of 16 years, unless the person is the child's parent. Of
course, the child's mother will have automatic parental responsibilities and
rights, regardless of her age. Norrie makes the somewhat puzzling assertion
that '[it] is difficult to imagine a situation in which it would ever be in the
child's interests to confer any parental responsibility or parental right on a
father under the age of 16'.[269] It is submitted that it is not difficult at all to
imagine such a situation. Take, for example, two mature, 14-year-olds who
engage in consensual, albeit underage, sexual intercourse. They are still 14
when their child is born.[270] Let us assume further that they decide that the

---

266 Section 11(2)(a).
267 It is possible, however, to bring a child to a children's hearing on the basis that he or she
   is, or is likely to become, a member of the same household as a person who has
   committed certain offences – s 52(2)(f). While this does not necessarily mean that the
   exercise of parental rights will be affected, it allows for enquiry where an individual's past
   behaviour raises doubt over the suitability of his or her living with any child. See chapter
   9, para 34 for a discussion of this provision.
268 Section 11(2)(b).
269 K. McK. Norrie, *Children (Scotland) Act 1995* (W. Green, 1995) at p 31.
270 The fact that the parties were underage when the child was conceived is no bar to the
   father being given parental responsibilities and rights. See for example, *McMillan* v
   Brady 1997 GWD 4–130, where the mother was 15 and the father was 34 when their child
   was born. He succeeded with his application for custody of the child at a later stage.

child should live with the young woman and her parents, who will help with childcare, and that the young man and his parents will also assist in caring for the baby. The young man turns out to be a model father and he and the young woman continue their relationship. The young man then has a disagreement with his girlfriend's parents and they stop him from seeing the child. Given her dependence on them, the young woman is reluctant to take a stand against her parents either in practical terms or by concluding a parental responsibilities and rights agreement. Arguably, he could make a very strong case that his continued contact with his child is in the child's best interests and that it should be secured by order of the court, if necessary.

A residence order[271]

5.92 The court may regulate with whom a child will live and specific provision is made for the child living with different people at different times. It was the usual practice under the common law and the previous legislation that, when parents were divorcing, one parent would be awarded custody and the other would be given access. This left the parent with access in a precarious position and often schools and the medical profession would doubt that such a parent had any rights to be fully involved in the child's life. All such divisive thinking is swept away by the 1995 Act. The starting point is now that each parent retains full parental responsibilities and rights, irrespective of divorce. If there is a need to regulate with whom the child is to live at given times, the court will do so, but such regulation should not be seen as an automatic step. Where regulation is required because, for example, the parents cannot agree, the court might provide that the child is to live with one parent from 6 pm on Sundays to 4.00 pm on Fridays and with the other parent from 4.00 pm on Fridays to 6.00 pm on Sundays. Of course, an infinite number of other arrangements might be made, with special provision being made for school holidays, birthdays, special events and the like. As we saw, applications in relation to parental responsibilities are not confined to parents and other people, like grandparents, other relatives and step-parents, might apply for residence orders for long or short periods of time. Where all a person wants is to keep in touch with the child and have him or her come to visit, the more appropriate request to make of the court is for a contact order.

A contact order[272]

5.93 Using this order, the court may regulate the arrangements for maintaining personal relations and direct contact between a child under 16 and a person with whom the child is not living. Again, such an order will often be unnecessary in the context of divorce, since both of the parents who were married will retain the obligation and the right to maintain contact unless it has been removed by order of the court. Regulation, in the sense of designating specific arrangements for contact, may be necessary, however, where the parents are in dispute over how it is to operate. It is not uncommon to find that the parent with whom a younger child is living will

271 Section 11(2)(c).
272 Section 11(2)(d).

allege that the child does not want to see the non-resident parent and that contact upsets the child. Often, the non-resident parent's response is that the child thoroughly enjoys their time together and it is the other parent who is obstructing contact. In many cases, each of the parents believes what he or she is saying and the truth is that the child is caught in the unenviable position of trying not to hurt either parent. Here a contact order might actually assist the child by taking all responsibility for the decision off the young person's shoulders. Of course, this is not always the case and the court will have to consider the evidence in the light of the overarching principles. A contact order may be of great value to persons other than parents who would like to maintain relations with the child and, again, the whole range of people may apply. One category of persons requires mention here: grandparents. It sometimes happens, once parents divorce, that the non-resident parent, who is usually the father, does not maintain contact. Depending upon the relationship they have had, the paternal grandparents in such a case may find that their former daughter-in-law obstructs their attempts to see their grandchild. If negotiation fails, their only avenue will often be an application for a contact order. The usual warning, that it will do nothing to enhance relations between the adults, should accompany advising this course of action.

A specific issue order[273]

5.94 In the words of the 1995 Act, this empowers the court to make an order 'regulating any specific question which has arisen, or may arise', in connection with parental responsibilities, parental rights, guardianship or the administration of a child's property. The provision is deliberately wide in its ambit and allows any interested parties including, of course, the child, to call on the court's assistance for the resolution of existing or prospective disputes. The court will reach its decision on the basis of the overarching principles. It is anticipated that this provision will be of particular use in resolving such difficult questions as what medical treatment a child might have and which school a child should attend. There is a similar provision, dealing with specific issue orders, in the Children Act 1989,[274] which applies in England and Wales. Since that legislation has been operating for longer than the 1995 Act, the courts there have had the opportunity to consider its application in a number of cases, including an application by a young woman for the court's sanction to her going on holiday to Bulgaria.[275] One benefit of the specific issue order is that it will enable the court to deal with

---

273 Section 11(2)(e). For a recent example of a specific issue order being sought (and refused) to enable the mother to take the children to live in Australia, against the wishes of the father, see *Fourman* v *Fourman* 1998 GWD 32–1638.

274 Section 8. For example, in *Dawson* v *Wearmouth* [1998] 1 All ER 271, an unmarried father who had parental rights was granted a specific issue order to the effect that his son should be known by the father's, rather than the mother's, last name. The decision was overturned, on the merits, by the Court of Appeal.

275 *Re C (A Minor) (Leave to Seek Section 8 Orders)* [1994] 1 FLR 26. It should be remembered that, in England and Wales, the young person not only has to satisfy a solicitor that he or she has the capacity to give instructions, the child must also obtain leave from the court to bring the action – 1989 Act, s 10(8) and *Practice Direction (Application by Children: Leave)* [1993] 1 All ER 820. Initially, the courts got into

a particular problem without having to encroach on parental responsibilities or rights any more than is necessary. This is entirely consistent with the overarching principle which requires the court not to make any order unless to do so will be better than not doing so.

An interdict[276]

5.95 This allows the court to order a person not to do a particular thing or, if doing it, to stop. In this context, it might be used to order parents not to proceed with consenting to a particular medical procedure, like the sterilisation of a young, learning-impaired, woman,[277] not to deal with the child's property in a particular way, or not to take the child to a particularly dangerous area of the world on vacation. As with specific issues orders, the circumstances in which interdict might be appropriate are infinite and, again, the power of the court to deal with a particular problem will ensure that it does not have to encroach on parental responsibilities or parental rights to a greater extent than is necessary.

An order appointing a judicial factor to manage a child's property or remitting the matter to the Accountant of Court to report on suitable arrangements for the future management of the child's property[278]

5.96 As we have seen, managing the child's property is normally part of the whole bundle of parental responsibilities and rights and there are some special rules which apply, where a child is about to acquire property.[279] Where the child already owns property, this provision allows the court to deal with the issue of management of that property.

An order appointing or removing any person as the child's guardian[280]

5.97 This provision allows for the court making such appointment and, of course, allows the court to remove any guardian, regardless of how he or she came to take up the office. Thus, parents, a guardian appointed by a parent, or a guardian appointed by the court, can be removed from office under this power.

In what kind of proceedings?

5.98 So far, we have seen who can apply and for what. Obviously, the application is to a court, but in what kind of proceedings? Applications in

---

something of a mess, with the court in *Re C* addressing the issue of welfare, as well as capacity, at this first stage. In *Re SC (A Minor) (Leave to Seek Residence Order)* [1994] 1 FLR 96, Booth J. assessed the child's capacity on the basis of her intellect and ability to cope with the stress inherent in litigation. The latter approach has prevailed in a subsequent case – *Re C (Residence: Child's Application for Leave)* [1995] 1 FLR 927. This difficulty is avoided in Scotland, since the child only has to convince the solicitor that he or she 'has a general understanding' of what it means to instruct a solicitor – Age of Legal Capacity (Scotland) Act 1991, s 2(4A).

276 Section 11(2)(f).
277 See *Re D (A Minor) (Wardship: Sterilisation)* [1976] 1 All ER 326, where an educational psychologist took a different route in England to intervene in such circumstances.
278 Section 11(2)(g).
279 Management of the child's property is discussed at paras 5.18–5.20, above.
280 Section 11(2)(h).

relation to parental responsibilities and rights may be made alone or ancillary to another action in either the sheriff court or the Court of Session.[281] In some cases, it will be appropriate to raise the action on its own. So, for example, an unmarried father, who does not have an agreement with the child's mother, may seek legal recognition of his role in the child's life by raising an action for parental responsibilities or rights. Depending upon whether he has been registered as the child's father, he may also have to raise an action for declarator of parentage[282] and, if he is doing that, his application in relation to parental responsibilities and rights can be a part of that action. Another relative, like a grandparent, may simply raise an action seeking a contact order. Many applications in respect of parental responsibilities and rights are raised in the context of divorce. In 1996, for example, 6,658 children were affected by divorce, being present in 34% of divorces.[283] While both the number of children involved and the percentage of divorces where they are present continues to fall,[284] the realisation that some six and a half thousand children were involved in one year alone, gives some idea of the magnitude of the impact of divorce on children.[285] In most of these cases, the issue will have arisen between the child's parents but, with the increase in remarriage and subsequent divorce, more step-parents have entered the picture.[286] In addition, there are the cases where the children's parents cohabited but, since they did not marry, can simply separate without divorcing. As we shall see, they can reach their own arrangements for the future care of any children and it is only where there is a dispute that the case comes to the court.

5.99 Given the large number of disputes over parental responsibilities and rights which come to the court in the context of divorce or, to a lesser extent, the separation of cohabiting parents, it is appropriate, at this point to consider some of the issues surrounding dysfunction in adult relationships and its impact upon children. It has long been recognised that the separation of a child's parents can have considerable impact on a child.[287] One of the leading studies in the field led its authors to conclude

281 Section 11(1).
282 See chapter 4, para 14.
283 Registrar General for Scotland, Annual Report 1996, p 128, Figure 8.1 and Table 8.8. Regrettably, the Annual Report 1997 no longer records details of children involved in divorce proceedings. While the Civil Judicial Statistics provide the statistics where orders were sought from or made by a court, these do not disclose the full impact of divorce on children. It is to be hoped that the Registrar General will return to the older practice in future Annual Reports.
284 In 1981 for example, 60% of divorces involved children under 16, while, in the peak year of 1985, twice as many children were involved.
285 As we shall see, it is the breakdown of the adults' relationship, rather than the actual divorce, that is significant for children – para 5.99, below.
286 In *Bradley* v *Bradley* 1987 SCLR 62, it was in the context of the aunt and uncle's divorce, that the issue of the child's future arose.
287 The parental obligation to provide financial support for a child is independent of the parent's marital status and, thus, it is not altered by divorce – see chapter 6, paras 29–31. However, on the breakdown of the adults' relationship, there will often be economic consequences for the child in terms of the standard of living of the household where he or she lives. For a discussion of the economic consequences of divorce and the adverse effects experienced most frequently by women and children, see chapter 14, para 27.

'We have learned that a child's early response to divorce and separation is not governed by any balanced understanding of the issues that led to the parents' decision. Nor are children much affected, if at all, by living in a community with a high incidence of divorce. Instead, at the time of the parental separation the child's attention is rivetted entirely on the disruption of his or her own family, and he is intensely worried about what is going to happen to him. Whatever its shortcomings, the family is perceived by the child at the time being as having provided the support and protection he needs. The divorce signifies the collapse of that structure, and he feels alone and very frightened'.[288]

While that study was conducted in California in the 1970s, similar findings have emerged from the, albeit limited, Scottish research.[289] Taken along with other research and literature, the findings of the early studies suggest that a number of factors should be borne in mind. First, it is the time of breakdown and separation, rather than the date of the divorce decree that is most significant for children.[290] This is a point stressed time and again in the literature and one is left with the impression that it took the adult world some time to accept what seems, on reflection, to be fairly obvious. After all, it is at the time of separation that children's lives are likely to change most noticeably. Not only will one parent have left the family home, but that home itself may now be in a new location and, as a result, the child may have moved school and be further away from friends and relatives. As the Scottish Law Commission noted when it was considering shortening the periods of separation required before spouses could divorce, since it is 'the marriage breakdown, and not the legal divorce, which is important', reducing the periods of separation would make no difference to children.[291] A second point to note is that, whatever the objective reasons which might justify a separation to adults, they are of little relevance to children. Third, irrespective of what parents think they have been doing, children frequently feel that they received little or no explanation of what was happening.[292]

5.100 What, if anything, can be done to reduce the burden on children? It

288 J. S. Wallerstein and J. B. Kelly, *Surviving the Breakup: How Children and Parents Cope with Divorce* (Basic Books, 1980), at p 35.

289 A. Mitchell, *Children in the middle: living through divorce* (Tavistock Publications, 1985).

290 In E. E. Maccoby and R. H. Mnookin, *Dividing the Child: Social and Legal Dilemmas of Custody* (Harvard University Press, 1994), at pp 19–58, the authors distinguish 'spousal divorce' (the ending of the intimate relationship between the husband and wife), 'economic divorce' (setting up of two households), 'parental divorce' (establishing new parenting roles), and 'legal divorce' (the decree). Irving and Benjamin make a similar point when they talk of the process of breakdown being a continuum and describe the 'phases or stages' of divorce – see H. H. Irving and M. Benjamin, *Family Mediation: Contemporary Issues* (Sage Publications, 1995), pp 17–48.

291 Report on Reform of the Ground for Divorce (Scot Law Com No 116, 1989) para 4.2. The Commission went on to note that, if the separation grounds were more attractive, spouses might use them rather than the behaviour ground and concluded, 'Indeed one of the main reasons for trying to reduce unnecessary use of the behaviour ground is to try to minimise unnecessary hostility in the interests of the children of the marriage'. Divorce reform is discussed in detail in chapter 13, paras 11–18.

292 Mitchell, n 289 above, at pp 54–80; Wallerstein and Kelly, n 288 above, at pp 39–41. Lack of communication is not confined to parent-child communication. Examining the picture

is sometimes suggested that married adults should be required to remain married until their children reach a particular age. Proponents of this view do not make clear whether they would require unhappy adults to continue to live together,[293] with the predictable resentment that would often accompany such an arrangement, or whether they would be permitted to live apart, in such other relationships as they might choose, but in a 'limping marriage'. It is unlikely that there would be any support for enforced cohabitation[294] and, as we have seen, it is separation, rather than divorce, which is significant for children. Assuming then, that we accept divorce as an option how can we arrange matters so as to do as little harm to the children as possible? The answer seems to lie in thinking about the children and their futures as early as possible. All too often, one or both of the adults involved will be experiencing pain, anger, frustration or, perhaps, depression. None of this helps these adults to focus on the children and, while we can all feel sympathy for these unhappy adults, they must be encouraged to confront this important matter. In addition, parents should be encouraged to explain what is happening and to allow the children to express the feelings, fears and views they have about both the present and the future. They are involved already and simply not talking about what is happening will not make it go away. Yet again, the value of seeking assistance through mediation is worth remembering. As we saw in chapter 1, mediation is often particularly suited to family disputes and a number of specialised mediation services are available to help in resolving disputes involving children.

Onus and standard of proof

5.101 Under the 1986 Act, which required that no order should be made unless the court was satisfied that to do so was in the child's interest, there was some doubt about where the onus of proof lay. Certainly, prior to that Act, the tendency had been that the parental right of access should be granted unless there was some reason to refuse it.[295] The question that arose was whether the 1986 Act had made any difference to that position. The view began to emerge that an applicant for any parental right had to demonstrate that the granting of the order would serve the child's interests; that is, that the onus of proof was placed on the applicant.[296] However, it

after divorce, Maccoby and Mnookin, above, at p 224 found that, when questioned separately, parents often had very different perceptions of how communication and shared decision-making (between the parents) was working in respect of their child.

293 It is worth noting that as long ago as 1983, the Scottish Law Commission recommended the abolition of decrees of adherence: a remedy which, in any event, could not be enforced. See Report on Outdated Rules in the Law of Husband and Wife (Scot Law Com No 76, 1983) at paras 3.1–3.6. The Commission's recommendation was given effect in the Law Reform (Husband and Wife) (Scotland) Act 1984, s 2(1).

294 Similar sorts of issues arise when it is suggested that the incidence of divorce could be reduced by making the whole process more difficult. For a discussion of divorce reform and the introduction of 'no fault' divorce, see chapter 13, paras 11–18.

295 *Blance* v *Blance* 1978 SLT 74; *Brannigan* v *Brannigan* 1979 SLT (Notes) 73.

296 *Porchetta* v *Porchetta* 1986 SLT 105; *Russell* v *Russell* (Sh Ct) 1991 SCLR (Notes) 429. In *Russell*, for example, the parents separated when their daughter was two years old. She lived with her mother and her father saw her regularly for about two years thereafter,

was not until *Sanderson* v *McManus*[297] that the question was put beyond doubt. There, the parents had lived together for several years, both before and after the birth of their son, separating on a number occasion's because of Mr Sanderson's violence towards his partner. After their final separation, he sought access (as it was then). The sheriff, the Sheriff Principal, the majority of the Inner House and the House of Lords, it is submitted quite correctly, concluded that the onus of proof was placed, quite firmly on the applicant, although it was acknowledged that, once the court had the evidence before it, 'the matter then becomes one of overall impression'.[298] It was agreed, again by the vast majority of the judges who considered the case, that the question of onus of proof would only be significant in 'an exceptional case'.[299] It was on this point that Lord McCluskey expressed his strongest dissent. While accepting that a parent had 'no absolute right' to access which could never be lost, he felt that what he described as the traditional Scottish approach, which favoured granting access to a parent unless a clear detriment to the child could be established, had not been altered by later cases, nor by the 1986 Act.[300] Addressing himself to these points, Lord Hope stressed that any decision on access did not sever all contact between the parent and child permanently in that it would always remain open to the parent to make a fresh application.[301] However, he was quite clear that, whatever the position had been at common law, the effect of the 1986 Act had altered any presumption in favour of parental contact.[302] Indeed, in his view, even prior to the 1986 Act, Lord Dunpark[303] had 'already recognised the fallacy in this approach, once the welfare of the child was made the paramount consideration'.[304] The 1995 Act reinforces that position by providing that the court

> 'Shall not make any order unless it considers that it would be better for the child that the order be made than that none should be made at all'.

---

until his visits were stopped by the mother. The sheriff acknowledged that there was nothing about the father which would disentitle him from exercising access. Indeed, he went as far as suggesting that the mother might have created the situation which caused problems over access. None the less, he felt bound to refuse access, since he could see no advantage which the child would derive from it, particularly in the light of distress which would surround it in the light of the parents' relationship.

297 1997 SC (HL) 55.
298 Lord Hope at p 62G. Lord Weir made a similar statement in the Inner House – see 1996 SLT 750, at p 765I–J.
299 1996 SLT 750, per Lord Weir at p 765I–J.
300 In the course of a spirited description of the value of the parent-child relationship, Lord McCluskey went on to place the importance of that relationship above other legal principles, including the rules of evidence. Some flavour of what he was saying can be gleaned from the following passage: '[The parent-child relationship] is recognised as a link which has abiding intrinsic value; it is a natural link, the importance of which is felt instinctively; it is a deep and abiding theme in literature, both religious and profane, and in social and political history. It is a link which is properly understood to have value quite independently of any supposed 'right' in a parent to obtain from a court of law an order allowing 'access' to his or her child' – 1996 SLT 750, at p 752C–D.
301 1997 SC (HL) 55, at p 63C–E.
302 1997 SC (HL) 55, at p 64A.
303 *Porchetta* v *Porchetta* 1986 SLT 105, a case decided under the legislation which preceded the 1986 Act.
304 1997 SC (HL) 55, at p 63F–G.

5.102 So much for the onus of proof, what of the standard to be satisfied by the individual discharging the onus? Again, this was a matter of some uncertainty under the 1986 Act, with at least one sheriff observing that the wording of the Act seemed 'to demand a standard of proof that is higher than the normal standard in civil matters',[305] and another doubting that anything other than proof on the balance of probabilities was required.[306] While the observations are *obiter*, the Inner House took the opportunity to clarify the matter in *F* v *F*,[307] where it confirmed that proof was, indeed, on the balance of probabilities. Neither the Commission nor the 1995 Act made any specific comment on the matter and it can be assumed that this remains the standard of proof.

5.103 Appeals present special problems in cases involving children. In *Sanderson*, for example, Lord Hope noted the difficulties caused by the delays inherent in a succession of appeals. He confirmed that an appeal court, which does not have the opportunity to see the witnesses nor form any impression of them, will 'be slow to disturb' the decision of the court of first instance.[308] In addition, he noted that, the greater the lapse of time, the stronger the case for the *status quo* will become. For this reason he suggested that it might be more appropriate after a lapse of time for the applicant to make a fresh application to the court of first instance, on the basis of a change of circumstances, rather than to pursue a succession of appeals. An additional complication with such a lapse of time is that circumstances may change.[309] In *D* v *D*,[310] a custody dispute began when the younger child was under a year old and before the second child was born. The decision of the sheriff, which was the subject of the appeal, was given when the children were six and three years old and, by the time of the appeal, the elder child was almost eight. In the light of Lord Hope's word in *Sanderson*, the appeal was not pursued vigorously.

Evidence

5.104 The usual rules of evidence apply in cases dealing with the future arrangements for children in the same way as they apply to all civil cases. However, the likelihood of the court being asked to consider something a child has said to a third party, requires a brief comment on the place of hearsay evidence from children. Since 1988,[311] hearsay evidence has been admissible in civil cases in Scotland. However, it is well established[312] that, where, as in the case of a very young child, the competency of the witness

---

305 *McEachan* v *Young* 1988 SCLR 98, at p 100.
306 *Sloss* v *Taylor* 1989 SCLR 407.
307 1991 SLT 357, at p 362.
308 1997 SC (HL) 55, at p 57H–58E.
309 By the time *Sanderson* reached the House of Lords, not only had Ms McManus married, but her new partner had started proceedings to adopt the child.
310 1998 SC 259.
311 Civil Evidence (Scotland) Act 1988, s 2.
312 *F* v *Kennedy (No 1)* 1993 SLT 1277.

has not been tested in accordance with the ordinary rules in such cases,[313] hearsay evidence is not admissible. Where a child whose competency has not been tested has made statements to which one party would like to refer, what is the court to do? If such statements cannot be treated as evidence, can any account be taken of them? To put it another way, must the court simply pretend that no such statement was made?

5.105 This was one of the problems which occurred in *Sanderson*. Both the sheriff and the Sheriff Principal had heard details of certain statements the child made to third parties after visits with his father. The Sheriff Principal was at pains to make clear that, while he accepted the child had made these statements, he was not treating them as evidence that the incident spoken to in them had actually taken place. The majority of the Inner House took the view that such statements could be considered as a part of the overall picture, a position endorsed by the House of Lords. In the words of Lord Hope

> 'It would have been artificial to leave out of account what the child said, so long as the evidence was that these statements were spontaneous. What the child said was simply another aspect of the child's behaviour which the court was entitled to take into account when having regard to his welfare'.[314]

Criteria for the court's decision

5.106 Unless the court is to be given complete discretion in reaching its decision on whether or not to grant an order, and in what terms, some guidance must be provided.[315] Nor is guidance helpful only to judges. It informs parents, and the lawyers and other professionals advising them, of the basis on which decisions are likely to be taken. The welfare principle, which is discussed more fully below, has been the foundation of the courts' decision-making for a very long time. As we shall see, what is relevant under that principle is not entirely uncontentious, but many of the important factors can be gleaned from past decisions. The real issue for the Scottish Law Commission, when it re-examined the whole matter of guidance to the courts, was whether anything more detailed was required. The Commission examined the idea of a statutory checklist of factors which the court would be required to consider – a solution favoured by the Law Commission in England and Wales[316] and adopted in the Children Act 1989.[317] After consultation,[318] that solution was rejected for Scotland on the

---

313 *Rees* v *Lowe* 1990 SLT 507. One Outer House decision suggests that the child must be examined in court to establish competency before any evidence from the child can be led – see *L* v *L* 1996 SLT 767. That this is the effect of the legislation has, it is submitted rightly, been doubted – D. H. Sheldon, 'Children's Evidence, Competency and the New Hearsay Provisions' 1997 SLT (News) 1.

314 1997 SC (HL) 55, at p 61B–C.

315 For a thought-provoking analysis, see R. H. Mnookin, 'Child Custody Adjudication: Judicial Functions in the Face of Indeterminacy' 39 Law & Contemp Prob 227 (1975).

316 Report on Guardianship and Custody (Law Com No 172, 1988), paras 3.17–3.21.

317 Section 1(3) and (4).

318 It is interesting that, while most respondents to the Commission's consultation favoured a statutory checklist, significant opposition came from legal consultees – Report on Family Law, para 5.23.

basis that such a checklist would be necessarily incomplete, might divert attention from other factors which ought to be considered, and might result in judges taking a mechanical approach to decision-making.[319] The Commission did consider one matter, the place of the child's own views, which had previously been viewed as part of the concept of welfare, to be of such magnitude that it should be mentioned in the legislation. As the Commission rightly pointed out

'These ... ought to be taken into account in their own right and not just as an aspect of welfare'.[320]

In addition, the Commission felt there was a need to strengthen the provision of the 1986 Act which sought to avoid unnecessary orders.[321]

5.107 As a result of these deliberations, the 1995 Act now provides that the court shall make decisions on the basis of the overarching principles. Already described as the child lawyers' mantra, the principles, which are explored in greater detail below are

The welfare of the child is the paramount consideration;

The child must be given the opportunity to express his or her views and account will be taken of these views in the light of the child's age and maturity;

The court will not make any order unless to do so will be better than making no order at all.

The welfare principle

5.108 In considering whether or not to make any order in respect of parental responsibilities, parental rights, guardianship, or the administration of a child's property the court is directed to 'regard the welfare of the child concerned as its paramount consideration'.[322] Before we move on to the thorny question of precisely *how* the court assesses welfare, several points should be noted. First, it is the welfare of the child concerned to which the court must address itself. It will often be the case that there are several children in one family on whose future care arrangements the court is being asked to pronounce. In such circumstances, it is essential that each child is seen as an individual and his or her particular needs are considered.[323] As we shall see, courts prefer not to separate siblings, provided that this is consistent with the welfare of each child. However, where the needs of each child are sufficiently diverse as to indicate different arrangements for different siblings, that solution should prevail. Second, the child's welfare is stated to be paramount and it is popular to say that the child's welfare prevails over all other factors. Thus, the comity which usually

---

319 Report on Family Law, paras 5.20–5.23.
320 Para 5.23.
321 Paras 5.16–18, rec 33(a) and draft Bill, clause 12(3).
322 Section 11(7)(a).
323 *Osborne v Matthan (No 2)* 1998 SC 682, where the custody of one child was at issue, the court indicated that it could not take account of the needs of another child in the family.

prevails in international law will take second place to the child's welfare.[324] Similarly, the status accorded to a person as a child's parent, while important, will not prevail over the child's welfare.[325] Thus, for example, a court was prepared to authorise the emigration to Australia of two boys so that they could accompany their mother and step-father, despite the fact that this all but eliminated the contact they could have with their father, a man who had shown himself to be reasonable and accommodating. As we have seen, in *Sanderson* v *McManus*,[326] the issue of any notional 'right' a parent might have to see his child was put firmly in second place to the child's welfare.[327]

5.109 While it is relatively uncontentious to accept that the child's welfare should be paramount in considering what, if any, orders the court should make, it is quite another matter to attempt to formulate what it is that promotes or detracts from a child's welfare. As Clive has said, '[t]he

---

324 In *Campins* v *Campins* 1979 SLT (Notes) 41, the court was quite willing to regard its responsibility to reach a decision in respect of the children as more important than showing the usual deference to a court of another country which had exercised legitimate jurisdiction. Since that case, increased international mobility and concern over international child abduction has resulted in the UK becoming a party to a number of international conventions and, as a result, the courts in Scotland are now bound to apply standard rules on jurisdiction, although these allow the court to intervene where there is concern for the child's welfare. In practice, the most significant conventions are the European Convention on the Recognition and Enforcement of Decisions concerning Custody of Children and on the Restoration of Custody of Children (1980, ITS (International Treaty Series) 35) and the Hague Convention on the Civil Aspects of International Child Abduction (1980, ITS 66), both of which are given effect to in the Child Abduction and Custody Act 1985. On 19 October 1996, the Convention on Jurisdiction, Applicable Law, Recognition, Enforcement and Co-operation in respect of Parental Responsibility and Measures for the Protection of Children (to be known as the Hague Convention on Children) was signed at the Hague. The UK has yet to ratify that Convention. International child abduction is discussed in chapter 6, paras 81–100.

325 *Sanderson* v *McManus* 1997 SC (HL) 55. See also, *Osborne* v *Matthan (No 2)* 1998 SC 682, where the First Division upheld the decision of the sheriff to grant custody of a little girl to the foster carer who had looked after her for several years rather than the child's mother who was due to return to Jamaica having recently completed a prison sentence for drug-dealing. While the case deals with points of statutory interpretation under the previous legislation, which are no longer live issues, the court emphasised the paramountcy of the child's welfare. The case also noted that the court could not consider the needs of this child's half-sister, whose future care was not at issue, and deals with the fact of racial difference between the child and the foster carer.

326 1996 SLT 750 (IH); 1997 SLT 629 (HL), discussed at para 5.101, above.

327 In *Franz* v *United States* 707 F 2d 582 (DC Cir, 1983), a court in the USA was faced with an interesting problem, in this context. When William and Catherine Franz divorced, Catherine was given custody of the children and William was allowed visitation rights which he exercised. Catherine subsequently remarried one Charles Allen, a contract killer employed by the leaders of organised crime. Charles agreed to testify in a criminal trial in return for relocation of, and protection for, himself, Catherine and the children, under the Witness Protection Program. Once they had been relocated, the US Marshall's Service refused to tell William where his children were, thus making it impossible for him to exercise his right of visitation. William raised an action against the US government, seeking damages and injunctive and declaratory relief. While much of the case turns on constitutional issues, the judgments provide an interesting analysis of the nature of the right to visitation (contact).

welfare of the child is not a technical legal concept'.[328] That is undoubtedly the case and, while it is stating the obvious to note that every case is unique, some indication of the factors a court might consider to be relevant, in determining what will serve a child's interests, can be gleaned from examining past decisions. Certain factors will be of greater significance in particular cases and individual members of the judiciary may attach greater or lesser importance to particular matters. Some of the older cases should be approached with particular caution, since what was considered impor- tant in one era may no longer hold sway. As we shall see, most of the cases relate to custody and access. While these concepts are no longer applicable under the 1995 Act, the factors which indicate what will serve a child's welfare remain relevant. The recognition of the continued involvement of both parents in the lives of children, even after divorce, and the fact that other adults may now play a significant role must be taken into account. None the less, disputes over residence and contact will continue and it is hoped that this exercise will throw some light on what is really meant by 'the welfare of the child'.

Relevant factors

Physical welfare

5.110　Clearly, a person who is wholly unable to take care of the physical needs of a young child would be unlikely to succeed in obtaining a residence order, unless the applicant could demonstrate that some other person would be available to assist with care. Thus, an applicant with serious physical or mental disability, or who was addicted to drugs or alcohol, might simply be unable to meet the child's needs. One might expect that a history of child abuse or neglect would sound alarm bells that would militate against the abusive or neglectful person being left with a child in his or her charge and usually that is the case.[329] What of the suggestion that the applicant poses a less direct but, none the less, significant, risk to the child's physical welfare?

5.111　In *Clayton* v *Clayton*,[330] the court was given ample opportunity to explore a whole range of issues which the father, a 72-year-old, retired academic, regarded as relevant to his son's welfare. He had raised these issues frequently with his soon-to-be ex-wife, with whom the child lived.

328 *The Law of Husband and Wife in Scotland* (4th edn, W. Green, 1997), at p 505. In earlier editions of this work, Dr Clive can be credited with providing one of the most comprehensive lists of factors which the courts have considered relevant in assessing welfare; a list which almost certainly informed the authors of other works, including this one. It is a reflection of Dr Clive's view of the non-legal nature of the welfare principle that he no longer includes such an enumeration of relevant factors. The decision was taken to include such a list here simply in the hope that it will be of assistance to students and practitioners. See also, Wilkinson and Norrie, n 1 above, at pp 208–225.

329 However, in *Early* v *Early* 1989 SLT 114, the father who had two convictions for child neglect did gain custody. The circumstances of neglect were somewhat unusual and the court was clearly more influenced by fact than sexual preference of the non-neglectful, lesbian mother.

330 1995 GWD 18–1000. The case is also available on Lexis and it is worth reading the full report.

While the active participation of the non-resident parent is now a central tenet of the 1995 Act, this particular father's conduct appears to have amounted to constant intervention, bordering on the controlling. The concerns included: the lead content in the water at the defender's flat (he offered to lend her money to have the pipes renewed); the fact that the defender had cats which he regarded (apparently as a species) as 'sources of fleas and dirt'; the fact that his estranged wife had taken in a lodger (he was concerned about his son being exposed to sexual deviants); the safety of his son taking a short bus ride to school (something the boy's mother had done along with the child, in order to assess his ability to cope with it); various issues of safety at his son's school; the competence of the school crossing guard (about whom he complained); and various matters associated with his son's education (he engaged in lengthy correspondence with the head teacher and other staff). Lord Gill's observation that '[h]is affection has become his preoccupation, particularly in the matter of education', can only be described as charitable in the extreme, although the strain placed on this generosity becomes apparent in the later statement that 'the pursuer regards any view of the defender which differs from his own as being erroneous'. In the event, the court was not persuaded that any of these concerns posed a danger to the child. The case was decided under the 1986 Act, which encouraged the award of parental rights to one parent, with little more than access (contact) being given to the other. Somewhat unusually in that case, the Minute of Agreement, concluded by the parents after separation, provided that, while the mother would have care and control of the boy, the father reserved his parental rights. It also provided that the parents would agree all major decisions affecting their son's welfare. Noting that the father 'has interfered on numerous matters which he ought to have left to the defender's own judgement and responsibility', Lord Gill took the view that 'the present state of affairs ought not to continue' and awarded custody to the mother. Effectively, the father's right to participate in decision-making was removed.[331] While the 1995 Act envisages the continued involvement of both parents in the child's life, regardless of divorce, one wonders if this might not be one of the very small number of unusual cases where the court might believe it to be better for the child that primary responsibility should be vested solely in one parent.

5.112 One kind of risk to a child's welfare which has been raised in courts in other jurisdictions is of the applicant who engages in the heinous offence of smoking cigarettes.[332] Should account be taken of exposing a child to the

---

331 It is worth noting that the mother had undertaken in evidence that she would consult with the father, were she to consider moving the boy from his present school. In the light of the father's past conduct, this seems to demonstrate a particularly generous attitude on her part. Of course, such an attitude is likely to elicit a favourable response from the court and, once the case has been decided, the court has no power to monitor compliance with promises, unless someone brings the case back to court.

332 In *Heck* v *Reed* 529 NW 2d 155 (ND 1995), the North Dakota Supreme Court reversed the decision of the trial court giving a wife-beating, but non-smoking, father custody of the children of the marriage in preference to the mother, a smoker. In *Smith* v *Smith* 1996 WL 591181 (Tenn Ct App 11 Oct 1996), a father was allowed visitation on the condition that he did not smoke in the child's presence. Within days of the decree, the mother

effects of secondary smoke? Needless to say, in *Clayton*, the fact that the mother had an occasional cigarette was one of a myriad of issues raised by the father, but the concern was not explored in any depth in the case. It might be relevant to distinguish between exposing an asthmatic child to such a pollutant and exposing a healthy child to one of the hazards of everyday life. Once we open the door to 'lifestyle' factors, other risks become relevant and, arguably, it is the degree of risk to the child that becomes important.[333] So, for example, exposing a child to an unhealthy diet to the extent that he or she became obese, would be relevant in examining the child's welfare, whereas supplying some sweets and the occasional hamburger and fries would not. This highlights the fact that how important a particular issue is in a given case will often be a matter of degree and, to some extent, judgment. While it is tragic that children occasionally die while engaging in sports or outward-bound activities, that is no reason to wrap every child in cotton wool and prevent him or her from taking calculated risks in pursuing hobbies. Indeed, to deny a child the opportunity to engage in the same activities as most of his or her peers would, arguably, be to fail to promote that child's development.

5.113 Older children have less immediate need for direct physical care, but the environment in which they would be living remains a consideration. Such factors as the accommodation available, the applicant's state of health and any childcare arrangements planned by a person out at work would also be relevant. In assessing the applicant's ability to care for the child, the court will consider any help which might be available. In the past, this has usually meant that, where a working father was applying for custody, the fact that he had a mother,[334] sister or fiancée[335] who was willing to help was viewed in a positive light.[336] Of course, in many cases, both parents will be in employment and the respective merits of the childcare arrangements they intend to make will be relevant. The courts appear to consider it preferable that a child should be cared for by a parent rather than a nanny,[337] although, in one case the issue came down to the respective merits of the nannies being offered by each party.[338] This raises the question of sending a child to boarding-school, as opposed to the child being educated as a day-pupil and staying at home. The courts do not appear to have been faced with the choice and it will be interesting to see how they resolve it. Is the provision of a boarding-school education a

returned to court complaining that the father had violated the condition and his visits were suspended. In *Unger* v *Unger* 644 A 2d 691 (NJ Super Ch, 1994), the court ordered a mother not to smoke in the presence of her children, nor to take them in a car where she had smoked within the previous ten hours. It can be expected that these cases represent the first whiff of a trend to come.

333 See for example, *Clayton* v *Clayton*, n 330 above, where, amongst the many matters over which the father took issue with the mother, was that of the lead content in the water in her home.
334 *Sloss* v *Taylor* 1989 SCLR 407, above; *Cowen* v *Brown* 1991 GWD 29–1718.
335 *Geddes* v *Geddes* 1987 GWD 11–349.
336 Indeed, in *Nessling* v *Nessling* 1991 GWD 31–1830, the fact that the father was no longer living with his girlfriend was one factor which prevented him from obtaining custody.
337 *Keshmiri* v *Keshmiri* 1991 GWD 4–195.
338 *Hogarth* v *Hogarth* 1991 GWD 30–1771.

financial commitment by a parent to ensure the child's development or is it an abdication of direct parental responsibility? Where both applicants are unemployed, then, other factors being equal, each of them is available to care for the child.

5.114 The importance of the relative affluence of competing applicants has often been stated not to be a factor, provided that each can provide the child with adequate surroundings, a point emphasised in *Casey v Casey*.[339] There, the dispute over the custody of two boys was between divorcing parents, each of whom had formed a new stable relationship. The mother was living in Surrey in relative affluence, while the father was living in Scotland and was dependent on state benefits. A number of issues influenced the decision,[340] but the Lord Ordinary attached significance to his belief that 'the children are likely to be offered better role models'[341] by the adults who just happened to be more affluent. In *Brixey v Lynas*, the sheriff's original award of custody to the unmarried father was influenced, in part, by his belief that he should not 'deprive the child of the advantages which the accident of her paternity make available to her ... there is a better chance of the father providing a stable background and a successful future for the child than there is of the mother doing so'.[342] Thus, while wealth is not a ticket to ensuring that an applicant will succeed, the apparent difficulty in divorcing 'role models' and 'opportunities', both perfectly legitimate factors in the welfare equation, from affluence, seems to work in favour of the better-heeled applicant.

5.115 Given that the first of the parental responsibilities is to safeguard and promote the child's health, development and welfare, the provision of adequate medical attention is important, particularly where the applicant is seeking to have the child live with him or her for substantial periods of time. Aspects of medical treatment may amount to exercising judgment, particularly where medical opinion itself is divided. An example here would be the decision whether or not to vaccinate a child against diseases almost unknown in Scotland today, where vaccination carries certain risks. However, the courts are wary of children being denied access to, generally accepted, mainstream, medical treatment. Nor is the fact that a parent's position is based on good faith or sincerely held beliefs sufficient to justify their straying from what the courts regard as within the normal parameters.

---

339 1989 SCLR 761.
340 These include the strong views of the elder child, the desire to keep the children together, and the mother's apparent sincerity in her willingness to facilitate the children's continued contact with their father but not, in this case, the *status quo*, nor the culpability of the adults as spouses. The range of factors considered in this case and the analysis of them makes it well worth reading.
341 1989 SCLR 761, at p 763.
342 1994 SLT 847 at p 849. That case is discussed more fully below in the context of the maternal preference, but the sheriff placed considerable emphasis on the very favourable impression created on him by the paternal grandmother, with whom the child and the father would be living, as opposed to either of the parents whom he clearly found to be fairly unimpressive. As we shall see, the sheriff's decision was overturned on appeal , but on a most unsatisfactory basis.

In *Finlayson (Applicant)*,[343] for example, the parents' opposition to their haemophiliac son receiving a blood transfusion was based, in part, on their fear of his contracting HIV as a result. Despite the sincerity of their concern, a children's hearing was still able to conclude that the boy was in need of compulsory measures of care and authorised treatment. In *McKechnie* v *McKechnie*,[344] the court refused to grant joint parental rights to a father where his religion prohibited certain kinds of medical treatment.

5.116 Obviously, some of these factors are less important when considering contact. Thus, for example, while the size of the applicant's home might be important if the child was to be living there, it would be less significant if the child merely visited or stayed overnight only occasionally. Similarly, alternative child-care arrangements need not be considered if the plan was for the child to spend time with the applicant only when he or she was not at work. Where the applicant is seeking only to be appointed as the child's legal representative, then clearly his or her ability to take care of the child's physical needs would be irrelevant, while such factors as judgment, experience and responsibility would hold greater sway.

Emotional welfare

5.117 The courts do consider the child's emotional welfare to be important, albeit it is more difficult to assess than physical welfare.[345] Thus, the person who provides a child with a stable, positive and secure environment is likely to prevail in a dispute over residence. How emotional welfare is assessed may involve hearing the child's views, but evidence that a child's appetite[346] or school work[347] have improved, in a particular setting, go some way to providing indicators of emotional welfare. Conversely, evidence of a deterioration in a child's behaviour after contact might suggest that the contact itself was having an adverse effect on the child.[348]

5.118 That sort of 'hard' evidence aside, how is a court to assess the emotional impact of a particular individual or circumstances upon a child? The task becomes all the more difficult when the court is attempting to assess the impact that such factors may have on the child in the future. The difficulty is well illustrated by the case of *Early* v *Early*,[349] where a lesbian

---

343 1989 SCLR 601. The children's hearings system is discussed in detail in chapter 9. For the present, it should be noted that the expression 'compulsory measures of care' applied in the context of this case, which was decided under the Social Work (Scotland) Act 1968. The equivalent expression in the 1995 Act is 'compulsory measures of supervision'.
344 (Sh Ct) 1990 SCLR (Notes) 153.
345 Indeed, it is sometimes somewhat artificial to separate emotional and physical welfare, since the two may be interrelated. A small child with unexplained stomach-ache, or one who begins to wet the bed, may have a physical illness, but it is just as likely that the symptoms are connected to the child's emotional state.
346 *Geddes* v *Geddes* 1987 GWD 11–349.
347 *Geddes* v *Geddes*, above; *O'Hagan* v *O'Hagan* 1989 GWD 8–319.
348 In *Sanderson* v *McManus*, above, the sheriff had been particularly impressed by the evidence given by the child's schoolteacher, who spoke of her own and her colleagues' concern over the child's uncharacteristically aggressive behaviour following visits with his father.
349 1989 SLT 114.

mother, who was living with her same-sex partner, sought to retain custody of her eight-year-old son in the face of opposition from his father. While the decision to award custody to the father was influenced by a number of factors, including the fact that the boy's sibling lived with him, the court took the view that the nature of the mother's relationship might cause the child 'unusual difficulties' and embarrassment. However, children may be teased about a great many things. Will the courts really attribute risk to a child's emotional welfare where for example, a parent's appearance or high public profile, might attract comment? If so, schoolteachers who teach at the school which their children attend should hold out little hope of having their children live with them, should any dispute arise. The suggestion that a parent's homosexuality or lesbianism will have any adverse effect on the child is disputed widely in the literature,[350] and has since been debunked, very soundly, by the Inner House.[351]

5.119 In this thorny field of assessing the emotional impact of particular factors, it must be tempting for the courts to seek refuge in the evidence of 'expert witnesses'. While less common in Scotland,[352] much use has been made of such evidence in other jurisdictions. However, it is worth sounding a note of caution in order that the courts do not simply abdicate the responsibility to exercise their judgment in favour of the so-called expert. Opinions vary widely in the fields of psychology and psychiatry and respected professionals in these fields may reach radically differing conclusions. It would be dangerous to allow a child's future to turn on the accidental selection of a particular expert or for cases to become nothing more than a battle between competing experts' opinions.

5.120 Given the fact that so many health-care professionals view continuity of care as being important for a child's emotional welfare,[353] it is not surprising that courts have tended to attach considerable significance to the

---

350 N. Polikoff, 'This Child Does Have two Mothers: Redefining Parenthood to Meet the Needs of Children in Lesbian and Other Nontraditional Families' 78 Geo L J 459 (1990); M. Strasser, 'Fit to be Tied: On Custody, Discretion and Sexual Orientation' 46 Am U L Rev 841 (1997); F. Tasker and S. Golombok, 'Children Raised by Lesbian Mothers' 1991 Fam Law 184.

351 *T, Petitioner* 1997 SLT 724, discussed in detail in chapter 8, para 17. In the earlier case of *Hill* v *Hill* 1991 SLT 189 the Scottish court returned a child to his homosexual father in Canada under the provisions of the Hague Convention. The court found that the boy had been wrongfully removed from Canada by the mother and was unwilling to accept that he would be exposed to harm by being returned. See also, *Meredith* v *Meredith* 1994 GWD 19–1150, where a father was permitted to have access to his children at the home he shared with his same-sex partner provided that open displays of affection between the adults were avoided.

352 Such evidence has been led in a number of cases. See for example, *Early* v *Early* 1989 SLT 114. For some of the difficulties which can arise, see *D* v *D* 1998 SC 259.

353 The classic work on this point is J. Goldstein, A. J. Solnit and A. Freud, *Beyond the Best Interests of the Child* (1st edn, 1973, revised edn, 1979, Free Press). The same authors went on to develop the idea of continuity of care and the least detrimental alternative in J. Goldstein, A. Freud and A. J. Solnit, *Before the Best Interests of the Child* (Free Press, 1979). The third book in the series is J. Goldstein, A. Freud, A. J. Solnit, and S. Goldstein, *In the Best Interests of the Child* (Free Press, 1986). Anna Freud participated in the writing of that book until shortly before her death in 1982. The theme of continuity of care has been taken up by countless authors since.

status quo.[354] If anything the trend has been more marked in recent years, even in the face of very questionable behaviour by some parents.[355] As ever, the courts focus on the welfare of the child and not the, sometimes reprehensible, conduct of parents. While the *status quo* will often prevail, other factors may be sufficiently strong so as to justify its being displaced.[356] As we have seen, the second of the overarching principles requires the court not to make any order unless it would be better for the child that the order be made than that none be made at all.[357] Does this mean that the *status quo*, as one facet of welfare, has been elevated by the 1995 Act into a guiding principle? Strictly speaking the answer is in the negative. *Status quo*, as just explored, relates to the *de facto* situation; that is the practical reality of where and with whom the child has been living. The instruction to the court in s 11(7)(a) deals with the *de jure* situation; that is, who has the legal responsibilities and rights and whether that should be altered by court order. The distinction can be clarified by an example. Let us take the case of unmarried parents who do not have any agreement giving the father parental responsibilities and rights but where, none the less, the father sees the child on a regular basis. They then fall out and the mother stops the father's visits. He applies to the court for a contact order. All other matters being equal (a highly unlikely state of affairs), the *de facto status quo*, his regular contact in the past, will assist him in showing that contact will serve the child's interest. However, the *de jure status quo*, his lack of any parental responsibilities and rights, means that, if he is to succeed, he will have to discharge the onus of proof showing that granting the order will be better than not doing so.

5.121 Mention should be made, at this point, of a central factor which has been described in the USA as the 'primary caretaker standard'.[358] The

---

354 In *Hannah v Hannah* 1971 SLT (Notes) 42, where the eight-year-old girl had lived with her father since she was one year old, the Lord Ordinary awarded custody to the child's mother, largely because the father was cohabiting with a new partner. That decision was reversed on appeal in recognition of the fact that the girl was happy and settled with her father. See also, *Whitecross v Whitecross* 1977 SLT 225 (father given custody of a young child whom he had looked after since the marital breakdown).

355 *Black v Black* 1990 SLT (Sh Ct) 42 (on appeal, father who had refused to return two boys to their mother after a visit, gained custody despite some serious questions about his lifestyle, because of 'the security of the life which they have with their father in familiar surroundings, with friends and at a school they know and like' (at p 46I)); *Breingan v Jamieson* 1993 SLT 186 (aunt, who had looked after the child with the help of other maternal relatives since the mothers' death, prevailed over the child's father and his new wife, despite their being able to provide a perfectly good home); *Sherwin v Trumayne* 1992 GWD 29–1683 (abducting father awarded custody).

356 *Casey v Casey* 1989 SCLR 761 (strong views of elder boy, mother and her new partner as better role models, and her willingness to facilitate contact with the father outweighed the *status quo*); *Early v Early*, n 352 above (lesbian mother lost custody of son to father who already had custody of the boy's siblings); *Hastie v Hastie* 1985 SLT 146 (mother gained custody from father and 62-year-old grandmother who had been indoctrinating the child against his mother); *Kyle v Stewart* 1989 GWD 14–580 (father prevailed over immature aunt who had been caring for the child).

357 Section 11(7)(a).

358 Goldstein *et al* prefer the term 'caregiver' to 'caretaker', since they believe it reflects the relationship more accurately – J. Goldstein, A. Freud, A. J. Solnit and S. Goldstein, *In the Best Interests of the Child* (Free Press, 1986), at p 63.

articulation of the primary caretaker standard is often credited to the Supreme Court of West Virginia in its decision in *Garsky* v *McCoy*.[359] Essentially, this standard involves looking at who had greater direct responsibility for looking after the child in the past, and giving preference to that person where there is a dispute over the child's care in the future. The precise indicator will vary with the age of the child and family circumstances but, in respect of a young child, who did the following would be relevant: got the child up in the morning; bathed and dressed the child; cooked and served meals; took the child to the doctor and dentist; helped to arrange the child's social life and knew the child's friends; arranged for alternative care; and put the child to bed at night. To some extent, recognition of the primary caretaker is similar to recognition of the *status quo*. Again, it can be argued that keeping things as much like they have been in the past will serve the child's welfare by creating a sense of continuity and stability. The standard has been attacked, however, as a thinly disguised variant of the maternal preference[360] and certainly, the effect of each is often the same.

Spiritual welfare

5.122 In the past, the courts have taken the view that it is preferable for a child to receive some religious instruction rather than none at all,[361] although they have been willing to accept that input on religious matters can be provided by a person other than the applicant.[362] Not surprisingly, the courts have refused to adjudicate between religions.[363] The cases in this area are all fairly old and involved what might be described as 'mainstream' religions commonly accepted in Scotland. Without wishing to get into the fascinating question of the difference between a cult and a religion, what attitude the courts might take to some of the more recently created or minority religions is not known.[364] Certainly, the fact that a small number

359 278 SE 2d 357 (1981).
360 R. Neely, 'The Primary Caretaker Parent Rule: Child Custody and the Dynamics of Greed' 3 Yale L & Pol Rev 167 (1984).
361 *McClements* v *McClements* 1958 SC 286, where the custody of a child was given to an adulterous mother (remember, this was in the 1950s), rather than an atheist father. There were a number of factors which led the court to this decision but, as Lord Justice-Clerk Thomson put it (at p 289), one of them was that the child 'ought not to be denied the opportunity of being brought up in the generally accepted religious beliefs of the society in which he lives'.
362 *McKay* v *McKay* 1957 SLT (Notes) 17. There, while the father was a communist and atheist, he had no objection to his mother, who lived with them, providing the child with a religious education. Perhaps not surprisingly, at one stage in the USA, the professing of communism seems to have been enough to lose a parent custody – *Eaton* v *Eaton* 191 A 839 (1937), where a communist, atheist mother lost custody and was granted visitation only on condition that she did not attempt to instil her beliefs in the children.
363 *McNaught* v *McNaught* 1955 SLT (Sh Ct) 9. Given the particular sensitivity of the issue in some parts of Scotland, the court's reluctance to act as referee on the question of whether a child should be raised in the Roman Catholic or Protestant faiths was to be expected. How a court could hope to make such a determination is difficult to see, although recognising the child's evolving capacity and listening to the child's views may provide assistance.
364 Certainly, the courts in England and Wales have been fairly wary of minority religions; *Hewison* v *Hewison* (1977) 7 Fam L 207 (father, who belonged to the Exclusive Brethren,

of people practise a particular religion, or that some of their beliefs are unusual, is no reason to suppose that the parent's religious preference will have an adverse impact on the child and that, after all, is what matters. A good example of the relevance of religion in a modern context can be found in *McKechnie* v *McKechnie*[365] where, as we have seen, the court expressed concern over the possible problems which could arise where a parent's religion prohibited medical treatment. It will be remembered that, while art 14 of the UN Convention on the Rights of the Child recognises the child's right to freedom of religion, it also recognises the right of parents and guardians to provide the child with guidance in this area, in a manner consistent with the child's evolving capacity.

Educational welfare

5.123 Given the parental responsibility to safeguard and promote the child's health, development and welfare, the child's educational development is a relevant factor. Again, however, what is the best choice for a particular child's education will often amount to no more than a matter of opinion. In *Clayton*, this was yet another of the concerns of the over-anxious father. He had strong views about a whole host of aspects of his son's education and sought an order of the court that his son should continue to attend a particular private school in Edinburgh. Lord Gill refused the order for a variety of reason, not least because he felt that

> 'while it may be appropriate to make an order regulating the education of a very young child, [it] is not appropriate to do so in the case of a child on the verge of adolescence whose own views on the subject will be increasingly important as his secondary education progresses'.

Applicant's behaviour

5.124 The applicant's behaviour is now regarded as significant only where it will have some effect on the child. Gone are the days when an adulterous parent could give up all hope of being allowed to care for a child.[366] The impact of parental behaviour on the child can sometimes be demonstrated to the court as, for example, where the mother's temper and generally uptight attitude was alleged to upset the child.[367] Similarly, where an applicant is addicted to alcohol or drugs, this conduct may have a significant effect on his or her ability to care for a child. However, while the

was deprived of custody because 'The mode of life and code of behaviour enforced by the sect upon its members and their children is ... harsh and restrictive' (at p 208)); *Re B and G (Minors) (Custody)* [1985] FLR 134 (Church of Scientology); *T* v *T* (1974) 4 Fam L 190 (mother's commitment as a Jehovah's Witness was fairly obsessive and she lost custody); *Re H (A Minor)* (1980) 10 Fam L 248 (custody was given to Jehovah's Witness mother who was prepared to allow father to celebrate birthdays and Christmas with the children).

365 (Sh Ct) 1990 SCLR (Notes) 153.

366 For the older, puritanical position, see *Lang* v *Lang* (1869) 7 M 445, where Lord Neave expressed the view (at p 447) that 'It is not that he has committed faults, but that he teaches, or is likely to teach, evil to [the children] and to corrupt their morals'. For the more modern approach, see *Geddes* v *Geddes* 1987 GWD 11–349; *Johnston* v *Johnston* 1947 SLT (Notes) 26; *McClements* v *McClements*, n 361 above.

367 *Geddes* v *Geddes*, above.

legal system may have become less moralistic, on a theoretical level, the problem remains of identifying precisely what conduct by a parent will have an adverse impact on a child. So, for example, the courts must still assess whether a parent's sexual preference and conduct, smoking, drinking, religious affiliation, career commitment, or fun-loving lifestyle,[368] will pose a threat to a child's welfare. In the end, this will come down to a matter of degree and, sometimes, the alternative on offer.

5.125 One particular aspect of a parent's behaviour merits special attention. Where there has been inter-spousal violence, but no overt violence towards the child, should this have any impact on the court's approach to future arrangements for the child? Let us focus the question by the use of an example. Let us suppose that the father of Ben and Daisy has a long history of violence towards the children's mother, who has raised an action for divorce on the basis of his behaviour. The father has never been violent towards either of his children and, indeed, is a loving parent. It is not practical for the children to live with him, but he would like to see them regularly. The children's mother wants this man out of her life and opposes contact. Taking a decision on the basis of the child's best interests might support continuing their established relationship with their father. Just to add to his case, let us suppose that the children want to see him. Do other factors outweigh these considerations? Clearly, a wife-beater is hardly a good role model, so does it matter whether he was violent in front of the children or only in private? Quite apart from what the children may have seen in the past, does his conduct say anything about his general personality and the attitudes to which he is likely to expose them? Should the court enquire whether he has been violent towards other partners and, therefore, might behave in a violent way in front of the children in the future? In focusing on the welfare of the children, should the court give any thought to Ben and Daisy's mother who may be genuinely and justifiably afraid of being anywhere near their father? Recent research in Denmark, England and New Zealand has drawn attention to the continuing danger to some women when their violent former partners misuse contact with the children as a means of continuing to control and terrorise these women.[369] It may be that any contact, in such cases, can be arranged through contact

---

368 In *Brixey* v *Lynas* 1994 SLT 847, it was clear that the sheriff was unimpressed by the behaviour of a young mother in respect of; frequenting public houses, getting drunk occasionally, past consumption of cannabis, fondness for male company, and brief recent association with another man. None the less, he did not accept that this conduct 'endangered' the child, as the father had alleged.

369 M. Hester and L. Radford, *Domestic violence in child contact arrangements in England and Denmark* (The Policy Press, 1996). For a discussion of the background to, and content of, the New Zealand legislation, see, R. Busch and N. Robertson, 'Innovative Approaches to Child Custody and Domestic Violence in New Zealand: the Effects of Law Reform on the Discourses of Battering' in P. Jaffe (ed), *Children Exposed to Domestic Violence* (Sage, 1998). New Zealand's Domestic Violence Act 1995 introduced a rebuttable presumption that a parent who had been violent to his or her partner or a child should not be permitted to have unsupervised access to the child unless the court was satisfied that the child would be safe with the violent parent. It also widened the definition of 'domestic violence' to include homosexual and lesbian relationships and violence towards members of the extended family.

centres or third party intermediaries, thus avoiding the parties having to meet each other. That, however, is not a complete solution since many women who have experienced domestic violence will not feel safe if their former partner has any idea where they live. In such cases, prohibiting contact may be the only answer.

The tender years doctrine or the maternal preference

5.126 The suggestion that a modern legal system might be driven by implicit gender bias in reaching decisions about the future arrangements for children is one which might be greeted with concern. That any legal system should be quite explicit in adopting this prejudice is astonishing. While the view that the mother is the natural custodier of young children held some sway in centuries past,[370] it was thought that such blind gender-based prejudice had been abandoned in favour of looking at the parents as individuals[371] and assessing what each had to offer the child. That was until *Brixey* v *Lynas*[372]. The case involved a dispute between unmarried parents over the custody of a two-year-old girl and, in overturning the earlier decision of the sheriff, who had granted custody to the father, the Inner House resurrected the maternal preference with the words, 'during her infancy the child's need for the mother is stronger than the need for the father'.[373] That such an approach runs counter to the current trend of looking at the unique facts of each case, considering the particular child and the applicants as individuals, and comparing what each applicant has to offer to the child, appears to have been ignored. Furthermore, this kind of prejudice flies in the face of the prohibition, stated quite explicitly in the UN Convention on the Rights of the Child, on discrimination based on the parent's sex. The Convention provides

370 *Martin* v *Martin* (1895) 3 SLT 150. The whole question of motherhood, fatherhood, and the changing nature of each, has generated a vast literature. The following are a small sample. In D. Blankenhorn, *Fatherless America: Confronting Our Most Urgent Social Problem* (Basic Books, 1995), the author argues that industrialisation 'led to the physical separation of home and work' and reduced men's involvement in family life. His view is that 'in some respects it has been downhill for fathers since the Industrial Revolution' (at p 12). In R. LaRossa, *The Modernization of Fatherhood: A Social and Political History* (The University of Chicago Press, 1997), the author disputes that the process was so straightforward and examines the emergence of the image of fatherhood in USA, including the way in which 'the current image of the father as economic provider, pal, and male role model all rolled into one became *institutionalized*' (p 1). In D. Friedman, *Towards a Structure of Indifference: The Social Origins of Maternal Custody* (Aldine de Gruyter, 1995), the author examines the legal change in the presumption of child custody from fathers to mothers in the USA and England (and other countries that permitted divorce) from 1880 to 1920 and why men gave up their rights without a fight. See also, M. A. Fineman, *The Neutered Mother, The Sexual Family* (Routledge, 1995).
371 The need to see each child as an individual had been emphasised in various reports, shortly before this case – see for example, Report of the Inquiry into the Removal of Children from Orkney in February 1991 (HMSO, 1992), para 3.40; Scotland's Children: Proposals for Child Care Policy and Law (Cm 2286, 1993), paras 2.6 and 2.7.
372 1994 SLT 847 (IH); 1996 SLT 908 (HL). For a detailed discussion of the case, see E. E. Sutherland, 'Mother Knows Best' 1994 SLT (News) 375; E. E. Sutherland, 'Neither a presumption nor a principle' 1996 JR 414 and E. E. Sutherland, 'The Unequal Struggle: Fathers and Children in Scots Law', 1997 CFLQ 191.
373 1994 SLT 847, at p 849I.

'The States Parties to the present Convention … shall respect and ensure the rights set forth in [this] Convention to each child within their jurisdiction *without discrimination of any kind, irrespective of the child's or his or her parent's* or legal guardian's race, colour, *sex*, language, religion, political or other opinion, national, ethnic or social origin, property, disability, birth or other status'.[374]

The father appealed to the House of Lords. Affirming the decision of the Inner House, their Lordships rejected the arguments about discrimination and endorsed the maternal preference. Lord Jauncey of Tullichettle's words give some idea of the thinking which prevailed

'Nature has endowed men and women with very different attributes and it so happens that mothers are generally better fitted than fathers to provide for the needs of very young children. This is no more discriminatory than the fact that only women can give birth'.[375]

It should be remembered that the House of Lords is not bound by its own previous decisions and there is always the possibility of a similar case being taken to the European Court of Human Rights.[376] For the present, however, the maternal preference holds some sway. In an individual case, the facts and circumstances may be such that the court is able to distinguish it from *Brixey*, something the courts appear to have been able to do.[377]

5.127 Given the sexist assumptions underlying the maternal preference, it may be that it will only apply where the mother conforms to the stereotype of the 'good mother'. Where a woman steps outside these parameters, she may be viewed all the more harshly, as both Ms Early[378] and Ms Brixey[379] discovered. Certainly, there are a host of cases from the USA where a mother's commitment to her career was often fatal to her claim to be able to provide adequate parenting in the post-divorce setting.[380] These cases are particularly graphic, since the fathers, who succeeded in gaining

---

374 Article 2(1), emphasis added.

375 1996 SLT 908, at p 911E.

376 Such a case would proceed on the basis of the European Convention on Human Rights which, again, prohibits discrimination (art 14) in recognising any of the rights it provides for. One of the rights dealt with in the Convention is the right to respect for privacy and one's own family life (art 8).

377 In *MacMillan* v *Brady* 1997 GWD 4–130, the Inner House refused to overturn the original decision of the sheriff to award custody of a young child to his father. The mother and father were 15 and 34 years old, respectively, when the child was born and the case reached the Inner House three years later. It would be fair to say that neither parent could be described as 'ideal'. The mother had an active social life, appears to have been drunk fairly regularly, sometimes while she was looking after the child. On other occasions she left the boy in the care of very young women. Her home appears to have been something of a 'party house' and, while she seems to have met the child's basic needs, the sheriff expressed concern that she was exercising insufficient supervision over her son. The father had a criminal record, experience of imprisonment and involvement with drugs. However, he appears to have been a very involved father throughout the child's life and he had since married and lived with his wife, her child by a previous relationship, and their child, in a stable family setting.

378 *Early* v *Early* 1989 SLT 114.

379 *Brixey* v *Lynas* 1994 SLT 847.

380 In *Prost* v *Greene* 652 A. 2d 621 (DC 1995), custody of the children was awarded to a full-time working father after the court decided that the mother was more devoted to her career and despite expert evidence that the children were more attached to her. In

custody, often had similarly demanding careers. Given the court's willingness to look at what the parent has to offer as a role model, it might be hoped that a similar prejudice against career women will not manifest itself in Scotland.

5.128 Since the prejudice focusing on the parent's gender and the child's age has been resurrected, is the child's gender of any significance? Are girls and young women better off with mothers? If so, are young men better off with their fathers? While the occasional case gives support to such a notion,[381] this form of facile prejudice is not widespread. In any event, the views of the child will be relevant and the older the child, the greater weight that will be attached to such views.

Links with other family members and continuity of established relationships

5.129 In one sense, recognising the continuity of relationships is a facet of favouring the *status quo*. However, another manifestation of it is the court's reluctance to separate siblings,[382] unless there is a good reason why they should live in different homes.[383] Certainly, a parent who was seeking residence would be well-advised to show a co-operative attitude to the other parent's participation in the child's future.[384] It is in the nature of some individuals and some relationships that parental hostility will make contact very difficult, particularly while the child is young and the resident parent will be required to participate in arranging it. In the most extreme cases, the resulting distress caused to the child may mean that it is better that there should be no contact at all. In *Russell* v *Russell*,[385] where the child became distressed when the father tried to visit, the sheriff went as far as

---

Richmond v *Tecklenberg* 396 SE 2d 111 (SC Ct App, 1990), custody of a six-year-old girl was awarded to the father whose work commitments were similar to the mother's busy schedule as a doctor. In D. K. Weisberg, 'Professional Women and the Professionalization of Motherhood: Marcia Clark's Double Bind' 6 Hastings Women's L J 295 (1995), Professor Weisberg uses O. J. Simpson prosecutor, Marcia Clark's, custody battle as an illustration of the problem. A similar case, this time from Canada and involving a high-profile politician, is discussed in S. E. Boyd, 'Looking Beyond *Tyabji*: Employed Mothers, Lifestyles, and Child Custody' in S. E. Boyd (ed), *Challenging the Public/Private Divide: Feminism, Law and Public Policy* (University of Toronto Press, 1997). See also, J. C. Murray, 'Legal Images of Motherhood: Conflicting Definitions from Welfare 'Reform', Family and Criminal Law' 83 Cornell L Rev 688 (1998).

381 In *Jordan* v *Jordan* 1983 SLT 539, for example, it was suggested that the mother might be a more appropriate custodier of teenage young women. See also, *Lewis* v *Lewis* 1992 GWD 27–1524; *Robertson* v *Robertson* 1981 SLT (Notes) 7.

382 In *Mason* v *Mason* 1987 GWD 27–1021, for example, this meant that the girl, who had particularly strong views, effectively determined not only her own custody but that of her younger brother who wanted to remain with her. See also, *Casey* v *Casey* 1989 SCLR 761; *Early* v *Early* 1989 SLT 114.

383 *Barr* v *Barr* 1950 SLT (Notes) 15; *Johnson* v *Johnson* 1972 SLT (Notes) 15.

384 In *Casey* v *Casey*, n 382 above, the court contrasted the mother's willingness to facilitate the father's residential access and to pay for the children's travel, with what it described as the father's 'late conversion' to the idea that the mother should have access. In *Clayton* v *Clayton* 1995 GWD 18–1000, the court was clearly impressed by the mother's willingness to consult the child's father in the future despite his high-handed and arrogant attitude in the past.

385 (Sh Ct) 1991 SCLR (Notes) 429.

suggesting that the mother had probably been instrumental in creating the problem. None the less, he felt bound to refuse access, since he could see no advantage which the child would derive from access, particularly in the light of the distress which would surround it. Clearly, this can amount to allowing one particularly intransigent adult to control the situation. While the courts should discourage this sort of attitude, the ultimate test is the child's welfare and there may be little that can be done in practice where one or both of the adults is sufficiently stubborn.[386] Again, various strategies, like the use of contact centres and third-party intermediaries, can be adopted to minimise the impact of adult conflict. A problem can arise where the person with whom the child is living is hostile to a parent and the concern over such a person 'turning the child against' a parent may be sufficiently great that it will result in a change in the child's living arrangements.[387]

The child's views

5.130 Even before the 1995 Act, it was widely accepted that the views of the child concerned were relevant in reaching a decision on the child's future in disputed cases,[388] although the courts quite properly took responsibility for the decision and, on occasions, declined to follow the child's preference.[389] In addition, the courts are aware of the potential for a child to be 'coached' by an influential adult.[390] It will be remembered that art 12 of the UN Convention on the Rights of the Child provides

> '1. States Parties shall assure to the child who is capable of forming his or her own views the right to express those views freely in all matters affecting the child, the views of the child being given due weight in accordance with the age and maturity of the child.
> 2. For this purpose the child shall in particular be provided the opportunity to be heard in any judicial and administrative proceedings affecting the child, either directly or through a representative or an appropriate body, in a manner consistent with the procedural rules of national law.'

If the UK was to comply fully with this provision of the Convention, taking children's views seriously could no longer be left to the discretion of

386 The decision of the Second Division in *Davidson* v *Smith* 1998 GWD 1–1, is interesting, in this context. There the parents had parted when their daughter was two years old and the mother refused to allow the father contact and prevented the child from receiving any presents or cards from him. Despite the fact that the child had not seen her father since just after the parental separation, contact was granted by the sheriff when the child was some six years old and the decision was upheld by the Sheriff Principal and the Inner House.

387 See for example, *Hastie* v *Hastie* 1985 SLT 146, where the paternal grandmother had demonstrated considerable hostility towards her former daughter-in-law and the fact that she had sought to pass this on to her grandson was a factor in his mother gaining custody.

388 See for example, *Fowler* v *Fowler* 1981 SLT (Notes) 9; *Fowler* v *Fowler (No 2)* 1981 SLT (Notes) 78 (where the child involved changed her mind); *Johnson* v *Johnson*, n 383 above (where siblings in the same family went to live with different parents); *Mason* v *Mason*, n 382 above (where one sibling had sufficiently strong views that she determined not only her own custody but that of her younger brother).

389 *Casey* v *Casey* (OH) 1989 SCLR 761 (Notes).

390 *Marco* v *Marco* 1989 GWD 5–190.

enlightened members of the legal profession and the judiciary; that is, having regard to the child's views could no longer be optional.

5.131 Thus it was that the Scottish Law Commission recommended[391] a specific provision, giving children the opportunity to have their views taken into account in the context of litigation.[392] When it is considering whether to make an order under s 11 and the terms of any such order, the court

> 'taking account of the child's age and maturity, shall so far as practicable –
> (i) give [the child] an opportunity to indicate whether he [or she] wishes to express his [or her] views;
> (ii) if he [or she] does so wish, give him [or her] an opportunity to express them; and
> (iii) have regard to such views as he [or she] may express'.[393]

On the face of it, this appears to put the child's views in a much more prominent position than they occupied in the past and, to some extent it does. Where the court is being asked to grant an order dealing with parental responsibilities, parental rights, guardianship or the administration of a child's property, the court is obliged to give the child the opportunity to express a view and to take any view expressed into account. However, there are a number of limitations on this apparent openness. Remember, we are dealing here, only with cases where there is a dispute and the case gets to a court. As we have seen, the procedure for ascertaining the child's views, which involves sending a form to the child and leaving the onus on the child to take matters further, is hardly child-friendly.[394]

5.132 It can be argued that, had the legislature been so minded, it could have done a great deal more to ensure that all children had the opportunity to have their views taken into account when the arrangements for their future care were being made. The Commission rejected the idea of a mandatory report on the child's views in every case on the grounds of cost. There is also the objection that to require every child to express a view would force children into making choices when they did not want that responsibility. The cost argument really comes down to 'putting one's money where one's mouth is'. Either we take children's rights seriously, and incur the cost involved, or we do not. Nor need asking a child about his or her views be handled so insensitively as to force a child to express a preference when the child does not want to do that. It may be that the Commission was accepting the political reality of what Parliament and the

---

391 Report on Family Law, paras 5.24–5.29, rec 34(a) and draft Bill, clause 12(5) and (6).
392 This is in addition to the obligation placed on any person who is taking a major decision, in the course of fulfilling parental responsibilities or exercising parental rights, to give the child an opportunity to express his or her views and to take those views into account – s 6. See chapter 6, paras 3–6. The real difficulty is that, since most arrangements for the care of children after divorce are made by the parents without detailed scrutiny by the court, there is no way of knowing whether the children were ever consulted at all.
393 Section 11(7)(b).
394 For a more detailed discussion of this point, see chapter 3, paras 45–49.

Treasury would agree to, but the result is something of a missed opportunity from a children's rights perspective.

5.133 In any event, the 1995 Act makes clear that the requirement to give the child the opportunity to express his or her views does not require the child to be legally represented if the child does not want to be.[395] Of course, a child who does wish to be represented has every right to instruct a solicitor and will have the capacity to do so provided that the child has a general understanding of what it means to do so.[396] Since most children have little or no property, they will be entitled to legal aid. At least one sheriff has expressed concern at the additional cost to the public purse when legal aid is provided for children to enter the process in their parents' divorce action,[397] suggesting that it may take some time for this, fairly modest, reform to be understood fully.

5.134 Procedural difficulties aside, the general scheme of empowering children applies and children aged 12 years old and over are presumed to have sufficient capacity to form a view.[398] As usual, this does not mean that a child below that age cannot form a view and there are numerous examples, prior to the 1995 Act, of the courts taking account of the views of children below the age of 12.[399] The direction to the court to take account of any view expressed, in the light of the child's age and maturity, certainly does not require the court to do what the child wants. This is consistent with the general principle of the UN Convention and the 1995 Act that participation is a child's right, but decision-making is an adult responsibility. Thus, it is for the court to determine what is in the child's best interests.

Presumption of non-intervention

5.135 The third of the overarching principles is the statutory equivalent of the popular aphorism, 'If it ain't broke, don't fix it'. In the words of the 1995 Act, the court

> 'Shall not make any ... order unless it considers that it would be better for the child that the order be made than that none should be made at all'.[400]

It has been described by Norrie as the 'presumption of minimum intervention', a misnomer which appears to have been accepted somewhat unquestioningly. In fact, the presumption in the second part of s 11(7)(a) is a presumption of non-intervention. The starting point for the court is that it should not intervene at all, unless to do so would be better than not doing so. Once the court has decided to intervene, it can do whatever will serve the child's best interests and is in no way required to take a minimalist approach.

---

395 Section 11(9).
396 Age of Legal Capacity (Scotland) Act 1991, s 2(4A).
397 *Henderson* v *Henderson* 1997 Fam LR 120.
398 Section 11(10).
399 *Fowler* v *Fowler* 1981 SLT (Notes) 9 (girl of ten); *O'Hagan* v *O'Hagan* 1989 GWD 8–319 (girl of 11); *MacKenzie* v *Hendry* 1984 SLT 322 (girl of eight); *Pow* v *Pow* 1931 SLT 485 (boy of eight, girl of ten); *Russell* v *Russell*, (Sh Ct) 1991 SCLR (Notes) 429 (girl of six).
400 Section 11(7)(a).

5.136 This principle has its roots in the 1986 Act which provided that the court was not to make an order unless it was 'satisfied that to do so would be in the interests of the child'.[401] As we have seen, this led to some debate about where the onus of proof lay in such cases; a debate which was finally resolved in *Sanderson* v *McManus*.[402] Arguably, the wording of the 1995 Act strengthens the weight to be attached to the *status quo* and increases the burden placed on anyone wishing to disturb it. Where married parents are in dispute over the future arrangements for their children, they will each usually enter the arena with the full range of responsibilities and rights.[403] Of course, in the light of the maternal preference, it can be argued that, even for married parents, the position of equality is entirely notional. However, any applicant who does not have parental responsibilities and rights, will not start from that, albeit notionally, equal position.

---

401 Law Reform (Parent and Child) (Scotland) Act 1986, s 3(2).
402 See the discussion of onus of proof at paras 5.101–5.103.
403 Where the existing arrangement is working, there may be no need for an order. In *Potter* v *Potter* (Sh Ct) 1992 SCLR (Notes) 788, which predates the 1995 Act, a five-year-old girl had lived with her mother and stayed overnight with her father for three weekends every month since her (married) parents separated. Although the arrangement appeared to work well, the mother sought custody in order to give legal recognition to the *de facto* position. The court refused to grant the order since it could see no obvious benefit to the child.

CHAPTER 6

FULFILLING PARENTAL RESPONSIBILITIES AND EXERCISING PARENTAL RIGHTS

6.1 So far, we have examined the nature of parental responsibilities and rights, who holds them automatically, and how the court deals with applications in respect of them. Of greater importance to children and their families is how these responsibilities and rights work in practice. In this chapter, we will consider how parental responsibilities and rights operate and will examine specific examples, before going on to look at how the legal system seeks to deal with financial responsibility for children and child abduction by family members.

THE GENERAL POSITION

6.2 As we have seen, parental responsibilities exist only insofar as practicable and in the child's interests[1] and parental rights exist only in order to enable the holder to fulfil his or her responsibilities.[2] Thus, the child's best interests lie at the heart of any action taken by a person in the course of fulfilling his or her parental responsibilities or exercising parental rights. Where more than one person has rights in respect of a child and, remember, that is a fairly common situation, the general rule is that each of the persons may exercise the right alone, without the consent of the other.[3] Where, for example, a young child requires surgery, either parent can normally consent to the operation being performed. There are two exceptions to this general rule. First, where the right itself has been conferred by any decree or deed, it may limit a person's freedom to act alone.[4] So, in the example of the child's operation, where the parents have divorced, the court decree regulating the exercise of parental rights may provide that both parents must participate in medical decisions. Second, the freedom to exercise parental rights alone does not entitle a person to remove a child from the UK without appropriate consent.[5] The problem of international child abduction has resulted in a plethora of international instruments and domestic legislation regulating the international movement of children. This provision is designed to prevent a parent, or third party with parental rights, from removing a child from the UK without

1 Children (Scotland) Act 1995, s 1(1).
2 Section 2(1).
3 Section 2(2).
4 Section 2(2).
5 Section 2(3).

having obtained the consent of other relevant persons. International child abduction and the national and international provisions aimed at combatting it are discussed below.[6]

The child's views

6.3 Traditionally, the place of the child's views in decision-making could be best described as variable. While there were examples of the child's views being determinative, as, for example, with the minor child's right to consent to or veto his or her own adoption, there was no general provision on the place of a child's views when other decisions were being taken.[7] As we have seen, in many cases, the child's preferences about his or her future care carried considerable weight when a court was reaching its decision. In examining the law on parental responsibilities and rights, the Scottish Law Commission was conscious of the provisions of the UN Convention on the Rights of the Child ('the UN Convention') and arts 5 and 12, in particular. It will be remembered that art 5 recognises the child's evolving capacity and art 12 gives the child the right to have his or her views taken into account in the decision-making process.[8] Thus it was that the Commission came to recommend two provisions which emphasise the place of the child's views,[9] recommendations which found their way into the Children (Scotland) Act 1995 ('the 1995 Act'). These provisions have already been discussed in chapter 3 but, such is their importance, that repeating their content and effect is warranted.

6.4 The first provision to note is s 6 of the 1995 Act which provides as follows

'(1) A person shall, in reaching any major decision which involves –

(a) his fulfilling a parental responsibility or the responsibility [the responsibilities of a person with care or control of a child]; or

(b) his exercising a parental right or giving consent by virtue of [being a person with care or control of a child],

have regard so far as is practicable to the views (if he wishes to express them) of the child concerned, taking account of the child's age and maturity, and of those of any other person who has parental responsibilities or parental rights in relation to the child (and wishes to express those views); and without prejudice to the generality of this subsection a child of twelve years of age or more shall be presumed to be of sufficient age and maturity to form a view.'

As might be expected, s 6(2) goes on to protect third parties who deal in good faith with a child's representative from a transaction being challenged

---

6 At paras 6.81–6.100.
7 Of course, the participation of the child, where he or she is old enough to have an input, has always been central to the children's hearings system – see chapter 9.
8 See chapter 3, paras 12–29 for a discussion of the Convention.
9 Report on Family Law, paras 2.60–2.66 and 5.24–5.29, recs 10 and 34 and draft Bill, clause 6 and 12(5) and (6).

on the ground that the appropriate views were not sought. On a cosmetic level at least, s 6 means that parents, and others fulfilling parental responsibilities or exercising parental rights, must give the child the opportunity to express his or her views and must take these views into account in the light of the child's age and maturity. Since the 1995 Act does not define 'major decision' and it has not been operating for long enough for a body of judicial decision to have been built up, we must resort to speculation. While what the family is having for dinner on a particular evening is not usually a major decision, trying to persuade a child, who has chosen to become a vegetarian, to eat meat begins to move into an area of greater significance. Arguably, such a lifestyle choice involves a major decision. Similarly, where the family takes a weekend break may not be a major decision, but whether the family should move to the other end of the country permanently, probably is.

6.5 What does this mean, in practice? Will this provision make any difference to the lives of children and their families? Firstly, it must be remembered that the parent is required only to take account of the child's view. Children are not being empowered to take over the decision-making function which is properly an adult responsibility. Secondly, it may take some time before parents and children become aware of s 6 and, in the meantime, little may change. Thirdly, even if everyone in Scotland became acutely aware of s 6, the practicalities of family life are such that it is doubtful that parents who formerly failed to consult their children will change their ways. None the less, the importance of s 6 should not be underestimated. It articulates a fundamental principle and one which, having been accepted by Parliament, now has the democratic seal of approval. If, as is sometimes suggested, law can shape attitudes and behaviour, this provision is moving us along in the right direction.

6.6 As we have seen, quite apart from this general duty to take account of children's views, the 1995 Act places the court under an obligation to take account of any views the child wishes to express and, again, a child of 12 or over is presumed to be capable of expressing a view. In the context of local authority care of children, court decisions designed to protect children and children deemed to be in need of compulsory measures of supervision, the child's views are, again, given a place.[10]

Delegation but not abdication

6.7 In restating what was the general position under the common law, the 1995 Act provides that, while a person who has responsibilities or rights may not surrender or transfer any part of these, the holder is permitted to arrange for them to be exercised or met by another person acting on the holder's behalf.[11] Such an arrangement can be made with another person who has parental responsibilities or rights in respect of the child. No

---

10 For a discussion of these 'public law' powers, see chapter 7.
11 Section 3(5).

arrangement of this sort affects a person's liability for failure to meet parental responsibilities.[12] This power to delegate covers a very wide range of possible situations. It would include, for example, an occasional baby-sitter, a full-time nanny, or day care, where the parent retains a high degree of involvement in the child's life.[13] In addition, it would cover substantial substitution for a parent's involvement as the following example indicates.

6.8   Take divorced parents where the mother has a residence order and a contact order has been made, giving the father the right to see his son every Saturday. The father takes a job abroad and is anxious that his son should maintain regular contact with the paternal side of the family. Would the 1995 Act permit him to delegate contact to his parents, the child's paternal grandparents? In order to answer this question, account must be taken of the important qualifications surrounding delegation. Firstly, if delegation is, in itself, a means of fulfilling parental responsibilities, the decision must be taken in the best interests of the child involved[14] and not simply for adult convenience. Secondly, since parental rights exist only to enable the fulfilment of parental responsibilities, the same consideration applies if delegation is a form of exercising parental rights. Thirdly, at least in the example above, it can be argued that the decision to delegate is a 'major decision' within the meaning of s 6. Thus, the child involved must be given the opportunity to express his or her views and to have those taken into account. Finally, since it is the delegation and not abdication of responsibilities that is permitted, delegation does not free the father of his own responsibility to maintain contact with the child so far as that is practicable.[15] Contact by way of letter, telephone, fax or e-mail might be appropriate here. It is submitted that it is only if all of the above qualifications are satisfied that delegation should be permitted. Provided that this is the interpretation placed on the 1995 Act, the flexibility offered by this provision seems both desirable and entirely consistent with the UN Convention.

Appointing a guardian

6.9   As we have seen, a child's guardian may make provision in a will appointing some other person to take over from him or her as the child's guardian in the event of the testator's death.[16] So, for example, a divorced woman might appoint her sister to take on her role as guardian to her children should the mother die. If the children's father also had parental responsibilities and rights at the time of the mother's death, he would continue to act as the children's guardian, along with the aunt.[17]

---

12 Section 3(6).
13 For a discussion of substitute care, its regulation and the obligations placed on the carer, see paras 6.21–6.24, below.
14 Section 1(1).
15 Sections 1(1) and 3(6).
16 Section 7.
17 Section 7(1)(b).

PARTICULAR PARENTAL RESPONSIBILITIES AND RIGHTS

6.10 Thus far, we have examined the acquisition, regulation and operation of parental responsibilities and rights in a general sense. As we so often find, the legal provision is of little consequence to the individual child and his or her family when everything is going well. It is when the happy family picture changes in some way that the law becomes important. It may be that the change is independent of the child, as when the parents divorce. However, the change need not be so dramatic. It may be that the family remains essentially intact, but the parents themselves, or the parents and the child disagree over a specific issue. Other family members may be involved in the dispute, as may third parties. In order to illustrate how the legal system works in such circumstances, it is useful to look at specific parental responsibilities and rights and how they operate. Some issues, like the choice of a child's name, consent to medical treatment and consent to adoption, are examined elsewhere, and will only be mentioned in passing here. Other issues, like the parental responsibility for financial support, will be considered in depth. In addition, we will take a brief look at an approach to parental responsibility found in some other jurisdictions but not in Scotland – parental criminal responsibility for the acts of their children.

Choice of name

6.11 As we have seen,[18] choosing the name of a new baby is a function of parental responsibilities and rights. Thus, in the case of married parents, each of them has this power. In the event of a dispute, it would be up to one of them to take the matter to the court for resolution.[19] Where the parents are not married to each other, it is the mother who can choose the child's name, unless the father has acquired parental rights, whether with her consent or by virtue of a court order. As with fulfilling any parental responsibility or exercising any parental right, the choice must be made in the best interests of the child. Arguably, it is not in a child's best interests to be burdened with a particularly silly name, such as Big Ears, or something unduly cumbersome, like the first names of all the members of the parents' favourite football team. While the registrar has no power to refuse to register a particular name, no matter how absurd the choice, any person with an interest may go to the court for resolution of the matter. Where the parents agree, the reality is that, often, there will be no person who is sufficiently motivated to intervene. Thus, even in Scotland, a child could be stuck with a name like Zowie or Heavenly Hirani until he or she was old enough to instigate a change. It is in the context of changing a child's name, often after the parents have divorced and one of them has remarried, that parental disagreement is more likely to reach the courts, although such disputes remain rare.[20] Again, both the original, parental decision and any

---

18 See the discussion of children's names in chapter 2, paras 58–61, above.
19 1995 Act, s 11.
20 For a rare example, see *GSF* v *GAF* 1995 SCLR 189. It should be noted that the case was decided under the law as it was prior to the Children (Scotland) Act 1995. Such disputes have been more common in the USA. See for example, *Halloran III* v *Kosta* 778 SW 2d 454 (1988, Tenn App) (in the child's best interests to keep her father's surname after her

decision by the court must be taken in the child's best interests. However, unlike the situation when a baby's name is being chosen, by the time any change of name is being considered, the child, himself or herself, may be in a position to express a view and this view must be taken into account. A child who wishes to change his or her name may raise an action to do so independently of the parents once the child is old enough to understand what is involved in instructing a solicitor and there is a presumption that a child of 12 years or older has sufficient understanding.[21] This may be the solution for such unfortunate children as Big Ears.

Residence

6.12 In the vast majority of families, the child's residence is an uncontentious issue. Children live with their parents and, regardless of the child's legal rights, most children move house, fairly unquestioningly, when their parents announce that such a move will happen. However, examining how the law will approach disputes provides a good illustration of the operation of parental responsibilities and rights in general. Let us take the example of Sarah, who lives with her (married) parents. In theory, each parent has the right to control her residence, but it does not become an issue until the parents decide to work in France when Sarah, a mature and articulate child, is eight years old. They would like her to go with them, but she does not want to leave her friends and the school she attends in Inverness, which offers both day and boarding facilities. She announces that she will not go with her parents but will stay with her best friend. The best friend's parents are willing to have her to stay, but Sarah's parents are not happy with this option because the friend's mother is known to have a problem with alcohol. At first instance, it is for Sarah's parents to decide whether to insist that she should accompany them to France or to make some other arrangement, like enrolling her as a boarder at her present school,[22] assuming they reject the option of her staying with her friend's family. Sarah's parents are aware of their obligation to give her the opportunity to express any views she has in respect of a major decision[23] but, having thought about what she has to say, they insist on Sarah accompanying them. She is not happy and, thanks to an excellent course at her school dealing with children's rights, she knows that she can instruct a solicitor, provided that she has a general understanding of what it means to do so.[24] She telephones the Child Law Centre and gets the name of a solicitor, to whom she explains the problem. The solicitor is satisfied of Sarah's capacity and indicates to her parents that further negotiation would seem

---

parents divorced); *Magiera* v *Luera* 808 P 2d 6 (Nev, 1990) (in the best interests of the child to keep the name of the parent she lives with). For a discussion of the history of last names and tests the courts have applied or might apply in the USA, see L. Kelly, 'Divining the Deep and Inscrutable: Towards a Gender-Neutral, Child-Centred Approach to Child Name Change Proceedings' 99 W Va L Rev 1 (1996).

21 Age of Legal Capacity (Scotland) Act 1991, s 2(4A); see chapter 3, para 42.

22 Remember, the parental right in respect of residence is to have the child living with them or otherwise to regulate the child's residence – s 2(1)(a).

23 Section 6.

24 Age of Legal Capacity (Scotland) Act 1991, s 2(4A).

to be a good idea, which failing, an action will be raised so that the matter can be resolved by the court.[25] An appointment with the local mediation service is arranged and, after further discussion, everyone agrees that Sarah should become a boarder at her present school and spend the holidays with her parents in France. Litigation has, thus, been avoided. Two years later, Sarah's parents return to live in Inverness and she moves back to live with them and becomes a day pupil at school. Later that year Sarah's father announces that he has formed a new relationship and her parents decide to divorce. Her mother plans to stay in Scotland but her father intends to emigrate to Canada, along with his new partner whom Sarah likes, where he has secured a well-paid job. By this time, foreign travel rather appeals to Sarah and she indicates that she would like to go to Canada with her father. Her mother is devastated and raises an action for a residence order. Her father opposes the application. Sarah telephones the solicitor she consulted before and is told that she can make her views clear to the court and can be separately represented. The court will then make a decision based on her welfare,[26] taking her views into account.[27] In this case, the court is unlikely to refuse to make an order of some kind, since it is not practical that each of her parents should have the right to determine residence since each of them would want to reach a different decision. It is possible that Sarah would be allowed to go to Canada with her father, not least because this is her preferred option.[28] In addition, the affluence of this particular family would make continued contact with her mother a realistic possibility. This may seem harsh on Sarah's mother but simply emphasises the point that it is the child's welfare that is paramount. Of course, in many cases were a child's residence is at issue, the family will not be as affluent as our fictional Sarah's and, as so often happens, poverty restricts the choices available.

Consent to medical treatment

6.13 In the case of a young child, who is not capable of understanding enough to be in a position to make choices for himself or herself, medical treatment can be described as both a parental responsibility and a parental right. The parental responsibility to safeguard and promote the child's health, development and welfare[29] means that parents, and anyone else who has the responsibility,[30] are obliged to ensure that the child receives adequate medical treatment. As we have seen, concern that a parent might prevent a child from having such treatment may result in the child's

---

25 The child concerned can raise an action for an order in relation to parental responsibilities and rights – s 11(5).
26 Section 11(7)(a). In assessing welfare the court might take any number of the factors discussed in chapter 5, paras 5.110–5.129 into account.
27 Section 11(7)(b).
28 In *Johnson* v *Francis* 1982 SLT 285, the court sanctioned two boys' emigration to Australia with their mother and step-father since it was impressed by the greater opportunities they would find there. This was in the face of opposition from the boys' father who felt that their departure would destroy any meaningful contact he could have with them.
29 Section 1(1)(a).
30 Where a person has the care and control of a person under the age of 16, he or she is required to *safeguard* the child's health, development and welfare, but is neither required

residence being given over solely to the other parent[31] or the state may step in to control treatment.[32] While medical decisions in respect of a child who cannot make the decision for himself or herself lie first with the persons who have parental rights, the legal system will not stand idly by when it is concerned that the parental decision is not in the child's interests. Where the situation attracts sufficient public concern, legislation may be passed to govern a particular practice. So, for example, female genital mutilation, a traditional practice in some African countries, sometimes erroneously presented as having a religious foundation, is prohibited by statute throughout the UK.[33] In other cases, either a state agency or a concerned individual will bring the matter before the court.[34] The child's role in consenting to or refusing medical treatment, and how this interacts with the parental role, has been discussed at length in chapter 3.[35]

Education

6.14 Such is the growth in the importance of education law[36] that it has generated a considerable body of literature to which reference should be

nor empowered to *promote* them – s 5(1). In addition, the carer may only consent to medical treatment if he or she does not know that the parent would refuse to consent – s 5(1)(b). The position of carers is discussed more fully below at para 6.24.

31 *McKechnie* v *McKechnie* (Sh Ct) 1990 SCLR (Notes) 153.
32 *Finlayson (Applicant)* 1989 SCLR 601.
33 Prohibition of Female Circumcision Act 1985.
34 See for example, the different conclusions reached by the courts in England in cases involving the sterilisation of mentally challenged young women – *Re D (A Minor) (Wardship: Sterilisation)* [1976] 1 All ER 326 and *Re B (A Minor) (Wardship: Sterilisation)* [1988] AC 199. On the issue of sterilisation and a mentally challenged adult in Scotland, see the decision of Lord McLean in *L, Petitioners* (OH) 1996 SCLR (Notes) 538.
35 See chapter 3, paras 67–71.
36 The field of education has been a rich source of litigation in the USA and has given the Supreme Court the opportunity to hand down such landmark decisions as *Pierce* v *Society of Sisters* 268 US 510 (1925) (state may not compel attendance at state schools where a private alternative is being provided), *Brown* v *Board of Education* 347 US 483 (1954) (racial integration) and *Wisconsin* v *Yoder* 406 US 205 (1972) (Amish parents exempted from requirement to send their children to school past the eighth grade in a case which explored the parents' right to religious freedom and various state interests, but did not deal with children's rights). Many other issues, including the following, have been litigated: the place of religion in state schools (*Engel* v *Vitale* 370 US 421 (1962); *Wallace* v *Jaffree* 472 US 38 (1985)); sex education (*Medieros* v *Kiyosaki* 478 P 2d 314 (Hawaii, 1970); teaching Darwin's theory of evolution, without giving equal billing to the biblical version (*Edwards* v *Aguillard* 482 US 578 (1987)); free distribution of condoms in schools (*Alfonso* v *Fernandez* 606 N Y S 2d 259 (1993); and home schooling. The very considerable body of literature generated includes: J. C. Cox, 'Parental Rights and Responsibilities of Control over Children's Education' 26 J L & Educ 179 (1990); D. W. Fuller, 'Public School Access: The Constitutional Right of Home-Schoolers to "Opt In" to Public Education on a Part-Time Basis' 82 Minn L Rev 1599 (1998); S. G. Gilles, 'Liberal Parentalism and Children's Educational Rights' 26 Cap U L Rev 9 (1997); L. L. Lane, 'The Parental Rights Movement' 69 U Colo L Rev 825 (1998); S. C. Thomason, 'Education Law' 20 U Ark Little Rock L J 453 (1998); C. Waters, 'A, B, C's and Condoms for Free: A Legislative Solution to Parents' Rights and Condom Distribution in Public Schools' 31 Val U L Rev 787 (1997); B. B. Woodhouse, 'A Public Role in the Private Family: The Parental Rights and Responsibilities Act and the Politics of Child

made on specific questions.[37] Parental involvement in a child's education is another example of something which is both a right and a duty. Parents, guardians and any person who has day-to-day care of a child are obliged to ensure that the child receives an education[38] and may face prosecution if they fail to do so.[39] In addition, a child may be in need of compulsory measures of supervision if he or she fails to attend school regularly without a reasonable excuse.[40] Usually, parents ensure that their child receives an education by sending the child to either a state-funded or a private school. However, there is nothing to prevent a parent educating a child at home, either himself or herself or by employing tutors, provided that an adequate standard of education is secured. There are numerous examples of successful home schooling, sometimes involving particularly gifted children, but the idea is not free from controversy. A child's overall development involves more than learning the subjects which form the core curriculum of formal education and, in particular, the acquisition of social skills, gained through a child's interaction with his or her peers and non-family adults, forms a part of that development. It can be argued that, where a child's home schooling minimises the opportunity for such interaction, his or her development is being impeded.

6.15 Parents also have the right to send their child to the state school of their choice, subject to a range of qualifications related to the suitability of the school to the child's particular needs and economic considerations.[41] The decision in *Harvey* v *Strathclyde Regional Council*,[42] which upheld the local authority's right to close a school despite widespread parental opposition, indicates the limits that can be placed on any real parental choice. The full impact of the House of Lords decision in *R* v *East Sussex County Council, ex parte Tandy*,[43] which concerned the provision of home tuition for a pupil suffering from myalgic encephalomyelitis (ME), has yet to be felt. However, it suggests that resource issues will no longer provide a local authority with the carte blanche excuse they have been hitherto. The local authority has a statutory duty to provide suitable education for pupils who, because of illness, are prevented from attending school. What is 'suitable education' is to be assessed by reference to the individual child. When the local authority cut Ms Tandy's home tuition from five hours per week to three, her mother challenged the decision. Concluding that the local authority was neither entitled to take its own budgetary constraints

Protection and Education' 57 Ohio St L J 393 (1996). In order to avoid confusion, the reader should be aware that the expression 'public school' is used in the USA to denote a school funded by the state (ie out of public funds).

37 A. Cleland, 'The Child's Right to Education' in Cleland and Sutherland *Children's Rights in Scotland* (W. Green, 1996); R. Marr and C. Marr, *Scots Education Law* (W. Green, 1995); *Stair Memorial Encyclopaedia*, vol 8.
38 Education (Scotland) Act 1980, ss 30–31.
39 *Wyatt* v *Wilson* 1994 SLT 1135.
40 Section 52(2)(h).
41 Education (Scotland) Act 1980, as amended by Education (Scotland) Act 1981. See A. Seager, 'Parental Choice of School' 1982 SLT (News) 29 and J. G. Logie, 'Parental Choice and the Courts' 1989 SLT (News) 417.
42 1989 SLT 612.
43 [1998] 2 All ER 769.

into account in assessing her need, nor in meeting it, Lord Browne-Wilkinson made the following observation

'To permit the local authority to avoid performing a statutory duty on the ground that it preferred to spend its money in other ways was to downgrade a statutory duty to a statutory power'.[44]

6.16 While the local authority is obliged to provide religious education in schools, it is open to parents to withdraw their children from that aspect of the curriculum.[45] Nothing in the legislation provides the child with any right to freedom of or, indeed, from, religion.[46] It is a curious feature of the education legislation that, while it recognises parental rights, it is silent on the rights of pupils. However, that does not mean that young people are without a host of rights in the field. When parents are making choices about education, they are fulfilling the responsibility to safeguard and promote the child's development and welfare and are, at least arguably, making a major decision. Consequently, they are obliged to give the child involved the opportunity to express his or her views and to take any such views into account.[47] Thus, the child is entitled to have an input into all such decisions. As is the case generally, the parent need not do what the child wants, but the child can challenge the parent's decision in court, if he or she satisfies the 'understanding' test. So, for example, a young person who finds private education politically unacceptable might challenge the parents' decision to send him or her to a private school.

6.17 Where two parents with responsibilities and rights disagree over a matter of education or, indeed, where any person with an interest is concerned, they can go to court and ask the court to resolve the matter. As we have seen, education was one of the many issues on which Mr Clayton disagreed with his long-suffering wife.[48] In that case, however, the court was not prepared to decree any particular arrangement for the child, nor was it prepared to restrict the mother's freedom of choice in the future. Of course, were Ms Clayton to remove her son from the private school he was attending, there is every likelihood that her ex-husband would raise an action for a specific issue order under s 11 of the 1995 Act.

Physical violence

6.18 As we shall see in chapter 7, the area of child abuse and neglect is a complex one which has attracted considerable national and international concern. Prosecution, under the criminal law, rightly follows on many cases of abuse of children by family members or strangers. Extensive regulation

---

44 At page 777.
45 Education (Scotland) Act 1980, ss 8 and 9.
46 Article 14 of the UN Convention on the Rights of the Child recognises the child's right to freedom of religion and the right of parents and guardians to provide the child with guidance, consistent with the child's evolving capacity. However, see J. G. Dwyer, *Religious Schools* v *Children's Rights* (Cornell University Press, 1998), where the author argues that education founded on the parents' religious preference is contrary to the child's civil rights.
47 Section 6.
48 *Clayton* v *Clayton* 1995 GWD 18–1000.

allows state agencies to step in to protect a child who is believed to be the victim of abuse and, ultimately, a child may be removed from a violent parent permanently. Distressing as it is to face the fact, the reality is that home is simply not a haven for some children. Thus, it falls to any responsible legal system to protect children and, in many respects, Scots law acquits itself reasonably well. However, the legal system demonstrates lamentable inadequacy when it permits physical violence against children under the euphemistic and vague umbrella of 'reasonable chastisement'.[49] It should be noted that children are the only category of persons against whom such violence is permitted.[50] The right to chastise a child stems from the notion of parental power[51] and, as such, can be delegated to others entrusted by parents with the care of the child.[52] What amounts to 'reasonable chastisement' is somewhat unclear, but depends on the circumstances of the individual case and, in particular, on the age of the child and the extent of the violence. Thus, for example, it has been held to be reasonable for a mother to hit her nine-year-old daughter with a belt,[53] but unreasonable for a mother to slap a two-year-old on the face with such force as to knock him over.[54] Where the 'reasonableness' test is satisfied, it provides a defence to a charge of assault.[55]

6.19 As early as 1990, the Scottish Law Commission sought views on the possible abolition or modification of the so-called right of 'reasonable chastisement'.[56] It received an unprecedented number of responses and, predictably enough, these spanned the spectrum of opinion. In its Report, the Commission recommended[57] reform of the law to clarify and restrict,

49 For an enlightened and enlightening discussion, see Newell, *Children Are People Too* (Bedford Square Press, 1989). For a USA perspective on the international position, see S. H. Bitensky, 'Spare the Rod, Embrace our Humanity: Toward a New Legal Regime Prohibiting Corporal Punishment of Children' 31 U Mich J L. Rev 353 (1998).

50 While robust physical contact is an inherent part of many sports, the criminal law remains applicable. See *Ferguson* v *Procurator Fiscal Glasgow*, unreported, 11 October 1995, where a football player who was convicted of assaulting another player on the pitch was sentenced to three months imprisonment.

51 Erskine, *Institutes*, I, v, 53.

52 *Stewart* v *Thain* 1981 JC 13. It should be noted that physical punishment within the context of education has been severely limited by statute – Education (No 2) Act 1986, s 48; Education Act 1993, s 295. See *Sutton London Borough Council* v *Davis* [1995] 1 All ER 53, where an English local authority refused to register Ms Davis as a childminder because she would not give an undertaking to refrain from hitting children in her care.

53 *B* v *Harris* 1990 SLT 208.

54 *Peebles* v *MacPhail* 1990 SLT 245.

55 Conversely, where the reasonableness test is not satisfied, the parent may face conviction. See the unreported case, cited in the Report on Family Law (para 2.67, n 3) where a father who had whipped and caned his children from the age of seven was sentenced to four years imprisonment. See also *C* v *HM Advocate* 1998 GWD 17–849, where a sentence of 12 months imprisonment was not found to be excessive in respect of a mother's conviction for assaulting her 11-year-old son to his severe injury by punching him, stamping on his head and biting him – all because she believed he had returned home late, while she was out.

56 Parental Responsibilities and Rights, Guardianship and the Administration of Children's Property (Scot Law Com Discussion Paper No 88, 1990), question 11.

57 Report on Family Law, paras 2.67–2.105, rec 11 and draft Bill, clause 4.The Commission's proposal was that, in both civil and criminal proceedings, it should not be a defence

but not to abolish, the parental right in this respect. However, even this modest reform proved too much for the legislature and the 1995 Act contains nothing on chastisement of children. Thus, the law remains in its present somewhat ambiguous state where the only thing that is clear beyond any shadow of a doubt is that Scots law fails to meet the standards of the UN Convention on the Rights of the Child which requires states parties to 'protect the child from all forms of physical or mental violence'.[58] Whether Scots law is also in breach of art 37(a) of the UN Convention, which requires states parties to ensure that 'no child shall be subjected to torture, or other cruel, inhuman or degrading treatment or punishment', was doubted by some commentators.[59] In its 'Concluding Observation on the United Kingdom', the Committee on the Rights of the Child was critical of the continued acceptance of corporal punishment of children in the UK.[60] What of the position under the European Convention on Human Rights? Article 3 of that Convention also prohibits 'inhuman or degrading treatment or punishment'. Having concluded, initially, that corporal punishment of children did not necessarily qualify as a breach, the European Court of Human Rights gradually edged its way towards countenancing the possibility that it might be so classified in particular circumstances.[61] In 1998, it took the final step in *A v United Kingdom*.[62] There, a nine-year-old boy had been caned by his stepfather with considerable force on a number of occasions. In 1994, while not denying the factual allegations, the stepfather argued that his actions amounted to 'reasonable chastisement' and was acquitted of the charge of occasioning actual bodily harm (broadly equivalent to assault, in Scotland). In a unanimous judgment, the European Court found that there had been a breach of the child's rights under art 3 and awarded him £10,000 in damages. That sum is payable by the UK government, rather than the stepfather, since it is the state's responsibility

that a person struck a child in the exercise of a purported parental right if he or she struck the child, (i) with a stick, belt or other object, (ii) in such a way as to cause or risk causing injury, or (iii) in such a way as to cause, or risk causing, pain or discomfort lasting more than a very short time.

58 Article 19(1).

59 L. Edwards and A. Griffiths, *Family Law* (W. Green, 1997) para 5.10. Cf Cleland and Sutherland at para 5.39.

60 Committee on the Rights of the Child, Concluding Observation on the United Kingdom, CRC/C/15/Add 34 (15 February 1995), para 16. The Committee's Concluding Observations are reproduced in Cleland and Sutherland at Appendix 3.

61 In *Campbell and Cosans v United Kingdom* (1982) 4 EHRR 293, the court rejected the argument that corporal punishment in schools was inhuman or degrading treatment or punishment. However, it did find that, where the parents opposed such an approach to discipline, it breached art 2 of the First Protocol to the European Convention on Human Rights, which requires respect for the parents' religious and philosophical convictions in the course of a child's education. It is unsurprising, perhaps, that the focus in the early 1980s should be on the parents', rather than the child's, rights. The change in the court's attitude can be seen clearly in *Costello-Roberts v United Kingdom* (1994) 19 EHRR 112, where the court concluded, by a five to four majority, that the child's rights under art 3 had not been breached in that case, because the minimum level of severity had not been reached. However, it made clear that corporal punishment could involve a breach of art 3. See also *Tyrer v United Kingdom* (1978) 2 EHRR 1.

62 23 September 1998, unreported, 100/1997/884/1096. The case can be found on the European Court's website.

to protect the child's human rights. As a result of disapproval from the European Court, Parliament was prepared to change its attitude to corporal punishment in schools. Let us hope that, in the face of this overwhelming condemnation, the concept of 'reasonable chastisement' will also be abolished. Public reaction at the time of the judgment varied from welcoming joy to outrage and horror, and it may be some time before it is accepted universally that children are entitled to the same protection from violence as are all other members of the community.

Religious upbringing

6.20 At the first instance, it is for the parents to provide such religious instruction, or none at all, as they consider appropriate as part of their general responsibility to safeguard and promote the child's health, development and welfare. As we have seen, while the courts have shown a preference for a child having some religious input in his or her life, as opposed to none at all, they are not prepared to adjudicate between religions.[63] It has already been noted that many of the cases on religion are rather old and it is most unlikely that a modern court would regard the failure to offer religion of some kind to be a noteworthy failing on the part of a parent. Indeed, where courts have taken note of religion at all in recent cases, it has been as a source of concern rather than benefit.[64] As a child ages and develops, his or her own views on religion will, of course, become more relevant. Whether a decision involving religion is a 'major decision' requiring the child to be given the opportunity to express views is a matter which will have to await judicial decision. However, presumably any parent who regarded religion as being of importance would regard a decision on the matter as fairly major and could be expected to consult the child accordingly.[65]

Substitute care

6.21 Many parents avail themselves of various kinds of assistance in caring for their children. This can range from an occasional babysitter to a full-time nanny or day care. In enlisting help in caring for their children, parents are both fulfilling their parental responsibilities and delegating some aspects of them. Thus, as with any parental responsibility, the parents must act in the child's best interests. In addition, the decision to hand over a significant amount of the child's care to another person may involve a

---

63 *McNaught* v *McNaught* 1955 SLT (Sh Ct) 9. Given the particular sensitivity of the issue in some parts of Scotland, the court's reluctance to act as referee on the question of whether a child should be raised in the Roman Catholic or Protestant faiths was to be expected. How a court could hope to make any such a determination is difficult to see, save for reliance on the child's own evolving capacity as an indicator of the right to determine the matter.

64 *McKechnie* v *McKechnie* (Sh Ct) 1990 SCLR (Notes) 153.

65 While art 14 of the UN Convention on the Rights of the Child recognises the child's right to freedom of religion, it also recognises the right of parents and guardians to provide the child with guidance, consistent with the child's evolving capacity. It is interesting to note that, when the 1995 Act deals with adoption, it is the child's religious persuasion, which becomes relevant – s 95.

major decision and, if the child is old enough to express a view, any such view must be taken into account in the light of the child's age and maturity. This provides us with a good example of the child's views and their place in decision-making. Obviously, a baby cannot articulate his or her views about a potential nanny, although even very young children can express a reaction to a particular person by, for example, unrelenting crying when left with that person. However, whether an older child should attend an after-school club until the parents get home from work, is something on which the older child may be able to express lucid views. As ever, the child's view must be taken into account and the child's welfare is paramount. However, that does not mean that the child's view will necessarily prevail. A child may not like a particular care arrangement, but his or her welfare may require that the parent works in order to provide the child with a home, clothing, piano lessons and foreign holidays. Obviously most parents would try to find something with which the child was happier but, failing a viable alternative and provided that the care arrangement was adequate, the child may have to put up with it.

6.22 Quite apart from the parents' responsibility in selecting and arranging for substitute care, the legal system accepts responsibility for regulating many aspects of such care. Essentially, Scots law approaches the issue from two different angles. First, is the obligation placed on local authorities to regulate the provision of child minding and day care under the Children Act 1989 ('the 1989 Act').[66] Second, there are the provisions of the 1995 Act governing the responsibilities and rights of the substitute carer and the impact of these on parental responsibilities and rights.

Regulation of childminders and day care

6.23 Anyone who looks after a child under the age of eight for reward on domestic premises (a 'child minder') or provides care on other premises ('day care') for more than two hours in any one day must register with the local authority.[67] The local authority can refuse registration if it believes the applicant or any person who would be likely to look after the child is not fit to care for a child.[68] In addition, it can refuse registration where it believes that any person living on the premises where the children would be cared for is unfit to be in the proximity of a child. In granting registration, the local authority must specify the requirements to be complied with in respect of the number of children that can be cared for, the premises, and such other matters as it considers reasonable.[69] Registration can be cancelled,[70] various offences are specified for breach of the 1989

---

66 That Scots law should be dealt with in a statute which applies largely only to England and Wales is a matter if historical accident. Part X of the 1989 Act replaced the Nurseries and Child-Minders Regulation Act 1948 which regulated the matter for the UK as a whole.

67 1989 Act, s 71. Parents, relatives, persons with parental responsibilities and nannies are exempted from the need to register.

68 See for example, *Sutton London Borough Council* v *Davis* [1995] 1 All ER 53, where an English local authority refused to register a child minder who declined to give an undertaking that she would not 'smack' a child.

69 1989 Act, ss 72 and 73.

70 1989 Act, ss 74 and 75.

Act[71] and there is a procedure for appeals against the decision of the local authority.[72] Thus, the machinery exists to ensure that such substitute care as is offered meets adequate standards. However, where there is inadequate provision of suitably approved day care, parents are driven to use unregistered carers. The 1989 Act attempted to tackle this shortcoming when it placed an obligation on each local authority to review the provision of child minding and day care within its area[73] and to make proposals for action to be taken as a result. In addition, the 1995 Act places the local authority under an obligation to provide day care for pre-school children and care outside school hours for older children, where the children are 'in need',[74] and each local authority must deal with such provision in its service plans.[75] Despite this, the provision for substitute care across Scotland remains uneven and affordable care is often inadequate.

Responsibilities and rights of substitute carers

6.24 In reviewing the position of a substitute carer, the Scottish Law Commission noted that, while anyone who cares for a child under the age of 16 was obliged to take reasonable care of that child and that criminal sanctions and the general principles of the law of delict applied, what more the carer could and ought to do was somewhat unclear. Accordingly, it recommended that specific provision should be made[76] and the 1995 Act now makes explicit, for the first time, that anyone who has the care or control of a person under the age of 16 must safeguard the child's health, development and welfare.[77] In particular, the carer may consent to medical or dental treatment, where the child is not able to give such consent. There are two important qualification on the carer's role. First, the carer may only consent if he or she does not know that the parent would refuse to consent. Second, it is worth noting that the carer's action is confined to 'safeguarding' the child's health and does not extend to 'promoting' it. This places the carer in a more restricted position than a parent. Schoolteachers are excluded from the category of carers with this power to consent and the reasoning behind the exclusion is interesting. The Commission was concerned to avoid such possibilities as a teacher consenting to the immunisa-

---

71 1989 Act, s 78.
72 1989 Act, s 77. See *Hogg* v *Inverclyde Council* 1998 GWD 12–583, where Ms Hogg appealed successfully against refusal to register her as a child minder. She lived with her husband, a gamekeeper, who kept firearms in the home for the purpose of his job. Despite the husband's excellent safety record and the fact that the guns were kept in a locked cabinet, the local authority felt that the presence of firearms posed an unacceptable risk. The appeal was allowed on the basis that the local authority was not required to give a cast-iron guarantee that the home was risk free and that it had failed to assess the risk in this particular case. It was observed that registration could be made subject to conditions and that revocation of registration remained a possibility, should any fresh concerns come to light.
73 1989 Act, s 19.
74 Section 27. The term 'in need' is defined in s 93(4) and is discussed in chapter 7. In addition, the local authority may provide these services to children who are not 'in need'.
75 1995 Act, s.19.
76 Report on Family Law, para 2.59, rec 9, draft Bill, clause 5.
77 Section 5.

tion of an entire class. While such action would be unreasonably high-handed, it might have been desirable to permit teachers to consent to minor medical procedures on behalf of young children, since many children sustain minor injuries at school. Of course, any school could invite parents to exercise the power of delegation provided for in the 1995 Act[78] in order to enable a teacher to consent to minor medical procedures, but it is more likely that such matters will continue to be dealt with on a practical basis without recourse to legal formalities.

Consent to adoption

6.25 Essentially, adoption severs the original child-parent relationship and creates a new relationship between the child and the adopters.[79] It is hardly surprising, then, that the general rule is that adoption requires parental consent. Broadly, this rule is subject to two qualifications. First, the unmarried father who has no parental responsibilities and rights has only a very limited opportunity to oppose adoption.[80] Second, the court has extensive powers to dispense with parental consent to adoption.[81] It should be noted that a child of 12 years old or over has the right to consent to or veto his or her own adoption[82] and a younger child has the right to have his or her views taken into account.[83] These matters are discussed fully in chapter 8.

Parental criminal responsibility

6.26 A few words should be said about a form of parental responsibility, largely unknown in Scots law,[84] but found in other jurisdictions. Known as 'parental responsibility' or 'parental liability' laws, these statutes hold parents criminally responsible if their children offend.[85] At the outset, it should be noted that the parent is not held responsible for the juvenile's offence, nor does the parent step into the offender's place as defender. The modern parental responsibility laws have their roots in parental vicarious

---

78 Section 3(5).
79 As we shall see in chapter 8, para 75, there is the possibility of continued contact between the child and birth relatives.
80 Adoption (Scotland) Act 1978, s 65(1), defining 'parent'.
81 Adoption (Scotland) Act 1978, s 16.
82 Adoption (Scotland) Act 1978, s 12(8) and 18(8). The court may dispense with the child's consent where he or she is incapable of giving it. It should be noted that, unlike the parent whose refusal can be overridden by the court, the competent child's refusal to consent is not subject to a reasonableness test.
83 Adoption (Scotland) Act 1978, s 6(1)(b)(i).
84 The exception here relates to a child's failure to attend school.
85 See N. R. Cahn, 'Pragmatic Questions about Parental Responsibility Statutes' Wis L Rev 399 (1996); J. E. Dimitrios, 'Parental Responsibility Statutes – And the Programs that must accompany them' 27 Stetson L Rev 655 (1997); T. Scarola, 'Creating Problems Rather Than Solving Them: Why Criminal Parental Responsibility Laws Do Not Fit With Our Understanding Of Justice' 66 Fordham L Rev 1029 (1997); P. W. Schmidt, 'Dangerous Children and the Regulated Family: The Shifting Focus of Parental Responsibility Laws' 73 N Y U L Rev 667 (1998).

civil liability for the acts of children[86] and statutes dealing with 'contributing to the delinquency of a minor'.[87] Where the modern laws differ from their older counterparts is in the fact that, simply by the child committing an offence, the parent is liable to be charged with a separate offence and it then falls to the parent to demonstrate one of a limited range of defences. In this respect, modern parental responsibility laws share a common ground with traditional truancy laws which frequently create automatic parental liability out of the child's failure to attend school. Among the modern parental responsibility laws which have attracted most attention are those passed in Oregon and Louisiana in 1995.[88] The Oregon statute renders a parent liable to prosecution where the child commits an act which brings him or her within the jurisdiction of the juvenile court, violates curfew or fails to attend school.[89] It is then up to the parent to demonstrate that he or she was the victim of the act, reported the act to the appropriate authorities, or took reasonable steps to control the child's conduct at the time of the act. The Louisiana statute is more narrowly framed and applies either to the commission by the child of specific offences (possession of illegal weapons, drug dealing, underage drinking, truancy) or where the parent allows the child to 'associate with a person known by the parent' to fall within certain categories (gang members, felons, drug dealers, and the like).[90] While the usual penalties of fines or imprisonment may be applied, parents may be required to take parenting classes or attend counselling, as an alternative.

6.27 Should Scots law consider adopting this reversal of 'visiting the sins of the fathers on the sons'? Undoubtedly, the same concern over juvenile crime that prompted the legislation in the USA would find some political supporters in Scotland. However, like most simplistic solutions, there are real drawbacks to legislation of this kind. Firstly, it would penalise parents for acts which they may have no prospect of controlling. It is a grave mistake to assume that, when a young person offends, the parent is necessarily indifferent. Parents may be doing all they can to steer a child away from crime and the child may simply be ignoring them. Secondly, such a law pits parents against their children. Where a child is manifesting his or her problems by offending, the co-operative, round-table, approach of the children's hearing, where family members, professionals and others work together to find a better way forward for the child, is an infinitely preferable, constructive, response. Thirdly, many young offenders come from economically disadvantaged backgrounds. Assuming parents are not to be imprisoned for their children's offences, does it make any sense to fine people who are already having a financial struggle? A fourth reason

---

86 Hawaii was the first state to impose civil liability on parents for the wrongs of their children and most states have enacted laws along these lines, although, unlike Hawaii, many limit recovery to sums in the region of $2,500.

87 Almost all states have specific legal provision dealing with this subject and governing anyone who is actively involved in promoting or encouraging a minor's criminality.

88 In addition to this kind of state-wide regulation, a host of municipalities have passed local laws along similar lines.

89 Act of 23 September 1995, codified at Or Rev Stat S 163.577 (1995).

90 Act of 21 June 1995, No 702, codified at La Rev Stat Ann S14:92.2 (West Supp 1997).

not to involve this kind of solution lies in the lengths to which some parents might be driven in the attempt to stop their children offending. There is a real risk that, out of desperation, some parents might resort to violence in the attempt to keep a child on the straight and narrow. In addition, of course, parental responsibility laws provide a malevolent child with a powerful weapon against his or her parents, assuming the child is sufficiently unconcerned about the consequences for himself or herself.

6.28 In 1985, the Scottish Law Commission invited views on whether automatic parental civil liability for the delictual acts of children ought to be introduced.[91] As a result of the comments it received, it very wisely recommended no change to the existing position whereby parents have no automatic liability in this respect.[92] Given the reluctance to extend civil liability, it seems we may be safe from the more dramatic step of criminal liability attaching to the parents of offenders. Of course, it must be remembered that, while the Commission does receive views from members of the public, the bulk of its responses come from lawyers.

FINANCIAL SUPPORT FOR CHILDREN

6.29 It is stating the obvious to note that it is expensive to meet the needs of children and it is widely acknowledged that families with children need considerably more resources than families without children, if they are to enjoy an equivalent standard of living.[93] At the most basic level, all children need to be fed, clothed and housed, and this is before we enter the realms of piano lessons, private education, designer trainers and foreign travel. Since most children have no financial resources of their own, the real issue is who will provide for this support. The UN Convention on the Rights of the Child approaches the issue, as it does others, by accepting that parents (and, possibly, other family members) have the first responsibility to provide for children, with the state having the residual responsibility where parents cannot meet their obligation.[94] This has always been the approach of Scots law. The parental obligation to provide financial support for children is firmly rooted in the common law,[95] but 'the state', first through local parishes and, later through central government, has always been there to provide for cases of need.[96]

6.30 The thrust of the modern debate about financial provision for children centres on how the balance should be struck between the parental

---

91 Legal Capacity and Responsibility of Minors and Pupils (Scot Law Com Consultative Memorandum No 65, 1985), para 6.12.
92 Report on the Legal Capacity of Minors and Pupils (Scot Law Com No 110, 1987), para 13.
93 P. Morgan, *Are Families Affordable? Tax, Benefits and the Family* (Centre for Policy Studies, 1996) at p 30; D. Utting, *Families and Parenthood: Supporting families, preventing breakdown* (Joseph Rowntree Foundation, 1995) at p 35.
94 See for example, arts 3(1), 4, 5, 18, 20, 24, 26 and 27.
95 Stair, *Institutions*, I, v, 1; Erskine, *Institutes*, I, vi, 56; Fraser, *Parent and Child* (3rd edn, 1906), at p 102.
96 See chapter 3, para 1 and the references cited therein.

obligation, on the one hand, and the state's obligation, on the other.[97] Within that debate, there is a further issue to be resolved: how the parental obligation should be allocated between parents, particularly where they are not living together with the child. Certain state provision, for example, of education and health care, are forms of indirect support for children and are accepted, at least for the time being, as the state's responsibility. Other matters, like foreign travel or private education, are items for which parents and other family members usually pay. The remaining needs of children are at the heart of the debate. Who provides for the cost of food, clothing and housing? The answer remains, either the parents or the state and, often, both. A complex system of state benefits is available to provide, in whole or in part, for the basic needs of children and families, where the adults cannot meet the full cost of doing so. It remains then to consider how parents and other family members become responsible for supporting children.

6.31 The common law on aliment was replaced by a statutory formulation which is currently found in the Family Law (Scotland) Act 1985 ('the 1985 Act').[98] The 1985 Act provides the framework for a court-administered system of alimentary obligations which make parents and certain other persons responsible for supporting a child. It embodies a flexible system for fixing the amount payable and allocating the responsibility between the various possible obligants. During the 1980s, amid much vague bleating about family values, that system came under attack. One of the system's strengths, its flexibility, had the inevitable result that awards appeared inconsistent. In addition, concern over the cost of state benefits and civil legal aid and so-called 'deadbeat fathers',[99] whose irresponsibility was exceeded only by their fertility, prompted calls for change.[100] Disquiet

---

97 The debate is not peculiar to the UK. Australia introduced a child support scheme in 1988, although it was significantly different to that introduced in the UK. Under the Australian scheme, the recipient gets to keep substantially more of the amount paid, even if he or she is receiving benefits and there is no element in the calculation to cover support of the carer. These differences may have made the scheme more palatable but, even so, criticism, amendment and further criticism, have ensued: M. Harrison, 'Australia's Child Support Scheme: Much Promised, Little Delivered' (1995) 42 Family Matters 7; G. T. Riethmuller, 'Reviewing the Method of Review: A Review of the Administrative Departure Procedures under the Child Support (Assessment) Act 1989' (1995) 9 AJFL 6. For a discussion of the position in the USA see W. J. Doherty, 'The Best of Times and the Worst of Times: Fathering as a Contested Arena of Academic Discourse' in A. J. Hawkins and D. C. Dollahite, *Generative Fathering: Beyond Deficit Perspectives* (Sage, 1997) and I. Garfinkel, *Assuring Child Support: an extension of social security* (Russell Sage Foundation, 1992).

98 For a discussion of the common law and the thinking behind the 1985 Act, see Report on Aliment and Financial Provision (Scot Law Com No 67, 1981) paras 2.8–2.55.

99 Experience from the USA suggests that non-payment of court-ordered child support is either not linked to gender or, if it is, women are less likely to pay than are men. Figures from the US Bureau of the Census show that 57.3% of non-resident mothers failed to pay, compared with 47.7% of non-resident fathers; Doherty, above.

100 Much the same concerns were instrumental in various changes in the system of calculating financial support for children in the USA. For an analysis of the development of the current system and the defects in its theoretical underpinnings, see M. Garrison, 'Autonomy or Community? An Evaluation of Two Models of Parental Obligation' 86 Cal L Rev 41 (1998).

focused particularly on lone mothers[101] who were receiving means-tested benefits, particularly where the child's father was making no or, at best, erratic, contributions towards the child's support.[102]

6.32 The government of the day produced a White Paper, 'Children Come First',[103] in which it set out the framework for the system which was designed to replace much of the existing law on aliment with a formula-driven, administrative, procedure, under which responsibility for the assessment and collection of financial support for children was to be passed over to the Child Support Agency (CSA). Despite widespread concern over many aspects of the proposed system, the Child Support Act 1991 ('the 1991 Act') was passed, implementing the proposals contained in the White Paper. Almost from the moment it began to operate on 5 April 1993, the system came in for unprecedented criticism. The legislation itself was found to produce very unfair results in some cases and the CSA was condemned for inefficiency and incompetence. As a result, changes were made to the regulations in 1994 and a second White Paper, 'Improving Child Support',[104] was produced, leading to further changes to the regulations and the Child Support Act 1995, which amended its predecessor.

6.33 In March 1998, the government indicated that it was reviewing the whole child support system[105] and, in July 1998, it published a Green Paper, 'Children First: a new approach to child support',[106] giving details of the proposals for reform. Essentially, the proposal is to replace the current, rather complicated, formulae, with liability based on a simple percentage of net income. There would be provision to take account of a potential payer having exceptional expenses and, as an incentive to resident parents co-operating with the system, they would be permitted to keep more of the sums paid in child support, even if they were in receipt of benefits. The intention is that the new system would be simpler to understand and would be administered in a more user-friendly and efficient manner. The government believed that these proposals 'provide the basis for a radically more

---

101 A survey of young women between the ages of 15 and 19, found 87% of children born to them in the UK were born outside marriage compared with 62% in the USA and 10% in Japan; Into a New World: Young Women's Sexual and Reproductive Lives (International Planned Parenthood Federation, 1998). While not all of these women are in receipt of means-tested benefits, many are. In addition, many lone mothers receiving benefit are over the age of 19.

102 Under the system then operating, where the mother was in receipt of supplementary benefit, the Department of Social Security was entitled to recover sums of money in respect of child maintenance from non-resident fathers – Supplementary Benefits Act 1976, s 17. That system has now been replaced by the child support system.

103 Cm 1264, 1990. As I have noted elsewhere, this would have been more accurately entitled The Taxpayer Comes First; Cleland and Sutherland, at p 91. Clearly, much the same view is shared by others; see for example, A. Garnham and E. Knights, *Putting the Treasury First: The Truth About Child Support* (Child Poverty Action Group, 1994).

104 Cm 2745, 1994.

105 It promised that it would conduct 'a "root and branch" review of the CSA [and would] announce proposals for fundamental reform'; New Ambitions for Our Country: A New Contract for Welfare, Cm 3805, 1998, chapter 7, para 17.

106 Cm 3992, 1998.

efficient and effective child support service'.[107] Wide consultation on the proposals is anticipated and, of course, the result might be that the original proposals will, themselves, be modified. What seems clear, however, is that the child support system, as an alternative to the courts, is here to stay for the foreseeable future. It is not anticipated that the proposals for reform will be operational until 2001 and we must return to the system, as it is at present.

6.34 What we have now are two systems for the assessment and allocation of responsibility for financial support for children.[108] Many parents will, of course, reach agreement on the matter and, provided that the person looking after the child is not claiming certain state benefits, he or she need not be troubled by the CSA. Even for such parents, what is provided for in both the 1985 and 1991 Acts is relevant, since their negotiations will often take place in the context of what they would be obliged to pay should they fail to reach agreement. In the absence of agreement and, in any event, where certain state benefits are being claimed, the 1991 Act governs financial support for children under the age of 16 and, in certain circumstances, under 19. The 1985 Act, embodying the concept of aliment, continues to apply to a whole range of cases and these are examined in detail below. It is necessary, therefore, to consider each system.

6.35 The distinction between the public law obligation to pay child support and the private law obligation of aliment does not tell the whole story. The Social Security Administration Act 1992 provides that parents are responsible for maintaining their children and, for this purpose, defines a child as not only a person under the age of 16 but also a person under the age of 19 where income support is being paid in respect of him or her.[109] Where income support is being paid in respect of a child, the Secretary of State can recover the cost from a parent, subject to that parent having sufficient resources to pay.[110] Thus, even under the public law provisions, a parent can be liable to support a child after the Child Support legislation has ceased to apply. If there is a decree of aliment in respect of the child in favour of one parent and that parent is in receipt of income support, the Secretary of State is empowered to enforce the decree irrespective of the entitled parent's wishes.[111] In addition, the fact that income support is being paid to the parent with whom the child is living makes the other parent liable to meet the cost of the resident parent's support as well.[112] Thus, for example, a man may be liable to support the mother of their child under

---

107 Cm 3992, 1998, at p iii.
108 This would appear to reflect a general trend noted by Glendon who observed, 'As the nature of interdependence between families and outside support systems changes, private law dealing with domestic relations tends to lose ground to or merge with a broad range of public laws and programs affecting the family. This is especially so in the more advanced welfare states' – M. A. Glendon, *The Transformation of Family Law*, at p 294.
109 1992 Act, s 78(6)(d).
110 1992 Act, s 106.
111 1992 Act, s 108.
112 1992 Act, s 107. This applies only where the child is under the age of 16 – 1992 Act, s 107(15).

these public law provisions despite the fact that he has never been married to her and, thus, has no private law obligation to aliment her.[113]

6.36　At the outset, and for the avoidance of doubt, a fundamental point should be noted. Supporting a child financially does not give a person any rights in respect of that child – nor should it. Where a child lives and with whom a child spends time are matters which are properly determined on the basis of what will serve the child's welfare best, taking due account, of course, of the child's views. Who pays money to support a child is determined according to statutory formulae, court decisions and parental agreement. While it will often be in the child's best interests to see a person who also supports him or her, there is no necessary correlation between the two. Research suggests that parents who do pay for the support of their children are more likely to maintain contact with them.[114] Children who are supported financially by non-resident parents 'do better' in terms of general well-being and educational achievement than children who are supported to the same economic level from other sources.[115] Undoubtedly, the support-contact connection is one which is exploited by some parents. For example, a mother may obstruct contact when support is not being paid or a father may stop payments when contact is not taking place. Interrelated though the two are, their separate goals must be appreciated. This is particularly true if the children who will not benefit from contact are to be protected, but the distinction is deeper than that. Children are not property in which a stake can be purchased. They are people with rights, needs and the right to have those needs protected. 'I paid for it, so it's mine' has no application in the context of children. Parents sometimes have difficulty grasping the distinction between financial support and contact and it is incumbent on legal and other advisers to make the position clear.[116]

Child support

6.37　Child support is the creature of the Child Support Act 1991[117] and it is administered by the many child support officers throughout the country

---

113 On the obligation that spouses, but not cohabitants, owe to each other, see chapter 11, para 49. An award of aliment for a child may now include an element for support of the carer – Family Law (Scotland) Act 1985, s 4(4).

114 Certainly, this has been the experience in the USA where there is a longer history of this kind of legislation – J. R. Dudley, 'Exploring Ways to Get Divorced Fathers to Comply Willingly' (1994) 14 J Divorce and Re-marriage 98.

115 A. Burgess, *A Complete Parent: Towards a new Vision for Child Support* (Institute for Public Policy Research, 1998), at p 5. See also, V. W. Knox, 'The Effects of Child Support Payments on Developmental Outcomes for Elementary School Age Children' (1996) 31 J Human Resources 4, where the author found this to be the case whether or not the non-resident parent maintained contact. While it is not cited, Burgess' research, in particular, appears to have informed the thinking behind the most recent Green Paper.

116 Parental misconception here can only have been encouraged by the suggestion in the first White Paper that, by improving the system and ensuring that fathers contributed to the support of their children, more fathers would be prompted to fulfil other responsibilities and maintain contact with their children. Another possibility, that impoverished fathers might actually resent their children, was never explored.

117 Throughout this section, references to 'the 1991 Act' are to this statute, as amended.

working for the CSA. They use a variety of concepts, with particular statutory meanings to apply a number of formulae set out in the 1991 Act, as amended, and the supporting regulations.[118]

The parties

6.38 For the 1991 Act to apply there must be a 'qualifying child', living with a 'person with care' and, somewhere in the picture, there must also be an 'absent parent'. 'Qualifying child' is defined in terms of the child's age, educational circumstances and living arrangements. First, the person must be a 'child' and, for this purpose, that means anyone

under the age of 16; or

under 18 who is registered for work on youth training and whose parent is still claiming child benefit in respect of him or her; or

under the age of 19 and receiving full-time education, not being advanced education.[119]

The educational component is subject to further definition, both in the 1991 Act and in regulations, but, broadly, it covers attendance at school or a further education college, but not university.[120]

6.39 A person who is married ceases to be a child, for the purpose of the 1991 Act, irrespective of age.[121] Second, in order to be a 'qualifying child', one or both of the parents must be an 'absent parent'.[122] Frequently, the child will be living with one parent, usually the mother, but the 1991 Act will also apply where the child is living with a third party, like a grandparent. There, the child will have two 'absent parents'.

6.40 A 'person with care' is one with whom the child has a home or who usually provides the day to day care for the child, not falling within certain prescribed categories.[123] There may be more than one person with care in respect of any child and this becomes important since, where any such person is in receipt of certain benefits, the 1991 Act will apply automatically. The person with care will often be one of the child's parents. Known as a 'parent with care', that parent is regarded by the 1991 Act as fulfilling his or her financial responsibilities to the child by providing the home and looking after the child. Once a maintenance assessment has been made under the 1991 Act, any child support maintenance will be payable by the absent parent and not the parent with care.

---

118 This is a complex area of the law and must, necessarily, be discussed in outline only here. For a detailed account of the system, see R. Bird, *Child Maintenance – The Child Support Act 1991* (3rd edn, Family Law, 1996); D. Burrows, *The Child Support Act 1991 – A Practitioner's Guide* (Butterworths, 1993); E. Knights and S. Cox, *The Child Support Handbook* (5th edn, Child Poverty Action Group, 1997).

119 Section 55(1).

120 A university student, if under the age of 25, may be able to claim aliment from parents and certain other persons. See chapter 6, paras 67–69, below.

121 Section 55(2). In addition, anyone who has gone through a ceremony of marriage falls outwith the definition of a child, even if the marriage is void or annulled subsequently.

122 Section 3(1).

123 Section 3(3).

6.41 The term 'absent parent' is particularly offensive and has connotations of indifference and neglect that are not inherent in the more objective term 'non-resident parent'. As part of a whole package of recommendations designed to encourage the payment of child support, Burgess suggests that the term should be replaced accordingly,[124] a suggestion taken up in the most recent proposals for reform. In any event, an absent parent is one who is not living in the same household as the child, where the child has a home with a person with care.[125] In defining 'parent', the 1991 Act restricts its application to 'any person who is in law the mother or father of the child'.[126] Thus, it covers birth parents, whether married to each other or not, and, where the child has been adopted, adoptive parents. It does not cover step-parents. Where parentage is in dispute, the 1991 Act contains special procedures for the determination of such disputes.[127]

When the system applies

6.42 Essentially, the child support system applies to two categories of people, those who must use it and those who choose to do so. Since the thrust of the 1991 Act was aimed at reducing the benefits bill, it is not surprising to find that, where a person with care is in receipt of certain state benefits, he or she must authorise the Secretary of State to take action to recover child support maintenance from the absent parent.[128] While the 1991 Act talks in terms of the Secretary of State, the system is administered through the CSA and the Department of Social Security and reference here will be to the child support officers who actually operate it. At present, the relevant benefits which trigger compliance are income support, family credit, disability working allowance and jobseeker's allowance. Since many lone parents are in receipt of one of these benefits, the effect is that the system introduced by the 1991 Act is compulsory for a very large number of people. Where a person is required to give such authorisation, he or she is obliged to co-operate in seeking a maintenance assessment and in providing the necessary information, in particular, that which will enable the absent parent to be traced.[129]

6.43 There are a number of non-resident parents, and particularly absent fathers, who, most emphatically, do not wish to be traced. The fear for many women is that, were they to co-operate in identifying and tracing such fathers, they would be exposing themselves and their children to the risk of hostility or violence. The 1991 Act provides that, where there are

---

124 Burgess Report, n 115 above, at p 7. She also suggests that 'parent with care' should be replaced with 'resident parent'. In addition, Burgess recommends a host of other measures designed to promote voluntarism in child support, including: allowing the parent on benefit to keep more of the money paid; recognising the rights and responsibilities of unmarried fathers; recognising and promoting the role of non-resident parents through better housing and employment provision; extending mediation to all separating couples, whether married or not; and providing 'couple-support' for all expectant and new parents.
125 Section 3(2).
126 Section 54.
127 Sections 26–28.
128 Section 6(1).
129 Section 6(5)–(9).

reasonable grounds for believing that co-operation in seeking a maintenance assessment would expose the mother, or any child living with her, to the risk of 'harm or undue distress', she will not be required to give authorisation.[130] The exemption is not confined to protection from threatened violence and might apply, for example, where the mother or child would be exposed to distress through payment being sought from the father of a child, where the child has resulted from rape or incest.[131] It appears that non-disclosure is not regarded as justified where, for example, the child's father is married and living with his wife and their children, albeit that family might well be disrupted by disclosure. The exemption provision is important since, unless the parent with care is exempted from co-operating under the 1991 Act, he or she risks substantial loss of benefit for refusal to co-operate.

6.44 Where a parent with care fails to co-operate as required by the 1991 Act as, for example, where a mother declines to identify the child's father and the child support officer does not consider that she has reasonable grounds for doing so, her benefits may be cut by up to 40% for up to three years, with possible extensions of this period for as long as she refuses to disclose the father's identity.[132] To reduce benefit payable to the mother is to reduce the income of the family unit and, thus, the money available for the support of the child. Given that benefit recipients exist in a situation of tight financial constraints when on full benefit, it is difficult to see how this provision can have anything other than a detrimental effect on the child involved. In exercising discretion under the 1991 Act, a child support officer is required to 'have regard to the welfare of any child likely to be affected by his decision'.[133] The child's welfare is not stated to be 'paramount', as in all other legislation affecting children and, as this provision illustrates, it can be displaced by fiscal considerations.

6.45 In addition to those who must use the child support system, it is available to many others. Anyone who qualifies as a person with care, whether a parent or not, may apply for a maintenance assessment under the 1991 Act, as can the absent parent.[134] Consistent with the general principles, recognising the empowerment of children aged 12 or over, any such child who is habitually resident in Scotland can apply for a main-

---

130 Section 6(2)–(3). While the exemption provision envisages a woman requiring protection under it, protection would apply equally to a father with care where the absent mother posed a similar risk. One feature of the 1991 Act is the curious use of gender. Some attempt is made to employ gender-neutral language, through references to 'the child' or 'the person with care', but every so often, this slips and children are referred to in the masculine (eg s 3(1)), as is the Secretary of State. It is as if the drafter was trying, but failed, to use gender-neutrality language consistently.

131 It is interesting that the spectre of such children was central to Parliament rejecting the Scottish Law Commission's recommendation that unmarried fathers should be treated like all other parents, when it would always have been possible to make special provision in respect of such cases. When it comes to recovering money, it seems, such exceptional cases can be accommodated.

132 Section 46 and Child Support (Miscellaneous Amendments) Regulations SI 1996 No 1945.

133 Section 2.

134 Section 4(1).

tenance assessment.[135] Where a qualifying child applies for a maintenance assessment, this can trigger an assessment in respect of other children who live with the same carer as that child and who share the same absent parent.[136] So, for example, where a 12-year-old, who lives with her father and younger siblings, applies for a maintenance assessment, the assessment can be made in respect of all the children at the same time, provided that they have the same absent mother. Applications for a maintenance assessment cannot be made where there is already an assessment in force.[137] Anecdotal evidence suggests that, in the course of negotiating financial settlements on divorce, some parents use the spectre of the CSA to encourage their partners to agree more generous provision for the support of the children. Clearly, it is important for solicitors to understand precisely what maintenance assessment would be made under the 1991 Act, in order to advise clients whether to pursue, or respond to, this line of negotiation.[138]

The 'maintenance assessment' and the formulae

6.46 The assessment of maintenance due by the absent parent is calculated according to a number of interrelated formulae set out in the 1991 Act and the regulations.[139] The key elements of the calculation are: the maintenance requirement; assessable income; the rate of deduction; and the protected income level. In its original form, the 1991 Act allowed for no deviation from its rigid formulation but, as a result of injustices and criticisms, a system of 'departures', allowing a modest amount of discretion, was introduced by the Child Support Act 1995 ('the 1995 Act').[140] If government proposals come to fruition, the basis on which child support is calculated will be altered substantially from the year 2001.[141]

The maintenance requirement

6.47 This is the basic amount of money required to support the child and is calculated using the income support allowance for each qualifying child living with the person with care and adding certain other premiums. Included in the maintenance requirement is an element for the support of the person with care.[142] The maintenance requirement is not necessarily the amount the absent parent will actually pay. If the absent parent's assessable income falls below a particular level, he or she will not have to pay all

---

135 Section 7(1).
136 Section 7(2).
137 Section 4(9).
138 Computer software is available to assist solicitors in making the necessary calculations.
139 Numerous examples of calculations under the 1991 Act are given in Bird, above, Burrows, above and Knights *et al*, n 118 above. Various personal allowances and premiums are used in the calculations and these can be expected to change at the beginning of each financial year. For accounts of the original formulae, from somewhat different perspectives, see W. A. Wilson. 'The Bairns of Falkirk: The Child Support Act' 1991 SLT (News) 417 and F. Wasoff, 'The New Child Support Formula: Algebra for Lawyers?' 1992 SLT (News) 389.
140 See paras 6.51–6.53.
141 Children First: a new approach to child support, Cm 3992, 1998.
142 A result of this is that, where a person would not normally be required to pay aliment or periodical allowance to a former cohabitant, where the former cohabitant is caring for

of the amount indicated in the maintenance requirement. If the absent parent's assessable income multiplied by the rate of deduction exceeds the maintenance requirement, he or she will be required to pay an 'additional element' in excess of the maintenance requirement. Thus, the maintenance requirement is only the first step in arriving at the amount paid by the absent parent.

Assessable income

6.48 Assessable income is calculated by taking a person's net income (ie after the deduction of tax, National Insurance and certain pension contributions) and deducting what is known as exempt income. Exempt income is the amount a person is entitled to keep in order to cover his or her own basic needs. Originally, exempt income was calculated by adding together the income support and social security allowances, applicable to the absent parent, and reasonable housing costs. No account was taken of the fact that an individual might have high costs in travelling to work or of property transferred in the course of a 'clean-break' divorce settlement.[143] As a result of criticisms of the inflexibility of that approach, an allowance is now made for such additional factors. So for example, where the absent parent's share in the family home has been transferred to the parent with care by agreement or by court order, an allowance is now made in calculating exempt income for a sum of money depending on the value of the property transferred. One factor which does not feature in exempt income is the extent to which the absent parent is supporting other persons, like a new partner and step-children. As we shall see, this becomes relevant later. Assessable income is calculated for both parents although only the absent parent (or both of them, if applicable) is required to pay child support.

The rate of deduction

6.49 We now have the maintenance requirement and the assessable income (net income minus exempt income) for each parent. The deduction rate, which is currently 50%, is then applied to the absent parent's assessable income to establish what sum of money is available to meet child support. Applying the current deduction rate, this means that the absent parent will not normally be required to pay more than half of his or her assessable income in child support. If half of the assessable income is less than the maintenance requirement, the absent parent pays the lesser sum. Where both the absent parent and the parent with care have assessable incomes, their shares are calculated in proportion to their assessable

their child, support will be provided indirectly. Where the non-resident parent is paying aliment for the child, rather than child support, an element for support of the carer can now be included in that – Family Law (Scotland) Act 1985, s 4(4) (added by the Child Support Act 1991, Sched 5, para 5).

143 For example, where a couple with children were divorcing, they might agree that the husband would transfer his share in the family home to the wife, so that she and the children would have somewhere to live. In return, she might agree to lower payments in respect of the children. If the CSA were to ignore such arrangements, as it did initially, substantial injustice could result for the husband who was then required to pay child support in full.

incomes. Where the absent parent has more than enough assessable income (after the deduction rate has been applied), then he or she pays a basic element of child support plus an additional element.

The protected income level

6.50 A further stage of calculating child support is required in order to ensure that the absent parent has enough left on which to live and with which to support any children living with him or her, a new partner and any step-children. This ensures the absent parent a level of protected income. There are two elements in calculating protected income. The first was introduced by the 1995 Act and provides that no absent parent can be required to pay more than 30% of his or her income in child support. The second element is more complicated to calculate but ensures, essentially, that the absent parent and his or her new family are no worse off than they would have been on income support.

If all of this sounds rather like asking you to think of a number, treble it, deduct half and subtract the number you first thought of, do not be alarmed. The above is simply an outline description of the process and applying it is easier, in practice, when there are firm figures with which to work. Having said that, it must be acknowledged that the system is far from simple and certainly, many people directly affected by it cannot use it. The complexity of the calculations almost certainly explains some of the problems experienced by the CSA itself.

Departures

6.51 Just as the court-administered system of aliment was criticised for the inconsistencies which resulted from its flexibility, the child support system has been criticised for being unduly rigid. As we have seen, in its original form, it failed to take account of such matters as the cost of a parent travelling to maintain contact with children, high costs incurred in travelling to work and settlements made in the pursuit of 'clean-break' divorces. These settlements were the very thing encouraged by the legislation in force at the time many of the settlements were made. While there was never any intention that a 'clean-break' divorce ended the parental obligation to children and, indeed, the Children (Scotland) Act 1995 enshrines the child's right (and the parent's obligation) to maintain contact, as far as money is concerned, negotiated settlements between divorcing spouses include, inevitably, elements of financial arrangements in respect of children. Where arrangements were made in good faith and served the needs of all concerned, it was regarded as unfair by many that the subsequent child support legislation took no account of such settlements. Quite rightly, this attracted much criticism and accusations of 'moving the goalposts'.

6.52 As a result, the 1995 Act introduced a system of 'departures', allowing child support officers to deviate from the rigid formula. That officials of this kind should be permitted to exercise discretion, the very discretion that was removed from the courts, raises fundamental questions about the nature of justice and government. However, the discretion can only be exercised within fairly strict guidelines and, in any event, appeal lies to the Child Support Appeal Tribunal and the courts. It may be that a more extensive system of departures, administered with appropriately exercised discretion, will alleviate some of the hardship caused by the child support system itself. Of course, discretion is the door which leads to inconsistency, the very evil the system was introduced to remove.

Reviews and appeals

6.53 Decisions on child support can be challenged through reviews and appeals. The original decision of the child support officer can be reviewed internally at the request of a person with care, an absent parent or the child, in order to challenge: (i) a refusal to make an assessment; (ii) a refusal to review; (iii) an existing assessment; or (iv) the cancellation of or refusal to cancel an assessment.[144] Such a review should be requested within 28 days of notification of the decision which is to be reviewed. Appeal lies thereafter to the Child Support Appeal Tribunal.[145] If the Tribunal finds in favour of the appellant, it refers the case back to the CSA for reconsideration by a different child support officer. Appeal lies, thereafter, 'on a question of law', to a Child Support Commissioner.[146] Further appeal to 'the appropriate court' is provided for and this would appear to be the Court of Appeal, unless the Commissioner directs that appeal should be to the Court of Session.[147] While the 1991 Act makes no specific provision in this respect, appeal on a point of law will lie to the House of Lords, thereafter.

6.54 In addition to review as the first stage in the appeal process, the 1991 Act provides for review in three other circumstances. The first is the automatic review of each case which will take place every two years to take account of changing allowance rates.[148] The second type of review may be requested by the person with care, the absent parent or the child, and is designed to take account of a change of circumstances.[149] Thirdly, a child support officer may instigate a review where he or she is satisfied that a decision in relation to child support was made in ignorance of a material fact, based on a mistake as to a material fact, or wrong in law.[150]

Enforcement

6.55 As we have seen, co-operation with the CSA is enforced through the threat of a reduction in benefits. Once a maintenance assessment has been

144 Section 18.
145 Section 20. Where the subject of the appeal is a reduced benefit direction, appeal from the original decision may go direct to the tribunal without the need to have an internal review first – s 46(7).
146 Section 24. In order to appeal to a Commissioner leave is required from the chairman of the tribunal or a Commissioner and the appeal must be made within 42 days of leave being granted.
147 Section 25. Such an appeal requires the permission of the Commissioner or, if refused, the court.
148 Section 16.
149 Section 17.
150 Section 19.

made, the CSA has further weapons in its armoury through deductions from earnings orders and liability orders. Deductions from earnings orders do not involve a court process and the absent parent need not even be in arrears. This is simply an order which requires the absent parent's employer to deduct the sum payable from wages or salary and pay it directly to the CSA.[151] Such an order will not be of great value where the absent parent is self-employed or moves jobs frequently. In such cases, the CSA can apply to a sheriff for a liability order after at least one payment has been missed.[152] The order can be enforced by the ordinary means of diligence, including, poinding of goods, inhibition and adjudication, but not by an arrestment of earnings.[153] Ultimately, imprisonment is the sanction for failure to pay child support.[154]

Child support and the courts

6.56 The main thrust of the 1991 Act is to exclude the courts from determining issues of financial support for children. Where a child support officer

> 'would have jurisdiction to make a maintenance assessment ... no court shall exercise any power which it would otherwise have to make, vary or revive any maintenance order'.[155]

A maintenance order is defined as 'an order which requires the making or securing of periodical payments to or for the benefit of the child'[156] under a variety of statutes, including the Family Law (Scotland) Act 1985. In short, the courts' former powers to regulate aliment are removed, subject to a number of exceptions. Before we explore the exceptions, it is worth noting that a child support officer need only have jurisdiction to make a maintenance assessment for the courts' jurisdiction to be excluded. It is not necessary that an assessment has been made and, indeed, the court is precluded from becoming involved even if the case is such that a child support officer would refuse to make an assessment if one were to be applied for.[157]

6.57 There are a host of exceptions to this general rule. Many of them are set out explicitly in the 1991 Act, others implicit in it. The explicit exceptions include: the court's power to revoke an existing maintenance order;[158] 'top up' awards, where a parent is particularly wealthy;[159] additional payments to cover educational expenses, like school fees;[160] and

---

151 Section 31.
152 Sections 33 and 38.
153 Section 38.
154 Section 40.
155 Section 8(1) and (3).
156 Section 8(11).
157 Section 8(2).
158 Section 8(4).
159 Section 8(6). Where the absent parent's income is high, application of the formulae for a maintenance assessment could result in an excessive award. In such cases, the 1991 Act contains a cut-off device and, where this operates, it is competent to go to the court to seek additional payments.
160 Section 8(7).

expenses attributable to a child's disability.[161] The court is not prevented from making an award against the person with care of the child.[162] In addition, the Lord Advocate may provide by statutory instrument that the court can make an order which is in substantially the same terms as an agreement by the absent parent to make payments in respect of the child.[163] The implicit exceptions turn on the requirement that, before the courts can be excluded, a child support officer must have jurisdiction. If that is not the case, the courts continue to hold sway. Where one of the parties is habitually resident abroad, the 1991 Act does not apply[164] and aliment can be claimed for a child in the ordinary courts. As we shall see, the Family Law (Scotland) Act 1985 ('the 1985 Act') defines a child for the purpose of aliment as a person under the age of 25,[165] in certain circumstances, whereas 1991 Act cuts off at the age of 19. Thus, a 20-year-old seeking aliment must apply to the courts under the 1985 Act. While the 1991 Act is concerned only with the collection of support from absent parents, the 1985 Act envisages that other people, like step-parents, may be liable to support a child and claims in respect of non-parents must be pursued in the courts.[166] How the courts approach the question of aliment is discussed below.

What child support achieves

6.58 From the point of view of the child and the family unit in which he or she lives, child support often achieves little or nothing. This can be illustrated by taking the example of a child living with a lone mother. If the mother is on income support and the child support payable is less than the amount she receives, she continues to receive income support and the child support paid is consumed by the CSA. She gains nothing. If she is in receipt of family credit, £15 of the child support is disregarded. That may mean her income is then such that she loses entitlement to family credit or, if she remains on family credit, that she is £15 better off each week. Of course, where the parents are in employment and the child support system has been used, she may end up better off, but these were not the cases at which the legislation was primarily aimed. In addition, it must be remembered that a mother who fails to co-operate with the CSA without what is deemed to be 'good reason' runs the risk of benefits being cut dramatically.[167]

6.59 The Child Support Act 1991 was passed to combat perceived problems and, in particular, inconsistent awards by the courts which were often not complied with, the rising cost of state benefits and legal aid and parental (for which, read 'paternal') irresponsibility. Has it achieved any of these goals?[168] Certainly, it has achieved consistency, but at the cost of such

161 Section 8(8) and (9).
162 Section 8(10).
163 Section 8(5).
164 Section 44. *McGeoch* v *McGeoch* 1996 GWD 29–1751.
165 1985 Act, s 1(5).
166 1985 Act, s 1(1)(d).
167 Section 46.
168 For a critique of the system based on a study of 123 cases, see R. Young, G. Davis, N. Wikeley, J. Barron and J. Bedward, *Child Support in Action* (Hart Publishing, 1998).

rigidity and injustice that further legislation was required. Whether the amendments have been enough to create a sufficiently flexible system is open to question. Legal aid to fund actions for aliment has been saved, and, where child support is being paid, a part of the benefits bill has been reduced. Of course, the cost of this has been the setting up, staffing and running of the CSA and the additional tribunals and Commissioners required to deal with appeals. Whether any money has been saved overall is doubtful. What of making parents, and particularly fathers, pay for the support of their children? Massive amounts of child support remain unpaid.[169] In addition, there are the human costs of the system.[170] It appears that the CSA made a wholly unacceptable number of mistakes, both in getting calculations wrong[171] and in erroneous identification of alleged fathers, and has an appalling backlog of cases still awaiting initial assessment.[172] Hardly a contribution to the sum of human happiness. While no accurate figures are available, it is widely accepted that many fathers, and particularly those with irregular employment, contributed to the support of their children voluntarily and sometimes generously, albeit erratically. Thus, for example, such a father might buy the child new shoes or give the mother money to do so. If the child was going on a school trip, he might hand over extra funds to cover the child's spending money. It seems less likely that such individuals will do so if they feel pursued by a government agency. While the approach of such parents was less than ideal, it embodied voluntarism; that is, an acceptance of responsibility. That had to be better for the child-parent relationship than what exists at present.

Aliment

6.60 At common law, the mutual obligation of aliment between parent and child was derived from natural law, enacted into civil law, and regarded as being of fundamental importance.[173] Fascinating though the common

---

169 In its Twenty-First Report, the House of Commons Committee on Public Accounts found that over £1 billion of child support was unpaid and the CSA did not expect to recover about three-quarters of it – House of Commons Committee on Public Accounts, Twenty-First Report: Child Support Agency: Client Funds Accounts 1996–97 (The Stationery Office, 1998), pp vi–vii.

170 The following comment sums up some of the publicly-voiced concern. 'The operation of the Act has brought hate mail and death threats to the Agency offices; six suicides of absent fathers were alleged to be related to claims; 1,000 men were disputing paternity by submitting to DNA tests, the cost of which have had to be reduced by the CSA; 11,000 single parents allegedly stopped claiming income support in order to avoid contact with fathers; and some men were even said to have sought artificial divorces in order to reduce the assessment.' – R. Deech, 'Property and Money Matters' in M. Freeman (ed), *Divorce: Where Next?* (Dartmouth, 1996) at pp 94–95.

171 One in six debt balances, representing money owed by absent parents, was wrong by more than £1,000 – Twenty-First Report: Child Support Agency: Client Funds Accounts 1996–97, above.

172 This was the position in respect of some 407,000 cases – Twenty-First Report: Child Support Agency: Client Funds Accounts 1996–97, above.

173 Stair, quoting from I Tim. 5:8, made the following observation, 'If he provide not for his own family, he is worse than an infidel'.

law is,[174] it is with the modern law of aliment, contained in the Family Law (Scotland) Act 1985 ('the 1985 Act'),[175] that we must concern ourselves. The 1985 Act provides an exclusive list of alimentary obligations and the reciprocal nature of child-parent aliment has been abolished. Children no longer owe an obligation of aliment to their parents.[176] As we have seen, parents are obliged to support their children through the mechanism of child support. Quite separately, they may owe an obligation of aliment.

Who may be obliged to aliment a child?

6.61 A child is owed an obligation of aliment by the following persons

- His or her mother[177]

6.62 As we saw in chapter 4, maternity has been unproblematic until fairly recently.[178] With the advent of assisted reproduction, the biological and social picture became slightly less certain but the legal position is clear. The woman who gives birth to the child is treated in law as the child's mother and no other woman is so treated.[179] Thus, it is the woman who gives birth who owes the obligation of aliment and not, for example, the woman who donated the ovum. Where a child has been adopted, the adoptive mother rather than the birth mother is treated by the legal system as the child's mother[180] and, thus, it is the adoptive mother who owes the obligation of aliment.

- His or her father[181]

6.63 Establishing the identity of the child's father may cause greater problems[182] but, in the ordinary case, once the father has been identified, he owes the child an obligation of aliment. It does not matter whether the parents have ever been married to each other. Where assisted reproduction has been used, the husband or, in certain circumstances, the partner of the woman who gave birth is usually treated as the child's father and he will, therefore, be liable to aliment the child.[183] Where a child has been adopted, the adoptive father becomes liable to aliment the child.[184]

---

174 For a discussion of the common law on aliment for children, see *Stair Memorial Encyclopaedia*, vol 10, paras 1229–1247.
175 Throughout this section, reference to the '1985 Act' are to this statute.
176 At common law, a child who had superfluous assets was obliged to aliment a parent, where the parent was in need and, failing the child, more remote descendants became liable: Stair, *Institutions*, I, 5, 8–9; *McCulloch v McCulloch* (1778) 5 Brown's Supp 376; *Muirhead v Muirhead* (1849) 12 D 356; *Thom v Mackenzie* (1864) 3 M 177. The Scottish Law Commission recommended the abolition of the obligation – Report on Aliment and Financial Provision (Scot Law Com No 67, 1981) paras 2.8–2.11.
177 Section 1(1)(c).
178 See chapter 4, paras 4–6.
179 Human Fertilisation and Embryology Act 1990, s 27(1), discussed in chapter 4, para 35.
180 Adoption (Scotland) Act 1978, s 39(1), discussed in chapter 8, para 67.
181 Section 1(1)(c).
182 See chapter 4, paras 8–13 for a discussion of the presumptions surrounding paternity.
183 Human Fertilisation and Embryology Act 1990, s 28, discussed in chapter 4, paras 36–38.
184 Adoption (Scotland) Act 1978, s 39(1), discussed in chapter 8, para 67. In the USA, the desire to avoid supporting the children lay behind one attempt to revoke an adoption

- Any person who has 'accepted' the child into his or her family[185]

6.64 The concept of 'accepting' a child into one's family is subtle, since acceptance implies both physical and psychological elements.[186] Simply tolerating a child living under the same roof does not suggest acceptance. On the other hand, treating a child as a member of the family by, for example, including him or her in family activities and family discussions about important decisions, does. Indeed, it might have been better if the Scottish statute had used the word 'treated' rather than 'accepted',[187] although each case is so dependent on its individual facts that much the same evidence would be led in either case. In any event, this provision means that an obligation of aliment may be owed to a child by other family members, like an aunt or uncle,[188] or a biologically unrelated person, like a step-parent or a parent's cohabitant. A person is not regarded as accepting a child where the child has been boarded out to that person by a local or public authority or a voluntary organisation.[189]

- The executor of a deceased person or any person has been enriched by succession to the estate of a deceased person owing obligation[190]

6.65 This is one of the few areas of the common law on aliment that has been preserved expressly by the 1985 Act. A person may owe an obligation of aliment to a child. That person dies. At common law, the obligation transmits to his or her executors and heirs, but only to the extent of both the deceased's liability and, in the case of an heir, to the extent that he or she has been enriched by succession.[191]

6.66 It is apparent, then, that a whole host of people may owe an obligation of aliment to a child. Take, for example, David, born to unmarried parents. Each parent owes him an obligation of aliment. They separate shortly after his birth and he lives with his mother and her parents, who take an active part in raising him and behave, for most purposes, like extra parents. In addition to David's mother and father, his grandparents have probably acquired responsibility to aliment him. David's mother marries and she and David move into a new home with her husband. The grandparents do not get along with their daughter's new husband and they

order – *Rich* v *Rich* 364 S E 2d 804 (Wva, 1987). Such a strategy would be ineffective for the purpose of avoiding aliment in Scotland if the pursuer had accepted the child into his or her family. It might work, however, in the context of child support.
185 Section 1(1)(d).
186 A number of English cases, interpreting the same phrase under the legislation applicable there at the time demonstrate the difficulty. Contrast *Snow* v *Snow* [1971] 3 All ER 833, where the step-father was found to have accepted the children, with *P* v *P* [1969] 3 All ER 777, where he was not. See also, *Watson* v *Watson* (Sh Ct) 1994 SCLR (Notes) 1097, where the question was whether a man could accept a child he erroneously believed to be his. In *Kirkwood* v *Kirkwood* [1970] 2 All ER 161, this point was decided differently.
187 This is the approach taken in other statutes. See for example, the Children (Scotland) Act 1995, s 12(4)(b).
188 *Inglis* v *Inglis* 1987 SCLR 608.
189 Section 1(1)(d).
190 Section 1(4).
191 Stair, *Institutions*, I, 5, 10; Erskine, *Institutes*, I, 6, 58; *Netherlie's Children* v *The Heir* (1663) Mor 415; *Aitkenhead* v *Aitkenhead* (1852) 14 D 584.

begin to see David only occasionally. David's step-father is a model parent and he and David form a close bond. Arguably, the grandparent's alimentary obligation may have ceased, since they are no longer 'accepting' him as a member of their family. However, David has now acquired a new person with an alimentary obligation, his step-father. Both of his birth parents, of course, remain obliged to aliment him. When David is 20 years old, his mother and step-father divorce. By then, he is at university studying for a law degree. The Child Support Act 1991 is no longer applicable. How is a court to resolve the issue of liability?

Who is a child?

6.67   For the purpose of aliment, a 'child' is a person

> under 18 years old,[192] or,

> under 25 years old, 'who is reasonably and appropriately undergoing instruction at an educational establishment, or training for employment or for a trade, profession or vocation'.[193]

The extent of aliment payable and how that is calculated will be discussed presently. For the moment it is important to note that the alimentary obligation can continue for quite some time and, certainly, well beyond what would normally be regarded as childhood. At first instance, it can last until the child is 18 although, of course, not every child will require support until then. Thereafter, it can continue until the 'child' is 25, but only if the conditions specified are met. Instruction at an educational establishment would certainly include taking a full-time course at college or university. Training for employment would include both training in an educational institution or 'on the job'. What is a trade, profession or vocation is not defined by the 1985 Act, but the fact that training for employment is also included probably means that training to do anything that might earn a living is covered. Arguably, it is not training for a trade, occupation or profession to learn how to serve hamburgers in a fast-food outlet, but it might well be training for employment. Unlike child support, the child's entitlement to aliment does not cease upon marriage, although the child's spouse will, thereby, join the group of possible obligants. It seems clear that David, in our example, falls within the ambit of the 1985 Act's definition of a 'child' despite the fact that he is 20 years old.

6.68   One point is clear. Where a child does not fall within the ambit of the conditions, the obligation to aliment ceases at 18. Thus, if an adult child is unemployed, there is no alimentary obligation. At common law, the alimentary obligation was potentially lifelong.[194] That is no longer the case. Thus, whereas parents in the past may have been obliged to support a

---

192 Section 1(5)(a).
193 Section 1(5)(b).
194 *Earl of Strathmore* v *Earl of Strathmore's Trustees* (1825) 1 W & S 402; *Beaton* v *Beaton's Trustees* 1935 SC 187. Where a child had been independent for a time, the obligation could revive if he or she became indigent thereafter; *Wallace* v *Goldie* (1848) 10 D 1510, where a father was found liable to support his married daughter, albeit he was permitted to discharge his obligation by offering to support her in his own home.

severely disabled adult child, that obligation is now incumbent on the state.[195] Of course, disability does not preclude instruction or training and where a disabled child under the age of 25 is continuing in education or training, he or she will benefit from the provisions on aliment.

6.69 More interesting, however, is what amounts to undergoing instruction or training 'reasonably and appropriately'. If they have supported their son through training as a hairdresser, are parents expected to continue to support him when he decides that he would rather be a car mechanic? Does it make any difference that there are no jobs in hairdressing in the area where they live, but there is a shortage of mechanics? To return to our example of David, assuming that he will graduate next year and has decided that he would like to go on to study for a master's degree, are the various people who may be obliged to support him expected to finance that? If so, can he then contemplate a doctorate at their expense? While each case will turn on its own facts, there must be a point at which parents (and other obligants) can say, 'Enough. No more'. With the recent changes in state support for further and higher education, there is no doubt that more students will be seeking support from family members and an increase in cases being brought by students against parents can be anticipated.[196]

No order of liability

6.70 Where more than one person owes an obligation to aliment, there is no automatic order of liability, although when aliment is being sought from one person, the obligations of other persons will be taken into account.[197] At common law, the obligation was primarily on the father, with the mother coming lower down the list of possible obligants.[198] That was swept away by the 1985 Act.[199] Now it is for the pursuer to decide against whom the action is to be raised and for the defender to raise the question of other possible obligants.[200] Thus, were David to raise an action against his step-

---

195 *McBride* v *McBride* (Sh Ct) 1995 SCLR 1021.
196 The process has already started – *Jowett* v *Jowett* (Sh Ct) 1990 SCLR (Notes) 348. Fear was struck in the hearts of many parents in October 1997 with the, much publicised, case of Mr Macdonald, a law student, who raised an action for aliment against his mother. Awarding interim aliment of £60 per month during term-time, Sheriff Robertson suggested that the student might consider getting a part-time job – *Macdonald* v *Macdonald* (1998) FLB 31–1. *The Scotsman* (15 May 1998, p 5) reported that the parties reached a settlement before the court had the opportunity to dispose of the case. Anyone contemplating an action against a parent in such circumstances should, of course, consider discussion and negotiation first. Litigation does nothing to improve family relations and, from a pragmatic point of view, may result in less generous treatment in the future when there is no longer an obligation of aliment.
197 Section 4(2).
198 In his *Institutes* (I, 6, 56), Erskine places the mother's obligation after those of all the paternal ascendants while, in his *Principles* (III, 1, 4), he places the mother directly after the father.
199 *Coyle* v *Coyle, Neilly* v *Neilly* 1981 SLT (Notes) 129.
200 *Inglis* v *Inglis* 1987 SCLR 608, where the father argued successfully that the sum sought from him should be reduced in the light of the fact that his daughter was living with her aunt and uncle who had accepted her into their family.

father, the step-father would be entitled to indicate both of David's parents and, possibly, his grandparents, as other potential obligants.

How much?

6.71 The obligation of aliment is to provide 'such support as is reasonable in the circumstances',[201] having regard to:

* The needs and resources of parties[202]

6.72 The present and foreseeable needs and resources of both the pursuer and defender are relevant here. Although many children will have no resources of their own, some do. Consequently, where a schoolgirl had a part-time job, her father was able to argue that the amount of aliment payable by him should be reduced.[203] In assessing the parties' respective needs and resources, the court will look at actual income and verifiable expenditure in respect of appropriate items and at evidence of an individual's lifestyle.[204]

* The earning capacities of parties[205]

6.73 It should be noted that it is not simply the actual earnings of the parties which are relevant, but their earning *capacities*. Where a person has a well-paid job and gives it up when confronted with a claim for aliment, what he or she was earning will usually be taken into account, as a reflection of earning capacity. Of course, earning capacity has to be approached reasonably. There is no point, for example, in looking at what a former miner used to earn, if all the mines in the area have closed and there is no prospect of a person being employed in that capacity. The earning capacity of a child raises an interesting question. As we saw, a schoolgirl's earnings were taken into account in reducing the amount of aliment payable by her father. Can every parent of an older child argue, therefore, that the child should seek part-time employment? It is submitted that, where the child is still at school, a case could be made for his or her need to concentrate on schoolwork and other related activities, like sport. However, where the young person had a job, but gave it up, the position would be less strong. Of course, it might be argued that the child gave the job up because schoolwork was suffering, rather than to avoid it being taken into account in the calculation of aliment. Certainly, given that so

---

201 Section 1(2).
202 Section 4(1)(a).
203 *Wilson* v *Wilson* 1987 GWD 4–106. Any young person in this position might be tempted to give up a part-time job in the light of this decision but, as we shall see, such a strategy would be risky.
204 See for example, *Joshi* v *Joshi* 1998 GWD 8–357, an application to vary aliment of £30 per week to nil. The payer had remarried and twins had been born to the new relationship. While the court accepted that this was a change of circumstances, it examined the payer's income and outlays and concluded that he had a good lifestyle, a conclusion reinforced by the fact that he had recently had a holiday in Kenya. In addition, the court noted that the payer's repayment of a bank loan would soon be complete, freeing more of his income, and refused to consider outlays in respect of *Sky Subscriber* to be expenditure which should take priority over the payment of aliment.
205 Section 4(1)(b).

many university students now have part-time employment, the courts might well attribute an earning capacity to them in computing aliment. Thus, returning to our hypothetical David, it might be that any award made to him would be premised on his having a part-time job.

- All the circumstances of the case[206]

6.74 This consideration acknowledges that every case will turn on its own facts. However, amongst other relevant circumstances mentioned in the 1985 Act is the fact that the defender is supporting another person, whether or not he or she is under an obligation to do so.[207] Given the fluidity of personal relationships, a person who owes an alimentary obligation to one group of children may have moved into a new relationship and be supporting a new partner and step-children. What he or she is doing, in fact, is relevant, even if it does not arise from any legal obligation. This amounts to no more than accepting reality. Turning again to David, assuming his mother made monthly payments to help her parents out, these would be taken into account in considering her ability to contribute towards his support. Clearly, a relevant circumstance to be considered by the court is that there are other people who owe an obligation of aliment to the pursuer.

6.75 A person's conduct is irrelevant unless it would be 'manifestly inequitable' to ignore it.[208] The 1985 Act, quite deliberately, does not define what sort of conduct would be taken into account and the courts have had only limited opportunity to explore the term. It can be argued that only conduct which had a bearing on resources should be relevant. Thus, the fact that a defender had a particularly extravagant lifestyle or has dissipated assets through, for example, gambling or alcohol abuse, might be relevant. On the other hand, can the court consider other conduct which might be relevant to the family circumstances? What of the obnoxious child who has been excluded from the family home for being thoroughly unpleasant and disruptive? In terms of 'other conduct' the courts have taken a sensible approach to date. For example, the fact that a woman had unprotected sex, was considered irrelevant when the father of her child tried to argue that the resulting pregnancy had been her responsibility.[209] On the other hand, the fact that a father lied about his income was considered relevant.[210]

Defences

6.76 The fact that a child is living with the defender is no bar to raising an action for aliment.[211] However, it is open to the defender to demonstrate that he or she if fulfilling the alimentary obligation by supporting the child

---

206 Section 4(1)(c).
207 Section 4(3)(a).
208 Section 4(3)(b).
209 *Bell* v *McCurdie* 1981 SC 64.
210 *Walker* v *Walker* 1991 SLT 649. Of course, lying about income goes to the heart of the resources available but, none the less, the fact of having lied was a consideration.
211 Section 2(6).

in his or her own home and that he or she will continue to do so.[212] In addition, where the child is over the age of 16, it is open to the defender to make an offer to maintain the child in his or her own household. Had the 1985 Act left it at that, a cynical defender might have defeated a claim for aliment by making wholly unrealistic offers to take the child into his or her home. For this reason, the 1985 Act provides that such an offer only constitutes a good defence where it would be reasonable to expect the child to accept the offer.[213] In assessing 'reasonableness', the court is directed to have regard to 'any conduct, decree or other circumstances'.[214] Clearly, where there has been a history of child abuse in the family, it would not be reasonable to expect the child to live in the same home as the abuser. On the other hand, it might be perfectly reasonable for a parent, who lived near to the university his or her child was attending, to make such an offer to the student, as a more economical way of providing support than financing the rent on a flat. In the case of David, his step-father might offer this defence and the fact that they had a good relationship throughout David's childhood might make acceptance reasonable. On the other hand, were David's birth father to offer the same defence, his lack of involvement in David's life to date might make acceptance less reasonable. Again, each case will turn on its own facts, including the dynamics of the individual family. An offer of this kind is no defence where the child is below the age of 16.[215]

How does the action proceed?

6.77 An action for aliment may be raised in either Court of Session or sheriff court,[216] and may be brought by way of an independent action or in the course of other proceedings.[217] The action may be raised by the child[218] or, on behalf of a child under 18, by a parent, a guardian, or a person with whom the child lives or who is seeking a residence order.[219] A woman may raise an action on behalf of her unborn child, but the action will not be

212 Section 2(7).
213 Section 2(8).
214 Section 2(9).
215 Section 2(8). To have allowed the defence to apply to younger children would have resulted in a return to the pre-1930 law as it affected children born outside marriage. Under the common law at that time, where the mother sought aliment from the child's father, he could defend the action by offering to support the child in his own household, once the child was past 'infancy' (seven years old). Not surprisingly, many lone mothers abandoned their actions in the face of such offers, despite the fact that many offers were not intended sincerely at all. An end was put to this kind of cynical manipulation by the Illegitimate Children (Scotland) Act 1930.
216 Section 2(1).
217 Section 2(2). While a claim for aliment can be raised in any proceedings the court considers appropriate, the issue is most likely to arise in the course of actions: for divorce, for financial provision, in respect of parental responsibilities and rights, and concerning parentage.
218 A person under the age of 16 has legal capacity to instruct a solicitor and to sue and defend in legal proceedings, where he or she has a general understanding of what it means to instruct a solicitor, and a child of 12 or older is presumed to have this capacity – Age of Legal Capacity (Scotland) Act 1991, s 2(4A) and (4B). See discussion in chapter 3, paras 63–64.
219 Section 2(4).

heard and disposed of until after the birth.[220] As we have seen, it is competent to raise an action against a person with whom the child is living.[221]

What the court can do

6.78 The court may grant decree in an action for aliment and, in so doing, may make two kinds of awards. The first, and most common, is to order the making of periodical payments for a definite or indefinite period or until a specific event happens.[222] Secondly, and as well, it can order the making of an alimentary payment of an occasional or special nature.[223] Such occasional awards may be for any purpose but might be appropriate, for example, to cover education expenses or special costs arising from a school trip or a holiday. Certainly, such awards are not to be used as a means of substituting a lump sum for a periodical payment.[224] In granting decree, the court can backdate an award[225] and a smaller sum than that sought may be awarded.[226]

6.79 Flexibility is inherent in the concept of aliment and the court retains the power to vary or recall an award.[227] Either the pursuer or the defender may request such variation or recall on showing that there has been a material change of circumstances.[228] Again, what is, or is not, a material change of circumstances will turn on the individual facts of each case and the only such circumstance spelt out in the 1985 Act is the making of a child maintenance assessment under the Child Support Act 1991.[229] The discovery by a man that he is not, in fact, the father of a child he has been found liable to aliment, would be a material change of circumstances.[230] The fact that the child is growing up and, thus, becoming more expensive to support might also be relevant, although an allowance for this might have been made in the original award.[231] The court has the power to backdate any

220 Section 2(5). Such an action may include a claim for inlying expenses – s 3(1)(b).
221 Section 2(6).
222 Section 3(1)(a).
223 Section 3(1)(b).
224 Section 3(2). By its very nature aliment covers continuing needs and changing circumstances. Thus, a person with liability should not be able to discharge the obligation by making a lump sum payment. Of course, a wealthy obligant might set up a trust fund for the support of a child. Effectively, this involves making a lump sum payment, but the trust would be expected to generate a continuing income and, in any event, future applications for aliment would be possible.
225 Section 3(1)(c). Backdating may be to the date of bringing of the action or a later date or, on special cause shown, to a date prior to the raising of the action.
226 Section 3(1)(d).
227 Section 5(1). *Nixon* v *Nixon* 1987 SLT 602; *Matheson* v *Matheson* 1988 SLT 238; *Macdonald* v *Macdonald* 1995 SLT 72.
228 In *Joshi* v *Joshi* 1998 GWD 8–357 while the court accepted that there had been a change of circumstances, occasioned by the birth of the payer's twins, it reviewed his financial provision and refused to vary the award of aliment which, in any event, had not been increased in line with inflation over the previous six years.
229 Section 5(2).
230 *Gallacher* v *Gallacher* 1997 GWD 26–1300.
231 *Kirkpatrick* v *Kirkpatrick* (Sh Ct) 1993 SCLR (Notes) 175; *Skinner* v *Skinner* (Sh Ct) 1996 SCLR (Notes) 334.

variation[232] and order repayment of sums paid under the original decree. In the course of considering variation or recall, it may make an interim award.[233]

Verdict on aliment

6.80 As we have seen, aliment, as a means of ensuring that parents supported their children, came under attack because it was believed that awards were inconsistent and, in any event, the sums awarded were often not paid. In addition, actions for aliment were often legally aided and, thus cost public money. It is questionable that child support provides a more effective mechanism for ensuring parental support or that it is a less expensive means of doing so. The real benefit of aliment lies in its flexibility. Awards can be tailor-made to meet the needs of individual cases. While this may produce apparent inconsistency, it may be more in line with reality than something which is formula-driven. Of course, the fact that an action is raised means that aliment no more embodies the valuable notion of voluntarism than does child support. As far as children under 16 are concerned, aliment is something of a dead letter for all but the wealthy and those with special circumstances, like disability. However, for offspring over the age of 19, it remains important and an increase in cases being brought by students and other young people undergoing training can be anticipated. In addition, aliment remains significant in recovering financial support from the wider family. With more children living in step-families and family breakdown continuing, aliment will remain a vital means of providing financial support for children and young people.

CHILD ABDUCTION

6.81 As we have seen, the legal system provides extensive machinery to regulate where a child may live and with whom. Despite that, a parent may be dissatisfied with the arrangements arrived at and may take the law into his or her own hands, either by taking the child away, in breach of an agreement or a court order, or by refusing to return the child after an authorised visit. Illegal removal of a child from a person entitled to control the child's residence is governed by both civil and criminal law, as is wrongful retention of the child. The aims of the law are: to deter parents and others from abducting children, either within Scotland or out of the country; to prevent such abduction; or, where abduction has taken place, to facilitate the return of the abducted child. At the outset, several points should be noted. Firstly, we are concerned here with the situation where a child is abducted by a parent or other family member,[234] rather than a stranger. Secondly, practicalities are often as important as law when it

---

232 Section 5(2).
233 Section 5(3).
234 Reference in the following discussion will usually be to a parent abducting a child, since this is the most common situation. However, it should be remembered that the abductor may be another family member, like a grandparent, or someone otherwise known to the child, like the non-resident parent's new partner. Usually, that person will be acting with the knowledge of the non-resident parent.

comes to preventing and dealing with international child abduction, although we are concerned primarily with the legal position. Thirdly, while the terms 'custody' and 'access' have been banished from the domestic scene, they continue to be used in international conventions.[235]

6.82 At the risk of stating the obvious, the child's destination is important in abduction cases. So, for example, where one parent takes the child from the other parent's home in Dundee to another part of that city, there may well be distress and concern, but return should be comparatively easy to effect. Similarly, as long as the child remains in Scotland and his or her whereabouts are known, the legal system provides a variety of mechanisms that should ensure a swift reunion with the parent who is entitled to control residence.[236] If the child is in another part of the UK, despite the fact that he or she is in a foreign jurisdiction, reunion should not be all that difficult to effect using the procedures devised to ensure mutual co-operation between the various UK jurisdictions.[237] It is when a child is taken to a foreign jurisdiction, outside the UK, that the matter becomes more complex.

6.83 Concerns over child abduction and the delays and difficulties involved in inter-jurisdictional disputes are not unique to Scotland. As a result of the very considerable international efforts aimed at minimising the distress caused to children and other family members by abduction, a number of international conventions have been concluded. At present, the most important are the Hague Convention on the Civil Aspects of International Child Abduction[238] ('the Hague Convention') and the European Convention on Recognition and Enforcement of Decisions concerning Custody of Children and on the Restoration of Custody of Children[239] ('the European Convention'), since they have been adopted into the UK through the Child Abduction and Custody Act 1985. We will return to the Conventions presently but, broadly, their impact is to create mutual obligations between contracting states to effect the speedy return of children to the appropriate country. Where a child has been abducted from Scotland to a Convention country, that is, one which is a party to either or both of the Conventions, the parent in Scotland can make use of the provisions. Conversely, the law provides for a child who has been brought to Scotland illegally being returned to his or her place of habitual residence. Where a child has been abducted to a country which is not a party to either Convention, the parent seeking to secure the child's return will have to rely on the domestic law of that country and, sometimes, the prospect of his or her being successful is very slim indeed. The Hague

---

235 While the relevant domestic legislation predates the Children (Scotland) Act 1995 and, indeed, the Children Act 1989 (England and Wales only), it has been amended to take account of the later statutes. So, for example, s 6(1)(a)(i) of the Child Abduction Act 1984, now refers to 'an order of a court in the United Kingdom awarding custody of the child to any person *or naming any person as the person with whom the child is to live*', the words in italics having been added by the 1995 Act.

236 See paras 6.90–6.91, below.

237 See para 6.92, below.

238 Signed at The Hague on 25 October 1980.

239 Signed in Luxembourg on 20 May 1980.

Convention on Jurisdiction, Applicable Law, Recognition, Enforcement and Co-operation in respect of Parental Responsibility and Measures for the Protection of Children,[240] signed at the Hague in October, 1996, has yet to be ratified by the UK, but ratification can be anticipated and the Convention's provisions will have an important impact on the issue in the future.

6.84 International child abduction, and the application of the European and Hague Conventions, have generated an enormous body of case-law and excellent literature.[241] Only a broad outline of the applicable law will be provided here and the reader is directed to the literature for further details. Before we consider child abduction, in its various geographic contexts, it must be remembered that it is often perfectly permissible for a parent or other person to take a child abroad.

Legal removal of a child from the jurisdiction

6.85 While the problems of international child abduction should not be underestimated, it would be unnecessarily intrusive for the legal system to require all parents to go through a formal legal procedure every time they wished to take their children out of the country. Even where the parents are divorced, the resident parent may be quite happy for the non-resident parent to take the child abroad on holiday. Either parent may remove a child from the jurisdiction, provided that there are no court orders prohibiting such removal and that the requisite consents have been obtained. However, the fact that a parent has any of the parental rights does not allow him or her to take a child who is habitually resident in Scotland out of the UK without the consent of the other parent.[242] Where the child is the subject of a residence order, anyone wishing to remove the child must obtain the consent of the child's parents, guardians and anyone who may determine the child's residence as a result of a residence order.[243] As we shall see, removal of a child by a 'connected person' without appropriate consent is a criminal offence.[244]

6.86 A parent or other person who wishes to remove a child from

240 The reader will be relieved to know that this Convention is generally referred to as the 'Hague Convention on Children'. For an excellent discussion of the Convention, see E. M. Clive, 'The New Hague Convention on Children' 1998 JR 169. Dr Clive was head of the UK delegation to the Hague Conference on Private International Law which concluded with the signing of the Convention, and was a member of the drafting committee.

241 See for example, I. L. S. Balfour, 'Child Abduction' in Cleland and Sutherland; E. B. Crawford, *Private International Law* (W. Green, 1998), paras 11.18–11.39; G. Jamieson, *Parental Responsibilities and Rights* (W. Green, 1995), chapters 22–33; Wilkinson and Norrie, chapter 10. This represents a small fraction of the available literature but refers the reader to further secondary sources and, in particular, to journal articles.

242 1995 Act, s 2(3)[and (6). The 1995 Act spells this point out in order to avoid the doubt, which existed under previous legislation, over whether one parent was entitled to so remove a child in the exercise of his or her own parental rights, despite opposition from the other parent.

243 Child Abduction Act 1984 (the '1984 Act'), s 6(3).

244 See paras 6.97–6.100, below.

Scotland, either temporarily or permanently, against the wishes of a person whose consent must be obtained may apply to the court for permission to do so.[245] Permission will only be granted if the court is satisfied that removal will be in the child's best interests and, in the course of making its decision, will take any views the child wishes to express into account in the light of the child's age and maturity.[246]

Preventing abduction

6.87 Nowhere is the cliché 'prevention is better than cure' more appropriately applied than in the context of child abduction. Information and advice on preventing the abduction of a child is available from the Scottish Courts Administration.[247] There are a number of steps which can be taken to prevent abduction. At the outset, it is helpful to have a court order dealing with residence. As we have seen, each parent usually has an automatic right to determine the child's residence. Consequently, it would be prudent to have the matter regulated formally where there is a dispute between them or the possibility of abduction. Any fear of abduction should be notified to the police. The police can use their national computer to pass the relevant information to all sea and airports throughout the UK with the aim of preventing the child being taken out of the country, where there is a real and imminent danger of this happening. Where there is the possibility of a child being abducted, the court may grant an interdict prohibiting removal of the child from Scotland[248] and may also order the surrender of any UK passport which contains particulars of the child,[249] although this will be of little value if the child is also entitled to a foreign passport.[250]

Illegal removal: the civil law

6.88 Four distinct, but sometimes overlapping, approaches to dealing with the problem of child abduction can be identified. Firstly, there are the ordinary provisions of domestic law. Secondly, there is provision for reciprocal enforcement of court orders throughout the UK. Thirdly, there are the provisions of the Hague Convention, dealing with the reciprocal enforcement of custody rights between signatory states and, finally, there

---

245 1984 Act, s 6(3)(a)(ii). An application for either a residence order or a specific issue order under the 1995 Act, s 11 would appear appropriate depending on what kind of removal was anticipated. Where the applicant planned to emigrate with the child, the former would be appropriate, whereas a short holiday abroad would be covered by a specific issue order.

246 1995 Act, s 11(7).

247 See Child Abduction from Scotland (Scottish Courts Administration, 1996). Reunite, a charitable organisation which seeks to prevent child abduction and to advise on the recovery of abducted children, produces a Child Abduction Prevention Pack and may be able to offer counselling to a parent whose child has been abducted. The addresses of the Scottish Courts Administration and Reunite can be found in the Appendix.

248 Family Law Act 1986 (the '1986 Act'), s 35(3).

249 1986 Act, s 37.

250 Where the parents are nationals of different countries, the child will often be entitled to a passport from each country or to appear on each parent's passport.

are the provisions of the European Convention, dealing with reciprocal enforcement of custody decisions. As has been noted, the Conventions apply only between states which are signatories to them, although some states, like the UK, are parties to both. It should be noted that the European Convention applies only where there has been a *decision* on custody, whereas the Hague Convention applies to the enforcement of *rights*. Thus, the latter can be used by parties who have never had a dispute adjudicated by a court. Enforcement of rights and decisions is conducted through the Central Authorities of the relevant states. In Scotland, the Central Authority is the Secretary of State for Scotland who operates through the Scottish Courts Administration for this purpose.

6.89 Which legal approach is appropriate depends on where the child is and whether or not there is a court decree dealing with residence.

Within Scotland

6.90 As we have seen, mothers and married fathers have parental responsibilities and rights from the time they become parents.[251] Unmarried fathers may acquire responsibilities and rights by agreement with the child's mother[252] or by court order.[253] Having a right to determine a child's residence or to have contact with a child does not give the parent the right to remove the child from the UK without the other parent's consent.[254] However, within Scotland, disputes over where the child will live, where the parents are not living together, are fairly common. Until a court removes a parent's parental rights, that parent retains them, irrespective of any change in the adults' living arrangements. In addition, it will be remembered that the court is directed not to make any order in relation to parental rights unless to do so would be better for the child than not making an order.[255] The effect of this is that many separated and divorced parents will retain their parental right to determine the child's residence.

6.91 This system works well for many families and reinforces recognition of the continued importance of both parents in a child's life, regardless of the breakdown of the adults' relationship with each other. However, it does mean that either parent with the right to determine the child's residence can do just that until the court determines otherwise. Where the parents cannot reach agreement, then, in order to avoid the threat or reality of tussles over where the child will live, a residence order should be sought.[256] An interim order should be considered as a means of regulating the matter in the meantime. Once one parent's right to determine residence has been removed, the other parent with the right to make such decisions controls where the child will live. If the non-resident parent then abducts the child, the police should be informed and they will usually assist in recovery of the child. The non-resident parent who abducted the child may be held to be in

251 1995 Act, s 3(1).
252 1995 Act, s 4.
253 1995 Act, s 11.
254 1995 Act, s 2(3) and (6).
255 1995 Act, s 11(7)(a).
256 1995 Act, s 11(1).

contempt of court, as may any person who knew of the decree and acted in defiance of it.[257] In addition, the court may ordain a person to deliver a child and failure to obey the order would again be contempt of court.[258]

Outwith Scotland but within the United Kingdom

6.92 A residence order in relation a child under the age of 16 made by any court in Scotland, England and Wales,[259] or Northern Ireland is recognised automatically throughout the UK as having the same effect as if it had been made by the court where recognition is sought.[260] Third parties can rely on such a court order. However, such an order can only be enforced once it has been registered. An order from England, Wales or Northern Ireland can be registered in Scotland by application to the court which granted it.[261] That court will then send a certified copy of the order, details of any variation of it, and a copy of the application to the Court of Session.[262] The order will then be registered.[263] Only orders relating to a child under the age of 16 can be registered and, once a child reaches the age of 16, registration ceases to have effect.[264] Where the original order is varied, recalled, or revoked, notice of this is given to the court where it is registered.[265] Once the order has been registered, a petition can be presented to the Court of Session for enforcement of it.[266] This scheme can be extended to certain dependent territories,[267] and has been so extended to the Isle of Man.

Under the Hague Convention[268]

6.93 The Hague Convention is concerned with the return of children removed or retained in violation of a person's right to determine a child's residence. Since such rights can arise without court intervention, it is not necessary to have a court decree in order to invoke the Hague Convention. It applies between states which are signatories[269] to it and was implemented for the whole of the UK by the Child Abduction and Custody Act 1985.

257 *Lord Advocate* v *The Scotsman Publications Ltd* 1989 SLT 705 (HL).
258 *Brown* v *Brown* 1948 SC 5; *Fowler* v *Fowler (No 2)* 1981 SLT (Notes) 78.
259 This includes orders made by the High Court in England and Wales in exercise of its wardship jurisdiction: 1986 Act, s 1(d).
260 1986 Act, ss 25 and 26.
261 1986 Act, s 27(1) and (2).
262 1986 Act, s 27(3).
263 1986 Act, s 27(4).
264 1986 Act, s 27(5).
265 1986 Act, s 28.
266 1986 Act, s 29.
267 Family Law Act 1986 (Dependent Territories) Order 1991, SI 1991 No 1723.
268 The text of the Convention can be found in the Child Abduction and Custody Act 1985, Sched 1.
269 States become parties to the Convention from time to time and, for the practitioner, it may be important to check the up-to-date position in respect of a particular country. The SCA can assist with this information. At the time of writing, the following states are signatories to the Hague Convention: Argentina, Australia, Austria, Bahamas, Belize, Bosnia-Herzegovina, Burkina, Canada, Chile, Colombia, Croatia, Cyprus, Czech Republic, Denmark, Ecuador, Finland, France, Georgia, Germany, Greece, Honduras, Hong Kong, Hungary, Iceland, Ireland, Israel, Italy, Liechtenstein, Luxembourg, Macedonia, Mauritius, Mexico, Monaco, Netherlands, New Zealand, Norway, Panama, Poland,

The fulcrum of the Hague Convention is the concept of a 'Central Authority' and anyone who claims that a child has been wrongfully removed or retained can apply, either to the Central Authority in the country of the child's habitual residence, or to the Central Authority of any contracting state. The Central Authority applied to will take steps to secure the return of the child[270] or, if the child is not within the Authority's jurisdiction, will pass the application on to the Central Authority of the state where the child is thought to be.[271] As we have seen, in Scotland, the Scottish Courts Administration carries out this function on behalf of the Secretary of State,[272] and it is one advantage of being in a small jurisdiction that it can provide an individual service on a case by case basis. Where possible, voluntary return of the child is attempted, but the Scottish Courts Administration will assist a party in finding a lawyer to initiate proceedings in the Court of Session.

6.94 Several issues are crucial in the process of recovering a child:

The removal or retention of the child must be wrongful[273]
To be wrongful, the removal or retention must breach the custody rights (or right to determine the child's residence) of another person under the law of the state in which the child was habitually resident immediately beforehand.

The person who had the right to determine the child's residence must either have been doing so or, but for the retention or removal, would have been doing so[274]

The period of time which has elapsed since removal or retention[275]
If less than one year has elapsed since the removal or retention of the child, the court is directed to return the child 'forthwith'. If more than one year has elapsed, the court must still order the child's return unless it can be shown that the child is now settled in his or her new environment.

If the person who had the right to determine the child's residence consented to the removal or retention or has acquiesced in it subsequently, the court need not return the child[276]

Portugal, Romania, Slovenia, South Africa, Spain, St. Kitts and Nevis, Sweden, Switzerland, Turkmenistan, UK, USA, Venezuela, Yugoslavia (Serbia and Montenegro) and Zimbabwe.
270 Hague Convention, arts 7,10 and 11.
271 Hague Convention, art 9.
272 Child Abduction and Custody Act 1985, s 3. It should be noted that the Scottish Courts Administration will supply an applicant with a certificate entitling him or her to legal aid without the usual need to consider income and reasonable cause.
273 Hague Convention, art 3(a).
274 Hague Convention, arts 3(b) and 13(a).
275 Hague Convention, art 12.
276 Hague Convention, art 13(a).

*If it can be established that there is 'grave risk that his or her return would
expose the child to physical or psychological harm or otherwise place the
child in an intolerable situation', the court need not return the child*[277]

Under the European Convention[278]

6.95 The European Convention applies to the reciprocal enforcement of
custody decisions between contracting states[279] and was implemented
throughout the UK by the Child Abduction and Custody Act 1985. The
term 'custody decisions' includes decisions relating to the care of a child,
the right of contact with a child and the right to decide where the child will
live.[280] Decisions are recognised in Scotland automatically,[281] but must be
registered with the Court of Session before they can be enforced.[282]
Recognition and enforcement can be refused in the following
circumstances.

*A change of circumstances rendering the original decision incompatible
with the welfare of the child*
Passage of time since the decision can constitute a change of circumstance,[283] but change of residence after an improper removal does not.
Before deciding the matter, the court must seek to ascertain the child's
views unless this is impracticable, particularly in the light of the child's age
and understanding.[284]

*The effects of the decision are manifestly incompatible with the
fundamental principles of the law relating to the family and children in the
state addressed*[285]
As we have seen, the overarching principles (the paramountcy of welfare,
participation by the child, and presumed non-intervention) determine
decisions about children in Scotland. It should be noted that the European
Convention allows the state addressed greater freedom in respect of its
domestic law than does the Hague Convention.

The defender was not given the opportunity to defend the original action[286]

---

277 Hague Convention, art 13(b). Contrast this with the position under the European
Convention.
278 The text of the Convention can be found in the Child Abduction and Custody Act 1985,
Sched 2.
279 As with the Hague Convention, states become parties from time-to-time and the SCA
can provide information on the up-to-date position. At the time of writing, the following
states have signed the Convention: Austria, Belgium, Cyprus, Denmark, Finland, France,
Germany, Greece, Iceland, Ireland, Italy, Luxembourg, the Netherlands, Norway,
Poland, Portugal, Spain, Sweden, Switzerland, and the UK.
280 European Convention, art 1(c).
281 1985 Act, s 15(2)(a).
282 1985 Act, s 15(2)(b).
283 European Convention, art 10(1)(b).
284 European Convention, art 15(1)(a).
285 European Convention, art 10(1)(a).
286 European Convention, art 9(1)(a).

The court granting the original decision did not have jurisdiction based on the habitual residence of one of the following: the defender, the child's parents or the child[287]

A decision has already been recognised in the state addressed which pre-dates the removal of the child[288]

The child has been brought to Scotland and neither Convention applies

6.96 Where a child is brought to Scotland in breach of a person's custody rights and neither of the Conventions apply, the Scottish courts recognise foreign custody orders based on the child's habitual residence,[289] and have shown themselves willing to return children to the appropriate jurisdiction.[290] None the less, a foreign custody order will not be followed blindly.[291]

Illegal removal: the criminal law

6.97 Scots common law has long recognised the criminal nature of taking a child away from the person who had custody or care of the child. With the increase in international child abduction, it was recognised that there was a need to deal with the special circumstances of that problem. It is conveni- ent to deal with the responses separately.

The general law

6.98 The offence of *plagium* is the stealing of a child from his or her parents.[292] It can be committed by anyone and the child's consent is no defence. Where a parent who has no right to determine the child's residence removes the child from the parent who has such a right, he or she commits *plagium*.[293] Where both parents have full parental responsibilities and rights, it is doubtful that either of them can commit *plagium*, since parental rights can be exercised by each of them alone.[294] The Scottish Law Commission has recommended the abolition of the offence of *plagium* and the creation of a new statutory offence of taking or detaining a child under the age of 16 from the control of any person having lawful control of that child.[295]

Removal of a child from the United Kingdom

6.99 It is an offence for a 'person connected with a child' to remove a

---

287 European Convention, art 9(1)(b).
288 European Convention, art 9(1)(c). See *Campins-Coll, Petitioner* 1989 SLT 33.
289 1986 Act, s 26.
290 *Sinclair* v *Sinclair* 1988 SLT 87.
291 *Campins* v *Campins* 1979 SLT (Notes) 41.
292 G. H. Gordon, *The Criminal Law of Scotland*, (2nd edn, W. Green, 1978), para 14–43; Wilkinson and Norrie, at pp 262–264.
293 *Downie* v *HM Advocate* 1984 SCCR 365.
294 1995 Act, s 2(2). This is subject to the provisions of s 2(3) and (6) governing the removal of a child from the UK.
295 Child Abduction (Scot Law Com Discussion Paper, No 67, 1985) and Report on Child Abduction (Scot Law Com No 102, 1987).

child from Scotland without the consent of the child's parents, guardians and any person who has custody of the child or has been named by a court as the person with whom the child is to live.[296] 'Connected person' includes the child's parents (including a person reasonably believed to be the child's father), the child's guardian and anyone who has been named by a court as the person with whom the child should live.[297]

6.100 It is a defence to show that the person who removed the child[298]

believed that he or she had the appropriate consent; or
believed that consent would have been given if all the circumstances had been known; or
took all reasonable steps to communicate with the relevant persons but had been unable to do so; or
did not know of any court order regulating residence.

A conviction under the 1984 Act, in summary proceedings, renders a person liable to imprisonment for up to three months, or a fine, or both. If the conviction is on indictment, the possible penalty is of imprisonment for up to two years, or a fine, or both.[299]

---

296 1984 Act, s 6.
297 1984 Act, s 6(2).
298 1984 Act, s 6(4).
299 1984 Act, s 8.

CHAPTER 7

CHILD PROTECTION

7.1 As we have seen, 'the state', in one form or another, is an ever-present force in the lives of children. Even before a child is born, the law regulates when a pregnancy may be terminated[1] and ante-natal conduct may be relevant to decisions taken about a child at birth or at a later stage in life.[2] Thereafter, there is detailed regulation of the duties that parents owe to their children and the rights they have in respect of them, with the emphasis being placed on parental responsibilities rather than parental rights.[3] Where parents cannot agree on arrangements for the care of their child, the state is present again, in the form of the courts, to determine what should happen. Children themselves may have recourse to the courts in this context, as may other private individuals. In addition, there is a whole panoply of legislation aimed at protecting children from specific dangers, from cigarettes to exploitative employment practices.[4] Nor is all regulation preventative in nature. The state accepts its obligation to provide for children through such mechanisms as financial support, health care and education. It is in child law that we find one of the clearest examples of the distinction between private and public law becoming blurred.

7.2 Given the array of possible forms of state intervention in the lives of children and their families, it would be all too easy to forget that the starting point is one of privacy in family life. The European Convention on Human Rights ('the European Convention') enshrines this principle in art 8[5] and the UN Convention on the Rights of the Child contains a host of provisions recognising the child's right to live within the family unless good reason is demonstrated for preferring some other arrangement.[6] However, both domestic and international law also recognise the state's obligation to provide for children and to protect them where they are not being adequately cared for in the home environment. Sometimes this involves the state itself in arranging alternative care, but it should be remembered that it may be possible for a particular child to remain at home with his or

---

1 See chapter 2, paras 22–26.
2 See chapter 2, para 19.
3 See chapters 5 and 6.
4 See chapter 3, paras 91–99.
5 Article 8 provides for the right to respect for privacy in family life.
6 See for example art 8 (child's right to preserve family relations), art 9 (child's right to live with his or her parents unless it is established that separation is necessary for the child's welfare), and art 18 (common parental responsibility for the care and upbringing of children).

her family, provided that the family is given additional support. In this chapter, we will begin by examining the central problem facing many children in Scotland today: child abuse or neglect. We will then consider the state's obligation, carried out through local authorities, to provide services for children and their families, before examining the various mechanisms available to the local authority where it is concerned about the welfare of a particular child. An inherent part of the whole system of child protection is the children's hearings system and, such is its importance, it warrants a chapter of its own.[7]

Child abuse and neglect

7.3 Child abuse and neglect is nothing new.[8] Traditional children's stories, bible tales and literature all provide ample evidence that some children have always been exposed to harm at the hands of the very people whom society expects to protect and nurture them.[9] Formal recognition of the problem can be seen in the founding of the Societies for the Prevention of Cruelty to Children in New York in 1874[10] and in England ten years later. While a number of local child protection societies had been in existence in Scotland for some time, what was to become the Royal Scottish Society for the Prevention of Cruelty to Children was founded in 1885.[11] In their early days, these organisations did excellent work, largely with what might be described as fairly obvious, or clear, cases of abuse and neglect.

7.4 By the 1920s, Caffey, a radiologist working in New York, became aware through X-rays of unexplained healed fractures to the bones of many children. Ultimately, he sought to draw attention to his concern that

---

7 See chapter 9.

8 For an account of the history of child abuse, see S. X. Radbill, 'Children in a World of Violence: The History of Child Abuse' in M. E. Helfner, R. S. Kempe and R. D. Krugman (eds), *The Battered Child* (5th edn, University of Chicago Press, 1997). Regarded as one of the most influential books on the subject, the first edition, edited by C. H. Kempe and R. E. Helfner, was published in 1968. See also, C. Lyon and P. De Cruz, *Child Abuse* (2nd edn, 1993).

9 See for example, Snow White (physical and emotional abuse and attempted murder by step-mother), The Pied Piper of Hamlyn (child-stealing), Jacob's willingness to sacrifice his son, Sir Walter Scott, *Heart of Midlothian* (1818) and R. L. Stevenson, *Kidnapped* (1886).

10 The founding of the Society in New York is usually attributed to the experience of Mary Ellen. A very moving account of the story of Mary Ellen can be found in B. Ashley, *A Stone on the Mantlepiece* (The Scottish Academic Press, 1985), at pp 21–23. Briefly, it appears that Mary Ellen's plight came to the attention of a volunteer missionary working in the Hell's Kitchen area of New York. Hearing that the child was beaten regularly by her parents, the missionary sought to rescue her and found the police and other authorities she approached were powerless to help. Finally, she discovered the New York Society for the Prevention of Cruelty to Animals and they were able to rescue the child, using animal protection legislation, by extending the definition of 'animal' to this 'little animal of the human race – a little animal which happened to have a soul'. A chilling reminder that many of the problems faced today are not new is found in the fact that Mary Ellen's 'parents' had fostered or adopted her (it is not clear which) from an institution charged with her care.

11 For a fascinating account of the founding and first hundred years of the RSSPCC, see B. Ashley, *A Stone on the Mantlepiece*, above. The early years of the Society saw much wrangling over the need for a separate Society for Scotland.

the fractures may have been caused by the carers of the children.[12] By the 1950s, Silverman, another radiologist, reinforced this view.[13] However, the landmark in modern recognition of child abuse and neglect can be traced to the multidisciplinary conference organised by Dr C. Henry Kempe on the 'Battered-Child Syndrome' in 1961 and the seminal article he and others wrote the following year.[14] Finally, the problem had been given a name and there would be no holding back the concern from the medical, and other, professions, thereafter. Strenuous efforts have been made around the world to predict, prevent and diagnose child abuse. Where a problem is found to be present, it is essential that the response to both the victim and the abuser is appropriate and effective. Unsurprisingly, consensus on many of these issues has proved elusive. Before we consider these matters, however, we must try to find working definitions of abuse and neglect.

Definitions of abuse and neglect

7.5 It will come as no surprise, when we come to examine the mechanisms for intervention in a child's or a family's life, that there are strict criteria for intervention. Thus, for example, before a court will consider granting a child assessment order, it must be satisfied of a number of things, including the fact that the local authority has reasonable cause to suspect that child 'is being so treated (or neglected) that he [or she] is suffering, or is likely to suffer, significant harm'.[15]

However, nowhere in the extensive definition section at the end of Part II of the Children (Scotland) Act 1995 is there any definition of either 'treatment' or 'neglect'. This is no accident. If the courts are to be in a position to deal with each case as it arises, a more flexible approach than that offered by precise and detailed definition is warranted. Secondly, the criterion for court-authorised intervention contemplated in the definition above, that the treatment of the child is likely to cause him or her 'significant harm', allows for intervention whether that treatment would generally be regarded as abusive or not. Thirdly, in the context of child protection, the courts are again bound by the overarching principles. As we have seen, the third of these principles is the presumption of non-intervention. That is, the courts are directed not to make an order unless the making of it would be better than not making it.[16] However, this does not help social workers and others who must make the day-to-day decisions. If they are to know when to consider closer investigation or

12 J. Caffey, 'Multiple Fractures in the Long Bones of Infants Suffering from Chronic Subdural Hematoma' 56 A J Roentgenol 163 (1946).
13 F. Silverman, 'The Roentgen Manifestations of Unrecognized Skeletal Trauma' 9 Am J Roentgenol Radium Ther Nucl Med 413 (1953).
14 C. H. Kempe, F. N. Silverman, B. F. Steele, W. Droegemueller and H. K. Silver, 'The Battered-Child Syndrome' 181 J Am Med Assoc 17 (1962).
15 Children (Scotland) Act 1995, s 55(1)(a), words in square brackets added. In the remainder of this chapter, references to the '1995 Act' are to the Children (Scotland) Act 1995 unless otherwise stated. Child assessment orders are discussed at paras 7.66–7.70, below.
16 1995 Act, s 16(3). The application of the overarching principles under Part II of the Act is a little more complicated than their application under Part I of the Act and is discussed more fully in paras 7.62–7.65, below.

further action, they must have some idea of what they are looking for. To put it another way, in order to ensure appropriate intervention, they must be given some kind of working definition. 'I know it when I see it' may work in the art world, but it has no place in the context of child protection.

7.6 Thus it is that we must look elsewhere for definitions of child abuse and neglect. In Scotland, the Scottish Office has provided general guidance, aimed at inter-agency co-operation, in 'Protecting Children – A Shared Responsibility: Guidance on Inter-Agency Co-operation'.[17] Before providing the more specific descriptions of the problem set out below, this document offers the general guidance that

> 'children may be in need of protection where their basic needs are not being met, in a manner appropriate to their stage of development, and they will be at risk of avoidable acts of commission or omission on the part of their parent(s), sibling(s) or other relative(s), or a carer'.[18]

This definition is offered in the context of considering whether it is appropriate to place a child's name on the Child Protection Register and care is taken to stress that the surrounding circumstances must be taken into account.[19] It is also noted that, while the categories of abuse and neglect defined below are well recognised, 'in practice, there may be overlap between categories'.[20] In England and Wales, the equivalent document is 'Working Together under the Children Act 1989'.[21] These two publications do not define abuse and neglect in identical terms and various professionals will often have other, more detailed, guidance available to them. In addition, there is an abundance of literature[22] on the subject and, in some cases, there is no unanimity on whether a particular form of abuse or neglect exists or the nature of its precise content. For our purpose, a number of different forms of the problem can be identified.

Physical injury

7.7 Physical abuse of children was probably amongst the earliest forms of child abuse to be identified and, in many cases, may be the easiest to detect. 'Protecting Children' highlights its existence rather than attempting a definition, when it describes it as

> '[A]n injury inflicted, or poisonous substance administered, or not knowingly prevented, by a person in charge of the child'.[23]

---

17 (Scottish Office, 1998), hereinafter referred to as 'Protecting Children'. This document replaces Effective Intervention: Child Abuse – Guidance on Co-operation in Scotland (Scottish Office, 1989) and takes account, not only of the Children (Scotland) Act 1995 and the UN Convention on the Rights of the Child, but of lessons learned in practice.
18 Annex C, para 2.
19 Annex C, para 3.
20 Annex C, para 4.
21 (Department of Health, 1991), hereinafter, referred to as 'Working Together'.
22 See Helfner, Kempe and Krugman, n 8 above; Lyon and de Cruz, n 8 above, pp 1–16; J. K. Mason (ed), *Paediatric Forensic Medicine and Pathology* (Chapman and Hall, 1989), chapters 14–18.
23 Annex C, para 4.

'Working Together' provides a slightly more detailed explanation of physical injury as being

> '[A]ctual or attempted physical injury to a child, or failure to prevent physical injury (or suffering) to a child including deliberate poisoning, suffocation or Munchausen syndrome by proxy'.[24]

Actions by the abuser may include hitting, biting, burning, scalding, choking or suffocating a child. Exposing a child to physical injury by, for example, leaving the child unsupervised near a stove with a pot of boiling water on top of it, may be abuse or neglect. It will be remembered that Scots law allows parents the defence of 'reasonable chastisement' when the issue of assaulting a child arises and, on one occasion, a court found that hitting a nine-year-old with a belt came within that defence.[25] As we have seen, the defence is likely to be removed or modified as a result of a recent decision of the European Court of Human Rights.[26]

7.8 Münchhausen syndrome by proxy (MSBP) is a curious condition which requires special mention, not least because of the attention it has attracted recently in Scotland. Münchhausen syndrome itself involves a patient who fabricates or deliberately induces illness in himself or herself. The element of proxy comes in when a carer, often the child's mother, deliberately engineers illness in a child or misleads health professionals about the child's state of health, so as to make them believe the child is ill.[27] It can be compared to the situation of an over-anxious parent who simply seeks medical assistance in circumstances, like the child having a mild cold, where many parents would simply let the condition take its course. There is no doubt that some parents do exhibit MSBP and that they may pose a danger to their children. However, there appears to be disagreement amongst the medical profession over diagnosis of MSBP and there is a concern that it is being over-diagnosed, with the result that some children are being removed from parents where they should not be, while others are not receiving treatment for conditions which they have.[28] Concern about over-diagnosis has emerged only recently and how this particular issue develops will be a matter for the future. It is the latest in a long line of indications that developments in the field of child abuse are never over.

Physical neglect

7.9 Rather than involving something active, neglect generally involves the

---

24 At para 6.40.
25 *B v Harris* 1990 SLT 208. For a full discussion of 'reasonable chastisement', see chapter 6, paras 18 and 19.
26 *A v United Kingdom* 100/97/884/1096.
27 D. Smallwood, 'Münchhausen Syndrome' [1996] Fam L 478. See also, *Re DH (A Minor) (Child Abuse)* [1994] 1 FLR 679, for a discussion of MSBP and the use of video surveillance in hospitals.
28 *The Scotsman*, 29 September 1998, devoted part of the front page, page 4 and part of the editorial to its own investigation and claimed that parents whose children were suffering from myalgic encephalomyelitis (ME) where particularly at risk of this kind of accusation. The suggestion of erroneous diagnosis has chilling echoes of what happened in Cleveland in 1987. See para 7.19, below.

failure to do something which the parent or other carer ought to be doing for the child. In the words of 'Protecting Children',

'This occurs when a child's essential needs are not met and this is likely to cause impairment to physical health and development. Such needs include food, clothing, cleanliness, shelter and warmth. A lack of appropriate care, including deprivation of access to health care, may result in persistent or severe exposure, through negligence, to circumstances which endanger the child'.[29]

While failure to provide adequate medical treatment may be neglect, given legitimate differences of opinion surrounding the appropriate treatment for particular conditions, parents are allowed a certain latitude in this respect. None the less, the fact that the parents were acting in good faith will not excuse their opposition to a form of treatment generally regarded as beneficial.[30] Whether leaving a child unattended constitutes neglect will depend on the age of the child and the other circumstances of the case.[31] Both 'Protecting Children' and 'Working Together' make specific reference to 'non-organic failure to thrive' in the context of child abuse.[32] More a consequence of abuse or neglect, failure to thrive involves a child who has shown a marked reduction or cessation in growth. It is not always an indicator of abuse or neglect but rather an indicator of a need for further investigation.[33]

Emotional abuse

7.10 While 'Protecting Children' provides a reasonable working description of emotional abuse as being 'failure to provide for the child's basic emotional needs such as to have a severe effect on the behaviour and development of the child',[34] its predecessor, 'Effective Intervention', provided considerably more guidance on both the problem and indicators that it might be present. It described emotional abuse as

'The severe impairment of social and emotional development, it is the (eventual) consequence of repeated and persistent: withholding of affection; criticism; verbal abuse; scapegoating for all the family's problems; rejection, or threat of rejection, to the child's distress; lack of contact and interaction with the child in

---

29 Annex C, para 4.
30 In *Finlayson (Applicant)* 1989 SCLR 601, for example, the parents' fear that their haemophiliac son might receive contaminated blood did not justify them in refusing to permit his treatment.
31 As we have seen, there is no fixed age at which a child may be left unattended and so, for example, it has been found not to be neglect where a father left his 13-year-old son alone for several hours – *D v Orr* 1994 SLT 908. Decisions here depend on the circumstances of the case and this explains the rather more surprising decision where it was held not to be neglect to leave a sleeping baby unattended in a car for 45 minutes – *M v Normand* 1995 SLT 1284.
32 'Protecting Children' (Annex C, para 4) describes this as being indicated by 'children who significantly fail to reach normal growth and developmental milestones (ie physical growth, weight, motor, social and intellectual development) where physical and genetic reasons have been medically eliminated and a diagnosis of non-organic failure to thrive has been established'.
33 See R. S. Kempe, C. Cutler and J. Dean, 'The Infant with Failure-to-Thrive' in Helfner, Kempe and Krugman, n 8 above.
34 Annex C, para 4.

play; lack of communication; wilful destruction of the child's confidence in his or her own competence; or berating the child in front of others'.[35]

While failure to thrive may indicate emotional abuse, this particular form of abuse may be more difficult to identify than physical injury or neglect, since there will often be no physical symptoms. 'Effective Intervention' provided the following useful indicators that emotional abuse might be present: over-anxiety in the child; avoidance of contact outside the home; low self-esteem; limited capacity for enjoyment; serious aggression; impulsive behaviour; or retardation of physical development through deprivation. Because of its nature, it may be that emotional abuse is under-diagnosed and lines are not always easy to draw here. For example, responsible parents want their child to develop his or her full potential, but at some stage active encouragement 'to do better' may become emotional abuse.

Sexual abuse

7.11 'Protecting Children' gives an indication of what will give rise to concern when it provides that

> 'Any child may be deemed to have been sexually abused when any person(s), by design or neglect, exploits the child, directly or indirectly, in any activity intended to lead to the sexual arousal or other forms of gratification of that person or any other person(s) including organised networks. This definition holds whether or not there has been genital contact and whether or not the child is said to have initiated, or consented to, the behaviour'.[36]

Specific examples of what may be involved include; incest, paedophilia, exhibitionism, molestation, sexual intercourse, rape, sexual sadism, child pornography, or child prostitution.[37] Regardless of the gender of the victim, the public perception is generally that sexual abusers are male. While this is accurate in some cases, it is far from a universal truth.[38]

7.12 A word must be said about organised, ritual and satanic abuse. It is, in part, a method by which the abuse may have occurred and, in part, concerned with the content or nature of the abuse itself. 'Working Together' discusses organised abuse;[39] that is, abuse organised by a number

---

35 Paragraph 2.6, where it is acknowledged that the description was drawn from Lothian Area Review Committee guidelines, April 1988.

36 Annex C, para 4.

37 R. and H. Kempe, *The Common Secret: Sexually Abused Children and Adolescents* (Freeman, 1984). See also K. Murray and D. A. Gough (eds), *Intervening in Child Sexual Abuse* (Scottish Academic Press, 1991).

38 See for example, *McIntosh v HM Advocate* 1998 GWD 21-1080 where a 26-year-old female care assistant at a children's home admitted two charges of shameless indecency in respect of sexual intercourse with a 15-year-old boy in the home and was unsuccessful in appealing against a sentence of nine months imprisonment. In the USA in 1997, the public was shocked (and sections of the press were fascinated) by the case of Mary Kay Letourneau, a 35-year-old schoolteacher. She was convicted of child-rape, having had sexual relations with a 13-year-old former pupil, and later gave birth to their first child. On release from prison, she resumed relations with him. She has now been returned to prison and has given birth to a second child, believed to be the couple's daughter.

39 At para 5.26.

of abusers, involving several children, and acknowledges that it may include ritualistic behaviour. However, it is at pains to point out that organised abuse covers 'a wide range of activity', and Lyon and de Cruz make the valid point that 'it is incorrect to simply classify ritualistic and organised abuse as one and the same form of child abuse'.[40] Sections of the media made much of the 'satanic' nature of the alleged abuse in the *Orkney Case*.[41] As we shall see, while the allegations certainly pointed towards a degree of organisation and the possibility of ritualistic elements being present, the way the case progressed and the approach of the inquiry into it were such that the accuracy of the allegations was never tested. 'Protecting Children' is alert to the possibility of organised networks or multiple abusers being involved in child abuse and gives detailed guidance on how suspicions may be investigated most effectively.[42]

7.13 The distinction, in definitional terms, between what might be regarded as abusive or neglectful and what warrants court intervention is important in understanding how the whole system of child protection works. For example, a field worker may be concerned about a particular child, but may not have enough evidence to warrant applying to a court for one of the available orders. However, the concern may justify a professional decision that something further needs to be done through; offering the family greater support, undertaking further investigation, or flagging up a particular child, as meriting special attention, through placing the child on the child protection register (known, colloquially, as the 'at risk' register). As we shall see, inter-agency co-operation is essential to effective child protection. Having generally accepted definitions of abuse assists in that co-operation.[43]

Prevention

7.14 The ultimate goal of any child protection policy must be to eliminate child abuse altogether. Realisation of this goal is unlikely in the foreseeable future, but much can be done in attempts at prevention. As we shall see, the local authority owes a host of duties to children and their families, expressed in the Children (Scotland) Act 1995 ('the 1995 Act') under the heading 'Support for Children and their Families',[44] with particular emphasis being placed on the obligations to 'children in need'. That term has a special technical meaning,[45] and at least some of these children may be at particular risk of abuse. Through the effective delivery of these forms of support, it is anticipated that much abuse will be prevented. 'Protecting Children' highlights the importance of being alert to the fact that a

---

40 At pp 6–7.
41 See paras 7.21–7.27 for a discussion of the case and the subsequent inquiry.
42 Paragraphs 5.14–5.24. Given that organised networks may operate over wide geographic areas, one avenue of investigation involves the use of the Home Office Large Major Enquiry System (HOLMES).
43 For stylistic convenience, in the remainder of this chapter, the term 'abuse' will be used to denote both abuse and neglect unless the context requires otherwise.
44 Part II, chapter 1.
45 See para 7.31 for a discussion of the term.

particular family is under stress or in need of help in bringing up children and points out that 'early support may enable a child or a family to tackle problems, improve coping and prevent the risk of significant harm'.[46] It emphasises the importance of listening to, and facilitating communication with, children and of acting upon concerns expressed by adults.[47]

Diagnosis and responses

7.15 Nowhere is the phrase 'damned if you do and damned if you don't' more accurately applied than to social workers, and other professionals, who are deciding whether or not to intervene in the life of a particular child. As we shall see, there have been a number of cases where, despite social workers being aware of concern about a particular child, the child has been left at home and has died at the hands of a parent or other family member. Sometimes, with the 20/20 vision afforded by hindsight, it is clear that warning signals went unheeded.[48] Had they been acted upon and the child removed, the tragedy could have been averted. In other cases, social workers and other professionals have been criticised for over-zealous intervention.[49] Understandably, parents whose children have been taken away, when there was insufficient evidence to warrant such action, are outraged. It must be remembered that, in such cases, it is not simply the parents' rights which have been infringed. Unjustified removal of children from their homes is a gross invasion of the children's rights. At its most extreme, it is a form of child abuse, with state agencies becoming the abusers. All of this simply serves to emphasise the obvious, that intervention in the name of child protection is a sensitive matter. Individual professionals are required to make decisions immediately. Is there sufficient evidence to warrant emergency removal of a child? Is it safe to leave the child at home pending further investigation? Remember the, often over-worked, professional will frequently be faced with conflicting evidence and versions of what is happening. He or she must exercise his or her judgment in good faith and can be assisted in that task by adequate training, guidance and support. The challenge for the legal system is to provide the machinery to ensure that children are protected at all times, whether by intervention or by remaining at home.

7.16 As its full title indicates, 'Protecting Children' acknowledges the vital importance of inter-agency communication and co-operation. It makes the point, quite unequivocally, that

> 'All agencies which work with children have a shared responsibility for protecting children and safeguarding their welfare. Each has a different contribution to make to this common task'.[50]

The fact that the initial referral may be to a number of agencies, including the social work department, the police or the Principal Reporter, highlights the need for agencies to share information and to co-ordinate their efforts

---

46 Paragraph 4.1.
47 Paragraphs 4.4–4.6.
48 See for example, the cases discussed in para 7.17 below.
49 The best-known recent examples took place in Cleveland and Orkney.
50 Paragraph 2.1.

from the stage of initial investigation onwards.[51] Similarly, efficient and effective record-keeping, with clear policy on the purpose and content of records, as well as procedures to enable ready access by appropriate individuals, is an essential element in child protection.[52] The central function of multi-agency case conferences in, considering abuse allegations, planning support for families, and assisting in understanding the possible impact of criminal proceedings on the victim, is stressed.[53] The case conference may decide that the child's name should be placed on the child protection register[54] and that an inter-agency protection plan should be drawn up for the child.[55] The initial short-term plan may be followed by a comprehensive assessment of the child's and the family's needs, leading to a more detailed child protection plan.[56] Where a child's name has been placed on the child protection register, it is anticipated that the first case conference to review the case will be held within three months and that subsequent reviews should take place at six-monthly intervals.[57] Where the risk to a particular child has been eliminated or reduced,[58] it is recommended that the child's name should be removed from the register, although removal should not lead to an automatic withdrawal or reduction in the services being offered to the child and the family.[59] The various agencies involved in child protection have developed clearly thought-out strategies. Nor has the law itself been static. However, it must be acknowledged that these attempts to establish a more effective system of child protection have often resulted from tragedies and mismanaged cases. In order to understand the lessons of the past it is appropriate to consider some of the errors which have occurred throughout the UK.

Developments in England, Wales and Northern Ireland[60]

7.17 While it was not appreciated at the time, the *Maria Colwell Report*[61] was to herald the first of many inquiries into how the child protection system had come to fail a particular child. Maria was killed by her step-father in 1972 at a time when the family's problems were well known to the local authority. She had been returned to the care of her mother and step-father, having been fostered by her aunt and uncle for the previous five

---

51 Protecting Children, paras 4.7–4.16.
52 Protecting Children, paras 4.26–4.29.
53 Protecting Children, paras 4.30–4.43.
54 For full details of the operation of the child protection register, see Protecting Children, Part 3.
55 Protecting Children, paras 3.1.
56 Protecting Children, paras 4.49–4.55. It is worth noting that a case conference may take place before a child is born if there is significant risk that he or she will suffer harm once born; para 4.56.
57 Protecting Children, paras 4.57–4.60.
58 The removal of the unfortunate phrase 'reduced to an acceptable level', used in 'Effective Intervention' (at para 3.37), is a welcome step.
59 Protecting Children, paras 3.10–3.11.
60 For a more detailed examination of the various inquiries in England and Wales, discussed below, see Lyon and de Cruz, n 8 above, at pp 23–58.
61 Report of the Committee of Inquiry into the Care and Supervision Provided in Relation to Maria Colwell (DHSS, 1974).

years. The inquiry which followed her death found that the local authority had failed to supervise her care in circumstances which should have alerted it to the need for vigilance. That report resulted in fundamental improvements in the approach to child protection but, as time was to demonstrate, the changes were not enough to save many other children from a fate similar to Maria's. A host of other inquiries were to follow[62] and the most influential were those into the deaths of Jasmine Beckford,[63] Tyra Henry[64] and Kimberly Carlile.[65] While inquiries may serve to point out what went wrong in particular instances, and to recommend how such failures can be avoided in the future, one is left with the inescapable conclusion that we are slow to learn from past mistakes. In looking at the catalogue of inquiries, we must never lose sight of the fact that these are not simply 'cases'. Each of these inquiries addressed events leading up to the death of an individual child in circumstances so horrific that what the child actually experienced goes beyond anything we can truly imagine.

7.18 A continuing theme to emerge from the various reports is the need for inter-agency co-operation in assessing both the needs of a particular child and the risks to which he or she may be exposed in a given environment. The failure to achieve this co-operation was fundamental to many of the deaths examined in the inquiries and it was found that case conferences, the most obvious mechanism for inter-agency co-operation, had not been used effectively. In addition, the need to monitor the health and care of children returned to their parents or left in the care of their parents, where there has been concern about their welfare, is essential if the child is to be protected adequately. It is no surprise to find that, as a result of public concern over their failure, child protection agencies became more vigilant and more proactive. That may be a partial explanation for what happened later in Cleveland. However, whereas the earlier cases related to physical abuse, the events in Cleveland were concerned with alleged sexual abuse and, as Lyon and de Cruz point out, the guidelines developed to deal with the problem 'were inadequate and inappropriate in the context of child sexual abuse'.[66]

7.19 The 'Cleveland Report'[67] was the response to an apparent epidemic

---

62 See *Child Abuse: A Study of Inquiry Reports 1973–1981* (HMSO, 1982), which examines the reports of 18 inquiries conducted during the period.
63 *A Child in Trust: Jasmine Beckford* (DHSS, 1985). Jasmine died at the age of four and a half as a result of a blow to her head inflicted by her step-father who was later convicted of manslaughter and sentenced to ten years imprisonment. Her mother was convicted of neglect. The post-mortem examination showed a catalogue of old, and more recent, injuries.
64 *Whose Child?* (DHSS, 1987). Tyra was murdered by her father at the age of 22 months.
65 *A Child in Mind: Protection of Children in a Responsible Society* (DHSS, 1987). Kimberley was also four and a half at the time of her death and, again, the cause of death was a blow to the head inflicted by her step-father. He was convicted of her murder and, again, the post-mortem examination showed a history of child abuse.
66 Above, at p 34.
67 For a full discussion of the events in Cleveland, see Report of the Inquiry into Child Abuse in Cleveland 1987 (HMSO, 1988, Cm 412), hereinafter, the 'Cleveland Report'. A journalist's account of the events can be found in S. Bell, *When Salem Came to the Boro'* (Pan Books, 1988).

of child sexual abuse in the Cleveland area in 1987, when the number of children being referred to hospital because of suspected sexual abuse reached an unprecedented level with some 125 children being involved.[68] From the point of view of the children and their parents, such inquiries are often unsatisfactory, since their focus is the mechanisms employed in child protection and not the truth or falsehood of the individual allegations.[69] None the less, the contribution made by such inquiries can be significant and the 'Cleveland Report' made a number of recommendations in respect of suspected child abuse and neglect and resulted in changes to both the law and practice. It found that differences in medical opinion over diagnosis,[70] and conflicts between police surgeons, who wanted to preserve evidence which might be required for criminal proceedings, and other doctors, who were more concerned with diagnosis and treatment of the children, led to a breakdown in professional co-operation. This had a disturbing impact on the children, many of whom were subjected to several examinations. Interview techniques used in the investigation were later called into question and, in some cases, discredited. The refusal to allow parents access to their children and the lack of communication with the parents were the subject of criticism. The Report recommended changes in the law which were largely incorporated in the Children Act 1989, while many of the practical suggestions have been incorporated into guides and codes of practice.[71]

7.20 That child abuse is not confined to the family setting became clear in a series of reports examining the treatment and abuse of children living in residential homes. Perhaps the best known of the inquiries arose from a punishment régime, more reminiscent of the Gulags than of a caring environment for young people, inflicted on children in residential care in Staffordshire,[72] and systematic sexual abuse of boys in residential care in Kincora.[73] Other reports concerned the overall provision for residential care,[74] self-harm by children in care[75] and sexual abuse.[76] These reports make disturbing reading, not least because the state had taken it upon itself

68 There appears to be some confusion over the precise number of children involved and the Cleveland Report itself gives the figure as 125 (para 64) and 121 (para 9.3.22).
69 As we shall see, the families in Orkney were to experience similar frustration as a result of the focus of the inquiry into events there. See para 7.24, below.
70 The use of reflex anal dilation (RAD) was accepted as a diagnostic technique by some of the doctors involved. It was discredited in the subsequent inquiry which recommended that it should be abandoned.
71 See for example, Working Together, above.
72 The Pindown Experience and the Protection of Children: The Report of the Staffordshire Child Care Inquiry (Staffordshire Social Services, 1991).
73 Report of the Committee of Inquiry into Children's Homes and Hostels (HMSO, 1985).
74 Choosing with Care: Report of the Committee of Inquiry into the Selection, Development and Management of Staff in Children's Homes (HMSO, 1992); Accommodating Children (Social Services Inspectorate and Social Information Systems, 1992); and People Like Us: The Report of the Review of Safeguards for Children Living Away from Home (Department of Health/Welsh Office, 1997).
75 Ty Mawr Community Home Inquiry (Gwent County Council, 1992).
76 Report of the Inquiry into the Conduct of Leeway's Children's Home (London Borough of Lewisham, 1985) and Castle Hill Report (Shropshire County Council, 1992).

to provide these children with more appropriate care than could their families. Having accepted that responsibility, it often failed to fulfil it. In effect, these children were frequently being abused (or, at least, inadequately cared for) for the second time in their lives and by their self-proclaimed protectors. Again, the reports resulted in legislation and changes in practice.

The Orkney Case

7.21 Public confidence in the child protection system in Scotland suffered a serious blow in 1991 when nine children were removed from the care of their families in what came to be known as the *Orkney case*.[77] The events in Orkney involved virtually all the agencies responsible for child protection and a series of references and appeals to the courts. While public scrutiny of the actions of state agencies is a cornerstone of democracy, the media attention attracted by the case, and the way in which it was reported by sections of the press, bordered on the sensational. A public inquiry followed and many of its recommendations contributed to reform of the law.[78] In the end, the children and their parents received damages from the local authority in an out-of-court settlement, albeit no liability was admitted.[79] What 'really happened' in Orkney will never be known fully but a brief outline of such facts as are known indicates the nature of the problem.[80]

7.22 As a result of earlier enquiries, Orkney Islands social work department became concerned about the welfare of nine children, aged between eight and 15, living on South Ronaldsay, one of the smaller of the Orkney Islands. In particular, the concern related to alleged sexual abuse of the children and the possibility that this had occurred in an organised or ritualistic manner. Warrants were granted, authorising the removal of the children to a place of safety[81] and, at about 7.00 am on 27 February 1991, the children were removed from their homes by social workers and RSSPCC officers, accompanied by police officers, and taken to the mainland. The children were referred to a children's hearing on two grounds.[82] It was alleged that they had been the victims of sexual abuse and that they were falling into bad associations or were being exposed to moral danger. At the first hearing, the children's presence was dispensed with; the

---

77 *Sloan* v *B* 1991 SLT 530.
78 See, Report of the Inquiry into the Removal of Children from Orkney in February 1991 (HMSO, 1992) (the Clyde Report), discussed at paras 7.24–7.27, below. As we shall see, the remit of the Inquiry was to examine how the case had been conducted and not to consider the allegations of abuse themselves.
79 *The Scotsman*, 5 March 1996 reported that each child had received £10,000 and each parent £5,000. It is a usual feature of out-of-court settlements that no liability is admitted.
80 For a more detailed discussion of the case, see E. E. Sutherland, 'The Orkney Case' 1992 JR 93.
81 The case took place in the context of the Social Work (Scotland) Act 1968 and the procedure for emergency protection of children, now found in the Children (Scotland) Act 1995, has been altered significantly, in part, as a result of this case.
82 The current grounds for referral to a children's hearing and the procedure to be followed are discussed in detail in chapter 9.

warrants to detain them in a place of safety were continued for 21 days; and, since the parents of the children did not accept the grounds of referral, the reporter was instructed to apply to the sheriff for a finding in fact as to whether the grounds of referral were established. A second children's hearing renewed the warrants to detain the children for a further 21 days, again having dispensed with the children's presence. The parents' appeal against this renewal was refused.

7.23 The sheriff heard the case on 3 April and, without hearing the evidence, he dismissed the reporter's applications for a finding on the facts as incompetent. He did so on the view that the proceedings were fundamentally flawed and he then went on to criticise the detention of the children and the quality of the evidence on which the case was based. The reporter appealed to the Inner House of the Court of Session against the sheriff's decision. On the advice of counsel, the reporter decided that, even if the appeals were allowed, the effect of the sheriff's attack on the proceedings and evidence, while incalculable, had so prejudiced the interests of justice that it would not be possible to proceed with the case. The children were returned home on 4 April, 37 days after their removal. The Inner House[83] heard the appeals and found in favour of the reporter. The sheriff's interlocutor was recalled and the court directed that any further proceedings were to be heard before a different sheriff. In the course of its decision, the court took the opportunity to examine a number of aspects of the case and to provide valuable guidance for the future operation of the system. In particular, the then relevant mechanism for emergency protection, the place of safety order, came under scrutiny, as did the issue of the child's right to participate in proceedings relating to his or her protection. Such was the concern about the case, at all levels, that examination of the events in Orkney was then handed over to a public inquiry. What is absolutely clear is that the child protection system operating at the time failed the children in this case. Either they were sexually abused, and have received neither protection nor counselling, or they were not, and they were deprived of their liberty without the reasons for that ever being justified in court.

The Clyde Report

7.24 At the outset, it is important to appreciate precisely what the Clyde Inquiry was set up to do. Its task was to examine the application of the law and procedures in the *Orkney case* and not whether the children had actually been abused. The subtlety of this distinction led to frustration, particularly amongst the children's parents who were seeking vindication. Running to 363 pages and containing 195 recommendations, the 'Report of the Inquiry into the Removal of Children from Orkney in February 1991' was published in October 1992.[84] It examined the conduct of all the agencies involved and the events which occurred as they were perceived by

---

83 *Sloan* v *B* 1991 SLT 530.
84 For a more detailed discussion of the Clyde Report, see E. E. Sutherland, 'Clyde and Beyond: The Report of the Inquiry into the Removal of Children from Orkney in February 1991', 1993 JR 178.

the various individuals who gave evidence. The nuances of understanding and interpretation of these recollections are fully explored and it is hard to imagine that anyone did not have the opportunity to put his or her point of view. What emerged was a picture of a lack of communication between individuals within various agencies, a lack of trust between certain individuals and agencies, an absence of any clear procedure, and a lack of clarity about the roles of individual agency members. Most tragic of all was the apparent failure to see the nine children involved as individual human beings.

7.25 While the Report made clear that the actual removal of the children was carried out with efficiency, criticism is levelled at various aspects of the children's treatment during the process and thereafter. Some of these criticisms were highlighted in the press at the time and, while the Report was not uncritical of the role of the media in the case, it must be accepted that some of the concerns it publicised were found to be justified. In particular, the following matters caused concern: the prohibition on the children taking personal possessions with them; the failure to explain their rights, at least to the older children; failure to get written consent to medical examination of the children from the parents; confusion over the medical examinations; separate placement of siblings; prohibition, without review, on access by the parents to the children and the children to each other; inadequate attention to the religion of some of the children; and a lack of planning for the educational needs of the children placed in Strathclyde. The interviewing of the nine children, after their removal, merits special attention. Again, there is a picture of confusion and ineptitude. No specific decision to interview the children was taken, nor was there a clear idea of the purpose of the interviews. There was a lack of co-ordination between agencies, the facilities and aids used in the interviews were not always fully understood by the interviewers and, perhaps most seriously of all, not all of the interviewers were adequately trained for the task in hand, assuming they knew what that was in the first place. While the reporter would have been entitled to continue with the case, he decided not to do so on the basis that the public statements of the sheriff who heard the case and the attendant publicity had so tainted the evidence as to make a fair hearing impossible. The Report is critical of this decision as one which was taken precipitately and which left the crucial matter of the truth or otherwise of the allegations unresolved.

7.26 The Report's greatest contribution to child protection lies in its recommendations for reform of the child protection system, a system which had so woefully failed the children in the *Orkney case*. These recommendations got off to a welcome start by giving prominence to the provisions of the UN Convention on the Rights of the Child, which, it should be remembered, was a fairly new instrument at the time, along with those of the European Convention on Human Rights. It was recommended that these should form an integral part of any reform of child law. The special nature of child sexual abuse was acknowledged and recommendations relating to investigation, procedures, and training and support for the personnel involved were made. Detailed national guidelines, prepared in an inter-disciplinary context, were proposed, as was the creation of a central resource to give expert advice and guidance. Given the concerns which arose in the *Orkney case*, it was not surprising that the Report devoted considerable attention to reform of the law and procedures relating to the removal of a child to a place of safety and the care and interviewing of the child thereafter. It recommended that place of safety orders should be replaced with child protection orders, with more stringent procedures being put in place for the granting of these orders. Similar recommendations were made for interim protection orders. The Report acknowledged the danger that, in the course of enquiries being carried out by several agencies, and particularly in cases of suspected multiple abuse, the individual child might cease to be the focal point of attention. The Report saw the appointment of a safeguarder as a valuable way of ensuring that sight is not lost of the individual child and recommended that the safeguarder's role should be enhanced and that consideration should be given to appointing a safeguarder in every child protection order application. It considered the idea of creating a new office, the 'child advocate', but felt that this might not be necessary if the role of the safeguarder were enhanced. Nor did it feel that there was a need to create a 'parent's advocate'.

7.27 It was recommended that the duty of the local authority to promote and safeguard the welfare of a child removed under a child protection order should be made explicit and that specific permission should be sought from a sheriff where the local authority wishes to take action beyond that encompassed within that general duty. The child's views should be considered in all matters affecting him or her. In terms of management, there were recommendations aimed at ensuring full communication and delineation of functions between agencies. In addition, the Report recommended the use of extensive guidelines on more specific matters, including; placement of siblings together, children retaining personal possessions, access (contact), medical examination, and interviewing of children. The Report concluded with various proposals relating to the children's hearing system, social work departments and the police. While some of these were consequential upon the new child protection orders, a number are concerned with training and resources. As we shall see, many of the Clyde Report's recommendations found statutory expression in the Children (Scotland) Act 1995, while many others are reflected in the guidance provided to various agencies and organisation.[85]

Towards the 1995 Act and beyond

7.28 Nowhere would complacency be more dangerous than in the child protection system. In Scotland, we had long been proud of the children's hearings system and it is sometimes suggested that an element of complacency may have crept into thinking about child protection. After all, we had not had the wealth of cases experienced by our near neighbours south

---

85 For example, many of the procedures and policies discussed in Protecting Children are directly referable to the Clyde Report.

of the border. Any suggestion of complacency is largely unfounded, since a thorough review of the child protection system had been undertaken in the late 1980s.[86] Before any of its recommendations could be implemented, not only did the *Orkney case* come to the fore, but other cases in Fife[87] and Ayrshire[88] emerged, leading to public inquiries, litigation and further consideration of exactly how the law on child protection should be reformed. In addition, aspects of the system were roundly criticised by the European Court of Human Rights in respect of child protection procedures which denied parents access to the various reports which were relevant to decisions being taken about their children.[89] There followed a discussion paper from the Scottish Office[90] and a White Paper[91] detailing proposals for legislative reform. The result was Part II of the Children (Scotland) Act 1995 ('the 1995 Act') and it is to the detailed provisions of that Act which we will turn shortly.

7.29 Critical analysis of the child protection system did not end with the passing of the 1995 Act. More recent concern has focused on children being looked after away from home, particularly under the auspices of the local authority, and two separate enquiries were commissioned in the UK. In 1997, the Kent Report, examining the arrangements for protecting children who are cared for away from home in Scotland[92] was published. In the course of making 62 recommendations, the Report left no doubt that all is far from well for many children. While the Report notes that there have been positive initiatives[93] and that some of the problems experienced in the past had been eradicated, the view is expressed that new problems are coming to the fore. Concern is expressed about a wide range of dangers facing young people being cared from away from home, including, physical and sexual abuse, bullying, racial issues, drugs and alcohol, running away, self-harm and prostitution. Poor practices in the running of some establishments remain a concern. It is recommended that improvements could be made in respect of: recording incidents of abuse; dealing with complaints from children and parents; the selection, recruitment and training of staff; and the inspection of facilities. It is suggested that a system of independent visitors should be introduced, with every child living away from home being allocated an independent person. Greater help for young abusers,

---

86 Review of Child Care Law in Scotland (HMSO, 1990). See also; Another Kind of Home: a review of residential child care (HMSO, 1992) (the Skinner Report); Reporters to the Children's Panel: Their Role, Function and Accountability (HMSO, 1992) (the Finlayson Report).

87 Report of the Inquiry into Child Care Policies in Fife (HMSO, 1992) (the Kearney Report).

88 *L, Petitioners (No 1)* 1993 SLT 1310 and *(No 2)* 1993 SLT 1342.

89 *McMichael* v *United Kingdom* 51/1993/446/525, ECHR, 24 February 1995.

90 Emergency Protection of Children in Scotland (SWSG, 1993).

91 Scotland's Children: Proposals for Child Care Policy and Law (HMSO, 1993).

92 R. Kent, *Children's Safeguards Review* (The Scottish Office, 1997). The remit of the Kent Report, which included young people living away from home in private boarding schools and the army as well as local authority care, was broader than the study undertaken in England and Wales; W. Utting, *Children and Violence* (Gulbenkian Foundation, 1997).

93 Particular reference is made to the Skinner Report (1992), the earlier Utting Report, Children in Public Care (1991) and the Warner Report, Choosing with Care (1992).

along the lines of the Halt Project in Glasgow and the Bridge Project in Dundee is suggested. Further research is called for. The Report is thorough and wide-ranging and culminates with the following plea.

'We must make 1997 a watershed when the protection of children entrusted to the care of others, be they boarding schools, children's homes, hospital or hostels, is improved. This will come about only by recognition of the extent of the problem, by the use of the appropriate formal structures, and through continued vigilance'.[94]

A reminder of just how badly the care experience can go wrong for children came later that year when two men, who had worked in local authority children's homes, were convicted of a catalogue of sexual offences against children in the 1960s and 1970s.[95] It was alleged that there had been a number of complaints about their conduct but, despite internal enquiries and police investigations, no action had been taken. Professor Marshall was appointed to chair an inquiry into the circumstances surrounding that case. Her report, *Edinburgh's Children*, published on 4 February 1999, found serious shortcomings in the way complaints by children against care workers were dealt with and makes 135 recommendations designed to ensure that children are not failed in this way in the future.

THE PEOPLE AND THE AGENCIES INVOLVED

The child

7.30 Clearly, the child is the most important person in the child protection system and it has been emphasised consistently that individuals, agencies and courts must view each child as an individual and consider that child's particular needs.[96] As we have seen, the legal system adopts different upper age limits for different purposes when defining 'a child'. In the context of child protection, a child is normally a person under the age of 16 years, unless the child is subject to a supervision order made by a children's hearing, in which case the person continues to fall within the definition of a child for as long as the supervision requirement lasts.[97] Similarly, where a person over the age of 16 is subject to a court order in England, Wales or Northern Ireland which falls to be regarded as equivalent to a supervision order, he or she will qualify as a child for the purpose of child protection on coming to Scotland.[98] A further exception relates to parental responsibilities orders. As we shall see, this is the mechanism whereby a court may vest parental responsibilities and rights in respect of a child in the local authority.[99] A child for this purpose is a person under the age of 18.[100]

---

94 At p 129.
95 *HM Advocate* v *Maclennan, Knott and Cull*, unreported, November 1997. A number of charges were found not proven in respect of the third accused.
96 See for example, the Clyde Report, para 3.40 and *Scotland's Children*, paras 2.6 and 2.7.
97 1995 Act, s 93(2)(b)(i) and (ii).
98 1995 Act, s 93(2)(b)(iii). Whether a court order from another part of the UK is so classified is determined by regulations made by the Secretary of State under s 33 of the 1995 Act.
99 1995 Act, s 86. See paras 7.89–7.93, below, for a discussion of parental responsibilities orders.
100 1995 Act, s 93(2)(a).

However, since all parental rights and most parental responsibilities terminate when a person reaches the age of 16,[101] this extension to 18 is of little practical significance.

7.31 As we shall see, the local authority is under a specific duty to provide for *children in need*. Essentially, these are children whose circumstances indicate that they may require priority attention. A child in need is one who is in need of care and attention because

> he or she is unlikely to achieve or maintain a reasonable standard of health or development unless services are provided for him or her by the local authority;
> his or her health or development is likely to be impaired significantly unless such services are provided;
> he or she is disabled;
> he or she is affected adversely by the disability of another member of his or her family.[102]

Relevant persons

7.32 'Relevant persons' are a creation of the Children (Scotland) Act 1995. What the Act sought to do was to indicate that people other than parents might be important in a child's life and to make those people part of the decision-making process. Previous legislation did that by defining the word 'parent' in a sufficiently broad way as to include at least some other persons.[103] Whether this new term really helps is open to question. It has always been a vain hope that children, and, indeed, most adults, would understand legislation in its raw form, but at least children had some notion of what parents were. It might have been better if the 1995 Act had continued to use the word 'parent', subject to a definition which encompassed the other categories of individuals included as relevant persons. It did not and, so, we must be clear about what it means by 'relevant persons'. They are

> any parent who has parental rights or responsibilities;
> any person in whom parental responsibilities or rights are vested by virtue of the Act; and
> any person who has appears to have charge of or control over a child, otherwise than in the course of employment.[104]

Local authority

7.33 As we shall see, a host of obligations and powers in respect of child protection are vested in the local authority[105] and many are carried out through the authority's social work department. However, many other agencies may be involved in a given case and inter-agency co-operation is central to child protection. Child Protection Committees (CPCs), made up

---

101 1995 Act, ss.1(2) and 2(7).
102 1995 Act, s 93(4)(a).
103 See for example the Social Work (Scotland) Act 1968, s 77, where 'parent' was defined, for the purpose of Part III of that Act, as including a guardian.
104 1995 Act, s 93(2)(b).
105 'Local authority' is defined as a council constituted under s 2 of the Local Government, etc. (Scotland) Act 1994.

of members of all the main agencies, provide a joint forum for the purpose of 'developing, promoting, monitoring and reviewing local child protection policies'.[106] In addition to inter-agency co-operation at the level of policy, case conferences are designed to provide a similar function in individual cases.[107] The detailed obligations and powers of the local authority are discussed more fully later in this chapter.

The Police

7.34 Police officers will often be the first people to encounter a situation where a child requires protection. In addition to their ordinary functions in ensuring public order and enforcing the criminal law, they will have to deal with the child's immediate need for protection and ensure that those responsible for the more long-term response are informed. The role of the police in both investigating suspected abuse and in planning for child protection is recognised in the Scottish Office guidance.[108] As we shall see, a police officer may take a child to a place of safety in an emergency, without any authority from a court, where it is not practicable to apply for a child protection order.[109]

Voluntary and religious organisations

7.35 The valuable contribution to child protection made by a host of voluntary organisations and religious groups is acknowledged in the Scottish Office guidance.[110] It is noted that children and families may seek assistance from these organisations and that they provide a wide range of services aimed at preventing or reducing the risk of abuse and at helping families to recover from abuse. Their assistance in providing advice and specialist services is also acknowledged, as is their increased professionalism which means that many of them now have detailed guidelines and training, both for their own workers and for children who may be confronted by abuse. While the Royal Scottish Society for the Prevention of Cruelty to Children receives no statutory recognition in the 1995 Act, nor is it mentioned by name in 'Protecting Children',[111] it is well known to members of the public and, in addition to preventive work, it is involved in a number of pioneering projects specialising in the treatment of child sexual abuse.[112]

---

106 Protecting Children, para 5.2. Full details of the requirements in respect of CPCs can be found in Child Protection: Local Liaison Machinery – Child Protection Committees, Circular No SWSG 14/97, which is reproduced as Annex A to Protecting Children.
107 See para 7.16, above.
108 See for example Child Protection, paras 2.4, 5.1–5.7 and Annex A.
109 1995 Act, s 61(5), discussed at para 7.88, below.
110 Protecting Children, para 2.10.
111 This can be contrasted with the express recognition of the Society's role in child protection found in Effective Intervention, Annex 5, paras 9 and 10.
112 See for example, the Overnewton Child Sexual Abuse Project in Glasgow which is funded by the local authority and other agencies; Effective Intervention, Annex 5, para 10.

Other professionals

7.36 It is in the nature of their work that members of other professions, including health-care professionals, school teachers, day carers and child minders, will encounter cases of suspected abuse. Unlike similar professionals in the USA, they are not directed by statute to take any particular course of action on the basis of their suspicions.[113] None the less, while a professional who fails to act on his or her suspicions will not face criminal sanctions, he or she may face civil liability or professional disciplinary proceedings.

Everyone else

7.37 There is no general obligation on a person without a specific duty towards children to do anything about child abuse. As we have seen, professionals dealing with children may face civil liability or professional censure for their failure to report abuse. Members of the public are not liable to any such sanctions.

Mandatory child abuse reporting laws

7.38 Since the late 1960s, every state in the USA has had a mandatory child abuse reporting law. While the precise content of the legislation varies from state to state, some common features emerge. If individuals are required to report abuse, there must be a clear definition of what it is that they are required to report, and the statutes contain definitions of abuse and neglect and usually the requirement is to report a reasonable suspicion to a specified state agency. In most states, the obligation is placed on all professionals who could be expected to come across abuse, including health-care professionals, social workers, teachers, child-care workers and law enforcement officers. Lawyers are normally exempt, as are religious leaders in some states. Members of the public are not normally subject to the reporting requirement. The obligation to report is reinforced by a carrot and a stick. The carrot is immunity from liability for erroneous reporting, provided that the report was made in good faith. The stick involves both civil and criminal liability for a failure to report. Mandatory reporting laws continue to be controversial, but they have resulted in a great increase in the number of cases of suspected abuse being reported.[114] Their strength lies in removing any ambiguity, whether resulting from professional ethics or otherwise, over the duty to report. Insofar as the law can influence public perceptions of morality, reporting laws may create a climate where there is acceptance of a more general responsibility for the welfare of children. However, reporting laws should not be seen as a panacea. They simply enable the first step to be taken. If they are to have any real value, the child protection system must be adequately resourced to enable each report to be investigated fully and for appropriate support and service to be provided.

113 See para 7.38, below.
114 See for example, M. Meriweather, 'Child Abuse Reporting Laws: A Time for Change' 20 Fam L Q 141 (1986).

LOCAL AUTHORITY RESPONSIBILITIES TOWARDS CHILDREN

7.39 In order to understand the general responsibility of local authorities towards children it is helpful to note first that the relevant part of the 1995 Act is entitled 'Support for Children and their Families'.[115] This sends out the clear message that, unless there is good reason why a child cannot live with his or her own family, the goal is to support that child *within that family*.[116] It is only where that option proves inappropriate that some other means of looking after a child should be considered. This message is reinforced by the Guidance,[117] issued under the 1995 Act, which talks of how to achieve 'partnerships with parents and children in the planning and delivery of services to children'.[118] A second point to note is that, in some cases, the 1995 Act refers simply to *children* and, in other cases, it deals with *children in need*. The distinction is important since the local authority's obligation to children in need is a general one – to safeguard and promote their welfare. In addition, there are specific duties placed on the local authority where the child is assessed as being in need. Where a child is not so assessed, the local authority's usual obligation is simply to indicate what services it will provide. Given the financial constraints on local authorities, it seems inevitable that this will have an impact on how the local authorities prioritise expenditure. Of course, sight should not be lost of the fact that a child who is not in need, at the moment, may enter this category if adequate preventive assistance is not provided. Inter-agency co-operation is central to effective service provision and so, for example, the 1995 Act provides that a local authority may request help from another local authority, a health board or a national health service trust.[119] Co-ordination of the local authority's own services, including social work, education and housing, and other agencies like health services, the police, the Benefits Agency and voluntary organisations, is a constant theme, running throughout the Guidance.[120]

Service plans

7.40 Planning, co-ordination and publicity of the precise services available are essential and local authorities are obliged to prepare, publish, and keep under review plans of the provision of services to children in their

---

115 Part II, chapter 1.
116 This message is reinforced by s 22(1)(b), which provides that the local authority shall promote the upbringing of children in need *by their families*, provided that this is consistent with its duty to safeguard and promote the children's welfare.
117 In addition to the 1995 Act, there are Regulations and Directions, made by the Secretary of State under the Act, and Guidance from the Scottish Office, fleshing out how the Act should work. These are collected together in *Scotland's Children: The Children (Scotland) Act 1995 Regulations and Guidance*, vol 1, *Support and Protection for Children and their Families* (2nd edn, 1997). There are two other volumes in the series, vol 2, *Children Looked After by Local Authorities*, and vol 3, *Adoption and Parental Responsibilities Orders*. References below to the 'Guidance' are to these materials.
118 Volume 1, chapter 2, para 23.
119 1995 Act, s 21.
120 See for example, vol 1, chapter 2, paras 35–37.

area.[121] The relevant services are those under the Social Work (Scotland) Act 1968[122] and Part II of the 1995 Act, and include services for children affected by disability,[123] the provision of accommodation to children,[124] the provision of day care for pre-school and other children,[125] and the provision of after-care and training for young people.[126] In the course of preparing its plan, the 1995 Act requires the local authority to consult every health board and national health service trust in its area, voluntary organisations which either provide services or represent users of services, the Principal Reporter, the chairperson of the children's panel for the area, and organisations which provide housing in the area.[127] In addition, the Secretary of State may direct that other persons should be consulted and the Guidance makes clear that consultation should go well beyond the bare bones of the statutory formulation. For example, it recommends that consultation should include children and their families who are using the services or have done so in the past[128] and that the local authority might consider using meetings, questionnaires and surveys as methods of obtaining feedback.[129] A good example of the process in action can be found in the City of Glasgow which published a preliminary draft of its 'Children's Services Plan' in August 1997.[130] This attractive, user-friendly, document was circulated widely, not only to organisations, but to the public, through libraries and other outlets, and comments were invited by mid-October. As a result of the consultation process, the final version was published in April 1998.[131]

7.41 Included in the Children's Services Plan must be details of which services the local authority intends to purchase from the private sector and which services it will be providing itself or in association with another local authority.[132] In addition to producing a plan, the local authority is obliged to publicise the services it provides for children in its area and the relevant services provided by other organisations.[133] Again, the Guidance indicates

---

121 1995 Act, s 19.
122 While substantial parts of the 1968 Act were repealed by the 1995 Act, significant portions remain in force. For our present purpose, s 5(1B)(a) to (o) lists local authority obligations, largely to children and persons with a disability, under a number of other statutes.
123 1995 Act, ss 23 and 24. A child may be affected by disability either as a result of his or her own condition or due to the disability of another family member – see paras 7.48–7.49, below.
124 1995 Act, s 25.
125 1995 Act, s 27.
126 1995 Act, ss 29 and 30.
127 1995 Act, s 19(5).
128 Volume 1, chapter 2, para 22. On consultation, see generally, paras 21–24.
129 Volume 1, chapter 2, para 23.
130 Children's Services Plan: Preliminary Draft (Social Work Department, City of Glasgow Council, 1997).
131 Local authorities were obliged to publish their Children's Services Plans by 1 April 1998 – The Plans for Services for Children Directions 1996, dir 3. The Directions are available in the Guidance, vol 1.
132 The Plans for Services for Children Directions 1996, dir 5.
133 1995 Act, s 20. See also, The Publication of Information about Services for Children Direction 1996. The Direction is available in the Guidance, vol 1.

ways in which this may be done effectively and suggests that the information should be available at places used by children and their families, like GPs' surgeries, Benefit Agencies and places of worship.[134] It highlights the importance of information being presented in a user-friendly form and accessible in languages other than English.[135]

Assessment

7.42 As we have seen, *children in need* is a term of art, and means children: who are unlikely to achieve or maintain a reasonable standard of health or development unless services are provided for them by the local authority; whose health or development is likely to be impaired significantly unless such services are provided; who are disabled; or who are affected adversely by the disability of another member of their families.[136] In order to decide whether a particular child is, indeed, a child in need, the local authority must assess the child's needs and family circumstances and consider how the needs can be best met. As the Guidance points out

> '[s]ome assessments will take relatively little time and can be carried out by social workers collecting and evaluating information from a small number of sources; others may be more complex and may take considerable time, involving meetings with family members and consultation and meetings with other professionals. Between these extremes can come a range of different levels of involvement'.[137]

In order that the number of assessments carried out in respect of a particular child is kept to a minimum, it is recommended that any assessment for the purpose of the 1995 Act should be carried out at the same time as any assessment required under other legislation.[138]

7.43 The Guidance goes on to require that the results of assessment should be recorded in writing and made available to families.[139] It is not stated expressly that the child should be told of the results and it is not clear whether he or she is viewed as part of the family to whom these results should be made available. Given the recognition throughout the 1995 Act of the child's place in the decision-making process, it is to be hoped that the information will be discussed with the child in an appropriate manner.[140] Certainly, when it comes to elaborating on how services should be provided for a child, the Guidance repeats the theme of 'partnership with

134 Volume 1, chapter 3, para 7.
135 Volume 1, chapter 3, para 6.
136 1995 Act, s 93(4)(a).
137 Volume 1, chapter 1, para 16. On assessment, generally, see paras 16–21.
138 Volume 1, chapter 1, para 17. For example, it may be appropriate to assess the child for the purpose of the Education (Scotland) Act 1980.
139 Volume 1, chapter 1, para 16.
140 While it would often be wholly inappropriate simply to give the child a copy of the report, the information contained in it might be explored sensitively in discussion with the child. See chapters 3 and 5, paras 36–39 and 130–134 respectively, for criticism of the way in which children's views are sought in the context of court proceedings under s 11 of the 1995 Act.

parents and children' and makes particular reference to all of the individuals involved having 'sufficient information, both orally and in writing, to make informed choices'.[141] If the outcome of the assessment is that the local authority considers the child to be suffering (or at risk of suffering) significant harm, it must consider the need to apply to the court under the various child protection procedures.[142] Alternatively, it may report the case to the Principal Reporter, who will consider the necessity of convening a children's hearing in respect of the child.[143] In either case, the child will then have a right to participate in the decision-making process by having any views he or she wishes to express taken into account in the light of his or her age and maturity.[144]

Promotion of the welfare of children in need

7.44 Fundamental to child protection is the local authority's obligation to safeguard and promote the welfare of children in need.[145] Insofar as it is consistent with safeguarding and promoting the child's welfare, the local authority is required to promote the upbringing of children by their own families.[146] The local authority is given considerable latitude in how it goes about fulfilling its duty to a child in need,[147] but it must have regard to each child's religious persuasion, racial origin, and cultural and linguistic background.[148] It may provide services for the child directly[149] and it may also provide services for another member of the child's family or for the family as a whole, if such provision is designed to safeguard or promote the child's welfare.[150] While it is envisaged that assistance will normally be given in kind, in exceptional circumstances, the local authority may provide assistance in cash and, where it does so, it may require some or all of the money provided to be repaid.[151] Before attaching a condition that money should be repaid, the local authority must consider the means of the child and the parents and it may not require repayment from any person who is receiving income support, family credit or jobseeker's allowance.[152]

7.45 Exactly what services are provided for, or in respect of, a particular child will depend upon the individual circumstances of the case, but it may include home helps or family aides, family centres offering child care, support to parents and education to improve parenting skills, suitable housing provision, occupational therapy, special equipment to help chil-

---

141 Volume 1, chapter 1, para 23.
142 See paras 7.66–7.88, below.
143 See chapter 9, below.
144 1995 Act, s 16(2).
145 1995 Act, s 22(1)(a).
146 1995 Act, s 22(1)(b).
147 For the range of services that it is envisaged the local authority might provide, see Guidance, vol. 1, chapter 2, Annex B.
148 1995 Act, s 22(2).
149 1995 Act, s 22(3)(a)(i).
150 1995 Act, s 22(3)(a)(ii) and (iii).
151 1995 Act, s 22(3)(b).
152 1995 Act, s 22(4).

dren with special needs and respite services.[153] As we shall see, day care and the provision of alternative accommodation for children are other services which the local authority may and, in some cases, must provide.

Day care for pre-school and other children

7.46 Day care provides young children with the opportunity to broaden their horizons while often giving parents a welcome break or the chance to engage in employment. Each local authority *must* provide day care for children in need in its area who are aged under five and have not yet started school and it *may* provide such care for children who are not classified as being in need.[154] The Guidance acknowledges that, while it is for each local authority to determine how much provision it will make for children who are not in need, day care services 'have an important role to play in preventing child abuse and neglect and avoiding the need for compulsory measures of supervision'.[155] While the goal is to provide 'good and safe basic care', it is envisaged that local authorities will work together with other providers in order to offer a range of services 'so that all parents can make informed choices about care for their child'.[156] Day care provision should be available to children who have a disability or special educational needs.[157] In addition, it should 'seek to reflect the ethnic make up of the community' served by the service.[158] As we have seen, the local authority oversees the provision of private day care of children under the age of eight, where it is provided through day care or child minding, through a system of registration.[159] The local authority may fulfil its obligation to provide day care by making use of registered day carers or child minders or by enlisting the assistance of the voluntary sector.[160] Where the local authority is providing day care, it may provide facilities, including, training, advice, guidance and counselling, for adults who care for children on a day-care basis or who accompany children to day care.[161]

7.47 The importance of providing care for school-age children, outside school hours and during school holidays, is recognised in Scotland and elsewhere.[162] Each local authority is obliged to provide care for children in need who are attending school outside school hours and during school

---

153 Guidance, vol 1, chapter 1, paras 25–28.
154 1995 Act, s 27(1). The government has expressed a commitment to improving the quality and availability of day care provision for all children; Meeting the Childcare Challenge: A Childcare Strategy for Scotland (The Stationery Office, 1998) (Cm 3958, 1998).
155 Guidance, vol 1, chapter 5, para 6.
156 Guidance, vol 1, chapter 5, paras 2 and 3.
157 Guidance, vol 1, chapter 5, para 5.
158 Guidance, vol 1, chapter 5, para 7.
159 Children Act 1989, Part X. The provisions on registration are discussed at para 6.23. It will be remembered that, where a person looks after a child in the parents' own home (a nanny), no registration is required. Relatives may also care for a child without the need to register even if they are being paid to do so.
160 Guidance, vol 1, chapter 5, paras 11–13.
161 1995 Act, s 27(2).
162 A commitment to providing adequate after-school care for all children was one of the central themes in President Clinton's State of the Union Address, delivered on 26 January 1998.

holidays.[163] While the 1995 Act refers to children 'who are in attendance at school', it makes sense to read this provision to mean children 'who ought to be attending school', whether they are truanting or not. In any event, the local authority should report truancy to the Principal Reporter so that a decision can be taken on whether a children's hearing should be convened for the child. Again, the local authority may provide care outside school hours and during school holidays for children who are not deemed to be in need.[164]

Children with disabilities and those affected by the disability of another person

7.48 Disability can have an impact on children in two distinct ways.[165] First, it may be the child who has a disability and requires special assistance or facilities.[166] Second, the child may be affected by the disability of another family member. In the latter case, a range of situations may give rise to the impact on the child. For example, it may be that the child's parent has a disability and is restricted in what he or she can do with the child or it may be that a sibling has a disability and requires additional parental attention.[167] It is for this reason that children with disabilities and those affected by the disability of others fall within the definition of children in need.[168] In all cases, the goal of local authority assistance is 'to minimise the adverse effect' of the disability on children[169] and to give them 'the opportunity to lead lives which are as normal as possible'.[170]

7.49 Where a child's parent or guardian asks the local authority to assess the child's disability or that of a member of the child's family, the local authority must carry out an assessment.[171] The purpose of such an assessment is to determine what the child's needs are. In addition, the carer of a child with a disability may ask the local authority to carry out an assessment of his or her ability to provide appropriate care.[172] Again, the local authority must make an assessment if requested to do so.

---

163 1995 Act, s 27(3).
164 1995 Act, s 27(3).
165 For this purpose, a person is 'disabled' if he or she is chronically sick or disabled or suffers from a mental disorder – 1995 Act, s 23(2).
166 It is estimated that there are some 33,000 children in Scotland with some form of disability; Guidance, vol. 1, chapter 6, para 8.
167 Guidance, vol 1, chapter 6, paras 20–22. The Guidance recognises that, where a parent has a disability, the parent and the child may be anxious that acknowledging a problem may lead to the break up of the family and that all concerned need reassurance that the local authority can provide a wide range of assistance to support families in bringing up their children.
168 1995 Act, s 93(4)(a)(iii) and (iv).
169 1995 Act, s 23(1)(a) and the Guidance, vol 1, chapter 6, para 4.
170 1995 Act, s 23(1)(b).
171 1995 Act, s 23(3).
172 1995 Act, s 24(1). Such a request may not be made where the carer is looking after the child by virtue of a contract of employment or as a volunteer for a voluntary organisation – 1995 Act, s 24(2).

Provision of accommodation for children

7.50 As a general rule, a child's welfare requires that there should be some adult on the scene to look after him or her. In the case of a young child, a parent or other carer should normally be on hand at all times.[173] On the other hand, a 14-year-old may be at no risk at all simply because his or her parents have gone out for the evening, leaving the child alone or with friends of the same age. The local authority's role in providing accommodation for children is, at first instance, a safety-net. Thus, the obligation to provide accommodation arises only where the child appears to require accommodation because

no-one has parental responsibilities for the child;
the child is lost or abandoned; or
the child's carer is prevented, whether or not permanently and for whatever reason, from providing suitable accommodation or care.[174]

It will be rare that no person has parental responsibilities for a child but such a situation might arise, for example, where a lone parent has died. Whether a child has been lost or abandoned will be a question of fact in each case, and the distinction between the two states depends on whether anyone is looking for him or her.[175] A child's parent may be prevented from looking after him or her for a host of reasons, including parental illness or imprisonment. A parent's inability to provide suitable accommodation may be due to the condition of the family home, whether that condition is a matter of a general state, like dirt, or caused by a recent event, like a fire or eviction.

7.51 For this purpose, a child is a person below the age of 18 and, thus, for example, the local authority must provide accommodation for a 16-year-old who has been thrown out of the parental home if the child appears to need accommodation. The obligation extends to children who reside or have been found in the local authority's area, so there is no opportunity to deny accommodation to a child who needs it simply because he or she usually lives in another local authority area.[176] In addition, the local authority may provide a child with accommodation if it considers that to do so would safeguard or promote the child's welfare.[177] So, for example, where the child has caring parents, the local authority may provide respite care if that would serve the child's welfare. The local authority has the power but, sadly, no obligation, to provide accommodation for 18-to 21-year-olds in similar circumstances, and the large number of young

173 Cf *M* v *Normand* 1995 SLT 1284.
174 1995 Act, s 25(1).
175 Lord Dunedin's description of a child being 'left to his fate' gives a good indication of what is meant by 'abandoned' – *Mitchell* v*Wright* (1905) 7 F 568, at p 574. See further, Wilkinson and Norrie, *Parent and Child* (W. Green, 1993) at pp 544–545.
176 1995 Act, s 25(1). Where the child is ordinarily resident in another local authority area, the accommodating authority must notify the other authority, in writing, that accommodation is being provided and the latter may take over accommodating the child at any time – 1995 Act, s 25(4).
177 1995 Act, s 25(2).

people sleeping rough is a testament to the inadequacy of local authority provision in this respect.[178]

7.52 The local authority's power and duty to provide accommodation under the 1995 Act replaces the old provision under the Social Work (Scotland) Act 1968,[179] and the latter was often referred to, colloquially, as 'voluntary care', although the accuracy of that description was often open to question.[180] To what extent is the provision of accommodation for a child under s 25 of the 1995 Act 'voluntary'? As far as the child is concerned, the local authority is obliged to take account of the child's views, in the light of his or her age and maturity and so far as practicable, before providing accommodation.[181] This is consistent with the general approach taken by the 1995 Act in facilitating the child's participation in the decision-making process. In essence, participation is the child's right, decision-making is an adult responsibility.[182] However, the responsibility for making the decision remains with adults, and a child may be provided with accommodation by the local authority against the child's wishes. What of the parents or other persons with parental responsibilities and rights? The general rule is that the local authority may not provide accommodation for a child if a person who has parental responsibilities and the rights to determine the child's residence and to exercise control over the child objects, provided that such a person is willing either to accommodate the child or to arrange accommodation for the child.[183] The person with responsibilities and rights may remove the child at any time.[184] This general rule is subject to two exceptions. First, where the child is aged 16 or over, and he or she has agreed to the accommodation being provided, parental opposition is irrelevant.[185] The second exception arises where a residence order has been made in respect of the child, and the person entitled to determine the child's residence has agreed to the local authority providing accommodation. Again, parental opposition is irrelevant.[186] In addition, the power to remove a child from local authority accommodation is subject to restriction. If the local authority has provided the child with accommodation for at least six months, the person entitled to determine the child's residence may not remove the child unless he or she has given the local authority 14 days notice of his or her intention to do so.[187]

178 1995 Act, s 25(3).
179 Section 15.
180 It has been suggested that, on occasions, it was put to parents that, unless they agreed to the local authority accommodating the child on a voluntary basis, the local authority would use its extensive powers to remove the child. As a result of the 1995 Act, the local authority no longer has the draconian powers it once had. See the discussion of the modern powers of the local authority below.
181 1995 Act, s 25(5).
182 For a discussion of the interaction of the two, see chapter 3, paras 19–22.
183 1995 Act, s 25(6)(a).
184 1995 Act, s 25(6)(b).
185 1995 Act, s 25(7)(a). The expression 'parental opposition' is used to denote opposition from any person with the requisite parental responsibilities and rights whether or not that person is the child's parent.
186 1995 Act, s 25(7)(b).
187 1995 Act, s 25(7).

7.53 Having established when the local authority must, or may, provide accommodation for a child, the next matter to consider is how it goes about doing so. The 1995 Act allows the local authority the widest possible range of options and, given the emphasis on recognising each child as an individual, this flexibility is desirable. Whatever option the local authority selects, it is obliged to produce a care plan, detailing what arrangements it intends to make for the child.[188] The accommodation may be provided in a family setting, by a relative of the child or someone unrelated to him or her. The extent to which there are fixed notions of a suitable setting for children is interesting. Both the 1995 Act and the regulations envisage a child being looked after by a single person and there seems to be no difficulty in accepting cohabiting heterosexual couples.[189] However, when we turn to consider the provision of foster care, it is clear that a household comprising a same-sex couple is not regarded as suitable.[190] This is particularly interesting in the light of the court's attitude to adoption where a child will be raised in such a household.[191] Alternatively, the child may be looked after in a residential establishment.[192] The local authority is empowered to make use of any services that would be available to a parent looking after his or her own child and so, for example, a local authority could arrange for a child to attend boarding school, if that was reasonable in the circumstances.[193] In arranging accommodation for a child, the local authority may send the child to live in England, Wales or Northern Ireland.[194]

7.54 One way in which the local authority may discharge its obligation to look after children is through the use of foster care.[195] Recruitment of

---

188 The Arrangements to Look After Children (Scotland) Regulations 1996, SI 1996 No 3262. See also, Guidance, vol 2, chapter 1.

189 1995 Act, s 26(1)(a). Concern over difficulties in recruiting and retaining foster carers led the Scottish Office to commission research. A report on the first phase of the research has been published– J. Triseliotis, M. Borland and M. Hill, Fostering Good Relations: A Study of Foster Care and Foster Carers in Scotland, Social Work Research Findings No 22 (Scottish Office, 1998).

190 The relevant regulation provides that the local authority shall not foster a child with a person except where the household of the person comprises, either 'a man and a woman living and acting jointly together' or 'a man or a woman living and acting alone' – Fostering of Children (Scotland) Regulations 1996, SI 1996 No 3263, r 12(4).

191 T, Petitioner (IH) 1996 SCLR 897, where an English local authority, which had experienced considerable difficulty in finding a suitable carer for a child with a number of disabilities, fostered him with Mr T in Scotland. The authority's choice proved to be an excellent one since, it will be remembered, Mr T went on to adopt the boy.

192 1995 Act, s 26(1)(b).

193 1995 Act, s 26(1)(c), referring back to s 17(1)(b). In these cash-strapped times it is difficult to imagine many local authorities preferring this option. However, were a child to show a particular talent for music or art, for example, the local authority might be persuaded to arrange for the child to attend a school which specialised in developing that talent even if it meant the child attending as a boarder.

194 1995 Act, s 26(2). An example of the reverse situation can be seen in T, Petitioner, above.

195 For completeness, it should be noted that parents may make private fostering arrangements and that they must notify the local authority of any such arrangements so that they can be subjected to scrutiny by the local authority – Foster Children (Scotland) Act 1984. For a discussion of both private and local authority fostering, see J. Fabb and T. G. Guthrie, Social Work Law in Scotland (2nd edn, Butterworths, 1997), at pp 132–138.

suitable foster carers is the responsibility of the local authority[196] and, before a person becomes a foster carer, he or she must undergo investigation by the local authority and its fostering panel.[197] The panel may approve a prospective foster carer for a particular child, for a category of children or for any children.[198] Once approved, the foster carer must enter into an agreement with the local authority (a foster carer agreement) governing such matters as the training of the foster carer, the responsibilities of the foster carer and an undertaking that the foster carer will not administer corporal punishment to the child.[199] Placement of a child with a foster carer may be on an emergency, immediate or more general basis. Emergency placement can be made only with approved foster carers and can last for up to 72 hours.[200] Immediate placement may be made with a relative or friend of the child who is not approved as foster carer, if the local authority is satisfied that the placement will be in the child's best interests and there are good reasons why the child should not wait in another placement while the home is approved.[201] Such placements may last for up to six weeks. In all other cases, the local authority must be satisfied that the placement is in the best interests of the particular child and the foster carer must have entered a further agreement covering the particular placement (a foster placement agreement).[202] Foster carers are usually paid by the local authority and detailed guidance is given on the calculation of payment.[203] It should be remembered that a child living with foster carers is still being 'looked after' by the local authority and its obligations to the child continue.

7.55 Once a child is being provided with accommodation by the local authority, what obligations does the authority have to the child? The local authority has a duty to safeguard and promote the welfare of every child it is looking after and the child's welfare must be its paramount concern.[204] That obligation includes providing advice and assistance to prepare the child for a time when the local authority is no longer looking after him or her.[205] In a sense, there is a parallel here with parenting. Just as a parent should prepare a child for independence, the local authority should prepare a child for a time when it no longer owes him or her obligations. Of course, there is no escaping the fact that, in a family, the parents will often be available to offer a child support and advice for many years to come. While the local authority may and, in some circumstances, must, continue to provide advice and assistance to children it has looked after, the obligation is time-limited and hardly parallels what a caring family could

196 Guidance, vol 2, chapter 3, paras 5–34.
197 Fostering of Children (Scotland) Regulations 1996, SI 1996 No 3263 (hereinafter, the 'Fostering Regulations 1996'), rr 4–7 and Guidance, vol 2, chapter 3, paras 41–49.
198 Fostering Regulations 1996, r 6(1).
199 Fostering Regulations 1996, r 8 and Sched 2 and Guidance, vol 2, chapter 3, paras 59–60.
200 Fostering Regulations 1996, r 13 and Guidance, vol 2, chapter 3, para 96.
201 Fostering Regulations 1996, r 14 and Guidance, vol 2, chapter 3, paras 97–100.
202 Fostering Regulations 1996, r 12 and Guidance, vol 2, chapter 3, paras 79–93.
203 Fostering Regulations 1996, r 9 and Guidance, vol 2, chapter 3, paras 73–78.
204 1995 Act, s 17(1)(a).
205 1995 Act, s 17(2).

provide.[206] Insofar as it is consistent with the child's welfare, the local authority must promote personal relations and direct contact on a regular basis between the child and any person with parental responsibilities in relation to the child.[207] In addition, the local authority must make use of services available to parents looking after their own children.[208]

7.56 As we have seen, when parents are making *any major decision* in the context of parental responsibilities and rights, they are required to give the child concerned the opportunity to express his or her views and to take account of these views in the light of the child's age and maturity.[209] Where a local authority is looking after a child, it must take reasonable steps to ascertain the child's views before making *any decision* with respect to the child and take those views into account, again, in the light of the child's age and maturity.[210] Arguably, a child being looked after by a local authority has a greater right to participate in the decision-making process than does a child who is being looked after by his or her family, although the practical difference is probably minimal.[211] In addition to seeking the child's views, before making a decision about the child, the local authority is obliged to ascertain the views of the child's parents, non-parents who have parental rights in respect of the child, and any other person the local authority considers relevant, and to take any views expressed by these persons into account.[212] In the course of making any decision about a child it is looking after, the local authority must have regard to the child's religious persuasion, racial origin, and cultural and linguistic background.[213] In fulfilling its obligations to the child, the local authority is permitted to act in a manner inconsistent with its duties under s 17 where such action is necessary to protect members of the public from serious harm.[214]

After-care for young people leaving care

7.57 Where a young person was being looked after by the local authority at the time he or she ceased to be of school age or at any time thereafter, the local authority is obliged to advise, guide and assist that young person until he or she reaches 19, unless the local authority is satisfied that the young person's welfare does not require it.[215] In addition, the young person

---

206 1995 Act, s 29, discussed at para 7.57, below.
207 1995 Act, s 17(1)(c). This local authority duty explains why every person with parental responsibilities to a child being looked after by local authority must inform the local authority of any change of address without unreasonable delay, subject to penalty for failure to do so – 1995 Act, s 18.
208 1995 Act, s 17(1)(b).
209 1995 Act, s 6, discussed in chapters 3 and 6, paras 36–38 and 3–6, respectively.
210 1995 Act, s 17(3)(a) and (4)(a).
211 In the case of a child living with his or her parents, there is a presumption that a child of 12 years old or older is capable of forming a view. No such presumption is stated in respect of a child being looked after by the local authority. Again, any practical difference is probably minimal.
212 1995 Act, s 17(3)(b)–(d) and (4)(b).
213 1995 Act, s 17(4)(c). It should be noted that it is the child's, rather than the parents', religious persuasion which is relevant here.
214 1995 Act, s 17(5).
215 1995 Act, s 29(1).

may request such advice, guidance and assistance until he or she is 21 and the local authority may provide it.[216] As we have seen, this is hardly the equivalent of the best that parents can offer, but it is better than nothing.

Financial assistance towards expenses of education or training

7.58 Where a young person was being looked after by the local authority at the time he or she ceased to be of school age or at any time thereafter, the local authority may make a grant to the young person to meet expenses connected with education or training or contribute towards accommodation or maintenance of such a young person while he or she is under 21.[217] Where a local authority has provided this form of assistance prior to the young person reaching the age of 21, it may continue to provide it thereafter.[218]

What the local authority may not do

7.59 For completeness, it should be noted that the local authorities may no longer do certain things they could do in the past. The discretionary power to guarantee the indentures or apprenticeships of young people that they have looked after has been abolished.[219] As we have seen, local authorities have a more general power to assist with the expenses of education and training of young people. Nor may the local authority arrange for the emigration of children.[220] While some local authorities made use of this power in the early part of this century, arranging for the emigration of children has long since been abandoned as a means of meeting the needs of children looked after by the local authority.[221]

THE ROLE OF THE COURT: ORDERS THE COURT MAY MAKE

7.60 Thus far, we have explored the ways in which the local authority can and, sometime, must, assist families in the care of children. These mechanisms are designed to ensure that as many children as possible can remain with their own families. However, it may be that the local authority is concerned that, despite its assistance, a child is at risk in the home environment. In other cases, the local authority's concern may go deeper than that. It may be convinced that a child is at risk in the family home. It must then consider what further steps to take and in this section we examine the various orders which may be sought from the court.

7.61 Prior to the 1995 Act, there were a number of problems with the law on child protection.[222] First, where there was serious concern about a

216 1995 Act, s 29(2).
217 1995 Act, s 30(1) and (2).
218 1995 Act, s 30(3).
219 This power was found in the Social Work (Scotland) Act 1968, s 25 and is abolished by the 1995 Act, s 24(1).
220 This power was found in the Social Work (Scotland) Act 1968, s 23 and is abolished by the 1995 Act, s 28.
221 For a discussion of the use of emigration, see J. Eekelaar, '"The Chief Glory": The Export of Children from the United Kingdom' (1994) 21 JLSS 487.
222 The relevant legislation was the Social Work (Scotland) Act 1968 and it is discussed in detail in Wilkinson and Norrie, at pp 418–444 and 457–461.

child's welfare, the only option was to remove that child from the home, pending the decision of a children's hearing. This 'all or nothing' response was sometimes inappropriate, not least where abuse or neglect was suspected and the opportunity to investigate and possibly gather evidence was all that was required. In addition, and regardless of what a child was told, some children would have perceived removal from the home as an indication that whatever may have happened was the child's fault. This is hardly the message to send to a child who may have been the victim of abuse. A second major problem, particularly in the wake of the *Orkney case*,[223] was the public perception that it was too easy for a local authority to engage in over-zealous removal of children from their families. Whether or not the perception was well-founded, the fact that it existed at all was cause for concern. The 1995 Act sought to deal with these problems by providing a broader range of intervention options and greater judicial scrutiny of emergency removal of children. Under the 1995 Act, four new orders may be sought from a sheriff: child assessment orders, exclusion orders, child protection orders and parental responsibilities orders

Overarching principles

7.62 When we examined the court's role in making decisions about parental responsibilities and rights, we saw that three overarching principles, described as the child lawyer's mantra, governed the court's approach.[224] These principles apply when a court is considering decisions in the context of child protection, subject to qualification. Similarly, the principles apply to a decision of a children's hearing.[225] The overarching principles, as they apply in the context of child protection, are as follows.

The welfare of that child throughout his or her childhood shall be the paramount consideration[226]

7.63 It is not surprising to find that the welfare principle applies throughout Part II of the 1995 Act, but it should be noted that it is welfare throughout the child's childhood, that is, until the child reaches the age of 18, that is relevant. This can be contrasted with the position in respect of parental responsibilities and rights, where welfare is not stated to be time-limited,[227] and decisions in the context of adoption, where it is welfare throughout the child's lifetime that is the paramount consideration.[228] It should be noted that welfare does not apply to all decisions in the context of child protection. As we shall see, where an application is made to a

---

223 Report of the Committee of Enquiry into the Removal of Children from Orkney in 1991 (HMSO, 1992) (the Clyde Report). See also, *Sloan* v *B* 1991 SLT 530.

224 1995 Act, s 11(7), discussed in chapter 5, paras 107–136.

225 It is interesting that the overarching principles are not stated to apply where other persons are taking decisions about children in the context of child protection. For example, when the Principal Reporter is considering whether to convene a hearing for a child, the paramountcy of welfare is not mentioned – 1995 Act, s 56. However, if a hearing is convened, the child's welfare comes into play.

226 1995 Act, s 16(1).

227 1995 Act, s 11(7)(a).

228 Adoption (Scotland) Act 1978, s 6, as amended by the 1995 Act.

sheriff to establish grounds of referral to a children's hearing, the sheriff's finding that the grounds are or are not established is not influenced by the child's welfare, although what happens thereafter at the hearing will be. Even where the child's welfare is the paramount consideration in the making of a decision, it is not absolute. It may be displaced 'for the purpose of protecting members of the public from serious harm'.[229]

The child must be given the opportunity to express his or her views in certain circumstances and regard must be had to those views[230]

7.64 The opportunity for the child to express his or her views and to have those views taken into account in the decision-making process features in this part of the 1995 Act and a child of 12 years old and older is presumed to be capable of expressing a view.[231] As we shall see, the child's participation has always been central to the children's hearings system, so this provision makes no real difference there. In the context of courts, this provision puts beyond all shadow of doubt that children must be given the opportunity to participate when decisions are being taken about them. However, it should be noted that, while the child's views are relevant to most decisions under this part of the 1995 Act, they need not be considered in all cases. For example, while they must be considered when a sheriff is deciding whether to vary or discharge a child protection order, they are not stated to be relevant in the initial decision to grant an order.

An order should be made unless making the order would be better than making no order at all[232]

7.65 The principle 'if it ain't broke, don't fix it' applies to certain decisions in the context of child protection. Presumed non-intervention applies to most decisions under Part II of the 1995 Act where a child's views are relevant. It does not apply where a children's hearing is advising a sheriff on whether a child protection order should be continued, nor to most appeals. As we shall see, the 1995 Act introduced the power of a sheriff, on hearing an appeal from the decision of a children's hearing, to substitute his or her own decision for that of the hearing.[233] The presumption of non-intervention applies to the sheriff's decision to exercise this power. Where presumed non-intervention applies, it determines whether an order should or should not be granted. Once an order has been granted, the appropriate level of intervention is not subject to any presumption of minimal intervention.

Child Assessment Orders (CAOs)

7.66 A child assessment order provides for the temporary removal of a child in order to assess whether the local authority's suspicion of abuse or

229 1995 Act, s 16(5). Similarly, in considering whether to detain a child in secure accommodation, one of the criteria is the likelihood of the child injuring himself, herself *or some other person* – 1995 Act, s 70(10)(b) (italics added).
230 1995 Act, s 16(2) and (4).
231 1995 Act, s 16(2).
232 1995 Act, s 16(3).
233 1995 Act, s 51(5)(c)(iii), discussed at para 9.28, below.

neglect is justified, where such assessment would not be possible without the court giving its authority.[234] Only a local authority may apply for a CAO and, before exercising his or her discretion to grant an order, the sheriff must be satisfied that

the local authority has reasonable grounds to suspect that the child is being so treated (or neglected) that he or she is suffering, or is likely to suffer, *significant harm*; and

such assessment is required to establish whether the child is being so treated or (neglected), and

such assessment is unlikely to be carried out, or be carried out satisfactorily, unless the order is granted.[235]

7.67 A CAO may be appropriate in a variety of circumstances. For example, it could be used to authorise medical examination of the child in the face of parental opposition. It should be noted, however, that Scots law empowers the child to consent to any medical treatment or procedure where the practitioner treating the child is satisfied that the child understands the nature and consequences of that treatment or procedure,[236] and the 1995 Act expressly preserves the child's right to consent to medical examination under the Act.[237] It is believed that, in Scotland, the power to consent to medical treatment carries with it the power to refuse.[238] If this analysis is correct, a CAO could be used to override parental opposition to medical examination, but it cannot be used to override the opposition of a child who understands what is involved.

7.68 A CAO cannot last for more than seven days[239] and it must specify when assessment is to begin.[240] It may specify that a child is to be taken to a particular place for assessment[241] and kept at that or any other place.[242] Any person who is in a position 'to produce the child' may be required to do so by the CAO and any such person must permit the assessment to be carried out and comply with any other conditions contained in the order.[243] Where a CAO results in the child's removal from home, he or she becomes a child being looked after by the local authority and the local authority acquires the responsibility for safeguarding his or her welfare.[244] In such circumstances, the CAO may regulate other matters, like the contact a child may have with other persons, like parents and siblings, while being assessed.[245] No appeal lies against the granting of a CAO. Given the short duration of the orders, it is difficult to see how any appeal could have been dealt with

---

234 1995 Act, s 55.
235 1995 Act, s 55(1).
236 Age of Legal Capacity (Scotland) Act 1991, s 2(4).
237 1995 Act, s 90.
238 See chapter 3, para 70, above, for a discussion of the child's right to refuse medical treatment.
239 1995 Act, s 55(3)(b).
240 1995 Act, s 55(3)(a).
241 1995 Act, s 55(4)(a).
242 1995 Act, s 55(4)(b).
243 1995 Act, s 55(3)(c).
244 1995 Act, s 17(1) and 17(6)(c).
245 1995 Act, s 55(5).

unless the CAO was not to take effect immediately. Where a CAO is sought and the sheriff finds that the more stringent grounds justifying the granting of a child protection order are satisfied, the 1995 Act provides that he or she 'shall' make the latter.[246] This is a rather odd provision, since the granting of a child protection order is, itself, discretionary.

7.69 CAOs have been available in England and Wales for some time under the Children Act 1989,[247] but have not proved popular. Even where an initial application has been made for an order, it has often been withdrawn, leading Cretney and Masson to conclude that '[i]t would seem that the order provides a framework for negotiation and is only obtained when this fails'.[248] Given that seven days is not normally long enough to carry out a comprehensive assessment of a child, the threat of a CAO may facilitate parental agreement to more thorough investigation. A hint that this effect may already be appreciated in Scotland can be found from the following observation from the Guidance. 'By giving enough information about the range of options available and possible outcomes, the local authority may help parents to agree to voluntary arrangements for assessment'.[249] As we have seen, it was always suspected that, under the 1968 Act, a parent sometimes agreed to a child being looked after by the local authority under threat of more dramatic intervention. The 1995 Act sought to remove this dishonesty by tightening up the arrangements for local authorities looking after children on a voluntary basis. It might be argued that CAOs have created a new avenue for subtle pressure to be applied to parents to ensure their co-operation with local authorities. On the one hand, any lack of transparency in state intervention is open to condemnation. On the other hand, the need to protect children from abuse and neglect is a powerful reason to warrant what may amount to an infringement of the rights of adults. Of course, sight must not be lost of the fact that removal of a child from his or her home, even for a relatively short period of time, is likely to be traumatic for the child and may be a breach of his or her rights, if removal is not fully justified.

7.70 Having assessed the child, the local authority will then be in a position to decide what, if any, further action it should take. It might conclude that its suspicions were unfounded and that no further action is required or that there is some cause for concern, but that voluntary arrangements can be made with the family to address the concern. However, the local authority may conclude that the case should be referred to the Principal Reporter[250] or that it should apply for an exclusion order or a child protection order.

---

246 1995 Act, s 55(2).
247 Section 43.
248 S. M. Cretney and J. M. Masson, *Principles of Family Law* (6th edn, 1996, Sweet and Maxwell), at p 825. See also J. Dickens, 'Assessment and control in social work: An analysis of the reasons for the non-use of child assessment orders' [1993] JSWFL 88 and R. Lavery, 'The child assessment order – a reassessment' [1996] CFLQ 41.
249 Guidance, vol 1, chapter 7, para 19.
250 Reference in the Act is to the Principal Reporter. As we shall see in chapter 9, the function is carried out on behalf of the Principal Reporter by a number of reporters located throughout Scotland. See chapter 9, paras 14–15.

Exclusion Orders

7.71 Under the law prior to the 1995 Act, where a member of the child's household was posing a real threat to the child, the only effective way to protect a child was to remove the child. That the alleged victim should be subjected to potentially damaging disruption always seemed unreasonable and it was likely that at least some children saw their removal as implying that the problem was somehow their fault. Since 1981, it has been possible for one of the parents to apply to have his or her partner excluded from the family home when exclusion is 'necessary for the protection of the applicant *or any child of the family*' from the partner's conduct.[251] However, while the provision has been used to protect adults from domestic violence, it has never been employed primarily as a child protection measure.

7.72 The 1995 Act introduced a new kind of exclusion order, modelled on the existing one, but available only on the application of the local authority.[252] A sheriff may exclude a named person from a child's family home if he or she is satisfied that

the child[253] has suffered, is suffering, or is likely to suffer, significant harm as a result of any conduct, or threatened or reasonably apprehended conduct, of the named person; and
the making of the order –
(i) is necessary to protect the child, irrespective of whether the child is residing in the family home at the moment, and
(ii) would better safeguard the child's welfare than removal of the child from the family home; and
if the order is made there will be someone specified in the application (an 'appropriate person') who is capable of looking after the child and any other family member who lives in the household and requires care and who is, or will be, residing in the family home.[254]

7.73 Again, the sheriff has a degree of discretion in granting an exclusion order, but the order must be refused if to grant it would be 'unjustifiable or unreasonable'.[255] In making this assessment, the sheriff is directed to consider all the circumstances of the case, including the conduct of the members of the child's family, the respective needs and financial resources of the members of that family, and the extent to which the home is used in connection with a trade, business or profession. In addition, he or she must take account of any requirement that the named person should reside in the family home. Such a condition may arise where the home is an agricultural holding[256] or where it is let or occupied by an employee as an

---

251 Matrimonial Homes (Family Protection) (Scotland) Act 1981, s 4(2), emphasis added. Exclusion orders under the 1981 Act, and the limits on their effectiveness, are discussed in chapter 12.
252 1995 Act, ss 57–60.
253 A child, for this purpose, is a person below the age of 16, unless he or she is between the ages of 16 and 18 and subject to a supervision order – 1995 Act, s 93(2)(b).
254 1995 Act, s 76(2).
255 1995 Act s 76(9)–(11).
256 What constituted an agricultural holding is defined in the Agricultural Holdings (Scotland) Act 1991.

incident of employment. The latter category would include a tied cottage, a police house, or a residence provided by a university to its Principal. In balancing these considerations, the sheriff must bear in mind that the child's welfare is the paramount consideration,[257] must take account of any views the child wishes to express[258] and should not make the order unless to do so would be better than not making the order.[259] Clearly, contested applications for exclusion orders will present members of the judiciary with quite a challenge.

7.74 An application for an exclusion order may not be determined finally unless the named person has been given an opportunity to be heard or represented before the sheriff.[260] In addition, certain other persons may be entitled to notice of the application for an exclusion order and they too have a right to be heard or represented.[261] Where the sheriff is satisfied that the conditions warranting an exclusion order have been satisfied, but that the appropriate persons have not been given sufficient opportunity to be heard, he or she may grant an interim exclusion order.[262] Where the appropriate persons have had the opportunity to be heard, an interim order may be granted pending final determination of the case.[263] Where an exclusion order is sought and the sheriff is satisfied that the conditions justifying a child protection order are satisfied, he or she may grant a child protection order.[264] The 1995 Act contains no provision for appeal against the sheriff's decision to grant or refuse an exclusion order and it must be assumed that the ordinary principles apply to permit appeals.

7.75 The effect of an exclusion order is to suspend the named person's right of occupancy in the home to which the order relates and to prevent him or her from entering that home except with the permission of the local authority which applied for the order.[265] It is interesting that only the local authority, and not the person caring for the child, may grant permission for the named person to enter the home. This might be to avoid pressure being put on the resident parent (or other family member) by the excluded parent or, indeed, to prevent the resident parent from nullifying the practical effect of the exclusion order. As we shall see, a strength of the older, matrimonial, exclusion orders lies in the ancillary orders which may be made along with the main order.[266] Under the 1995 Act, the court may, again, make ancillary orders. It may: grant a warrant for summary ejection of the named person; grant an interdict prohibiting the named person from entering the home without the permission of the relevant local authority; grant an interdict prohibiting the named person from removing relevant

257 1995 Act, s 16(1).
258 1995 Act, s 16(2) and (4)(b)(i).
259 1995 Act, s 16(3) and (4)(b)(i).
260 1995 Act 76(3)(a).
261 1995 Act, ss 76(3)(b) and 91(3)(d).
262 1995 Act, s 76(4).
263 1995 Act, s 76(6).
264 1995 Act, s 76(8). It is interesting to note that, where a child protection order is sought, the sheriff has no power to substitute an exclusion order.
265 1995 Act, s 77(1).
266 See chapter 12.

items from the home without the written consent of the local authority, the appropriate person or by order of the sheriff; grant an interdict prohibiting the named person from entering or remaining in a specified area within the vicinity of the home; grant an interdict prohibiting the named person from taking any specified steps in relation to the child; or make an order regulating contact between the named person and the child.[267] This very wide range of ancillary orders should ensure that an exclusion order can be tailor-made to the needs of the individual case. At any time when an exclusion order is in force, the local authority may apply to the sheriff for a power of arrest to be attached to it.[268] Again, this parallels the provision on attaching a power of arrest found in the older, matrimonial, exclusion orders. An exclusion order under the 1995 Act lasts for no longer than six months and may last for a shorter period of time where that is specified in the order itself.[269] In addition, it ceases to have effect where permission to occupy the home is withdrawn by a third party whose consent to occupation is required or where the order is recalled by the sheriff.[270] Unlike those available under the 1981 Act, exclusion orders under the 1995 Act may not be renewed. Where an exclusion order has expired at the end of the six-month period, there would be nothing to prevent a local authority from applying for another exclusion order, provided that it can satisfy the relevant conditions.

7.76 The introduction of the new exclusion order is to be welcomed but it is defective in a number of respects. Only a local authority can apply for an order excluding a suspected abuser from the home, and why applications should be confined to local authorities is not clear. The fact that the order is modelled on similar orders available to individuals under the 1981 Act means that the alleged abuser cannot be removed immediately. Thus, in cases of real emergency, children will still have to be removed pending the granting of an exclusion order. In considering whether exclusion would be 'unjustified or unreasonable' the court is being asked to compare a child's needs with those of an adult. This is simply not comparing like with like. It is surprising to note that the controversy generated in the press by the creation of this new exclusion order did not relate to its limitations and shortcomings, but rather to the idea that a suspected abuser might be excluded from his or her home before the case against him or her has been proved. Since the alternative is the removal from the home of a child, against whom no wrong is alleged, one can be forgiven for wondering where the protesters' priorities lay. In any event, a similar debate had already been exhausted in respect of matrimonial exclusion orders.

Child Protection Orders (CPOs)

7.77 Under the law prior to the 1995 Act, emergency protection of children was effected through the mechanism of a place of safety order.

267 1995 Act, s 77(3).
268 1995 Act, s 78.
269 1995 Act, s 79(1) and (2)(a).
270 1995 Act, s 79(2)(b) and (c).

These orders were open to a number of criticisms,[271] not least because of their inflexibility, and the CPOs, introduced by the 1995 Act, are designed to be more flexible, simpler to operate and, in particular, to last for no longer than is necessary. This last goal has resulted in a tight timetable within which the various steps related to CPOs must be taken and the result is a procedure which is anything but simple, at least on a first reading. In this section, we will consider the conditions for the granting of a CPO before we go on to consider the procedural steps to be followed. At the end of our discussion, an excellent diagram outlines the procedure.[272]

7.78 Two separate sets of conditions exist for the granting of a CPO. Under the first, any person may apply to the sheriff for a child protection order.[273] Thus, a police officer, a relative of the child or the child, himself or herself, may apply, although it is anticipated that the vast majority of applications will come from the local authority. The sheriff has a discretion to grant a CPO where he or she is satisfied that there are reasonable grounds to believe that

> the child is being so treated (or neglected) that he or she is suffering significant harm or that he or she will suffer such harm if not removed to and kept in a place of safety or if he or she does not remain in the place where he or she is being accommodated;[274] and
>
> the order is necessary to protect the child from such harm (or further harm).[275]

The second of these requirements signals a significant shift from the earlier law which seemed to presume that removal of the child was usually the solution. With the addition of child assessment orders and the new exclusion orders to the battery of protective options, it may be that another solution is more appropriate in a given case. Similar provisions operating in England and Wales suggest that local authorities have made little use of CAOs, preferring to apply for CPOs, and it remains to be seen whether the same approach will be taken in Scotland.

7.79 The second set of conditions under which a CPO may be sought relates to obstruction of enquiries into child abuse or neglect and is open only to the local authority.[276] It must satisfy a sheriff that it has reasonable grounds to suspect that

> the child is being so treated (or neglected) that he or she is suffering, or will suffer significant harm, and

271 For a discussion of the shortcomings of place of safety orders, see the Clyde Report, n 78 above, paras 16.1–16.13 and Scotland's Children: Proposals for Child Care Policy and Law (Cm 2286, 1993), paras 5.8–5.18
272 This diagram is reproduced with grateful thanks to Professor Kenneth McK Norrie who devised the diagram and published it first in *Children's Hearings in Scotland* (W. Green, 1997), Appendix 1.
273 1995 Act, s 57(1). An applicant must give notice to the local authority in the area where the child resides (where that local authority is not the applicant) and the Principal Reporter of the application for a CPO – 1995 Act, s 57(5).
274 1995 Act, s 57(1)(a).
275 1995 Act, s 57(1)(b).
276 Notice of the application must be given to the local authority in the area where the child resides (where that local authority is not the applicant) and the Principal Reporter of the application for a CPO – 1995 Act, s 57(5).

it is making enquiries to allow it to decide whether it should take any action to safeguard the welfare of the child, and

its enquiries are being frustrated by access to the child being unreasonably denied, such access being required as a matter of urgency.[277]

Again, the sheriff has a discretion to grant a CPO and it remains to be seen what the courts regard as unreasonable denial of access of such magnitude as to frustrate enquiries.

7.80 In reaching his or her decision, the sheriff must regard the child's welfare as the paramount consideration.[278] There is no requirement to take the child's views into account, although how the child feels about the possibility of being removed from home or detained elsewhere will be relevant in considering whether the order will serve the child's welfare. The sheriff must make an immediate decision on an application for a CPO and there is no scope for giving a decision at a later date.[279] There is no appeal against the sheriff's decision to grant or refuse a CPO.[280] A CPO is much more flexible than the old place of safety order. Not only can it authorise the removal and retention of a child, it can provide that a child should not be removed from a specified place, require a person to produce the child, and provide that the location of the child's whereabouts should not be disclosed to particular persons.[281] Where he or she decides to grant a CPO, the sheriff must consider whether it is necessary to make a direction on contact between the child and any person or class of persons, like parents or persons with parental responsibilities to the child.[282] The sheriff may make such direction as he or she believes appropriate, but may consider prohibiting contact or making contact subject to such conditions as are appropriate to safeguard and promote the child's welfare.[283] At the same time as the application for a CPO is made, the applicant may apply for a direction as to the exercise of parental rights or the fulfilment of parental responsibilities and, in particular, may seek direction in relation to examination, assessment or interview of the child or any treatment the child might require.[284]

7.81 Since the intention is that a CPO provides for emergency protection of children and should last for no longer than is necessary, there are detailed provisions on implementation, review, duration, recall and variation of a CPO. If the requisite steps are not taken within the strict time-limits set out in the 1995 Act, the CPO ceases to have effect. Thus, there should be no possibility of a child drifting within the system. Nor should any child be removed from home for longer than is absolutely necessary before a further decision is taken on his or her future. The steps involved

---

277 1995 Act, s 57(2).
278 1995 Act, s 16(1).
279 Act of Sederunt (Child Care and Maintenance Rules) 1997, r 3.31.
280 1995 Act, s 51(15).
281 1995 Act, s 57(4).
282 1995 Act, s 58(1). It will be remembered that one of the issues which arose in the *Orkney case* was the local authority's prevention of contact between the children and their parents and the children with each other.
283 1995 Act, s 58(2).
284 1995 Act, s 58(3) and (4).

once a CPO has been granted are set out below and are presented in diagrammatic form thereafter.[285]

Implementation

7.82 Once granted, a CPO ceases to have effect if no attempt to implement it has been made within 24 hours.[286] The attempt need not be successful and time starts to run from the time of successful implementation.[287] Thus, where the CPO authorises removal of a child and the local authority makes several attempts to implement it but is only successful more than 24 hours after the CPO was granted, its effective implementation is the time when the clock starts. Of course, some CPOs will provide for situations where it is not possible to demonstrate active implementation. For example, where the CPO authorises a child to be kept at a place of safety where the child is already living, apart from actually providing for the child, there is no active implementation unless the child tries to leave or someone tries to remove him or her. In such cases, implementation is contemporaneous with the granting of the order.[288] This provision is not intended to force the local authority's hand and, indeed, there is a clear direction in the Act that a CPO should only be implemented where there is a reasonable belief that implementation is necessary to safeguard and promote the child's welfare.[289] Since any directions made by the sheriff on granting a CPO are dependent on it, they fall if the CPO itself ceases to have effect.[290]

Review

7.83 Where a CPO has resulted in a child being taken to a place of safety or kept in such a place, it must be subject to review on the second working day after implementation.[291] Review can come about in one of two ways. First, an application may be made to the sheriff to set aside or vary the CPO. Such an application may be made by the child concerned,[292] a person who has parental rights in respect of him or her, a relevant person,[293] any person to whom notice of the original application was given under the rules, or the applicant for the order. No other person may apply for a CPO to be varied or set aside. If the application for review relates to a CPO made under s 57 or a direction made under s 58, it must be made before the commencement of a children's hearing arranged to review the CPO.[294] If

285 In our exploration, we will assume that the local authority applied for the CPO.
286 1995 Act, s 60(1).
287 1995 Act, s 59(5)(a).
288 1995 Act, s 59(5)(b).
289 1995 Act, s 57(6).
290 1995 Act, s 58(7)(b).
291 'Working day' is defined as every day except Saturday and Sunday, 25 and 26 December and 1 and 2 January – 1995 Act, s 93(1).
292 The child may have capacity to make the application or may require another person to make it on his or her behalf – Age of Legal Capacity (Scotland) Act 1991, s 2(4A) and (4B).
293 'Relevant person' is defined in s 93(2)(b) and discussed at para 7.32, above. Since the definition includes a person who has parental rights in respect of the child, it is not clear why such persons are mentioned separately in s 60(7)(b).
294 1995 Act, s 60(8)(a).

the application relates to an order or direction continued by virtue of s 59, it must be made within two days of the continuation being authorised.[295] No deviation from these strict time-limits appears to be permitted. The Principal Reporter must be notified of the application[296] and the Principal Reporter may arrange a children's hearing, in order to offer advice to the sheriff, at any time before the sheriff has reached a decision on the application.[297] The hearing by the sheriff, which must determine the application within three working days, then acts as a review of the CPO.[298] The sheriff must hear the parties to the application and, if he or she wishes to make representations, the Principal Reporter.[299] The sheriff must then determine whether the conditions for the making of a CPO are satisfied or, where the application relates to a direction under s 58, whether the direction should be varied or cancelled.[300] Where the sheriff determines that the conditions for a CPO are satisfied, he or she may confirm or vary the CPO or any term or condition on which it was granted, confirm or vary any direction given under s 58, or continue the CPO in force along with any conditions attached to it.[301] In these circumstances, the CPO will continue in force until the hearing arranged under s 65(2) takes place. Where the sheriff is not satisfied that the conditions for a CPO are satisfied, he or she must recall the order and cancel any attached directions.[302]

7.84 In the absence of an application to the sheriff to vary or recall the CPO, it is reviewed by means of an initial hearing. Where a child has been taken to a place of safety or detained in such a place, the Principal Reporter must arrange an initial hearing to determine whether the CPO should be continued.[303] The hearing must take place on the second working day after implementation of the CPO and failure to hold a hearing timeously will result in the CPO lapsing.[304] Where the hearing is satisfied that the conditions for a CPO are satisfied, it may continue the CPO and any direction made under s 58[305] and there is no appeal from the hearing's decision.[306] In these circumstances, the CPO will continue in force until the hearing arranged under s 65(2) takes place. While a hearing may vary any direction or condition attached to the original CPO, it appears it may not impose fresh directions or conditions.

295 1995 Act, s 60(8)(b).
296 1995 Act, s 60(9).
297 1995 Act, s 60(10).
298 1995 Act, s 59. If the application to the sheriff is not determined within this period, the CPO lapses – 1995 Act, s 60(2).
299 1995 Act, s 60(11).
300 1995 Act, s 60(11). Unlike the sheriff's original decision and that of an initial hearing, there is no prohibition on appealing against the sheriff's decision to vary or recall a CPO. It can be argued that, where an appeal is not prohibited, it is permitted. However, if the review is seen as continuing the process of an application under s 57, the prohibition on appeals against decisions under that section may apply – 1995 Act, s 51(15).
301 1995 Act, s 60(12).
302 1995 Act, s 60(13).
303 1995 Act, s 59(1) and (2).
304 1995 Act, s 59(3) and (4).
305 1995 Act, s 59(4).
306 1995 Act, s 51(15).

Second review by means of an application to the sheriff

7.85 Where the review has been by means of an initial hearing, rather than an application to the sheriff, there is the possibility of a second review, since an application for variation or recall may be made to the sheriff within two working days of the initial hearing which continued the CPO.[307] This application is the same, in all essential respects, as making an application to the sheriff before the initial hearing has taken place.

Eighth working day hearing

7.86 As we have seen, the CPO is intended as a short-term emergency measure and no CPO can remain in force beyond the eighth working day after implementation.[308] If, as will usually be the case, it is felt that there may be a need for further measures to be considered in order to protect the child, a children's hearing must be arranged for no later than the eighth working day after implementation of the CPO. At that hearing, if it is believed that the child should remain in a place of safety, the hearing may grant a warrant under s 66(1) or 69(7). It will be very unusual for this hearing to take the alternative step of making a supervision requirement, at this stage, since there will not normally have been time to make available the relevant reports.

Emergency protection where a CPO is not available

7.87 In urban areas of Scotland there should be little difficulty in finding a sheriff to hear an application for a CPO. However, in rural areas, sheriffs are less numerous and it is possible that no sheriff will be available to hear the application. Children cannot be left at risk of serious harm in these circumstances and s 61 provides two mechanisms for emergency protection of children where a CPO cannot be obtained. First, where it is not practicable for the application for a CPO to be made to a sheriff, a justice of the peace may consider the application.[309] He or she may then grant a special kind of short-lived CPO, if persuaded that the conditions for the granting of a CPO are satisfied.[310] The applicant must implement the CPO as soon as is reasonably practicable and must inform a range of people that the CPO has been implemented, where the child is being accommodated, the reason for the granting of the CPO, and any other steps taken to safeguard the child's welfare.[311] A CPO granted by a justice of the peace has much the same effect as a CPO granted by a sheriff, but it cannot last for longer than 24 hours and it is envisaged that an application for a full CPO will be made in the interim.[312]

---

307 1995 Act, s 60(7).
308 1995 Act, s 60(6) and 65(2).
309 1995 Act, s 61(1)(b) and 61(2)(b).
310 1995 Act, s 61(1) and 61(2).
311 The Emergency Child Protection Measures (Scotland) Regulations 1996, SI 1996 No 3258, rr 7–9. Where the applicant considers it necessary for the child's protection, he or she may withhold information relating to the child's whereabouts – r 10.
312 1995 Act, s 61(3) and (4).

Child Protection Order Flowchart *

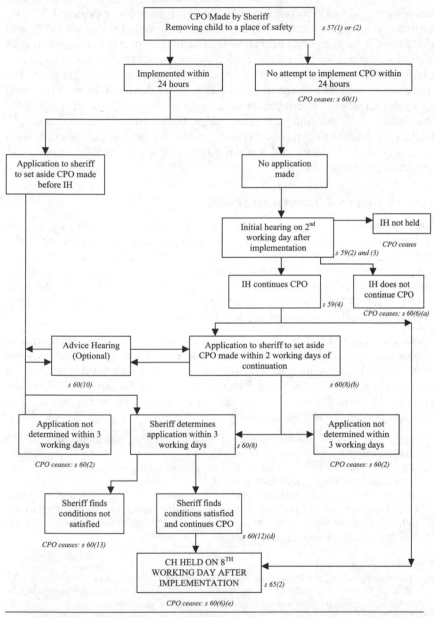

CPO : child protection order
CH : children's hearing
IH : initial hearing

N.B. s 60(6)(c): CPO ceases to have effect when a reporter decides not to arrange a children's hearing
s 60(6)(d): CPO ceases to have effect when a reporter considers that the conditions for its granting are no longer satisfied

*This diagram is reproduced with grateful thanks to Professor Kenneth McK. Norrie.

7.88 The second mechanism whereby emergency protection can be effected without an application to a sheriff allows a police officer to take a child to a place of safety in certain circumstances. Where a police officer has reasonable cause to believe that the conditions for making a CPO are satisfied, that it is not practicable to make an application to a sheriff, and that in order to protect a child from significant harm, it is necessary to take a child to a place of safety, the police officer may take the child to such a place of safety.[313] As soon as is reasonably practicable thereafter, the officer must inform a range of people that he or she has removed the child to a place of safety, where the child is being accommodated, the reason for the child's removal and any other steps taken to safeguard the child's welfare.[314] A child may not be kept at a place of safety under this provision for longer than 24 hours and it is envisaged that a CPO will be applied for, if necessary, within that time.[315]

Parental Responsibilities Order (PRO)

7.89 Under the law prior to the 1995 Act, the local authority had, in certain circumstances, the power to assume parental rights in respect of a child in its care.[316] It could carry out the whole procedure by administrative act and, only once the process was completed, did it have to inform the child's parents. The onus then fell on the parents to challenge the decision in court. Of all the people involved, many of these parents were the least able to make effective use of the legal system.

7.90 The 1995 Act has abolished this invidious, largely administrative, procedure, and replaced it with a judicial procedure which requires the local authority to seek the transfer of parental responsibilities to it by means of an application for a PRO, prior to that transfer.[317] Before the sheriff may grant the order, he or she must be satisfied, in respect of each relevant person,[318] that he or she

> freely, and with full understanding of what is involved, agrees unconditionally that the order be made; or
> is not known, cannot be found, or is incapable of giving consent; or
> is withholding consent unreasonably; or
> has persistently failed without reasonable cause to fulfil the parental responsibility to safeguard and promote the child's health, development and welfare or, if the child is not living with him or her, has failed to maintain personal relations and direct contact on a regular basis; or,

---

313 1995 Act, s 61(5).
314 The Emergency Child Protection Measures (Scotland) Regulations 1996, SI 1996 No 3258, rr 3 and 4. Where the applicant considers it necessary for the child's protection, he or she may withhold information relating to the child's whereabouts – r 5.
315 1995 Act, s 61(6).
316 Social Work (Scotland) Act 1968, s 16. For a discussion of the old law and its shortcomings, see Wilkinson and Norrie, n 175 above, at pp 418–444.
317 1995 Act, s 86. See also, *Scotland's Children: The Children (Scotland) Act 1995 Regulations and Guidance*, vol 3, *Adoption and Parental Responsibilities Orders*, chapter 2.
318 For the purpose of this section, a relevant person is any person who has parental rights in relation to the child – 1995 Act, s 86(4).

has seriously ill-treated the child and the child's reintegration into the household is unlikely.[319]

That these conditions are similar to those required for dispensing with parental agreement to adoption is no accident.[320] While the effects are different, the two concepts may form part of the overall, long-term planning for a particular child. It is worth noting, however, that the fact that one of the above conditions is satisfied does not require the sheriff to grant the PRO, since he or she must also be satisfied that to do so would be consistent with the child's welfare.[321] There is no express requirement to take the child's views into account in the granting or refusal of a PRO, but the child's views would be relevant to assessing welfare. Again, the 1995 Act contains no provision on appeals against a sheriff's decision to grant or refuse a PRO and it must be assumed that appeals are competent.

7.91 The transfer is of 'the appropriate parental rights and responsibilities' and these are defined as all parental responsibilities and rights except the right to consent to an order freeing a child for adoption or an adoption order.[322] Thus, the effect is to remove almost all parental responsibilities, except those relating to adoption, from everyone who had them before the order was made.[323] Since each of these people must either have agreed to the order or have fallen foul of one of the other conditions, this seems unobjectionable. In granting a PRO, the sheriff may make it subject to conditions as he or she considers appropriate.[324] Detailed provision on the contact a child may have with certain persons is dealt with in a separate section and this suggests that the kind of conditions envisaged in s 86(5) relate to other matters like where the child should live and medical treatment. While the 1995 Act does not state the point expressly, it is reasonable to suppose that parental responsibilities transferred to the local authority last only as long as these responsibilities and rights would have lasted if held by parents or other persons. Thus, it is only the responsibility to offer direction and guidance which lasts past the child's 16th birthday.[325] While a PRO is in force, the local authority must fulfil the responsibilities transferred to it,[326] but this does not prevent it from allowing the child to live with a parent, guardian, relative or friend if such an arrangement would be for the benefit of the child.[327] However, the local authority may require any such person to return the child by giving notice in writing to him or her.[328]

---

319 1995 Act, s 86(2).
320 For a more detailed discussion of these conditions, in the context of adoption, see chapter 8, paras 40–55. The parallel is reinforced by the provision for curators *ad litem* and reporting officers to be appointed to fulfil the role in respect of PROs that they already fulfil in respect of adoptions – 1995 Act, s 87(4) and (5).
321 1995 Act, s 16(1).
322 1995 Act, s 86(3).
323 1995 Act, s 86(3).
324 1995 Act, s 86(5).
325 1995 Act, ss 1(2) and 2(7).
326 1995 Act, s 87(1).
327 1995 Act, s 87(2).
328 1995 Act, s 87(3).

7.92 Under the previous law, there were difficulties over parental access to children when the local authority had assumed parental rights. This led to the 1968 Act being amended to prevent local authorities terminating access without giving the parents notice of their intention to do so and giving the parents the right to apply to a sheriff for an access order.[329] The 1995 Act takes a different approach. It starts from a position of presuming contact will be permitted and provides that the local authority shall allow reasonable contact between the child and any person who was either a responsible person prior to the granting of the PRO, or any person in whose favour a residence order or contact order was in force prior to the PRO being granted.[330] In addition, the child, the local authority or any person with an interest may apply for a contact order[331] and the sheriff may make a contact order without any such application being made.[332] A contact order may be varied or discharged by the sheriff on the application of the child, the local authority or any person with an interest,[333] and shall cease to have effect if the PRO to which it is referable terminates.[334]

7.93 A PRO may be varied or discharged by the sheriff on the application of the local authority, the child, a person who was a relevant person prior to the making of the order, or any person claiming an interest.[335] If it is not so discharged, a PRO ceases to have effect when the child or young person: reaches the age of 18; is adopted; is freed for adoption; is the subject of an order for return under the Child Abduction and Custody Act 1985; or when an order for access under that Act is registered in respect of the child.[336]

---

329 Social Work (Scotland) Act 1968, ss 17A and 17B (added by the Health and Social Services and Social Security Adjudications Act 1983, s 7(2)).
330 1995 Act, s 88(2).
331 1995 Act, s 88(3).
332 1995 Act, s 88(4).
333 1995 Act, s 88(5).
334 1995 Act, s 88(6).
335 1995 Act, s 86(5).
336 1995 Act, s 86(6).

CHAPTER 8

ADOPTION

8.1 Adoption can best be described as the process which creates the relationship of parent and child by order of the court.[1] It was not until 1930 that what we now recognise as adoption existed in Scotland at all. However, arrangements by which a child was placed with another family to be cared for by that family on a relatively permanent basis had long been known. Celtic law recognised the concept of fosterage,[2] whereby a child, often of high rank, was sent to live with another person. The arrangement could be for payment or for affection, and contracts, detailing the obligations of everyone involved, were often drawn up. It appears that fosterage was often used to create alliances at a time when the rule of law was weak and, since it did not sever the child's link with his or her birth family, it cannot be seen as the forebearer of modern adoption.

8.2 The courts first had the opportunity to address the effects of a private adoption agreement in 1901 in *Kerrigan* v *Hall*.[3] There, Ms Kerrigan, a single woman, had handed her child over to a married couple, the Halls, to be cared for by them and had agreed to make a monthly contribution towards the child's support. Whether it was agreed that the arrangement should be permanent was a matter of dispute and Ms Kerrigan failed to make the agreed payments. When Ms Kerrigan later married, she sought the return of her child and the Halls refused. They argued that there had been a binding agreement to transfer the child, that the pursuer was unfit to care for the child, and, quite incredibly, that they had a right to retain the child until the arrears in respect of support payments were made.[4] The issues of the mother's fitness and the right of retention were dismissed fairly swiftly by the court. On the issue of adoption as a way of effecting a binding transfer of the child, the court was quite clear that such a notion had no place in Scots law and, indeed, that it would 'come very near to

---

1 *J and J* v *C's Tutor* 1948 SC 636 per Lord President Cooper, at 641.
2 J. Cameron, *Celtic Law* (W. Hodge, 1937) at pp 62–67. The Gaelic text, a facsimile and a translation of the Contract of Fosterage by Sir Roderick MacLeod can be found at pp 222–225.
3 (1901) 4 F 10.
4 The claim in respect of retention appears to have been based on drawing a parallel with the right to retain property until a debt is paid, along the lines of the hotelier's right to hold on to a guest's property until the guest pays his or her bill. Given the modern emphasis on children's rights, it is quite astonishing to encounter such an argument being made in respect of a child.

sanctioning the sale of a child by its parents'.[5] However, the court did accept that private care arrangements were permissible and that agreements in respect of payment for them were enforceable.

8.3 By 1911, the word 'adoption' was being used by the court without further discussion.[6] Welcoming the Adoption of Children (Scotland) Act 1930, one commentator observed, 'for a long time there has been no doubt that the law relating to the adoption of children required amendment'.[7] Given that the severing of the parent-child bond had already been viewed by the courts as impossible, it must be concluded that what was being described as adoption was what we would now describe as private fostering arrangements. Adoption, properly so-called, was introduced by the Adoption of Children (Scotland) Act 1930, enacted four years after similar legislation was introduced for England and Wales.[8] It has been suggested that the impetus to introduce a formal adoption law, at least in England and Wales, was to meet the needs of children orphaned as a result of the First World War. If that is so, the legislation throughout the UK arrived too late for many of its intended beneficiaries but, then, delay in turning policy into legislation may be nothing new. The legislation has undergone considerable reappraisal over the years and the current statute governing adoption is the Adoption (Scotland) Act 1978 ('the 1978 Act'),[9] itself amended in a number of significant respects, most recently, by the Children (Scotland) Act 1995. The recent amendments were preceded by extensive

---

5 Per Lord President Kinross, at p 13. As A. B. Wilkinson and K. McK. Norrie observe in *Parent and Child* (at p 514), 'This lack of any equivalent in Scots law for the Roman law *adoptio* or *adrogatio* has sometimes been thought remarkable in a system which has been heavily influenced by Roman law institutions. The omission is, however, consistent with other legal systems within the Civilian legal tradition.'

6 *Briggs* v *Mitchell* 1911 SC 705.

7 Anonymous, 'The Adoption of Children (Scotland) Act 1930', 1930 SLT (News) 153.

8 Adoption of Children Act 1926. Cretney and Masson describe adoption as being introduced in England and Wales 'reluctantly'. As they point out, the Report of the Committee on Child Adoption (1921, Cmd 1254) (Hopkinson Report) was followed by six unsuccessful Bills, before the further recommendations of the Report of the Child Adoption Committee (1926, Cmd 2401, 1925) (Tomlin Report) were enacted – S. M. Cretney and J. M. Masson, *Principles of Family Law* (6th edn, Sweet & Maxwell, 1997) at p 876. In the USA, the first adoption law was passed in Alabama in 1850 and a host of other states followed suit fairly quickly – J. Zainaldin, 'The Emergence of a Modern American Family Law: Child Custody, Adoption and the Courts, 1796–1851' 73 Northwestern U L Rev 1038 (1979). Prior to that, individual adoptions were effected by legislative acts and Friedman attributes the move, from this rather clumsy device to more general provision, to the needs of the sizeable land-owning middle class. As he says, '... the point of adoption, as a *legal* device, is not love, but money; nobody needs a formal adoption paper to love a child desperately; inheritance of property from a 'father ' or a 'mother' is another matter. Adoption is not a requirement amongst the landless poor. Thus the need felt for general adoption laws is yet another reflex of the master fact of American law and life; the enormous bulk of the landed middle class' – L. M. Friedman, *A History of American Law* (2nd edn, Simon and Schuster, 1985) at p 212.

9 References in this chapter are to the 1978 Act, as amended, unless otherwise stated. The Act should be read along with the Regulations made under it and the relevant Scottish Office Guidance – see *Scotland's Children: The Children (Scotland) Act 1995 Regulations and Guidance*, vol 3, *Adoption and Parental Responsibilities Orders* (Scottish Office, 1997).

consultation and a UK-wide examination of adoption.[10] In addition, the Human Fertilisation and Embryology Act 1990 created a new form of adoption, available in certain circumstances, where a child has been born as a result of a surrogacy arrangement.[11] Adoption has received considerable European[12] and international attention,[13] culminating in the Hague Convention on Adoption in 1993.[14] An extensive body of literature exists dealing with the law and practice relating to adoption.[15]

8.4 In its purest form, adoption severs the ties between a child and his or her birth family and transplants the child into the new, adoptive family. We shall see presently that many adoptions, particularly step-parents' adoptions, do not conform to this simple model. Even where the adopters are biologically or socially unrelated to the child, there is residual legal recognition of the child's link to his or her biological family through, for example, the prohibition on marriage between the child and a birth parent.[16] In addition, practical arrangements may be made for a child to have continued contact with birth relatives. In order to understand the, often subtle, developments in adoption law and practice, it is necessary to understand the changing social context of adoption.

10 The changes introduced by the 1995 Act were preceded by considerable discussion and consultation. As part of the Inter-Departmental Review of Adoption Law, two background papers were commissioned: E. France, International Perspectives (Department of Health, 1990) and J. Thorburn, Review of Research Relating to Adoption (Department of Health, 1990). The Scottish Office produced four Discussion Papers: The Nature and Effect of Adoption (Discussion Paper No 1, 1990, Scottish Office); Agreement and Freeing (Discussion Paper No 2, 1992, Scottish Office); The Adoption Process (Discussion Paper No 3, 1991, Scottish Office); and Intercountry Adoption (Discussion Paper No 4, 1992, Scottish Office). See also, The Future of Adoption Law in Scotland: A Consultation Paper (SWSG, 1993). For the parallel discussion in England and Wales, see *Adoption: The Future* (HMSO, 1993).
11 1990 Act, s 30. See para 8.34 and chapter 4, paras 53–62 for a full discussion of the provision.
12 See for example, the European Convention on the Adoption of Children, ETS No 58, 1967.
13 The UN Convention on the Rights of the Child is somewhat guarded in its approach to adoption but recognises the concept, none the less. See Article 21.
14 That Convention was preceded by the 1965 Hague Convention on Jurisdiction, Applicable Law and Recognition of Decrees Relating to Adoptions, TS 94 (1978); Cmnd 7342. Sadly, the 1965 Hague Convention did not attract much support, although it was given effect in the UK by the Adoption Act 1968 (now substantially re-enacted in the 1978 Act). It may be that the pressing need to regulate international adoption was not fully recognised in the 1960s: a theory given credence by the greater enthusiasm that has been shown for the 1993 Convention.
15 For further details of adoption law, taking account of the 1995 Act, see P. G. B. McNeill, *Adoption of Children in Scotland*, (3rd edn, W. Green, 1998). Much of what is contained in texts dealing with adoption prior to the 1995 Act amendments to the legislation remains relevant: see, Wilkinson and Norrie, *Parent and Child*, pp 514–558; *The Laws of Scotland: Stair Memorial Encyclopaedia*, vol 10, paras 1188–1216. For an excellent discussion of the more theoretical and practical issues, see J. Triseliotis, J. Shireman and M. Hundleby, *Adoption: Theory, Policy and Practice* (Cassell, 1997), which contains an excellent bibliography. British Agencies for Adoption and Fostering (BAAF) publishes a journal, Adoption and Fostering, a newsletter, Adoption and Fostering News, regular Practice Notes and a range of monographs on particular topics in the field.
16 Adoption (Scotland) Act 1978, s 41(1), discussed at para 8.69, below.

Changing social context of adoption

8.5 When adoption was introduced in Scotland, the typical case for which it was designed was of the single mother, like Ms Kerrigan, who was unable to keep her child because of the social and economic circumstances prevailing at the time. Childless couples, like the Halls, promised a better future for the child and the norm was for babies to be adopted at an early stage by such couples and to have no further contact with birth families. The picture began to change dramatically in the 1960s, with the changes continuing to the present.[17] The increased efficiency of contraception, the access to lawful abortion and the greater acceptance of single motherhood have resulted in a dramatic reduction in the number of children, and particularly babies, available for adoption.[18] During 1969, the year in which adoptions peaked, 2,268 children were adopted.[19] By 1997, the figure had fallen to 471.[20] Of the 471 children adopted, only 62 were aged between six months and two years old, while the largest single group, the five- to nine-year-olds, accounted for 192 adoptions, with a further 116 children being aged between ten and 17.[21] The fact that comparatively few babies are available for adoption has resulted in an increased interest in international adoptions. While this can be beneficial to the children involved, international adoption carries with it a number of problems and should not be seen as an easy answer to the needs of childless couples and individuals.[22]

8.6 The fact that the majority of adoptions involve children (and often older children) rather than babies is both a cause and an effect of the changing nature of adoption itself. The dramatic increase in step-parent adoption is a partial explanation of the number of older children being adopted and we will return to step-parent adoption presently. As far as adoption by non-relatives is concerned, the fact that older children are involved indicates that adoption is now a part of long-term planning for children who can no longer be cared for by their parents or other family members. However, many of these children will have an established relationship with birth relatives, including, of course, their parents. This has focused debate on the possibility of continued contact between the child

---

17 Even within the last 20 years, there have been changes. The following statement is taken from *Scotland's Children: The Children (Scotland) Act 1995 Regulations and Guidance*, vol 3, at para 2, 'Since the 1978 Act came into force, the number of children placed for adoption by adoption agencies has fallen but the level of difficulty and disability of the children placed have grown considerably. Services which were predominantly designed to find adoptive placements for healthy babies have changed and developed into family finding services for some of the most disadvantaged children in Scotland'.

18 Fortunately, individuals and couples who are experiencing difficulty in having children now have a greater range of options open to them through assisted reproduction – see chapter 4, paras 28–73.

19 Registrar General Scotland, Annual Report 1995, Table 9.1 was the most recent to give the figures back to 1930. Given the novelty of the concept, it is not surprising that there were only three adoptions that year.

20 See Registrar General Scotland, Annual Report 1997 (hereinafter, the 'Annual Report 1997') (General Register Office for Scotland, 1998), p 140, Table 9.1.

21 Annual Report 1997, Table 9.2.

22 See para 8.89, below.

and his or her birth family and the whole notion of 'open adoption'.[23] Traditionally, Scotland operated a system of 'closed adoption', whereby there was no such continued contact. However, in some cases, continued contact may be beneficial to the child and how this can be done is discussed below.[24]

The purpose of modern adoption: the child's welfare throughout his or her life

8.7 Before we examine how adoption operates and the procedure involved, it is important to be quite clear about the purpose of modern adoption. While it may bring benefits to the various adults involved, adoption exists to serve the needs of children. The birth parents may gain by knowing that they have enabled their child to live in a secure family environment that they were unable to offer.[25] Some childless individuals or couples will be given the opportunity to become parents. A step-parent may be given full legal recognition of the role he or she has been playing in the child's life, prior to the adoption. Ideally, adoption should bring benefits to all concerned. However, we must not lose sight of the fact that the child's welfare is the overriding concern in adoption. The 1978 Act, as amended, is quite unambiguous on this point. Section 6(1) provides that

'... in reaching any decision relating to the adoption of a child, the court or adoption agency shall have regard to all the circumstances but –
(a) shall regard the need to safeguard and promote the welfare of the child throughout his [or her] life as the paramount consideration'.[26]

The Children (Scotland) Act 1995 ('the 1995 Act') made substantial amendments to s 6(1) of the 1978 Act. These amendments are not simply of historical interest, since they ensure greater compliance with the UN Convention on the Rights of the Child ('the UN Convention') and, thus, evidence the legislature's desire to meet our international obligations under that instrument.[27] In addition, certain caution should be exercised before placing reliance on older decisions under the pre-amendment legislation. The first change to note brings us back to a variant on the old debate surrounding 'primacy' and 'paramountcy' of welfare since, in the past, s 6 provided that the child's welfare was the 'first consideration' in adoption decisions.[28] Despite the fact that the UN Convention uses the

---

23 See Inter-Departmental Review of Adoption Law, Discussion Paper No 1: The Nature and Effects of Adoption (Scottish Office, 1990); and Triseliotis *et al*, n 15 above.
24 See paras 8.74–8.77.
25 As we shall see, not all birth parents are happy for an adoption to go ahead. In certain circumstances, the court may dispense with the birth parents' agreement – see paras 8.45–8.55, below.
26 The words in square brackets have been added to achieve a non-sexist formulation.
27 For an excellent discussion of the Scots law on adoption, the changes introduced by the 1995 Act, and the UN Convention – see J. M. Scott, 'Adoption' in Cleland and Sutherland *Children's Rights in Scotland* (W. Green, 1996).
28 For discussion of how this phrase was interpreted – see *P v Lothian Regional Council* 1989 SLT 739; *L v Central Regional Council* 1990 SLT 818; *Lothian Regional Council v A* 1992 SLT 858; Wilkinson and Norrie, *Parent and Child*, at pp 550–553.

phrase '*a primary* consideration' in other respects, when it deals with adoption, it makes the child's welfare '*a paramount* consideration'.[29] Semantics aside, by making the child's welfare '*the* paramount consideration', Scots law at least meets the UN Convention's standard. In addition, it achieves internal consistency when other legislation affecting children is considered.[30] As we shall see presently, there are various different stages in the adoption process and s 6(1) makes clear that the child's welfare is the paramount consideration at all stages of that process.

8.8 A second innovation, introduced by the 1995 Act is the direction to the adoption agency and the court to consider the child's welfare *throughout the adopted person's life*, and not simply *during childhood*, as was the case in the past. Again, this is consistent with the UN Convention and acknowledges the profound and lifelong importance of adoption.[31]

8.9 Given the paramountcy of the child's welfare in adoption decisions, it follows that an adoption order may be granted despite the fact that it may have adverse effects on others. In *Osborne* v *Matthan (No 2)*,[32] the fact that a decision relating to the residence rights of one child in the family may have an adverse effect on another child in that family will not prevent the court from making an order when it is considering the first child's welfare. By analogy, it can be assumed that, where adoption will best serve the welfare of the first child, the fact that it may cause distress to a second child will not prevent the adoption from going ahead.

8.10 As we shall see, the court has the power, in certain circumstances, to dispense with parental consent to adoption and, clearly, a parent whose child has been adopted against his or her wishes will often suffer considerable distress as a result of the decision. None the less, the child's welfare must prevail. A particularly graphic example of this principle in operation can be found in *Angus Council Social Work Department, Petitioner*,[33] a case which takes account of the amendments made to the 1978 Act by the 1995 Act. There, the adoption agency applied for an order freeing H, a five-year-old girl, for adoption in the face of opposition from her mother. 'Tragic' may be a much over-used term, but it applied, in its fullest sense, to the mother in this case. She had a long history of personality disorders, self-mutilation, suicide attempts and psychiatric care, probably connected to

---

29 Article 21.
30 Courts and children's hearings are directed to regard the child's welfare as the paramount consideration when making decisions about a child in other contexts – 1995 Act, ss 11(7)(a) and 16(1).
31 For an excellent discussion of the importance of adoption and of what it can offer to children, see Triseliotis *et al*, n 15 above, chapters 1–3.
32 1998 SC 682. Of course, any existing relationship between children is a part of assessing each child's welfare and involves striking a delicate balance between recognising that relationship and seeing each child as an individual. This point is clearly appreciated in the Scottish Office Guidance when it provides: 'The needs of each child in a family group and the quality of the relationship between them should be assessed. The effect of past experience needs to be taken into account': *Scotland's Children: The Children (Scotland) Act 1995 Regulations and Guidance*, vol 3, *Adoption and Parental Responsibilities Orders*, para 12.
33 1998 GWD 23-1148.

her own disturbed childhood. After her daughter was born, she gave birth to another child prematurely and he died the following day. The effect of the mother's problems was that she was frequently unable to provide H with adequate care and, as a result, H had spent large portions of her life being looked after by others, either on a formal or informal basis. While the mother had maintained contact, her visits often disturbed H and, on occasions, she had used contact as an opportunity to abduct the child. The adoption agency was confident of finding suitable adopters for H and expert opinion from social workers and child psychologists supported her being settled in a new environment as quickly as possible and, preferably, before she started school. In a considered and detailed judgment, Lord Penrose explained his decision to grant the order freeing the child for adoption and making no provision for continued contact with the child's mother. He was aware that the decision might have an adverse effect on the mother's fragile mental health, but the overwhelming evidence supporting adoption as the only course of action which would serve H's welfare left him no alternative.

Assessing welfare

8.11 As we have seen in the context of residence and contact, assessing what will serve a particular child's welfare is a matter fraught with difficulty and, often, differences of opinion. Just as each question of residence or contact is unique, so too is each stage of deciding whether adoption by the prospective adopter or adopters is the best option for a particular child. Having directed the adoption agency and the court to regard the child's welfare as the paramount consideration, s 6(1) of the 1978 Act goes on to provide that the agency and the court

'(b) shall have regard so far as practicable –
(i) to his [or her] views (if he [or she] wishes to express them) taking account of his [or her] age and maturity, and
(ii) to his [or her] religious persuasion, racial origin and cultural and linguistic background'.[34]

Again, this statutory provision warrants closer examination. Unlike the requirement to regard the child's welfare as paramount, regard is to be had to the factors in s 6(1)(b) only 'so far as practicable'. As we shall see, while there may be good reason to disregard these factors on occasions, courts have sometimes interpreted the phrase in a way that affords them questionable latitude.

8.12 The requirement to have regard to any views the child wishes to express, in the light of the child's age and maturity, is nothing new in the context of adoption. However, the statutory presumption, expressed in s 6(2), that a child of 12 years of age or more shall be sufficiently mature to form a view is another innovation of the 1995 Act and is consistent with other provisions of that statute. What is unfortunate is that nothing was done, by way of amendment, to clarify the position with regard to the information available to the child when he or she expressed or, indeed,

---

34 Words in square brackets added.

refrained from expressing, a view. The problem was highlighted by the decision *C, Petitioners*,[35] which concerned the adoption of a six-year old boy, C. The applicants were his mother and her husband, who was not C's father.[36] C's mother and the male applicant had had a relationship prior to his conception and had married two weeks after his birth. In the meantime, C's mother had a brief relationship with C's father but had not seen him since she was two months pregnant and had no contact with him. C believed that both of the applicants were his birth parents and they had no intention of ever telling him the truth. The social work department felt unable to provide the report required by the Act because it believed that the applicants' refusal to disclose the true facts to C made it impossible to ascertain his wishes and feelings. The court appointed a reporting officer and curator *ad litem* who duly submitted a report dealing with the family circumstances and the applicants' reasons for not wishing to disclose the truth to the child. Granting the adoption order, the court found that it was not practicable to ascertain the wishes and feelings of the child. To grant an order in such circumstances is a regrettable reflection on taking the views of children seriously. To say that it is 'not practicable' to ascertain a child's views, simply because adults with an interest choose to deceive the child, is to misunderstand the statutory provision. These words are intended to cover cases where the child is too young to form or express a view. While it may be regarded as either trite or naive to say so, courts are about trying to get at the truth and should not become parties to deception, however good the motive. Nor was the court without another avenue in this case. As we shall see, courts may refuse the adoption order but still recognise a step-parent's role in the child's life by granting him or her parental responsibilities and rights. That, it is submitted, is the correct course for any court faced with this sort of case. If the applicant and his or her spouse do not feel that this is adequate, the solution is in their hands. They can always tell the child the truth – a truth that he or she will inevitably discover later when access to birth records becomes possible.[37]

8.13 The requirement to take account of the child's views must be read along with the Age of Legal Capacity (Scotland) Act 1991, which gives a child of 12 years old and over the right to veto or consent to his or her own adoption.[38] A parent's consent to the adoption of his or her child can be dispensed with in a number of circumstances, including the fact that parental consent is being withheld unreasonably.[39] The consent of a child

35 1993 SLT (Sh Ct) 8. A similar case arose in England in *Re S (A Minor) (Adoption)* [1988] 1 FLR 418, where the court participated in deceiving a 13 year-old girl as to the truth about her maternity. For a discussion of these cases and other problems in ascertaining the child's views in adoption, see E. E. Sutherland, 'Adoption: The Child's View' 1994 SLT (News) 37.
36 Until the law was amended by the Children (Scotland) Act 1995, the only way for a step-parent to adopt a child was by applying to adopt jointly with the birth parent. This absurd and offensive procedure and the newer approach to step-parent adoption are discussed in paras 8.31–8.32, below.
37 On reaching the age of 16 (formerly 17), an adopted person is entitled to access to his or her birth records – Adoption (Scotland) Act 1978, s 45(5).
38 Section 2(3). See also, 1978 Act, s 12(8) (adoption orders) and s 18(8) (freeing orders).
39 1978 Act, s 16(2)(b) (adoption orders) and s 18(1)(b) (freeing orders).

aged 12 or over is not subject to any such 'reasonableness test' and the court has no power to dispense with the consent of a competent child. However, where the court is satisfied that the child is 'incapable of giving consent to the order' it may dispense with that consent.[40]

8.14 The 1978 Act now requires the adoption agency and the court to have regard to *the child's* 'religious persuasion, racial origins and cultural and linguistic background'.[41] Formerly, it was only the wishes of the child's *parents or guardians* as to the child's religious upbringing to which the adoption agency was required to have regard and this continues to be a relevant consideration.[42] The new, and additional, provision is significantly different. Firstly, it is child-centred rather than parent-centred and the practical effect of this may be considerable. For example, while parents may have had strong views about the religious upbringing of a baby, that baby can hardly be described as having had the opportunity to form a 'religious persuasion'. Secondly, the provision gives effect to the UN Convention on the Rights of the Child which requires states to respect the child's right to preserve his or her identity.[43]

8.15 Thirdly, the factors about the child which are to be considered are a great deal wider than simply religion. There has been much debate about the importance of placing children with adopters from the same ethnic and cultural group as the child and, clearly, transracial adoption raises the question of ethnic identity.[44] The issue of transracial adoption first came to the fore, in the USA, over the adoption of Native-American children by persons who did not share their ethnic background and led to the passing of the Indian Child Welfare Act in 1978.[45] The focus of attention in the USA has now shifted to the adoption of African-American and Hispanic-American children by ethnically different adopters, and opinion on the wisdom or otherwise of such a course of action is strongly divided.[46]

---

40 1978 Act, s 12(8) (adoption orders) and s 18(8) (freeing orders).
41 Section 95 of the Children (Scotland) Act 1995, inserting new s 6 of 1978 Act.
42 Adoption (Scotland) Act 1978, s 7.
43 Article 8. 'Identity' is stated to include nationality, name and family relations, but is not confined to these elements. Obviously many adoptions will not preserve the child's original family relations but this is permitted by Article 21.
44 The term 'transracial' is being used to denote adoption where the adopter and adoptee belong to different ethnic groups but are nationals of the same country. Definition here is not without its problems, since bi-racial children seem to be treated by most commentators as belonging to the minority group to which they are connected. The reason for this appears to be that belonging to a minority group is what may occasion disadvantage. However, to ignore any part of a child's identity poses problems and is not in line with the UN Convention. 'Inter-country' adoptions will often be 'transracial' but they present additional issues and international adoption is considered below at paras 8.89–8.91.
45 The adoption of Native American children is subject to a system which differs from that applying to all other American children. Despite possible constitutional objections to such different treatment of a particular group, the US Supreme Court upheld the Act in *Mississippi Band of Choctaw Indians* v *Holyfield* 490 US 30 (1989).
46 For a broad range of opinion, see the papers delivered at the Symposium on Transracial Adoption, published in 6 B U Pub Int L J (1997). For differing views, see H. Fogg-Davis, 'A Race-Conscious Argument for Transracial Adoption' 6 B U Pub Int L J 385 (1997) and R-A. W. Howe, 'Transracial Adoption: Old Prejudices and Discrimination Float Under A New Halo' 6 B U Pub Int L J 409 (1997).

Transracial adoption has occasioned less comment in Scotland, probably because it occurs less frequently.[47] However, Parliament was sensitive to the issue when it amended the Adoption (Scotland) Act 1978 to provide that both the adoption agency and the court are required to have regard, where practicable, to the child's religious persuasion, racial origin and cultural and linguistic background.[48] However, racial and ethnic matching is not mandated. If it were, the result might be that children for whom an appropriate 'match' could not be found would remain in foster care, rather than being adopted by people who were suitable on the basis of all other criteria. Ultimately, therefore, the test must be the child's welfare overall, without adherence to absolute rules on racial or ethnic matching and that is what the provision in the 1978 Act seeks to achieve. Certainly, the First Division concluded in one case that, while the child's ethnic background differed from that of the applicant for a residence order, the difference was not fatal to the application.[49] While obtaining a residence order is a less radical step than granting an adoption order, similar reasoning might be applied to adoption cases.

8.16 Thus, beyond the limited guidance the court is given in assessing welfare, it is left to approach each case on the basis of its own particular facts and circumstances. That this should be the approach reinforces the fact that each child is an individual with particular needs and that a suitable adopter or adopters should be found for that child. In *T, Petitioner*[50] the Inner House took the opportunity to stress that there were no rules about who might adopt and what would serve the child's welfare beyond those laid down by statute.[51] In particular, it sought to dispel some of the myths surrounding homosexual parenting. It appears, then, that the trend in Scotland is to reject any kind of blanket assumptions: a trend which can only be welcomed by older individuals and couples and those who do not fit within the strict parameters of traditional relationships.

8.17 Given the importance of the decision in *T, Petitioner*, not least because it demonstrates a real willingness by the court to consider a broad range of evidence, it merits examination in some detail. It concerned an application by a single man to adopt a five-year-old boy whom he had looked after for the previous 18 months. The child had a number of special needs, being profoundly deaf, unable to walk unaided, and sight-impaired. He had been born in England, had never lived with his mother, and his

---

47 For a discussion of transracial adoption in the UK context, see Triseliotis *et al*, n 15 above, chapter 8.

48 1978 Act, s 6(1)(b)(ii).

49 *Osborne* v *Matthan (No 2)* 1998 SC 682.

50 1996 SCLR 897, discussed in: K. McK. Norrie, 'Parental Pride: Adoption and the Gay Man' 1996 SLT (News) 321 and E. E. Sutherland, 'Another Unfounded Assumption Laid to Rest?' 1997 JR 373. *T, Petitioner* was considered in England in *Re W (A Minor) (Adoption: Homosexual Adopter)* [1997] 3 All ER 620, where the court concluded that there was no prohibition on the adoption of a child by a 49-year-old lesbian who planned to raise the child in family with her long-term partner.

51 However, the 1978 Act lays down a host of precise rules about who may and may not adopt. See paras 8.26–8.33, below.

father was unknown. The local authority responsible for his care sought a permanent home for the boy but, because of his special needs, experienced considerable difficulties. Eventually he was placed with Mr T, a nurse who subsequently gave up his job to look after the child. It was in this setting that Mr T applied to adopt the boy. Mr T, who was living in a stable homosexual relationship of some ten years standing with a partner who was in full-time employment, made it clear that it was his intention that they should raise the child together. The various reports from social workers and the reporting officers appointed by the court were consistent in affirming that the boy was happy with the couple, well cared for by them and, indeed, that Mr T was particularly suited to meet his special needs. The Lord Ordinary refused to grant the adoption petition, in part[52] because he felt there was a fundamental question of principle, due to the fact that the applicant proposed to raise the child in a homosexual relationship. On appeal, that decision was unanimously overturned by the Inner House. Lord President Hope made the forthright observation that he did not see this case as raising a matter of fundamental principle.[53] He rightly pointed out that, under the statute as it applied at the time, first consideration had to be given to safeguarding and promoting the welfare of the child throughout his childhood[54] and that, in order to assess what would be conducive to that, all the circumstances of the case had to be considered. While the applicant's sexual orientation and his intention to raise the child in a homosexual relationship were relevant circumstances, they should not prevail over the many other circumstances present in the case. He noted that neither the existing legislation nor the European Convention on the Adoption of Children prohibited adoption by a person who was cohabiting, whether in a heterosexual or homosexual relationship, nor had any attempt been made to introduce such a restriction when the Children (Scotland) Act 1995 was passed.[55] Demonstrating a welcome openness of mind, Lord Hope considered research studies[56] on the effect on a child of living in a homosexual relationship and concluded that '[t]here is a sharp difference between attitudes which are informed by preconceptions about homosexuality on the one hand and the results of a study of the systematic evidence on the other'.[57] The courts have not always shown themselves to be open to

---

52 The Lord Ordinary was also concerned about the failure of the child's mother to participate in the proceedings, albeit numerous attempts had been made to contact her. This point is discussed at para 8.55, below.

53 1996 SCLR 897, at p 907E.

54 The Children (Scotland) Act 1995, s 95 amended s 6(1)(a) the Adoption (Scotland) Act 1978 to provide that the child's welfare *throughout his or her life* is the *paramount consideration*.

55 In the course of the extensive consultation which preceded the Children (Scotland) Act 1995, views were sought on homosexual adoption and no recommendations to amend the law were made.

56 1996 SCLR 897, at p 912F–913D. In particular, he considered expert evidence led in *B v B (Minors) (Custody, Care and Control)* [1991] 1 FLR 402 and the, very considerable, research evidence provided in the leading Canadian case, *Re K and B* [1995] 125 DLR 4th 653.

57 1996 SCLR 897, at p 913D.

accepting the diversity of human relationships,[58] but this decision, at least, is a step in the right direction.

The third of the overarching principles: presumed non-intervention

8.18 As we have seen, in the context of child law, the paramountcy of welfare is one of the three overarching principles governing decision-making; the others being the child's right to participate in the decision-making process and the presumption of non-intervention. We have explored the way in which statutory recognition is given to the place of the child in the decision-making process. On the one hand, we have seen that courts are sometimes prepared to place a very singular interpretation on what it means to take a child's views into account. On the other hand, a child aged 12 or over is given considerably more control over decision-making in the context of adoption. What then, of presumed non-intervention?

8.19 The principle receives recognition in two distinct ways. First, a new s 6A has been added to the 1978 Act, which places an obligation on adoption agencies to consider whether adoption is the best way to meet the needs of the child or whether 'there is some better, practicable, alternative'. The agency is required to address this issue 'before making any arrangements for the adoption of a child' and, if a better alternative presents itself, not to make any adoption arrangements.[59] Arguably, this is not a presumption of non-intervention but it is very close in creating a positive duty to consider the other options available. Second, the court is directed not to make an adoption order, or an order freeing a child for adoption, 'unless it considers that it would be better for the child that it should do so than that it should not'.[60] It may be that this requirement adds little beyond a certain statutory tidiness, in demonstrating that all three of the overarching principles are being observed in the context of adoption in the same way as they are observed elsewhere. Its practical significance would appear to be minimal, since the requirement to regard the child's welfare as the paramount consideration achieves the same result.

Adoption and the child's sense of identity

8.20 Precisely which factors contribute to an individual's sense of identity, and how that identity develops over time, are complex and controversial

---

58 See for example, *Early* v *Early* 1990 SLT 221, where custody of a nine-year-old boy was granted to his father, who had convictions for child neglect, rather than his lesbian mother with whom he had always lived.

59 In *Angus Council Social Work Department, Petitioner*, n 33 above, Lord Penrose was at pains to note that the adoption agency had explored other options before taking the decision to look for prospective adopters for the child and, in his judgment, explains why such possibilities as care of the child by other relatives and long-term foster care would not be the appropriate solution in that case. He also noted that 'the child has a remarkably mature insight into her present position and future .... She has expressed a wish to have a new mother and father'.

60 1978 Act, s 24(3).

questions.[61] However, we can get a sense of some of the factors which are regarded as relevant, in the legal context, and believed capable of legal regulation, from the provisions of the UN Convention on the Rights of the Child. It recognises the child's right to a name,[62] nationality[63] and identity,[64] along with the right of the child not to be separated from the family except in limited circumstances[65] and to family reunification.[66] As Bissett-Johnson notes, '[t]hese conveniently tie in with the European Convention's right to respect for family life, save for such interventions by the state as are necessary in a democratic society'.[67] Given the very dramatic legal impact of adoption, in its simplest form, it might be argued that adoption runs counter to many of these rights.[68] However, societies around the world accept that adoption, or a similar concept, may best provide a secure family environment for a child. Indeed, the UN Convention recognises the possibility of adoption[69] and the European Convention on the Adoption of Children is devoted to the concept.

8.21 What, then, does Scots law do to foster the child's sense of identity in the context of adoption? As we shall see presently, the whole process of adoption is highly regulated, with attention being paid to such matters as the selection of prospective adopters for a particular child and placement arrangements. There are a host of possibilities, ranging from the simple passing of information and photographs to direct contact, which can enable a child to keep in touch with members of his or her birth family. The issue of transracial adoption is one which raises the issue of the child's ethnic identity and, while the legislation takes account of the issue, no hard and fast rules are applied in this respect. Once the adopted person reaches the age of 16, he or she is entitled to access to his or her adoption records.[70] An adopted person who indicates that he or she wishes to exercise this right must be advised that counselling is available,[71] although accepting

---

61 This is a recurring theme in Triseliotis, *et al*, n 15 above. See also J. Goldstein, A. J. Solnit and A. Freud, *Beyond the Best Interests of the Child* (1st edn, 1973, revised edn, 1979, Free Press); Triseliotis, *In Search of Origins* (Routledge and Kegan Paul, 1973); and J. M. Masson and C. Harrison, 'Identity: Mapping the Frontiers' in N. V. Lowe and G. Douglas (eds), *Families Across Frontiers* (Martinus Nijhoff, 1996).
62 Article 7.
63 Articles 7 and 8.
64 Article 8.
65 Article 9.
66 Article 10.
67 A. Bissett-Johnson, 'Name, Nationality and Identity' in Cleland and Sutherland, n 27 above, at p 37. Professor Bissett-Johnson's chapter provides an excellent discussion of the extent to which Scots law meets the standards set in both the UN Convention and the European Convention on Human Rights in respect of name, nationality and identity.
68 See the decision of the European Commission on Human Rights in *Soderback* v *Sweden* 33124/96, 22 October 1997, where the Commission found a violation of an unmarried father's rights under art 8 of the European Convention on Human Rights.
69 Article 21.
70 1978 Act, s 45(5). The age at which a person can gain access to his or her own adoption records was reduced from 17 to 16 by the Children (Scotland) Act 1995, Sched 2, para 22.
71 1978 Act, s 45(6). Local authorities and approved adoption societies are obliged to provide counselling – s 45(6A) and (6B).

counselling is not a prerequisite of access to the records. Given that sensitive information may be disclosed by the original records and that some adopted people take the matter further by attempting to trace birth relatives, it is probably advisable to take up the offer of counselling.

Adoption and money

8.22 In one sense, adoption is not wholly divorced from the issue of money. Sometimes a mother's decision to place her baby for adoption will be prompted, at least in part, by poverty. She may believe her economic circumstances are such that the baby would have a better future with other, more affluent, parents. Sometimes, the parents' inability to continue to look after a child will be part of a general picture of economic and social deprivation. Of course, adoption agencies make no guarantees about the wealth of prospective adopters, but it can be expected that they will be able to provide the basic material comforts, at the very least. It is no secret that children being looked after by the local authority are a great deal more likely to come from economically deprived backgrounds than from comfortable middle-class homes. Some of these children will be placed for adoption. None of this is intended to suggest that poverty precludes good parenting. It is simply a recognition that poverty may contribute to children being placed for adoption. Nor should it be assumed that the most affluent parents will be selected automatically as prospective adopters. Certainly, the fact that prospective adopters can offer a child more, in material terms, than can the child's parents, is not the basis on which adoption decisions proceed.[72] As we shall see, adoption agencies are required to operate under strict guidelines and wealth is not a criterion in assessing the suitability of prospective adopters. In an article published in 1979, two academics applied a strict economic analysis to adoption.[73] They took the view that, since there was already a black market in adoption, it might be preferable to have open and regulated transactions. Such was the force and, on

---

72 In *Re M (A Minor) (Adoption or Residence Order)* [1998] 1 FLR 570, the disparity between what the mother, who had a history of troubled relationships and problems with alcohol and drugs, and the prospective adopters, two comfortable, married academics, who had provided an eight-year-old girl with stability, security and support in her personal and intellectual development, was clear. The mother's appeal against the adoption order, made by the county court, was successful and a residence order was made, requiring the child to live with the couple who had applied to adopt her. This case is interesting in a number of respects. It appears that the child herself expressed some opposition to the adoption. In addition, the prospective adopters indicated that, if the adoption did not go ahead, they would no longer be able to offer the child a home.

73 E. Landes and R. A. Posner, 'The Economics of the Baby Shortage' 7 J Legal Studies 323 (1978). To put the article in perspective, the authors were probably engaging in the kind of intellectual game that is admired only by others who engage in the same amusing, but unproductive, sport. Some ten years later, by which time Professor Posner had been appointed to the US Court of Appeals for the Seventh Circuit, he affirmed his position in another article; R. A. Posner, 'Regulation of the Market in Adoptions' 67 B U L Rev 59 (1987). The second article opens with the rather sad claim to fame, 'Whenever critics of the law-and-economics movement want an example of its excesses they point to what is popularly known as the "baby selling article" which Dr. Elisabeth Landes and I wrote almost a decade ago'.

occasions, virulence, of the responses,[74] that it became clear, beyond a shadow of doubt, that the overwhelming majority of writers on the subject rejected this approach to adoption.

8.23 'Baby selling' is simply not permitted under the 1978 Act which provides

'[I]t shall not be lawful to make or give to any person any payment or reward for or in consideration of –
(a) the adoption by that person of a child;
(b) the grant by that person of any agreement or consent required in connection with the adoption of a child;
(c) the transfer by that person of the care and possession of a child with a view to the adoption of the child; or
(d) the making by that person of any arrangements for the adoption of a child'.[75]

8.24 However, there are a number of circumstances in which the payment of money in the adoption setting is permitted. Payment to an adoption agency in respect of expenses reasonably incurred, including expenses in respect of foreign adoption, is permitted.[76] In certain circumstances, a local authority or an adoption society may make payments to adopters or prospective adopters under the Adoption Allowances Schemes.[77] The Schemes are subject to extensive regulation by the Secretary of State.[78] In other cases, while the payment or receipt of money in connection with adoption may be an offence and may attract criminal penalties,[79] it will not necessarily invalidate the adoption.[80]

THE PARTIES INVOLVED IN ADOPTION

Who may be adopted?

8.25 Since the concept of adoption is used, in Scotland, to provide for the welfare of children, only children may be adopted here.[81] Any person under the age of 18 who has never been married may be adopted,[82] and an

---

74 Many articles have been written in response. One of the most considered is: J. R. S. Prichard, 'A Market for Babies?' 34 U Toronto L J 341. It is hardly surprising that the very idea of selling children generated a degree of passion; see M. G. Kelman, 'Consumption Theory, Production Theory and the Ideology of the Coase Theorem' 52 S Cal L Rev 669.
75 1978 Act, s 51(1).
76 1978 Act, s 51(3) and (4).
77 1978 Act, ss 51(5), 51A and 51B.
78 See: the Adoption Allowance (Scotland) Regulations 1996 SI 1996 No 3257; The Adoption Allowance Schemes Direction 1996; and *Scotland's Children: The Children (Scotland) Act 1995 Regulations and Guidance*, vol 3, *Adoption and Parental Responsibilities Orders*, pp 30–38.
79 1978 Act, s 51(2).
80 See *C v S* 1996 SLT 1387, which explores the effect of the prohibition on payment under the Adoption (Scotland) Act 1978 and the Human Fertilisation and Embryology Act 1990, with curious results. The case is discussed in chapter 4, para 59.
81 In the USA, the concept has been used, with mixed success, as a mechanism by which adult homosexuals might gain some recognition of their relationship. For a discussion of this application of adoption, see chapter 10, para 3.
82 1978 Act, s 12(1) and (5).

adopted child may be the subject of a subsequent adoption order.[83] Provided that the proceedings began before the child's 18th birthday, the petition can be granted after he or she reaches 18.[84] As we have seen, a competent child of 12 or over must consent before he or she can be adopted[85] and the adoption agency and the court must take account of any views that younger children wish to express.[86]

Who may adopt?

8.26 Despite the court's recent openness in refusing to accept some unfounded assumptions about the suitability or otherwise of categories of individuals as adopters, the 1978 Act provides a precise and detailed set of rules on who may adopt. It is premised on the notion of married (by definition heterosexual) couples as adopters, albeit single people are permitted to adopt. We have seen that there is a special, expedited procedure which can be used in some surrogacy cases. The Children (Scotland) Act 1995 amended the 1978 Act and greatly improved the mechanism and thereby, the conceptual framework for step-parent adoptions. Before we return to these special cases, let us consider the more general provisions governing who may adopt a child.

The general requirements for applicants

8.27 Where two people apply to adopt a child together, they must be married to each other and each must be at least 21 years old,[87] unless one of the applicants is the child's parent, in which case it is sufficient that he or she is 18 or over.[88] One party must be domiciled in a part of the UK, the Channel Islands or the Isle of Man[89] or the couple must have been resident in one of these places for at least a year immediately prior to their application.[90] The requirement of domicile or residence does not apply to Convention adoptions.[91]

8.28 Aside from the case of a birth parent adopting his or her own child, which we will consider presently, one person alone may make an adoption

---

83 1978 Act, s 12(7).
84 1978 Act, s 12(1). Prior to the amendment of the 1978 Act, by the 1995 Act, Sched 2, para 7, the adoption petition had to be granted before the person to be adopted reached the age of 18. The fear that the whole process might be rushed, in such circumstances, has been removed by this amendment.
85 1978 Act, ss 12(8) and 18(8). The court may dispense with the consent of a child where it is satisfied that the child is incapable of giving consent.
86 1978 Act, s 6(1)(b)(i).
87 1978 Act, ss 14(1) and (1A).
88 1978 Act, ss 14(1) and (1B). The new procedure for step-parent adoption, introduced by the Children (Scotland) Act 1995, has removed the need for the birth parent to whom the step-parent is married to adopt the child at all and is discussed in paras 8.31–8.32, below. None the less, the old procedure remains competent.
89 1978 Act, s 14(2)(a).
90 1978 Act, s 14(2)(c).
91 1978 Act, s 14(2)(b). 'Convention adoption order' means an adoption order made in accordance with s 17(1), and 'the Convention' means the Hague Convention on Jurisdiction, Applicable Law and Recognition of Decrees Relating to Adoptions – 1978 Act, s 65(1). See paras 8.90–8.91, below.

application and, again, he or she must satisfy the requirements as to age[92] and domicile or residence.[93] A sole applicant for adoption must satisfy the court either, that he or she is unmarried,[94] or if married, that (i) his or her spouse cannot be found, or (ii) that the couple have separated and are living apart with the likelihood that the separation will be permanent, or (iii) that his or her spouse is incapable, by reason of ill-health (whether physical or mental) of making an application for an adoption order.[95]

8.29 The requirement that two people adopting together must be married to each other, precludes cohabiting heterosexual and homosexual or lesbian couples from adopting a child. In the case of heterosexual couples, the only argument which might be made to preclude them from adoption is that, somehow, cohabitation outside marriage is an indicator of instability in the relationship and such instability does not create the optimum environment in which to raise a child. In any event, supporters of the existing law might argue that the remedy is there for the couple: they can simply marry. Since marriage is certainly no indicator of stability in a relationship, the time has come to challenge any presumption of instability which may attach to cohabitation. When we turn to consider lesbian and homosexual couples, the option of marriage is absent.[96] Thus, however stable the relationship, the law will not permit a joint adoption by the couple. As we have seen, it is only under the provision permitting adoption by a single person, that homosexual and lesbian couples can enter the adoption picture at all. In two recent cases,[97] one in Scotland, the other in England, each court noted, not only the fact that the applicant was living with a same-sex partner, but the stability and duration of the relationship. We must conclude that the stable relationship and, at least to some extent, the partner, were viewed positively by the court. Why then, should the partner not be recognised as having a legal relationship with the child? Of course, he or she could apply for parental responsibilities and rights[98] assuming, of course, that the couple had sufficient resources to fund the application. Again, why make people jump through legal hoops when a more reasonable approach to who may adopt would be a simpler solution?[99]

Adoption by birth parent alone

8.30 While it was seen as a way to avoid the stigma of illegitimacy in the past, there is little reason for a birth parent to adopt his or her own child today. However, very occasionally, there may be cases where, due to the

---

92 1978 Act, s 15(1).
93 1978 Act, s 15(2).
94 1978 Act, s 15(1)(a).
95 1978 Act, s 15(1)(b).
96 A purported marriage between persons of the same sex is void – Marriage (Scotland) Act 1977, s 5(4)(e). See chapter 10, para 72.
97 *T, Petitioner* 1996 SCLR 897 and *Re W (A Minor) (Adoption: Homosexual Adopter)* [1997] 3 All ER 620.
98 Children (Scotland) Act 1995, s 11. See chapter 5 for a discussion of applications for parental responsibilities and rights.
99 See J. F. Davies, 'Two Moms and a Baby: Protecting the Nontraditional Family Through Second Parent Adoptions' 29 New Eng L Rev 1055 (1995).

particular provisions of a trust or a will, some benefit will accrue (usually to the child) from such an adoption. In any event, a birth parent may adopt his or her own child provided that:[100] (i) the other parent is dead or cannot be found, or (ii) by virtue of the Human Fertilisation and Embryology Act 1990, s 28, there is no other parent,[101] or (iii) there is some other reason justifying the exclusion of that other parent.[102] It is difficult to imagine a case where the third of these conditions would be satisfied. Taking an extreme case of the rapist-father and assuming that he was not also married to the child's mother, he would have no parental responsibilities or rights automatically. Since the mother presumably would not consent to his being given responsibilities or rights he would have to apply to a court for them and his application would almost certainly be unsuccessful. Thus, the mother could ensure that he had no part in the child's life. It is not clear what she would gain by having all legal recognition of him eradicated by adopting her child. Indeed, all that would be achieved would be to terminate any right the child might have in respect of aliment or succession and, since the court is required to give paramount consideration to the child's welfare throughout his or her life in adoption decisions, this might be fatal to her case. Even in the context of child support, this would be one of the cases where the Child Support Agency could be expected to exercise discretion in ignoring the father.

Step-parent adoption

8.31 One effect of the increase in the divorce rate is that there are more parents who are in a position to remarry and many do. These marriages create step-families. As we have seen, many children are born to unmarried women. While a number of them will be living with the child's father and, indeed, may go on to marry him, others will not. However, the mother may marry someone else and, if she does, a step-family is created. Step-families, like birth-families, are enormously varied but, in a practical sense, many step-parents become 'parents' to their step-children. In some families, everyone is happy with the *de facto* situation and do not seek legal recognition of the step-parent's role. However, the only mechanism by which a step-parent and step-child can establish a full legal child-parent relationship, with the attendant consequences for such matters as succession, is through adoption. Prior to the Children (Scotland) Act 1995, the only way in which such adoptions could be effected was by the step-parent and the birth parent to whom he or she was married applying to adopt the child together. The absurdity about the whole procedure was that the birth parent had to adopt his or her own child, a situation which many birth parents found distressing and offensive. As step-parent adoption became

---

100 1978 Act, s 15(3).

101 Virgin births and cloning aside, there will always be another biological parent. It is interesting that the Act uses the word 'parent' here when s 28 of the 1990 Act deals solely with paternity. What is being addressed here is the situation where a woman has had a child using one of the assisted reproductive techniques and the legal system does not recognise any man as the child's father – see chapter 4, paras 28–73.

102 Where the court concludes that there is good reason justifying the exclusion of the other parent and grants the adoption order, it must record its reason– 1978 Act, s 15(3)(b).

more common,[103] it was apparent that something had to be done to bring the law into line with common sense. The 1995 Act[104] introduced a new procedure whereby it is only the step-parent who has to apply to adopt.[105] The parent to whom the step-parent is married retains his or her original status, with all the parental responsibilities that he or she had prior to the adoption.[106]

8.32 A difficulty with step-parent adoptions has always been that, once the adoption takes place, it severs the child's legal link with the 'other' birth parent, ie the birth parent who is not married to the step-parent.[107] For this reason, s 53 of the Children Act 1975 provided that, when a court was considering an application for adoption, it could simply give parental rights to the step-parent instead. This acknowledged the step-parent's position as a significant person in the child's life, without severing the child's link with the other birth parent. Section 53 was repealed by the Children Act 1995,[108] since the same result is achieved through the court's general obligation to consider whether making the adoption order would be better than not making it.[109] Thus, when a step-parent seeks an adoption order, the court may, instead, make a residence order or it may make no order at all.[110] In addition, it will be remembered that the adoption agency is directed to consider whether an alternative to adoption would better serve the welfare of the child.[111] Where the 'other' parent is opposed to the step-parent's adoption of a child, the court may dispense with the parent's consent, but it will not do so lightly.[112]

Adoption by other relatives

8.33 Adoption by other relatives is comparatively rare[113] and, often, where the relative looking after the child would like the matter to be regulated in a formal legal sense, a residence order will suffice. Where a relative does apply to adopt a child, the court may grant a residence order instead under the provision discussed above in respect of step-parents.

---

103 It will be remembered that almost half of all adoptions are step-parent adoptions – Registrar General for Scotland, Annual Report 1997, above, at p 141.
104 Section 97.
105 1978 Act, s 15(1)(aa).
106 1978 Act, ss 12(3A) and 39(1).
107 In addition, the link with other birth relatives, like grandparents, from one side of the family is also severed.
108 Sched 4, para 26 and Sched 5.
109 1978 Act, s 24(3).
110 In *Soderback* v *Sweden* 33124/96, 22 October 1997, the Commission found that an unmarried father's rights under art 8 of the European Convention on Human Rights had been violated when a Swedish court authorised a step-parent adoption in the face of his opposition. The repercussions of this case could be enormous if the European Court of Human Rights takes the same view.
111 1978 Act, s 6A.
112 *A* v *B* 1987 SLT (Sh Ct) 121; and *HQ and LQ* v *CG*, unreported, 16 October 1992, IH and *AB and CD* v *EF* 1991 GWD 25–1420.
113 In 1997, only nine of the sole adoptions, and 18 of the joint adoptions, involved relatives – Registrar General for Scotland, Annual Report 1997, above, Table 9.1.

Surrogacy and parental orders

8.34 As we saw in chapter 4, there is an expedited and less regulated form of adoption available to some couples who commission a child though the use of a surrogate, provided that they meet an extensive list of conditions.[114] Briefly, only married couples who satisfy the usual domicile or residence requirement for adoption, and are each at least 18 years old, may apply for a parental order. One of the applicants must be the genetic parent of the child. The child concerned must have been carried by a woman other than the wife as a result of the placing in her of an embryo or sperm and eggs or of her artificial insemination. The application must be made within six months of the child's birth and the child must be living with the couple at the time the application is made. It is essential that the surrogate consents and, unlike ordinary adoption, her agreement cannot be dispensed with by a court. As with ordinary adoption cases, her consent is ineffective if given within six weeks of the birth. Any man who would be treated as the child's father by virtue of s 28 of the Human Fertilisation and Embryology Act 1990 must also consent. In addition, the court must be satisfied that no money, other than for expenses reasonably incurred, has been involved. Such a parental order will result in the child being treated as a child of the marriage and has the same effect as adoption. Where a parental order cannot be obtained, it is open to the commissioning couple to apply to adopt the child in the ordinary way. As *C v S*,[115] illustrates, it is possible for a commissioning couple who have paid a fairly large sum of money to the surrogate and thus become ineligible for a parental order on that ground alone, to secure an ordinary adoption order in the face of the surrogate's opposition.

The role of the child's birth parents

8.35 It is fundamental to any free society that children are not removed from their parents and placed in other families against the wishes of the parents unless a good reason for doing so is established before an independent tribunal. This is recognised by both the European Convention on Human Rights[116] and the UN Convention on the Rights of the Child.[117] Thus in Scots law, the general position is that, before an adoption order can be granted, it must be the case that each parent or guardian of the child 'freely, and with full understanding of what is involved, agrees unconditionally to the making of an adoption order'.[118] It does not matter whether the identity of the applicants for adoption is known to the parent or guardian. A parallel provision requires the consent of each of the child's parents or guardians to an order freeing the child for adoption.[119] In both cases, the

---

114 Human Fertilisation and Embryology Act 1990, s 30. For a more extensive discussion of the conditions and how they apply, see chapter 4, paras 53–62.

115 1996 SLT 1387. The case is discussed in chapter 4, para 57.

116 Article 8 (respect for private and family life).

117 Articles 9 (right not to be separated from the family except in limited circumstances), 10 (right to family reunification) and 21 (adoption permitted, but only in accordance with certain requirements).

118 1978 Act, s 16(1)(b).

119 1978 Act, s 18(1)(a).

mother's consent is ineffective if it is given less than six weeks after the child's birth.[120] As we shall see, the general rule requiring full and free consent is subject to exceptions. First, a court may make an order declaring the child free for adoption. While this will often be done with the consent of the child's parents, their agreement may, in certain circumstances, be dispensed with by a court. Once a child is declared free for adoption, no further parental consent is required. Second, where a child has not been freed for adoption, the court may again dispense with parental consent, in certain circumstances, and make the adoption order. Given the magnitude of the decision to dispense with the agreement of a child's parent or guardian, in the adoption process, it is hardly surprising that it is subject to detailed statutory regulation and has generated a considerable body of case-law. For this reason, we will consider parents' and guardians' agreement, and the dispensing with it, separately.

Other family members

8.36 Other family members, who are not also guardians of the child, are given no place at all in adoption proceedings. The difficulties which can result from such an approach are illustrated by *F* v *F*,[121] a case which predates the 1995 Act but remains relevant, none the less, in a number of important respects. There, two boys, aged 6 and 7 were being looked after by the local authority and it concluded, eventually, that they should be adopted. There was no opposition from the children's parents, but the boys' paternal grandparents wanted to provide them with a home and the local authority was aware of this. Since grandparents who are not also the child's guardians have no standing in adoption proceedings, the only option for them was to apply for parental rights in order to attain the relevant status.[122] In this case, the grandparents faced the added delay of having to apply for legal aid and, in the meantime, the local authority proceeded to apply for an order freeing the children for adoption and to place them with prospective adopters. When the grandparents' application for parental rights reached the court, they were granted custody (as it was then) and the local authority appealed against the decision. What had happened was that two separate sets of proceedings, in different sheriff courts, were being conducted in respect of the future arrangements for the same children. The proceedings came together before the Inner House and a host of issues were resolved. What the case highlights is the absurdity of such a situation. It is regrettable that, in the course of amending the legislation, little regard was had to the role of other relatives in such a situation. However, the 1995 Act did add the requirement that the adoption agency must give active consideration to any alternative to adoption and whether that would better serve the child's best interests.[123]

---

120 1978 Act, s 16(4) (adoption orders) and s 18(4) (freeing orders).
121 1991 SLT 357.
122 At the time of this case, their application was made under the Law Reform (Parent and Child) (Scotland) Act 1986. The application would now be made under s 11 of the 1995 Act.
123 1978 Act, s 6A, added by the Children (Scotland) Act 1995, s 96.

Thus, even where a relative is not the child's guardian, if the relative is offering to look after the children, the local authority is now obliged to assess that offer and its suitability prior to applying to have a child freed for adoption and, certainly, prior to placing a child with prospective adopters.

The Scottish Adoption Service and Adoption Agencies

8.37 Adoption is a serious matter and one which requires rigorous scrutiny. For that reason, adoptions cannot be arranged privately and anyone, other than an adoption agency, who arranges an adoption is liable to prosecution, as is anyone who makes the placement or anyone who receives the child in such circumstances.[124] There are two exceptions to this rule. First, where the adopter is a relative of the child, making the arrangements and placing the child need not be undertaken by an adoption agency.[125] Second, a children's hearing may make it a condition of supervision that a child should live with people who are prospective adopters.[126] These exceptions aside, adoption arrangements must be made by a local authority or an approved adoption society, these organisations being known, for this purpose, as 'adoption agencies'.

8.38 Every local authority is obliged to establish and maintain a service designed to meet the needs of adopted children, their parents and guardians, and adopters or potential adopters.[127] These services are known collectively as the Scottish Adoption Service.[128] The services which must be provided include: arrangements for assessing children and prospective adopters and placing children for adoption; counselling and assistance to children who have been adopted; and counselling for persons with problems relating to adoption.[129] These must be provided in conjunction with the local authority's other social services and approved adoption societies in the area in order to achieve a co-ordinated approach.[130] If a local authority does not have an adoption service of its own, it may use the services of an approved adoption society.[131]

8.39 Any voluntary organisation may apply for approval from the Secre-

---

124 1978 Act, s 11(1) and (3).
125 1978 Act, s 11(1). It should be noted that the adopter and the child must be related. The person making the arrangements need not be related to either of them.
126 Children (Scotland) Act 1995, s 70(3).
127 1978 Act, s 1(1).
128 1978 Act, s 1(4). 'Local authority' means a council constituted under the Local Government, etc. (Scotland) Act 1994, s 2: 1978 Act, s 65(1).
129 1978 Act, s 1(2).
130 1978 Act, s 1(3).
131 1978 Act, s 1(1)(c). As a result of local authority reorganisation in the 1990s, it was anticipated that some local authorities would be too small to offer a full adoption service. Hence the provision for buying in a particular service from an approved adoption society. At the time of writing, it is understood that this has been done by a number of local authorities and, for example, the City of Edinburgh has contracted out adoption, in respect of children under the age of five, to the Scottish Adoption Society. Were a local authority to contract out all of its adoption service, it might face problems, since certain steps, like applying for an order to have a child freed for adoption, may only be taken by a local authority.

tary of State to act as an adoption society.[132] While some approved adoptions societies offer the whole range of adoption services, others offer specific, specialist services.[133] If the Secretary of State is satisfied that the organisation is likely to make an effective contribution to the Scottish Adoption Service, taking into account a number of specific factors and any other relevant considerations, approval must be given for the organisation to act as an adoption society.[134] The Secretary of State is specifically directed to consider: the applicant's adoption programme; its complaints procedure; the number and qualifications of its staff; its financial resources; and the organisation and control of its operations.[135] Where the applicant is likely to operate extensively within the area of a particular local authority, the Secretary of State is required to seek, and take into account, the local authority's view of the application.[136] Where the applicant is already an approved adoption society, the Secretary of State is obliged to take its past record and reputation into account.[137] The Secretary of State may grant or refuse the application to act as an adoption society or for renewal of such status, and must notify the applicant of the decision.[138] Where approval has been granted, this lasts for three years unless it is withdrawn by the Secretary of State[139] prior to the expiry of that period.[140]

THE AGREEMENT OF A CHILD'S PARENTS AND GUARDIANS

Parents and guardians

8.40 As we have seen, the starting point in adoption is that each parent and guardian of the child must freely, and with full understanding of what is involved, agree unconditionally to the making of the adoption order.[141] In order to appreciate how the consent requirement operates, it is important to understand what is meant by a 'parent' or a 'guardian', in this context. 'Guardian' is given the straightforward, if circular, definition of 'a person appointed by deed or will or by a court of competent jurisdiction to be the guardian of the child'.[142] When we turn to consider the meaning of 'parent', however, we find the following definition in the 1978 Act

132 1978 Act, s 3(1). At the time of writing, the following organisations are approved adoption societies: Barnardo's (specialising in older and children with special needs), Family Care (counselling only), the Scottish Adoption Association, St Andrews Aid Society and St Margaret's Adoption Society.
133 Before the Children (Scotland) Act 1995 amended s 3(1) of the 1978 Act, applicants had to offer the whole range of services. The amendment recognises the valuable contribution made by some organisations in respect of specialist services. For example, Family Care offers counselling only.
134 1978 Act, s 3(2).
135 1978 Act, s 3(3).
136 1978 Act, s 3(4).
137 1978 Act, s 3(5).
138 1978 Act, s 3 (2) and (6).
139 On withdrawal of approval, see 1978 Act, s 4.
140 1978 Act, s 3(7).
141 1978 Act, s 16(1). A similar provision requires the parents' and guardians' consent to the making of a freeing order – s 18(1). The mother's agreement is ineffective if given less than six weeks after child's birth; ss 16(4) and 18(4).
142 1978 Act, s 65(1).

'(a) the mother of the child, where she has parental responsibilities or rights in relation to him [or her];
(b) the father of the child, where he has parental responsibilities or rights in relation to him [or her];
(c) both parents where they both have parental responsibilities or rights'.[143]

This means that a parent who has any parental responsibility or right qualifies as a parent for the purpose of the adoption legislation. Thus, a parent with nothing more than the right to occasional contact with the child must consent to the adoption order in the first instance. Since each parent may normally exercise parental rights alone, s 65(1) makes it absolutely clear that, where both parents have responsibilities or rights, *both* of them must consent to adoption. This would have been the case, in any event, because the 1978 Act refers specifically to the consent of *each* parent or guardian, but it appears to have been thought necessary to put the matter beyond all doubt. The parental right here is stated to apply irrespective of whether or not the parents have ever been married to each other and, at first glance, the 1978 Act appears to show a refreshing, and rare, acceptance of the unmarried father. However, his position warrants closer examination.

The position of the unmarried father

8.41 Where the child's unmarried father has any parental responsibilities in respect of the child, his consent to the child's adoption is required. However, unmarried fathers are the only group of parents who do not acquire these rights and responsibilities automatically.[144] Where the child's mother does not agree to his acquiring them,[145] he may apply to the court. Whether he is successful will depend on his satisfying the court that an order giving him some degree of recognition will serve the child's welfare and that it would be better that the order was made than that no order was made at all.[146] Should he fail, his consent to his child's adoption is not required. The number of unmarried fathers making parental responsibilities and rights agreements with the child's mother or acquiring responsibilities and rights through the courts is relatively small. Thus, there are many fathers who take no part in the adoption process. It should be noted, however, that before a court may make an order freeing a child for adoption, it must satisfy itself of the following, in respect of any person claiming to be the child's father: (i) that he does not intend to apply for an order in respect of parental responsibilities or rights; (ii) that if he did apply, it is likely that the order would be refused; (iii) that he has no intention of entering into a parental responsibilities and rights agreement with the child's mother; and (iv) that regardless of his intention, such an agreement is unlikely to result.[147] For some unmarried fathers, the problem

---

143 1978 Act, s 65(1), word in square brackets has been added. This definition was added by the Children (Scotland) Act 1995, s 98(1) and Sched 2, para 29.
144 Children (Scotland) Act 1995, s 3(1)(b). See chapter 5, paras 44–67 for a full discussion of the position of the unmarried father.
145 Children (Scotland) Act 1995, s 4.
146 Children (Scotland) Act 1995, s 11.
147 1978 Act, s 18(7).

may be that they are not aware that they are fathers at all at the time adoption is being considered. If such a father discovers the fact of his paternity after the child has been freed for adoption, but before the adoption order is granted, can he intervene at that time? What if the child has already been adopted? Since these questions require some understanding of the procedure for freeing for adoption and dispensing with parental consent, they are dealt with separately below.[148]

Parents whose parental responsibilities and rights have been removed

8.42 What of parents or guardians[149] who have had parental responsibilities or rights at one time, but have lost them? Is their consent to adoption required? It is submitted that this may depend on how they lost their parental responsibilities and rights. First, they may have done so as a result of a local authority obtaining a parental responsibilities order.[150] Such an order is stated to transfer 'the appropriate parental responsibilities and rights' from the parents to the local authority.[151] However, one right which is not transferred is the right to agree to or decline to agree to the granting of an adoption order or an order freeing a child for adoption.[152] Thus, even after a parental responsibilities order is granted, the parents retain their rights in respect of consent to adoption.

8.43 The second way in which a parent may have lost parental responsibilities and rights is through the operation of s 11 of the Children (Scotland) Act 1995. The court has enormous latitude in the making of orders in relation to parental responsibilities and rights under this provision. However, any order depriving a person of parental responsibilities or rights does so 'only in so far as the order expressly so provides and only to the extent necessary to give effect to the order'.[153] It is arguable that, just as the innominate right to consent to adoption survives a parental responsibilities order granted to a local authority, it survives a s 11 order because it is neither specified therein, nor is it necessary to give effect to the deprivation of other rights, like the right to determine residence or to have contact with a child.[154] However, when we turn to the definition of a 'parent' in s 65(1) of the 1978 Act, we find that the only people who qualify as such are those who have any of the responsibilities or rights as specified in ss 1 and 2 of the 1995 Act. If a person does not have any of these rights,

148 See, The Problem of The Suddenly-Appearing Father, paras 8.83–8.88, below.
149 For ease of expression, reference below to consent, in the context of parents, applies equally to the guardian's consent and 'parental consent' should be read accordingly.
150 Children (Scotland) Act 1995, ss 86–89, discussed in chapter 7, paras 89–93.
151 1995 Act, s 86(1).
152 1995 Act, s 86(3).
153 1995 Act, s 11(11).
154 Some support for this interpretation can be found in s 11(12) of the 1995 Act. It provides that, where the court makes a residence order requiring the child to live with a person who had did not have full responsibilities or rights prior to the order, the person will have the full set, as a result of the order. However, the 'full set' of responsibilities and rights, in this context, is stated to be those detailed in ss 1 and 2 of the 1995 Act and does not include the right to consent to adoption of the child.

he or she is no longer a parent for the purpose of the 1978 Act and his or her consent to a child's adoption is not required. This is, indeed, a curious result and one wonders if it is what Parliament intended.

8.44 Let us take the example of a boy whose father is unknown and whose mother has had various problems with drug addiction and depression. Her sister, the boy's aunt, has looked after him since he was a baby. His mother has returned to the scene periodically and threatened to take him away and, finally, in order to prevent this happening, the aunt has applied for, and been given, full parental responsibilities and rights. All parental responsibilities and rights were removed from the mother, since it was felt that even contact with her would be detrimental to the boy. The mother becomes estranged from the family due to disagreement over the case. Two years later, the aunt applies to adopt her nephew. In the meantime, the boy's mother has recovered fully from her problems and wishes to resume caring for him. Would it be reasonable that an adoption should proceed without her consent being required? The mother could apply to the court for parental responsibilities and rights and re-enter the picture in that way. However, given her estrangement from the family, she may not have known about the adoption plans. Leaving aside the issue of whether adoption or a parental responsibilities and rights order is the best way to deal with this problem, the point is that the mother may be denied any role in the adoption because her responsibilities and rights have been removed by a section 11 order, when that would not have been the result had the local authority been granted a parental responsibilities order. There seems to be no good reason to treat the two situations differently.

Dispensing with parental agreement

8.45 Thus far, it has been stressed that parental consent to adoption is central to respect for family integrity. However, there are circumstances where the parents are unable or wholly unsuited to fulfil any active role as parents. In such circumstances, it can be argued that the child's best interests would be served by his or her finding a new family and being placed with that family as a full member. Balancing the child's best interests with the rights of parents who do not want their child to be adopted is far from simple and it must be stressed that parental consent is not dispensed with by simply applying the welfare test. Instead, the court must be satisfied that the parents' consent should be dispensed with for one of a list of specific grounds. Thus, dispensing with parental consent involves a two-stage process.[155] First, it must be established, as a matter of fact, that one of the grounds for dispensing with parental consent exists. Only then is the court in a position to move to the second stage – deciding whether it *should* make such a dispensation. As with all decisions in the adoption, the court must decide this second stage by applying the welfare test. Parental

---

155 1978 Act, s 16(1)(b). See *P* v *Lothian Regional Council* 1989 SLT 739 and *L* v *Central Regional Council* 1990 SLT 818.

consent may be dispensed with only where one of the following four grounds is satisfied.[156]

The parent or guardian is not known, cannot be found or is incapable of giving agreement[157]

8.46 It will be very rare that the identity of a child's mother is not known but, occasionally, babies are abandoned and the mother is never traced. In such cases, this provision makes it possible for the baby to be adopted by dispensing with the unknown mother's consent. As we have seen, a married woman's husband is presumed to be the father of her child unless the contrary is proved.[158] Thus, there is no scope for an unknown married father, assuming that the mother of the child is known. Since unmarried fathers have no right in adoption proceedings unless they have acquired parental responsibilities or rights, or are likely to do so, the fact that the father is unknown is immaterial for adoption purposes.

8.47 Before the court will conclude that a parent cannot be found, it will require evidence of the efforts made to locate the parent. The dearth of Scottish authority on this point suggests that it has not given rise to problems. Clearly, establishing a negative is not easy and the court will apply common sense to the facts before it.[159] Establishing that a parent is incapable of consenting to the adoption will normally require medical evidence of incapacity. Where parental incapacity is of a temporary nature, it is unlikely that a court would dispense with the parent's consent immediately.

The parent or guardian is withholding agreement unreasonably[160]

8.48 Of all the grounds for dispensing with parental consent to adoption, this has proved the most contentious. On the one hand, it might be argued that the bond between a parent and child is so strong that no parent would want that connection to be severed. Since adoption severs the legal link between the child and the birth parent, it follows that, whatever problems the parent has had in parenting, it would always be reasonable for the parent to hold on to the link. Were the courts to accept this argument, it would never be 'unreasonable' for a parent to withhold agreement to

---

156 1978 Act, s 16(2). The current s 16(2) is a result of amendment by the Children (Scotland) Act 1995. Previously there were six grounds for dispensing with parental consent and they contained an element of overlap. Thus the law has been simplified but not altered in any substantial way.
157 1978 Act, s 16(2)(a).
158 Law Reform (Parent and Child) (Scotland) Act 1986, s 5(1)(a), discussed in chapter 4, para 9.
159 In *Re A (Adoption)* [1966] 2 All ER 613, for example, the court was prepared to dispense with parental consent in order to permit the adoption of R, a 20-year-old escapee from an unspecified totalitarian régime. R had been living with the applicant and the applicant's children, who were about the same age, in England since leaving his home country illegally. While his parents remained there, they were not viewed favourably by the régime and it was feared that any attempt to contact them would expose them to risk or disapproval. It should be remembered that the adoption legislation operating in England at the time permitted adoption of a person under the age of 21.
160 1978 Act, s 16(2)(b).

adoption and this ground for dispensing with parental agreement could never be satisfied. It is hardly surprising that the courts have not taken this approach, since it must be presumed that Parliament intended a statutory provision to have a workable purpose when it passed the relevant legislation. Instead, the approach adopted by the courts is based on the premise that parents want the best for their children. Thus, a reasonable parent would agree to adoption in certain circumstances and, if those circumstances are present in the instant case, any parent who withholds agreement is doing so 'unreasonably'. It is not simply the reaction of the parent before the court that is being considered – his or her reaction is judged against that of a hypothetical 'reasonable parent'.[161]

8.49 It is in respect of this ground for dispensing with parental consent that the two stages of the decision-making process can most often become confused, since separating the facts and circumstances which make a decision unreasonable, from the parent's approach to agreement, is not always easy.[162] At the same time and because of its complexity, this ground affords a good opportunity to explore the nature of the two-stage process itself. In assessing the reasonableness of the parent's refusal to agree (the first stage), the court must look at all the circumstances of the case, including the interests of the child, the birth parents and the prospective adopters.[163] Given the circumstances in which contested adoptions arise, it is not surprising that factors about the parent's lifestyle will often be addressed.[164] The fact that a birth parent has changed his or her mind on the matter may indicate unreasonableness,[165] although the courts appreciate that this is a difficult time for a parent and will not necessarily attach too much weight to vacillation.[166] Certainly, it cannot be concluded that agreement has been withheld unreasonably simply because the adoption

161 *A* v *B and* C 1971 SC (HL) 129 per Lord Reid, at p 141; *D and D* v *F* (IH) 1994 SCLR 417; *P* v *Lothian Regional Council*, n 155 above, per Lord Justice-Clerk Ross, at p 741.

162 The difficulty is summed up by the following statement from Lord Justice-Clerk Ross in *AB and CB, Petitioners* (IH) 1990 SCLR (Notes) 809 at p 813 – 'In our opinion, if the respondent was acting reasonably he would have put the welfare of the children first, and if he did, he would not withhold consent'. See also *Central Regional Council* v *M* (IH) 1991 SCLR 300, per Lord McCluskey, at pp 302–303 where he highlights the difficulty in separating the decision to dispense with parental consent from the decision on the adoption itself.

163 *P* v *Lothian Regional Council*, n 155 above, per Lord Justice-Clerk Ross, at p 741K. In *A* v *B and C*, n 161 above, at p 141, Lord Reid explained why the interests of all three parties mattered. Having noted the importance of the child's interests, he went on to say – 'But I see no reason why the claims of the natural parents should be ignored. ... And the adopting family cannot be ignored either. ... We are dealing largely with future probabilities for the decision once made is irrevocable. ... That seems to me to be an additional reason for giving considerable weight to ... to the claims of the natural parents and the adopting parents'.

164 See for example, *Angus Council Social Work Department, Petitioner*, n 33 above (mother's mental instability); *Re D (An Infant)* [1977] AC 602 (father's homosexual relationships with under-21-year-olds which were illegal at that time); *Lothian Regional Council* v *A* 1992 SLT 858 (mother's self-destructive behaviour); *R* v *Lothian Regional Council* 1987 SCLR 362 (alcoholic mother who had failed to stop drinking).

165 *AC and CB, Petitioners* 1963 SC 124, per Lord President Clyde, at p 137.

166 *Re W (An Infant)* [1971] AC 682, per Lord Hailsham, at p 700.

would be good for the child.[167] Courts in the future may take both comfort and warning from the following explanation given by Lord Hailsham

'Two reasonable parents can perfectly reasonably come to opposite conclusions on the same set of facts without forfeiting their right to be regarded as reasonable. The question in any given case is whether a parental veto comes within the band of possible reasonable decisions and not whether it is right or mistaken. Not every reasonable judgment is right, and not every mistaken exercise of judgment is unreasonable. There is a band of decisions within which no court should seek to replace the individual's judgment with its own'.[168]

Where the court has concluded that a parent is withholding agreement unreasonably, it *may* dispense with parental consent (the second stage).[169] In deciding whether to do so, it has a slightly easier task since, at this stage, it must apply the welfare test.[170]

The parent or guardian has persistently failed, without reasonable cause, to fulfil one or other of the following parental responsibilities in relation to the child –
(i) the responsibility to safeguard and promote the child's health, development and welfare; or
(ii) if the child is not living with him, the responsibility to maintain personal relations and direct contact with the child on a regular basis[171]

8.50 This ground for dispensing with parental agreement to adoption replaces the pre-1995 ground, in similar terms. The old ground referred to persistent failure to discharge any of the parental duties. Of course, prior to the 1995 Act, parental responsibilities were not clearly defined. It was thought necessary, therefore, to specify which parental responsibilities were of sufficient magnitude that persistent failure to discharge them warranted dispensing with a parent's consent to adoption. The responsibility to safeguard and promote the child's health, development and welfare and the responsibility to maintain personal relations and direct contact were selected as the two most important parental responsibilities for this purpose. Thus, a parent's persistent failure to provide direction and guidance or to act as the child's legal representative will not warrant dispensing with parental agreement to adoption. Persistent failure to fulfil either of the parental responsibilities specified in s 16(2)(c)(i) or (ii) will be enough to justify a court in considering whether it ought to dispense with parental consent. However, in *Angus Council Social Work Department,*

---

167 *Re W (An Infant)*, above, per Lord Hodson, at p 818.
168 *Re W (An Infant)* [1971] AC 682, per Lord Hailsham, at p 700.
169 1978 Act, s 16(1)(b)(ii).
170 1978 Act, s 6(1)(a). See *Lothian Regional Council v A*, n 164 above, per Lord President Hope, at p 863B.
171 1978 Act, s 16(2)(c). Because of the length of time it may take to hear appeals, disputed adoption cases have continued across the transition period when the amendments to the 1978 Act, introduced by the 1995 Act, came into force. The relevant legislation is that which applied at the time the application was made – SI 1997 No 744, discussed in *B v C*, 10 July 1998, 2nd Div, 1998 GWD 29-1457. That case, which concerned a successful adoption application by a couple who had looked after the four-year-old child for over two and a half years, is of interest in discussing the application of the welfare principle where the child's mother seems to have overcome her earlier addiction to heroin.

Petitioner,[172] Lord Penrose expressed the view that 'the branches of section 2(c) are not mutually exclusive'[173] and could occur in the same case. It is submitted that, not only is that view correct, it might not be all that unusual given the way in which cases of this kind arise. Let us suppose that the child has come to be looked after by the local authority because of concern over parental neglect. The local authority places the child with foster carers and provision is made for the child's mother to have regular contact. Let us suppose further that she frequently fails to appear at the times arranged for contact. In such a case, she may have failed persistently to discharge her responsibility under section 16(2)(c)(i), while the child was in her care, and may have gone on to fail persistently to discharge her obligation under section 16(2)(c)(ii), once the child was being looked after by the local authority.

8.51 Nor is the court obliged to look only at the present in assessing whether this ground is established. In *Angus Council Social Work Department, Petitioner*, the mother had been reasonably diligent in maintaining contact with the child once she was with foster carers. The concern about her parenting related primarily to the period of time when her daughter lived with her. Thus, the parent's persistent failure to discharge his or her parental responsibilities involved looking at past conduct. Indeed, the very use of the word 'persistent' requires that there must have been a course of failure on the parent's part. For example, an isolated instance of leaving a young child at home alone may warrant investigation and, possibly, intervention, but it is not 'persistent'. The phrase 'persistently failed' has a certain judgmental resonance about it, but this is not to suggest that the parent's failure must necessarily be culpable. The standard to be applied is an objective one and brings us back to that mythical figure the 'reasonable parent'. Where the parent has failed to meet the responsibility as a reasonable parent would have done, then the fact that there was some reason why the failure might not have been the parent's fault, will not necessarily prevent the ground being established.[174] Depending upon the explanation, it might affect the second stage of the court's decision, whether it does actually dispense with the parent's agreement.

8.52 Parental explanation for failure to discharge their responsibilities may, of course, amount to a reasonable excuse. To some extent, there is overlap between the fact that conduct need not to be culpable for it to qualify as persistent failure, justifying the court in moving on to the second stage of its decision, and finding it to be a 'reasonable excuse', which would prevent the court from reaching that stage. Certainly, the line between the two is not easy to draw. In any event, parental ill-health might be thought to be a reasonable excuse for a failure to meet the standard of the reasonable parent, while callous disregard would not. What of parental addiction to drugs or alcohol? It might be argued that the problem is of the

---

172 Referred to as *Angus Council v C* 1998 GWD 23–1148.
173 The full text of the opinion is reported on Lexis.
174 See for example, *Central Regional Council v B* 1985 SLT 413, where the mother explained her persistent failure on the basis of her own poor health and her husband's ill-treatment of her.

parent's own making and, as such, is not a reasonable excuse. On the other hand, it can be argued that an addict is no longer exercising free will, by reason of the addiction, and, as such, addiction is a reasonable excuse. Almost certainly, the courts will prefer the former view. Is parental imprisonment a reasonable excuse for failure to maintain direct contact? Aside from the fact that prisoners may write letters, make telephone calls and receive visitors, thus making contact possible, imprisonment may be viewed as an obstacle which the parent ought to have foreseen or as an unfortunate result that the parent did not expect. Of course, provided a court does not view the particular parental conduct negatively, it may not matter that it fails to qualify as a reasonable excuse, since the court can take it into account in the second stage of the decision-making process when it is considering whether it should dispense with parental consent.

The parent or guardian has seriously ill-treated the child, whose reintegration into the same household as the parent or guardian is, because of the serious ill-treatment or for other reasons, unlikely.[175]

8.53 The phrase 'serious ill-treatment' is unfortunate since any ill-treatment of a child is, arguably, serious, and all the more of a concern when it is meted out by the very person who ought to be caring for the child, the parent or guardian. To put it another way, it is difficult to imagine what would amount to 'trivial ill-treatment'. It should also be noted that serious ill-treatment itself is not enough to warrant a finding that this ground is established, the child's reintegration into the family must also be unlikely and we will return to this point presently. When we considered abuse and neglect of children, we saw that the former is generally positive, in the sense of something actively done, while the latter is usually negative, or passive.[176] Both constitute ill-treatment, whether physical, emotional or sexual in nature.

8.54 Once serious ill-treatment has been established, the court must consider the likelihood of the child's reintegration into the family. Where the child's reintegration is unlikely, the reason is not important. It may be connected to the ill-treatment. For example, where a child has been abused in a particular household, he or she may have been so affected by the experience that reintegration is no longer possible, despite the fact that the abuser no longer lives there. However, the problem over reintegration may be wholly unconnected with the ill-treatment, as, for example, where the parent has become ill or has remarried, and no longer feels able to care for the child.

Postscript on dispensing with parental agreement

8.55 The scenarios discussed above envisage a parent who is actively opposing the adoption. Not only would such a parent normally make his or her feelings known, he or she will usually participate in the proceedings where dispensing with parental agreement is being considered. What of the

175 1978 Act, s 16(2)(d).
176 See chapter 7, paras 5–13.

parent who simply lies low and refuses to communicate? Can parental agreement be dispensed with in these circumstances? This was the problem faced by the court in *T, Petitioner*.[177] Despite attempts by two successive reporting officers to make contact with her, the child's mother failed to respond, having previously indicated to social workers that she wanted nothing further to do with the child. The Lord Ordinary took the view that he was unable to dispense with the mother's agreement to the adoption, since he was not satisfied that she understood the full implications of the application.[178] The Inner House took a different view and made clear that, while parental understanding is fundamental to *giving consent* to adoption, it is not relevant to *dispensing with that consent*. In the words of Lord President Hope, '[i]f it were otherwise, the parent would be able to frustrate the whole process by declining to have anything to do with it'.[179]

DECLARING A CHILD FREE FOR ADOPTION

8.56 A special procedure exists which allows the court to declare a child free for adoption. The value of this procedure is best understood by highlighting the problems which can occur in its absence. Before an application for an adoption order can be made, the child must live with the prospective adopters for a period of time. While the birth parents may have indicated that they agree to the child being adopted, it is always possible that they will change their minds before the adoption order is made and this leaves the prospective adopters in a precarious position. Arguably, the uncertainty creates insecurity and hampers the process of the child and the prospective adopters settling down fully as a secure family unit. For this reason, the Houghton Committee[180] recommended the 'freeing procedure' which was introduced by the Children Act 1975 and now forms a part of the 1978 Act. Broadly, the effect of an order freeing the child for adoption (a 'freeing order') is to vest all parental responsibilities and rights in the adoption agency and obviating the need for the birth parents to have any further involvement in the adoption process. This gives the prospective adopters greater security since, once a freeing order has been obtained, the birth parents cannot normally prevent the adoption from going ahead. In addition, the birth parents may choose to have no further involvement in the adoption process,[181] thus enabling them to get on with their lives. As one would expect, there are various conditions for the granting, and qualifications on the effects, of a freeing order.

8.57 Only a local authority adoption agency may apply for a freeing order and the procedure is not available to approved adoption societies.[182] In the

---

177 (IH) 1996 SCLR 897.
178 It will be remembered that this was only one of the grounds on which the order was refused, the other being the fact that the prospective adopter was living in a same-sex relationship.
179 At p 903A.
180 Report of the Departmental Committee on the Adoption of Children (Home Office and Scottish Office, 1972) (Houghton Committee), paras 221–225.
181 1978 Act, s 18(6).
182 1978 Act, s 18(1). This suggests that a local authority which has contracted out all of its adoption services will not be able to use the freeing procedure.

first instance, each parent and guardian of the child must agree to the granting of a freeing order.[183] The consent of the child's mother is ineffective if given less than six weeks after the child's birth.[184] Where a parent or guardian does not agree, the adoption agency may apply to have the parent or guardian's consent dispensed with, but only where the child is in the care of the local authority.[185] The court may dispense with the agreement of a parent or guardian in the same way as it can dispense with parental agreement to an adoption order but, in the case of freeing orders, there are two additional requirements. First, it must be satisfied that the child has already been placed for adoption or that it is likely that the child will be so placed.[186] Second, it will be remembered that, where the child's parents are not married and the unmarried father has no parental responsibilities and rights, the court must be satisfied that he does not intend to apply for them or that, if he does, it is likely that his application would be unsuccessful.[187] Where the child is 12 years old or older, his or her consent is required before a freeing order may be granted.[188] Where the child is below the age of 12, any views he or she wishes to express must be taken into account by the court, in the light of the child's age and maturity.[189]

8.58 In considering whether or not to grant a freeing order, the court must regard the need to safeguard and promote the welfare of the child throughout his or her life as the paramount consideration.[190] In addition to having regard to the views of a child under 12, it must consider the child's religious persuasion, racial origin and linguistic and cultural background.[191] Prior to granting the order, the court must satisfy itself that each parent or guardian of the child who can be found has been given an opportunity to make a declaration that he or she prefers not to be involved in any future questions concerning the adoption of the child and any such declaration must be recorded by the court.[192]

8.59 The effect of the granting of a freeing order is to vest all parental rights and duties, including the right to agree to the child's adoption, in the adoption agency.[193] Once a freeing order has been granted, it is competent for the court to transfer these parental rights and duties from one adoption agency to another.[194] Where a freeing order is made in respect of a child

183 1978 Act, s 18(1)(a).
184 1978 Act, s 18(4).
185 1978 Act, s 18(2).
186 1978 Act, s 18(3).
187 1978 Act, s 18(7). The court must also be satisfied that there is no realistic prospect of his making a parental responsibilities and rights agreement with the child's mother.
188 1978 Act, s 18(8). The court may dispense with the child's consent, but only where the child in incapable of giving it.
189 Section 18 makes no mention of the views of children under 12 years old, but the decision is one 'relating to the adoption of a child' and, as such, is governed by the general provision requiring the child's views to be taken into account – 1978 Act, s 6(1)(b)(i).
190 1978 Act, s 6(1)(a).
191 1978 Act, s 6(1)(b).
192 1978 Act, s 18(6).
193 1978 Act, s 18(5).
194 1978 Act, s 21.

who is subject to a supervision order, the court may terminate the supervision order.[195]

8.60 As we have seen, each parent or guardian of the child will have been given the opportunity to declare that he or she prefers to have no future involvement in the child's adoption. Where a parent or guardian either did not do so or, having made such a declaration, has withdrawn it, he or she is entitled to a progress report from the local authority one year after the freeing order has been granted.[196] The progress report should indicate whether or not the child has been adopted and, if not, whether or not the child has been placed for adoption.[197] If the child has not been adopted or placed for adoption, the parent or guardian may apply for revocation of the freeing order.[198] Interpreting a similar provision in the adoption legislation applying in England and Wales, the House of Lords concluded that, even where the parent was not fit to have unfettered responsibility for the child, it was competent to revoke the freeing order none the less, since the child's welfare could be protected under other legislative provisions.[199]

THE ADOPTION PROCESS

8.61 The adoption process begins with adoption being considered as one of the options for a child who cannot live with his or her birth family. It might be thought that it ends with the court granting the adoption order, but that would be inaccurate in terms of both law and practice. For example, the obligation to provide counselling to those involved in adoption extends beyond that time and, years after the adoption itself has taken place, the adopted person may decide to exercise his or her right to see the adoption records. Nor should the legal system's part in the process be seen in isolation, since adoption involves input from other disciplines, including social work, psychology, psychiatry and medicine. There is a vast body of literature dealing with all of these aspects of adoption and the process will be considered here only in outline.[200]

---

195 1978 Act, s 18(9).

196 1978 Act, s 19.

197 1978 Act, s 19(2). The adoption agency has 14 days after the expiry of the 12 months from the granting of the freeing order in which to make the report.

198 1978 Act, s 20.

199 *Re G (A Minor) (Adoption: Freeing Order)* [1997] 2 All ER 534. In that case, it was accepted that suitable adopters might never be found for the child.

200 For details of the legal procedures involved, see not only the 1978 Act but the relevant regulations, including – the Adoption Agencies (Scotland) Regulations 1996, the Adoption Allowances (Scotland) Regulations 1996 and the Adoption Allowance Schemes Direction 1996. These, along with the Scottish Office guidance are available in a single volume: *Scotland's Children: The Children Scotland Act 1995 Regulations and Guidance*, vol 3, *Adoption and Parental Responsibilities Orders* (The Scottish Office, 1997). For a detailed discussion of the procedures involved, see P. G. B. McNeill, *Adoption of Children in Scotland* (3rd edn, W. Green, 1998). While the discussion of the procedure in Wilkinson and Norrie pre-dates amendments to the Act introduced by the Children (Scotland) Act 1995, much of it reflects the current position and, of course, when the new edition of that work is published in 1999, it will provide a valuable resource. For a discussion of the theory and practice, see Triseliotis *et al*, n 15 above.

Placement

8.62 A child may only be placed for adoption after all the options available for the child's future have been explored and local authorities usually have adoption panels which consider this matter.[201] Once it is established that adoption is the best option for the particular child, the selection of suitable adopters requires consideration being given to the child's racial, religious, cultural and linguistic profile.[202] Thought should be given to whether there is a need to place the child in the same home as siblings and whether there should be continued contact with birth parents.[203] As the guidance from the Scottish Office points out '[c]areful preparation of the child can maximise the chance of success of a placement' and '[l]inking a child with prospective adopters is a sensitive process'.[204] The local authority must visit within one week of the child being placed with prospective adopters and, thereafter, should visit as often as it considers necessary and whenever a visit is requested by the child or the adopters.[205] During this time, the birth parents should be offered support and counselling and given information explaining the adoption process. They should be made aware of their role in agreeing to the child being freed for adoption and to the adoption.[206]

8.63 Private placement of children for adoption is prohibited unless the child and the adopters are related and most placements are now undertaken by an adoption agency.[207] If the child has been placed for adoption privately, the applicant for adoption must give the local authority notice of the intention to adopt at least three months before date of the order and the local authority must investigate the case and report to the court.[208] Where either the applicant or one of the applicants is a parent, step-parent or relative of the child, or the child has been placed with the applicant by an adoption agency, the adoption order may not be made until the child is 19 weeks old and unless the child has had a home with the applicants for the preceding 13 weeks.[209] In all other circumstances, no adoption order may be made until the child is 12 months old and unless the child has had a home with the applicants for the preceding 12 months.[210] Before granting the adoption order the court must be satisfied that sufficient opportunity has been afforded to either the adoption agency which placed the child or

201 1978 Act, s 6A. See *Scotland's Children: The Children Scotland Act 1995 Regulations and Guidance*, vol 3, *Adoption and Parental Responsibilities Orders* (The Scottish Office, 1997) (hereinafter 'Regulations and Guidance') paras 8 and 9.
202 1978 Act, s 6(1)(b)(ii) and Regulations and Guidance, para 10.
203 Adoption Agencies (Scotland) Regulations 1996 (hereinafter the '1996 Regulations'), reg 11(2)(b).
204 Regulations and Guidance, paras 13 and 17.
205 1996 Regulations, reg 19(2)(F).
206 Regulations and Guidance, paras 31–32.
207 1978 Act, s 11(1).
208 1978 Act, s 22.
209 1978 Act, s 13(1).
210 1978 Act, s 13(2).

the local authority in whose area the home is situated to see the child with the applicant or applicants in the home environment.[211]

Restrictions on removal of child pending adoption

8.64 Where a local authority has placed a child with a person with a view to adoption and the parents of the child have consented to the placement, it is an offence for any person to remove the child without the permission of the adoption agency or the court.[212] Where a person who has provided a home for a child for five years gives notice to the local authority of his or her intention to apply to adopt the child, it is an offence to remove the child from that person's care either prior to the making of the application for an adoption order or for a period of three months after the receipt by the local authority of the notification of intention, whichever occurs first.[213] Where the child was in the care of the local authority prior to having a home with the applicant or prospective adopter and remains in local authority care, the local authority can only remove the child in accordance with the procedure for return of a child placed for adoption or with the leave of a court.[214] In addition, the child's removal may be authorised by a children's hearing.[215]

Application to court

8.65 The application for an adoption order is competent in either the Court of Session or the sheriff court, with most adoption orders being dealt with in the sheriff court,[216] and the proceedings will be in private unless the court directs otherwise.[217] A curator *ad litem* will be appointed to safeguard the child's interest and a reporting officer will be appointed to witness agreements to adoption.[218] Employees of the adoption agency which placed the child for adoption or, in the case of an application for a freeing order, the adoption agency which has applied for the order, or an adoption agency which has parental responsibilities and rights in respect of the child, are precluded from acting as curators *ad litem* or reporting officers.[219]

8.66 The court[220] grants or refuses the adoption and may make it subject to such conditions as it thinks fit.[221] In addition, the court may postpone the determination of the adoption application and make an order vesting

---

211 1978 Act, s 13(3).
212 1978 Act, s 27.
213 1978 Act, s 28.
214 1978 Act, ss 28(3), 30 and 31.
215 1978 Act, s 28(4).
216 In 1997, only one adoption petition was lodged with the Court of Session, while 369 adoption orders were granted in the sheriff court, with a further eight petitions being refused and 15 being withdrawn. Two petitions for freeing for adoption were lodged with the Court of Session, compared with 96 being granted, 11 refused and four withdrawn, in the sheriff court. See, Civil Judicial Statistics Scotland 1997, Tables 2.8 and 3.12.
217 1978 Act, ss 56 and 57.
218 1978 Act, s 58(1).
219 1978 Act, s 58(2).
220 1978 Act, s 56.
221 1978 Act, s 12(6).

parental responsibilities and rights in respect of the child in the applicants for a probationary period of up to two years.[222] Where the court refuses to grant the adoption order the child is returned to the adoption agency.[223] All adoptions are registered in the Adopted Children's Register.[224]

THE EFFECTS OF ADOPTION

8.67 As we have seen, the goal of adoption has traditionally been to find a new family for the child. For that reason, an adoption order vests all parental responsibilities and rights in relation to the child in the adopters[225] and, as a general rule, the child is no longer regarded as the child of his or her birth parents.[226] Where a child is adopted by a married couple, he or she is treated by the legal system as the legitimate child of the couple.[227] Where the adopter is a single person, the child is regarded as that person's child.[228] It will be remembered that, in the case of step-parent adoption, only the step-parent actually adopts the child and the birth parent to whom the step-parent is married retains his or her original status. The effect is that the child is treated as the child of that couple.[229] Where a child has been adopted by one of his or her parents and that person subsequently marries the other birth parent, the adoption does not prevent the child's subsequent legitimation.[230] Thus, the general effect of adoption is to create a new family unit with all the attendant legal consequences.

8.68 As ever, if that simple position was all there was to it, the law would fail to take account of other important considerations and thus, there are exceptions to, and qualifications on, the general rule. As we have seen, the adoption order itself may have conditions attached to it. In addition, there is the possibility of continued contact between the child and birth relatives, which we consider presently. First, let us consider a number of respects in which adoption has no, or only limited, effect.

The prohibited degrees for purposes of marriage

8.69 The adoption order does not terminate the relationship between the child and birth relatives for the purpose of the prohibited degrees of marriage.[231] Thus, where a woman has two children and each of them is adopted into separate families, the prohibition on the children marrying each other remains in force. In addition, marriage between an adopted child and an adoptive parent falls within the prohibited degrees. Surprise is

---

222 1978 Act, s 25.
223 1978 Act, s 30(3).
224 1978 Act, s 45.
225 1978 Act, s 12(1). The position stated here applies to all adoptions taking place on or after 1 January 1976.
226 1978 Act, s 39.
227 1978 Act, s 39(1)(a).
228 1978 Act, s 39(1)(b).
229 1978 Act, s 39(1)(c).
230 1978 Act, s 39(2).
231 1978 Act, s 41(1) and the Marriage (Scotland) Act 1977, s 2 and Sched 1. For a full discussion of the prohibited degrees, see chapter 10, paras 26–31.

often the reaction when it is appreciated that two children adopted into the same family, but otherwise unrelated, may marry.

Incest

8.70 Similarly, adoption has no effect for the purpose of the law of incest insofar as birth relatives are concerned, but relations between the adoptive child and the adoptive parent are prohibited.[232]

Pensions and certain insurance policies

8.71 If a child is entitled to receive a pension, adoption does not terminate that entitlement.[233] Where the birth parent has taken out an insurance policy with a friendly society or certain other institutions, the policy is not terminated by adoption but is transferred to the adoptive parents who acquire the rights and liabilities under the policy.[234]

Succession

8.72 Initially, adoption had no effect on the law of succession. The law was altered radically by the Succession (Scotland) Act 1964 which, essentially, treated the adopted child as a child of the adopters, effective from 10 September 1964.[235] Certain transitional provisions apply and subsequent statutes have altered the position further,[236] but the modern position is that the adopted child takes a full place in his or her adoptive family for succession purposes,[237] subject to the remaining exception that adoption has no effect on succession to titles, honours and coats of arms.[238]

Nationality or immigration

8.73 A child who is a citizen of the UK and colonies retains that status even if adopted by persons who are not.[239] Where a foreign child is adopted by a UK citizen the child acquires UK nationality.[240]

Open adoption and adoption with contact

8.74 When most adoptions followed the traditionally-accepted model of babies being adopted by childless couples, the idea of all contact between the child and his or her birth family being severed, at least until the adopted person took the decision to find out more about his or her birth family, may have made some sense. Thus, Scots law adopted the model of 'closed adoption'. As recently as 1972, the Houghton Committee supported

---

232 1978 Act, s 41(1) and Criminal Law (Consolidation) (Scotland) Act 1995, s 1.
233 1978 Act, s 42.
234 1978 Act, s 43.
235 1964 Act, s 23(1).
236 See for example, the Law Reform (Miscellaneous Provisions) (Scotland) Act 1966, s 5, governing deeds coming into operation on or after 1 January 1976.
237 See chapter 14, paras 176–196 for a discussion of the law on succession. See also, *Laws of Scotland, Stair Memorial Encyclopaedia*, vol 25, paras 713–714.
238 Succession (Scotland) Act 1964, s 37(1)(a). The Lord Lyon King of Arms has a discretion to permit the use of a coat of arms.
239 1978 Act, s 41(2).
240 British Nationality Act 1981, s 1(5). Should the adoption cease to have effect, the child does not lose British nationality – 1981 Act, s 1(6).

closed adoption unequivocally.[241] However, as we have seen, adoption increasingly involves older children who already know their birth relatives. In step-parent adoptions the child will often know a host of birth relatives. In these cases, it may be unreasonable and, sometimes, wholly unrealistic, to expect that the child will no longer have contact with some members of his or her birth family. Even in the case of babies or young children, there are arguments supporting a degree of openness in adoption.

8.75 The term 'open adoption' should be used with care, since it may mean many different practical arrangements in different circumstances.[242] At a minimum, it may involve the exchange of information between the birth parents and the adopters in the early stage, with the exchange continuing, in some cases, but no direct contact between the birth parents and the child. However, it may involve direct contact between the child and his or her birth parents or other birth relatives and such an arrangement is known, for obvious reasons, as 'adoption with contact'. Opinion is divided on the wisdom of open adoption, particularly openness involving contact. The disadvantages usually stated are that it prevents the child settling into his or her new family fully and is confusing for the child. However, research suggests that even very young children are capable of dealing with attachment to more than one set of adults at the same time. In addition, it is argued that openness in adoption may help children to deal with the feelings of rejection sometimes associated with adoption and, thus, help the child to develop a stronger sense of identity. Open adoption may also reduce the risk of the child from idealising (or demonising) the birth parent. Open adoption was touched upon in the review of adoption conducted in the early 1990s, but opinion was sufficiently divided and the experience of it was so limited, that the only conclusion reached was that more research was required.[243] For the present, all that can be said is that various forms of open adoption do operate in Scotland.[244] It may be that the issue of open adoption is like so many other issues in child law. It is simply a matter of finding the right arrangements for the individual child. However, the attitude of the adopters will usually be crucial in making an openness work.

8.76 When the court makes an adoption order it may attach 'such terms

241 Report of the Departmental Committee on the Adoption of Children (Home Office and Scottish Office, 1972) (Houghton Committee) para 29. The Committee went as far as to suggest that the right of children, in Scotland, on reaching the age of 17 (now reduced to 16) to gain access to their adoption records should be removed. In the event, far from Scots law being altered, the right was extended to children in England and Wales by the Children Act 1975. Closed adoption is supported by the European Convention on the Adoption of Children (1967, Cmnd 3673), art 10 of which provides for adoption vesting 'rights and obligations of every kind' in the adopters.
242 For an excellent discussion of open adoption, the relevant research and literature, and how it may operate, see Triseliotis et al, n 15 above, chapter 4.
243 The Future of Adoption Law in Scotland (Scottish Office, 1993).
244 Adoption with contact is accepted as a possibility by the Adoption Agencies (Scotland) Regulations 1996, SI 1996 No 3266, regulation 11(2)(b) of which provides that, where the adoption panel recommends continued contact between the child and a birth parent, it must give reasons for its recommendation.

and conditions as the court thinks fit'.[245] After some initial doubt,[246] the courts in Scotland accepted that this power could be used, as it had been in England,[247] to provide for contact between a child and a birth parent or parents, where this would be of some benefit to the child.[248] Of course, that does not mean that every parent who wishes to retain some contact with a child after adoption will be allowed to do so. The test for continued contact is the child's welfare and, sometimes, contact will not be in the child's interests.[249]

8.77 Where contact has not been built into the adoption order, certain persons may apply to the court for a contact order. This option is not available to most birth parents. Where a person has had parental responsibilities and rights, and these have been removed by a freeing order or an adoption order, that person may not apply to the court for an order relating to parental responsibilities or rights under s 11 of the Children (Scotland) Act 1995.[250] However, a person who has never had parental responsibilities is not prevented by this provision from applying for any parental responsibility or right, including contact. In some cases, the unmarried father will be such a person. Certainly, it means that all other birth relatives, like siblings and grandparents, may apply, provided that they have not had any parental responsibility or right removed by the freeing order or the adoption order. It must be remembered that application is simply the first step. Whether they will be allowed contact will be determined on the basis of the overarching principles.[251]

Can an adoption order be revoked?

8.78 The 1978 Act contains provision for the revocation of an adoption order in certain limited circumstances. Where a child has been adopted by one of his or her parents and the parents subsequently marry each other, they may apply to the court for revocation of the adoption order.[252] There is provision for an overseas adoption to be annulled.[253] An adopted child may be adopted subsequently and, thus, the first adoption is superseded by the second. However, those situations aside, the 1978 Act contains no

---

245 1978 Act, s 12(6).
246 *A v B* 1987 SLT (Sh Ct) 121.
247 *Re C* (A Minor) (Adoption Order: Conditions) [1988] 1 All ER 705.
248 In *B v C* 1996 SLT 1370, a condition providing for supervised contact between a child and her birth parents was made where the reason behind the adoption was the fact that the parents suffered from a degenerative illness which the child was likely to inherit.
249 See for example, *Angus Council Social Work Department, Petitioner*, unreported, 12 June 1998, OH, where Lord Penrose observed, in refusing to order contact between the birth mother and the child – 'It appears to me to be a legitimate consideration whether continued contact would be beneficial to [the child]. [The mother] is a disruptive influence in the child's life. Contact would inhibit the formation of new family ties. It would create and sustain anxiety in the child and uncertainty about her place in the new family and her relationship with [her birth mother]'.
250 Section 11(4)(a) and (b). See chapter 5, paras 78–82 for a full discussion of this provision and the developments which led to it.
251 1995 Act, s 11(7).
252 1978 Act, s 46.
253 1978 Act, s 47.

statement on revocation of adoption. Certainly, the intention is that the child should take a full part as a child in the adoptive family and that adoption should be permanent.

8.79 It is interesting that there appears to be only one case in Scotland where the adopters sought to reduce an adoption order.[254] In *J and J* v *C's Tutor*,[255] a married couple adopted a baby boy whom they believed to be a healthy child. It became apparent later that the child had sustained injury at birth resulting in serious and permanent mental disability. The couple sought reduction of the adoption order on the basis that they had entered the adoption under essential error, induced by the innocent misrepresentations of the mother's agents. They also argued that some of the formalities for adoption had not been complied with. Their action was dismissed by the Inner House. Observing that an adoption order is neither a decree *in foro* nor a decree in absence, Lord President Cooper went on to express the view that adoption was not a matter of contract and was, therefore, not open to reduction on the ground of error. While a failure to comply with formal requirements might have criminal consequences, he did not accept that it made the adoption voidable. However, the Lord President did not close the door completely on actions for reduction of an adoption order when he said 'I reserved the case (probably theoretical) of mistaken identity as to the adopted child; and I deliberately abstain from generalising more widely than is necessary for the decision of the case'.[256]

8.80 To permit reduction for 'quality related defects' would be to reduce the adopted child to the status of a commodity and the Inner House is to be applauded for its refusal to do so in *J and J* v *C's Tutor*.[257] None the less, it appears that an adoption order might be reduced in certain circumstances. As Lord President Cooper suggested, one such circumstance might be error as to the identity of the child. Let us suppose that two babies born at the same hospital on the same day were switched by mistake.[258] One of them is adopted subsequently. When that child's birth parents discover the error later, could they have the adoption order reduced and reclaim their child? That will be a matter for a future court but, if reduction of an

---

254 In the USA some states permit revocation of adoption where, unknown to the adopters, the child suffered from a particular condition, like epilepsy or mental disability, at the time of the adoption. See for example, *In Re Lisa Diane G* 537 A 2d 131 (RI, 1988), where a couple sought to reverse an adoption because they had not been told that the eight-year-old girl they adopted had a history of emotional problems and the Department of Children and their Families, who placed her with them, had been advised that she was unsuitable for adoption. Their action was held to be competent. That case can be contrasted with *Rich* v *Rich* 364 SE 2d 804 (Wva, 1987), where a man, who had adopted his wife's children by a previous marriage, sought to have the adoption orders revoked when he and the mother divorced later. His aim was to avoid paying child support. The court refused his application on the basis that there had been no fraud in the adoption process.
255 1948 SC 636.
256 1948 SC 636, at p 644.
257 As Lord President Cooper observed (at p 642) – 'There were occasions in the course of the debate when it appeared as if an adoption were a contract between natural parent and adopter for the sale of goods subject to a warranty of quality'.
258 As we have seen (chapter 4, paras 5–6) babies have been so swapped.

adoption order is a 'decision relating to adoption', the court would have to make its decision on the basis that the child's welfare was paramount, taking account, of course, of the child's views.[259]

8.81 Revocation of adoption can be contrasted with the adopters raising an action for damages against an adoption agency which has induced them to adopt a child by concealing relevant information about a child. No action of this type appears to have been raised in Scotland but, in the USA, they have been successful. *Burr* v *Board of County Commissioners of Stark County*[260] provides a particularly graphic example of such a case. There, the adopters had been told by the adoption agency that the child's mother was an 18-year-old single woman who was moving out of the state in search of employment and who could not care for him. In fact, she was a 31-year-old patient in the state mental hospital and, while the father was unknown, it was thought that he was another patient. The child was diagnosed as uneducable and as having severe mental disabilities and Huntington's disease. The adopters were awarded substantial damages in their action against the adoption agency. It is submitted that such an action would be competent in Scotland in these circumstances.

Equitable adoption

8.82 For completeness, it should be noted that Scots law has no concept of equitable adoption. The concept has been used in the USA to secure inheritance rights to a child who has lived as a child of the family but has never been adopted.[261] Similarly, it has been used to impose an obligation to support a child financially.[262] Scots law has no need of the concept for the purpose of imposing an alimentary obligation, since a person who has accepted a child into his or her family already acquires a duty to aliment the child.[263] However, a child accepted into the family gains none of the succession rights accorded to other children, nor would the Scottish Law Commission's recommendations for reform of the law of succession create such a right.[264]

THE PROBLEM OF THE SUDDENLY-APPEARING FATHER

8.83 It is quite possible that a father will be unaware of the fact of his paternity. Since the married father has automatic parental responsibilities and rights, his consent is built into the adoption process and there is no real potential for him to appear 'out of the blue'. The unmarried father, who is given no parental responsibilities or rights automatically, might not be identified at an early stage of the adoption process. Can he become

---

259 1978 Act, s 6.
260 491 NE 2d 1101 (Ohio, 1976).
261 *Singer* v *Hara* 522 P 2d 1187 (Wash App, 1974); *Deveroux* v *Nelson* 517 SW 2d 658 (Tex Ct App, 1974). The court in Maryland refused to apply the concept to relieve a person of the duty to pay inheritance tax on property inherited form a 'quasi parent' – *McGarvey* v *State* 533 A 2d 690.
262 *Wener* v *Wener* 35 A 2d 50 (1970).
263 Family Law (Scotland) Act 1985, s 1(1)(d), discussed in chapter 6, para 64.
264 Report on Succession (Scot Law Com No 124, 1990) paras 3.13–3.14.

involved later? This question is worth considering in the light of a much-publicised case in the USA. The trend there has been towards greater recognition of the rights of unmarried fathers, at least where they have shown some commitment to fatherhood.[265] However, the whole question of the unmarried father's position in adoption cases came under the media spotlight in what came to be known as the 'Baby Jessica' case.[266]

8.84 Briefly, the facts are as follows. Cara Clausen, a single woman, gave birth to a baby girl, in Iowa, in February 1991. Within days, she and the man she named first as the baby's father released her for adoption and the baby went home to Michigan with her prospective adopters, the DeBoers. Ms Clausen soon began to have doubts about giving up her child and sought to reverse the termination of her parental rights. More significantly, for the first time, she named the baby's real father as Daniel Schmidt, a matter later confirmed by tests.[267] Mr Schmidt quickly sought legal advice and instituted proceedings to prevent the adoption going ahead. Meanwhile, the DeBoers were caring for the baby, whom they named Jessica, in Michigan. There followed two years of litigation in Iowa and Michigan and, undoubtedly, the case was complicated by the fact that two jurisdictions were involved. During this time, Ms Clausen and Mr Schmidt married each other. In September 1992, the Iowa Supreme Court concluded that Jessica should be returned to her birth parents and, after a period of further wrangling, the same conclusion was reached by the Michigan Supreme Court, largely on jurisdictional grounds.

8.85 The US Supreme Court refused a stay of enforcement and, on 3 August 1993, to the horror of the television-viewing public, Jessica, whom the Clausens had renamed Anna, was removed from the DeBoers to be handed over to the Clausens.[268] By this time Anna was two and a half years old. Was it in this child's best interests to be removed from the only home she had known and where she was happy and well-settled? According to the Iowa Supreme Court, that was not the issue. Whether a particular adoption would serve the child's best interests was a matter to be determined once the child was available for adoption. Until either the appropriate consent to her adoption had been obtained, or a court had terminated parental rights, the question of adoption did not arise. Since Mr Schmidt had not been informed of the fact of his paternity until rather late in the day, he could not have abandoned his daughter, so there was no reason for a court to terminate his parental rights, and his consent to her

---

265 *Stanley* v *Illinois* 405 US 645 (1972); *Quilloin* v *Walcott* 434 US 246 (1978); *Caban* v *Mohammed* 441 US 380 (1979); *Lehr* v *Robertson* 463 US 248 (1983).

266 *Deboer* v *Schmidt (In re Clausen)* 501 NW 2d 193 (Mich, 1993).

267 Apparently, at the time of the birth, Ms Clausen thought it was easier to name her current partner as the child's father, rather than Mr Schmidt, her ex-boyfriend. Doubtless, as events unfolded she realised that this had not been a wise decision, but one wonders how many women would have acted as she did in the same position. It may be that there are a host of time bombs ticking away with regard to fathers who had no opportunity to participate in an adoption decision.

268 As a member of that television-viewing public, I can confirm that the child's obvious distress was a reason for horror. The fact that television cameras were there at all was another reason.

adoption had never been sought. Unsurprisingly, the case generated considerable academic comment and has contributed to the more general debate on how decisions about a child's future ought to be taken.[269] As so often happens in cases involving children, one is left with a profound sadness and a feeling that 'there has got to be a better way to deal with this'. Of course, the challenge for lawyers and legislators is to find the 'better way' in a manner consistent with having due regard for the rights of everyone involved.

8.86 Such a case could arise, very easily, in Scotland. Were a father, who had been unaware of his paternity, to discover that he was a child's father and attempt to prevent the adoption going ahead, how would Scots law respond? If he marries the child's mother, he acquires parental responsibilities and rights, which makes him a parent for the purpose of consent to adoption.[270] Let us suppose, however, that he does not marry the child's mother. If a freeing order has been granted before the father discovers his paternity, the court may have discharged its obligation in respect of every person 'claiming' to be the child's father and have satisfied itself that no issue of his acquiring parental responsibilities or rights would arise.[271] While there is provision for revocation of a freeing order, it does not meet this situation.[272] It appears, then, that the court could not revoke the freeing order. The father's only remedy might be to petition the *nobile officium* of the Court of Session, since there is clearly a lacuna in the law. It might be argued that the court would be making a decision 'relating to the adoption of a child' and, as such, would be bound to regard the best interests of the child as the paramount consideration.[273] On the other hand, since the father's agreement to the granting of a freeing order could not have been dispensed with by simply applying the welfare test, it might be argued that the court must address the issue of whether his agreement should be dispensed with. If the latter view is preferred, the Court of Session would find itself in exactly the same position as was the Supreme Court in Iowa. That is to say, the welfare test does not fall to be applied until the child is available for adoption. The child is not available for adoption until either the parents have agreed or their agreement has been dispensed with. Assuming that the father's consent was not dispensed with, there would seem to be a strong case for revocation of the freeing. That would buy the father time to apply for parental responsibilities and rights in order to put him in a position to contest the adoption itself. There would be the opportunity for the court to dispense with his consent to

---

269 T. L. Craig, 'Establishing the Biological Rights Doctrine to Protect Unwed Fathers in Contested Adoptions' 25 Fla St U L Rev 391 (1998); K. Korn, 'The Struggle for the Child: Preserving the Family in Adoption Disputes Between Biological Parents and Third Parties' 72 N C L Rev 1279 (1994); E. P. Miller, 'DeBoer v Schmidt and Twiggs v Mays: Does the 'Best Interests of the Child' Standard Protect the Best Interests of Children?' 20 J Contemp L 497 (1994); B. Weaver-Catalana, 'The Battle for Baby Jessica: A Conflict of Interests' 43 Buff L Rev 583 (1995).
270 Children (Scotland) Act 1995, s 3(1)(b).
271 As it is required to do under s 18(7) of the 1978 Act.
272 1978 Act, s 20, discussed at para 8.88.
273 1978 Act, s 6(1).

adoption but, again, it could only do so on the basis of one of the grounds set out in s 16(2) of the 1978 Act.

8.87 What if the adoption order has been granted by the time the father becomes aware of his paternity? Can a father come forward at that stage and seek to have the adoption order reduced? As we have seen, reducing an adoption order will not be done lightly, but it is probably not impossible.[274] Let us take the case of a mother who lies about the identity of the child's father in order to facilitate the adoption and that man indicates that he has no intention of seeking parental responsibilities or rights. For whatever reason, the real father later discovers the truth. We have seen that the Inner House did not view adoption as a matter of contract,[275] but can fraud be relevant to an issue of status? Certainly, it has been accepted that an action to reduce a decree of divorce was competent where fraud was alleged, although Lord President Dunedin made it clear that 'it is absolutely necessary that there should be conclusive proof of the fact that something was concealed from the Court'.[276] By analogy, a case for the competency of reduction of an adoption order can certainly be made.

8.88 If the father cannot revoke the adoption order, can he at least seek contact with the child? Since such a father will never have had parental responsibilities and rights, they have not been removed by the adoption order and he may apply for contact with the child.[277] Bearing in mind that the decision on contact will be taken on the basis of the overarching principles, the suddenly-appearing father may face considerable difficulty. He has no established relationship on which to base any claim that the child's welfare would be served by contact with him. The courts do not accept that simple paternity is sufficient to warrant any assumption that contact should be allowed. In seeking to demonstrate that it would be better to make a contact order than that none should be made, it is difficult to see what other argument he could pull out of the hat. Were the child of sufficient age to express a view, it might be that the child's curiosity would afford him some support. None the less, the father's prospects are not good. This may seem harsh on a father who, through no fault of his own, was unaware of the fact of his paternity, but it simply demonstrates the fundamental, and correct, approach to issues involving children. The welfare of the child is the paramount consideration.

INTER-COUNTRY AND FOREIGN ADOPTION

8.89 As a result of the small number of children available for adoption in Scotland and of sympathy for the plight of children who are suffering

---

274 See para 8.78, above.
275 *J and J* v *C's Tutor* 1948 SC 636.
276 *Walker* v *Walker* 1911 SC 163, at p 170. In the event, the pursuer failed to produce sufficient proof. See also, *Begg* v *Begg* (1889) 16 R 550, where a proof before answer was allowed but, again, the pursuer failed to produce sufficient evidence.
277 He is not prevented from applying by the Children (Scotland) Act 1995, s 11(4)(a) and (b).

deprivation in other parts of the world, inter-country adoption has gained popularity.[278] It poses a number of special problems. Firstly, there is a danger that the full and free agreement of the birth parents may not have been obtained prior to the child being offered to the prospective adopters. Secondly, the ethnic and cultural dimension of such adoption must be considered. Thirdly, it would be wholly unacceptable that persons who were regarded as unfit to adopt a child in Scotland could do so by going abroad, since all children should be entitled to the protection afforded to Scottish children. Fourthly, there is a concern that financial inducements may play a greater part in adoptions outside the UK than is permitted here. That is not to suggest that inter-country adoption is undesirable. Provided that adequate safeguards surround it, adoption of a foreign child by a couple in Scotland may offer a child the chance to have a secure and loving home when the child would have been denied such a home otherwise.

8.90 International concern over inter-country adoption resulted in the Hague Convention on Jurisdiction, Applicable Law and Recognition of Decrees Relating to Adoptions.[279] While the Convention did not attract much support,[280] the UK did ratify it and enacted legislation to give effect to it.[281] The relevant provisions are now found in s 17 of the 1978 Act which deals with 'Convention adoption orders'. Given the very small number of countries which have ratified the Convention, it is hardly surprising that it has not given rise to litigation in the UK. It is expected that the more recent Hague Convention on Adoption of 1993, which utilises the mechanism of central authorities, already proven to be effective in the context of international child abduction, will attract greater support and the Adoption Bill, currently before Parliament, will give effect to its provisions.[282]

8.91 At present, the real control of foreign adoption is exercised through immigration law and the recognition of non-Convention adoptions.[283] An adoption order made in England, Wales, Northern Ireland, the Isle of Man or any of the Channel Islands is an adoption order within the meaning of the 1978 Act and is recognised as such.[284] 'Overseas adoptions' are recognised in Scotland and are regulated by the statutory instruments in force governing 'adoptions of children appearing to [the Secretary of

278 As Rosenblatt points out – 'International adoptions are not always inter-country *per se*, in that they do not always involve the respective procedures of two separate countries'; Rosenblatt, *International Adoption* (Sweet and Maxwell, 1995) at p 1.
279 TS 94 (1978); Cmnd 7342.
280 Apart from the UK, the Convention has only been ratified by Austria and Switzerland.
281 Adoption (Scotland) Act 1978.
282 See the Consultation Paper, Proposals for Intercountry Adoption (Scottish Office, 1996) which considered how the 1993 Hague Convention might be implemented in Scotland.
283 See E. Crawford, *Private International Law* (W. Green, 1997), chapter 11; Rosenblatt, above; J. M. Scott, 'Adoption' in Cleland and Sutherland, n 27 above; Wilkinson and Norrie, *Parent and Child*, pp 576–588; *Butterworth's Scottish Family Law Service*, paras C1504–C1526.
284 1978 Act, s 38(1)(c).

State] to be effected under the law of any country outside Great Britain'.[285] Where an adoption does not fall within one of these categories, it may still be recognised at common law and certainly, the 1978 Act countenances recognition of other kinds of adoptions.[286]

285 1978 Act, ss 38(1)(d) and 65(2). See SI 1973 No 19 as amended by SI 1995 No 1614.
286 1978 Act, s 38(1)(e).

CHAPTER 9

THE CHILDREN'S HEARINGS SYSTEM

9.1 A child may be referred to the Principal Reporter who decides whether it is necessary to convene a children's hearing to examine the child's case, where it appears that the child may be in need of compulsory measures of supervision.[1] Before examining how the system works, it is necessary to take a brief look at its history and philosophy, how it has worked, and at the personnel involved in its operation.

HISTORICAL BACKGROUND

9.2 Scots law has long provided mechanisms aimed at child protection and at dealing with juvenile offenders. The children's hearings system[2] resulted from the Kilbrandon Committee, set up in 1961 with the following remit: 'to consider the provisions of the law of Scotland relating to the treatment of juvenile delinquents and juveniles in need of care and protection or beyond parental control, and, in particular, the constitution, powers, and procedure of the courts dealing with such juveniles and to report'.[3] The Committee reported in 1964, its proposals were largely accepted by the government of the day[4] and appropriate legislation duly followed.[5] That comparatively speedy and simple process, which is the envy of modern law reformers, gave Scotland a system for providing additional

---

1 As we have seen, a court may refer a case to the Principal Reporter when it is considering parental responsibilities or rights (chapter 5, para 87) and the local authority is bound to do so in a variety of circumstances (see chapter 7).
2 R. Breustedt, B. Kearney, A. Stevens and E. E. Sutherland, 'The Evolution of the Children's Hearings System over the Last Twenty-five Years', (1997) 2 SLPQ 73; A. Gordon, 'The Role of the State', in E. E. Sutherland and A. Cleland (eds), *Children's Rights in Scotland* (W. Green, 1996); *B. Kearney, *Children's Hearings and the Sheriff Court* (W. Green, 1987) (new edition in preparation); A. Lockyer and F. M. Stone (eds), *Juvenile Justice in Scotland: Twenty-Five Years of the Welfare Approach* (1998, T & T Clark); K. McK. Norrie, *Children's Hearings in Scotland* (W. Green, 1997); *The Laws of Scotland, Stair Memorial Encyclopaedia* vol 3; paras 1261–1387; *A. B. Wilkinson and K. McK. Norrie, *Parent and Child* (W. Green, 1993), Ch 17. While the publications marked *discuss the hearings system as it was under the 1968 Act, they are none the less valuable sources.
3 Report of the Committee on Children and Young Persons, Scotland, Cmnd 2306, 1964, para 1, usually referred to as the 'Kilbrandon Report' or simply 'Kilbrandon'.
4 Social Work and the Community, Cmnd 3065, 1966.
5 The Social Work (Scotland) Act 1968, Part III, hereinafter, the '1968 Act'. The system did not become operational until 1971 and the delay can be attributed to local government reorganisation, the need to set up the necessary infrastructure, and training of personnel.

help and guidance to children and young people who appeared to need it, whether the need was demonstrated by their own actions or by the behaviour of others.

9.3 It would not be an overstatement to say that the hearings system has attracted enormous support both at home and abroad, and it has been variously described as 'remarkable and unique'[6]; 'a model for restructuring juvenile justice systems'[7]; 'this reform which has earned so much praise'[8]; and 'a vastly superior way of dealing with children and their problems than ever the old courts were'.[9] Nowhere would complacency be more misplaced than in the field of child law and this radical reform has itself been subject to intense scrutiny and critical appraisal.[10] Aspects of the system have received criticism – on one occasion from no less a body than the European Court of Human Rights.[11] Furthermore, the way the hearings system operated made it necessary for the UK to enter a reservation (now withdrawn) when ratifying the United Nations Convention on the Rights of the Child.[12] Sometimes, perceived shortcomings were dealt with by specific legislation.[13] However, the Children (Scotland) Act 1995 ('the 1995 Act') presented the opportunity to repeal the old legislation governing the system, to re-enact and consolidate much of it, and to introduce some reform measures. None the less, and despite the reforms introduced, the philosophy of the Kilbrandon Committee remains the foundation of the modern children's hearings system.

9.4 The use made of the hearings system has changed over the years.[14] In 1972, 92% of referrals were on the ground that the child was alleged to have committed an offence while only 8% were care and protection cases. By 1996–97, the corresponding figures were 69% and 31% respectively.[15]

---

6 George Younger (then Secretary of State for Scotland) in the foreword to F. M. Martin and K. Murray (eds), *The Scottish Juvenile Justice System* (Scottish Academic Press, 1982).

7 S. Fox, *Children's Hearings and the International Community*, 1991 Kilbrandon Child Care Lecture (Scottish Office, 1991) at p 17.

8 *Sloan* v *B* 1991 SLT 530, per Lord President Hope at p 548.

9 Twenty-one Years of Children's Hearings (The Scottish Office, 1993), at p 24.

10 Review of Child Care Law in Scotland (HMSO, 1990); Report of the Inquiry into the Removal of Children from Orkney in February 1991 (the 'Clyde Report', HMSO, 1992); Report of the Inquiry into Child Care Policies in Fife (the 'Kearney Report', HMSO, 1992); Another Kind of Home: a review of residential child care (the 'Skinner Report', HMSO, 1992); Reporters to the Children's Panel: Their Role, Function and Accountability (the 'Finlayson Report', HMSO, 1992); Emergency Protection of Children: Consultation Paper on Proposals for Change (HMSO, 1993); Scotland's Children: Proposals for Child Care Policy and Law (Cm 2286, 1993).

11 *McMichael* v *United Kingdom* [1995] 20 EHRR 205.

12 Reservation F was withdrawn on 18 April 1997. See chapter 3, para 14.

13 See, for example, the Children Act 1975, s 66, which introduced safeguarders (discussed later in this chapter) into the system, and the Solvent Abuse (Scotland) Act 1983, which addressed the public concern of the time surrounding children sniffing glue and other substances. See, J. M. Watson, *Solvent Abuse – The Adolescent Epidemic?* (1986).

14 See, R. Breustedt, B. Kearney, A. Stevens and E. E. Sutherland, 'The Evolution of the Children's Hearings System over the Last Twenty-five Years' (1997) 2 SLPQ 73.

15 Initially the statistics on children's hearings were published as part of the *Social Work Statistics* (HMSO) and from 1976 to 1996, they were published annually by the Scottish Office in a separate publication, *Statistical Bulletin: Referrals of Children to Reporters and*

There are a number of possible explanations for this movement in the types of cases which form the bulk of the system's caseload. Initially, it may have been that the system was perceived by the public and the various agencies involved with children as being concerned primarily with children who offended. Over the last 25 years, however, there has been a radical increase in the awareness of the extent of child abuse and neglect in Scotland. This increased awareness has, in turn, led to a greater appreciation of the need to recognise the problem and to respond to it in an appropriate manner. It is one of the strengths of the hearings system that it has been able to respond to the changing demands being placed upon it. In addition, the actual number of children being referred to the reporter has doubled in real terms.[16] While some of this increase can be explained by the greater awareness of child abuse and neglect and, indeed, may reflect a degree of faith in the way the system operates, the fact that so many children may require compulsory intervention in their lives is cause for concern.

THE KILBRANDON PHILOSOPHY

9.5 What, then, were the Kilbrandon Committee's recommendations and the thinking behind them? There are essentially three strands to the Kilbrandon philosophy. First, when assessing the child's needs, the Committee concluded that there was little practical difference between children who offended and those who were in need of protection from others, since the 'normal up-bringing process' had 'fallen short'[17] in all of the cases. Thus, it concluded, it would be appropriate to deal with both types of cases in the same forum. This idea of treating 'children who did wrong' along with 'children who were being wronged' is often seen as the most radical departure from what had gone before, and there were concerns that innocent children might be stigmatised by sharing a forum with offenders. However, since the essence of the Kilbrandon philosophy is treatment, rather than punishment, in respect of offenders, that fear was misplaced. That the Committee should have recommended such a child-centred approach to all children, some 21 years before the UN Convention is both remarkable and encouraging.

9.6 Second, Kilbrandon believed that, in both situations, 'special measures of education and training' were required to overcome the child's problems.[18] This heralded the advent of a system which was whole-heartedly dedicated to applying the non-punitive treatment model to

Children's Hearings. The Scottish Children's Reporters Administration (SCRA) assumed responsibility for the relevant statistics from April 1997 and the *Statistical Bulletin: Referrals of Children to Reporters and Children's Hearings 1996/97* (No SCRA/IM/1998/21) covers the period 1 April 1996 to 31 March 1997. Throughout this chapter, statistics quoted will be derived from this source unless otherwise stated and it will be referred to simply as the 'Statistical Bulletin'. It is worth noting that these statistics predate the implementation of Part II of the 1995 Act but, none the less, they give a flavour of how the system operates.

16 Whereas, in 1972, 17,950 children (12.2 per 1,000 children under 16) were referred to the reporter, the number had risen to 25,862 (26.13 per 1,000 children under 16) by 1996/97.

17 Kilbrandon Report, n 3 above, para 15.

18 Above, para 15.

juvenile offenders. While the previous system had embraced education as one of its goals, these recommendations sought to strengthen the treatment element. In respect of both offenders and children in need of protection, the emphasis was to be on examining the whole circumstances of the child's life with a view to finding a positive way to proceed. Although the modern term 'holistic approach' is not found in the Kilbrandon Report, it was clearly in the minds of the committee members when they recommended that decisions on disposal should be made in the light of a variety of factors: the whole circumstances of the child's case; involvement of and co-operation from the child's family; and ensuring the continued involvement of the decision-makers in the child's life in order that the measures initially applied could be varied in the light of the child's response to them.[19]

9.7 The third strand of the Kilbrandon philosophy drew a distinction between determination of the facts – for example, whether the parents did leave a child unattended or whether a particular child stole from a shop – and the decision on disposal, ie what should happen to the child.[20] While, in cases of disputed facts, the former is a matter with which courts are ideally suited to deal, the latter could be dealt with more appropriately in some other setting. Indeed, since the involvement of the child's family and the continued involvement of the decision-makers was to be central to the new approach, courts would be singularly unsuited to handling such matters. The Committee therefore recommended the creation of panels of individuals, drawn from the community, who would sit together in groups of three to explore the whole circumstances of the case and determine the disposal.[21] Central to the proposed system, and the full participation by all concerned that was inherent in it, is the informality which such lay panels could offer when compared with courts. Essential to 'full, free and unhurried discussion'[22] of all the circumstances involved is the private nature of hearings. Thus, hearings are not open to the public, and while members of the press may be present, it is an offence to publish any material which would identify the child or the child's address or school.[23] A further Kilbrandon recommendation was that hearings should take place in 'relatively simple accommodation of the committee-room type, preferably in reasonably modern buildings, the room itself combining an atmosphere of simplicity and unobtrusive and unostentatious dignity ... in premises ... dissociated entirely from the criminal courts and police stations'.[24] This recommendation was taken up and, in order that all the individuals present should participate as fully as possible, it is important that they should feel comfortable and not be intimidated by their surroundings, as so often happens in courts. Since the new measures represented considerably more

---

19 Above, paras 12–33 and 77–79.
20 Above, para 72.
21 Above, para 73.
22 Above, para 109.
23 Children (Scotland) Act 1995, s 44. The Secretary of State may dispense with the prohibition on publicity in respect of a children's hearing in the interests of justice. Where related proceedings are in the sheriff court or the Court of Session, the courts may dispense with the prohibition on publicity.
24 Kilbrandon Report, n 3 above, para 226.

intrusion in the lives of the children concerned and their families, it was recognised that there was a need to provide for appeals to the courts over matters of disposal and for regular review of each child's case.[25]

PERSONNEL OF THE HEARINGS SYSTEM

9.8 The child concerned is the central person in the hearings system. Other family members will, of course, also play a crucial role in most cases. However, in order to understand the structure of the system, it is helpful to view the personnel involved in its operation from a different perspective.

Secretary of State for Scotland

9.9 In terms of the organisation of the system, overall control lies with the Secretary of State for Scotland,[26] who is responsible for a whole range of matters associated with it, including: making regulations under the 1995 Act; making rules for the conduct of hearings;[27] appointing and dismissing members of the children's panel for each area;[28] and prescribing the qualifications for reporters.[29] Appointment of panel members takes place after consultation with the Children's Panel Advisory Committee in each area.[30] In the past, a reporter could only be dismissed with the consent of the Secretary of State. However, this is no longer the case, although appeal against dismissal lies to the Secretary of State.[31]

Children's Panel Advisory Committee

9.10 Each local authority[32] in Scotland must establish a Children's Panel Advisory Committee (CPAC), consisting of two members nominated by the local authority and three nominated by the Secretary of State, who also appoints the chairman.[33] Essentially, the function of the CPAC is to advise

25 Above, para 197.
26 At present, the Scottish Office Minister for Children's Issues also has considerable involvement in the system. The children's hearings system will be one of the devolved matters after the Scottish Parliament is established; Scotland's Parliament, (Cm 3658, 1997) p 4; Scotland Act 1998. It may be that any new Minister for Children's Issues will take over the function currently discharged by the Secretary of State.
27 Children (Scotland) Act 1995, s 42.
28 Section 39(2) and Sched 1, para 1.
29 Section 40(1).
30 Schedule 1, para 6.
31 Local Government (Scotland) Act 1994, s 129(1) and Reporters (Appeals against Dismissal) (Scotland) Regulations 1997 (SI 1997 No 729).
32 Children (Scotland) Act 1995, Sched 1, para 3. Two or more local authorities may form a joint CPAC, provided that they have the written consent of the Secretary of State – Sched 1, para 8. This was intended to enable small local authorities to pool resources and benefit from the economies of scale in terms of both resources and personnel. Clackmannan, Falkirk and Stirling, for example, have taken advantage of the opportunity to do so.
33 Schedule 1, para 5. The local authority may ask the Secretary of State to increase the number of people serving on the CPAC and, where the request is granted, each additional member is nominated alternately by the Secretary of State or the local authority – Sched 1, para 4.

the Secretary of State on the appointment of panel members and, if requested to do so, on the general administration of the panels.[34]

The Local Authority

9.11 Local authorities play an important part in the hearings system in terms of administration, support and in implementation of the hearings' decisions. In addition to establishing a CPAC, each local authority must make arrangements to assist the CPAC in finding potential panel members and in training them.[35] The local authority is responsible for publishing a list of the names and addresses of the panel members for its area and making that list available for public inspection.[36] While the Secretary of State determines the level of expenses to be paid, it is the local authority which actually meets the expenses of panel members, potential panel members, members of the CPAC and its sub-committees, and safeguarders.[37]

Children's Panel and Panel Members

9.12 Each local government area in Scotland has a children's panel, made up of individual members of the community who have been appointed by the Secretary of State, including the chairman and deputy chairman.[38] At first instance, potential panel members are self-selecting, in that people volunteer. However, these volunteers are interviewed and screened before they embark on a rigorous programme of training.[39] Given the extensive powers of a children's hearing to determine the future arrangements for a particular child, it is essential that selection and training of panel members should be as thorough as possible. Although appointment lies solely in the hands of the Secretary of State, a panel member can only be dismissed by the Secretary of State with the consent of the Lord President.[40] To date, no panel member has ever been dismissed although some have, for a variety of reasons, not had their appointment renewed. Once appointed, a panel member becomes eligible to sit on a children's hearing. Panel members are unpaid, although their expenses are met by the local authority.

9.13 A children's hearing is made up of three members of the children's panel[41] and each hearing must have one male and one female serving on

---

34 Schedule 1, para 6. The CPAC may submit the names of potential panel members and, if requested to do so, advise the Secretary of State on the suitability of persons referred to him or her as potential panel members.
35 Schedule 1, para 10.
36 Schedule 1, para 12.
37 Schedule 1, para 11 and s 41(4). While panel members and members of the CPAC are only paid expenses, safeguarders receive a fee in addition to their expenses.
38 Section 39.
39 At present, training is funded by each individual local authority, with a number sharing resources on an informal or ad hoc basis. Plans are afoot to develop a national training programme, although it is envisaged that delivery of training will remain at a local level. The Scottish Office presently funds a small network of independent training organisers based at the Universities of Aberdeen, Edinburgh, Glasgow and St Andrews.
40 Tribunals and Inquiries Act 1992, s 7(1)(e) and Sched 1, Part II, para 61.
41 Children (Scotland) Act 1995, s 39(3).

it.[42] One member of the hearing will serve as chairman and, while that person has no greater say in the final decision than the other two members, he or she has a variety of duties to carry out in the course of the hearing. These will be explored when the various stages of the hearing are examined below. It is the children's hearing, as constituted in each case, that is responsible for reaching a decision in respect of an individual child.

The Reporter

9.14 The 1995 Act refers to various functions being the responsibility of the Principal Reporter. He or she is the chief officer of the Scottish Children's Reporter Administration (SCRA), the national service which appoints, employs and manages the deployment of the individual reporters throughout Scotland.[43] In reality, and in terms of the 1995 Act,[44] the responsibilities associated with the hearings system are usually carried out by these individual reporters and that term will be used here. The Secretary of State may prescribe the qualifications of reporters and, while they may be legally qualified, they need not be.[45] Where a reporter is not legally qualified, he or she may still appear in court, subject to regulations prescribed by the Secretary of State and the Lord Advocate.[46] Subject to the general provisions of employment law, a reporter can be dismissed by SCRA, but appeal against dismissal lies to the Secretary of State.[47]

9.15 The reporter's role in the hearings system is central to its operation, since it is through the reporter that children come to hearings. The reporter's functions are: to receive information about children who may be in need of *compulsory measures of supervision*;[48] to investigate the case,[49] drawing upon other agencies for further information; to decide whether a hearing needs to be convened and, if so, to arrange a hearing.[50] Thus, the reporter's role is both one of decision-making and one of administration and the various aspects of this role will be explored more fully later.

Safeguarders

9.16 Safeguarders were not part of the original children's hearings system and were a creation of the Children Act 1975,[51] although it was not until

---

42 Section 39(5).
43 In 1995, there were 133 reporters employed throughout Scotland; Statistical Bulletin, p 27.
44 Section 40(5) and s 93(1).
45 Section 40(1).
46 Section 40(4). The Reporters (Conduct of Proceedings before the Sheriff) (Scotland) (Amendment) Regulations 1997 (SI 1997, No 1084). A reporter who does not have a practising certificate may, none the less, appear in court after having gained at least one year's experience as a reporter. See *Elizabeth Templeton v ME* (Sh Ct) 1998 SCLR 672, at p 679B.
47 Local Government (Scotland) Act 1994, s 129(1) and Reporters (Appeals against Dismissal) (Scotland) Regulations 1997 (SI 1997 No 729).
48 Children (Scotland) Act 1995, s 53(1).
49 Section 56(1).
50 Section 65(1).
51 Section 66 of the 1975 Act added s 34A to the Social Work (Scotland) Act 1968.

1984[52] that the relevant provision was brought into force. Like its predecessor, there is no mention in the 1995 Act of the word 'safeguarder' and instead, it simply refers to 'a person to safeguard the interests of the child'.[53] Safeguarders are appointed by the local authority, after consultation with the Sheriff Principal and the chairman of the children's panel for the area, and the appointment is for three years, with the possibility of reappointment on one occasion. The Secretary of State is empowered to make regulations with respect to their functions,[54] and access to information[55] and the procedure for their appointment.[56] Payment of safeguarders, at a level well below that of curators *ad litem*, is a local authority responsibility.[57]

9.17 A children's hearing or a court must consider whether it is necessary to appoint a person to safeguard the interests of the child and, if it is, must appoint a safeguarder, subject to such terms and conditions as are thought appropriate.[58] Thus, the hearing or the sheriff must be satisfied that a third party is needed to protect the child's interests in the proceedings; that is to say that the function fulfilled by the hearing or the sheriff may not, in itself, be enough to provide that protection. This requirement, which was one of the preconditions for appointment under the Social Work (Scotland) Act 1968 ('the 1968 Act'), may have contributed to some initial reluctance to appoint safeguarders.[59] The various reports which preceded the 1995 Act supported an enhanced role for the safeguarder[60] and the language of the 1995 Act is more directive than was previously the case.[61] It is anticipated that greater use will be made of safeguarders in the future.

9.18 To describe the role of the safeguarder as being 'to safeguard the

52 Social Work (Panels of Persons to Safeguard the Interests of Children) (Scotland) Regulations 1984, SI 1984 No 1442 (S119). An attempt was made in 1996 to draft new regulations governing safeguarders but it did not come to fruition; see draft Panel of Safeguarders, Reporting Officers and Curators *ad litem* (Scotland) Regulations 1996.
53 Children (Scotland) Act 1995, s 41(1)(a).
54 Section 42(2)(f).
55 Ibid.
56 Section 42(2)(e).
57 Section 41(4) and (5).
58 Section 41(1). A safeguarder may not be appointed in proceedings to consider the granting of a child protection order (see, chapter 7, para 77) and the safeguarder's role in appeals is somewhat ambiguous (see, para 9.99).
59 Under the previous legislation, there was a further explanation for the low rate of appointment of safeguarders. The hearing or the sheriff had to be satisfied not only that the appointment of a safeguarder was necessary to protect the interests of the child, but also that there was or was likely to be a conflict of interest between the child and the parents, before an appointment could be made – the 1968 Act, s 34A. Even with such restrictive conditions for appointment, the use of safeguarders was becoming slightly more frequent. Whereas in 1987, a safeguarder was appointed in only 1.2% of cases, the figure had risen to 5.7% by 1996/97. However, this global figure masks enormous regional variations, with a safeguarder being appointed in 14.2% of cases in SCRA's eastern region but only 1.9% of cases in the south east; *Statistical Bulletin*, Tables 12C and 12D.
60 See, Review of Child Care Law in Scotland, n 10 above, Recommendation 85; Report of the Inquiry into the Removal of Children from Orkney in February 1991, n 10 above, paras 17.10–17.15; Scotland's Children: Proposals for Child Care Policy and Law, n 10 above, para 6.20.
61 While the 1968 Act made it mandatory to consider the need to appoint a safeguarder, it was simply permissive on the matter of actually making the appointment. While it was

interests of the child' is somewhat tautologous and, indeed, there is a degree of ambiguity about the precise role of the safeguarder.[62] Essentially, the safeguarder has two functions. The first is to provide an independent, and often fresh, analysis of what will serve the child's best interests. The second is to assist the child in expressing his or her views and, where the child is not present at the hearing, actually conveying these views.[63] While doubt has been expressed that one person can fulfil both functions adequately, particularly where the safeguarder's conclusion on what will serve the child's best interests conflicts with the child's views, such doubt is unfounded.[64]

'Relevant Persons'

9.19 Again, the user-unfriendly term 'relevant person', is found in the context of children's hearings. It has the same meaning and is open to the same objections as were discussed in chapter 7. Briefly, a relevant person is anyone who has parental responsibilities or rights in respect of the child, or who ordinarily (other than by reason of employment) has charge of, or control over, the child.[65] Frequently, this will mean that the relevant persons will be the child's parents, if they are or have been married to each other, but it would include another relative or a parent's cohabitant, if that individual was actually involved in caring for the child. Foster carers would often qualify,[66] since they are not employed to care for a child, but a childminder would not.

9.20 One category of person requires special mention – the so-called 'genetic father'. An unmarried father who has not acquired parental responsibilities or rights and is not caring for the child is not a relevant person.[67] However, if he is living with the child's mother, the Children's

probably of lesser significance in practice, it is worth noting that, while the 1968 Act placed the responsibility for the decision on the chairman of the hearing, the 1995 Act talks in terms of the whole hearing.

62 Initially, this problem was exacerbated by the lack of training available to them, vagueness as to their precise powers and their isolation within the system. Isolation was perhaps inevitable, given the necessarily independent role of the safeguarder. The formation of the Scottish Safeguarders Association has gone some way towards addressing the problem. In addition, the Secretary of State has made regulations governing the training, function and powers of safeguarders – see n 52 above.

63 Children's Hearings (Scotland) Rules 1996 SI 1996 No 3261 ('the 1996 Rules'), r 15(4)(c) recognises the role of the safeguarder in conveying the child's views.

64 See chapter 3, para 43 and E. E. Sutherland, 'The Role of the Safeguarder', in Representing Children: Listening to the Voice of the Child (Scottish Child Law Centre, 1996).

65 Children (Scotland) Act 1995, s 93(2). See chapter 7, para 32 for a fuller discussion of relevant persons.

66 The position of a foster carer will depend, to some extent, on the nature and duration of the care. While an emergency foster carer who had been looking after the child for a very short period cannot be described as 'ordinarily' caring for the child, a person who has been the child's carer for a period of years can be so described. Where the dividing line will be drawn remains to be seen.

67 In *McMichael* v *United Kingdom*, [1995] 20 EHRR 205, the European Court held that denying an unmarried father any right to participate in the hearing process was justifiable.

Hearings (Scotland) Rules 1996 ('the 1996 Rules'), rather than the 1995 Act, accord him a special position in the hearings system, with the right to receive copies of all the same documents as a relevant person does[68] and to attend the hearing.[69] None the less, since he is not a relevant person, he has no right to accept or deny the grounds of referral, appeal against the hearing's decision, or call for a review – a situation which is bound to confuse some of the beneficiaries of the provision. On the basis that half a loaf is better than none at all, it can be said that at least some recognition is being afforded to some unmarried fathers, but the number who will benefit from this recognition will be extremely small. If the father is living with the mother, one would assume that he would have some responsibility for the child's care and control. Thus, the only situation in which this provision will apply is where the parents are living together and the child is living elsewhere.

9.21 The 1995 Act does not make clear who decides whether an individual is a relevant person but such a decision comes within the chairman's overall control of procedure at hearings.[70] Preventing attendance by a relevant person would be a ground for appeal against the hearing's decision.[71] While the chairman has a duty to keep the number of people present at a hearing to a minimum,[72] this does not affect a relevant person's right to attend. The general rule is that each relevant person has both the right and the duty to attend a hearing.[73] The right to attend is subject to the possibility of a person being excluded from part of a hearing where the person's presence is likely to inhibit the child in expressing his or her views and is causing, or is likely to cause, significant distress to the child.[74] The hearing may free an individual from the obligation to attend if it would be unreasonable to expect such attendance or if it would be unnecessary for the proper consideration of the case.[75] So, for example, the hearing might decide that it was not essential that a parent should return from a far-flung corner of the world where he or she was working when the other parent could be present. The fact that a parent was in prison in Scotland would not present such an obstacle as to make attendance unreasonable and, in any event, would not remove the parent's right to attend.

The child

9.22 The child is, of course, the central person in the hearings system. Thus, it is unsurprising that the child has both the right and the duty to attend his or her own hearing.[76] The child can be freed from the obligation

---

68 1996 Rules, r 5(3)(b).
69 1996 Rules, r 12(1).
70 1996 Rules, r 10(3). A business meeting may be required to determine whether a particular person is a relevant person for the purpose of notification of a hearing; s 64 and 1996 Rules, r 4(2)(a).
71 Section 51.
72 Section 43(1).
73 Section 45(8).
74 Section 46.
75 Section 45(8).
76 Section 45(1).

to attend, if, in respect of certain grounds of referral,[77] his or her presence is deemed to be unnecessary, or, in any case, where such presence would be detrimental to his or her interests.[78] However, the child cannot be prevented from attending the hearing if he or she wishes to do so. If the reporter can show cause, the hearing may issue a warrant to find the child, to keep him or her in a place of safety, and to bring the child to a hearing.[79] Similarly, a warrant can be issued at the reporter's request or at the hearing's discretion where the child has failed to attend a hearing.[80] A child can be detained for up to seven days under such a warrant although it will expire on the first day the hearing sits to consider the case if that is earlier.[81]

HOW CHILDREN'S HEARINGS WORK

9.23 The hearings system provides for children who are in need of *compulsory measures of supervision* but sometimes the needs of a particular child can be met in another way. For example, parents may have left a young child unattended on occasions but, once they have discussed the matter with a social worker, they may have appreciated that such conduct is inappropriate and the reporter may be satisfied that they will not leave the child alone in the future. In such a case, the reporter may decide that a hearing is unnecessary. Similarly, a child may have been truanting regularly but, once the reporter learns of the progress made in discussions between the child, the parents, and the school, he or she may again decide that a hearing is unnecessary. The crucial point to bear in mind is that the hearings system is there to provide for the needs of each individual child.

9.24 The hearings system is governed, subject to one exception, by the overarching principles found throughout the 1995 Act. Decisions of both the hearing and the sheriff are governed by the paramountcy of the welfare principle, except where the need to protect members of the public from serious harm warrants another course of action. A child of sufficient age and maturity has a right to have his or her views taken into account, and the principle of not intervening unless intervention will be better applies. While reiteration of these principles is always valuable, they were already fundamental to the hearings system before the 1995 Act was passed.

Grounds of referral

9.25 Before a case can proceed to a hearing, the reporter must be satisfied that there is a *prima facie* case, satisfying at least one of the grounds of referral.[82] Since the grounds of referral are the trigger which suggest that a child may be in need of compulsory measures of care, they warrant close

---

77 These are the grounds of referral involving the allegation that a person other than the child has committed any of the offences listed in Schedule 1 of the Criminal Procedure (Scotland) Act 1995.
78 Children (Scotland) Act 1995, s 45(2).
79 Section 45(4).
80 Section 45(5).
81 Section 45(6).
82 Section 52(1).

examination. Of course, some children are referred to the reporter on more than one ground. Most of the grounds of referral are identical to, or substantially the same as, those found in the original legislation, although some changes have been made.

(a) the child is beyond the control of any relevant person[83]

9.26 The fact that this is one of the more self-explanatory grounds for referral is evidenced by the dearth of litigation surrounding it. We have already seen that, where a person has responsibilities for children, he or she will normally have corresponding rights in order that the responsibilities can be met. Thus, the responsibilities to safeguard and promote the child's health, development and welfare and to provide appropriate direction and guidance has the corresponding right to control, direct or guide the child's upbringing in a manner appropriate to the child's stage of development. Where the necessary control is not being exercised, for whatever reason, then the fear is that the responsibilities might not be met. Obviously, the degree of control that is appropriate in respect of an individual child will vary and such factors as age, developmental level, and special circumstances (for example, behavioural problems) will be relevant. While the lack of control will often be due to the child's failure to co-operate, it may be caused by some other factor, for example, the relevant person's health problems.

(b) the child is falling into bad associations or is exposed to moral danger[84]

9.27 This ground contains two, sometimes separable, conditions, and satisfying either alone is sufficient for a referral. However, in respect of each, the essence of this ground is the impact which the associations or danger might have on the child, in terms of actual harm or learned behaviour and attitudes, regardless of whether such effect is actually manifesting itself at present. In respect of 'bad associations', the fact that the child is spending time with a disruptive group of teenagers might be enough, even if the child has not done anything wrong as a result of the association. Exposure to moral danger might be constituted by the fact that the parents' home is frequented by alcoholics or drug addicts or by the fact that a parent carries out his or her occupation as a prostitute from the home. Where the only evidence supporting an allegation that a child is exposed to moral danger is the child's own criminal conduct, that conduct must be proved beyond reasonable doubt.[85] The value-laden terms 'bad' and 'moral danger' are, perhaps, unfortunate, since they carry with them the risk of socio-economic or cultural prejudices being expressed.

---

83 Section 52(2)(a).
84 Section 52(2)(b).
85 *Constanda* v *M* 1997 SCLR 510. In that case, a 14 year-old boy was referred to a hearing on the ground that he was exposed to moral danger. The only evidence was that he had committed various lewd acts in the presence of his ten year-old female cousin. In the absence of corroboration, the court refused to find the ground of referral established. Clearly, had there been corroborative evidence, the boy could have been referred to the hearing on the simpler ground that he had committed an offence.

*(c) the child is likely – (i) to suffer unnecessarily; or (ii) be impaired
seriously in his or her health or development, due to a lack of parental
care[86]*

9.28 The test for this ground is an objective one, that is to say, whether a
reasonable person looking at the circumstances would conclude that the
lack of parental care was likely either to cause the child unnecessary
suffering or to cause serious impairment to health or development.[87] The
suffering or impairment need not be physical, and emotional or psychological harm is also relevant.[88] Although the term 'parental care' is used, it
applies to anyone with parental responsibilities and rights, whether a
parent or not. It is not necessary that the parents' lack of care should be
motivated by their malice or indifference, since parental illness or ignorance may just as easily put the child at risk. Indeed, the fact that the
parental motive is a protective one is irrelevant.[89] Where a parent provides
inadequate substitute care, thereby risking causing the child unnecessary
suffering or serious impairment, that, in itself, would satisfy this ground of
referral. A parent's lack of care may be evidenced by a failure to protect
the child from the actions of others.[90] Actual harm need not have occurred
– it is the likelihood of harm that is relevant here and so, for example, the
ground may apply where a baby has never lived with the parents whose
past conduct is thought to put the child at risk.[91]

*(d) the child is a child in respect of whom any of the offences mentioned in
Schedule 1 to the Criminal Procedure (Scotland) Act 1995 has been
committed[92]*

9.29 The offences listed in Schedule I are as follows:

(i) any offence under the Criminal Law (Consolidation) (Scotland) Act
1995, Part I (sexual offences);
(ii) offences under the Children and Young Persons (Scotland) Act
1937, s 12 (cruelty to persons under 16), s 15 (causing or allowing a
person under 16 to be used for begging), s 22 (exposing a child under 7
to the risk of burning), or s 33 (causing or allowing a person under 16 to
take part in a dangerous performance);
(iii) any other offence involving bodily injury to a child under the age of
17 years;
(iv) any offence involving the use of lewd, indecent or libidinous practice
or behaviour towards a child under the age of 17 years.

9.30 A further group of offences, relating to the taking, distributing,

86 Section 52(2)(c).
87 *M* v *McGregor* 1982 SLT 41, per Lord Justice-Clerk Wheatley, at p 43.
88 *F* v *Suffolk County Council* [1981] 2 FLR 208.
89 *Finlayson, Applicant* 1989 SCLR 601, where the parents' refusal to allow their haemophiliac son to be treated with donated plasma was prompted by their fear that he might
contract HIV from it.
90 *Kennedy* v *S* 1986 SLT 679, where it was the father's cohabitant who ejected the child
from the home at night.
91 *McGregor* v *L* 1981 SLT 194.
92 Section 52(2)(d).

possessing or publishing of indecent photographs of a person under the age of 16 years, is still found in the Civic Government (Scotland) Act 1982, s 52(1). That Act refers to them as Schedule 1 offences for the purpose of the, now repealed, Criminal Procedure (Scotland) Act 1975.[93] Their omission from its successor, the Criminal Procedure (Scotland) Act 1995, would appear to be a drafting oversight.

9.31 This ground of referral is concerned, as are the others, with the needs of children and not with the conviction of offenders, albeit the two matters are not unconnected.[94] It is satisfied where it is established that one of the specified offences has been committed against a child, and it is not necessary that any individual should have been charged with the offence, far less that there should have been a conviction.[95] It does not matter that the offence was committed outwith Scotland.[96] Since children's hearings are civil,[97] rather than criminal, proceedings, establishing that one of the above offences has been committed against a child requires proof on the balance of probabilities and not beyond reasonable doubt.[98]

(e) the child is, or is likely to become, a member of the same household as a child in respect of whom any of the offences referred to in paragraph (d) above has been committed[99]

9.32 Where one child has suffered harm in a particular environment, it is reasonable to question whether another child should be placed at the same risk. The offences here are as set out in (d) above, and it must be established that another child (the first child) was the victim of such an offence, before the ground can apply to a child in the instant case (the second child).[100] What amounts to a 'household' for the purpose of this ground has been subject to very wide interpretation by the courts. Clearly, where the second child would be living in the same home as the first, the ground would be satisfied. However, living under the same roof is not essential and, where the second child will be living in the same family unit or group of individuals as the first child, that will suffice, even if the first child has been removed from the group.[101] This interpretation makes eminent sense, given that the household in which the second child is living

---

93 Civic Government (Scotland) Act 1982, s 52(7).

94 *Kennedy* v *B* 1992 SCLR 55.

95 *McGregor* v *K* 1982 SLT 293; *Kennedy* v *F* 1985 SLT 22. In each of these cases, the child had suffered multiple injuries which the doctors who examined them did not consider to have been caused accidentally. In neither case was the individual who was alleged to have inflicted the injuries named.

96 *S* v *Kennedy* 1996 SLT 1087, where the relevant events took place in Germany. It was argued that, since criminal law does not generally have extra-territorial effect, events in Germany could not constitute an offence in Scotland. This argument was rejected by the court.

97 *McGregor* v *D* 1977 SLT 182, at p 184; *W* v *Kennedy* 1988 SLT 583.

98 *Harris* v *F* 1991 SLT 242, per Lord Justice-Clerk Ross, at p 245E–F.

99 Section 52(2)(e).

100 See *McGregor* v *H* 1983 SLT 626, where a certified copy of the sheriff's interlocutor finding the grounds to be established was regarded as sufficient proof. Cf *M V Constanda* 1999 SCLR 108.

101 Above, per Lord President Emslie, at p.628. In that case, the first child had been removed from the home under compulsory measures of supervision.

is one where either the adult members failed to protect the first child from the offence or at least one of the adult members committed the offence against the first child. Even steps taken by a parent to remove the second child from the offender's presence may not be enough to break the bond that constitutes a household.[102] Any other approach could make it all too easy for parents to frustrate the protective purpose of the legislation and, in any event, there has still been a failure to protect the first child from the offence. Even the passage of time may not be sufficient to change the nature of a household.[103]

(f) *the child is, or is likely to become, a member of the same household as a person who has committed any of the offences referred to in paragraph (d) above*[104]

9.33 Whereas ground (e) was premised on the environment in which a child might be at risk, this ground anticipates the situation where the child is living with, or is likely to live with, the person who actually committed the offence. The relevant offences and the meaning of 'household' are as discussed above. While proof of the conviction of an individual will be sufficient evidence, conviction itself is not essential, again because the standard of proof required to establish a ground of referral is the civil standard of balance of probabilities. The offence itself need not have been committed against the child.[105] This ground of referral raises some of the questions which were discussed earlier in the context of sex offenders being kept away from children.[106] However, the fact that there is a *prima facie* case establishing this ground of referral merely indicates to the reporter that the child may be in need of compulsory measures of supervision and, even if the case does proceed to a hearing, will not necessarily result in the child being separated from the offender.

(g) *the child is, or is likely to become, a member of the same household as a person in respect of whom an offence under sections 1 to 3 of the Criminal Law (Consolidation) (Scotland) Act 1995 (incest and intercourse with a child by a step-parent or a person in a position of trust) has been committed by a member of that household*[107]

9.34 This ground is designed to achieve the purposes of both grounds (e) and (f) above, but in the context of incest or sexual intercourse in breach of trust. Its similarity with ground (e) lies in the fact that it seeks to protect one child because of something that happened to another child, while the similarity with ground (f) lies in seeking to protect a child from a (usually)

---

102 *Kennedy* v *R's Curator ad litem* 1993 SLT 295, where the mother left the father who had committed the offence against the first child, taking the second child with her. Lord President Hope expressed the view that 'the criterion is that of relationship rather than locality', at p 300A–B.

103 *A* v *Kennedy* 1993 SLT 1188, where the first child had died, as a result of being wilfully assaulted and mistreated at his parents' home, eight and a half years before the second child was born.

104 Section 52(2)(f).

105 It is the presence of the offender in the child's household that raises concern here.

106 See chapter 3, para 100.

107 Section 52(2)(g).

known offender. Its origins lie in the prior legislation, although the corresponding provision gave protection only to girls and young women. However, since the offences referred to here are contained in the Criminal Procedure (Scotland) Act 1995, Schedule 1, any child to whom this ground applies would be covered by ground (f). Given, amongst other factors, the need to explain the grounds of referral to the child at the beginning of the hearing, Norrie wisely opines that '[R]eporters should avoid this paragraph like the plague'.[108]

(h) the child has failed to attend school regularly without reasonable excuse[109]

9.35 As we saw earlier, parents (and certain other persons) are obliged to ensure that their children attend school, unless they are making adequate alternative provision for the child's education, and a parent who fails to do so is guilty of an offence.[110] Where a child is not attending school, this may indicate that the child is in need of compulsory measures of supervision, regardless of whether the failure is a product of parents failing to discharge their parental responsibilities or the child's own choice. Education is not only a child's right, but is regarded as an essential part of promoting the child's development. Failure to attend school may indicate other problems in the child's life, including bullying at school. Accordingly, the situation at least warrants examination.

9.36 Some indication of what constitutes a reasonable excuse can be gleaned from defences available to parents in respect of their failure to send a child to school and include the child's illness and the lack of a school place within a reasonable distance of the child's home.[111] The child's exclusion from school, at least in the absence of proven conduct on the child's part warranting exclusion, is a reasonable excuse and, in logic, it is difficult to reach any other conclusion.[112] The ground of referral makes no mention of provision of education by alternative means, for example, by educating the child at home, but such provision would almost certainly constitute a reasonable excuse. Less clear is the, apparently common, practice of some parents, who take children on holiday during the school term. Since other examples of the child's failure to attend school being prompted by parental convenience, for example to help on a farm, would almost certainly not be regarded as a reasonable excuse, it is difficult to see why the parents choosing term-time for the family holiday would. An interesting, but untested, question arises where a young woman's reason for failing to attend school is that she is fulfilling her parental responsibilities by looking after her own child. It might be that, in bringing her to the reporter's attention, her own right to education could be met at the same time as providing alternative child care arrangements. None the less,

108 Children's Hearings, n 2 above at p 26.
109 Section 52(2)(h).
110 See chapter 6, para 14.
111 Education (Scotland) Act 1980, s 35.
112 *D v Kennedy* 1988 SLT 55. The court did not indicate whether a different conclusion would have been reached had the child's conduct warranted exclusion.

were she to refuse such a solution, the issue of whether she had a reasonable excuse remains unanswered.

(i) the child has committed an offence[113]

9.37 It will be remembered that one of the fundamental tenets of the Kilbrandon philosophy was that children who offended were no different to children who were offended against when it came to meeting the individual child's needs and that, accordingly, both groups of children could be dealt with in the same setting. Thus, almost all[114] children who commit an offence come within the ambit of the hearings system. This ground of referral can only apply to a child of eight years or older, since criminal responsibility does not attach until a child reaches that age.[115] If either the child or any of the relevant persons do not accept that the child committed the offence, it must be established before the sheriff according to the criminal standard, that is, proof beyond reasonable doubt. However, once the ground is established, the case proceeds in exactly the same way as all others with the needs of the child being the focus. Neither punishment of offenders nor deterrence of others has any place in the hearings system.

(j) the child has misused alcohol or any drug, whether or not a controlled drug within the meaning of the Misuse of Drugs Act 1971[116]

9.38 This ground of referral is one of the innovations of the 1995 Act although previously a child who misused drugs or alcohol could have been referred to the reporter on a variety of grounds, including being beyond parental control, being in moral danger or a lack of parental care. However, increased concern over drug and alcohol misuse amongst the young was felt to warrant specific reference to it[117] and, in any event, establishing this ground is more straightforward. It is the misuse, rather than the use, of alcohol or drugs that is relevant here. Thus, a child taking medication in accordance with the instructions where it has been prescribed by his or her doctor would not be included. While a 14-year-old who has a glass of champagne at a family celebration is arguably not *misusing* alcohol, the same young person getting drunk with a group of friends probably is. Where a child is plied with alcohol by an adult, it can be argued that the child is not misusing alcohol. Such a situation would be covered by ground (b) or, where the alcohol was provided by a relevant person, ground (c).

113 Section 52(2)(i).
114 It is competent for a child to be tried in the ordinary criminal courts in certain circumstances; see chapter 3, para 86.
115 Criminal Procedure (Scotland) Act 1995, s 41. See, *Merrin* v *S* 1987 SLT 193 where a seven-year-old boy was referred on the ground that he had committed the offences of wilful fire-raising and wasting police time. The sheriff refused to find the grounds established without hearing the evidence and his decision was upheld by the Inner House.
116 Section 52(2)(j).
117 Article 33 of the UN Convention on the Rights of the Child requires states to take all appropriate measures to protect children from the illicit use of drugs and this too prompted specific reference to drugs in the grounds of referral.

(k) the child has misused a volatile substance by deliberately inhaling its vapour, other than for medicinal purposes[118]

9.39 This ground was introduced in 1983 to deal with the problem of glue-sniffing and other misuse of volatile substances[119] and, at the time, was criticised as being something of a knee-jerk reaction to the latest problem to emerge in respect of children. The criticism was directed at the narrow ambit[120] of the ground and, to some extent, has been met by the creation of ground (j), above. The incidence of glue-sniffing has been overtaken by other concerns, but, none the less, it remains a dangerous practice, resulting in a number of fatalities every year, and one which justifies further inquiry into whether a child may be in need of compulsory measures of supervision.

(l) the child is being provided with accommodation by a local authority under section 25, or is the subject of a parental responsibilities order obtained under section 86, of this Act and, in either case, his or her behaviour is such that special measures are necessary for his or her adequate supervision in his/her interest or the interest of others[121]

9.40 As we have seen,[122] the local authority has a range of responsibilities to children who have no-one else to look after them. Where the local authority is discharging these duties, it may be that the child's behaviour is such that the local authority believes additional measures, including the use of secure accommodation, may be necessary in order to protect the child from his or her own actions or to protect others from the child's conduct.[123] Except in an emergency, it would clearly be a violation of the child's rights[124] if such measures were imposed without impartial adjudication of the matter and this ground enables a child to be brought to a hearing where his or her needs can be explored fully.

9.41 The above discussion of the grounds of referral concentrated on what they are. Some sense of the concerns arising in respect of children can be gleaned from examining the use made of the individual grounds for referral. While the most recent statistics available are for 1996/97 and, thus, cover the grounds of referral found in the previous legislation, they give some idea of the operation of the system and, in any event, it is not anticipated that the changes made to the grounds will make a significant difference in this respect.

9.42 As Table 1 illustrates, it is still the case that males are more likely to

---

118 Section 52(2)(k).
119 Solvent Abuse (Scotland) Act 1983.
120 It was felt that the opportunity should have been taken to introduce a ground of referral which tackled the wider range of ways in which children can do harm to themselves, including drug and alcohol misuse and playing 'chicken' on road or playing on railway lines.
121 Section 52(2)(l).
122 Chapter 7.
123 See Secure Accommodation (Scotland) Regulations 1996 (SI 1996 No 3255).
124 Article 37(b) of the UN Convention on the Rights of the Child requires that no child shall be deprived of his or her liberty unlawfully or arbitrarily, while Art 3 of course, requires that the child's best interests shall be a primary consideration in the making of decisions.

Table 1. Reason for referral to the reporter[125]

	males (%)	females (%)
Beyond control	4	7
Moral danger	2	5
Lack of parental care	8	17
Victim of offence	8	24
At risk	1	3
Same household as incest victim	0	0
Non-attendance at school	7	13
Solvent abuse	0	0
Offence	69	30

be referred to the reporter on the offence ground, while females are more likely to be referred to the reporter as victims. Why this is so merits a book in its own right, but either it says something about different patterns of behaviour by or treatment of young males and females in Scotland today, or it reflects a difference in official attitudes to young people depending on their gender.

OPERATION OF THE SYSTEM

9.43 As with any legal process, there are a number of different stages in the operation of the hearings system, each with its own requirements and subtleties. The flowchart at the end of this chapter shows the operation of the system and its various stages. The flowchart takes a relatively simple trip through the procedure and does not include all possible permutations and nuances, so the text should be read for explanations in greater detail.

Information received by the Principal Reporter

9.44 Information comes to the reporter from a variety of sources. A local authority has a duty to investigate cases where information is received suggesting that a child might be in need of compulsory measures of supervision and, if the inquiry tends to confirm the suspicion, to pass the information on to the reporter.[126] Usually, information provided by the local authority will have come from its own social work or education departments. The police have a similar duty to pass information on to the reporter.[127]

9.45 Where a child comes to the attention of a civil court in a whole range of proceedings – for example, divorce, applications for parental responsibilities and rights and adoption – it may refer the child to the reporter if it

---

125 Statistical Bulletin, Tables 4(i) and (ii).
126 Section 53(1). The local authority is not obliged to investigate a case where it is satisfied that such investigation is unnecessary and this provision would include cases where it was already dealing with the particular problem or where it believed allegations to be malicious.
127 Section 53(2)(a) and (3).

appears that one of the grounds of referral, other than the offence ground, is satisfied.[128] In addition, after conviction, a criminal court can remit the case to the reporter for disposal.[129] It is worth remembering that anyone can contact the reporter if he or she believes that a child may be in need of compulsory measures of supervision[130] and, indeed, it may be the child's parents who seek help in this way. Some idea of how cases come to the attention of the reporter can be gleaned from looking at the figures for 1996–97 set out in Table 2.

Table 2. Source of referrals[131]

	%
Law enforcement agencies	79
Social work departments	9
Educational sources	10
Parents	1
Other	1

Initial investigation by the reporter

9.46 Having received information about a particular child, the reporter must consider what further investigation is necessary. Particularly where the case has been referred by the local authority, it may be that the reporter already has sufficient information to consider the need for a hearing and he or she may decide that no further investigation is required. Where further investigation is required, the reporter will normally request a social background report from the local authority, and the local authority is obliged to provide this report.[132] In addition, the reporter may request information from other persons, including the child's school, the medical profession and the police. While co-operation is the hallmark of the hearings system, these other persons are not obliged to comply with the reporter's request. Having gathered together the necessary information, the reporter is in a position to decide whether to arrange a hearing.

Will a hearing be arranged?

9.47 In assessing the need for a hearing, the reporter must be satisfied on two points. First, he or she must be satisfied that there is a *prima facie* case establishing one of the grounds of referral. If no ground of referral applies to the child, a hearing is incompetent.[133] Second, the reporter must believe that compulsory measures of supervision may be necessary. It may

128 Section 54.
129 Criminal Procedure (Scotland) Act 1995, s 49.
130 Section 53(2)(b).
131 *Statistical Bulletin*, Table 3. As in any tabulation, the rounding up or down of figures may mean that the total is not 100%. In 1996, 6 reports were made to reporters by the RSSPCC, an insufficient number to reach 1% but, none the less important.
132 Section 56(2) and (3).
133 Section 52(1).

frequently be the case that, while a ground of referral exists, the reporter is satisfied that the child's needs can be met by other means or, indeed, that no action is necessary at all.[134] The reporter has enormous discretion in reaching his or her decision and, while the 1995 Act does not make any direction on this point,[135] will be guided by what will serve the child's welfare. The only exception to the reporter's discretion arises when a court remits the case to the hearing for disposal where a child has either pled guilty to, or been found guilty of, an offence.[136] The reporter must arrange a hearing in these circumstances. Where the reporter decides not to arrange a hearing, he or she must take certain specified action (see, para 48 below). Where the reporter decides that a hearing is necessary, then he or she will go on to make the necessary arrangements[137] (see paras 49–53 below). In either case, where the referral has come from the local authority or the police, the reporter must inform the local authority or the chief constable, as the case may be, of the decision.[138]

No hearing to be arranged

9.48 Where the reporter decides not to arrange a hearing, he or she must inform the child, relevant persons and the person who brought the case to his or her attention of the decision.[139] In addition, the reporter may refer the case to the local authority with a view to it providing advice, guidance and assistance to the child and the family.[140] Where the reporter decides that a hearing is not required, he or she cannot later convene a hearing based solely on the information obtained during the initial investigation.[141]

Arranging a hearing

9.49 Where the reporter has not already done so, he or she must request a social background report from the local authority and, in any case, may request an additional report.[142] Again, the local authority is obliged to comply with the request and may supply any other information it considers relevant.[143] In addition, the reporter must notify a range of individuals of the time, date and place of the hearing and provide them with certain documents. Where the reporter considers that disclosing the whereabouts

---

134 Section 56(4). In 1996/97, 59% of referrals to reporters resulted in no formal action being taken. Of these, compulsory intervention was deemed unnecessary in 36% of the referrals, while, in a further 16%, the child was already under supervision; *Statistical Bulletin*, Table 7.
135 While s 16(1) directs the court and the children's hearing to regard the child's welfare throughout childhood as the paramount consideration, no similar direction is given to the reporter.
136 Criminal Procedure (Scotland) Act 1995, s 49.
137 Children (Scotland) Act 1995, s 56(6).
138 1996 Rules, r 3(2)(b).
139 Section 56(4)(a).
140 Section 56(4)(b). In 1996/97, 10% of cases were so referred; *Statistical Bulletin*, Table 7.
141 Section 56(5).
142 Section 56(7).
143 Ibid.

of the child or any relevant person may place that person at risk of serious harm, he or she may withhold the information and give the person's address as that of the Principal Reporter.[144]

9.50 Once the chairman of the children's panel has decided which panel members will sit on a particular hearing,[145] the reporter must notify them of the time and place of the hearing, wherever practicable, at least seven days before the hearing is to take place.[146] Each panel member must also be provided with the following documents (if applicable): the report on the child and his or her social background; a statement of the grounds for referral; any judicial reference or remit or any reference by the local authority; any supervision requirement to which the child is subject; any safeguarder's report; any views the child has given in writing to the Principal Reporter; and any other information or document which is material to consideration of the case.[147]

9.51 Notification in writing of their right and obligation to attend the hearing and the time, date and place of it, must be given to the relevant persons, along with copies of all the documents supplied to the members of the hearing.[148] This notice must be given at least seven days before the hearing,[149] except in specified circumstances where arranging a hearing more quickly is required.[150] Giving copies of the documents to relevant persons is an innovation of the 1995 Act and the provision is a result of the criticisms levelled at the system by the European Court of Human Rights.[151]

9.52 The child is entitled to receive notification in writing of the time, date and place of the hearing and of his or her right and obligation to attend.[152] Again, notice should be given at least seven days prior to the hearing, except in the specified circumstances which warrant a hearing

---

144 1996 Rules, r 9.
145 1996 Rules, r 10(1). The selection of a chairman and the members of a particular hearing from the panel for the area is a matter for the chairman of the children's panel, whom failing, his or her deputy, or by the operation of standing arrangements made by the chairman after consultation with the reporter and possibly other panel members.
146 1996 Rules, r 5(1). While the Rules require notification of the time and place of the hearing to the members, the child and the relevant persons are entitled to notice of the *date*, time and place (rr 6(1) and 7(1)). It is not anticipated that this drafting error causes any problems in practice.
147 1996 Rules, r 5(1). These documents should be provided to the members of the hearing as early as practicable and, if possible, at least three days before the hearing. The additional information document may be provided at any time before the hearing; 1996 Rules, r 5(2).
148 Section 45(8) and (9) and the 1996 Rules, r 7(1) and (3).
149 1996 Rules, r 7(4).
150 1996 Rules, r 6(2). Examples include arranging a hearing where an absconding child has been found or a child protection order has been implemented.
151 *McMichael* v *United Kingdom*, n 11 above. Previously, all that was required was that the substance of what was contained in such documents should be disclosed to the family by the chairman at the hearing. That this was a breach of natural justice was always a concern. The concern now is that writers of reports may be unduly cautious in what they write.
152 Section 45(1) and the 1996 Rules, r 6(1).

taking place earlier.[153] Where the hearing has decided to relieve the child of the obligation to attend,[154] the reporter must, none the less, inform the child of his or her right to attend.[155] While the child is entitled to receive a copy of the statement of the grounds of referral,[156] he or she is not entitled to receive copies of the other relevant documents supplied to the other parties. Consistent with the 1995 Act[157] and the UN Convention,[158] the child is given the opportunity to express his or her views within the hearing system generally, and a special additional opportunity to do so is intimated to the child at the time of notification of the hearing.[159] Any views expressed to the reporter, prior to the hearing, will be intimated to the members of the hearing, the relevant persons and any safeguarder who has been appointed. There is a certain irony in giving the child a special opportunity to express his or her views when the child is provided with less background information than anyone else present on which to comment. While sending a full set of the documents relating to the hearing to a toddler would be absurd, a teenager might well have valuable comments to make on, for example, the social background report or a school report. Denying such children access to these documents is arguably a breach of the child's right to express his or her views, since a person can hardly fully express views on a situation in the absence of all the relevant information.

9.53 Any safeguarder appointed by the hearing must be notified of the time, date and place of the hearing and must be provided with copies of all the documents provided to the members of the hearing, irrespective of the date of the safeguarder's appointment.[160] He or she must also receive a statement of the reasons for his or her appointment.[161] The chief social worker of the appropriate local authority must also be informed of the date, time and place of the hearing and the name, date of birth and address, so far as known, of the child whose case will be considered.[162]

Business meeting preparatory to a hearing

9.54 Before the 1995 Act, there was no provision in the legislation for any kind of meeting to resolve administrative or procedural matters prior to the hearing itself. However, such meetings did take place, at least in some parts of the country, and their existence was one of the issues which caused debate in the *Orkney Case*.[163] While the court concluded that, provided they were confined to matters of a purely administrative nature, they were permissible as involving no unfairness, the opportunity was taken in the

153 1996 Rules, r 6(2).
154 Section 45(2).
155 1996 Rules, r 6(3).
156 1996 Rules, r 18(1)(b).
157 Section 16(2).
158 Article 12 of the UN Convention on the Rights of the Child.
159 1996 Rules, r 6(4).
160 1996 Rules, r 14(2) and (5).
161 1996 Rules, r 14(2).
162 1996 Rules, r 8.
163 *Sloan* v *B* 1991 SLT 530.

1995 Act to put these meetings on a statutory basis and their appropriate ambit is now defined.[164]

9.55 Prior to the hearing, the reporter may arrange a business meeting with three panel members[165] to discuss procedural and other matters.[166] The 1995 Act simply talks in terms of 'procedural and other matters' and the giving of 'direction or guidance' to the reporter as being matters to be considered by a business meeting. The 1996 Rules are a little more helpful in fleshing this out and provide that a business meeting *shall* determine the following, if they are referred to it by the reporter: who should be notified as a relevant person; whether a child should be notified that he or she has been freed from the obligation to attend a hearing; and whether a relevant person should be notified that he or she has been freed from the obligation to attend a hearing.[167] All of these are couched in terms of the reporter's duty to notify particular individuals and it would always be open to the hearing itself to come to a different conclusion in respect of an individual's attendance.[168] Where a person had been notified by the reporter that he or she was not obliged to attend and a hearing decided that the person's attendance is required, the individual would not, presumably, have committed an offence under the 1995 Act by failing to attend.

9.56 Unlike the unofficial meetings held before the 1995 Act regulated the matter, a business meeting must be notified to the child, the relevant persons, and any safeguarder, at least four days before it takes place.[169] While they have no right to attend the meeting, they must be informed of the matters which will be considered, and of their right to make their views on any of these matters known to the reporter, who will present their views to the meeting.[170] Once the business meeting has reached a decision or given guidance to the reporter, the reporter must inform the child, the relevant persons and any safeguarder of the results.[171]

The hearing: who may be present?

9.57 This brings us to the point when the hearing actually meets for the first time. The conduct of the hearing is a matter for the chairman of each hearing.[172] However, the chairman is directed to permit attendance only by persons whose presence is necessary for the proper consideration of the case and, in any event, to take all reasonable steps to keep the number of persons present to a minimum.[173] This is designed to provide the child, and the relevant persons, with an atmosphere conducive to their full participation. However, certain persons have a right to attend the particular

---

164 Section 64 and 1996 Rules, r 4.
165 These need not and, indeed, often will not, be the panel members who will make up the hearing, but must include one man and one woman; 1996 Rules, r 4(1).
166 Section 64(1) and 1996 Rules, r 4(1).
167 1996 Rules, r 4(2).
168 Section 45.
169 Section 64(2) and 1996 Rules, r 4(3).
170 1996 Rules, r 4(4)–(6).
171 1996 Rules, r 4(8).
172 1996 Rules, r 10(3).
173 Section 43 and 1996 Rules, r 13.

hearing, others have a right to attend hearings generally, and yet others may attend with the permission of the chairman. The persons who will or may be present are:

The child

9.58 As we have seen, the central person in the hearings system, the child, is both entitled, and (usually) obliged, to attend the hearing.[174]

The relevant persons

9.59 Subject to possible exclusion from part of a hearing, the relevant persons have both a right and (usually) a duty to attend.

The genetic father

9.60 The genetic father, who is not a relevant person, has a right, but no obligation, to attend, provided that he is living with the child's mother.[175]

The members of the hearing

9.61 For a hearing to be constituted at all, the panel members selected to serve on it must be present.

The reporter

9.62 While there is no mention in the 1995 Act or the 1996 Rules of the reporter's right to attend, attendance is implied, not least because the reporter is obliged to make a record of the hearing[176] and he or she may be able to offer assistance in explaining or clarifying legal and administrative matters.

Any safeguarder appointed by the hearing

9.63 Any safeguarder appointed by the hearing is entitled to attend[177] and, arguably, in order to discharge his or her duties fully, should be present.

A social worker

9.64 While there is no provision in the 1995 Act or the 1996 Rules giving a local authority social worker the right to attend a hearing, given the local authority's duty to provide a social background report and to implement any supervision requirement,[178] it is not surprising that a social worker is usually present and, indeed, is likely to participate in discussions.

Legal and other representatives

9.65 The child and each relevant person may be accompanied by a person

174 Section 45.
175 1996 Rules, r 12(1).
176 1996 Rules, r 31.
177 Where the safeguarder has been appointed by the sheriff, he or she has no automatic right to attend a subsequent hearing but may be permitted to do by the chairman; 1996 Rules, r 13. For the position under the 1968 Act, see *Catto* v *Pearson* 1990 SLT (Sh Ct) 77.
178 Section 71.

to assist them at the hearing.[179] While the representative may be legally qualified, the absence of legal aid to pay for representation at hearings means that lawyers rarely appear at hearings. A representative may assist more than one person at the hearing and the child and the relevant person may all be assisted by the same person.[180] It is important to establish precisely who the representative is assisting, since a relevant person's representative may be excluded from the hearing, while the child's representative may not be.[181]

Journalists

9.66 The right of members of the press to be present at a hearing is subject to the hearing's power to exclude such persons.[182]

Other persons with a right to attend

9.67 A police officer or prison officer who has a person entitled to attend a hearing in his or her lawful custody has a right to be present at the hearing for the purpose of escorting that person.[183] Members of the Council on Tribunals, or its Scottish Committee, have the right to attend a hearing, subject to the hearing's power to exclude them on the same basis as a journalist may be excluded.[184]

Other persons who may attend at the chairman's discretion

9.68 A host of other persons may be permitted to attend a hearing at the chairman's discretion.[185] In terms of discussing the child's case, a particular individual may have a valuable contribution to make and so, for example, the child's school teacher may be present. The chairman may use his or her discretion to allow an unmarried father to attend when he would not be entitled to do so otherwise.[186] Given that the aim of the hearing is to explore all the relevant circumstances of the child's life as fully as possible, the attendance of 'unqualified persons' will often be entirely reasonable. In addition, members of the local CPAC and the clerk to the CPAC of the local authority, trainee panel members and their instructors, trainee social workers, and others engaged in research may be permitted to attend[187] and, where any of these persons does so, he or she will simply observe the proceedings and will take no part in them.

9.69 Obviously, if all those who might attend were present at once, the child would be faced with a very crowded room indeed, and the chairman is bound to ensure that such a scenario does not occur. None the less, when

179 1996 Rules, r 11(1).
180 1996 Rules, r 11(3).
181 Section 46(1) .
182 Section 43(3)(b) and 43(4).
183 1996 Rules, r 12(2).
184 Section 43(3)(a) and 43(4).
185 1996 Rules, r 13(d).
186 See, *L* v *H* 1996 SLT 612, at p 617 E–F, where Lord Justice-Clerk Ross expressed the hope that this would be done, at least where the father had contact with the child.
187 1996 Rules, r 13(a)–(c).

one considers all the people who are entitled to attend, it becomes apparent that a child may find a sizeable adult gathering at a hearing.

The hearing: preliminary procedures

9.70 The hearing begins with the chairman introducing the members of the hearing to the child and the relevant persons and it would be normal, at this stage for everyone present to be introduced and his or her presence explained, if necessary.[188] The purpose of the hearing, for example, whether it is to consider grounds of referral or to review an existing supervision requirement, will then be explained, usually by the chairman.[189] Inquiry will then be made as to the child's age, since the hearing can only have jurisdiction where there is a child whose needs are to be considered.[190] If the hearing is one at which grounds of referral will be considered, the next stage is central to the whole proceedings.

9.71 Since it is only where the child and the relevant person accept the grounds of referral that the hearing can proceed at this stage, explaining the grounds of referral is of immense importance.[191] This is sometimes described as 'putting the grounds' to the family and that phrase is unfortunate, since it fails to capture the essence of what should be done. Simply reading out the formal ground or grounds stated by the reporter is not enough, and the chairman must explain what these mean in language designed to facilitate the family's understanding of what is being alleged. The child and the relevant persons must then be asked if they accept the grounds of referral[192] and, depending on their responses, various things can happen with different results.

The child will not understand or has not understood the grounds of referral

9.72 Where the hearing is satisfied either that the child will not *understand* the ground as, for example, in the case of a baby or toddler, or, having attempted to explain them, that the child has not understood the grounds, the hearing can either discharge the referral or direct the reporter to apply to the sheriff for a finding as to whether any of the grounds of referral is established.[193]

9.73 There is no provision in either the 1995 Act or the Rules governing the situation where the hearing takes the view that any of the relevant persons has not understood the grounds of referral. However, it can be argued that a person cannot 'accept' something which he or she does not understand, and, thus, the hearing should treat a failure by a relevant

---

188 Quite apart from simple courtesy, it may help a child (and the relevant persons) to know just why various people are there and what their function is. For example, to know that Ms Jones is a trainee social worker who will not be taking any part in the proceedings, might enable the child to ignore her presence.
189 1996 Rules, r 20(2) and r 22(2).
190 Sections 47 and 93.
191 Section 65(4).
192 Ibid.
193 Section 65(9).

person to understand the grounds of referral in the same way as it would treat non-acceptance.

The child or any of the relevant persons do not accept the grounds of referral

9.74 Where the child or any of the relevant persons do not *accept* the grounds of referral the hearing can either discharge the referral or direct the reporter to apply to the sheriff for a finding as to whether any of the grounds of referral are established.[194] Where a relevant person is not present at the hearing, his or her acceptance of the ground is not required.[195]

The child or the relevant persons accept the grounds in part

9.75 Where the child and any of the relevant persons *accept only part* of the grounds of referral, the hearing can proceed in respect of those grounds,[196] or it can discharge the referral, or direct the reporter to apply to the sheriff for a finding as to whether any of the grounds of referral are established.[197]

The child and the relevant persons accept the grounds of referral as stated

9.76 Where the child and the parents accept the grounds of referral, the hearing proceeds to the next stage.[198] While the process will often be continuous, a subsequent hearing may take place where such is necessary for a full consideration of the case or for further investigation.[199] The hearing may require the child to stay at or attend a particular place – for example, a hospital, clinic or other establishment – for up to 22 days in order that further investigation be carried out and may grant a warrant to enforce such attendance.[200] Throughout the proceedings of a children's hearing, the members must bear in mind that it may be necessary to appoint a safeguarder and, if so, to make such an appointment.[201] Where a safeguarder has been appointed, the hearing will normally be continued pending the availability of the safeguarder's report.[202]

Discharging the referral

9.77 The decision to discharge the referral is determined by the welfare principle.[203] By the time the hearing meets, it may be apparent that the child is not, after all, in need of *compulsory measures of supervision* because the issue giving rise to concern is no longer present. For example, the family circumstances may have changed significantly. Alternatively, the family may not accept the grounds of referral and the hearing may decide that there is no need to proceed. Whatever the reason, the hearing may

---

194 Section 65(7)(a).
195 Section 65(10).
196 Section 65(6).
197 Section 65(7)(b).
198 Section 65(5).
199 Section 69(2).
200 Section 69(3)–(9). This warrant does not affect the child's right to refuse medical or other treatment under s 90 of the 1995 Act.
201 Section 41.
202 1996 Rules, r 14(4).
203 Section 16(1).

discharge the case and no further action can be taken in relation to that ground of referral.

Application to the sheriff

9.78 Where the grounds of referral are not understood by the child or not accepted by the child or any of the relevant persons, the hearing may direct the reporter to apply to the sheriff for a finding as to whether any of the grounds of referral is established. This is the practical manifestation of the point, fundamental to the Kilbrandon philosophy, that courts are the appropriate place for the determination of facts, since it is in a court that the rights of all the parties involved can be protected by representation and by the rules of evidence and procedure.[204] The chairman must explain to the family why the application to the sheriff is being made and must inform the child of his or her obligation to attend.[205]

9.79 Where the reporter has lodged an application, it must be heard by the sheriff within 28 days of being lodged.[206] Proof is on the balance of probabilities, except where it is alleged that the child has committed an offence, in which case, proof beyond reasonable doubt is required.[207] The child is both obliged and entitled to attend the proof and, again, while the sheriff can relieve the child of this obligation in certain circumstances, he or she cannot override the child's right to attend.[208] If the child fails to attend, the sheriff may grant an order to find the child and keep him or her in a place of safety until the case can be disposed of or the expiry of 14 days, whichever is the earlier.[209] Relevant persons also have a right to attend and the child and the relevant persons may be represented by a lawyer or a person who is not legally qualified.[210] Unlike proceedings at the hearing, legal aid is available to fund legal representation before the sheriff and, consequently, it is more likely that the parties will be legally represented. In addition, the sheriff must consider whether it is necessary in order to protect the child's interest, that a safeguarder should be appointed and, if it is, to appoint a safeguarder for the child.[211]

9.80 If, in the course of hearing the application, the child and the relevant persons accept grounds which were not formerly accepted, the sheriff must dispense with hearing the evidence.[212] Where members of the family change their minds in this way, there is no longer anything for the sheriff to determine. However, where the child is incapable of understanding the

204 *McGregor* v *D* 1977 SLT 182.
205 Sections 65(8) and 68(4) and (5). The reporter must also give the child and the relevant persons written notice of the fact that an application is being made to the sheriff; 1996 Rules, r 19.
206 Section 68(2)
207 Section 68(3). This applies to proof of the child's allegedly criminal conduct even where the child has not been referred on the offence ground; *Constanda* v *M* 1997 SCLR 510.
208 Section 68(4) and (5).
209 Section 68(6) and (7).
210 Section 68(4). See also Child Care and Maintenance Rules 1997 (SI 1997 No 291), r 3.21.
211 Section 41.
212 Section 68(8)(a).

grounds of referral and the relevant persons accept them, the sheriff may dispense with hearing the evidence, unless he or she is satisfied that the evidence should be heard.[213] Dispensing with hearing the evidence in the case of a child's lack of understanding as, for example, in the case of a baby, is not automatic. There may be good reason to hear the evidence where, for example, the sheriff questions whether the facts alleged satisfy a ground of referral or there is doubt over the relevant person's understanding of what he or she is accepting.

9.81   Where the sheriff finds that none of the grounds of referral has been established, he or she must dismiss the application, discharge the referral, cancel any warrant, and that is the end of the particular proceedings.[214] Where the sheriff finds any of the grounds of referral established, he or she will remit the case back to the reporter to arrange for a hearing to determine the case.[215] The sheriff may order that the child should be kept in a place of safety, pending the hearing, if he or she considers that to do so would be in the child's best interests or that there is reason to believe that the child will run away before the hearing.[216]

The hearing: consideration of the case

9.82   Where the grounds of referral are accepted by the child and the relevant persons or are established before the sheriff, the hearing moves on to consider the case. In the case of accepted grounds, the whole process will usually be continuous. The hearing considers not only the grounds of referral but also any available reports and other relevant information.[217] Specific mention is made of social background reports and the report from any manager of a residential establishment where the child is living.[218] While these will obviously provide valuable information to the hearing, it is the whole picture which should be examined and all relevant information should be explored. The chairman is directed to inform the child and the relevant persons of the substance of any reports, if he or she considers the information material to the case and is satisfied that disclosure would not be detrimental to the interests of the child.[219] So far as the relevant persons are concerned, this is a curious provision, since they will have copies of reports and, indeed, the requirement to disclose may be left over from the 1968 Act which did not require them to be given copies of any reports at all. Explanation may be helpful where the hearing questions the extent to which any relevant person has understood the reports fully. Of course, since the child has no right to receive the documents sent to adults, the provision dealing with explanation of the content of reports is relevant.

9.83   It is of the essence of the hearings system that everyone involved should have the opportunity to participate freely in seeking a positive way

---

213 Section 68(8)(b).
214 Section 68(9).
215 Section 68(10)(a).
216 Section 68(10)(b).
217 Section 69(1) and 1996 Rules, rr 5 and 20(6).
218 1996 Rules, r 20(3)(a) and (b).
219 1996 Rules, r 20(4).

forward for the child and the hearing is directed to discuss the case with the child, the relevant persons, any representative and any safeguarder.[220] Where a child is old enough to participate, and even young children are capable of some degree of participation, the 1995 Act and the 1996 Rules acknowledge that special steps may be required to facilitate this participation in what, after all, is a room full of adults. Any safeguarder who has been appointed has a role in helping a child to put forward his or her views. In addition, it is acknowledged that it may be necessary to exclude some or all of the relevant persons from the hearing, in order to give the child as much opportunity to participate and express his or her views.

Exclusion of a relevant person

9.84 The possibility of excluding a relevant person was introduced by the 1995 Act and recognises that a child's right to participate in his or her own hearing might be inhibited by the presence of a particular adult.[221] For example, the child might be reluctant to talk about past abuse by a parent or an unwillingness to return to live with a parent, if that parent is present. Exclusion is relevant only after the grounds have been accepted or established, and any relevant person or the person's representative can be excluded in certain circumstances.[222] Exclusion is permitted in two situations: either it must be necessary in order to obtain the child's views, or, the person's presence must be causing, or be likely to cause, significant distress to the child. While a relevant person's representative may be excluded from the hearing, there is no provision for exclusion of the child's representative. Since the same person may represent the child and the relevant persons, this means that a representative who could have been excluded in his or her capacity as the relevant persons' representative, can remain in the hearing, if he or she is also representing the child.

9.85 Once the excluded person returns to the hearing, the chairman is obliged to explain to him or her the substance of what has taken place in his or her absence.[223] The knowledge that what is said during the period of exclusion will be passed on to the excluded person may inhibit some children, but natural justice requires that the information should be disclosed.

The hearing's decision

9.86 Having considered the case fully, the hearing will then decide on the appropriate disposal of the case.[224] The disposal must be made in the light of the welfare principle[225] and the following options are open to the hearing.

---

220 1996 Rules, r 20(3)(c) and (d) and r 22(3)(b) and (c).
221 Section 46(1). Prior to the 1995 Act, parents and others with a right to be present were sometimes 'invited to withdraw' from the hearing to facilitate discussion with the child. While they were not obliged to comply with the request, most did.
222 Section 46(1).
223 Section 46(2).
224 Section 69(1).
225 Section 16.

Continue the case

9.87 The members of a hearing may, on occasions, feel that they have insufficient information on which to reach a decision in the child's best interests. In such cases, the hearing will be continued to allow for the relevant information to be gathered.[226] The hearing should indicate the reasons for the continuation and these might include, for example, the need for further information regarding a possible disposal and its suitability for a particular child. Where the hearing decides to appoint a safeguarder, a continuation will be required to allow the safeguarder time to undertake the necessary investigation and prepare a report. And a case may be continued on more than one occasion. It should be noted that continuation is inappropriate where the disposal would be the same, regardless of any further information that might become available.

Discharge the referral

9.88 Unless the hearing is satisfied that the child is in need of *compulsory* measures of supervision it must discharge the referral[227] and all orders, requirements and warrants issued in connection with the ground of referral so discharged cease to have effect.[228]

Make a supervision requirement

9.89 Where the hearing is satisfied that the child is in need of compulsory measures of supervision it may make a supervision requirement.[229] The nature of the supervision requirement will be determined by the welfare principle. From its inception, the hearings system has been based on a treatment model, aimed at overcoming the problems in the child's life and, as such, punishment of children who have committed offences, has no place in it. As we shall see, the hearing may require the child to live in a residential establishment and, regardless of the motive of the adults in reaching this decision and the explanation given to the child for it, some children may perceive this or, indeed, any type of supervision requirement, as a form of punishment. Decisions of the hearing relate to the child and, while they may have an impact on the adult family members (where, for example, the exercise of parental responsibilities is limited to the extent that such exercise would be inconsistent with a supervision requirement),[230] the hearing has no power to order adults to comply with particular conditions.[231] However, where the relevant persons do not co-operate with a supervision requirement, the case may be brought back to a hearing for

---

226 Section 69(2).
227 Sections 69(1)(b) and (12).
228 Section 69(13).
229 Sections 69(1)(c) and 70(1).
230 Section 3(4).
231 Expressing a view that would undoubtedly find support in some quarters today, the Kilbrandon Committee recommended that the hearing should be able to order parents to find caution for the good behaviour of their children; para 159. This recommendation was not implemented.

review and the supervision requirement can be varied. Supervision requirements may be in the following terms.

- Require the child to live at a specified place[232]

9.90 While a hearing may decide that a child should live with his or her parents, the power to require a child to live at a specified place is very wide-ranging indeed, and may mean that the child goes to live with other relatives, foster carers or in a residential establishment. The decision of a hearing supersedes any court order governing the child's residence[233] and, where the hearing decides that the child should live somewhere other than with the parents, suspends the parental right to decide the child's place of residence. While the specified place will usually be in Scotland, it may be in England or Wales.[234] The place where the child is to live must be named expressly,[235] if the place is not the child's home, and the hearing will not normally name a particular residential establishment unless it has been informed that there is a place available for the child at that establishment.[236] Consistent with the principle of presumed non-intervention, where the child will be living with someone other than a relevant person, the hearing must consider a social background report indicating why the child's needs will be better served by this option.[237]

9.91 Given its highly intrusive nature, it is hardly surprising that special rules surround the decision to place a child in secure accommodation, that is, accommodation in a residential establishment 'for the purpose of restricting the liberty' of the child.[238] Before a hearing can specify that a child should be placed and kept in secure accommodation, one of two conditions must be satisfied. The first, aimed solely at protecting the child, requires that the child has absconded from a residential establishment at least once before and is likely to do so again, such absconding being likely to put his or her physical, mental or moral welfare at risk.[239] The second, alternative, condition is not confined to protecting the child, and covers the situation where, if the child absconds, there is a likelihood of the child injuring himself, herself, or some other person, unless he or she is kept in

---

232 Section 70(3)(a).
233 *Aitken* v *Aitken* 1978 SLT 183.
234 Section 70(4).
235 *R* v *Children's Hearing for the Borders Region* 1984 SLT 65, where requiring the child to live 'in a pre-adoptive home chosen by the local authority' was not sufficiently specific.
236 There is nothing to prevent a hearing naming an establishment when no place is available, particularly where it believes that the local authority ought to be making greater efforts in, or devoting more resources to, the provision of suitable accommodation. However, the smooth running of the hearings system relies on co-operation between all the agencies involved. For a discussion of the problems that can occur when the co-operative relationship breaks down, see *Report of the Inquiry into Child Care Policies in Fife*, n 10 above.
237 1996 Rules, r 20(6). In addition, the local authority must indicate that the Fostering of Children (Scotland) Regulations 1996 (SI 1996 No. 3263) have been complied with.
238 Section 93(1). The accommodation may be managed by the local authority, a voluntary organisation or some other person but must, in any event, be approved by the Secretary of State; Secure Accommodation (Scotland) Regulations 1996 (SI 1996 No 3255) r 3.
239 Section 70(10)(a).

secure accommodation.[240] Clearly, this allows the hearing to derogate from the principle that the child's welfare is paramount.[241] Having named the place where the child will reside and specified that the child should be placed in secure accommodation, it is then for the chief social worker of the relevant local authority to determine how long the child should be kept in the secure accommodation.[242] Hearings have been sparing in employing secure accommodation in the past, although the incidence of its use has increased.[243]

9.92 Where a child is living in a residential establishment, with no direction on secure accommodation, the chief social worker and the person in charge of the establishment can decide to place the child in secure accommodation provided that they agree that such placement will be in the child's interest, and that one of the two conditions set out above is satisfied. In addition, the chief social worker must be satisfied that the particular accommodation is appropriate to the child's needs. Having decided to place the child in secure accommodation, the chief social worker must inform the reporter, giving details of and reasons for the placement, within 24 hours. Thereafter, the reporter must arrange a hearing to review the child's case, no later than 72 hours from the time of the placement in secure accommodation.[244]

9.93 The local authority is bound to implement the supervision requirement determined by the hearing.[245] If the child cannot be received into the named establishment immediately, the local authority can accommodate him or her in some other suitable place for up to 22 days.[246] If it becomes apparent that the child cannot be accommodated at the named accommodation within that period, the local authority must inform the reporter who will convene a review hearing.[247] Where the child is to live in residential accommodation other than that provided by the local authority, the authority is bound to investigate whether any conditions imposed by the hearing are being met and, if they are not, to take reasonable steps to overcome the problem.[248] This might include requesting a review hearing.

240 Section 70(10)(b).
241 See the interaction between this provision and the power to derogate from the paramountcy of welfare in order to protect the public from serious harm, contained in s 16(5). In England and Wales, the child's welfare, while a relevant consideration, is not regarded as paramount when considering secure accommodation: *Re M (A Minor) (Secure Accommodation Order)* [1995] 2 WLR 302.
242 Section 70(9)(b).
243 In 1996/7, the use of secure accommodation was authorised on 110 occasions and authorisation was continued on a further 140 occasions. The cases involved 155 males and 95 females and 81% of the young people were aged 14 and 15; *Statistical Bulletin*, Table 17.
244 Secure Accommodation (Scotland) Regulations 1996 (SI 1996 No 3255) r 6.
245 Section 71(1).
246 Children's Hearings (Transmission of Information etc) (Scotland) Regulations 1996 (SI 1996 No. 3260), r 4(1).
247 Ibid, r 4(2) and (3).
248 Section 71(2)(b).

- Require the child to comply with any other condition[249]

9.94 The hearing has the power to impose any other condition that is consistent with the general principles of Part II of the 1995 Act. Any condition must be stated in unambiguous language along with the reasons for its imposition.[250] As we have seen, punishment is no part of the hearings system and conditions must, therefore, be aimed at meeting the child's needs, in the broadest sense. While the range of possible conditions is not limited to them, two particular conditions are mentioned expressly in the 1995 Act. The first requires the child to submit to any medical examination or treatment.[251] However, the hearing has no power to impose a condition which would limit the child's general right to consent to or refuse such treatment, where the child is of sufficient maturity to understand what it involves.[252] The second condition mentioned in the 1995 Act is one which regulates the child's contact with any specified person or class of persons.[253] While contact will not be an issue in every case, clearly 'regulating contact' might include 'regulating it to zero', that is, prohibiting contact. Where a child is living away from the family home, the regulation of contact may be of enormous importance to the child and the family and this is one of the clearest examples of a condition, imposed on the child, which can have a direct impact on other family members. Even where the child does remain at home, regulation of contact may be significant where, for example, the hearing prohibits contact between the child and named individuals who are thought to have had a bad influence on the child.

9.95 Where a child is subject to a supervision requirement and a relevant person intends to take the child to live outwith Scotland, the relevant person must give the reporter and the local authority 28 days notice of his or her intention and the reporter must arrange a review hearing.[254] This provision is designed to ensure that, where a hearing has decided that a child needs compulsory measures of supervision, these measures cannot be defeated by the removal of the child from the hearings system's jurisdiction. It applies where the intention is to take the child *to live* outside Scotland and does not apply to holidays, although the distinction between an extended holiday and going to live abroad is not entirely clear-cut. In any event, the 1995 Act provides no penalty for failure to comply with this requirement.[255]

9.96 A supervision requirement may have a dramatic impact on the life of the child and his or her family and, quite properly, is subject to a variety of controls. Once the hearing has reached its decision, the chairman must

---

249 Section 70(3)(b) and (5).
250 *D* v *Strathclyde Regional Council* (Sh Ct) 1991 SCLR (Notes) 185; *Kennedy* v *M* 1995 SLT 717.
251 Section 70(5)(a).
252 Section 90 preserves the child's rights under the Age of Legal Capacity (Scotland) Act 1991, s 2(4). On consent to medical treatment, see chapter 3, para 67.
253 Section 70(5)(b).
254 Section 73(7) and (8)(a)(iv).
255 Neither the Child Abduction Act 1984 nor the Child Abduction and Custody Act 1985 apply to determination of a child's place of residence by a children's hearing.

inform the child, the relevant persons, any safeguarder and any representative, of the hearing's decision, the reasons for it, and their right to appeal against the decision.[256] In addition, the reporter must send this information to them in writing, along with a copy of any supervision requirement.[257] Any person with whom the child is living must be informed of the decision of the hearing, as must the appropriate chief constable, if the information leading to the child's case was given by a police officer.[258] Pending the hearing of any appeal against the decision of a hearing to make a supervision requirement, the child or any relevant person may apply for suspension of the supervision requirement and the reporter must arrange a hearing to consider the application.[259] Subject to the special provisions on protection of the public, the aim of a supervision requirement is to meet the child's needs and, once that has been achieved, there is no justification for further involvement in his or her life. Consequently, no supervision requirement should continue for longer than is necessary in the interests of promoting or safeguarding the child's welfare,[260] none remains in force for longer than one year, although there is the possibility of variation or continuation,[261] and supervision ends, in any event, when the young person reaches the age of 18.[262]

- Require that the place where the child is to live should not be disclosed to a specified person or class of persons[263]

9.97 This provision was introduced by the 1995 Act, but neither the Act nor the Rules give any indication of when it would be appropriate for the hearing to order that the child's address should not be disclosed to specified persons. Clearly the child's welfare would be relevant here, but non-disclosure might serve to protect foster carers or prospective adopters from harassment by, for example, a parent. In order to justify a non-disclosure direction, the hearing should probably be satisfied, first, that it would be undesirable for the specified person to have unrestricted opportunities to contact the child, and, second, that there is reason to believe that the specified person would seek to make contact if he or she knew where the child was.

- Require that the supervision requirement shall be reviewed at a particular time[264]

9.98 No supervision requirement can last for more than one year from the time it was made, continued or varied[265] but, prior to the 1995 Act, a hearing had no power to mandate a review at an earlier time, and all it could do was express the hope that the local authority would request a

256 1996 Rules, r 20(5).
257 1996 Rules, r 21(1).
258 1996 Rules, r 21(2).
259 Section 51(9) and (10) and the 1996 Rules, r 23.
260 Section 73(1).
261 Section 73(2).
262 Section 73(3).
263 Section 70(6).
264 Section 70(7).
265 Section 73(2). On reviews, see below.

review at such an earlier time. It is not anticipated that hearings will make extensive use of this provision, but it might be considered where it is thought that the child's needs could be met with a short-term plan. An interesting use could be made of this provision where a child will reach school-leaving age within the year and the hearing is considering terminating the supervision requirement. If the supervision requirement is continued until after the child reaches school-leaving age, the local authority is obliged to provide him or her with guidance and assistance up to the age of 19 years.

Appeals

9.99 While appeals from the decision of a children's hearing are infrequent,[266] the fact that appeal is possible is important in reinforcing the legality of what is a lay system of decision-making.[267] The child has a right to appeal against the decision of a children's hearing, although his or her ability to do so effectively will be subject to the child's general capacity.[268] Any relevant person has standing to appeal, whether or not the person actually attended the hearing.[269] Subject to the general rules on qualifying for it, legal aid is available to fund representation for an appeal. A genetic father, who is not also a relevant person, has no right to appeal. Where a safeguarder has been appointed by a hearing, there is no mention of his or her right to appeal against the hearing's decision. It can be argued that it is part of the safeguarder's function, in safeguarding the interests of the child,[270] that he or she ought to be able to appeal against a decision where he or she does not believe that the decision serves that interest. In any event, a safeguarder may sign an appeal on the child's behalf.[271] This suggests that, at least, the safeguarder can act as the child's representative in respect of appeals where the child is not of sufficient age and maturity to instruct a solicitor. However, where the child has capacity and decides not to appeal against the hearing's decision it is doubtful that the safeguarder can raise an independent appeal. The reporter has no standing to appeal against the decision of a hearing.

9.100 The appeal must be lodged within three weeks, beginning with the date of the hearing's decision[272] and the date assigned for hearing the appeal must be no more than 28 days after the date the appeal was

---

266 In 1996/7, while 7,452 cases were disposed of by children's hearings, there were only 145 appeals to the sheriff; *Statistical Bulletin*, Section 10.
267 This is particularly important in the light of art 37(d) of the UN Convention on the Rights of the Child which requires that every child who is deprived of his or her liberty should have prompt access to legal and other appropriate assistance and the right to challenge the legality of the deprivation of his or her liberty before a court or other competent, independent and impartial authority. See chapter 3 for a discussion of the UK reservation to the Convention and withdrawal thereof.
268 See chapter 3, para 60.
269 Section 51(1). The person concerned must have been a relevant person at the time of the hearing decision and becoming a relevant person at a later date will not bring with it the right to appeal; *Kennedy v H* 1988 SLT 586.
270 Section 41(1)(a).
271 Child Care and Maintenance Rules 1997 (SI 1997, No 291), r 3.53(3).
272 Section 51(1)(a).

lodged.[273] The reporter must ensure that all the reports available to the hearing, the report of the proceedings at the hearing, and the reasons for the decision, are lodged with the sheriff clerk.[274]

9.101 With the exception of the decision to continue a child protection order, the 1995 Act provides that an appeal can be taken to the sheriff against any decision of a hearing.[275] This is somewhat misleading. The wording permitting appeals under the 1995 Act is the same as that found in the 1968 Act and case-law developed under the latter identified a range of decisions, largely of a procedural nature, as non-appealable.[276] Arguably, they will continue to be non-appealable. None the less, the decisions which really matter to the child and the family – for example, the imposition of a supervision requirement and its terms, any decision to continue or vary such a requirement, or the granting of a warrant to detain the child – can be appealed against.

9.102 At the outset, and throughout the appeal, the sheriff must consider whether it is necessary to appoint a safeguarder[277] and, where appointed, the safeguarder has the same rights and duties as a curator *ad litem*.[278] The safeguarder must intimate to the sheriff clerk whether or not he or she intends to become a party to the proceedings.[279] The sheriff is directed to allow the appeal if he or she is satisfied that the hearing's decision is 'not justified in all the circumstances of the case'.[280] For example, failure to allow the child or the relevant persons the opportunity to participate, or proceeding on the basis that grounds of referral had been accepted when they had not,[281] have all been accepted as legitimate grounds for appeal. Procedural irregularities may justify overturning the hearing's decision,[282] but only if the irregularity has a significant impact on the case.[283] Since *all the circumstances of the case* are relevant, the sheriff is probably entitled to consider changes in circumstances which have occurred since the hearing. This could result in overturning a decision which was reasonable at the time it was made. None the less, given that the whole system is aimed at meeting the needs of the child, and those needs will depend on the

---

273 Child Care and Maintenance Rules 1997 (SI 1997, No 291), r 3.54(5).
274 Section 51(2).
275 Section 51(1) and (15).
276 See B. Kearney, n 2 above, at pp 303–306.
277 Section 41(1).
278 Child Care and Maintenance Rules 1997, (SI 1997, No 291), r 3.8.
279 If the safeguarder decides to become a party, he or she may appear personally or may instruct a lawyer. If the safeguarder decides against entering appearance, he or she must submit a written report, detailing the enquiries he or she has made and his or her conclusions in respect of the child's interests – Child Care and Maintenance Rules 1997 (SI 1997, No 291), rr 3.6–3.10.
280 Section 51(5).
281 *M* v *Kennedy* 1993 SLT 431, where the hearing proceeded on the basis that the sexual abuse of the child had taken place in the 'family home' when those words had been struck out by the sheriff when the grounds were established.
282 *O* v *Rae* 1993 SLT 570.
283 See, for example, *McGregor* v *A* 1982 SLT 45, where, despite the fact that the wrong statute was cited in the grounds of referral, no substantial injustice resulted.

prevailing circumstances at a given time, any other solution would be indefensible.

9.103 In considering the appeal, the sheriff may hear evidence from the parties, or their representatives. In addition, he or she may examine the reporter, examine the compilers of any reports, and call for any further reports which may be of assistance.[284]

Sheriff's decision-making powers in an appeal

9.104 Having heard all the evidence, the sheriff will allow or dismiss the appeal. If the appeal is dismissed, the sheriff must confirm the decision of the hearing.[285] Where the appeal is against the decision of a review hearing and the sheriff finds it to be frivolous, he or she can order that no further appeal be heard for one year.[286] If the sheriff allows the appeal, he or she has a number of options. The sheriff may either, remit the case back to the hearing, with reasons for allowing the appeal, so that the hearing can reconsider the case,[287] or he or she may discharge the child from any further hearing in relation to the grounds of referral.[288] The 1995 Act introduced a further, controversial, option. Where a sheriff allows an appeal, he or she may now substitute any disposal that the children's hearing could have made without any need to refer the case back to a hearing.[289] This allows the sheriff to substitute his or her own disposal for that of the hearing and this has been condemned in some quarters. Given that the Kilbrandon Committee believed that, while establishing disputed facts was appropriate for the courts, disposals were a matter for hearings, this is, indeed, a departure from the original philosophy. Such provision for judicial involvement was essential, however, if the hearings system was to comply with the UN Convention. To date, sheriffs have been extremely reluctant to exercise their power to discharge the child when allowing appeals[290] and it is anticipated that they will show similar restraint in exercising this power. Where the sheriff substitutes his or her disposal for that of the hearing, the decision will be treated as if it were a decision of the hearing.[291] Where the successful appeal is against the granting of a warrant to find, keep or detain a child in a place of safety the sheriff must recall the warrant.[292] Similarly, where a successful appeal relates to a supervision requirement, with the condition that the child should reside in secure accommodation, that condition falls.[293]

9.105 Further appeal lies by way of stated case from the sheriff to the

284 Section 51(3).
285 Section 51(4).
286 Section 51(7).
287 Section 51(5)(c)(i).
288 Section 51(5)(c)(ii).
289 Section 51(5)(c)(iii).
290 Of the 145 appeals to the sheriff in 1996/97, 100 failed and the hearing's disposal was confirmed; 39 were upheld and the case was remitted back to the hearing for further consideration, and only six were upheld and discharged; *Statistical Bulletin*, Section 10.
291 Section 51(6).
292 Section 51(5)(a).
293 Section 51(5)(b).

Sheriff Principal and, with leave from the Sheriff Principal, to the Court of Session, on a point of law or in respect of any irregularity in the conduct of the case.[294] Permitting appeal to the Sheriff Principal is an innovation of the 1995 Act and has attracted criticism.[295] Such appeals are open to the child, any relevant person and the reporter on behalf of the children's hearing[296] and the application to state a case for the purpose of the appeal must be made within 28 days of the decision being made.[297] Again, appeals are not permitted in respect of child protection orders.[298] There is no appeal to the House of Lords.[299]

REVIEW OF ESTABLISHED GROUNDS OF REFERRAL: NEW EVIDENCE

9.106 The 1968 Act made no provision for a challenge to established grounds of referral where new evidence emerged after the appeal process had been exhausted. Initially, it was thought that even the last resort of a petition to the *nobile officium* could not be used to cure this defect in the procedure.[300] However, in what came to be known as the *Ayrshire Case*,[301] the Inner House granted a petition to the *nobile officium*, and ordered a sheriff to examine the grounds of referral afresh in the light of the new evidence. Thereafter, it was up to the Inner House to consider what to do about the case, but without the benefit of the statutory authority that a hearing would have had. This left the law in an uncertain[302] and highly unsatisfactory state, and the 1995 Act introduced a statutory framework for dealing with new evidence relating to the grounds of referral.

9.107 Challenging established grounds of referral is available only to the child and the relevant persons and, even then, only in certain restricted circumstances.[303] The grounds under challenge must have been established before the sheriff, that is, either the child or any of the relevant persons must have refused to accept the grounds or there must have been a failure to understand on the part of the child.[304] In addition, the applicant must

---

294 Section 51(11).
295 Sheriff Mitchell, speaking as a private individual rather than in his judicial capacity, has made the following comment 'An appeal from one judge to another judge is just plain bad jurisprudence', J. K. Mitchell, 'Appeals, Disposals and Warrants', Legal Services Agency seminar, 26 October 1995. That may be so, but it is the norm in civil appeals in the sheriff court.
296 Section 51(12).
297 Section 51(13).
298 Section 51(15).
299 Section 51(11)(b).
300 *R, Petitioner* 1993 SLT 910, where the child retracted her earlier allegations of sexual abuse.
301 *L, Petitioners* (*No 1*) 1993 SLT 1310 and (*No 2*) 1993 SLT 1342, where the disputed allegations of sexual abuse were challenged on the basis of new expert evidence, and the increased awareness of the need to be careful in the manner of questioning adopted in cases of this kind.
302 A subsequent case, *H, Petitioners* 1997 SLT 3, followed the decision in *R, Petitioner* 1993 SLT 910.
303 Section 85(1) and (4).
304 Section 85(1) and (2).

claim: to have evidence which was not considered by the sheriff in the original application and which might have materially affected that application; that this evidence is likely to be credible and reliable and would have been admissible in respect of the original application; and that there is a reasonable explanation of the failure to lead the evidence during the original application.[305]

9.108 If the sheriff is not satisfied that the claims made are established, he or she must dismiss the application and the hearing's disposal stands.[306] Where the sheriff is satisfied that the claims made in the application for review are established, there are two possibilities. Either, the challenge is such that all of the grounds of referral are struck down by it, or, while some of the grounds are no longer established, others remain valid. Where any ground of referral remains established, the sheriff may remit the case to the reporter to arrange a hearing and, pending the hearing, may order that the child be kept in a place of safety.[307] Where none of the grounds remains established, there is no longer any valid reason for a supervision requirement. However, the 1995 Act acknowledges that it might be precipitate simply to return the child to the family without any arrangements for transition.[308] Thus, while the sheriff may terminate the supervision requirement immediately, he or she may also postpone such termination.[309] In addition, where the supervision requirement is terminated, the sheriff may direct the local authority to give the child supervision or guidance but, where the child is of sufficient age and maturity to do so, the child can reject such help.[310] There is yet another, albeit unlikely, possibility to consider. Where the new evidence strikes down some or all of the original grounds of referral, it may disclose new grounds. Where this happens, the sheriff may find the new grounds established[311] and remit the matter to the reporter to arrange a fresh hearing to determine the case.[312]

REVIEW OF THE SUPERVISION REQUIREMENT

9.109 In line with the general thrust of the 1995 Act, the hearings system seeks to recognise that its goal is to meet the needs of the child, recognising that these needs may change, sometimes rapidly, and that intervention in a child's life should only continue for as long as it is better than non-intervention. Thus, for example, there is provision that no child should be subject to supervision for longer than is necessary[313] and that any change in

---

305 Section 85(3).
306 Section 85(5).
307 Section 85(6)(b).
308 In the *Ayrshire Case*, (*L, Petitioners*, n 301 above) the children had not been living with their families for a number of years prior to the successful challenge to the grounds of referral. In these circumstances, the court recognised that the return home of the children would be eased by a period of transition.
309 Section 85(7)(a). If the supervision requirement is to continue in effect, the sheriff may order that the child's whereabouts should not be disclosed to certain persons; s 85(8).
310 Section 85(9) and (10).
311 Section 85(7)(b).
312 Section 68(10).
313 Section 73(1).

circumstances should be considered as quickly as possible, in order to assess any change in the child's needs. The mandating and availability of reviews should ensure that no child is left to drift in the system.

9.110 Unless a supervision requirement is reviewed within one year of its being made, it ceases to have effect.[314] In addition, the local authority must refer a case to the reporter in certain circumstances, with a view to a review hearing being arranged, and the child and any of the relevant persons may request a review hearing within certain periods of time. Where a child is subject to a supervision requirement, the local authority must refer the case to the Principal Reporter where it is satisfied that the requirement ought to cease to have effect or be varied; that a condition contained in the requirement is not being complied with; or the best interests of the child would be served by their applying for a parental responsibilities order, applying for an order freeing the child for adoption, or placing the child for adoption.[315] The child or any relevant person may apply for review of a supervision requirement at any time three months after, either, the date when the requirement was made, or, the date of the most recent continuation or review of a requirement.[316]

9.111 A hearing to review a supervision requirement operates much like the original hearing and can continue the review hearing to allow for further investigation, terminate the supervision requirement, vary the requirement, insert in the requirement any other requirement it could have made, or continue the requirement.[317]

THE CHILDREN'S HEARINGS SYSTEM IN THE FUTURE

9.112 The 1995 Act introduced a number of changes to the system and it was feared in some quarters that these changes would undermine the Kilbrandon philosophy. The 1995 Act replaced the notion of a child being in need of 'compulsory measures of care' with 'compulsory measures of supervision' as the criterion for a child being referred to a hearing at all. While the latter certainly sounds less benevolent, it simply reflects the true nature of what was always the essence of the decision made by a hearing.

9.113 Other reforms introduced by the 1995 Act arguably strengthen the Kilbrandon philosophy. This is particularly true in respect of improving the child's ability to take a meaningful part in the proceedings. Safeguarders have been given a much expanded role, thus enabling more children to be assisted in participating in the hearing. The 1995 Act introduced the possibility of a person being excluded from all or part of the hearing and this may make it easier for children to express views that they believe a particular adult might not like and, thus, reduce the stress the child might experience. Of course, the knowledge that the substance of what he or she has said will be relayed to the excluded adult when he or she returns may

314 Section 73(2).
315 Section 73(4).
316 Section 73(6).
317 Section 73(9).

be an inhibiting factor for some children, but the provision achieves some improvement for the child's right to express views in a manner consistent with natural justice.

9.114 Some of the reforms introduced by the 1995 Act and the 1996 Rules were essential if the hearings system was to conform to international standards. Thus, for example, providing copies of all documents to relevant persons meets a criticism levelled at the system by the European Court of Human Rights in *McMichael*. The increased role of the sheriff in appeals has improved judicial oversight and enabled the UK to withdraw its reservation to the UN Convention in respect of children's hearings.[318]

9.115 Defects in the system remain and they are often the result of problems found in the legal system as a whole. Children's ignorance of the law, in general, and their rights, in particular, coupled with the fact that most children will not have a safeguarder, must inhibit some children from participating as fully as they might in what is, after all, a very adult setting. A thorough-going review of practical ways in which children can be informed about and enabled to participate in the legal system is long overdue. The fact that children do not receive copies of the reports that are sent to the other participants in the hearing is regrettable, particularly in respect of older children. It may be that some of what is contained in a social background report would be distressing to a child, particularly if the child is simply sent the report and left to read it alone. That may be reason to provide the child with reports in a setting different to that appropriate to an adult, but it is not a reason for the legislation as it stands.

9.116 A further, fundamental, problem – the position of the unmarried father – is, again, not peculiar to the hearings system. Consistent with the rest of the law, unmarried fathers, unlike mothers and married fathers, do not have an automatic right to participate in the hearings system unless they have some parental responsibilities and rights by virtue of a parental rights agreement or a court order. The genetic father's position has been improved slightly by the 1996 Rules, but the essential discrimination continues. The absence of legal aid to enable parents to be represented at hearings means that most parents are effectively denied legal representation. While the informal nature of children's hearings is one of its strengths, it would be a mistake to assume that lawyers, and particularly those who specialise in child law, are incapable of understanding the nature of the system and of contributing to it.

9.117 None the less, the hearings system represents an enlightened and compassionate way to meet the needs of children. Perhaps most encouraging of all, is the fact that it remains subject to rigorous scrutiny.[319] Given the very considerable support for the hearings system, it has been suggested that its jurisdiction could be expanded to embrace all cases concerning

---

318 Reservation F was withdrawn on 18 April 1997.

319 See, for example, Just in Time: Report on Time Intervals in Children's Hearings Cases (Scottish Children's Reporter Administration, 1997), which, as its title suggests, analyses all stages of processing a case through the system and makes a number of recommendations aimed at reducing delays. The remit of the Working Group, chaired by Sally

children, including decisions on residence, contact and adoption. To move decision-making in all such cases from the courts to the hearings might require further modification of the hearings system including, perhaps, the introduction of a legally qualified chairperson. Undoubtedly, greater resources would be required by any such new system. The alternative of a Family Court should not be dismissed, but this possible use of hearings presents an interesting challenge.

Kuenssberg, has been extended to include consideration of how its recommendations might be implemented; Consultation on Inter-agency Code of Practice and National Standards for the Processing of Children's Cases (Scottish Children's Reporter Administration, 1998).

The Children's Hearing System: Steps in the procedure

Information received by the principal reporter	
Initial investigation – First stage	
Is there a prima facie case establishing one of the grounds of referral?	No → Case does not proceed
Yes → Initial investigation – Second stage	
Does it appear that the child is in need of compulsory measures of supervision?	No → No formal action
Yes → Convening a hearing: who must or may be present	
Is it necessary to call a business meeting	Yes → Business meeting called
No → Should the referral be discharged?	Yes → Discharge the referral
No → Should a safeguarder be appointed	Yes → Appointment of a safeguarder
No → Hearing – First stage:	

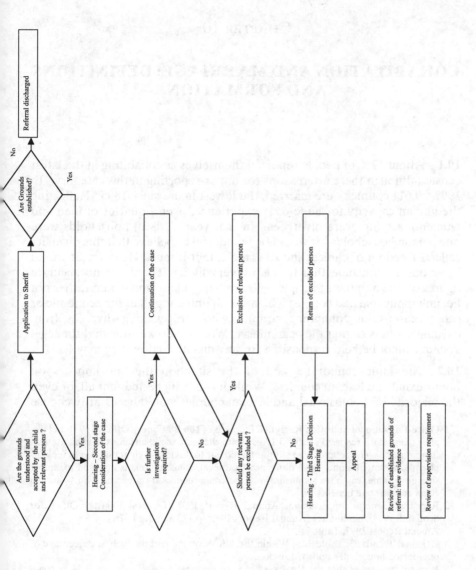

431

CHAPTER 10

COHABITATION AND MARRIAGE: DEFINITIONS AND FORMATION

10.1 About 17% of people reported themselves as cohabiting in the latest census, although there are reasons for under-reporting in this category.[1] In 1997, 29,611 couples were married, the lowest figure since 1895.[2] Reflecting the human capacity for hope over experience, over a quarter of men and women marrying, were divorcees.[3] In that year, 31% of households were one person households.[4] It would be wonderful to believe that this diversity reflects freedom of choice, and to some extent it must. However, it would be wrong to conclude that this is universally so. There are no accurate figures on the number of people who are living alone and would rather not be, unhappily married couples who are remaining together for economic or other reasons, or cohabiting couples who are awaiting divorces from existing spouses so that they can marry. What we do know is that the legal system cannot be held responsible for any dissatisfaction they may feel.[5]

10.2 The same cannot be said of the situation the law imposes on homosexual and lesbian couples.[6] While it is not suggested that all, or even the majority of, homosexual and lesbian couples would necessarily choose

1 Office for National Statistics, Regional Trends 33 (The Stationery Office, 1998), hereinafter 'Regional Trends 33', Table 3.17. Despite changing social attitudes to cohabitation, there may be some couples who still preferred not to disclose their status due to feelings of embarrassment alone. On a more practical level, cohabitation, as opposed to simply sharing a home, can have significant adverse consequences for a person who wishes to claim certain state benefits.
2 Registrar General for Scotland, Annual Report 1997 (General Register Office for Scotland, 1998), hereinafter 'Annual Report 1997', p 122 and Table 7.1.
3 Annual Report 1997, Table 7.4.
4 Regional Trends 33, Table 3.19. Within the UK, Scotland had the highest percentage of one-person households outside London.
5 It might be argued that the legal system is responsible for the delay in at least some divorces from former spouses.
6 It is unfortunate that the Scottish Law Commission expressly excluded such relationships when it was considering reform of the law on cohabitation: The Effects of Cohabitation in Private Law (Scot Law Com Discussion Paper No 86, 1990), para 1.13 and Report on Family Law (Scot Law Com No 135, 1992) para 16.3. It may be that, had this controversial matter been included, any discussion of the reforms proposed would have concentrated on the issue of homosexual and lesbian relationships and might have resulted in reforms affecting all cohabitants being rejected. The Commission felt free, none the less, to spell out that, not only should same-sex marriage be prohibited in Scotland, but that no domiciled Scot should be permitted to marry a person of the same sex anywhere in the world, see draft Family Law (Scotland) Bill, cl 20. Arguably, this is no more than a restatement of the present law.

marriage rather than cohabitation, the option is simply not available to them.[7] Nor does Scots law countenance the possibility of transsexualism. Essentially, an individual retains his or her birth gender irrespective of steps taken to change that.[8] Where a person has changed his or her sex, in terms of the practical manifestations thereof, his or her capacity to marry will remain tied to his or her birth gender. Thus, where a person begins life as a male, he can undergo any amount of hormone treatment and sex realignment surgery, regard himself as having become female and appear as such to the world at large. None the less, he will still be unable to marry a male person, since the law will continue to regard him as male. As we shall see, heterosexual cohabiting couples do not get many of the benefits automatically available to married couples, including the right to aliment from a partner, financial provision on the termination of the relationship or succession rights on intestacy. However, their relationships are recognised for other purposes including limited protection in the family home and damages on the wrongful death of a partner. None of these rights is extended to lesbian or homosexual couples. In *Grant* v *South-West Trains*,[9] the European Court of Justice reached the disappointing conclusion that discrimination based on sexual orientation does not constitute sex discrimination and, thus, that employers are not obliged to offer the same benefits to same-sex partners as they offer to other partners.

10.3 In other jurisdictions, some same-sex couples have sought to overcome the legal system's failure to recognise their relationship by employing other legal mechanisms including, adoption,[10] powers of attorney, cohabitation contracts and wills, so far, with mixed success.[11] The problem with trying to mould other legal concepts to accommodate a personal relationship is that they will often provide an imperfect solution. Thus, for example, a power of attorney will not meet problems between the parties if they separate and cohabitation contracts risk being struck down on public

---

7 Marriage (Scotland) Act 1977, s 5(4)(e).
8 *X, Petitioner* 1957 SLT (Sh Ct) 61; *Corbett* v *Corbett* [1971] P 83; and A. Campbell, 'Successful Sex in Succession: Sex in Dispute – the Forbes-Sempill Case and Possible Implications' 1998 JR 257 and 325. See chapter 2, paras 70–73.
9 [1998] IRLR 207.
10 In *Matter of Adoption of Adult Anonymous* 106 Misc 2d 792 (NY, 1981), a 22-year-old man adopted his 26-year-old male partner and in *In re Adult Anonymous II* 452 NYS 2d 198 (1982), a 43-year-old man adopted his 32-year-old male partner. However, the courts in New York seem to have had a change of attitude and in *In re Adoption of Robert Paul P* 471 NE 2d 424 (NY, 1984), the court rejected a similar adoption application, stating that adoption 'is plainly not a quasi-marital vehicle to provide non-married partners with a legal imprimatur for their sexual relationship' (at p 425). The concept of adoption cannot be used to create a legally recognised relationship between same-sex partners in Scotland since only persons under the age of 18 can be adopted here, see Adoption (Scotland) Act 1978, ss 12(1) and 65(1).
11 L. Anderson, 'Property Rights of Same-Sex Couples: Towards a New Definition of Family' 26 J Fam L 357 (1987); M. N. Cameli, 'Extending Family Benefits to Gay Men and Lesbian Women' 68 Chi-Kent L Rev 447 (1992); D. L. Chambers, 'What if? The Legal Consequences of Marriage and the Legal Needs of Lesbian and Gay Male Couples' 95 Mich L Rev 447 (1996).

policy grounds.[12] Another mechanism, the notion of domestic partnership, has been explored in the USA.[13] Essentially, this involves extending the concept of a business partnership to cover a personal relationship.[14] Denmark was the first country to pass legislation in 1989, providing for registered partnership.[15] It was followed by Sweden and the Netherlands, and a number of other countries are considering similar legislation,[16] although Scotland is not among them. Typically, the registered partnership is available only to persons who cannot marry and gives some, but not all, of the benefits of marriage to couples who register their partnership.[17] It should be noted that a registered partnership is not marriage. Since it requires the formal step of registration, nor is it simple cohabitation. It creates a third category of adult relationships and one which could apply equally to heterosexual as well as lesbian and homosexual couples. Recent legislation in Canada has extended the rights of same-sex partners in respect of child custody and financial support and, to a limited extent, in respect of family property. Of course, another option is to provide for same-sex marriage and that option is discussed later in this chapter.[18] What all of this makes clear is that there is no reason for the legal system to go on denying choice and recognition to various groups within society. The solutions are out there if we want to find them.

10.4 Whether as a matter of choice or because it is the only option open to them, a number of couples live together while others marry. The extent to which these various relationships are recognised socially will often depend on the couple's friends and families, although it is probably fair to say that it is more difficult to ignore a spouse than a cohabitant. As we shall see in chapters 11 and 12, marriage is a relationship recognised by the legal system as having certain, albeit limited, consequences. That is not to say that cohabitation is devoid of all legal consequences and, where cohabitation does have such consequences, they will often mirror those attaching to marriage and will only arise in heterosexual marriage-like relationships.

12 See chapter 11, para 93 for a discussion of cohabitation contracts and the Scottish Law Commission's view that, at least so far as heterosexual couples are concerned, they are not against public policy. It is worth noting that the Commission recommended, none the less, that legislation should clarify the validity of such contracts.

13 R. C. O'Brien, 'Domestic Partnership: Recognition and Responsibility' 32 San Diego L Rev 163 (1995).

14 The Partnership Act 1890 and the Limited Partnerships Act 1907 define partnership as the relationship which subsists between 'persons carrying on a business in common with a view of profit' – 1890 Act, s 1(1). Thus, the concept of partnership as understood in Scots law, could not be adapted readily to accommodate personal relationships.

15 For a discussion of the introduction of registered partnerships in Denmark and the comparative developments in Sweden, see D. Bradney, *Family Law and Political Culture* (Sweet & Maxwell, 1996), pp 151–155.

16 Belgium, Finland, France, Luxemburg, Portugal and Spain are currently considering such legislation – see P. L. Spackman, 'Grant v South-West Trains: Equality for Same-Sex Partners the European Community' 12 Am J Int'l L and Pol'y 1063 (1997), at pp 1097–1098.

17 In Denmark, Norway and Sweden registered partners gain all the rights acquired by married couples except the opportunity to adopt children, to assistance with reproduction and to church weddings. In the Netherlands, registered partners cannot currently adopt children but the prohibition is being reconsidered – see Spackman, above, at pp. 1093–1097.

18 At para 10.19–10.21.

Thus, for example, a cohabitant may gain the protection of the Matrimonial Homes (Family Protection) (Scotland) Act 1981, but only if the couple have been living together as if they were man and wife.[19] The consequences of cohabitation will be explored in chapters 11 and 12.

10.5 Popular usage suggests that there is some confusion surrounding what is often described as 'common law marriage'. References in the media to a 'common law' wife or husband are often references to a cohabitant rather than a spouse. However, Scots law continues to permit one kind of irregular marriage, marriage by cohabitation with habit and repute. Here, a valid marriage can be created without the parties complying with any of the formalities required for a regular marriage and, indeed, there will usually be no ceremony at all. Such a marriage can more properly be described as common law marriage. Marriage by cohabitation with habit and repute and the other, now obsolete, forms of irregular marriage are discussed later in this chapter.[20]

COHABITATION

10.6 Here, we are concerned with what might be described as 'cohabitation proper'; that is, the situation where a couple live together quite openly without any pretence that they are, in fact, married. Undoubtedly, there has been a dramatic increase in the number of couples cohabiting and changing attitudes to cohabitation mean that couples are much less likely to feel any need for secrecy. What often distinguishes cohabitation from marriage is the issue of clarity of definition. Aside from the special case of irregular marriage, each marriage begins and ends on specific, easily identifiable, dates, the latter being either the date of death of one of the spouses or the date that the divorce decree is granted. Marriage has clear parameters marked by certificates, recorded in registers. In short, marriage comes in a neat package. Cohabitation, on the other hand, can be more difficult to pin down both in terms of the nature of the relationship and its duration. Take, for example, two students who start the term sharing a flat as platonic friends. As time goes by, their friendship develops into a romantic and sexual relationship and eventually they occupy the same bedroom every night. Has their relationship become one of cohabitation and, if so, when did they begin to cohabit? Where two people have separate homes but one of them stays overnight regularly at the other's house and has moved in quite a number of personal belongings, can they be viewed as cohabiting? If they are, when did the cohabitation begin? The Scottish Law Commission was well aware of the difficulties surrounding any definition of cohabitation and the injustice that might result from defining it in terms of arbitrary time limits.[21]

10.7 In its examination of cohabitation, the Commission considered why people cohabit rather than marry and, not suprisingly, found a variety of

---

19 Section 18(1). In order to determine this, the court is directed to consider a variety of factors including the duration of the cohabitation and whether there are any children of the relationship.
20 Paras 10.75–10.80.
21 The Effects of Cohabitation in Private Law (Scot Law Com Discussion Paper No 86, 1990), para 1.2 and Report on Family Law (Scot Law Com No 135, 1992) para 16.4.

reasons for cohabitation.[22] One might question the legitimacy of this inquiry. After all, we rarely ask why people get married, so why should we question the motive behind cohabitation? However, the Commission's question was asked in the context of considering whether the law should attach greater consequences to cohabitation than it does at present. Thus, if people cohabit with the express intention of avoiding the consequences of marriage, it is relevant to know that before we consider whether cohabitation should be treated more like marriage. In some cases, couples cohabit because one or both of them is not free to marry and in many such cases they plan to marry when that option becomes possible. Other couples cohabit as a kind of trial marriage, just to see how living together will work out for them. If all goes well, these couples plan to marry in the future. Other couples choose cohabitation as an alternative to marriage. Sometimes these people have been married before and do not wish to repeat an experience which they found to be less than satisfactory. In other cases the couple, or at least one of them, may be rejecting the notion of marriage and its consequences quite expressly. In yet other cases, cohabitation may be prompted by inertia: the couple started living together and have simply done nothing further.

10.8 In terms of legal regulation of cohabitation, there is comparatively little to say since there is virtually no regulation. There are no legal restrictions on who may cohabit apart from the general provisions of the criminal law which outlaw certain types of sexual relationships. Thus, where either party is below the age of consent or where the relationship between the parties amounts to incest, sexual relations between them will be criminal and, thus, the cohabitation might be described as illegal. It is stating the obvious to note that there are no formalities to be observed for a couple to cohabit.

ENGAGEMENT TO MARRY

10.9 For many couples, getting engaged is the usual preliminary to getting married. Often accompanied by the man giving a ring to the woman, the couple throwing a party, and friends and family giving presents, the social significance of an engagement lies in people giving public expression to something they regard as being an important event. At one time, promising to marry someone had considerable legal significance as well. While the courts would not order a person to go through with the marriage,[23] an action for damages for breach of promise to marry lay at the instance of the innocent party.[24] With the passage of time, such actions became extremely rare, although there was no way to know how many actions were

---

22 The Effects of Cohabitation in Private Law (Scot Law Com Discussion Paper No 86, 1990), para 1.4.

23 Specific implement will not normally be granted in respect of personal relationships, see D. M. Walker, *The Law of Civil Remedies in Scotland* (W. Green, 1974) at p 280. However, see the discussion in respect of enforcing the parental obligation to maintain contact with a child at chapter 5, paras 28 and 29.

24 Damages were recoverable not simply for pecuniary loss but also for hurt feelings. In *Hogg* v *Gow* May 27, 1812, FC, where a man was persuaded by the children of his

threatened and settled without resort to litigation. In any event, the Scottish Law Commission reviewed this area of the law and concluded that, where a person had doubts about entering a particular marriage, it is better that they should be free to withdraw, unfettered by the fear of an action for damages.[25] Accordingly, the Commission recommended the abolition of such actions and that recommendation found statutory expression in the Law Reform (Husband and Wife) (Scotland) Act 1984 ('the 1984 Act') which provides

> 'No promise of marriage or agreement between two persons to marry one another shall have effect under the law of Scotland to create any rights or obligations; and no action for breach of any such promise or agreement may be brought in any court in Scotland, whatever the law applicable to the promise or agreement'.[26]

Thus, it is no longer possible for the jilted party to raise an action in Scotland for damages for breach of promise of marriage. It should be noted that this provision covers agreements made in Scotland and elsewhere, irrespective of the proper law applying to the agreement. Of course, a person could raise such an action in a foreign court, provided that the foreign law permits such actions and that the foreign court accepts jurisdiction.[27]

10.10 While actions for damages for breach of promise are now obsolete, other actions remain competent in the context of promised marriages which do not take place. The use of the word 'obligations' in the 1984 Act suggests that actions in delict are barred. Thus, a promise to marry, made with a callous disregard for sincerity, would not appear to give any ground for an action for damages founded in delict. However, actions founded on unjustified enrichment would appear possible. Thus, where property was transferred by one party to the other in contemplation of marriage, such property could be recovered using the *condictio causa data causa non secuta*.[28]

10.11 A question, much loved by law examiners although probably of less significance in practice, is what happens to gifts the parties have given to each other in anticipation of or during the engagement. While the usual presumption against donation applies, there are no special rules here and where one party has given an unconditional gift to the other, the donee is entitled to keep it even if he or she is the person who ends the relationship. Thus, for example, there would usually be no need to return birthday

previous marriage not to go ahead with a later marriage, his fiancee was awarded £500 (later increased to £700). Lord Meadowbank (at p 656) gives some idea of the thinking prevalent at the time when he refers to Ms Gow's 'loss of market' and says, 'Her heart is used; it is worn; she is less attractive to others.'

25 Report on Outdated Rules in the Law of Husband and Wife (Scot Law Com No 76, 1983), paras 2.1–2.12 and rec 1.

26 Section 1(1). This provision is retrospective – s 1(2).

27 Such actions were abolished in England and Wales by the Law Reform (Miscellaneous Provisions) Act 1970, s 1(1), but only in so far as contractual remedies are concerned. Only a minority of jurisdictions in the USA still permit such actions. In Illinois, for example, the statute limits recovery to pecuniary loss.

28 For the limits of applying this remedy, see *Grieve* v *Morrison* 1993 SLT 852 and *Shilliday Smith* 1998 SLT 976.

presents. However, where the gift is given subject to an express or implied condition that the marriage will take place, then it must be returned if the condition is not fulfilled. There is conflicting sheriff court authority on how engagement rings should be regarded. In one case,[29] the ring was treated as an unconditional gift, and the woman was permitted to keep it, while in another case,[30] it was treated as a conditional gift and, thus, the man who had given it was entitled to get it back. Given that an engagement ring is usually given in recognition of the engagement, with another ring being given at the time of marriage, it might be argued that engagement rings should normally be viewed either as unconditional gifts[31] or as gifts where the condition, that is, the engagement itself, has already been fulfilled. However, where the ring in question is a family heirloom which has been in the man's family for some time, it might be argued that there is an implied condition that it will remain in the family and, thus, that it is given subject to the condition that the woman will become a member of that family through marriage. In such circumstances, failure to fulfil the condition would require the return of the ring.

10.12 In the event that the marriage does not take place, the legal position of gifts given to the couple by third parties will again depend on the circumstances in which the gifts were given. Arguably, where a gift is given to mark the engagement, any condition attaching to it has been fulfilled by the engagement itself and, thus, it is not subject to return simply because the marriage does not proceed.[32] Wedding presents, on the other hand, can be viewed as having been given subject to the condition that the wedding will take place. Thus, if there is no wedding, the donors are entitled to have the gifts returned to them. In practice, most people would probably prefer to avoid embarrassment and forget all about modest wedding presents. After all, who needs another toaster? However, where a wedding present is of greater value as, for example, where the couple has been given a house by the parents of one of them, the possible conditional nature of the gift may be significant.

RESTRICTIONS ON MARRIAGE

10.13 Scots law has always regarded marriage as important. In common with other western, Judeo-Christian societies,[33] the significance of marriage can be attributed to its various functions, at least in the past, in defining the roles of individuals within the group, marking alliances between different groups, determining succession to property and power and, latterly,

---

29 *Gold* v *Hume* (1950) 66 Sh Ct Rep 85.
30 *Savage* v *McAllister* (1952) 68 Sh Ct Rep 11.
31 In England and Wales, there is a rebuttable presumption that the engagement ring is given unconditionally, see Law Reform (Miscellaneous Provisions) Act 1970, s 3(2).
32 A parallel might be drawn with wedding presents where the marriage does actually go ahead. In such circumstances, the condition attaching to the gift has been fulfilled and wedding gifts are not subject to return if the couple subsequently divorce.
33 Marriage is important, of course, in non-western, non-Judeo-Christian societies. Any reluctance to discuss the position in such societies is based solely on the author's belief that she has inadequate knowledge of them to comment in a fully-informed way.

providing what is often thought to be the optimum environment for procreation and the raising of children. The religious, as well as the social, significance of marriage was and, for some, still is, considerable.[34] In the later 20th century, the emerging importance of the individual, autonomy and personal fulfilment, have resulted in emphasising the role of marriage in providing support and comfort to individuals, although its place as a forum for child-rearing remains significant.

10.14 For these reason, the legal system, from Celtic law,[35] though the period of canon law,[36] then through the secular (or, at least, a quasi-secular) legal system, has always sought to regulate marriage.[37] Thus, who can marry at all, who can marry whom and the formalities required for a valid marriage are all clearly set out. In some respects, regulation of marriage is aimed at protecting the individual. Thus, a minimum age for marriage is laid down to protect the young from embarking on this form of commitment prematurely. Similarly, a marriage may be void where one of the parties was coerced into entering it. However, the legal system's enthusiasm for regulating marriage derives, at least in part, from the belief that marriage is not simply a personal matter and that there is some general societal interest in it. Thus, certain individuals are prohibited from marrying because it is believed that they are too closely related. The formal requirements for marriage allow the opportunity, at least in theory, for members of the public to lodge objections and for official review of the individuals' capacity to marry. These requirements also assist in public record-keeping. In short, the law regulates marriage *because* it is regarded as important at the same time as it *contributes* to the importance of marriage by attaching consequences to it.

10.15 Restrictions on marriage sometimes reflect the prevailing cultural, religious or social mores of the time and, thus, they may vary between societies and over time. It is worth taking a brief look at some restrictions on marriage found elsewhere, either in the past or the present, that have not found their way into Scots law. Many legal systems require parental consent before young people below a particular age may marry. Scots law has never embraced such a requirement and this, combined with the low age of capacity to marry, made Scotland something of a haven for young runaways whose pursuit of true love was being blocked by parents in

---

34 Thus, Stair was able to comment, 'The first obligations God put upon man towards man, were the conjugal obligations, which arose from the constitution of marriage before the fall.... Though marriage seem to be a voluntary contract by engagement ... marriage itself and the obligations thence arising are *jure divino*' – Stair, I, iv, 1. When Stair refers to 'man' he is using the word to mean 'person' rather than a male person.

35 See J. Cameron, *Celtic Law* (Hodge, 1937) and W. D. H. Sellar, 'Marriage, Divorce and Concubinage in Gaelic Scotland', *Transactions of the Gaelic Society of Inverness*, vol 51 (1978–80), 464.

36 See J. C. Barry (trs and ed), *William Hay's Lectures on Marriage* (1967, vol 24, Stair Society).

37 For a discussion of the history of regulation of the law on husband and wife, see E. M. Clive, *The Law of Husband and Wife in Scotland* (4th edn, W. Green, 1997) at pp 1–16.

England and elsewhere.[38] Nor has Scots law adopted prohibitions on marriage between members of different religious[39] or ethnic[40] groups– prohibitions which, happily, are now increasingly rare in other jurisdictions. Unlike the position in many other countries, persons intending to marry in Scotland do not have to undergo a blood test for a variety of medical conditions or diseases. Where such tests are required, their purpose varies. In most cases, they are simply designed to inform the individual of the current state of his or her health and the results are not disclosed to the prospective spouse, nor is the marriage prohibited where particular conditions are found to be present.[41] Given the limited use made of such tests elsewhere, it is doubtful that we are losing anything by not having them.[42] For completeness, it should be noted that one form of marriage permitted in some other jurisdictions, the proxy marriage, is not permitted in Scotland. Here, both parties must be present at the ceremony, regardless of whether it is civil or religious in nature.[43]

10.16 Before we examine the detailed provisions governing marriage, it is worth noting the distinctions between prohibited, void and voidable marriages. Clive very usefully examines these concepts from both their prospective and retrospective perspectives; that is, he considers them both from the point of view of someone wishing to get married and from the point of view of someone who has gone through a ceremony of marriage despite an obstacle being present.[44] As he points out, certain impediments, for example, non-age or a prior subsisting marriage, are such that they have the effect of prohibiting marriage altogether and will prevent a marriage from going ahead if they are discovered prior to the ceremony taking place. Should the ceremony proceed in ignorance of the impediment the marriage will be void.[45] Other impediments, for example, such deficiency in a party's

38 A. E. Anton and P. Francescakis, 'Modern Scots "Runaway Marriages"' 1958 JR 253. The Marriage (Scotland) Act 1977 introduced certificates of no impediment in the attempt to reduce the number of runaway marriages – see para 10.54.
39 While not prohibiting bi-religious marriage, the provision of 19 Geo II c 13, s 1, which rendered any marriage between two Protestants or a Protestant and a Catholic null and void if performed by a Catholic priest, was restrictive of such marriages. Bi-religious couples could, of course, have sought the services of a member of the Protestant clergy for the ceremony, but that might not have accommodated the Catholic partner fully. The provision is discussed in *Yelverton* v *Longworth* (1864) 2 M (HL) 49 at p 54–55.
40 In the USA, in the celebrated and aptly-named case, *Loving* v *Virginia* 388 US 1 (1967), the Supreme Court struck down a Virginia statute prohibiting marriage between people of different racial groups and, thus, brought an end to the miscegenation laws there and in the other fifteen states which had them at the time.
41 The Uniform Marriage and Divorce Act 1970, which gives model legislation which individual states in the USA may adopt, in whole or in part, provides only an optional subsection dealing with pre-marital medical examination. In France, where pre-marital blood-testing is required, the results are made known only to the individual tested.
42 A considerably more intrusive possibility would be tests for particular conditions, for example, HIV, where the results were disclosed to a prospective spouse or marriage was prohibited. While disclosure might be justified on the basis of protecting another person, there seems no justification for a prohibition on marriage.
43 Marriage (Scotland) Act 1977, ss 13(1)(b) and 19(2)(b).
44 Clive, n 37 above, at paras 03.001–03.013 and 07.001–07.077.
45 Clive also highlights the distinction between a void marriage and a non-existent marriage, although he accepts that the distinction is not particularly useful in Scots law since it has

capacity to comprehend the nature of the ceremony that he or she does not understand what is going on, will again prevent the marriage from going ahead if identified in advance. This usually arises, however, in the context of a later challenge to the validity of the marriage. As Clive points out, prohibited marriage and void marriage 'are overlapping but not co-extensive'[46] concepts. Thus, while a celebrant is prohibited from performing a marriage ceremony where certain formalities have not been complied with, such marriages are rarely void. While a marriage may be void for a whole host of reasons, the sole ground on which a marriage is voidable in Scotland is the incurable impotency of one of the parties.[47] Void and voidable marriages are discussed later in this chapter along with the Scottish Law Commission's proposals for reform of the existing law.[48]

10.17 As we have seen, the various restrictions on marriage and requirements for the proper execution of a marriage ceremony can be analysed and rationalised in a variety of ways. Here they will be examined under the headings of capacity, consent and formal requirements. The main statute governing marriage is the Marriage (Scotland) Act 1977 ('the 1977 Act').

Capacity

Age

10.18 Scots common law recognised a minor as having the capacity to marry and, thus, girls could marry at 12 years old and boys at 14. By the beginning of this century, marriage at such an early age was rare and, in 1929, the minimum age for marriage was raised to 16 for both males and females.[49] The 1977 Act takes a two-pronged approach to the issue of age. First, it provides that no person domiciled in Scotland may marry before reaching the age of 16.[50] Essentially, domicile is the link between an individual and a legal system and what this provision means is that where a domiciled Scot goes through a ceremony of marriage abroad before his or her 16th birthday, the marriage will not be recognised here, regardless of what the law might permit in the other country. Second, the 1977 Act

---

no practical consequences – para 07.001. It is worth noting, however, that where a court grants a declarator of nullity of marriage, it may make the same orders for financial provision as it could have made in the context of divorce, see Family Law (Scotland) Act 1985, s 17(1). Where a person wishes to be freed from another's assertion that a marriage exists when it does not, the appropriate remedy is an action for declarator of freedom and putting to silence which does not empower the court to make any financial provision.

46 Clive at para 07.002.

47 In England and Wales, a marriage is voidable on the following grounds: inability to consummate, wilful refusal to consummate, lack of consent, mental disorder, venereal disease, pregnancy by a man other than the marriage partner, see Matrimonial Causes Act 1973, s 12. For a discussion of these grounds of nullity, see N. V. Lowe and G. Douglas, *Bromley's Family Law* (9th edn, Butterworths, 1998) at pp 87–101 and S. M. Cretney and J. M. Masson, *Principles of Family Law* (6th edn, Sweet and Maxwell, 1997) at pp 54–71.

48 See para 10.72–74.

49 Age of Marriage Act 1929. For a discussion of the background to the Act, see E. M. Clive, 'The Minimum Age for Marriage' 1968 SLT (News) 129.

50 Section 1(1).

provides that a marriage solemnised in Scotland, where either of the parties is under 16, shall be void.[51] Thus, no one can contract a valid marriage in Scotland if either of the parties is under 16, irrespective of what the law of the individuals' domiciles provides. As we saw earlier, parental consent has no place in Scots marriage law. Once a person reaches the age of 16, he or she has the capacity to marry and not only is parental consent not required, parental opposition is irrelevant. In reviewing the law on void marriages, the Scottish Law Commission recommended no change to the present law in respect of age.[52]

Male and female

10.19 Marriage is an option available only in the context of heterosexual relationships;[53] that is, the parties must be respectively male and female. There is a legal impediment to marriage where both parties are of the same sex.[54] As we have seen, the law does not recognise the possibility of a person changing sex, regardless of whether the change occurs naturally[55] or is brought about by surgical or other intervention.[56] While the Scottish Law Commission noted that there was some support for a change in the law to allow same-sex marriage and to accommodate recognition of transsexualism, it was unwilling to make any recommendation in its 1992 Report.[57]

10.20 Opposition to same-sex marriage comes from certain religious groups,[58] what might be described as traditionalists, proponents of the argument that it is legally impossible and homophobics. Traditionalists argue that our society has always viewed marriage as something between a man and a woman and sometimes find support in the notion that procreation is central to marriage. The fact that we have always done something in a particular way is not a reason to continue blindly on that path. As we have seen, procreation and child-rearing are only part of the modern functions of marriage, and recognition of the relationships adults have with each other is another, equally valid, function. In any event, lesbians and homosexuals can procreate[59] and raise children.[60] Same-sex marriage is only legally impossible because that is how marriage is defined at present. There is nothing to prevent us changing that definition. In short, if there is a will to permit same-sex marriage, it can be done.

---

51 Section 1(2).
52 Report on Family Law, n 21 above, para 8.4 and rec 44.
53 For a fascinating discussion of a number of pre-modern western cultures and non-western cultures which accepted same-sex unions as valid, see W. N. Eskridge, 'A History of Same-Sex Marriage' 79 Va L Rev 1419 (1993).
54 Marriage (Scotland) Act 1977, s 5(4)(e).
55 *X, Petitioner* 1957 SLT (Sh Ct) 61.
56 *Corbett* v *Corbett* [1971] P 83. See chapter 2, paras 70–73.
57 Report on Family Law, n 21 above para 8.5 and rec 45. The Commission's reluctance to make any firm recommendation on this point is unsurprising since it did not explore these issues in the earlier discussion papers.
58 For example, support for viewing marriage as confined to heterosexuals can be found in the bible: Leviticus 18.22, Romans 1:26–32.
59 Donor insemination and surrogacy provide obvious examples of how this can be achieved; see chapter 4, paras 44–46 and 53–58.
60 See for example, *T, Petitioner* 1997 SLT 724, discussed at chapter 8, para 17.

10.21 The issue of same-sex marriage has attracted considerable attention in other jurisdictions. In the USA, recent developments suggest an uncertain prognosis for such unions there. In *Baehr* v *Lewin*,[61] three same-sex couples applied for marriage licences in Hawaii. When the licences were refused, they filed complaints with the court alleging violation of their rights to privacy, due process and equal protection of the law, as protected by the Constitution of Hawaii. Ultimately, the ban was declared unconstitutional and the way appeared open for same-sex marriage at least in Hawaii.[62] Just as one door opened, another closed. Having gained substantial majorities in the House of Representatives and the Senate,[63] the Defense of Marriage Act[64] was signed by President Clinton on 21 September 1996.[65] Broadly, that Act provides that no state is obliged to recognise a same-sex marriage performed in another state and that the Federal government will not do so. Much of the literature surrounding the *Baehr* decisions and the Act concentrates on constitutional issues which need not detain us here. None the less, the debate has produced cogent arguments, largely supporting legal provision for same-sex marriage.[66] Legislation designed to achieve just that is currently being considered in the Netherlands. How long it will take Scots law to follow suit is a matter for speculation but, given the inertia which has surrounded the implementation of the Scottish Law Commission's modest proposals to extend the rights of heterosexual cohabitants, any rapid movement seems unlikely.

Prior subsisting marriage

10.22 As a general rule, only monogamous marriage is recognised in

61 852 P 2d 44 (Haw, 1993). See also, *Baehr* v *Miike* 910 P 2d 112 (Haw, 1996), where the Church of Jesus Christ of Latter-Day Saints made an unsuccessful attempt to intervene in the case. The defender's name changes in the course of the *Baehr* cases due to the appointment of a new State Director of Health in Hawaii in the course of the litigation.

62 *Baehr* v *Miike*, Haw Cir Ct, 3 December 1996.

63 The House passed the Bill by 342–67 on 12 July 1996 (142 Cong Rec H7485–86) and the Senate by 85–14 on 10 September 1996 (142 Cong Rec S10129).

64 Pub L No 104–199, SS2–3, 110 Stat 2419 (1996) (codified as 28 USC S 1738C and 1 USC S7).

65 Such was the controversy surrounding the legislation that the President is alleged to have signed it at midnight 'to minimise public attention and contain any political damage just forty-five days before the election'; P. Baker, 'President Quietly Signs Law Aimed At Gay Marriages' *The Washington Post*, 22 September 1996 at A21. Judging by press coverage and the academic literature generated in response to the Act, the attempt to minimise public attention failed. However, the President did win the election.

66 L. Kramer, 'Same-Sex Marriage, Conflict of Laws, and the Unconstitutional Public Policy Exemption' 106 Yale L J 1965 (1997); M. A. Provost, 'Disregarding the Constitution in the Name of defending Marriage: The Unconstitutionality of the Defense of Marriage Act' 8 Seton Hall Const L J 157 (1997); B. A. Robb, 'The Constitutionality of the Defense of Marriage Act in the Wake of Romer v Evans' 32 New Eng L Rev 263 (1997); and L. J. Silberman, 'Can the Island of Hawaii Bind the World? A Comment on Same-Sex Marriage and Federalism Values' 16 Quinnipiac L Rev 191 (1996). Not all of the literature supports legal provision for same-sex marriage; see L. D. Wardle, 'A Critical Analysis of Constitutional Claims for Same-Sex Marriage' 1996 BYU L Rev 1, which contains an appendix listing a number of articles in favour of, or opposed to, such provision.

Scotland. A person may only be married to one spouse at a time although, of course, an individual may marry any number of times in the course of a lifetime. While a marriage remains valid, there is a legal impediment which prevents either spouse from contracting another valid marriage.[67] This is true regardless of whether the first marriage was a regular or an irregular marriage. Not only will the prior subsisting marriage render a subsequent attempt at marriage void, but anyone who attempts to marry again, in the knowledge that a prior marriage remains valid, commits a criminal offence.[68] The Scottish Law Commission recommended that a prior subsisting marriage should continue to render a later marriage void.[69]

10.23 Where one of the parties to a bigamous marriage was unaware of his or her partner's prior subsisting marriage, the second ceremony creates what is known as a putative marriage.[70] This is not a marriage in any real sense, but a child born as a result of such a union is deemed in law to be legitimate. Effectively, the fact that one of the child's parents was innocent is regarded as sufficient to avoid the stigma of illegitimacy attaching to the child. Since the parents' marital status is now of much less importance than used to be the case, the effects of the doctrine of putative marriage are minimal. However, it does have one interesting result. Whereas an unmarried father normally has no automatic parental responsibilities or rights, the father in a putative marriage will gain the benefits of a married father and this is so even where he was the parent who was aware of the bigamous nature of the purported marriage; yet more evidence, if any were needed, of the absurdity inherent in the present law on the position of unmarried fathers.

10.24 Any discussion of the monogamous nature of marriage raises the question of polygamous[71] marriage, a practice widely accepted in other jurisdictions. While at one time it was thought that Scots law did not recognise polygamous marriages,[72] statute intervened long ago to provide

---

67 Marriage (Scotland) Act 1977, s 5(4)(b). See for example, *Burke* v *Burke* 1983 SLT 331.
68 Clive takes the view that '[a]n erroneous but bona fide belief on reasonable grounds that a first marriage had been dissolved by divorce would probably be a good defence to a charge of bigamy' (at para 18.024). See the discussion of the *McMahon* case, unreported, *The Scotsman* 15 November 1997, p 8 discussed at chapter 11, para 76. Even where sexual intercourse is procured by bigamy, the victim will not be entitled to compensation under the Criminal Injuries Compensation Scheme in respect of 'a crime of violence' – *Gray* v *Criminal Injuries Compensation Board* 1993 SLT 28 (OH). *The Scotsman*, 31 October 1998, p 3, reported that Ms. Gray's appeal to the Inner House was unsuccessful.
69 Report on Family Law, n 21 above, para 8.3 and rec 43.
70 A putative marriage requires that one of the parties entered it under an error of fact and in the belief that the marriage was valid. The error must be one of fact and not of law – *Purves' Trustees* v *Purves* (1895) 22 R 513.
71 Polygamy means having more than one spouse at the same time although, strictly speaking, polygyny is the correct term for a man having more than one wife, while polyandry covers the situation where one woman has more than one husband. The term polygamy is widely used to refer to men with multiple wives, probably because polyandry is virtually unknown. Why polyandry is so rare has fascinated feminist anthropologists but one obvious explanation would seem to be that while polygyny is likely to increase the number of children born within marriage, polyandry will not have this effect.
72 *Muhammad* v *Suna* 1956 SC 366.

recognition of such marriages in certain circumstances.[73] The precise circumstances for recognition and the effects of a polygamous marriage will be discussed in chapter 11 when we examine the effects of marriage. For the present purpose, it should be noted that a subsisting polygamous marriage, whether actually or potentially so, will be sufficient to prevent a subsequent valid marriage in Scotland.[74]

Prohibited degrees of relationship

10.25 Scots law has always prohibited marriage between persons who are closely related to each other and, originally, the prohibitions were derived from the Old Testament[75] and passed on through the canon law. Quite apart from the simple religious imperative being regarded as enough, in itself, to justify such restrictions, they have found support in what might be described as a 'biological rationale'. Essentially, this is founded in a fear that procreation by close relatives increases the likelihood of genetic defects being passed on to future generations.[76] In addition, there was, and still is, considerable support for the idea that individuals have clearly defined positions within the family structure and that family harmony is best maintained by supporting and reinforcing these individual roles. The 'family integrity rationale' for the prohibited degrees emphasises that sexual relations between certain family members is not acceptable. Thus, siblings should see each other as companions but not as potential sexual partners. A father-in-law should see his daughter-in-law as an ally and quasi-child but, again, not as a potential lover. With the advent of adoption, adoptive relationships were, to some extent simply slotted in to this general image of family relationships. Over time, legislation removed a variety of the prohibitions in a piecemeal fashion[77] and the current prohibitions are now contained exclusively in the 1977 Act.[78] Thus, if marriage is not

73 The Matrimonial Proceedings (Polygamous Marriages) Act 1972 allowed the Scottish courts to grant a variety of decrees in respect of polygamous marriages and the Private International Law (Miscellaneous Provisions) Act 1995, s 7(2) accords the same status to a marriage which is in fact monogamous, although it was entered into under a system which permits polygamy, as any other monogamous marriage.

74 Clive (at para 09.010, n 28) cites the case of *Mohammed Shafi*, reported in *The Scotsman*, 18 August 1977, who had a wife and five children in Pakistan and was convicted of bigamy in Glasgow Sheriff Court having gone through a ceremony of marriage with a woman in Scotland.

75 Leviticus, 18:6–24.

76 As Glendon points out in *The Transformation of Family Law* (at p 57), 'A genetic explanation is popular but too facile. Many of the prohibitions involve people who are not blood relatives. Furthermore, no country forbids marriage between unrelated persons (such as haemophiliacs) whose mating is also problematic from a genetic point of view.'

77 See for example, the Deceased Wife's Sister's Marriage Act 1907, the Deceased Brother's Widow's Marriage Act 1921, the Marriage (Prohibited Degrees of Relationship) Act 1931 (which removed the prohibition on marriage to a deceased spouse's nephew, niece, uncle or aunt) and the Marriage (Enabling) Act 1960 (which substituted the word 'former' for 'deceased' in the earlier legislation, opening the way to marriage where the previous union had been terminated by divorce rather than death).

78 The 1977 Act has, itself, been amended, most notably for the purpose of the prohibited degrees, by the Marriage (Prohibited Degrees of Relationship) Act 1986.

prohibited by the Act, it is permitted,[79] provided, of course, that there is no other bar to it. As was the case with non-age, prohibited marriages are void, not only if solemnised in Scotland, but also in respect of a domiciled Scot anywhere in the world.[80] Despite the fact that the prohibited degrees of relationship were modified as recently as 1986, anomalies persist.[81] The Scottish Law Commission has recommended only a minor change to the existing law.[82]

10.26 Broadly, marriage is not allowed between persons who are regarded as being too closely related to each other by reason of a blood relationship (consanguinity), a family relationship through marriage (affinity), or a relationship created by adoption.[83] Some of the prohibited degrees are mirrored in the law of incest, while others are not.[84] Thus, for example, not only is marriage between a parent and his or her child prohibited, any sexual relationship between the parties would amount to incest. On the other hand, while marriage between a man and his former mother-in-law is prohibited in certain circumstances, sexual relations between them does not amount to incest. While prohibitions on marriage for reasons of consanguinity are absolute, prohibitions founded on affinity are not. The prohibited degrees of relationship are set out in Schedule 1 of the 1977 Act, which is reproduced opposite, and the various prohibitions are discussed below.

10.27 First, Table 1, part 1 sets out the prohibited degrees of relationships by reason of consanguinity. A man may not marry any of the persons mentioned in part 1, column 1, and a woman may not marry the persons mentioned in part 1, column 2. What this means is that you cannot marry your parent, grandparent, great grandparent, child, grandchild, great grandchild, brother or sister, nephew or niece, or aunt or uncle. Relations of the half blood are treated in the same way as relations of the full blood[85] and whether individuals were born to married or unmarried parents is irrelevant. Thus, where a man and woman have the same father but different mothers, the prohibition on marriage applies to them in exactly the same way as a couple who have both parents in common. These are the only blood relatives to whom marriage is prohibited and so, for example, marriage between first cousins is permitted.[86]

---

79 Irregular marriages are not governed by the prohibited degrees contained in the 1977 Act since it refers to marriages being 'solemnised.' However, Clive (at para 03.006, n 26) takes the view that irregular marriages are subject to the same prohibitions by virtue of the common law.
80 Marriage (Scotland) Act 1977, s 2(1).
81 Such anomalies are not unique to Scotland. See Glendon, n 76 above pp 55–58, where the distinction between the incest taboo and prohibitions on marriage are discussed along with the rational and irrational bases for them.
82 Report on Family Law, paras 8.6–8.13 and rec 46.
83 Marriage (Scotland) Act 1977, s 2 and Sched 1.
84 See paras chapter 11, paras 77–80.
85 Marriage (Scotland) Act 1977, s 2(2).
86 The Scottish approach is not one which finds favour throughout the world. In the USA, for example, about half of the states permit first cousin marriage, while the other half prohibit such unions and the issue is one which attracts considerable debate. See Moore, 'A Defense of First Cousin Marriage' 10 Clev Mar L Rev 139 (1961).

Table 1: Prohibited degrees of relationship

Column 1   Column 2

1: Relationships by consanguinity

Column 1	Column 2
Mother	Father
Daughter	Son
Father's mother	Father's father
Mother's mother	Mother's father
Son's daughter	Son's son
Daughter's daughter	Daughter's son
Sister	Brother
Father's sister	Father's brother
Mother's sister	Mother's brother
Brother's daughter	Brother's son
Sister's daughter	Sister's son
Father's father's mother	Father's father's father
Father's mother's mother	Father's mother's father
Mother's father's mother	Mother's mother's father
Mother's mother's mother	Mother's father's father
Son's son's daughter	Son's son's son
Son's daughter's daughter	Son's daughter's son
Daughter's son's daughter	Daughter's son's son
Daughter's daughter's daughter	Daughter's daughter's son

2: Relationships by affinity referred to in section 2(1A)

Column 1	Column 2
Daughter of former wife	Son of former husband
Former wife of father	Former husband of mother
Former wife of father's father	Former husband of father's mother
Former wife of mother's father	Former husband of mother's mother
Daughter of son of former wife	Son of son of former husband
Daughter of daughter of former wife	Son of daughter of former husband

2A: Relationships by affinity referred to in section 2(1B)

Column 1	Column 2
Mother of former wife	Father of former husband
Former wife of son	Former husband of daughter

3: Relationships by adoption

Column 1	Column 2
Adoptive mother or former adoptive mother	Adoptive father or former adoptive father
Adopted daughter or former adopted daughter	Adopted son or former adopted son

10.28 The implications of assisted reproduction for the prohibited degrees of relationship have not been properly explored and the result is that the law, as it stands at present, produces some anomalous results. The woman who gives birth to a child, and no other woman, is regarded as the child's mother.[87] Thus, where ova are donated by A and used to enable B to bear a male child, C, marriage between B and C is prohibited but marriage between A and C is permitted, despite the fact that A is C's genetic mother. Where a woman has a child by donor insemination, her husband is treated in law as the child's father and no other man is so treated.[88] Thus, assuming the child to be a girl, she cannot marry her mother's husband, with whom she has no genetic relationship, but she can marry the donor, her genetic father. Furthermore, the artificially created child-parent relationships are stated to apply 'for all purposes'[89] and the result is that the child forms relationships within the prohibited degrees with other family members in the birth family but not in the genetic, non-birth, family.

10.29 Second, Table 1, parts 2 and 2A sets out prohibited degrees of relationship by reason of affinity. Relationships through affinity do not necessarily bar a marriage and the circumstances which serve to lift the prohibition differ depending on the precise relationship involved.[90] A man may not marry the persons listed in column 1 of part 2 and a woman may not marry persons listed in column 2 of part 2 unless

> (a) both parties have attained the age of 21 at the time of marriage; and
> (b) the younger party has not at any time before attaining the age of 18 lived in the same household as the other party and been treated by the other party as a child of the family.[91]

Thus, you cannot marry the son or daughter of a former spouse, the former spouse of a parent, the former spouse of a grandparent or the grandchild of a former spouse, unless these two conditions are satisfied. The reason for the general prohibition on such marriages is the desire to avoid relationships between people who may have been in a quasi child-parent relationship. However, where the parties have never actually had that kind of relationship, there is no rational basis to prevent them from marrying. In addition, by requiring that each of the parties should be at least 21 years old, the law attempts to ensure an increased opportunity for mature reflection.[92]

10.30 Similarly, a man may not marry the persons listed in column 1 of part 2A and a woman may not marry persons listed in column 2 of part 2A unless

> (a) both parties have attained the age of 21, and
> (b) each party's former spouse is dead.[93]

---

87 Human Fertilisation and Embryology Act 1990, s 27(1). For further discussion, see chapter 4, para 35.
88 1990 Act, s 28(2). For further discussion, see chapter 4, para 36.
89 1990 Act, s 29(1). For further discussion, see chapter 4, para 34.
90 See D. Nichols, 'Step-daughters and Mothers-in-law' 1986 SLT (News) 229.
91 Marriage (Scotland) Act 1977, s 2(1A).
92 When it considered this prohibition and the exception to it, the Scottish Law Commission concluded that, while different views might be held, the law as it stands is not 'manifestly unreasonable' and, thus, that there was no reason to reopen the debate – *Report on Family Law*, n 21 above, para 8.7.
93 Marriage (Scotland) Act 1977, s 2(1B).

Thus, you cannot marry the parent of a former spouse or the former spouse of a child unless these conditions are satisfied. The only circumstances in which a man may marry his former mother-in-law is where both his former wife and his former father-in-law are dead. The rationale behind this prohibition is what was described earlier as 'family integrity' and it is aimed at ensuring that family members do not regard each other's spouses in an inappropriate way. The exception provides for marriage where each party's former spouse is dead and there are no longer other relationships to be protected and, again, the higher age limit is intended to ensure that the parties involved have gained a greater degree of maturity. Examining this prohibition and the exception to it, the Scottish Law Commission found the law to be 'odd and unreasonable' and explored a number of hypothetical examples of how it might apply in order to demonstrate this conclusion. Essentially, the Commission's objection was to the fact that the former spouses of each party wishing to marry must be dead and that marriage is not permitted where the parties are simply divorced from their former spouses. As it pointed out, a relationship between such divorced former in-laws would not amount to incest and all that the law does is to prevent them from getting married. It concluded that the remaining restriction on marriage between divorced, as opposed to widowed, former in-laws should be abolished.[94]

10.31 The prohibited degrees of relationship in respect of adoption are set out in part 3 of Table 1. These provide that a person may not marry an adoptive parent or former adoptive parent, nor an adopted child or former adopted child. Two children adopted into the same family may marry each other provided that no other prohibition applies. While there is no genetic link between such children, it seems very odd indeed that two children who may have been raised as brother and sister can marry. While adoption has the general effect of severing the legal relationship between the adopted child and his or her birth relatives, the prohibition on marrying birth relatives remains even after adoption.[95] Thus, where a boy and girl were born to the same mother and each of them was adopted into separate families, they cannot marry later.

Consent

10.32 That each party should consent freely and with full understanding of what he or she is embarking upon is essential to the whole notion of marriage as a consensual relationship. Anything, whether it be a natural condition or the effects of alcohol or drugs, that diminishes a party's capacity to understand the nature of the ceremony or, indeed, marriage itself, has an impact on that individual's apparent consent. Similarly, such factors as error or duress impact upon the true and free nature of any apparent consent. In addition, a person's motive for entering a marriage,

---

94 Report on Family Law, n 21 above, paras 8.7–8.13 and rec 46.
95 Adoption (Scotland) Act 1978, s 41(1).

for example, the desire to subvert immigration rules, may be such that it effectively vitiates consent. Going through a ceremony of marriage with a mental reservation as to its effect or validity might also be viewed as negating any true consent. While complete incapacity can be distinguished from defective consent, there are subtle gradations within the whole notion of impaired capacity and this, in turn, raises the question of what ought to be its effect on the validity of the marriage. Clive discusses the respective benefits of viewing such marriages as void, that is, simply invalid, or voidable, that is, capable of being reduced on application to the court,[96] and concludes that the existing rule of Scots law whereby the absence of true consent renders a marriage void 'is probably as good as any, provided the nullifying defects of consent are kept within properly narrow bounds'.[97] A further issue to consider is personal bar. Where a person's consent has been diminished at the time of the ceremony, but the person recovers and continues life as if the marriage was valid in the full knowledge of what happened, should he or she be barred from challenging the marriage at a later date?[98] The Scottish Law Commission reviewed defects in consent and their effect on the validity of marriage and recommended a number of clarifications and amendments to the existing law.[99] These are discussed below in the context of the various forms of defective consent.

Mental illness or defect

10.33 Where one of the parties is incapable, by reason of mental illness or defect, of understanding the nature of the marriage ceremony or of giving consent to marriage, the marriage is void.[100] However, a person may be of limited intelligence and still be quite capable of understanding the nature of marriage and of consenting to it and a heavy burden of proof lies on the person seeking to challenge the validity of such a marriage.[101] Where insufficient capacity can be demonstrated prior to the ceremony, an objection can be lodged and such an impediment will prevent it from going ahead.[102] The Scottish Law Commission has recommended that mental incapacity should continue to render a marriage void, subject to the caveat that, where the incapacity is temporary and the incapax has not sought to

---

96 The distinction between void and voidable marriages is discussed below at paras 10.72–10.74.
97 At para 07.030.
98 For an excellent discussion of this point, see Clive, para 07.062.
99 Report on Family Law, n 21 above, paras 8.16–8.20 and rec 48.
100 *Long* v *Long* 1950 SLT (Notes) 32.
101 In *Long* v *Long*, above, Lord Strachan put the position thus: 'It does not follow from the fact that the defender is a mental defective that she was incapable of understanding the nature of marriage or of giving consent thereto.' The language used may be brutal and unacceptable today, but the point is clear. See also, *Scott* v *Kelly* 1992 SLT 915, where a woman sought to challenge the validity of her deceased sister's marriage on the basis of her late sister's incapacity to consent, facility and circumvention and alleged undue influence. The last two of these grounds were struck out at the procedure roll stage as not being grounds on which a marriage could be declared void.
102 Marriage (Scotland) Act 1977, s 5(4)(d).

challenge it within a reasonable time of regaining capacity, the marriage should be treated as valid from the time it took place.[103]

Intoxication

10.34 If taken in sufficient quantities, the effects of alcohol or drugs may be such as to render a person incapable of understanding the nature of the marriage ceremony and, where an individual's capacity to consent is affected in this way, the marriage will be void.[104] The degree of intoxication would have to be fairly extreme for this to be the case and it is hard to imagine any celebrant going ahead with a marriage in such circumstances. The accepted view[105] is that the intoxicated person is required to challenge the validity of the marriage on regaining his or her senses[106] and this view would be reinforced if the reform recommended by the Commission were enacted into legislation.

Error and fraud

10.35 Only a very limited range of serious errors surrounding marriage will render the marriage void. Error as to the nature of the ceremony or the identity of the other party will have this effect.[107] In a modern context, it is unlikely that such errors would occur but it is conceivable, where one party had only limited English, that he or she might mistake the ceremony itself for one of engagement. Error as to identity might arise in the case of identical twins where, for example, a woman thought she was marrying one twin and, in fact, went through the ceremony with the other.[108] Error as to other factors, such as the qualities of the spouse or what life after the marriage will be like, do not vitiate a marriage.[109] Thus, assuming that the events took place in Scotland, if Cinderella had discovered after the marriage that, far from being charming and wealthy, her prince was an impoverished boor, she could not have challenged the validity of the marriage.[110] The fact that the other party fraudulently induced the error is

---

103 Report on Family Law, n 21 above, rec 48(b).

104 A clear example of such intoxication can be found in *Johnston* v *Brown* (1823) 2 S 495, a case involving an irregular marriage, where the woman was so drunk as to be incapable of giving consent, not only at the time of the marriage, but for three days thereafter.

105 See Clive, para 07.032.

106 Clive, paras 07.032 and 07.062.

107 Stair, I, 9, 9; *Lang* v *Lang* 1921 SC 44.

108 In the past, when women were heavily veiled during the ceremony, there may have been greater potential for error as to identity. The bible gives an early example of such an error in the story of Jacob who worked for seven years in order to marry Rachel. He was duped into going through a ceremony with her sister Leah and had to toil for a further seven years before he was allowed to marry his true love; Genesis, 29: 5–28.

109 Stair, above; *Lang* v *Lang*, above; *MacDougall* v *Chitnavis* 1937 SC 390.

110 It is worth remembering that the parties are not necessarily stuck with a disastrous marriage indefinitely. If the prince was sufficiently boorish as to make it intolerable for Cinderella to continue to live with him, she might have grounds for divorce on the basis of his behaviour and, failing that, she might seek a divorce based on separation after two or five years. For the grounds for divorce see chapter 13.

also irrelevant.[111] In *Lang* v *Lang*,[112] a woman induced a man to marry her by telling him that he was the father of the child she was expecting. When he discovered that another man was the child's father, he sought to have the marriage reduced on the basis of both error and fraudulent misrepresentation. The court rejected his action on both grounds.

10.36 As Clive points out, '[t]he distinction between error as to identity and error as to attributes is not always easy to draw'[113] and the point is illustrated well by the case of *McLeod* v *Adams*.[114] There, an army deserter used a false name and pretended to a woman that he was a sergeant in the Black Watch. After the marriage ceremony he deserted the woman and she sought to have the marriage declared void. Her action founded on error failed because she had intended to marry the person standing next to her, regardless of the fact that she was mistaken as to a number of attributes or qualities that he was supposed to have.[115] There is a clear parallel here with error in other contractual settings[116] and it might be said that the analysis and solution is no more satisfactory. Indeed, many other legal systems allow for nullity of marriage over a considerably broader range of circumstances than is permitted in Scotland.[117] The Scottish Law Commission did not recommend any extension of the circumstances in which

---

111 In his article, 'The Stolen Heiress: or The Biter Bit' (1927) 39 JR 233, William Roughead recounts the remarkable tale of a 15-year-old English heiress, Ellen Turner, lured from boarding school in 1826 by one Edward Gibbon Wakefield and induced to go through an irregular marriage in Scotland with him in the mistaken belief that this would save her father from financial ruin, an eventuality which was not in prospect at all. Wakefield was later convicted of abducting the young woman and sentenced to three years imprisonment, after which he went on to become a colonial statesman and the founder of New Zealand. At the trial, an advocate, Duncan (later Lord President) McNeill gave evidence that neither Ms Turner's error nor Mr Wakefield's fraud would render the marriage void under Scots law. It does not appear that he was asked about the possible effects of duress. His opinion was greeted with both incredulity and horror in the court and the English media. In the event, the marriage was subsequently declared void by an Act of Parliament and Ms Turner went on to marry a prominent local man, only to die in childbirth two years later.

112 Note 107 above. The issue was thought to be of sufficient importance that a court of seven judges sat and the decision in *Lang* overruled *Stein* v *Stein* 1914 SC 903, where a marriage was held to be void in similar circumstances.

113 At para 07.034.

114 1920 1 SLT 229.

115 Declarator of nullity was granted, however, due to the fact that the groom never intended marriage at all and, thus, only pretended to consent. It should be noted that personal bar would prevent the guilty party from founding on his or her own unilateral mental reservation, see paras 10.47–48, below.

116 Contrast, for example, the cases of *Morrisson* v *Robertson* 1908 SC 332 and *Mcleod* v *Kerr* 1965 SC 253. For a discussion of error in contract, see W. W. McBryde, *The Law of Contract in Scotland* (W. Green, 1987), chapter 9 and D. M. Walker, *The Law of Contract and Related Obligations in Scotland* (3rd edn, T & T Clark, 1995), chapter 14.

117 This is the case, for example, in England and Wales, where nullity may be granted on a whole range of grounds including the fact that the woman was pregnant by another man at the time of the marriage or that one of the parties was suffering from a communicable venereal disease – Matrimonial Causes Act 1973, s 12. See para 10.72.

nullity of marriage should be allowed,[118] largely because it felt that the possibility of divorce was sufficient to resolve any problems.

Duress and force and fear

10.37 As a matter of practice, it may be a great deal more common for relatives and friends to try to dissuade a person from going through with a marriage than it is for anyone to exert pressure in order to bring about a marriage. Given the formalities required for marriage, the opportunities for a 'shotgun wedding'[119] are greatly diminished. None the less, the fact that the Scottish courts have had recent opportunity to consider cases involving allegations of duress, suggests that the problem is not as much of a dead letter as one might think. In addition, these cases have allowed the courts to give a statement, in a modern context, of what is required, in terms of pressure or duress, in order for a marriage to be rendered void.

10.38 Essentially, what is required is that such duress or other pressure, for example, moral blackmail, was exerted on one of the parties that his or her will was overcome and he or she gave the appearance of consenting to the marriage when that would not have happened had the pressure not been exerted. In short, what appears to be consent cannot be regarded as such because it was not given freely. The kind of threat is not confined to physical harm to the individual consenting and can include the threat of imprisonment,[120] social ostracism or harm to another person. Whether a potential spouse's threat to commit suicide if the marriage does not go ahead can create sufficient duress appears to be untested but, given the other forms of pressure regarded by the courts as sufficient in the cases discussed below, it seems that it probably would be. The test is a subjective one and depends on the individual concerned. What would be enough to overcome the will of one person may be insufficient to overcome the will of another, more resilient and determined, individual.

10.39 Whether a distinction should be drawn between a justified and legal threat and one which is unjustified or illegal is open to question. In *Buckland* v *Buckland*,[121] an Englishman was accused of sexual corruption of a minor in Malta. While he protested his innocence, he was persuaded that his chances of a fair trial were minimal and that, in all likelihood, he would be convicted and imprisoned. By marrying the young woman, he was

---

118 Report on Family Law, n 21 above, rec 48(c). The Commission recommended that only errors as to the identity of the other party or the nature of the ceremony should render a marriage void and explicitly excludes errors as to the name or qualities of the other party from having this effect. Again, the Commission recommended that the person in error should raise the action for nullity as soon as is reasonably practicable after the error is discovered and that failure to do so should render the marriage valid from the time of the ceremony.

119 Clive (para 07.038, n 1) cites a fascinating example of this sort of marriage in Arkansas in 1928, where the groom was accompanied to the ceremony by the bride's father who was literally carrying a shotgun. In *Lee* v *Lee* 3 SW 2d 672 (1928) the bride had given birth to a child and had named the groom as the child's father, something he did not deny when questioned by her father before the ceremony.

120 *Buckland* v *Buckland* [1968] P 296; *Szechter* v *Szechter* [1971] P 286.

121 Ibid.

able to avoid this outcome and, on his return to England, he successfully petitioned to have the marriage declared null. However, the court attached an important qualification to granting the declaration of nullity. It noted that his reasonably apprehended fear had arisen from no fault on his part and made clear that he would not have succeeded if he had been guilty of corrupting the young woman. As Clive rightly points out, the distinction the court drew is hard to justify since 'consent is no more free, and a forced marriage no more desirable, if the fear is justly imposed'.[122] It might be that the court was importing some notion of personal bar or, more correctly since the case was English, estoppel, which would deny the remedy of a declaration of nullity to a person who had brought the problem on himself or herself.

10.40 Two recent cases have involved parties claiming that they were coerced into going through with arranged marriages and it is important to note at the outset that the fact that a marriage has been arranged by family members is not, of itself, any reason to conclude that either party has been subject to duress. Family involvement in finding suitable marriage partners, while not commonplace for the majority of Scots, is an accepted part of parental responsibility for some members of particular religious or ethnic groups. In general, the role of the family members is simply to suggest suitable partners and effect introductions and does not involve subjecting the parties to any pressure at all. However, as these recent cases demonstrate, parental enthusiasm for a particular marriage can result in one or both of the parties being subjected to such pressure that his or her apparent consent is vitiated.

10.41 In *Mahmood* v *Mahmood*,[123] a 21 year-old woman was successful in seeking a declarator of nullity due to the duress placed on her to get her to go through with the marriage ceremony. The marriage had been arranged by her parents some five years earlier, but she had not been told of the plans at the time. When she indicated that she would not comply with their wishes, her parents threatened to disown her, a threat that had some credibility since they had already disowned two of her siblings who had refused to go through with arranged marriages, and to cut her off financially, a particular hardship since she worked in their shop and was completely financially dependent on them. They also threatened to send her to live in Pakistan and impressed on her that she would bring shame on her family and community if she persisted in refusing to marry the man of their choice. Despite informing her prospective husband that she did not want to marry him, she went through with the ceremony and the couple lived together for a few months and had fairly minimal sexual relations. While the court was at pains to point out that parental pressure and the threat of disapproval would alone be insufficient,[124] it took the view that all the circumstances of this case indicated consent resulting from duress. A

---

122 At para 07.039.
123 1993 SLT 589.
124 Thus, in the absence of other factors, where a man marries his pregnant partner simply, '[t]o do the decent thing', it is unlikely that the general (and, arguably, misguided) social pressure which may have prompted him to act in this way will constitute duress.

similar approach was taken a year later in *Mahmud* v *Mahmud*,[125] where a 31-year-old man experienced similar family pressure and went through a marriage ceremony with a woman from Pakistan, despite the fact that he was already living with a woman in Scotland and they were expecting a child. Again, in the circumstances, the court concluded that the apparent consent was vitiated by the relentless family pressure.

Sham marriages

10.42 Another situation where apparent consent may be so tainted as to be invalid arises where the parties go through what seems to be a valid ceremony of marriage, but for some purpose other than getting married. The most frequent ulterior motive for such marriages is to subvert immigration laws and, while it is understandable that courts are unhappy about letting people benefit by their attempts to 'circumvent the law of the land',[126] one should remember, perhaps, that the reason why people try to avoid the rigours of UK immigration law is sometimes to escape fairly intolerable economic conditions elsewhere.[127] In addition, there are instances of sham marriages where the parties went through the ceremony for what the courts might regard as more noble and pressing reasons.[128]

10.43 The modern Scottish cases on sham marriages all contain common elements. In each case, there was a civil ceremony despite the fact that the parties had strong religious convictions, the marriage was not consummated and, in most of the cases, the intention was to enable one of the parties to stay in the UK. In *Orlandi* v *Castelli*[129] both parties were Roman Catholics who regarded a religious ceremony as essential to a valid marriage. None the less, they went through the civil ceremony in order to enable the man, an Italian national, to remain and work in Scotland.[130] By the time the woman raised an action for declarator of nullity three years later, the man had returned to Italy and did not lodge defences. Defences were lodged, however, by the Lord Advocate. Allowing a proof before answer, Lord Cameron took the view that, if it could be established that there was 'no true matrimonial consent and that the ceremony was only

---

125 1994 SLT 599.
126 *Akram* v *Akram* 1979 SLT (Notes) 87, per Lord Dunpark, at p 89, where he expressed the view that personal bar might be invoked to prevent the nullifying effects of a lack of consent where this was the only motive for the parties going through the marriage ceremony.
127 Economic migrants are often distinguished from, and treated much less favourably than, refugees, who are fleeing persecution. While the plight of the latter merits maximum accommodation, the plight of the former is frequently dismissed as nothing other than pursuit of the 'main chance.' Arguably, seeking a home where one will avoid abject poverty and all that goes with it, is a legitimate and entirely understandable goal.
128 See, for example, *Szechter* v *Szechter* [1971] P 286, where a man divorced his wife and went through a ceremony of marriage with his secretary. The marriage was part of an elaborate ruse to enable the secretary to escape intolerable conditions as a political prisoner in Poland. Once the couple reached England, the man applied to have the marriage declared null so that he could remarry his first wife. The court granted the nullity, analysing the case in terms of defective consent resulting from externally caused duress and was thus able to avoid any need to condone the misuse of the legal process.
129 1961 SC 113.
130 This case predates the European Union provisions on free movement of labour.

designed as a sham or as an antecedent to true marriage'[131] it could be set aside.

10.44 In *Mahmud* v *Mahmud*,[132] a Moslem couple went through a civil ceremony, in the belief that they would not be truly married until a religious ceremony had been performed and, again, the court took the view that this was sufficient to vitiate any consent to marriage. Much the same view was taken in *Akram* v *Akram*,[133] where Lord Dunpark was at pains to point out that it was the lack of consent to marriage that justified him in granting the decree and not what he saw as the pursuer's second motive, that of enabling the defender to apply for an extension of his residential permit. Had the latter point been the only consideration, he indicated that he would have refused the decree on public policy grounds and that the pursuer might have been personally barred from founding on her own misuse of the system. The fact that the 'marriages' in these cases were not consummated is not crucial, in so far as consummation is not a prerequisite of a valid marriage, nor is non-consummation necessarily a ground for nullity[134] or divorce.[135] None the less, it does provide an indication that these religious people did not regard themselves as married.

10.45 The whole area of sham marriages is fraught with problems. For example, Clive draws a distinction between parties who go through an empty ceremony and couples who have an ulterior motive but, none the less, intend to get married for a particular limited purpose.[136] In the first case he would not regard them as married, whereas in the second case he would. Conceptually, this distinction is quite valid and, as an intellectual exercise, it is stimulating. However, as he admits, '[w]hether parties to a sham marriage will draw this distinction clearly in their minds may be doubted'. Nor does the notion of personal bar provide a satisfactory solution to the problem of sham marriages. Permitting declarator of nullity where the parties' religious beliefs are such that they went through a ceremony that they did not regard as valid for the purpose of marriage and, thereby, achieving some other purpose, while barring couples who cynically use the trappings of the legal system to achieve an ulterior motive, suggests that one form of misuse of the system is acceptable while the other is not. Respect for religion is one thing, using it as some kind of all-encompassing excuse is quite another.

10.46 In England and Wales,[137] the courts take a very different view of sham marriages, simply regarding them as valid and leaving it to the parties

---

131 At p 120.
132 1977 SLT (Notes) 17.
133 Note 126 above.
134 Permanent incurable impotency at the time of the marriage renders a marriage voidable, rather than void, and one of the spouses would have to raise an action for declarator – see para 10–73.
135 Wilful refusal to consummate a marriage may constitute a ground for divorce, but only if the parties choose to make an issue of the matter – see chapter 11, para 14.
136 At para 07.047.
137 *H* v *H* [1954] P 258; *Silver* v *Silver* [1955] 2 All ER 614.

to seek a divorce if they do not wish to be married.[138] Such a solution has much to commend it in terms of simplicity and the Scottish Law Commission has recommended that a marriage should no longer be rendered void simply because one or both parties goes through a ceremony with a tacit mental reservation as to its effect.[139]

Unilateral mental reservation

10.47 Sham marriages might be described as ceremonies where there are bilateral mental reservations. Here we turn to the situation where one party believes that he or she is getting married but the other party is acting subject to a unilateral mental reservation and does not believe that a valid marriage will result from the ceremony. Such a situation could arise where one of the parties simply does not accept that a valid marriage can result from a civil ceremony or where one of the parties has no intention of getting married and is simply using the ceremony to achieve some ulterior purpose.[140] For an example of unilateral mental reservations, nothing can compare with the activities of one Mr Risi, whose enthusiasm for marriage ceremonies appears to have been equalled only by his lack of concern for the niceties of the law.[141]

10.48 Where one party has a unilateral mental reservation to marriage, there is no effective consent to the marriage and, certainly, the innocent party can seek a declarator of nullity. Personal bar would seem to preclude the guilty party from founding on his or her own mental reservation in order to avoid the marriage. Again, the whole situation is somewhat unsatisfactory and the Commission's recommendations for reform, if enacted, would mean that unilateral mental reservations had no effect on the validity of a marriage.[142]

Joke marriages

10.49 Where apparent consent to marriage is given in the context of a

---

138 A similar approach has been taken by the Canadian courts; P. M. Bromley, 'The Validity of 'Sham Marriages' and Marriages Procured by Fraud' 15 McGill LJ 319 (1969), F. Bates, 'Limited and Extraneous Purpose Marriages' 4 Anglo-American LR 69 (1975).

139 Report on Family Law, rec 48(e).

140 See, for example, *McLeod* v *Adams*, discussed at para 10.36 above, where the marriage ceremony was simply a part of the man's overall scheme to get access to the widow's money and abscond with it.

141 *McEwan* v *Risi*, 25 March 1964, unreported, and *Scott* v *Risi*, 26 March 1965, unreported. These cases and the implications of the facts disclosed therein are discussed extensively by Clive at para. 07.053. Between September 1958 and June 1963 Mr Risi married four women in succession without bothering to secure divorces. His first wife divorced him in 1962, but he did not become aware of the divorce until after he had gone through two further marriage ceremonies. Undaunted by a conviction for bigamy, he went through a fourth marriage ceremony. The trail seems to go cold at that point, although this is certainly one of those cases where one is curious about what happened to him (and the unfortunate women he met) thereafter.

142 Report on Family Law, n 21 above, rec 48(e).

joke, there is no true consent to marriage and thus no marriage.[143] Given the formalities surrounding regular marriage, it is difficult to imagine that the preliminaries and ceremony would be completed in such a context and the issue is probably something of a dead letter.

FORMALITIES OF MARRIAGE

10.50 As we saw, public control of marriage requires not only that capacity and consent should be regulated, but that certain procedure for marriage should be laid down. In the past, regulating the formalities of marriage was a matter for the Roman Catholic church and, after the Reformation, for the Reformed church and the Commissary Court.[144] During the period of the Commissaries, it appears that such regulation of marriage as existed, in theory, was applied somewhat unevenly, in practice.[145] Apparently, it was not unusual for session clerks to issue certificates of proclamation of banns when no banns had been proclaimed.[146] In addition, there was no national system of registration of births, marriages and deaths and the local parish registers were somewhat unreliable.[147] In post-Reformation Scotland only ministers of the Church of Scotland could perform marriages, with the privilege being extended to certain Episcopalian ministers in 1711.[148] Of course, the possibility of irregular marriage meant that Scots law always recognised civil marriage, although irregular marriages were themselves a source of some disquiet.[149] The 19th and early 20th centuries saw gradual reform of the law on marriage, often as a result of considered reflection by specially appointed committees.[150] The range of religious celebrants who could perform marriages was expanded in 1834[151] and the possibility of civil notice of intention to marry was introduced in

---

143 *Dunn* v *Dunn's Trustees* 1930 SC 131. While courts in the USA have usually taken a similar approach, this was not the case in *Hand* v *Berry* 154 SE 239 (Ga, 1930) where, despite the fact that the couple dared each other to marry 'in a spirit of hilarity and without serious intent', the court found that there had been no fraud and upheld the validity of the marriage.

144 For a discussion of the law at this time, see J. Fergusson, *A Treatise on the Present State of the Consistorial Law in Scotland* (Bell and Bradfute, 1829) and M. Lothian, *The Law, Practice and Styles peculiar to the Consistorial Actions transferred to the Court of Session* (Black, 1830).

145 Lothian, above, at p 255.

146 Fergusson, above, at p 124.

147 A national system of registration was introduced by the Registration of Births, Deaths and Marriages (Scotland) Act 1854.

148 While, in theory, other religious celebrants were liable to prosecution for performing marriages, Clive (at para. 01.013, n 68) expresses the view that such prosecutions were rare.

149 For a discussion of the various types of irregular marriage and some of the reaction to them, see paras 10.75–80, below.

150 See, Report of the Royal Commission on the Laws of Marriage (1868); Report of the Committee on the Marriage Law of Scotland (the Morison Committee) (Cmd 5354, 1937) and, later, the Report of the Committee on the Marriage law of Scotland (the Kilbrandon Committee) (Cmnd 40111, 1969).

151 Marriage (Scotland) Act 1834 allowed ministers and priests who did not belong to the Church of Scotland to perform marriages. However, it was not until the Marriage (Scotland) Act 1977 that non-Christian celebrants were given this power – see para 10.51, below.

1878.[152] Civil regular marriage was introduced in 1939, when two of the three forms of irregular marriage were abolished.[153]

10.51 The current law on the formalities required for marriage is contained in the Marriage (Scotland) Act 1977 ('the 1977 Act') and, so well does it seem to be working, that there has been little movement to make any changes to it.[154] The preliminary procedures are common to both civil and religious marriages and are not particularly arduous. Marriage can be celebrated in either a civil or a religious ceremony, with most religious groups being accommodated. The ceremony itself can be very simple and only the parties, two witnesses and the celebrant, need be present. Registration of the marriage is, again, straightforward. Of course, celebration of marriage can be a much more elaborate affair, but that choice is left to the parties or, frequently, one suspects, their families. The various formal requirements for marriage will be discussed in the paragraphs which follow. At the end of this section, there is a diagram (Table 2) illustrating the formal steps leading to the conclusion of a valid marriage[155] and the numbers on the diagram correspond to the numbers in square brackets below.

Notice of intention to marry [1]

10.52 Each party intending to marry in Scotland must submit notice of intention to marry, using a standard form and known as the 'marriage notice', to the district registrar in the district where the marriage is to be solemnised.[156] Each marriage notice must be accompanied by the prescribed fee,[157] a copy of the individuals' birth certificates and, where a person has been married before, by a copy of the decree dissolving the previous marriage[158] or a copy of the previous spouse's death certificate.[159] If either party is unable to submit any of the required documents, he or she may make a declaration stating that fact and the reasons why it is impracticable for the relevant document to be produced. In addition, he or she must provide the district registrar with such information about the content of the document, and other documentary evidence in support of that information, as the district registrar may require.[160] Where any

---

152 Marriage Notice (Scotland) Act 1878.
153 Marriage (Scotland) Act 1939.
154 The possibility of civil marriages being celebrated by persons other than registrars was mooted in 1985, but nothing came of the idea; Consultation Paper: Marriage in Scotland (Registrar General for Scotland, 1985). In February 1998, in response to a request from COSLA, the Registrar General issued a Consultation Paper on Civil Marriages outwith Registration Offices (12 February 1998, available on: http://www.open.gov.uk/gros/cmoro.htm), exploring the possibility of civil marriage ceremonies being performed at places other than registration offices. See para 10.59, below.
155 Compliance with the required formalities will result in the marriage being valid in the formal sense. Any marriage may be challenged, of course, on other grounds.
156 1977 Act, s 3(1). There are currently some 250 offices throughout Scotland with a registration officer.
157 The fee is currently £10.00; SI 1993 No 3153.
158 1977 Act, s 3(1)(a).
159 1977 Act, s 3(1)(b).
160 1977 Act, s 3(2).

document submitted to the district registrar is in a language other than English, a certified translation must be submitted along with it.[161]

10.53 There is no difficulty about a person or a couple coming from abroad to get married in Scotland. Most of the arrangements can be made on their behalf by someone else and the marriage notice and other documents can be submitted by post or by that other person. Unlike many other jurisdictions, there is no requirement that the prospective spouses should live in Scotland for a period of time before they marry.[162] As we will see, at least 14 days must elapse between the marriage notices being lodged and the marriage schedule being issued and couples travelling from abroad who plan to lodge their own marriage notices should bear this in mind. If the couple has opted for a religious marriage, one of them must collect the marriage schedule from the district registrar,[163] but this can be done shortly before the wedding is to take place. In addition to the documents everyone must submit along with the marriage notice, a person who is domiciled outside the UK may be required to provide a 'certificate of no known impediment'.[164]

10.54 As we saw earlier, Scotland developed a reputation as the home of the runaway marriage, in part, because of the relatively low age of consent to marriage and the lack of any requirement for parental consent. It can be argued that, while Scots law should reflect what is acceptable to the indigenous population, there is less justification for providing a haven for others to flout the requirements of their own domestic law, particularly when such requirements are not manifestly unreasonable.[165] In addition, there is the problem that such a marriage might be declared void in the couple's home country where, for example, there had been a lack of the parental consent required there. To facilitate the creation of 'limping marriages', valid in one country but not in another is, at the very least, messy. In any event, to play the role of a haven for runaways did little for Scotland's standing in the international legal community. Following the recommendations of the Kilbrandon Committee,[166] the 1977 Act intro-

---

161 1997 Act, s 3(3).
162 In some other jurisdictions, there is a residence requirement. For example, in England and Wales, a residence requirement is part of the preliminaries for most marriages. However, it is possible to obtain a special licence in certain circumstances and, thus, avoid the residence requirement. See, Lowe and Douglas, n 47 above, pp 38–48 and Cretney and Masson, n 47 above, pp 17–25.
163 1977 Act, s 6(3).
164 1977 Act, s 3(5). The Act itself does not give this certificate a name and it is sometimes referred to as a 'certificate of capacity.' This is somewhat misleading. The certificate does not guarantee capacity, it merely indicates that the issuing authority is not aware of any impediment. Where, for example, one of the parties has been coerced into agreeing to the marriage, such a certificate will not cure the defective consent.
165 The position would be different if the foreign law contained a prohibition on certain marriages which offended against public policy here. For example, a bar on marriage between people of different racial or ethnic groups might prevent the parties from obtaining a certificate of no incapacity from their home country but, once the reason was explained, would not prevent the marriage going ahead here.
166 Report of the Committee on the Marriage law of Scotland (Cmnd 4011, 1969), paras 73–101.

duced the requirement that persons who are domiciled outside the UK must provide a certificate of no known incapacity from a competent authority in the country of their domicile, 'if practicable'.[167] The certificate should state that the person 'is not known to be subject to any legal incapacity (in terms of the law of that state)'. Where a person has been resident in the UK for two years or longer immediately prior to lodging the marriage notice he or she need not provide such a certificate.[168] Where a person's divorce is recognised in Scotland, but not by the law of his or her domicile, the marriage can go ahead in Scotland without the certificate.[169] It should be noted that the requirement for certificates does not apply to persons domiciled in other parts of the UK[170] and, indeed, young people do occasionally run away from other parts of the UK to get married in Scotland. As we shall see, the failure to provide a certificate of no known impediment will not render a marriage void, assuming that the couple somehow manage to get away with it despite district registrars having a reputation for considerable vigilance. None the less, the introduction of these certificates has reduced the number of runaway marriages taking place in Scotland.

Marriage notice book and display on list of intended marriages [2]

10.55 On receiving the marriage notice, the district registrar must enter the prescribed particulars in the marriage notice book[171] and, as soon as is practicable, enter the names of the parties and the proposed date of the marriage[172] in a list which is displayed in a conspicuous place at the registration office and remains there until the date for the marriage has passed.[173] Any person who claims that he or she might have reason to submit an objection to an intended marriage may inspect the marriage

---

167 1977 Act, s 3(5). Not all jurisdictions issue such certificates, something anticipated by the words of the Act. Thus, for example, persons domiciled in any state in the USA, where there is no authority, either centrally or in each state, which will issue these certificates, can marry in Scotland without producing a certificate. Where, according to the law of a person's domicile, his or her personal law is that of another foreign state, the certificate may be issued by a competent authority in that other state – s 3(5)(i).

168 1977 Act, s 3(5)(ii)(a).

169 1977 Act, s 3(5)(ii)(b).

170 There is provision for a person who lives in another part of the UK to submit 'an approved certificate' issued there in lieu of a marriage notice and the documents which are required along with it – 1977 Act, s 3(4).

171 1977 Act, s 4(1).

172 The addresses of the parties are not displayed on the list of intended marriages, although this information is entered in the marriage notice book. This change was recommended by the Kilbrandon Committee which received evidence that some young couples were pestered by traders who used the list as an opportunity to contact potential customers.

173 1977 Act, s 4(2). The 'conspicuous place' depends on the particular registration office. Where the office is in shop-front premises, the notice is usually displayed in the window, and where the office is in a building set in its own grounds, there is usually a noticeboard at the edge of the grounds and visible from the street. Such display is meant to give public notice of the intended marriage, so that anyone with an objection can make it known. In a small community, this may work, although there, it is likely that the residents know of the intended marriage anyway. In a large city, it is doubtful that display of the list of intended marriages serves any purpose at all.

notice book, free of charge, at any time when the registration office is open for public business.[174]

Objections to a proposed marriage [3]

10.56 Prior to a marriage taking place, any person may submit an objection in writing to the district registrar.[175] Where the objection relates to the capacity of one of the parties to understand the nature of the marriage ceremony or of consenting to marriage, the objection must be accompanied by a medical certificate.[176] What happens next depends on the nature of the objection. If the district registrar is satisfied that the objection relates to nothing more than a misdescription or inaccuracy in the marriage notice,[177] he or she will notify the parties, make enquiries and, subject to the approval of the Registrar General, make the necessary correction to documents.[178] In all other cases, the district registrar must: inform the Registrar General and suspend issuing the marriage schedule, pending consideration of the objection; where the marriage schedule has already been issued to the parties, in the case of a religious marriage, attempt to notify the celebrant and advise him or her not to solemnise the marriage, pending consideration of the objection.[179]

10.57 The Registrar General then considers whether or not there is a legal impediment to the marriage. A legal impediment exists where the marriage would be void because the parties are within the prohibited degrees of relationship set out in s 2 and Sched 1 of the 1977 Act;[180] one of the parties is, or both are, already married; one or both of the parties will be under the age of 16 on the date the marriage is intended to be solemnised; one or both of the parties is incapable of understanding the nature of the marriage ceremony or of consenting to marriage; both parties are the same sex; or, one or both of the parties is, or are, not domiciled in Scotland and the marriage would be void *ab initio* under the law of the

---

174 1977 Act, s 4(3).
175 1977 Act, s 5(1).
176 1977 Act, s 5(1).
177 Such an inaccuracy might relate, for example, to the misspelling of a name, although it is unlikely that the district registrar would have failed to notice such an error when comparing the marriage notice with the birth certificate and, in any event, one wonders why anyone would bother to object in such circumstances. Where a person erroneously described herself as single, when she was, in fact, divorced, the mistake could again be corrected.
178 1977 Act, s 5(2)(a).
179 1977 Act, s 5(2)(b).
180 As we saw, the Marriage (Prohibited Degrees of Relationship) Act 1986 permits marriage between a person and the parent or child of a former spouse, but only where both parties have reached the age of 21 and, prior to the younger reaching the age of 18, they have not lived in the same household in a child-parent relationship (see para 10.29, above). There may be disagreement over whether a particular couple satisfies the conditions which would allow them to marry. Thus, the 1977 Act provides that, regardless of whether or not any objection to their marriage has been lodged, such a couple may seek a declarator from the Court of Session that they have satisfied the conditions – s 2(5). Such a declarator is conclusive for the purpose of satisfying the Registrar General that no impediment to marriage exists – s 5(3A).

domicile of the party or parties.[181] Where the Registrar General is satisfied that an impediment to the marriage exists, he or she will direct the district registrar to take all reasonable steps to ensure that the marriage does not take place and shall notify the parties, or direct the district registrar to notify the parties, accordingly.[182] Where the Registrar General is satisfied that there is no legal impediment, he or she shall inform the district registrar accordingly.[183] A person who has submitted an objection may withdraw it at any time, although this does not prevent the Registrar General from continuing to look into any matter raised in it.[184] The 1977 Act provides no mechanism for appeal against the decision of the Registrar General that an impediment does or does not exist. As Clive[185] points out, a disappointed objector has the remedy of interdict and a disappointed applicant can apply to the court for declarator.

The marriage schedule [4]

10.58 Once the district registrar has received a marriage notice from each of the parties and is satisfied that no impediment to the marriage exists, or has been so informed by the Registrar General, he or she completes a marriage schedule.[186] This document serves as the basis for registration of all regular marriages. Where the marriage is to be a civil one, the district registrar simply retains it until the ceremony. Where the marriage is to be a religious one, it is collected by one of the parties[187] and acts as authority for the celebrant to perform the marriage. Various time limits surround the completion and, in the case of a religious marriage, the issuing, of the marriage schedule. Usually, the district registrar may not issue a marriage schedule until 14 days have elapsed since the marriage notices were lodged.[188] However, the parties may make a written application for the schedule to be issued within the 14-day period, stating their reasons for the request, and the Registrar General may authorise the district registrar to issue the schedule on an earlier date.[189] Parallel provisions allow for civil marriages taking place within the 14-day period.[190] In addition, the schedule will not normally be issued more than seven days before the ceremony is due to take place, but, again, the Registrar General may waive this

---

181 1977 Act, s 5(4).
182 1977 Act, s 5(3)(a).
183 1977 Act, s 5(3)(b).
184 1977 Act, s 5(5).
185 At para 04.010.
186 1977 Act, s S.6(1).
187 1977 Act, s S.6(3).
188 1977 Act, s S.6(4)(a).
189 1977 Act, s 6(4)(a)(i) and (ii). The Registrar General would appear to have complete discretion in reaching a decision here, subject only to the possibility of judicial review. Since having the 14-day period waived would presumably involve a matter of some urgency, it might be that judicial review would not provide an aggrieved party with much of a remedy. In any event, it is unlikely that the Registrar General would authorise early issue of a marriage schedule unless the parties offered a good reason and what would constitute such a reason is a matter of speculation. The imminent death of one of the parties, the sudden posting to a war zone of a member of the armed forces or, possibly, the imminent birth of the parties' child, might be regarded as sufficiently good reason.
190 1977 Act, s 19(1).

requirement.[191] If more than three months has elapsed since the marriage notices were lodged, the Registrar General may instruct the district registrar not to complete a marriage schedule until fresh marriage notices have been submitted.[192] It is at this point that the formalities for marriage follow different courses, depending on whether the ceremony is to be a civil one or a religious one.

Civil marriage [5]

10.59 Only district registrars or assistant district registrars appointed by the Registrar General may solemnise a civil marriage[193] and usually the ceremony must take place at the registration office.[194] However, a registrar may solemnise a marriage at another location within his or her registration district or, with the permission of the Registrar General, in another registration district where there is no authorised registrar in certain, very limited, circumstances.[195] In order to benefit from this latitude, one of the parties must apply for the marriage to be solemnised other than in the registrar's office, stating the reason why they cannot attend at the office.[196] If the registrar is satisfied that the party is unable to attend at his office because of serious illness or serious bodily injury and that there is good reason why the marriage cannot be delayed until the person can so attend, then he or she can comply with the request.[197] If the registrar is not persuaded that the conditions are satisfied, he or she must consult the Registrar General, who may or may not grant permission for the ceremony to go ahead as requested.[198] The parties are responsible for any additional expense incurred by the registrar where a marriage is solemnised outside the registrar's office.[199] No hours within which marriages can take place are stated, although they are normally performed within the office hours of the registration office. As we saw, the parties cannot usually marry within a 14-day period of lodging the marriage notices.

10.60 For the ceremony to proceed, both parties must be present, along with two witnesses 'professing to be 16 years of age or over', the registrar must have the marriage schedule and the prescribed fee must have been paid.[200] Thereafter, there is no form laid down for the ceremony, but Clive

191 1977 Act, s 6(4)(b).
192 1977 Act, s 6(2). It is curious that the time limits within which the marriage schedule may not be issued, and discussed above, apply unless dispensed with, whereas this time limit only applies if the Registrar General so instructs. There does not appear to be any reason for the difference in approach.
193 1977 Act, ss 8(1)(b) and 17. A persons must be at least 21 years old to be so appointed.
194 1977 Act, s 18(1). A registrar must normally solemnise marriages only at his or her own registration office but may, with the permission of the Registrar General, solemnise marriages at the registration office of another registrar – s 18(2).
195 1977 Act, s 18(3).
196 1977 Act, s 18(3) and (4)(a).
197 1977 Act, s 18(4)(b).
198 1977 Act, s 18(5).
199 1977 Act, s 18(3).
200 1977 Act, s 19(2). The fee is currently £40; SI 1993 No 3153. Since each party's marriage notice must be accompanied by a fee of £10, the minimum cost of a civil marriage is therefore £60.

provides a detailed account of the procedure which is usually followed, based on information supplied to him by the General Register Office.[201] Essentially this involves the registrar in explaining the nature of the proceedings and impediments to marriage, establishing that the parties know of no such impediments and accept each other as spouses and declaring them to be married. It will often be possible for the parties to custom-make the ceremony, within reason. The services of an interpreter may be used at the marriage ceremony if the registrar considers it necessary or desirable, the cost of such services being borne by the couple.[202] After the various declarations have been made, the parties, the witnesses and the celebrant sign the marriage schedule[203] and the particulars are entered in the register of marriages.[204]

10.61 It is apparent from the provisions discussed above that, apart from the special case of illness or physical injury, there is no possibility of having a civil marriage ceremony at a place of the couples choosing. Thus, couples cannot be married at home, nor can two keen mountaineers be married on top of Ben Nevis. Such a couple may try to find a religious celebrant who will perform the ceremony at the place of their choice, but they may not want a religious marriage. This very serious limitation on civil ceremonies in Scotland was addressed by the Registrar General in 1998 when he issued a Consultation Paper exploring the possibility of approving venues other than registration offices for the solemnisation of civil marriages, subject to couples meeting any additional costs incurred.[205] While the Consultation Paper did not address the issue, it would be worth considering broadening the range of people who can perform civil ceremonies. If, however, possible celebrants were subject to no restrictions, there might be a danger of the whole process becoming rather lax. None the less, other jurisdictions allow members of the judiciary to fulfil this role and, given that sheriffs play an active part in the dissolution of marriage, they might welcome the opportunity to participate in the more cheerful end of the matrimonial process.[206]

---

201 At para 04.024.
202 1977 Act, s 22. Neither a party to the marriage nor one of the witnesses may act as interpreter. Before the ceremony, the interpreter must sign a statement that he or she understands, and is able to converse in, any language which he or she will interpret during the ceremony. After the ceremony, the interpreter must provide a certificate, in English and signed, that he or she has faithfully acted as interpreter during the ceremony.
203 1977 Act, s 19(3).
204 1977 Act, s.19(4).
205 Civil Marriages outwith Registration Offices (12 February, 1998, available on: http://www.open.gov.uk/gros/cmoro.htm). The Consultation Paper expressed the view that the state has a specific interest in the arrangements for civil marriage in respect of recording the relationship, the seemliness and dignity of the ceremony and the 'reasonableness' of the venue. It is clear that the Las Vegas-style wedding chapel is not being envisaged for Scotland. The Marriage Act 1994, which applies in England and Wales, provides for approval of specific venues for the celebration of marriages there.
206 Such an idea is not entirely without precedent. The, now obsolete, form of irregular marriage, whereby the parties exchanged consent, was often followed by the couple seeking a warrant from the sheriff in order to register the marriage. Such marriages were popularly known as 'marriage before the sheriff', although the marriage itself took place when consent was exchanged – see para 10.76, below.

Religious marriage [6]

10.62 At one time, the range of persons who could celebrate religious marriages in Scotland was very narrow indeed. In particular, there was no possibility of marriage according to the forms of a number of non-Christian faiths. Thus, Muslims, Hindus and Sikhs had to go through a civil ceremony in order to be validly married here and many couples belonging to these religions also had a religious ceremony, often regarding the latter as marking the time when they were truly married. The possibility that a couple might go through one ceremony, which they did not regard as constituting a valid marriage, then go through another ceremony, which had no standing in the eyes of the law but which the couple regarded as valid, raises the question of whether such couples were ever married. More fundamentally, in a multi-cultural, multi-religious, society like ours, it is highly offensive to suggest that marriage by the forms of one religion is legally binding, while marriage according to the forms of another religion counts for nothing at all. For these reasons, the Kilbrandon Committee recommended that the range of religious celebrants who could perform marriage ceremonies should be broadened and this recommendation was taken up in the 1977 Act.

A religious marriage can be solemnised by a person who is

A minister of the Church of Scotland,[207] *or*
A minister, clergyman, pastor, priest or other marriage celebrant of a religious body prescribed by regulations made by the Secretary of State[208]

10.63 Any celebrant permitted by a religion on the prescribed list may solemnise marriages. The regulations currently in force cover all the main Christian denominations and the Hebrew Congregation.[209]

Nominated by some other body as a marriage celebrant and registered as such by the Registrar General under s 9 of the 1977 Act[210]

10.64 Religious bodies other than those covered by the previous provisions may nominate individual members for the purpose of solemnising marriages, provided that the nominees are aged 21 or older.[211] A religious body is defined as 'an organised group of people meeting regularly for common religious worship'[212] and obviously includes non-Christian religions. In addition, the nominee can be any member of the group and need not be a minister, pastor or priest. The Registrar General must reject a nomination if he or she is of the opinion that the nominating body is not a religious body; the marriage ceremony used by that body is not of an

---

207 1977 Act, s 8(1)(a)(i).
208 1977 Act, s 8(1)(a)(ii).
209 The Marriage (Prescription of Religious Bodies) (Scotland) Regulations 1977 (SI 1977 No 1670).
210 1977 Act, s 8(1)(a)(iii).
211 1977 Act, s 9(1).
212 1977 Act, s 26(2).

appropriate form;[213] the nominee is not a fit and proper person to solemnise marriage; or, there are already enough nominees of that religious body registered to meet the needs of the body.[214] If the Registrar General rejects a nomination, he or she must inform the nominating body in writing of the decision and the reasons for it.[215] The nominating body may appeal to the Secretary of State within 28 days and the Secretary of State may direct the Registrar General to accept the nomination or may confirm the rejection.[216] In the latter case, the nominating body may appeal to the Court of Session within 42 days but only in respect of a determination of whether it is a religious body. Where the Registrar General accepts the nomination, he or she must decide how long the nominee will be registered for and whether the person's authority should be subject to any geographic limits[217] and inform the nominee and the nominating body of the acceptance and the conditions attaching to it.[218] In addition, the Registrar General must enter the name of the nominee, the nominating body and other relevant particulars in a register kept for that purpose and available for public inspection free of charge.[219] The Registrar General may remove a person's name from the register if that person so requests; the nominating body so requests; the marriage ceremony used by the body is no longer of an appropriate form; or, the person is now deemed unsuitable , for a variety of reasons.[220] In the case of the last two grounds, the individual and the nominating body may appeal against the decision to the Secretary of State within 28 days of being informed of the decision.[221]

10.65 While the possibility of religious groups nominating celebrants is an improvement on the pre-1977 position, when such groups could not conduct marriage ceremonies at all, it implies two tiers of religion – those

---

213 In order to be 'of an appropriate form', the marriage ceremony must include a declaration by the parties, in the presence of each other and two witnesses, that they accept each other as husband and wife and a declaration by the celebrant, thereafter, that they are husband and wife. In addition, nothing in the ceremony must be inconsistent with these declarations. In order to assess compliance with this requirement, the Registrar General may require the nominating body to produce in writing the form of words to be used – 1977 Act, s 9(3).
214 1977 Act, s 9(2).
215 1977 Act, s 9(5)(b).
216 1977 Act, s 9(6).
217 1977 Act, s 9(4).
218 1977 Act, s 9(5)(a)(i).
219 1977 Act, s 9(5)(a)(ii). The nominating body is required to inform the Registrar General, within 21 days if practicable of any of the following events; any change in the name or address of the body or its amalgamation with another religious body, the death of one of its approved celebrants, any change of name, address or designation of one of its approved celebrants, or the cessation of an approved celebrant to exercise such functions. The Registrar will then amend the register accordingly – 1977 Act, s 11.
220 1977 Act, s 10(1). The celebrant will no longer be regarded as suitable if he or she has been convicted of an offence under the Act, has been carrying on a business, solemnising marriages for gain; is not a fit and proper person; or 'for any other reason, should not be so registered' – s 10(1)(d). In such a case, the Registrar General must give the person 21 days notice in writing of the decision and the reasons for it and must consider any representations made by the person within that period – s 10(2) and (3). During that time, the celebrant must not solemnise marriages – s 10(5).
221 1977 Act, s 10(4).

which can be trusted to organise marriages generally and those which must nominate celebrants on an individual basis. The time has come to treat all religions equally. Of course, the answer might be to provide that the only form of marriage recognised by the legal system is a civil ceremony and leave it to individuals to add any religious element they feel appropriate thereafter. At present, this would raise the problem of individuals who did not feel that a non-religious service could be used to constitute a marriage but, if the Scottish Law Commission's proposal are accepted, such a mental reservation would not render the marriage void.[222]

Temporarily authorised by the Registrar General under s 12 of the 1977 Act[223]

10.66 The Registrar General may grant any person, who is 21 years old or over, temporary authorisation to solemnise marriages. This can be done for a single wedding or for a period of time and may be subject to such terms and conditions as the Registrar General considers appropriate.[224]

10.67 As we saw, the marriage schedule will not usually be issued within a 14-day period of lodging the marriage notices. Subject to the restrictions imposed by the particular religious body, religious marriage provides much greater flexibility in terms of the time and place of marriage than does civil marriage. The ceremony should be performed on the date and at the place specified in the marriage schedule[225] and there is provision for the district registrar to accommodate any change in plans after the schedule has been issued.[226]

10.68 For many people, the choice of a religious marriage is prompted, in part, by the content of the ceremony. None the less, the 1977 Act lays down certain requirements. For the ceremony to proceed, both parties must be present, along with two witnesses 'professing to be 16 years of age or over', and the celebrant must have been given the marriage schedule.[227] In addition, ministers in the Church of Scotland and celebrants whose religious body has blanket approval must use the form of ceremony approved by that religious body.[228] Individually nominated and temporarily approved celebrants must use a form of ceremony which includes a declaration by the parties, in the presence of each other and two witnesses, that they accept each other as husband and wife and a declaration by the celebrant, thereafter, that they are husband and wife. Nothing in the ceremony must be inconsistent with these declarations.[229] The services of an interpreter may be used at the marriage ceremony if the celebrant considers it necessary or desirable, the cost of such services being borne by

---

222 See para 10.32, above.
223 1977 Act, s 8(1)(a)(iv).
224 1977 Act, s 12.
225 1977 Act, s 6(5).
226 A new marriage schedule may be issued or the original amended to take account of a change of date or place – 1977 Act s 6(6) and (7).
227 1977 Act, s 13(1).
228 1977 Act, s 14(a).
229 1977 Act, s 14(b).

the couple.[230] Immediately after the marriage has been solemnised, the parties, the witnesses and the celebrant sign the marriage schedule.[231] Within three days the parties must deliver the marriage schedule to the registrar or arrange for its delivery[232] and, on receipt, the registrar will enter the particulars in the register of marriages.[233] What happens if the marriage schedule is lost or destroyed after the ceremony? The drafters of the 1977 Act thought of this and, provided that the Registrar General is satisfied that the marriage has been properly solemnised and that the marriage schedule was duly signed, he or she can direct the district registrar to complete a copy of the original marriage schedule, arrange for signature by the people who signed the original, where that is practicable, and enter the particulars in the marriage register.[234] If, after 21 days have elapsed from the date of the marriage, the registrar has not received the marriage schedule, he or she may serve notice on either of the parties to the marriage requiring production of the marriage schedule within eight days.[235] If this notice is not complied with, the registrar may serve a second notice on the party requiring him or her to attend personally at the registration office within eight days to deliver the marriage schedule.[236]

Non-compliance with formalities

10.69 What is the effect of failing to comply with any of these formalities? What if, after the ceremony, the couple discover that the celebrant was not authorised or that one of the witnesses was, in fact, only 15 years old? What if the ceremony was performed at a place other than that specified in the marriage schedule? When the 1977 Act was passed, these question caused much speculation. While certain breaches of the statute, for example, one of the parties being under the age of 16 or the couple being related within the prohibited degrees, are stated to render the marriage void, in its original form the 1977 Act was silent on the effect of non-compliance with the various formalities required. The uncertainty prompted the passing of an amendment to the 1977 Act adding s 23A.[237] It provides that, subject to the invalidating effects of non-age or relationship within the prohibited degrees, the validity of a marriage shall not be questioned because of non-compliance with the formalities set out in the 1977 Act, provided that certain conditions are met. The conditions are that both parties were present at the ceremony and that the marriage has been registered. Thus, assuming these conditions are satisfied, the validity of a marriage cannot be

---

230 1977 Act, s 22. Neither a party to the marriage nor one of the witnesses may act as interpreter. Before the ceremony, the interpreter must sign a statement that he or she understands, and is able to converse in, any language which he or she will interpret during the ceremony. After the ceremony, the interpreter must provide a certificate, in English and signed, that he or she has faithfully acted as interpreter during the ceremony.
231 1977 Act, s 15(1).
232 1977 Act, s 15(2).
233 1977 Act, s 15(3).
234 1977 Act, s 15(4).
235 1977 Act, s 16(1).
236 1977 Act, s 16(2).
237 Law Reform (Miscellaneous Provisions) (Scotland) Act 1980, s 22(1)(d).

questioned simply because the celebrant was not authorised, or the marriage was performed at a place or on a date other than that specified in the marriage schedule, or because one of the witnesses was under age, or, indeed, because there were no witnesses at all. It should be noted that this provision does not cure other fundamental defects in a person's capacity to marry. Thus, the fact that a marriage has been registered will not validate a marriage which is otherwise void due to a lack of capacity or a lack of true consent. Nor does s 23A affect the criminal liability of any person who has committed an offence under the 1977 Act.

10.70   The Scottish Law Commission has made two recommendations in respect of the formalities of marriage.[238] First, it takes the view that a distinction ought to be drawn between essential and non-essential formalities. It recommends that the following requirements should be stated to be essential: the giving of notice of intention to marry, the production of a marriage schedule, the presence of both parties, the presence of two witnesses professing to be over 16 years old, the presence of an authorised celebrant and an outward exchange by the parties of consent to marriage. Failure to comply with any of these requirement, except that relating to the presence of the parties, would be curable by registration along the same lines as is presently provided for in s 23A. Second, it recommends that failure to comply with other formalities, for example, forgetting to produce one of the required documents, would not render the marriage void although criminal penalties might apply.

Offences

10.71   Irrespective of the validity of the marriage, the 1977 Act provides that various kinds of conduct, usually by the parties or the celebrant, will constitute an offence. There are two broad categories of offences, their respective severity being reflected in the possible penalties. Any person who falsifies or forges a marriage schedule or declaration described in the 1977 Act; knowingly uses any false or forged marriage schedule, certificate, declaration or other document mentioned in the 1977 Act; being an approved celebrant, solemnises a marriage without a marriage schedule; not being an approved celebrant or authorised registrar, conducts a marriage ceremony in such a way as to lead the parties to believe that he or she is solemnising a valid marriage; or being an approved celebrant or authorised registrar, solemnises a marriage without both parties being present, commits what is regarded as a more serious offence.[239] Any person who solemnises a marriage in contravention of restrictions applying to his or her authorisation; solemnises a marriage while under notice that his or her registration as a celebrant is being considered for removal; solemnises a marriage using other than the approved form of ceremony; or, being a

238 Report on Family Law, n 21 above, paras 8.14–8.15, rec 47(a) and (b) and draft Family Law (Scotland) Bill, clause 21.
239 1977 Act, s 24(1). On conviction on indictment, the maximum penalty is a fine or imprisonment for up to two years, or both. On summary conviction, the maximum penalty is a fine not exceeding level 3 on the standard scale or imprisonment for up to three months, or both.

Table 2: Formal requirements for a regular marriage

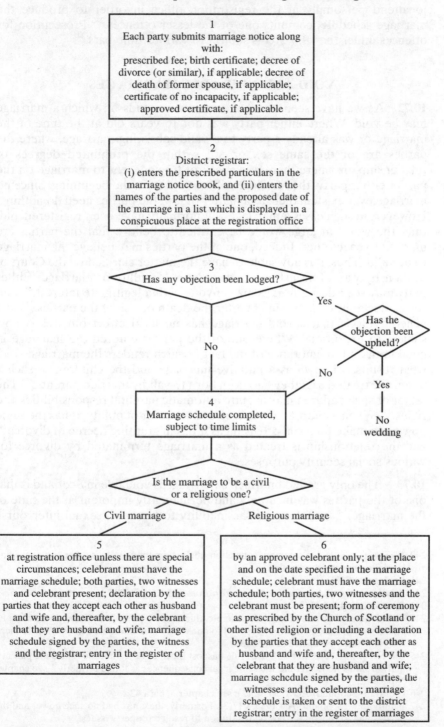

1
Each party submits marriage notice along with:
prescribed fee; birth certificate; decree of divorce (or similar), if applicable; decree of death of former spouse, if applicable; certificate of no incapacity, if applicable; approved certificate, if applicable

2
District registrar:
(i) enters the prescribed particulars in the marriage notice book, and (ii) enters the names of the parties and the proposed date of the marriage in a list which is displayed in a conspicuous place at the registration office

3
Has any objection been lodged?

Yes

Has the objection been upheld?

No

Yes

4
Marriage schedule completed, subject to time limits

No
wedding

Is the marriage to be a civil or a religious one?

Civil marriage

Religious marriage

5
at registration office unless there are special circumstances; celebrant must have the marriage schedule; both parties, two witnesses and celebrant present; declaration by the parties that they accept each other as husband and wife and, thereafter, by the celebrant that they are husband and wife; marriage schedule signed by the parties, the witness and the registrar; entry in the register of marriages

6
by an approved celebrant only; at the place and on the date specified in the marriage schedule; celebrant must have the marriage schedule; both parties, two witnesses and the celebrant must be present; form of ceremony as prescribed by the Church of Scotland or other listed religion or including a declaration by the parties that they accept each other as husband and wife and, thereafter, by the celebrant that they are husband and wife; marriage schedule signed by the parties, the witnesses and the celebrant; marriage schedule is taken or sent to the district registrar; entry in the register of marriages

party to a marriage, fails to comply with a notice from the district registrar to attend personally at the registration office in order to produce the marriage schedule, commits one of the lesser offences.[240] Prosecution for offences under the 1977 Act is subject to various time bars.[241]

VOID AND VOIDABLE MARRIAGES

10.72 As we have seen, there are various grounds on which a marriage may be void. Where either party was not 16 years old at the time of the marriage or was already a party to a valid subsisting marriage, where the parties are of the same sex or are within the prohibited degrees of relationship, or where there was a lack of true consent to marriage on the part of either party, the marriage will be void from the beginning. Since no marriage ever existed, then, as a matter of law, the parties need do nothing. However, in such cases a marriage will normally have been registered and, thus, the world at large would be entitled to believe that the parties are married to each other. Indeed, one of the parties may believe the marriage to be valid. Thus, it is advisable to have the matter clarified by the Court of Session by way of an action for declarator of nullity of marriage. Either party may seek declarator, as may anyone with a legitimate interest,[242] and such a declarator can be sought after the death of one of the parties.[243] The general rule is that a void marriage has no legal effect but this is now subject to exceptions. Where one of the parties entered the marriage in good faith and in ignorance of the fact[244] which renders the marriage void, what results is known as a putative marriage and the children of such a union are treated as if they had been born to validly married parents.[245] The father of such children may acquire automatic parental responsibilities and rights.[246] When a court grants decree of declarator of nullity, it has the same powers to make financial provision as it has in granting decree of divorce[247] and the relationship is treated as a marriage terminated by divorce for various social security purposes.

10.73 The only ground on which a marriage is voidable in Scotland is that one of the parties was incurably and permanently impotent at the time of the marriage.[248] Impotency is the inability to have full sexual intercourse

---

240 1977 Act, s 24(2). On summary conviction, the maximum penalty is a fine not exceeding level 3 on the standard scale.
241 1977 Act, s 24(3).
242 *Administrator of Austrian Property* v *Von Lorang* 1926 SC 598.
243 *Scott* v *Kelly* 1992 SLT 915.
244 The error must be one of fact (for example, thinking the other party to be single when he or she was, in fact, married) as opposed to one of law (for example, believing uncle-niece marriage to be permitted in Scotland).
245 *Burke* v *Burke* 1983 SLT 331. This rule has lost much of its significance since the parents' marital status no longer has the same legal consequences as it had formerly – see chapter 5, para 42.
246 Children (Scotland) Act 1995, s 3(2); see chapter 5, para 42.
247 Family Law (Scotland) Act 1985, s 17(3). Formerly, the court had no such power and the parties had to rely on the law on restitution to resolve property issues.
248 *CB* v *AB* (1884) 11 R 1060; affirmed (1885) 12 R (HL) 36.

and its cause may be physical[249] or psychological.[250] It should be distinguished from sterility and wilful refusal to have sexual relations.[251] Various complications surround the question of whether the impotency is curable and, if so, the effect of the sufferer refusing to seek a cure.[252] The general position is that the sufferer is entitled to the opportunity to attempt a cure[253], although he or she is not obliged to seek one.[254] Only the parties to a voidable marriage have title to sue and a party may found on his or her own impotency.[255] After all, if the situation is acceptable to the parties, what interest does the rest of the world have?[256] The parties themselves may be personally barred from raising the action where, for example, they have adopted a child.[257] Delay in raising the action will not necessarily act as a bar,[258] nor will an ulterior motive.[259] A voidable marriage remains valid until declarator of nullity is granted, whereupon, the decree has retrospective effect,[260] subject to a number of exceptions. The father of a child resulting from a voidable marriage has automatic parental responsibilities and rights[261] and the child is treated as if he or she had been born to married parents. In granting decree of declarator of nullity, the court may make the same orders for financial provision as it could have made on granting decree of divorce.[262]

10.74 Actions for declarator of nullity in respect of voidable marriages are extremely rare and most couples would probably prefer to seek a consensual divorce on the basis of two years separation. As Clive has pointed out, '[t]he concept of the voidable marriage is an unfortunate

---

249 *L* v *L* 1931 SC 477.
250 *AB* v *CB* (1906) 8 F 603; *M* v *W or M* 1966 SLT 152.
251 *J* v *J* 1978 SLT 128. Neither sterility nor wilful refusal to consummate is a ground for nullity, although the latter might be a ground for divorce – Divorce (Scotland) Act 1976, s 1(2)(b).
252 See Clive, para 07.066–07.068.
253 *WY* v *AY* 1946 SC 27.
254 If the impotent party is the defender, refusal to seek treatment will result in the decree being granted – *WY* v *AY*, above. Where the impotent party refusing treatment is the pursuer, decree would probably not be granted – *M* v *W or M*, n 250 above. Where treatment is available, but would involve danger to life or intolerable pain, a person would not be expected to undergo it and the impotency would be treated as incurable – *C* v *M* (1876) 3 R 693.
255 *F* v *F* 1945 SC 202.
256 It can be argued that other people may have an interest. For example, children of an earlier marriage of one of the parties may have a financial interest in terms of succession. None the less, as a matter of policy, it is entirely defensible to deny them title to sue.
257 *AB* v *CB* 1961 SC 347.
258 *Allardyce* v *Allardyce* 1954 SLT 334.
259 *CB* v *AB* (1885) 12 R (HL) 36.
260 For the difficulties which could arise where one of the parties goes through another marriage ceremony before the voidable marriage is declared null, see Clive, para 07.011. See also, *Mason* v *Mason* [1944] NI 134 and *Wiggins* v *Wiggins* [1958] 1 WLR 1013.
261 Children (Scotland) Act 1995, s 3(2). Apart from children resulting from premarital intercourse or donor insemination, it is unlikely that children would result from such a union, but see, *Snowman* v *Snowman* [1934] P 186.
262 Family Law (Scotland) Act 1985, s 17(3). Formerly, the court had no such power and the parties had to rely on the law on restitution to resolve property issues.

one'[263] and the Scottish Law Commission has recommended that it should be abolished.[264] As we have seen, the Commission has also recommended that the factors rendering a marriage void should be placed on a statutory basis, that a mental reservation as to the effect of a ceremony should not have this effect, and that marriage between a person and the parent of his or her former spouse should be permitted.[265]

IRREGULAR MARRIAGE

10.75 Mention has been made of irregular marriage, a Scottish institution which has attracted considerable attention at home and abroad, particularly in England. There were three types of irregular marriage; marriage by declaration of present consent (*per verba de praesenti*), marriage by promise followed by sexual intercourse (*per verba de futuro subsequente copula*), and marriage by cohabitation with habit and repute. A Royal Commission recommended abolition of these forms of marriage in 1868,[266] prompted, at least in part, by the celebrated case of *Longworth* v *Yelverton*,[267] which kept the courts busy for some six years. The facts of the case are the stuff that novels are made of and, indeed, it prompted a whole *genre* of literature in the mid-19th century.[268] Despite this, the first two of the forms of irregular marriage survived until 1940[269] and the third remains valid today.

10.76 Marriage by declaration of present consent required nothing more than a genuine exchange, in Scotland, of consent to immediate marriage.[270] There was no need to have a celebrant or witnesses, although the latter would certainly have been of assistance in providing evidence in any later dispute. There did not need to be express verbal consent by both parties and a gesture or conduct could be sufficient to indicate consent.[271] Whether consent could be exchanged by proxy is unclear, but there was no need for subsequent cohabitation or sexual intercourse, the exchange of consent itself being sufficient to constitute marriage. The availability of this form of irregular marriage no doubt contributed to Scotland's attraction for

263 At para 07.003. See also, K. McK. Norrie, 'Transsexuals, the Right to Marry and Voidable Marriages in Scots Law' 1990 SLT (News) 353.
264 Report on Family Law, n 21 above, paras 8.21–8.30 and recs 49 and 50.
265 Report on Family Law, paras 8.1–8.19 and recs 43–48.
266 Report of the Royal Commission on the Laws of Marriage (1868), p xxviii.
267 (1862) 1 M 161; (1864) 2 M (HL) 49; (1865) 3 M 645; (1867) 5 M (HL) 144; (1868) 7 M 70.
268 The most famous of these is probably Wilkie Collins', *Man and Wife* (OUP, 1870, now available in paperback 1995), although the fashion was started by Theresa Longworth herself, when she wrote *Martyrs to Circumstance* (1861).
269 Marriage by declaration of present consent and marriage by promise followed by sexual intercourse were abolished by the Marriage (Scotland) Act 1939, s 5, which came into force on 1 July 1940. An attempt was made to abolish marriage by cohabitation with habit and repute at the same time, but this was abandoned.
270 For a detailed discussion, see Clive, paras 05.002–05.007.
271 *McAdam* v *Walker* (1813) 1 Dow 148, where the man expressed his consent verbally and the woman curtsied in response. The man shot himself a few hours later.

runaways hoping to marry quickly and, in the attempt to stem the tide, the Marriage (Scotland) Act 1856[272] imposed a 21-day residence requirement. Marriage by declaration of present consent was finally abolished by the Marriage (Scotland) Act 1939.[273]

10.77 The theory behind marriage by promise followed by sexual intercourse,[274] appears to be that where there was a promise of future marriage and, in reliance on that promise, the woman permitted sexual intercourse, the sexual act is seen as an exchange of consent to marriage. Discussing this theory in *N* v *C*,[275] Lord Sands seems to have drawn a distinction, depending on social status. When considering the knight and the lady, he seems prepared to accept that promise followed by intercourse amounts to an exchange of consent to marriage. However, in a later passage, he seems to doubt that this theory held good for 'those sections of the community in which antenuptial fornication is most apt to occur'.[276] Certainly, a modern explanation for this kind of marriage might be personal bar. In any event, there had to be a serious promise of marriage followed by sexual intercourse, both in Scotland.[277] Again, this form of marriage was finally abolished by the Marriage (Scotland) Act 1939 ('the 1939 Act').[278]

10.78 Marriage by cohabitation with habit and repute is the only remaining valid form of irregular marriage. It probably has its roots in pre-tridentine canon law, later acknowledged by a 1503 statute dealing with widows' terce. Whether it was simply a method of *proving* that consent to marriage had been exchanged or was developed into a method of *constituting* marriage has been the subject of considerable debate[279] and, prior to the abolition of marriage by present consent, the distinction was largely unimportant in terms of the result. However, it can be argued that, if cohabitation with habit and repute was simply evidence of an exchange of consent, it would have been abolished by the 1939 Act. Since many marriages have been declared since then, it is now accepted that this is a method of constituting marriage. While it is often helpful to seek declarator of marriage from the courts, such a declarator is simply confirmation that the marriage exists and not something which creates it, a point best illustrated by the fact that many declarators are granted after the death of one of the spouses. Establishing a date on which such a marriage was constituted caused some problems in the past and the difficulty was largely

---

272 Section 1. Clive (at para 01.016) expresses the view that the device 'was not entirely successful.'
273 Section 5.
274 For a detailed discussion, see Clive, paras 05.008–05.018.
275 1933 SC 492.
276 At p 501.
277 *Longworth* v *Yelverton* (1864) 2 M (HL) 49.
278 Section 5.
279 See Clive, paras 05.022–05.027; D. I. C. Ashton-Cross, 'Cohabitation with Habit and Repute' (1961) JR 21; D. P. Sellar, 'Marriage by cohabitation with habit and repute: review and requiem?' in D. Carey Miller and D. Meyers, *Comparative and Historical Essays in Scots Law* (1992).

remedied by the 1977 Act,[280] which provides for registration of the marriage.[281]

10.79 For a valid marriage by cohabitation with habit and repute to exist, all of the following conditions must be satisfied.

- The couple must live together *as husband and wife*, rather than as lovers, employer and housekeeper, or what the older cases describe as 'man and mistress'.[282] What starts out as cohabitation in one capacity, for example, where the woman was initially the man's housekeeper, can become cohabitation as husband and wife.[283] In all logic, where the parties plan to marry at a later date, it can be argued that they are not living as husband and wife prior to that date, but the courts have not always taken this view.[284] Clearly, were the parties to make it clear that they had rejected the institution of marriage, they would not satisfy this requirement and, in any event, the element of repute, discussed below, would be lacking. The modern acceptance of cohabitation without marriage, has increased the likelihood of open cohabitation and, arguably, has reduced the likelihood of this requirement being met.

- The cohabitation must be *in Scotland*.[285]

- The cohabitation must be for *a sufficiently long time*. Nowhere can the watering-down of a requirement be illustrated more clearly than here. While no minimum duration for the cohabitation was ever established, the older cases suggest that a period of several years would be required.[286] It has been emphasised consistently that there is no hard and fast rule and that the quality of the cohabitation and repute are what matters.[287] Thus, it has been possible for courts to accept periods of cohabitation of less than a year as being sufficient.[288]

- The parties must be *reputed to be husband and wife* and 'although repute need not be universal it must be general, substantially unvarying and consistent and not divided'.[289] As Clive points out, '[t]he law on sufficient

280 See Clive, paras 05.040–05.048 for a discussion of the problem and the solution.
281 Marriage (Scotland) Act 1977, s 21. Where a decree of declarator of marriage has been granted, the Principal Clerk of Session transmits the relevant particulars to the Registrar General who arranges for the marriage to be registered.
282 *Cunningham* v *Cunningham* (1814) 2 Dow 482; *Campbell* v *Campbell* (1866) 4 M 867; *Petrie* v *Petrie* 1911 SC 360; *Nicol* v *Bell* 1954 SLT 314.
283 *Nicol* v *Bell*, above.
284 *Mackenzie* v *Scott* 1980 SLT (Notes) 9 (couple had discussed getting married, declarator refused); *Shaw* v *Henderson* 1982 SLT 211 (couple had made arrangements for a wedding, declarator granted); *Dewar* v *Dewar* 1995 SLT 467 (couple had discussed formal ceremony, declarator granted).
285 *Dysart Peerage Case* (1881) LR 6 App Cas 489, per Lord Watson, at pp 537–538.
286 *Mackenzie* v *Mackenzie* 8 March 1810 FC (ten years was enough); *Campbell* v *Campbell*, n 282 above, (views expressed that three years would probably be enough but one year would not); *Wallace* v *Fife Coal Company* 1909 SC 682.
287 *Shaw* v *Henderson*, n 284, above; *Kamperman* v *MacIver* 1994 SLT 763.
288 *Shaw* v *Henderson*, n 284 above (11 months sufficient); *Mullen* v *Mullen* 1991 SLT 205 (six months enough); *Kamperman* v *MacIver*, above (six months not 'necessarily insufficient').
289 *Low* v *Gorman* 1970 SLT 356, per Lord Robertson, at p 359.

repute is difficult to apply in contemporary conditions',[290] since non-marital cohabitation is widespread and the names used by individuals can no longer be regarded as conclusive. Certainly, it is not fatal that some people knew the couple were not married, even where those individuals are relatives.[291] On the other hand, where a substantial number of friends and relatives knew that the parties were not married this may be fatal to the pursuer's case.[292] Where it is widely known that the relationship began as a non-marital one, it may be difficult, but not impossible, to displace the original illicit repute.[293]

- The parties must have *capacity to marry*. Where the parties are within the prohibited degrees of relationship, for example, they will never have the necessary capacity and no marriage by cohabitation with habit and repute can be established. However, where there is an impediment to marriage at the beginning of the cohabitation and it is removed subsequently, a case for marriage by cohabitation with habit and repute can be established. Only the period of time during which the parties had capacity to marry can be considered. Thus, where the woman was under the age of 16 when the parties began living together, only the period of cohabitation after her 16th birthday will be considered relevant. As a number of the cases illustrate, cohabitation begun while one or both of the parties was married to someone else cannot be considered, but once each of them is free to marry, the clock can begin to run.[294]

10.80 Marriage by cohabitation with habit and repute is open to a number of criticisms. The very idea that some couples can gain the benefits of marriage by misleading the world at large, while couples who cohabit openly and honestly cannot, smacks of injustice. The uncertainty surrounding what amounts to cohabitation for a sufficient length of time or adequate repute is undesirable. The potential hazard which such irregular marriages pose to subsequent regular marriages is probably more theoretical than real, given the tiny number of irregular marriages actually created. In addition, there is a belief that the concept has been stretched out of all recognition, particularly in cases where the couple has planned a wedding ceremony and the operative period of cohabitation has been very short. Ironically, it is sometimes in such cases that marriage by cohabitation with habit and repute gives the court the opportunity to achieve compassionate justice where that would not be possible otherwise. This is particularly true where one of the parties has died and the declarator of marriage enables the surviving spouse to gain benefits or compensation. Arguably, this situation simply militates in favour of greater recognition of all cohabitants. Undoubtedly, the existence of this kind of marriage has benefits for the very small number of people who marry abroad and cannot produce

---

290 At para 05.034.
291 *Shaw* v *Henderson*, n 284 above; *Donnelly* v *Donnelly's Executor* 1992 SLT 13; *Gow* v *Lord Advocate* 1993 SLT 275. It is worth remembering that family members may have a pecuniary interest in disputing the marriage of a deceased relative.
292 *Petrie* v *Petrie*, n 282 above; *Mackenzie* v *Scott*, n 284 above.
293 *Shaw* v *Henderson*, n 284 above; *Gow* v *Lord Advocate*, n 291 above.
294 *Campbell* v *Campbell*, n 282 above; *Shaw* v *Henderson*, n 284 above.

evidence of the marriage or those whose attempt at regular marriage transpires later to be invalid for a reason that does not bar marriage by cohabitation with habit and repute. The Scottish Law Commission has recommended the prospective abolition of this kind of marriage.[295] However, this recommendation should be read along with the Commission's other recommendations on void marriages and the rights of cohabitants, since they form part of an inter-related package.

GETTING MARRIED ABROAD

10.81 The Foreign Marriages Acts provide a long-established procedure for marriage ceremonies being conducted at British consular offices or embassies where at least one of the parties is a UK national.[296] Special provisions enable marriages to be performed abroad by armed forces chaplains where at least one of the parties is a serving member of the armed forces or the child of such a person.[297] In addition, it is possible to get married abroad in a ceremony performed by a local celebrant according to local laws.

10.82 Getting married abroad has become increasingly popular, with many Scots couples taking a package holiday which includes the arrangements for the wedding. Of course, there is no need to arrange one's marriage abroad through a travel company and all the parties need to be clear about are the formalities required in the place where the marriage ceremony will be performed. Provided that each of the parties has the capacity to marry according to the law of his or her domicile and that the local formalities for marriage are complied with, the marriage will be valid, assuming no other vitiating factors like duress to be present. If the foreign jurisdiction requires certificates dealing with the parties' capacity to marry, like the certificates of no known impediment required of foreigners planning to marry in Scotland, these can be obtained from district registrars here.[298] Each party submits a marriage notice and the supporting documents to the district registrar in the district where he or she lives. If the district registrar is satisfied that the person is not subject to any incapacity under Scots law, a certificate can be issued after 14 days. After the marriage, what the couple will receive, of course, is a foreign marriage certificate which may look very different to a Scottish certificate. This normally presents no problems and is usually accepted in Scotland as proof

---

295 Report on Family Law, n 21 above, paras 7.1–7.13 and rec 42. The Commission emphasised that a marriage contracted prior to any legislation implementing its abolition should be valid, whether or not declarator had already been obtained.

296 Foreign Marriage Acts 1892 and 1947. Originally the marriage was conducted in accordance with English law and the consent required there was required even if the parties were domiciled in Scotland. This anomaly was removed after recommendations from the Scottish and English Law Commissions; Foreign Marriages (Amendment) Act 1988, s 2. For a full discussion of the procedures for these marriages, see Clive, paras 09.028–09.034.

297 Foreign Marriage Act 1892.

298 Marriage (Scotland) Act 1977, s 7.

of the marriage.[299] Should the couple be unable to provide evidence of the foreign marriage, for example, because they have lost the marriage certificate and cannot get a copy of it, they can go through a second ceremony in Scotland.[300] Essentially, they have to go through the usual preliminary formalities and a ceremony but, when the marriage schedule is completed, a statement is appended to it to the effect that the couple declare that they have gone through a marriage ceremony abroad on a specified date. Where a foreign marriage is invalid by reason, for example, of a lack of compliance with the local formalities, and the couple return to Scotland and live here as husband and wife for a period of time and are generally regarded as a married couple, they may become validly married by virtue of the doctrine of marriage by cohabitation with habit and repute.

ROYAL MARRIAGES

10.83 Certain descendants of George II are required to give notice to the Privy Council and to obtain the consent of the sovereign prior to marrying and failure to comply with these requirements may render the marriage void.[301]

COURT ORDERS RELATING TO MARRIAGE

10.84 As this chapter illustrates, there are a variety of circumstances in which a court might be called upon to pronounce on the validity of a marriage or some related matter. Different remedies apply and the most common are set out below by way of summary.

Declarator of marriage: a statement from the court that a marriage exists.

Declarator of nullity of marriage: a statement from the court that a marriage either has never existed between two parties (void marriage) or no longer exists (voidable marriage).

Declarator of freedom and putting to silence: a statement from the court that a particular relationship does not exist and instructing the defender to stop claiming that it does. Most frequently, it will be used to indicate that the pursuer is not married to the defender and order the defender to stop claiming that the parties are married, but it has been used to stop false assertions of a father-child relationship.[302]

Interdict: order from the court telling someone not to do something or, if doing it, to stop.

---

299 My own, rather splendid, marriage certificate, bearing a large gold seal and issued in El Paso, Texas, has been accepted without problem, although not without comment, in Scotland.
300 1977 Act, s 20.
301 Royal Marriages Act 1772.
302 *Imre* v *Mitchell* 1958 SC 439.

CHAPTER 11

COHABITATION AND MARRIAGE: THE CONSEQUENCES

11.1   As we saw in chapter 10, in order to create a valid marriage the parties must normally comply with a variety of formalities and there will be a record of the marriage having taken place. Cohabitation on the other hand, requires no such formalities and there will be no official record of the relationship. This alone might explain why the legal system attaches significantly fewer consequences to cohabitation than to marriage. However, there are numerous other explanations including the desire, whether for religious or other reasons, to indicate that marriage, rather than cohabitation, is the approved form of adult relationship. When marriage itself is denied to a particular group, as is the case with lesbian and homosexual couples, it may indicate a reluctance on the part of the legal system and sections of society to recognise the relationship at all. As we saw, a number of mechanisms can be used by cohabiting couples to gain some degree of recognition for their relationships. It is worth remembering that to attach the same consequences to cohabitation as attach to marriage effectively denies heterosexuals the choice over what kind of relationship they want to have. Thus, treating the two states differently can be argued to liberate individuals and promote freedom of choice.[1] Of course, this argument only holds good where the individuals not only have the choice available to them, but exercise the choice freely. There is no doubt that, in some cases, couples cohabit when one, but not the other, would prefer them to be married. None the less, it would be possible to provide that both marriage and cohabitation had identical legal consequences or to remove all legal significance from either or both of them.[2]

11.2   In this chapter, the consequences of marriage will be explored and where the same or similar consequences attach to cohabitation, they too will be examined. On occasions, consequences which resulted from marriage in the past will be mentioned, if only to clarify that they no longer

---

1   S. Cretney, 'The law relating to Unmarried Partners from the Perspective of a Law Reform Agency', R. Deech, 'The Case Against Legal Recognition of Cohabitation' and D. MacDougall, 'Policy and Social Factors affecting the Legal Recognition of Cohabitation without Formal Marriage' in J. M. Eekelaar and S. N. Katz (eds), *Marriage and Cohabitation in Contemporary Societies* (Butterworths, 1980); M. D. A. Freeman and C. Lyon, *Cohabitation without Marriage* (1983); M. L. Parry, *The Law Relating to Cohabitation* (3rd edn, Sweet and Maxwell, 1993).

2   E. M. Clive, 'Marriage: An Unnecessary Legal Concept', B. Hoggett, 'Ends and Means – The Utility of Marriage as a Legal Institution' in J. Eekelaar and S. Katz (eds), above,

apply. In many respects, marriage has fewer consequences than it once did, while the recognition of cohabitation has grown. At the end of this chapter, how individuals can regulate their own relationships is explored, along with the Scottish Law Commission's proposals for reform of the law as it affects cohabitants. Given the fact that the legal consequences of marriage are diminishing, if we were to maximise the extent to which individuals were able to regulate their own relationships, while extending a minimal level of protection and equitable guarantees to cohabitants, we might find the distinction between different forms of adult relationship had all but disappeared. Effectively, the legal significance of marriage would have been removed.

11.3 First, however, the legal consequences themselves must be explored. For ease of use, they have been subdivided into personal consequences, obligations, property, aliment, state benefits, taxation, judicial proceedings and criminal law. Many of these subjects merit books in their own right and relevant publications are cited throughout. The family or matrimonial home is considered in chapter 12 and the allocation of a separate chapter is a reflection both the importance of the home itself and the very specific régime provided by the Matrimonial Homes (Family Protection) (Scotland) Act 1981 and other legislation. Financial provision on divorce and succession are discussed in chapter 14.

PERSONAL CONSEQUENCES

Name

11.4 As we saw earlier, marriage has no automatic consequences for a person's name.[3] The practice which leads some wives to take their husbands' last names on marriage is no more than a convention, and one which was only adopted relatively recently in Scotland. Provided that no fraud is intended, the parties may call themselves by any name they choose. Thus, each spouse may retain his or her last name, both may use the last name of one of them or the couple may adopt some combination of both names. Equally, cohabitants are free to use any names they choose, again provided that no fraud is intended.

Where a person lives and with whom

11.5 The common law imposed on spouses the notional duty to 'adhere'; that is, to live together. However, the courts would not enforce the obligation and actions for adherence were usually simply a device to enable the pursuer to obtain an award of aliment against the defender. Actions of adherence were abolished by statute in 1984.[4] Refusal to live with a

---

and 'Matchings' in B. Hale (The Hon Mrs Justice, formerly Professor Brenda Hoggett), *From the Test Tube to the Coffin: Choice and Regulation in Private Life*, The Hamlyn Lectures, Forty-Seventh Series (Sweet and Maxwell, 1996).
3 This point is discussed at length in chapter 2 at paras 62–63.
4 Law Reform (Husband and Wife) (Scotland) Act 1984, s 2(1). The Act implemented the Scottish Law Commission's recommendations contained in the Report on Outdated Rules in the Law of Husband and Wife (Scot Law Com No 76, 1983).

blameless spouse (assuming such a creature exists) who is prepared to live together will entitle the innocent spouse to seek divorce for desertion after a period of two years.

11.6 At common law, the husband had the right to choose the place of the matrimonial home and, provided his choice was genuine or reasonable,[5] a wife who refused to live there was regarded as being in desertion. This prerogative of the husband was abolished by statute in 1984,[6] with one curious and interesting result. Where a married couple are happy to live with each other but cannot agree on the location of the home, arguably, neither of them is in desertion. Were one of them to decide later that divorce[7] was the only answer, he or she would have to proceed on the basis of separation for two years, if the other spouse agreed, or wait for five years, if the requisite consent was not forthcoming.

11.7 A person's ordinary or habitual residence may be important in particular contexts. For example, a person can raise an action to have his or her spouse declared dead in the sheriffdom where the missing person was last known to reside or where the pursuer has resided for the previous 40 days[8]. The concept of habitual residence is increasingly used in the context of jurisdiction and recognition of decrees. Residence is a question of fact and, thus, the same rules apply to married persons, cohabitants and, indeed, hermits.

Children

11.8 Obviously, it is a good idea for a couple to discuss and agree the issue of whether they will try to have children in the future. Even so, people sometimes change their minds. In the case of a married couple, radical disagreement over this matter may entitle either spouse to seek a divorce on the basis of the other's behaviour or simply by waiting for the two or five year separation to expire. Where a woman terminates a pregnancy in the face of her husband's opposition, he would almost certainly be successful in seeking a divorce.[9] Equally, were she to conceive using donor insemination without consulting him, her action could be seen as going sufficiently to the heart of the marriage as to warrant divorce. Were a husband to become a sperm donor without consulting his wife, or in the face of her opposition, again, his conduct might enable her to obtain a divorce, although it is possible to distinguish the two situations. In the case of the wife having donor insemination, she would be introducing a child into their relationship and one where her husband would be treated as the father, at least until he could demonstrate his lack of consent. In the case of the husband-donor, no further involvement by him would normally be anticipated.

11.9 As we saw earlier, while parental marital status is of minimal

5 *Stewart* v *Stewart* 1959 SLT (Notes) 70.
6 Law Reform (Husband and Wife) (Scotland) Act 1984, s 4.
7 Divorce, and the circumstances in which it may be granted, are discussed fully in chapter 13.
8 Presumption of Death (Scotland) Act 1977, s 1(4). See chapter 2, paras 51–55.
9 See *Kelly* v *Kelly* 1997 SLT 896 and the discussion in chapter 2, para 25.

importance in terms of children's rights, the same cannot be said of parental rights. While a woman's husband is presumed to be the father of her child, an unmarried father must be registered as such (a process which requires the mother's agreement) before any presumption arises.[10] Whereas mothers and married fathers have parental responsibilities and rights automatically, unmarried fathers must apply to the court unless they can reach agreement with the mother.[11] The injustice of this particular form of discrimination against children born to unmarried parents and to unmarried fathers was discussed fully in chapter 5.

11.10 Married couples may find it easier to gain access to services aimed at assisted reproduction than unmarried couples and particularly same-sex couples.[12] Of course, some of the techniques do not require medical assistance and, thus, can be carried out by the parties themselves. The legal system is moving some way towards accepting diversity in adult relationships by providing not only that a woman's husband will be treated as the father of any child she bears as a result of assisted reproduction, but that the unmarried male partner of a single woman will benefit from a similar approach if the treatment has been provided to the couple together.[13] As yet, the law has not accommodated same-sex couples in this respect, but the recent shift of attitude in respect of adoption is encouraging.

11.11 Broadly, only two categories of persons can apply to adopt a child – unmarried persons and married couples.[14] Certain exceptions permit an application by a married person alone where his or her spouse is missing or incapable of applying or where the couple are separated on a permanent basis. Couples who are cohabiting, but unmarried, cannot adopt a child together and that is so irrespective of their sexual orientation. The decision in *T, Petitioner*,[15] where the Inner House not only permitted a single man to adopt a child, where he had made clear his intention to raise the child in family along with his homosexual partner, but also debunked some of the myths surrounding homosexual parenting, is again a step along the road to recognition of diversity.

Remarriage and cohabitation

11.12 A married person cannot enter into another marriage while the first marriage remains in existence.[16] Once the first marriage is dissolved by divorce or the death of a spouse, individuals are free to remarry and, of course, a person can marry any number of times over his or her lifetime.[17]

---

10 Law Reform (Parent and Child) (Scotland) Act 1986, s 5(1). See chapter 4, paras 7–13.
11 Children (Scotland) Act 1995, ss. 3 and 4. See chapter 5, paras 40–67.
12 For a discussion of assisted reproduction and the techniques available, see chapter 4, paras 28–73.
13 Human Fertilisation and Embryology Act 1990, s 28. See chapter 4, para 37.
14 Adoption (Scotland) Act 1978, ss. 14 and 15. See chapter 8, paras 26–34.
15 1996 SCLR 897. This case is discussed fully in chapter 8, para 17.
16 Marriage (Scotland) Act 1977, s 5(4)(b). See chapter 10, paras 22–24.
17 As Glendon puts it, 'The fundamental right to marry ... has now to be understood as the right to marry, and marry and marry'; M. A. Glendon, *The New Family and the New Property* (Butterworths, 1981) at p 72.

Marriage to certain relatives of a former spouse is restricted or prohibited.[18] While a married person is not prevented from cohabiting with someone other than his or her spouse, such a relationship will almost certainly be grounds for divorce. If a sexual element to the cohabitation can be established, the aggrieved spouse could raise an action of divorce based on adultery and, if such evidence cannot be found, an action based on behaviour would be competent. Where a couple's relationship is one of unmarried cohabitation, either party may cohabit with, or, indeed, marry, someone else with impunity.[19]

Personal relations

11.13 Under the older common law, marriage placed the wife under a duty of obedience to her husband with the result that he could control various aspects of her behaviour, including her friendships and contacts.[20] This notion, coupled with the husband's right of chastisement 'has now gone without trace'.[21] Now, each spouse is free to choose his or her own friends and to spend time with other people. It is a rare spouse indeed who shares the same level of enthusiasm for every one of his or her partner's friends. Were either spouse to spend unreasonable amounts of time with friends or family, particularly where the spouse was not included in these gatherings, this might constitute behaviour justifying the neglected spouse in seeking a divorce. Each spouse is free to take up the occupation of his or her choice and to behave as they wish in other respects, although certain conduct, while legal, again, might constitute grounds for divorce. It is worth noting that there is no longer any liability in delict for inducing one spouse to leave the other.[22] Cohabitants are unfettered by the law in terms of how they spend their time or with whom.

Sexual relations

11.14 While incurable impotence makes a marriage voidable[23] and wilful refusal to have sexual relations may justify divorce, the law views this as a private matter for the parties and does not intervene unless the spouses choose to make an issue of any lack of sexual activity in a marriage. Similarly, it is for one of the parties to allege excessive sexual demands, as conduct justifying a divorce, before the law will intervene. While the idea of sexual fidelity, as an inherent part of marriage, remains, and adultery constitutes a ground for divorce, the husband's right to claim damages from his wife's paramour was abolished in 1976.[24] While homosexual relations

18 See chapter 10, para 29.
19 This assumes that the cohabitation was truly that and was not such as to create the belief that the parties were, in fact, married. In the latter case, there is the risk of a marriage by cohabitation with habit and repute being declared later – see chapter 10, paras 78–80.
20 Stair, I, 4, 9; *Lady Cadboll v Her Husband* (1758) 5 Supp 475.
21 Clive, *The Law of Husband and Wife in Scotland* (4th edn, W. Green, 1997) para 11.018.
22 Law Reform (Husband and Wife) (Scotland) Act 1984, s 2(2).
23 See chapter 10, para 73.
24 Divorce (Scotland) Act 1976, s 10(1), implementing the recommendation contained in the Report on Liability for Adultery and Enticement of a Spouse (Scot Law Com No 42,

do not amount to adultery, such conduct and, indeed, certain heterosexual conduct amounting to less than adultery, will almost certainly justify the non-participating spouse in seeking a divorce.

11.15 At one time it was thought that a wife gave blanket consent to sexual intercourse with her husband simply by marrying, with the consequence that a husband could not rape his wife.[25] This absurd notion was struck down, first, in cases where the spouses were separated,[26] and, eventually, in *S v HM Advocate*,[27] where the parties were living together. As Lord Justice-General Emslie put it, '[n]owadays it cannot seriously be maintained that by marriage a wife submits herself irrevocably to sexual intercourse in all circumstances'.[28] Again, the surprise is not that the common law position was rejected, but that the rejection was so long in coming.[29] Of course, where the spouses are living together, it may be very difficult to produce sufficient evidence to secure a conviction.[30]

Nationality and Immigration[31]

11.16 The impact of marriage on a woman's nationality appears to have varied throughout history,[32] but the current position is that marriage has no automatic effect on either spouse's nationality. A British national does not lose his or her nationality by marrying a foreigner, nor does a foreign spouse acquire nationality by marrying a British citizen. However, the foreign spouse of a British citizen can acquire nationality by naturalisation more easily than can other persons[33] based on residence for three years. Cohabitation has no effect on nationality.

11.17 Marriage is important, however, for immigration purposes.[34] Spouses normally anticipate that they will live together and, thus, it is only reasonable that immigration rules should accommodate this usual consequence of marriage. At one time, the rules operating in the UK were discriminatory, favouring the wives of British citizens. After criticism by

1976). There is no reported case of a wife claiming damages against her husband's paramour in such circumstances and the Commission thought it unnecessary to deal with the possibility in legislation.
25 Hume, I, 306.
26 *HM Advocate* v *Duffy* 1983 SLT 7; *HM Advocate* v *Paxton* 1985 SLT 96.
27 1989 SLT 469.
28 At p 473.
29 The courts in England accepted the possibility of marital rape in *R* v *R* [1991] 3 WLR 767. In the USA, some states allow prosecution where the couple are living apart – see the landmark cases, *Smith* v *State* 426 A 2d 38 (NJ, 1981) and *Commonwealth* v *Chretien* 417 NE 2d 1203 (Mass, 1981). In only a few states is prosecution competent where spouses were living together at the time of the alleged rape.
30 In *S* v *HM Advocate*, n 27 above, for example, the jury found the charge not proven.
31 See D. C. Jackson, *Immigration: Law and Practice* (Sweet and Maxwell, 1996), chapters 11 and 12; I. R. MacDonald and N. Blake, *MacDonald's Immigration Law and Practice* (Butterworths, 1995), chapter 11.
32 At common law, the effect of marriage was, at most, minimal. By the 19th-century, a married woman's nationality followed that of her husband, but the rule was modified in the 20th century and eventually abandoned. See Clive, para 11.003.
33 British Nationality Act 1981, s 6.
34 See Clive, paras 11.005–11.008.

the European Court of Human Rights,[35] the rules were changed and the current rules[36] no longer discriminate on the ground of sex. A foreign spouse should obtain an entry clearance certificate and, provided that he or she satisfies a number of conditions, will be admitted to the UK for a period of up to 12 months. Fiancés and fiancées can gain admission for shorter periods of time under similar provisions and, while the rules do not apply to cohabitants, they are admitted on a discretionary basis. Nationals of member states of the European Economic Area and their spouses are not governed by these rules and have a much easier time gaining admission to the UK and staying here.

Domicile[37]

11.18 Domicile is the link between an individual and a legal system and can be particularly important for personal purposes like the capacity to marry and succession to moveable property. Increasingly, ordinary or habitual residence is now used as the connecting factor for civil purposes. At common law, a wife acquired a domicile of dependence on marriage based on that of her husband[38] and she had no capacity to acquire any other domicile even if the parties were separated.[39] This produced anomalous results and the rule was finally abolished with effect from 1974.[40] Thus, a married woman now acquires and changes her domicile in the same way as all other persons. Cohabitation has no automatic effect on domicile although, of course, moving to a particular place with the intention of settling there will effect the acquisition of a domicile of choice.

OBLIGATIONS

Contract[41]

11.19 Initially, under the common law, marriage removed a woman's independent contractual capacity.[42] On marriage, the husband became his wife's curator (legal guardian), whose consent was usually required for her to contract at all. Initially, this curatory was lifelong. This was in addition to the husband's *jus mariti* and *jus administrationis*, which are discussed below in the context of property. It appears that exceptions developed even under

---

35 *Abdulaziz, Cabales and Balkandali* v *UK* (1985) 7 EHRR 471.
36 Statement of Changes in Immigration Rules (1994 HC 388), amended by the Statement of Changes in Immigration Rules (Cm 3365, 1996) and the Statement of Changes in Immigration Rules (1997 HC 26).
37 See A. E. Anton, *Private International Law* (2nd edn, W. Green, 1991); P. M. North, *The Private International Law of Matrimonial Causes in the British Isles and the Republic of Ireland* (Martinus Nijhoff, 1977).
38 Stair, I, 4, 9; *Warrender* v *Warrender* (1835) 2 Sh and MacL 154.
39 *Low* v *Low* (1891) 19 R 115.
40 Domicile and Matrimonial Proceedings Act 1973, s.1. The Act came into force on 1 January 1994 and has prospective effect only. The Act contains transitional provisions for women who had acquired domiciles of dependence as a result of the previous law.
41 See W. W. McBryde, *The Law of Contract in Scotland* (W. Green, 1987); D. M. Walker, *The law of Contracts and Related Obligations in Scotland* (3rd edn, T&T Clark, 1995).
42 Stair, I, 4, 16.

the common law, not least to accommodate deserted wives.[43] That the restrictions on married women's capacity to contract and to control their own property were interrelated is evidenced by the fact that the legislation which removed various restrictions often dealt with both areas of the law. The Married Women's Property (Scotland) Act 1920 essentially put married women on an equal contractual footing with other adults and provided that the husband's curatory should be confined to any period while his wife was in minority.[44] The Law Reform (Husband and Wife) (Scotland) Act 1984 abolished the husband's curatory over his minor wife.[45] The wife's *praepositura rebus domesticus*, whereby she was presumed to be the domestic manager of the home, with authority to bind her husband to pay for goods and services acquired in that capacity, was abolished by the same statute,[46] as was a husband's liability for his wife's antenuptial debts.[47]

11.20 The present law is summed up in the Family Law (Scotland) Act 1985 ('the 1985 Act'), which provides that marriage 'shall not of itself affect ... the legal capacity of the parties'.[48] As a general statement of the law, this reflects the current position accurately and spouses can contract with third parties, and with each other, as independent individuals.[49] While they can act as agents for each other, there is no presumption that this is the case. However, the neutral position of marriage insofar as it affects an individual's activity, in the contractual context, is subject to two qualifications. The first is quite rightly described by Clive as 'not very important in modern practice'.[50] As we will see shortly, spouses are obliged to aliment each other, subject to certain conditions. Where a spouse owes the obligation to aliment and fails to fulfil it, anyone who supplies the other spouse with necessaries may seek recompense from the non-alimenting spouse on the basis of unjustified enrichment.

11.21 The second qualification to the general rule results from a recent decision of the House of Lords which drove a coach and horses through the Scots law of cautionary obligations and is likely to have more far-reaching

---

43 See Clive, at paras 13.001–13.002.
44 Section 3(1) and 2. The Act also abolished the *jus administrationis*, the *jus mariti* having been abolished by the Married Women's Property (Scotland) Act 1881, s 1(1). While a minor male who married a woman of full age did not pass into his wife's curatory on marriage, there is some doubt about whether he was forisfamiliated by the marriage itself. That the husband was forisfamiliated by marriage is supported by Stair, I, 5, 13 and *Harvey* v *Harvey* (1860) 22 D 1198 at p 1208 per Lord Justice-Clerk Inglis. However, support for proposition that marriage did not have this effect can be found in Bankton, *Institute*, I, 6, 8 and *Anderson* v *Anderson* (1832) 11 S 10.
45 Section 3.
46 Section 7.
47 Section 6.
48 Section 24(1)(b).
49 A good example of husbands and wives contracting can be seen in the number of spouses who practice law in partnership together. There is, of course, a certain risk in putting all the domestic eggs in one basket.
50 At para 13.006.

implications.[51] In *Smith v Bank of Scotland*,[52] Ms Smith alleged that she had been induced to grant a standard security in favour of the Bank over the matrimonial home, which she co-owned with her husband, by misrepresentations made by her husband as to the effect of such a security. The security was required to enable her husband to obtain overdraft facilities to provide further finance for his business, a business in which Ms Smith had no direct interest.[53] Ms Smith alleged that she had no opportunity to consider the documents relating to the standard security before she signed them, was not supplied with copies of them and was not advised by the Bank to seek independent legal advice as to their effect. When the Bank sought to realise the security, Ms Smith raised an action of reduction based on her husband's misrepresentations and argued that, since the Bank was aware that the security related to her husband's business, it could be held to have constructive knowledge of any misrepresentation made by him. Dismissing the action, the Inner House affirmed the established position in Scots law at the time. First, there was no presumption of undue influence in transactions involving husbands and wives and none was created simply because the transaction was not to the wife's advantage. Second, something more than the nature of the parties' relationship would be required before constructive knowledge of undue influence could be imputed to the Bank. That this differed from the position in England and Wales was acknowledged by the then Lord President (Hope) when he refused to extend an earlier decision of the House of Lords in an English appeal[54] to Scotland.[55] Allowing Ms Smith's appeal, the House of Lords seems to have been guided by little more than policy considerations and, while it sought to confine the ambit of the decision to cautionary obligations and warned expressly against clothing every person who transacted with a wife with constructive knowledge of the husband's undue influence or misrepresentation, that is precisely the effect the decision will have.[56] Nor is it confined to spouses. In all likelihood it will be extended at least to cohabitants.

11.22 It might be argued that there are policy considerations justifying this decision. Instinctively, one feels far greater sympathy for a person who

---

51 In the course of discussing *Smith*, below, and its possible limits, Gretton comments, 'The decision has implications for the law of contract, for conveyancing, for banking law and for constitutional law'; G. L. Gretton, 'Sexually Transmitted Debt' 1997 SLT (News) 195, at p 196.

52 1997 SLT 1061.

53 In the Inner House, Ms Smith's action was conjoined with that of the wife of her husband's business partner who had consented to their home being used as security for the business overdraft, the house being owned solely by the husband in their case. That decision is reported as *Mumford and Smith v Bank of Scotland* 1996 SLT 392. Ms Mumford did not appeal against the decision of the Inner House.

54 *Barclays Bank plc v O'Brien* [1994] AC 180. See also *CIBC Mortgages plc v Pitt* [1994] 1 AC 200, a case involving a joint mortgage, which was decided differently, and *Royal Bank of Scotland v Etridge (No 2)* [1998] 4 All ER 705.

55 1996 SLT 392, at p 398G-I.

56 Gretton, n 51 above, at p 195, reports that, as a result of *O'Brien*, banks in England no longer simply advise a spouse to seek independent legal advice, they require separate representation and deal with the spouse through that representative. Of course, the additional cost is not borne by the bank.

is about to lose her home than for a large financial institution. Most banks operate throughout the UK and there may be some merit in uniformity in banking law. However, neither of these reasons outweighs other considerations. Quite apart from sacrificing the principled approach of Scots law to instant expediency, there are the implications for the nature of personal relationships and the role of women within them. Increasingly, marriage is seen as a union of independent individuals. To deny that it often creates a, highly desirable, special relationship between people who will do more for each other than either of them would do for strangers is unrealistic. However, to presume that marriage will result in carte-blanche for undue influence, which will be misused, is to revert to a view that married people are barely individuals at all. While the decision will apply equally to the husbands of entrepreneurial wives, this case suggested what the Inner House saw was 'the assumption by the husband of quasi-fiduciary responsibility over his wife's affairs, such as to deprive her of her own power of decision making':[57] hardly a modern view of the husband-wife relationship. As the Inner House rightly pointed out, what was required was 'detailed consideration of all the issues by the Scottish Law Commission'[58] rather than this hasty extension of English law to Scotland.

Delict[59]

11.23 At common law, spouses could not sue each other in delict. In part, the prohibition was founded on the notion of spouses as one person, but it also derived from the belief that an action in delict would produce no benefit to the couple, particularly in the days when wives were less likely to have any independent income. The absurdity of the prohibition became apparent, not only as spouses were increasingly seen as individuals, but due to the proliferation of motor vehicles. The most common kind of delict to occur between spouses happens when one of them is injured while he or she is a passenger in a car driven by the other. Since the driver will normally be covered by insurance, the insurer, rather than the driver, pays any damages awarded. Thus, in 1962, statute intervened to provide that

> 'Subject to the provisions of this section, each of the parties to a marriage shall have the like right to bring proceedings against the other in respect of a wrongful or negligent act or omission, or for the prevention of a wrongful act, as if they were not married'.[60]

11.24 Thus, spouses acquired the capacity to sue each other in delict. However, this power was subject to the court's power to dismiss the action where 'it appears that no substantial benefit would accrue to either party from the continuation of the action' and, indeed, the court is placed under an obligation to consider such dismissal at an early stage in the proceedings.[61] It should be noted that the power to dismiss is couched in terms of

---

57 1996 SLT 392, at p 398E.
58 Ibid, at p 398I.
59 J.M. Thomson, *Delictual Liability* (Butterworths, 1994), chapter 13.
60 Law Reform (Husband and Wife) Act 1962, s 2(1).
61 1962 Act, s 2(2). The power to dismiss does not apply to the Matrimonial Homes (Family Protection) (Scotland) Act 1981, s 21.

individual benefit. The fact that an award of damages made against one spouse will effectively transfer assets from one spouse to the other, with no overall gain to the family unit, will not justify dismissing the action. This limitation on inter-spousal litigation is anomalous. Aside from the provision of legal aid, where the Legal Aid Board must be satisfied of probable cause, it is usually up to potential litigants to decide whether to raise the action and actions are not dismissed simply because defendants have no assets. Perhaps the most persuasive reason to repeal the dismissal provision is the Scottish Law Commission's finding that it does not appear to have been considered in any case.[62] The Commission recommended that the provision dealing with the court's power to dismiss such actions should be repealed.[63]

11.25 Spouses have no automatic liability for each other's delictual conduct, nor do cohabitants. In either case, the operation of the usual rules on vicarious liability may render one partner liable for the acts or omissions of the other but such liability does not derive from their personal relationship as spouses or cohabitants.[64]

11.26 The special nature of the relationship of married couples has long been recognised in the context of delictual claims arising from the death of a spouse. The current law is found in the Damages (Scotland) Act 1976 ('the 1976 Act'), as amended,[65] and provides that, where a person dies as a result of the delictual act or omission of another person, the bereaved spouse can claim damages in respect of the following: loss of support;[66] distress and anxiety caused by contemplating the deceased's suffering prior to death; grief and sorrow caused by the deceased's death; the loss of the deceased's society and guidance[67]; and funeral expenses.[68] In addition, the surviving spouse may claim for loss of the deceased's services.[69]

11.27 In assessing the quantum of a claim for loss of support, the extent to which the claimant has actually suffered financial loss is relevant. Thus, where a widow has always had a successful career and is self-supporting, she will have less of a claim in respect of loss of support.[70] However, the court is specifically prohibited from taking account of a widow's prospects of remarriage when assessing an award of damages.[71] While this provision ensures that counsel do not engage in a distressing (at least for the widow)

---

62 The Commission searched Lexis for reported and unreported cases in the Court of Session and the sheriff court and found no case in which s 2(2) had been referred to – Report on Family Law (Scot Law Com No 135, 1992), para 10.6.

63 Report on Family Law, paras 10.1–10.8 and rec 54.

64 *McIver* v *Tait* (1925) 41 Sh Ct Rep 21; *Turnbull* v *Frame* 1966 SLT 24.

65 The most significant amendments to the 1976 Act are contained in the Administration of Justice Act 1982 and the Damages (Scotland) Act 1993.

66 Section 1(3).

67 Section 1(4). The provision for an award covering distress and anxiety, grief and sorrow and loss of the deceased's society and guidance was added by the Damages (Scotland) Act 1993 and replaces the older loss of society award.

68 Section 1(3).

69 Administration of Justice Act 1982, s 9, discussed at para 30, below.

70 *Mitchell* v *Gartshore* 1976 SLT (Notes) 41.

71 Law Reform (Miscellaneous Provisions) Act 1971, s 4.

debate of a woman's 'marketability', as Clive points out,[72] it produces anomalies since there is no equivalent provision in respect of widowers, divorced spouses or cohabitants and the fact that the widow is cohabiting need not be ignored.[73] The Scottish Law Commission has recommended that this provision should be re-examined.[74] The fact that a woman married, knowing that her partner was suffering from the terminal condition which resulted in his death, did not preclude her from claiming for loss of support.[75] Claims in respect of emotion are, necessarily, difficult to quantify and awards will depend on the circumstances of each case. Loss of services includes those rendered by a now-deceased homemaker.[76]

11.28 In 1982,[77] the legislation was extended to a cohabitant of the deceased, defined as 'any person, not being the spouse of the deceased, who was immediately before the deceased's death, living with the deceased as husband or wife'. It would be entirely possible for an individual deceased to leave behind both a spouse and a cohabitant and, provided that he or she was living with the cohabitant immediately prior to death, then both of the bereaved survivors could claim damages. The precise wording of this provision makes it clear that only heterosexual cohabitants can benefit from its terms. Other family members may have a claim and the heads under which they can recover depends on their relationship to the deceased. Members of the deceased's immediate family may claim under all the heads of damages available to a spouse or cohabitant,[78] immediate family being defined as including a parent, child or any person accepted by the deceased as a child of his or her family.[79] Other specified relatives, including more remote ascendants and descendants, siblings, nieces and nephews, aunts and uncles and cousins may claim for funeral expenses and loss of support, but not under the other, 'emotional', heads of damages.[80] A somewhat curious provision allows for the possibility of a surviving divorced spouse claiming for loss of support and funeral expenses.[81] Members of the deceased's immediate family and the more remote specified relatives may claim for loss of the deceased's gratuitous services.[82] Reviewing the range of individuals involved and their various claims, it

---

72 At para 13.014.
73 *Morris* v *Drysdale* 1992 SLT 186.
74 Report on the Law Relating to Damages for Injuries Causing Death (Scot Law Com No 31, 1973) para 92.
75 *Phillips* v *Grampian Health Board* 1989 SLT 538; 1992 SLT 659.
76 *Brown* v *Ferguson* 1990 SLT 274.
77 Administration of Justice Act 1982, s 14(4).
78 Damages (Scotland) Act 1976, s 1(3) and (4).
79 Section 10(2) and Sched 1.
80 Section 1(3) and Sched 1.
81 Sched 1, para 1(f). This provision is undoubtedly a relic of the time when a former spouse (most often an ex-wife) might well have been awarded a periodical allowance until her death or remarriage. Thus, she would have suffered financial loss on the death of her former husband. Awards of periodical allowance are not normally made for such extended periods of time now. See chapter 14, para 112.
82 Administration of Justice Act 1982, s 9. Compensation in respect of gratuitous services is discussed at para 11.30 below.

becomes apparent that causing the death of another person may result in very considerable liability.[83]

11.29 In addition to the claim a relative may have under the various heads discussed above for the death of a family member, it is worth remembering that relatives may also be the deceased person's executors, beneficiaries under the deceased's will or beneficiaries under the rules on intestacy. This is relevant here because, where the deceased's death has been caused by the delictual act or omission of a third party, the deceased's claim may transmit to the executor and, thereafter, any damages become part of the deceased's estate and of interest to the beneficiaries. Where the deceased is killed outright, his or her executor cannot raise any claim. However, if the deceased survives the delictual event and dies later as a result of his or her injuries, the deceased's right of action now transmits to his or her executors, who may raise an action for damages or continue any action the deceased had time to raise.[84] The claim could include both patrimonial loss, like the deceased's loss of earning, and *solatium* for the pain and suffering experienced by the deceased.

11.30 Traditionally, the law has drawn a distinction between delictual acts causing death and those causing personal injury. Where injury results, the general rule is that only the victim has any claim[85] and, in the past, the victim could not claim for losses sustained by another person.[86] The Scottish Law Commission examined various aspects of the law in respect of personal injuries and, as a result of its recommendations,[87] the Administration of Justice Act 1982 ('the 1982 Act') was passed. Broadly, the 1982 Act provides for payment of damages, first, for services rendered to the injured person by a partner or relative as a result of the injuries sustained[88] and, second to compensate for services which the injured person can no longer provide to a partner or other relative.[89] Relative, in this context, covers not only immediate family but the more remote distant family members listed above.[90] Turning to the first of these situations, the injured person (the pursuer) can claim for the reasonable remuneration of a relative who provides services the pursuer now requires as a result of his or her injuries and, depending on the nature of the pursuer's injuries, such services might include assistance with bathing and dressing, driving the pursuer, shopping and cooking for the pursuer and cleaning the home. The pursuer then accounts to the relative by paying for the services.[91] Initially, recovery was

---

83 For an example of how the calculations were carried out, see *Wotherspoon* v *Strathclyde Regional Council* 1992 SLT 1090. While this case was decided before the amendments introduced by the 1993 Act it gives the general idea.

84 Damages (Scotland) Act 1976, s 2A, as inserted by s 4 of Damages (Scotland) Act 1993. This applies where the deceased died on or after 16 July 1992.

85 *Robertson* v *Turnbull* 1982 SC (HL) 1; Administration of Justice Act 1982, s 9(4).

86 *Edgar* v *Lord Advocate* 1965 SC 67, where the wife gave up her job to nurse her husband and her loss of earnings were held not to be recoverable.

87 Report on Damages for Personal Injuries (Scot Law Com No 51, 1978).

88 Sections 7 and 8.

89 Section 9.

90 Section 13.

91 Section 8(2).

only permitted for such services up to the date of the action[92] but subsequent amendment to the 1982 Act now allows for services that will be rendered after the action.[93] Claims for services rendered to the injured person are excluded where the relative agrees expressly to provide the services free of charge.[94] The second situation governed by the 1982 Act covers the situation where the injured person has rendered services to a relative free of charge but, as a result of his or her injuries, is no longer able to do so. An obvious example here would be of a homemaker, who is no longer able to provide unpaid child care, make the family meals or clean the home, but the 1982 Act also applies to unpaid home maintenance or assistance which was given by an adult child to an older parent.[95] While the person's contribution to the family was unpaid in the past, the law now recognises that compensation must be provided when that contribution can no longer be made.

PROPERTY

11.31 Under the common law which prevailed until the second half of the 19th century, the system applied to matrimonial property was one of 'community of property',[96] as that term was understood at the time.[97] It was, however, very different to any modern meaning that might be ascribed to that term. Almost all of the wife's moveable property passed to her husband on marriage, under the *jus mariti*, and was his to do with as he wished. Similarly, all property she acquired subsequently became his. The only moveable property the wife retained was that under alimentary provisions in a marriage contract and what was known as her *paraphernalia*, essentially her clothes, jewellery and the receptacles in which they were kept.[98] While the wife retained ownership of her heritable property, the *jus administrationis* gave her husband the right to administer it on her behalf and, of course, any rents or other income derived from the heritage became his as moveable property. Special rules governed what happened to the property in the event of death or divorce and these largely reflected a redistribution of community property. The *jus mariti* and the *jus*

---

92 *Forsyth's Curator Bonis* v *Govan Shipbuilders* 1989 SLT 91.
93 The Law Reform (Miscellaneous Provisions) (Scotland) Act 1990, s 69 added s 8(3) to the 1982 Act. Unlike s 8(2), the pursuer is not obliged to account to the relative for sums recovered under this head.
94 Administration of Justice Act 1982, ss 8(1) and (3).
95 *Ingham* v *John G. Russell (Transport) Limited* 1991 SLT 739.
96 Stair, I, 4, 9.
97 See Clive, paras. 14.001–14.006; G. P. Paton, 'Husband and Wife, Property Rights and Relationships' in *An Introduction to Scottish Legal History* (Stair Society, 1958, vol 20).
98 F. P. Walton, *A Handbook of Husband and Wife According to the Law of Scotland* (3rd edn, W. Green, 1951) at pp 219–221, considers *paraphernalia* in considerable detail. There is also a discussion, at pp 221–222, of 'pin-money', an English legal term which found its way into some Scottish marriage contracts. It denoted an allowance paid by the husband to the wife 'for her pocket-money and to buy dress suitable to the rank and position of the husband' and was the wife's separate property. Presumably this is the source of later use of the term to denote modest earnings by a wife which were not regarded as essential to the household budget. Such distinctions are no longer relevant.

administrationis were abolished in 1881[99] and 1920,[100] respectively, and throughout the latter half of the 19th century, legislation removed most of the vestiges of the old system.[101] The process was completed this century, most notably by the Succession (Scotland) Act 1964[102] and the Family Law (Scotland) Act 1985.

Separate property

11.32 The modern Scots law on matrimonial property, as expressed in the Family Law (Scotland) Act 1985,[103] is essentially a system of separate property. The 1985 Act provides that

> 'marriage shall not of itself affect ... the respective rights of the parties to the marriage in relation to their property'.[104]

Thus, each spouse keeps the property he or she brings into the marriage or acquires subsequently and, broadly, can do with it as he or she pleases. As a general rule, the fact that two people are married to each other is irrelevant so far as their property is concerned. As usually happens with any apparently simple rule, there are both complexities in applying it and exceptions to it; complexities and exceptions which warrant far more explanation than the rule itself.

11.33 The fact that a married couple will usually be living together and running their lives on a co-operative and mutually supportive basis, can create all sorts of complications in the fair resolution of property disputes. An additional problem is caused by the fact that any disputes only come to light when the couple decide to separate or divorce. It is as well to bear in mind that the principles and rules being examined here are concerned with property *while the parties are married to each other*. A whole separate set of principles and rules apply to *financial provision on divorce or separation* and to the right of a spouse to *succeed to a partner's property on death*. These are discussed in chapter 14. During the marriage one spouse may purchase a particular item for himself or herself, as a gift for the other spouse or for their joint use, without thinking about the question of ownership at all. The purchase price may have come from that spouse's own funds, from the other spouse or from a joint bank account to which they each contribute, in equal shares or in different proportions. How the law deals with the ownership of the property may be determined by the

99 Married Women's Property (Scotland) Act 1881, s 1(1).
100 Married Women's Property (Scotland) Act 1920, s 1.
101 The various statutory provisions are discussed in Clive, paras 14.007–14.017.
102 As its title suggests, the Act dealt with succession but it also replaced the old system for financial provision on divorce, whereby an innocent wife got one half or one third of her husband's moveable estate (what she would have got if he had died), with one based on discretionary awards of a periodical allowance or a capital sum or both. These provisions have now been superseded by those in the Family Law (Scotland) Act 1985.
103 The Scottish Law Commission examined a variety of systems which might be adopted – Consultative Memorandum on Matrimonial Property (Scot Law Com Cons Memo No 57, 1983). After consultation and discussion, it recommended the system which forms the basis of the 1985 Act – Report on Matrimonial Property (Scot Law Com No 86, 1984).
104 Section 24(1)(a).

nature of the property, the presence or absence of documentary title or, simply, the evidence available of the intention of the parties. Spouses sometimes find that the ownership of property is not as they thought it would be and, looking at the overall picture of contributions and benefits, it is undoubtedly the case that injustice can result. In this context, injustice stems from at least two distinct sources.

11.34 The first source might be described as the hurly-burly of life and the common failure of people to consider the legal consequences of their actions and to plan accordingly. When a relationship is going well, spouses (and other family members) will do things for each other willingly and cheerfully and it is only when the relationship begins to sour that the property issues assume importance. Typical cases include one spouse buying property and the other contributing towards the purchase price and one spouse using his or her skill and effort to improve the property of the other. How can the contributor get financial recognition of the contributions? One mechanism to consider is that of agency. It might be argued that the purchaser was acting, not only for himself or herself, but also as agent for both spouses. Another possibility is to argue that the property was held in trust by the purchaser on behalf of both spouses. With the removal of some of the problems surrounding proof of trusts,[105] it may be that the Requirements of Writing (Scotland) Act 1995 ('the 1995 Act')[106] has opened the way for the Scottish courts to make greater use of trusts than has been the case in the past. It might be argued that, in order to establish a trust of this kind, no writing is required, thus allowing non-owning spouses and other partners to lead other evidence of the agreement between the parties. On the other hand, since an interest in land[107] will normally be involved, it might be argued that the agreement itself must be in writing. If the latter view is taken, it would still be open to the pursuer to demonstrate that he or she qualified under the provisions on personal bar contained in the 1995 Act and that the agreement should be upheld despite the lack of writing.[108] The position is far from clear and it will be for the courts to provide the definitive answer. What of the concept of constructive trust,

---

105 The Blank Bonds and Trusts Act 1696 which required proof of trust to be by the writ or oath of the alleged trustee proved a formidable obstacle to establishing trusts – see for example, *Newton* v *Newton* 1923 SC 15. There the man took heritage in the name of his fiancée intending that it should be held for him. He failed to establish trust, but did recover sums in respect of improvements made to the property under the principle of recompense. For a discussion of why the 1696 Act need not have been an obstacle in all cases, see K. McK. Norrie, 'Proprietary Rights of Cohabitants' 1995 JR 209. In any event, the 1696 Act was repealed by the Requirements of Writing (Scotland) Act 1995, s 11.

106 For an excellent discussion of the law as it was before the 1995 Act and the likely effects of the Act itself, see R. Rennie and D. J. Cusine, *The Requirements of Writing* (Butterworths, 1995). See also, I. J. S. Talman (ed), *Halliday's Conveyancing Law and Practice in Scotland* (2nd edn, W. Green, 1996), chapter 3.

107 A contract or unilateral obligation for the creation, transfer, variation or extinction of an interest in land must be in a written document and properly subscribed (1995 Act, s 1(2)(a)(i)), as must the creation, variation or extinction of an interest in land (1995 Act, s 1(2)(b)).

108 Where the requirements of writing have not been complied with, the pursuer can still seek to have the obligation upheld by satisfying the requirements of personal bar, as defined in the 1995 Act (s 1(4) and (5)).

employed extensively in other jurisdictions in order to achieve justice between cohabitants?[109] It may be that this concept brings with it at least as many problems as it solves[110] and that Scots law should steer clear of taking on board an alien and problematic solution. Another avenue for recovery is through the concept of unjustified enrichment.[111] Where one spouse contributed to the purchase price of the property, a claim for repetition of the contribution may lie, provided that he or she can show that the owner of the property was enriched, that there was no intention to donate and that there was a mistaken belief on the contributor's part as to ultimate ownership of the property.[112] Similarly, where one spouse has contributed time and effort to improve the other spouse's property, without any intention of donating that effort, a claim of recompense in respect of the owner-spouse's enrichment might be appropriate.[113]

11.35 The second source of injustice attaching to property is more systemic and relates to the position of women in society and typical female roles within the family.[114] As we saw in chapter 1, average female earnings are lower than average male earnings. Homemaking, child-care and the care of older relatives are more often done by women and frequently on an unpaid basis.[115] The result is that women often have less opportunity to acquire property of their own and the separate property rule magnifies this distinction between men and women within marriage. Reviewing the systems of matrimonial property operating in western Europe and the USA in the 1970s, Rheinstein and Glendon[116] sought to establish the extent to which spousal equality was being promoted and the role of the spouse who worked inside the home was being recognised. They found that separate property systems and community property systems had 'partially converged insofar as separate property systems had adopted devices to

---

109 S. Wong, 'Constructive trusts over the family home: lessons to be learned from other Commonwealth jurisdictions' (1998) 18 LS 369.
110 See N. V. Lowe and G. Douglas, *Bromley's Family Law* (9th edn, Butterworths, 1998) at pp 137–163 and S. Cretney and J. Masson, *Principles of Family Law* (6th edn, Sweet and Maxwell, 1997) at pp 126–148.
111 For an excellent and detailed discussion of the concept of enrichment, see N. Whitty, 'Indirect Enrichment in Scots Law' 1994 JR 200 and 239.
112 See *Scanlon v Scanlon* 1990 GWD 12–598, where a cohabitant was able to recover payments she had made towards the purchase of a car, payments made in the erroneous belief that she would become the joint owner.
113 *Newton v Newton*, n 105 above; cf *Rankin v Wither* (1886) 13 R 903.
114 This point has been discussed extensively in the literature. See M. A. Glendon, *The New Family and the New Property* (Butterworths, 1981); C. Smart, *The Ties that Bind: Law, Marriage and the Reproduction of Patriarchal Relations* (1984); S. M. Okin, *Justice, Gender and the Family* (Basic Books, 1989); M. F. Brinig and S. M. Crafton, 'Marriage and Opportunism' 23 J Legal Stud 869 (1994); F. Olsen, 'The Family and the Market: A Study of Ideology and Legal Reform' 97 Harv L Rev 1497 (1983); M. Minow, 'Consider the Consequences' 94 Mich L Rev 900 (1986).
115 Again, the literature on this subject is extensive. See for example, N. Glazer, *Women's Paid and Unpaid Work* (Temple University Press, 1991); P. Armstrong, 'Women's Paid and Unpaid Work' in S. B. Boyd, *Challenging the Public/Private Divide: Feminism, Law and Public Policy* (University of Toronto Press, 1997); K. O'Donovan, *Sexual Divisions and the Law* (Weidenfeld and Nicolson, 1985), chapter 2.
116 M. Rheinstein and M. A. Glendon, 'Interspousal Relations' in A. Chloros (ed), *International Encyclopaedia of Comparative Law* (1980) 31 at p 169.

increase sharing of property between spouses, and community property systems had adopted devices to provide for more independence in management'.[117] In addition, they found a growing divergence between the different systems according to the emphasis placed on the solidarity of the spouses or their independence. 'In some countries, shared ownership and control of property has been seen either as required by one interpretation of the principle of equality, or as desirable in itself. ... In other countries, law reforms have emphasised the independence of the spouses, either because it corresponds to a different notion of equality, or because it was thought to be desirable in itself.' Reviewing the situation from the perspective of the 1980s, Glendon concluded that '[n]either one trend nor the other has clearly prevailed; they are interacting in each system'.

11.36 The Scottish Law Commission was aware of these issues when it reviewed the then current position in Scotland in 1983[118] and recommended reforms a year later.[119] As a result, the Family Law (Scotland) Act 1985 is not blind to the difficulty in accommodating independence and an equitable approach to matrimonial property and, in particular, the needs of homemakers. While it is not suggested that either specific exceptions to the separate property rule, or the provisions which effectively limit the whole idea of spousal property being separate, eradicate the systemic injustice, they do go some way towards alleviating some of its effect.

11.37 The clearest exceptions to the separate property rule are found in the presumptions that household goods[120] and money or property derived from a housekeeping allowance[121] belong to both spouses in equal shares. While ownership is not affected, the special provisions governing who can occupy, and be excluded from, the matrimonial home affect the property rights of the spouses.[122] This different treatment of the matrimonial home can have an impact on the rights of third parties, both generally, and when the spouse-owner is facing sequestration.[123] The power of the court to transfer tenancies[124] and the legislation governing succession to tenancies[125] create situations that are not wholly consistent with the notion of separate property. Insofar as they infringe on an individual's unfettered discretion to deal as he or she wishes with his or her own property, the obligation to aliment a spouse,[126] the provisions governing financial provision on

---

117 M. A. Glendon, *The Transformation of Family Law; State, Law and Family in the United States and Western Europe* (The University of Chicago Press, 1989) at p 117.

118 *Consultative Memorandum on Matrimonial Property* (Scot Law Com Cons Memo No 57, 1983). The Commission explored the whole range of property régimes operating elsewhere and, in the light of these, considered both radical and more modest reform of Scots law. In addition, it commissioned a study of the actual and perceived ownership of family property – A. J. Manners and I. Rauta, Family Property in Scotland (HMSO, 1981).

119 Report on Matrimonial Property (Scot Law Com No 86, 1984).

120 See para 11.39.

121 See para 11.43.

122 See chapter 12, paras 10–12.

123 See chapter 12, paras 40–42.

124 See chapter 12, para 30.

125 See chapter 12, para 30.

126 See para 11.48.

divorce[127] and the law of succession,[128] all present some qualification on the separate property rule.

Moveable property

11.38 Applying the separate property rule, all property bought or acquired by either spouse belongs to that spouse. Where spouses buy property together, they are treated no differently to strangers and they own the property in proportion to their contributions to the price. Of course, the problem with a married couple is that resources may be pooled and individual spouses may buy items without discussing ownership of particular goods. If any dispute only arises after a lapse of time, receipts will have been lost and individual recollections of events may vary. As we saw earlier, there are various mechanisms that one spouse can use to share in property bought by the other. That does not overcome the gender difference that can arise in respect of acquisition of property. In order to alleviate problems over the most common household property special rules provide presumptions about its ownership. It should be remembered that these are simply presumptions and they can be rebutted by evidence.

Household goods

11.39 The Family Law (Scotland) Act 1985 created a presumption that household goods are owned by the spouses in equal shares.[129] The Act provides

> 'If any question arises (whether during or after the marriage) as to the respective rights of ownership of the parties to a marriage in any household goods obtained in prospect of or during the marriage other than by gift or succession from a third party, it shall be presumed, unless the contrary is proved, that each had a right to an equal share in the goods in question.'[130]

As we saw earlier, the provision was amended at the committee stage in the House of Commons to add the qualification relating to goods acquired prior to the marriage or by gift or succession from a third party. Clive points out that the provision, as originally recommended by the Scottish Law Commission, would have been more useful 'because it would have applied to all the household goods as they stood, without there being any need to ask in the first instance when or how they were acquired'.[131] Even without the amendment, proof that particular goods were owned prior to the marriage or had been inherited by one party would usually have been enough to rebut the presumption. None the less, the provision is useful in according with what appears to be most spouses' perception of the ownership of household goods.[132] Goods acquired prior to the marriage can

---

127 See chapter 14, para 24.
128 See chapter 14, paras 185 and 191.
129 Section 25. All of the 1985 Act, except s 25, came into force on 1 September 1986; SI 1986 No 1237. Section 25 came into force on 30 November 1988; SI 1988 No 1887.
130 Section 25(1).
131 At para 14.097.
132 Manners and Rauta (p 6 and Table 2.9), n 118 above, found that, when asked who owned particular items in the home, the majority of respondents thought that items like

come within the ambit of the provision where they were purchased in contemplation of marriage. This will cover the situation where the couple do not live together prior to marriage, but start buying items for the matrimonial home and include the contents of the 'bottom drawer'. Once the couple are married and living together, the fact that a particular item was bought by one of them alone or by both of them, but in unequal shares, will not prevent the item becoming household goods.[133]

11.40   Household goods are defined as

> 'any goods (including decorative or ornamental goods) kept or used at any time during the marriage in any matrimonial home for the joint domestic purposes of the parties to the marriage, other than -
>   (a) money or securities;
>   (b) any motor car, caravan or other road vehicle;
>   (c) any domestic animal'.[134]

In each case, it will be a question of fact whether a particular item qualifies. It should be noted that it is the use to which goods are put that is significant, not the spouse who actually uses them. Thus, the fact that the husband always does the laundry will not prevent the washing machine being household goods. Only gifts from third parties are excluded. Where the husband gives his wife a food processor for her birthday and she uses it for their 'joint domestic purposes' (rather than starting divorce proceedings), this again, may bring it within the ambit of the provision.[135] Conversely, acquisition of a particular item by one spouse for his or her sole use will put that item outside the presumption, provided the pattern of use remains sole use. Thus, where the wife buys herself a set of golf clubs and the husband buys himself an bicycle, in each case to pursue their own hobbies, these items will not be household goods. In the case of a two-lawyer couple, when the wife buys a set of law reports and each of the spouses uses them when working at home, the law reports do not become household goods, since they are being used for a professional, rather than a domestic, purpose.

11.41   Certain goods are expressly excluded. Money and securities are discussed below. At first sight, the exclusion of cars and other motor vehicles may seem curious, since the 'family car' is often bought with pooled resources and is probably the second largest investment (after the home) that most couples make. The justification for the exclusion appears

---

> furniture, the refrigerator, the cooker and the washing machine were owned jointly. 14% of respondents thought that the wife owned the washing machine, while 58% thought the husband owned the power drill. Perhaps the question to ask is whether attitudes have changed since 1981 and, if so, how.

133 Section 25(2).
134 Section 25(3). A special warning for students, rather than practitioners, is appropriate at this point. It should be noted that s 25(3) provides the definition of 'household goods' for the purpose of determining ownership during the marriage. The definition of 'matrimonial property' for the purpose of financial provision on divorce is found in s 10 of the Act and is different. Students will save themselves a great deal of confusion if they take the distinction on board fully from the outset.
135 In such a case, the fact that the food processor was a gift to the wife might be argued to rebut the presumption of shared ownership.

to be twofold. First, a car is one of the few items of corporeal moveable property where there is a registered title, indicating ownership. Third parties dealing with a spouse selling a car are entitled to believe what is on the face of the title and, of course, the title can be taken jointly. Second, according to Manners and Rauta, spouses seemed to perceive the car as belonging to one or other of them. The exclusion of domestic pets may reflect the particular emotion people feel for the animals living with them, although problems of ownership seem particularly likely when one considers the number of domestic pets that are not bought, but rather, acquired, by the animal moving in. Where the animal is 'found a good home' by a previous owner, it will be a question of fact whether it was donated to the couple or one spouse alone. In any event, Nermal the cat will not be regarded as household goods despite the fact that he is used for the joint domestic purpose of mousing.

Savings from housekeeping allowance

11.42 At common law, where the husband gave his wife a housekeeping allowance and, due to her skill as a housekeeper or her using her own money to buy household supplies, she saved some of the money, that money belonged to the husband none the less.[136] In an attempt to alleviate the injustice of such a wife deriving no benefit from her frugality or generosity, statute intervened in 1964 to provide that, where a wife made savings from a housekeeping allowance made to her by her husband, the savings were presumed to be owned by them jointly in the absence of any agreement to the contrary.[137] The provision applied only to wives and househusbands gained no benefit from it.

11.43 The current law, similar to its predecessor, but with the sexist element removed, provides

> 'If any question arises (whether during or after a marriage) as to the right of a party to a marriage to money derived from any allowance made by either party for their joint household expenses or for similar purposes, or to any property acquired out of such money, the money or property shall, in the absence of any agreement between them to the contrary, be treated as belonging to each party in equal shares.'[138]

Straightforward savings from a housekeeping allowance present no problems. They are presumed to be held in equal shares. What is meant by money 'derived from' such an allowance is less clear and, on the basis of what little authority there is, seems to be subject to a somewhat stingy interpretation. In *Pyatt* v *Pyatt*,[139] a wife used savings from housekeeping to provide the stake for her to do the football pools. She won £14,000 and her husband claimed half. In considering whether her winnings were 'derived from' the housekeeping allowance, the court concluded that they had resulted from two

---

136 *Smith* v *Smith* 1933 SC 701; *Preston* v *Preston* 1950 SC 253.
137 Married Women's Property Act 1964, s 1.
138 Family Law (Scotland) Act 1985, s 26.
139 1966 SLT (Notes) 73. For the common law position in England and Wales, see *Hoddinott* v *Hoddinott* [1949] 2 KB 406.

elements, one being the stake and the other being her luck or skill in predicting the outcome of the football matches. Since the stake had been essential to her participation, it concluded that the winnings were derived from the housekeeping allowance and, thus, that Mr Pyatt was entitled to half of the proceeds. Success with football pools is normally regarded as more a matter of luck than of skill and one wonders if the reasoning in *Pyatt* would be applied to cases where the input of talent or skill was greater. Take, for example, the wife who buys canvass and oils and creates a masterpiece or the husband who buys a word processor and paper and writes a best-selling novel. Where the raw materials were purchased from a housekeeping allowance, will the courts really overlook the individual's skill, talent and industry in awarding a half share of the proceeds to the creator's spouse?

11.44 Whether money was 'for their joint household expenses or for similar purposes' may give rise to problems in some cases, particularly where the spouse remits sums of money without making the purpose clear.[140] Where the money is provided for mortgage payments, the authorities give conflicting views on how they are to be regarded.[141] Certainly, money paid by way of aliment or simply handed over as a gift[142] will not come within the ambit of the section.

Wedding presents

11.45 Who owns the wedding presents is determined by the intention of the donor. In the unlikely event that the donor expressed an intention,[143] there is no problem. However, where no intention was expressed, it may be inferred from circumstances like the nature of the gift.[144] Caution should be exercised over attaching too much importance to the place of delivery of the gift.[145] The practical solution suggested in one sheriff court case,[146] that the spouse whose friends or relatives gave the gift should be regarded as the owner, has the merit of simplicity but does not accord with the common

---

140 See for example, *Logan* v *Logan* 1920 SC 537, where the husband sent home the whole unspent balance of his earnings, and *Ireland* v *Ireland* 1954 SLT (Notes) 14, where the husband handed over all of his earnings and received only a modest spending allowance back. In neither of these cases can it be assumed that all of the money paid over was meant for housekeeping expenses. On the other hand, in *Preston* v *Preston*, n 136 above, the money remitted was treated as a housekeeping allowance.

141 *Tymoszczuk* v *Tymoszczuk* (1964) 108 SJ 676; *Johns' Assignment Trusts, Re Niven* v *Niven* [1970] 2 All ER 210.

142 Where for example, one spouse gives money to the other with the words, 'get yourself something for your birthday'.

143 *Traill* v *Traill* 1925 SLT (Sh Ct) 54.

144 In *Duncan* v *Gerrard* (1888) 4 Sh Ct Rep 246, the following statement, much loved by law students, is found – '[w]ere a pair of earrings sent to the intended bridegroom, or a set of law reports sent to the intended bride, I should have no difficulty in holding that the earrings were intended for the bride and the law reports for the bridegroom'. How times have changed.

145 In *Duncan* v *Gerrard* , above, the court concluded that the presents belonged to the wife because they had been delivered to her father's house. Where the couple do not live together, this could probably be regarded as nothing more than a convention or convenience. After all, the gifts have to be delivered somewhere.

146 *McDonald* v *McDonald* 1953 SLT (Sh Ct) 36, where, in the event, the parties reached agreement and decree was granted of consent.

practice of giving the gift to the couple jointly, nor does it deal with the problem where the donor was friendly with both spouses. Clive's view that, in the absence of other evidence, 'it is a fair inference ... that the donors intended the gifts to be given jointly to the two parties'[147] accords with the reality in most cases and, of course, it is always open to one spouse to seek evidence from the donor of a contrary intention. It will be remembered that the exclusion of wedding gifts, which are also household goods, from the presumption of shared ownership resulted from an amendment to the 1985 Act made at committee stage in the House of Commons.[148] Had the Scottish Law Commission's original scheme been left unaltered, the problem over many wedding presents would have been avoided.

Gifts between spouses

11.46 Most married couples give each other presents. These may be to mark special occasions, like birthdays or anniversaries, or for no reason at all, as, for example, when one of the spouses brings home a book or flowers for the other or pays for a meal they have shared. None the less, the presumption against donation applies between spouses,[149] although the nature of their relationship and the affection assumed to go with that, has probably reduced the presumption's strength.[150] Transfer of property requires both intention[151] and delivery. Proof of intention to donate can be inferred from the surrounding evidence and, particularly if the alleged transfer took place at a time like a birthday, will be reasonably simple to establish. However, given that spouses will usually be living together, evidence of delivery may present problems. Many of the older cases here involved disputes with creditors and the question of revocability of gifts between spouses.[152] The rule that donations between husband and wife were revocable has long since been abolished.[153] Gifts between spouses, unlike gifts from third parties, are not excluded from the presumption of equal ownership of household goods. It can be argued that, by giving a household item to a spouse, the donor is putting it beyond his or her ownership and, thus rebutting the presumption of equal shares. On the other hand, if the item is used for joint domestic purposes, then it may fall within the presumption. While it would be fascinating to see how a court would resolve such a dispute, it is likely that, where the disagreement between the spouses had reached that stage, they would be seeking a divorce and property issues would be resolved by applying the rules on financial provision on divorce.

---

147 At para 14.041.
148 At para 14.038, n 85. Section 25(1) excludes gifts from the presumption of shared ownership
149 *Jamieson* v *McLeod* (1880) 7 R 1131; *Smith* v *Smith's Trustees* (1884) 12 R 186.
150 *Ballantyne's Trustees* v *Ballantyne's Trustees* 1941 SC 35.
151 A, possibly apocryphal, story comes to mind here. It was reported that, having lost substantial property in their earlier divorce, the actor, Richard Burton, made clear that various valuable pieces of jewellery which he bought and allowed Elizabeth Taylor to wear during their subsequent marriage, were on loan to her and were not gifts.
152 See Clive, paras 14.042–14.047.
153 Married Women's Property (Scotland) Act 1920, s 5. It is interesting that there was probably never any presumption against donation between parent and child; Stair, I, 8, 2.

Money and bank accounts

11.47 Money and securities are expressly excluded from the definition of household goods[154] and, thus, there is no presumption that they are owned in equal shares by the spouses. The separate property rule applies to them and, where, for example, a husband opens a bank account or buys shares in his own name, *prima facie*, the money or shares belong to him. Where his wife claims that the money was wholly or partly her's and that her husband was acting on her behalf, it is open to her to produce evidence of agency or trust and she will have the benefit of the presumption against donation. Many couples have joint bank accounts and the terms of agreement with the bank will normally entitle each of them to draw on the account. In the absence of any warning or agreement, this is usually sufficient to protect the bank where one spouse empties the joint account without the other's knowledge or permission. As between the spouses, the names in which the account is held will not be conclusive of ownership, since it may have been opened for domestic convenience. The source of deposits in the account will be relevant, as will the intention of one spouse to donate to the other. Where each spouse contributed something to the account, Clive takes the somewhat generous view that the intention to create equal shares would be 'fairly readily inferred' since 'spouses operating such an account will rarely, if ever, intend that it should later be picked meticulously apart to discover the precise share of each'.[155] In addition, it is worth remembering that savings from a housekeeping allowance are presumed to be owned by the spouses in equal shares.[156]

ALIMENT

11.48 At common law, a husband was bound to aliment his wife provided that she was willing to adhere and was not guilty of any matrimonial fault justifying his non adherence, even if she had an independent income and could afford to support herself.[157] Wives did not acquire the obligation to aliment their husbands until 1920 and, even then, the obligation only arose where the husband had insufficient resources of his own.[158] At a time when state support was even more niggardly than it is now, the obligation to provide financial support fell on the wider family and, in addition to the husband's duty to support his wife (and, later, her duty to support him), there were mutual obligations of support owed between parents and children and grandparents and grandchildren.

Current position

11.49 The Family Law (Scotland) Act 1985 swept away the old obligations of aliment and now only those persons listed in the Act are required to provide financial support and, then, within the parameters set out in the

154 Family Law (Scotland) Act 1985, s 25(3)(a).
155 At para 14.069.
156 1985 Act, s 26.
157 *Donnelly* v *Donnelly* 1959 SC 97.
158 Married Women's Property (Scotland) Act 1920, s 4.

statute. We saw earlier that children can expect to be supported by their parents and by persons who have accepted them into the family. For our present purpose, it is the mutual obligation of aliment between spouses that is relevant. No similar obligation of support exists between cohabitants.[159] Each spouse[160] is obliged to provide the other with 'such support as is reasonable in the circumstance'[161] and how that is determined will be considered presently. From 1 September 1986,[162] all alimentary obligations arising by operation of law or from a court decree only continued in effect so far as they were consistent with the Act.[163] However, any arrears due remained payable.[164]

Extent of the obligation

11.50 The crucial question, once a spouse realises that he or she is obliged to aliment his or her partner (or is entitled to receive aliment from that person) is how much? The 1985 Act provides for reasonable support in the circumstances, reasonableness being determined with regard

(a) to the needs and resources of the parties;
(b) to the earning capacities of the parties;
(c) generally to all the circumstances of the case'.[165]

Clearly, each case will turn on its own individual facts. However, some guidance can be gleaned from previous cases, always bearing in mind that, even where they are not inconsistent with the Act itself, some of the older cases may have limited application to very changed social conditions.

11.51 The needs of the parties include those of the payer and payee and would include such elements as food, clothing, accommodation, travel and entertainment. Whether a court should take account of a party's needs in terms of a standard of living that was only acquired after the pursuer started to live with the defender is open to question. Certainly, there is older authority to support the proposition that a wife was entitled to 'be supported decently in the position which she occupies in virtue of her husband's position'.[166] However, particularly where a marriage has been

---

159 Under the Child Support Acts 1991 and 1995, the payment includes an element to cover support for the parent with care of the child – see chapter 6, paras 35–41. Similarly, where a court awards aliment for a child it may include reasonable provision for expenses incurred by the person who has care of the child – 1985 Act, s 4(4). The cohabitation rules for social security purposes assume support from a cohabitant – see para 11.66.

160 1985 Act, s 1(1)(a) and (b). Spouses include the parties to a polygamous marriage – s 1(5).

161 1985 Act, s 1(2).

162 All of the 1985 Act, except s 25, came into force on that date; SI 1986 No 1237. Section 25 came into force on 30 November 1988; SI 1988 No 1887.

163 1985 Act, s 1(3).

164 1985 Act, s 1(4).

165 1985 Act, s 4(1).

166 Walton, above at p 151. The passage quoted continues, 'It would not be right that she should be reduced to a bare pittance, while her husband is living in affluence'. While such a rationale might hold good today, subject to the removal of gender bias, it could be argued that wives no longer have any derivative status on which to found.

relatively short, it is submitted that a court would be reluctant to award a generous amount of aliment on the basis of a recently acquired standard of living alone. As we shall see, when the court comes to consider all the circumstances of the case, it may take account of the fact that the defender is supporting another person in his or her household, whether or not the defender is obliged to aliment that person.[167]

11.52 The resources of each party include earned income and income from capital.[168] State benefits which are not means-tested form part of a person's resources but benefits, like income support which are means-tested do not, since the latter will not be paid if the aliment awarded takes the claimant's income over the prescribed level. Both actual and foreseeable resources are relevant. Actual resources would include the case where a person is receiving an allowance as a result of another person's generosity, even where the payer is not obliged to make the payment. Take, for example, the case of an employed woman who leaves her unemployed husband and goes to live with another man. The cohabitant has no obligation to support her but he makes a good living and contributes generously to their joint household. When the husband claims aliment from his wife, the fact that the cohabitant was contributing to the household would be relevant in assessing resources available to the wife. However, the cohabitant's income itself would not form part of the calculation since to include it would indirectly impose on him an obligation to aliment his cohabitant's husband.[169] Where a person receives benefits in kind, like free meals at work or a company car, these benefits are relevant as part of his or her overall resources but, since they are not available to meet a claim for aliment, they should not be assessed simply on their cash value.[170] Before foreseeable resources will be taken into account, it must be clear that they will materialise. Thus, payments under an insurance claim or for likely redundancy are relevant. In cases of doubt, it will always be open to the person seeking an award of aliment to return to the court later to seek a variation on the basis of a change of circumstances. As we shall see, in addition to its usual powers, the court may order either party to provide details of his or her resources or those relating to an incapax on whose behalf he or she is acting.[171]

11.53 The court is directed to take account not only of an individual's actual earnings but his or her earning capacity.[172] Thus, where a spouse voluntarily gives up a well-paid job in order to avoid paying aliment, the court can take account of what he or she might have been earning. Of course, the court should make this assessment with an eye to reality. The fact that a person is an experienced miner does not create an earning capacity if all the mines in the area have closed down and there is no employment in the field.

167 1985 Act, s 4(3)(a), discussed at para 54, below.
168 *Alexander v Alexander* 1957 SLT 298.
169 *Munro v Munro* 1986 SLT 72.
170 *Semple v Semple* (Sh Ct) 1995 SCLR (Notes) 569.
171 1985 Act, s 20.
172 1985 Act, s 4(1)(b).

11.54 In the attempt to provide a system for assessing aliment which is sufficiently flexible, the court is directed to have regard to all the circumstances of the case.[173] While this means exactly what it says, the 1985 Act provides further guidance on other relevant circumstances. First, the court may take account of the fact that the defender is supporting another person in his or her household, whether or not the defender is obliged to aliment that person.[174] Take, for example, a married man who leaves his wife and children and goes to live with a woman and her two children. He is not obliged to support his cohabitant and it is unlikely that he has accepted her children into his household such that he has acquired any obligation to aliment them. None the less, he contributes a large part of his earnings towards the family budget in his new household. In assessing the claim by his wife and children for aliment, the court will take account of his contributions in the new household. It might be asked why his first family should suffer financially because he has chosen to become part of and support a new family and, indeed, the question is asked by many first families. The answer lies in accepting reality. Few individuals earn enough money to support two families. In short, the pie is not big enough to go round. Which family, then, should the breadwinner support, the one with whom he or she is living or the one with whom there is less contact? As a practical matter it may be easier to provide for support to apply where the person is living. In addition, there is the argument that the second relationship will have a better chance of lasting if it is not faced with poverty while watching much of the household income being sent to support another family. Of course, such arguments do not find much sympathy with the first families who may be forced to seek state support. Essentially, what the law tries to do here is to make the best of a bad situation and, arguably, it does a reasonable job in the circumstances. It should be noted that it is only support given in the defender's household that is specifically mentioned. Where, for example, a woman makes payments to help out her elderly mother who does not live with her, the payment is not covered by this subsection. However, it is a relevant circumstance which the court may consider.

11.55 When considering other relevant circumstances for an award of aliment, the court is directed that it, 'shall not take account of any conduct of a party unless it would be manifestly inequitable to leave it out of account'.[175] As we shall see, at least in theory, fault has played a diminishing role in divorce and financial provision on divorce. While aliment is a concept that only applies between spouses while they are married to each other (periodical allowance being the post-divorce payment), questions of aliment often arise in the period immediately prior to divorce, when the parties are considering the possibility and may be marshalling their own versions of which of them 'is to blame'. It would be inconsistent with the general approach to matrimonial problems if fault was to play a large part in decisions on aliment. On the other hand, there may be circumstances

173 1985 Act, s 4(1)(c).
174 1985 Act, s 4(3)(a).
175 1985 Act, s 4(3)(b).

where one party's conduct has had a very significant effect on the resources available. Thus, for example, where one spouse has given property away or arranged for his or her earnings to be paid to a limited company, in order to minimise his or her spouse's claim for aliment, this conduct is relevant and will be taken into account.[176] Similarly, where one spouse has dissipated resources by excessive gambling or adopting an extravagant lifestyle, such conduct is relevant. Whether conduct which has no impact on resources is ever relevant is open to question. It is submitted that, in general, it is not. While the fact that one spouse has been violent towards the other or has committed adultery is relevant in the context of divorce, it is not relevant in the context of aliment. None the less, one can understand the decision of an English court which felt it could not ignore the fact that the wife had encouraged her husband's attempted suicide.[177]

No order of liability

11.56 As we saw when considering aliment for children, a number of people may have an obligation to aliment a particular child. Where this happens, there is no automatic pecking order of liability and the court is required to look at all of the obligations.[178] Examples of multiple alimentary obligations being owed to a spouse are very much more unusual but, where this happens, the court is again required to have regard to all of them. Take, for example, a 22-year-old married student. His wife is employed and owes an obligation of aliment to him but so too may his parents.[179] Assuming that his parents divorced while he was a child and his step-mother accepted him as a child of her family, she too may owe him an obligation of aliment. Thus, were he to raise an action for aliment against any one of them, the obligations of the others would be relevant, as of course would the needs, resources and earning capacity of the student himself.

DEFENCES TO A CLAIM FOR ALIMENT

11.57 There are two defences to a claim for aliment. Claims for aliment are competent even where the parties are living in the same household.[180] The first defence is that the parties are doing just that and the defender is fulfilling the obligation to aliment and intends to continue doing so.[181] This defence will come down to proof of facts and any real dispute is likely to be over the adequacy of any payments being made. The second defence to a claim of aliment arises in the more common situation where the spouses

---

176 Where one spouse attempted to mislead the court about his assets, his conduct was held to be such that it would be inequitable to leave it out of account – *Walker v Walker* 1991 SLT 649.
177 *Kyte v Kyte* [1987] 3 WLR 1114.
178 1985 Act, s 4(2).
179 Under s 1(1)(c) and (5) of the 1985 Act the parental obligation can continue until a child reaches the age of 25 where he or she is 'reasonably and appropriately undergoing instruction at an educational establishment'.
180 1985 Act, s 2(6).
181 1985 Act, s 2(7).

are no longer living together. Here the defender may make an offer to receive the claimant into his or her own household and aliment the person there.[182] Obviously such an offer will often be unattractive to a claimant, particularly if there has been violence or acrimony in the past. For this reason, the 1985 Act provides that such an offer only constitutes a good defence where it would be reasonable to expect the claimant to accept the offer to be housed in the defender's household and, in particular, the court is directed to have regard to 'any conduct, decree or other circumstances'.[183] Thus, where there is an interdict ordering the defender not to molest the pursuer, a claim for aliment could not be met by an offer from the defender to support the pursuer in the defender's household. The fact that the parties have agreed to live apart is not of itself conclusive that it is unreasonable to expect the pursuer to accept the offer.[184] None the less, where the parties believe that this is the best solution for them, the court might conclude quite reasonably that the defender's change of mind is designed solely to avoid paying aliment.

Raising an action

11.58   An action for aliment can be raised in the Court of Session or the sheriff court.[185] It can be raised alone or along with other proceedings, including actions for separation, divorce, declarator of marriage or declarator of nullity of marriage.[186] In granting decree for aliment, the court may

> (a) order the making of periodical payments, whether for a definite or indefinite period or until the happening of a specified event;
> (b) order the making of alimentary payments of an occasional or special nature;
> (c) backdate an award of aliment
>   (i) to the date of the bringing of the action or to such later date as the court thinks fit, or
>   (ii) on special cause shown, to a date prior to the beginning of the action;
> (d) award less than the amount claimed even if the claim is undisputed.[187]

11.59   The essence of an award of aliment is the continuing duty of support between spouses and, thus, the payments envisaged are ongoing in nature. While there is provision for occasional, special payments, it is not intended that a lump sum should be substituted for periodical payments. The costs of raising an action for aliment are not 'necessaries' for which the other spouse is liable.[188] Often where there has been an award of aliment, the couple will divorce later. As we shall see, at that time, the desire to provide for a 'clean break' means that different principles apply to financial provision on divorce.

---

182 1985 Act, s 2(8).
183 1985 Act, s 2(8) and (9).
184 1985 Act, s 2(9).
185 1985 Act, s 2(1).
186 1985 Act, s 2(2).
187 1985 Act, s 3(1).
188 1985 Act, s 22.

11.60 Pending a decision on aliment[189] the court has the power to award interim aliment and, whether any claim for aliment is disputed or not, the court may award a lesser sum by way of interim aliment than that sought or it can make no award at all.[190] The guidelines for assessing aliment apply to claims for interim aliment.[191] Since aliment is an obligation owed by one spouse to the other, it is surprising to find that a party can seek interim aliment in an action for nullity of marriage where he or she is denying the existence of the marriage.[192] While the court can vary or recall an award of interim aliment, the variation or recall can only have prospective effect.[193] However, in order for an award of interim aliment to be varied or recalled, it is not imperative to show a change of circumstances.[194]

Variation and recall of an award

11.61 Once an award of aliment has been made either party can go back to the court seeking to have the order varied or recalled provided that 'since the date of the decree there has been a material change of circumstances'.[195] Often the change will relate to the income of one or both parties. Thus, where the spouse who is receiving aliment gets a substantial increase in salary or moves in with a wealthy partner, the paying spouse might apply for the award to be reduced or terminated. Where the paying spouse is made redundant, he or she might make a similar application. Curiously, where the award has been made on the basis of an error, there is no change of circumstances and, thus, no ground for variation.[196] The 1985 Act was amended to provide that the making of a maintenance assessment with respect to a child for whom an award of aliment had been made was a material change of circumstance.[197] However, the Act is silent on the effect of a maintenance assessment on other awards of aliment. Since the assessment will usually involve an individual in making fresh payments, it is submitted that it will normally be a material change of circumstances. In varying or recalling an award of aliment, the court may backdate its order and order any sums paid under the original decree to be repaid.[198]

Enforcement of a decree for aliment

11.62 For some pursuers getting the court decree for aliment is just the first step. Actually collecting the money can prove to be more difficult. The

---

189 1985 Act, s 6(1).
190 1985 Act, s 6(2).
191 *McGeachie v McGeachie* 1989 SCLR 99.
192 1985 Act, s 17(2). It has also been held that an action for interim aliment was competent after the decree of divorce had been granted but while the claim for financial provision was still pending – *Neill v Neill* 1987 SLT (Sh Ct) 143.
193 *McColl v McColl* 1993 SLT 617.
194 1985 Act, s 6(4). See *Bisset v Bisset* (Sh Ct) 1993 SCLR 284.
195 1985 Act, s 5(1).
196 *Walker v Walker* 1995 SLT 375. Prior to the 1985 Act, such a variation was competent – *Dickinson v Dickinson* 1952 SC 27.
197 1985 Act, s 5(1A), inserted by SI 1993 No 660, with effect from 5 April 1993.
198 1985 Act, s 5(4).

ability to enforce a decree for aliment depends on the defender having resources and, to some extent, on where the defender and the resources are located. If the defender is in Scotland, arrears of aliment are recoverable as an ordinary debt.[199] In addition, if the debtor fails to pay under the decree, a current maintenance arrestment can be obtained which requires the debtor's employer to deduct a sum of money from the debtor's wages or salary and pay it to the creditor.[200] Civil imprisonment remains possible where a person fails to pay in accordance with a decree for aliment and the threat of pursuing such a course of action may prove effective, at least in respect of debtors who are in a position to pay but are showing a reluctance to do so.[201] Before civil imprisonment can be effected, it is necessary to apply to a sheriff for a warrant to commit to prison and these proceedings are the creditor's responsibility, a factor which may explain why the remedy is not used more often. While imprisonment does not wipe out the alimentary debt and new warrants for imprisonment can be sought every six months, the fact that a person's ability to earn a living while in prison is clearly diminished, may be further explanation for creditors' reluctance to pursue this option. In addition, and as a practical solution, the creditor is often better off seeking income support and leaving the Secretary of State to pursue the errant spouse.[202]

11.63 Where the debtor-spouse is in England, Wales or Northern Ireland, the Maintenance Orders Act 1950 improved the procedure for recovery of aliment awarded in Scotland greatly and the statute has undergone various amendments which have refined the procedure further.[203] Essentially, the Scottish decree is registered in the appropriate High Court or magistrates court and can then be enforced. Similarly, where the decree has been granted in England, Wales or Northern Ireland, its enforcement in Scotland can be effected through registration. Further afield, the procedure for enforcement of a Scottish decree and the prospect of success depend on the country involved. At least in theory, the Maintenance Orders (Reciprocal Enforcement) Act 1972 provides the framework to enable the enforcement of decrees for aliment on a worldwide basis. Where the system works, it means that Scottish decrees can be enforced abroad and foreign decrees can be enforced here. Essentially, the Act classifies countries as being in one of three categories;[204] reciprocating countries,[205] convention coun-

---

199 Debtors (Scotland) Act 1987, ss 46(1) and 73(1).
200 1987 Act, ss 51–57. Four weeks must have elapsed since the decree was intimated to the debtor.
201 Civil Imprisonment (Scotland) Act 1882, s 4.
202 Social Security Administration Act 1992, s 106.
203 The 1950 Act has been amended by various subsequent statutes including, the Maintenance Orders Act 1958, the Administration of Justice Act 1977, the Civil Jurisdiction and Judgments Act 1982, and the Maintenance Enforcement Act 1991. For a detailed discussion of the enforcement procedure, see Clive, paras 12.071–12.086.
204 A fourth category would be countries where we have no arrangements in place and, in such cases, the only option for enforcement would be through the courts in that country, assuming that domestic law provided for such enforcement.
205 These are largely Commonwealth countries.

tries[206] and those which are neither, but with which the UK has an arrangement.[207]

Termination of aliment

11.64 The obligation to aliment a spouse ends when the marriage terminates, either by divorce or on the death of one of the spouses. A widow, but not a widower, has a right to temporary aliment from the estate of the deceased partner,[208] a right the Scottish Law Commission has recommended should be abolished.[209] In addition, when it makes an award of aliment the court may provide that periodic payments are payable for a definite or indefinite period or until a specified event happens.[210]

STATE BENEFITS[211]

11.65 When we turn to the payment of state benefits, it becomes apparent that this aspect of public law shows a greater capacity to understand the diversity of adult relationships than it does in the context of private law. The modern successor to the Poor Law, the Social Security Administration Act 1992 provides that spouses are liable to maintain each other and parents are liable to maintain their children[212] and the responsible person becomes a 'liable relative'. Where income support is paid to or in respect of a person, the Secretary of State is empowered to recover the cost from the liable relative.[213] In addition, where income support is being paid to one parent of a child, the Secretary of State can recover this from the other parent,[214] regardless of the fact that these adults are not and possibly never have been, married to each other. The effect is that one adult can be responsible for maintaining another through the mechanisms of public law when that is not the case through private law. As we saw, there are similar provisions in the Child Support Act 1991.

11.66 The state's willingness to look more broadly at relationships than does private law applies too in the context of entitlement to non-contributory income-related benefits. The relevant benefits are income support, family credit, housing benefit and the job-seekers allowance and their aim is to assist people in various circumstances whose income falls below specified minimum levels. For these benefits, the family is seen as a unit, with resources being aggregated and heterosexual cohabiting couples are treated in the same way as married couples. Of course, taking the

---

206 Countries which have acceded to the United Nations Convention on the Recovery Abroad of Maintenance. The current list can be found in Clive at para 12.090, n 35.
207 The procedure for enforcement in each case is discussed extensively by Clive at paras 12.087–12.175.
208 Stair, I, 4, 22. For a discussion of this right, see Clive, paras 30.010–30.017.
209 Report on Succession (Scot Law Com No 124, 1990), para 9.10, rec 56 and draft Succession (Scotland) Bill, clause 27.
210 1985 Act, s 3(1).
211 State benefits encompass a vast field and they will be discussed in outline only here.
212 1992 Act, s 78(6).
213 1992 Act, s 106.
214 1992 Act, s 107.

overall household income into account is more often likely to disentitle families from benefit than to open the way to its payment. When we turn to contributory benefits, including incapacity benefit, widow's benefit and retirement pensions, marriage, as opposed to cohabitation, emerges as significant in entitling a person to benefit. Thus, a woman can claim a variety of benefits on the basis of her husband's national insurance contributions while a female cohabitant cannot.[215] Men gain little from a wife's contributions, although there is provision for a man relying on these to increase his entitlement to a retirement pension. Cohabiting men gain no such advantage. A widow loses her entitlement to widow's benefits on remarriage or where she cohabits with a man.

11.67 Thus, the effect of the state's capacity to grasp diversity in relationships is somewhat inconsistent. In respect of non-contributory benefits, it usually results in responsibility for an individual's financial support being placed on another individual rather than the state or to reduce entitlement to benefit. Marriage opens the door for women, and to a lesser extent, men, to gain access to certain benefits although often cohabitation will terminate them. Depending on the benefit involved, people in same-sex relationships may, for once, be winners in the legal system. Neither the rules on liable relatives nor those on aggregation of income apply to them and, in this sense, their entitlement to non-contributory benefits is less limited. However, they gain no entitlement to contributory benefits.

TAXATION

11.68 While spouses have increasingly come to be treated as individuals for tax purposes,[216] marriage brings with it a number of benefits including the married couple's allowance, the treatment of savings for tax purposes and inheritance tax.

JUDICIAL PROCEEDINGS

Criminal cases

11.69 While prosecution in criminal cases is normally the province of the Crown Office, private prosecution remains possible in Scotland. There would seem to be no authority that would prevent one spouse from instituting proceedings against the other. Private prosecution requires either the concurrence of the Lord Advocate or the permission of the High Court and it is unlikely that either would consider the fact of marriage to present a bar to prosecution.

---

215 The benefits include the widow's payment, widowed mother's allowance, widow's pension and category B retirement pension – Social Security Contributions and Benefits Act 1992. It should be noted that the older system of national insurance contributions, whereby a married woman could opt out of paying contributions and rely instead on those of her husband, was abolished, subject to transitional provisions by the Social Security Pensions Act 1975.

216 Initially, a married woman's income was treated as that of her husband for tax purposes, as were capital gains accruing to her. The system was changed with effect from 1990–91, subject to transitional provisions – Finance Act 1988.

11.70 The idea of spouses giving evidence against each other in the context of criminal cases provides copious material for theoretical debate and for movie-makers. Whether one spouse may give evidence against the other (competency), as opposed to whether such a spouse can be called by the prosecution or a co-accused to give evidence when the former does not want to (compellability),[217] may raise different issues. However, in either case, the questions go to the heart of the marital relationship and the nature of marriage. At common law, one spouse was not a compellable witness against the other unless the witness-spouse was the alleged victim of the crime or had been injured by it.[218]

11.71 The current position is that a spouse is a competent witness in all cases;[219] that is, he or she may give evidence. However, a spouse cannot be compelled by a co-accused or by the prosecution to give evidence, unless that spouse was the victim of the alleged crime or was injured by it.[220] Nor can a spouse be compelled to disclose any communication made between the spouses during marriage.[221] It should be noted that the privacy attaching to inter-spousal communications belongs to the witness and not the accused. Thus, while the accused can compel his or her spouse to give evidence, the spouse-witness cannot be compelled to give evidence of inter-spousal communication.[222] Neither the prosecution nor the defence may comment upon a spouse's failure to give evidence.[223] The protection given to a husband or wife who does not want to give evidence against a spouse stems from marriage and, consequently, a person who is a spouse by the time of the trial cannot be compelled to give evidence even if he or she was not married to the accused at the time of the relevant alleged incidents.[224] However, ante-nuptial communications will not be protected.[225] It is doubtful that any protection is offered to a former spouse once the marriage has ended, although the position on confidential communications is less clear.[226] Cohabitants are both competent and compellable witnesses against each other.

11.72 Should spouses be protected from having to give evidence against each other? Clive examines three possible justifications for such protection and finds 'none of them very satisfactory'.[227] The first is that spouses ought

---

217 To talk of a 'compellable witness' is somewhat misleading. A person can be made to appear before the court, if necessary, by the use of warrants and physical compulsion. However, once there a person cannot be made to give any evidence at all. The legal system can attempt to secure co-operation by, for example, the threat of imprisonment, but it cannot make an individual utter one word.

218 *Harper v Adair* 1945 JC 21.

219 Criminal Procedure (Scotland) Act 1995, s 264(1).

220 1995 Act, s 264(2)(a).

221 1995 Act, s 264(2)(b).

222 1995 Act, s 264(2)(b).

223 1995 Act, s 264(3).

224 Thus, the Hollywood scenario where the gangster marries his moll just before the trial, in order to prevent her being called as a witness, has some validity.

225 These are not communications 'made between the spouses during marriage'.

226 For different views, see Clive, para 18.013 and A. G. Walker and N. Walker, *The Law of Evidence in Scotland* (T&T Clark, 1984) at p 380.

227 At para 18.014.

to be able to confide in one another and know that the communication will be protected. He dismisses this justification on the ground that the logical result here would be to give the privilege to the accused and not, as the law does, to the potential witness.[228] The second justification is that there is something repulsive about using inter-spousal communication. If this were so, he argues, then all evidence of such communications would be barred. The third argument is based on an aversion to using confidential communications. As Clive rightly points out, why, then, do we not protect other such communications like those between cohabitants? Perhaps a fourth justification, based on pragmatism rather than principle, can be put forward for inter-spousal privilege. There is great practical value in not forcing individuals into a situation where they will feel a strong urge to lie. The legal system should not send out invitations to commit perjury. Were spouses compellable witnesses, some would be driven, by affection, loyalty or, perhaps, fear, to lie. Of course, this line of argument provides equal justification for offering similar immunity to cohabitants, to parents and children, to siblings, to very close friends and, in the case of fear, to the vulnerable or easily intimidated. Going far enough down that road might leave the officious bystander as the only compellable witness and, of course, he or she is unlikely to need compulsion.

Civil cases

11.73   At common law, the notion that husband and wife became one upon marriage[229] severely restricted the possibility of inter-spousal litigation. While it was not true that all such litigation was barred,[230] it seems to have been restricted to consistorial and quasi-consistorial actions. Thus while actions relating to marriage contracts, aliment, separation and divorce were competent, spouses could not sue each other in contract or delict. The Married Women's Property (Scotland) Act 1920 provided that a married woman would be capable of suing as if she were not married.[231] Initially, the courts took the view that this had not lifted the bar on inter-

---

228   In addition, Clive questions how many people know about the law on this point. The answer there is probably a small proportion of the general population but a large number of seasoned criminals.

229   See for example, *Young v Young* (1903) 5 F 330, where a husband raised an action for defamation against his wife some 18 months after she allegedly said he induced her to take arsenic. Dismissing the action, the court approved *dicta* in *Phillips v Barnett* [1876] 1 QB 436, to the effect that the husband and wife were regarded as one in law. However, it is clear from the following statement from Lord President Kinross (at p 330) that the Scottish court found a certain pragmatic value in limiting inter-spousal litigation: 'One can see that if such an action were allowed it would not contribute to domestic peace, but open the door to claims which had much better be left to sleep. If every domestic squabble were followed by an action for defamation there would be a large addition to the business of the Court'.

230   The statement in *Hamilton v Her Husband* (1625) Mor 6048, that 'no action would be sustained betwixt husband and wife while the marriage stands', was overstating the position.

231   1920 Act, s 3(1).

spousal litigation in delict[232] but later allowed actions in contract.[233] It was not until 1962 that actions in delict between spouses became competent and, even then, they were subject to the court's discretion to dismiss the action where 'it appears that no substantial benefit would accrue to either party'.[234] As we saw earlier, the Scottish Law Commission has recommended the abolition of this, apparently never used, discretion.[235] Thus, with the exception of the court's power of dismissal, it appears that marriage no longer has any effect on the spouses' capacity to litigate against each other. Cohabitants have always been free to litigate against each other without restriction.

11.74 The general common law position was that spouses were not competent witnesses against each other. In 1853 statute intervened, although the provision is not free of ambiguity.[236] The position is most probably that spouses are both competent and compellable witnesses against each other in civil proceedings subject to an exemption in respect of confidential communications. Where one spouse has communicated information to another during the marriage, the recipient cannot be compelled to disclose that confidential communication. Whether the spouse may make such a disclosure if he or she wishes is not completely clear but, in practice, such disclosure has been permitted. While it is competent for a spouse to give evidence relating to whether sexual intercourse took place between them, statute protects them from being compelled to do so.[237] Former spouses do not appear to be protected from giving evidence against each other, nor are cohabitants.

CRIMINAL LAW

11.75 As we have seen, marriage, but not cohabitation, is relevant to the criminal law since spouses are not normally compellable witnesses against each other. However, the criminal law treats spouses in other contexts as if they were strangers. Thus, spouses can steal from one another[238] and a husband can rape his wife.[239] Perhaps the most common offence to occur within the domestic setting, whether married or cohabiting, is that of assault. While the assault itself is a crime like any other assault, the special protection offered by the Matrimonial Homes (Family Protection) (Scotland) Act 1981 is recognition of the special position of partners. Thus, while the general rule is that marriage has little effect on the criminal law, certain offences require special mention in the context of marriage and, in some cases, cohabitation.

---

232 *Harper* v *Harper* 1929 SC 220, where the court rehearsed all the arguments against allowing spouses to sue each other, including, the special relationship between spouses and the family disharmony that could be caused by permitting litigation.
233 *Horsburgh* v *Horsburgh* 1949 SC 227.
234 Law Reform (Husband and Wife) Act 1962, s 2(2).
235 Report on Family Law, paras 10.1–10.8 and rec 54. See para 11.24 above.
236 Evidence (Scotland) Act 1853, s 3. See Clive, paras 18.015–18.017.
237 Law Reform (Miscellaneous Provisions) Act 1949, s 7(2).
238 *Harper* v *Adair* 1945 JC 21.
239 *S* v *HM Advocate* 1989 SLT 469.

Bigamy

11.76 Bigamy is an obvious case in point. It is an offence for a married person to go through a second ceremony of marriage while his or her first marriage is still in existence. Where the first marriage was void, there is no offence, since there is no valid pre-existing marriage. There is some debate surrounding the status of a voidable marriage as a defence to a charge of bigamy and this turns on whether the marriage had been avoided by the time of the trial.[240] It is a defence to a charge of bigamy that the accused acted in good faith and had reasonable grounds to believe his or her spouse was dead[241] or that the previous marriage had been dissolved by divorce. As a recent case illustrates, for the defence to apply, the accused must be acting on a reasonable belief that the previous marriage has been dissolved rather than simply failing to find out the true position.[242] Where a married person simply cohabits with someone other than his or her spouse, no offence is committed and, of course, cohabitation presents no obstacles to subsequent marriage to a new partner.

Sexual offences

11.77 At common law, marriage increased considerably the circle of people with whom sexual intercourse amounted to incest. Incest is now governed by the Criminal Law (Consolidation) (Scotland) Act 1995 ('the 1995 Act') and, as we shall see, the range of prohibited sexual relationships has been narrowed in respect of adults, although both marriage and cohabitation are relevant when sexual relations with a partner's offspring enter the picture. The 1995 Act provides for three distinct offences: incest, intercourse with a step-child and intercourse in breach of trust.

11.78 Intercourse with certain blood relatives constitutes incest and the specified relatives are ascendants, descendants, aunts or uncles, and nieces or nephews.[243] This applies whether the relationship is through the half- or full-blood[244] and regardless of the marital status creating the relationship.[245] In addition, sexual intercourse with an adoptive parent or former adoptive parent, or an adopted child or former adopted child, is defined as incest.[246]

---

240 See Clive, para 18.023.

241 *Macdonald* (1842) 1 Broun 238.

242 Mr McMahon, a divorcee, married his second wife in England. They separated and he came to Scotland where he went through his third marriage ceremony, using the decree from his first divorce to satisfy the district registrar that he was free to marry. He argued that he thought his second wife had divorced him although he does not appear to have made any special effort to inquire about the alleged divorce. In fact, she had not divorced him and he was convicted of bigamy in Paisley Sheriff Court. The fact that the court did not regard the matter as particularly heinous is reflected by the sentence. Mr McMahon was fined £1,000. While the case illustrates a failure to make enquiries, Mr McMahon's use of his first divorce decree to enable him to go through the third ceremony raises questions about his good faith. See *The Scotsman*, 15 November, 1997, p 8.

243 1995 Act, s 1(1). So far as men are concerned, the list of relatives with whom intercourse constitutes incest is: mother, daughter, grandmother, grand-daughter, sister, aunt, niece, great grandmother and great granddaughter. For women, there is a parallel list.

244 Section 2(a).

245 Section 2(b).

246 Section 1(1). See n 243 above.

Sexual intercourse with relatives not specified in the 1995 Act is not incest.[247] Thus, it is not incest for a woman to have sexual intercourse with her great great grandfather. Nor is it incest for two children, adopted into the same family, but otherwise unrelated, to have sexual relations. This is not surprising, since the adoptive siblings could marry. On the other hand, while a man may not marry his former mother-in-law while either his ex-wife or his former father-in-law is alive, sexual intercourse with his mother-in-law is not incest.[248] It is a defence to a charge of incest for the accused to prove that he or she did not know and had no reason to suspect that he or she was related to the other person in the degree specified;[249] did not consent to sexual intercourse;[250] or was married to the other person at the time sexual intercourse took place by a marriage entered into outside Scotland and recognised as valid under Scots law.[251]

11.79 The law has long recognised that, while there is no blood-tie, the relationship between a step-parent and step-child may be such that the child is open to the possibility of exploitation. However, given the fluidity of family relationships, it may be that the individuals concerned have never lived together nor has any bond, along the lines of the child-parent relationship, ever been created. Thus, the 1995 Act provides that it is an offence for a step-parent or former step-parent to have sexual intercourse with a step-child or former step-child, but only in certain circumstances.[252] These are, first, that the step-child is under the age of 21[253] or, second, that prior to the age of 18, the step-child has lived in the same household as the step-parent and been treated as a child of the step-parent's family. It is a defence for the accused to prove that he or she did not know and had no reason to believe that the person with whom sexual intercourse took place was a step-child or former step-child;[254] believed on reasonable grounds that the other person was over the age of 21;[255] did not consent to sexual

---

247 Section 1(3).
248 The Scottish Law Commission recommended that the bar to such marriages should be removed – Report on Family Law, rec 46, discussed at chapter 10, para 30.
249 Section 1(1)(a).
250 Section 1(1)(b). Thus, a rape victim would not be guilty of incest where the rapist was a relative within the prohibited category.
251 Section 1(1)(c). The fact that the marriage must be recognised under Scots law is an important qualification. Where a domiciled Scotswoman married her uncle abroad, the marriage itself would be invalid and the defence would not apply. On the other hand, were such a couple domiciled in Israel, where such marriages are permitted, the marriage would be recognised and the defence would apply to sexual relations between them in Scotland.
252 Section 2.
253 When the Scottish Law Commission recommended the creation of this offence, it confined it to persons under the age of 16 – Report on the Law of Incest in Scotland (Scot Law Com No 69, 1981) paras 4.24–4.26. Its recommendation, in that respect, was rejected by Parliament when it enacted the predecessor to the current legislation – see the Incest and Related Offences (Scotland) Act 1986 which added s 2B to the Sexual Offences (Scotland) Act 1976. Section 2B was identical in its terms to the current provision.
254 Section 2(a).
255 Section 2(b).

intercourse;[256] or was married to the other person at the time sexual intercourse took place by a marriage entered into outside Scotland and recognised as valid under Scots law.[257]

11.80 Given the increased incidence of cohabitation, there are many people who, while not step-parents, are in much the same kind of relationship with their partner's children. Thus, one might expect to find an offence, similar in its terms to having sexual intercourse with a step-child, to exist. There is no such full equivalent. However, it is an offence for a person over the age of 16 to have sexual intercourse with a child under the age of 16 where the parties are members of the same household and the older person is in a position of trust or authority in relation to the child.[258] It is a defence for the accused to prove that he or she believed on reasonable grounds that the child was over the age of 16; did not consent to sexual intercourse; or was married to the other person at the time sexual intercourse took place by a marriage entered into outside Scotland and recognised as valid under Scots law. Of course, it is an offence for any man to have sexual intercourse with a girl under the age of 16,[259] but the provision of this specific offence serves as a signal to cohabitants that sexual intercourse in breach of trust is likely to attract additional opprobrium which will be reflected in sentencing.

Domestic violence

11.81 Whatever else it is, domestic violence is not a natural, nor is it an inevitable, consequence of relationships. Indeed, one commentator has described the term as the 'ultimate oxymoron'.[260] However, it is in the context of relationships that it can arise and, where it does, it is more often during the currency of the relationship, although in some cases it continues after divorce or separation. Awareness of the problem increased in the 1970s and the literature on its early recognition and continued presence is extensive.[261] The Matrimonial Homes (Family Protection) (Scotland) Act 1981 ('the 1981 Act') sought to address some aspects of domestic violence, most significantly through the creation of exclusion orders. Undoubtedly, the 1981 Act has provided a remedy in cases where none existed before.[262] However, it has not solved the problem. The threat of exclusion from the home is, alone, not enough to stop all domestic violence. Nor are interdicts always effective. The criminal law has a panoply of remedies which may

256 Section 2(c).
257 Section 2(d).
258 Section 3(1).
259 Section 5. For a discussion of sexual offences against children, see chapter 3, paras 96–100.
260 Carson makes the following comment – 'The juxtaposition of the words 'domestic' (the intimate relations of a family group living together) and 'violence' (the exertion of physical force so as to injure or abuse) punctuates the incongruity of what most believe is an increasingly frequent and serious problem occurring in a place that traditionally was thought to be tranquil, supportive and safe'; W. P. Carson, Jr, 'Domestic Violence: The Ultimate Oxymoron' 33 Willamette L Rev 767, at 767 (1997).
261 See chapter 12, para 2 and footnotes thereto.
262 The impact of the 1981 Act and its limits are discussed in chapter 12.

apply to domestic violence, including charges of breach of the peace, assault (with various aggravations), culpable homicide and murder. Again, the threat of a criminal sanction is insufficient to prevent a significant amount of domestic violence.

Stalking

11.82 Stalking can be defined as 'intentionally harassing, threatening and/ or intimidating a person by following them about, sending them letters or articles, telephoning them, waiting outside their place of abode and the like'.[263] Essentially, it involves the stalker showering unwanted attention on the victim and one difficulty with it is drawing the line between legitimate romantic pursuit and conduct which the victim finds threatening or offensive. Indeed, stalking shares with harassment the difficulty of having that very element of being victim-defined. Stalking is nothing new,[264] nor is it confined to people who know each other at all. Far less is it limited to people who have had a relationship. Indeed, the problem gained attention through the experiences of a number of high-profile victims who did not know the stalkers.[265] However, it merits discussion in the context of personal relationships because it can arise where people have had a relationship, either because one partner cannot accept that the relationship is over or, even if he or she accepts that, because one partner demonstrates a desire for continued direct or indirect, but unwelcome, contact of some kind.

11.83 The police and the courts in Scotland have always had the capacity to deal with the problem using a charge of breach of the peace, an offence whose very flexibility makes it ideally suited to adapt to new concerns.[266] However, it has been argued that the creation of a specific offences covering stalking afford greater protection to victims[267] and legislation in other jurisdictions has met with some success.[268] Following consultation by the Home Office and the Lord Chancellor's Department,[269] the Protection from Harassment Act 1997 ('the 1997 Act') was passed. While it created

---

263 Goode, 'Stalking: Crime of the Nineties' (1995) 19 Crim LJ 21, at p 22.
264 The behaviour of Lady Caroline Lamb, in pursuing Lord Byron after he had ended their relationship, provides a fairly dramatic example of stalking in earlier times.
265 Perhaps the most extreme examples are those of Mark Chapman, who both stalked and killed John Lennon, and John Hinckley, who shot Ronald Reagan, in part, to impress Jodie Foster whom he was stalking.
266 A. Bonnington. 'Stalking and the Scottish courts' 1996 NLJ 1394.
267 R. Mays, S. Middlemiss and J. Watson, ' "Every breath you take ... Every move you make" – Scots Law, The Protection from Harassment Act 1997 and the Problem of Stalking' 1997 JR 331.
268 E. F. Sohn, 'Anti-stalking statutes: Do they actually protect victims?' 30 CLB 203 (1994) and S. A. Strikis, 'Stopping Stalking' 18 Georgetown LJ (1993) 2771. Inevitably, much of the literature in the USA has questioned the constitutional validity of anti-stalking laws there, but the concerns expressed, particularly in relation to vagueness, are relevant to the UK – see for example, M. K. Boychuk, 'Are Stalking Laws Unconstitutionally Vague or Overboard?' 88 Northwestern U LR (1994) 769.
269 Consultation Paper, Stalking: the Solutions (Home Office, 1996).

two new offences in England and Wales,[270] as well as providing for civil remedies, it takes a different approach as far as Scotland is concerned. Here, the victim has the possibility of raising an action for harassment and seeking damages, interdict, interim interdict or a non-harassment order.[271] If the stalker breaches a non-harassment order, he or she can face a fine or imprisonment of up to six months, on conviction in a summary case, or five years, if convicted on indictment.[272] A non- harassment order can also form part of the sentence where an accused has been convicted of breach of the peace provided that the offence falls within the 1997 Act's definition of harassment.[273]

11.84 Whether the new provisions will effect greater protection for the victims of stalking is unproven, as yet. Certainly, it sends out a clear message that certain kinds of conduct are unacceptable and this, combined with the penalties a stalker might face, should serve as a deterrent to potential stalkers. As with all legislation of this kind, it will only be effective if it is combined with sufficient enthusiasm from the police, prosecutors and the courts. In the domestic arena, where the stalker and victim have had some past relationship, it is another weapon in the arsenal which may help to combat continued abuse. The criminal law already contributes to that arsenal and, as we shall see in chapter 12, the Matrimonial Homes (Family Protection) (Scotland) Act 1981 takes a different approach.

Other possible offences

11.85 Clive[274] discusses a number of offences where the marital relationship may have an impact. He examines propositions from Alison who, it should be remembered, was writing in the early nineteenth century. The first is to the effect that a wife cannot be convicted of reset for concealing goods brought home by her husband, unless she makes a business of dealing in stolen goods or has disposed of them.[275] The second is more general in nature and absolves a wife of liability where she protects her husband, regardless of the seriousness of the offence he has committed.[276] In both cases, her lack of liability is founded in her duty to protect and cherish her husband. Clive rightly points out, not only the sexist nature of the approach, since it does not provide a husband with similar immunity, but the illogicality of the whole approach. If the older approach of the criminal law to marital rape is now regarded, quite correctly, as indefen-

---

270 Section 2 creates the offence of 'harassment' and s 4 creates the offence of 'putting people in fear of violence'. That the latter is a more serious offence is reflected in the penalties, with s 4 attracting the possibility of up to five years imprisonment.
271 1997 Act, s 8.
272 1997 Act, s 9.
273 1997 Act, s 11, amending the Criminal Procedure (Scotland) Act 1995 to add s 234A.
274 At paras 18.034–18.037.
275 A. J. Alison, *Principles and Practice of the Criminal Law of Scotland*, I, 670–671.
276 Alison, above, I, 669.

sible in the light of modern marital relationships, so too should be the idea that a wife is incapable of making rational judgments about her husband's behaviour. Love is no longer blind, although sometimes it may be a little short-sighted.

COHABITANTS

11.86 Very few of the consequences of marriage, discussed above, apply to cohabitants. Where marriage itself has no significant consequences, as is the case with nationality, domicile and contractual obligations, cohabitation and marriage are treated alike. However, the rules designed to recognise the marital relationship or to protect the spouses are more often than not denied to cohabitants. Thus, there is no presumption in respect of household goods or any housekeeping allowance, no obligation to aliment, no special rules on the competency or compellability of partners as witnesses. Cohabitants do receive recognition for the purpose of delictual liability and, to a limited extent, in the context of the family home.[277] In addition, cohabitation is recognised for the purpose of certain state benefits, but not others. Where recognition is accorded, the effect of the legislation is usually to minimise the burden on the public purse and pass it on to an individual, rather than to extend pension entitlement to cohabitants. Thus, a cynic might argue, the legal system is quite capable of recognising cohabitation when it suits a particular end, most notably, saving public money.

11.87 The cases for and against equating cohabitation and marriage were considered at the beginning of this chapter, as was the possibility of a third type of relationship, the registered partnership. The Scottish Law Commission considered the position of heterosexual cohabitants in 1990[278] and, after consultation, had its impression 'that this is a subject on which widely differing views are held'.[279] It received submissions representing very varied points of view from those supporting dramatic reform of the law on cohabitation to those who recommended no change in the law on the basis that cohabitants could make their own arrangements. The Commission wisely rejected the notion of complete self-regulation, doubting 'whether it is realistic to expect all cohabiting couples to make adequate private legal

---

277 See chapter 12, para 35 for a discussion of cohabitants and the family home and para 11.88 for a discussion of the Scottish Law Commission's proposals for reform.
278 The Effects of Cohabitation in Private Law (Scot Law Com, Discussion Paper No 86, 1990).
279 Report on Family Law, n 62 above, para 16.1. The Commission also received submissions regarding recognition of same-sex relationships and, while it acknowledged the case being made, felt that reform should concentrate on heterosexual relationships 'on pragmatic grounds' – para 16.3 and see the definition of cohabitants in the draft Family Law (Scotland) Bill, clause 33. As has been noted earlier, this may be a wise approach if there is to be any hope of getting the recommended reforms through Parliament. There is no reason to suppose that the Scottish Parliament will necessarily be any more tolerant of diversity than Westminster has shown itself to be.

arrangements'.[280] However, it favoured only modest changes to the existing law[281] and stated the purpose of legal intervention in this area as follows:

> 'It should neither undermine marriage, nor undermine the freedom of those who have deliberately opted out of marriage. It should be confined to the easing of certain legal difficulties and the remedying of certain situations which are widely perceived as being harsh and unfair'.[282]

11.88 The Commission recommended that the presumption of equal ownership of household goods[283] and savings from any housekeeping allowance[284] should apply to cohabiting couples, subject to the necessary statutory modifications. It also recommended that, for the avoidance of doubt, it should be made clear that a cohabitant has an insurable interest in the life of his or her partner.[285] During the currency of the relationship, the Commission did not recommend any further reform of the law. In particular, it did not recommend introducing any obligation of aliment for cohabitants.[286] The Commission's thinking on this is interesting. It felt that, during the relationship, such an obligation is largely irrelevant. This argument might be made, with equal validity, about married couples. Once the relationship has broken down, the Commission found an obligation of aliment between cohabitants to be objectionable, not least because it could never be terminated by divorce. In addition, it believed that, where the couple had a child and the relationship had ended, the provisions on child support were adequate to provide for the parent with care of the child. As we shall see,[287] the Commission recommended that the courts should have limited powers to make a financial award on the termination of the relationship while the parties are alive and for succession, in the event that one of the cohabitants dies intestate. Given the very modest nature of the recommendation, the Commission did not feel there was any need to provide for opting out of them.[288] While the proposals give greater recognition than the present law, they represent a minimalist, and largely non-interventionist, approach to cohabitation. Scots cohabitants would remain in the position of having opted out of marriage and most of its consequences, retaining freedom of choice but at what price? The party in the weaker bargaining position, who will often also be the economically weaker party, gains only minimal protection. All the more important, then, that the opportunity to negotiate an alternative package is available,

---

280 Ibid.
281 Report on Family Law, paras 16.1–16.47, recs 80–87 and draft Bill, clauses 33–42.
282 Report on Family Law, para 16.1.
283 Report on Family Law, paras 16.7–16.11, rec 80 and draft Bill, clause 34.
284 Report on Family Law, paras 16.12–16.13, rec 81 and draft Bill, clause 35.
285 Report on Family Law, para 16.41, rec 85 and draft Bill, clause 40. In addition, it recommended that the provisions of the Married Women's Policies of Assurance (Scotland) Act 1880, s 2, as amended, which enables a spouse to take out a policy of assurance on his or her own life for the benefit of his or her spouse without the need for intimation or delivery, should be extended to cohabitants – paras 16.42–16.45, rec 42 and draft Bill, clause 41.
286 Report on Family Law, paras 16.5–16.6.
287 See chapter 14, paras 174 and 199.
288 Report on Family Law, para 16.47.

although, as we shall see, a cohabitation contract may not be the panacea for the economically weaker party.

INDIVIDUAL ARRANGEMENTS: CUSTOM-MADE MARRIAGE AND COHABITATION

11.89 As we have seen, a host of consequences flow automatically from the fact of being married or of cohabiting. In some cases, the parties can reject these consequences. The presumption that household goods are shared equally by the spouses is rebuttable, simply by showing that this was not the intended effect. In other cases, rejection of the automatic régime requires the parties to do something more. Thus, for example, before a spouse can renounce his or her occupancy rights in the matrimonial home, the renunciation must be in writing and made before a notary public.[289] In yet other cases, the protective provisions of the law do not permit of contracting out. Thus, a person cannot waive his or her right to seek a matrimonial interdict. However, what of the couple who want to clarify the details of their relationship before they embark upon it, either to avoid some or all of the automatic consequences of marriage or to determine, in advance, what should happen if they divorce[290]? Can they execute a contract to cover all eventualities? If they can, is such a contract available to cohabitants? The ability to reach a binding agreement would be attractive to many heterosexual cohabitants since, at present, they benefit from so few of the rules governing matrimonial property, are excluded from the régime governing financial provision on the dissolution of their relationship while they are alive, and have no automatic succession rights if their partners die intestate. The attraction of binding agreements for same-sex cohabitants would be even greater.

11.90 So far as married partners are concerned, ante-nuptial and, to a lesser extent, post-nuptial, marriage contracts have a long history.[291] During the 19th century they were used extensively by the wealthy to avoid the usual consequences of marriage, particularly for property. When one remembers that the wife's moveable property and the management of her heritage passed to her husband on marriage, the attraction of such contracts for women (and often their families) is clear. In addition, they provided useful protection from creditors. Such contracts fell from favour, in part, because of the changes in the legal effects of marriage on property, but also because of fiscal and other considerations. However, there is nothing to prevent a couple from executing such a contract to govern their own relationship and certainly such contracts are becoming increasingly popular in the USA.[292]

289 Matrimonial Homes (Family Protection) (Scotland) Act 1981, s 1(5) and (6). See chapter 12, para 11.
290 We are concerned here with agreements made prior to marriage or shortly thereafter. How couples can take control of the divorce process, and reach their own agreements governing the consequences of divorce, is discussed in chapter 14, at paras 155–158.
291 See Clive, paras 17.001–17.007.
292 At one time, such agreements were used largely by couples marrying later in life who employed them to regulate succession. There was considerable doubt about the validity of contracts which attempted to govern property during the couple's marriage and in the

11.91 Whereas the purpose of the old marriage contracts was often to protect the woman's property from her husband's profligacy, the modern marriage contract is ideally a freely negotiated bargain between equal individuals. Needless to say, such an ideal is not always reflected in the cases when a contract is challenged later. As with any contract, it is possible that one of the parties has not understood the nature of the contract, its terms, or that one party signed under duress.[293] The problem with marriage contracts is that, by virtue of being made in the context of an emotional relationship, they may present great opportunity for inequality of bargaining power to arise, particularly if one party is anxious to marry and the other is less enthusiastic.[294] In addition, marriage or cohabitation contracts are not for everyone, nor should they be seen as the panacea where the law

event of divorce. The decision in *Posner* v *Posner* 233 So 2d 381 (Fla, 1970), removed the presumption that there was an automatic public policy objection to agreements which sought to regulate property on divorce. The Uniform Premarital Agreement Act 1983, which had been adopted in a large number of states, applies only to agreements made prior to marriage and provides that they are not contrary to public policy. The possibility that a couple might reach an agreement which freed one party from future support obligations, thus shifting the burden onto the state, was anticipated to some extent. Consequently, the Act provides that any right to child support cannot be adversely affected by the agreement (s 3). For a discussion of premarital agreements in the USA, see L. Weitzman, *The Marriage Contract* (1981); L. Becker, 'Ethical Concerns in Negotiating Family Law Agreements' 30 Fam L Q 587 (1996); T. M. Featherston and A. E. Douthitt, 'Changing the Rules by Agreement: The New Era in Characterisation, Management and Liability of Marital Property' 49 Baylor L Rev 271 (1997); A. A. Marston, 'Planning for Love: The Politics of Prenuptial Agreements' 49 Stan L Rev 887 (1997).

293 The Uniform Premarital Agreement Act requires the agreement to be in writing and signed by the parties (s 2). In addition, there is a fairly wide-ranging provision (s 6) governing the conditions that will render a purported agreement unenforceable. The agreement will not be enforced where one party did not execute it voluntarily or where the agreement was unconscionable at the time it was made, unconscionability being presumed where there was a lack of full disclosure of property or obligations. While the fact that one party did not receive independent legal advice is not a prerequisite for reducing an agreement, it is a relevant factor in determining whether other vitiating factors were present.

294 In *DeLorean* v *DeLorean* 511 A 2d 1257 (NJ, 1986), the wife was a 23 year-old with limited business experience in the modelling and entertainment industries and the husband was a 48 year-old senior executive with General Motors when the woman signed a premarital agreement hours before the wedding ceremony. She refused to sign the agreement initially but, after discussing it with her future spouse, who threatened to cancel the wedding if she did not sign, she did so, thereby giving up very substantial property rights. Mr DeLorean had provided an attorney, who advised against signing. This agreement was upheld on the basis that there had been neither fraud nor duress and that the agreement was not unconscionable, albeit it was not a good bargain from Ms DeLorean's point of view. Significantly, the court noted that she would not be left destitute and, thus, would not become a charge on the public purse. In *Simeone* v *Simeone* 525 A 2d 162 (Pa, 1990), the wife was a 23 year-old unemployed nurse and the husband was a 39 year-old neurosurgeon when she signed a prenuptial agreement, in the presence of the man's attorney, on the eve of the wedding. Ms Simeone had no independent legal advice and the agreement limited the amount of financial support she would be entitled to after the marriage and in the event of divorce. Again, the agreement was upheld when she sought to challenge it in the course of divorce proceedings. See also; *Fletcher* v *Fletcher* 628 NE 2d 1343 (Oh, 1994) where what is meant by independent legal advice is discussed.

proves inadequate. Many people give little or no thought to the legal consequences of the way they currently arrange their lives and such people are unlikely to go to the trouble of executing a marriage contract. None the less, where each of the parties receives independent legal advice[295] and agrees freely to the terms, there is no reason why such a contract should not be used by sufficiently organised individuals. Given the recent willingness of the House of Lords to impose a fiduciary relationship on spouses,[296] it will be interesting to see if a similar approach is taken to the pre-nuptial context.

11.92 Certainly, the couple should be warned that such contracts are not watertight. Quite apart from all the usual grounds on which any contract may be reduced, the Family Law (Scotland) Act 1985 contains specific provision for the setting aside or variation of any ante-nuptial or post-nuptial marriage settlement in the context of divorce.[297] Either party may ask the court to set aside or vary the agreement and the court is directed only to exercise its power where it would be consistent with the guiding principles governing financial provision on divorce and reasonable in the light of the parties' resources.[298] Where the contract contains 'an agreement as to financial provision to be made on divorce', it may also be subject to reduction or variation under s 16 of the 1985 Act in the event of divorce. The test to be applied here is whether the agreement was 'fair and reasonable at the time it was entered into'.[299] For a person who had the foresight to conclude a comprehensive agreement governing property during marriage and financial provision on divorce, the test applicable for reduction or variation would appear to be different depending on which of the provisions is being addressed. Take, for example, a couple who concluded the agreement when they were modestly comfortable school teachers. They agree that they will not have children, each will continue to work and be essentially self-supporting and that their property will be kept entirely separate during the marriage. They agree further that neither of them will seek any settlement from the other in the event of a divorce. Over the next ten years, the wife goes on to develop a very successful career as a folk singer and amasses considerable wealth while the husband continues in his original job. If he applies to have their agreement set aside as a marriage settlement, he gets the benefits of its being inconsistent with the principles laid down for financial provision on divorce and can have the current resources of each of them taken into account. If he challenges the contract as an agreement as to financial provision on divorce, it will be judged on the basis of whether it was fair and reasonable at the time it was made which, arguably, it was.

---

295 On the basis of cases where the agreement at issue was a joint minute, arrived at in anticipation of a divorce, the fact that the parties received independent legal advice will not necessarily prevent it being set aside – see *McAfee* v *McAfee* (OH) 1990 SCLR (Notes) 805 and *Gillon* v *Gillon (No 1)* 1994 SLT 978.
296 See *Smith* v *Bank of Scotland* 1997 SLT 1061, discussed at paras 11.21–11.22.
297 1985 Act, ss 8(1)(c) and 14(2)(h).
298 1985 Act, s 8(2).
299 1985 Act, s 16(1)(b).

11.93 Turning to cohabiting heterosexual couples, the position is less clear. The problem is that a contract between cohabitants might be struck down as illegal and unenforceable on public policy grounds because its object was 'the furtherance of illicit sexual intercourse'.[300] However, as the Scottish Law Commission pointed out when it examined the issue,[301] the cases supporting such a view of cohabitation contracts date from the 19th century or earlier and it is to be hoped that such a view would not be taken today. Further support for the validity of cohabitation agreements can be found in the fact that the law already recognises cohabitation for a variety of purposes, the changed nature and increased incidence of cohabitation itself and the recommendation of the Committee of Ministers of the Council of Europe that such agreements should be upheld.[302] Thus, it is less likely that cohabitation agreements would be struck down by the courts. None the less, the Commission felt that it would be wise to put the matter beyond doubt and recommended that legislation should provide

> 'A contract shall not be void or unenforceable solely because it is a contract between cohabitants or between prospective cohabitants who entered into the contract in contemplation of cohabiting with each other'.[303]

11.94 Cohabitation contracts and same-sex couples raise two issues. First, if, as the Commission thought likely, the courts would now be prepared to recognise cohabitation contracts between heterosexual cohabitants, would the same approach be taken if the couple in question were of the same sex? At present, the law does not accord any recognition to such relationships, so that aspect of the 'times have changed' line of argument is of little assistance. Certainly, the Council of Ministers' recommendation makes no reference to sexual preference and, thus, can be seen as supporting such cohabitation agreements. None the less, if there was scope for doubt over the attitude of the courts to heterosexuals' cohabitation agreements, the scope increases in this context: all the more reason why legislation should be quite explicit in allowing for cohabitation agreements between same-sex couples. Which brings us to the second question. Will the Commission's proposal accommodate such agreements? The draft legislation proposed makes no mention of the sex of the cohabitants. However, clause 33 of the draft Bill defines cohabitants as 'a man and a woman who are not married to each other but who ... are living together as if they were husband and wife'.[304] Thus, the Commission's proposal would be of no help to same-sex couples who would be thrown back onto the courts' interpretation of how far we have come and what constitutes an illicit relationship. Furthermore, were the Commission's proposal to be enacted into legislation, it might be argued that the exclusion of same-sex couples from that legislation, when

---

300 W. M. Gloag, *The Law of Contract* (2nd edn, W. Green, 1929) at p 562.
301 The Effects of Cohabitation in Private Law (Scot Law Com, Discussion Paper No 86, 1990) para 9.1; Report on Family Law, para 16.46, rec 87.
302 On 7 March 1988, the Committee recommended that member states should take steps along the lines ultimately recommended by the Commission – rec (88)3.
303 Draft Family Law (Scotland) Bill, clause 42.
304 It will be remembered that the Commission has explicitly excluded same-sex relationships from the scope of its inquiry. Consequently, the definition of cohabitation is in line with what it examined and on which it consulted.

specific provision was being made for upholding cohabitation agreements, militated against upholding cohabitation contracts between same-sex couples.

11.95 So much for express contract, but what of implied contract? Where a couple cohabit and make no express written agreement, is it possible to imply contractual intent from the way they conduct or, more often, conducted, their relationship? This issue came to the fore in the USA in *Marvin* v *Marvin*,[305] a long-running battle between the actor Lee Marvin and his former cohabitant Michelle Triola Marvin, and was the case which added the word 'palimony'[306] to the media's vocabulary. The couple had lived together for some seven years, had never married and had no children together. Mr Marvin was married to someone else for the first two years of the cohabitation. Ms Marvin had changed her name and had been Mr Marvin's constant companion until they separated. She alleged that he had promised to support her in the future in consideration of her companionship and that, even if she could not establish an express contract, there was an implied contract for future support or, at least, for a rehabilitative award.[307] The court held that an action based on express or implied contract arising from a cohabitation relationship was competent and that, where no express contract could be established, it should inquire into the conduct of the parties to see if any contract could be implied. It further concluded that the doctrine of *quantum meruit* and the concept of trust could be used to provide a remedy for cohabitants. Subsequent courts, while not disturbing the principles elaborated by the first court, concluded that Ms Marvin had established neither express contract nor implied contract, nor did the circumstances justify a rehabilitative award.[308] In short, what has been hailed as the cohabitants' charter netted Ms Marvin absolutely nothing. Concern about the case focussed on the idea of implied contract being used and the searching inquiries which the court might undertake in order to establish the nature of the parties relationship.[309]

---

305 The cases are usually cited as follows: *Marvin I* 557 P. 2d 106 (Cal, 1976), *Marvin II* 5 Fam L Rep (1979) and *Marvin III* 179 Cal Rptr 555 (Cal Ct App, 1981). It is often said in the literature that these cases have been misunderstood but they have now been re-explained so often that any lingering misunderstanding must be minimal.

306 'Alimony' in the USA refers to the periodic payments due by one spouse to the other during marriage and after divorce, although it is most often used in the post-divorce context. See for example, the derogatory term 'alimony drone', meaning a former spouse who lives solely on the money provided by his or her former partner. 'Palimony' was the term coined to cover payments sought by one ex-partner from the other after the relationship has ended, where the couple had cohabited rather than married.

307 Californian law allows a spouse who has been dependant on the other spouse in the past to seek an award to allow him or her time to acquire the necessary skills in order to become self-supporting. A similar provision is found in Scotland in the Family Law (Scotland) Act 1985, s 9(1)(d).

308 The trial court had awarded Ms Marvin $104,000 as an equitable award to allow for rehabilitation but this was struck down on appeal – see *Marvin III*, n 305 above, at p 559, finding that there was 'no basis whatsoever, either in equity or in law' for the award.

309 Glendon, *The Transformation of Family Law* (University of Chicago Press, 1989) notes that a number of cases involving well-known cohabitants have been settled out of court to avoid just this kind of inquiry – see p 279.

Courts in Georgia,[310] Illinois[311] and New York,[312] have rejected the concept of non-marital implied contract, while it has been accepted, in principle, in Oregon[313] and Wisconsin.[314] To date, the Scottish courts have not had the opportunity to explore this application of implied contract and how the concept might be developed will be interesting. For now, the advice to people in Ms Marvin's situation in Scotland should be, 'don't spend the money yet'.

COHABITANTS AND LAW REFORM PROPOSALS

11.96 As we have seen, the Scottish Law Commission considered how the legal system treats cohabitants[315] and consulted on possible reform.[316] As a result of the responses it received, it has recommended very modest reforms, aimed at removing some of the worst injustices that can face cohabitants. In the draft Family Law (Scotland) Bill, which embodies its proposals for reform, cohabitants are defined as 'a man and a woman who are not married to each other but who (whether or not they represent to others that they are married to each other[317]) are living with each other as if they were husband and wife'.[318] The Commission rejected the idea of attaching a minimum period of time to its definition of cohabitation and, 'given the nature and limited extent of [its] proposals',[319] saw no need to make provision for opting out of the consequences which it recommended should attach to it.

11.97 What then, did it suggest should be done? The Commission recommended that the rebuttable presumptions of equal shares in household goods and in money and property derived from a housekeeping allowance, which currently apply to spouses, should be extended to cohabitants. A comprehensive scheme for the division of the couple's

310 *Rehak* v *Mathis* 238 SE 2d 81 (Ga, 1977).

311 *Hewitt* v *Hewitt* 394 NE 2d 1204 (Ill, 1979).

312 *Morone* v *Morone* 413 NE 2d 1154 (NY, 1980), where the court described the implied contract theory as 'conceptually so amorphous as practically to defy equitable enforcement'.

313 *Beal* v *Beal* 4 Family Law Reporter 2462 (Ore, 1978).

314 *Watts* v *Watts* 13 Family Law 1367 (Wis, 1987).

315 The Effects of Cohabitation in Private Law (Scot Law Com Discussion Paper No 86, 1990).

316 In addition to the usual consultation process through responses to the Discussion Paper, the Commission held two public meetings (organised by the Faculty of Law, Glasgow University and the Legal Services Agency) to discuss its proposals and arranged for System Three Scotland to carry out a public opinion poll – Report on Family Law, paras 1.3–1.4.

317 It will be remembered that the Commission recommended the abolition of marriage by cohabitation with habit and repute – draft Bill, clause 22.

318 Clause 33. The narrow ambit of this definition has been discussed at length earlier in this chapter and in chapter 10.

319 Report on Family Law, para 16.47. In relation to some of the consequences, like those aimed at the prevention of domestic violence, it felt that opting out was inappropriate and should not be possible. Other consequences, like those on household goods, raise only a rebuttable presumption and can be avoided simply by evidence of a contrary intention, while yet others, like insurance policies and cohabitation contracts, require opting in, in the first place.

property where they split up, similar to that which applies on divorce, was rejected.[320] The only proposal for financial provision where the parties are alive would enable one of the partners to apply to the court for an award of a capital sum. The court could only make such an award if it was satisfied that it is fair and reasonable in all the circumstances of the case *and* that the other former partner 'has derived economic advantage from contributions by the applicant, or that the applicant has suffered economic disadvantage in the interests of the other former cohabitant or their children'.[321] The application would have to be made within a year of the cohabitation ending and the court would be empowered to order that the capital sum should be paid by instalments or that payment should be deferred. Where one of the cohabitants dies, it is recommended that the surviving partner should be able to apply to the court for a discretionary award from the deceased's estate.[322] In addition, the Commission recommended other statutory provisions aimed at avoiding the doubt which currently surrounds cohabitation and its place in the legal system. It is recommended that each cohabitant's insurable interest in the life of the other should be recognised[323] and that the validity of a cohabitation contract should not be questioned solely because it is concluded between parties who are cohabiting or are about to do so.[324] The Commission specifically rejected the creation of any obligation of aliment between cohabitants, comprehensive financial provision on the termination of the relationship and automatic succession rights for cohabitants.

11.98 Undoubtedly the Commission's proposals had the support of whole sections of the legal establishment and some sections of the public.[325] What is recommended is only slightly removed from what is often presented as the libertarian view of leaving people a choice between marriage and cohabitation, each having very different consequences. Proponents of this view argue that, in any event, individuals who want their cohabitation to have consequences other than those provided by law can always execute an agreement, encapsulating their chosen form of relationship. In a world populated only by wholly rational and organised lawyers, these lines of argument are highly persuasive, if complete equality of bargaining power is also built into the fantasy. But the real world is not like that. It is populated by whole hosts of people who: do not know what the law provides; do not think about the legal consequences of their actions; do not plan ahead; and,

---

320 Report on Family Law, paras 16.14–16–16. In the period between the publication of the Discussion Paper and the Report, the Child Support Act 1991 had made provision governing the support of a former partner who has future child care responsibilities.

321 Draft Bill, clause 36, discussed in the Report on Family Law, paras 16.17–16.23 and rec 82.

322 Draft Bill, clauses 37 and 38, discussed in the Report on Family Law, paras 16.24–16.37 and rec 83. In an earlier report, the Commission had rejected the idea of replacing the system of fixed legal rights for spouses and children and of introducing discretionary awards – Report on Succession (Scot Law Com No 124, 1990).

323 Report on Family Law, para 16.41, rec 85(a) and draft Bill, clause 40.

324 Report on Family Law, para 16.46, rec 87 and draft Bill, clause 42.

325 In the Report on Family Law, the Commission details responses from various consultees and the results of the public opinion poll showing clear support for the scheme it has proposed.

frequently, are not bargaining from positions of equal strength. For many of these people, the fact that cohabitation has virtually no legal consequences will not be something of which they are conscious until their relationship ends, either through separation or death. At the very time when they are at their most emotionally vulnerable, the reality of what the legal system is not providing will dawn on them. It would have been infinitely better if the law were to put cohabitation and marriage on an equal footing and then allow sufficiently organised individuals to contract out of some of the provision. That would ensure, on the one hand, a minimal level of protection for all and, on the other hand, the opportunity for freedom of choice for the very small number of people who actually organise the details of their lives.

CHAPTER 12

THE MATRIMONIAL OR FAMILY HOME

12.1 As we have seen, the position at common law, whereby the wife's heritable property was administered by her husband was altered radically by statute.[1] This, combined with the separate property rule, meant that, where a spouse owned heritage, that spouse could do with that property as he or she liked. As a general rule, that remains the position. Two specific problems arose where the heritage in question was also the family home. First, it meant that the owning spouse could treat the other spouse like a stranger and could evict him or her at will.[2] Similar difficulties arose where one spouse was the tenant, rather than the owner, of the family home and the other was not. That people should be placed in this precarious position in relation to the roofs over their heads warranted, at the very least, further inquiry.

12.2 Second, the property régime was wholly inadequate in meeting the legitimate needs of the victims of domestic violence. While not new,[3] there had been increasing worldwide awareness of the problem of domestic violence throughout the 1970s,[4] and the time was ripe, in Scotland as

---

1 The Married Women's Property (Scotland) Act 1920 abolished the *jus administrationis*.
2 *MacLure* v *MacLure* 1911 SC 200; *Millar* v *Millar* 1940 SC 56.
3 Cruelty, a concept which encompassed domestic violence, had been a ground for divorce since the Divorce (Scotland) Act 1938. Thus, the courts had long been familiar with the physical and non-physical violence to which a spouse could subject his or her partner.
4 Report from the Select Committee on Domestic Violence in Marriage (1974–75) HC 533; Observations on the Report from the Select Committee on Domestic Violence in Marriage, Cmnd 6690, 1976; R. E. Dobash and R. Dobash, *Violence Against Wives: A Case Against the Patriarchy* (Open Books, 1979); E. Pizzey, *Scream Quietly or the Neighbours Will Hear* (Penguin, 1974); M. A. Strauss, 'Measuring intrafamilial conflict and violence: The Conflict Tracts (CT) Scale' 41 *Journal of Marriage and the Family* 75 (1979); J. M. Eekelaar and S. N. Katz (eds), *Family Violence* (Butterworths, 1978). More recent literature on the subject includes the following: M. L. Clark, 'Feminist Perspectives on Violence Against Women and Children' 3 *Canadian Journal on Women and the Law* 421 (1989); B. J. Hart, 'State Codes on Domestic Violence: Analysis, Commentary and Recommendations' 43 Juv & Fam Ct J (1992); E. Schneider, 'The Violence of Privacy' in M. Fineman and R. Mykitiuk (eds), *The Public Nature of Private Violence* (Routledge, 1994); S. K. Steinmetz, 'Family Violence: Past, Present and Future' in M. B. Sussman and S. K. Steinmetz, *Handbook of Marriage and the Family* (Plenum, 1987); M. A. Strauss and R. J. Gelles, 'Societal changes and change in family violence from 1975 to 1985 as revealed in two national surveys' 48 *Journal of Marriage and the Family* (1986); G. Walker, *Family Violence and the Women's Movement: The Conceptual Politics of Struggle* (University of Toronto Press, 1990); K. Yllo and M. Bograd, *Feminist Perspectives on Wife Abuse* (Sage, 1988); 'Developments in the Law: Legal Responses to Domestic Violence' 106 Harv L Rev 1498 (1993). For an excellent review of the progress

elsewhere, to attempt to tackle a problem which had all too often been swept under the carpet. So far as the family home was concerned, the fact that a spouse who was neither owner nor tenant lived there at the discretion of the other spouse put the former in an invidious position where he or she was a victim of domestic violence. Even where the spouses were joint owners or joint tenants of the home, the victim of domestic violence faced a dreadful dilemma, since the violent partner had a right to live there too. Either the victim had to remain in the home and risk further violence, or he or she had to leave the home, a choice which was made all the more difficult if the victim had children to consider as well. A cohabitant experienced the same difficulties as a spouse, having no right to live in the home, if he or she was neither owner nor tenant, when faced with domestic violence.

THE MATRIMONIAL HOMES (FAMILY PROTECTION) (SCOTLAND) ACT 1981

12.3 After consultation on its provisional proposals,[5] the Scottish Law Commission published its Report on Occupancy Rights in the Matrimonial Home and Domestic Violence[6] in 1980. The Commission's proposals formed the basis of the Matrimonial Homes (Family Protection) (Scotland) Act 1981 ('the 1981 Act'),[7] which attempts to address the issues discussed above. It deals with occupancy rights in the matrimonial home, subsidiary and consequential matters, regulatory orders in respect of the home, exclusion from the home, transfer of tenancy, interdicts and powers of arrest and the rights of cohabitants in the family home. The 1981 Act treats spouses and cohabitants differently in a number of important respects and the special position of cohabitants is considered at the end of this chapter, along with the Scottish Law Commission's proposals to improve their position.

12.4 Some of the limits of the 1981 Act should be clarified at the outset. It is concerned, not with the ownership of the home, but with the use of it, either through occupancy rights or exclusion from the home. Ultimately, ownership remains unaffected.[8] With the exception of the court's power to transfer tenancy, the protection offered by the 1981 Act applies during marriage. The 1981 Act ceases to have effect on divorce and it is important

of Federal legislative efforts aimed at domestic violence, see G. B. Stevenson, 'Federal Antiviolence and Abuse Legislation: Towards Elimination of Disparate Justice for Women and Children' 33 Willamette L Rev 847 (1997).

5 Occupancy Rights in the Matrimonial Home and Domestic Violence (Scot Law Com Cons Memo No 41, 1978).

6 Scot Law Com No 60, 1980.

7 The Commission's proposals were not accepted in their entirety and, where Parliament preferred a different approach, that will be noted in the discussion that follows. The 1981 Act has been subject to amendment on a number of occasions, including those contained in the Law Reform (Miscellaneous Provisions) (Scotland) Acts 1985 and 1990. References below are to the 1981 Act, as amended.

8 Where a home does not fall within the definition of a 'matrimonial home' the 1981 Act does not apply to it and it will be governed by the ordinary rules of property, as each spouse's separate property – Family Law (Scotland) Act 1985, s 24(1)(a).

to bear this in mind in negotiating a divorce settlement or seeking financial provision from the court.[9] As a tool to counter domestic violence, the 1981 Act is useful, but of limited effect, not least because a violent spouse who has been excluded from the home knows exactly where to find his or her partner. Interdicts and powers of arrest are, again, valuable tools, but they do not necessarily prevent a violent partner from kicking down a door. Having noted the 1981 Act's limits, it should be stressed that having it is infinitely better than not having it. What, then, does the 1981 Act provide?

What is a 'matrimonial home'?

12.5   The 1981 Act defines the matrimonial home as

> 'any house, caravan, houseboat or other structure which has been provided or has been made available by one or both of the spouses as, or has become, a family residence and includes any garden or other ground or building attached to, and usually occupied with, or otherwise required for the amenity or convenience of, the house, caravan, houseboat or other structure but does not include a residence provided or made available by one spouse for that spouse to reside in, whether with any child of the family or not, separately from the other spouse'.[10]

This rather lengthy definition merits exploration.

12.6   First, let us consider the nature of the structure itself. Most people live in houses or flats and these are included within the definition, as are the more unusual kinds of homes like caravans or houseboats. Caravans are included whether they are of the easily moveable type or affixed to the land in a semi-permanent way. Interestingly, a couple can have more than one matrimonial home and an obvious example would be having a house in town and a weekend retreat in the country.[11] Where both residences have been made available for family use, they will both be matrimonial homes. While there is a connection with the notion of 'family residence', the home need not actually have been used as such. Thus, a holiday cottage on Lewis, bought with the *intention* that it would be used by the family, would be covered even if no family holidays had ever been taken there. Perhaps most important of all is that it does not matter which of the spouses acquired the property or when. As we saw when we looked at household goods, as opposed to matrimonial property, it is important to distinguish between the régime applicable during the marriage and that which applies on divorce. The distinction arises again in the context of the matrimonial home. A flat bought by one of the spouses, many years before the couple met each other, will still be a matrimonial home under the 1981 Act if it became a family residence. Should the couple divorce subsequently, that flat will not be matrimonial property for the purpose of financial provision

---

9   As we shall see in chapter 14, when dealing with financial provision on divorce, the court has very wide powers and, for example, it can transfer property from one spouse to the other and regulate the occupation of the matrimonial home – Family Law (Scotland) Act 1985.

10   Section 22.

11   *O'Neill* v *O'Neill* 1987 SLT (Sh Ct) 26.

on divorce. In chapter 1, we saw that there can be a variety of definitions of 'family'. In the context of 'family residence', 'family' includes a couple with no children. As we shall see when we examine the rights of cohabitants under the 1981 Act, a home can be treated as a 'matrimonial home' where the couple living in it are not married to each other and, thus, no matrimony is involved at all.

12.7 What, then, is not a matrimonial home? Any home acquired by one spouse for his or her own use is not included under the 1981 Act. Thus, where a woman acquires a studio where she can go to paint undisturbed, the studio will not become a matrimonial home. Similarly, where a separated spouse acquired a home for his or her use (whether with children or not), separately from the other spouse, that home is not governed by the 1981 Act. Where one spouse provides a home for the other spouse to live in, with or without the children, the precise wording of the 1981 Act leaves some doubt about whether this is a matrimonial home or not. The Outer House has held that such a home is not a matrimonial home[12] and the Scottish Law Commission has recommended that the 1981 Act should be amended to put the matter beyond doubt.[13]

12.8 The matrimonial home includes ground or buildings attached to or coupled with the home itself and 'required for the amenity or convenience' of the home. Obvious examples are a garage attached to the house or the garden around it. Again, there is some ambiguity over this aspect of the provision, caused, this time, by the punctuation. The Scottish Law Commission has recommended amendment to make it clear that non-attached ground or buildings are included as part of the matrimonial home, where they are required for the amenity or convenience of the home.[14] This proposal would clarify, for example, how a garage, situated a short distance from the home, would be treated.

'Entitled' and 'non-entitled' spouses

12.9 Central to the 1981 Act is the concept of 'entitled' and 'non-entitled' spouses. An entitled spouse is one who has a right to occupy the matrimonial home, whether because he or she is the owner or tenant or because he or she is allowed by a third party to occupy it[15] on some other basis including, for example, under a liferent.[16] A spouse with no such right is a 'non-entitled' spouse. Thus, where the wife bought the home and it has been used by the couple, she is the entitled spouse and her husband is the non-entitled spouse. Where the husband inherited a holiday cottage from his grandmother and this was used by himself and his wife, he would be the

---

12 *McRobbie* v *McRobbie*, unreported, (1984) 29 JLSS 5.
13 Report on Family Law, (Scot Law Com No 135, 1992) para 11.46, rec 63 and draft Bill, clause 28(b).
14 Report on Family Law, para 11.47, rec 64 and draft Bill, clause 28(a).
15 For example, where the home is occupied with the permission of a trustee in bankruptcy. Where the third party who allows occupancy is the spouse's employer and the spouse is required to live in the home, this can have implications for obtaining an exclusion order – s 4(3)(b). These are discussed below in the context of exclusion orders – para 22.
16 Section 22, which refers back to s 1(1).

entitled spouse and his wife would be the non-entitled spouse. Where one spouse is allowed to occupy the house with some other person, he or she is only an entitled spouse if the third party has waived the right to occupy in favour of the now-entitled spouse.[17] Thus, if the grandmother in the previous example had left the holiday cottage to all six of her grandchildren, the husband would not be the entitled spouse unless his siblings and cousins had waived their rights to occupy. None of this covers the very common situation where married couples take the home in joint names,[18] are joint tenants or are both permitted to occupy the home by a third party. Occupancy rights under the Act do not apply to such cases but, as we shall see, the 1981 Act does deal with other aspects of such homes.

Occupancy rights

12.10 The 1981 Act gives the non-entitled spouse a right to live in the matrimonial home. It does this by providing first, that where the non-entitled spouse is in occupation of the home, he or she has the right to continue to occupy it[19] and, second, where the spouse is not in occupation, that he or she has a right to enter and occupy the home.[20] These rights can be exercised along with any child of the family,[21] a term defined very widely in the 1981 Act.[22] It would be all too easy, almost twenty years on, not to grasp the magnitude of what the 1981 Act has done, simply by creating these occupancy rights and the extent to which it places the needs of people above simple property rights. Rights on paper are one thing, enforcing them may be quite another. The 1981 Act deals with this by providing that, where the non-entitled spouse is not in occupation and the entitled spouse will not allow him or her into the home, the occupancy right can only be enforced with leave of the court.[23]

12.11 A non-entitled spouse may renounce his or her occupancy rights but this is subject to various conditions aimed at protecting that spouse's position.[24] Firstly, the renunciation must be in writing and, secondly, at the time of renunciation, the non-entitled spouse must swear before a notary

---

17 Section 1(2). *Murphy* v *Murphy* (Sh Ct) 1992 SCLR 62.
18 In 1978–79, 78% of property bought by married couples was taken in joint names – Manners and Rauta, *Family Property in Scotland* (OPCS, 1981), at p 4. At present, it is thought that the corresponding figure would be in excess of 90%. I am grateful to Professor Robert Rennie for providing this figure.
19 Section 1(1)(a).
20 Section 1(1)(b).
21 Section 1(1A).
22 Section 22 defines the term to include 'any child or grandchild of either spouse, and any person who has been brought up or accepted by either spouse as if he or she were a child of that spouse, whatever the age of such a child, grandchild or person may be'. Thus, the 1981 Act embraces the idea of 'family' as being wider than the nuclear family and 'child' as extending beyond the childhood of children. So, for example, a non-entitled spouse might exercise her occupancy rights along with her adult step-son and his child. Such exercise might, however, be subject to a regulatory order – see para 12.16, below.
23 Section 1(3). The factors the court will take into account here are considered under regulatory orders, discussed below at para 12.17.
24 Section 1(5) and (6).

that it is made freely and without coercion.[25] Thirdly, renunciation must be in respect of a particular home. Thus, for example, a person cannot give a blanket renunciation of occupancy rights in all matrimonial homes which the couple may have in the course of their marriage.

12.12 Occupancy rights arise by virtue of marriage and end on divorce[26] or the death of one of the parties. Where the entitled spouse is permitted by a third party to occupy and that third party withdraws permission, the occupancy rights of the non-entitled spouse end. The 1981 Act contains extensive provisions to protect the non-entitled spouse from dealings that the entitled spouse may have with third parties in respect of the matrimonial home and, in most cases, it will not be possible for the non-entitled spouse's rights to be avoided by such dealings. Occupancy rights can continue for as long as the marriage lasts, even if one of the spouses has not been living in the home for some time – once a matrimonial home, always a matrimonial home.[27] The Scottish Law Commission examined this point and believed that it could result in injustice in some cases.[28] Thus, it recommended that the occupancy rights of the non-entitled spouse should come to an end where the parties had been separated for a continuous period of two years or more and the non-entitled spouse has not occupied the home during that time.[29]

Subsidiary and consequential matters

12.13 Having the right to live in the matrimonial home is a step in the right direction, but the effective content of the right would have been greatly diminished if the non-entitled spouse had nothing further. It is unlikely that a building society or a landlord would permit occupation to continue where the mortgage or rent remained unpaid for some time. A home without any appliances or furniture or one where water cascaded through a hole in the roof would be of limited use. Thus, the 1981 Act provides that the non-entitled spouse may do certain things, regarded as subsidiary to or consequential upon occupancy rights.[30] It also provides for the apportioning of

25 The entitled spouse is not required to come to Scotland to swear or affirm before a notary. This can be done abroad before a person authorised to administer oaths or receive affirmations in that country.

26 When granting a decree of divorce, the court has the power to regulate the occupation of the former matrimonial home and exclusion from it – Family Law (Scotland) Act 1985, s 14(2)(d) and (3). However, the court will only exercise this power in the context of its extensive powers to make other arrangements for financial provision on divorce – see chapter 14, paras 14–127.

27 This general proposition is subject to some qualification. For example, s 6(3)(b), which addresses dealings with third parties, does cover the situation where a spouse has not been in occupation for five years or more – see para 12.26.

28 Report on Family Law, paras 11.24–11.28. The Commission was aware of the danger of providing that occupancy rights should terminate after only a short period of non-occupation where, for example, the entitled spouse had so terrorised the non-entitled spouse as to drive him or her out. However, it contrasted this with the situation of spouses who had been separated for 15 or 20 years.

29 Recommendation 56, draft Family Law (Scotland) Bill, clause 25.

30 Section 2(1).

expenditure[31] and deals with related problems where the spouses are not respectively, entitled and non-entitled.[32] In addition, either spouse may apply to the court for a variety of orders regulating occupancy rights and the possession and use of furniture and plenishings in the home.[33]

12.14 For the purpose of securing his or her occupancy rights, the non-entitled spouse may do the following without the permission of the entitled spouse[34]

make any payment due by the entitled spouse in respect of rent, rates, secured loan instalments, interest or other outgoings (not being outgoings on repairs or improvements);

perform any other obligation incumbent on the entitled spouse (not being an obligation in respect of non-essential repairs or improvements);

enforce performance of an obligation by a third party which that third party has undertaken to the entitled spouse to the extent that the entitled spouse may enforce such performance;

carry out such essential repairs as the entitled spouse may carry out;

carry out such non-essential repairs or improvements as may be authorised by court order, being such repairs or improvements as the entitled spouse may carry out and which the court considers to be appropriate for the reasonable enjoyment of the occupancy rights;

take such other steps, for the purpose of protecting the occupancy rights of the non-entitled spouse, as the entitled spouse may take to protect the occupancy rights of the entitled spouse.

12.15 Where one spouse is an entitled spouse and the other is a non-entitled spouse, the court may make an order apportioning expenditure on the first four of these items or in respect of any expenditure the non-entitled spouse incurred with the consent of the entitled spouse.[35] Where both spouses are entitled or permitted to occupy the matrimonial home, each of them will normally be entitled to make necessary payments and instruct essential repairs and either of them may apply to the court for permission to carry out non-essential repairs.[36] Again, the court is empowered to apportion expenditure between them.[37] As we shall see, the court is empowered to regulate the possession and use of furniture and plenishings. Whether or not such an order has been made, either spouse may make payments in respect of such furniture and plenishings, owned, hired or acquired by the other, and carry out essential repairs without the permission of the other spouse.[38] Again, the court can apportion the expenditure so incurred between the spouses.[39] Applications for apportionment of expenditure must be made within five years of payment being made.[40]

31 Section 2(3) and (5).
32 Section 2(4).
33 Section 3.
34 Section 2(1).
35 Section 2(3).
36 Section 2(4).
37 Section 2(4).
38 Section 2(5)(a).
39 Section 2(5)(b).
40 Section 2(7).

Regulatory orders

12.16 Thus far, we have seen that a spouse may have a right to occupy the matrimonial home by virtue of being the owner or tenant of the home or by virtue of the 1981 Act. Obviously, that means that each spouse may have rights in respect of the same home and how they operate together may be problematic. For this reason, the 1981 Act provides that either spouse may apply to the court for an order regulating occupancy rights and associated matters. This part of the 1981 Act applies not only where there is a non-entitled and an entitled spouse, but where the spouses are both entitled or permitted to occupy the home.

12.17 The court is bound to declare occupancy rights if it appears that the application relates to a matrimonial home. That is to say, it has no discretion in terms of stating the basic rights of each spouse as provided by the common law and the 1981 Act.[41] Having an occupancy right declared is the essential first step before other regulation of occupancy rights can be sought.[42] Thereafter, the court has a discretion in respect of orders it may make – enforcing the applicant's right of occupation, restricting the non-applicant's occupancy rights, and regulating the exercise of occupancy rights by either of them.[43] However, under this section, the court cannot make an order where its effect would be to exclude the entitled spouse from the home.[44] Exclusion orders are dealt with in s 4 of the 1981 Act and will be considered presently. The court is given guidance on regulatory orders. It is obliged to make such an order as appears 'just and reasonable having regard to all the circumstances of the case, including'[45]

> the conduct of the spouses in relation to each other and otherwise;
> the respective needs and financial resources of the spouses;
> the needs of any child of the family;
> the extent (if any) to which,
> (i) the matrimonial home, and
> (ii) any relevant item of furniture and plenishings,
> is used in connection with a trade, business or profession of either spouse; and
> whether the entitled spouse offers or has offered to make available to the non-entitled spouse any suitable alternative accommodation.

As we shall see, the above criteria are used again in the 1981 Act and are central to the court's decision-making in respect of the home. Provided that the non-applicant spouse has been given the opportunity to be heard, the court has the power to grant such interim regulatory orders as it considers to be necessary or expedient.[46] Compensation may be awarded to the spouse whose occupancy rights have been lost or impaired.[47]

---

41 That requires, of course, that a spouse does have occupancy rights. Where, for example, a spouse has renounced his or her occupancy rights, then there are no rights to be declared.
42 *Welsh* v *Welsh* 1987 SLT (Sh Ct) 30.
43 Section 3(1).
44 Section 3(5). This may explain, at least in part, why regulatory orders are not used very often.
45 Section 3(3).
46 Section 3(4).
47 Section 3(7).

Exclusion orders

12.18 As we saw at the beginning of this section, one of the problems for a spouse faced with domestic violence was that, even if he or she had a right to live in the family home, continuing to do so might no longer be an option because of the prospect of the violence being repeated. A major goal of the 1981 Act was to improve the protection that the law gave to victims of domestic violence. The introduction of the exclusion order is central to affording improved protection. Essentially, it allows a court to order a person to leave the matrimonial home, regardless of his or her rights as owner, tenant or non-entitled spouse. It is not intended as punishment of a spouse who has behaved badly. Rather, it seeks to provide a safe living environment for a spouse and, often, children, who need it. An exclusion order will not always be the answer, however, particularly where there is a real prospect that the abuser will return to the home. Matrimonial interdicts are discussed below and they provide yet another attempt to combat domestic violence, although some abusers remain undeterred by the threat of arrest and imprisonment. Despite all of this, an exclusion order can provide an effective remedy in some cases.

12.19 The court is directed that it

'*shall* make an exclusion order if it appears ... that the making of the order is *necessary* for the protection of the applicant or any child of the family from *any conduct or threatened or reasonably apprehended conduct* of the non-applicant spouse which is or would be *injurious to the physical or mental health* of the applicant or child'.[48]

However, the court is also directed not to grant an exclusion order if it would be unjustified or unreasonable, having regard to all the circumstances of the case, including those set out in s 3(3) of the 1981 Act.[49]

12.20 Early judicial hostility to the whole notion of an exclusion order was palpable. Initially, some courts interpreted the statutory provision in a very restrictive way and demanded that applicants should satisfy such stringent requirements that Parliament's intended remedy was rendered inaccessible to many victims of domestic violence. In *Bell* v *Bell*,[50] the Inner House indicated that the test of necessity was a 'high and severe'[51] one and that there must be '*real immediate danger* of *serious* injury or *irreparable damage*'.[52] In addition, it was suggested that an exclusion order should not be granted unless the applicant was living in the home at the time of the application[53] and that such an order should not be granted if an interdict would provide adequate protection.[54] Fortunately, judicial interpretation is not static and subsequent courts proved less hostile to the idea of excluding

---

48 Section 4(2), emphasis added. Why these words have been emphasised will become apparent when we see how the courts interpreted the provision initially.

49 Section 4(3)(a). The criteria in s 3(3) are set out in para 12.17, above. The interaction of ss 4(2) and 3(3) is considered below.

50 1983 SLT 224. See also *Smith* v *Smith* 1983 SLT 275.

51 Lord Robertson, at p 230.

52 Lord Justice-Clerk Wheatley, at p 228, emphasis added.

53 *Bell* v *Bell*, above.

54 *Bell* v *Bell*, above, and *Smith* v *Smith*, above.

an abuser from his or her home. Indeed, a number of the early errors were corrected fairly quickly. The operation of exclusion orders has come a long way from the early restrictive approach.

12.21 Either spouse can apply for an exclusion order 'whether or not that spouse is in occupation at the time of the application'.[55] The applicant need not have applied for an interdict before applying for an exclusion order,[56] although it will depend on the circumstances of each case whether an interdict will be viewed as providing adequate protection.[57] The appropriate test to apply is that of necessity, as defined and explained in the 1981 Act, and without the addition of the higher standards set out in cases like *Bell*.[58] Perhaps the clearest guidance on how the court should approach an application for an exclusion order was given by Lord Dunpark, when he said that the court should consider the following four questions

> '1. What is the nature and quality of the alleged conduct?
> 2. Is the court satisfied that the conduct is likely to be repeated if cohabitation continues?
> 3. Has the conduct been or, if repeated, would it be injurious to the physical or mental health of the applicant or to any child of the family?
> 4. If so, is the order sought necessary for the future protection of the physical or mental health of the applicant or child?'.[59]

In the context of a threat to the physical or mental health of the child, two points are worth noting. It will be remembered that the 1981 Act (as amended) gives a very broad definition of 'child' and one which extends beyond childhood indefinitely.[60] However, an exclusion order under this statute cannot be justified solely on the basis that to grant it would serve the best interests of the child.[61]

12.22 As we have seen, the court is directed not to make an exclusion order where making an order would be 'unjustified or unreasonable' having regard to all the circumstances of the case, including the matters

---

55 1981 Act, s 4(1), as amended by s 13(5) of the Law Reform (Miscellaneous Provisions) (Scotland) Act 1985. Lord Justice-Clerk Wheatley had attempted to correct earlier misinterpretation when he said, '[i]f there is any misconception that following *Bell* v *Bell* an interim exclusion order will only be granted if the parties are both occupying the matrimonial home, the sooner that misconception is removed the better' – *Colagiacomo* v *Colagiacomo* 1983 SLT 559, at p 562. See also *Brown* v *Brown* 1985 SLT 376.
56 *Colagiacomo*, above; *Ward* v *Ward* 1983 SLT 472 (history of alcohol-related violence, interdict granted); *Brown* v *Brown*, above; *McCafferty* v *McCafferty* 1986 SLT 650; *Millar* v *Millar* (Sh Ct) 1991 SCLR (Notes) 649.
57 *Nasir* v *Nasir* 1993 GWD 30–1909 (exclusion order refused, in part, because interdict thought to be adequate); *Pryde* v *Pryde* 1996 GWD 39-2245 (exclusion order refused, interdict and power of arrest thought to be adequate).
58 See *McCafferty*, above, where the Inner House expressed the view that some of the statements in *Bell* were an unnecessary gloss on the 1981 Act.
59 *McCafferty*, above, at p 656.
60 This was not so in the Scottish Law Commission's original scheme and Clive (at para 15.048) is critical of the inclusion of adult offspring.
61 *Hampsey* v *Hampsey* 1988 GWD 24–1035. The local authority has a separate right to apply for an exclusion order in the context of child protection – Children (Scotland) Act 1995, s 76. For a discussion of exclusion orders under that Act, see chapter 7, para 71–76.

specified in s 3(3).[62] However, the court is also directed that it shall grant an exclusion order where it is 'necessary for the protection' of the applicant or a child.[63] It is not surprising, then, that Lord Dunpark 'had difficulty in envisaging circumstances in which an order which is necessary for the protection of the spouse may be 'unjustified or unreasonable'.[64] Clive[65] suggests that the relationship between the two subsections can be understood on the hypothesis that both spouses are in the home. He cites the example of a violent wife whose exclusion might, none the less, be unreasonable if the home was also her place of business and the husband could readily find suitable alternative accommodation. Another example suggested by him is of a violent couple, where exclusion of both of them might be justified but such a course of action would hardly be reasonable. The 1981 Act makes specific provision for agricultural holdings and tied houses and the court is directed, in such cases, not to make an exclusion order if it would be unjustified or unreasonable having regard to the requirement that the spouse must live in the home and the likely consequences of exclusion.[66]

Protection of occupancy rights against dealings

12.23 The value of occupancy rights would be greatly diminished if the entitled spouse could sell the home to a third party and the third party could then come along and evict the non-entitled spouse. For this reason, the 1981 Act contains provisions designed to protect the non-entitled spouse from the entitled spouse's dealings with third parties. The non-entitled spouse's rights under the 1981 Act cannot be prejudiced by the entitled spouse's dealings[67] with the property.[68] Nor can a third party acquire a right to occupy the property as a result of such dealings.[69] Thus, were the entitled spouse to sell the matrimonial home to a third party and, as we shall see, this would be difficult in itself, not only would the non-entitled spouse's occupancy rights remain valid, the purchaser would acquire no right to live in the home. Under the original scheme recommended by the Scottish Law Commission, a spouse who wanted protection from dealings with third parties would have been required to register a matrimonial home notice in the property registers.[70] That requirement was rejected by Parliament. Since there is no register of occupancy rights there

---

62 Section 4(3)(a).
63 Section 4(2).
64 *Brown* v *Brown* 1985 SLT 376, at p 378.
65 At para 15.050.
66 Section 4(3)(b).
67 'Dealings' include the sale or lease of the home, the granting of a standard security over it and the creation of a trust, but not where the property is transferred as a result of compulsory purchase by a public authority or transfer by operation of law (for example, on bankruptcy) – s 6(2). Where a person engineers his or her own bankruptcy, known as a 'contrived sequestration or adjudication', the Court of Session may recall the sequestration or order the reduction of a decree of adjudication and can make an order to protect the occupancy rights of a non-entitled spouse – Bankruptcy (Scotland) Act 1985, s 41.
68 Section 6(1)(a).
69 Section 6(1)(b).
70 Occupancy Rights in the Matrimonial Home and Domestic Violence, n 5 above.

is no way to be absolutely certain that none exists. What this means is that a third party may buy a home in good faith, completely unaware that there is a non-entitled spouse with occupancy rights in respect of it. Not surprisingly, solicitors acting for the purchasers of residential property are very careful in order to protect their clients' interests.[71]

12.24 There are a host of exceptions to the general rule on dealings with third parties. Dealings which predate the 1981 Act[72] or the entitled spouse's marriage[73] are unaffected by rights acquired subsequently by a non-entitled spouse. So, for example, where the owner-spouse granted a standard security over the home before he or she got married, the creditor will be able to sell the home if loan repayments are not made, and the non-entitled spouse will lose occupancy rights. As we saw, the non-entitled spouse can renounce his or her occupancy rights in a particular home and, provided that this is done in accordance with the requisite formalities, there will be no occupancy rights to trouble a purchaser.[74] Similarly, the non-entitled spouse may consent to the dealing and, provided this is done in writing and in the prescribed form, the purchaser will be protected.[75] Where the home is occupied by permission of a third party and the entitled spouse relinquishes his or her occupancy rights, the non-entitled spouse is no longer protected.[76] Where the entitled spouse occupies the property along with a third party, the non-entitled spouse is not protected against dealings by them.[77]

12.25 An important qualification on the non-entitled spouse's occupancy rights is the court's power to dispense with his or her consent to dealings by the entitled spouse. If the non-entitled spouse will not give consent, the court may dispense with that consent in certain circumstance and, where it grants such a dispensation, the non-entitled spouse will no longer be protected against dealings.[78] The entitled spouse or anyone with an interest may apply to the court for an order dispensing with the non-entitled spouse's consent. The grounds for the application are:[79] that consent is being withheld unreasonably;[80] that consent cannot be given by reason of physical or mental disability; that the non-entitled spouse cannot be found after reasonable steps have been taken to trace him or her; or that the non-

---

71 Clive, at para 15.061, has criticised the provision thus: 'In order to guard against a very small risk, which would have materialised in very few cases, it introduces extra expense and inconvenience into many ordinary conveyancing transactions.'
72 Section 6(3)(d). The 1981 Act came into force on 1 September 1982.
73 Section 6(3)(c).
74 Section 6(3)(a)(ii).
75 Section 6(3)(a)(i). The form is prescribed by the Matrimonial Homes (Form of Consent) (Scotland) Regulations 1982, SI 1982 No 971.
76 Section 6(2).
77 Section 6(2).
78 Section 6(3)(b).
79 Section 7(1).
80 Consent will be regarded as being withheld unreasonably if either, the entitled spouse has been led to believe that consent would be forthcoming and there has been no change of circumstances, or, having tried, the entitled spouse cannot get an answer to the request for consent – s 7(2).

entitled spouse is under 16 years of age.[81] In reaching its decision, the court has a discretion and must consider all the relevant facts, including the factors set out in s 3(3). It has been suggested that the proposed dealing must have reached the stage of firm negotiations as to such matters as price and conditions, before an application can be made.[82] This means that the entitled spouse cannot seek to have consent dispensed with prior to putting the property on the market. The Scottish Law Commission has proposed that it should be possible to dispense with consent at an earlier stage, provided that the dispensation relates to a sale for not less than a specified price and within a specified time, or the granting of a heritable security for a loan of not more than a specified amount to be executed within a specified time.[83] In addition, it has recommended that, where the court refuses to dispense with the non-entitled spouse's consent to a dealing, the court should have the power to order the non-entitled spouse to make payments in lieu of rent and to attach other conditions to the continued occupation of the home.[84]

12.26 From the point of view of the ordinary purchaser of a home, perhaps the most important exception to the rule against dealings by an entitled spouse with a third party is that specifically designed with a purchaser in good faith in mind. Where such a third party receives an affidavit from the seller, declaring that the subjects of the sale are not a matrimonial home in which a spouse of the seller has occupancy rights, or a renunciation of occupancy rights, or a consent to the dealing, then the purchaser will not be prejudiced by any occupancy rights of the seller's spouse.[85] 'Good faith' is not defined in the 1981 Act and it is not clear what, if any, inquiries a prospective purchaser would be expected to make.[86] Some further protection is offered to the good faith purchaser who did not obtain the necessary affidavit, renunciation or consent. Where the entitled spouse has permanently ceased to be entitled to occupy the home and, for a continuous period of five years, the non-entitled spouse has not occupied the home, the non-entitled spouse's occupancy rights cease to be protected.[87] The Commission has recommended that this period of time should be reduced to two years.[88]

81 This problem will only arise, of course, in respect of a marriage celebrated abroad.
82 *Fyfe* v *Fyfe* 1987 SLT (Sh Ct) 38. See also, *Longmuir* v *Longmuir* 1985 SLT (Sh Ct) 33 for the procedure to be adopted in applications.
83 Report on Family Law, paras 11.13–11.15, rec 55(c) and draft Family Law (Scotland) Bill, clause 26(2).
84 Report on Family Law, para 11.15, rec 55(d) and draft Family Law (Scotland) Bill, clause 26(2).
85 Section 6(3)(e). In the course of consultation, the Scottish Law Commission received submissions to the effect that the need for an affidavit sworn or affirmed before a notary caused considerable inconvenience, particularly to people living in rural areas. It has recommended that the reference to affidavits should be replaced by a reference to written declarations subscribed by the seller – Report on Family Law, paras 11.16–11.18, rec 55(f) and draft Family Law (Scotland) Bill, Sched 1, paras 70 and 71.
86 Clive explores the possibilities extensively at para 15.076.
87 Section 6(3)(f).
88 Report on Family Law, paras 11.6 and 11.11, rec 55(b) and draft Family Law (Scotland) Bill, clause 26(1)(b).

12.27 It is in the nature of residential property that it may change hands on a number of occasions. Where the entitled spouse has sold the property to a third party and that third party sells it on to a fourth party, are the non-entitled spouse's occupancy rights still protected? To put it another way, when a person is buying a home, how many transactions does he or she have to go back in the search for possible non-entitled spouses with occupancy rights? This is the question of 'double dealing' and respected commentators have arrived at completely different answers.[89] It remains for the courts to provide the definitive answer. The Scottish Law Commission has recommended that the 1981 Act should be amended to prevent a non-entitled spouse exercising occupancy rights against a person who had acquired his or her interest, in good faith and for value, from a person other than the entitled spouse. Anyone deriving title from a person so protected would also be protected.[90] Effectively, then, the position of the second, third and fourth purchasers would be clarified.

Protection where both spouses are entitled to occupy the home

12.28 Increasingly, spouses who buy their homes do so in joint names. This means that there is neither an entitled, nor a non-entitled, spouse. Each spouse will have the right to live in the home and neither can bring an action of ejection against the other.[91] Each spouse can carry out essential repairs and, as a result of the 1981 Act, can carry out non-essential repairs and the court can apportion expenditure between them.[92] It should be remembered that, where the spouses are co-owners of the home, the court can still regulate occupancy under s 3 and grant exclusion orders under s 4.

12.29 So much for the use of the home, but what of sale or other dealings, for example, the granting of a heritable security? Where each spouse has a *pro indiviso* share in the property he or she can sell or mortgage his or her share and can apply for a decree of division and sale in order to force the sale of the whole property. If no additional protection were provided this could compromise the occupancy rights of the other spouse. For this reason, the 1981 Act addresses each aspect of the problem. Where one spouse sells his or her share in the home to a third party, the other spouse's occupancy right will not be affected, nor will the third party acquire a right of occupancy.[93] Very few purchasers would want to buy property on such terms. While one spouse may still apply for a decree of division and sale, the court has a discretion to refuse the decree, to postpone it, or to grant it subject to conditions.[94] In reaching its decision, the court is directed to

---

89 For the view that the non-entitled spouse is protected against subsequent purchasers see D. Nichols and M. M. Meston, *The Matrimonial Homes (Family Protection) (Scotland) Act 1981* (2nd edn, W. Green, 1986), para 6.05. For the opposite view see Clive, paras 15.080–15.081.

90 Report on Family Law, paras 11.10–11.12, rec 55(a) and draft Family Law (Scotland) Bill, clause 26(1)(a).

91 Section 4(7). This clarifies earlier doubt raised in *Price* v *Watson* 1951 SC 359.

92 Section 2(4)(a) and (b) and (6).

93 Section 9(1). Other dealings by an owner are also covered by this provision.

94 Section 19.

consider all the circumstances of the case, including the factors set out in s 3(3), the conduct of the parties and, whether the spouse bringing the actions has offered suitable alternative accommodation to the other spouse.[95] It is unclear where the onus of proof lies in such cases. It can be argued that, since individuals have a *prima facie* right to sell their property, the onus lies on the spouse wishing to prevent the sale.[96] On the other hand, the effect of a decree is to force the non-applicant to sell his or her property unwillingly and, thus, arguably the onus should be on the party applying for the decree.[97] Whatever the onus of proof, the court will usually refuse or postpone the decree where the needs of a spouse and the children indicate that the home is required by them.[98] Decree may be postponed until after a date when the marriage will be dissolved.[99] Thus, for example, a court might postpone the decree until after the youngest child reached the age of 18. It is important to note that s 19 applies only where the co-owners are spouses. If the spouse waits until after the divorce has been granted, decree of division and sale must be granted. By this time, property issues should have been resolved in the course of the divorce itself.

Tenancy transfer orders

12.30 Many spouses are joint tenants in their home while, in other cases, only one spouse is the tenant. In either case, the court can regulate occupancy under s 3 and grant an exclusion order under s 4. However, the 1981 Act empowers the court to do a great deal more than that. It can transfer the tenancy from one spouse to the other[100] or, where both spouses are tenants, vest the tenancy in one of them alone[101] and provide for just and reasonable compensation to be paid to the deprived former tenant.[102] In reaching its decision, the court is directed to consider all the circumstances of the case, including the factors in s 3(3), the applicant's suitability to become a tenant and the applicant's capacity to perform the obligations under the lease.[103] A copy of the application must be served on the landlord, who must be given an opportunity to be heard before the court

---

95 The offer of alternative accommodation must be specific and a general offer to help the other spouse to find such accommodation is insufficient – *Hall* v *Hall* 1987 SLT (Sh Ct) 15.
96 *Berry* v *Berry* 1988 SCLR 296.
97 *Hall* v *Hall*, above.
98 *Crow* v *Crow* 1986 SLT 270 (needs of the family resulted in postponement of the sale); *Berry* v *Berry*, above, (no children, decree granted); *Rae* v *Rae* 1991 SLT 45 (home required for wife and children, sale refused).
99 In both *Berry* v *Berry* and *Crow* v *Crow*, divorce actions were pending.
100 Section 13(1). Under the Housing (Scotland) Act 1987, Sched 3, the landlord of a secure tenancy may apply to the court to recover possession of the property because he or she wants to transfer the tenancy to the spouse, former spouse or former cohabitant of the tenant.
101 Section 13(9).
102 In assessing compensation, no account is to be taken of the loss of any right to purchase a home at a discount – s 13(11).
103 Section 13(3). In *McGowan* v *McGowan* 1986 SLT 112, for example, the court thought that it would be a 'travesty of justice' for the violent adulterous husband to retain the tenancy while his wife and their son lived in overcrowded conditions with her married daughter.

grants the transfer.[104] The court can transfer tenancy even where the landlord does not agree and he or she will be notified of the transfer by the court.[105] On the transfer of a tenancy, the tenancy vests in the non-entitled spouse (or former co-tenant) and he or she acquires all rights and liabilities under the lease, subject to one important qualification.[106] Where the transferee was a non-entitled spouse (that is, was not a joint tenant) he or she is not liable for arrears of rent and these remain the responsibility of his or her spouse. Certain kinds of tenancy cannot be transferred by the court.[107] These include: a tied house, an agricultural holding, a croft, the subject of a cottar, a statutory small tenancy, a let on a long lease, or a tenancy-at-will.[108]

Matrimonial interdicts

12.31 Interdict is a remedy of long standing and, essentially, what it involves is the court telling a person not to do something or, if doing a particular thing, to stop.[109] Because it limits a person's freedom of action, an interdict must be precise in its terms and no wider than is necessary[110] so that the person knows exactly what he or she is prohibited from doing. Interdict can be used to protect persons or property rights.[111] There were two problems with interdict under the common law as a means of securing protection from domestic violence. First, in order to establish that breach of interdict had taken place, a petition and complaint had to be brought with the concurrence of the Lord Advocate or the procurator fiscal.[112] Second, and more seriously, since interdict is a civil remedy, the police had no power to make an arrest simply for breach of interdict. Of course, where an offence has occurred the police can respond to that and it is not unusual for conduct which amounts to a breach of the peace to accompany a breach of interdict.[113]

12.32 The 1981 Act sought to meet the problem by introducing the term 'matrimonial interdict' and providing that a power of arrest must, in certain circumstances, be attached to such interdicts. Where a power of arrest has been attached, a police officer may arrest a person where there is reasonable cause to suspect that the person is in breach of interdict. What the 1981 Act actually did is best summed up by Clive, who said, '[t]he Act

104 Section 13(4).
105 Section 13(6).
106 Section 13(5).
107 Section 13(7) and (8).
108 The precise meaning of each of these terms is defined in the relevant statute and the relevant statutes are referred to in the 1981 Act.
109 D. M. Walker, *The Law of Civil Remedies in Scotland* (W. Green, 1974), at pp 214–246.
110 See for example, *Murdoch* v *Murdoch* 1973 SLT (Notes) 13, where interdict, prohibiting a husband from telephoning his wife or calling at her house, was refused as being too wide.
111 See for example, *MacLure* v *MacLure* 1911 SC 200, where a husband obtained interdict preventing his wife from entering a hotel he owned which had also been the matrimonial home.
112 *Gribben* v *Gribben* 1976 SLT 266.
113 See for example, *Dow* v *Hamilton* 1992 GWD 19–1096.

does not create a new remedy: it merely strengthens an old'.[114] 'Matrimonial interdict' for this purpose means an interdict, including an interim interdict, which

(a) restrains or prohibits any conduct of one spouse towards the other spouse or a child of the family, or
(b) prohibits a spouse from entering or remaining in a matrimonial home or in a specified area in the vicinity of the matrimonial home'.[115]

Arguably, paragraph (b) of this definition is too narrow. For example, it does not apply to a refuge where the spouse is staying temporarily, nor to his or her place of work, nor to a child's school. Accordingly, the Scottish Law Commission has recommended that the definition should be broadened to include such places.[116] An application for interdict can be made while the spouses are living together.[117] However, the courts have emphasised that interdict should not be used as a back-door method of obtaining an exclusion order.[118]

12.33 As we saw, the procedure following a breach of interdict is somewhat cumbersome. In the case of domestic violence, something rather more immediate is required. Thus it was that the 1981 Act came to introduce the idea of a power of arrest being attached to certain interdicts. There was a suspicion that the courts might be reluctant to attach such a power and the 1981 Act provides that, where requested to do so, the court *shall* attach a power of arrest

'(a) to any matrimonial interdict which is ancillary to an exclusion order, including an interim order,
(b) to any other matrimonial interdict where the non-applicant spouse has had the opportunity of being heard by or represented before the court, unless it appears to the court that in all the circumstances of the case such a power is unnecessary'.[119]

The power of arrest does not take effect until a copy of the interdict and the attached power of arrest have been served on the interdicted spouse. There is no provision for a power of arrest lasting for a specified time and it ceases to have effect on the termination of the marriage unless it has been recalled earlier.[120]

114 At para 15.104.
115 Section 14(2).
116 Report on Family Law, paras 11.30–11.31 and 11.33, rec 57(c) and draft Family Law (Scotland) Bill, clause 27(1).
117 Section 14(1) provides that '[i]t shall not be incompetent for the court to entertain an application by a spouse for a matrimonial interdict by reason only that the spouses are living together as man and wife'. The Commission has recommended that this should be couched in positive terms – Report on Family Law, paras 11.32–33, rec 57(a) and draft Family Law (Scotland) Bill, clause 27(1).
118 *Tattersall v Tattersall* 1983 SLT 506, at p 509. Again, the Commission has recommended amendment to the Act in order to clarify the interaction between interdict and exclusion – Report on Family Law, para 11.33, rec 57(b) and draft Family Law (Scotland) Bill, clause 27(1).
119 Section 15(1).
120 Section 15(2). The Commission has recommended that the power of arrest should not cease to have effect on the termination of the marriage but that it should cease to have

12.34 Where a power of arrest has been attached to an interdict, a police officer may arrest the interdicted spouse without a warrant where the officer has reasonable cause to suspect there has been a breach of interdict.[121] Where the spouse is arrested, he or she will be taken to a police station and may be liberated if the officer in charge is satisfied that there is no likelihood of violence towards the other spouse.[122] If the spouse is not liberated, he or she will be brought before the sheriff and may, in certain circumstances,[123] be detained for a period not exceeding two days. There-after, proceedings for breach of interdict may follow. The Scottish Law Commission has recommended simplification of the procedure following arrest.[124]

Cohabiting couples

12.35 The 1981 Act applies to heterosexual cohabitants, subject to two, very important, qualifications. First, a cohabitant who is neither owner nor tenant of the home has no automatic occupancy rights in the home.[125] He or she must apply to the court and, if the rights are granted, they may be of relatively short duration. As we saw, while marriage has a clearly defined beginning and end, cohabitation is a more fluid concept. This has an impact for occupancy rights. It is often the case with married couples that the court's intervention in respect of occupancy of the home is a temporary measure, until the whole issue of property is regulated in the course of the divorce. If the occupancy and other rights of cohabitants were not subject to any limit, in theory, they could go on indefinitely or until one partner returned to the court.[126] Second, the protection against dealings afforded to spouses does not apply in the case of a cohabitant.[127] In addition, and fairly obviously, the terminology used in the 1981 Act when dealing with spouses

effect, whether or not there is a divorce, three years after it was granted, unless it is recalled earlier – Report on Family Law, paras 11.37–39, rec 60 and draft Family Law (Scotland) Bill, clause 27(3).

121 Section 15(3). The Commission considered the possibility of requiring arrest for suspected breach of interdict and concluded that it was preferable to retain police discretion – Report on Family Law, para 11.36, rec 59.

122 Section 16(1).

123 Section 17(5).

124 Report on Family Law, paras 11.41–45, rec 62 and draft Family Law (Scotland) Bill, clause 27(4).

125 In the discussion paper, the Scottish Law Commission invited views on whether cohabitants should be given automatic occupancy rights. There was widespread opposition to the idea, not only from lawyers, financial institutions and the police, but also from Scottish Women's Aid who felt that such a change in the law would jeopardise the position of many women who are sole tenants in their homes. Accordingly, the Commission recommended no change – Report on Family Law, para 16.38.

126 Of course, it might be argued that, in the case of a married couple, property issues are only resolved in the divorce because one of the spouses went back to court to seek a divorce. Perhaps another reason for the distinction is, then, that cohabitation is seen as something less than marriage. See for example, the following statement, 'marriage is a status, which continues regardless, until it is brought to an end by divorce, whereas, and by contrast, cohabitation does not involve any status and must simply be a question of fact' – *Armour* v *Anderson* 1994 SLT (Sh Ct) 14 at p 15.

127 Section 18(5) expressly provides that nothing in s 18 prejudices the rights of any third party who has an interest in the home.

must be adapted when being applied to cohabitants. Thus, where applicable, they are known as entitled and non-entitled 'partners'. Of course, both partners may be entitled to occupy the home, but the court may still be called upon to regulate occupancy rights or to grant an exclusion order.

12.36 A cohabiting couple is defined as 'a man and woman who are living with each other as if they were man and wife'.[128] At one time, the use of the present tense in the definition was thought to limit the 1981 Act's application to couples who were actually cohabiting at the time of the application.[129] Fortunately, the courts have rejected this approach and the 1981 Act is now applied to couples who were cohabiting when the relevant events occurred regardless of the fact that they are no longer doing so.[130] This development is particularly important when one considers that the cohabitation may have ceased because one of the partners has fled from the violence of the other. If the courts were not to offer protection to such a partner, one of the fundamental goals of the 1981 Act would have been defeated. As Lord President Hope pointed out

> 'It clearly would be absurd if [section 18] had to be construed in a way which would make it impossible for one partner of a couple who had previously been cohabiting to obtain the benefits of its provision for herself and any child of the relationship without having to expose herself and the child to the risk of further abuse and injury'.[131]

In assessing whether a particular individual qualifies as a cohabitant under the 1981 Act, the court is directed to consider all the circumstances of the case including the duration of the cohabitation and whether there are any children of the relationship.[132]

12.37 How, then, does the 1981 Act operate in respect of cohabitants? Where a cohabitant is non-entitled, he or she can apply for occupancy rights in the home[133] and, initially, these may be granted for a period of up

---

128 Section 18(1).
129 *Verity* v *Fenner* (Sh Ct) 1993 SCLR (Notes) 223; *Crossley* v *Galletta* (Sh Ct) 1993 SCLR (Notes) 780.
130 *Armour* v *Anderson* (IH) 1994 SCLR 642. It is worth noting that both partners were entitled to occupy the home in that case.
131 *Armour* v *Anderson*, above, at p 647.
132 Section 18(2). This applies only to determining cohabitation for the purposes of s 18(1) and not for the purposes of s 18(3); *Armour* v *Anderson*, above, per Lord President Hope, at p 647.
133 In *McAlinden* v *Bearsden and Milngavie District Council* 1986 SLT 191, it was held that a cohabitant who had not applied for occupancy rights did not qualify as 'homeless' for the purposes of the Housing (Homeless Persons) Act 1977, s 1. Since a cohabitant has no rights until they are granted by the court, the logic of this decision may be doubted. In addition, it would appear to be somewhat inconsistent with the most recent code of guidance issued to local authorities by the Secretary of State, albeit the code is not binding on the courts – Tackling Homelessness (Scottish Office, 1994). In determining whether a person is homeless, the local authority is directed to take account of any risk of violence to which a person would be exposed if he or she occupied a particular home. Even the fact that an exclusion order has been granted is not to be regarded as establishing that it is safe for a person to return to the home. For a discussion of the 1981 Act and its interaction with housing legislation see Clive, paras 15.133–15.138.

to six months.[134] Thereafter, any number of extensions of up to six months each may be granted indefinitely. It should be noted that a cohabitant cannot apply for interim occupancy rights.[135] Where both partners are entitled to occupy the home, there is no need to apply for occupancy rights and the 1981 Act applies as if such rights had been granted.[136] Where the partners have occupancy rights, whether because they are both entitled partners or because occupancy rights have been granted to the non-entitled partner by the court, the provisions of the 1981 Act governing subsidiary and consequential rights, regulation of occupancy, exclusion orders and matrimonial interdicts, become available to them.[137] Thus, for example, such a partner can ask the court to regulate occupancy, apportion the cost of repairs, and exclude the other partner, just like a spouse.

12.38 As we saw, cohabitants with occupancy rights are not protected from a partner's dealings with third parties and the Scottish Law Commission has recommended no change to the law in this respect.[138] However, the Commission has recommended reform of the law to remedy a deficiency in the 1981 Act as it stands at present. Where one partner is entitled to occupy the home and the other is not, the entitled partner cannot apply for a matrimonial interdict with the power of arrest attached where the non-entitled partner has not applied for occupancy rights.[139] This closes off a whole avenue of protection to such an entitled partner and the Commission has recommended that the provisions on matrimonial interdicts be extended to cohabitants through what will be called a 'domestic interdict' and that the provisions of powers of arrest should apply to such interdicts.[140]

12.39 The definition of a cohabiting couple contained in the 1981 Act makes it clear that it does not apply to lesbian or homosexual couples. Thus, partners in such relationships remain in the precarious position of occupying the home at the discretion of a partner, where only one partner is the owner or tenant, and cannot seek the limited protection afforded to other cohabitants by the 1981 Act. Domestic violence in lesbian and homosexual relationships has received less attention than similar behaviour in heterosexual relationships.[141] None the less, the problem exists and,

---

134 Section 18(1).
135 *Smith-Milne* v *Gammack* (Sh Ct) 1995 SCLR 1058. While Clive (at para 15.118, n 67) rightly takes the view that there is a need for reform of the law on this point, the Scottish Law Commission has made no such recommendation.
136 Section 18(3).
137 The following provisions of the Act apply: s 2 (subsidiary and consequential rights), s 3 (regulatory orders), s 4 (exclusion orders), s 5(1) (variation or recall of orders), s 13 (tenancy transfer orders), s 14 (matrimonial interdicts), s 15 (attachment of power of arrest to a matrimonial interdict), s 16 (procedure after arrest), s 17 (interdict) and s 22 (interpretation).
138 Report on Family Law, para 16.39.
139 *Bell* v *Lorimer* 1989 SCLR 759. An entitled partner cannot obtain an exclusion order against a non-entitled partner who had not applied for occupancy rights, since the non-entitled partner has no right to occupy – *Clarke* v *Hatten* 1987 SCLR 527.
140 Report on Family Law, para 16.40, rec 84(a) and draft Family Law (Scotland) Bill, clause 39.
141 There is a growing body of literature, none the less. See, for example, P. G. Barnes, '''It's Just A Quarrel'': Some States Offer No Domestic Violence Protection to Gays' 84 ABA

where this is the case, partners are left in the vulnerable position of having to 'put up, or ship out'. Given that the legal system is prepared to offer some protection from domestic violence to heterosexual couples, it is wholly indefensible that it is not offered to all couples. Of course, ordinary interdicts and the criminal law are available to offer protection to everyone but, as we have seen, the legal system itself has accepted the inadequacy of these remedies in dealing with the problem of domestic violence.

Debt, sequestration and the family home

12.40 Where the spouse who owns or co-owns the home becomes insolvent, the family home may be one of his or her main assets. Clearly, the trustee in the sequestration may want to sell the home for the benefit of creditors. If the home were to be treated just like any other asset, the debtor's family would risk losing the roof over their heads. For this reason, the family home receives special treatment under the Bankruptcy (Scotland) Act 1985 ('the 1985 Act'). 'Family home' in this context is more narrowly defined than under the 1981 Act, being the home which was occupied as a residence on the day before sequestration by the debtor and spouse, or by the debtor's spouse or former spouse, or by the debtor and a child of the family.[142] We saw that there can be more than one 'matrimonial home' for the purpose of the 1981 Act. Can a debtor have more than one 'family home' which receives special treatment? Applying the definition from the 1985 Act, this certainly seems possible. For example, a debtor may be living with her husband and their children in one home, while another home is occupied by her ex-husband and the children of that marriage. Both homes would appear to be covered. As we shall see, when it is deciding how to treat the home, the court is directed to consider a number of factors, including the interests of the creditors, and it has considerable discretion. So, while a debtor may have more than one family home, the court's willingness to protect more than one of them may be curtailed by the interests of the creditors. It should be noted that the home of a debtor living alone, or a debtor living with a cohabitant and no children, does not receive special treatment.

J 24 (1998); K. F. Duthu, 'Why Doesn't Anyone Talk About Gay and Lesbian Domestic Violence?' 18 Thomas Jefferson L Rev 23 (1996); S. E. Lundy, 'Abuse That Dare Not Speak Its Name: Assisting Victims of Lesbian and Gay Domestic Violence in Massachusetts' 28 New Eng L Rev 273 (1993); C. M. Da Luz, 'A Legal and Social Comparison of Heterosexual and Same-Sex Domestic Violence: Similar Inadequacies in Legal Recognition and Response' 4 S Cal Rev L & Women's Stud 251 (1994); N. E. Murphy, 'Queer Justice: Equal Protection for Victims of Same-Sex Domestic Violence' 30 Val U L Rev 335 (1995); and R. Robson, 'Lavender Bruises: Intra-Lesbian Violence, Law and Lesbian Legal Theory' 20 Golden Gate U L R 567 (1990).

142 Bankruptcy (Scotland) Act 1985, s 40(4)(a). 'Child of the family' is also defined slightly differently from the definition in the 1981 Act. Where the child is not a child or grandchild of the debtor or spouse, the 1985 Act requires that the child has been 'accepted' as a member of the family (s 40(4)(b)), whereas, the 1981 Act required that such a child had been 'treated' as a member of the family. Arguably, while treatment can be assessed on objective criteria, acceptance involves a psychological and subjective element. While conceptually interesting (see chapter 6, para 64), the distinction may be of no great practical significance in this context.

12.41 The trustee in sequestration may not sell a family home without the consent of the debtor's spouse or former spouse or the permission of the court.[143] The court may refuse the application, grant it subject to conditions[144] or postpone the granting of it for up to a year. In reaching its decision, the court is directed to have regard to all the circumstances of the case, including, the needs and financial resources of the debtor's spouse or former spouse, the needs and resources of any child of the family, the interests of the creditors, and the length of time that the residence has been used as a family home.[145] As Clive points out, '[a]s the needs of the spouse will very often be diametrically opposed to the interests of the creditors, and as the Act gives no indication of the weight to be attached to each, this will be a very difficult discretion to exercise'.[146]

12.42 As we saw earlier, if the sequestration is simply a contrivance by the debtor to defeat a spouse's occupancy rights, the spouse can apply to the court to have the sequestration recalled.[147] Since the spouse has a fairly short time in which to make such an application,[148] the trustee in sequestration is obliged to inform him or her of the right to challenge.[149]

12.43 When we looked at the matrimonial home, we saw that the legislation recognised that a home without furniture or essential kitchen items was of limited use. Similarly, the Debtors (Scotland) Act 1987[150] recognises the importance of such items in exempting them from poinding where such goods are located in the dwelling-house of the debtor and reasonably required for use there by the debtor or a member of his or her household.[151] It should be noted that this provision *does* protect the household goods of a debtor living alone or with a cohabitant. Again, the definition of exactly what is protected differs between the 1981 Act and the 1987 Act, the latter providing a detailed list of, largely, practical household items.[152] These items do not pass to the trustee if the debtor is sequestrated.[153] Where such items are co-owned by the debtor and his or spouse,

143 Section 40(1). The procedure differs depending on whether the debtor is the owner or co-owner of the home. If the debtor is the owner, the trustee makes a summary application. If the debtor is a co-owner, the trustee should raise an action of division and sale and the court is directed to consider the same factors as apply to an application to sell – s 40(3). See, *Salmon's Trustees* v *Salmon* 1989 SLT (Sh Ct) 49.
144 *McMahon's Trustee* v *McMahon* 1997 SLT 1090.
145 Section 40(2).
146 At para 16.023. He goes on to observe that often the only way to give weight to both factors might be to postpone granting the application in order to allow the spouse to find alternative accommodation. For this reason, he suggests (not very strongly) that the court's power to refuse the application should, perhaps, be abolished.
147 Section 41(1)(b).
148 The statutory time limit is 10 weeks from the date of sequestration.
149 Section 41(1)(a).
150 Debtors (Scotland) Act 1987, s 16.
151 Certain other goods, including the debtor's clothing and the tools of his or her trade, are exempted from poinding regardless of where they are located – s 16(1).
152 It includes such items as: beds and bedding, chairs or settees, tables, food, cooking utensils, articles used for safety in the dwelling-house (eg a smoke detector) and tools used for maintenance of the dwelling-house.
153 Bankruptcy (Scotland) Act 1985, s 33(1)(a).

it is thought that they are exempt from poinding.[154] So far as other, non-exempt goods are concerned, where the debtor co-owns them with a spouse, they can be poinded, but the co-owner may buy out the debtor's share by paying the appropriate sum of money to an officer of the court. If the debtor is sequestrated, his or her share of co-owned goods passes to the trustee who can then apply for division and sale and, unlike applications to sell the family home, the court has no discretion to refuse or postpone the decree when the application relates to other property. Given that essential household goods are exempt, this may not seem particularly harsh. After all, people can get by without the television, the stereo and, at a stretch, the computer. However, when one considers that the family car, which has always been used for taking the children to school and leisure activities, might be lost, the disruption of family life becomes apparent.

SPECIAL TREATMENT OF THE FAMILY HOME

12.44 As this chapter illustrates, the home is not treated in the same way as other property. While actual ownership is not affected, marriage and, to a lesser extent, cohabitation, have an impact on the spouse's or cohabitant's free use of this particular kind of property. Indeed, an individual's personal relationship may result in that person being excluded from the home altogether. That the law should take this approach is a matter of policy, reflecting both the importance of having a home and where priorities will be placed should domestic violence occur. Not only are the provisions of the ordinary criminal law available in the fight against domestic violence, the 1981 Act seeks to provide additional protection tailor-made to meet the particular context in which the domestic violence is present. Attempts continue to ensure that awareness of the problem does not abate, as evidenced most recently by the Zero Tolerance and Scottish Office[155] campaigns and it is essential that we should not let up in getting over the very simple message that domestic violence is wholly unacceptable. The scale of the problem remains enormous. Scottish Women's Aid received 49,717 requests for information, support or safe refuge in the one-year period 1996–97.[156] This represents 136 women asking for help in Scotland every day. Only a fraction of the female victims[157] of domestic

---

154 See, Clive at para 16.027 and W. J. Stewart, 'Non-Debtor Spouses and the Contents of Houses' 1989 SLT (News) 180.
155 See S. MacAskill and D. Eadie, An Evaluation of the Scottish Office Domestic Violence Media Campaign (HMSO, 1995).
156 Scottish Women's Aid Annual Report 1996–97, p 6. This was an increase of 19% on previous year's figures. While it is encouraging that victims of domestic violence seek help from Women's Aid and other resources, thus demonstrating that victims are no longer prepared to put up with the intolerable, the fact that the problem is so widespread is horrifying.
157 It is acknowledged that there are male victims of domestic violence and, of course, that domestic violence perpetrated against men is every bit as unacceptable as that perpetrated against women. The reported incidence of domestic violence and the literature suggest, however, that women make up a far higher proportion of victims than do men, even allowing for under-reporting by men.

violence approach Women's Aid.[158] The policy considerations in which the 1981 Act is rooted reach beyond the spouses, cohabitants and the children involved, and can have an impact on the rights of third parties and, in particular, on purchasers of heritable property and creditors. In this respect the law must balance competing and, often, incompatible, interests. The system developed is not perfect and, even if the Scottish Law Commission's recommendations are implemented, injustice will result in individual cases. None the less, the special treatment afforded to the family home represents a real attempt to tackle some of the most pressing problems of modern child and family law.

158 The Scottish Needs Assessment Programme (SNAP) found that up to 750,000 women in Scotland are victims of domestic violence and treating these victims costs £110 million per year. Of course, that sum is for medical treatment only and does not include the many other cost implications of domestic violence, including, dealing with the impact on the health of the many children who witness domestic violence; housing; police time; legal aid and court time; *The Scotsman*, 28 October 1997, p 8.

CHAPTER 13

SEPARATION AND DIVORCE

13.1 Much is made of the fact that Scots law permitted divorce in certain limited circumstances from the time of the Reformation,[1] some 300 years before judicial divorce was possible in England and Wales.[2] That Scots law allowed some spouses to escape marriages at an early stage in our legal history may be a matter of pride, but we should be careful about over-emphasising our ground-breaking position. Firstly, divorce was only available to the 'innocent' spouse and, even then, only where his or her partner had committed the matrimonial offences of adultery or desertion. Secondly, the prevailing economic conditions made divorce less of an option than it is today. Most women were in no position to support themselves and, unless their husbands had sufficient property to enable the court to provide for support, the practicalities effectively precluded divorce.[3] As we shall see in chapter 14, the whole system for financial provision on divorce was very different.[4] Thirdly, not only were the grounds for divorce very limited, but the social climate did not make it the widely-accepted solution to marital dissatisfaction that it has become. For the majority of the

1 The Kirk Sessions of the reformed church took it upon themselves to grant divorce for adultery as early as 1559, although the Act of 1573 (c 55) permitted an innocent spouse to seek a divorce in the civil courts for adultery or desertion. See, *An Introduction to Scottish Legal History* (Stair Society, vol 20).

2 Prior to the Matrimonial Causes Act 1857, which introduced judicial divorce (for adultery only) in England and Wales, the only way to obtain a divorce was by private Act of Parliament, an expensive process and, thus, one which was inaccessible to all but a few. Given that Scots law only required the defender to reside here for 40 days in order to found jurisdiction, one might have expected a cross-border trade in divorce, parallel to the market in runaway marriages. It does not appear that this happened, not least because of a refusal on the part of courts south of the border to recognise such divorces. For a discussion of the history of divorce in England and Wales, see N. V. Lowe and G. Douglas, *Bromley's Family Law* (9th edn, Butterworths, 1998), at pp 225–227 and S. M. Cretney and J. M. Masson, *Principles of Family Law* (6th edn, Sweet & Maxwell, 1997) at pp 305–306.

3 Access to divorce itself was not dependent upon resources, however, since the poor's roll made free legal services available to the very poor from the 15th century onwards. The Legal Aid (Scotland) Act 1949 introduced civil legal aid, along the lines we know today. Given the current, savage cuts in legal aid and the possibility that further economies may be in the pipeline, we may find that free or, at least, assisted, divorce will be less accessible in the future than it was in the past.

4 Until 1964, financial provision on divorce was based on the fiction that the defender had died at the date of the decree of divorce. This meant that the pursuer could receive an award out of any available capital but there was no provision for the award of a periodical allowance. For the majority of couples who had no capital, this meant that the pursuer gained no financial provision. See chapter 14, paras 14–15.

Scottish people, it is only comparatively recently that divorce lost its, fairly considerable, social stigma.[5]

13.2 A further point is worth noting, in the context of the world scene. Divorce is an ancient concept and was available, for example, under Roman law.[6] Nor were other jurisdictions as slow as England and Wales to make provision for divorce. The availability of divorce in the USA varied considerably depending on location but, during the colonial period, while divorce was not available in the south, Pennsylvania enacted legislation permitting divorce for adultery as early as 1682 and later expanded the grounds to include incest, bigamy and homosexuality. After Independence, regional variation continued, but divorce was available in a number of states.[7] In France, the ethos of the Revolution and the attendant notion of individual liberty resulted in divorce becoming available by mutual consent, albeit this liberal law was fairly short-lived.[8] Even where divorce was not available, legal systems often accommodated marital disharmony through the concepts of nullity or separation. Prior to the Reformation, both were possible in Scotland, with nullity being granted on a broader range of grounds than is presently the case.[9] Of course, while nullity leaves each spouse free to remarry, separation does not have this effect.[10] In addition, where divorce is not possible spouses will often separate in fact and, indeed, may go on to cohabit with new partners.[11]

13.3 None the less, the Act of 1573 marked the first statutory recognition of the post-Reformation common law acceptance of divorce.[12] As we have

5 One need go no further than consulting grandparents and, perhaps, parents, to find this view expressed. Even amongst the aristocracy, where different social norms sometimes applied, divorce could still attract salacious interest and disapproval – see, for example, *Argyll* v *Argyll* 1962 SC 140 and 1962 SC (HL) 88 and the abdication of Edward VII following his decision to marry Wallis Simpson, a divorcee.

6 Of course, Roman law spans a broad spectrum but by the time of the late republic, divorce was a reasonably common occurrence, at least amongst the upper classes; see H. F. Jolowicz, *Historical Introduction to the Study of Roman Law* (2nd edn, Cambridge University Press, 1967) at p 245.

7 New York's law of 1785 allowed divorce for adultery only, while Vermont's law of 1787 included adultery, impotence, intolerable severity, three years desertion, and a long absence with a presumption of death, as grounds for divorce. New Hampshire allowed divorce if a spouse joined the Shaker sect, a provision described by Friedman as 'not an unreasonable rule, since the Shakers did not believe in sexual intercourse' – L. M. Friedman, *A History of American Law* (2nd edn, Simon and Schuster, 1985) at p 206.

8 The provisions of the 1792 law disappeared with the Civil Code in 1804 – see M. A. Glendon, *The Transformation of Family Law: State, Law and Family in the United States and Western Europe* (University of Chicago Press, 1989) at pp 159–160.

9 P. Fraser, *Husband and Wife According to the Law of Scotland* (2nd edn, W. Green & Son, 1976–78), II, 1129–1139.

10 For a discussion of the modern law on separation, see paras 13.5–13.10.

11 See, for example, the discussion of the position in Italy where 'many Italians followed the age-old custom of dissolving their unions by departure' – Glendon, n 8 above, at pp 17–18. For a discussion of the position in Ireland see, W. Duncan, 'The Divorce Referendum in the Republic of Ireland: Resisting the Tide' (1988) 2 International Journal of Law and the Family 62.

12 See Clive, at para 20.001, where he describes the Reformers as 'basing themselves precariously on two scriptural passages' in concluding that adultery and desertion justified divorce.

seen, divorce was available to the innocent spouse on the grounds of his or her partner's desertion for four years or adultery. Thus, initially, the whole concept of divorce was centred on the notion of fault, with an innocent spouse being entitled to seek divorce because his or her partner had committed one of these specific matrimonial offences. These remained the grounds for divorce until 1938 when cruelty, sodomy, bestiality and incurable insanity were added.[13] This marked a slight, but only slight, departure from fault as the central concept in divorce. With the addition of a partner's incurable insanity as a ground for divorce, there was recognition of what we now accept as a marriage having broken down due to circumstances where no blame was being attributed. The Divorce (Scotland) Act 1976 ('the 1976 Act') was the next landmark in the history of divorce in Scotland and it provides for the circumstances in which a divorce can be obtained today.[14] It purports to provide that divorce is available only where the marriage has broken down irretrievably. However, as we shall see, this is not the reality of the current law, since irretrievable breakdown itself can only be established by proving one of five factual circumstances: adultery; behaviour; desertion followed by two years non-cohabitation; two years non-cohabitation with consent; and five years non-cohabitation.[15] If one of these circumstances is established, breakdown will be accepted, whether or not that has happened, in fact. If the pursuer cannot satisfy one of the five circumstances, no amount of pleading that the marriage has broken down irretrievably will lead to decree of divorce being granted. Furthermore, while the phrase 'irretrievable breakdown' suggests a move towards a system of no-fault divorce, what we have is a mixed or part-fault system, with fault being at the heart of two of the grounds (adultery and desertion), no-fault being central to two others (two or five years non-cohabitation) and a third ground, behaviour, containing elements of both.

13.4 There is a tendency in looking at the law on adult relationships to discuss marriage and cohabitation, on the one hand, and move on swiftly to consider separation and divorce, on the other. It is as if there is nothing in between and, for the lawyer, that may often be true of his or her professional contribution. For individuals involved in personal relationships, however, there is a great deal between these two points. Not all relationships which experience problems end in divorce or separation. Some couples, whether married or cohabiting, overcome the problems, repair the damage and may go on to live happily ever after. In this context,

---

13 Divorce (Scotland) Act 1938, which enacted the recommendations of the Royal Commission on Divorce and Matrimonial Causes (Gorrell Commission) (Cd 6478, 1912). Clearly, delay in implementing enlightened law reform proposals is not a wholly new phenomenon. The Act also reduced the period of desertion from four years to three. Similar legislative provision had been made for England and Wales in the Matrimonial Causes Act 1937.

14 In its original form, the 1976 Act provided for both the grounds of divorce and financial provision on divorce. As far as financial provision is concerned, the 1976 Act has been superseded by the Family Law (Scotland) Act 1985 which now governs financial provision on divorce and is discussed in chapter 14.

15 Divorce (Scotland) Act 1976, s 1(2).

there are a host of professional and other organisations and individuals which can offer assistance.[16] While it might be both patronising and paternalistic for a lawyer to discuss the possibility of reconciliation with every client, it is helpful to bear the possibility in mind. As we shall see, the law not only accepts reconciliation attempts as part of the general divorce picture, it encourages them.[17] Where reconciliation is not an option or the attempt does not work, it is worth remembering, none the less, that the breakdown of a relationship is very rarely sudden. It is a continuum[18] and most people seeking a divorce bring considerable baggage with them. Ideally, the practitioner in this area of the law should be not only sensitive and tactful, he or she should have considerable inner resources as well.

SEPARATION

De facto separation

13.5 At the outset, it important to distinguish between *de facto*, or factual, separation and *de jure*, or legal, separation. *De facto* separation involves the couple in simply distancing themselves from each other, often by having separate accommodation, and is more commonly known as 'splitting up'. While it will usually involve considerable emotional and psychological elements, it is essentially a practical state, and a variable one at that. It may be temporary or permanent. Some couples use this arrangement to see if they can work through difficulties they are experiencing. Others intend the separation to be permanent and, in addition, may plan to divorce. It may be total or partial. Some separated couples live in different homes and do not communicate at all. Others continue to see each other. Yet others occupy the same home but lead fairly distant lives. The point here is that this kind of separation does not involve any legal process.

13.6 Since cohabitants are not required to go through any legal procedure in order to terminate their relationship, *de facto* separation is all that is required of them to achieve that end and, indeed, for some people, this is one of the attractions of cohabitation. However, they may still have a host of ancillary matters to resolve, particularly if they have children or have

---

16 Couples Counselling (formerly the Scottish Marriage Counselling Service – the Scottish equivalent of the organisation Relate, in England and Wales) is, perhaps, the best-known organisation in this field. Other organisations include Family Mediation and Scottish Marriage Care (formerly, the Catholic Marriage Advisory Service). See the Appendix for details of these organisations. In addition, there are a variety of private counselling services and therapists who work in the area of family relationships.

17 See paras 13.30–13.31.

18 For an excellent discussion of the continuum and what the authors describe as the 'phases or stages' of divorce see, H. H. Irving and M. Benjamin, *Family Mediation: Contemporary Issues* (Sage Publications, 1995), pp 17–48. While this book concentrates on the position in Canada and the USA, much of its content can inform discussion here. Much the same point is made by Maccoby and Mnookin when they draw distinctions between 'spousal divorce' (the ending of the intimate relationship between the husband and wife), 'economic divorce' (setting up of two households), 'parental divorce' (establishing new parenting roles), and 'legal divorce' (the decree) – E. E. Maccoby and R. H. Mnookin, *Dividing the Child: Social and Legal Dilemmas of Custody* (Harvard University Press, 1994) at pp 19–58.

acquired property together. If they cannot agree on these matters, they will have to go to court for a resolution of disputed issues. For married couples, *de facto* separation has no effect on their legal relationship, although it may form the basis of their divorce after two or five years. They will continue to have all the rights and obligations of married persons and so, for example, if one of them forms a new relationship, the other may raise an action for divorce on the basis of adultery. Again, any disputes over children or property may be resolved by the parties themselves or in the courts.

13.7 Where married partners separate and reach agreement on ancillary matters, they may prefer to formalise their decision in a written separation agreement.[19] As Clive[20] points out, such agreements have a number of disadvantages. If it is intended that the separation will only be temporary, a formal agreement may simply entrench positions and reinforce the separation. If the parting is permanent, a separation is a much less efficient way to recognise breakdown than is divorce. In either case, since this is simply a form of contract, the weaker party is at the mercy of the stronger, whether that strength comes from economic, personal or other factors. Separation agreements are revocable while the parties are alive[21] and can be varied by the court in respect of children[22] and aliment.[23]

Judicial separation

13.8 Judicial separation is a remedy which applies only to married couples and involves the court in granting a decree ordaining the spouses to live apart. It is an ancient remedy and has its rationale in a time when husbands controlled their wives property, actions of adherence were competent, aliment was only available to a spouse who was willing to adhere, and divorce was only available on limited grounds. Every legal reason for its existence has now disappeared. As we have seen, husbands and wives are treated on an equal basis as far as control and ownership of their property is concerned,[24] actions of adherence have been abolished[25] and aliment is not subject to a willingness to adhere.[26] A decree of separation is available on precisely the same grounds, and subject to the

---

19 For a detailed discussion of separation agreements see, Clive, paras 19.003–19.041. The content of such agreements has been covered comprehensively for the practitioner in I. L. S. Balfour, *Separation Agreements* (W. Green, 1997), available in software format.
20 At para 19.003.
21 *Palmer* v *Bonnar* 25 January 1810, FC; *McKeddie* v *McKeddie* (1902) 9 SLT 381.
22 The court has to make decisions on the basis of the child's best interests regardless of agreements made by, for example, the parents or its own previous decisions – Children (Scotland) Act 1995, s 11. Of course, this requires that someone brings the case to court.
23 Family Law (Scotland) Act 1985, s 7(2).
24 The *ius maritii* and the *ius administrationis* were abolished by the Married Women's Property (Scotland) Acts 1881 and 1920 respectively.
25 Law Reform (Husband and Wife) (Scotland) Act 1984, s 2(1).
26 Family Law (Scotland) Act 1985, s 2. It is only a defence to an action of aliment by a person over the age of 16 that the defender is willing to support him or her in the defender's household if it would be reasonable to expect the pursuer to accept such an offer. If the pursuer had grounds for a separation, it would not normally be reasonable to expect the pursuer to live in the defender's household.

same defences, as is a decree of divorce.[27] Most ironic of all is the fact that most couples have, in fact, already separated when the court ordains them to do just that.

13.9 In the course of considering the abolition of judicial separation,[28] the Scottish Law Commission asked the Central Research Unit of the Scottish Office to carry out empirical research into its use.[29] The research found that the use of judicial separations had been falling steadily[30] and that most actions were raised in the Glasgow area.[31] Most actions raised involved craves for other remedies as well, usually relating to such matters as children, aliment and the family home.[32] Since all of these matters can be dealt with independently of an action for separation, one wonders why the remedy is used at all. Platts' research suggests a number of reasons[33] and others can be surmised. A pursuer might have economic or personal reasons, like wanting to preserve the right to aliment or a pension or simply to delay divorce as long as possible.[34] Some pursuers want a record of 'who was to blame' for the breakdown of the relationship, without taking what they see as the drastic step of divorce. In other cases, the use of judicial separation may be premised on the pursuer's incomplete or erroneous understanding of the law. An individual might oppose divorce on religious grounds, but that does not explain why he or she would seek a decree of separation.

13.10 For completeness, it is worth noting that, apart from putting a legal stamp of approval on the parties' factual separation, a decree of separation does little to alter the parties' legal position. It does not convert a spouse into a single person. It does not remove the obligation to aliment. It makes no difference to the parties' rights in respect of the matrimonial home. It makes little difference to succession.[35] Little wonder, then, that the Scottish Law Commission has recommended the abolition of this anachronistic remedy.[36]

27 Divorce (Scotland) Act 1976, ss 1 and 4.
28 The idea of abolition was first mooted in the Discussion Paper Family Law: Pre-consolidation Reforms (Scot Law Com Disc Paper No 85, 1985), paras 7.1–7.8.
29 A. Platts, The Use of Judicial Separation (Scottish Office, Central Research Unit, 1992). For research on the use of judicial separation in England and Wales, see. S. Maidment, Judicial Separation (Centre for Socio-Legal Studies, 1982).
30 Between 1985 and 1989, the number of decrees granted fell from 234 to 116 – Platts, chapter 2, para 2.
31 Platts, chapter 2, para 3.
32 Platts, chapter 2, paras, 7, 11 and 12.
33 Platts interviewed a number of solicitors who used separation actions and their comments are interesting – Platts, chapter 3.
34 As we shall see, the defender in such actions can seek divorce after five years regardless of his or her spouse's opposition.
35 Where a wife (but not a husband) dies intestate after she has obtained a decree of separation, all property acquired by her after the decree does not pass to her husband – Conjugal Rights (Scotland) Amendment Act 1861, s 6. The narrow ambit and sexist nature of this provision can be explained by historical reasons which no longer provide justification for it.
36 Report on Family Law (Scot Law Com No 135, 1992), paras 12.1–12.19, rec 66 and draft Bill, clause 29.

DIVORCE

What kind of divorce provision might we have?

13.11 With few exceptions, divorce law has been based historically on the concept of one party being to blame for the breakdown of a marriage. Where a fault-based system permitted any exception, it normally related to divorce where a spouse was insane or, at least, the conduct complained of was prompted by mental illness or disorder. This was a reflection of the importance attached to marriage as a social and economic institution and, in some cases, as a religious act. In the context of legal theory, marriage was seen as a status and, thus, required serious reason to be undone, or it was a contract, and breach of the contract required it to be shown that one or other party had failed to fulfil his or her obligations under it. Changing social attitudes and the very fact that divorce was a remedy being used more frequently prompted questioning of the whole fabric of our value systems, in general, and of divorce law, in particular.

13.12 Throughout the 1960s, fault-based divorce came under attack for a number of reasons. Firstly, marriages break down for a host of reasons and, while it is possible to focus on the conduct of one party, it is rarely the case that that party's conduct is the sole cause of the marital breakdown. The other partner will often have contributed something to the whole process. Thus, to centre a divorce solely on the 'guilty party's' behaviour is often both inaccurate and unfair. Secondly, relationships develop and change, sometimes positively, sometimes negatively, often with a combination of both aspects. Where a couple decide that, on balance, their relationship has more negative than positive aspects and they wish to end it, why should the legal system make them point fingers and accuse each other of short-comings? Such an approach can only increase conflict, cause or, at least, exacerbate, acrimony, and frequently results in much unnecessary washing of dirty laundry in public. If one function of the legal system is to provide for the resolution of disputes in a compassionate and efficient way, a fault-based system is not the way to approach divorce. In addition, such a system does nothing to facilitate future co-operation between the parties – something which is crucial if there are children involved. Of course, this argument was viewed by some as carrying less weight where only one party wanted a divorce. Where the other spouse wished the marriage to continue and had 'done nothing wrong', it might be argued that he or she should feel secure in the knowledge that the marriage would continue. On the other hand, what purpose would this serve? Only a naive and overbearing legal system would attempt to force people to live together and, even then, it would be powerless to make one person be pleasant to, far less, love, another. Thirdly, if fault had to be established before a divorce could be granted, some couples might be driven to collude in manufacturing the necessary evidence or simply perjuring themselves, in order to be free of each other.[37] Arguably, no legal system should encourage such action if it is to retain credibility.

---

37 There is ample anecdotal evidence that adultery was used in this way by couples anxious to divorce prior to the 1976 Act.

13.13   In the face of such opposition, one might ask whether the notion of fault has any place in divorce at all. It can be argued that some behaviour, and particularly violence,[38] may be so reprehensible that, not only should the law condemn it unequivocally, but the victim should be able to make as swift an exit from the marriage as possible. However, the legal system does condemn violence within marriage by providing that the offender will face criminal sanctions.[39] The criminal law may provide inadequate protection for some victims but, if the threat of imprisonment cannot achieve that end, it is difficult to see how the civil remedy of divorce can. If helping the victim to escape from a violent marriage is the goal, then it can be achieved in other ways by, for example, providing for a quick and efficient system of divorce in all cases. A second reason that is sometimes presented for the retention of fault is the bolstering of marriage by indicating what is and is not acceptable behaviour. In a sense the 'taking marriage seriously' argument suggests that the law has a role in laying down moral parameters and in letting people know the rules. The consequence is that innocent spouses can feel secure in the knowledge that they cannot be divorced against their will and guilty spouses know that there will be penalties, in terms of divorce and, possibly, the economic consequences of divorce, if they break the rules. A third argument for fault is that it helps innocent spouses to feel vindicated and lays blame squarely at the door of the guilty spouse. Of course, this assumes that the breakdown of the marriage is clearly attributable to one spouse, something that has already been questioned here. Even where one party is clearly responsible for the breakdown, it must be questioned whether a finding of 'guilt' in a decree of divorce really serves any purpose. Very few people are likely to see it. Sometimes it is suggested that the religious significance of marriage requires either no divorce at all or some place for fault in the process. That may be an argument for how individuals who subscribe to a particular religion choose to run their lives. It is not, however, any argument at all for the way in which a legal system, catering to a multi-cultural society, ought to approach any issue.

13.14   The impact of the debate from the 1960s was interesting. In England and Wales, the Divorce Reform Act 1969[40] introduced divorce along much the same lines as are found currently in the Divorce (Scotland) Act 1976. The proponents of no-fault divorce had their first victory in the USA in 1969 in, perhaps unsurprisingly, California. By the 1970s every state had rejected what might be called 'full-fault' divorce: that is, a system whereby divorce could only be granted by one party establishing that the other had done something that breached the marital obligation. While

---

38 Whether a similar argument can be made for other forms of matrimonial misconduct, like adultery or desertion, is open to question. It might be argued that we took the decision that adultery was a private rather than a public matter when it was de-criminalised. It is questionable that the public perception of either form of behaviour puts it on the same footing as violence.

39 For a discussion of domestic violence and the legal system's responses to it see chapter 12, paras 31–34.

40 The Act was a product of proposals emanating from the Law Commission there – Reform of the Grounds of Divorce: The Field of Choice (Cmnd 3123, 1966). These

some states abandoned fault altogether, others retained it, either as an alternative ground for divorce or in decisions on ancillary matters, most often property disputes. As we have seen, the Divorce (Scotland) Act 1976 was part of the same trend in retaining fault but permitting divorce on no-fault grounds as well.[41] While divorce for fault remains competent and, as we shall see, reasonably popular, consensual divorce became available after two years separation and unilateral divorce became possible after five years non-cohabitation.

13.15 Sir Isaac Newton was not simply articulating a law of physics when he noted that, for every action, there is an equal and opposite reaction. He could have been commenting on prevailing attitudes to legal issues, in general, and the law on divorce, in particular. In the USA a veritable war is currently being waged between proponents and opponents of no-fault divorce,[42] with some strange bedfellows emerging.[43] No-fault divorce is blamed for moral decline, the post-divorce poverty of women and children,[44] juvenile crime and even the increase of domestic violence within marriage.[45] The law on divorce in England and Wales was altered radically

proposals were themselves a response to the proposals of a group appointed by the Archbishop of Canterbury – Putting Asunder: A Divorce Law for Contemporary Society (Society for Propagation of Christian Knowledge, 1966).

41 As we saw earlier, the Family Law (Scotland) Act 1985 governs financial provision on divorce. It banishes fault from the calculation in making such financial provision and will be discussed in chapter 14.

42 Without wishing to do the authors the injustice of over-simplification or compartmentalisation of their positions, the following are a selection of articles from the current debate. Opponents of no-fault divorce: M. F. Brinig and S. M. Crafton, 'Marriage and Opportunism' 23 J Legal Stud 869 (1994); C. E. Schneider, 'Marriage, Morals and Law: No-Fault Divorce and Moral Discourse' 1994 Utah L Rev 558 (1994); L. D. Wardle, 'Divorce, Violence and the No-Fault Divorce Culture' 1994 Utah L Rev 741 (1994); M. Zelder, 'The Economic Analysis of the Effect of No-Fault Divorce Law on the Divorce Rate' 16 Harv J L and Pub Pol'y 241 (1993). Supporters of no-fault divorce: I. M. Ellman, 'The Place of Fault in a Modern Divorce Law' 28 Ariz St L J 773 (1996); I. M. Ellman and S. Lohr, 'Marriage as Contract, Opportunistic Violence and Other Bad Arguments for Fault Divorce' 1997 U Ill L Rev 719; E. S. Scott, 'Rehabilitating Liberalism in Modern Divorce Law' 1994 Utah L Rev 687.

43 For example, some feminists find themselves opposing no-fault divorce, albeit for different reasons, alongside religious fundamentalists and members of the far-right. For a variety of feminist perspectives on divorce see: G. Blumberg, 'Reworking the Past, Imagining the Future: On Jacob's Silent Ladder' 16 L & Soc Inquiry 115 (1991); Brinig and Crafton, above; M. A. Fineman, *Illusion of Equality: The Rhetoric and Reality of Divorce Reform* (University of Chicago Press, 1991); S. A. M. Gavigan, 'Paradise Lost, Paradox Revisited: The Implications of Family Ideology for Feminist, Lesbian and Gay Engagement to Law' 31 Osgoode Hall L J 589 (1993); H. H. Kay, 'Equality and Difference' 56 U Cin L Rev 1 (1987); M. Regan, 'Divorce Reform and the Legacy of Gender' 90 Mich L Rev 1453 (1992); Scott, above.

44 The phrase 'the feminization of poverty' emerged in the USA in the 1980s, largely as a result of the work of L. J. Weitzman – see, L. J. Weitzman, 'The Alimony Myth: Does No-Fault Divorce Make a Difference?' 14 Fam L Q 141 (1980) and L. J. Weitzman, *The Divorce Revolution: The Unexpected Social and Economic Consequences for Women and Children in America* (Free Press, 1985). Professor Weitzman's work has whipped up an academic storm in the USA. See chapter 14, para 27.

45 Ellman and Lohr, above, present a direct challenge, not only to the reasoning of Brinig and Crafton, but to their statistical analysis showing that no-fault divorce increases domestic violence. The argument that no-fault divorce causes domestic violence can be

by the Family Law Act 1996 amid acrimonious debate both inside and outside Parliament.[46] There is a delicious irony in the fact that, while divorcing couples are criticised for failure to approach the resolution of their problems in a reasonable and calm manner, the process of reforming the law on that very subject can produce such an intellectual fist-fight.

13.16 Divorce has been blamed for much the same ills in Scotland as have been attributed to it elsewhere but, to date, the debate has been much more measured. In the light of concern surrounding the deficiencies in the existing law, the Scottish Law Commission explored possible reform. What the deficiencies in the present law are will be discussed fully when we turn to consider the grounds for divorce in detail. Broadly, the problem lies in the length of time parties have to wait if they want to use the no-fault grounds of two or five years non-cohabitation. It is believed that this causes the fault grounds, and in particular behaviour, to be used where they might not otherwise be. There is also some concern that parties might be driven to commit perjury, for example, over the length of time for which they have not been cohabiting, in order to speed up the divorce process.[47] The Commission put forward the following options for consideration:[48] introducing a period of separation as the sole ground of divorce; introducing notice, followed by a period of time, as the sole ground of divorce; permitting divorce by mutual consent only; and keeping the present system, subject to modification.[49] These proposals were subject to the usual process of consultation and, in addition, a public opinion survey was conducted, in order to assess the reaction of a broader body of people than would normally respond to a Discussion Paper.[50]

13.17 While debate in Scotland has been calm and balanced, it is clear

put in a nutshell as follows. If divorce is simple, non-judgmental and carries no adverse economic consequences for the perpetrators of domestic violence (men), they have no incentive to behave well in marriage. They will, therefore, feel free to abuse their wives. It is premised on a frighteningly cynical view of human nature and human relationships – one which assumes, essentially, that people prefer behaving badly to behaving well and will exploit a position of strength at every opportunity.

46 Proposals for reform had been put forward by the Law Commission in England and Wales – The Ground for Divorce (Law Com No 192, 1990). Essentially, the Commission proposed delayed divorce on demand, with the process taking just over a year from one party filing notice to decree being granted. While what the legislation provides for takes up that broad idea, many compromises were reached. What has resulted is considerably more complicated and less satisfactory than the original model proposed. See S. M. Cretney and J. M. Masson, n 2 above, pp 324–383.

47 Scottish Law Commission, Discussion Paper, The Grounds of Divorce: Should the law be changed? (Scot Law Com Disc Paper No 76, 1988), pp 1–7 and Scottish Law Commission, Report on Reform of the Grounds of Divorce (Scot Law Com No 116, 1989), paras 1.1–2.11.

48 The Grounds of Divorce: Should the law be changed?, pp 7–20.

49 Variations on these options were also considered including the possibility of retaining some of the fault grounds to accommodate hardship where, for example, unilateral divorce after a period of time or notice, would not meet that end.

50 Report of a Survey on Proposed Changes to the Divorce Law (System Three Scotland, 1988). A summary of the findings can be found in the Report on Reform of the Grounds of Divorce, Appendix D. It is interesting that whereas, prior to the reform of 1976, it was church organisations, and particularly the Church of Scotland, which contributed what

that views about divorce vary just as widely here as elsewhere, as the following observation from the Commission's final Report demonstrates

> 'No reform of the law of divorce will please everyone. We received, for example, comments suggesting, at one extreme, divorce on demand at registrar's offices and, at the other extreme, a return to the pre-1938 position where the only grounds for divorce were adultery and desertion and where not even extreme cruelty was a ground for divorce'.[51]

In the light of the responses it received and its own further consideration of the matter, the Commission preferred fairly modest reform over the more radical options.[52] Again, these recommendations will be examined in detail along with the existing law to which they apply. In a nutshell, however, what is proposed is to reduce the two-year and five-year periods of non-cohabitation to one and two years respectively. The other spouse's consent would still be required before divorce would be granted after the shorter of the periods of non-cohabitation. Since the period of non-cohabitation before a divorce could be granted without the other spouse's consent would be the same as that required for desertion, it was thought that desertion need no longer be a ground for divorce and its abolition was recommended. Adultery and behaviour would remain grounds for divorce. In the case of adultery, this was retained largely in deference to public opinion and, in the case of behaviour, its retention was aimed primarily at enabling victims of domestic violence to end the marriage as quickly as possible. We would still be left with a divorce law that claimed to grant divorce on the sole ground of irretrievable breakdown, but that manifestly did not do that.[53] The real difference would be that the law would work better in meeting the needs of the Scottish people.

13.18 These proposals for reform, dating from 1989, were repeated in 1992[54] and still await legislative action. It may be that they will not find their way on to the statute book until after the Scottish Parliament has been set up. Perhaps at that stage the whole debate will take on the more contentious tone found elsewhere and, who knows, some of the more radical options considered and rejected by the Commission may resurface and find support. All that is for the future. For now, we must turn to the law as it is at present.

---

might be perceived as the view of the general public, public opinion surveys are now used. While all religious groups can, of course, be part of the debate on law reform, it is a more democratic reflection of the nature of modern Scottish society that the public as a whole should have an input.

51 Report on Reform of the Grounds of Divorce, para 1.3.
52 Report on Reform of the Grounds of Divorce, paras 2.12–3.7.
53 The Commission addressed this point but observed that it could be met by the argument that '[i]t did not matter if the law was misleading in this respect. It was just a matter of words which did not affect what actually happened'. Few consultees seemed concerned about it – Report on Reform of the Grounds of Divorce, para 2.15.
54 Scottish Law Commission, Report on Family Law (Scot Law Com No 135, 1992). In the draft Family Law (Scotland) Bill, found at the end of the Report, the Commission includes its proposals for reform of the grounds for divorce and deals with new proposals for reform of the defences to an action for divorce.

Irretrievable breakdown the sole ground for divorce

13.19 Strictly speaking, the sole ground on which decree of divorce will be granted in Scotland today is that the marriage has broken down irretrievably.[55] However, irretrievable breakdown can only be established by satisfying one of the five factual circumstances set out in the Divorce (Scotland) Act 1976.[56] In colloquial terms, they are: adultery; behaviour; desertion followed by two years non-cohabitation; two years non-cohabitation with consent; and five years non-cohabitation. This formulation of what will warrant a decree of divorce has two consequences. First, where the spouses believe that their marriage has broken down irretrievably, but they cannot satisfy one of the five factual circumstances, they cannot get divorced. Of course, such spouses are in the best possible position to make that determination, and there is a degree of absurdity in claiming that irretrievable breakdown is the ground of divorce when that is not the case in reality. Second, provided that the pursuer can establish one of the five factual situations, he or she will be entitled to decree, even if the marriage has not actually broken down irretrievably. So, for example, where a husband has committed adultery once, his wife can get a divorce. It might be that, had the couple taken some time and worked their problems through, their marriage could have been salvaged. In that sense, it has not broke down *irretrievably*. Of course, the fact that the pursuer raised the action does not auger well for such an outcome, but, aside from opportunities for reconciliation which are considered later,[57] the court is not concerned with retrieving marriages once the factual circumstances justifying divorce have been established. It is hardly surprising, then, that the five factual situations themselves have come to be known as the 'grounds for divorce'.[58]

13.20 Before we look in detail at the grounds for divorce, it is helpful to examine the popularity of each of them. Table 1 indicates the number of divorces granted on each ground in 1997.[59] The current position, with

Table 1

adultery	909
behaviour	3,081
desertion	33
two years non-cohabitation with consent	5,769
five years non-cohabitation	2,424
Total	12,222[60]

---

55 Divorce (Scotland) Act 1976, s 1(1).
56 Section 1(2).
57 See paras 13.30–13.31.
58 Both the Scottish Law Commission and Clive use this term and it will be adopted here.
59 Registrar General for Scotland, Annual Report 1997 (The Stationery Office, 1998), hereinafter, 'Annual Report 1997', Table 8.1.
60 The more numerate reader will have noticed that the figures under each ground do not add up to the total. Four stray divorces are classified under 'other grounds' in the Annual

slightly less than half of divorces being granted on the basis of two years non-cohabitation with consent, represents a change, even in recent times. Between 1981 and 1997,[61] the incidence of the use of this ground rose from 25% to 47%, while the use of non-cohabitation for five years increased from 14% to 20% and divorces based on adultery fell from 17% to 7%. Behaviour, the most popular ground for divorce in 1981, when it accounted for 41% of cases, lost popularity but, none the less, still accounts for about 25% of divorces. Since the introduction of two years separation with consent, desertion has ceased to have much statistical significance, currently accounting for only 0.25% of divorces. Of course, for the 33 pursuers who used it in 1997, it was of considerable importance.

13.21 In 1997,[62] 12,222 decrees of divorce were granted,[63] the lowest figure since 1989.[64] Youth at the time of marriage is undoubtedly a factor which increases the likelihood of divorce and, in 37% of divorces, one or both of the parties had been under 21 at the time of marriage.[65] However, experience is no guarantee of success,[66] since some 14% of men and women divorcing had been divorced before.[67] Religious or cultural differences between the parties may increase the likelihood of divorce, although there is no evidence that these particular divergences are any more significant than, for example, spouses having radically different political views.[68] When are marriages particularly at risk? While a significant number of marriages last for less than five years, there appears to be some truth in the conventional wisdom surrounding the 'seven year itch'.[69] Once a marriage has lasted for 20 years, the likelihood of divorce decreases although, of

Report 1997, but there are no other grounds for divorce in Scotland. Clive points out (para 20.006, n 27) a further problem with the reliability of statistics in this area. Sometimes there are discrepancies between those collected by the Registrar General and those in the Civil Judicial Statistics. None the less, the data available gives a good flavour of what is happening.

61 Annual Report 1997, p 132.
62 The divorce statistics for 1989–1991 are analysed in detail in S. Morris, S. Gibson and A. Platts, Untying The Knot: Characteristics of Divorce in Scotland (Scottish Office Central Research Unit, 1993).
63 Annual Report 1997, Table 8.1.
64 While the number of divorces in 1997 dropped by 86 on the previous year, the overall picture in the last decade is relatively stable and we have probably reached the 'levelling out' of the divorce rate experienced in other jurisdictions like Canada, England and Wales and the USA.
65 Annual Report 1997, Table 8.6.
66 To judge the 'success' of a marriage on the sole criterion of the spouses 'staying the course' is obviously far too simplistic. Take, for example, the couple who stay together for economic reasons but lose no opportunity to express the hostility they feel towards each other with the result that each of them is miserable. Such a marriage can hardly be regarded as a success for them or, indeed, the unfortunate children who live in such a strife-torn atmosphere.
67 Annual Report 1997, Table 8.4.
68 The Annual Report 1997, Table 8.7, analyses divorces in terms of the method of celebration of the marriage.
69 The Annual Report 1997, Table 8.5 gives a detailed breakdown of divorce by duration of marriage and the following groupings emerge: 0–4 years (1,793), 5–9 years (3,224), 10–14 years (2,385), 15–19 years (1,804), 20–24 years (1,380), 25–29 years (952), and 30 years and longer (684).

course, more marriages of this duration will be terminated by the death of one of the spouses. Whether cohabitation prior to marriage makes divorce less likely is open to question. However, it is undoubtedly the case that where couples cohabit and decide not to remain together, they have avoided both marriage and divorce and reduced the overall number of potential divorces.

13.22 Scots Law has never embraced the requirement, found in other jurisdictions,[70] that divorce proceedings cannot be started until the parties have been married for a period of time. In Scotland, at least in theory, a divorce can be started on the day of the wedding.[71] What, then, is involved in establishing the various grounds for divorce?

Grounds for divorce

Adultery

13.23 This is the oldest of the grounds for divorce and the 1976 Act provides that irretrievable breakdown will be established if, 'since the date of the marriage the defender has committed adultery'.[72] Various elements of the statutory provision and the definition of adultery itself warrant closer examination.

What is adultery?

13.24 Adultery is voluntary sexual intercourse with a person of the opposite sex who is not one's spouse and requires penetration of the vagina by the penis.[73] Ejaculation is not essential. It is not adultery for a woman to have donor insemination[74] without her husband's consent, even if a child results.[75] Since sexual intercourse is essential to adultery, it is not adultery for a spouse to form a close association with a person of the opposite sex that stops short of that particular activity. Nor is it adultery to have a lesbian or homosexual affair. The act must be voluntary. Thus, a woman who is raped is not guilty of adultery.[76] Where the woman is so drunk or

---

70 In England and Wales, for example, divorce proceedings cannot be started within the first year of marriage – Family Law Act 1996, s 8(2).

71 As we shall see, the only grounds which could apply so quickly are adultery or behaviour and, in practice, both of these grounds require the pursuer to consult a solicitor, assuming, of course, that the pursuer is not legally qualified. None the less, that first stage of the process could conceivably be completed on the same day as the marriage took place.

72 Divorce (Scotland) Act 1976, s 1(2)(a).

73 *MacLennan* v *MacLennan* 1958 SC 105, per Lord Wheatley, at p 114.

74 For a discussion of donor insemination and the view that, where a woman pursued such a course of action without her husband's consent, he would almost certainly succeed in obtaining a divorce on the basis of her behaviour see chapter 4, paras 44–46, above.

75 *MacLennan* v *MacLennan*, above. There, a woman returned from a stay in the USA with a child that her husband could not have fathered. Her defence to his action for divorce based on her adultery was that she had conceived the child by donor insemination. The court accepted that this was a valid defence and gave her the opportunity to produce evidence of the donor insemination. In the event, she produced no such evidence and decree of divorce was granted.

76 *Stewart* v *Stewart* 1914 2 SLT 310. On the other hand, a married man who commits rape is guilty of adultery.

drugged as to be incapable of consenting, her actions cannot be described as voluntary. However, where the consumption of the debilitating substance is voluntary, an argument can be made that she is personally barred from founding on her own irresponsible conduct.[77] Only sexual intercourse which takes place after the marriage is relevant and pre-marital conduct, however promiscuous, is irrelevant. The wording of the statute makes clear that one act of adultery will be sufficient. Good faith is no defence and, thus, where a woman has sexual intercourse with a third party in the mistaken belief that her spouse is dead, her conduct would be construed as adulterous.[78] Where do polygamous marriages fit into the concept of adultery? If adultery is sexual intercourse with a person other than one's marriage partner, is it adultery for a man to have sexual relations with both of the women to whom he is married? Clive presents an interesting argument, emphasising the idea of adultery as a breach of the spousal duty of fidelity. He concludes that, at least where the first marriage was monogamous until the husband acquired the capacity to contract the second polygamous marriage, the first wife can found on the subsequent conduct as a breach of this original obligation of fidelity. As he concedes, this 'means that intercourse between a man and one wife can sometimes be adultery in relation to another wife. This is a novel proposition, but divorce actions against polygamists present a novel problem'.[79]

Defences

13.25 An action for divorce on the ground of adultery can be met by the following defences: *lenocinium*, condonation or collusion, and the Scottish Law Commission has recommended reform of each of them.

13.26 The 1976 Act provides that decree of divorce will not be granted for adultery if the adultery 'has been connived at in such a way as to raise the defence of *lenocinium*'.[80] This ancient common law defence has its origins in the time when adultery was a crime and arose in the context of a husband who promoted or encouraged his wife's prostitution. At one time it was thought that the defence of *lenocinium* applied only where a husband had profited from his wife's prostitution.[81] However, no such profit is required and Lord President Inglis defined it as occurring '[w]hen a husband is accessory to the crime of adultery by his wife, or is a participant in the crime, or is the direct occasion of her lapse from virtue'.[82]

13.27 For a successful plea of *lenocinium*, there must be three elements:

---

77 Clive (at para 21.005) takes this view and cites a number of English cases where the courts were unsympathetic to the 'incapacitated' individual. Indeed, he cites *Yarrow* v *Yarrow* [1892] P 92, where the court took the view that insanity would be no defence, a somewhat extreme position.

78 *Hunter* v *Hunter* (1900) 2 F 771, where the woman, believing her husband to be dead, had remarried. The same principle applies where a person believed himself to be divorced – *Sands* v *Sands* 1964 SLT 80.

79 At para 21.008.

80 Divorce (Scotland) Act 1976, s 1(3).

81 G. Mackenzie, *Criminal Law*, I, 17.6. It is worth remembering that *lenocinium*, like adultery, was a crime at that time.

82 *Weymss* v *Weymss* (1866) 4 M 660, at p 662.

the pursuer must actively and seriously encourage the defender to commit adultery; the defender must take the encouragement seriously; and the pursuer's encouragement must have caused the adultery.[83] Examining each element in turn gives a clearer idea of what is involved. The pursuer must take an active and serious part in promoting the adultery. Thus, a suggestion made in jest or anger is not enough.[84] Nor is it enough where a spouse suspects the other's infidelity and either turns a blind eye or feigns ignorance and takes the opportunity to gather evidence of adultery.[85] The defender must believe the pursuer meant the suggestion to be taken seriously. Where the defender knew that the pursuer's suggestion was a joke but went off and committed adultery none the less, the defence will not apply. The pursuer's suggestion must be the operative cause of the adultery.[86] It is not enough that the defender was having an affair anyway and that this was likely to continue.[87] While *lenocinium* would apply to cases involving prostitution, it would apply equally to encouraging one's partner to participate in a spouse-swapping party, group sex or, simply, where the parties agree to have an 'open marriage', with neither of them using the other's adultery to found an action for divorce. The Scottish Law Commission has recommended that the statutory reference to *lenocinium* should be replaced by a reference to adultery 'actively promoted or encouraged by the pursuer',[88] effectively taking the concept as it has developed and rendering it into modern language.

13.28 The second defence arises where the adultery 'has been condoned by the pursuer's cohabitation with the defender in the knowledge or belief that the defender has committed the adultery'.[89] The defence of condonation existed at common law but caution should be exercised in relying on some of the older cases, since the formulation in the 1976 Act is not

83 *Hunter* v *Hunter* (1883) 11 R 359, per Lord President Inglis, at p 365.
84 In *Hunter* v *Hunter*, above, in the course of an argument, the husband brought up his wife's past as a former prostitute and angrily suggested she return to that livelihood. This was insufficient and the case can be contrasted with *Marshall* v *Marshall* (1881) 8 R 702, again a case involving a man married to a former prostitute, where the husband's similar suggestion was made on more than one occasion and, the court accepted, seriously intended.
85 In *Thomson* v *Thomson* 1908 SC 179, a husband who suspected his wife's adultery gave her the money for a trip she claimed she was making to Stirling and instructed detectives to watch her in Gateshead where she proved his suspicions to be true. Her plea of *lenocinium* was unsuccessful.
86 This is illustrated by the sad saga of the Gallachers. The couple had already separated when the husband wrote to his wife suggesting that she 'do something' so that they could get a divorce. She was able to found on this letter in her plea of *lenocinium* in respect of her adultery three months later – *Gallacher* v *Gallacher* 1928 SC 586. However, when she again committed adultery, some years later, the plea was repelled since the lapse of time suggested no causal link between the letter and her actions – *Gallacher* v *Gallacher* 1934 SC 339. The introduction of divorce after two years separation with consent seems designed for such couples, but, collusion aside, the fact that Mrs Gallacher raised the defence suggests she was not all that keen on the divorce being granted. None the less, a modern Mr Gallacher could, at least, rely on five years separation in his action. See also, *Riddell* v *Riddell* 1952 SC 475.
87 *Hannah* v *Hannah* 1931 SC 275 and *Riddell* v *Riddell*, above.
88 Report on Family Law, paras 13.2–13.4, rec 67 and draft Bill, clause 30(1).
89 Divorce (Scotland) Act 1976, s 1(3).

identical to the concept of condonation as it developed at common law. In addition, the modern statutory provision must be read along with the provision allowing for resumed cohabitation aimed at facilitating reconciliation. None the less, the whole concept of condonation has the same underlying rationale in both its common law and statutory forms. Essentially, it is designed to provide for a fresh start, encouraging couples who can do so to put adultery behind them and get on with their lives. It can also be seen as preventing the aggrieved spouse holding the adultery over the other's head.

13.29 Clearly in order to condone the adultery, the pursuer must know of it. At common law, the degree of knowledge which the pursuer was required to have was not entirely clear. The 1976 Act clarifies the position by requiring cohabitation in the knowledge of 'the adultery'. While the pursuer need not have all the details of what happened, a general understanding of what is being condoned is essential. Thus, where a wife has confessed to adultery with a particular rugby player in the local team, the husband will not be barred, by reason of condonation, from obtaining a divorce when he discovers that she engaged in similar conduct with other members of the team. On the other hand, where a husband confesses to having had an affair with a particular colleague and his wife continues to live with him for a further six months, the fact that she did not know how often adultery was committed or where will not prevent a plea of condonation being upheld. At common law, an element of mental forgiveness was required in addition to continued cohabitation and knowledge.[90] Mental attitude, being essentially a private matter, is difficult to ascertain and even more difficult to prove. The 1976 Act swept away this requirement and the test is now a wholly factual one. Condonation is no less so simply because it is conditional. Where, for example, the factual test is satisfied, condonation will be established regardless of the fact that the pursuer required the defender not to see his or her lover again, even if the defender does not honour the undertaking.[91]

13.30 Despite the Scottish Law Commission's scepticism,[92] the 1976 Act contains provisions aimed at encouraging the parties to attempt reconciliation. As we have seen, condonation is a defence to an action for divorce based on adultery. Without the provisions of the 1976 Act on reconciliation attempts, were the parties to resume cohabitation as husband and wife in the attempt to patch things up, the pursuer would be running the risk that,

---

90 *McKellar* v *McKellar* 1977 SLT (Notes) 70, a case decided on the law prior to the 1976 Act.

91 Of course, if the defender commits adultery again, the pursuer will have a fresh cause of action.

92 The Commission took the view that, 'once the action has been raised, reconciliation is pretty well out of the question. At an early stage, however, while the dispute is still in the hands of the family solicitor, he may be able to compose petty differences which might have blown up into a serious division between the parties' – *Divorce: The Grounds Considered*, (Scot Law Com 1967 Cmnd 3256), para 32. Albeit the language reflects a bygone era, this comment demonstrates that, in 1967, solicitors were playing a role in resolving family disputes which is sometimes presented today as innovative.

if the reconciliation attempt failed, he or she would have foregone the possibility getting a divorce. Some potential pursuers might be unwilling to take that risk and, so the thinking goes, the opportunity to save some marriages would be lost. The 1976 Act allows the parties to resume cohabitation without running the risk of prejudicing the original ground for divorce and contains two kinds of provisions. The first provides for court-sanctioned reconciliation attempts and provides that, where the court considers that there is a reasonable prospect of a reconciliation between the parties, it *shall* continue, or further continue, the action for such period as it thinks proper to enable attempts to be made to effect such a reconciliation. If, during such continuation the parties cohabit with one another, no account shall be taken of such cohabitation for the purposes of that action.[93] This applies to all the grounds for divorce and is not subject to any time limits other than those any court may lay down in an individual case.

13.31 The second kind of permitted reconciliation attempt requires no sanction of the court and the periods of resumed cohabitation permitted depend on the ground for divorce being used. In the case of adultery, resumed cohabitation is not treated as condonation provided that the pursuer has not cohabited with the defender at any time after the end of the period of three months from the date on which such cohabitation was continued or resumed.[94] Unlike earlier provisions on resumed cohabitation attempts, the 1976 Act does not require the resumed cohabitation to be 'with a view to effecting reconciliation',[95] although the heading to s 2 is 'Encouragement of reconciliation'. Clearly, while the aim of the provision is reconciliation, any resumed cohabitation within the time-limit is protected, regardless of the parties' motives. The provisions on reconciliation attempts read like a bad translation from a foreign language. It is unfortunate that, while the Scottish Law Commission has recommended that a number of other provisions should be rendered into more readily-intelligible form, they made no suggestions in respect of reconciliation attempts.

13.32 The third defence to an action for divorce for adultery applies to all the other grounds as well. The accepted definition of collusion is 'an agreement to permit a false case to be substantiated or to keep back a good defence'.[96] Collusion requires conspiracy between the parties. It has been doubted that collusion serves any useful purpose. If the court discover that a false case has been put forward or that a good defence has been withheld, it will refuse the decree. In addition, perjury or subornation of perjury (inciting someone else to commit perjury) are offences in their own right and punishable as such. It is hardly surprising, then, that the Scottish Law

---

93 Divorce (Scotland) Act 1976, s 2(1).
94 Divorce (Scotland) Act 1976, s 2(2).
95 Divorce (Scotland) Act 1964.
96 *Walker* v *Walker* 1911 SC 163. It is sometimes defined in terms of the oath of calumny, an oath administered in consistorial causes and having its origins in the ecclesiastical courts. It was abolished by the Divorce (Scotland) Act 1976, s 9. However that section also provides that 'nothing in this section shall affect any rule relating to collusion'.

Commission has recommended the abolition of collusion as a separate bar to divorce.[97] The Commission recommended, however, that it should be expressly provided that a court should not grant decree of divorce if it is satisfied that the pursuer has put forward a false case or the defender has withheld a good defence.[98]

Proof

13.33 As with all divorce actions, proof is on balance of probabilities.[99] The pursuer can found on the defender's criminal conviction in a UK court, for example, of rape or incest, as evidence of adultery, provided that a third party identifies the defender as the convicted person.[100] Where the defender's adultery has been proved in earlier matrimonial proceedings, the defender can use this in later proceedings and again, a third party must identify the defender as the person concerned.[101]

Reform

13.34 The Scottish Law Commission has recommended that adultery be retained as a ground for divorce.[102]

Behaviour

13.35 The second of the grounds for divorce, behaviour, includes the older notions of cruelty, under the earlier law, but, as we shall see, it is a fresh ground for divorce and goes a great deal further. The 1976 Act provides that irretrievable breakdown will be established if

> 'since the date of the marriage the defender has at any time behaved (whether or not as a result of mental abnormality and whether such behaviour has been active or passive) in such a way that the pursuer cannot reasonably be expected to cohabit with the defender'.[103]

Again, this provision warrants closer examination.

When?

13.36 Only behaviour after the marriage is relevant and the discovery that one's sweet, loving spouse was, in fact, a violent, drunken, promiscuous axe-murderer, before the marriage, is no ground for divorce. When we looked at error as a ground for nullity of marriage, we saw that error as to a spouse's qualities or attributes was insufficient.[104] The fact that only behaviour after the marriage is relevant to divorce is consistent with this approach.[105] That a single act may constitute sufficient behaviour is

---

97 Report on Family Law, paras 13.5–13.8, rec 68(b) and draft Bill, clause 30.
98 Report on Family Law, paras 13.5–13.8, rec 68(a) and draft Bill, clause 30. Since the court would have the power to do this, in any event, this provision is arguably unnecessary.
99 Divorce (Scotland) Act 1976, s 1(6). Prior to the 1976 Act, divorce for adultery required proof beyond reasonable doubt, reflecting the formerly criminal nature of adultery.
100 Law Reform (Miscellaneous Provisions) (Scotland) Act 1968, s 10.
101 Law Reform (Miscellaneous Provisions) (Scotland) Act 1968, s 11.
102 Report on Reform of the Grounds for Divorce, para 1.1.
103 Divorce (Scotland) Act 1976, s 1(2)(b).
104 See chapter 10, para 35.
105 See, *Hastings* v *Hastings* 1941 SLT 323, discussed below at para 13.51.

indicated by the words 'at any time'. Thus, if the defender has struck the pursuer once, this will be sufficient if its effect on the pursuer is such that he or she can no longer reasonably be expected to cohabit.

A mental element?

13.37 The use of the word 'behaved' creates some difficulty, at least from a theoretical perspective. As Clive[106] points out, the 1976 Act could have provided that irretrievable breakdown was established where the pursuer could not reasonably be expected to cohabit with the defender *for any reason*, but it does not do that. Behaviour is something more than a condition or state of affairs. Certainly, behaviour can be 'active or passive',[107] but must there be some mental element? The words 'whether or not as a result of mental abnormality' may preclude an insanity defence here, but they do not get us any further in assessing the mental element for behaviour. It is submitted that Clive's conclusion that behaviour requires 'some minimal mental element'[108] must be correct and the example he cites of a person in a coma not 'behaving' is highly persuasive. Having said that, it is important to remember that, while a person's condition may be involuntary, it may result in behaviour which is such that the pursuer cannot reasonably be expected to cohabit with the defender.[109]

Not necessarily unreasonable behaviour

13.38 As we have seen, behaviour may be active or passive and thus, coldness, indifference or taciturnity can constitute behaviour. It is important to remember that the behaviour itself need not be reprehensible. It is the effect it has on the pursuer that is relevant. So, for example, a committed social worker who is working long hours and, in addition, is involved in a host of political and other groups, may be contributing much to the community. However, if the result is that he is rarely at home and has no time to share with his spouse, she may establish that she can no longer reasonably be expected to cohabit.[110] Nor need the conduct be directed at the other spouse. Under the old law on cruelty, the courts struggled with such notions as whether the behaviour went to the root of the marriage and, thus, a woman whose husband had been convicted of murder might be denied decree.[111] Now it is the impact of the conduct

---

106 At para 21.013.
107 *Fullarton* v *Fullarton* 1976 SLT 8; *Gollins* v *Gollins* [1964] AC 644; *Thurlow* v *Thurlow* [1976] Fam 32.
108 At para 21.013.
109 *Purdie* v *Purdie* 1970 SLT (Notes) 58; *Fullarton* v *Fullarton,* above; *Thurlow* v *Thurlow,* above. Since the 1976 Act creates the behaviour ground, caution should be exercised in looking at pre-1976 cases where the pursuer was seeking to establish cruelty for the purpose of divorce; *Grant* v *Grant* 1974 SLT (Notes) 54; *H* v *H* 1968 SLT 40.
110 See, *O'Neill* v *O'Neill* [1975] 3 All ER 289, a case which generates much mirth in lectures. There, the husband's well-intentioned enthusiasm for improving the family home had the result that, in a two-year period, the floorboards were often up, there was no door on the bathroom for about eight months, 30 tons of rubble were removed from under the floorboards and dumped in the garden and it was not possible to hang curtains. The wife left, taking the children with her, and got a divorce.
111 *Smith* v *Smith* 1976 SLT (Notes) 26, at p 27, where Lord Stewart took the view that the murder conviction might 'detract from the husband's quality as a reputable citizen but it

which will be relevant. Conduct towards other family members may be of significance here as, for example, where one spouse was particularly hostile to a partner's child who was living with them. On the other hand, one is not expected to embrace every one of a spouse's relatives with unbridled enthusiasm.

The impact of the behaviour

13.39 The essence of this ground is that the behaviour must be such that 'the pursuer cannot reasonably be expected to cohabit with the defender'. There are two points to note here. First, it is the particular pursuer with which the court is concerned, not a hypothetical reasonable pursuer.[112] In this sense, the test is subjective. Behaviour that one person does not mind or finds faintly irritating, might drive another person to distraction. Of course, the pursuer does not have to demonstrate injury to mental health,[113] far less that he or she was, indeed, driven to distraction. None the less, while the individual pursuer is the focus, the court is called upon to decide whether that pursuer can reasonably be expected to cohabit with that defender. In this sense, the test is objective. A court could conclude, quite competently, that it was not unreasonable to expect cohabitation to continue and, thus, that decree should be refused. While any other solution would turn this ground for divorce into one that was self-defined by pursuers, it is rare for courts to refuse decree.[114] It can be argued that, where a pursuer goes to the trouble of raising an action, he or she is demonstrating that he or she is unhappy with the behaviour, the first step, but only the first step, towards establishing this ground.

13.40 That brings us to the second point. The time at which the test is to be applied is the date of the proof and, by then, the spouses may not have been living together for some time. An interesting question is whether there must be a causal link between the behaviour and the pursuer's lack of willingness to cohabit. That is to say, must it be unreasonable to expect the pursuer to cohabit *because of* the behaviour, rather than there being some

does not necessarily detract from his conduct as a husband'. This case can be contrasted with *White* v *White* 1966 SLT (Notes) 52, where the husband's conviction for an act of gross indecency in a public toilet was sufficient to enable the wife to obtain a divorce for cruelty. See also *Waite* v *Waite* 1961 SLT 375.

112 In *Meikle* v *Meikle* 1987 GWD 26–1005, for example, the wife, who had previously lived in the city, obtained a divorce on the basis that her husband spent a great deal of time out on the farm and she could not adapt to life in the country.

113 This was required under the old law on cruelty.

114 See, *Graham* v *Graham* 1992 GWD 38–2263, where the sheriff refused decree on the basis that the pursuer had tolerated the defender's behaviour for 30 years and, therefore, could reasonably be expected to continue to tolerate it. In the event, it transpired that the couple had been married for only three years and the sheriff principal was denied the opportunity to explore this interesting point. It is submitted, however, that the sheriff was wrong in principle. After all, even the proverbial worm turns. To suggest that a person who has put up with a situation he or she did not enjoy is thereby barred from eventually deciding that he or she has had enough, is absurd. It fails to recognise that people develop, change and may go through a process of consciousness-raising. Were this sort of informal time-bar to apply, then the logical conclusion would be that every spouse should start divorce proceedings earlier rather than later; hardly an approach conducive to encouraging people to work their problems through.

other clear cause for the pursuer's unwillingness to cohabit, like being involved with someone else? Clive is quite emphatic in his view that the behaviour need not be the cause of marital breakdown and, as usual, cites a highly persuasive example.[115] However, that is not the same as asking whether the behaviour must be the cause of it being unreasonable to expect the pursuer to cohabit with the defender. The paradigm case here is where the behaviour itself has ceased. Suppose that a wife's absence from home and irritable behaviour, when she was there, was caused by the stress resulting from her demanding job as a solicitor. She has changed careers and is now a happy, calm, legal academic. There is no longer behaviour that makes it unreasonable to expect her husband to cohabit with her and, arguably, he has no case.[116] However, it may be that past conduct has had such an impact on the relationship that it has been destroyed beyond repair and, in such circumstances, not only would it be unreasonable to expect continued cohabitation, but there is a real causal link between past behaviour and the current feelings of the pursuer.[117] Causation was stretched to and, arguably, beyond, its limits in *Findlay* v *Findlay*.[118] There, the wife had left her husband because of his behaviour. She then formed a new relationship and, by the time of the proof, was living with another man. In her action for divorce on the basis of her husband's behaviour, Lord Prosser took the view that the new relationship could be viewed 'as arising in a sense from the earlier conduct and separation, and as being a relevant factor in considering whether, at the date of the proof, the pursuer can reasonably be expected to cohabit with the defender'.[119] While this was certainly seeing the whole history of the marriage in its totality, it amounts to treating something which was, in truth, a *novus actus interveniens*, as if it was the product of a chain of causation.

What kind of behaviour?

13.41 Behaviour is certainly the most flexible of all the grounds for divorce and this may explain its great popularity in the past and its significant, although reduced, use, today. There is behaviour which creates something of a *prima facie* case for divorce, if the pursuer chooses to found on it, and domestic violence is an obvious example. However, it would be a rare spouse indeed who never did anything that caused his or her partner

---

115 At para 21.022, he says, '[t]here is no warrant whatsoever in the words of section 1(2)(b) for saying that a divorce can be granted only if the behaviour caused the breakdown, or the continued breakdown, of the marriage'. He gives the example of a woman who leaves her husband to live with another man. Her husband then threatens to kill her. As Clive quite rightly points out, while she would be entitled to a divorce on the basis of such behaviour (the threats), the marriage had broken down well before and for another reason.

116 Clive (at para 21.018, n 31) cites an unreported case, *Johnston* v *Johnston*, from August 1988 in Arbroath Sheriff Court, where it was alleged that the husband's behaviour had been caused by exposure to chemicals in sheep-dip and that the cause had been identified and removed. Proof before answer was allowed.

117 In *Hastie* v *Hastie* 1985 SLT 146, for example, the wife had accused her husband of having an incestuous relationship with his niece. While, by the time of the proof she accepted that the accusations were unfounded, decree was granted.

118 1991 SLT 457.

119 At p 461.

some irritation. Such conduct as: putting empty cartons back in the refrigerator; leaving a host of pairs of shoes lying around the bedroom floor; doing the crossword in a partner's newspaper; or raising one's voice to the cat, may be irksome, but will normally be regarded as trivial. Of course, few people would consider pursuing a divorce because of that kind of behaviour and it is most unlikely that a court would grant decree on the basis of it. While it is not possible to provide a comprehensive list of the kinds of behaviour which may raise the inference that the pursuer can no longer be expected to cohabit with the defender, cases from the past provide useful illustrations. The following may be relevant:[120] actual, threatened or attempted physical violence; non-physical behaviour, including, verbal or economic abuse; controlling behaviour; humiliation and nagging; certain kinds of sexual behaviour, including, excessive sexual demands, wilful refusal to engage in sexual activity, insistence on sexual practices abhorrent to the pursuer, sodomy or bestiality, and homosexuality or lesbianism; neglectful behaviour, indifference and taciturnity; obsessive behaviour; habitual drunkenness or drug abuse; exposure to risk of disease; and certain kinds of behaviour towards third parties, including criminal conduct in certain contexts.

Behaviour and the other grounds for divorce

13.42 How behaviour interacts with the other grounds for divorce is interesting. Clearly, adultery would be one form of behaviour which might well make it unreasonable to expect the pursuer to cohabit with the defender, as might some form of lesser sexual relationship or, indeed, a non-sexual association with a member of the opposite sex.[121] Where a pursuer has a strong suspicion of a partner's adultery, but does not have sufficient evidence, he or she might found the action on the defender's close relationship with the third party. A spouse who absents himself or herself from the home without reasonable cause may, again, be behaving in a way that makes continued cohabitation by the other spouse unreasonable to expect. Desertion followed by two years non-cohabitation is a separate ground for divorce and has a specific meaning in this context. Were a pursuer allowed to found on desertion followed by non-cohabitation for less than two years, the effect would be to undermine the desertion ground itself. Thus, simple desertion for such a lesser period of time will not alone be sufficient to justify a divorce on the behaviour ground.[122] Desertion can, however, be founded on along with other conduct as part of the overall picture which makes it unreasonable to expect the pursuer to cohabit with the defender.[123]

---

120 Broadly, these are the categories adopted by Clive and he discusses them in greater detail at paras 21.025–21.034.
121 *Stewart* v *Stewart* 1987 SLT (Sh Ct) 48, where the husband explained the fact that he came home late by indicating a relationship with another woman. See also, *MacLeod* v *MacLeod* 1990 GWD 14–767; *Pinder* v *Pinder* 1954 SLT (Sh Ct) 15; *Richardson* v *Richardson* 1956 SC 394.
122 *Stringfellow* v *Stringfellow* [1976] 1 WLR 645; *Gray* v *Gray* 1991 GWD 8–477.
123 See for example, *Rose* v *Rose* 1964 SLT (Notes) 15, a case under the old law where persistent desertion and criminal activity were found to be cruelty.

Defences

13.43 Unlike adultery, no specific defences are mentioned in respect of behaviour, although collusion[124] would apply here as it does in all divorce cases. There are no specific provisions on resumed cohabitation or reconciliation attempts in this context, although the court's general power to continue a case would require it to do so where it appeared that there was a reasonable prospect of a reconciliation.[125] Since behaviour relates to whether it is reasonable to expect the pursuer to continue to cohabit with the defender at the time of the action, the fact that the couple has resumed cohabitation, at some stage, for the purpose of reconciliation or, indeed, for any reason, will not destroy the pursuer's case if he or she continues the action.

Proof

13.44 Again, proof of this ground is on balance of probabilities.[126]

Problems with behaviour as a ground

13.45 While no divorce is immediate, proceedings on the behaviour ground can be started right away and, if a pursuer has no other 'fault' ground to use, this may make behaviour more attractive than waiting for the two or five year periods to expire before a divorce based on the non-cohabitation grounds can be obtained. Some forms of behaviour, like violence, may be such that the pursuer's desire to end the marriage is completely understandable. However, where one spouse is simply not getting along with the other, there must sometimes be a temptation for a person who is anxious to get his or her divorce as quickly as possible to produce every shred of the partner's thoughtless, inconsiderate or other behaviour, in the hope of amassing enough to convince a court that it is no longer reasonable to expect continued cohabitation. Such a raking over of past shortcomings is undesirable and wholly inappropriate in a system which claims to grant divorces on the basis of irretrievable breakdown. It can only create acrimony and cannot foster future co-operation between the parties over such matters as the children. There is already evidence of a reduction in the use of behaviour and an increase in the use of two years non-cohabitation with consent, and this suggests that at least some spouses are prepared to wait a little longer and thereby avoid the accusations and acrimony. Were the period of separation to be reduced to one year, as the Scottish Law Commission has recommended, it is anticipated that far fewer spouses would use behaviour, since the difference in the time it would take to get a divorce would be negligible.

Reform

13.46 The Scottish Law Commission has recommended that behaviour should be retained as a ground for divorce.[127]

---

124 For a discussion of collusion, see para 13.32, above.
125 Divorce (Scotland) Act 1976, s 2(1).
126 Section 1(6).
127 Report on Reform of the Ground for Divorce, para 1.1.

Desertion

13.47 The 1976 Act provides that irretrievable breakdown will be established if

> 'the defender has wilfully and without reasonable cause deserted the pursuer; and during a continuous period of two years immediately succeeding the defender's desertion –
> (i) there has been no cohabitation between the parties, and
> (ii) the pursuer has not refused a genuine and reasonable offer by the defender to adhere'.[128]

Desertion has been a ground for divorce since 1573 but, as we shall see, the definition of what amounts to desertion has changed over the years and caution should be exercised in using some of the older cases. It is probably best to analyse desertion under the current law as being comprised of two distinct elements, first, the initial desertion and, second, a period of two years non-cohabitation during which time the pursuer has not refused a genuine and reasonable offer to adhere.

Initial act or acts

13.48 The defender's initial desertion must be 'wilful' and, clearly, this requires some intention on the defender's part to end married life. Thus, where the defender is incapable of forming an intention, for example, as a result of insanity or unconsciousness, the necessary mental element is missing and there can be no desertion. Similarly, where a person is taken to hospital, albeit voluntarily, or imprisoned, but intends to resume married life on release, his or her actions do not amount to desertion. It might be argued that, where one spouse has a history of criminal activity and imprisonment, he or she ought to realise that continued criminal activity will result in future imprisonment. Thus, by continuing to offend he or she is showing at least a foolish or wilful disregard for the possibility of future non-cohabitation. However, the intention is not to leave the marriage and the criminal's spouse would have to rely on behaviour or the non-cohabitation grounds in order to obtain a divorce.[129]

13.49 Nor is it desertion for one spouse to leave the other voluntarily, but for some purpose other than leaving the relationship. Were a woman to attend a one-week residential conference even in the face of her husband's opposition, her conduct could hardly be regarded as desertion. Similarly, were a man to 'get on his bike' in search of employment and leave the home for several weeks, the intention to desert his marriage would not be demonstrated. Nor, it can be argued, would longer periods of absence amount to desertion where there is a legitimate reason. Thus, an oil worker who works abroad on six month contracts would not normally be viewed as being in desertion. Of course, it is possible for a spouse's initial departure to be legitimate, but for subsequent conduct to amount to desertion. Where a woman went to stay with her aunt on holiday she was not in desertion initially. However, when she wrote to her husband three weeks later,

128 Section 1(2)(c).
129 *Rose* v *Rose*, above.

indicating that she did not intend to return, she was.[130] Aside from such a clear case, there must be a point at which leaving a partner, where no specific intention to end the marriage is made clear, amounts to desertion. Were a scientist to sign up for a three year expedition to a remote jungle region in the face of spousal opposition, there might be a case for arguing that the length of time combined with the disregard for his or her partner's feelings amounts to desertion. As Clive puts it, '[i]t is a question of fact and degree when an intention to leave temporarily against the wishes of the other spouse becomes an intention to desert'.[131]

13.50 While desertion normally involves practical separation, with the deserting spouse often leaving the home, lesser forms of separation may suffice. Thus, the parties may remain under the same roof but one may withdraw from all the practical elements of cohabitation to the extent that he or she is effectively in desertion. Simple refusal of sexual intercourse will not suffice[132] although, as we have seen, this may contribute towards a divorce on the ground of behaviour. Indeed, it is not always the person who leaves the home who is in desertion. If one spouse ejects the other or locks him or her out,[133] it is the spouse who takes this action and, thus, ends the cohabitation, who is in desertion despite the fact that he or she may remain in the home.[134] Simply ordering a spouse from the home or behaving in such a way as to drive one's partner out is not desertion and, thus, there is no such thing as constructive desertion. However, such conduct would normally warrant a divorce on the behaviour ground and the obvious attraction for the pursuer is that he or she could start proceedings immediately rather than waiting for the two years non-cohabitation to expire.

'Reasonable cause' for deserting

13.51 Desertion is only a ground for divorce where the defender has acted 'without reasonable cause'. What amounts to reasonable cause for desertion will, of course, depend on the facts of the particular case. Almost certainly, anything that would amount to behaviour making it unreasonable to expect the pursuer to cohabit with the defender for the purpose of s 1(2)(b) of the 1976 Act would constitute reasonable cause for desertion. For a long time, however, the doubt over the question of whether conduct that would not be sufficient ground for a judicial separation, could be a defence in the context of desertion. Eventually, in a pre-1976 decision,[135] the Inner House took the view that lesser conduct could be reasonable cause for desertion, provided that it was 'grave and weighty'.[136] That

130 *Macaskill v Macaskill* 1939 SC 187.
131 Para 21.041.
132 *Lennie v Lennie* 1950 SC (HL) 1.
133 In most cases, the ejected spouse would have the right to gain re-entry to the home and might be able to exclude the aggressor under the Matrimonial Homes (Family Protection) (Scotland) Act 1981 but, as we saw in chapter 12, this might not always provide a viable, practical solution for a victim of domestic violence.
134 *McMillan v McMillan* 1962 SC 115; *Burgess v Burgess* 1969 SLT (Notes) 22.
135 *Richardson v Richardson* 1956 SC 394.
136 In the event, the court did not regard the husband's refusal to end a platonic friendship with a female colleague as sufficiently grave or weighty conduct.

decision remains of some importance, in a modern context, since it allows a defender to use conduct which would not justify divorce as a reason for desertion. This would include pre-marital conduct[137] and what amounts to a condition, rather than behaviour.[138] Some doubt remains over a further issue. Did the defender have to know of the 'reasonable cause' at the time of desertion, in order to found on it as a defence? Clive[139] explores the question at length, noting that the leading relevant House of Lords decision[140] could be used to justify either an affirmative or a negative answer to the question. His conclusion that the defender's knowledge is essential here is infinitely preferable to the alternative on the grounds of both logic and common sense.

13.52 All that the 'reasonable cause' defence does is to enable a spouse who was aggrieved by a partner's behaviour to leave at the same time as delaying the divorce until the five year period of non-cohabitation has elapsed. Take, for example, a wife who commits adultery. Her husband storms out on discovering this and, a few months later, she goes to live with her new partner. She would now like to get a divorce as soon as possible in order to remarry, but her husband refuses to co-operate by raising an action for divorce on the ground of adultery. After two years, she raises an action for divorce based on his desertion. He founds on her adultery as reasonable cause for his desertion.[141] She must therefore wait for five years before she can obtain a divorce, assuming he continues to withhold his consent.

Deserted spouse's state of mind

13.53 So much for the deserting spouse's state of mind and conduct. What of the pursuer's state of mind? To what extent must the pursuer have been willing to live with the defender at the time of the initial desertion and subsequently? This problem, known as 'willingness to adhere', is one 'which has haunted the Scottish law on desertion since the sixteenth century'[142] and has been resolved, to a large extent, by the current legislation. At one time desertion was a bilateral offence which required a spouse withdrawing from cohabitation, on the one hand, and the other spouse not only being willing to adhere at the time of desertion, but for the whole of the relevant period of time thereafter, on the other.[143] This early

---

137 For example, in *Hastings* v *Hastings* 1941 SLT 323, it was held to be good cause for desertion that the wife had persuaded her husband to marry her by pretending that the child she was carrying was his when this was not, in fact, the case. He would not have been able to obtain a divorce based on adultery, since the conduct was prior to the marriage, nor could he avoid the marriage due to this error – *Lang* v *Lang* 1921 SC 44.

138 For example, in *AB* v *CB* 1959 SC 27, where the husband had killed a child of the marriage while insane, the court did not dwell on the fact that he was suffering from a condition in finding good cause for non-adherence.

139 At paras 21.051–21.053.

140 *Wilkinson* v *Wilkinson* 1943 SC (HL) 61.

141 Of course, were the husband to withhold a good defence, his action would amount to collusion. For a discussion of the problems surrounding collusion see para 13.32, above.

142 Clive, at para 21.035.

143 The development of the law on this point is discussed more fully by Clive at paras 21.035–21.038.

view of desertion was subsequently modified and the current position, as reflected in the very careful wording of the statute, is that the pursuer must have been willing to adhere at the time of desertion. This is simply a question of fact and the pursuer is not required to demonstrate any great enthusiasm for such adherence.

13.54 Thereafter, there must be a period of two years non-cohabitation during which the pursuer has not refused the defender's genuine and reasonable offer to adhere. Thus, where the defender makes no such offer, the pursuer's state of mind during the subsequent two-year period is irrelevant. Similarly, where the defender's offer is not genuine or is unreasonable, the pursuer's refusal will not bar the divorce. Whether the offer is, in fact, disingenuous or unreasonable will depend on the circumstances of the case. For example, where the offer is simply a ruse, designed to prevent the divorce going ahead, it is unlikely to be genuine. The danger here is that the offer and the pursuer's response can become something of a game of poker and the only way the pursuer may be able to demonstrate the disingenuous nature of the offer is by accepting it. Certainly, if the offer were then to be withdrawn, the pursuer could argue it was never intended seriously.

13.55 In terms of the reasonableness of an offer, the cases tend to turn on very individual circumstances but it can be concluded that, where for example, the accommodation offered was wholly inadequate or in some distant location, unknown to the pursuer, it would probably be regarded as unreasonable.[144] As we saw, at one time the husband had the right to choose the place of the matrimonial home. The abolition of this right in 1984[145] means that neither spouse has a greater right than the other to select the place of the home. Where each wishes to live at a different location, neither can be regarded as being in desertion by sticking firmly to his or her guns, since there is no real intention to desert the spouse. In such a case, were either spouse to seek a divorce, he or she would have to rely on the non-cohabitation grounds.

Two years non-cohabitation

13.56 The initial desertion must be followed by a period of two years non-cohabitation. Cohabitation is defined in the 1976 Act as 'in fact living together as man and wife'[146] and non-cohabitation is, fairly obviously, not doing that. Exactly what this means will be discussed presently[147] but, suffice to say at this point, that it involves a degree of separation, but not necessarily living in different homes. As we saw with the other grounds for divorce, the legislation encourages attempts at reconciliation and, in the context of desertion, there are two relevant provisions. Reading them together and applying them requires taking a few deep breaths before one starts. First, in considering whether any period of time required has been

144 *Muir* v *Muir* (1879) 6 R 1353; *McMillan* v *McMillan* 1962 SC 115.
145 Law Reform (Husband and Wife) (Scotland) Act 1984, s 4, discussed in chapter 11, at para 6.
146 Divorce (Scotland) Act 1976, s 13(2).
147 At paras 13.61–13.62, below.

continuous, no account shall be taken of any period or periods not exceeding six months in all during which the parties have cohabited with one another. However, no such period of resumed cohabitation counts towards the period of non-cohabitation.[148] Second, a divorce for desertion *will* be barred if, after the expiry of the requisite two years the pursuer has resumed cohabitation with the defender and has cohabited with the defender at any time after the end of the period of three months from the date on which the cohabitation was resumed.[149]

Defences

13.57 It is apparent that an action for divorce based on desertion can be met by the plea that the pursuer refused a genuine and reasonable offer from the defender to adhere, that offer being made within two years of the initial desertion. As we saw, the defender can argue that he or she had reasonable cause to behave as he or she did. In addition, any such action would be barred on the ground of collusion.[150] While the 1976 Act does not use the word 'condonation' in the context of desertion, this is the concept being applied when it provides for resumed cohabitation that will not bar a divorce.

Proof

13.58 Again, proof of this ground of divorce is on balance of probabilities.[151]

Reform

13.59 The Scottish Law Commission has recommended the abolition of desertion as a ground for divorce.[152] If the periods for divorce after a period of non-cohabitation were reduced from two and five, to one and two years, respectively, anyone who might have used desertion in the past would be able to obtain a divorce just as quickly and without the need to establish the various aspects inherent in a divorce for desertion.

Two years non-cohabitation and the defender's consent

13.60 The 1976 Act provides that irretrievable breakdown will be established if

> 'there has been no cohabitation between the parties at any time during a continuous period of two years after the date of the marriage and immediately preceding the bringing of the action and the defender consents to the granting of the decree of divorce'.[153]

This ground, along with divorce after five years non-cohabitation, was introduced by the 1976 Act and together they represent a massive departure from the notion of fault inherent in the previous law. For the first

---

148 Divorce (Scotland) Act 1976, s 2(4).
149 Section 2(3).
150 For a discussion of collusion see para 13.32, above.
151 Divorce (Scotland) Act 1976, s 1(6). Prior to the 1976 Act, divorce for adultery required proof beyond reasonable doubt, reflecting the formerly criminal nature of adultery.
152 Report on Reform of the Grounds for Divorce, paras 1.1 and 2.16.
153 Section 1(2)(d).

time, couples who agree that divorce is the correct solution for them were freed from the need to rake over past misdeeds or collude in fabricating grounds for divorce. There are no statistics available on how many couples use this ground where fault grounds do exist but it would be safe to assume that many do. As we shall see when we consider divorce procedure, couples with no children below the age of 16 who have agreed on any financial provision to be made, can take advantage of the do-it-yourself procedure for their divorce if they are founding it on two years non-cohabitation. The financial saving involved for such co-operative couples will be considerable. Little wonder, then, that this is now the most commonly used ground for divorce. If the Scottish Law Commission's recommendation[154] that the period of non-cohabitation be reduced from two years to one is accepted, it can be anticipated that the use of this ground will increase still further.

Non-cohabitation

13.61 As we saw when considering desertion, 'the parties to a marriage shall be held to cohabit with one another only when they are in fact living together as man and wife'.[155] The very careful wording here was designed to avoid the difficulty which arose in England where the equivalent legislation used the phrase 'living apart'. There, the Court of Appeal[156] took the view that it was not enough that the parties were physically separated, at least one of them must have believed the marriage to be at an end. This was arguably an erroneous interpretation of the English statute. In any event, the phraseology used in the 1976 Act would appear to have avoided this problem.[157]

13.62 Non-cohabitation is a factual state and can be inferred from a whole host of circumstances. Ultimately, each case will turn on its own unique combination of facts. The fact that two people may be living under the same roof and yet not cohabiting is illustrated by the somewhat unusual English case of *Fuller* v *Fuller*.[158] There, the husband left the home and the wife formed a sexual relationship with the lodger. After the husband had a heart attack, he required assistance with domestic tasks and he returned to live in the spare bedroom in the family home and paid rent, while his wife took care of such matters as his laundry and meals. She continued her relationship with the (first) lodger and they shared a bedroom. The court was quite prepared to accept that, although the spouses were living in the same home, they were not doing so as marriage partners and the decree was granted. Of course, in many cases, the parties will live in separate accommodation although, again, this is not conclusive. Other relevant factors in assessing whether the parties are cohabiting *as husband and wife* will include: spending time together, showing affection and mutual support, having sexual intercourse, sharing child care, sharing financial responsi-

---

154 Report on Reform of the Grounds for Divorce, para 1.1.
155 Divorce (Scotland) Act 1976, s 13(2).
156 *Santos* v *Santos* [1972] Fam 247.
157 For an excellent discussion of why requiring mental rejection of the marriage would create enormous problems see Clive at paras 21.070–21.074.
158 [1973] 1 WLR 730.

bilities, and taking holidays together. The very fact that many good friends and, indeed, divorced couples do a number of these things simply makes the point that it is the overall picture of the particular relationship which must be assessed. Since divorce on this ground will only be granted where the defender consents, it is difficult to see who is going to object to the assertion that, whatever consideration the parties may have shown to one another, they were, none the less, not cohabiting as husband and wife.

Continuous period of two years

13.63 The 1976 Act requires that non-cohabitation should be 'for a continuous period of two years'. Consistent with the theme of the 1976 Act, no account is taken of periods of resumed cohabitation for the purpose of attempting reconciliation. As we saw earlier, court-sanctioned reconciliation attempts are not subject to any time limit.[159] In addition, in considering whether any period of time required has been continuous, no account shall be taken of any period or periods not exceeding six months in all during which the parties have cohabited with one another. Again, no such period of time counts towards the two years non-cohabitation.[160]

The defender's consent

13.64 The defender must consent to decree of divorce being granted and the use of the present tense in the statute makes clear that any consent given can be withdrawn at any time prior to decree.[161] In addition, in the words of Lord Maxwell, 'it is perfectly open to the defender to withhold consent for any reason he thinks fit or for no reason'. In that case,[162] the husband was withholding consent unless the wife agreed not to seek any financial award or expenses and clearly consent can be used as a counter in the bargaining process over financial awards and, rather more worryingly, the children. Of course, as far as the future arrangements for children are concerned, the court is bound to reach its decision having regard to their welfare but the extent to which consent could be used privately between the parties should not be underestimated. One wonders if there is any point at which a court would regard a condition as so objectionable that it would accept the consent, but delete the condition. Suppose, for example, that a man has left his wife of 20 years and their three children for a much younger woman. He is keen to get a divorce, marry his new love and start a second family. Anxious to protect her children's succession rights, his wife makes her consent to divorce conditional upon his having a vasectomy. Can the husband salvage the consent element, without complying with the condition? It is submitted that, objectionable as the condition is, he cannot. If Lord Maxwell was correct, and it is submitted that he was, the defender can consent or not and can add any conditions she likes. The only solution

159 Divorce (Scotland) Act 1976, s 2(1).
160 Section 2(4).
161 *Taylor* v *Taylor* 1988 SCLR 60.
162 *Boyle* v *Boyle* 1977 SLT (Notes) 69.

for the husband would be to wait for five years for the divorce and, in the meantime, start the family anyway.[163]

Defences

13.65 Apart from any failure to comply with the statutory requirements of this ground for divorce – for example, that the defender alleges that he or she does not consent – the only defence which applies here is collusion.[164] There would appear to be great opportunities for collusion, particularly in the context of affidavit evidence. If the spouses say that they have not been cohabiting for two years and provide a supporting affidavit from a third party, there is normally no further enquiry. Of course, anyone who participates in such deception, including the third party, risks civil and criminal penalties. It goes without saying, that no one should provide such a false affidavit for a relative or friend, however close, and however urgent the divorce may seem.

Proof

13.66 Again, proof of this ground is on balance of probabilities.[165]

Five years non-cohabitation

13.67 The 1976 Act provides that irretrievable breakdown is established if

> 'there has been no cohabitation between the parties at any time during a continuous period of five years after the date of the marriage and immediately preceding the bringing of the action'.[166]

This is the second of the wholly innovative grounds for divorce introduced by the 1976 Act and, subject to a very limited defence, provides for unilateral divorce after a period of non-cohabitation.

No cohabitation for a continuous period of five years

13.68 The elements for establishing this ground for divorce are identical to those required for a divorce after two years non-cohabitation, with two important exceptions. First, and fairly obviously, the period of non-cohabitation required is five years. In computing the five years, the same periods of resumed cohabitation are permitted as were discussed in respect of two-year divorces. The second difference between the two grounds is that the defender's consent is not required in this case. As we shall see, this ground for divorce allows for an additional defence.

Defences

13.69 A court is not bound to grant decree in respect of this ground 'if in the opinion of the court the grant of decree would result in grave financial hardship to the defender'.[167] Hardship is defined as including the loss of the

---

163 As we saw in chapter 4, the consequences for any children born outside marriage are minimal.
164 Collusion is discussed at para 13.32, above.
165 Divorce (Scotland) Act 1976, s 1(6).
166 Section 1(2)(e).
167 Section 1(5).

chance of acquiring any benefit. This provision was designed to protect older spouses, and particularly older wives, who had been in long marriages where they had become financially dependant on their husbands, often because they had not pursued a career in order to raise children and run the home. Such women risk the loss of enjoying a share in their husbands' pensions and various benefits if they are widowed. The position is particularly difficult for a woman whose husband has contributed to a pension scheme which will provide generously for retirement and widowhood. Since financial provision on divorce treats pension entitlement as a form of accrued saving and, thus, it is taken into account in calculating an award, it is really the benefits payable to widows that matter, since the divorcee will lose her entitlement.

13.70 In order to establish a case here, the defender must establish that the grave financial hardship will result from the divorce, rather than the fact that the marriage has broken down or the parties have separated.[168] It should be noted that the court is not obliged to refuse decree if grave financial hardship is established; it simply has a discretion to do so. Sometimes the court can use this discretion to continue the case and suggest that the pursuer goes away to consider making better financial provision for the defender.[169] The objection to refusing decree on this basis is that, whatever the function of divorce law is, it is not to provide for financial security in old age. That is a matter for the state or, increasingly, individuals. The Scottish Law Commission has recommended that the provision on grave financial hardship should be repealed.[170]

13.71 Collusion[171] would, again, apply to this ground of divorce but, unlike two years non-cohabitation, there is far less opportunity for collusion. Here, there is a defender who is not consenting to the decree of divorce and, thus, the person in the best position to collude is also in the best position to raise any issues concerning whether the conditions set out in the ground have been met.

13.72 The fact that the defender has some other reason for opposing the granting of the decree, for example, sincere moral or religious opposition to divorce, is irrelevant.[172]

---

168 Contrast *Boyd* v *Boyd* 1978 SLT (Notes) 55, where the wife's financial loss resulted from the fact that the parties were no longer living together and pooling their limited resources, with *Nolan* v *Nolan* 1979 SLT 293, where the wife stood to lose a substantial pension entitlement if widowed.

169 See for example, *Nolan* v *Nolan*, above.

170 Report on Family Law, paras 13.9–13.12, rec 69 and draft Bill, clause 30(3).

171 Collusion is discussed at para 13.32, above.

172 In *Waugh* v *Waugh* 1992 SLT (Sh Ct) 17, the defender in a simplified divorce case, based on five years non-cohabitation, wrote to the court to say, 'I simply do not want a divorce. Married in Church, I took vows, and an oath made my commitment'. The court dismissed his objection as 'frivolous' although the Sheriff Principal was at pains to point out that the word was being used in its strict legal sense and the sincerity of the defender's views was not being doubted.

Proof

13.73 Again, proof of this ground is on balance of probabilities.[173]

Usefulness and reform

13.74 Albeit the period of non-cohabitation required is rather long at present, the significance of this provision, as a departure from the fault-based system of divorce, cannot be ignored. In addition, the very fact of this ground's existence may prompt greater use of the two years separation ground. Take the example of a husband who leaves his wife for another woman and wants a divorce in order to marry the new person in his life. His wife refuses to raise an action for divorce based on his adultery and indicates that she will not consent to a divorce after two years. Understandably she is angry, hurt and in no mood to co-operate. She may even hope that he will return to her. After a year, it becomes apparent that he will not return and she begins to rebuild her life too. By the time two years have elapsed since his departure, they may have worked out co-operative arrangements in respect of the children, she may take a very different view of matters and she may indicate that she will consent to a divorce, with or without some financial inducement. This seems to be a much more satisfactory arrangement for all concerned. If the Scottish Law Commission's recommendation[174] that the period of non-cohabitation here should be reduced from five years to two years finds its way into legislation, the ground will become even more useful.

Mediation

13.75 Where a couple decide to divorce, they may be able to reach agreement over such matters as the future arrangements for the care of their children and property. Where they cannot reach agreement by themselves, mediation offers an opportunity for them to get assistance in exploring their options, with a view to reaching some consensus. The development of, and present provision for, mediation is discussed in chapter 1.

The Procedure

13.76 Older lawyers in Edinburgh still tell tales of the Saturday morning divorces. In those days, divorce, as an issue of status, was regarded as being of such magnitude that all decrees of divorce were granted by the Court of Session. Even in undefended cases, the pursuer had to be present and give evidence, along with a witness. Divorce could be dealt with on any day that the court sat, but Saturday morning was largely given over to undefended divorce.

13.77 It was not until the late 1970s that the procedure for divorce underwent a number of radical changes. So dramatic were the changes that the face of divorce practice was altered beyond recognition. 1978[175] saw the

---

173 Divorce (Scotland) Act 1976, s 1(6).
174 Report on Reform of the Grounds for Divorce, para 1.1.
175 Act of Sederunt (Rules of Court Amendment No 1) (Consistorial Causes) 1978.

introduction of affidavit evidence in divorce cases and now, in almost all undefended actions, it is not necessary for the pursuer and the witnesses to appear in court at all. For tens of thousands of Scots, the trek to Edinburgh on a Saturday morning has been avoided. Five years later, the Divorce Jurisdiction, Court Fees and Legal Aid (Scotland) Act 1983 introduced two further reforms. First, it brought to an end the Court of Session's monopoly on divorces and actions became competent in the sheriff court.[176] Second, it introduced the simplified procedure for a limited range of cases which enables the spouses to complete the paperwork themselves, without the need to employ solicitors. Not surprisingly, this has come to be known as the 'do-it-yourself' procedure.[177] The other significant change in the whole divorce landscape has been the increased recognition and use of mediation as a prelude to divorce.

13.78 The question facing the legal system now is whether courts are the appropriate forum for divorces to take place at all.[178] When the only way to obtain a divorce was by a formal procedure in open court, it may be that the legal system was attempting to reflect some perceived social need to mark the serious nature of divorce with these official trappings. The use of affidavit evidence and the introduction of the simplified procedure brought an end to this. Now, it can be argued, the only meaningful role for the court is the resolution of matters which are actually in dispute. This suggests a distinction should be drawn between different kinds of divorce actions. While a court may be appropriate to a defended action, most undefended actions are dealt with by a sheriff in chambers without the parties being present. Is it necessary to use up so much shrieval time in this way? It is worth remembering that the failure to defend a divorce action is not necessarily the same thing as consenting to the divorce, since the former may be prompted by a lack of funds, recognition that the marriage is over anyway or, simply, inertia. None the less, at least in divorces where there is consent, would an administrative process not work just as well?

13.79 Where the divorce is defended, it is far more likely that the dispute will be over an ancillary matter, rather than the divorce itself. Most often, these disputes are over the future arrangements for the care of the children, financial provision, or both of these matters. Issues concerning children and property disputes are dealt with all the time in the courts in independent actions. They could be dealt with in a similar way where the parties are divorcing. Just when we have made great steps away from viewing children as something akin to the property of their parents, it would be a mistake to assume that their futures can be dealt with along with other 'ancillary matters'. Separating divorce from decisions about children's futures might recognise the free-standing and important nature of decisions being taken about children. Of course, their futures are

---

176 Section 1.
177 See Evidence in Divorce Actions (Scotland) Order 1989, SI 1989 No 582.
178 For an interesting debate from the USA about the place of the courts in the divorce process see J. C. Sheldon, 'The Sleepwalker's Tour of Divorce Law' 48 Me L Rev 7 (1996) and C. Kadock, 'Five Degrees of Separation: A Response to Judge Sheldon's The Sleepwalker's Tour of Divorce Law' 49 Me L Rev 321 (1997).

inexorably tied to how their parents live and the resources available to finance these arrangements, but that does not mean that residence and contact need be decided in the course of a divorce action. As we saw in chapter 3, there is a range of ways we might approach issues affecting children and improve upon the present system. So far as divorce procedure is concerned, suffice it to say that the fact that children are involved is not a justification for the present procedure for divorce. How divorce procedure might develop is a matter for future, considered and unhurried, debate. For the present, it is worth noting how the existing procedures are used, before we move on to consider the procedures themselves.[179]

13.80 Women are far more likely to raise the action for divorce than are men.[180] Almost half of all divorces are now granted on the basis of two years non-cohabitation with consent and, in such cases, it does not matter which spouse is the pursuer and which is the defender. They are, in a sense, interchangeable. None the less, when we turn to divorce based on adultery, we find 68% of actions being raised by the wife, with the corresponding figures for behaviour and desertion being 91% and 82% respectively. Why this is so must be a matter for speculation. Certainly, it is not a phenomenon peculiar to Scotland and the following observation has been made

'Wives more than husbands tend to be more willing to confront marital problems and be more articulate in their expression. By contrast, husbands may be unaware of the problems or at least unwilling to discuss them openly. Consequently, those husbands who subconsciously wish to leave the relationship but are unwilling to initiate it themselves may encourage their wives to do so'.[181]

Jurisdiction

13.81 Both the Court of Session[182] and the sheriff court[183] now have jurisdiction to grant divorce, although most actions are now raised in the sheriff court.[184] The Court of Session has jurisdiction if either party is domiciled in Scotland or has been habitually resident here for one year immediately preceding the raising of the action.[185] The sheriff court will only have jurisdiction if one of these conditions is satisfied and one of the parties has either, been resident in the sheriffdom for 40 days preceding the raising of the action, or has been so resident for at least 40 days ending

179 Divorce in the Court of Session and the sheriff court are governed by the Rules of the Court of Session and the Ordinary Cause Rules, respectively. For a more detailed discussion of divorce procedure and the Rules see Clive, paras 27.001–27.120 and S. A. Bennett, *Divorce in the Sheriff Court* (5th edn, W. Green, 1997).
180 62% of actions reaching final judgment in the Court of Session, and 70% of those completed in the sheriff court, in 1996, were raised by women – Civil Judicial Statistics 1996, (The Stationery Office, 1997), Tables 6.2 and 6.3.
181 H. H. Irving and M. Benjamin, *Family Mediation: Contemporary Issues* (Sage Publications, 1995) at p 24.
182 Court of Session Act 1830. Prior to this, divorce actions were dealt with in the Commissary Court.
183 Divorce Jurisdiction, Court Fees and Legal Aid (Scotland) Act 1983, s 1.
184 In 1996, 98% of divorces were granted in the sheriff court – Civil Judicial Statistics 1996, Table 6.1.
185 Domicile and Matrimonial Proceedings Act 1973, s 7(3).

within 40 days of the raising of the action.[186] Proceedings in the Court of Session are more expensive than in the sheriff court and the only reason to raise the action in the former would be if neither party was resident in Scotland.

13.82 The fact that divorce actions may be raised in any of the sheriff courts throughout Scotland and the Court of Session gives rise to the possibility of concurrent proceedings in respect of the same marriage and, in addition, there may be proceedings underway in a foreign jurisdiction. Parties to proceedings are obliged to inform the court of concurrent proceedings which could affect the validity of the marriage and there is provision for mandatory and discretionary sists.[187] The court must sist proceedings if, prior to the proof, proceedings for divorce or nullity of marriage have begun in a 'related jurisdiction' (ie England and Wales, Northern Ireland, Jersey, Guernsey, or the Isle of Man).[188] In addition, the court has a discretion to sist an action.[189]

The parties

13.83 Only one of the parties to a marriage can raise an action for divorce and there is no provision for such actions being raised on behalf of an incapax.[190] The action must be raised against the other party to the marriage. Where the defender is suffering from a mental disorder, a curator *ad litem* will be appointed to protect the defender's position.[191] Both parties must be alive when decree of divorce is granted. Where an action is raised and either party dies before that stage, the marriage is ended by death and divorce is no longer an option.[192]

13.84 The Lord Advocate has the right to intervene in any divorce

---

186 Domicile and Matrimonial Proceedings Act 1973, s 8(2).
187 Domicile and Matrimonial Proceedings Act 1973, Sched 3. Nothing in the Act restricts the courts' other powers to sist an action – s 11.
188 For a sist to be mandatory, the following conditions must also be satisfied: (a) the parties must have lived together; (b) they must have resided together in the related jurisdiction when the Scottish action was begun or, if they were not living together then, their last place of common residence must have been the related jurisdiction; and (c) either of them must have been habitually resident in the related jurisdiction for one year immediately prior to the raising of that action.
189 A discretionary sist may be granted where, prior to the Scottish action being raised, (a) any other proceedings affecting the validity of the marriage are continuing in another jurisdiction outside Scotland, and (b) the balance of fairness requires that those proceedings should be completed before further steps are taken in Scotland.
190 *Thomson* v *Thomson* (1887) 14 R 634. This is to be contrasted with nullity of marriage where the action can be raised by anyone having an interest – *Scott* v *Kelly* 1992 SLT 915.
191 For the part played by the curator *ad litem* see, Rules of the Court of Session (RSC), r 49 and the Ordinary Cause Rules (OCR), r 33. Where the divorce is being sought on the basis of two years non-cohabitation with consent, the Mental Welfare Commission, will be notified with a request to indicate whether it believes the defender to be capable of giving consent.
192 As we shall see, spouses have certain automatic rights in succession. Death of one of the parties in the course of divorce proceedings can, therefore, produce results which the deceased spouse might not have wished. All the more important, then, that anyone who is separated or contemplating divorce should make a will, thus minimising the extent to which property will pass to the spouse.

proceedings, although this is rarely done.[193] Where it is alleged that the defender committed adultery with a named defender, the action must be intimated to that person, who has a right to intervene in order to deny the averments of adultery.[194] A similar provision applies if sodomy is alleged with a named third party. Divorce cases involving children may also require intimation to relevant third parties.[195] Where any order is sought in respect of the child under s 11 of the Children (Scotland) Act 1995, the action must be intimated to the child, although this can be dispensed with by the court. If intimation is not dispensed with, a special form of notice is used rather than sending a copy of the initial writ or summons to the child.[196] Where a request has been made under s 8 of the Family Law (Scotland) Act 1985, the action must be intimated to any creditor with security over the property.[197]

Ordinary procedure

13.85 The action begins with the drafting of the summons (Court of Session) or initial writ (sheriff court) which sets out the pursuer's case and the remedies being sought.[198] This is served upon the defender and other interested parties. The defender then has 21 days, if living within Europe, or 42 days, if living outside Europe, in which to seek legal advice and to consider the appropriate response. This period of time is known as the *induciae*. If the defender does not intend to defend the action, it will normally proceed under the affidavit procedure. If the defender intends to defend the action on any aspect of it, he or she must intimate this to the court and lodge defences. If the divorce is based on two years non-cohabitation with consent, the defender should intimate consent. The court can hear any preliminary motions to deal with such matters as sisting the action, interim residence and contact, or interim aliment. Like any civil action, an options hearing will be fixed to deal with various procedural and other matters.

13.86 If the divorce involves a dispute in respect of children, two additional points should be noted. The first is confined to the sheriff court,

---

193 Court of Session Act 1988, s 19; Sheriff Courts (Scotland) Act 1907, s 38B. See, *McDonald* v *McDonald* 1921 1 SLT 280.

194 The need to intimate to the third party is dispensed with where the pursuer is founding on rape or incest by the defender.

195 Where the child: (i) is being looked after by the local authority; (ii) is the child of one party to the marriage who has been accepted as a family member by the other spouse and is liable to be maintained by that spouse; and (iii) is in the care and control of a third party, the relevant third parties must receive intimation of the action if the court may make an order under the Children (Scotland) Act 1995, s 11. This provision is designed to ensure that the court has all relevant information before it.

196 Any other course of action might risk children being exposed to sensitive information in a highly inappropriate way. For a discussion of children and the court process, see chapter 3.

197 Similarly, any third party whose consent to the transfer is required must receive intimation and, where the pursuer is seeking to set aside or interdict any transfer of property, there must be intimation to interested third parties.

198 A decree of divorce will always be sought and, in addition, the pursuer may be seeking other remedies, for example, a residence order in respect of a child or various orders for financial provision.

and raises the possibility of an additional step in the proceedings, known as the child welfare hearing.[199] These hearings were introduced in 1996 in an attempt to resolve disputes involving children more quickly, provided that this can be done in a manner consistent with the child's welfare. The idea here is to gather the disputing parties together and see if some or all of the disputed matters can be resolved without the need for a full proof. A child welfare hearing will be arranged automatically if there is any dispute over the future arrangements for the children and, in any case, can be ordered by the sheriff at any time, at his or her own instance. The sheriff clerk fixes a date for the hearing on the first suitable court date not earlier than 21 days from the lodging of the notice to defend. The parties, including any child who has expressed the wish to be present, must attend in person, except on showing cause why this is not possible, and all parties are obliged to provide the sheriff with sufficient information to enable him or her to conduct the hearing. The sheriff then seeks to ensure the resolution of the disputed matters and takes a more interventionist role than is usually the case in court proceedings. The sheriff may order such steps to be taken, make such an order, or order such further procedure, as he or she thinks fit. It may be that, as a result of the hearing, the parties can reach agreement over matters of residence and contact and this can be encapsulated in either an order from the court or a joint minute. Of course, disputed matters may remain so even after the hearing and the matter will then proceed to proof at a later date. More than one child welfare hearing can be arranged in a case and, in practice, some sheriffs use multiple hearings in particularly contentious cases, as a way of overseeing interim arrangements in respect of the children and providing an opportunity to defuse disputes and tailor-make fresh interim arrangements, should this prove necessary. The second point to note is that, where parental responsibilities and rights are in dispute in the divorce action, the court may refer the dispute on that point to a mediator accredited to a specified family mediation organisation at any stage.[200]

13.87 As we have seen, proof in divorce actions is on balance of probabilities.[201] Corroboration is no longer required in civil proceedings.[202] However, in establishing a ground of divorce, evidence from someone other than a party to the marriage is required.[203] The Lord Advocate has exercised his statutory power[204] to elide the requirement of third party evidence in respect of undefended divorce actions based on the non-cohabitation grounds, provided: that there are no children of the marriage under the age of 16; that neither party is applying for an order for financial provision; and that neither party suffers from a mental disorder.[205] Hearsay evidence is permitted in civil proceedings provided that the party who

---

199 Options hearings are governed by ORC, r 33.22A.
200 RSC, r 49.23; OCR, r 33.22. See, *Harris* v *Martin* (IH) 1995 SCLR (Notes) 580.
201 Divorce (Scotland) Act 1976, s 1(6).
202 Civil Evidence (Scotland) Act 1988, s 1(1).
203 1988 Act, s 8(3).
204 1988 Act, s 8(4) and (5).
205 Evidence in Divorce Actions (Scotland) Order 1989 (SI 1989, No 582).

made the statement would have been a competent witness.[206] Evidence of what occurred in the course of mediation conducted by an accredited family mediator is usually inadmissible.[207]

13.88 At the end of defended proceedings the court a grants decree of divorce, if the pursuer is successful, or a decree of absolvitor if the defender is successful, thus rendering the matter *res judicata*. If the action has not been defended and the pursuer has not proved his or her case, the court grants a decree of dismissal. Of course, either party is free to raise a subsequent divorce action at any time in the future, but not on the basis of matters which have already been adjudicated.

Affidavit procedure

13.89 Where the action is not defended, the affidavit procedure can be used and this means that there is no need for the pursuer or the witnesses to appear in court.[208] While not as cheap as the do-it-yourself procedure, it is less expensive than an ordinary proof. Unlike the do-it-yourself procedure, the affidavit procedure can be used for any of the grounds for divorce. The action begins in the same way as the ordinary procedure, with the summons or initial writ being drafted and served upon the defender. Upon expiry of the *induciae*, the sworn affidavits of the pursuer and at least one witness are submitted along with other relevant documents and either a minute from counsel (Court of Session) or, more usually, a minute signed by the pursuer's solicitor (sheriff court). The court can then grant decree and the date of divorce is the date when the granting of the divorce appears in the rolls of court.

Simplified or 'do-it-yourself' procedure

13.90 Where the divorce is based on five years separation or two years separation with consent, there is a simplified procedure which enables spouses to obtain a divorce without the need to consult a solicitor at all.[209] The applicant fills out a form, available from any sheriff court, and submits it to the court along with a copy of the marriage certificate, his or her statement sworn before a notary, and the prescribed fee.[210] Where appropriate, the other spouse indicates consent by signing the form. Unfortunately, this cheap and simple procedure is restricted to a fairly narrow range of cases since it is only available where

  (a) the application is based on one of the separation grounds;
  (b) there are no children of the marriage under 16 years of age;
  (c) neither party is seeking an order for financial provision;
  (d) there are no other proceedings pending which could affect the validity of the marriage; and
  (e) neither party suffers from a mental disorder.

206 1988 Act, s 2(1).
207 Civil Evidence (Family Mediation) (Scotland) Act 1995.
208 RSC, r 49.29; OCR, r 33.28.
209 Divorce Jurisdiction, Court Fees and Legal Aid (Scotland) Act 1983, s 2. Evidence in Divorce Actions (Scotland) Order 1989, SI 1989 No 582.
210 The fee is currently £56.

A decree of divorce granted under this procedure cannot be reclaimed against.

Reconciliation

13.91 Where the court believes there is a reasonable prospect of reconciliation between the parties it must continue the action for such time as it thinks necessary to enable the parties to attempt reconciliation[211] and no such attempt acts as a bar to divorce. As we saw, there are also specific provisions in the 1976 Act relating to permitted periods of resumed cohabitation in respect of the individual grounds for divorce. However, neither the court nor solicitors are required to pursue or promote the idea of reconciliation. There is no provision for mandatory counselling in divorce actions in Scotland nor, it is submitted, should there be.

Cross-actions for divorce

13.92 It is possible, although rare, for each spouse to raise an action for divorce against the other. This is not a matter of one spouse defending the action raised against him or her, whether on the merits or on an ancillary matter. It arises where each spouse wants to be divorced but is alleging that the irretrievable breakdown arose out of the other's adultery, desertion, behaviour or the fact that they have not been cohabiting for the previous five years. Such couples could take the less confrontational course of agreeing to a divorce after two years non-cohabitation and, short of the dubious desire to blame one's spouse for the marital breakdown, there is little reason for pursuing this line. Where cross-actions are raised, they are usually disposed of together.[212]

Appeals and reclaiming motions

13.93 Appeals from the sheriff court are heard by the Court of Session and reclaiming motions from the Outer House of the Court of Session are heard by the Inner House. Appeal to the House of Lords is possible, although rare. A decree of divorce takes effect immediately. This avoids the difficulties which can arise where a jurisdiction issues a decree *nisi*, which is then followed by a decree absolute.[213] Since a Scottish decree of divorce may be reclaimed against or appealed, an extract decree of divorce will not normally be issued until the time for appeal has expired.[214] Once an appeal has been lodged, the decree of divorce is suspended until the appeal is dealt with.[215]

Publicity

13.94 In a defended action, proof is in open court and can be reported by

---

211 Divorce (Scotland) Act 1976, s 2(1).
212 *Pringle* v *Pringle* 1967 SLT (Notes) 60.
213 *De Thoren* v *Wall* (1876) 3 R (HL) 28; *Re Seaford, Seaford* v *Seifert* [1968] P 53.
214 RSC, r 7.2(1); OCR, r 30.4.
215 *Fowler* v *Fowler (No.2)* 1981 SLT (Notes) 78.

the media, subject to certain restrictions aimed at protecting public morals[216] and children.[217]

Registration

13.95 All divorces granted in Scotland on or after 1 May 1984 are registered in the Register of Divorces and an extract from the register can be obtained on payment of the prescribed fee.

Recognition of divorces, annulments and judicial separations granted in other jurisdictions

13.96 As we have seen in respect of other aspects of child and family law, international mobility makes it more important now than ever before that, so far as is possible, a court decree granted in one country is recognised abroad. In the context of divorce, it could create problems if a person had been divorced in Scotland, but was still regarded as married in a foreign jurisdiction. For example, such a person might go through a marriage ceremony in that foreign jurisdiction, only to discover that he or she had committed bigamy there. Whether a decree of the Scottish courts will be recognised abroad will depend, of course, on the particular jurisdiction and its law. The corollary of this point is that, in Scotland, we should be reasonably accommodating in our recognition of divorces granted elsewhere. Consequently, we have developed a system to provide for such recognition in a way that is consistent with our own system's fundamental values.[218] The Family Law Act 1986 is the current relevant statute. A new Convention on this subject is under consideration within the European Union.

Divorces granted in the United Kingdom

13.97 A divorce, annulment or judicial separation granted by a court of civil jurisdiction anywhere in the UK since 1 January 1974 will be recognised throughout the UK.[219] A non-judicial divorce[220] obtained in the UK prior to that date may still be valid under common law. Such divorces are no longer possible.

Divorces granted outside the United Kingdom

13.98 Recognition in Scotland of a divorce, annulment or legal separation, obtained outside the UK, will depend on whether or not it was granted in proceedings. 'Proceedings' are defined as 'judicial or other

216 Judicial Proceedings (Regulation of Reports) Act 1926.
217 The Children and Young Persons (Scotland) Act 1937, s 46, as amended by the Children and Young Persons Act 1963, s 57. On the protection of children from publicity see chapter 3, paras 56–58.
218 For a more detailed discussion of this matter and of other international private law aspects of divorce see Clive, paras 28.001–28.065, A. E. Anton and P. R. Beaumont, *Private International Law* (2nd edn, W. Green, 1990); E. B. Crawford, *Private International Law in Scotland* (W. Green, 1998).
219 Family Law Act 1986, s 44, replacing the relevant parts of the Domicile and Matrimonial Proceedings Act 1973. Divorces granted prior to that date will be governed by recognition under the common law.
220 For example, a Catholic annulment, a Jewish *gett*, or a Moslem *talak*.

proceedings'[221] and must be instituted and concluded in the same country.[222] Recognition can be refused if it would be 'manifestly contrary to public policy'[223] and where there has been a lack of notice to the parties or a lack of documentary evidence of the divorce.[224] Since the rules for recognition are the same for divorces, annulments and separations, reference below to 'divorce' applies to all these forms of dissolution of marriage.

13.99 Where a divorce has been obtained overseas in proceedings, it will be recognised in Scotland if it was valid under the law of the place where it was obtained[225] and, at the time when the proceedings were begun, either party to the marriage was habitually resident in that country, or domiciled in that country, or a national of that country.[226] A divorce obtained overseas, but not in proceedings, will be recognised in Scotland if it was valid under the law of the place where it was obtained[227] and, either, each party was domiciled in that country, or, either party was domiciled in that country and the other party was domiciled in a country under whose law the divorce was valid. In addition, it is essential that neither party was habitually resident in the UK for one year immediately preceding the divorce being obtained.[228]

Financial provision after a foreign divorce or annulment

13.100 It would be possible for one spouse could go abroad to obtain a divorce which would be recognised here, for example, by using his or her nationality to found jurisdiction. If the foreign decree made no, or what appears here to be, grossly inadequate, financial provision and the courts here could do nothing further, the spouse left in Scotland would not be receiving a level of justice accepted by our legal system. The Matrimonial and Family Proceedings Act 1984, Part IV, attempts to provide for such an eventuality. An action for financial provision can be raised in the Court of Session or the sheriff court after a foreign divorce which is recognised here provided that

(a) the applicant was domiciled or habitually resident in Scotland on the date when the application was made; and
(b) the other party to the marriage –
(i) was domiciled or habitually resident in Scotland on the date when the application was made; or
(ii) was domiciled or habitually resident in Scotland when the parties last lived together as husband and wife; or
(iii) on the date when the application was made, was an owner or tenant of, or

---

221 1986 Act, s 54(1).
222 *R v Secretary of State for the Home Department, ex parte Fatima* [1986] AC 527.
223 1986 Act, s 51(3)(c).
224 1986 Act, s 51(3)(a) and (b).
225 1986 Act, s 46(1)(a).
226 1986 Act, s 46(1)(b).
227 1986 Act, s 46(2)(a).
228 1986 Act, s 46(2)(b) and (c).

had a beneficial interest in, property in Scotland which had at some time been a matrimonial home of the parties.[229]

In addition, a further set of criteria must be met. These are: the other party to the marriage initiated the divorce proceedings; the application for financial provision was made within five years of the divorce taking effect; a court in Scotland would have had jurisdiction to entertain an action for divorce … immediately before the foreign divorce took effect; the marriage had a substantial connection with Scotland; and both parties are living at the time of the application.[230] Once jurisdiction is established, Scots law on financial provision, which is discussed in the following chapter, will apply, subject to the necessary modifications.[231]

---

229 1984 Act, s 28(2)(a) and (b). If the action is being raised in the sheriff court, there are additional jurisdictional requirements relating to the particular sheriffdom – s 28(2)(c).
230 1984 Act, s 28(3).
231 1984 Act, s 29(1).

CHAPTER 14

TERMINATION OF ADULT RELATIONSHIPS: THE CONSEQUENCES

14.1 Adult relationships come to an end in one of two ways, through either choice or death. Either the partners or, at least, one of them, choose to end their relationship or one of them dies. As we have seen, while a relationship continues, cohabitation and marriage are not all that different. It is when we turn to consider the consequences of the relationship ending, that we find very marked differences between cohabitation and marriage.

14.2 On the termination of marriage by divorce, a whole range of legal provision is in place to assist the parties or the court in reaching decisions on financial provision. Where a marriage comes to an end due to the death of one of the spouses, the survivor will have various succession rights, depending on whether or not the deceased left a will. The legal system is designed to cope with both eventualities. It is 'there' for former spouses. Cohabitants have no right to seek financial provision on the termination of the relationship and former cohabitants must use the general provisions of the law to separate their property and resolve any disputes. Should either of them die, the survivor has no right to succeed to the former partner's property, unless the deceased has made a will to that effect. The legal system is, quite emphatically, not 'there' for them. While former cohabitants can rely on the general provisions of the law in resolving property matters where they are both alive, the law is something of a blunt instrument in dealing with such disputes.[1] In treating former cohabitants largely as strangers, it fails to accommodate the special nature of the relationship they have had. As we have seen, the non-regulation of cohabitation is one of its attractions for some couples and the fact that cohabitation may be begun and ended without the intervention of the legal system makes it a true alternative form of relationship. However, the sophisticated legal régime for financial provision on divorce is an acknowledgement that, in order to do justice to former spouses, the history of their relationship and their future prospects and responsibilities are relevant. As we shall see, this protects spouses who, for example, have sacrificed their

---

1 See chapter 11, paras 89–95 for a discussion of ways in which cohabitants can seek to regulate relationships. It will be remembered that the decision in *Shilliday* v *Smith* 1998 SLT 976, where a former cohabitant was awarded some £9,000 in respect of renovations to her former partner's home for which she had paid, turned on the very narrow fact that her expenditure was made on the understanding that they would get married. Thus, the case is of no help to cohabitants who have not planned to marry.

careers for the partnership or will have continuing responsibilities for the day-to-day care of children.[2] No such protection is afforded to former cohabitants. Given the widespread incidence of cohabitation, the legal system's failure to provide for breakdown is nothing short of dereliction of duty and the Scottish Law Commission has recommended modest reform of the law in this respect. Arguably, the suggested reforms do not go far enough and they will be discussed in due course. The reforms proposed apply only to heterosexual cohabitants and, when it is remembered that marriage is not an option for same-sex couples, the legal system's neglect in this respect becomes all the more apparent.

14.3 Fortunately, the legal system does not take a similarly cavalier attitude towards the children. Regardless of whether the parents have been married to each other, the arrangements for their future care will be agreed between the parents or, failing agreement, resolved in court and this matter is discussed fully in chapter 5. As we saw, the unmarried father is discriminated against and, unless he has concluded a parental rights agreement with the child's mother, he may be disadvantaged in terms of future involvement in his child's life. None the less, at least such fathers can call upon dedicated legal provisions in resolving disputes. Both parents have a continuing obligation to support their children and this may include an element of support for the person who is looking after the child. Generally, children's succession rights are unaffected by their parents' marital status.[3]

14.4 It follows from the discussion above, that much of this chapter will be concerned with the termination of marriage. However, where the absence of provision for cohabitation has particular significance, this will be noted, and what the law might provide for will be discussed. In addition to the legal consequences of divorce, it is worth remembering the significant social, emotional and economic consequences which accompany relationship breakdown To a large extent these apply equally to cohabitation and marriage. Even for partners who agree that their relationship is over, this is a stressful time. Where one partner did not want the relationship to end, coping with the separation and adjusting to the changes inherent in it, can present continuing problems for him or her. For the partner who wanted the separation, guilt may be a factor. Again, a variety of organisations and individuals can help here.[4]

---

2 Child support calculations and awards of aliment for children do contain an element of support for the child's carer but that is not the same thing as including recognition of the loss of future career opportunities. See para 14.84.

3 The general rule, acknowledging equality of children, is subject to exceptions in respect of succession to titles and honours and the right of legitim out of the estate of any person who died before the commencement of the Act – Law Reform (Parent and Child) (Scotland) Act 1986, s 9(1). See chapter 5, para 49.

4 Most of the organisations which assist couples with problems during the currency of their relationship are happy to help divorced persons – see chapter 13, para 4, n 16. A search of the worldwide web using the word 'divorce' produced over 200 sites. Some of these deal with practical issues like future arrangements for children or financial provision, while others are concerned with the more emotional dimension. There is considerable focus on the USA.

PERSONAL CONSEQUENCES

14.5 As we saw in chapter 11, marriage has few remaining personal legal consequences. Thus, from a legal point of view, divorce makes no difference to such matters as: the name a person may use; where a person lives; habitual residence, domicile and nationality.

Freedom to marry

14.6 Perhaps the most obvious personal consequence of divorce is that each of the parties is free to remarry.[5] One might think that, having just been released from a marriage that was, at least latterly, less than satisfactory, this would be the last thing on a newly-divorced person's mind and, for many, that is so. However, as we saw, over a quarter of men and women marrying in 1997, were divorcees.[6] Indeed, every solicitor with any significant divorce practice will be all too familiar with the client who is desperate to get a divorce as quickly as possible, in order to remarry. Of course, the lapse in time between the marriage actually breaking down and the divorce decree being granted frequently allows ample time for the formation of new relationships. It should be remembered that, after divorce, certain restrictions are placed on marriage between persons who were formerly members of the same extended family.[7] Thus, for example, a woman may not marry the child of her former spouse if, prior to either of them reaching the age of 18, they lived together as a family.[8] Nor can a man marry his former mother-in-law, unless they are both over the age of 21 and both his ex-wife and her father are dead.[9] There is no legal restriction placed on remarriage between former spouses.[10] At one time, a person who had been divorced for adultery could not later marry his or her paramour where the paramour had been named in the decree.[11] The prohibition was repealed by statute in 1964,[12] although it is arguable that it had fallen into desuetude long before then.[13]

14.7 Since cohabitation does not restrict either partner's freedom to marry, separation has no special consequences in this respect. The restrictions placed on a divorced person marrying a member of his or her former

---

5 Unlike some other legal systems, Scots law does not prohibit remarriage within a specified period of time after divorce.
6 Registrar General for Scotland, *Annual Report 1997* (The Stationery Office, 1998), hereinafter the 'Annual Report 1997', Table 7.4.
7 See chapter 10, paras 25–31 for a full discussion of the restrictions and the proposals for reform of the law.
8 Marriage (Scotland) Act 1977, s 2(1A).
9 Marriage (Scotland) Act 1977, s 2(1B).
10 For example, in *Mitchell* v *Mitchell* 1995 SLT 426, the parties not only married each other twice, they divorced twice, with interesting consequences for what constituted matrimonial property. See also *Mullen* v *Mullen* 1991 SLT 205, where a marriage by cohabitation with habit and repute was established between previously divorced partners.
11 The common law contained no such prohibition, but it was introduced by the Act of 1600, c 20. Since the paramour had to be named in the decree, as opposed to the summons, the practice grew up of not so naming paramours.
12 Statute Law Revision (Scotland) Act 1964.
13 In 1951 Walton observed: 'There appears to be no modern decision on the subject, and Mr Bell doubts if it is now in force.' *Husband and Wife* at p 10.

partner's family do not apply to cohabitants. Thus, for example, a man may marry the daughter of his former cohabitant, despite the fact that they all lived together as a family and he adopted a quasi-parental role in respect of the younger woman.

Other consequences

14.8 Since individuals are free to call themselves what they wish, marriage and divorce have no effect on a person's name. Some people who changed their last name on marriage revert to a former name, others do not. The decision may be prompted by the length of time for which any changed last name has been used or a desire to have the same last name as one's children. In any event, divorce makes no difference to the freedom to use a chosen name. Similarly, death has no impact on the surviving partner's choice of name.

14.9 As we saw, marriage does not give either spouse the right to choose the place of the family home, nor, aside from the provisions on desertion, does it require spouses to live together. Thus, divorce can be said to make no difference. However, one point should be noted. Where the couple has children, future freedom of movement may be restricted for the person with whom the children live. While a parent's right to effective contact is not sacrosanct, a parent with whom the children live cannot simply take the children and move out of the country, without sanction of the court or the other parent's agreement. This is so where parental responsibilities and rights apply, whether the parents have been married or not and, thus, is a function of parenthood, rather than of marriage or divorce.

14.10 Marriage has an effect on the extent to which one spouse can be compelled to give evidence against the other in both civil and criminal proceedings.[14] The older authorities suggest that these effects continue, at least in the context of criminal proceedings, after divorce.[15] However, Clive[16] doubts that this is the case and suggests that the earlier view is based on a number of old English cases whose worth is now doubted there. The position remains to be tested in the Scottish courts and this would seem to be a case for clear legislative provision.

14.11 As a general rule, the former spouses lose the right to benefit from legislation reserved for married couples. Thus, for example, neither spouse can enforce occupancy rights in the former matrimonial home, nor can the provisions on exclusion orders be used.[17] It is important, therefore, to plan for future accommodation when considering financial provision on divorce.[18] In terms of protection from domestic violence, the full range of

---

14 See chapter 11, paras 70–72.
15 F. P. Walton, *Husband and Wife*, (3rd edn, W. Green & Son, 1951) at p 287.
16 At paras 18.013 and 18.017.
17 Matrimonial Homes (Family Protection) (Scotland) Act 1981.
18 The court has the power to make an order regulating the post-divorce occupation of the matrimonial home – Family Law (Scotland) Act 1985, s 14(2)(d). See para 14.110, below.

civil and criminal remedies are available to former spouses although, as we have seen, their effectiveness may be limited.

14.12 The right to a widow's pension and certain other benefits ceases on divorce. Pension rights under a spouse's occupational pension cease on divorce and it is important to build this in to the calculation of financial provision on divorce.[19]

14.13 Since divorce ends the marriage, former spouses are generally denied the rights they had in that capacity. Thus, former spouses do not have any right to succeed to each other's property on intestacy. However, divorce does not revoke prior testamentary writings. Where a testator has made a will leaving property to a spouse, and they divorce, whether the former spouse may still benefit is a matter of construction. Even where the former spouse is described as 'my wife, Ms Mary Smith', further interpretation is required. On the one hand, the phrase may be interpreted as meaning that the bequest was made to Ms Smith in her capacity as a wife and, thus, after divorce, she is no longer entitled to benefit.[20] On the other hand, it may be viewed as simply a way of describing a particular individual and, in such a case, divorce makes no difference.[21] Given this uncertainty, any testator who does not want a former spouse to benefit should make a fresh will at the time of or, preferably, prior to, divorce. The Scottish Law Commission has recommended that divorce should have the effect of revoking a testamentary provision in favour of a former spouse, unless the contrary intention appears.[22] Such an approach would appear to be more in accordance with the intention of most divorcees and would remove the present uncertainty.

FINANCIAL PROVISION ON DIVORCE

14.14 The common law on financial provision on divorce provided only for the 'innocent' spouse and was premised on the fiction that the 'guilty' spouse had died at the date of the decree. While this was subject to a number of exceptions, the effect was that the old succession devices of the *ius relictae*, terce and courtesy were used.[23] Since the husband's *ius relicti* had a statutory foundation which referred to the death of the wife, it did not apply.[24] When the grounds for divorce were extended by statute in 1938, the common law rules on financial provision were applied to them.[25] The only exception was where divorce was granted for incurable insanity.[26] The effect of this approach to financial provision on divorce was that,

---

19 See paras 14.114–14.119, below.
20 *Pirie's Trustees* v *Pirie* 1962 SC 43.
21 *Henderson's Judicial Factor* v *Henderson* 1930 SLT 743.
22 Report on Succession (Scot Law Com No 124, 1990) paras 4.34– 4.45, rec 17 and draft Succession (Scotland) Bill, clause 14.
23 These terms are discussed at para 14.188.
24 *Eddington* v *Robertson* (1895) 22 R 430.
25 Divorce (Scotland) Act 1938, s 2.
26 There, the court had the power to order the pursuer to pay a capital sum or a periodical allowance for the benefit of the defender and any children of the marriage – 1938 Act, s 2(2).

where the defender had considerable capital, the pursuer would be well provided for. However, where this was not the case, the pursuer got nothing. Bearing in mind that divorce was a remedy sought by a number of the less affluent, income was likely to be the defender's only resource and this meant that many pursuers received no financial provision. Reviewing the position in 1950, the Mackintosh Committee concluded that where the husband had an income but no capital, the result could be that 'a wronged wife' might be prevented from seeking a divorce 'because she would be left entirely unprovided for'.[27] It made a number of recommendations for reform of the law.

14.15 The Morton Commission[28] endorsed the Mackintosh Committee's proposals and added a number of its own, although it was not until 1964 that the proposals were implemented in the Succession (Scotland) Act of that year ('the 1964 Act'). The 1964 Act swept away the old common law provisions and replaced them with something a little more akin to modern notions of financial provision. While it remained the case that only the 'innocent' spouse could seek an award, the court was given discretion to award a capital sum or a periodical allowance, or both. For the first time, a pursuer could receive a continuing payment from the defender's income.[29] In making an award, the court was directed to consider 'the respective means of the parties to the marriage and to all the circumstances of the case'.[30] The next landmark in the history of reform was the Divorce (Scotland) Act 1976 ('the 1976 Act'). Since it provided, at least in theory, that divorce was based on irretrievable breakdown rather than fault, there were no longer 'innocent' and 'guilty' spouses. The illusory nature of irretrievable breakdown has been discussed[31] but, none the less, the introduction of the non-cohabitation grounds meant that notions of guilt and innocence lost some of their sway. The truly innovative aspect of the 1976 Act was that it provided for *either* spouse seeking financial provision.[32] For the first time, a spouse at whom the finger of fault was being pointed could receive a capital sum, a periodical allowance, or both. However, awards continued to be made on the same discretionary basis as before,[33] and there is no doubt that fault played a part in the decision-making process for many, but not all, judges. The shortcomings of the 1976 Act will be discussed presently but, lest we get caught up in critical analysis, sight should not be lost of the enormous advances achieved. In a little over 20 years, Scots law moved from a system of financial provision based on the

27 Report of the Departmental Committee on the Law of Succession in Scotland (Mackintosh Committee) (Cmd 8144, 1950) at pp 20–21.

28 Report of the Royal Commission on Marriage and Divorce 1951–55 (Morton Commission) (Cmd 9678, 1956).

29 As the Scottish Law Commission noted, courts continued to consider what the spouse would have received at common law and this is 'perhaps the explanation for the tendency, discernible in the cases reported after 1964, to award a wife between a third and a half of her husband's capital' – Report on Aliment and Financial Provision (Scot Law Com No 67, 1981) para 3.10.

30 1964 Act, s 26(2).

31 See chapter 13, paras 19–22.

32 Divorce (Scotland) Act 1976, s 5(1).

33 1976 Act, s 5(2).

notional death of the 'guilty' spouse to one where either spouse could seek financial provision through awards of a capital sum or a periodical allowance or both.

What should the law seek to do?

14.16 In reviewing the law on financial provision on divorce in 1981, the Scottish Law Commission[34] noted a defect in the approach of both the Mackintosh Committee and Morton Commission. Neither gave extensive consideration to the purpose of financial provision on divorce. What financial provision on divorce should seek to achieve is fundamental to the type of legal provision governing it and lies at the heart of any discussion of the subject. Of course, what must be appreciated, at the outset, is that two households are more expensive to run than one. For the wealthy, this may be of no great consequence. There are few Scottish examples[35] of the very large awards found in other jurisdictions.[36] Why this is so is a matter for speculation. It may be that there are fewer very wealthy Scots living and divorcing in Scotland. It may be that such individuals value their privacy and are prompted to reach agreement and avoid both the publicity and the cost involved in litigation.[37] Certainly, such cases often attract considerable publicity, sometimes because the people involved are well known, and, sometimes because of the sums of money and the value of the property transferred. The point is that the individuals involved had affluent lifestyles before divorce and, by any standard except, perhaps, their own, continue to do so. Most such couples will reach agreement on financial provision and, in any event, it would be a mistake to devise a legal system based on such exceptional cases. For individuals living on means-tested benefits, the economic effects of divorce may not be substantial and they will often have little or no property to distribute.

14.17 However, for most divorcing couples who fall between these two extremes, divorce means that they will experience a diminution in their standard of living. In short, the pie is not big enough.[38] The result is fierce debate about how this inadequate pie should be divided, with competing

---

34 Report on Aliment and Financial Provision, para 3.8.
35 For an example of a relatively large award, in Scottish terms, see *MacLean* v *MacLean* 1996 GWD 22–1278, where the wife was awarded £235,000. Considerable assets were involved in *De Winton* v *De Winton* 1996 GWD 29–1752, but, because much of the property was not matrimonial property, the wife received an award of only £30,000. In *Wilson* v *Wilson* 1999 SLT 249 the award to the wife of £408,609, by way of capital sum, and £200 per week for 30 months, is fairly large by Scottish standards but must be understood in the context of a husband worth in excess of £2 million. Again, many of the assets were not matrimonial property.
36 For examples of substantial awards in England, see *Dart* v *Dart* [1996] 2 FLR 286; *F* v *F* *(Ancillary Relief: Substantial Assets)* [1995] 2 FLR 45.
37 In *De Winton* v *De Winton*, above, where a protracted dispute resulted in an award of £30,000 to the wife, she was unsuccessful in seeking the expenses of her action which she estimated at £20,000 – *De Winton* v *De Winton* 1997 SLT 1118. For an example of the cost involved in litigation in England where considerable assets were at stake, see *F* v *F* *(Costs: Ancillary Relief)* [1995] 2 FLR 702.
38 The problems are expressed slightly differently by Mary Ann Glendon in her, somewhat pessimistic, observation: 'No country has completely solved the economic problems

claims being premised on, sometimes inconsistent, goals. None the less, the Scottish Law Commission[39] rightly addressed the question of what financial provision on divorce should seek to achieve. It is only through establishing clear goals that coherent legal provision can be formulated. Establishing the goals of financial provision on divorce is not the same as devising the mechanisms by which these goals may be achieved. However, the two are not wholly separable. For example, continued support may be a goal of financial provision, insofar as it reflects expectations of the parties. On the other hand, an award of a periodical allowance may be no more than a mechanism by which a particular goal of financial provision is achieved. For this reason some of the mechanisms are discussed below along with a number of possible aims.

Is conduct relevant?

14.18 The benefits and disadvantages of fault as the basis of divorce itself are discussed in chapter 13. Divorce is now based on irretrievable break-down of marriage, albeit the notion of fault has a lingering presence. Thus, in theory, fault has no role in the granting or refusal of a decree of divorce and, increasingly, spouses are choosing the no-fault grounds as the way to secure divorce.[40] Arguably, in such a climate, fault has no place in determining financial provision on divorce. We have moved well beyond the simplistic notion that marriages break down because one spouse was guilty of a matrimonial offence and that it is therefore appropriate to punish the wrongdoer. To allow fault to play any role is simply to open the door to all its attendant disadvantages and, in particular, to a rehashing of past grievances. It would be regrettable if what was not admitted through the front door could sneak in through the back door. None the less, it would be possible to devise a system which did not permit fault to be an issue in divorce itself, but admitted evidence of it on the question of financial provision, if reasons for doing so were persuasive. A school of

associated with marriage breakdown. The modest income and assets of most families, the frequency of marriage dissolution and the formation of new families, the many dis-advantages of working single mothers in the job market and the marriage market, and the strained resources of all welfare states make it unlikely that an entirely satisfactory solution to these problems can be found' – M. A. Glendon, *The Transformation of Family Law* (University of Chicago Press, 1989), at p 237.

39 Report on Aliment and Financial Provision, paras 3.35–3.64. The Commission's discus-sion merits reading in full since, despite the passage of time, it still contains one of the best examinations of the possible options. The aims considered are derived, in large part, from the Consultative Memorandum produced by the Commission, which included an examination of systems operating in other jurisdictions, and the responses it received to it – Memorandum on Aliment and Financial Provision (Scot Law Com Cons Memo No 22, 1976). In addition, the Commission was able to draw on empirical research it had commissioned – B. Doig, The Nature and Scale of Financial Provision on Divorce (1981, CRU) and A. J. Manners and I. Rauta, *Family Property in Scotland* (HMSO, 1981). It was also informed by The Financial Consequences of Divorce: The Basic Policy (Law Com No 103, 1980, Cmnd 8041).

40 In 1997, 67% of divorces were granted on the basis of non-cohabitation. Between 1981 and 1997, non-cohabitation for two years, coupled with the other spouse's consent, increased in popularity from 25% to 47%, while the use of non-cohabitation for five years increased from 14% to 20%; Registrar General for Scotland, Annual Report 1997 (General Register Office for Scotland, 1998), Table 8.1.

thought exists, most notably in the USA, which takes the view that, where the law fails to penalise reprehensible behaviour at some stage in the divorce process, either through fault as the basis for the divorce itself or through expressing disapproval in the making of financial awards, it actually increases the incidence of such behaviour.[41] No-fault divorce, so the argument goes, both increases unacceptable behaviour, like domestic violence, within marriage, and increases the incidence of divorce itself. That view is far from widely accepted.[42]

14.19 However, there may be some justification for admitting some aspects of conduct to decisions on financial provision. This requires, first, that we draw the subtle distinction between discussing conduct and allocating fault. Where the conduct has had a clear impact on the resources available, there may be good reason to take account of that, but only that, conduct, in dividing up the remaining assets. Thus, for example, where one spouse has dissipated assets through gambling, it may seem fair to the other spouse that this conduct should not be ignored. However, where the gambler was also violent, that conduct should not be considered in the context of financial provision since, arguably, it had no impact on resources.[43] The conclusion would seem to be that, while fault has no place generally in decision-making on financial provision, certain narrow aspects of conduct may be relevant. While financial provision should not be used as a means of 'punishing the guilty', it ought to take account of conduct which had a bearing on the financial picture.

Continuing support? Transitional or permanent?

14.20 Marriage creates a mutual obligation of aliment between spouses.[44] How that obligation operates was discussed in chapter 11 but the fundamental point is that, when individuals marry, they can expect spousal support should they require it, always assuming the other spouse has sufficient resources. Are spouses, therefore, entitled to assume lifelong financial support? Divorce is readily available and unilateral divorce can be obtained after five years non-cohabitation. Thus, we accept that marriages end. This suggests that the obligations attaching to them should be capable of termination as well. On a conceptual level, there is something untidy about continuing support. The Scottish Law Commission received strong

41 See for example, M. F. Brinig and S. M. Crafton, 'Marriage and Opportunism' 23 J Legal Stud 869 (1994) and L. D. Wardle, 'Divorce, Violence and the No-Fault Divorce Culture' 1994 Utah L. Rev 741 (1994).

42 For a particularly thorough response to Brinig and Crafton see I. M. Ellman and S. Lohr, 'Marriage as Contract, Opportunistic Violence and Other Bad Arguments for Fault Divorce' U Ill L Rev 719 (1997).

43 Of course, it might be argued that a spouse who is the victim of domestic violence may have suffered a diminution in earning capacity because of the physical or psychological effects of the violence. Where such a case is established, there may be reason to take the violent conduct into account. The alternative would be for the victim to raise an action for damages for the loss suffered. Such an approach has been pursued in the USA in states where there is no inter-spousal tort immunity – Scherer, 'Tort Remedies for Victims of Domestic Abuse' 43 S C L Rev 543 (1992).

44 Family Law (Scotland) Act 1985, s 1(1)(a) and (b).

criticism of lifelong support, from a variety of quarters. Men, the usual payers in this context, saw it as an intolerable burden on their future resources, as did second wives. The resentment is particularly strong where there were children in the new relationship and the second couple were struggling to make ends meet. Many former wives did not like the continued dependency and, it must be said, any hope of a person getting on with her life must be diminished by such a continuing link. In short, continuing support is inconsistent with clean-break[45] divorce. In addition, there are all the attendant problems of non-payment and its impact on receipt of state benefits.

14.21 However, there are instances where a case can be made for continuing financial support. In marriage, financial support is part of the parties' expectations. They may, therefore, plan their lives accordingly. If the law were not to take account of such planning, injustice might result. Two examples illustrate this point. First, take the couple who decide to have children and believe that the best person to look after the children on a day-to-day basis is a parent. They agree that the wife, who is the higher-earning spouse, will continue with her career, while the husband will stay at home with the children. He sacrifices career advancement, but runs the home and looks after the children very well. If, on divorce, all financial support for him were to terminate, he might find himself unable to find a job immediately and would have to carry the full financial burden of what was a mutual decision. The issue of the financial implications of future child care responsibilities will be addressed presently. Without taking that into account, the husband in our example is, none the less, facing disadvantage because of past mutual decisions. This does not necessarily make a case for life-long support, but it does suggest a need for transitional provision. Other examples around this theme can be found, but the basic point is clear. In some cases, there is a need to provide for financial support to enable a former spouse to adjust to single life in the hope that such a person will become self-supporting.

14.22 The second example centres on the changing nature of society and the rapidity with which that change has taken place. Thirty years ago, it was common, at least in middle class families, for couples to regard the wife's paid employment as secondary to the husband's. It was often the case that, either on marriage or, at least, when the children were born, the wife would cease employment and devote herself full time to running the home and looking after the children. It was not that she 'gave up work'. Homemaking became her job. Even after the children went to school and left home, many such women continued to be full-time homemakers. These women are now in their fifties and have no recent experience of working outside the home. Realistically, their employment prospects are not good. If

---

45 As the Commission noted, the term 'clean break' gained considerable popularity, although it 'seems more applicable to techniques than to objectives' – Report on Aliment and Financial Provision, para 3.44, n 83.

financial support for them were to cease on divorce, they would often be left in a disadvantageous financial position, while their former husbands might have considerable income. It may be that the solution here is through the distribution of accrued assets, and this will be considered presently. Where that option will not produce an equitable result, there appears to be a case for continued financial support. The kind of transitional provision that might work in the first example might not be enough here. Where people made decisions that were reasonable in a particular social and economic context, it would amount to 'moving the goalposts' if we failed to accommodate them simply because times have changed. In some cases, this may justify lifelong support. However, such cases will dwindle and ultimately disappear. Perhaps no one marrying today should assume that marriage will be permanent and, thus, lifelong support may be less defensible in the future. For the time being, however, the results of a bygone era must be accommodated.

Equitable adjustment of economic advantages and disadvantages arising from the marriage and acknowledgement of non-economic contributions?

14.23 The discussion of instances where some degree of continuing financial support may be justified is one aspect of a bigger question. As we saw, people plan their lives on the basis of expectations which may be valid at the time they are made and, often, on the assumption of a lasting relationship. Frequently, this involves living life as a co-operative venture or partnership where each spouse contributes, in varying degree, not only economically, but in terms of time, sacrifice and compromise. Ideally, each spouse also benefits from the arrangement, sometimes in different ways. Should the marriage be ended by divorce, there would seem to be good reason to take all such contributions and benefits into account. On the one hand, there is the total amount of economic advantage accrued during marriage and, on the other, there is what went into making the acquisition possible. Within these two categories, there is room for manoeuvre. Perhaps it will not be appropriate to consider all property accrued during the marriage in every case and, for example, inherited property or gifts from an outside source may be seen as having nothing to do with the marriage at all. Equally, not everything a person did while married is referable to the marriage, nor to the acquisition of assets. For example, one spouse may have given up his or her job because he or she found it boring. Such action is neither referable to the marriage nor a sacrifice which contributed to the acquisition of assets. However, in the cases of the homemaker husband and the older wife, discussed above, what the individuals in the economically weaker position did can be seen as both referable to the marriage and making a contribution in that context. Advantages and disadvantages, on the one hand, and contributions and sacrifices, on the other, are subtle and will create a degree of uncertainty. Discussion of them may even be used as an opportunity to dredge up old grievances. None the less, taking account of them would appear to be a reasonable goal in assessing financial provision. It should be remembered, however, that while some couples will have assets which can be divided using these criteria, many will not. This consideration will not necessarily obviate the need for some kind of continuing support.[46]

Division of property?

14.24 Whatever may be said in the course of marriage ceremonies about sharing property, the position under modern Scots law is one of separate property, subject to a small number of exceptions. It might be argued, therefore, that the parties ought to have no expectation of sharing in each other's property. However, as we saw when discussing the notion of continuing support, the spouses may organise their lives in such a way that one of them has a greater opportunity to acquire property than does the other. The opportunity may be increased by the role the other spouse is fulfilling in the relationship. While the marriage is going well, the ownership of particular property may be of no practical consequence. Indeed, the couple may view the property as belonging to them both. It may only be when divorce looms that the ownership of the home, cars, bank accounts and other assets takes on any significance. Where this property has been acquired while the spouses were engaged in a co-operative venture, it can be argued that they each have a moral stake in it. Thus, the opportunity to redistribute such property may achieve justice in terms of both the parties' expectations and the way the property was acquired. While it is acknowledged that, in many marriages, there will be little or no property and, thus, nothing to redistribute, many couples will have some assets. Just what property should be eligible for redistribution will be discussed in the context of the Family Law (Scotland) Act 1985 ('the 1985 Act').

Restitution

14.25 A possible goal of financial provision on divorce might be to put the spouses in the position they would have been in had they not married. The existing provisions on restitution could be applied, subject to modification. Of course, the longer the marriage subsists, the more difficult the process would become. It can probably be assumed that happy couples are often fairly careless about keeping records of everything they have done for each other. The point here is that the marriage has taken place. Divorce does not nullify marriage, it terminates it: that is, it brings to an end something which not only existed, but endured for a period of time. During that time many factors may have affected not only the parties' property, but their whole lifestyle. It is simply not practical to try to unpick all of that. The idea of recognising advantages and disadvantages, along with contributions and sacrifices, discussed above, takes account of changes which have come about as a result of the marriage, but without the difficulties inherent in seeking to effect restitution.

Provision for children

14.26 The future physical, emotional, psychological and other needs of

---

46 Where assets exist, but they are not readily realisable as, for example, where the only asset is a business which cannot be sold without cutting off future income, it would be possible to recognise contributions and disadvantages, but make any award payable over a period of time. This possibility is explored in greater depth presently.

any children involved in the divorce process are of paramount importance. As the individuals caught in an unfortunate situation, not of their own making, first consideration must be given to them. As we saw in chapter 5, extensive machinery, through mediation and the courts, exists to determine the future arrangements for their care. In addition, both parents and, sometimes, step-parents, have a continuing financial responsibility to them. However, financial provision on divorce is arguably a separate issue.[47] Clearly, any system that was solely concerned with arrangements that would work best for children would fail to provide for the many divorcing couples who do not have children. Even where children are present, any rigid formulation which tied property awards to them would have the inherent danger that parents would fight, tooth and nail, to have the children live with them, not because they felt they could look after them better, but because of the economic advantage.

14.27 The connection between a substantial responsibility for caring for children and economic disadvantage is well established. Since it is usually women with whom the children live after divorce, the whole process has come to be known, at least in the USA, as the 'feminization of poverty'.[48] The likely effect of taking care of the children after divorce is a diminution in earning capacity or an increase in expenditure to provide for substitute care and, sometimes, both. Thus, it seems reasonable that the future

47 In England and Wales, the Matrimonial Causes Act 1973, s 25(1) (as amended) provides that in exercising its powers to make financial provision on divorce, the court must 'have regard to all the circumstances of the case, first consideration being given to the welfare while a minor of any child of the family who has not attained the age of 18'. This provision resulted from the view of the Law Commission there that the law should 'emphasise as a priority' the need to safeguard the welfare and maintenance of the children – Financial Consequences of Divorce (Law Com No 112, 1980) para 24. For a discussion of the limits of this approach, see S. M. Cretney and J. M. Masson, *Principles of Family Law* (6th edn, Sweet and Maxwell, 1997) at pp 428–434.

48 The phrase 'the feminization of poverty' emerged in the USA in the 1980s, largely as a result of the work of L. J. Weitzman – see L. J. Weitzman, 'The Alimony Myth: Does No-Fault Divorce Make a Difference?' 14 Fam L Q 141 (1980) and L. J. Weitzman, *The Divorce Revolution: The Unexpected Social and Economic Consequences for Women and Children in America* (Free Press, 1985). See also J. B. McLindon, 'Separate But Equal: The Economic Disaster of Divorce for Women and Children' 21 Fam L Q 351 (1987). In what is probably one of the most ferocious academic battles of recent times, the accuracy of Weitzman's statistical studies has been questioned, first by analysts who did not have access to Weitzman's unpublished data – G. J. Duncan and S. D. Hoffman, 'Reconsideration of the Economic Consequences of Marital Dissolution' 22 Demography 485 (1985) and S. D. Hoffman and G. J. Duncan, 'What are the economic consequences of Divorce' 25 Demography 641 (1988). Later, what remained of the data was analysed, leading to further criticism, and an admission by Professor Weitzman of certain statistical errors which she attributed to computer experts involved in the research. Professor Weitzman, however, stands by her original conclusions. See R. R. Peterson, 'A Re-evaluation of the Economic Consequences of Divorce' 61 Am Sociological Rev 528 (1996), L. J. Weitzman, 'The Economic Consequences of Divorce Are Still Unequal: Comment on Peterson' 61 Am Sociological Rev 537 (1996) and R. R. Peterson, 'Statistical Errors, Faulty Conclusions, Misguided Policy: Reply to Weitzman' 61 Am Sociological Review 539 (1996). Marigold Melli has observed that the real divorce revolution has been the growing awareness of 'the failure of our divorce system to apportion fairly the economic burdens of marital dissolution' – M. S. Melli, 'Constructing a Social Problem: The Post-Divorce Plight of Women and Children' 1986 ABF Research Journal 759, at p 771.

economic effects of caring for children should be taken into account. One caveat should be made here. If future child care is to be a consideration in financial provision on divorce, it is imperative that the decision on where the children will live be made first on the basis of the welfare principle and any views the children wish to express. Economic consequences should then be dealt with around that decision.

Relief of the public purse?

14.28 A possible goal of financial provision on divorce is to ensure that, where a former spouse needs to be supported, the obligation falls on his or her former partner, rather than the state and, thereby, the taxpayer. This consideration has been taken into account, openly and unashamedly, by some courts in the USA. However, it is wholly inconsistent with the idea of divorce ending the marital relationship and its attendant obligations. It may be that a policy decision has already rejected this concept, since social security law does not require a person to support a former spouse.[49] Certainly, the Scottish Law Commission found 'no support ... for the view that the objective of financial provision on divorce should be to save the public purse'.[50]

Apportionment by means according to a formula?

14.29 The obvious attraction of devising some kind of formula for the division of assets and possible future support lies in the predictability of such a system. Assuming a flexible formula could be devised to take account of as many variables as possible, it might be thought that, not only could a great deal of time be saved, but many more couples could reach agreement without going to court at all. However, people's lives are infinitely variable and it is highly unlikely that any formula could do justice in all cases. As the Scottish Law Commission pointed out: 'Predictability of results ceases to be a virtue if the results are predictably unsatisfactory and unjustifiable'.[51] It would be interesting to know whether the drafters of the child support system read the Commission's Report.

A place for judicial discretion?

14.30 Perhaps all that we can ask of a system for financial provision on divorce is that it should do 'justice' in the instant case. In order to achieve this, we might leave it to the judiciary to exercise discretion. That was, in essence, what the Divorce (Scotland) Act 1976 did. However, there is a danger either of unpredictability and inconsistency or of the development of unsatisfactory rules of thumb.[52] To leave the judges with no guidance, or guidance that is so general that it is not helpful, was described by the Law

---

49 The position on former spouses can be contrasted with the treatment of cohabitants for social security purposes.
50 Report on Aliment and Financial Provision, para 3.45.
51 Report on Aliment and Financial Provision, para 3.52.
52 In cases under the 1976 Act, a 'one-third rule', whereby the wife received a periodical allowance amounting to one-third of the husband's income in addition to a capital award, held some sway. However, such a rule would clearly be unsatisfactory in many cases and, in any event, does not explain why such a proportion would be appropriate.

Commission in England and Wales as 'an abdication of responsibility by Parliament in favour of the judiciary'.[53] It seems clear that some form of reasonably detailed guidance is necessary if the legislators' goals are to be conveyed to those who have to work with the system, not only in the courts, but in advising clients who may be seeking to negotiate an agreement. That is not to say that all judicial discretion should be removed. Individual cases will present their own unique circumstances and it is unlikely that rules could be devised which were both sufficiently clear and sufficiently flexible so as to meet every eventuality.

One goal or several?

14.31 It is apparent from this discussion that financial provision on divorce may seek to achieve a number of goals. In addition to devising a system which would be regarded as reasonable by the parties and non-sexist in nature, the Scottish Law Commission sought one which would

'be capable of applying to many different types of marriage – whether long or short, with children or without children, with property or without property, whether housewife marriages or two-career marriages, whether entered into one year ago or forty years ago'.[54]

This was no small task and it became apparent that no single goal would satisfy such diverse needs. The Commission appreciated that, while setting out a number of principles to be applied would result in provision which was 'more complex legislatively than one which simply directs the court to make such order as it thinks fit', the practical application of such a system would be no more difficult.[55] In addition, it saw the need to retain an element of discretion to offset cases where the application of particular principles would produce unreasonable results.

Defects in the law prior to 1985

14.32 An overwhelming defect in the law prior to the 1985 Act was that it relied on judicial discretion at the expense of clarity and predictability. While judicial discretion was not wholly unfettered,[56] it was extensive, since the court was directed to make such an award 'as it thinks fit'.[57] This left

---

53 Discussion Paper on The Financial Consequences of Divorce: The Basic Policy, above, at para 69.
54 Report on Aliment and Financial Provision, para 3.63.
55 Report on Aliment and Financial Provision, para 3.61.
56 The usual rule on the exercise of discretion applied. Thus, an award would only be overturned on appeal where the lower court, 'failed to take into account matters relevant and necessary ... or has taken into account irrelevant or improper considerations or has misdirected itself in law' or where the amount awarded 'is so unreasonable ... as to take it outside the field of discretion altogether' – *Gray* v *Gray* 1968 SC 185, per Lord Cameron, at p 197.
57 1976 Act, s 5(2). This was in contrast to the position in England and Wales at the time where, however questionable it might appear now, the courts were at least given a clear indication of the objective to be achieved. The courts were directed to make an award which would 'place the parties, so far as is practicable and, having regard to their conduct, just to do so, in the financial position in which they would have been if the marriage had not broken down and each had properly discharged his or her financial obligations and responsibilities towards the other' – Matrimonial Causes Act 1973, s 25(2).

much to individual judges, their particular views on human behaviour and their own analysis of what financial provision was designed to achieve. Inevitably, inconsistency resulted and it was anticipated that the opportunity for inconsistency could only increase when divorce jurisdiction was extended to the sheriff courts.[58] Rules of thumb developed, although the Inner House refused to give approval to them.[59] Not only could solicitors advising clients give little clear indication of the likely award, the opportunity to negotiate settlements was impeded. The Scottish Law Commission concluded: 'Such a system does nothing to help the parties to arrange their affairs in a mature and amicable way. It is calculated to increase animosity and bitterness'.[60]

14.33 In addition, the courts were very restricted in the kind of awards they could make. They could award payment of a periodical allowance or a capital sum, payable at once. There was no power to order the transfer of property or to regulate the occupation of the matrimonial home after divorce. Where the court awarded a periodical allowance, it could not make the award subject to any time-limit. In short, the courts were not armed with the tools to enable them to meet the needs of the diverse range of cases being presented.

14.34 When the Scottish Law Commission began to consider financial provision on divorce, there was a remarkable lack of reliable information about the amounts being sought and awarded. Accordingly it arranged for a study to be carried out under the auspices of the Central Research Unit of the Scottish Office.[61] This enabled the Commission to assess what was happening on the basis of rather better information than anecdotal evidence. Having established what financial provision should seek to achieve, the Commission formulated firm proposals for reform, embodying a number of guiding principles and elements of discretion. These proposals were adopted, almost unchanged, and are contained in the Family Law (Scotland) Act 1985.

The Family Law (Scotland) Act 1985

14.35 The 1985 Act[62] gives courts a wide range of options in making orders for financial provision and provides clear guiding principles to be applied in granting the orders. The orders and principles are discussed in detail below. Broadly, what the 1985 Act does is to provide for a system of dividing property on the basis of deferred community of acquests. It recognises both economic and non-economic contributions, allows for a period of post-divorce adjustment, accepts the economic consequences of caring for children and, ultimately, provides a safety net for cases where all of these considerations will still not produce a just result. In line with these

---

58 This was achieved by the Divorce Jurisdiction, Court Fees and Legal Aid (Scotland) Act 1983, s 1.
59 *McRae* v *McRae* 1979 SLT (Notes) 45.
60 Report on Aliment and Financial Provision, para 3.37.
61 B. Doig, *The Nature and Scale of Financial Provision on Divorce* (CRU, 1981).
62 References in this section are to the Family Law (Scotland) Act 1985 unless otherwise stated.

principles, the court is empowered to order one spouse to do any or all of the following: pay a capital sum to the other; transfer property to the other; or pay a periodical allowance. In addition, it can make a range of 'incidental orders' and can require the trustees or managers of pension funds to pay sums to one of the spouses in the future. All in all, it is a highly sophisticated system. Without wishing to adopt the 'here's tae us, wha's like us' approach, found all too often throughout Scotland, it can be asserted that what we have is one of the most developed systems for financial provision on divorce to be found anywhere in the world. It balances clarity of objectives with the appreciation of diversity, and guidance with flexibility. Certainly, solicitors who have experience of working with the 1985 Act view it favourably and found 'it had produced greater clarity generally and a frame of reference which did not exist previously'.[63] What, then, does the 1985 Act provide?

14.36 Either spouse may apply to the court for a variety of orders in respect of financial provision on divorce and the general guidance given to the court is to make such orders as are *both* justified by the principles set out in the 1985 Act *and* reasonable having regard to the resources of the parties.[64] Thus, it is not enough that the award satisfies the principles, it must also pass the reasonableness test. While the court cannot make an award greater than that justified by the principles, it can reduce what the principles would indicate on the basis of available resources.[65] This two-pronged approach enables the court to take account of dramatic changes in individual fortunes. As we shall see, the property available for division is valued at what is known as 'the relevant date'. This is either the date when the parties ceased to cohabit or the date of the raising of the divorce action, whichever is earlier. There is often quite a delay between the parties separating and the divorce action coming to court, particularly if they are in dispute. The value of heritable property may fluctuate or a successful business may head toward the rocks[66] in the meantime. Thus, looking to the resources of the parties at the time of divorce enables the court to take account of such fluctuations. For this purpose, 'resources' are those of either party and are not restricted to the property which falls within the definition of 'matrimonial property'. So, for example, where the wife had been given a flat by a third party, it was not matrimonial property.[67] It was,

---

63 F. Wasoff, R. E. Dobash and D. S. Harcus, *The Impact of the Family Law (Scotland) Act 1985 on Solicitors' Divorce Practice* (Scottish Office, 1990) at p 63. Sixty per cent of solicitors expressed this view. Where reservations were expressed, many of these related to uncertainty over how the court would interpret what were, at the time of the study, fairly new legislative provisions.

64 Section 8(2).

65 *Latter* v *Latter* 1990 SLT 805; *Millar* v *Millar* (Sh Ct) 1990 SCLR (Notes) 666; *Welsh* v *Welsh* 1994 SLT 828. Certain statements made in the House of Lords in *Wallis* v *Wallis* 1992 SLT 676; 1993 SLT 1348, suggested problems with the operation of s 8(2). As Clive has observed (at para 24.012), 'It is fortunate that these *obiter dicta* are not binding on anyone'.

66 See for example, *Crockett* v *Crockett* (OH) 1992 SCLR 591.

67 What constitutes matrimonial property is discussed below, see para 14.41.

however, part of her resources and had the effect of reducing the capital sum to which she would have been entitled.[68]

Conduct of parties

14.37 As we saw in examining the possible goals of financial provision, there are widely differing views on whether the conduct of the parties should be taken into account. The 1985 Act steers something of a middle course here. As a general rule, the court is directed to take no account of the conduct of either party unless 'the conduct has adversely affected the financial resources which are relevant to the decision'.[69] Thus, only conduct which has an economic impact may be considered. This is entirely consistent with the clear goals set out in the first three principles of the 1985 Act. For example, the third principle seeks to achieve a fair sharing of the economic burden of caring for children in the future. Past conduct is simply not part of that equation. However, that is not to say that certain conduct is wholly irrelevant. In the context of the first principle, which seeks to ensure fair sharing of matrimonial property, conduct which affected that property may be relevant. Indeed, as we shall see, one of the circumstances which the court may take into account in deviating from equal sharing is destruction, dissipation, or alienation of property by one of the parties. In applying the second principle under the 1985 Act and seeking to balance advantages, disadvantages and contributions, where they are correlated, it may be that one party's conduct is part of the overall picture.

14.38 In the attempt to cover all possibilities, the 1985 Act goes on to provide that, in the context of the fourth (facilitation of adjustment) and fifth principles (alleviation of hardship), it must disregard conduct 'unless it would be manifestly inequitable to leave the conduct out of account'.[70] To date, this does not appear to have opened the doors to the undesirable parade of past mis-deeds.[71] Thus, while the 1985 Act minimises the relevance of conduct and, arguably, relegates it to its proper place, conduct is not wholly irrelevant.

The principles to be applied

14.39 In order to understand the principles to be applied by the court, each must be examined individually and in detail. Often only some of the principles will apply in a given case. For example, and to state the obvious, in a childless marriage, there is no need to consider sharing the economic burden of future child care. Indeed, it would be most unusual to find all of the principles applying in any case. Having understood each of the principles, it is then important to appreciate their interaction and to analyse the instant case in terms of that interaction. In assessing the system itself, it is necessary to see the principles as a whole in order to understand

---

68 *Buczynska* v *Buczynski* 1989 SLT 558.
69 Section 11(7)(a).
70 Section 11(7)(b).
71 *Brunton* v *Brunton* 1986 SLT 49; *Kavanagh* v *Kavanagh* 1989 SLT 134; *Skarpaas* v *Skarpaas* 1991 SLT (Sh Ct) 15 (husband's alcoholism taken into account); *White* v *White* 1990 GWD 12–616 (financial provision 'on the basis of economic practicalities rather than the attribution of fault').

how they can be used to accommodate the diverse range of cases which may arise.

Principle 1: *The net value of the matrimonial property should be shared fairly between the parties to the marriage*[72]

14.40 As we saw in chapter 11, Scots law operates what is essentially a system of separate property during marriage, subject to a number of exceptions.[73] The approach to property changes dramatically when the issue becomes one of financial provision on divorce. Provided that the property in question falls within the definition of matrimonial property, it is subject to 'fair sharing'. As a general rule, 'fair sharing' means 'sharing equally' but, as we shall see, this can be subject to exceptions where special circumstances warrant some other division.[74]

Matrimonial property

14.41 For the purpose of financial provision on divorce, 'matrimonial property' means all the property belonging to the parties or either of them at the relevant date, which was acquired by them, otherwise than by way of gift or succession from a third party

'(a) before the marriage for use by them as a family home or as furniture or plenishings for such a home; or
(b) during the marriage but before the relevant date'.[75]

The formulation creates two categories of property, each subject to different time-frames. How this definition applies to different kinds of property is explored below in respect of particular, commonly-held, types of property.

14.42 Certain property falls outwith the definition of matrimonial property. Anything acquired by the parties after the relevant date, usually the date of separation, is excluded although, as we have seen, such property is relevant to the broader question of a spouse's resources.[76] In addition, property acquired 'by way of gift or succession from a third party' is specifically excluded by the statutory definition itself. Thus, where one spouse inherits property, that is his or hers alone. Again, such assets may count as resources when the overall award is considered. Gifts from third parties are excluded. As far as gifts[77] are concerned, the qualifying words

---

72 Section 9(1)(a).
73 See chapter 11, paras 32–37.
74 Section 10(1) and (6). See para 14.49, below.
75 Section 10(4). It is important to note that this definition is not the same as the definition of household goods for the purpose of presumed equal shares during marriage – s 25(3). Consequently, the special treatment of money and securities, motor vehicles and domestic pets has no application here. The distinction between the treatment of different kinds of property during marriage and on divorce is fundamental and one which has caused difficulty for many students over the years.
76 *Petrie* v *Petrie* 1988 SCLR 390. Such property is not necessarily irrelevant in the overall calculation of financial provision since it may be part of the spouses resources – *Buczynska* v *Buczynski*, n 68 above.
77 Of course, the same caution does not arise in respect of inheritance from a spouse. In such a case, divorce is not an issue.

from a third party are important to note here. Gifts from one spouse to the other are matrimonial property for the purpose of financial provision on divorce. Of course, it will often be the case that such gifts will have been purchased out of monies which would themselves have been matrimonial property. Treating such inter-spousal gifts as matrimonial property does not, therefore, change the overall picture. However, a gift may have been bought with money inherited from a third party and, in that case, while the money itself would have been excluded, the gift bought with it will not.

14.43 The rule on inherited property and gifts from third parties is subject to one, very important qualification. Where the inheritance or gift is converted into other property,[78] it loses its protected status. Thus, for example, when donated money is used to buy heritable or moveable property, like a house or a painting, the house or painting becomes matrimonial property.[79] Where a family heirloom is sold and the proceeds are used to buy a car, the car becomes matrimonial property. This avoids the need to address the problem of 'tracing',[80] that is, following the path taken by a particular asset as it is converted into a series of different assets. It might be argued that this approach could produce very unfair results. Take, for example, a couple where each spouse inherits £20,000 from relatives. The husband uses his inheritance to improve the family home by having a conservatory built and the kitchen modernised. The wife deposits her inheritance in a high-interest savings account. The husband's inheritance has become matrimonial property, but the wife's has not. The fact that most couples probably have no idea that this would be the effect would exacerbate the apparent injustice, were it not for the court's discretion to look at the source of the funds used to buy a particular asset. As we shall see, in derogating from the general rule that fair sharing means sharing equally, one of the special circumstances the court may consider is the

---

78 Whether the property has, if fact, been converted into other property is normally unproblematic. However, in the context of shares in a company, the question is not always so clear, as is illustrated by two cases. In each case, the original shares were not matrimonial property since they had either been bought prior to the marriage or acquired by way of gift from a third party. In *Latter* v *Latter* 1990 SLT 805, the original shares were held in a number of family companies. During the marriage, company reconstruction resulted in the shares being held in one parent company. This change was sufficient to render the shares a holding in a new company and, as such, matrimonial property. In *Whittome* v *Whittome (No 1)* 1994 SLT 114, the original private company became a public limited company in the course of the marriage. There, however, the change was regarded as nominal and the shares remained individual property. See Clive, paras 24.032–24.033 for a discussion of company reconstruction, bonus issues and rights issues.
79 In *Latter* v *Latter* 1990 SLT 805, the wife's parents paid a sum of money to her solicitor and that money was used to purchase a house in the wife's name. The court concluded that the gift to her was the house rather than the money. This would seem to be a questionable analysis. How could her parents have given her a house they had never owned? It may be the court was seeking to do 'substantial justice', but that result could have been achieved by applying the special circumstance on the source of funds which justifies derogation from the principle of fair sharing meaning equal sharing which is discussed below.
80 For a different approach to tracing assets, see the Proceeds of Crime (Scotland) Act 1995, s 2(2) and the Criminal Law (Consolidation) (Scotland) Act 1995, Part V.

source of the funds used to acquire a particular asset.[81] Thus, the court may look at the fact that the husband used his inheritance to increase the value of the home.

Value of property

14.44 Property is valued on the basis of 'net value' at the 'relevant date'. 'Net value' is the value of the property after the deduction of certain permitted debts. The outstanding debts of either or both parties may be deducted depending on the nature of the debt and the time at which it was incurred. If the debt relates to matrimonial property, it can be deducted whether it was incurred prior to or during the marriage.[82] All other debts (ie those not relating to matrimonial property) may only be deducted if they were incurred during the marriage.[83] Only debts which are outstanding at the relevant date fall within the statutory definition. Thus, debts which have already been settled fall outwith the calculation. The use of the word 'outstanding' is not without problems. The preferred view is that a debt is outstanding even if it is not instantly payable and this is the approach the courts have usually taken.[84] However, in some cases, the courts have disregarded future debts.[85]

14.45 The 'relevant date' is

'Whichever is the earlier of –
(a) ... the date on which the parties ceased to cohabit;
(b) the date of service of the summons[86] in the action for divorce'.[87]

The benefit of having a clearly identifiable date for valuation of property lies in its simplicity. It also avoids the need to have property re-valued if the proceedings take time to come to court. However, these benefits must be understood in the light of difficulties which can arise.

14.46 The first difficulty can arise with couples who separate and then have one or more reconciliation attempts and this complication is anticipated in the 1985 Act. It provides

'no account shall be taken of any cessation of cohabitation where the parties

---

81 1985 Act, s 10(6)(b). While that provision talks in terms of the source of funds used to 'acquire' a particular asset, any reasonable interpretation would require the same approach to be taken to increasing the value of an existing asset.
82 Section 10(2)(a).
83 Section 10(2)(b).
84 *Buchan* v *Buchan* (Sh Ct) 1992 SCLR (Notes) 766 (where income tax on earnings during the marriage was deducted although it was not calculated until after the relevant date); *Mackin* v *Mackin* 1991 SLT (Sh Ct) 22 (where the house was purchased subject to a financial penalty if resold within five years, the value was calculated taking account of the penalty).
85 *McCormick* v *McCormick* (OH) 1994 SCLR (Notes) 958 (where the estimated tax liability on the husband's business profits was not deducted); *Latter* v *Latter*, n 79 above, (where the notional value of capital gains tax was not deducted from the value of shares).
86 Of course, if the divorce action was raised in the sheriff court, it would have been started by the service of an initial writ. The Scottish Law Commission recommended the appropriate amendment to the 1985 Act – Report on Family Law, draft Bill, Sched 1, para 82.
87 Section 10(3).

thereafter resumed cohabitation, except where the parties ceased to cohabit for a continuous period of 90 days or more before resuming cohabitation for a period or periods of less than 90 days in all'.[88]

Clive may be understating the problem when he describes this provision as 'difficult to understand at first reading'[89] and his attempt to explain it by the use of a worked example is an idea which is adopted, with thanks, here. Suppose the spouses separate on 5 November 1998 and resume cohabitation on February 14 1999. They separate again, one month later, on 14 March. The period of resumed cohabitation is less than 90 days and, thus, too short to take into account. The relevant date remains, therefore, 5 November. Let us suppose further that they make a second attempt at reconciliation on 4 July 1999 and, this time, remain together until 30 October 1999, when they part for good. The second period of resumed cohabitation exceeds 90 days and, thus, the relevant date becomes 30 October 1999.

14.47 The second difficulty with the relevant date, as defined in the 1985 Act, arises when property increases in value after the relevant date but before the action is heard. As we saw, diminution in value will be taken into account in examining the resources available to each party.[90] However, where matrimonial property increases in value during this time no similar accommodation is provided for in the 1985 Act. This resulting problem is exemplified in *Wallis* v *Wallis*, which generated considerable debate on the 1985 Act and the interpretation of s 9(1)(a).[91] The couple there co-owned the family home which was worth £44,000 at the relevant date and £64,000 at the time of the divorce.[92] The husband wanted to remain in the home since he used it in the course of his business. He could have bought his wife's share from her at whatever value they agreed and, incidentally, saved a tidy sum by using the simplified divorce procedure, but that was not the approach he took. Instead, he sought an order from the court transferring his wife's share in the property to him, using the relevant date as the basis for valuing the home. The sheriff rejected this approach, used the current market value of the home in his calculations and, adjusting the figures to take account of other property, made an award of a capital sum to the wife which reflected the increase in value. On appeal, this decision was confirmed by the Sheriff Principal. In the Inner House, Lord Hope rejected this basis for valuation and pointed out that, in terms of the 1985

---

88 Section 10(7). This provision is not to be confused with periods of resumed cohabitation as they affect the grounds for divorce.
89 At para 24.022.
90 Section 8(2)(b).
91 E.M. Clive, 'Financial Provision on Divorce' 1992 SLT (News) 241; J. M. Thomson, 'Financial Provision on Divorce: Not Technique but Statutory Interpretation' 1992 SLT (News) 245; 'Dr Clive Replies' 1992 SLT (News) 247. See also, A. Bissett-Johnson and J. M. Thomson, 'Sharing Property in a Fluctuating Market' 1994 SLT (News) 248, which considers the House of Lords decision.
92 At both dates the outstanding loan on the house was £26,600 and there was other property, namely, the furniture and plenishings in the home and a car, to be considered. For simplicity, we will concentrate on the value of the home, which was the real issue in the case.

Act, it was the net value of property *at the relevant date* that mattered.[93] Effectively, the husband received property worth £32,000 for £22,000. That decision was confirmed in the House of Lords.[94] This seems a wholly unreasonable result. As Clive points out, since the question of increases in value are not covered by the 1985 Act, they are governed by the common law. Thus, increases in value belong to the owners and, where property is owned in common, the increase in value should benefit both of them. 'This fundamental common law principle that the owner gets the benefit of increases in value between two dates is not, and could not be, affected by *Wallis* v *Wallis*'.[95] The sheriff's award was, in fact, made up of two elements – the wife's share of the net value at the relevant date (awarded under s 9(1)(a)) and an award to buy out her share of the increase in value since the relevant date (to which she was entitled under the common law). There is nothing in the 1985 Act to say that, in putting a value on property *for the purpose of a property transfer order* (which might, of course, cover non-matrimonial property) anything other than the current value should be used. That this ought to be the result is undoubtedly so, but must have been of little consolation to Ms Wallis.

14.48 The solution to this problem has been found by courts applying a different technique in such cases. Where the parties do not arrange the transfer without invoking the court's assistance, then, arguably, the court should not grant simple transfer. Mr Wallis gained from not taking the negotiation route, since it would have involved the use of the current market value. It is open to either spouse to raise an action for division and sale[96] when, again, current market value would prevail. However, it is undesirable that there should be a proliferation of court actions[97] and the better course would be for the court to make an incidental order, in the course of the divorce, for the sale of the property and the division of the proceeds between the parties.[98] This might not have suited Mr Wallis, since he wanted to remain in the home. However, if threatened with sale, he would then have had every incentive to negotiate a fair price for the transfer.

Special circumstances

14.49 As we have seen, the thrust of the first principle of financial provision on divorce is that matrimonial property should be shared fairly between the parties. It must be remembered that this first principle, embodied in s 9(1)(a), must be read along with the other principles, with

93 1992 SLT 676, at p 679D.
94 1993 SLT 1348.
95 At para 24.028.
96 *Mackenzie* v *Mackenzie* 1991 SLT 461; *Crockett* v *Crockett* (OH) 1992 SCLR 591.
97 In *Jacques* v *Jacques* 1995 SLT 963, the sheriff refrained from making an order for the transfer of property in order to avoid the kind of problem which arose in *Wallis*. The Inner House (at p 966) made clear that, rather than leave the parties to seek division and sale, the appropriate course would have been to make an incidental order.
98 In *Lewis* v *Lewis* (Sh Ct) 1993 SCLR 32, this approach was not found to be inconsistent with *Wallis* and the approach was endorsed by the House of Lords in *Jacques* v *Jacques* 1997 SLT 459.

the result that equal sharing may be deviated from because of them. None the less, the starting point is that 'fair sharing' means 'sharing equally'. Within the ambit of the first principle itself, the 1985 Act provides that it may be appropriate that property is shared 'in such other proportions as are justified in special circumstances'.[99] Section 10(6) of the 1985 Act gives examples of special circumstances which might justify deviation from the principle of equal sharing. It should be noted, however that these are simply illustrations and do not provide an exhaustive list.[100] The special circumstances identified in the 1985 Act are as follows

The terms of any agreement between the parties on the ownership or division of any of the matrimonial property[101]

14.50 As we saw in chapter 11, some couples may seek to 'custom-make' their marriage by executing an antenuptial or postnuptial marriage agreement which may include provisions relating to the possibility of divorce. While the court has a limited power to vary the terms of such agreements, it may decline to do so.[102] In any event, such an agreement may address how particular items of matrimonial property are to be treated. While any form of written agreement would provide useful evidence,[103] there is no requirement of this level of formality and other evidence would be admissible in establishing the agreement. Increasingly, couples take the title to property, and particularly the home, in joint names. It has sometimes been argued that this displaces another agreement as to the treatment of that particular property.[104] Evidence of title is not conclusive, however, since there may be other factors justifying a division which is not in accordance with that provided for in the title.[105] As with any agreement, it can be set aside where it has been made as a result of duress, fraud, or the like. In any event, agreements are only an example of circumstances which give the court the opportunity to exercise its discretion and deviate from the principle of equal sharing. The court is not given carte blanche to deviate from the fundamental principle of fair sharing and, indeed, taking account of any agreement, is designed to achieve just that end.

The source of the funds or assets used to acquire any of the matrimonial property where those funds or assets were not derived from the income or efforts of the parties during the marriage[106]

14.51 When we examined the exclusion of property acquired by gift or succession from a third party from the definition of matrimonial property,

---

99 Section 10(1).
100 For example, the fact that a marriage has been a short one may be relevant – *Kerrigan* v *Kerrigan* 1988 SCLR 603.
101 Section 10(6)(a).
102 Section 16, discussed at paras 14.157–14.158, below.
103 *Anderson* v *Anderson* 1991 SLT (Sh Ct) 11.
104 *Jacques* v *Jacques*, n 97 above; *Reynolds* v *Reynolds* (Sh Ct) 1991 SCLR (Notes) 175; *Wallis* v *Wallis*, n 65 above.
105 For example, in *Kerrigan* v *Kerrigan* 1988 SCLR 603, the brevity of the marriage was also taken into account as, in *Farrell* v *Farrell* (Sh Ct) 1990 SCLR 717, was the fact that one party had assumed the other's mortgage liability.
106 Section 10(6)(b).

we saw the injustice that might result when that property was converted to some other kind of property, since 'tracing' of assets is not permitted. In our example of the beneficiary couple, where the husband used his inheritance to improve the home and the wife put her inheritance into a savings account, it appeared that his action would result in loss to him. In order to avoid that type of injustice, the court is permitted to look to the source of such property. Thus, in deviating from equal sharing of the value of the home, it could look to the fact that the money for home improvements came wholly from money inherited by the husband. Similar considerations apply where one spouse is given money by his or her family and uses it to buy matrimonial property.[107] This ability to look at the source of property, where it has not come from the efforts of the parties, has been applied to property given to one spouse by members of his or her family,[108] to pre-marital property[109] and to property acquired by succession,[110] where it was then used to acquire other property.

Any destruction, dissipation or alienation of property by either party[111]

14.52 During the marriage, each spouse's property belongs to him or her and spouses may manage their property in very different ways. Let us take the example of a couple where each spouse earns the same excellent salary. Suppose the husband uses his income to pay the mortgage and the bills and has invested the excess wisely. The wife, on the other hand, has spent her income on wining, dining, travelling and having a thoroughly good time. The husband does not participate in these activities. When they reach the point of divorce (which might come as no surprise in such a case), a substantial part of the matrimonial property has been amassed as a result of the husband's frugality and the wife has contributed very little. It may be that some of this imbalance would be dealt with under the second principle for financial provision, which seeks to balance advantages gained by one party through contributions made by the other.[112] That aside, however, the court's power to take account of dissipation of property is another avenue of flexibility built into the system. What amounts to dissipation is not entirely clear-cut. Normal run-of-the-mill events, like the failure of a business, have been held not to be dissipation,[113] although circumstances might be imagined where a spouse's continued losses in disastrous business schemes might amount to that. Failure to pay a mortgage has also been held not to be dissipation[114] whereas forging a spouse's signature in order

107 This approach is preferable to contorting the definition of a gift in order to achieve the same result – see *Latter* v *Latter* 1990 SLT 805.
108 *Buczynska* v *Buczynski*, n 68 above; *Kerrigan* v *Kerrigan*, above; *MacLean* v *MacLean* 1996 GWD 22–1278; *Milne* v *Milne* 1994 GWD 11–666.
109 This might be relevant, for example, where one spouse owned a home prior to the marriage and the proceeds from its sale were used to buy the current matrimonial home. See *Budge* v *Budge* 1990 SLT 319; *Buchanan* v *Buchanan* 1989 GWD 26–1166; *Jesner* v *Jesner* 1992 SLT 999; *Phillip* v *Phillip* 1988 SCLR 427.
110 *Davidson* v *Davidson* 1993 GWD 31–2000.
111 Section 10(6)(c).
112 Section 9(1)(b).
113 *Russell* v *Russell* 1996 GWD 15–895.
114 *Park* v *Park* 1988 SCLR 584.

to burden the property has.[115] So much for dissipation, what of destruction or alienation? These words can be given their ordinary meaning and set in the context of reasonable actions. Thus, deliberately wrecking the contents of the home would arguably be destruction, while the accidental dropping of an ornament would probably not be. Giving away large sums of money might amount to alienation, while the giving of reasonable birthday gifts might not. Again, the discretionary nature of the court's power here allows it to take actions into account when it is reasonable to do so and disregard other events, when appropriate. It should be noted that taking account of destruction, dissipation or alienation of property is not a matter of the court deciding who behaved 'well' or 'badly' in the course of the marriage and is, thus, not an inquiry into conduct. It is simply a matter of taking account of actions that had specific effects on property.

The nature of the matrimonial property, the use made of it (including use for business purposes or as a matrimonial home) and the extent to which it is reasonable to expect it to be realised or divided or used as security[116]

14.53 Some matrimonial property is capable of being sold and the proceeds can then be divided. Often, this is what the spouses agree in respect of the home. In other cases, the spouses can reach agreement that certain items of property will be taken by each spouse and set-off against each other. Thus, one may take the kitchen appliances while the other takes the dining-room suite. However, the nature of the property may be such that it does not permit readily of such division. If the spouses cannot reach agreement, taking into account the relevant valuations, the court has a discretion to take account of special circumstances in respect of property.

14.54 It may be that particular property cannot be realised or, at least, that realisation is not a reasonable economic option. This can arise where the asset in question is a business, property inexorably linked to the business, a pension, or an insurance policy.[117] Thus, for example, the sale of a farm might amount to 'killing the goose that lays the golden eggs'. Similarly, early surrender of an insurance policy will usually produce a very poor return. In such circumstances, the court usually has the option of awarding a capital sum but deferring payment or ordering payment to be made by instalments, rather than ordering the sale of the property.

14.55 It may be that the spouse with whom any children will be living would like to keep the home in order to minimise the disruption to the children. If they remain in the home they will be near to their school, friends and relatives. In such a case, the court might transfer the non-resident parent's share in the home to the parent with whom the children are living.[118] The extent to which the non-resident parent may be compen-

---

115 *Short* v *Short* 1994 GWD 21–1300.
116 Section 10(6)(d).
117 *Davidson* v *Davidson*, n 110 above; *Gray* v *Gray* 1979 SLT (Notes) 94. Pensions are discussed in detail – see para 14.63, below.
118 *Cooper* v *Cooper* 1989 SCLR 347; *Farrell* v *Farrell* (Sh Ct) 1990 SCLR 717; *Peacock* v *Peacock* 1994 SLT 40.

sated for the transfer will often depend on the other assets available and whether the spouse who will get the home is in a position to make mortgage payments and raise additional funding.[119] One option is to grant a standard security over the home in favour of the non-resident spouse, making it repayable when the house is sold, which failing, when the youngest child reaches the end of his or her schooling.[120] It should not be assumed, however, that 'he or (usually) she who gets the children gets the home', since other circumstances may render such a solution inappropriate.[121] Similarly, particular property might be used for business purposes where, for example, a veterinary surgery is part of the same structure as the family home. Again, the court has the power to consider this circumstance in reaching a decision in respect of the property, and again, the discretionary nature of the court's power must be appreciated.

The actual or prospective liability for any expenses of valuation or transfer of property in connection with the divorce[122]

14.56   This special circumstance simply allows the court to take account of the fact that valuation and transfer of property is often an unavoidable expense of the whole process and to enable it to ensure that the burden does not fall unreasonably on either party.

Orders under principle 1

14.57   In making an award under this principle, the court may only order the payment of a capital sum, whether payable as a lump sum or by instalments, or order the transfer of property.[123] In addition, the special treatment of future pension entitlement is an important subtlety in the division of matrimonial property. Since principle 1 is concerned with the fair sharing of property already accrued, the court cannot order the payment of a periodical allowance.[124] As we shall see, other principles do allow for periodical allowance to be awarded in certain circumstances.

Application of principle 1 to particular property

14.58   In order to demonstrate how the principle in s 9(1)(a) operates, it is useful to look at examples of specific types of property and explore what the courts have, or might have, done.

The home

14.59   For many owner-occupier couples the home will be their biggest single asset. Scotland has a long history of reliance on rented property as providing the family home, but the trend is changing. Whereas, in 1979, Manners and Rauta[125] found 37% of the homes in their study to be owner-

---

119 *Cooper* v *Cooper*, above; *Peacock* v *Peacock*, above.
120 *Murley* v *Murley* (OH) 1995 SCLR (Notes) 1138.
121 *MacKenzie* v *MacKenzie* 1991 SLT 461; *Thom* v *Thom* (OH) 1990 SCLR (Notes) 800.
122 Section 10(6)(e).
123 Sections 8(1) and 12(3).
124 Section 13(2).
125 Family Property in Scotland, Table 2.1.

occupied, the figure for the country as a whole was 59% by 1996.[126] Thus, how the home is dealt with on divorce is not simply a middle-class concern although usually, the wealthier the couple, the more valuable the home is likely to be.

14.60 The first issue to consider is when the home is and is not matrimonial property. As we saw, the definition of matrimonial property normally restricts it to property acquired since the date of the marriage. Clearly, a home acquired, otherwise than by gift or succession from a third party, after the date of the marriage, but before the relevant date, is matrimonial property. A home acquired after the relevant date will not be matrimonial property although, as we have seen, its value may be taken into account in assessing one party's resources.[127] It should be noted that, as far as this part of the definition is concerned, all homes acquired within the time-frame are matrimonial property, irrespective of the use to which they are put. This can be contrasted with the definition of the 'matrimonial home' for the purpose of the Matrimonial Homes (Family Protection) (Scotland) Act 1981. Where, after marriage but before separation, the wife buys a flat which she uses exclusively for painting and the husband buys a cottage which he rents out, both are matrimonial property.

14.61 In addition, the 1985 Act provides that property acquired before the date of the marriage by either or both of the parties 'for use by them as a family home or as furniture or plenishings for such a home' will be matrimonial property.[128] Thus, certain property acquired before the marriage may be matrimonial property provided the condition on use is met. Here, the purpose for which the property was bought is important. In *Maclellan* v *Maclellan*,[129] the husband bought a croft before the marriage, for his own use. When he later married, his wife moved into the croft and they lived there for 26 years. While it had become the family home, it had not been bought for that purpose and, thus, was not matrimonial property. A spouse in Ms Maclellan's position may, however, gain something under the second of the principles where he or she can show a contribution to enhancing the value of the property, albeit the property itself is not matrimonial property. In *Budge* v *Budge*,[130] for example, the wife's efforts in enhancing the value of a croft were recognised in the capital award she received.[131] In *Buczynska* v *Buczynski*,[132] a man bought a home for himself

126 Regional Trends 33 (Office for National Statistics, 1998), Table 6.3. Despite this increase in owner-occupation, Scotland still lags behind the rest of the UK. In England, the figure is 68%, in Wales, 71%, and, in Northern Ireland, 69%. It should be noted that the statistics from this report do not compare squarely with those found by Manners and Rauta but looking at the two can give a general impressionistic flavour.
127 *Petrie* v *Petrie* 1988 SCLR 390. Such property is not necessarily irrelevant in the overall calculation of financial provision since it may be part of the spouses resources – *Buczynska* v *Buczynski*, n 68 above.
128 Section 10(4)(a).
129 1988 SCLR 399.
130 1990 SLT 319.
131 See also, *Ranaldi* v *Ranaldi* 1994 SLT (Sh Ct) 25, aff'd 1992 GWD 26–1486. The apparent lack of synchronisation in the dates here is due to the fact that the original decision was in March 1992 and there was simply a delay in the case reaching the law reports.
132 Note 68 above.

and his new partner at a time when he was still married to his first wife. He and his partner cohabited in the home and continued to live there after they married. Since the home had been bought for them to live in, it was matrimonial property for the purpose of their subsequent divorce, regardless of the fact that they were not free to marry at the time the home was bought. Not only is the purpose of the purchase important, it must be 'person-specific'. Thus, if Mr Buczynski had bought the home in question for use by himself and his first wife and then lived in it with his second wife, it would not have been matrimonial property in the second divorce.[133]

14.62 It is the 'net value' of property that is relevant under the 1985 Act.[134] Heritable property is particularly prone to price fluctuations, usually in an upward direction. Indeed, the leading cases on property increasing in value between the date of separation and the date of divorce are concerned largely with heritage.[135] As we have seen, because of *Wallis* v *Wallis*, greater justice can often be achieved between the parties by an award of a capital sum or by an order for division and sale, than by property transfer. Any loans secured on the home must be deducted before the value of the home can be ascertained and, thus, any outstanding mortgage or other loans secured in this way must be subtracted from any valuation. For many couples, what looked like a very valuable asset becomes much less so in an instant. Thereafter, applying the first principle, the net value of the home will be shared fairly between the spouses. While this may mean that it should be shared equally, this will not always be the case and the special circumstances relating to the source of the funds from which the house was purchased and the use made of it are particularly applicable in the context of the home.[136] For example, the fact that the home is needed for the future care of the children, or for the continuation of a business, may be relevant.

Pensions

14.63 Pension provision forms an increasingly important part of the assets of many individuals and couples today. Scotland, in common with other post-industrial countries, faces an increase in the proportion of the population who are older people and this trend will increase in the future.[137] One result of the demographic changes is that a smaller pool of working population will have to support a growing number of older people if the latter do not make provision for their own support in old age. Consequently, successive governments have encouraged individuals to make

---

133 The person-specific nature of this provision is illustrated further by the, somewhat unusual, case of *Mitchell* v *Mitchell* 1995 SLT 426. The home was purchased as the matrimonial home during the parties' first marriage. They divorced and later remarried. The original home was matrimonial property when they divorced for the second time.
134 Section 10(2).
135 See para 14.47, above.
136 See para 14.42, above.
137 The 1996-based projections estimate that the number of children under the age of 15 will fall to 83% of the 1996 level by the year 2021 while the number of people over pensionable age will increase by 7% – Registrar General for Scotland, Annual Report 1997, pp 16–17.

provision for themselves through the mechanism of pension schemes and plans, both by mandating pension provision and offering tax incentives. In 1979, Manners and Rauta found that 56% of the people they interviewed had pension provision of some kind[138] and it can be expected that the figure is higher today. The hope of the individual is that, through putting money into such a scheme while he or she is working, a financially secure old age can be assured without the need to rely unduly on state benefits. The idea that such financial security can be achieved adequately simply through National Insurance payments is now no more than a forlorn hope. A variety of different schemes and plans exist for pension provision and, apart from the State Earnings Related Pension Scheme (SERPS), the most popular are occupational pension schemes and personal pension plans.[139] Many schemes include not only provision for pensions but also for lump-sum payments to members on their retirement or provision for widows and widowers, should the member die in service.

14.64 It is worth remembering that, in some two-career couples, each of them will have made pension provision. In such cases, it may be that each spouse's pension entitlement cancels out the other and there will be no need to make special arrangements on divorce. However, for many other couples, only one of them will have had the opportunity to make any significant pension provision and, where this is the case, it is frequently the husband rather than the wife who will have done so.[140] This is another example of the way in which the traditional breadwinner-homemaker model of family arrangement provides men, rather than women, with the opportunity to acquire assets during such a marriage.[141] Since fair sharing of accrued assets is fundamental to the scheme established by the 1985 Act, it is essential that the value of pension entitlement and related benefits is recognised and appropriate arrangements are made for fair sharing.

14.65 The 1985 Act, as amended, makes it clear that pension provision is part of the picture when considering matrimonial property, when it provides that

> '[t]he proportion of any rights or interests of either party ... in any benefits under a pension scheme which either party has or may have (including such benefits payable in respect of the death of either party) ... which is referable ... [to the relevant period] ... shall be taken to form part of the matrimonial property'.[142]

138 Family Property in Scotland, Table 2.14.
139 For a discussion of the various kinds of pension provision available, see A. C. Page and R. B. Ferguson, *Investor Protection* (Weidenfeld and Nicolson, 1992), chapters 13 and 14.
140 For many women who have been in contributory pensions, career breaks taken to have and care for children will reduce the amounts to which they are entitled.
141 A UK survey found that, of the married women surveyed, 38% were contributing to a pension scheme – J. Field and G. Prior, *Pensions and Divorce* (DSS, 1996), at p 66. See also, J. Field and G. Prior, *Women and Pensions* (DSS, 1996). The tentative findings of a study of division of pension benefits in the USA suggest that equitable division is not always the result – J. M. Krauskopf and S. B. Seiling, 'A Pilot Study on Marital Power as an Influence in Division of Pension Benefits at Divorce of Long Term Marriages' 1996 Disp Resol 169.
142 Section 10(5) as amended by the Pensions Act 1995, s 167(2) and the Family Law Act 1996, s 17.

'Pension scheme' is defined widely to include an occupational pension scheme; a personal pension scheme; a retirement annuity contract; or an annuity or insurance policy purchased or transferred for the purpose of giving effect to a pension scheme.[143] It should be noted that 'any benefits under a pension scheme' includes 'any benefits by way of pension, whether under a pension scheme or not'.[144] This would cover the case, for example, where payments were made to a retired partner by the remaining partners in a firm in terms of the partnership agreement without there being any pension scheme in place at all. Under the previous law, problems arose, in the context of divorce, in respect of 'death in service' benefits payable to the widow or widower of a member of a pension scheme and it was doubted that this element of the benefits formed part of matrimonial property.[145] The amendment to the 1985 Act (by the Pensions Act 1995) has put this matter beyond doubt and it is now clear that such benefits, where referable to the appropriate period, form part of the value to be taken into account.

14.66 So much for the types of pension and related interests which are relevant. How is the value of this particular kind of matrimonial property to be ascertained? This question raises two separate, but related, matters – valuation of the pension rights and establishing what proportion of that valuation falls to be regarded as matrimonial property. In terms of valuing the pension right, the older method (continuing service method) was based on assuming that the scheme member would continue in the scheme until retirement and ascertaining the value by, often expensive, actuarial evidence. Regulations[146] have replaced this with the 'cash equivalent transfer value' (CETV), which calculates the value of the pension, assuming the member leaves the scheme at the relevant date.[147] The regulations provide further guidance on valuation depending on the kind of pension scheme involved and whether the member is still an active member of the scheme at the relevant date.[148] The benefit of using CETV is that it is a simple, well-established, method and one with which scheme managers are familiar, since it is routinely used when scheme members are transferring their pensions between different schemes. Since scheme managers are obliged to provide information on the CETV on request to a member who is involved

---

143 Section 10(10).
144 Pensions Act 1995, s 167(10).
145 *Brooks* v *Brooks* 1993 SLT 184; *Crosbie* v *Crosbie* (Sh Ct) 1995 SCLR 339; *Gribb* v *Gribb* 1994 SLT (Sh Ct) 43 (unaffected by *Gribb* v *Gribb* 1996 SLT 719); *Welsh* v *Welsh* 1994 SLT 828.
146 Divorce etc (Pensions) (Scotland) Regulations 1996 ('1996 Regulations'), SI 1996 No 1901, as amended by the Divorce etc (Pensions) (Scotland) Amendment Regulations 1997, SI 1997 No 745. See also, A. Bissett-Johnson, 'Recent Changes in Valuation and Division of Pensions on Divorce' 1996 SLT (News) 295; S. Eden, 'Pensions on Divorce' 1996 Fam LB 22–3 and 23–3; and Clive at paras 24.038–24.039.
147 1996 Regulations, reg 3(2). Regulation 3(5) provides for departure from this method of calculation in certain circumstances. Eden (1996 Fam LB 23–3) suggests that the discretion to depart is fairly broad, while Clive (para 24.039, n 19) takes the view that departure is only permitted in very narrow circumstances.
148 1996 Regulations, regs 3(2) and 4.

in a divorce action,[149] it is not surprising that it was the method of calculation selected in the regulations.[150]

14.67 Having established the value of the pension rights, it then becomes necessary to establish what proportion of the value is matrimonial property. It should be remembered that it is only that part of the pension right which falls between the date of the marriage and the relevant date which can reasonably be regarded as matrimonial property. Again, the 1996 Regulations provide a simple method based on the following formula

$$A \times \frac{B}{C}$$

where A is the value of the member's interest in the scheme at the relevant date, B is the period between the date of the marriage and the relevant date, and C is the period the member has been in the scheme prior to the relevant date. A worked example illustrates the application of this formula. Let us suppose that the husband joined the scheme in 1976 and got married in 1992. The relevant date is in year 2000.[151] He will have been in the scheme for 24 years at the relevant date (C), but only 8 of these years relate to the time between marriage and the relevant date (B). Thus, only eight twenty-fourths, or one-third, of the value of his interest in the pension scheme (A) is matrimonial property.

14.68 Like all other matrimonial property, the pension rights or, rather, the portion of them that is matrimonial property, will then be subject to fair sharing. The difficulty with pensions is that they are not capable of being realised immediately or, if it is possible to cash them in, the amount realised is only a fraction of what would have been available at a later date. Prior to the Pensions Act 1995 ('the 1995 Act'), the courts sought to deal with the problem by awarding a capital sum, and leaving the payer to find the money from other assets, or by deferring payment or ordering that it should be made by way of instalments. The 1995 Act has added new powers to the battery of orders a court can make and the court can now order pension fund managers to pay lump sums directly to a former spouse when they become due.[152] Further reform of the law on the treatment of pensions on divorce can be anticipated, with 'pension-splitting' becoming the way of the future.[153]

---

149 1996 Regulations, reg 4.

150 The Treatment of Pension Rights on Divorce, Cm 3345, 1996.

151 Obviously, the specific date on which events occurred will be relevant to the calculation in individual cases, but the example conveys the general idea.

152 1985 Act, s 12A, as amended by the Pensions Act 1995, s 167(3), discussed at para 14.116.

153 Pension-splitting is anticipated by the The Family Law Act 1996, s 17. For a discussion of the history and futility of this provision, see Clive, para 24.037, n 13. At the time of writing, the consultation process on pension-splitting has reached an advanced stage – see Pension sharing on divorce: reforming pensions for a fairer future (Department of Social Security, 1998), Part I of which contains a statement of the government's aims and policy on the matter, with Part II providing the draft Pension Sharing Bill.

Award of damages and redundancy payments

14.69 Whether an award of damages will be treated as matrimonial property raises interesting analytical questions relating more to the law of delict than to matrimonial property. Where both the injury and the payment of damages occur after the marriage but before the relevant date, damages are matrimonial property.[154] Where the injury occurred before the marriage but the damages claim was settled during the marriage, two views might be taken of the money paid. On the one hand, the interest arose prior to marriage and should be regarded as separate property. On the other hand, separate property becomes matrimonial property when it changes nature, since 'tracing' of assets is not permitted. Thus, the claim may have been individual, but the actual money paid is not. Where the injury occurred during the marriage and the damages were paid after the relevant date, does this mean that, applying the same rules, the damages are separate property? Apparently not, since the right of action accrued during the marriage. In addition, it must be remembered that the solatium element of damages is, by definition, personal in nature and often damages contain an element for loss of future earnings. If they were treated as matrimonial property, subject, at first instance to equal sharing, the result might be inconsistent with the whole purpose of those elements of the award. This is a prime case for the application of the idea of special circumstances justifying a division that is unequal or, indeed, no division at all. Where the injury occurs after the relevant date, any damages awarded are not matrimonial property, although they will count as part of the recipient's resources. Similar principles would appear to apply to criminal injuries compensation[155] and redundancy payments.[156]

Spouse's career

14.70 In the USA, courts have wrestled with the issue of whether a spouse's professional degree or other career advancement is matrimonial property.[157] This is quite separate to the issue of considering a spouse's income. Take the case of a wife[158] who works to support her husband while he completes college and goes on to obtain a medical degree.[159] She sacrifices her own aspirations to study in order to support them both and to

---

154 *Skarpaas* v *Skarpaas* 1991 SLT (Sh Ct) 15; *Petrie* v *Petrie* 1988 SCLR 390.
155 *McGuire* v *McGuire's Curator Bonis* 1991 SLT (Sh Ct) 76.
156 *Smith* v *Smith* 1989 SLT 668; *Tyrrell* v *Tyrrell* 1990 SLT 406. A payment made on leaving the army after the relevant date has been held not to be matrimonial property – *Gibson* v *Gibson* 1990 GWD 4–213.
157 See, J. Singer, 'Husbands, Wives and Capital: Why the shoe won't fit' 31 Fam L Q 119 (1997).
158 In many of the cases, it is the wife who worked to support the husband. However, treating career development as matrimonial property is a principle capable of gender-neutral application. In *Golub* v *Golub* 139 Misc 2d 440 (NY, 1988), the court took the view that the increased value during the marriage of the wife's career as a model and actress was matrimonial property in the light of the husband's contributions to her career in acting as her lawyer and financial adviser. In *Elkus* v *Elkus* 572 NYS 2d 901 (NY, 1991) the court took a similar view of a husband's contribution to his wife's career as an opera singer.
159 Law, medicine and dentistry are all graduate degrees in the USA and require that students already hold a previous degree. In addition, state funding is generally less

finance his education. The husband duly graduates and goes on to start what becomes a very profitable practice. When they divorce some years later, the wife claims his medical licence as matrimonial property in which she is entitled to share. It might be argued that a professional licence entitles the holder, and only the holder, to practice in the particular profession and that such licences cannot be bought and sold. However, *O'Brien* v *O'Brien*,[160] a decision of the highest appellate court in New York state, was the first of many decisions there to hold that such a qualification was matrimonial property and, thus, its value was subject to division on divorce. While the decision has been followed consistently in that state,[161] other states have rejected this approach. Where they have done so, they have often found some other mechanism to enable them to recognise the supporting spouse's contribution.[162] In Scotland, the issue of a spouse's direct interest in the other spouse's professional qualification or career has not been founded upon in this way. The reason lies in the second principle under the 1985 Act, which requires the court to take account of advantages gained by one spouse as a result of contributions made by the other. This principle will be considered presently.

14.71 A related but separate issue is whether the goodwill in a spouse's business, built up in the course of the marriage, is matrimonial property. Let us suppose that the wife has built up a successful practice as a dentist over the last 20 years, while her husband remained at home caring for the children. As with any such business, its value is not confined to the equipment in the surgery but includes an element of 'goodwill' representing loyal patients who will continue to use the practice and speak well of it in the local community, thus attracting other patients. The asset has been built up in the course of the marriage and, therefore, it has been argued, it is matrimonial property and subject to division. Again, views on this point

generous than in the UK. As a result, qualifying in any of these professions is more expensive than it is here and takes longer. Since the students are generally older, a greater proportion of them are married.

160 489 NE 2d 712 (NY, 1985). There, the husband filed for divorce two months after he obtained his licence to practice medicine, his wife having supported him through the final portion of his undergraduate degree and medical school.

161 *Elkus* v *Elkus*, n 158 above; *Golub* v *Golub*, n 158 above; *McAlpine* v *McAlpine* 539 NYS 2d 680 (NY, 1989) (fellowship in Society of Actuaries); *McGowan* v *McGowan* 535 NYS 2d 990 (NY App Div, 1988) (master's degree). See, S. E. Keller, 'The Rhetoric of Marriage, Achievement and Power: An Analysis of Judicial Opinions Considering the Treatment of Professional Degrees as Marital Property' 21 Vt L Rev 409 (1996) and K. W. Meighan, 'For Better or For Worse: A Corporate Finance Approach to Valuing Educational Degrees at Divorce' 5 Geo Mason L Rev 193 (1997).

162 See for example, *Mahoney* v *Mahoney* 453 A 2d 527 (NJ, 1982), where the concept of 'reimbursement alimony' was used to award the supporting spouse a sum equal to that spent on support and education. A similar approach was taken in *Bold* v *Bold* 574 A 2d 552 (Pa, 1990). Other courts have taken the supporting spouse's contributions and the benefiting spouses's enhanced earning capacity into account in awarding alimony or dividing property. An early statement of this approach can be found in *In re Marriage of Graham* 574 P 2d 75 (Colo, 1978) although there, the wife had not sought alimony. See also, *Downs* v *Downs* 574 A 2d 156 (Vt, 1990); *Lowery* v *Lowery* 413 SE 2d 731 (Ga, 1992); *In re Marriage of Francis* 442 NW 2d 59 (Iowa, 1989); *Roberts* v *Roberts* 670 NE 2d 72 (Ind Ct App 1996).

in the USA have varied from state to state, with community property states tending to treat goodwill as community property.[163] Where the notion of goodwill as matrimonial property has been rejected it has been on the basis that: any element of goodwill is personal to the practitioner;[164] it would be inequitable to require payment of a judicially-determined sum which could not be realised;[165] or, it would result in 'double counting' since it was reflected in the spouse's income.[166] How do the Scottish courts view such an asset? Since it is property acquired by one of the spouses during the marriage, goodwill in a business falls clearly within the scope of s 9(1)(a). However, the court can deviate from equal sharing or, indeed, any sharing at all of such an asset, where circumstances warrant deviation. One of the circumstances – the use made of the property and the readiness with which it can be realised – might be argued to warrant special treatment of goodwill. In addition, other circumstances, not mentioned specifically in the 1985 Act, may warrant deviation. Taking the US cases as examples, it might be argued that deviation was warranted by the personal nature of goodwill or on the basis of the 'double counting'.

Animal companions

14.72 The law treats animals as property and domestic animals fall to be treated as any other property in the context of divorce. Whether a pet or, more correctly, animal companion, is matrimonial property thus depends on the time and means by which the animal came to join the household. Where one spouse had the animal as a companion prior to marriage, the animal is not matrimonial property at all. That spouse can therefore continue to have the companion after divorce. Where the animal arrives after the marriage, other than by way of gift or succession from a third party, it is matrimonial property. Thus, where either party buys the animal for himself or herself, or as a gift for the other spouse, the ordinary rules apply. Where the animal simply arrives and stays, again, it is matrimonial property. In any of these cases, the value of the animal is subject to fair sharing and, in economic terms, that means equal sharing unless special circumstances justify deviation from this norm. Where the animal has a pedigree, with valuable breeding potential, and that is the issue, a financial accommodation may be made, as with any other property. However, in the context of family pets, the issue may be personal rather than economic. It may be that each spouse wants the animal with him or her. How is the court to resolve the issue with negotiation and mediation having failed? Certainly, the court might be persuaded that 'the nature of the matrimonial property' and 'the extent to which it is reasonable to expect the property to

---

163 *Dugan* v *Dugan* 457 A 2d 1 (NJ, 1985) (law firm); *Golden* v *Golden* 75 Cal Rptr 735 (Cal Ct App, 1969) (private medical practice); *In re Marriage of Nichols* 606 P 2d 1314 (Colo Ct App, 1980) (dental practice). By analogy with the goodwill of a professional practice, a court in New Jersey recognised 'celebrity goodwill' as matrimonial property – *Piscopo* v *Piscopo* 557 A 2d 1040 (NJ Super Ct App Div, 1989).
164 *Powell* v *Powell* 648 P 2d 218 (Kan, 1982) (private medical practice); *Travis* v *Travis* 795 P 2d 96 (Okla, 1990) (law firm).
165 *Holbrook* v *Holbrook* 309 NW 2d 343 (Wis Ct App, 1981) (law firm).
166 *Holbrook* v *Holbrook*, above.

be realised or divided or used as security', is a special circumstance warranting deviation from the presumption that fair sharing means sharing equally, but that does not really get us any further. It may be that the only solution lies along the lines of an incidental order, mirroring residence and contact orders. To date, the courts have not been confronted with this issue.[167]

Principle 2: *Fair account should be taken of any economic advantage derived by either party from contributions by the other, and of any economic disadvantage suffered by either party in the interests of the other party or of the family*[168]

14.73 Such is the hurly-burly of relationships that no rigid application of property law or of a formula could take account of all the relevant circumstances and do justice in all cases. Another approach might be to allow complete judicial discretion and, while this has the benefit of flexibility, the costs are either unpredictability and inconsistency or arbitrary rules of thumb. In the attempt to build flexibility into the system at the same time as retaining a principled approach with identifiable goals, the 1985 Act elaborates four further principles to guide the courts. The second principle recognises the diversity of relationships and the fact that individuals make both economic and non-economic contributions and may sacrifice their own economic position for the good of the other spouse or the family as a whole.

14.74 Perhaps the paradigm case here is where the family is organised on the homemaker-breadwinner model, with one spouse staying at home to look after the children and the domestic needs of the family and the other spouse engaging in employment in the workplace. Variants on this theme are where the homemaker is in part-time employment and the spouse who stays at home to care for older relatives. However, principle 2 is capable of accommodating a wider range of cases. One spouse may have worked throughout the marriage to support the other while the latter gained valuable qualifications. A spouse may have expended considerable effort improving property that was owned jointly or solely by the other spouse. The aim here is to have a principle that is capable of accommodating diversity. However, in order that it does not become a back door to complete judicial discretion, it is subject to further definition and refinement.

What are economic advantages, disadvantages and contributions?

14.75 'Economic advantage' is defined as 'advantage gained whether before or during the marriage and includes gains in capital, in income and in earning capacity' and 'economic disadvantage' has the corresponding meaning.[169] 'Contributions' means 'contributions made whether before or

167 In *Bell* v *Sommers*, unreported, *The Scotsman*, 13 April 1996, p 8, the dispute between two couples over the ownership of a Burmese cat was settled before the court had the opportunity to explore the matter fully. However, issues of custody, care and DNA profiling were discussed.
168 Section 9(1)(b).
169 Section 9(2).

during the marriage; and includes indirect and non-financial contributions and, in particular, any such contribution made by looking after the family home or caring for the family'.[170]

14.76 The first point to note here is that it is not only actions during the marriage which are relevant. Advantages and disadvantages sustained, and contributions made, before the marriage can be taken into account. Given the very clear parameters largely restricting matrimonial property to that acquired in the period between marriage and separation, this seems, at first sight, to be curious. However, the Scottish Law Commission felt that there were situations where what had happened prior to the marriage might be relevant.[171] It gave the example of a wife who gave up a job or a tenancy in anticipation of marriage. Clearly, she may have suffered economic disadvantage. To disregard it simply because of the timing, when it was so clearly referable to the marriage, seemed to the Commission to be unjust. Driven by an English case,[172] recent at the time of the Commission's deliberations, it considered the case of spouses who had cohabited for a considerable period prior to marrying. Whether the Scottish courts would have taken account of a lengthy period of pre-marital cohabitation was unclear.[173] In any event, the Commission felt both that the ante-nuptial period might be relevant and that the law should be clarified in this respect. Given the very large number of couples who cohabit prior to marriage and the fact that, if anything, the practice has increased since the Commission's proposals, this provision can be seen as not only reasonable but, to some extent, prophetic. The Commission itself noted that an anomaly would remain in that no financial provision could be made for cohabitants who separate, never having married, but it felt that this was a matter to be addressed in the future.[174]

14.77 Economic advantages and disadvantages are defined as widely as possible and have enabled the courts to take account of advantage gained, for example: by having housekeeping and childcare provided;[175] by having mortgage payments made in respect of one's home;[176] by receiving gifts

---

170 Section 9(2).
171 Report on Aliment and Financial Provision, para 3.98.
172 *Kokosinski* v *Kokosinski* [1980] 1 All ER 1106, where the parties had cohabited for 24 years before the husband was divorced by his wife in Poland and married his cohabitant. The second marriage lasted for only a short time. During the period of cohabitation, the female cohabitant had made substantial economic and non-economic contributions which benefited her partner. Wood J. took the view that he could and should have regard to what had happened during the cohabitation since to do otherwise would be unjust.
173 In *Fraser* v *Fraser* 1976 SLT (Notes) 69, where the ante-nuptial cohabitation was much shorter, Lord Grieve refused to take it into account on the basis that 'a wife who divorces her husband is not entitled to any financial award for the period when she was her husband's mistress' (at p 70).
174 The Commission later addressed the whole question of what financial provision the law might provide for applying to former heterosexual cohabitants – The Effects of Cohabitation in Private Law (Scot Law Com Discussion Paper No 86, May 1990) and Report on Family Law, paras 16.14–16.23. Its proposals are discussed below – see paras 14.171–14.175.
175 *Jesner* v *Jesner* 1992 SLT 999; *McVinnie* v *McVinnie (No 2)* 1997 SLT (Sh Ct) 12.
176 *Kerrigan* v *Kerrigan* 1988 SCLR 603.

from a spouse;[177] by taking a spouse's property;[178] where one spouse provides money for the other's business;[179] and from spousal earnings.[180] The disadvantage most often recognised is the loss of career opportunities, earnings and pension entitlement when a spouse stayed at home.[181] In this respect, the courts do not confine themselves to past losses but take account of difficulty in resuming a career.[182] As we shall see presently, the courts are often required to balance a whole range of advantages and disadvantages which have occurred within the context of the relationship. In considering contributions, the court is directed to look not only at those of an economic nature but non-economic contributions as well. Thus, recognised contributions have included home-making and child care, assistance in a business context and caring for a spouse in time of illness.[183] In particular, it is directed to take account of caring for the family. Caring for one's spouse and any children are obviously included here, but what of caring for one's own, or one's spouse's, sick or older relative? Indeed, does it matter whose relative is being cared for? Is such a person part of 'the family'[184]? There is a certain irony in the fact that, in a statute called the Family Law (Scotland) Act 1985, the only definition of a 'family' indicates that it 'includes a one-parent family'.[185] However, this is not surprising. As we saw in chapter 1, what we mean by a 'family' produces a host of possible answers, but none that is universally satisfactory. It can be argued that caring for any family member certainly ought to be taken into account as a contribution in the wider context of 'the family'. The Scottish Law Commission has recommended narrowing the definition of 'contributions' in such a way that care of other family members might no longer be so readily included and its recommendation is discussed below.[186]

14.78 While the value of s 9(1)(b) often lies in its recognition of non-economic contributions, it is not confined to them. Let us return to the example, given under principle 1, of the couple where the husband used his inheritance to finance home improvements and investments while the wife spent hers on having fun. As we saw, that might have justified a deviation from equal sharing of the matrimonial property and so there might be no outstanding imbalance. Assuming that the court had not treated the wife's action as dissipation of matrimonial property, justice could still be achieved by the application of principle 2. The husband's contributions to the

---

177 *Davidson* v *Davidson* 1993 GWD 31–2000.
178 *Tahir* v *Tahir (No 2)* 1995 SLT 451.
179 *De Winton* v *De Winton* 1996 GWD 29–1752.
180 *Ranaldi* v *Ranaldi* 1994 SLT (Sh Ct) 25.
181 *Adams* v *Adams (No 1)* 1997 SLT 144; *Kelly* v *Kelly* 1992 GWD 36–2130; *Little* v *Little* 1989 SCLR 613; *Louden* v *Louden* 1994 SLT 381; *McCormick* v *McCormick* 1994 GWD 35–2078; *Miller* v *Miller* 1995 GWD 23–1248.
182 *Toye* v *Toye* (Sh Ct) 1992 SCLR 95.
183 *Skarpaas* v *Skarpaas* 1991 SLT (Sh Ct) 15.
184 Section 9(2).
185 Section 27(1).
186 The Commission has recommended that the definition be amended to provide that a contribution should include 'looking after the family home or caring for *the children of the parties*'; Report on Family Law, para 16.23, rec 82(a), draft Bill, Sched. 1, para 81. See the discussion at paras 14.80 below.

improvement of the matrimonial property will have increased the value of the wife's property. She has, therefore, gained an economic advantage resulting from her husband's economic disadvantage in spending his money. The fact that he too has gained some economic advantage by enhancing his share of the matrimonial property is relevant, of course, but the gain to the wife must also be taken into account. In considering an award here, the court is directed to disregard the conduct of either party unless it has adversely affected the financial resources relevant to the decision.[187]

When does principle 2 apply?

14.79 It should be noted that, while the 1985 Act requires some correlation between the economic advantage sustained by one party and the contributions of the other, it will take account of economic disadvantage suffered by one party where it was sustained in the interests of the other spouse *or of the family*. What is the importance of this distinction? Let us consider first the correlation between economic advantage and disadvantage. Where one party gains economic advantage, but this is unrelated to the other spouse, the court cannot take account of it. Thus, for example, where one spouse's property increased in value after the relevant date, due to a rise in property prices or inflation, the other spouse has no right to share in the increase since he or she had no part in it.[188] Similarly, where one spouse suffers some disadvantage, like ill-health, but it produces no advantage for the other spouse, it will not come within the first part of s 9(1)(b) and is not relevant.[189] Certainly, looking after the couple's children and running the home, will normally provide corresponding disadvantages and advantages. Indeed, it can be argued that anything done that enhances a spouse's general well-being puts that person in a better position to earn a livelihood and, thus, confers economic advantage.[190]

14.80 Turning to disadvantages suffered as a result of contributions made in the interests of the children or the family, any disadvantage suffered in this context is relevant whether or not it benefited the other spouse. One's own illness would again be excluded from the equation since, while serious illness might well produce economic disadvantage, it was not sustained in the interests of the family. Whether there ought to be scope to consider it under principle 5 – dealing with serious financial hardship – will be discussed presently. None the less, caring for children would normally be

---

187 Section 11(7).
188 *Carroll* v *Carroll* 1988 SCLR 104; *Phillip* v *Phillip* 1988 SCLR 427; *Muir* v *Muir* 1989 SCLR 445; *Tyrrell* v *Tyrrell* 1990 SLT 406.
189 *Barclay* v *Barclay* (Sh Ct) 1991 SCLR (Notes) 205; *Haughan* v *Haughan* 1996 SLT 321.
190 In *Ranaldi* v *Ranaldi*, n 180 above, the court appears to have applied a very restrictive view of contributions. There, the wife used her resources to pay the children's school fees and to enhance the family's overall standard of living. Clearly, she had made a contribution and had suffered economic disadvantage by so doing. The court did not accept that the husband had gained economic advantage because he could have paid the school fees himself and the other enhancements to the standard of living were regarded as luxuries. It is submitted that this view is unduly restrictive. The wife's contributions were made in the interests of the family and, as such, it should not have been essential that the husband gained advantage from them.

covered under the second part of s 9(1)(b) as well as the first. In addition, caring for a sick or older relative is relevant. If the other spouse had to gain some benefit, caring for the other spouse's relatives might, arguably, count as a benefit to that person. Caring for one's own relatives would not. However, this does not matter, since the other spouse need not gain anything, provided that the disadvantage has been incurred *in the interests of the family*. Assuming that 'family' is given a sufficiently broad definition, such care would qualify. The Scottish Law Commission has recommended that the definition of 'contributions' should be amended to provide that a contribution should include 'looking after the family home or caring for *the children of the parties*.[191] It would seem that, were this proposal to be accepted, caring for one's own older relatives would no longer be a contribution. The suggested amendment would also appear to exclude caring for step-children unless the carer could demonstrate that an advantage was sustained by the other spouse (who would be the parent of the step-children). This narrowing of the concept of the family, arguably in the face of social reality, cannot be described as one of the Commission's better recommendations.

14.81 When the court is considering s 9(1)(b), it is directed to have regard to the extent to which

'(a) the economic advantages or disadvantages sustained by either party have been balanced by the economic advantages or disadvantages sustained by the other party, and
(b) any resulting imbalance has been or will be corrected by a sharing of the value of the matrimonial property or otherwise'.[192]

Essentially, the court is being directed to look at the whole picture here. It may be that one party has foregone lucrative employment and the opportunity to build up pension entitlement by staying at home to raise a family, but that spouse may have enjoyed an affluent lifestyle, free access to considerable funds and foreign travel. In short, while the spouse was giving a lot, he or she was also getting a lot. Thus, in *Welsh* v *Welsh*,[193] for example, the economic advantage gained by the husband in terms of housekeeping and child care, and the wife's corresponding disadvantage through career loss, were offset by the advantage the wife gained by the husband paying the mortgage and the bills. There are cases, however, where the lifestyle enjoyed by a spouse will not be sufficient to offset economic disadvantages and, in such a case, the financial award will be adjusted accordingly.[194]

14.82 Having done a basic accounting, insofar as that is possible, the court

191 Report on Family Law, para 16.23, rec 82(a), draft Bill, Sched. 1, para 81. The effect would be that, while care of sick or older relatives might still be relevant, anyone founding on it would be required to demonstrate that the other spouse had sustained economic advantage or some other benefit, as a result.
192 Section 11(2).
193 1994 SLT 828. In that case, further adjustment was required to take account of the fact that the husband occupied the house after separation. See also, *Budge* v *Budge* (OH) 1990 SCLR (Notes) 144 and *Petrie* v *Petrie* 1988 SCLR 390.
194 *Louden* v *Louden* 1994 SLT 381 where the wife was awarded more than half of the matrimonial property.

is directed to consider the extent to which any imbalance can be dealt with by the sharing of matrimonial property. This gives the court a clear indication that the first stop, in considering financial provision on divorce, is principle 1. If the balancing of advantages, disadvantages and contributions can be achieved through the division of matrimonial property, either equally or unequally, then it should be. Only if that will not achieve a satisfactory result, should principle 2 be applied to make further adjustments. The result is that in many cases, while one spouse may have suffered economic advantage as a result of the other spouse's disadvantage or contributions, the whole imbalance can be put right through the division of property, either in equal shares or some other proportions.[195] However, it may be that there is insufficient matrimonial property to achieve a satisfactory correction to the imbalance. In such cases, principle 2 enables the court to make an award out of non-matrimonial property.[196] Where there is no significant matrimonial capital, the court can still make a capital award, payable by instalments out of income.[197]

Orders under principle 2

14.83 In making an award under this principle, the court may only order the payment of a capital sum, whether payable as a lump sum or by instalments, or order the transfer of property.[198] It cannot order the payment of a periodical allowance.[199] The thrust behind s 9(1)(b) is the balancing of past advantages, disadvantages and contributions. Once the adjustment has been made, the notion of a clean break applies and there is no justification for a continuing payment. An early problem with the 1985 Act was the court's reliance on the old familiar remedy of periodical allowance. Given that it had been the cornerstone of financial provision on divorce prior to the 1985 Act, this is, perhaps, unsurprising. However, since a periodical allowance cannot be awarded under principle 2, the result was that the principle itself was underutilised, with the court preferring to rely on principle 5 which, as we shall see, seeks to alleviate financial hardship.

Principle 3:   *Any economic burden of caring, after divorce, for a child of the marriage under the age of 16 years should be shared fairly between the parties*[200]

14.84 Principles 1 and 2 are concerned with the past, albeit, they seek to make arrangements for the future and, in the case of principle 2, take account of the impact of past events on the future. Principle 3 is concerned, quite squarely, with the future. It recognises that the children of the marriage will need to be cared for in the future and that caring for children has economic consequences. The relationship between the responsibility to support one's children and the fact that caring for children will have economic consequences is a subtle one. On the one hand, the parental

---

195 *Louden* v *Louden*, above.
196 *De Winton* v *De Winton* 1996 GWD 29–1752; *Ranaldi* v *Ranaldi*, n 180 above.
197 Section 12(3).
198 Sections 8(1) and 12(3).
199 Section 13(2).
200 Section 9(1)(c).

responsibility to support a child is clear and distinct and quite unrelated to marriage or divorce. However, as we saw in chapter 6, in awarding aliment in respect of a child or assessing child support, the court or the Child Support Agency may include provision for the person looking after the child.[201] Given that the carer will usually be a parent, the impact of child care on the parent is, thus, already recognised. Where the parents have been married, what principle 3 seeks to do is to share the future economic impact of child care between the parties to the marriage. The result is that, while support of children and support of former partners are distinct, they are not wholly separable in law. In this, the law is simply reflecting practical reality.

Child of the marriage

14.85 For the purpose of principle 3, a 'child of the marriage' includes not only children of both spouses but any child who has been 'accepted by the parties as a child of the family'.[202] As we have seen, the whole notion of accepting a child into one's family is not without problems.[203] However, the 1985 Act envisages that a child of either spouse or a child who has come to live with them[204] may trigger the application of s 9(1)(c), if the necessary acceptance can be demonstrated. Given the incidence of divorce and remarriage, recognition of the fact that step-children often form part of the picture in the context of divorce is essential.

14.86 The 1985 Act is concerned only with the economic burden created by children under the age of 16. While children over that age often continue to live with a parent, the need for the parent to be present (or to make alternative child care arrangements) is ended and, thus, the impact on the parent's ability to earn a living is reduced. None the less, the parent must still provide a home large enough to accommodate any such child and the additional cost of this should not be ignored. Take, for example, the increasingly common case of a child who decides to go to a local university in order to keep costs to a minimum. She has lived with her mother since her parents divorced and will continue to do so. Of course, her mother is not obliged to house her, but they agree that it is the best arrangement. The solution here is for the daughter to claim aliment from her father and include therein an element to cover the cost of accommodation. She can then pay her mother something towards her accommodation.

Assessing the economic burden

14.87 The thinking behind principle 3 predates the Child Support Act 1991 but, none the less, the fact that provision for the child is not wholly separable from provision for the former spouse who will be caring for the

---

201 Family Law (Scotland) Act 1985, s 4(4); Child Support Act 1991, Sched 5, para 5.
202 Section 27(1).
203 See chapter 6, para 64, above, for a discussion of 'acceptance' in the context of aliment.
204 Any child boarded out with either or both of the parties by a local or public authority or a voluntary organisation is excluded – s 27(1).

child is reflected in the factors to which the court must have regard in considering an award under s 9(1)(c). They are[205]

> any decree or arrangement for aliment for the child;[206]
> any expenditure or loss of earning capacity caused by the need to care for the child;
> the need to provide suitable accommodation for the child;
> the age and health of the child;
> the educational, financial and other circumstances of the child;
> the availability and cost of suitable child-care facilities or services;
> the needs and resources of the parties; and
> all the other circumstances of the case.

In addition, the court may take account of the fact that the person who will have to make financial provision (the payer) is, in fact, supporting another person in the payer's household, whether or not there is any legal obligation to support that person.[207] In considering an award here, the court is directed to disregard the conduct of either party, unless it has adversely affected the financial resources relevant to the decision.[208]

14.88 The Child Support Act 1991 now provides that the needs of the child's carer may form part of the assessment of child support or an award of aliment.[209] As a result, there may be less need to make provision under principle 3. Consequently, the use made of s 9(1)(c) has decreased. None the less, it is still a valuable provision.[210] Future income may be part of supporting a child but keeping a roof over the heads of both the child and the carer may result in a greater capital award to the carer.[211]

Orders under principle 3

14.89 In making an award under this principle, the court has the full panoply of orders at its disposal. Not only may it order the payment of a capital sum,[212] whether payable as a lump sum or by instalments, or order the transfer of property, it can order the payment of a periodical allowance.[213] It is worth noting that, while it is the economic burden of caring for a child under the age of 16 that triggers this principle, any periodical allowance payable as a result need not terminate when the child reaches

---

205 Section 11(3).
206 Such an arrangement would include that made under the Child Support Act 1991.
207 Section 11(6).
208 Section 11(7).
209 In *Millar* v *Millar* (Sh Ct) 1990 SCLR 666, the award of aliment in respect of the child was held to be sufficient to achieve fair sharing of the economic burden of childcare. See also, *Adams* v *Adams (No 1)* 1997 SLT 144.
210 *Maclachan* v *Maclachan* 1998 SLT 693.
211 *Morrison* v *Morrison* 1989 SCLR 574.
212 *Macdonald* v *Macdonald* (OH) 1993 SCLR (Notes) 132; *Morrison* v *Morrison*, above; *Shipton* v *Shipton* (Sh Ct) 1992 SCLR 23.
213 *McCormick* v *McCormick* 1994 GWD 35–2078 (periodical allowance awarded for five years); *Monkman* v *Monkman* 1988 SLT (Sh Ct) 37; *Toye* v *Toye* (Sh Ct) 1992 SCLR 95 (periodical allowance awarded for three years).

16.[214] Where a person suffers loss of earning capacity as a result of caring for a child, he or she is unlikely to experience an instant economic recovery on the child's 16th birthday.

> **Principle 4:** *A party who has been dependent to a substantial degree on the financial support of the other party should be awarded such financial provision as is reasonable to enable him to adjust, over a period of not more than three years from the date of the decree of divorce, to the loss of that support on divorce*[215]

14.90 The thinking behind much of the 1985 Act was centred on the notion of a clean-break divorce. However, as we saw in discussing the possible goals of financial provision on divorce, to expect a spouse who has been dependent on his or her partner to become self-supporting immediately may be unrealistic and unreasonable. Here, we are not thinking of the two-career couple where each of them has always been self-sufficient. Nor are we dealing with the cases where, due to the fact that marital breakdown is a process rather than a one-off event, the parties have established independent lives and become self-supporting by the time of the divorce itself.[216] In addition, it is only where the division of property under the first three principles would not provide sufficiently for adjustment that s 9(1)(d) comes into play. Typically, principle 4 addresses itself to the spouse (often the wife) who has sacrificed employment opportunities to stay at home and care for the children. If she is to become self-supporting, she may need a 'buffer' to help her through the period of adjusting to independence. However, s 9(1)(d) is sufficiently flexible to accommodate other cases of past dependence. So, for example, provision may be made under it to allow a spouse to adjust where there are no children or where a spouse would suffer a dramatic diminution in his or her standard of living, were past dependence not taken into account.[217] Indeed, provision may be made under this principle where there is no prospect of the spouse achieving financial independence at all.[218]

---

214 *Monkman* v *Monkman*, above. There, the defender's capacity to pay a periodical allowance was such that the pursuer would not have been compensated for the economic loss resulting from child care if payment stopped when the child reached 16 and, accordingly, if a periodical allowance was awarded that would be payable for several years thereafter.

215 Section 9(1)(d).

216 In *Gray* v *Gray* (Sh Ct) 1991 SCLR (Notes) 422, the court took the view that, despite her past dependence, the wife had not sought financial support from her husband since the separation and had adjusted, therefore, no award was made under s 9(1)(d).

217 *Atkinson* v *Atkinson* 1988 SCLR 396. In *Wilson* v *Wilson* 1998 SCLR 1103 a wife was awarded £200 per month for 30 months (in addition to a capital award of £408,609). She intended to attend college and the award under s 9(1)(d) was based on Lord Marnoch's view at 1109 that there was 'no guarantee that the pursuer will be eligible for a grant during the period of re-training and, even if she were so eligible, there is no possibility that it would maintain her in the standard of life to which she has become accustomed while married to the defender'.

218 In *Barclay* v *Barclay* (Sh Ct) 1991 SCLR (Notes) 205, for example, the wife was suffering from multiple sclerosis and was resident in a nursing home. It was not envisaged that she would ever resume life in the community.

Relevant factors

14.91 The underlying rationale of a 'period of adjustment' is that it is intended to be transitional and, as such, short-term. In assessing what, if any, order to make for financial provision under this principle, the court is directed to have regard to[219]

the age, health and earning capacity of the party who is claiming the financial provision;
the duration and extent of the dependence of that party prior to divorce;
any intention of that party to undertake a course of education or training;[220]
the needs and resources of the parties;[221] and
all the other circumstances of the case.

In addition, the court may take account of the fact that the person who will have to make financial provision (the payer) is, in fact, supporting another person in the payer's household, whether or not there is any legal obligation to support that person.[222]

Conduct

14.92 In the context of principle 4, how the court is to treat the conduct of either of the parties changes from the system adopted up to this point. The general rule remains that the court should take no account of conduct.[223] As was the position under principles 1, 2 and 3, the court may take conduct into account if it has adversely affected the financial resources relevant to the decision.[224] In addition, however, the court is given greater latitude to consider conduct where it would be 'manifestly inequitable to leave the conduct out of account'.[225] The uncharacteristically strong language used in the 1985 Act suggests that, for conduct to qualify for consideration here, it would have to be fairly extreme. Clive expresses the view that '[a] spouse who had been wholly responsible for the breakdown of the marriage could not normally claim successfully under section 9(1)(d)'.[226] This is probably correct, but the statement should not be misunderstood. It does not mean that, where a divorce is granted on one of the fault grounds, the defender will be precluded automatically from receiving an award under s 9(1)(d). Indeed, awards have been made to defenders in these circumstances. Being the defender in a divorce action does not necessarily make a person 'wholly responsible' for the breakdown of the marriage. As we have seen,

---

219 Section 11(4).
220 An award under s 9(1)(d) is particularly suited to accommodating a period of retraining or education which will enable the recipient to earn a living: *Buckle* v *Buckle* (Sh Ct) 1995 SCLR (Notes) 590 (periodical allowance awarded for one year to a wife who planned to take a one-year course in office technology); *Louden* v *Louden* 1994 SLT 381 (similar provision to allow for retraining); *Wilson* v *Wilson* 1993 GWD 38–2521 (similar provision to enable the wife to take a teacher training course); *Wilson* v *Wilson* 1998 SCLR 1103 (award of £200 per week while wife took additional training as a hotel receptionist).
221 As before, 'needs' are defined as 'present and foreseeable needs' and 'resources' as 'present and foreseeable resources' – s 27(1).
222 Section 11(6).
223 Section 11(7).
224 Section 11(7)(a).
225 Section 11(7)(b).
226 At para 24.075.

marriages break down for a host of reasons and breakdown is usually attributable to a number of causes. Even where each spouse may have grounds on which an action could be raised, the benefit of cross-actions is highly questionable. This highlights the problem of allowing conduct to be taken into account at all. It can be argued that, since irretrievable breakdown is the sole ground for divorce, at least in theory, the notion of fault has no place in any aspect of the divorce. Raising issues of conduct which had an impact on resources may be sufficiently narrow as to keep any allegations within a limited ambit. However, once other conduct becomes relevant, we are getting very close to reopening the whole can of worms associated with fault. On the other hand, if the law is to make an attempt to reflect the public perception of 'fairness', there is no doubt that particularly heinous conduct ought to be considered. Bearing in mind that s 9(1)(d) is there to provide for financial provision where the first three principles have not done so adequately, the possibility of considering conduct is not as dangerous as it might have been.

Orders under principle 4

14.93 Section 9(1)(d) envisages a period of up to three years from the date of the divorce decree as the time-frame. Three points should be stressed here. Firstly, an award under this principle is not confined to an order for periodical allowance and the court may make an award of capital or order the transfer of property.[227] In practice, however, periodical allowance is usually used in the context of principle 4 and the award may be in addition to other division of property.[228] Secondly, a periodical allowance is only appropriate where an award of capital or the transfer of property would be inappropriate or insufficient to satisfy the requirements of the case.[229] Thirdly, where a periodical allowance is awarded it may be for up to three years, but it may be for a much shorter period of time.[230]

Principle 5: *A party who at the time of the divorce seems likely to suffer serious financial hardship as a result of the divorce should be awarded such financial provision as is reasonable to relieve him of hardship over a reasonable period*[231]

14.94 Principle 4 envisaged a short-term period of adjustment to independence. Principle 5 addresses the injustice which could result from the divorce, but over the longer term. The paradigm case here would be of a fairly long marriage which has operated on the homemaker-breadwinner

---

227 Section 8(1).
228 See for example, *Tyrrell* v *Tyrrell* 1990 SLT 406, where the wife who had received considerable capital on separation, financial support for the seven years between the separation and the proof and further capital in the divorce, was awarded periodical allowance under s 9(1)(d). Her claim for an award under s 9(1)(e) was not successful.
229 Section 13(2).
230 *Dever* v *Dever* 1988 SCLR 352 (periodical allowance awarded for six months from the date of decree); *Louden* v *Louden* 1994 SLT 381 (periodical allowance awarded for one year from date of decree); *Petrie* v *Petrie* 1988 SCLR 390 (periodical allowance awarded for one year from the date of decree); *Sheret* v *Sheret* (Sh Ct) 1990 SCLR (Notes) 799 (periodical allowance awarded for 13 weeks from the date of decree).
231 Section 9(1)(e).

model, where one spouse has stayed at home to care for the children and has either not been part of the paid workforce or has had only minimal employment. While this principle, like all the others, applies equally to husbands and wives, it is most often women who claim under it. Thirty years into the marriage, when divorce looms, a wife who has adopted the homemaker role may no longer be caring for the now grown-up children, but her prospects of becoming economically self-supporting at the level she currently enjoys, is not a likely one. As we saw when we considered lifelong financial support, it was not popular with either the payers or, to a lesser extent, the recipients. In addition, it is inconsistent with any notion of clean-break divorce. However, for many women who married 30 years ago, the homemaker-breadwinner model was the norm and was consistent with social expectations at the time. They traded financial independence for the expectation of lifelong support. If law reform were not to take account of the context in which the arrangement was made, then it could be accused of moving the goalposts so far as such women are concerned. Nor is the problem simply a transitional one, where all we need to do is wait for these cases to filter through the system. Some couples marrying today still plan to organise their lives around the idea of one homemaker and one bread-winner, albeit there is greater acceptance that either spouse may adopt either role. Thus, it is essential that the legal system should provide for such cases and that is precisely what the fifth of the principles is designed to do.

A last resort

14.95 It is important to note that s 9(1)(e) is intended as a last resort.[232] Any financial hardship which might result from the divorce should be dealt with under the other principles, where that is possible. Thus, it may be that adequate financial provision can be made through the sharing of the matrimonial property, allowing for adjustment to take account of economic advantages and disadvantages sustained.[233] If there are children under 16 involved, taking account of the economic burden of childcare can be factored in. Where the application of the first three principles will not overcome the problem of financial hardship, it may be that providing for a period of adjustment will.[234]

14.96 This raises the question whether it is appropriate to make an award under both s 9(1)(d) and s 9(1)(e). The simplest answer is that, since the 1985 Act does not express any prohibition on such dual awards, they are

---

232 In recommending this principle, the Scottish Law Commission described it as 'a long-stop'. It noted that 'grave financial hardship' is a defence to divorce on the ground of five years non-cohabitation and suggested that if it was built into financial provision on divorce, there might be less need to resort to the defence. See, Report on Aliment and Financial Provision, para 3.110. It is a reflection of the coherence of the Commission's recommendations over the years that it has now recommended the abolition of grave financial hardship as a defence to divorce – Report on Family Law, paras 13.9–13.12, rec 69 and draft Bill, clause 30(3), discussed in chapter 13, at para 70, above.

233 *Buckle* v *Buckle* (Sh Ct) 1995 SCLR (Notes) 590; *Savage* v *Savage* 1993 GWD 28–1779.

234 *Muir* v *Muir* 1989 SLT (Sh Ct) 20 (award under s 9(1)(d) for one year regarded as sufficient and claim under s 9(1)(e) refused); *Tyrrell* v *Tyrrell*, n 228 above.

competent. Certainly, on occasions the courts have made awards under both principles 4 and 5.[235] Assuming that the other arrangements for financial provision leave a spouse facing serious financial hardship, it may be that the court sees justification for an award under principle 5. That may offset the serious hardship but, none the less, the claimant may be facing a dramatic reduction in his or her standard of living. In order to allow for transition from dependence, the court may ease the way by providing a buffer under principle 4. This simply recognises that a transitional award may be appropriate despite the fact that the recipient will not be in the same financial position as he or she enjoyed during the marriage, even after a period of transition.

Relevant factors

14.97 In assessing what, if any, order to make for financial provision under this principle, the court is directed to have regard to[236]

the age, health and earning capacity of the party who is claiming the financial provision;[237]
the duration of the marriage;[238]
the standard of living of the parties during the marriage;[239]
any intention of the claimant to undertake a course of education or training;
the needs and resources of the parties; and
all the other circumstances of the case.

It should be noted that, while there is some overlap with the circumstances which are relevant in considering an award under s 9(1)(d), the lists are not identical. In addition, the court may take account of the fact that the person who will have to make financial provision (the payer) is, in fact, supporting another person in the payer's household, whether or not there is any legal obligation to support that person.[240]

14.98 The extent to which the court can take account of a spouse's conduct, under principle 5, is the same as that under principle 4. Just to recap, this means that, as a general rule, the court should take no account

---

235 See for example, *Stott* v *Stott* 1987 GWD 17–645, where the court awarded a periodical allowance of £75 per week for three years under s 9(1)(d) and a periodical allowance of £55 per week under s 9(1)(e) for a further four years.
236 Section 11(5).
237 *Barclay* v *Barclay*, n 218 above; *Haughan* v *Haughan* (OH) 1996 SCLR (Notes) 170.
238 In some cases, the combination of the claimant's age, the duration of the marriage and, sometimes, other factors, have resulted in orders for payment of a periodical allowance until the claimant's death or remarriage: *Bell* v *Bell* 1988 SCLR 457 (42 year-old wife, 24 year marriage); *Gribb* v *Gribb* 1994 SLT (Sh Ct) 43, aff'd 1996 SLT 719 (62 year-old wife, 38 year marriage); *Haughan* v *Haughan*, above (51 year-old wife with health problems, 26 year marriage); *Johnstone* v *Johnstone* 1990 SLT (Sh Ct) 79 (35 year-old wife suffering from epilepsy, 13 year marriage).
239 The fact that someone suffers a drop in his or her standard of living will not necessarily mean that he or she will suffer serious financial hardship – *Atkinson* v *Atkinson* 1988 SCLR 396. On the other hand, the court may take a dramatic drop in standard of living into account when assessing the seriousness of any hardship. See for example, *Davidson* v *Davidson* 1993 GWD 31–2000, where the husband was awarded a capital sum in recognition of the 'considerable financial discomfort' he would suffer through the loss of a wealthy wife.
240 Section 11(6).

of conduct.[241] However, it may take conduct into account either if it has adversely affected the financial resources relevant to the decision[242] or where it would be 'manifestly inequitable to leave the conduct out of account'.[243] The same observations on conduct as were made in the context of principle 4 apply here.[244]

When does principle 5 apply?

14.99   Before s 9(1)(e) can apply, the claimant must be facing the prospect of serious financial hardship in the future. Thus, for example, where a person will have a reasonable income and capital, principle 5 has no application.[245] In addition, the financial hardship must be 'serious'. It is always tempting to explain such a qualification in terms of a synonym, like 'significant', but that does not get us any further. Certainly, the court is directed to consider the standard of living of the parties during the marriage, so subsistence-level poverty is not a prerequisite for an award. In looking at the prospect of financial hardship, the court takes into account not only private resources, but any entitlement to state benefits.[246] As we saw when we looked at the possible goals of financial provision on divorce, the Commission squarely rejected any notion that it was designed to avoid claims on the public purse.

14.100   The Act makes clear that the serious financial hardship must be *as a result of the divorce* and not, for example, due to some other misfortune.[247] One line of argument should be explored, if only to dismiss it. Marriage brings with it a right to be supported financially, within certain circumstances, since spouses owe an obligation of aliment to each other.[248] If the marriage is ended, that obligation falls. Thus, it might be argued, any loss of aliment results from divorce and should be covered by s 9(1)(e). However, that is not the purpose of the 5th principle. It is part of the whole mechanism for ensuring fair financial provision *on divorce*. Financial provision on divorce is premised on the marriage, and all its attendant

241   Section 11(7).
242   Section 11(7)(a).
243   Section 11(7)(b).
244   See para 14.92, above.
245   *Murray* v *Murray* 1993 GWD 16–1058; *Tyrrell* v *Tyrrell*, n 228 above.
246   *Barclay* v *Barclay*, (Sh Ct) 1991 SCLR (Notes) 205.
247   In *Barclay* v *Barclay*, above, where the wife was suffering from multiple sclerosis and was resident in a nursing home, any financial hardship was due to her condition rather than the divorce. This was not the result the Commission anticipated. Discussing its view that financial hardship should be assessed at the time of divorce, it acknowledged that the imposition of a strict dividing line might produce harsh results and gave the following example: '[T]he spouse whose progressive disease was diagnosed before the divorce would have a claim but the spouse whose disease was first diagnosed after the divorce would not' – Report on Aliment and Financial Provision, para 3.110. *Barclay* can be contrasted with the decision in *Haughan* v *Haughan*, n 237 above, where the wife, who had various physical health problems and suffered from depression had been living on benefits since the separation. There was no matrimonial property or capital, but the husband had significant earnings. The court made an award under s 9(1)(e) for payment of a periodical allowance until her death or remarriage.
248   Sections 1(1) and 4, discussed in chapter 11, at para 49.

obligations, being at an end. Thus, it is not designed to provide for what a person would have been entitled to, were he or she still married.

14.101 It follows from the fact that financial hardship must be as a result of the divorce that it must be assessed at the time of the divorce itself. The Commission was anxious to ensure that it did not become 'a gateway to support after divorce in all cases just as if the marriage had not been dissolved. ... It should therefore be made clear in the legislation that it is only where the likelihood of grave financial hardship is established *at the time of the divorce* that a claim will arise under this principle'.[249] Thus, once the divorce occurs, no amount of financial hardship will found a claim under principle 5.

Orders under principle 5

14.102 Awards under s 9(1)(e) may result in an order for the payment of a capital sum or the transfer of property, but the most common approach taken by the courts is to make an order for the payment of a periodical allowance. Sometimes the order will be for payment of a periodical allowance until the death or remarriage of the recipient, but principle 5 should not be understood as the ticket to lifelong financial support. In many cases an award for a shorter period of time has been made. It was a fundamental part of the Scottish Law Commission's thinking that the system it proposed should provide for financial provision on divorce that did not rely on the old notion of financial support for life. Recognising that, in some cases, injustice would result from strict adherence to that principle, it created principle 5. The question is whether the courts have overused s 9(1)(e).

Orders the court may make

14.103 As we have seen, one of the shortcomings of the law under the previous legislation was that the court could only make orders within a fairly limited range and thus, was not able to meet all eventualities. Under the 1985 Act, either party may now apply for one or more of the following, much wider, range of orders.

An order for the payment of a capital sum to him or her by the other party to the marriage[250]

14.104 An order for payment of a capital sum can be made on the granting of the divorce or within a period of time specified when the divorce is granted.[251] Normally, financial provision and divorce are dealt with together but, exceptionally, there may be some urgency for the divorce despite the fact that financial provision will take longer to resolve.

---

249 Report on Aliment and Financial Provision, para 3.110, emphasis added. The Commission cited the example of a husband who was made redundant at the age of 52 being precluded from claiming against a wife whom he had divorced 30 years before.
250 Section 8(1)(a).
251 Section 12(1).

Clive[252] cites the example of one spouse being anxious to remarry because a child is on the way and wisely points out the dangers inherent in such an approach. Once divorced, the former spouse has no legal rights in his or her former partner's estate. Thus, if the former partner dies, the surviving ex-spouse may have no claim. In any event, the desire to rush a divorce in order that a child can be born in wedlock must be fairly minimal, since parental marital status is of almost no legal significance for children[253] and, provided that they do marry eventually, of no legal significance at all for parents.[254] In addition, where one spouse learns that the other is anxious to obtain a divorce for such a pressing personal reason, the former may use this knowledge in order to secure a more advantageous agreement on financial provision.

14.105 A degree of flexibility can be built into an order to pay a capital sum by the use of two different mechanisms. First, the order can be made effective from a specified future date;[255] that is, it can be made but its operation delayed. Where, for example, certain assets will have to be realised in order that the capital sum can be paid, but these assets would fetch a great deal more if the sale was delayed by a year, the court might make payment effective from an appropriate later date. Similarly, payment might be postponed until after the vesting of a pension entitlement[256] or after a house has been sold.[257] This provision may be of particular value where one spouse wishes to continue to live in the family home until the children grow up, but is not in a position to compensate the other spouse for his or her share. In such circumstances, the payment of a capital sum could be deferred until the youngest child reaches 18, whereupon the house may be sold.

14.106 The second mechanism allowing for flexibility in relation to the payment of a capital sum is that the court may order payment by instalments. This power is of particular value where either the available capital is tied up in an income-generating asset, like a business, or where a spouse has little or no capital but does have a high income.[258] Payment of a capital sum by instalments is quite distinct from payment of a periodical allowance, since the former relates to a finite sum, whereas the latter is subject to variation. In the mind of the payer, this may be important. As we shall see, there have been cases where the court has awarded a periodical allowance, where it could have awarded a capital sum payable by instalments. In such circumstances, the latter course of action would have been

---

252 At para 24.092.
253 Law Reform (Parent and Child) (Scotland) Act 1986, s 1(1).
254 While the unmarried father has no automatic parental responsibilities or rights, if he marries the child's mother at a later stage, he acquires the full range of parental responsibilities and rights – Children (Scotland) Act 1995, s 3(1)(b).
255 Section 12(2).
256 *Gracie* v *Gracie* 1997 SLT (Sh Ct) 15.
257 *Symon* v *Symon* (Sh Ct) 1991 SCLR (Notes) 414.
258 *Buckle* v *Buckle* (Sh Ct) 1995 SCLR (Notes) 590; *Dorrian* v *Dorrian* (Sh Ct) 1991 SCLR (Notes) 661; *Gracie* v *Gracie*, above; *McEwan* v *McEwan* 1997 SLT 118.

more consistent with the principles and mechanisms set out in the 1985 Act.[259]

14.107 The general rule is that a capital award cannot be varied at a later date. However, this is subject to one exception. Where there is a material change of circumstances, either party can apply to the court to have the date or method of payment varied.[260] Where, for example, payment of a capital sum had been ordered by way of instalments because the payer's only substantial asset was a business and the payee discovers that the payer is about to sell the business, it might be reasonable for the payee to apply to the court for all of the sum to become payable on completion of the sale.

An order for the transfer of property to him or her by the other party to the marriage[261]

14.108 An order for the transfer of property is conceptually very similar to an order for the payment of a capital sum and most of the same rules apply where they are capable of so doing. Thus, an order for the transfer of property can be made on the granting of the divorce or within a period of time specified when the divorce is granted[262] and can be made effective from a future date.[263] In addition, either party can apply to the court to have the date of the transfer of property varied on demonstrating a material change of circumstances.[264]

14.109 One special provision applicable to the transfer of some property is the need to protect the interests of any third party who has an interest in the property. Where a third party's consent is required before property can be transferred, the court cannot order transfer until the requisite consent has been obtained.[265] This provision will normally apply where the property is subject to a standard security since the security holder will usually have reserved the right to consent to transfer of the property.[266] Where the property is subject to a security which does not reserve the right to consent to any transfer, the court may not order transfer until the creditor has been given the opportunity to be heard.[267]

14.110 A property transfer order is of particular value when one spouse wishes to remain in the family home with the children after the divorce. However, the displaced spouse will also require a home and, where resources permit, the solution may lie in transfer of the home to one spouse

---

259 Section 13(2)(b) provides that a court should not make an order for the payment of a periodical allowance unless an order for the payment of a capital sum or for the transfer of property 'would be inappropriate or insufficient to satisfy' the fundamental principles of the Act.
260 Section 12(4).
261 Section 8(1)(aa).
262 Section 12(1).
263 Section 12(2).
264 Section 12(4).
265 Section 15(1).
266 *MacNaught* v *MacNaught* (Sh Ct) 1997 SCLR 151.
267 Section 15(2).

and a capital award to the other.[268] As a result of the decision of the House of Lords in *Wallis* v *Wallis*,[269] a problem, known as the 'Wallis trap', has emerged. The difficulty created by this decision relates to the time at which property is valued and the extent to which increases in value can be taken into account. The complexities of the problem are discussed below but, for the present, it should be noted that there are cases where it is more equitable for the court not to order the transfer of property in exchange for payment of a capital sum but, rather, to leave the parties to reach an equitable settlement by themselves. If they cannot do this, the court can order the sale of the home and the division of the proceeds.[270]

An order for the making of a periodical allowance to him or her by the other party[271]

14.111 As we saw when we looked at the possible goals of financial provision on divorce, the continuing responsibility, on the part of the payer, and the continued dependence, on the part of the payee, may make a periodical allowance unpopular with both. It was a fundamental tenet of the Scottish Law Commission's proposals for reform of the law on financial provision that the parties should experience a clean break, in economic terms, on divorce, where that was possible. However, it was always acknowledged that a periodical allowance might be the only way to achieve justice in particular cases. The 1985 Act carried that thinking into effect and the court is directed only to make an order for the payment of a periodical allowance where orders for the payment of a capital sum or the transfer of property would be inappropriate or insufficient in the circumstances.[272] In addition, a periodical allowance may only be provided for where it is justified by any one or more of three of the five principles set out in the 1985 Act. The principles are discussed in detail below but, briefly, a periodical allowance cannot be awarded unless it is justified as a means of: sharing the economic burden of future child-care responsibilities; providing a spouse who has been substantially dependent on the other with the opportunity to adjust to the loss of support on divorce; or, avoiding serious financial hardship which would otherwise result from the divorce. Thus, the thrust of the 1985 Act is that a periodical allowance should be the exception rather than the norm.

14.112 Like orders for the payment of a capital sum or the transfer of property, an order for the payment of a periodical allowance by one party to the marriage to the other can be made on the granting of the divorce[273]

---

268 At one stage, doubt was expressed as to whether it was competent to order the transfer of property and payment of a capital sum in the same action: *Little* v *Little* 1990 SLT 230; *Walker* v *Walker* 1990 SLT 229, 1991 SLT 157. The Law Reform (Miscellaneous Provisions) (Scotland) Act 1990, Sched 8, para 34 amended s 8(1) of the 1985 Act to make it clear that both orders were competent in the same action.
269 1993 SLT 1348.
270 Section 14(2)(a).
271 Section 8(1)(b).
272 Section 13(2)(b).
273 Section 13(1)(a).

or within a period of time specified when the divorce is granted.[274] However, an order for periodical allowance can also be made after the decree is granted, where no such order has been made previously and there has been a change of circumstances.[275] An order for payment of a periodical allowance can be made for a definite or indefinite period or until the happening of a specified event.[276] In some cases, a periodical allowance may be awarded until the death or remarriage of the payee,[277] but the courts are increasingly using this power to award a periodical allowance for a much shorter period of time.[278]

14.113 On showing a material change of circumstances, an order for payment of a periodical allowance may be varied or recalled[279] by the court or an order for the payment of a capital sum or the transfer of property can be substituted for it.[280] Variation or recall can be backdated and the court may order money already paid to be repaid.[281] Where the payer dies, the obligation to pay a periodical allowance continues against the deceased's estate, but it is open to the deceased's executor to apply for variation or recall of the order on the basis of a change of circumstances.[282] On the death or remarriage of the payee, an order for periodical allowance ceases to have effect.[283]

An order relating to pension benefits[284]

14.114 This order was not available to the courts under the 1985 Act in its original form.[285] It was added by the Pensions Act 1995 ('the 1995 Act') to meet the special problems created where pensions entitlements formed part of the property in the particular case. The difficulty with pensions is that they are not capable of being realised immediately or, if it is possible to cash them in, the amount realised is only a fraction of what would have been available at a later date. Until the 1995 Act, the courts sought to deal

---

274 Section 13(1)(b).
275 Section 13(1)(c).
276 Section 13(3).
277 In some cases, the combination of the claimant's age, the duration of the marriage and, sometimes, other factors, militates in favour of such an award: *Bell* v *Bell* 1988 SCLR 457; *Gribb* v *Gribb* 1994 SLT (Sh Ct) 43, aff'd 1996 SLT 719; *Haughan* v *Haughan* 1996 SLT 321; *Johnstone* v *Johnstone* 1990 SLT (Sh Ct) 79.
278 *Dever* v *Dever* 1988 SCLR 352 (periodical allowance awarded for six months from the date of decree); *Louden* v *Louden* 1994 SLT 381 (periodical allowance awarded for one year from date of decree); *Petrie* v *Petrie* 1988 SCLR 390 (periodical allowance awarded for one year from the date of decree); *Sheret* v *Sheret* (Sh Ct) 1990 SCLR (Notes) 799 (periodical allowance awarded for 13 weeks from the date of decree).
279 Section 13(4)(a).
280 Section 13(4)(c).
281 Section 13(4)(b).
282 Section 13(7)(a). Clearly, the death of the payer is, in itself, a fairly dramatic change of circumstance.
283 Section 13(7)(b).
284 Section 8(1)(ba).
285 The Scottish Law Commission did consider the question of pension rights but made no recommendation since it believed the matter was more properly one that should be considered as a whole by the Occupational Pensions Board and, in any event, felt that the scheme it proposed could accommodate any accrued pension rights – Report on Aliment and Financial Provision, para 3.132.

with the problem by awarding a capital sum, and leaving the payer to find the money from other assets, or by deferring payment or ordering that it should be made by way of instalments.

14.115   The new powers, added by the new section 12A to the 1985 Act, enable the court to make an order against the trustees and managers of pension schemes requiring them to pay lump sums as directed by the court when they fall due. Thus, the court can order payment of a lump sum, or any part of it, to the former spouse of a member of the pension scheme. Before a s 12A order can be made, three conditions must be satisfied.[286] Firstly, the court must have made an order for the payment of a capital sum by a party to the marriage ('the liable party'). Secondly, the liable party must have rights or interests in benefits under a pension scheme which are matrimonial property. Thirdly, the benefits must include the payment of a lump sum either to the liable party or on his or her death.

14.116   Where the lump sum is payable to the liable party, the court may order the trustees or managers of the pension scheme to pay all or part of it to the other party to the marriage ('the other party').[287] Where the lump sum is payable on the death of the liable party, precisely what the court may order depends on the nature of the scheme. If the trustees or managers of the scheme have the power to determine the payee of the lump sum, the court may require them to pay part or all of it to the other party when it falls due.[288] If the liable party has the power to nominate the payee, the court may require him or her to nominate the other party as the payee of all or part of the lump sum.[289] In other cases, the court may order the trustees or managers to pay all or part of the lump sum to the other party instead of to such other person as would have been entitled to receive it.[290] Any payment made by the trustees in accordance with such a court order discharges the trustees' liability to the liable party to the extent of the sums paid[291] and is treated as payment of the capital sum by the liable party.[292]

14.117   Section 12A orders are subject to variation or recall at the instance of an interested party, where the liable party's liability has been discharged other than by payment by the trustees or managers of the pension scheme.[293] It may be that the liable party would prefer to pay the capital sum before payment becomes due under the pension scheme. For example, a male liable party whose pension rights have been made subject to such an order may have remarried and may wish the pension provision to be available to his new wife. If he has the resources available, he can pay off the capital sum due and apply to the court to have the s 12A order recalled. It is possible that the sum payable eventually under the scheme will be less

---

286   Section 12A(1).
287   Section 12A(2).
288   Section 12A(3)(a).
289   Section 12A(3)(b).
290   Section 12A(3)(c).
291   Section 12A(4)(a).
292   Section 12A(4)(b).
293   Section 12A(5).

than was anticipated at the time of the divorce. To cover this eventuality, Clive wisely counsels that '[i]t will therefore be prudent to ensure that the form of the capital sum order is such as to preserve the deferred liability of the liable party or his or her estate'.[294]

14.118 A feature of pension schemes is that rights under them can usually be transferred to another scheme, often when the member moves jobs. To take account of this possibility, regulations require the trustees or managers of the first scheme to notify the trustees or managers of the new scheme of the s 12A order.[295] The trustees or managers of the new scheme then become liable under the order[296] and the same procedure applies to subsequent transfers.[297] The other party is also entitled to notice of any transfer of pension rights.[298]

14.119 While the extension of the court's powers in respect of pensions are an interesting development and one which recognises the importance of pensions as a part of family property, it should be noted that they do not amount to the same thing as the much-publicised idea of 'pension-splitting'. This would involve the more radical option of taking a part of the liable party's pension entitlement and putting it into a separate pension scheme, either with the same company or elsewhere, for the benefit of the other party.[299] In this way, the other party would acquire a pension entitlement in his or her own right which could be enhanced by fresh contributions from that other party. Certainly, it is an option which has attracted considerable public support, not least from 'first wives' facing the end of a longer-term marriage which has been organised on the traditional breadwinner-homemaker model. Reform along these lines seems likely and, indeed, appears to have been anticipated by the provisions of s 17 of the Family Law Act 1996.[300]

An incidental order[301]

14.120 In formulating what was to become the 1985 Act, the Scottish Law Commission expressed the view that

---

294 At para 24.100.
295 Divorce, etc. (Pensions) (Scotland) Regulations 1996, SI 1996 No 1901 (as amended by the Divorce etc (Pensions) (Scotland) Amendment Regulations 1997, SI 1997 No 745), reg 5.
296 1985 Act, s 12A(6) and (8).
297 1996 Regulations, reg 6.
298 1996 Regulations, regs 6 and 7. The other party is required to notify the relevant trustees or managers of any change in his or her name or address within 14 days of the change and notice sent to the last known address of the other party is deemed to have been received on the seventh day after posting – 1996 Regulations, regs 8 and 9.
299 See, The Treatment of Pension Rights on Divorce (Cm 3345, 1996).
300 Section 17 amends s 10 of the 1985 Act (by adding a new subsection 5A) to provide that the court may not make an order which would allow assets to be removed from an unfunded pensions scheme earlier than would otherwise be the case. As Clive points out (at para 24.104), '[i]t is strange to introduce a limitation on the exercise of a power before the power itself is conferred'.
301 Section 14.

'Firmness of principle and flexibility of technique should, in our view, character-ise the law on financial provision'.[302]

It believed, therefore, that the court should have a very wide range of orders available to it so that it could implement the principles set out in the 1985 Act in an effective way. The incidental orders, provided for in s 14, are set out below. Some are self-explanatory, both in terms of the order and why it might be necessary, while others require a little more exploration.[303] In many cases, the orders will be unnecessary or inapplicable. For example, in divorces where there is no property, there will be nothing to value. Even where there is substantial property, most spouses will arrange for the valuation of the property themselves. However, where spouses prove intransigent or special circumstances present themselves, the incidental orders ensure that the court will not be impotent when faced with these difficulties.

14.121 Any of these orders, except those relating to the occupation of the matrimonial home and associated expenses, may be granted before, on or after the granting or refusal of a decree of divorce.[304] While the orders are called 'incidental orders', the term is simply one of convenience, since there need not be a 'main order' for financial provision like, for example, an order for the transfer of property. Incidental orders are, none the less, orders for financial provision and, as such, must be justified under the principles set out in s 9 and are subject to the limitation of being reasonable in the light of the parties resources.[305] They are as follows.

(*a*) An order for the sale of property.[306]

14.122 While the court can exercise this power at any time, it would not normally be competent to order sale of the home during the course of divorce proceedings.[307]

(*b*) An order for the valuation of property.

(*c*) An order determining any dispute between the parties to the marriage as to their respective property rights by means of a declarator thereof or otherwise.

(*d*) An order regulating the occupation of the matrimonial home or the use of furniture and plenishings therein or excluding either party to the marriage from such occupation.

14.123 As Clive rightly points out, this 'is probably the most important of

302 Report on Aliment and Financial Provision, para 3.128.
303 For a more detailed discussion of the incidental orders, see Clive, paras 24.113–24.126.
304 Section 14(1).
305 A suggestion to the contrary was made in *Demarco* v *Demarco* (OH) 1990 SCLR 635, at p 638. Were incidental orders not subject to the same overall restrictions as other orders under the Act, the effect would be to open the way to unfettered judicial discretion, something rejected in the Act as a whole.
306 The court could use this power to ensure that the home was sold and the proceeds divided equally between the parties: *Larkin* v *Larkin* (Sh Ct) 1992 SCLR 130; *Jacques* v *Jacques* 1995 SLT 963, aff'd 1997 SLT 459; *Reynolds* v *Reynolds* (Sh Ct) 1991 SCLR (Notes) 175.
307 *McKeown* v *McKeown* 1988 SCLR 355.

the court's incidental powers'.[308] As we saw, occupancy rights under the Matrimonial Homes (Family Protection) (Scotland) Act 1981 ('the 1981 Act') end on divorce. However, it may be that continued occupation of the home by one spouse and the children would be the best way to give effect to the guiding principles of the 1985 Act. In such cases, the court is given this flexible power and may order continued occupation for a specified or unspecified time.[309] Where the order is granted, most, but not all, of the provisions in relation to occupancy rights found in the 1981 Act apply.[310] It should be noted that the provisions of the 1981 Act in relation to dealings with third parties do not apply. If the occupying spouse is concerned that his or her former partner might sell the home, an interdict should be sought. The court may only exercise this power, and that governing the regulation of expenses in relation to the home, on or after the granting of a decree of divorce.[311]

(e) An order regulating liability, as between the parties, for outgoings in respect of the matrimonial home or furniture or plenishings therein.[312]

(f) An order that security shall be given for any financial provision.[313]

(g) An order that payments shall be made or property transferred to any curator bonis or trustee or other person for the benefit of the party to the marriage by whom or on whose behalf application has been made.

(h) An order setting aside or varying any term in an antenuptial or postnuptial marriage settlement.[314]

(j) An order as to the date from which any interest on any amount awarded shall run.

14.124 As we have seen, the court may defer payment of a capital sum. In such circumstances, the court has the power to provide for interest to be payable on the deferred sum.[315] In addition, the court may order that interest should run from a date prior to the date of the decree.[316]

(k) Any ancillary order which is expedient to give effect to the principles set out in section 9 or to any order made under section 8(2) of the Act.

308 At para 24.119.
309 In *Symon* v *Symon* (Sh Ct) 1991 SCLR (Notes) 414, for example, the right to occupy was only until the home was sold.
310 See s 14(5).
311 Section 14(3).
312 In *McCormick* v *McCormick* 1994 GWD 35–2078, this power was used to order one party to make loan repayments until a share in the home was transferred.
313 In *Macdonald* v *Macdonald* 1995 SLT 72, the husband was ordered to grant a standard security over his share of the home against payment of a capital sum at a future date. In *Murley* v *Murley* (OH) 1995 SCLR (Notes) 1138, the husband was ordered to transfer his share in the home to the wife and she was required to take out a standard security over the home to the value of sums that would become payable to him at a later date.
314 'Settlement' includes a policy of assurance under the Married Women's Policies of Assurance (Scotland) Act 1880; s 14(6).
315 *Bannon* v *Bannon* 1993 SLT 999.
316 Initially, there was some doubt about the possibility of such backdating of interest payments – *Carpenter* v *Carpenter* 1990 SLT (Sh Ct) 68 and *Skarpaas* v *Skarpaas* 1991 SLT (Sh Ct) 15. The matter was clarified by the Inner House in *Geddes* v *Geddes* 1993

14.125 This 'catch-all' power enables the court to ensure that the principles set out in s 9 can be given effect to and could be used to order one party to repay a secured loan by a certain date[317] or to effect the conveyance of a property where a party refused to co-operate with a property transfer order.[318]

An anti-avoidance order

14.126 Such is the animosity between some spouses that they will go to incredible lengths to defeat a soon-to-be ex-partner's claims for financial provision. Some spouses will attempt to hide assets and, despite the court's powers in respect of disclosure,[319] will be successful in doing so. Other spouses will attempt to alienate property by putting it in the name of a relative, friend or new partner, selling it, or giving it away.[320] In the attempt to combat such behaviour, the court is armed with wide powers to interdict, vary or set aside transactions aimed at defeating a claim for financial provision.[321] However, the powers conferred are not unfettered. The application for variation or setting aside of a transaction or interdict must be brought within a year of the claim for financial provision being disposed of.[322] A challenger is not permitted to go back into the mists of time, since only transactions or transfers which took place within five years preceding the claim for financial provision may be varied or set aside.[323] In order to be successful, it is for the challenger to establish that the transaction or transfer has had, or is likely to have, the effect of defeating, in whole or in part, any claim for financial provision.[324] In addition, the court's powers are discretionary and will not be used to restrict one party's freedom of action unnecessarily. Clearly, regard must be had to the legitimate interests of innocent third parties who risk being caught in the middle of this process. Where a third party has acquired rights in property in good faith and for value, the court is directed not to make any order prejudicing such rights.[325] Similarly, the interest of anyone deriving title from such a third party is protected.

14.127 The powers may be exercised in the course of a claim for financial

SLT 494, where Lord President Hope pointed out (at p 500) that this power is analogous with the common law power where possession of land has been given prior to transfer and, indeed, is consistent with the general principles of unjustified enrichment. See also, *Welsh* v *Welsh* 1994 SLT 828.

317 *McConnell* v *McConnell* 1993 GWD 34–2185.
318 See, D. J. Cusine, 'Property Transfer Orders: Some Conveyancing Imponderables' (1990) 35 JLSS 52 and E. M. Clive, 'Property Transfer Orders' (1990) 35 JLSS 118.
319 See para 14.160, below.
320 Clive (at para 24.128, n 17) cites the, fairly extreme, case of *Robertson* v *Robertson* 1996 GWD 3–167, where a husband appealed against a sentence of 60 days imprisonment for breach of interdict, the breach in question being his drinking away of over £8,000.
321 Section 18.
322 Section 18(1).
323 Section 18(1)(i).
324 Section 18(2).
325 Section 18(3). A third party claiming that he or she might be affected has a right to make representations – *Harris* v *Harris* 1988 SLT 101.

provision or within one year thereof.[326] However, since an action for a periodical allowance may be raised after the decree of divorce has been granted, in certain limited circumstance,[327] an application for an anti-avoidance order may be appropriate well beyond one year from the original resolution of financial claims. Where the court varies or reduces a transaction or transfer, it may include in any order it makes 'such terms and conditions as it thinks fit and may make any ancillary order which it considers expedient to ensure that the order is effective'.[328] Clive expresses the view that this would enable the court to get round the problem that it may only award a capital sum or order the transfer of property on granting the decree of divorce or within a specified time thereafter. It appears that, once the court has varied or set aside a transaction or transfer, it can then make an order for financial provision taking its own action into account. Anti-avoidance orders represent a valuable weapon in the arsenal at the court's disposal, not least because the sanctions attaching to them are the usual sanctions for breach of interdict and include imprisonment.

Tax consequences of marital breakdown[329]

14.128 Typically, three sorts of tax consequences flow from legal separation or divorce.[330] The first are consequences which arise simply by virtue of the fact of physical separation or the changed legal relationship of the spouses. The second and third kinds of tax consequences flow from the changes in the economic circumstances of the spouses which typically result on separation or divorce, particularly as a result of orders under s 8 of the 1985 Act. The second set of tax consequences flow from the creation of on-going liability to make support payments of some sort in respect of the spouse or former spouse or children of the marriage. The third set result from the one-time transfer of assets between spouses.

14.129 When speaking of 'tax', we are in fact referring to several different taxes arising under a number of different taxing statutes. The following discussion will focus primarily on three separate taxes: income tax, charged on individuals under the Income and Corporation Taxes Act 1988 (TA 1988); capital gains tax, charged on individuals under the Taxation of Chargeable Gains Act 1992 (TCGA 1992); and inheritance tax, charged on individuals under the Inheritance Tax Act 1984 (IHTA 1984). The first and second sorts of tax consequences described in the preceding paragraph generally involve income tax, although inheritance tax considerations may arise under the second sort as well. The third sort of tax consequences largely involve capital gains and inheritance tax considerations. Finally, two other taxing statutes may be relevant to a very limited number of cases

---

326 Section 18(1).

327 Section 13(1)(c).

328 Section 18(4). In *Tahir* v *Tahir (No 2)* 1995 SLT 451, where a loan was found to be fictitious, the court used its power to set aside a decree pronounced against a former husband for payment of the loan.

329 I am grateful to my colleague, Rob Dunbar, Lecturer in Private Law at the University of Glasgow for contributing this section on the tax consequences of marital breakdown.

330 See, generally, G. Saunders (ed), *Tolley's Tax Planning* (Tolley Publishing Co, 1997) and J. Tiley (ed), *UK Tax Guide 1998–99* (17th edn, Butterworths).

involving the transfer of certain assets, both capital assets and trading assets, of unincorporated businesses. These are the Value Added Tax Act 1994 (VATA 1994), under which value added tax (VAT) is charged, and the Capital Allowances Act 1990 (the CAA 1990).

Tax consequences arising by virtue of the fact of separation or divorce

14.130 As noted above, a small number of tax consequences flow merely from the fact of legal separation or divorce, and will arise regardless of whether the marital breakdown also involves on-going payment obligations or asset transfers between spouses or former spouses. In general, we are only concerned here with the availability of certain allowances and other reliefs which are relevant in computing a taxpayer's taxable income or tax payable in respect of *income tax* under the TA 1988.

14.131 The TA 1988 presently offers taxpayers a limited number of allowances and other reliefs which they may deduct in computing their income taxes. Generally, such allowances are based on a recognition that a taxpayer's personal circumstances may be such that he or she must incur expenditures over which he or she has little control. Failure to give the taxpayer some relief from income tax in these circumstances would be considered to impose a hardship on the taxpayer. Thus, for example, all individual income taxpayers are entitled to a *basic personal relief* of £4,195 for the 1998/99 taxation year.[331] Taxpayers who are 65 years of age or older at any time in the taxation year are entitled to a higher personal relief of £5,410[332] and those who are 75 years of age or older at any time in the taxation year are entitled to an even higher basic personal relief of £5,600.[333] The basic personal relief takes the form of a deduction in computing a taxpayer's income that is subject to tax, therefore, by virtue of this relief, the first £4,195 of income of every UK taxpayer (or £5,410 or £5,600, as the case may be) is effectively exempt from income tax. Again, the idea is to ensure that a certain measure of each taxpayer's income is free from tax.

14.132 The basic personal allowance is available to every taxpayer, regardless of marital status, and is not affected by changes in living arrangements or marital status. There are two other allowances, however, which are affected by marital breakdown. The first is the *married couple's allowance*.[334] In the first instance this allowance is available to a married man, although the value of the allowance can be shared with the wife. In order to claim the allowance, the man must, throughout at least part of the taxation year, be married and living together with his wife. A man and wife are automatically treated as 'living together' for these purposes unless either, they are legally separated under an order of a court or by deed of separation, or if they are actually separated in such circumstances that the separation is likely to be permanent.[335] Unlike the personal allowance,

---

331 TA 1988, s 257(1).
332 TA 1988, s 257(2).
333 TA 1988, s 257(3).
334 TA 1988, s 257A.
335 TA 1988, s 282.

which reduces the amount of a taxpayer's income subject to tax, this married couple's allowance reduces the taxpayer's tax liability itself. The amount of the allowance for the 1998–99 year of assessment is £285 (strictly speaking, it is £1,900 multiplied by 15%); this is the amount by which the claimant may reduce his tax payable. If either spouse is 65 or over at any time in the year of assessment, the allowance is worth £495.75, and if either is 75 or over, it is worth £501.75, subject to reductions where the claimant's total income exceeds £16,200. While the married couple's allowance goes to the husband in the first instance, the wife can elect to claim one half of this allowance[336] or the husband and wife can elect together that the wife claim the whole allowance.[337] These elections must be made before the start of the year of assessment in respect of which the claim is being made. It is advisable to make this election in cases in which the husband's tax bill is not large enough for the allowance to be fully utilised.

14.133 With respect to marital breakdown, the key point to note is that the loss of this married couple's allowance can be triggered by separation. The allowance continues to be available in the year of assessment in which the married couple cease living together, but not in any subsequent year, even if they happen still to be legally married in that subsequent year. It should be noted that, if a husband separates and is divorced, then remarries in the same year of assessment, he is still only entitled to claim one married couple's allowance.[338] In addition, it should be noted that, if a husband and wife ceased to live together before 6 April 1990, but ever since then they have remained married and the wife has been wholly maintained by the husband, the husband is not entitled to any tax deductions for the maintenance payments he makes, but he may claim the married couple's allowance.

14.134 The second allowance which is affected by marital breakdown is the *additional personal allowance for children*.[339] Generally, both spouses may be able to claim this allowance if they have a dependant child living with them who is a 'qualifying child', within the special definition given to that term under the TA 1988. There are some differences between the treatment of men and women, however. With respect to the wife, she may be entitled to claim this allowance in the year of separation, even if she is not yet divorced. This is because s 259(1)(a) of TA 1988 provides that a woman will be able to claim the allowance only if she is not both married *and* living with her husband throughout the whole of the taxation year. Similarly, if the woman remarries, she will be able to claim this allowance in the year of remarriage, because she will not have been both married and living with her new husband throughout that year. With respect to the husband, however, the allowance will not be available until the first taxation year immediately after he is both separated and divorced. No allowance is available in the year of separation, nor in the year of divorce, if

336 TA 1988, s 257BA(1).
337 TA 1988, s 257BA(2).
338 TA 1988, s 257A(6).
339 TA 1988, s 259.

the year of divorce is later than the year of separation. This is because s 259(1)(b) of the TA 1988 provides that a man is only entitled to the allowance if he is not married and living with his wife for any part of the taxation year. Similarly, if he should remarry, he would not be entitled to claim the allowance at all for the taxation year of the remarriage, because he would have been married and living with the new wife for at least a part of that taxation year.

14.135 In order to claim this allowance, the taxpayer must also have a 'qualifying child' residing with him or her for at least part of the taxation year. There are two parts to the definition of 'qualifying child', both of which must be met. First, the child must either be born in the taxation year, or have been under the age of 16 at the start of the taxation year, or, if over 16 at the start of the year, have been in full-time instruction at university, college, secondary school or some other educational establishment. Second, the 'qualifying child' must be a child of the taxpayer claiming the allowance. For these purposes, the word 'child' is defined to include a step-child, an illegitimate child if at some point after that child's birth, the taxpayer actually married the other parent, and an adopted child, if the child was younger than 18 when adopted.[340] Even if the child is not a 'child' of the taxpayer within this meaning, for example, if the child is a foster-child, the taxpayer may still be entitled to claim this allowance if the child is born in the taxation year or was under 18 at the start of the year and has been maintained by the taxpayer for all or part of that taxation year.

14.136 Like the married couple's allowance, this additional personal allowance reduces the taxpayer's tax liability itself, and the amount of this allowance for the 1998–99 year of assessment is also £285 (strictly speaking, it is £1,900 multiplied by 15%). This is the amount by which the claimant may reduce his or her tax payable. If the taxpayer has more than one qualifying child, he or she is still only entitled to claim this allowance once.[341] Both ex-spouses may qualify as persons who may potentially claim this additional personal allowance; the wife in the taxation year in which the separation takes place, the husband in the first year after separation and divorce.[342] Similarly, both could claim the allowance if each had a qualifying child residing with him or her for at least part of the taxation year. It is possible for two taxpayers to claim the allowance in respect of the same qualifying child, but the 1988 Act requires that the total allowance of £285 be apportioned between the taxpayers.[343] The apportionment can be made on any basis agreed by the taxpayers and, if the taxpayers reach no agreement, the apportionment will be in proportion to the length of periods of residence of the qualifying child with each taxpayer.[344]

Tax consequences in respect of on-going payment obligations arising on separation or divorce

340 TA 1988, s 259(8).
341 TA 1988, s 259(3).
342 TA 1988, s 259(1).
343 Section 260(1).
344 TA 1988, s 260(3).

14.137 The tax treatment of on-going payment obligations on marital breakdown is not nearly as generous to the payer as it was prior to 15 March 1988. Numerous commentators have noted that these changes have tended to encourage taxpayers to move towards a reduction of on-going support payments to one-time transfers of assets. In any case, the narrowness of the new rules means that the scope for the use of support payments to achieve some tax benefit to the payer or payee has virtually been eliminated. The new rules are contained in s 347B of the 1988 Act and apply in respect of nearly all arrangements arrived at after 14 March 1988, with the exception of a limited range of arrangements finalised after this date to which the old rules apply. Like the married couple's allowance and the additional personal allowance, the provision for tax relief in respect of maintenance payments provides for a reduction in the taxpayer's tax liability itself rather than a deduction in computing the taxpayer's income subject to tax. The maximum amount of the allowance for the 1998–99 year of assessment is limited to £285 (again, £1,900 multiplied by 15%).[345] Thus, even if the amount of maintenance payments made during the taxation year which qualify for this tax allowance, defined in s 347B as 'qualifying maintenance payments', exceed £1,900, which will often be the case, the maximum relief is limited to an amount calculated by reference to £1,900. If the amount of qualifying maintenance payments for the taxation year is less than £1,900, the amount of the reduction of tax is limited to that lesser amount multiplied by 15%.[346] This is obviously not a very generous relief for taxpayers who are under an obligation to make such payments. The taxpayer making qualifying maintenance payments is not entitled to deduct such payments in calculating his income subject to tax, but gets this limited reduction in tax payable. The recipient, however, is not required to pay any tax on the entire amount of the payments received.[347] Because the recipient is not taxable, there is no requirement on the payer to withhold any tax from the payment, as was the case under the pre-15 March 1988 rules. Thus, the maintenance payments are to be made gross. Obviously, when parties to a separation agreement or divorce are attempting to agree on a quantum in respect of the payments, this tax treatment must be borne in mind.

14.138 The making of maintenance or other on-going payments under a separation agreement or support order in a divorce can potentially have *inheritance tax* consequences under the IHTA 1984, but for three provisions in this Act, which have the effect of ensuring that inheritance tax should not, in most cases, arise. The name 'inheritance tax' suggests a tax which is only imposed on death. This is not the case. The IHTA 1984 brings within its scope a number of transfers which are made during a taxpayer's lifetime and therefore it must be considered whenever such transfers occur. Inheritance tax may apply whenever, by virtue of a transfer of an asset or assets by an individual, the value of the transferor's estate has been reduced.

345 Section 347B(3) and (5A).
346 Section 347B(2) and (3).
347 Section 347A(1).

14.139 'Estate' is defined very broadly to include all property to which an individual is beneficially entitled.[348] Inheritance tax is only charged where an individual has made a 'chargeable transfer'.[349] In order to have made such a transfer, the taxpayer must have made a 'transfer of value' which is not an 'exempt transfer'. Thus, if a transfer made by a taxpayer is either not a 'transfer of value' or is an 'exempt transfer', no inheritance tax is chargeable. A 'transfer of value' is defined as a disposition which results in a reduction in the value of the transferor's estate.[350] Thus, dispositions between persons dealing at arm's length for consideration will generally not be subject to inheritance tax because the value of the transferor's estate is generally not reduced in such sales. Furthermore, there will be no transfer of value for inheritance tax purposes if the disposition was made without gratuitous intent.[351] In particular, a disposition is not a transfer of value if it was not intended to confer any gratuitous benefit. To benefit from this provision, the IHTA 1984 requires that the disposition either was made in an arm's length transaction between persons who are not connected with each other or was a disposition which might be expected to be made in such a transaction between such persons. A husband and wife would be connected persons, even if they were legally separated, but would cease to be so on the granting by the court of a divorce.[352] The Inland Revenue has indicated in a Statement of Practice,[353] that it considers that transfers of money or property pursuant to a court order granting a divorce or nullification of a marriage will generally be regarded as exempt from inheritance tax by virtue of the fact that such transfers are not intended to confer any gratuitous benefit to the recipient. It is not clear from this Statement of Practice, however, whether such transfers made prior to the granting of the divorce, for example, a transfer pursuant to a separation agreement, would similarly be exempt from inheritance tax. While such gifts would also seem to lack gratuitous intent, they are ones which are made between connected persons, because the husband and wife would still be married. Therefore, it would have to be argued that the disposition was one which might be expected to be made in an arm's length transaction between persons who are not connected with each other. In the context of a legal separation, particularly one made in contemplation of eventual divorce, there seems to be a strong argument that this condition is met. Unfortunately, the Inland Revenue has not clarified this point, and taxpayers cannot be certain that a transfer pursuant to a separation agreement will necessarily be free from inheritance tax under this provision.

14.140 Fortunately, there are other provisions which should free most arrangements made on separation or divorce from inheritance tax. The IHTA 1984[354] provides that a disposition will not be a transfer of value, and

348 IHTA 1984, s 5(1).
349 As defined in s 2(1) of the IHTA 1984.
350 IHTA 1984, s 3(1).
351 IHTA 1984, s 10(1).
352 IHTA 1984, s 270.
353 SP E12.
354 IHTA 1984, s 11(1).

therefore cannot give rise to inheritance tax, if it is made by one party to a marriage in favour of the other or in favour of a child of either party. The payment must, however, be for the maintenance of the other party or for the maintenance, education or training of the child, where the child is 18 or under or, if over 18, is in full-time education or training. This exception also applies in respect of payments made by persons who were formerly married for the maintenance of the former spouse or for the maintenance, education or training of a child of theirs.[355] Thus, most maintenance payments for the support of a spouse or former spouse or for the support of children, whether made pursuant to a separation agreement entered into before divorce or to a divorce decree, should be exempt from inheritance tax as they would not be 'transfers of value'.

14.141 In addition, even if a disposition is a transfer of value because neither ss 10 nor 11 apply, the transfer will still be exempt from inheritance tax if the transfer is made to the transferor's spouse.[356] If the spouse is not domiciled in the UK, however, the maximum amount that could be transferred to the spouse exempt from inheritance tax is limited to £55,000. This exemption applies even if the spouses are legally separated, but ceases to apply once the spouses are divorced. Thus, the section should exempt from inheritance tax any transfers made by one spouse to another under a separation agreement, but may not apply to such transfers made in pursuance of a divorce decree.

14.142 As noted, these three provisions should allow most maintenance payments, and, indeed transfers of capital assets made pursuant to either a separation agreement or divorce, to be free from inheritance tax. Even if a party to a separation or divorce cannot rely on any of these provisions, however, there is a strong likelihood that no inheritance tax will be payable. Most transfers made by individuals to other individuals (as opposed to trusts or corporations, for example) since 18 March 1986 are generally not subject to inheritance tax unless the person making the transfer should die within seven years of the making of the transfer. These transfers are called 'potentially exempt transfers' (or 'PETs'). One important condition that must be met in order for a transfer to be considered a PET, however, is that the transfer must be by way of 'gift'. As noted earlier in the discussion of the potential application of s 10 of the IHTA 1984 in respect of transfers on marital breakdown, the Inland Revenue takes the view that such transfers are generally not made with 'gratuitous intent'. It may be the case, therefore, that the Inland Revenue would view any transfer made in the context of a separation agreement or divorce as not being a 'gift', and therefore as not qualifying as a PET. If a transfer made during the transferor's lifetime is not a PET, it will generally be subject to inheritance tax immediately as a 'chargeable transfer'. Even if such a transfer were chargeable, inheritance tax is charged at a rate of 0%, effectively meaning that the transfer is free of inheritance tax liability, if it, together with all other chargeable transfers made during a seven-year

355 IHTA 1984, s 11(6).
356 IHTA 1984, s 18(1).

period of which the time of the transfer forms a part, do not exceed £223,000.

14.143 Finally, it should be noted that there are a limited range of reliefs which are available in respect of transfers of certain types of assets. The most important of these reliefs is in respect of transfers of assets which qualify as 'relevant business property'.[357] The relief works by reducing the 'value transferred', which is essentially the value on which any inheritance tax will be calculated, by either 100% or 50%, thereby effectively either eliminating, or reducing by half, the taxpayer's liability. Assets giving rise to the 100% reduction include: a business or part of a business; shares of a company not quoted on a stock exchange which, by themselves or with other shares of the transferor, gave the transferor control of the company before the transfer; and, shares of a company not quoted on a stock exchange which, by themselves or with other shares of the transferor, gave the transferor at least 25% of the voting power. Generally, such assets must have been owned by the transferor throughout the two-year period preceding the transfer, and the relief does not apply in cases in which the business carried out by the company or unincorporated business consists mainly in dealing in securities, stocks, shares, land and buildings, and in other financial assets, or in which the business consists primarily in the holding of investments. Thus, the business property relief is generally only available in cases in which the business is an active business rather than an investment business.

Tax consequences in respect of transfers of assets on separation and divorce

14.144 Aside from on-going maintenance payments, the most important economic consequence of separation or divorce is the transfer of assets which may occur as part of a separation agreement or pursuant to a court order. Often, for example, there will be a transfer of an interest in the family home, which is for most people their single most important financial asset, from one party to the other. Equally, however, there may be transfers of ownership of personal property, including vehicles, furniture and appliances, jewellery and art, and of intangible property, such as financial instruments (for example, company shares, bonds, interests in trusts, or in investment funds). Generally, all such assets will be capital assets of the taxpayers, rather than business or trading assets, and therefore may have capital gains and inheritance tax, rather than income tax, consequences for the person making the transfer.

14.145 The nature of inheritance tax was outlined above. The one-time transfer of assets on separation or divorce may result in a 'transfer of value',[358] because it will result in the reduction in the value of the transferor's estate. Once again, unless such a transfer is deemed not to be a 'transfer of value',[359] or, if the transfer is a 'transfer of value', it is an 'exempt transfer', the taxpayer may be liable for inheritance tax. As with

357 As defined in ss 103–106 of the IHTA 1984.
358 IHTA 1984, s 3(1).
359 Due to the provisions of the IHTA 1984, ss 10 or 11.

on-going maintenance payments, it is likely that one-off transfers of assets pursuant to a separation agreement or divorce would be made by the transferor without the requisite gratuitous intent, and would therefore not be considered to be a 'transfer of value' and the earlier comments with respect to s 10(1) of the IHTA 1984 also apply here. It is less clear that s 11(1), which provides that certain types of maintenance payments are not considered to be 'transfers of value' and therefore not subject to inheritance tax, is relevant to one-off transfers of capital assets. However, the transfers of certain assets, such as rental properties or other investment properties, which produce a stream of income for the recipient, may be considered to be maintenance payments of the sort described in s 11.

14.146 In most cases, however, s 18(1) of the IHTA 1984 will be the provision of most importance in respect of one-off transfers of assets. As noted above, it provides that such transfers will be exempt from inheritance tax if they are made to the transferor's spouse. As a practical matter, most of the one-off transfers of capital assets made pursuant to a separation agreement or divorce will be from one spouse or former spouse to the other. Again, if the spouse is not domiciled in the UK, the maximum amount that can be transferred to the spouse exempt from inheritance tax is limited to £55,000. In addition, this exemption applies even if the spouses are legally separated, but ceases to apply once the spouses are divorced. Thus, the section should exempt any transfers made by one spouse to another under a separation agreement from inheritance tax, but may not apply to such transfers made pursuant to a divorce decree. Finally, it should be remembered that, even if the transferor cannot rely on any of these provisions to ensure that no inheritance tax applies on the transfer of assets, the transferor may be able to make use of other provisions under the IHTA 1984, of the sort described in the preceding paragraphs, which have the effect of relieving the transferor from inheritance tax liability.

14.147 The other major tax which could apply on the one-off transfer of assets on separation or divorce is capital gains tax ('CGT') chargeable under the Taxation of Chargeable Gains Act 1992 (the 'TCGA 1992'). CGT can arise on the disposal of capital assets by individuals resident or ordinarily resident in the UK. The transfer of ownership of assets pursuant to a separation agreement or on divorce would be such a disposal. CGT will apply in respect of 'chargeable gains'.[360] Such gains generally arise where the consideration received by a person making a disposal of capital assets exceeds the value of the consideration originally paid (or deemed to be paid) by the transferor on the acquisition of the assets, together with certain other costs associated with the original acquisition and the ultimate disposal by the transferor.[361] From 31 March 1982, the amount of any such gain can be reduced by an 'indexation allowance'; essentially, a deduction in computing the chargeable gain which is made to give the transferor credit for the effects of inflation on the ultimate disposal price of capital

360 TCGA 1992, s 1(1).
361 TCGA 1992, s 38.

assets. The TCGA 1992 seeks to tax only 'real' economic gains, rather than gains that result as a result of price inflation.

14.148   On the transfer of assets on separation or divorce, consideration will generally not pass from the recipient of the transfer to the transferor, since the purpose of such transfers is to ensure that the economic relationship between the parties is adjusted. Even in the absence of consideration, however, CGT may apply. This is because s 17(1) of the TCGA 1992 deems certain disposals to be for consideration equal to the 'market value' of the asset at the time of the transfer where the disposal of the asset has been other than by way of a bargain made at arm's length. 'Market value' is defined to mean the price which the asset might reasonably be expected to fetch on a sale in the open market.[362] While s 17(1) does not define what is meant by a disposal made 'other than by way of a bargain ... at arm's length', it gives examples of such bargains which include a disposal by way of a gift or a transfer of an asset by a settler in a settlement. Thus, where a transfer is made on separation or divorce for the benefit of a former spouse or others, s 17(1) would deem such a transfer to have been made at arm's length. As noted above, in respect of s 10 of the IHTA 1984, it is doubtful that transfers of assets made on separation or divorce are made with the requisite gratuitous intent, and such transfers are therefore not likely to be considered 'gifts' of the sort which would attract s 17(1).

14.149   The reason that s 17(1) may apply in respect of most transfers made on separation and might apply in respect of transfers made on divorce, is due to the provisions of s 18(2) of the TCGA 1992. It provides that where a person making a disposition is 'connected' with the person acquiring the asset, the transaction is deemed not to be at arm's length. As a result, such a disposition would, pursuant to s 17(1), be deemed to take place at market value. A husband and wife are treated as 'connected persons',[363] with the result that any transfer of assets between a husband and wife will be treated as having taken place at the market value of the asset, regardless of what, if any, consideration was actually exchanged between them. It should be noted that, upon divorce, the man and woman cease to be husband and wife, with the result that they are no longer connected persons and, thus, s 17(1) no longer applies. A person is also connected with a 'relative', defined as including lineal descendants.[364] The result is that a one-off transfer of assets to a child of the marriage will also be considered, by virtue of ss 18(2) and 17(1) of the TCGA 1992, as having taken place at market value. To the extent that the capital assets being transferred have appreciated in value since their acquisition by the transferor, CGT could therefore arise even without the transferor receiving any consideration for the transfer.

14.150   Unlike under the IHTA 1984, there is no exception from potential CGT liability where the transfer is made without the requisite gratuitous

362 TCGA 1992, s 272(1).
363 TCGA 1992, s 286(2).
364 TCGA 1992, s 286(8).

intent or for the purposes of maintenance. There are, however, a number of exceptions and reliefs under the TCGA 1992 which should allow the transferor to avoid CGT liability in many cases. The most important of these provides that, if a husband and wife are married and living together at any point in a particular taxation year, the disposal of a capital asset by one spouse to the other is deemed to take place at a consideration that is such as to ensure that no CGT arises.[365] Thus, the spouse making the transfer will realise no gain or loss on the disposal, and the other spouse will acquire the asset at the same price that is used to ensure no gain or loss to the transferor. A husband and wife are treated as living together unless they are separated under an order of a court or by deed of separation, or if they are in fact separated in such circumstances that the separation is likely to be permanent.[366]

14.151 Where a transfer of assets is made prior to the conclusion of a separation agreement and prior to actual permanent separation, the spouse making the transfer should be able to rely on the protection discussed in the foregoing paragraphs. While the transfer will be to a connected person, and is therefore deemed to occur at market value, the transfer is deemed to occur at such a value as to ensure that no chargeable gain arises to the transferor. Problems arise, however, if the transfer takes place after the year in which separation occurs, but prior to divorce. In such circumstances, the transfer will still be a transfer to a connected person, and therefore will be deemed to be at market value, because the spouses are still married. However, the spouse making the transfer will not be entitled to rely on the relief described above, because the spouses are not living together in the taxation year. Therefore, a chargeable gain may arise to the transferor, with CGT potentially applying. As a result, spouses will generally wish to ensure that any transfers of capital assets take place in the year of separation and while they are still married, so as to ensure that the spouse making the transfer will benefit from the relief from CGT.

14.152 Where the above relief does not apply, or where the transfer of assets is to another connected person, such as a child of the marriage, a chargeable gain could result, with CGT implications to the transferor. It is still possible that the transferor could rely on a number of other reliefs available under the TCGA 1992 to ensure that no CGT arises. The most important of these will be the exemption from CGT which is available on the disposal of a private residence. This exemption is set out in ss 222 to 226 of the TCGA 1992 and provides that a gain on the disposal of a taxpayer's only or main residence will generally not be treated as a chargeable gain, and will therefore result in no CGT liability. For a fuller description of this exemption, reference can be made to the *UK Tax Guide*. It is important to note, however, that a taxpayer can have only one main residence and, therefore, if the spouse is transferring ownership in more than one residential property pursuant to a separation agreement or divorce, the

---

365 TCGA 1992, s 58.
366 TCGA 1992, s 288(3) which refers to the Income and Corporation Taxes Act 1988, s 282.

exemption will be available in respect of only one of the properties. Given that a matrimonial home will often be the single most important asset in which interests are being transferred, this exemption is obviously of great practical importance.

14.153 It is also important to remember that, where ownership of tangible moveable property, such as furniture or motor vehicles, is transferred on separation or divorce, no chargeable gain is treated as having occurred, and therefore no CGT liability will arise, where the amount or value of consideration or deemed consideration on the disposal does not exceed £6,000. Many items of tangible moveable property will have a market value of less than this amount, and can therefore be transferred free of CGT. Even where the taxpayer has realised a chargeable gain which is potentially subject to CGT, the first £6,800 of such gains made each year by the taxpayer is not subject to CGT.[367]

14.154 In conclusion, while CGT, like inheritance tax, can potentially arise on the one-time transfer of assets on separation or divorce, there are a range of exemptions and reliefs which will generally allow the spouse who is making the transfer to avoid adverse tax consequences. The rules can be complicated, however, and taxpayers can fall into traps if the separation agreement or divorce is not structured carefully. It is always advisable, therefore, for separating and divorcing spouses to seek professional tax advice, preferably prior to separating and, in any event, prior to finalising the financial arrangements of the separation or divorce.

Agreement on financial provision

14.155 When we were considering the consequences of cohabitation and marriage, we looked at the possibilities for custom-making a marriage. As we saw, some couples conclude an agreement prior to getting married covering both the currency of the marriage and what will happen in the event of divorce. Quite apart from the usual methods by which any agreement may be challenged, the court has the power to vary antenuptial marriage settlements in the course of divorce.[368] More often, however, couples will not embark on marriage anticipating divorce or, at any rate, will not articulate such thoughts as they may have on the matter. Faced with a marriage that is not working out, what, then, can the couple do? To what extent can they agree the terms of their own divorce? How should they go about reaching agreement? We have seen that 'bargaining in the shadow of the law' or 'private ordering' is becoming increasingly well-recognised and mediation is a particularly popular form of alternative dispute resolution. The development, benefits and potential pitfalls of mediation are discussed in chapter 1.[369] It will be remembered that organisations like Family Mediation and Comprehensive Accredited Lawyer Mediators (CALM) are of particular relevance in this context.

14.156 Clearly, it is highly desirable that spouses contemplating divorce

367 TCGA 1992, s 3.
368 1985 Act, ss 8(1)(c) and 14(2)(h).
369 Chapter 1, paras 45–50.

should sit down and talk to each other calmly and reasonably about the divorce itself, any children involved and financial provision. They may find it helpful to involve a third party in the course of their discussions and organisations like Family Mediation Scotland and CALM are particularly experienced at assisting in the process. Of course, the divorce itself is not something that they can arrange without recourse to the legal system, since divorce is a legal process and requires the sanction of the court. However, there is nothing to stop a couple deciding that, while one of them has grounds for an action based on the other partner's adultery, they will simply allow the period of two years non-cohabitation to elapse and seek divorce by consent. As we have seen, it is neither permitted[370] nor desirable that the parents should resolve the future arrangements on residence and contact without consulting the children involved and, in any event, the court has at least a theoretical duty to be satisfied as to these arrangements.[371] As far as financial provision on divorce is concerned, couples are free to make their own arrangements.

14.157 As a matter of practice, the agreement should be as comprehensive as possible and each party should have received independent legal advice. To put it bluntly, a generous, reasonable, but ill-informed person might be taken to the cleaners by a spouse who was better informed and not playing by the same rules. Assuming that the couple reach agreement, they need do nothing further. However, it is common to record the terms of the agreement. Where the divorce is being pursued under the affidavit procedure or by ordinary proof, it is usual to present the agreement in a minute, or joint minute, of agreement and ask the court to interpone its authority to it. If the parties are pursuing a divorce by the do-it-yourself procedure, the agreement should be recorded in the Books of Council and Session.

14.158 While couples are encouraged to make their own financial arrangements, the court retains the power to set aside or vary an agreement, or any term of it, where it was not fair and reasonable at the time it was entered into.[372] The court can exercise this power on granting decree of divorce, or, within a time specified when the decree was granted.[373] The whole circumstances of the agreement, including non-disclosure of information and the legal advice each party received, are relevant to assessing its reasonableness.[374] In addition, the court has the power to vary or set aside an agreement in respect of a periodical allowance in three distinct

---

370 The Children (Scotland) Act 1995, s 6 requires that children be given the opportunity to express their views if they want to when a decision is being taken on the exercise of parental responsibilities or rights and the decision-maker is obliged to give due weight to these views in the light of the child's age and maturity. How much this actually happens in the family setting is, of course, open to question.

371 1995 Act, s 12. This is discussed fully in chapter 3 at paras 36–37 and chapter 6 at paras 3–6.

372 1985 Act, s 16(1)(b).

373 Section 16(2)(b).

374 *Anderson* v *Anderson* 1989 SCLR 475; *Gillon* v *Gillon (No 1)* 1994 SLT 978; *Gillon* v *Gillon (No 2)* 1994 SLT 984; *Gillon* v *Gillon (No 3)* 1995 SLT 678; *McAfee* v *McAfee* (OH) 1990 SCLR (Notes) 805.

circumstances. Firstly, where the agreement expressly provides that a term relating to periodical allowance can be varied or set aside by the court,[375] the court can vary the term or set it aside at any time.[376] Secondly, where the party obliged to pay a periodical allowance under the agreement has been sequestrated, declared bankrupt or has executed a trust deed for the benefit of his or her creditors, since the agreement was made, the court can vary or set aside the term relating to the periodical allowance.[377] Thirdly, where a maintenance assessment has been made under the Child Support Act 1991, the court may vary or set aside the term relating to periodical allowance.[378]

Procedural matters

14.159 Financial provision can be sought by either party in a divorce action[379] in either the Court of Session or the sheriff court,[380] although actions are now usually dealt with in the sheriff court.[381] While significant numbers of couples still rely on litigation in order to resolve financial provision on divorce, increasing numbers resolve the matter by agreement.

14.160 Prior to 1985, the only way to force the other spouse to disclose his or her financial position was by means of a commission and diligence. While that procedure remains available, the 1985 Act introduced a simplified procedure for requiring either party to disclose details of his or her resources.[382] Unlike a commission and diligence, the court may not inquire into the extent of disclosure[383] and, while the party complying with the requirement to disclose must give a value for each asset listed, he or she is not required to produce documentation proving the value.[384] In Scotland, where either party is required by the court to provide details of his or her resources, whether under a commission and diligence or under s 20, failure to do so is contempt of court and is punishable as such.

---

375 Section 16(1)(a). See *Mills* v *Mills* (Sh Ct) 1990 SCLR 213; *Ellerby* v *Ellerby* (Sh Ct) 1991 SCLR 608.
376 Section 16(2)(a).
377 Section 16(3).
378 Section 16(3)(d). As Clive points out (at para 24.139), there is a strange reference in the provision to a maintenance assessment relating to a child 'for whose benefit periodical allowance is paid'.
379 The court has the same powers to make financial provision on granting a decree of nullity of marriage – s 17. In addition, the court has certain limited powers in respect of financial provision where a divorce has been granted abroad – Matrimonial and Family Proceedings Act 1984, discussed in chapter 13 at para 100, above.
380 Sections 8(1) and 27(1).
381 Divorce has been competent in the sheriff court since 1 May 1984 – Divorce Jurisdiction, Court Fees and Legal Aid (Scotland) Act 1983. In 1996, 98% of divorces were granted in the sheriff court – Civil Judicial Statistics 1996 (The Stationery Office, 1997), Table 6.1.
382 Section 20.
383 Where it is suspected that a spouse is concealing assets, it may, therefore, be preferable to seek the granting of a commission and diligence.
384 *Nelson* v *Nelson* (Sh Ct) 1993 SCLR (Notes) 149.

14.161 Scotland has no equivalent to the so-called Thyssen, or million-aires', defence,[385] available to wealthy spouses in England and Wales. Essentially, the defence exempts a party from complying with the usual requirement to complete a questionnaire detailing his or her assets, where that party provides an affidavit to the effect that the assets are such that any order the court might make can be complied with. It does not entitle a wealthy spouse to refuse any question about his or her financial position, particularly where they are of a broad general nature. None the less, the benefit of this defence is that it enables a spouse to retain a degree of privacy. However, it is wholly inapplicable in the Scottish system where the court is directed to ensure that the net value of matrimonial property is divided fairly. In order to do that, it must know what property there is and what it is worth.

Enforcement

14.162 Lawyers the world over are all too familiar with the problem of having obtained financial provision for a client on divorce and then finding that the decree is being ignored by the former spouse. A Scottish decree can be enforced within Scotland using all the usual methods of debt recovery. While civil imprisonment remains possible for failure to pay aliment, a periodical allowance payable after divorce is not aliment and thus, threats of imprisonment, while sometimes effective against an ignor-ant errant former spouse, cannot be carried out.

14.163 The problem becomes even greater when the former spouse has left the jurisdiction.[386] Over the years, efforts have been made to facilitate international enforcement of court orders for financial provision. Recipro-cal enforcement throughout the UK is reasonably straightforward. There-after, enforcement depends on whether or not the foreign jurisdiction is a 'reciprocating country', a 'convention country'[387] or a country where the Hague Convention on the Recognition and Enforcement of Decisions Relating to Maintenance Obligations 1972 applies.

Verdict on the 1985 Act

14.164 The aim of the 1985 Act was to provide a principled approach to financial provision on divorce, combining guidance to the courts on what they should be trying to achieve and how, with sufficient flexibility to accommodate the enormous variety of human situations presenting them-selves. The legislation sought to assist the courts further by widening the range of tools at the courts' disposal. Undoubtedly, it has fulfilled its aims. As with any new legislation, it was inevitable that it should take the courts a little time to work through its application. However, we have now reached a point where the principles underlying the 1985 Act, and how

---

385 The defence takes its name from *Thyssen-Bornemisza* v *Thyssen-Bornemisza (No 2)* [1985] 1 All ER 328. See also, *Dart* v *Dart* [1996] 2 FLR 286 and *F* v *F (Ancillary Relief: Substantial Assets)* [1995] 2 FLR 45.
386 For an excellent discussion of international enforcement, see Clive, paras 12.063–12.175.
387 One which has acceded to the United Nations Convention on the Recovery Abroad of Maintenance 1956.

they apply, are reasonably clear. The range of orders the courts may make appear to maximise flexibility. Indeed, the courts have sometimes shown themselves to be capable of inspired interpretation of the 1985 Act. The limited criticism of the 1985 Act has focused on the courts over-use of s 9(1)(e) to award periodical allowances.[388] In a number of cases,[389] the other principles, and particularly s 9(1)(b), could have been used to award a capital sum, payable by instalments, achieving justice in the instant case and retaining the integrity of the 1985 Act as it was intended originally.

14.165 To quote a popular riposte, 'hard cases make bad law', but hard cases have emerged from the 1985 Act. Thus, for example, the definition of matrimonial property means that, where a home belonged to one spouse before the marriage and was not acquired for the couple's use, it does not go into the pot for division, regardless of how long they have lived in it.[390] The rule against 'tracing' assets that change their nature over time can produce anomalous results.[391] Increase in the value of separate property during the marriage can produce apparently unjust results where the increase cannot be linked by a contribution by the non-owning spouse.[392] Chronically sick or disabled spouses seem to get a raw deal in some cases,[393] but not in others.[394] However, such is the coherence and internal integrity of the 1985 Act that we should exercise care before rushing to amend it in response to perceived hard cases. That the legislation does not provide a satisfactory solution in all cases is often due to the fact that there is insufficient property to meet the needs of the parties adequately. As such, the problem is social and economic, rather than legal, in nature and any solution lies in the political, rather than the law reform, arena.

14.166 How the 1985 Act is perceived as working in practice is important. A study into the impact of the 1985 Act on solicitors' divorce practice, conducted within a few years of the Act coming into force[395] reflected

---

388 See for example, J. M. Thomson, 'Financial Provision on Divorce – the Current State of Play' 1989 SLT 17 and 33 and J. M. Thomson, *Family Law in Scotland* (3rd edn, Butterworths, 1996) at p 140.

389 This was particularly true is the early days of the Act's operation. See for example, *Stott* v *Stott* 1987 GWD 17–645.

390 *Maclellan* v *Maclellan* 1988 SCLR 399.

391 Contrast *Latter* v *Latter* 1990 SLT 805 and *Whittome* v *Whittome (No 1)* 1994 SLT 114.

392 In *Wilson* v *Wilson* OH, unreported, 9 June 1998, the Lord Ordinary repeated his earlier criticism (in *Latter* v *Latter*, above) that the Act failed to distinguish corporeal and incorporeal property, with the result that 'company property' could not be regarded as 'matrimonial property'. None the less, by applying ss 9(1)(b) and (d), he was able to make a substantial award to the wife.

393 *Barclay* v *Barclay* (Sh Ct) 1991 SCLR (Notes) 205.

394 *Haughan* v *Haughan* 1996 SLT 321.

395 F. Wasoff, R. E. Dobash and D. S. Harcus, The Impact of the Family Law (Scotland) Act 1985 on Solicitors' Divorce Practice (Central Research Unit, hereinafter CRU, 1990). The Act came into force on 1 September 1986 and the research for the report was conducted two to three years thereafter. It took the form of in-depth interviews with 58 solicitors practising in or near Edinburgh and focused on simulated first interviews with clients presenting typical cases.

general satisfaction amongst practitioners.[396] While keeping lawyers happy should not be seen as a primary objective of legislation, it is important that professionals who use any system find that the system is, in fact, workable. The researchers concluded that

'The principles and concepts introduced by the Act had a major impact in setting the agenda or framework for early discussion of financial arrangements'.[397]

In addition, the research found that: while the 1985 Act provided a common agenda for solicitors, it did not result in a uniform approach; it encouraged negotiated settlements; solicitors gave more emphasis to the principle of a clean break than the researchers felt was warranted by the Act; and that the Act had little application to couples with few resources. While too much emphasis should not be placed on a small study conducted some time ago in a restricted locality, these results are encouraging. That a statute which was intended to give clear guidance is actually doing that is to be welcomed, as is the fact that it does not appear to have resulted in undue uniformity. Encouraging negotiated settlements is a desirable result in embodying voluntarism and reducing the need to resort to acrimonious litigation. The fact that the 1985 Act has little application to divorces where the spouses have little income or property is hardly surprising, since its focus is property.

14.167 More recent research found that couples were increasingly reaching their own settlements on financial matters either informally or through the use of Minutes of Agreement or Joint Minutes of Agreement.[398] The fact that spouses are able to reach agreement without the need for litigation may, itself, be a tribute to the 1985 Act. Where the principles to be applied are clear, this provides the necessary certainty to enable negotiation to be a realistic option. Bargaining in the shadow of the law may, thus, be encouraged by clear legal provision.

14.168 Further research is underway to examine the volume of court business in the sheriff courts in Cupar, Edinburgh, Falkirk and Glasgow and, thus, representing both urban and rural areas, courts with both a high and a low volume of cases, and what are described as 'any east/west differences'. While the research is aimed at assessing the impact of the Child Support Act 1991 on court business, its results will disclose changes in the approach to financial provision on divorce. The research involves a two-stage process, with the first stage, which has been completed,[399]

---

396 Sixty per cent of the solicitors expressed the view that the 1985 Act 'represented an improvement to the legislative framework governing divorce'; a few believed that it 'had produced greater clarity generally and a frame of reference which did not exist previously'; several thought it had simply put into legislative form things that solicitors were doing anyway but that 'it was nevertheless better to have that practice in statutory form'; while 29 cited specific examples of improvements resulting from the Act and over half of them stated the benefit of having a set of guidelines – The Impact of the Family Law (Scotland) Act 1985 on Solicitors' Divorce Practice, at pp 63–64.

397 At p 1.

398 S. Morris, S. Gibson and A. Platts, Untying the Knot: Characteristics of Divorce in Scotland (CRU, 1993) and F. Wasoff, A. McGuckin and L. Edwards, Mutual Consent: Written Agreements in Family Law (CRU, 1997).

399 MVA Consultancy, Survey of Family Business in the Scottish Courts (CRU, 1997).

involving the examination of cases reaching final decree in 1992, and the second stage repeating the process for 1994.

14.169 What of the creator of the 1985 Act? The Scottish Law Commission felt little need to recommend amendment of the Act when it had the opportunity. Such amendment as it did recommend resulted largely from its, now implemented, recommendations on parental responsibilities and rights and was fairly minor. However, one recommendation, which appears to have escaped the notice of commentators to date, arguably makes a subtle but important change to the second principle of financial provision, contained in s 9(1)(b). As we saw, contributions could be made by 'looking after the family home or caring for the family'.[400] In discussing this, it was suggested that this would include caring for sick or older family members as well as caring for children. The Commission has recommended that the definition be amended to provide that a contribution should include 'looking after the family home or caring for *the children of the parties*'.[401] The effect would be that, while care of sick or older relatives might still be relevant, anyone founding on it would be required to demonstrate that the other spouse had sustained economic advantage or some other benefit, as a result. While caring for a spouse's own sick or older relatives would still be covered, caring for one's own relatives might not. On one view this change is reasonable, since, arguably, the spouse gains no benefit from a person looking after his or her own relatives. However, on any broader view of 'family' and taking account of the fact that older family members are an increasingly large group of people, this change does appear to be a retrograde step.

14.170 It is always a tribute to a legislation when its reputation is such that it attracts positive attention from abroad.[402] In 1998, the Lord Chancellor's Advisory Group on Ancillary Relief focused on the Scottish system, along with that operating in Denmark, as a possible model when it was considering reform of the law in England and Wales.

FINANCIAL PROVISION AND FORMER COHABITANTS

14.171 Essentially, the legal system treats former cohabitants as strangers, should their relationship end. The sophisticated machinery provided for financial provision on divorce by the Family Law (Scotland) Act 1985 is inapplicable to cohabitants. On occasion, they may find assistance in the concept of unjustified enrichment, implied contract or the law of trusts but these other mechanisms cannot be adapted to provide a comprehensive régime for former cohabitants.[403] The Scottish Law Commission addressed

---

400 Section 9(2).
401 Report on Family Law, para 16.23, rec 82(a), draft Bill, Sched 1, para 81.
402 Recently, a South African court was required to apply the Act in respect of a couple who were divorcing there – *Hassan* v *Hassan* 1998 (2) SA 589. The case involved a marriage of substantial duration with accrued capital and pension rights and it appears that the court had no difficulty in using the Act, although it may have awarded the periodical allowance for rather longer than a Scottish court would have done in the circumstances.
403 For a discussion of the concepts cohabitants have employed and their limited application, see chapter 11, paras 89–95.

itself to the whole question of how the legal system approaches cohabitation in its Discussion Paper on 'The Effects of Cohabitation in Private Law'.[404] Conscious of the very considerable public, as well as professional, interest in the matter, the Commission held public meetings[405] and arranged for a public opinion survey to be carried out.[406] As a result of the views which emerged both from these avenues of inquiry and from the more formal responses to the Discussion Paper, the Commission set out fairly modest proposals for reform in its 'Report on Family Law', published in 1992. The proposals await legislative action.

14.172 In considering what, if any, financial provision should be available to former cohabitants, the obvious starting point for the Commission was the system available to divorcing spouses. However, the Commission came down heavily against simply amending the provisions and applying them wholesale to former cohabitants. It felt that fair sharing of accrued assets was unwarranted since the parties may have cohabited rather than married in order to avoid this very consequence of marriage.[407] It also rejected any short- or long-term financial support for cohabitants along the lines provided for in s 9(1)(d) and (e) of the 1985 Act. The Commission's position was consistent with the views expressed by those who responded to the Discussion Paper and the public opinion survey.[408] That left only two of the principles on financial provision – those dealing with the economic burden of future childcare and the adjustment of economic advantages and disadvantages – to be considered. After the Commission published its Discussion Paper, but before publication of its Report, the Child Support Act 1991 amended the Family Law (Scotland) Act 1985 to provide that any award of aliment for a child might include an element of support for the carer.[409] The child support scheme itself allows for such an element to be built into the assessment of child support.[410] Thus, the Commission's provisional proposal,[411] which would have allowed for provision to be made in this respect, was overtaken.

14.173 In the context of financial provision on divorce, it will be remem-

---

404 Discussion Paper No 86, 1990.
405 The meetings were organised by the Faculty of Law at the University of Glasgow and the Legal Services Agency, Glasgow.
406 The public opinion survey was carried out by System Three Scotland.
407 Report on Family Law, para 16.15.
408 In the survey, respondents were shown a card which read, 'Suppose that a couple cohabited for five years and then separated. They have no children. Should the one who is better off financially be bound to pay aliment (maintenance) to the other?'. Seventy-six per cent did not favour an alimentary obligation. While the Commission acknowledged that this question does not relate directly to s 9(1)(d) or (e), it concluded, quite reasonably, that the responses indicated the general feeling about an alimentary obligation between former cohabitants. Of course, the Commission also took account of the views of those who responded to the Discussion Paper, 'almost all' of whom opposed extending these principles to former cohabitants – Report on Family Law, para 16.15.
409 Child Support Act 1991, Sched 5, para 5 adding s 4(4) to the Family Law (Scotland) Act 1985.
410 Child Support Act 1991, s 11.
411 Discussion Paper, para 5.16.

bered that the 1985 Act provides, as the second of the guiding principles, that

'Fair account should be taken of any economic advantage derived by either party from contributions by the other, and of any economic disadvantage suffered by either party in the interests of the other party or of the family'.[412]

The Commission concluded that this principle was capable of application in the context of former cohabitants[413] and this view was supported by respondents and the public opinion survey.[414] The Commission makes a number of persuasive arguments for allowing former cohabitants the benefit of this sort of economic reckoning. Perhaps none is more compelling than the observation that to do so

'would not be to impose on cohabitants a solution based on a particular view of marriage. It would merely be to give them the benefit of a principle designed to correct imbalances arising out of the circumstances of a non-commercial relationship where the parties are quite likely to make contributions and sacrifices without counting the cost or bargaining for a return'.[415]

It noted further that, as the law stands, cohabitants who marry are permitted to have economic advantages and disadvantages, sustained during the pre-marital cohabitation, taken into account. Thus, at present, former cohabitants whose marriage lasts for only a short time gain the use of the provision, whereas cohabitants who never marry do not. The Commission was conscious of the argument that those who reject marriage should accept the consequences of their action. Quite correctly, it did not find this argument persuasive. It recognised the reality that many people do not know what the law provides for and do not make special arrangements. In addition, to deny cohabitants the opportunity to have advantages and disadvantages balanced out would allow a knowledgeable and unscrupulous partner to benefit from the other partner's ignorance or generosity. No legal system can seriously claim the moral high-ground if it participates in such exploitation.

14.174 The Commission has recommended that, where cohabitation terminates other than by death, a former cohabitant should be able to apply to a court, within one year of the cohabitation terminating, for financial provision on the basis of s 9(1)(b). The court would have the power to award a capital sum and to make an interim award. It will be remembered that the Commission also recommended that the validity of a cohabitation contract should not be questioned solely because it is concluded between parties who are cohabiting or are about to do so.[416] Thus,

---

412 Section 9(1)(b).
413 Discussion Paper, para 5.15.
414 In the survey, respondents were given the scenario of a couple who have cohabited for some years and have no children. One partner has worked to build up the other's business but has not been paid. Were the couple to split up, respondents were asked whether the contributing partner should have a financial claim. Eighty-five per cent supported the person having a financial claim, with only 13% expressing opposition – Report on Family Law, para 16.19.
415 Report on Family Law, para 16.18.
416 Report on Family Law, para 16.46, rec 87 and draft Bill, clause 42.

cohabitants who are sufficiently knowledgeable, organised and practical still have the opportunity to put their cohabitation on a formal footing.

14.175 The Commission's proposals, while welcome as a step in the right direction, arguably do too little to protect heterosexual cohabitants.[417] In addition, it should be noted that the draft Family Law (Scotland) Bill, which embodies the proposals for reform, defines cohabitants as

'a man and a woman who are not married to each other but who (whether or not they represent to others that they are married to each other)[418] are living with each other as if they were husband and wife'.[419]

Thus, the proposals do nothing for same-sex couples. Whether contracts concluded by such couples would be viewed favourably by the courts is, at least, unclear.[420]

SUCCESSION

14.176 As Glendon has observed

'Inheritance law has an ever-dwindling role to play in family wealth transmission. Increasingly, family wealth is passed on through lifetime transfers; children receive their 'inheritance' in advance in the form of educational and other assistance in their formative years, and spouses provide for each other through survivorship arrangements, life insurance and so on'.[421]

None the less, succession remains a significant method by which assets are transmitted. There is something distinctly distasteful about families squabbling over the property of a deceased relative but, sadly, such behaviour is not uncommon. 'But Grandma promised me that brooch' is an all-too-familiar refrain. To some extent, the deceased can reduce the opportunity for family feuds by leaving a will, although this does not always prevent challenges to the validity of the will itself[422] and, certainly, it will not prevent those who feel they have not been given their just desserts from feeling aggrieved. All of that is part of the rich tapestry of human relations and it might be argued that there is nothing the law can do about it. What the legal system can do, however, is to make provision that is simple, clear and accords with the way most people would want their property to be distributed on death.

417 For a discussion of the overall position of cohabitants, see chapter 11, paras 96–98.
418 It will be remembered that the Commission recommended the abolition of marriage by cohabitation with habit and repute – draft Bill, clause 22.
419 Clause 33. The narrow ambit of this definition has been discussed at length earlier in this chapter and in chapter 10.
420 On the law's neglect of same-sex couples, see the discussion in chapters 10 and 11 at paras 2–4 and 10, respectively.
421 M. A. Glendon, *The Transformation of Family Law*, at pp 238–239. See also, J. H. Langbein, 'The Twentieth Century Revolution in Family Wealth Transmission' 86 Mich L R 722 (1988).
422 Newspapers have reported that the late Gene Rodenberry, the creator of *Star Trek*, left a will providing that any beneficiary who challenged any aspect of the will would lose the inheritance that he or she would have received otherwise. One of his daughters mounted a challenge, none the less, and is reputed to have lost a very large sum of money as a result.

14.177 Through the common law and legislation the legal system provides a whole package of mechanisms for dealing with a person's property after death.[423] Before we examine the provisions, a few general points are worth noting. What happens will depend on two factors. The first is whether the deceased died testate or intestate; that is, whether or not he or she left a valid will. The second is whether the deceased is survived by a widow or widower, children or other relatives. It is convenient to deal with the rights of the surviving spouse along with those of children, since the two are connected. Even where the deceased did leave a will, this will not necessarily determine what happens to all of his or her property. Certain expenses and the deceased's debts are deducted from the estate before anything further happens to it. Thereafter, it is helpful to examine the respective positions on testate and intestate succession. It should be noted that the Scottish Law Commission has recommended extensive reform of the law on succession[424] and the recommendations await legislative action.

'Unworthy heirs'

14.178 Before looking at these various points, it is worth clarifying the position as regards what are known in other jurisdictions as 'unworthy heirs'. Scots law has no general concept of 'unworthy heirs' who are barred from succession. Thus, a child who ignores an elderly parent has the same succession rights as a child who has cared for the parent for years, if the parent dies intestate. Even where the parent leaves a will leaving everything to the caring child, the neglectful child will still be able to claim legal rights. A parent has no power to disinherit a child, although there are various mechanisms which can be employed to minimise the amount available to be claimed. Equally, these mechanisms can be used to defeat a spouse's legal rights. For example, a person could convert all of his or her property into heritage, thus defeating a claim for legal rights which are only exigible from the deceased's moveable estate. This is hardly a realistic option for most people. Similarly, a person could give away all of his or her property, thus leaving nothing to be inherited. Any transfer of property must be genuine and a 'mere simulate or sham transaction will not defeat

---

423 For a discussion of termination of marriage by death, including succession, see Clive, chapter 30. On succession, generally, see: A. R. Barr, J. M. H. Biggar, A. M. C. Dalgleish and H. J. Stevens, *Drafting Wills in Scotland* (Butterworths, 1994); D. R. Macdonald, *Succession* (2nd edn, W. Green, 1994); M. C. Meston, *The Succession (Scotland) Act 1964* (4th edn, W. Green, 1993).

424 Report on Succession (Scot Law Com No 124, 1990) which includes a draft Succession (Scotland) Bill containing the Commission's proposals. The Commission's Report was preceded by three Consultative Memoranda: Intestate Succession and Legal Rights (No 69); The Making and Revocation of Wills (No 70); and Some Miscellaneous Topics in the Law of Succession (No 71). The Commission's work on the Consultative Memoranda was also informed by A. J. Manners and I. Rauta, Family Property in Scotland (HMSO, 1981) and a public opinion survey carried out in 1986 by System Three Scotland on 'Attitudes towards Succession Law in Scotland'. The results of the survey are published in Consultative Memorandum No 69, Appendix II. After the Memoranda were published, further research became available – Succession Law: A Report to the Scottish Law Commission about estates passing on death in Scotland (CRU, 1989).

legal rights'.[425] Obviously, such a dramatic option is unattractive to most people, not least because it leaves them in a financially precarious position. However, Scots law does embrace the notion that a person might forfeit his or her right to inherit in certain narrow circumstances.

Forfeiture

14.179 Where a claimant has culpably killed the deceased, the general rule that a person should not benefit from his or her crime, prevented the killer from succeeding to the deceased's property. As Clive points out, '[u]ntil 1979 there was a surprising lack of decisions on the question'.[426] In that year, a sheriff applied the principle of forfeiture to bar a widow who had been convicted of the manslaughter of her husband from succeeding to his estate.[427] Six years later, the Court of Session applied the rule to prevent a widow who had stabbed her violent husband from claiming a widow's allowance.[428] It is in cases of this kind, where the long-standing victim of domestic violence finally turns on the abuser, that the rule appears particularly harsh. For this reason, the Forfeiture Act 1982, which allows a court to modify the rule, was passed. If the claimant has been convicted of murdering the deceased, he or she is prevented from succeeding to the deceased's property and the Act is of no assistance to him or her.[429] However, if the conviction is for a lesser form of causing death, the offender may apply to the court, within three months of conviction,[430] for relief from the rule.[431] The court will grant or refuse relief having regard to the conduct of the offender and the deceased and all the circumstances of the case.[432] If it is satisfied that relief from forfeiture is warranted, it may grant such relief in respect of some, but not all, of the interests in property that the wrongdoer would have had.[433] The Scottish Law Commission has recommended amendment to the forfeiture rule and the situations in which application for relief may be made.[434] In particular, its recommendation would apply the rule to a conviction for murder, culpable homicide or manslaughter in a British court and equivalent convictions in foreign courts. Relief from forfeiture could be sought by the convicted person in all cases within six months of conviction.

Payment of debts

14.180 Even where there is a will, certain rules apply automatically before any remaining property is distributed according to the provisions of the

---

425 Clive, at para 30.068. See also the cases cited thereat.
426 Para 30.077.
427 *Smith, Petitioner* 1979 SLT (Sh Ct) 35.
428 *Burns* v *Secretary of State for Social Services* 1985 SLT 351.
429 Forfeiture Act 1982, s 5.
430 1982 Act, s 2(3).
431 1982 Act, s 1.
432 *Paterson, Petitioner* 1986 SLT 121; *Gilchrist, Petitioner* 1990 SLT 494.
433 1982 Act, s 2(4) and (5).
434 Report on Succession, paras 7.1–7.27, recs 34–38, draft Succession (Scotland) Bill, clauses 19 and 20.

will. In cases of both testacy and intestacy the following must be paid before the rest of the estate is distributed

Deathbed and funeral expenses

14.181 These include outstanding medical expenses relating to the deceased's last illness,[435] the cost of burial or cremation,[436] and, according to one rather old case,[437] a reasonable sum for the post-funeral party. The cost of mourning clothes for a widow, but not a widower, is regarded as a privileged debt and takes precedence over debts owed to other creditors of the deceased.[438] There is a dearth of modern case-law on the point[439] and the Scottish Law Commission has recommended the abolition of the right to mournings.[440]

Debts of the deceased

14.182 The deceased's debts are paid in the following order – debts secured over property, preferred debts (including some taxes and certain employees' wages), and ordinary debts. Payment of debts is automatic and, while it is common to do so, it is not necessary to provide for this in a will.

14.183 The deceased's widow and children have a right to temporary aliment from the deceased's estate.[441] The prevailing view is that such debts rank along with other ordinary debts of the deceased and cannot be met if the estate is clearly insolvent.[442] Where the estate is not clearly insolvent, the executors are entitled to pay temporary aliment to the widow and children prior to confirmation. The amount of aliment payable will depend on the circumstances of each case, but some guidance can be given by the standard of living enjoyed by the widow and children while the deceased was alive. Since temporary aliment is an ancient right, having its roots in the widow's right to heritable property, the older authorities suggest that it was tied to the times at which rents on land became payable. Obviously, such a notion is of little assistance in determining the duration of temporary aliment in a modern context and six months seems to have emerged as an acceptable period.[443] While there is no case-law to support a widower's right to temporary aliment, Clive[444] rightly points out that, since aliment itself is now a reciprocal obligation, such a claim would probably be competent where, for example, the widower had been receiving aliment

435 *Sanders* v *Hewat* (1822) 1 S 333.
436 Cremation Act 1902.
437 *Glass* v *Weir* (1821) 1 S 163.
438 *Sheddan* v *Gibson* (1802) Mor 11855.
439 For a discussion of the requirements surrounding mournings, as expressed by the institutional writers, see Clive, para 30.008.
440 Report on Succession, para 9.3, rec 54, draft Succession (Scotland) Bill, clause 25.
441 *Barlass* v *Barlass's Trustees* 1916 SC 741. For a more detailed discussion, see Clive, paras 30.010–30.017.
442 *Buchanan* v *Ferrier* (1822) 1 S 323. Contrary views were expressed in *Barlass* v *Barlass's Trustees*, above.
443 *MacCallum* v *MacLean* 1923 SLT (Sh Ct) 117.
444 At para 30.016.

from his wife prior to her death. In its Consultative Memorandum,[445] the Scottish Law Commission reserved its position on the abolition of temporary aliment and simply sought views. Consultation produced a division of opinion, with the Law Society of Scotland initially favouring retention of temporary aliment and then rejecting it in favour of payments to account.[446] In the end, the Commission concluded that '[a]bolition of this little known, and little used, right would simplify the law without causing hardship or inconvenience' and recommended abolition.[447]

Claim for continuing aliment

14.184 Where a person has a right to aliment from the deceased, he or she may claim aliment from the deceased's executor or any person enriched by succession to the deceased's estate. The result is that the widow and children have a continuing right to aliment from the executor or the deceased's successor. The origins of this provision lie in the old law of succession under which the eldest son succeeded to the heritable estate. If there was little moveable property, this meant that the younger children might be left unprovided for and it was therefore reasonable that the eldest son should take over his father's obligation to support the other children. The eldest son no longer has this primary right of succession and the rationale for the rule has thus disappeared in respect of children. It remains the case that a deceased could have converted all his assets into heritage and made a will leaving the heritage to a third party, perhaps with the intention of defeating the widow's or the children's claim to legal rights. When it was considering reform of the law on aliment, the Scottish Law Commission recommended that this right should be retained, pending full consideration of the law on succession[448] and it was retained expressly in the Family Law (Scotland) Act 1985.[449] In the light of the Commission's wide-ranging recommendations for reform of the law of succession, it has now suggested that the right to continuing aliment should be abolished.[450]

Devolution of property on intestacy

14.185 It might be argued that, since everyone aged 12 or older[451] has the right to make a will, where a person fails to do so, he or she has abdicated the right to decide what should happen to his or her property on death. However, the whole notion of relying on people to participate actively in the legal process in order to achieve what they want is flawed. The truth is that many people do not make a will for a variety of reasons. Some may be happy with the rules on intestacy although, one suspects, few people will

---

445 Some Miscellaneous Topics in the Law of Succession (Scot Law Com Cons Memo No 71), para 8.6.
446 Report on Succession, para 9.10.
447 Report on Succession, para 9.10, rec 56 and draft Bill, clause 26.
448 Report on Aliment and Financial Provision, para 2.153. The Commission made a similar recommendation in respect of widow's mournings – para 2.154.
449 Section 1(4).
450 Report on Succession, paras 9.4–9.5, rec 55 and draft Bill, clause 27.
451 Age of Legal Capacity (Scotland) Act 1991, s 2(2).

even know what they are. Others may be driven or, more accurately, not driven, by inertia. Many probably mean to make a will but do not get round to it. Perhaps the biggest single force behind intestacy is a reluctance to address the reality of one's own demise. In any event, research found that about one third of the estates examined in 1986–87 were intestate.[452] For these reasons it is important that what the law provides for in the event of intestacy should accord as closely as possible with what people would want.

14.186 Where a person dies intestate, his or her property will be distributed in the following order after the payment of deathbed and funeral expenses and debts

Prior rights

14.187 The deceased's spouse has certain prior rights to inherit the deceased's property. The surviving spouse is entitled to claim three kinds of property under his or her prior rights: a dwelling house,[453] furniture and plenishings, and a sum of money. He or she inherits the deceased's interest in the dwelling house in which the survivor was ordinarily resident at the time of death up to a value of £130,000.[454] If the surviving spouse was ordinarily resident in more than one home, he or she has six months in which to elect which house is to be subject to prior rights. If the value of the dwelling house exceeds £130,000, the spouse is entitled to £130,000 instead.[455] The surviving spouse is also entitled to the furniture and plenishings of a dwelling house in which he or she was ordinarily resident, up to a value of £22,000.[456] If the furniture and plenishings are worth more than £22,000, the surviving spouse may elect which items to take, up to that value. In addition to the house and furniture, the surviving spouse is entitled to a sum of money from the estate.[457] If the deceased left descendants, the sum is currently £35,000, otherwise it is £58,000.[458] If the

---

452 Succession Law: A Report to the Scottish Law Commission about estates passing on death in Scotland (CRU, 1989), para 3.5.

453 'Dwelling house' is not confined to the structure of the house itself and includes the garden – Succession (Scotland) Act 1964, s 8(6)(a). When we considered the 'matrimonial home', as defined by the Matrimonial Homes (Family Protection) (Scotland) Act 1981, s 22, we saw that it included caravans and houseboats. It is unclear whether such homes are included for succession purposes.

454 1964 Act, s 8. This figure was last revised by the Prior Rights of Surviving Spouse (Scotland) Order 1999, SI 1999 No 445. If the deceased died before 1 April 1999, earlier statutory instruments provide for lower limits.

455 1964 Act, s 8(1). Where the dwelling house forms only part of the subjects comprising one tenancy, the surviving spouse is entitled to only the value of the deceased's interest up to £130,000 – 1964 Act, s 8(2)(a). Similarly, where the dwelling house was used by the deceased for carrying on a trade, profession, or occupation, and the value of the estate would be substantially diminished if the house were disposed of separately, the surviving spouse may claim only the value of the deceased's interest up to the maximum of £130,000.

456 1964 Act, s 8(3). Again, this sum was last revised in the Prior Rights of Surviving Spouse (Scotland) Order 1999, SI 1999 No 445. It does not matter that the deceased had no interest in the dwelling house where the furniture and plenishings are located.

457 1964 Act, s 9.

458 Again, these figures were set by the Prior Rights of Surviving Spouse (Scotland) Order 1999, SI 1999 No 445.

estate is worth less than the relevant sum, the surviving spouse is entitled to the whole of the estate. Where the estate is worth more, the spouse's entitlement is paid out of the heritable and moveable parts of the estate in proportion to the amounts of these parts,[459] since this will have an impact on the legal rights of other claimants. For completeness, it is worth noting that a surviving cohabitant has no prior rights.[460]

Legal rights

14.188 Legal rights give the surviving spouse and children certain automatic rights in the deceased's estate[461] and can be claimed only after the prior rights have been satisfied. Prior to the Succession (Scotland) Act 1964 ('the 1964 Act'), different legal rights applied to both moveable and heritable property. Now legal rights are confined to moveable property (the rights formerly applying to heritable property having been abolished) and comprise the right of the surviving spouse, or relict, to *ius relictae* (if a widow) or *ius relicti* (if a widower) and the right of children to legitim or 'bairn's part'. Legal rights cannot be defeated by any testamentary disposition by the deceased and are the source of the view that a person cannot disinherit his or her spouse or children. Since they apply only to the moveable estate, this is not necessarily true. While alive, a person could convert all of his or her property into heritage and leave that heritage to a third party, thus ensuring that there is no moveable property out of which legal rights could be claimed. It should be noted that it is only the deceased's children who are relevant in the calculation of legal rights. The notion of 'accepting' a child into the family, found in the law on aliment, has no application here. In addition, where any child of the deceased has died leaving issue, the grandchildren step into the deceased parent's place for succession purposes.[462]

14.189 The surviving spouse is entitled to one half of the remaining moveable estate if there are no surviving children, or one third if there are.[463] If there is a surviving spouse, the children are entitled to one third of the remaining moveable estate to be divided between them. If there is no surviving spouse, the children's portion becomes one half. When it is remembered that prior rights take precedence over legal rights, it becomes apparent that the whole of a modest estate left by a person with a surviving spouse may be consumed before legal rights become relevant.

Division of the free estate

14.190 The remainder of the estate, known as the 'free estate' goes to the

---

459 1964 Act, s 9(3).
460 The position of cohabitants and the Scottish Law Commission's recommendations for reform are discussed in paras 14.197–14.200, below.
461 Strictly speaking, legal rights are not succession rights and have been described as 'in the nature of debts which attach to the free succession after the claims of onerous creditors have been satisfied' – *Naismith* v *Boyes* (1899) 1 F (HL) 79 at p 81. Of course, that case predates the introduction of prior rights by the 1964 Act and these must now be taken into account.
462 1964 Act, s 11.
463 1964 Act, s 10.

first group of the deceased's relatives on the following list: widow or widower; children; brothers and sisters; parents and siblings (each share half between them); parents; aunts and uncles and grandparents.[464]

Devolution of property if there is a will

14.191 As we have seen, legal rights cannot be defeated regardless of what the deceased has provided for in his or her will. Thus, the relict and any children will be entitled to claim legal rights from the deceased's moveable estate. If the deceased has failed to provide for any one of them, there is no problem. However, each individual provided for in the will must choose between the legacy and legal rights.[465] A person cannot claim both. Once this matter has been resolved, the deceased's property is distributed according to the will.

14.192 It will be remembered that neither marriage nor divorce has the effect of revoking a prior will. Where property has been left to a 'husband' or 'wife', it is a matter of construction whether that refers to the spouse at the time the will was made or the spouse at the time of death.[466] Similarly, if the spouse is described as a 'husband' or 'wife' and actually named, it is a matter of construction whether the property was left to the named person in his or her capacity as a spouse or as an individual.[467] *De facto* separation has no effect on succession and judicial separation is only relevant to a wife's (but not a husband's) property acquired after the granting of the decree of separation and only if she dies intestate. Clearly, individuals should be advised to make a new will each time they marry, separate or divorce. The Scottish Law Commission has recommended that divorce should have the effect of revoking a will insofar as it provides for a former spouse, but not in any other respect, and has recommended repeal of the statutory provisions on separation.[468]

Power of the court to order financial provision from the deceased's estate

14.193 Unlike the position in England and Wales, the Scottish courts have no jurisdiction to make provision for family members and other dependents where the deceased failed to do so. However, where the deceased left children, they may have a right to claim aliment from the deceased's executor or any person enriched by succession to the deceased's estate.[469]

Reform

14.194 Conscious of a number of problems with the law on succession, the Scottish Law Commission undertook a detailed review of the law and has

---

464 1964 Act, s 2(1).
465 1964 Act, s 13.
466 *Burns's Trustees, Petitioners* 1961 SC 17.
467 *Pirie's Trustees* v *Pirie* 1962 SC 43; *Henderson's Judicial Factor* v *Henderson* 1930 SLT 743.
468 Report on Succession (Scot Law Com No 124, 1990), paras 4.45 and 7.33.
469 Family Law (Scotland) Act 1985, s 1(4).

recommended substantial reform in respect of both testate and intestate succession. As we have seen, it recommended the abolition of the right to mournings and temporary and continuing aliment.[470] Taken in isolation, these proposals, and particularly those on continuing aliment, might seem harsh. As ever, the Commission's proposals for reform must be read as a whole since they provide for a new scheme which differs radically from the existing law. In addition, it should be remembered that the sums of money recommended by the Commission were set in 1990, prior to the increase in the appropriate values introduced by the most recent statutory instrument in 1993. Thus, figures recommended by the Commission should be read as notional, since they are likely to be increased substantially in any legislation. The brief outline of the Commission's proposals provided below cannot hope to do justice to the subtleties of the scheme and a thorough reading of the 'Report on Succession' is recommended.[471]

14.195 Essentially, the Commission recommends the abolition of prior rights, the replacing of legal rights with a new system of legal shares and largely abolishes the distinction between moveable and heritable property. How would the new system work? Turning first to cases of intestacy, the Commission has recommended that, instead of prior and legal rights, the surviving spouse would be entitled to the first £100,000 of the deceased's estate and it would not matter whether the estate consisted of moveable or heritable property.[472] He or she could choose to take the house and furniture in satisfaction, or partial satisfaction, of the legal share. If there was property remaining thereafter, the spouse would receive all of it if there were no surviving issue[473] of the deceased and half of the remainder if there were, with the balance being divided among the children.[474] If there was no surviving spouse, the children would inherit the whole estate.[475]

14.196 The new concept of legal shares would apply only to protect family members against disinheritance. Any surviving spouse or child who was dissatisfied with what he or she had been left under the deceased's will would have to apply for his or her legal share within two years of the deceased's death.[476] A surviving spouse would be entitled to claim 30% of the first £200,000 of the deceased's estate and 10% of the remainder.[477] What children could claim would depend on whether there was a surviving spouse. If there was, the first £100,000 of the estate would already have been set aside and they could claim 15% of the next £200,000 of the

---

470 Report on Succession, paras 9.3–9.10, recs 54–56 and draft Bill, clauses 25–27.
471 A more detailed discussion can be found in Meston, n 423 above, at pp 123–130.
472 Draft Succession (Scotland) Bill, clause 1(2)(a).
473 There is provision for representation of the deceased's predeceasing children by their own children in the same terms as are provided currently – clause 2. Arguably, this reproduces a defect in the current law which begins representation only at the nearest class of surviving relative. See Meston, n 423 above, at p 127.
474 Draft Succession (Scotland) Bill, clause 1(2)(b).
475 Draft Succession (Scotland) Bill, clause 1(3)(a). In the absence of a spouse and children, other relatives succeed, broadly along the lines of the present rules for division of the remaining estate on intestacy – clause 1(3).
476 Draft Succession (Scotland) Bill, clauses 5 and 6.
477 Draft Succession (Scotland) Bill, clauses 5 and 7(1).

deceased's estate and 5% of the remainder.[478] If there was no surviving spouse, the proportions would increase to 30% and 10% respectively.[479] It should be noted that this simply produces a pot from which children can claim. If there are a number of children, each child only gets a proportion of the pot. Clive expresses the view that, '[t]he scheme would be conceptually, and practically, very much simpler than the present law'.[480]

SUCCESSION AND FORMER COHABITANTS

14.197   At present, cohabitants have no right to succeed to a partner's estate on intestacy. Of course, it is open to either partner to leave a will[481] but relying wholly on individuals to do so amounts to dereliction of duty by the legal system. That the law's failure to accommodate cohabitants produces injustice can be demonstrated by any number of examples. Here, one will suffice. Suppose a couple have been living together for 20 years. The man was married and has three grown-up children, but he has had no contact with them since he divorced their mother many years ago. He owns the house in which he and his cohabitant live and the relationship has been organised on the traditional homemaker-breadwinner model, with the man working, earning and amassing savings and the woman running the home and being financially dependent on her partner. If he dies intestate, his children will inherit his property and his former cohabitant will be entitled to absolutely nothing from his estate. It is doubtful that he would have wanted such an outcome. Of course, he should have made a will. However, that will be of little comfort to his former cohabitant as she is forced to move out of the home and rely on state benefits.

14.198   One problem here is the great range of cases to be considered. The Scottish Law Commission was conscious of this diversity when it addressed the issue of succession on intestacy as part of its more general consideration of the position of cohabitants. In the Discussion Paper, 'The Effects of Cohabitation in Private Law', it examined a whole range of cohabitation relationships, noting distinguishing features. Such features as the duration of the cohabitation; whether there were children of that relationship; whether the deceased left a surviving spouse; whether the deceased was survived by other children or relatives, had some relevance to what, if anything, consultees felt the surviving cohabitant should receive. Unlike the responses it received in respect of financial provision on the ending of cohabitation, the responses here were inconclusive. This is hardly surprising, given the diversity to be accommodated.

14.199   It was this very diversity that persuaded the Commission to

478 Draft Succession (Scotland) Bill, clauses 5 and 7(2).
479 Draft Succession (Scotland) Bill, clause 7(2). The first £100,000 would not be discounted in this case.
480 At para 30.073.
481 The Commission recommended that each cohabitant's insurable interest in the life of the other should be given statutory recognition – Report on Family Law, para 16.41, rec 85(a) and draft Bill, clause 40. The Commission was told by the Association of British Insurers that several insurance companies already regard cohabitants as having such an interest.

recommend provision for the surviving cohabitant to apply to the court for a discretionary award from the deceased's estate.[482] In considering such an application the court is directed to have regard to all the circumstances of the case, including: the length of the cohabitation; the existence of any children resulting from the relationship of the applicant with the deceased; the size and nature of the net estate of the deceased; any benefit received, or to be received, by the applicant from a third party on, or as a result of the deceased's death; the nature and extent of any other rights against, or claims on, the deceased's net estate; the nature and extent of any contribution made by the applicant from which the deceased has derived economic advantage; the nature and extent of any economic disadvantage suffered by the applicant in the interests of the deceased or of their children.[483] The court would be able to make an order for a capital payment and to transfer property.[484]

14.200 One aspect of the Commission's proposal does seem rather harsh on the surviving cohabitant. A claim must be made within six months of the death of the deceased.[485] The court would be permitted to entertain claims outwith this time-limit 'on cause shown'. Given that the death of one's partner will be a traumatic experience for most people, it would be understandable if the bereaved was not operating at maximum efficiency in the months immediately after the partner's death. Of course, the Commission was conscious of the need to avoid delay in the winding up of estates.[486] It is to be hoped that the courts exercise their power generously in hearing claims after the six-month period has elapsed.

---

482 Draft Bill, clauses 37 and 38, discussed in the Report on Family Law, paras 16.24–16.37 and rec 83. In an earlier report, the Commission had rejected the idea of replacing the system of fixed legal rights for spouses and children and of introducing discretionary awards – Report on Succession, paras 3.3–3.12, recs 5 and 6 – (Scot Law Com No 124, 1990).
483 Draft Bill, clause 37(1).
484 Draft Bill, clause 38(1).
485 Draft Bill, clause 37(3).
486 The draft Bill, clause 37(4) exempts the executor from liability for having distributed the estate after six months have elapsed. This is without prejudice to any power to recover any part of the estate which has been distributed.

CHAPTER 15

OLDER MEMBERS OF THE FAMILY

15.1 People are living longer than ever before. Whereas the average male born in 1900 had a life expectancy of 44.7 years, his counterpart born in 1997 can expect to live to be 72.6 years old.[1] The corresponding figures for women are 47.4 years and 78 years respectively, and it is a consistent feature of the statistics that women have a longer life expectancy than men.[2] Not only does this increased life expectancy have significant consequences for the older members of the community themselves, it may have implications for other family members and for professionals dealing with older clients and patients. One result of the increase in life expectancy, when combined with falling birth rates, is that older people will make up an increasing percentage of the population.[3] This has enormous social and economic consequences for society as a whole and, since the needs of at least some older people will have to be met by a smaller proportion of the working population, has led to older people being lumped together and perceived as a burden.[4] The good news here is that the increased awareness of older members of the community has resulted in older people organising themselves as a lobbying force; what is known in the USA as 'gray power'.[5]

1 Registrar General for Scotland, Annual Report 1997 (General Register Office for Scotland, 1998), Table 5.4.
2 This, in turn, means that women make up a higher proportion of older people. In 1997, 58% of the population aged 60 or over were women, with the proportion of women rising to 66% in the over-75 age group – Annual Report 1997, Table 2.1. The comparative longevity of women is a world-wide phenomenon. For a fascinating examination of the comparative lifestyles and positions of older women in Europe, see Age becomes her: Older Women in the European Union, The Women of Europe Dossier No 45 (European Commission, 1997). See also, L. Aitken and G. Griffin, *Gender Issues in Elder Abuse* (Sage, 1996), chapter 1, 'Thinking in Numbers – The Feminization of Old Age and its Conditions'.
3 People over 60 years old currently make up some 20% of the population of Scotland. Projections, prepared by the Government Actuary in consultation with the Registrar General for Scotland, suggest that, by the year 2021, the number of people over pensionable age will increase by 7%, with the number of people over 75 increasing by 27%. See Annual Report 1997, p 16 and Table 2.1.
4 As early as 1979, Kalish identified different kinds of negative thinking surrounding older people – R. A. Kalish, 'The New Ageism and the Failure Models: A Polemic' (1979) 19 The Gerontologist 398. For a more recent discussion, see B. Penhale, 'The Abuse of Elderly People: Considerations for Practice' (1993) 23 British Journal of Social Work 95.
5 The obvious analogy here was taken a step further when a pressure group for older people adopted the name 'Gray Panthers'. See for example, *Schweiker v Gray Panthers*

15.2 Terminology in this area is not without its problems. Clearly, neither 'the aged' nor 'the elderly' is acceptable, since each carries with it the same notion of a homogeneous mass, as does the now-defunct term 'the disabled'.[6] On that basis, it might be argued that any group-term denies individuality and, while that may be true, such terms are convenient for the purpose of discussion, provided we remember that we are dealing with individual people. 'People' would seem to be the key here and the term used in this chapter is 'older people'. The term 'elders' has a certain attraction, connoting, as it does, members of a group who, by virtue of their age, hold a revered status. It was rejected for two reasons.[7] First, 'elderly' has come to have a technical meaning in some circles, denoting people over the age of 80. Second, useful debate is not stimulated by sentimental notions which, on closer examination, are often not observed in practice.

15.3 What is absolutely clear is that 'older family members' and 'older people' are classifications which encompass very diverse groups of people. It would be a grave mistake to assume that old age necessarily brings with it incapacity. Many older people are both physically and mentally able to care for themselves, albeit, sometimes with some modest assistance with such matters as domestic chores. However, for a significant number of older people, the impairment of physical or mental capacity can be more marked. Where the incapacity is solely physical, this raises questions of how and where the older person can be given assistance with day-to-day care. Can he or she remain at home and be cared for by a spouse or partner, who will often be an older person too? What further support can be provided in the home? Should the older person go to live with relatives? What assistance will they require? Should residential or nursing care be considered? Who will pay for such services as are provided? Who really makes the decisions about the older person's future care? Where mental incapacity is involved, the issue becomes one of how the legal system can protect the older person from his or her own actions and those of others, at the same time as ensuring the maximum autonomy and dignity for the individual concerned. Achieving this balance may be particularly difficult where the older person is completely lucid at some times, but not at others, especially given the conservative attitude of the medical profession to issues of capacity. The existence of abuse of older people, both in the home and in institutional care, is now well recognised. Age Concern Scotland has a number of user-friendly fact sheets giving information on a whole range of issues affecting older people, options they might consider and details of what assistance is available.[8]

---

453 US 34 (1981), which involved a constitutional challenge to legislation requiring a far-from-affluent spouse to pay for the medical care of the other spouse who was in residential care.

6 Cf. The Royal Commission on Long-term Care of the Elderly, established in December 1997, discussed at para 15.25.

7 Since abuse of older people has come to be known, almost universally, as 'elder abuse' that term will be used here.

8 The Fact Sheets are available at a nominal charge and the addresses for Age Concern Scotland and other organisations mentioned in this chapter can be found in the Appendix.

15.4 The greatest challenge to the legal system, and other relevant agencies, is the great diversity of circumstances which must be accommodated if we are to provide for the needs and resources, abilities and disabilities, of every individual older person. While a full discussion of all the issues which arise in this context merits a book in itself, and some of the many books available are mentioned in this chapter,[9] a number of the issues are highlighted and discussed briefly below. The intention is to provide a starting point for anyone who is interested in what has, hitherto, rarely been included in discussions of family law.[10]

DAY-TO-DAY LIVING ARRANGEMENTS

The options

15.5 Many older people have a strong preference to remain in their own homes. The advantages of privacy and autonomy cannot be underestimated and assistance may be available to retain this option for the older person who needs some extra help. Fundamental to the régime of community care currently operating is the idea that people should be given such assistance as they need to enable them to live in their own homes rather than in institutional care. The government White Paper, 'Caring for People: Community Care in the Next Decade and Beyond',[11] states this as one of the primary objectives of community care and the National Health Service and Community Care Act 1990 sought to implement that policy.[12] For those with adequate resources, private arrangements can be made for cleaning, laundry and shopping. In addition, every local authority is obliged to provide domiciliary services[13] to households where a person in need is

9   In addition to the works cited on specific issues, see: G. J. Agich, *Autonomy and Long-term Care* (OUP, 1993); S. Arber and M. Evandrou, *Ageing, Independence and the Life Course* (Jessica Kingsley, 1993); K. Blakemore and M. Boneham, *Age, Race and Ethnicity: as a Comparative Approach* (OUP, 1994); R. Hugman, *Ageing and the care of older people in Europe* (Macmillans, 1994); C. Phillipson and A. Walker, *Ageing and Social Policy: a critical assessment* (Gower, 1986); A. Walker and L. Warren, *Changing Services for Older People* (OUP, 1996); N. Wells and C. Freer, *The ageing population: burden or challenge?* (Macmillans, 1988).
10 A notable exception here is the Sixth World Conference of the International Society on Family Law, held in Tokyo in April 1988. A selection of the papers given at that conference, looking at a variety of jurisdictions and covering the whole range of issues affecting older people, their families and society can be found in J. M. Eekelaar and D. Pearl (eds), *An Aging World: Dilemmas and Challenges for Law and Social Policy* (Clarendon Press, 1989).
11 Cm 849, 1989, para 1.11. The White Paper was a response to the Community Care: Agenda for Action (the Griffiths Report) 1988.
12 The 1990 Act made substantial amendments to the Social Work (Scotland) Act 1968, in respect of community care and related matters, essentially transferring responsibility for long-term care of older people from the National Health Service to local authorities. References in this chapter are to the 1968 Act, as amended, unless otherwise stated.
13 Domiciliary services are defined as those services which are provided in the home which, in the opinion of the local authority, are necessary to enable a person to lead as independent a existence as is practicable – Social Work (Scotland) Act 1968 Act, s 94, as amended by the National Health Service and Community Care Act 1990, Sched 9, para 10(14)(a). The 1990 Act amended the 1968 Act substantially.

living.[14] Who is 'a person in need' and how those needs are assessed is discussed below.[15] Briefly, however, what this means is that an older person who could stay at home, provided that he or she had a home help or a laundry service, for example, can request the local authority to carry out an assessment of the situation. If that assessment confirms the need, the local authority is obliged to provide the relevant services although the question of the financial burden may be a different matter. The Social Work (Scotland) Act 1968 ('the 1968 Act') requires the local authority 'to provide' (or make provision for) these services. An ordinary reading of the relevant section might lead to the conclusion that such provision should be free of charge, but the 1968 Act does not actually say that and, in fact, local authorities often charge for the services, depending on the individual's financial resources. In addition to assistance with domestic chores, meals can be delivered. Modifications can be made to the home by, for example, raising the height of power points for ease of access or installing hand-rails, and aids, like sticks or bath seats, can be provided.

15.6 Where the older person feels that he or she would like the security of knowing that help is always on hand, but wishes to sacrifice as little privacy and autonomy as possible, sheltered housing is an option worth considering. Typically, sheltered housing provides self-contained flats for one or two[16] occupants, where the resident can continue to take care of himself or herself, with or without the assistance of a home-help. The block of flats will usually have a full-time, resident, manager-caretaker and each room in every flat will have a bell-pull to summon assistance from the manager-caretaker. Each block of flats will often have additional communal facilities, such as a residents' lounge or a laundry room, which residents can choose to use or not. Again, this kind of accommodation is available in the private sector to purchase or lease and through the local authority. When considering private provision, it is worth remembering that the initial outlay is only part of the cost and there will often be fairly high on-going charges. Since this kind of accommodation is intended for use by older people only, there are restrictions on the age of residents, which have implications for the resale of such a flat.[17] Local authorities also have a certain amount of sheltered housing as part of the housing stock but this is subject to the usual problems of availability, which varies from area to area. An older person living in sheltered accommodation may qualify as a person in need and, once his or her needs have been assessed, may be entitled to receive domiciliary services from the local authority.[18]

15.7 Another option is for the older person to go to live with relatives. For some families, multi-generational living provides benefits for all involved. The older person has the security of knowing that help is always

---

14 Section 14.
15 See paras 15.10–15.14.
16 Sheltered housing may be large enough to accommodate two people and such accommodation would be suitable for a married (or unmarried) couple, two siblings or two friends.
17 The restrictions are laid down as burdens on the title to the property.
18 Section 14.

on hand and can contribute to family life by providing much needed assistance with childcare. Grandchildren have another adult on hand to talk to and learn from. However, unless everyone involved shows an almost saintly level of consideration and tolerance, tensions are inevitable. It is essential to explore whether a given family can accommodate these tensions before embarking on such an arrangement. In addition, it is worth remembering that the individual family members may change. Toddlers, who go to bed early, may become music-loving, teenage, night-owls. Homemakers may become career-people. Active older people may become infirm or vulnerable. Again, where an older person is living with relatives, the local authority can be required to assess the person's needs and to provide domiciliary services.[19]

15.8 Yet another option, and one which many older people find unattractive, at least initially, is residential care.[20] At the outset, simple residential care should be distinguished from arrangements where nursing, medical or psychiatric care is provided. The primary reason for distinguishing these two distinct types of care is so that an individual older person's situation can be accommodated fully. If a person requires nursing care, his or her needs would not be adequately met by living in residential accommodation where the staff are not appropriately trained. Equally, were a healthy, competent older person to find himself or herself living in accommodation where many of the other residents were receiving psychogeriatric care, it could be argued that the accommodation was not suited to the needs of that individual and, indeed, that specialist resources were not being used as well as they might be. A second reason for distinguishing the types of care relates to the local authority's responsibilities and powers. Local authorities are obliged to provide residential accommodation to persons in need who require assistance[21] and needing care and assistance by reason of age or infirmity is specifically mentioned in the 1968 Act.[22] However, while a local authority may arrange accommodation with nursing care, it must make the arrangement with a nursing home or certain other agencies, rather than provide that accommodation itself.[23] A third distinction between the types of accommodation available relates to registration requirements where residential accommodation is being provided by the private sector, as is increasingly the case. Residential homes must register with the local authority which has extensive powers of inspection and supervision. Nursing homes must be registered with the health board. Where both types of accommodation are being provided in one establishment, it must be registered with both the local authority and the health board. In 1992 the Social Work Services Inspectorate was established and it

---

19 Section 14.
20 That such arrangements may seem unattractive is hardly surprising when one considers that residential facilities are often described as 'old folks homes' or even 'granny farms'.
21 Section 12(1). The local authority may make cash payments to secure suitable accommodation in certain circumstances – s 12(3) and (4). Section 12 provides a fairly spectacular example of convoluted, barely-comprehensible, drafting.
22 Section 94(1).
23 Section 13A.

has the power to inspect residential homes run by the local authority as well as those run by voluntary or private organisations.

15.9 When older people and their families are considering residential care, they often do so with a degree of reluctance, fear and, as far as family members are concerned, guilt. 'Putting granny in a home' is a phrase resonant with the worst Dickensian notions of institutionalisation. A catalogue of recent cases where residents have been abused or neglected in such care has done nothing to alleviate the problem.[24] Undoubtedly residential care can present risks of exploitation and it is only through rigorous regulation and monitoring that the risk can be minimised. This, in turn, requires adequate funding for not only care itself, but also for the monitoring bodies.

Assessment of needs[25]

15.10 Mention has been made of 'persons in need' and 'assessment of needs'. The Social Work (Scotland) Act 1968 ('the 1968 Act'), as amended, includes within the definition of persons in need, persons who 'are in need of care and attention arising out of infirmity, youth or age'.[26] The local authority is obliged to carry out an assessment of the needs of anyone who appears to be in need of community care services[27] and to provide such services as are required, subject to the financial constraints discussed below.[28] The 1968 Act makes an effort to ensure the co-ordination of service provision between different agencies, such co-ordination being essential if individuals are not to 'slip through the net'. Before the local authority reaches a decision on the provision of nursing care to a person, it must consult a medical practitioner.[29] If it appears that the person being assessed is a disabled person, the local authority must consider the person's specific needs in that respect.[30] If, in the course of carrying out an assessment, it appears to the local authority that the person may require services which are supplied by the health board or another local authority, it is required to inform the board or the authority.[31]

---

24 In August 1997, *The Sunday Times* launched the 'Who Cares?' campaign, to explore the adequacy of residential and nursing care currently being provided for older people in the UK. The newspaper received a deluge of correspondence alleging inadequate, neglectful and abusive practices across the country. It also received correspondence from owners of homes and staff who work in them who felt they were doing a professional and compassionate job.

25 For a more detailed discussion of the law and practice here, see J. Fabb and T. G. Guthrie, *Social Work Law in Scotland* (2nd edn, Butterworths, 1997), chapter 6. For a detailed discussion of the practical issues in carrying out an assessment of needs, see B. Hughes, *Older People and Community Care* (OUP, 1995), chapter 5.

26 Section 94(1).

27 Section 12A. Every local authority must publish community care services plans, detailing the arrangements for providing community care services in its area, and must keep these plans under review – s 5A.

28 Section 12A(1).

29 Section 12A(2).

30 Section 12A(4). Such needs are governed by the Disabled Persons (Services, Consultation and Representation) Act 1986.

31 Section 12A(3).

15.11 The relevance of local authority resources to the provision of services was a matter of some debate for a time but appears to have been resolved, albeit in a wholly unsatisfactory way. The question is whether, in the course of assessing an individual's needs, the local authority can take its own budgetary limitations into account. In *R v Gloucestershire County Council, ex parte Barry*, the Court of Appeal[32] took the logically preferable view that such considerations were not relevant either in assessing an individual's needs, nor in deciding whether to provide services to meet those needs. The House of Lords[33] overturned that decision. Thus, it appeared, local authority resources formed part of the needs assessment and the criteria used in determining eligibility for services.[34]

15.12 However, that decision must be read in the light of the later unanimous decision of the House of Lords in *R v East Sussex County Council, ex parte Tandy*,[35] which concerned the provision of home tuition for a pupil suffering from myalgic encephalomyelitis (ME). The local authority had a statutory duty to provide suitable education for pupils who, because of illness, were prevented from attending school. What is 'suitable education' is to be assessed by reference to the individual child. When the local authority cut Ms Tandy's home tuition from five hours per week to three, her mother challenged the decision. Concluding that the local authority was neither entitled to take its own budgetary constraints into account in assessing her need, nor in meeting it, Lord Browne-Wilkinson made the following observation

'To permit the local authority to avoid performing a statutory duty on the ground that it preferred to spend its money in other ways was to downgrade a statutory duty to a statutory power'.

He went on to note that, when it is a matter of the local authority deciding how to use its scarce resources in the exercise of its statutory powers, the matter becomes much more difficult to challenge. Thus, the distinction between statutory duties and statutory powers is an important one. Applying this reasoning to the case of assessment of needs, the local authority has a statutory duty to assess the needs of an individual. Thereafter, it is required to decide whether that person's needs call for the provision of services. The decision on services is to be made with reference to the individual who has been assessed, just as the decision on educational provision must be individual-specific. In reaching its decision, the local authority is required, in certain circumstances, to notify or liaise with a whole range of other individuals and agencies, but nowhere are its own resources mentioned in the 1968 Act.

15.13 A very loud and long note of caution should be inserted before drawing the happy conclusion that *R v Gloucestershire County Council, ex*

---

32 [1996] 4 All ER 421.
33 [1997] 2 All ER 1.
34 See T. G. Guthrie, 'The Significance of Resources in Community Care Assessments' (1997) 2 SLPQ 149 and T. G. Guthrie, 'The House of Lords and Community Care Assessments' (1997) 2 SLPQ 225.
35 [1998] 2 All ER 769.

parte Barry has effectively been overruled. In *Tandy*, Lord Browne-Wilkinson made express reference to *Barry* and, while he acknowledged that both cases concerned 'the extent to which a local authority can take account of its own lack of resources in carrying out its statutory duty',[36] he went on to observe that 'that is the limit of the similarity between the two cases'. The learned Law Lord felt able to distinguish the nature of the decisions being taken under the respective pieces of legislation, although it might be argued that the distinction is so fine that it is barely discernable. It may be that this point will be the subject of further litigation although, given the uncertainty which the recipients (or non-recipients) of local authority services must suffer in the meantime and the time and cost involved in such litigation, it would be preferable if Parliament were to resolve the matter.[37]

15.14 Once a person's needs have been assessed, a care plan will be drawn up detailing the services to be provided to that individual and, thereafter, services cannot be withdrawn without a further assessment being carried out.[38]

Paying for accommodation

15.15 Who will pay for the care of an older person and any additional services required is a matter of great concern to older people themselves and their families. Aside from the case of wealthy older people, who can make provision for themselves, the question of meeting the cost of present and future care looms large in decision-making and is one with which, in an ideal society, the older members of our community would not be troubled. Back in the real world, it is worth remembering that children have not been obliged to aliment to their parents since 1985,[39] nor do more remote descendants owe such an obligation. Thus, there is no binding requirement on a child to pay for a parent's residential care. Of course, many children with sufficient assets are only too happy to provide the best possible care. Where an older person has no resources with which to provide for his or her own care, and no one else is able or willing to do so, it falls to the state, through the local authority and other agencies, to make adequate pro-

---

36 At p 776.
37 The government's commitment to the Better Government for Older People Programme which aims 'to improve public services for older people by better meeting their needs, listening to their views, and encouraging and recognising their contribution' suggests that legislation ought to find support from that quarter. See Cabinet Office press release 'Giving Older People a Voice' on http://www.coi.gov.uk/coi/depts/GCO/coi2350e.ok
38 *R v Gloucestershire County Council, ex parte RADAR*, 21 December 1995, unreported, but discussed in Fabb and Guthrie, above, at pp 194–195.
39 The Family Law (Scotland) Act 1985, s 1, limits the obligation of aliment to spouses, parents, people who have accepted a child into the family, and person's enriched by succession to property belonging formerly to a person owing such an obligation. Previously, a child who had superfluous assets was obliged to aliment a parent, where the parent was in need and, failing the child, more remote descendants became liable: Stair, *Institutions*, I, 5, 8–9; *McCulloch* v *McCulloch* (1778) 5 Brown's Supp 376; *Muirhead* v *Muirhead* (1849) 12 D 356; *Thom* v *Mackenzie* (1864) 3 M 177. See, *Report on Aliment and Financial Provision* (Scot Law Com No 67, 1981), paras 2.9–2.11, for a discussion of the thinking behind the abolition of the child's obligation to aliment a parent.

vision. Between wealthy older people, who can make their own arrangements, and the truly indigent, lie the majority of older people who have some assets, but fear that these may be insufficient to meet their needs. Essentially, a person is required to pay for his or her own care, sometimes by realising assets such as the home,[40] until the individual's capital falls below a specified statutory level. Thereafter, the local authority is responsible for paying, unless the care resident is married. Since husbands and wives are obliged to aliment each other,[41] a spouse may be obliged to contribute to the costs of his or her partner's care.

15.16 Sometimes, the only significant asset an older person has is the family home and this may be co-owned and occupied along with a partner. In such circumstances, sale of the home is not required.[42] We have not yet reached the point where healthy older people are thrown out of their homes to pay for the care of a partner. None the less, many older people would prefer that their home should pass to their children or other family members, rather than be sold to provide for their care. Various strategies can and, arguably, should, be considered by anyone advising such a person.[43] It should be made clear that we are not considering anything fraudulent here, but rather, the management of property in a way which benefits the client most and may achieve what the client wants within the bounds of the law. There can sometimes be difficult professional questions for solicitors in these cases. Very often what is desired is that the property should be transferred from the older person to his or her children, but that the older person should remain entitled to possession of the property. Adequately protecting all parties' interests in such a transaction may be difficult. The most obvious solution would be for the older person to convey the property to himself or herself in liferent and the children in fee. Another suggestion would be to convey the property to a family trust, again reserving a liferent. The difficulty with such complicated suggestions is that the local authority may not be prepared to treat such a restricted disposal as a proper disposal and may challenge the disposal as a device. Very often the family solicitor acts for all parties in the transaction, even where there is a simple transfer without reserving the right to occupy. In such circumstances, the practitioner must ensure that all parties understand the nature of the transaction and, in particular, that the older person understands that an absolute transfer means exactly what it says. There have been cases where the transferee child has been made bankrupt and

---

40 Should the older person not wish to sell the home, the local authority is empowered to create a charge on the property which it can use to recoup its costs when the property is sold – Health and Social Services and Social Security Adjudications Act 1983, s 23.
41 Family Law (Scotland) Act 1985, s 1(1)(a) and (b).
42 Health and Social Services and Social Security Adjudications Act 1983. This provision protects the occupancy of a spouse, an unmarried partner, a relative over the age of 60 or a relative who is incapacitated. In addition, the local authority has a discretion to disregard the home if it is occupied by another person who does not fall into one of these categories and this might include, for example, a friend who gave up his or her own home to look after the care resident.
43 See J. Heritage (pen name), *Residential Care Fees: Don't Let Them Grab The House* (Spinning Acorn, 1997).

the permanent trustee has forced the older person to vacate his or her home so that the trustee can sell what has become, in effect, simply an asset of the bankrupt child. A solicitor should record the transaction in writing for all parties and, where he or she acts for all parties, should ensure compliance with the conflict of interest rules.[44]

15.17 In assessing an individual's eligibility to have the cost of accommodation met, state agencies are aware that claimants may try and arrange their affairs in such a way as to maximise entitlement. For this reason, legislation and regulations allow the local authority to look behind the transfer of property under two separate provisions. The first is the Health and Social Services and Social Security Adjudications Act 1983 (HASSASSA) and it is concerned only with property transferred within the six months prior to the older person moving into residential care. Where a person has deprived himself or herself of property with the intention of reducing or avoiding liability to pay for accommodation, the local authority may claim sums owing for the cost of accommodation from the person who received the property.[45] However, the local authority can only recover sums up to the value of the property transferred and only where no, or inadequate, consideration was given for the property.

15.18 The second provision is contained in regulation 25 of the National Assistance (Assessment of Resources) Regulations 1992[46] and deals with the way a person's capital is calculated in order to assess what, if anything, he or she must pay towards residential accommodation. Where a person has deliberately deprived himself or herself of property 'for the purpose of decreasing the amount that [he or she] may be liable to pay for [his or her] accommodation', the local authority can, none the less, take the value of the property into account in calculating the resident's (or potential resident's) 'notional capital'. In effect, the local authority can deem the former owner to be the owner of the divested property. While the timing and the motive behind the transfer of property is relevant in determining whether there has been 'deliberate deprivation' of assets, there are no hard and fast rules. Unlike the provision in HASSASSA, no time-limit is stated in the regulations and so there is nothing to prevent a local authority from applying the regulations in respect of an alienation of property more than six months before the transferor moved into residential care.[47] What is more striking, however, is the fact that there is no power to recover money

---

44 Solicitors (Scotland) Practice Rules 1986.
45 1983 Act, s 21.
46 SI 1992 No 2977.
47 In *Yule* v *South Lanarkshire Council* 1998 SLT 490, Mrs Yule disponed her house to her granddaughter 'for love, favour and affection' and retained a liferent in it for herself. Over a year later, she went to live in a nursing home. The local authority sought to treat the value of her house as 'notional capital' which would have rendered her, rather than the local authority, liable for the nursing home fees. Mrs Yule challenged the *vires* of the local authority's decision on the basis that its powers under HASSASSA precluded it from using regulation 25 of the National Assistance (Assessment of Resources) Regulations 1992. The court rejected this argument and the decision is unsurprising, since there is nothing in either of the provisions to suggest exclusion of the other. It should be noted, however, that the issue of whether Mrs Yule had, in fact, deliberately deprived herself of

from the recipient of the property. All a finding of 'deliberate deprivation' of assets will do is render the resident liable to pay more than he or she would have been liable to pay otherwise. It does not exempt the local authority from its responsibility to provide accommodation. Clearly the local authority will proceed on the basis of HASSASSA, where the transfer of property fell within the required six month time-limit since, if it is successful, it will be able to recover from the recipient of the property or register a charge against the property. It is only if the alienation fell outwith that the six-month period that it would rely on what are, to the local authority, the less useful provisions in the 1992 Regulations.

15.19 Both of the above provisions apply equally to the alienation of moveable or heritable property. Thus, where the older person gives away money, jewellery or antiques, the provisions could apply in the same way as they would apply to the alienation of an interest in the home. That is not to say that every time an older person gives a gift to a family member, he or she should be concerned about the provisions. In each case the prerequisite is phrased slightly differently but, in both cases, the alienation must be aimed at avoiding paying for accommodation. There are many other, perfectly reasonable, motives for the transfer of assets to a relative. An older man may feel that he is no longer happy to drive and give his car to his daughter. A grandmother may give a particular piece of jewellery to a granddaughter on the occasion of the latter's 21st birthday. Many religious festivals are seen as times when family members exchange presents. An older person may want to help a young relative with the financial burden now inherent in receiving a university education. Gifts are also routinely made as potentially exempt transfers for the purposes of inheritance tax. Since the home is often the most valuable asset, transfer of it may attract greater suspicion and it is worth considering whether any of a whole range of possible strategies is appropriate in a particular case.

Outright conveyance of the home to a relative

15.20 What the older person does here is to convey his or her home to a relative so that the asset no longer belongs to the older person. Such an arrangement will usually be coupled with an agreement, whether in writing or not, that the relative will take care of the older person's needs. The advantage may be that the older person will become eligible for assistance in paying for residential or nursing accommodation when that would not have been the case if he or she had owned a home. The relative is then simply topping up local authority provision and the house remains in the family. While there are no statistics available, it is thought that this kind of arrangement has worked well for many families. However, there are dangers. The most obvious is that not all people behave honourably and families fall out. Thus, having conveyed the home to a relative, the older person runs the risk of the relative failing to honour the agreement. Variations on this theme include the possibility, already noted, of the

an asset, was not before the court. For a discussion of the case and how it was misrepresented in the press, see J. Heritage (pen name), 'Residential Care Fees: Protection of Assets' 1998 SLT (News) 105.

relative becoming bankrupt, and being unable to help the older person, or the death of the relative. The latter case can be anticipated by providing that, on the relative's death, the home passes to the older person (with further provision that it should pass to other specified relatives in the event that the older person has already died) and, while this would defeat the overall purpose of the original arrangement, at least the older person would get the asset back. It should be remembered, however, that most wills are revocable. Were such an arrangement to be entered into in the six months immediately prior to the older person entering residential care, it would almost certainly fall foul of the HASSASSA provision discussed above. However, such arrangements could be made well before a person showed any signs of needing care although it should also be borne in mind that regulation 25 may be invoked by the local authority. If the relatives are divorced, it is unlikely that the home would be treated as matrimonial property for the purpose of division of assets if it is clear that the property was, in fact, a gift.[48]

Conveyance of the home in fee to a relative with the older person retaining a liferent

15.21 The home could be conveyed to a relative in fee, with the older person retaining a liferent in the property. This protects the older person's right to remain in the home as long as he or she is able to do so. Were such an older person to need residential care, only the liferent interest in the home would be his or her property, thus increasing the likelihood of eligibility for assistance with the cost of care. Where the older person was still competent, and the fee-holder agreed, the home could be sold to meet the cost of care, but that rather defeats the point of such arrangements. The real problem here is that, where the older person becomes incompetent, the relative would have difficulty in selling the property because the older person, having lost legal capacity, will be unable to discharge the liferent or consent to the sale. Thus, the relative might be unable to provide the luxuries that he or she might wish to give to the older person. In any event, HASSASSA and regulation 25 may, again, present problems.[49]

Conveyance of the home to a trust with the older person retaining a right to live in the home rent-free

15.22 A third option would be to convey the property to a trust with the older person being given a beneficial interest to remain in the home. This might work as long as the person was able to live there but, again, there is the problem of realising the asset if the capital was needed and, depending upon the timing, the possibility that the arrangement would be viewed as a simulate device for deliberate deprivation.

Payment for care by the local authority, subject to the local authority being given a standard security over the home

15.23 Where an older person needs to live in residential care but the

48 Family Law (Scotland) Act 1985, s 10(4). See chapter 11, para 33.
49 See *Yule* v *South Lanarkshire Council*, above.

home is still required to provide accommodation for his or her spouse, an unmarried partner, a relative over the age of 60, or a relative who is incapacitated, it will be disregarded by the local authority. This does not exempt a spouse from his or her alimentary obligation,[50] unmarried partners and other relatives having no such obligation. The extent of the obligation to aliment is only what is regarded as reasonable in the circumstances but, were a contribution to the cost of care to be required from the spouse, payment might be deferred by the local authority being given a standard security over the home. In this way, the local authority would recover the sum owed when the home is eventually sold. In addition, the local authority has a discretion to disregard the home if it is occupied by another person who is not a partner or specified kind of relative. Again, it might be that the local authority would permit such a person to continue living in the home, subject to a standard security being executed.

15.24 Moveable assets, for example, money and investments, allow less scope for flexibility. The older person could give such assets to a relative, on the understanding that the relative will take care of the person's needs in the future, but such an arrangement requires a very considerable amount of trust and is open to the same problems as were discussed in respect of outright conveyance of the home. Again, depending on the kind of property transferred, the timing and the older person's intention, the transfer might fall foul of the anti-alienation provisions of HASSASSA and regulation 25. It is not possible to create a trust for one's own support.[51]

15.25 There is no doubt that providing appropriate and affordable accommodation for older people is a pressing contemporary concern and, in December 1997, Sir Stewart Sutherland was appointed to chair the Royal Commission on Long-term Care of the Elderly,[52] with the following remit

> 'To examine the short and long term options for a sustainable system of funding of long-term care for elderly people, both in their own homes and in other settings and, within 12 months, to recommend how and in what circumstances, the cost of such care should be apportioned between public funds and individuals'.

The remit then lists a number of factors to which the Royal Commission should have regard in its deliberations.[53] In addition to accepting written

50 Family Law (Scotland) Act 1985, s 1(1)(a) and (b).
51 *Ker's Trustee* v *Justice* (1866) 5 M 4; *Wilson and Others, Petitioners* 1968 SLT (Notes) 83.
52 It was most unfortunate that the term 'the elderly' was used and it would have been better if the UN term 'older people' or, even, 'elderly people' had been selected instead when the government was taking the welcome step in addressing the matter of long-term care.
53 The rather lengthy list of factors is as follows: the number of people likely to require various kinds of long-term care both in the present and through the first half of the next century, and their likely income and capital over their lifetime; the expectations of elderly people for dignity and security in the way in which their long-term care needs are met, taking account of the need for this to be secured in the most cost-effective manner; the strengths and weaknesses of the current arrangements; fair and efficient ways for individuals to make any contribution required of them; constraints on public funds, and

submissions, public hearings were held in a variety of towns and cities in the UK and a site was established on the worldwide web, in the attempt to give interested parties, including older people and carers, the opportunity to present their views.[54] It may be a reflection of the urgency with which the issue is viewed that a time-limit formed part of the remit itself and the Royal Commission's report was presented to Parliament in March 1999.

Who decides?

15.26 A crucial question is who decides where an older person should live. Where the older person is competent, there can be only one answer to that question. Competent adults, regardless of their age and whether infirm or not, are entitled to make decisions for themselves. Of course, this does not mean that older people can always do what they want any more than any other adult can. An older person can only live with relatives if such an arrangement is acceptable to the relatives. The availability and suitability of particular residential accommodation will determine whether a place can be found for an older person who wants to live there. Family members frequently become involved in advising older people about what might be the best option, but it is important that the emphasis must be on what the older person wants and needs, rather than the convenience of others. Where an older person's physical or mental capacity deteriorates, the family may feel that residential care or some other option would be beneficial, although the older person might disagree. This might be a good time to seek a needs assessment from the local authority, in order to involve someone else in exploring the options with the older person. Where the older person becomes incompetent, the decision must be taken by others and, again, the involvement of the local authority social work department and a medical practitioner may be helpful.

15.27 One factor which is often left out of account when an older person transfers his or her home to a relative is that, even if the transfer is successful in its aim of forcing the local authority to pay for residential or nursing home care, the local authority will only pay up to a certain limit. If the older person's assets have been so depleted that he or she cannot contribute anything towards the cost of care, the actual choice of home, be it residential or nursing, will be severely restricted. Older people should bear this in mind when considering transfer of the home to a relative. If the older person retains ownership of the home then, although the home may have to be sold to pay for care, the older person is likely to have a wider choice than if the local authority is solely responsible for the charges.

earlier work done by various bodies on this issue. Two other matters which 'the Royal Commission should also have regard to' are the deliberations of the Government's comprehensive spending review, including the review of pensions; the implications of their recommendations for younger people who by reason of illness or disability have long-term care needs.

54 The site is: http://www.open.gov.uk/doh/elderly/elderly.htm and the variety of methods of communicating with the Royal Commission represent a real effort to enable participation to be as wide as possible, a matter mentioned in the remit itself.

DIMINISHING PHYSICAL AND MENTAL CAPACITY

15.28 The significance of diminished physical or mental capacity for adults is discussed in chapter 2, since the issues are not confined to older people.[55] However, the problems associated with diminishing or diminished capacity are faced by a significant number of older people and their families.[56] As we saw, physical incapacity alone has little impact on an individual's ability to handle his or her own affairs and to make decisions, although it will be significant when assessing a person's needs and in providing for them. In the case of mental incapacity, the law provides for a, sometimes bewildering, array of guardians who may be empowered to look after the person of the incapax, manage some or all of his or her property,[57] or to fulfil both functions. The Scottish Law Commission has made extensive recommendations for reform of the law both in respect of personal guardians and management of property.[58] The Lord Chancellor's Department is currently examining proposals for reform of the law on personal decision-making on behalf of incapable adults and, as a part of its deliberations, is considering whether the same system as is proposed for England and Wales should operate throughout the UK.[59]

ABUSE AND NEGLECT

15.29 It is now widely accepted that some older people are abused or neglected, both in the home and in residential care, by partners, other family members, or paid or voluntary carers. Like child abuse, it is often pointed out that the problem itself is not new. It is simply that we have named it, are more aware of it and, thus, identification of its incidence has increased. There is also a greater readiness to report it. Assuming this to be true, there is no comfort to be drawn from such a view unless we can go on to prevent this form of abuse and protect people from it. Defining what we mean by abuse or neglect is problematic, as is establishing the incidence of the problem. The national organisation, Action on Elder Abuse, includes within its definition, physical abuse, psychological abuse, sexual abuse, material abuse and active and passive neglect. The Social Services Directorate defines such abuse as

> 'Physical, sexual, psychological or financial. It may be intentional or unintentional or the result of neglect. It causes harm to the older person, either temporarily or over a period of time'.

55 See chapter 2, paras 81–93.
56 The Scottish Law Commission was particularly aware of the special problems of mental incapacity associated with dementia. Age Concern Scotland and Alzheimer Scotland: Action on Dementia have produced a number of helpful publications on the subject.
57 For an excellent discussion, see David Nichols, 'Legal Arrangements for Managing the Finances of Mentally Disabled Adults in Scotland' 1992 (3) J Soc Wel & Fam L 193.
58 Scottish Law Commission, Report on Incapable Adults (Scot Law Com No 151, 1995); Scottish Law Commission, Report on Vulnerable Adults: Public Authority Powers (Scot Law Com No 158, 1997).
59 Consultation Paper, Who decides? Making decisions on behalf of incapable adults (Lord Chancellor's Department, 1997) paras 1.10–1.13. The question is asked after it is made clear that the Scottish Law Commission has already made proposals, which are different in a number of respects, for reform of the law in Scotland.

The parallels with child abuse are apparent immediately and the only form of abuse which separates the two is that of material abuse, that is, the illegal or improper exploitation or use of the older person's funds or resources. That this difference exists is hardly surprising, since children rarely have property while older people often do. However, what of the similarities?

15.30 As with the recognition of child abuse and neglect, the USA led the field in research into what has come to be known as 'elder abuse'.[60] Initially, research concentrated on abuse by relatives in the home, a fact which is explained by Aitken and Griffin thus

'it is cheaper to fund and research on supposedly dysfunctional families and to discover that they have a problem than it is to review pension schemes and care structures to provide adequately for older people'.[61]

The first work in the UK was that of Eastman[62] who had extensive experience as a social worker working with older people and who believed that others must be experiencing the phenomenon he had observed. Again, the parallel with the early writers on child abuse is uncanny.[63] Much of the early work concentrated on abuse by female carers, often middle-aged women, of an older person in the home,[64] but it is now well understood that the issues are a great deal broader. By the 1990s an awareness of abuse in residential homes and day centres had emerged.[65] Action on Elder Abuse was founded in 1993, to provide advice, information and guidance on preventing elder abuse and to raise awareness of the problem and promote research. It now operates a telephone helpline and was instrumental in the campaign, conducted in *The Sunday Times* newspaper in 1997, which sought to highlight the problem of abuse in the residential sector. Given the widespread discussion of the problem at all levels, the attempt to raise awareness has had a degree of success.

15.31 Assessing the real incidence of elder abuse presents difficulties, not least because under-reporting is almost certainly a feature. In addition, more than one form of abuse or neglect may be present at the same time in respect of the same individual. The findings of Block and Sinnott are often

---

60 See for example, M. Block and J. Sinnott (eds), *The Battered Elder Syndrome: An Exploratory Study* (University of Maryland Press, 1979) and K. Pillemer and R. Wolf (eds), *Elder Abuse: Conflict in the Family* (Auburn House, 1986). For more contemporary comment, see J. Blair, ' "Honor Thy Father and Thy Mother" – But for How Long? – Adult Children's Duty to Care For and Protect Elderly Parents' 35 U Louisville J Fam L 765 (1996–97) and J. C. Skabronski, 'Elder Abuse: Washington's Response to a Growing Epedemic' 31 Gonz L Rev 627 (1995–96).

61 Above, at pp 32–33.

62 *Old Age Abuse* (Age Concern, 1984). Ten years later, the same author published *Old Age Abuse – A New Perspective* (Chapman and Hall, 1994), which, while described as a second edition of the first, is an edited work, raising new issues and involving other experts in the field.

63 See chapter 7, para 4, where the early work of Caffey, Helfner and others in identifying child abuse, is discussed.

64 For a discussion of the impact of caring on daughters, see J. Lewis and B. Meredith, *Daughters Who Care* (Routledge, Chapman and Hall, 1988).

65 Aitken and Griffin, above, Eastman (1994) above, and S. Biggs, C. Phillipson and P. Kingston, *Elder Abuse in Perspective* (OUP, 1995) discuss abuse in the residential setting.

quoted and suggest that about 4% of older people experience some kind of abuse or neglect, although Aitken and Griffin point out that their research was based on a very poor response rate of only 17%. Indeed, it is a feature of research here (and in attempts to quantify child abuse) that all findings seem to be questioned by other researchers, usually on methodological grounds. Other studies in Britain have suggested figures of 5%[66] and, in Canada, of 4%.[67] Whatever the true figures, it is clear that a significant number of older people experience abuse or neglect and sometimes both. The question is how to deal with the problem.

15.32 Addressing this issue requires consideration of both prevention of abuse and protection of victims at the earliest possible time. In order to prevent something from happening, it is essential to know why it happens and this demonstrates the need to understand the causes of elder abuse. As with the causes of other forms of abuse and, indeed, with crime itself, there is no unanimity of opinion. However, it is widely accepted that the causes differ depending on whether the abuse is taking place in the home or in residential or nursing home care and on the differing relationship between the older person and the abuser. Where the abuser and victim are related and the abuse takes place in the home, often-cited causes include: a history of a poor relationship between the parties; the inability of the abuser to provide the level of care required; a lack of necessary support; and the role reversal sometimes involved when, for example, a child becomes a carer.[68] Abuse in a residential setting suggests deficiencies in the way the particular home is run. Recruitment and training, as well as supervision and support of staff, all play a central role here. In addition, the overall climate in the facilities and real opportunities for older people and their families to make concerns known and to have complaints taken seriously and dealt with, are important.[69] The issue of whether the very fact of an older person's dependency is a central explanation for abuse occurring is at the heart of the current debate.[70] In addition, abuse occurs in the wider community and the extent to which this is caused by a more general problem of ageism, in itself as a form of abuse, has begun to be explored.[71]

15.33 Prevention of abuse in the home requires consideration of, first, whether that form of care, by the particular carer, is the best option. If it is, the necessary information and support for all involved is essential. In a residential setting, clear regulation of recruitment and training, as well as of support and supervision of staff, will go a long way towards the elimination

---

66　J. Ogg and G. Bennett, 'Elder Abuse in Britain' (1992) 305 BMJ 998, found that one in 20 older people reported experiencing some kind of abuse, with one in fifty reporting physical abuse.

67　E. Podnieks, 'National survey on abuse of the elderly in Canada' (1992) 4 Journal of Elder Abuse and Neglect 5.

68　Aitken and Griffin, above, chapter 5; Biggs et al, above, chapter 5; Eastman (1994) above, chapter 2.

69　Aitken and Griffin, above, chapter 4; Biggs et al, above, chapter 6; Eastman (1994) above, chapter 7.

70　Aitken and Griffin, above, pp 127–132; Biggs et al, above, pp 67–70; Eastman (1994) above, chapters 5 and 6.

71　Aitken and Griffin, above, chapter 3.

of abuse. Rigorous inspection and effective complaints procedures, backed up by effective sanctions, are also crucial.

15.34 Where abuse occurs it falls to the legal system and other agencies to provide effective protection for the victim from future abuse. This requires that the abuse itself must be identified. Thereafter, the criminal law will often provide a sanction. For example, physical and sexual abuse will usually constitute an assault and material abuse may constitute fraud. However, while prosecution of the offender may be entirely appropriate, the criminal law may often be something of a blunt instrument. Psychological abuse or neglect may not readily suggest any offence. Even where an offence can be identified, problems over gathering evidence, asking the victim to give evidence, and delay, all reduce the likelihood of a conviction. Furthermore, conviction of the offender may do little to help the victim. At present, there are inadequacies in the civil law provision for protecting older people and other vulnerable groups from abuse and the Scottish Law Commission's proposals for reform,[72] if implemented, would do much to improve the situation.

THE WAY AHEAD

15.35 The increase in Scotland's ageing population presents special challenges for the community as a whole. For family members, these challenges have always been present, but changing family structures have implications here, as they do for other areas of family life. How we should meet these challenges, as a society and as family members, is a matter of on-going debate. One thing is clear. We have no excuse if we fail. The statistics are there for all to see. We have been given more than adequate notice.

15.36 In considering how to approach the various issues involved, it is tempting to see parallels between children and older family members. We are presented with two identifiable groups. In each case, there may be vulnerability and, thus, some justification for seeing the role of family members and the state as a protective one. If that means that we might learn from mistakes made in the past in respect of providing for the needs of children, the parallel is positive. For example, the recognition that individuals within a 'category', be the category children or older people, are individuals whose particular needs must be met, is a lesson which may be transferred very usefully. Similarly, the need to co-ordinate assistance and services being provided to an individual and to consider what the individual wants are common themes. However, older adults are not children, they are people who have been used to running their own lives. Children expect to be looked after and accept that decisions will be taken by others, albeit they have a right to have any views they wish to express taken into account.[73] Adults generally take responsibility for themselves and expect to make their own decisions, often without having to justify

---

72 Report on Vulnerable Adults (Scot Law Com No 158, 1997), discussed in chapter 2 at para 92.
73 Children (Scotland) Act 1995, ss 6, 11(7)(b) and 16(2)(a).

them to others. Older people have had the time to develop preferences and idiosyncrasies, whether wholly rational or not, which we all expect to be free to pursue as adults. Thus, while learning lessons from the law and practice relating to children has benefits, we must remain vigilant so that we retain our awareness of the distinct situation of older people.

15.37 In terms of enabling older people to live as fully and autonomously as possible, at the same time as ensuring that those with special additional needs are accommodated, the legal system and the services available have many positive aspects, but more needs to be done. In some respects, this will require funding and is a political issue. Real impetus for change will come from improved public awareness of exactly what the needs of older people are and where the present system is deficient. While progress has been made in raising public awareness, there remains a degree of ignorance to be overcome. In other respects, for example, personal guardianship and the protection of property, proposals for reform of the law are on the table and simply need to be enacted. As ever, further research is required in a whole host of areas, most notably into elder abuse and both gender and ethnic issues as they impact upon older people.

15.38 Unlike people with disabilities, women and children, older people received scant attention from the international community.[74] That began to change in 1990, when the General Assembly of the United Nations designated 1 October as the International Day of Older Persons and with the adoption, in 1991, of the United Nations Principles for Older Persons.[75] The Principles call for action in a number of areas and make specific mention of the following: independence, participation, care, self-fulfilment and dignity. Conscious that the ageing of the world's population 'represents an unparalleled, but urgent, policy and programme challenge to Governments, non-governmental organisations and private groups', the United Nations General Assembly[76] decided to observe 1999 as the Year of Older Persons, to use it as a vehicle to promote the Principles,[77] and to encourage states to take advantage of it to increase awareness of both the challenge of ageing societies and the contributions made by older people.[78] Bearing in mind the way in which children's rights have developed in an international context, and the resulting impact on the national scene, it is to be hoped that the rights of older persons will be similarly developed by the international attention being given to the matter. Who knows, the UN Convention on the Rights of Older Persons may not be far off.

---

74   While Article 2 of the Universal Declaration of Human Rights 1948 prohibits discrimina-
     tion on a variety of grounds including race, sex, religion, birth or other status, nothing is
     said of discrimination on the basis of age, and no mention of the special needs of older
     people until Article 25 which deals with the right to an adequate standard of living.
75   General Assembly Resolution 46/91.
76   General Assembly Resolution 47/5 (16 October 1992).
77   The Year's unifying theme is 'Towards a society for all ages', a concept which grew out of
     the broader notion of a 'society for all', promoted by the World Summit for Social
     Development in Copenhagen in March 1995.
78   General Assembly Resolution 52/80 (30 January 1998).

APPENDIX

Useful Organisations: Addresses, Telephone Numbers and Websites
If the organisation you are looking for does not seem to be listed, try under the organisation's name prefixed by the word 'Scottish'. Where a particular organisation has a central office, its address and telephone number are given and the central office can advise on local services.

Action on Elder Abuse
Astral House
1268 London Road
London SW16 4ER
Tel: 0181 764 7648
Helpline: 0800 7314141

Age Concern Scotland
113 Rose Street
Edinburgh EH2 3DT
Tel: 0131 220 3345

Alzheimer Scotland – Action on Dementia
22 Drumsheugh Gardens
Edinburgh EH3 7RN
Tel: 0131 243 1453
24-hour freephone helpline:
0800 317 817
Web site: http://www.alzscot.org

Barnardos
235 Corstorphine Road
Edinburgh EH12 7AR
Tel: 0131 334 9893
Web site: http://
www.barnardos.org.uk

British Agencies for Adoption and Fostering (BAAF)
40 Shandwick Place
Edinburgh EH2 4RT
Tel: 0131 225 9285
Web site: http://
www/vois.org.uk/baaf

Capability Scotland (formerly the Scottish Council for Spastics)
22 Corstorphine Road
Edinburgh EH12 6HP
Tel: 0131 337 9876

Advice Service Capability Scotland (ASCS)
11 Ellersly Road
Edinburgh EH12 6HY
Tel: 0131 313 5510

Catholic Marriage Advisory Council
See Scottish Marriage Care

Child Support Agency
Parklands
Callendar Business Park
Callendar Road
Falkirk FK1 1XT
Tel: 0345 133133
Web site: http://www.dss.gov.uk/csa

Child Support Commissioners
23 Melville Street
Edinburgh EH3 7PE
Tel: 0131 225 2201
Web site: http://
www.hywels.demon.co.uk/commrs

Childline
Tel: 0800 1111

Children 1st
41 Polwarth Terrace
Edinburgh EH11 1NU
Tel: 0131 337 8539
Campaign Office: 0131 346 4552

Children in Need (BBC Appeal)
Broadcasting House
5 Queen Street
Edinburgh EH2 1JF
Tel: 0131 469 4225

Children in Scotland
Special Needs Forum
Princes House
5 Shandwick Place
Edinburgh EH2 4RG
Tel: 0131 228 8484

Children's Hospice Association for Scotland (CHAS)
18 Hanover Street
Edinburgh EH2 2EN
Tel: 0131 226 4933

Children's Panel Advisory Committee
c/o City Chambers
High Street
Edinburgh EH1 1YJ

Citizens Advice Bureau
58 Dundas Street
Edinburgh EH3 6QZ
Tel: 0131 557 1500
See under 'Citizens Advice Bureau' in your telephone directory for the address and telephone number of your local branch.

Enable (formerly Scottish Society for the Mentally Handicapped)
7 Buchanan Street
Glasgow G1 3HL
Tel: 0141 226 4541

Ethnic Minorities Law Centre
41 St. Vincent Place
Glasgow G1 2ER
Tel: 0141 204 2888

European Commission
Directorate-General V–E2
Rue de la Loi 200
B–1049 Bruxelles
Tel: (32 2) 299 0482
Fax: (32 2) 299 0509
Web site: http://europa.eu.int/comm

Faculty of Advocates
Advocates' Library
Parliament House
Edinburgh EH1 1RF
Tel: 0131 226 5071

Family Care
21 Castle Street
Edinburgh EH2 3DN
Tel: 0131 225 6441

Family Law Association
c/o Aitkens
17 Grampian Court
Beveridge Square
Livingston EH54 6QF
Tel: 01506 417737

Family Mediation Scotland
127 Rose Street, South Lane,
Edinburgh EH2 4BB
Tel: 0131 220 1610
See also under 'Mediation' in your local telephone directory for services offered locally.

Gingerbread
Gingerbread Scotland
Maryhill Community Central Halls
304 Maryhill Road G20 7YE
Tel: 0141 353 0953

Gingerbread Edinburgh & Lothian Project Ltd
Gingerbread House
19 Chester Street

Edinburgh EH3 7RF
Tel: 0131 220 1585

Fife Federation
17 Tolbooth Street
Kirkcaldy
Tel: 01592 200967

Helping Parents Helpline
Centre House
14 Basil Avenue
Armthorpe
Doncaster DN3 2AT
Tel: 01302 833596

Health Education Board for Scotland
Woodburn House
Canaan Lane
Edinburgh EH10 4SG
Dementia Helpline: 0800 317817
Tel: 0131 536 5500
Web site: http://
www.hebs.scot.nhs.uk

International Society of Family Law
Paul Vlaardingerbroek
Treasurer
Den Hooiberg 17
4891 NM Rijsbergen
The Netherlands
E-mail:
P.Vlaardingerbroek@kub.nl
Web site: http://www.law.byu.edu/
ISFL/Main.html

Law Society of Scotland
26 Drumsheugh Gardens
Edinburgh EH3 7YR
Tel: 0131 226 7411
Dial-a-law: 0990 455554
Web site: http://
www.lawscot.org.uk

Marriage Counselling Scotland
105 Hanover Street
Edinburgh EH2 1DJ

Mental Welfare Commission for Scotland
25 Drumsheugh Gardens
Edinburgh EH3 7RB
Tel: 0131 225 7034

National Council for One Parent Families
255 Kentish Town Road
London NW5 2LX
Tel: 0171 428 5400

National Foster Care Association
1 Melrose Street
Glasgow G4 9BJ
Tel: 0141 332 6655
Web site: http://
www.kidsource.com/nfpa

National Stepfamily Association
3rd Floor, Chapel House
18 Hatton Place
London EC1N 8RU
Tel: 0171 209 2460
    0990 168388

One Plus Parent Families
55 Renfrew Street
Glasgow G2 3BD
Tel: 0141 333 1450

Parentline
Endway House
The Endway
Hadleigh SS7 2AN
Tel: 01702 559900

Penumbra
Gogar Park
167 Glasgow Road
Edinburgh EH12 9BG
Tel: 0131 317 1337

Registrar General for Scotland
General Register Office for Scotland
Ladywell House
Ladywell Road
Edinburgh EH12 7TF
Tel: 0131 314 4243
Web site: http://www.open.gov.uk/
gros/groshome.htm

Relate
Relate operates in England and
Wales. In Scotland, see Marriage
Counselling Scotland, above and
'Lothian Marriage Counselling
Service' etc. in your local telephone
directory.

Reporter
See under Scottish Children's
Reporter Administration, below,
and under 'Children's Reporter' in
your local telephone directory.

Reunite
National Council for Abducted
Children
PO Box 4
London WC1X 3DX
Tel: 0171 404 8356

**Royal Scottish Society for the
Prevention of Cruelty to Children
(RSSPCC)**
41 Polwarth Terrace
Edinburgh EH11 1NL
Tel: 0131 337 8539

**St. Andrew's Children's Society
Ltd., Adoption, Fostering
Agency**
113 Whitehouse Loan
Edinburgh EH9 1BB
Tel: 0131 452 8248

**St. Margaret of Scotland Adoption
Society**
274 Bath Street
Glasgow G2 4JR
Tel: 0141 332 8371

Scottish Adoption Advice Service
16 Sandyford Place
Glasgow G3 7NB
Tel: 0141 339 0772

Scottish Adoption Association Ltd.
2 Commercial Street
Leith
Edinburgh EH6 6JA
Tel: 0131 553 5060

**Scottish Association of Children's
Curators**
c/o Penman Gordon & Co
Solicitors
175 Saracen Street
Glasgow G22 5JM
Tel: 0141 336 6647

Scottish Child Law Centre
Cranston House
108 Argyle Street
Glasgow G2 8BH
Tel: 0141 226 3737
Advice line: 0800 317500
Web site: http://www.salc.org.uk

**Scottish Children's Reporter
Administration (SCRA)**
Ochil House
Springkerse Business Park
Stirling FK7 7XE
Tel: 01786 459500
See also under 'Children's
Reporter' in your local telephone
directory.

Scottish Courts Administration
Hayweight House
23 Lauriston Street
Edinburgh EH3 9DQ
Tel: 0131 229 9200

Scottish Law Commission
140 Causewayside
Edinburgh EH9 1PR
Tel: 0131 668 2131

Scottish Legal Aid Board
44 Drumsheugh Gardens
Edinburgh EH3 7SW
Tel: 0131 226 7061
Web site: http://www.slab.org.uk

Scottish Low Pay Unit
24 Sandyford Place
Glasgow G3 7NG
Tel: 0141 221 4491

Scottish Marriage Care
50 Greenock Road
Paisley PA3 2LE
Tel: 0141 849 6183

196 Clyde Street
Glasgow G1 4JY
Tel: 0141 204 1239

Scottish Office
St. Andrews House
Regent Road
Edinburgh EH1 3DG

Victoria Quay
Edinburgh EH6 6QQ
Tel: 0131 556 8400
Enquiry line: 0345 741741
Web site: www.scotland.gov.uk

Scottish Safeguarders' Association
c/o The Secretary
100 Spoutwells Drive
Scone
Perth PH2 6PQ
Tel: 01738 551985

Scottish Women's Aid
12 Torphichen Street
Edinburgh EH3 8JQ
Tel: 0131 221 0401
See also under 'Women's Aid' in
your local telephone
directory.

Shakti
31 Albany Street
Edinburgh EH1 3QN
Tel: 0131 557 4010

BIBLIOGRAPHY

CHAPTER 1

Books

Alison, A J *Principles and Practice of the Criminal Law of Scotland* (1832–33)

Boyd, S E (ed) *Challenging the Public/Private Divide: Feminism, Law and Public Policy* (University of Toronto Press, 1997)

Brophy, J and Smart, C *Women-in-law: Explorations in Law, Family and Sexuality* (Routledge, 1985)

Brunet, E and Craver, C B *Alternative Dispute Resolution: The Advocate's Perspective* (Michie, 1997)

Davidson, H A and Ray, L E (eds) *Alternative Means of Family Dispute Resolution* (American Bar Assocation, 1982)

Eekelaar, J M and Nhlapo, T (eds) *The Changing Family: Family Forms and Family Law* (Hart Publishing, 1998)

Eekelaar, J M and Katz, S N *The Resolution of Family Conflict* (Butterworths, 1984)

Folberg, H J and Taylor, A *Mediation: A Comprehensive Guide to Resolving Disputes without Litigation* (Jossey-Bass, 1984)

Fortin, J *Children's Rights and the Developing Law* (Butterworths, 1998)

Freeman, M (ed) *Children's Rights: A Comparative Perspective* (Dartmouth, 1996)

Fukuyama, F *The End of Order* (The Social Market Foundation, 1997)

Glendon, M A *The Transformation of Family Law: State, Law and the Family in the United States and Western Europe* (University of Chicago Press, 1989)

Hester, M and Radford, L *Domestic Violence in Child Contact Arrangements in England and Denmark* (The Policy Press, 1996)

Irving, H H and Benjamin, M *Family Mediation: Contemporary Issues* (Sage Publications, 1995)

Jaffe, P *Children Exposed to Domestic Violence* (Sage, 1998)

The Laws of Scotland: Stair Memorial Encyclopaedia (Butterworths)

Leach, P *Children First* (Michael Joseph, 1990)

O'Donovan, K *Sexual Divisions in Law* (Weidenfeld and Nicolson, 1985)

Parkinson, L *Conciliation in Separation and Divorce* (Croom Helm, 1986)

Smith, T B *A Short Commentary on the Law of Scotland* (W. Green & Son, 1962)

Smout, T C *A Century of the Scottish People 1830–1950* (Fontana Press, 1969)

Stair *Institutions of the Law of Scotland* (1681)

Trachete-Huber, E W and Huber, S K *Mediation and Negotiation: Reaching Agreement in Law and Business* (Anderson Publishing Co, 1998)

Walker, D M *Principles of Scottish Private Law* (4th edn, Oxford University Press, 1988)

Wilson, the late W A, Forte, A D M, Earlsferry, The Lord Rodger of, Paton, A, Dunlop, L, Hood, P and Young, A R W *Gloag and Henderson, The Law of Scotland* (10th edn, W. Green, 1995)

Articles

Bottomley, A 'What is Happening to Family Law? A Feminist Critique of Conciliation' in Brophy and Smart *Women-in-law: Explorations in law, family and sexuality* (Routledge, 1985)

Bruch, C 'And how are the children? The effects of ideology and mediation on child custody and children's well-being in the United States' (1995) Int J L and Fam 106

Busch, R and Robertson, N 'Innovative Approaches to Child Custody and Domestic Violence in New Zealand: the Effects of Law Reform on the Discourses of Battering' in Jaffe (ed) *Children Exposed to Domestic Violence* (Sage, 1998)

Campbell, K 'Human Rights Brought Home' 1998 SLT (News) 269

Clive, E 'Family Law Reform in Scotland: Past Present and Future' 1989 JR 133

Clark, B and Mays, R 'The Legal Profession and ADR' 1996 JR 389

Cretney, S M 'Family Law – A Bit of a Racket?' (The Joseph Jackson Memorial Lecture) (1996) NLJ 91

Dick, A H and Jeffrey, M 'Lawyer Mediator: Interface or Interloper' 1995 SLT (News) 305

Dyer, A 'The Internationalization of Family Law' 30 UC Davis L Rev 625 (1997)

Freeman, A and Mensch, E 'The Politics of Virtue: Animals, Theology and Abortion' 25 Ga. L. Rev. 923 (1991)

Freeman, M 'The Convention: An English Perspective' in Freeman, M (ed) *Children's Rights: A Comparative Perspective* (Dartmouth, 1996)

Fuller, L L 'Mediation: Its Forms and Functions' 44 S Cal L Rev 305 (1970)

Gavison, R 'Feminism and the Public/Private Distinction' 45 Stan L Rev (1992)

Grillo, T 'The Mediation Alternative: Process Dangers for Women' 100 Yale LJ 1545 (1991)

Hart, B J 'Gentle Jeopardy: The Further Endangerment of Battered Women and Children in Custody Mediation' 7 Mediation Quarterly 317 (1990)

Lacey, L J. 'Mimicking the Words, But Missing the Message: The Misuse of Cultural Feminist Themes in Religion and Family Law Jurisprudence' 35 BC L Rev 1 (1993)

Lehrman, L 'Mediation of Wife Abuse Cases: the Adverse Impact of Informal Dispute Resolution on Women' 7 Harvard Women's Law Journal 57

Leitch, M L 'The Politics of Compromise: A Feminist Perspective on Mediation' 14 Mediation Quarterly 163 (1986)

Majury, D 'Unconscionability in an Equality Context' (1991) 7 Fam LQ 123

Mnookin, R H and Kornhauser, L 'Bargaining in the Shadow of the Law' 88 Yale LJ 950 (1979)

Olsen, F 'The Myth of State Intervention in the Family' 18 U Mich. J L R 835 (1985)

Rifkin, J 'Mediation from a Feminist Perspective: Promise and Problems' 2 Law and Inequality 21 (1984)

'Roundtable: Opportunities for and Limitations of Private Ordering in Family Law' 73 Ind LJ 535 (1998)

Schneider, C E 'Moral Discourse and the Transformation of American Family Law' 83 Mich L Rev 1803 (1985)

'Towards a Feminist-Informed Model of Therapeutic Family Mediation' in Irving and Benjamin, *Family Mediation: Contemporary Issues* (Sage Publications, 1995)

Woods, L 'Mediation: A Backlash to Women's Progress on Family Law Issues' 19 Clearinghouse Review 431 (1985)

Reports

Alternative Dispute Resolution in Scotland (CRU, 1996)

Discussion Paper on Confidentiality in Family Mediation (Scot Law Com, No 92, 1991)

Family Mediation Scotland: Eleventh Annual Report 1997–98 (Family Mediation Scotland, 1998)

Giving Children a Voice in Family Mediation (National Family Mediation and the Gulbenkian Foundation, 1994)

Looking to the Future: Mediation and the Grounds of Divorce – the Government's Proposals, Cm 2799 (1995)

Report on Evidence: Protection of Family Mediation (Scot Law Com No 136, 1992)

Report on Family Law (Scot Law Com No 135, 1992)

CHAPTER 2

Books

Bainham, A (ed) *The International Survey of Family Law 1996* (Martinus Nijhoff, 1998)

Bainham, A (ed) *The International Survey of Family Law 1995* (Martinus Nijhoff, 1997)

Clive, E M *The Law of Husband and Wife in Scotland* (4th edn, W. Green, 1997)

Degener, T *Human Rights and Disabled Persons* (Martinus Nijhoff, 1994)

Forbes *The Institutes of the Law of Scotland*

Francione, G L *Animals, Property and the Law* (Temple U Press, 1995)

Francione, G L *Rain Without Thunder: The Ideology of the Animal Rights Movement* (Temple U Press, 1996)

Gardner, R (ed) *Animal Rights: The Changing Debate* (New York U Press, 1996)

Gordon, G H *The Criminal Law of Scotland* (2nd edn, W. Green, 1978)

Hagen, J and Kay, F *Gender in Practice: A Study of Lawyers' Lives* (OUP, 1995)

Kennedy, I and Grubb, A *Medical Law* (2nd edn, Butterworths, 1994)

The Laws of Scotland: Stair Memorial Encyclopaedia (Butterworths)

McBride, W W *Bankruptcy* (2nd edn, W. Green, 1995)

Mason, J K and McCall Smith, R A *Law and Medical Ethics* (4th edn, Butterworths, 1996)

Mason, J K and McCall Smith, R A *Butterworths Medico-Legal Encyclopaedia* (Butterworths, 1987)

Mason, J K *Forensic Medicine for Lawyers* (3rd edn, Butterworths, 1995)

Mason, J K *Medico-Legal Aspects of Reproduction and Parenthood* (2nd edn, Dartmouth, 1998)

Roberts, D *Killing the Black Body: Race, Reproduction and the Meaning of Liberty* (Pantheon, 1997)

Roberts, D *Women, Pregnancy and Substance Abuse* (Center Women's Policy, 1991)

Singer, P *Animal Liberation* (2nd edn, Avon Books, 1990)

Singer, P and Regan, T (eds) *Animal Rights and Human Obligations* (Prentice Hall, 1989)

Smith, T B *A Short Commentary on the Law of Scotland* (W. Green, 1962)

Smout, T C *A History of the Scottish People 1560–1830* (Fontana Press, 1969)

Stair *Institutions of the Law of Scotland* (1681)

Sutherland, E E and McCall Smith, R A (eds) *Family Rights: Family Law and Medical Advance* (EUP, 1990)

Talman, I J S (ed) *Halliday's Conveyancing Law and Practice in Scotland* (2nd edn, W. Green, 1996)

Ward, A D *The Power to Act: The Development of Scots Law for Mentally Handicapped People* (Scottish Society for the Mentally Handicapped, 1990)

Wilson, W A *The Scottish Law of Debt* (2nd edn, W. Green, 1991)

Articles

Bell, R D 'Prenatal Substance Abuse and Judicial Intervention in Pregnancy: Winnipeg Child and Family Services *v* G (DF)' 55 U Toronto Fac L Rev 321 (1997)

Best, S L 'Fetal Equality?: The Equality State's Response to the Challenge of Protecting Unborn Children' 32 Land and Water L Rev 193 (1997)

Epstein, C F, Saute, R, Oglensky, B and Gever M 'Glass Ceilings and Open Doors: Women's Advancement in the Legal Profession' 64 Fordham L Rev 291 (1995)

Fortin, J E S 'Is the "Wrongful Life" Action Really Dead?' (1987) JSWL 306

Glaze, C L 'Combatting Prenatal Substance Abuse: The State's Current Approach and the Novel Approach of Court-Ordered Protective Custody of the Fetus' 80 Marq L Rev 793 (1997)

Griffiths, J 'Recent Developments in The Netherlands Concerning Euthanasia and other Medical Behaviour that Shortens Life' (1994) 1 Medical Law International 137

Hale, B (The Hon Mrs Justice, formerly Professor Brenda Hoggett) 'Dispatchings' in *From the Test Tube to the Coffin: Choice and Regulation in Private Life* The Hamlyn Lectures, Forty-Seventh Series (Sweet and Maxwell, 1996)

Halevy, A and Brody, B 'Brain Death: Reconciling Definitions, Criteria and Tests' Annals of Internal Medicine 119 (1993) 519

Hunt, C 'Criminalizing Prenatal Substance Abuse: A Preventive Means of Ensuring the Birth of a Drug-Free Child' 33 Idaho L Rev 451 (1997)

Kelly, L 'Divining the Deep and Inscrutable: Towards a Gender-Neutral, Child-Centred Approach to Child Name Change Proceedings' 99 W Va L Rev 1 (1996)

Kramer, L 'Same-Sex Marriage, Conflict of Laws, and the Unconstitutional Public Policy Exemption' 106 Yale L J 1965 (1997)

Laurie, G T 'The Most Personal Information of All: An Appraisal of Genetic Privacy in the Shadow of the Human Genome Project' 10 Int J Law, Policy and the Family (1996) 74

Leonard, A M 'Fetal Personhood, Legal Substance Abuse and Maternal Prosecutions: Child Protection or "Gestational Gestapo"?' 32 New Eng L Rev 615 (1998)

Mason, J K 'United Kingdom *v* Europe: Current Attitudes to Transsexualism' (1998) 2 Edinburgh Law Review 107

Mason, J K and Laurie, G T 'The Management of the Persistent Vegetative State in the British Isles' 1996 JR 263

Mills, M D 'Fetal Abuse Prosecutions: The Triumph of Reaction over Reason' 1998 DePaul L Rev 989 (1998)

Nichols, D 'Legal Arrangements for Managing the Finances of Mentally Disabled Adults in Scotland' 1992 (3) J Soc Wel & Fam L 193

Provost, M A 'Disregarding the Constitution in the Name of Defending Marriage: The Unconstitutionality of the Defense of Marriage Act' 8 Seton Hall Const L J 157 (1997)

Pullen, I 'Patients, Families and Genetic Information' in Sutherland and McCall-Smith (eds), *Family Rights: Family Law and Medical Advance* (EUP, 1990)

Robb, B A 'The Constitutionality of the Defence of Marriage Act in the Wake of Romer *v* Evans' 32 New Eng L Rev 263 (1997)

Roberts, D 'Punishing Drug Addicts Who Have Babies: Women of Color, Equality and the Right of Privacy' 104 Harv L Rev 1419 (1991)

Rodger, A 'Report of the Scottish Law Commission on Antenatal Injury' 1974 JR 83

Spackman, P L 'Grant *v* South-West Trains: Equality for Same-Sex Partners in the European Community' 12 Am U J Int'l L & Pol'y 1063 (1997)

Sutherland, E E 'Regulating Pregnancy: Should We and Can We?' in Sutherland and McCall-Smith (eds) *Family Rights: Family Law and Medical Advance* (EUP, 1990)

Truog, R D 'Is It Time to Abandon Brain Death?' Hastings Centre Report 27, No 1 (1997) 29

Van Bueren, G 'Annual Review of International Family Law' in Bainham (ed) *The International Survey of Family Law 1995* (Martinus Nijhoff, 1997)

Ward, A D 'Revival of Tutors-Dative' 1987 SLT (News) 69

Ward, A D 'Tutors to Adults: Developments' 1992 SLT (News) 325

Wise, J 'When Life Saving Treatment Should be Withdrawn in Children' (1997) 315 Brit Med J 834

Woolfrey, J 'Why Law Firms Cannot Afford to Maintain the Mommy Track' 109 Harv L Rev 1375 (1996)

Woolfrey, J 'What Happens Now? Oregon and Physican-Assisted Suicide' 28 Hastings Center Report 9 (1998)

Reports

Caring For People: Community Care in the Next Decade and Beyond (White Paper: Cm 849, 1989)

Consultation Paper, Managing the Finances and Welfare of Incapable Adults (Scottish Office, 1997)

Consultation Paper, Who Decides? Making Decisions on Behalf of Mentally Incapable Adults (December 1997, Lord Chancellor's Department)

Discussion Paper on Mentally Disabled Adults: Legal Arrangements for Managing their Welfare and Finances (Scot Law Com No. 94, 1991)

Discussion Paper on Mentally Disordered and Vulnerable Adults: Public Authority Powers (Scot Law Com No 96, 1993)

Legal Capacity of Minors and Pupils (Scot Law Com Consultative Memorandum No 65, 1985)

More than a Box of Toys (Save the Children Scotland, 1997)

Report on Incapable Adults (Scot Law Com No 151, 1995), Cmnd 2962

Report on Injuries to Unborn Children (Law Com No 60, 1974)

Report on the Legal Capacity of Minors and Pupils (Scot Law Com No 110, 1987)

Report on Liability for Antenatal Injury (Scot Law Com No 30, 1973), Cmnd 5371

Scotland's Parliament (Cm 3658, 1997)

Social Work Services and Prisons Inspectorate for Scotland, Women Offenders – A Safer Way: A Review of Community Disposals and the Use of Custody for Women Offenders in Scotland (The Scottish Office, 1998)

CHAPTER 3

Books

Alison, A *Principles of the Criminal Law of Scotland* (The Law Society of Scotland and Butterworths (1832 reprinted 1989)

Alston, P, Parker, S and Seymour, J (eds) *Children, Rights and the Law* (Clarendon Press, 1992)

Bishop, D and Frazier, C *Juvenile Justice: Juveniles Processed in Criminal Court and Care Dispositions* (US General Accounting Office, 1995)

Cavadino, P *Children Who Kill* (Waterside Press, 1996)

Clark, N J and Stephenson, G M (eds) *Children, Evidence and Procedure* (British Psychological Society, 1993)

Cohen, C P and Davidson, H A (eds) *Children's Rights in America: UN Convention on the Rights of the Child Compared with United States Law* (American Bar Association, 1990)

Craig *Jus feudale* (1655)

Davies, G M and Noon, E *An Evaluation of the Live Link for Child Witnesses* (Home Office, 1990)

Edwards, L and Griffiths, A *Family Law* (W. Green, 1997)

Farson, R *Birthrights* (Penguin, 1978)

Flekkoy, M G and Kaufman, N H *Rights and Responsibilities in Family and Society* (Jessica Kingsley, 1987)

Fortin, J *Children's Rights and the Developing Law* (Butterworths, 1998)

Fraser *A Treatise on the Law of Scotland Relating to Parent and Child* (1906)

Freeman, M D A *The Rights and Wrongs of Children* (Frances Pinter, 1983)

Freeman, M *Children's Rights: A Comparative Perspective* (Dartmouth, 1996)

Gallacher, R *Children and Young People's Voices on the Law, Legal Services and Systems in Scotland* (Scottish Child Law Centre, 1998)

Holt, J *Escape from Childhood* (Penguin, 1975)

Howell, J C (ed) *A Sourcebook: Serious, Violent, Chronic Juvenile Offenders* (Sage, 1995)

Hume, D *Commentaries on the Law of Scotland Respecting Crimes* (The Law Society of Scotland, 1819, reprinted 1986)

Lavalette, M, McKechnie, J, Hobbs, S and Murray, J *The Forgotten Workforce: Scottish Children at Work* (Scottish Low Pay Unit, 1991)

The Laws of Scotland: Stair Memorial Encyclopaedia (Butterworths)

Le Blanc, L J *The Convention on the Rights of the Child: United Nations Lawmaking on Human Rights* (University of Nebraska Press, 1995)

Listening to the Voice of the Child (Scottish Child Law Centre, 1995)

Mackay, G A *Practice of the Scottish Poor Law* (1907)

McCain, B, Bonnington, A J and Watts, G A *Scots Law for Journalists* (6th edn, W. Green, 1995)

MacCormick, N *Legal Right and Social Democracy: Essays in Legal and Political Philosophy* (Clarendon Press, 1982)

McKechnie, J, Lindsay, S and Hobbs, S *Still Forgotten: Child Employment in Dumfries and Galloway* (Scottish Low Pay Unit, 1994)

Marshall, K *Children's Rights in the Balance* (The Stationery Office, 1997)

Mason, J K and McCall Smith, R A *Law and Medical Ethics* (4th edn, Butterworths, 1996)

Murray, K *Live Television Link: An Evaluation of its Use by Child Witnesses in Scottish Criminal Trials* (Scottish Office, 1995)

Murray, K and Asquith, S (eds) *Children's Evidence and Technology* (University of Glasgow, 1992)

Nicholls, G *A History of the Scotch Poor Law* (1856)

Norrie, K McK *Children (Scotland) Act 1995* (W. Green, 1995)

The Rights of the Child: A European Perspective (Council of Europe Publishing, 1996)

Robinson, J A (ed) *The Law of Children and Young Persons in South Africa* (Butterworths, 1997)

Smith, T B *A Short Commentary on the Law of Scotland* (W. Green & Son, 1962)

Spencer, J and Flin, R *The Evidence of Children: the Law and the Psychology* (2nd edn, Blackstone, 1993)

Stair *Institutions of the Law of Scotland* (1681)

Sutherland, E E and Cleland, A (eds) *Children's Rights in Scotland: Scots Law Analysed in the Light of the UN Convention on the Rights of the Child* (W. Green, 1996)

Van Bueren, G *The International Law on the Rights of the Child* (Martinus Nijhoff, 1995)

Veerman, P *The Rights of the Child and the Changing Image of Childhood* (Martinus Nijhoff, 1992)

Whitney, L and Cook, A *The Use of Closed-Circuit Television in New Zealand: The First Six Trials* (New Zealand Department of Justice, 1990)

Wilkinson, A B and Norrie, K McK *Parent and Child* (W. Green, 1993)

Articles

Bainham, A 'The Judge and the Competent Minor' (1992) 108 LQR 194

Bentovim, A and Simons, J 'Withholding Consent to Life-Saving Treatment: Three Cases' (1995) 310 Brit Med J 373

Chen, G Z 'Youth Curfews and the Trilogy of Parent, Child and State Relations' 72 NYUL Rev 131 (1997)

Cleland, A 'Representing Children – A Global View' 1994 JLSS 366

Cohen, C P 'A Guide to Linguistic Interpretation of the UN Convention on the Rights of the Child' in Cohen and Davidson *Children's Rights in America: UN Convention on the Rights of the Child Compared with United States Law* (American Bar Association, 1990)

Cohen, C P 'The Role of Non-Governmental Organisations in the Drafting of the Convention on the Rights of the Child' 12 Human Rights Quarterly 137 (1990)

Dickens, D M 'The Modern Function and Limits of Parental Rights' (1981) 97 LQR 462

Eekelaar, J 'The Emergence of Children's Rights' (1986) 6 Oxford L Stud 161

Federle, K H 'Children Curfews and the Constitution' 73 Wash U L Q 1315 (1995)

Fox, S J 'Beyond the American Legal System for the Protection of Children's Rights' 31 Fam L Q 237 (1997)

Freeman, M D A 'Laws, Conventions and Rights' (1993) 7 Children and Society 37

Giampetro-Meyer, Brown, T and Kubasek, N 'The Exploitation of Child

Labor: An Intractable Legal Problem?' 16 Loy L A Int'l & Comp L J 657 (1994)

Grant, J P and McLean S A M 'Police Contact with Children under Eight Years of Age' 1981 J Soc Welf L 140

Grant, J P 'Could Do Better: The Report on the UK's Compliance with the Convention on the Rights of the Child' 1995 JR 533

Guggenheim, M 'Reconsidering the Need for Council for Children in Custody, Visitation and Child Protection Proceedings' 29 Loy U Chi L J 299 (1998)

Hafen, B 'Children's Liberation and the New Egalitarianism: Some Reservations about Abandoning Youth to their Rights' BYUL Rev 605 (1976)

Kiernan, K 'Lone Motherhood, Employment and Outcomes for Children' (1996) Int'l J Law and the Family 231

Kizer, S A 'Juvenile Curfew Laws: Is There a Standard?' 45 Drake L Rev 749 (1997)

Klein, E K 'Dennis the Menace or Billy the Kid: An Analysis of the Role of Transfer to Criminal Court in Juvenile Justice' 35 Am Crim L Rev 371 (1998)

MacCormick, N 'Children's Rights: A Test Case' in MacCormick *Legal Rights and Social Democracy: Essays in Legal and Political Philosophy* (Clarendon Press, 1982)

Margulies, P 'The Lawyer as Caregiver: Child Client's Competence in Context' 64 Fordham L Rev 1473 (1996)

Minow, M 'Rights for the Next Generation: A Feminist Approach to Children's Rights' 9 Harv W L J 1 (1986)

Moran, M 'Ending Exploitative Child Labor Practices' 5 Pace Int'l Rev 287 (1993)

Muntarbhorn, V 'The Convention on the Rights of the Child: Reaching the Unreached?' (1992) 91 Bulletin of Human Rights 66

Norrie, K. McK 'The *Gillick* Case and Parental Rights in Scots Law' 1985 SLT (News) 157

Rentelin, A D 'Who's Afraid of the CRC: Objections to the Convention on the Rights of the Child' 3 ILSA J Int'l & Comp L 629 (1997)

Rosato, J L 'The Ultimate Test of Autonomy: Should Minors have the Right to Make Decisions Regarding Life-Sustaining Treatment?' 49 Rutgers L Rev 1 (1996)

Shear, L E 'Children's Lawyers in California Family Law Courts' 34 Fam and Conciliation Courts Review 256 (1996)

Sheldon, D H 'Children's Evidence, Competency and the New Hearsay Provisions' 1997 SLT (News) 1

Shepherd, R E Jr 'Juvenile Justice' 12 Crim Just 43 (1997)

Sutherland, E E 'A Voice for the Child and the Children (Scotland) Act 1995, Part I' 1996 JLSS 391

Sweeting, H and West, P 'Family Life and Health in Adolescence: A Role for Culture in the Health Inequalities Debate' (1995) 40 Soc Sci Med 163

Sweeting, H, West, P and Richards, A 'Teenage Family Life, Lifestyles and Life Chances: Association with Family Structure, Conflict with Parents and Joint Family Activity' 12 Int'l J Law, Policy and the Family 15 (1998)

Thomson, J M 'The *Gillick* Case and Parental Rights in Scots Law: Another View' 1985 SLT (News) 223

Wald, M 'Children's Rights: A Framework for Analysis' 12 UC Davis L Rev 225 (1979)

Reports

Consultation Paper on Further Measures to Support Child Witnesses in Civil and Criminal Proceedings (Scottish Courts Administration, 1997)

Consultation Paper on Identification of Children: Proposals to Amend Section 47 of the Criminal Procedure (Scotland) Act 1995 (Scottish Office, 1996)

Final Report of the [Oslo] International Conference of Child Labour (ILO, 1997)

Legal Capacity and Responsibilities of Minors and Pupils (Scot Law Com Consultative Memorandum No 65, 1985)

Report of the Committee on Children and Young Persons, Scotland (Cmnd 2306, 1964)

Report of the Departmental Committee on Protection and Training (HMSO, 1928)

Report on the Evidence of Children and Other Potentially Vulnerable Witnesses (Scot Law Com No 125, 1990)

Report on the Legal Capacity and Responsibility of Minors and Pupils (Scot Law Com No 110, 1987)

Sex Offenders: A Ban on Working With Children (Home Office and Scottish Office Consultation Paper, 1997)

The Use of Closed-Circuit Television for Child Witnesses in the ACT (Report for the Australian Law Commission, 1992: Cashmore and De Haas)

CHAPTER 4

Books

Cleland and Sutherland (eds) *Children's Rights in Scotland: Scots Law Analysed in the Light of the UN Convention on the Rights of the Child* (W. Green, 1996)

Corea, G *The Mother Machine: Reproductive Technologies from Artificial Insemination to Artificial Wombs* (Perennial Library, 1985)

Cotton, K and Wynn, D *Baby Cotton: for love and money* (Dorling Kindersley, 1985)

Cusine, D J *New Reproductive Techniques: A Legal Perspective* (Gower, 1988)

Dworkin, A *Right-Wing Women* (Perigree Books, 1983)

Eekelaar, J and Sarcevic, P (eds) *Parenthood in Modern Society: Legal and Social Issues for the Twenty-First Century* (Martinus Nijhoff, 1993)

Hale, B (The Hon Mrs Justice, formerly Professor Brenda Hoggett) *From *the Test Tube to the Coffin: Choice and Regulation in Private Life*, The Hamlyn Lectures, Forty-Seventh Series (Sweet and Maxwell, 1996)

The Laws of Scotland: Stair Memorial Encyclopaedia (Butterworths)

McLean, S A M (ed) *Law Reform and Human Reproduction* (Gower, 1992)

Mason, J K (ed) *Paediatric Forensic Medicine and Pathology* (Chapman and Hall, 1989)

Mason, J K *Forensic Medicine for Lawyers* (3rd edn, Butterworths, 1995)

Mason, J K *Medico-Legal Aspects of Reproduction and Parenthood* (Dartmouth, 1998)

Mason, J K and McCall Smith, R A *Law and Medical Ethics* (4th edn, Butterworths, 1994)

Ochiltree, G *Children in Stepfamilies* (Prentice Hall, 1990)

Smout, T C *A Century of Scottish People 1830–1950* (Fontana Press, 1969)

Sutherland, E E *Grandparents and the Law in Scotland* (Age Concern Scotland, 1993)

Triseliotis, J *In Search of Origins* (Routledge and Kegan Paul, 1973)

Wilkinson A B and Norrie, K McK *Parent and Child* (W. Green, 1993)

Articles

Barratt, C L R and Cooke, I D 'Risks of Donor Insemination' (1989) 299 BMJ 1178

Baunach, C G 'The Role of Equitable Adoption in a Mistaken Baby Switch' 31 U Louisville J Fam L 501 (1992/93)

Berry, J J 'Life After Death: Preservation of the Immortal Seed' 72 Tul L Rev 231 (1997)

Bissett-Johnson, A 'Name, Nationality and Identity' in Cleland and Sutherland (eds) *Children's Rights in Scotland: Scots Law Analysed in the Light of the UN Convention on the Rights of the Child* (W. Green, 1996)

Byers, K A 'Infertility and *In Vitro* Fertilisation: A Growing Need for Consumer-Oriented Regulation of the *In Vitro* Fertilisation Industry' 18 J Legal Med 265 (1997)

Cannon, S 'Finding Their Own "Place To Be": What Gregory Kingsley's and Kimberley Mays' "Divorces" from their Parents have done for Children's Rights' 39 Loy L Rev 837 (1994)

Chester, R 'To Be, Be, Be ... Not Just To Be: The Legal and Social Implications of Cloning for Human Reproduction' 49 Fal L Rev 303 (1997)

Hale, B (The Hon Mrs Justice, formerly Professor Brenda Hoggett) 'Hatchings' in *From the Test Tube to the Coffin: Choice and Regulation in Private Life*, The Hamlyn Lectures Forty-Seventh Series (Sweet and Maxwell, 1996)

Harlow, H H 'Paternalism Without Paternity: Discrimination Against Single Women Seeking Artificial Insemination by Donor' 6 S Cal Rev & Women's Stud 173 (1996)

Katz, K D 'Ghost Mothers: Human Egg Donation and the Legacy of the Past' 57 Alb L Rev 733 (1994)

King, A E 'Solomon Revisited: Assigning Parenthood in the Context of Collaborative Reproduction' 5 UCLA Women's L J 329 (1995)

Kuo, L 'Lessons Learned from Great Britain's Human Fertilisation and Embryology Act: Should the United States Regulate the Fate of Unused Human Embryos?' 19 Loy L A Int'l & Comp I J 1027 (1997)

MacDonald, P M 'DNA Profiling – Less than the Whole Truth' 1990 SLT (News) 285

McLean, J 'Human Cloning: A Dangerous Dilemma' (1998) 43 JLSS 24

Mcmillen, J 'Begging the Wisdom of Solomon: Hiding Behind the Issue of Standing in Custody Disputes to Treat Children as Chattel without Regard for their Best Interests' 39 St Louis U L J 699 (1995)

Miller, E P *Deboer* v *Schmidt* and *Twigg* v *Mays*: Does the "Best Interests of the Child" Standard Protect the Best Interests of Children?' 20 J Contemp L 497 (1994)

Newman, S A 'Human Cloning and the Family: Reflections on Cloning Existing Children' 13 N Y L Sch J Hum Rts 523 (1997)

Nolan, L C 'Posthumous Conception: A Private or Public Matter?' 11 B Y U J Pub L 1 (1997)

Norrie, J K 'Legal Regulation of Human Reproduction in Great Britain' in, McLean, S A M (ed) *Law Reform and Human Reproduction* (Gower, 1992)

Paine, S J, Moore, P K and Hill, D L 'Ethical Dilemmas in Reproductive Medicine' 18 Whittier L Rev 51 (1996)

O'Donovan, K 'Right to Know One's Parentage' 1988 Int'l J of Law and the Family 27

Rankin, J J 'DNA Fingerprinting' (1988) 33 JLSS 124

Rao, R 'Reconceiving Privacy. Relationships and Reproductive Technology' 45 UCLA L Rev 1077 (1998)

Richards, J L 'Redefining Parenthood: Parental Rights versus the Rights of the Child' 40 Wayne L Rev 1227 (1994)

Robertson, J A 'Liberty, Identity and Human Cloning' 76 Tex L Rev 1371 (1998)

Schiff, A R 'Arising from the Dead: Challenges of Posthumous Procreation' 75 N C L Rev 901 (1997)

Sera, J M 'Surrogacy and Prostitution: A Comparative Analysis' 5 Am U J Gender & L 315 (1997)

Snyder, R S 'Reproductive Technology and Stolen Ova: Who Is The Mother?' 16 Law and Ineq 289 (1998)

Steinberg, D I 'Divergent Conceptions: Procreational Rights and Disputes over the Fate of Frozen Embryos' 75 BU Pub Int L J 315 (1997)

Swanson, H S W 'Donor Anonymity in Artificial Insemination: Is It Still Necessary?' 27 Colum J L & Soc Probs 151 (1993)

Reports

A Critique of Human Cloning: Report and Recommendations of the National Bioethics Advisory Commission (1997)

Consent and the Law: Review of the Current Provisions of the Human Fertilisation and Embryology Act 1990 (Department of Health, 1997)

Group of Advisers on the Ethical Implications of Biotechnology to the European Commission, Ethical Aspects of Cloning Techniques (1997)

Evidence: Blood Group Tests, DNA Tests, and Related Matters (Scot Law Com Discussion Paper No 80, 1988)

HFEA Code of Practice (2nd revision, 1995)

Human Fertilisation and Embryology: A Framework for Legislation (White Paper: Cm 259, 1987)

Registrar General for Scotland, Annual Report 1997 (General Register Office for Scotland, 1998)

Registrar General for Scotland, Annual Report 1996 (General Register Office for Scotland, 1997)

Report of the Committee of Inquiry into Human Fertilisation and Embryology (Cmnd 9314, 1984)

Report on Evidence: Blood Group Tests, DNA Tests, and Related Matters (Scot Law Com No 120, 1989)

Report on Succession (Scot Law Com No 124, 1990)

Review of the Consent Provisions of the Human Fertilisation and Embryology Act 1990 (Department of Health, 1998) (McLean Report)

Review of the Guidance on the Resarch Use of Foetuses and Foetal Material (the Polkinghorne Report) (Cmd 762, 1989)

Surrogacy Review for Health Ministers of Current Arrangements for Payments and Regulation (Cm 4068, 1998)

CHAPTER 5

Books

Bankton *An Institute of the Law of Scotland* (1753)

Blankenhorn, D *Fatherless America: Confronting Our Most Urgent Social Problem* (Basic Books, 1995)

Boyd, S E (ed) *Challenging the Public/Private Divide: Feminism, Law and Public Policy* (University of Toronto Press, 1997)

Clive, E M *The Law of Husband and Wife in Scotland* (4th edn, W. Green, 1997)

Craig *Jus feudale* (1655)

Erskine *Institutes* (1773)

Fineman, M A *The Neutered Mother, The Sexual Family* (Routledge, 1995)

Fraser, Lord *Parent and Child* (3rd edn, J. Clark (ed), 1906)

Friedman, D *Towards a Structure of Indifference: The Social Origins of Maternal Custody* (Aldine de Gruyter, 1995)

Goldstein, J, Freud, A and Solnit, A J *Before the Best Interests of the Child* (Free Press, 1979)

Goldstein, J, Freud, A, Solnit, A J and Goldstein, S *In The Best Interests of the Child* (Free Press, 1986)

Goldstein, J, Solnit, A J and Freud, A *Beyond the Best Interests of the Child* (rev edn, Free Press, 1979)

Hester, M and Radford, L *Domestic Violence in Child Contact Arrangements in England and Denmark* (The Policy Press, 1996)

Hope *Major Practicks* (Stair Society)

Irving, H H and Benjamin, M *Family Mediation: Contemporary Issues* (Sage Publications, 1995)

LaRossa, R *The Modernization of Fatherhood: A Social and Political History* (The University of Chicago Press, 1997)

The Laws of Scotland: Stair Memorial Encyclopaedia (Butterworths)

Maccoby, E E and Mnookin, R H *Dividing the Child: Social and Legal Dilemmas of Custody* (Harvard University Press, 1994)

Mitchell, A *Children in the Middle: Living Through Divorce* (Tavistock Publications, 1985)

Norrie, K McK *Children (Scotland) Act 1995* (W. Green, 1995)

Stair *Institutions of the Law of Scotland* (1681)

Wallerstein, J S and Kelly, J B *Surviving the Breakup: How Children and Parents Cope with Divorce* (Basic Books, 1980)

Wilkinson, A B and Norrie, K McK *Parent and Child* (W. Green, 1993)

Articles

Abraham, D L 'California's Stepparent Visitation Statute: For the Welfare of the Child, or a Court-Opened Door to Legally Interfere with Parental Autonomy: Where are the Constitutional Safeguards' 7 S Cal Rev L & Women's Studies 125 (1997)

Boyd, S E 'Looking Beyond *Tyabji*: Employed Mothers, Lifestyles, and Child Custody' in Boyd (ed) *Challenging the Public/Private Divide: Feminism, Law and Public Policy* (University of Toronto Press, 1997)

Cannon, S A 'Finding Their Own "Place To Be": What Gregory Kingsley's and Kimberley Mays' "Divorces" from their Parents have done for Children's Rights' 39 Lov L Rev 837 (1994)

Clive, E M 'Legal Aspects of Illegitimacy in Scotland' 1979 SLT (News) 233

Mnookin, R H 'Child Custody Adjudication: Judicial Functions in the Face of Indeterminacy' 39 Law & Contemp Prob 227 (1975)

Murray, J C 'Legal Images of Motherhood: Conflicting Definitions from Welfare "Reform", Family and Criminal Law' 83 Cornell L Rev 688 (1998)

Neely, R 'The Primary Caretaker Parent Rule: Child Custody and the Dynamics of Greed' 3 Yale L & Pol Rev 167 (1984)

Polikoff, N 'This Child Does Have Two Mothers: Redefining Parenthood to Meet the Needs of Children in Lesbian and Other Nontraditional Families' 78 Geo L J 459 (1990)

Sheldon, D H 'Children's Evidence, Competency and the New Hearsay Provisions' 1997 SLT (News) 1

Strasser, M 'Fit to be Tied: On Custody, Discretion and Sexual Orientation' 46 Am U L Rev 841 (1997)

Sutherland, E E 'Mother Knows Best' 1994 SLT (News 375

Sutherland, E E 'Neither a Presumption Nor a Principle' 1996 JR 414

Sutherland, E E 'The Unequal Struggle: Fathers and Children in Scots Law' 1997 CFLQ 191

Tasker, F and Golombok, S 'Children Raised by Lesbian Mothers' 1991 Fam Law 184

Weisberg, D K 'Professional Women and the Professionalization of

Motherhood: Marcia Clark's Double Bind' 6 Hastings Women's L J 295 (1995)

Reports

Family Law: Illegitimacy (Scot Law Com Consultative Memorandum No 53, 1982)

Into a New World: Young Women's Sexual and Reproductive Lives (International Planned Parenthood Federation, 1998)

Parental Responsibilities and Rights, Guardianship and the Administration of Children's Property (Scot Law Com Discussion Paper No 88, 1990)

Registrar General for Scotland, Annual Report 1996 (Registrar General for Scotland, 1997)

Registrar General for Scotland, Annual Report 1997 (Registrar General for Scotland, 1998)

Report on Family Law (Scot Law Com No 135, 1992)

Report on Guardianship and Custody Law (Law Com No 172, 1988)

Report on Illegitimacy (Scot Law Com No 82, 1984)

Report of the Inquiry into the Removal of Children from Orkney in February 1991 (HMSO, 1992)

Report on the Legal Capacity and Responsibility of Minors and Pupils (Scot Law Com No 110, 1987)

Report on Outdated Rules in the Law of Husband and Wife (Scot Law Com No 76, 1983)

Report on Reform of the Ground for Divorce (Scot Law Com No 116, 1989)

Scotland's Children: Proposals for Child Care Policy and Law (Cm 2286, 1993)

Second Report on Illegitimacy (Law Com No 157, 1986)

CHAPTER 6

Books

Bird, R *Child Maintenance – The Child Support Act 1991* (3rd edn, Family Law, 1996)

Burgess, A *A Complete Parent: Towards a New Vision for Child Support* (Institute for Public Policy Research, 1998)

Burrows, D *The Child Support Act 1991 – A Practitioner's Guide* (Butterworths, 1993)

Cleland and Sutherland *Children's Rights in Scotland: Scots Law Analysed in the Light of the UN Convention on the Rights of the Child* (W. Green, 1996)

Crawford, E B *Private International Law* (W. Green, 1998)

Dwyer, J G *Religious Schools v Children's Rights* (Cornell University Press, 1998)

Edwards, L and Griffiths, A *Family Law* (W. Green, 1997)

Erskine *Institutes* (1773)

Erskine *Principles* (1754)

Fraser *Parent and Child* (3rd edn, J. Clark (ed), 1906)

Freeman, M (ed) *Divorce: Where Next?* (Dartmouth, 1996)

Garfinkel, I *Assuring Child Support: An Extension of Social Security* (Russell Sage Foundation, 1992)

Garnham, A and Knights, E *Putting the Treasury First: The Truth About Child Support* (Child Poverty Action Group, 1994)

Glendon, M A *The Transformation of Family Law*

Gordon, G H *The Criminal Law of Scotland* (2nd edn, W. Green, 1978)

Hawkins, A J and Dollahite, D C *Generative Fathering: Beyond Deficit Perspectives* (Sage, 1997)

Jamieson, G *Parental Responsibilities and Rights* (W. Green, 1995)

Knights, E, Garnham, A and McDowell, J *The Child Support Handbook* (3rd edn, Child Poverty Action Group, 1995)

Knights, E and Cox, S *The Child Support Handbook* (5th edn, Child Poverty Action Group, 1997)

Laws of Scotland: Stair Memorial Encyclopaedia, vol. 8 (Butterworths)

Marr, R and Marr, C *Scots Education Law* (W. Green, 1995)

Morgan, P *Are Families Affordable? Tax, Benefits and the Family* (Centre for Policy Studies, 1996)

Newell *Children Are People Too* (Bedford Square Press, 1989)

Stair *Institutions of the Law of Scotland* (1681)

Utting, D *Families and Parenthood: Supporting Families, Preventing Breakdown* (Joseph Rowntree Foundation, 1995)

Wilkinson, A B and Norrie, K McK *Parent and Child* (Scottish Universities Law Institute Ltd, 1993)

Young, R, Davis, G, Wikeley, N, Barron, J and Bedward, J *Child Support in Action* (Hart Publishing, 1998)

Articles

Balfour, I L S 'Child Abduction' in Cleland and Sutherland *Children's Rights in Scotland: Scots Law Analysed in the Light of the UN Convention on the Rights of the Child* (W. Green, 1996)

Bitensky, S H 'Spare the Rod, Embrace our Humanity: Toward a New Legal Regime Prohibiting Corporal Punishment of Children' 31 U Mich J L Rev 353 (1998)

Cahn, N R 'Pragmatic Questions about Parental Responsibility Statutes' Wis L Rev 399 (1996)

Cleland, A 'The Child's Right to Education' in Cleland and Sutherland *Children's Rights in Scotland: Scots Law Analysed in the Light of the UN Convention on the Rights of the Child* (W. Green, 1996)

Cox, J C 'Parental Rights and Responsibilities of Control over Children's Education' 26 J L & Educ 179 (1990)

Deech, R 'Property and Money Matters' in Freeman (ed) *Divorce: Where Next?* (Dartmouth, 1996)

Dimitrios, J E 'Parental Responsibility Statutes – and the Programs that Must Accompany Them' 27 Stetson L Rev 655 (1997)

Doherty, W J 'The Best of Times and the Worst of Times: Fathering as a Contested Arena of Academic Discourse' in Hawkins and Dollahite *Generative Fathering: Beyond Deficit Perspectives* (Sage, 1997)

Dudley, J R 'Exploring Ways to Get Divorced Fathers to Comply Willingly' 14 J Divorce and Re-marriage 98 (1994)

Fuller, D W 'Public School Access: The Constitutional Right of Home-Schoolers to "Opt In" to Public Education on a part-Time Basis' 82 Minn L Rev 1599 (1998)

Garrison, M 'Autonomy or Community? An Evaluation of Two Models of Parental Obligation' 86 Cal L Rev 41 (1998)

Gilles, S G 'Liberal Parentalism and Children's Educational Rights' 26 Cap U L Rev 9 (1997)

Harrison, M 'Australia's Child Support Scheme: Much Promised, Little Delivered' (1995) 42 Family Matters 7

Kelly, L 'Dividing the Deep and Inscrutable: Towards a Gender-Neutral, Child-Centred Approach to Child Name Change Proceedings' 99 W Va L Rev 1 (1996)

Knox, V W 'The Effects of Child Support Payments on Developmental Outcomes for Elementary School Age Children' (1996) 31 J Human Resources 4

Lane, L L 'The Parental Rights Movement' 69 U Colo L Rev 825 (1998)

Logie, J G 'Parental Choice and the Courts' 1989 SLT (News) 417

Riethmuller, G T 'Reviewing the Method of Review: A Review of the Administrative Departure Procedures under the Child Support (Assessment) Act 1989' (1995) 9 AJFL 6

Scarola, T 'Creating Problems Rather Than Solving Them: Why Criminal Parental Responsibility Laws Do Not Fit With Our Understanding of Justice' 66 Fordham L Rev 1029 (1997)

Schmidt, P W 'Dangerous Children and the Regulated Family: The Shifting Focus of Parental Responsibility Laws' 73 N Y U L Rev 667 (1998)

Seager, A 'Parental Choice of School' 1982 SLT (News) 29

Thomason, S C 'Education Law' 20 U Ark Little Rock L J 453 (1998)

Wasoff, F 'The New Child Support Formula: Algebra for Lawyers?' 1992 SLT (News) 389

Waters, C 'A, B, C's and Condoms for Free: A Legislative Solution to Parents' Rights and Condom Distribution in Public Schools' 31 Val U L Rev 787 (1997)

Wilson, W A 'The Bairns of Falkirk: The Child Support Act 1991' 1991 SLT (News) 417

Woodhouse, B B 'A Public Role in the Private Family: The Parental Rights and Responsibilities Act and the Politics of Child Protection and Education' 57 Ohio St L J 393 (1996)

Reports

Child Abduction (Scot Law Com Discussion Paper No 67, 1985)

Children Come First (White Paper: Cm 1264, 1990)

Children First: a new approach to child support (Green Paper: Cm 3992, 1998)

House of Commons Committee on Public Accounts, Twenty-First Report: Child Support Agency: Client Funds Accounts 1996–97 (The Stationery Office, 1998)

Improving Child Support (White Paper: Cm 2745, 1994)

Into a New World: Young Women's Sexual and Reproductive Lives (International Planned Parenthood Federation, 1998)

Legal Capacity and Responsibility of Minors and Pupils (Scot Law Com Consultative Memorandum No 65, 1985)

New Ambitions for Our Country: A New Contract for Welfare (Cm 3805, 1998)

Parental Responsibilities and Rights, Guardianship and the Administration of Children's Property (Scot Law Com Discussion Paper No 88, 1990)

Report on Aliment and Financial Provision (Scot Law Com No 67, 1981)

Report on Child Abduction (Scot Law Com No 102, 1987)

Report on Family Law (Scot Law Com No 135, 1992)

Report on the Legal Capacity of Minors and Pupils (Scot Law Com No 110, 1987)

CHAPTER 7

Books

Ashley, B *A Stone on the Mantlepiece* (The Scottish Academic Press, 1985)

Bell, S *When Salem Came to the Boro'* (Pan Books, 1988)

Cretney, S M and Masson, J M *Principles of Family Law* (6th edn, 1996, Sweet and Maxwell)

Fabb, J and Guthrie, G T *Social Work Law in Scotland* (2nd edn, Butterworths, 1997)

Kempe, R S and H *The Common Secret: Sexually Abused Children and Adolescents* (Freeman, 1984)

Kempe, R S and Krugman, R D (eds) *The Battered Child* (5th edn, University of Chicago Press, 1997)

Lyon, C and De Cruz, P *Child Abuse* (2nd edn, 1993)

Mason, K (ed) *Paediatric Forensic Medicine and Pathology* (Chapman and Hall, 1989)

Murray, K and Gough, D A (eds) *Intervening in Child Sexual Abuse* (Scottish Academic Press, 1991)

Norrie, K *Children's Hearings in Scotland* (W. Green, 1997)

Articles

Caffey, J 'Multiple Fractures in the Long Bones of Infants Suffering from Chronic Subdural Hematoma' 56 A J Roentgenol 163 (1946)

Dickens, J 'Assessment and Control in Social Work: An Analysis of the Reasons for the Non-Use of Child Assessment Orders' [1993] JSWFL 88

Eekelaar, J '"The Chief Glory": The Export of Children from the United Kingdom' (1994) 21 JLS 487

Hempe C H, Silverman F N, Steele B F, Droegemueller W and Silver, H K 'The Battered-Child Syndrome' 181 J Am Med Assoc 17 (1962)

Kempe, R S, Cutler, C, and Dean J 'The Infant with Failure-to-Thrive' in Helfner, Kempe and Krugman (eds) *The Battered Child* (5th edn, University of Chicago Press, 1997)

Lavery, R 'The Child Assessment Order – A Reassessment' [1966] CFLQ 41

Meriweather, M 'Child Abuse Reporting Laws: A Time for Change' 20 Fam LQ 141 (1986)

Radbill S X 'Children in a World of Violence: The History of Child Abuse' in Helfner, Kempe and Krugman (eds) *The Battered Child* (5th edn, University of Chicago Press, 1997)

Silverman, F 'The Roentgen Manifestations of Unrecognized Skeletal Trauma' 9 Am J Roentgenol Radium Ther Nucl Med 413 (1953)

Smallwood, D 'Münchhausen Syndrome' [1996] Fam L 478

Sutherland, E E 'The Orkney Case' 1992 JR 93

Sutherland, E E 'Clyde and Beyond: The Report of the Inquiry into the Removal of Children from Orkney in February 1991' 1993 JR 178

Reports

Accommodating Children (Social Services Inspectorate and Social Information Systems, 1992)

Another Kind of Home: a review of residential child care (the 'Skinner Report') (HMSO, 1992)

Castle Hill Report (Shropshire County Council, 1992)

Child Abuse: A Study of Inquiry Reports 1973–1981 (HMSO, 1982)

A Child in Mind: Protection of Children in a Responsible Society (DHSS, 1987)

Child Protection: Local Liaison Machinery – Child Protection Committees (Circular No SWSG 14/97)

A Child in Trust: Jasmine Beckford (DHSS, 1985)

Children in Public Care (the 'Utting Report') (1991)

Choosing with Care: Report of the Inquiry into the Selection, Development and Management of Staff in Children's Homes (HMSO, 1992)

Effective Intervention: Child Abuse – Guidance on Co-operation in Scotland (Scottish Office, 1989)

Emergency Protection of Children in Scotland (SWSG, 1993)

Kent, R Children's Safeguards Review (The Scottish Office, 1997)

Meeting the Childcare Challenge: A Childcare Strategy for Scotland (The Stationery Office, 1998) (Cm 3958, 1998)

People Like Us: The Report of the Review of Safeguards for Children Living Away from Home (Department of Health/Welsh Office, 1997)

The Pindown Experience and the Protection of Children: The Report of the Staffordshire Child Care Inquiry (Staffordshire Social Services, 1991)

Protecting Children – A Shared Responsibility: Guidance on Inter-Agency Co-operation (Scottish Office, 1998)

Report of the Committee of Inquiry into the Care and Supervision Provided in Relation to Maria Colwell (DHSS, 1974)

Report of the Committee of Inquiry into Children's Homes and Hostels (HMSO, 1985)

Report of the Committee of Inquiry into the Removal of Children from Orkney in February 1991 (the 'Clyde Report') (HMSO, 1992)

Report of the Inquiry into Child Abuse in Cleveland 1987 (the 'Cleveland Report') (HMSO, 1988, Cm 412)

Report of the Inquiry into Child Care Policies in Fife (the 'Kearney Report') (HMSO, 1992)

Report of the Inquiry into the Conduct of Leeway's Children's Home (London Borough of Lewisham, 1985)

Reporters to the Children's Panel: Their Role, Function and Accountability (the 'Finlayson Report') (HMSO, 1992)

Review of Child Care Law in Scotland (HMSO, 1990)

Scotland's Children: The Children (Scotland) Act 1995 Regulations and Guidance, vol 1, Support and Protection for Children and their Families (2nd edn, 1997). [Also in the series, vol 2, Children Looked After by Local Authorities, and vol 3, Adoption and Parental Responsibilities Orders]

Scotland's Children: Proposals for Child Care Policy and Law (HMSO, 1993)

Triseliotis, J, Borland, M and Hill, M Fostering Good Relations: A Study of Foster Care and Foster Carers in Scotland. Social Work Research Findings No 22 (Scottish Office, 1998)

Ty Mawr Community Home Inquiry (Gwent County Council, 1992)

Whose Child? (DHSS, 1987)

Working Together under the Children Act 1989 (Department of Health, 1991)

CHAPTER 8

Books

Butterworth's Scottish Family Law Service, paras C1504–C1526

Cameron, J *Celtic Law* (W. Hodge, 1937)

Cleland, A and Sutherland, E E (eds) *Children's Rights in Scotland: Scots Law Analysed in the Light of the UN Convention on the Rights of the Child* (W. Green, 1996)

Crawford, E *Private International Law* (W. Green, 1997)

Cretney, S M and Masson, J M *Principles of Family Law* (6th edn, Sweet and Maxwell, 1997)

Friedman, L M *A History of American Law* (2nd edn, Simon and Schuster, 1985)

Goldstein, J, Solnit, A J and Freud, A *Beyond the Best Interests of the Child* (1st edn, revised edn, Free Press, 1973/1979)

The Laws of Scotland: Stair Memorial Encyclopaedia (Butterworths)

Lowe, N V and Douglas, G (eds) *Families Across Frontiers* (Martinus Nijhoff, 1996)

McNeill, P G B *Adoption of Children in Scotland* (3rd edn, W. Green, 1998)

Rosenblatt *International Adoption* (Sweet and Maxwell, 1995)

Triseliotis, J *In Search of Origins* (Routledge and Kegan Paul, 1973)

Triseliotis, J, Shireman, J and Hundleby, M *Adoption: Theory, Policy and Practice* (Cassell, 1997)

Wilkinson, A B and Norrie, K McK *Parent and Child* (W. Green, 1993)

Articles

Anonymous 'The Adoption of Children (Scotland) Act 1930' 1930 SLT (News) 153

Craig, T L 'Establishing the Biological Rights Doctrine to Protect Unwed Fathers in Contested Adoptions' 25 Fla St U L Rev 391 (1998)

Davies, J F 'Two Moms and a Baby: Protecting the Nontraditional Family Through Second Parent Adoptions' 29 New Eng L Rev 1055 (1995)

Fogg-Davis, H 'A Race-Conscious Argument for Transracial Adoption' 6 B U Pub Int L J 385 (1997)

Howe, R-A W 'Transracial Adoption: Old Prejudices and Discrimination Float Under a New Halo' 6 B U Pub Int L J 409 (1997)

Kelman, M G 'Consumption Theory, Production Theory and the Ideology of the Coase Theorem' 52 S Cal L Rev 669

Korn, K 'The Struggle for the Child: Preserving the Family in Adoption Disputes Between Biological Parents and Third Parties' 72 N C L Rev 1279 (1994)

Landes, E and Posner R A 'The Economics of the Baby Shortage' 7 J Legal Studies 323 (1978)

Masson, J M and Harrison, C 'Identity: Mapping the Frontiers' in Lowe and Douglas (eds) *Families Across Frontiers* (Martinus Nijhoff, 1996)

Miller, E P 'DeBoer v Schmidt and Twiggs v Mays: Does the "Best Interests of the Child" Standard Protect the Best Interests of Children?' 20 J Contemp L 497 (1994)

Norrie, K McK 'Parental Pride: Adoption and the Gay Man' 1996 SLT (News) 321

Posner, R A 'Regulation of the Market in Adoptions' 67 B U L Rev 59 (1987)

Prichard, J R S 'A Market for Babies?' 34 U Toronto L J 341

Scott, J M 'Adoption' in Cleland and Sutherland (eds) *Children's Rights in Scotland: Scots Law Analysed in the Light of the UN Convention on the Rights of the Child* (W. Green, 1996)

Sutherland, E E 'Adoption: The Child's View' 1994 SLT (News) 37

Sutherland, E E 'Another Unfounded Assumption Laid to Rest?' 1997 JR 373

Weaver-Catalana, B 'The Battle for Baby Jessica: A Conflict of Interests' 43 Buff L Rev 583 (1995)

Zainaldin, J 'The Emergence of a Modern American Family Law: Child Custody, Adoption and the Courts, 1796–1851' 73 Northwestern U L Rev 1038 (1979)

Reports

Adoption: The Future (HMSO, 1993)

The Adoption Process (Discussion Paper No 3, 1991, Scottish Office)

Agreement and Freeing (Discussion Paper No 2, 1992, Scottish Office)

Consultation Paper, Proposals for Intercountry Adoption (Scottish Office, 1996)

France, E. International Perspectives (Department of Health, 1990)

The Future of Adoption Law in Scotland (Scottish Office, 1993)

Intercountry Adoption (Discussion Paper No 4, 1992, Scottish Office)

The Nature and Effect of Adoption (Discussion Paper No 1, 1990, Scottish Office)

Registrar General Scotland, Annual Report 1995 (General Register Office for Scotland, 1996)

Registrar General Scotland, Annual Report 1997 (General Register Office for Scotland, 1998)

Report of the Child Adoption Committee (the 'Tomlin Report') (Cmd 2401, 1925)

Report of the Committee on Child Adoption (the 'Hopkinson Report') (Cmd 1254, 1921)

Report of the Departmental Committee on the Adoption of Children (the 'Houghton Committee') (Home Office and Scottish Office, 1972)

Report on Succession (Scot Law Com No 124, 1990)

Scotland's Children: The Children (Scotland Act 1995 Regulations and Guidance, vol 3, Adoption and Parental Responsibilities Orders (Scottish Office, 1997)

Thorburn, J Review of Research Relating to Adoption (Department of Health, 1990)

CHAPTER 9

Books

Cleland, A and Sutherland, E E (eds) *Children's Rights in Scotland: Scots Law Analysed in the Light of the UN Convention on the Rights of the Child* (W. Green, 1996)

Fox, S *Children's Hearings and the International Community*, 1991 Kilbrandon Child Care Lecture (Scottish Office, 1991)

Kearney, B *Children's Hearings and the Sheriff Court* (W. Green, 1987)

The Laws of Scotland: Stair Memorial Encyclopaedia (Butterworths)

Lockyer, A and Stone, F M *Juvenile Justice in Scotland: Twenty-Five Years of the Welfare Approach* (T & T Clark, 1998)

Martin, F M and Murray K (eds) *The Scottish Juvenile Justice System* (Scottish Academic Press, 1982)

Norrie, K McK *Children's Hearings in Scotland* (W. Green, 1997)

Watson, J M *Solvent Abuse – The Adolescent Epidemic?* (1986)

Wilkinson, A B and Norrie, K McK *Parent and Child* (W. Green, 1993)

Articles

Breustedt, R, Kearney, B, Stevens A, and Sutherland, E E 'The Evolution of the Children's Hearings System over the Last Twenty-Five Years' (1997) 2 SLPQ 73

Gordon, A 'The Role of the State' in Cleland and Sutherland (eds) *Children's Rights in Scotland: Scots Law Analysed in the Light of the UN Convention on the Rights of the Child* (W. Green, 1996)

Sutherland, E E 'The Role of the Safeguarder' in *Representing Children: Listening to the Voice of the Child* (Scottish Child Law Centre, 1996)

Reports

Another Kind of Home: A Review of Residential Child Care (the 'Skinner Report') (HMSO, 1992)

Consulation on Inter-Agency Code of Practice and National Standards for the Processing of Children's Cases (Scottish Children's Reporter Administration, 1998)

Emergency Protection of Children: Consultation Paper on Proposals for Change (HMSO, 1993)

Just in Time: Report on Time Intervals in Children's Hearings Cases (Scottish Children's Reporter Administration, 1997)

Report of the Committee on Children and Young Persons, Scotland (the 'Kilbrandon Report') (Cmnd 2306, 1964)

Report of the Inquiry into Child Care Policies in Fife (the 'Kearney Report') (HMSO, 1992)

Report of the Inquiry into the Removal of Children from Orkney in February 1991 (the 'Clyde Report') (HMSO, 1992)

Reporters to the Children's Panel: Their Role, Function and Accountability (the 'Finlayson Report') (HMSO, 1992)

Review of Child Care Law in Scotland (HMSO, 1990)

Scotland's Children: Proposals for Child Care Policy and Law (Cm 2286, 1993)

Scotland's Parliament (Cm 3658, 1997)

Social Work and the Commmunity (Cmnd 3065, 1966)

Statistical Bulletin: Referrals of Children to Reporters and Children's Hearings 1996/97 (No SCRA/IM/1998/21)

Twenty-one Years of Children's Hearings (The Scottish Office, 1993)

CHAPTER 10

Books

Barry, J C (trs and ed) *William Hay's Lectures on Marriage* (Stair Society, 1967)

Bradney, D *Family Law and Political Culture* (Sweet & Maxwell, 1996)

Bromley, P M and Lowe, N V *Family Law* (8th edn, Butterworths, 1992)

Cameron, J *Celtic Law* (Hodge, 1937)

Carey Miller, D and Meyers, D *Comparative and Historical Essays in Scots Law* (1992)

Clive, E M *The Law of Husband and Wife in Scotland* (4th edn, W. Green, 1997)

Collins, W *Man and Wife* (OUP, 1995)

Cretney, S M and Masson, J M *Principles of Family Law* (6th edn, Sweet & Maxwell, 1997)

Fergusson, J *A Treatise on the Present State of the Consistorial Law in Scotland* (Bell and Bradfute, 1829)

Glendon, M A *The Transformation of Law: State, Law and Family in the United States and Western Europe* (University of Chicago Press, 1989)

Longworth, T *Martyrs to Circumstance* (1861)

Lothian, M *The Law, Practice and Styles Peculiar to the Consistorial Actions Referred to the Court of Session* (Black, 1830)

Lowe, N V and Douglas, G *Bromley's Family Law* (9th edn, Butterworths, 1998)

McBryde, W W *The Law of Contract in Scotland* (W. Green, 1987)

Stair *Institutions of the Law of Scotland* (1681)

Walker, D M *The Law of Civil Remedies in Scotland* (W. Green, 1974)

Walker, D M *The Law of Contract and Related Obligations in Scotland* (3rd edn, T & T Clark, 1995)

Articles

Anderson, L 'Property Rights of Same-Sex Couples: Towards a New Definition of Family' 26 J Fam L 357 (1987)

Anton, A E and Francescakis, P 'Modern Scots "Runaway Marriages"' 1958 JR 253

Ashton-Cross, D I 'Cohabitation with Habit and Repute' (1961) JR 21

Baker, P 'President Quietly Signs a Law Aimed at Gay Marriages' *The Washington Post*, 22 September 1996

Bates, F 'Limited and Extraneous Purpose Marriages' (1975) 4 Anglo-American LR 69

Bromley, P M 'The Validity of "Sham Marriages" and Marriages Procured by Fraud' (1969) 15 McGill LJ 319

Cameli, M N 'Extending Family Benefits to Gay Men and Lesbian Women' 68 Chi-Kent L Rev 447 (1992)

Chambers, D L 'What If? The Legal Consequences of Marriage and the Legal Needs of Lesbian and Gay Male Couples' 95 Mich L Rev 447 (1996)

Clive, E M 'The Minimum Age for Marriage' 1968 SLT (News) 129

Eskridge, W N 'A History of Same-Sex Marriage' 79 Va L Rev 1419 (1993)

Kramer, L 'Same-Sex Marriage, Conflict of Laws, and the Unconstitutional Public Policy Exemption' 106 Yale L J 1965 (1997)

Moore 'A Defense of First Cousin Marriage' 10 Clev Mar L Rev 139 (1961)

Nichols, D 'Step-daughters and Mothers-in-law' 1986 SLT (News) 229

Norrie, K McK 'Transsexuals, the Right to Marry and Voidable Marriages in Scots Law' 1990 SLT (News) 353

O'Brien, R C 'Domestic Partnership: Recognition and Responsibility' 32 San Diego L Rev 163 (1995)

Provost, M A 'Disregarding the Constitution in the Name of Defending Marriage: The Unconstitutionality of the Defense of Marriage Act' 8 Seton Hall Const L J 157 (1997)

Robb, B A 'The Constitutionality of the Defense of Marriage Act in the Wake of Romer v Evans' 32 New Eng L Rev 263 (1997)

Roughead, W 'The Stolen Heiress: or The Biter Bit' (1927) 39 JR 233

Sellar, D P 'Marriage by Cohabitation with Habit and Repute: Review and Requiem?' in Carey Miller and Meyers *Comparative and Historical Essays in Scots Law* (1992)

Silberman, L J 'Can the Island of Hawaii Bind the World? A Comment on Same-Sex Marriage and Federalism Values' 16 Quinnipiac L Rev 191 (1996)

Spackman, P L 'Grant v South-West Trains: Equality for Same-Sex Partners in the European Community' 12 Am J Int'l L and Pol'y 1063 (1997)

Wardle, L D 'A Critical Analysis of Constitutional Claim for Same-Sex Marriage' 1996 BYU L Rev 1

Reports

The Effects of Cohabitation in Private Law (Scots Law Com Discussion Paper No 86, 1990)

Office for National Statistics, Regional Trends 33 (The Stationery Office, 1998)

Registrar General for Scotland, Annual Report 1997 (General Register Office for Scotland, 1998)

Report of the Committee on the Marriage Law of Scotland (the Morison Committee) (Cmd 5354, 1937)

Report of the Committee on the Marriage Law of Scotland (the Kilbrandon Committee) (Cmd 4011, 1969)

Report on Family Law (Scot Law Com No 135, 1992)

Report on Outdated Rules in the Law of Husband and Wife (Scot Law com No 76, 1983)

Report of the Royal Commission on the Laws of Marriage (1868)

Chapter 11

Books

Alison, A J *The Principles and Practice of the Criminal Law of Scotland*

Anton, A E *Private International Law* (2nd edn, W. Green, 1991)

Bankton *An Institute of the Law of Scotland* (1753)

Boyd, S B *Challenging the Public/Private Divide: Feminism, Law and Public Policy* (University of Toronto Press, 1997)

Chloros, A (ed) *International Encyclopaedia of Comparative Law* (1980)

Clive, E M *The Law of Husband and Wife in Scotland* (4th edn, W. Green, 1997)

Cretney, S M and Masson, J M *Principles of Family Law* (6th edn, Sweet and Maxwell, 1997)

Eekelaar, J M and Katz, S N (eds) *Marriage and Cohabitation in Contemporary Societies* (Butterworths, 1980)

Freeman, M D A and Lyon, C *Cohabitation without Marriage* (Gower, 1983)

Glazer, N *Women's Paid and Unpaid Work* (Temple University Press, 1991)

Glendon, M A *The New Family and the New Property* (Butterworths, 1981)

Glendon, M A *The Transformation of Family Law; State, Law and Family in the United States and Western Europe* (The University of Chicago Press, 1989)

Gloag, W M *The Law of Contract* (2nd edn, W. Green, 1929)

Hale, B (The Hon Mrs Justice, formerly Professor Brenda Hoggett) *From the Test Tube to the Coffin: Choice and Regulation in Private Life*, The Hamlyn Lectures, Forty-Seventh Series (Sweet and Maxwell, 1996)

An Introduction to Scottish Legal History (The Stair Society, 1958)

Jackson, D C *Immigration: Law and Practice* (Sweet and Maxwell, 1996)

Lowe, N V and Douglas, G *Bromley's Family Law* (9th edn, Butterworths, 1998)

MacDonald, I R and Blake, N *MacDonald's Immigration Law and Practice* (Butterworths, 1995)

Manners, A J and Rauta, I *Family Property in Scotland* (HMSO, 1981)

McBryde, W W *The Law of Contract in Scotland* (W. Green, 1987)

North, P M *The Private International Law of Matrimonial Causes in the British Isles and the Republic of Ireland* (Martinus Nijhoff, 1977)

O'Donovan, K *Sexual Divisions and the Law* (Weidenfeld and Nicolson, 1985)

Okin, S M *Justice, Gender and the Family* (Basic Books, 1989)

Parry, M L *The Law Relating to Cohabitation* (3rd edn, Sweet and Maxwell, 1993)

Rennie, R and Cusine, D J *The Requirements of Writing* (Butterworths, 1995)

Smart, C *The Ties that Bind: Law, Marriage and the Reproduction of Patriarchal Relations* (1984)

Stair *Institutions of the Law of Scotland* (1681)

Talman, I J S (ed) *Halliday's Conveyancing Law and Practice in Scotland* (2nd edn, W. Green, 1996)

Thomson, J M *Delictual Liability* (Butterworths, 1994)

Walker, A G and Walker, N *The Law of Evidence in Scotland* (T & T Clark, 1984)

Walker, D M *The Law of Contracts and Related Obligations in Scotland* (3rd edn, T & T Clark, 1995)

Walton, F P *A Handbook of Husband and Wife According to the Law of Scotland* (3rd edn, W. Green, 1951)

Weitzman, L *The Marriage Contract* (Free Press, 1981)

Articles

Armstrong, P 'Women's Paid and Unpaid Work' in Boyd, *Challenging the Public/Private Divide: Feminism, Law and Public Policy* (University of Toronto Press, 1997)

Becker, L 'Ethical Concerns in Negotiating Family Law Agreements' 30 Fam L Q 587 (1996)

Bonnington, A 'Stalking and the Scottish Courts' 1996 NLJ 1394

Boychuk, M K 'Are Stalking Laws Unconstitutionally Vague or Overboard?' 88 Northwestern U LR (1994) 769

Brinig, M F and Crafton, S M 'Marriage and Opportunism' 23 J Legal Stud 869 (1994)

Carson, W P Jr 'Domestic Violence: The Ultimate Oxymoron' 33 Willamette L Rev 767 (1997)

Featherston, T M and Douthitt, A E 'Changing the Rules by Agreement: The New Era in Characterisation, Management and Liability of Marital Property' 49 Baylor L Rev 271 (1997)

Goode 'Stalking: Crime of the Nineties' (1995) 19 Crim LJ 21

Gretton, G L 'Sexually Transmitted Debt' 1997 SLT (News) 195

Marston, A A 'Planning for Love: The Politics of Prenuptial Agreements' 49 Stan L Rev 887 (1997)

Mays, R, Middlemiss, S and Watson, J '"Every breath you take ... Every move you make" – Scots Law, The Protection from Harassment Act 1997 and the Problem of Stalking' 1997 JR 331

Minow, M 'Consider the Consequences' 94 Mich L Rev 900 (1986)

Norrie, K McK 'Proprietary Rights of Cohabitants' 1995 JR 209

Olsen, F 'The Family and the Market: A Study of Ideology and Legal Reform' 97 Harv L Rev 1497 (1983)

Sohn, E F 'Anti-stalking Statutes: Do They Actually Protect Victims?' 30 CLB 203 (1994)

Strikis, S A 'Stopping Stalking' 18 Georgetown LJ (1993) 2771

Whitty, N 'Indirect Enrichment in Scots Law' 1994 JR 200

Wong, S 'Constructive Trusts Over the Family Home: Lessons to be Learned from Other Commonwealth Jurisdictions' (1998) 18LS 369

Reports

The Effects of Cohabitation in Private Law (Scot Law Com Discussion Paper No 86, 1990)

Manners, A J and Rauta, I Family Property in Scotland (HMSO, 1981)

Report on Damages for Personal Injuries (Scot Law Com No 51, 1978)

Report on Family Law (Scot Law Com No 135, 1992)

Report on the Law of Incest in Scotland (Scot Law Com No 69, 1981)

Report on the Law Relating to Damages for Injuries Causing Death (Scot Law Com No 31, 1973)

Report on Liability for Adultery and Enticement of a Spouse (Scot Law Com No 42, 1976)

Report on Matrimonial Property (Scot Law Com No 86, 1984)

Report on Outdated Rules in the Law of Husband and Wife (Scot Law Com No 76, 1983)

Report on Succession (Scot Law Com No 124, 1990)

Statement of Changes in Immigration Rules (1994 HC 388)

Statement of Changes in Immigration Rules (Cm 3365, 1996)

Statement of Changes in Immigration Rules (1997 HC 26)

CHAPTER 12

Books

Dobash, R E and Dobash, R Violence Against Wives: A Case Against the Patriarchy (Open Books, 1979)

Eekelaar, J M and Katz, S N (eds) Family Violence (Butterworths, 1978)

Fineman, M and Mykitiuk, R (eds) *The Public Nature of Private Violence* (Routledge, 1994)

Macaskill, S and Eadie, D *An Evaluation of the Scottish Office Domestic Violence Media Campaign* (HMSO, 1995)

Manners A J and Rauta, I *Family Property in Scotland* (OPCS, 1981)

Nichols, D and Meston, M M *The Matrimonial Homes (Family Protection) (Scotland) Act 1981* (2nd edn, W. Green, 1986)

Pizzey, E *Scream Quietly or the Neighbours Will Hear* (Penguin, 1974)

Sussman, M B and Steinmetz, S K *Handbook of Marriage and the Family* (Plenum, 1987)

Walker, D M *The Law of Civil Remedies in Scotland* (W. Green, 1974)

Walker, G *Family Violence and the Women's Movement: The Conceptual Politics of Struggle* (University of Toronto Press, 1990)

Yllo, K and Bograd, M *Feminist Perspectives on Wife Abuse* (Sage, 1998)

Articles

Barnes, P G '"It's Just A Quarrel": Some States Offer No Domestic Violence Protection to Gays' 84 ABA J 24 (1998)

Clark, M L 'Feminist Perspectives on Violence Against Women and Children' 3 Canadian Journal on Women and the Law 421 (1989)

Da Luz, C M 'A Legal and Social Comparison of Heterosexual and Same-Sex Domestic Violence: Similar Inadequacies in Legal Recognition and Response' 4 S Cal Rev L & Women's Stud 251 (1994)

'Developments in the Law: Legal Responses to Domestic Violence' 106 Harv L Rev 1498 (1993)

Duthu, K F 'Why Doesn't Anyone Talk About Gay and Lesbian Domestic Violence?' 18 Thomas Jefferson L Rev 23

Hart, B J 'State Codes on Domestic Violence: Analysis, Commentary and Recommendations' 43 Juv & Fam Ct J (1992)

Lundy, S E 'Abuse That Dare Not Speak Its Name: Assisting Victims of Lesbian and Gay Domestic Violence in Massachusetts' 28 New Eng L Rev 273 (1993)

Murphy, N E 'Queer Justice: Equal Protection for Victims of Same-Sex Domestic Violence' 30 Val U L Rev 335 (1995)

Robson, R 'Lavender Bruises: Intra-Lesbian Violence, Law and Lesbian Legal Theory' 20 Golden Gate U L E 567 (1990)

Schneider, E 'The Violence of Privacy' in Fineman and Mykitiuk (eds) *The Public Nature of Private Violence* (Routledge, 1994)

Steinmetz, S K 'Family Violence: Past, Present and Future' in Sussman and Steinmetz *Handbook of Marriage and the Family* (Plenum, 1987)

Stevenson, G B 'Federal Antiviolence and Abuse Legislation: Towards Elimination of Disparate Justice for Women and Children' 33 Willamette L Rev 847 (1997)

Stewart, W J 'Non-Debtor Spouses and the Contents of Houses' 1989 SLT (News) 180

Strauss, M A and Gelles, R J 'Societal Changes and Change in Family Violence from 1975 to 1985 as Revealed in Two National Surveys' 48 Journal of Marriage and the Family (1986)

Strauss, M A 'Measuring Intrafamilial Conflict and Violence: The Conflict Tracts (CT) Scale' 41 Journal of Marriage and the Family 75 (1979)

Reports

An Evaluation of the Scottish Office Domestic Violence Media Campaign (HMSO, 1995)

Observations on the Report from the Select Committee on Domestic Violence in Marriage (Cmnd 6690, 1976)

Occupancy Rights in the Matrimonial Home and Domestic Violence (Scot Law Com, Consultative Memorandum No 41, 1978)

Report on Family Law (Scot Law Com No 135, 1992)

Report on Occupancy Rights in the Matrimonial Home and Domestic Violence (Scot Law Com No 60, 1980)

Report from the Select Committee on Domestic Violence in Marriage (1974–75) HC 533

Scottish Women's Aid Annual Report 1996–97

CHAPTER 13

Books

Anton, A E and Beaumont, P R *Private International Law* (2nd edn, W. Green, 1990)

Balfour, I L S *Separation Agreements* (5th edn, W. Green, 1997)

Bennett, S A *Divorce in the Sheriff Court* (5th edn, W. Green, 1997)

Crawford, E B *Private International Law* (W. Green, 1997)

Cretney, S M and Masson, J M *Principles of Family Law* (6th edn, Sweet and Maxwell, 1997)

Fineman, M A *Illusion of Equality: The Rhetoric and Reality of Divorce Reform* (University of Chicago Press, 1991)

Fraser, P *Husband and Wife According to the Law of Scotland* (2nd edn, 1876–78)

Friedman, L M *A History of American Law* (2nd edn, Simon and Schuster, 1985)

Glendon, M A *The Transformation of Family Law: State, Law and Family in the United States and Western Europe* (University of Chicago Press, 1989)

An Introduction to Scottish Legal History (vol 20, Stair Society)

Irving, H H and Benjamin, M *Family Mediation: Contemporary Issues* (Sage Publications, 1995)

Jolowicz, H F *Historical Introduction to the Study of Roman Law* (2nd edn, Cambridge University Press, 1967)

Lowe, N V and Douglas, G *Bromley's Family Law* (9th edn, Butterworths, 1998)

Maccoby, E E and Mnookin, R H *Dividing the Child: Social and Legal Dilemmas of Custody* (Harvard University Press, 1994)

Mackenzie, G *Criminal Law* (Edinburgh, 1678)

Weitzman, L J *The Divorce Revolution: The Unexpected Social and*

Economic Consequences for Women and Children in American (Free Press, 1985)

Articles

Blumberg, G 'Reworking the Past, Imagining the Future: On Jacob's Silent Ladder' 16 L & Soc Inquiry 115 (1991)

Brinig, M F and Crafton, S M 'Marriage and Opportunism' 23 J Legal Stud 869 (1994)

Duncan, W 'The Divorce Referendum in the Republic of Ireland: Resisting the Tide' (1988) 2 International Journal of Law and the Family 62

Ellman, I M and Lohr, S 'Marriage as Contract, Opportunistic Violence and Other Bad Arguments for Fault Divorce' U Ill L Rev 719 1997

Ellman, I M 'The Place of Fault in a Modern Divorce Law' 28 Ariz St L J 773 (1996)

Gavigan, S A M 'Paradise Lost, Paradox Revisited: The Implications of Family Ideology for Feminist, Lesbian and Gay Engagement to Law' 31 Osgoode Hall L J 589 (1993)

Kadock, C 'Five Degrees of Separation: A Response to Judge Sheldon's "The Sleepwalker's Tour of Divorce Law"' 49 Me L Rev 321 (1997)

Kay, H H 'Equality and Difference' 56 U Cin L Rev 1 (1987)

Regan, M 'Divorce Reform and the Legacy of Gender' 90 Mich L Rev 1453 (1992)

Schneider, C E 'Marriage, Morals and Law: No-Fault Divorce and Moral Discourse' 1994 Utah L Rev 558

Scott, E S 'Rehabilitating Liberalism in Modern Divorce Law' 1994 Utah L Rev 687

Sheldon, J C 'The Sleepwalker's Tour of Divorce Law' 48 Me L Rev 7 (1996)

Wardle, L D 'Divorce, Violence and the No-Fault Divorce Culture' 1994 Utah L Rev 741

Weitzman, L J 'The Alimony Myth: Does No-Fault Divorce Make a Difference?' 14 Fam L Q 141 (1980)

Zelder, M 'The Economic Analysis of the Effect of No-Fault Divorce Law on the Divorce Rate' 16 Harv J L and Pub Pol'y 241 (1993)

Reports

Discussion Paper Family Law: Pre-consolidation Reforms (Scot Law Com Discussion Paper No 85, 1985)

Divorce: The Grounds Considered (Scot Law Com 1967, Cmnd 3256)

The Ground for Divorce (Law Com No 192, 1990)

The Grounds of Divorce: Should the law be changed? (Scot Law Com Discussion Paper No 76, 1988)

Maidment, S. Judicial Separation (Centre for Socio-Legal Studies, 1982)

Morris, S, Gibson, S, and Platts, A Untying the Knot: Characteristics of Divorce in Scotland (Scottish Office Central Research Unit, 1993)

Platts, A. The Use of Judicial Separation (Scottish Office, Central Research Unit, 1992)

Putting Asunder: A Divorce Law for Contemporary Society (Society for Propagation of Christian Knowledge, 1966)

Reform of the Grounds of Divorce: The Field of Choice (Cmnd 3123, 1966)

Report on Family Law (Scot Law Com No 135, 1992)

Report on Reform of the Grounds of Divorce (Scot Law Com No 116, 1989)

Report of a Survey on Proposed Changes to the Divorce Law (System Three Scotland, 1988)

Royal Commission on Divorce and Matrimonial Causes (Gorrell Commission) (Cd 6478, 1912)

CHAPTER 14

Books

Barr, A R, Biggar, J M H, Dalgleish, A M C and Stevens, H J *Drafting Wills in Scotland* (Butterworths, 1994)

Cretney, S M and Masson, J M *Principles of Family Law* (6th edn, Sweet and Maxwell, 1997)

Glendon, M A *The Transformation of Family Law* (University of Chicago Press, 1989)

MacDonald, D R *Succession* (2nd edn, W. Green, 1994)

Meston, M C *The Succession (Scotland) Act 1964* (4th edn, W. Green)

Page, A C and Ferguson, R B *Investor Protection* (Weidenfeld and Nicolson, 1992)

Rauta, I *Family Property in Scotland* (HMSO, 1981)

Saunders, G (ed) *Tolley's Tax Planning* (Tolley Publishing Co, 1997)

Thomson, J M *Family Law in Scotland* (3rd edn, Butterworths, 1996)

Tiley, J (ed) *UK Tax Guide 1998–99* (17th edn, Butterworths)

Walton, F P *Husband and Wife* (3rd edn, W. Green & Son, 1951)

Weitzman, L J *The Divorce Revolution: The Unexpected Social and Economic Consequences for Women and Children in America* (Free Press, 1985)

Articles

Brinig, M F and Crafton, S M 'Marriage and Opportunism' 23 J Legal Stud 869 (1994)

Bissett-Johnson, A and Thomson, J M 'Sharing Property in a Fluctuating Market' 1994 SLT (News) 248

Bissett-Johnson, A 'Recent Changes in Valuation and Division of Pensions on Divorce' 1996 SLT (News) 295

Clive, E M 'Financial Provision on Divorce' 1992 SLT (News) 241

Clive, E M 'Dr Clive Replies' 1992 SLT (News) 247

Clive, E M 'Property Transfer Orders' (1990) 35 JLSS 118

Cusine, D J 'Property Transfer Orders: Some Conveyancing Imponderables' (1990) 35 JLSS 51

Duncan, G J and Hoffman, S D 'Reconsideration of the Economic Consequences of Marital Dissolution' 22 Demography 485 (1985)

Eden, S 'Pensions on Divorce' 1996 Fam LB 22–3 and 23–3

Ellman, I M and Lohr, S 'Marriage as Contract, Opportunistic Violence and Other Bad Arguments for Fault Divorce' U Ill L Rev 719 (1997)

Hoffman, S D and Duncan, G J 'What are the Economic Consequences of Divorce' 25 Demography 641 (1988)

Keller, S E 'The Rhetoric of Marriage, Achievement and Power: An Analysis of Judicial Opinions Considering the Treatment of Professional Degrees as Marital Property' 21 Vt L Rev 409 (1996)

Langbein, J H 'The Twentieth Century Revolution in Family Wealth Transmission' 86 Mich L R 722 (1988)

McLindon, J B 'Separate But Equal: The Economic Disaster of Divorce for Women and Children' 21 Fam L Q 351 (1987)

Meighan, K W 'For Better or For Worse: A Corporate Finance Approach to Valuing Educational Degrees at Divorce' 5 Geo Mason L Rev 193 (1997)

Melli, M S 'Constructing a Social Problem: The Post-Divorce Plight of Women and Children' 1986 ABF Research Journal 759

Peterson, R R 'A Re-evaluation of the Economic Consequences of Divorce' 61 Am Sociological Rev 528 (1996)

Peterson, R R 'Statistical Errors, Faulty Conclusions, Misguided Policy: Reply to Weitzman' 61 Am Sociological Review 539 (1996)

Scherer 'Tort Remedies for Victims of Domestic Abuse' 43 S C L Rev 543 (1992)

Singer, J 'Husbands, Wives and Capital: Why the Shoe Won't Fit' 31 Fam L Q 119 (1997)

Thomson, J M 'Financial Provision on Divorce: Not Technique but Statutory Interpretation' 1992 SLT (News) 245

Thomson, J M 'Financial Provision on Divorce – the Current State of Play' 1989 SLT 17 and 33

Wardle, L D 'Divorce, Violence and the No-Fault Divorce Culture' Utah L Rev 741 1994

Weitzman, L J 'The Alimony Myth: Does No-Fault Divorce Make a Difference?' 14 Fam L Q 141 (1980)

Weitzman, L J 'The Economic Consequences of Divorce are Still Unequal: Comment on Peterson' 61 Am Sociological Rev 537 (1996)

Reports

Doig, B *The Nature and Scale of Financial Provision on Divorce* (CRU, 1981)

The Effects of Cohabitation in Private Law (Scot Law Com Discussion Paper No 86, May 1990)

The Financial Consequences of Divorce: The Basic Policy (Law Com No 103, 1980, Cmnd 8041)

Financial Consequences of Divorce (Law Com No 112, 1980)

MVA Consultancy, Survey of Family Business in the Scottish Courts (Central Research Unit, 1997)

Manners, A J, Rauta, I. Family Property in Scotland (HMSO, 1981)

Morris, S, Gibson, S and Platts, A. Untying the Knot: Characteristics of Divorce in Scotland (Central Research Unit, 1993)

Report on Aliment and Financial Provision (Scot Law Com No 67, 1981)

Report of the Departmental Committee on the Law of Succession in Scotland (Mackintosh Committee) (Cmd 8144, 1950)

Report on Family Law (Scot Law Com No 135, 1992)

Report of the Royal Commission on Marriage and Divorce 1951–55 (Morton Commission) (Cmd 9678, 1956)

Report on Succession (Scot Law Com No 124, 1990)

Succession Law: A Report to the Scottish Law Commission about estates passing on death in Scotland (Central Research Unit, 1989)

The Treatment of Pension Rights on Divorce (Cm 3345, 1996)

Wasoff, F, Dobash, R E and Harcus, D S The Impact of the Family Law (Scotland) Act 1985 on Solicitors' Divorce Practice (Central Research Unit, 1990)

Wasoff, F, McGuckin A and Edwards, L. Mutual Consent: Written Agreements in Family Law (Central Research Unit, 1997)

CHAPTER 15

Books

Aitken, L and Griffin, G *Gender Issues in Elder Abuse* (Sage, 1996)

Agich, G J *Autonomy and Long-term Care* (OUP, 1993)

Arber, S and Evandrou, M *Ageing, Independence and the Life Course* (Jessica Kingsley, 1993)

Biggs, S, Phillipson, C and Kingston, P *Elder Abuse in Perspective* (OUP, 1995)

Blakemore, K and Boneham, M *Age, Race and Ethnicity: as a Comparative Approach* (OUP, 1994)

Block, M and Sinnott, J (eds) *The Battered Elder Syndrome: An Exploratory Study* (University of Maryland Press, 1979)

Eastman, M *Old Age Abuse* (Age Concern, 1984)

Eastman, M *Old Age Abuse – A New Perspective* (Chapman and Hall, 1994)

Eekelaar, J M and Pearl, D (eds) *An Aging World: Dilemmas and Challenges for Law and Social Policy* (Clarendon Press, 1989)

Fabb, J and Guthrie, T G *Social Work Law in Scotland* (2nd edn, Butterworths, 1997)

Freer, C and Wells, N *The Ageing Population: Burden or Challenge?* (Macmillans, 1988)

Heritage, J *Residential Care Fees: Don't Let Them Grab the House* (Spinning Acorn, 1997)

Hughes, B *Older People and Community Care* (OUP, 1995)

Hugman, R *Ageing and the Care of Older People in Europe* (Macmillans, 1994)

Lewis, J and Meredith, B *Daughters Who Care* (Routledge, Chapman and Hall, 1988)

Phillipson, C and Walker, A *Ageing and Social Policy: A Critical Assessment* (Gower, 1986)

Pillemer, K and Wolf, R (eds) *Elder Abuse; Conflict in the Family* (Auburn House, 1986)

Stair *Institutions of the Laws of Scotland* (1681)

Walker, A and Warren, L *Changing Services for Older People* (OUP, 1996)

Articles

Blair, J 'Honor Thy Father and Thy Mother – But for How Long? – Adult Children's Duty to Care For and Protect Elderly Parents' 35 U Louisville J Fam L 765 (1996–97)

Guthrie, T G 'The Significance of Resources in Community Care Assessments' (1997) 2 SLPQ 149

Guthrie, T G 'The House of Lords and Community Care Assessments' (1997) 2 SLPQ 225

Heritage, J 'Residential Care Fees: Protection of Assets' 1998 SLT (News) 105

Kalish, R A 'The New Ageism and the Failure Models: A Polemic' (1979) 19 The Gerontologist 398

Nichols, D 'Legal Arrangements for Managing the Finances of Mentally Disabled Adults in Scotland' 1992 (3) J Soc Wel & Fam L 193

Ogg, J and Bennett, G 'Elder Abuse in Britain' (1992) 305 BMJ 998

Penhale, B 'The Abuse of Elderly People: Considerations for Practice' (1993) 23 British Journal of Social Work 95

Podnieks, E 'National Survey on Abuse of the Elderly in Canada' (1992) 4 Journal of Elder Abuse and Neglect 5

Skabronski, J C 'Elder Abuse: Washington's Response to a Growing Epidemic' 31 Gonz L Rev 627 (1995–96)

Reports

Age becomes her: Older Women in the European Union, The Women of Europe Dossier No 45 (European Commission, 1997)

Caring for People: Community Care in the Next Decade and Beyond (Cm 849, 1989)

Community Care: Agenda for Action (the Griffiths Report) 1988

Report on Incapable Adults (Scot Law Com No 151, 1995)

Report on Vulnerable Adults: Public Authority Powers (Scot Law Com No 158, 1997)

INDEX